POLITICS AND DIPLOMACY
OF PEACEMAKING

Containment and Counterrevolution
at Versailles, 1918–1919

POLITICS
and
DIPLOMACY
of
PEACEMAKING

Containment and
Counterrevolution at Versailles,
1918-1919

❧❦

ARNO J. MAYER

1967

Alfred · A · Knopf : NEW YORK

First Edition

Library of Congress Catalog Card Number: 67–18598

Acknowledgment is hereby made for permission to quote from the following:

Woodrow Wilson and World Settlement by Ray Stannard Baker, by permission of Rachel Baker Napier; *Organization of American Relief in Europe, 1918–1919,* edited by S. L. Bane and R. H. Lutz, Copyright 1943 by the Board of Trustees of Leland Stanford Junior University, by permission of Stanford University Press; *The Aftermath* by Winston S. Churchill, Odhams Press Limited proprietors of the copyright in Great Britain, by permission of Odhams Press Limited and Charles Scribner's Sons; *The Truth About the Peace Treaties* by David Lloyd George, © Copyright 1960 Beaverbrook Newspapers Ltd., by permission of The Beaverbrook Foundation; *Les Délibérations du Conseil des Quatre* (March 24–June 25, 1919) by Paul Mantoux, 1955, by permission of Centre National de la Recherche Scientifique; *Lord Riddell: Intimate Diary of the Peace Conference and After, 1918–1923,* by Lord George Riddell, by permission of Victor Gollancz Ltd.; *Opera Omnia di Benito Mussolini* edited by Edoardo and Duilio Susmel, Copyright 1953 by La Fenice, Florence.

For my sons Carl and Daniel

Preface

IN THIS STUDY of peacemaking after the First World War I am not concerned with the day-by-day negotiations of the territorial, military, financial, and legal clauses that made up the Versailles Treaty. These final terms of settlement were hammered out in committees by experts acting on instructions from their respective heads of delegation. By virtue of their position and assignment most of these experts were shielded from the political and ideological pressures that swirled around the Big Four and their first-echelon advisers. This book specifically focuses on the political and diplomatic context and climate in which the principal peacemakers dealt with critical issues and problems involving fundamental policy considerations. My primary interest is with those major questions that usually came directly to the Big Four, without predigestion by experts, and that reflected the intersection of the ending of a gigantic military conflict with the opening of a universal international civil war.

In terms of chronology and method this study of peacemaking is a sequel to my *Political Origins of the New Diplomacy, 1917–1918*. In both books I have restricted the chronological scope in order to be able to encompass a wide range of national developments and policies and subject them to comparative analysis from the perspective of contemporary world history. Moreover, in both books I have stressed the intense interplay of domestic and international politics, which is characteristic of contemporary mass, revolutionary, and counterrevolutionary politics. Whereas in 1917–18, in the heat of the war, the Allied "parties of movement" (predominantly the Left) put their imprint on the diplomacy of the world crisis, in 1918–19, while peace was being made, the "parties of order" (predominantly the Right) reclaimed their primacy in the victor nations. To document this right-wing resurgence I have had to dwell at great length—occasionally at excessive length—on those internal developments that became the mainsprings of foreign policy and diplomacy. At other places I have made detailed probes of the impact of international politics on domestic affairs. Particularly in my treatment of the Italian and Hungarian questions it was difficult to strike a satisfactory balance between the internal and external aspects.

Hajo Holborn first inspired me to study peacemaking at Versailles and encouraged my resolve to break away from the restrictive approach of conventional diplomatic history. E. H. Carr read through most of the manuscript, giving me the full benefit of his unsurpassed mastery and understanding of recent world and Russian history. Richard Ullman reviewed the chapters dealing with Allied intervention in Russia, while Henry Winkler read the materials pertaining to England and the British Labour Party. With my colleague Arthur Link I had many instructive discussions about American politics and diplomacy. Felix Gilbert, in addition to sharing with me his passion for the scholarly study of contemporary history, patiently answered many questions about postwar Italy. My conception of the age of the Russian Revolution owes much to Robert Palmer's treatment of an earlier revolutionary age, which we discussed while we were colleagues at Princeton, where he is now returning. At various stages Gerald Feldman, Hanna Hastings, and especially John Weiss enthusiastically assisted me with my research, for which I am in their debt.

Students of contemporary history are particularly prone either to avoid crucial controversial issues or to treat them in terms consonant with the current conventional wisdom. To the extent that I resisted both temptations much of the credit goes to Stringfellow Barr, E. H. Carr, Erich Kahler, Herbert Marcuse, Carl Schorske, Ernst Simon, and Stanley Stein. Although I assume full responsibility for all factual errors and untenable interpretations, I cannot absolve these fellow internal exiles from having fortified my critical outlook with their warm friendship, civic courage, and spirited conversation.

It is a pleasure to acknowledge the assistance of the staffs of Firestone Library at Princeton, Widener Library at Harvard, Sterling Memorial Library at Yale, New York Public Library, the Bibliothèque Nationale, and the Bibliothèque de Documentation Internationale Contemporaine. I also wish to thank the curators of manuscript and special collections in the United States at Columbia, Princeton, Stanford, Yale, the Library of Congress, and the National Archives; in London at the British Museum Library, the Foreign Office Library, the Public Record Office, the Archives of the Labour Party at Transport House, and the Research Library of the Conservative Party; in Amsterdam at the International Institute for Social History; and in Milan at the Instituto Giangiacomo Feltrinelli. In Princeton John W. Davidson made available to me a transcribed copy of Ray Stannard Baker's unpublished diary; in Paris J.-B. Duroselle and Stuart Schramm gave me restricted access to state papers relating to French policy toward Soviet Russia in 1918–19. And finally I must record my gratitude for financial support from the American Council of Learned Societies, the Rockefeller Foundation, the Social Science Research Council, and the Research Committee of Princeton University.

ARNO J. MAYER

Princeton
December 1966

Contents

POLITICS AND DIPLOMACY
OF PEACEMAKING

Containment and Counterrevolution
at Versailles, 1918–1919

ABBREVIATIONS

A.F. OF L.: American Federation of Labor

CGT: Confédération Générale du Travail

CGL: Confederazione Generale del Lavoro

DR,APS: *Daily Review of the Foreign Press,* Allied Press Supplement

F.R.: *Papers Relating to the Foreign Relations of the United States, 1918–19*

F.R.,P.C.,1919: *Papers Relating to the Foreign Relations of the United States. The Paris Peace Conference, 1919*

G.F.M.: German Foreign Ministry (microfilm of records)

ILP: Independent Labour Party

ISP: Partito Socialista Italiano (Italian Socialist Party)

JO: Journal Officiel de la République Française, Chambre des Députés, *Débats Parlementaires,* Session Ordinaire, 1918–19.

LP: Labour Party

PD: House of Commons, *Parliamentary Debates,* 5th series, 1918–19.

SFIO: Section Française de l'Internationale Ouvrière (French Section of the Workers' International, or French Socialist Party)

SPD: Sozialdemokratische Partei Deutschlands (German Social Democratic Party)

T.U.C.: Trades Union Congress

UDC: Union of Democratic Control

USPD: Unabhängige Sozialdemokratische Partei Deutschlands (German Independent Social Democratic Party)

Prologue

For quite some time reasoning by historical analogy has been the stock in trade of modern statesmen and their advisers, particularly when confronted with big questions. In 1918–19 the history of the Congress of Vienna was considered to be the most pertinent guide to the making of peace; and the history of the French Revolution, including Europe's reaction to it, the most pertinent guide to dealing with the Russian Revolution. Of course, each statesman's interpretation of these paradigms was marked by his own ideological preferences, national interest calculations, political exigencies, and personal tastes. But all alike searched the history of the Vienna Congress and the French Revolution for policies to be emulated, shunned, or applied in modified form. All participants both used and abused historical analogies precisely because then as now such analogies were vital aids in the analysis and discussion of the quagmire of contemporary history.

The peacemakers of 1814–15 and 1918–19 convened to settle the accounts of a multilateral, unlimited, and ideological conflict; to legalize a new territorial status quo; to agree on safeguards and sanctions against future transgressions by the major defeated enemy; and to explore ways of putting the peace and concert of Europe on more enduring foundations. In both Vienna and Paris each statesman pursued these overarching objectives while simultaneously striving to maximize the national interest of his own country.

These two sets of constantly jarring objectives were pursued within a framework of power politics. Conflicting national interests were accommodated through mutual compensations and concessions. In 1814–15 as in 1918–19 the major powers assumed responsibility for bringing and maintaining in balance the international system of sovereign states. They arrogated to themselves the right to settle all basic territorial, military, economic, and political issues before securing approval for their decisions from the plenary congress or conference. The secondary and minor powers were cast in the role of suitors, suppliants, or satellites. They promoted their interests primarily by deftly capitalizing on the jockeyings, rivalries, and needs of the big powers.

Not surprisingly, on the eve of the Paris Peace Conference Charles

K. Webster urged the British Foreign Office to look for precedents to the negotiations that had concluded the Napoleonic Wars. At Vienna the assembled statesmen had upheld the cardinal distinction between major and minor powers; had adjusted borders according to the dictates of the balance of power; and had agreed on diplomatic procedures to be followed in the future.[1] Shortly after the Conference Webster also claimed that "however puny" the problems of 1814–15 appeared next to those of 1918–19, the Vienna settlement was the only one which in "scope and importance" could be compared to the Versailles settlement: "the boundaries of almost every state in Europe were re-modelled; a barrier was erected against and reparations were inflicted upon the dominant military power; colonial territories were redistributed; new international organizations were erected; and even schemes for the perpetuation of world peace were considered."[2]

As a conventional diplomatic historian with a passion for the functional, procedural, and technical aspects of peacemaking, Webster tendered advice to a foreign office dominated by practitioners of the Old Diplomacy, most of whom were of gentlemanly background.[3] These and other factors predisposed him to stress the important but in the last analysis surface similarities between Vienna and Paris.

At the turn of the century Woodrow Wilson had joined the New Historians in their rebellion against this one-dimensional political and legal history. He was interested "not so much in what happened as in what underlay the happening; not so much in the tides as in the silent forces that lifted them." For him law and government were "regulative rather than generative," and he refused to be satisfied with legal and political history that got at "the surface only, not at the heart of affairs."[4]

In any case, given his progressive *Weltanschauung*, which was solidly rooted in this New History, Wilson was bound to probe into the direction in which a re-enactment of history was likely to take the world. Early in the deliberations he explicitly rejected the Congress of Vienna as a valid precedent. His reasons were that this Congress had

[1] Charles K. Webster: *The Congress of Vienna, 1814–1815* (London: G. Bell and Sons; 1945). Webster completed this handbook for the Historical Section of the Foreign Office in August 1918; it was first published in 1919. See also Pertinax: "L'Exemple du Congrès de Vienne," *Echo de Paris,* December 18, 1918.

[2] Webster: "The Congress of Vienna 1814–15 and the Conference of Paris 1919: A Comparison of their Organization and Results," The Historical Association *Leaflet No. 56* (London, 1923), 2. See also Sir Ernest Satow: "Peacemaking Old and New," *The Cambridge Historical Journal,* I:1 (1923), 23–60; and F. S. Marston: *The Peace Conference of 1919: Organization and Procedure* (London: Oxford; 1944), 56–7.

[3] See Rupert Wilkinson: *Gentlemanly Power: British Leadership and the Public School Tradition* (London: Oxford; 1964).

[4] Woodrow Wilson: "The Variety and Unity of History," in Howard J. Rogers (ed.): *Congress of Arts and Science: Universal Exposition, St. Louis, 1904* (Boston: Houghton Mifflin; 1906), II, 3–20.

presided over a vast restoration, both national and international, and had charted the Holy Alliance which sought to "extend the system of monarchical and arbitrary government in the world." Wilson impassionately begged that "such would not be the purpose of the present conference."[5]

Ideologically and temperamentally the President would readily have reconciled himself to an enlightened restoration calculated to head off a White reaction. But a restoration had been difficult to launch and sustain after 1814–15, at the end of a revolutionary cycle. How much more difficult to launch and sustain one in 1918–19, at the beginning of such a cycle! In 1814–15 the peacemakers were secure in having the support of powerful and influential political, social, economic, and administrative strata which craved domestic order and international stability; they could build on governmental organisms which had survived almost intact; and they needed concern themselves almost exclusively with territorial divisions.

The peacemakers at Paris were not nearly so well served. To begin with, in 1918–19 the leaders and forces favoring moderate reconstruction at home and abroad were fatally buffeted by *enragés* of the Left as well as of the Right. This erosion of conservative liberalism had been well advanced by 1914; the war and revolution merely exacerbated it. Moreover, in Germany, throughout the Danubian basin, in the Balkans, and in Turkey governmental structures were shaky, in ruins, or embryonic. Also, though by no means least important, in both defeated and victor Europe questions of economic and social reconstruction and reform were generating intense political heat. Needless to say, these divisive and explosive domestic conditions were bound to affect the work of the Peace Conference, thereby complicating the assignment of the assembled statesmen far beyond what had faced their predecessors after Napoleon's fall.[6]

According to Ferrero, the Big Four were confronted with a Himalayan task.

> Everything was destroyed, commercial treaties and treaties of alliance, conventions between State and State relating to the most jealously guarded interests, the public and private law of every single State. The elite of the greater European nations, and more especially its youth who would have been called to govern in ten or fifteen years' time, were mown down. The Prussian, no less than the English and French, aristocracy were decimated. The same was true of the middle classes both in France and Germany. The better part of the Russian nation was dispersed or dead. Everywhere the balance of wealth was upset; vast fortunes were made without labour by ignorant, incapable, or cowardly persons, while the flower

[5] *F.R.,P.C.,1919,* III (January 28, 1919), 751, 753.
[6] Pertinax, writing in *Echo de Paris,* November 16, 1918.

of the population was ruined or perished in the trenches. The national fortune even of the richest peoples, was heavily mortgaged in order to meet gigantic war obligations. It is by no means rash to estimate these burdens as amounting to more than half their total possessions. Finally, during the war there was revealed to all eyes the double soul—which wishes for power and at the same time for justice—of the State created by the French Revolution and by the nineteenth century. In this war all the most generous sentiments which make life dear to men were exalted; but at the same time the most terrible offensive weapons which the world has ever seen were brought into action. The States of Western Civilization finally dared to do what to previous ages would have seemed madness if not a crime, and that was, to arm the masses.

Ferrero went on to warn that the apprenticeship of the successor states, which would be arduous and tedious even under the most favorable of circumstances, would be doubly difficult in the "midst of a Europe devastated, bled white, convulsed, and impoverished by the war."[7] *The New Europe* refused to share this pessimism, even though it conceded that Central Europe was "as nearly a *tabula rasa* as a civilized continent could be."[8]

This awareness of the unparalleled scope and complexity of peacemaking in the wake of the world war and the world revolution was widespread. According to Villard of *The Nation,* the statesmen were charged not with simply closing a war but with fully recasting the inherited world order. Notwithstanding Wilson's ecumenical promise, at this juncture the world was "less safe for democracy than at any previous period in modern times . . . and the whole modern order of society was on trial for its life."[9] For the Paris correspondent of the *Philadelphia Ledger* the Conference had to balance and square "the accounts of a whole epoch, the deeds and misdeeds of an exhausted civilization."[1]

As early as May 1918 H. G. Wells, who in September 1914 had held out the promise of *The War That Will End War,* could "conceive no such Peace Congress as those that had settled up after other wars settling up after this War." There were no precedents to go by because this war had been "enormously bigger than any other war . . . and had struck deeper at the foundations of social and economic life." With commendable candor Wells confessed that he doubted that the Western intelligentsia and political class even began "to realize how much of the

---

[7] Guglielmo Ferrero: *Problems of Peace: From the Holy Alliance to the League of Nations* (New York: G. P. Putnam; 1919), 260–2.

[8] *The New Europe,* November 14, 1918, 98–100.

[9] Oswald Garrison Villard: "The Truth about the Peace Conference," *The Nation* (April 26, 1919), 647. This was Villard's first article after his return from Europe.

[1] E. J. Dillon: *The Inside Story of the Peace Conference* (New York: Harper; 1920), 5. See also "The Scope of the Settlement," *The Nation* (November 23, 1918), 618.

old system was dead today, how much had to be remade."[2] This doubt was confirmed once the Paris Conference began to flounder. Wells promptly joined thirty prominent Western intellectuals who compared themselves to those "gloomy prophets and the first apostles" who in experiencing the "agony of Babylonia and Imperial Rome" had cried out that the decomposition of these great powers "was due less to the choc of [external] invasion than to the weight of their own [internal] crimes." These modern brainworkers saw themselves as more "despairing and paralyzed" than the witnesses of past political cataclysms because the decadence confronting them was "more universal, more profound, and more incurable" than that of ancient Greece and Rome.[3]

These and similar expressions of the post-Armistice *Weltschmerz, crise de conscience,* or failure of nerve serve to call attention to the deep and multivarious crisis that, starting in 1917, the Great War precipitated throughout the world: the Bolshevik Revolution in Russia, the nationalist rebellions throughout the Dual Monarchy, the November Revolution in Germany, the post-Armistice neurasthenia in the Allied nations, the Kemalist revolution in Turkey, the rice riots in Japan, the May Fourth Movement in China, and Gandhi's first Swaraj campaign in India. In each of these countries an old order was being jostled by a new one; in some, revolution and counterrevolution were squaring off. It was with this crisis-torn world, particularly with a crisis-torn Europe, swirling about them, that the Big Four were expected to negotiate a lasting diplomatic settlement.

As of the mid-nineteenth century the inseparability of strain or defeat in war and reform or revolution became increasingly apparent. Russia's defeat in the Crimean War was followed by the reforms of the sixties; Austria's defeat at Sadowa led to the compromise of 1867; France's defeat in 1870–1 brought first the fall of the Second Empire, then the Commune, and eventually the birth of the fragile Third Republic; China's defeat in the Sino-Japanese War stimulated an outburst of anti-imperialist nationalism and prepared the ground for the "Hundred Days" of 1898; Russia's defeat in the war with Japan contributed to the revolution of 1905, followed by the Octobrist reforms; and, finally, Russia's exhaustion in the Great War precipitated first the March uprising and then the November Revolution of 1917.

The Russian Revolution came as a timely reminder of the costs of military exhaustion and defeat under conditions of mounting political tensions. Otherwise both the Allies and the Central Powers might well have held out for unconditional surrender. Had it not been for the

[2] H. G. Wells: *In the Fourth Year: Anticipations of a World Peace* (London: Chatto and Windus; 1918), 11.
[3] See Henri Barbusse: *La Lueur dans l'abîme: Ce que veut le Groupe Clarté* (Paris: Editions Clarté; 1920), 5, 148.

demonstration effect of the Bolshevik Revolution neither side would have considered the Wilsonian points as an acceptable basis for armistice negotiations. In the event the Armistice was concluded just in time to limit the political consequences of military defeat in Central and East Central Europe to less than revolutionary proportions. But even with this eleventh-hour finish the legacy of disruption and convulsion was far from negligible.

Granted, neither Germany nor Austria went Spartacist; and Hungary remained Bolshevik for only 133 days. Even so, particularly since Allied policies contributed to this outcome, it would be wrong to dismiss the danger of revolution as having been at best a sham or at worst a conspiracy. Admittedly, the social and political carriers as well as the precipitants of unrest varied in composition and intensity from country to country, and from month to month. But, the fact remains that there were grave disorders, rebellions, and strikes throughout defeated Europe, notably because politicians and labor leaders had ready-made organizational weapons with which to capitalize on political instability, unemployment, food shortages, and runaway prices.

In her diary Beatrice Webb raised a question that haunted Europe's political class, including the chief statesmen, throughout the Peace Conference: "Are we confronted with another Russia in Austria, possibly even in Germany—a Continent in rampant revolution . . . ?"[4] For General Smuts Europe was reduced to her "original atoms," with no hint of the "new political forms" within which these might be joined.[5] Curiously, it was the conservative liberal and legalistic David Hunter Miller who stressed, quite properly, that whereas the peacemakers of 1814–15 only had to reconcile disputes "between well-known and established powers," those of 1918–19 had to bring about "order out of chaos in practically all of Europe east of the Rhine, and north of the Danube, as well as restoration and a new life in various other parts of Europe and Asia."[6] Likewise, Walter Lippmann noted the absence of "stable government anywhere east of the Rhine," warning that no one knew "what Germany would be, nor Russia, nor the twenty odd nationalities of Eastern Europe and New Asia."[7] With good reason Woodrow Wilson acknowledged the wisdom and necessity of postponing the Conference "until there were governments in Germany and Austria-Hungary which could enter into binding agreements."[8] While Smuts exuberantly proposed that the League be made the trustee of the

---

[4] Margaret I. Cole (ed.): *Beatrice Webb's Diaries, 1912–1924* (London: Longmans, Green; 1952), 133–4, entry of November 4, 1918.

[5] Cited in David Hunter Miller: *My Diary at the Conference of Paris*, 21 vols. (privately printed; New York: Appeal Printing Company; 1924), III, 36.

[6] Memorandum by Miller, dated November 21, 1918, cited in *F.R.,P.C.,1919*, I, 354–7.

[7] Walter Lippmann: *The Political Scene: An Essay on the Victory of 1918* (New York: Holt; 1919), 31.

[8] Wilson to Edward Mandell House, November 10, 1918, cited in *F.R.,P.C.,1919*, I, 128.

politically untrained peoples "left behind by the decomposition of Russia, Austria, and Turkey,"[9] Wilson and his advisers did their best to press the Allies into helping the "receiver" and successor governments of the defeated empires to consolidate themselves.

Of course, even without the force of the Soviet Russian example and the activities of local Bolshevik parties this chaos would have developed and caused concern. But as it was, the Bolshevik regime, by its mere survival as well as through its flaming manifestoes, provided encouragement to all far-Left radicals and stirred especially Independent Socialists into greater militancy. In addition, Lenin offered food to the Ebert-Scheidemann government, sent the Radek mission to Berlin, charted the Third International in early March 1919, and built up the Red Army. Counterrevolutionaries in particular vastly exaggerated the scope and aggressive nature of these steps, thereby making the specter which was haunting Europe doubly terrifying.

Naturally not only the Big Four or Five but also the experts within each delegation differed among themselves in their estimates of the nature and seriousness of the revolutionary threat, and hence in their prescriptions for containing it. Moreover, as in 1792–4, the coherence and unity of the counterrevolutionary crusade were undermined by rival national interests, uneven material capabilities, and shifting domestic pressures. Even so, in spite of these grave dissonances, the Paris Peace Conference made a host of decisions, all of which, in varying degrees, were designed to check Bolshevism: the victors made territorial concessions to Poland, Rumania, and Czechoslovakia for helping to stem the revolutionary tide beyond their own borders; they gave military assistance and economic aid to these and other border lands as well as to the Whites for their armed assault on Soviet Russia and Hungary; they stepped up their direct military intervention in Russia; they rigorously enforced the blockade against Bolshevik Russia and Hungary; they rushed economic assistance to Austria and the successor states to help stabilize their governments; and they drafted the charters of the International Labor Organization (I.L.O.) and the League of Nations with a view to immunizing the non-Bolshevik Left against the ideological bacillus of the Bolshevik Revolution.

Some of these measures constituted a defensive containment policy, a *cordon sanitaire* calculated to prevent the Revolution from spreading beyond Bolshevik-controlled areas; other measures were aimed at the outright overthrow of Lenin and Béla Kun. But all alike were decided, orchestrated, sanctioned, or condoned by the peacemakers in Paris. Furthermore, all alike—intentionally or unintentionally—contributed to sparing defeated Europe further revolutionary infections. During the pivotal year of 1918–19, when defeated Europe was most vulnerable, the armed intervention, reinforced by the blockade, forced Lenin to

[9] Cited in Miller· *Diary,* III, 36.

exhaust his scarce military and economic resources in defensive operations. Outside Russia he was reduced to countering the massive material intervention by the Allies with ideological appeals.

At the time, the outcome of this first round in the international civil war of the twentieth century seemed to be very much in the balance. According to Ray Stannard Baker, "at all times, at every turn in the negotiations, there rose the specter of chaos, like a black cloud out of the east, threatening to overwhelm and swallow up the world. There was no Russia knocking at the gates of Vienna! At Vienna, apparently, the revolution was securely behind them; at Paris it was always with them."[1] At one time or another every delegation played on this fear of the Bolshevik specter for its own purposes, thereby making the threat even more pervasive than it needed have been.

The uses and abuses of this spuriously inflated bogy of Bolshevism were as numerous then as they are today. With intermittent support from Lloyd George, President Wilson sought to convince Georges Clemenceau that Germany would succumb to Spartacism unless the Allies promptly lifted the blockade and proffered moderate peace terms. Back home, when Congress threatened to refuse his first major foreign aid bill, Wilson reluctantly but successfully frightened Capitol Hill with tales of the horrors of Bolshevism sweeping over the entire European continent.

Naturally, the vulnerable "receiver" governments of Germany, Austria, and Hungary were the most boisterous advocates of this Wilson line, insisting that should their countries be swallowed up by Bolshevism the advancing flood would not stop at the borders of the victor nations. Ironically, the German government itself diminished the blackmail value of Spartacism by repressing it sternly at home and by fighting Bolshevism eagerly in the *Baltikum*. On the other hand, Count Michael Károlyi invited the Bolsheviks into the Hungarian government in order to make his threats more credible. As for the Poles and the Rumanians, they received vast amounts of financial, economic, and military aid from the Allies for their assault on Soviet Russia and Soviet Hungary. Roman Dmowski and John Brătianu, supported by Ferdinand Foch and Winston Churchill, styled themselves as selfless champions of anti-Bolshevism, all the time extorting exorbitant territorial annexations for their counterrevolutionary services. Even Eleutherios Venizelos, whom Harold Nicolson mysteriously paired with Lenin as "the only two great men in Europe,"[2] was not above trading on the Bolshevik scare; neither were Thomas Masaryk and Eduard Beneš.

In brief, at one time or another most delegations at the Paris Peace Conference wielded the specter of Bolshevism as a weapon and a

[1] Ray Stannard Baker: *Woodrow Wilson and World Settlement,* 3 vols. (Garden City, N.Y.: Doubleday, Page; 1923), I, 102.
[2] Harold Nicolson: *Peacemaking, 1919* (New York: Harcourt, Brace; 1939), 271.

threat. In each instance the assault on or containment of Bolshevism was calculated to advance a government's foreign policy goals while at the same time fortifying its political position at home. *Contra communismo saepe; pro patria et politica semper.*

This twin assignment of stabilizing governments throughout defeated Europe and of containing if not destroying the Russian Revolution called for day-to-day consultations, decisions, and directives. Here, then, was one of the chief sources of that "vast quantity of executive work which was thrust upon the Conference of Paris and which found no parallel at Vienna."[3] Once the Paris Conference is placed in its historical context this executive work can no longer be deplored as a festering diversion from the real stuff of diplomacy, from negotiations of frontier adjustments, colonial redistributions, and reparations. In fact, this diversion, which vastly complicates diplomacy, may yet turn out to be the essence of peacemaking in an era of international civil war. It certainly deserves more than passing mention that the peacemakers of 1918–19 manipulated blockades, wielded military and economic aid, and ordered counterrevolutionary military interventions. Properly to carry out this assignment of preventing Europe "from going to smash under [their] feet," they established the Supreme Economic Council, the Directory for Relief, the Blockade Committee, and the Supreme Council.[4]

The tight interlocking of international and domestic policies in both defeated and victor nations complicated the diplomacy of peacemaking still further.

Since in the defeated nations governments had to be formed before plenipotentiaries could be sent to the Paris Peace Conference, foreign policy platforms became decisive weapons in the struggle for political control. In November 1917 the Bolsheviks had seized power in Russia primarily though not exclusively on a promise of immediate peace; and they were determined to maintain themselves in power without external aid until fellow revolutionary regimes could come to their rescue.

After the Armistice, in Germany, Austria, Hungary, and the successor states, rival political parties, notably those which eventually formed or controlled the governments, claimed that they were best qualified to secure favorable terms from the Big Four. The essential corollary of this pledge was the insistence that successful performance in the peace negotiations was the passkey to domestic rehabilitation, reconstruction, and reform.

But whereas in Russia the Bolsheviks had seized power from below,

---

[3] Webster: "The Congress of Vienna 1814–15 and the Conference of Paris 1919," 6.
[4] Baker: *World Settlement,* II, 365. Cf. André Tardieu: *La Paix* (Paris: Payot; 1921), 118–19; Winston Churchill: *The Aftermath* (London: Macmillan; 1941), 143–4; Nicolson: *Peacemaking,* 117–18, 139; Paul Birdsall: *Versailles Twenty Years After* (New York: Reynal and Hitchcock; 1941), 57.

in Germany, Austria, and Hungary inveterate power elites invited the leaders of the nonrevolutionary forces of movement to act as receivers for bankrupt regimes. They pressed Friedrich Ebert, Friedrich Adler, and Károlyi into accepting these receiverships, not only because at home each was an ideal foil against revolutionary and anarchist excesses, but above all also because each was alone likely to inspire confidence in the Allies, notably in Wilson.

The promise and, in the case of Austria, the fulfillment of Allied goodwill and aid played a crucial role once these provisional governments tried to transform their receiverships from above into popular mandates from below. The Social Democrats and their collaborators forewarned the electorates—and the Allies punctuated these warnings —that in case of chaos or revolution their countries could expect neither food, nor credits, nor favorable peace terms, with the result that there would be massive starvation, especially in the large cities. On the other hand, they promised that provided order was maintained and reformist republican regimes established the victors, under pressure from Wilson and the Allied Left, would provide economic aid and grant moderate peace terms. By mid-January the triumph of the parties of the July Coalition in the campaign for the German Constituent Assembly best attested to the nature and successful application of this political formula. Within two months Károlyi's withdrawal in favor of Béla Kun, which was precipitated by the peremptory Vix Note, demonstrated the failure of the same formula in Hungary.

Just as the peacemakers could ill afford to ignore this interplay of national and international politics in the defeated countries, they could not ignore it in their own. In 1814–15 the peace was negotiated "in elegant and ceremonious privacy . . . [by] a group of Aristocrats, life-trained as statesmen or diplomats,"[5] who considered themselves responsible to crowned sovereigns and barely worried about partisan pressures. The situation was not so serene a century later, when seasoned party politicians of *petit-bourgeois* background—two professors, a journalist, a solicitor—gathered around the conference table. The Big Four were responsible to parliaments, and they never seriously considered insulating themselves from the political parties, pressure groups, mass media, and mass electorates, which were highly agitated over the peace question. To be sure, compared to Metternich, Castlereagh, and Talleyrand, the Big Four were "amateur" diplomats. It does not follow, however, that because they aligned the methods and procedures of diplomacy with the prevailing requirements of party and mass politics they understood less about international affairs than their illustrious predecessors.

Churchill rightly emphasized that the peacemakers of 1918–19 were orators, mass leaders, and men of action, "each of whom had to

[5] Churchill: *Aftermath,* 120. Cf. Satow: "Peacemaking Old and New," 52–3.

produce a triumph for himself and his Party and give satisfaction to national fears and passions well founded or not." But why go on and call them "embarrassed demagogues," as Churchill did?[6] Probably nostalgia for both cabinet diplomacy and status politics accounts for the still widely espoused defamation that these "plenipotentiaries were essentially politicians, old parliamentary hands, and therefore expedient-mongers whose highest qualifications for their own profession were drawbacks which unfitted them for their self-assumed [diplomatic] mission."[7]

Even during the prewar decades the growth of party, mass, and crisis politics had substantially eroded cabinet diplomacy, with politically based foreign policy actors superseding professional diplomats. By 1918–19 this erosion of the methods, procedures, style, and personnel of the Old Diplomacy was completed. There was no going back, least of all at the opening of a revolutionary era with soaring class and party strife at home and abroad. And yet, the very day the Conference was formally inaugurated the *Temps* called on the Central Powers not to allow party conflicts to disturb international relations; not to use foreign intervention "to upset the internal equilibrium of nations"; and not to bring into play party polemics in the peace deliberations. At the same time it inveighed against making partisan use of half-accurate information about these negotiations.[8] *Mirabile dictu.*

With the Armistice the political truce burst wide open in the victor nations, the forces of order and reaction seizing the offensive. In the United States the congressional elections of November 1918 returned a Republican Senate, thereby undermining domestic support for Woodrow Wilson's moderate peace project; in England the coupon election of mid-December 1918 returned a grim House of Commons, resolved to hold Lloyd George to a Carthaginian course; in Italy, in late December, Leonida Bissolati, Italy's foremost Wilsonian, resigned from Orlando's cabinet. Heartened by these developments, on December 29 Clemenceau defiantly proclaimed his skepticism of the Wilsonian program, certain that the war-hardened Chamber of 1914 was determined to have a punitive settlement.

According to Nicolson this upsurge of vindictiveness was a spontaneous prolongation of wartime passions into the post-Armistice period. Irrational hatreds swelled up and consumed "alert but ignorant electorates," which thereafter made it "impossible even for supermen to devise a peace of moderation and righteousness."[9] But was this outburst of revengeful jingoism all that spontaneous? And, if it was, did the governments and their supporters, which had known how to mobilize

6 Churchill: *Aftermath,* 120–1.
7 Dillon: *Inside Story,* 99.
8 *Le Temps,* January 18, 1919.
9 Nicolson: *Peacemaking,* 7, 63–5.

these hatreds, do anything to revaluate these mass sentiments?

There are numerous indications that the clamor for a punitive peace was stirred up as part of a vast political design. Except for the protofascist new Right the leaders, parties, pressure groups, patriotic leagues, and newspapers that sparked this agitation also favored rigorously conservative or outright reactionary social and economic policies. In fact, the forces of order appear to have taken advantage of the intoxication of victory either to preserve or advance their class interests and status positions under an ideological cover which was a syncretism of jingoist nationalism, baleful anti-Wilsonianism, and rabid anti-Bolshevism. Whoever was not a superpatriot was denounced as a fellow traveler of the Bolsheviks and stood accused not only of disloyalty but also of advocating a sellout peace.

The revolutionary segments of the Socialist and labor movements were not the primary target of the jingoist *cum* anti-Bolshevik campaign. Its aim was to rout and disconcert the very core of the forces of change, to do so now, pre-emptively, before the fast-growing Left had a chance to rally around Wilson and to make political gains from the high cost of living, rising taxes, and the strains of reconversion. In addition to championing a Wilsonian peace, this Left—this non-Communist Left—was battling for the forty-eight-hour week, collective bargaining, graduated income taxes, and social welfare measures.

Already in the prewar decade the Left and the Right in Britain, France, and Italy had faced each other with mounting bitterness over these same issues. Compared to then, of course, in 1918–19 the economic and fiscal crisis was infinitely more acute; the membership and following of the labor movement was vastly greater; the Russian Revolution stood forth both as an invigorating and a frightening example; and the Right was able to claim credit for timely preparedness as well as victory. But notwithstanding these important permutations and mutations the continuities with the prewar situation were all too apparent. Specifically, in the struggle over labor, tax, and welfare issues, the extremists of the Right frightened Conservatives into inflexibility by deliberately exaggerating the revolutionary posture and the foreign policy pacifism of the Left. In turn, this creeping inflexibility played into the hands of the radical Left, which charged the Right with domestic reaction and warmongering. By mid-1914 the moderate leaders of both camps were rapidly becoming hostages to their respective extremists, with the result that the politics of compromise and accommodation became increasingly deadlocked. Witness the threatened strike by the Triple Industrial Alliance and the Ulster crisis in Britain, the impasse over the three-year law in France, and Red Week in Italy.

The war merely sharpened this polarization of politics and labor-management relations, at the expense of the conservative-reformist center. Victory strengthened, hardened, and emboldened the refractory Right; the Russian Revolution had a similar impact on the militant Left. Both extremes left indelible marks on the politics and diplomacy of the victor powers in 1918–19. Because the jingoist Right had champions or sympathizers in the legislatures, foreign offices, interior ministries, armed services, conservative parties, and editorial offices, its preemptive thrust was felt in a vast range of developments: in America, in the November elections, in congressional obstruction of a Wilsonian peace, in the Red Scare, and in the drive for "normalcy"; in England, in the coupon election, in Parliamentary opposition to the appeasement of Germany and Soviet Russia, and in the government's sham reconstruction program; in France, in the gestation of the *chambre bleu horizon,* in Clemenceau's intransigence toward Germany and Soviet Russia, in the resolute repression of strikes, and in Parliament's obstinate refusal to approve nonregressive taxes; and in Italy, in Sidney Sonnino's domination of the peace delegation, in Gabriele d'Annunzio's expedition to Fiume, in the growth of the *Fasci de combattimento,* and in Orlando's failure to check inflation.

Except for frightening established governments and societies and serving as a pretext for the excesses of the avant-garde of anti-Bolshevism, the extreme Left had no leverage outside the labor movement. Its leaders, most of them nationally unknown, concentrated their organizational, propagandist, and conspiratorial activities on the rapidly expanding Socialist parties and trade unions, making special efforts to enlist the new recruits. They fed on each and every grievance, sparked local strikes, participated prominently in mass demonstrations, and worked their propaganda presses overtime. In 1918–19 these zealots helped generate a mood of impatience among the rank and file, thereby goading their Majoritarian and Independent rivals into a greater sense of urgency about the labor cause. These political and syndicalist militants should not be denied their share of the credit for the enactment of the forty-eight-hour week by the Allied parliaments and for the labor movement's concerted and partially successful opposition to direct military intervention in Russia.

Without this impatience and activism on the Left Woodrow Wilson's moderating influence would have been completely nullified. As it was, precisely because the moderate forces of movement were so decisively checked even before the start of the Conference, Wilson had only limited leverage. Moreover, he was hesitant to appeal to the Left for help for fear that the militants would seize the initiative for themselves. Wilson was condemned to labor in a political field, both national and international, in which measured reformism, so essential to the achievement of his diplomatic aims, was fatally emasculated.

Wilson's principles and aims, like all such pronunciamentos, were destined to be honored in the breach. The conditions that had prompted their formulation and acceptance in early 1918 had passed into history: there was no longer any need to restrain the Soviet government from signing a separate peace with the Central Powers; with the success of the revolution from above in Berlin the rebellion against the Kaiser and Erich Ludendorff no longer required encouragement; and after the Armistice the Allied Governments could dispense with the support of their own forces of movement. Above all, the Allied cabinets were much less prone to bend to the ideological and diplomatic wishes of the Wilson Administration once victory had drastically reduced their dependence on American military and economic power. Besides, no programmatic guidelines had complicated the labors of the peacemakers of 1814–15.

Even so, the President's Fourteen Points and subsequent pronouncements were not simply shunted aside. By making their two reservations with regard to the freedom of the seas and reparations the Allies conceded that Wilson's prescriptions had crystallized into a public touchstone for the coming peace negotiations; and the pre-Armistice exchanges with Germany even endowed them with a measure of contractual force.[1]

But quite apart from any moral or legal obligation to Germany, until May 1919 the Allied Governments could not afford to disavow Woodrow Wilson publicly. The President's ideology and America's economic bounty were expected to exercise a moderating influence on revolutionary conditions in defeated Europe and on the post-Armistice neurasthenia in the victor nations. Without the still potent spell of Wilsonianism the swing toward Leninism within the Left might well have assumed considerable proportions. Especially the Independents, but also the Majoritarians, trusted in the President to block a punitive peace, thereby thwarting the offensive of the Allied Right, consolidating the reformist regimes in the defeated nations, and giving the lie to Lenin's charge that Wilsonianism was but an insidious bourgeois-capitalist smoke screen.

The frenzied enthusiasm that greeted the President upon his arrival in Europe was not without political and class overtones. While Socialist, labor, and radical-bourgeois leaders and their followers wildly cheered him, their opponents berated them for apotheosizing Wilson for selfish, partisan purposes. On the eve of the Conference the Allied Governments were sufficiently apprehensive about this united front of Wilson and the Left that they purposely obstructed contacts between them. On the other hand, the governments of the defeated nations continued to profess their faith in Wilson until well after they knew that his cause was lost. As for the governments of the successor states, they courted Wilson's favor in their bid for favorable frontiers and economic

1 Webster: "The Congress of Vienna 1814–15 and the Conference of Paris 1919," 8–9.

aid. In sum, throughout most of the Conference the President and his arsenal of spiritual and material resources were considered indispensable by each delegation as well as by the Berne International. Significantly, even Clemenceau was careful not to risk a break with Wilson; and notwithstanding his anti-Wilsonian tirades, Lenin was eager for the President to blunt the military edge of the counterrevolutionary intervention.

At the time of the Congress of Vienna Tsar Alexander I certainly did not play such a pivotal role as did Wilson. Quite apart from the fact that the League of Nations was to serve as an instrument for peaceful change in the international arena while the Holy Alliance was designed to freeze the new status quo at home and abroad, the Tsar had considerably less leverage than Wilson. Whereas Alexander was confined to cooperation with fellow sovereigns and to military means of intervention. Wilson could marshal popular support for the League and dispose of substantial economic and financial resources which were of critical importance to the exhausted nations of Europe.[2]

R. S. Baker quite rightly stressed that the use of the "economic weapon" to achieve diplomatic and political ends "was only in its crude beginnings at Paris," and that the world would get "a fuller taste of it in the future."[3] During the Conference all nations—large and small, old and new—brought their economic resources into play; and the Conference as a whole, supported by the neutrals, enforced a strict blockade against Bolshevik Russia and Hungary.

But America's use of the economic weapon was particularly noteworthy. She had a vast reservoir of instantly available capital, food, and manufactures, and her delegation had a precocious understanding of economic power as an instrument of control in the international politics of this dawning era of civil war.

The Armistice was not signed as yet when U. S. officials in Europe advised Washington that since America's "economic and financial support would be essential to the Allies in the post-war period" material pressures might be used to force an acceptable interpretation of "our own principles and policies."[4] Wilson himself chose Armistice Day solemnly to declare that it would be America's "fortunate duty to assist by example, by sober, friendly counsel and by *material aid* in the establishment of a just democracy throughout the world";[5] and he may well

[2] See Satow: "Peacemaking Old and New," 37; and H. W. V. Temperley: "Attempts at International Government in Europe: The Period of the Congress of Vienna (1814–25) and the Period Since the Treaty of Versailles (1919–22)," Historical Association *Leaflet No. 56* (London, 1923), 16–17.

[3] Baker: *World Settlement,* II, 349.

[4] George McFadden, representative of the War Trade Board in Europe, to Robert Lansing, November 9, 1918, cited in *F.R.,P.C.,1919,* II, 729–31.

[5] Cited in *F.R.,P.C.,1919,* I, 1.

have had the economic weapon in mind when he told his advisers, during the crossing to Europe, that the U.S. would fight for a new order "agreeably if we can, disagreeably if necessary."[6]

Colonel House shared the view of many U. S. officials and business leaders that the Allies were "vitally interested in what manner we propose to use our great strength" in finance, commerce, shipping, raw materials, and food.[7] As for D. H. Miller, he confidently predicted that Wilson's covenant would be accepted without any American concessions because "Europe was bankrupt financially and her Governments were bankrupt morally . . . [and] the mere hint of the withdrawal of America . . . would see the fall of every government in Europe without exception, and a revolution in every country of Europe with one possible exception."[8]

Members of the British Delegation confirmed this diagnosis. According to Keynes, in early 1919 "Europe was in complete dependence on the food supplies of the United States; and financially she was even more absolutely at their mercy." In Nicolson's judgment this economic dependence made the Allies "entirely subservient to the dictates of Washington" and gave Wilson an "overwhelming force of compulsion." In retrospect, both Keynes and Nicolson recall that it never occurred to them that, "if need arose, Wilson would hesitate to use" America's economic and financial power, and both attribute this hesitancy to his having been a prophet instead of a man of power.[9]

In actual fact, the American Delegation played a leading role in the formulation and implementation of diplomatically and politically intended economic policies toward Soviet Russia, Bolshevik Hungary, the successor states, and the new regimes in Germany and Austria. But whereas Wilson readily used the economic weapon to strangle Bolshevism, to support fledgling nations, and to stabilize the governments of the defeated nations, he hesitated to exert pressure on the Allies. This hesitation, however, was due to political considerations, both domestic and foreign, rather than to his prophetic disposition.

At home influential senators, the patriotic leagues, the jingoist press, and select interest groups mounted a campaign against the use of the economic weapon for a Wilsonian peace of the sort advocated by the European Left. To make matters worse, the three Allied premiers were well informed about this opposition and proposed to foster and harness it for their own purposes. By early December 1918 the London *Spec-*

6 Cited in Charles Seymour: *The Intimate Papers of Colonel House,* 4 vols. (Boston: Houghton Mifflin; 1928), IV, 282.
7 House to Lansing, November 23, 1918, cited in *F.R.,P.C.,1919,* I, 170. See also Patrick Hurley to Wilson, December 12, 1918, cited in *F.R.,P.C.,1919,* II, 662.
8 Miller: *My Diary,* III, 259.
9 John Maynard Keynes: *The Economic Consequences of the Peace* (New York: Harcourt, Brace; 1920), 38–9; and Nicolson: *Peacemaking,* 41–2.

tator assured its readers that Wilson did not have the "least chance of getting any treaty ratified which was repugnant to the sentiments of the Republican party"; and that since the opinions of that party were "framed in unreserved support of Great Britain and France" the Allies could approach the Conference "with all confidence."[1] Within a month the Boston *Transcript* (independent Republican) hinted that since the Allied statesmen were familiar with the American opposition as well as with the American Constitution they might be "inclined to heed rather the view of the American majority than that of a President whose general policies had been discredited by the popular vote."[2] Meanwhile Senator Henry Cabot Lodge set out to encourage the Allied Carthaginians to join him in standing up to Wilson.[3]

As the *Springfield Republican* suggested, in order to "neutralize the influences working against him in his own country" the President would have "to rally sympathetic elements in Great Britain, France and Italy."[4] In fact, the Right on both sides of the Atlantic was apprehensive about the progressive *domestic* implications of a peace of reconciliation, just as the Left was nervous about the conservative domestic consequences of a vindictive settlement.

Radical publicists called attention to this political struggle "not between nations but between parties whose constituency transcended all national boundaries." For the purposes of peacemaking "the progressive wings of the American parties, British labor and liberals, French and Italian and Belgian liberals and socialists were one party; the Lodges and Milners and Carsons and Clemenceaus and their following of imperialists and protectionists constituted the opposing party."[5] To be sure, Radicals were blind to the broad popular support of the Right and crudely divided the political spectrum into two monolithic blocs. But except for these blind spots this characterization of the transnational political confrontation had considerable merit, not least because it acknowledged the inevitability of the politics of intervention. Frederick Jackson Turner quite rightly anticipated that the

---

[1] Cited in *The New Republic* (December 14, 1918), 176.

[2] Cited in *The Literary Digest* (January 11, 1919), 10.

[3] "I am sending you a copy of the speech which I made on Saturday [December 21, 1918, in Congress] which was intended chiefly for the benefit of the Allies." Lodge to Theodore Roosevelt, cited in Roger Burlingame and Alden Stevens: *Victory Without Peace* (New York: Harcourt, Brace; 1944), 204. See also Lodge's letter to Henry White on the eve of White's departure for Paris, cited in Allan Nevins: *Henry White* (New York: Harcourt, Brace; 1944), 172.

[4] *Springfield Republican*, December 15, 1918, forwarded by Tumulty to Wilson, December 17, 1918, in Wilson Papers, VIII A:3.

[5] *The New Republic* (December 21, 1918), 212. By March 21, 1919, in discussing the outburst of Republican opposition to Wilson, the *Daily News* (London) commented that "the lines of division today run not perpendicularly between nations, but horizontally through nations."

conservative forces of different nations were on the verge of cooperating internationally, in imitation of their Socialist rivals.[6]

Theoretically the Right indignantly and violently objected to external intervention in the internal affairs of nations. In practice, however, it championed counterrevolutionary intervention in Bolshevik countries and relied on informal transnational contacts elsewhere. Naturally Lenin and Karl Radek disdainfully rejected this principle of the nonintervention in the internal affairs of other nations[7] and proceeded to devise organizational mechanisms with which to maximize the effectiveness of their predesigned interference abroad. Meanwhile, Wilson searched for political support for the material and ideological intervention for which he was so much better equipped than Lloyd George, Clemenceau, Orlando, and even Lenin.

As noted before, his supporters were in retreat in the United States as well as in Europe. In America *The New Republic, The Nation,* the League of Free Nations Society, the Committee of 48, segments of organized labor, and internationally minded businessmen and financiers were fighting a rear-guard battle against onrushing conservatives, superpatriots, and anti-Communists. Simultaneously in the Allied nations the non-Communist Left and the radical bourgeoisie were in disarray. Perhaps this narrow political base at home and in the Allied countries accounts for Wilson's hesitancy to go over the heads of the Big Three. The hardening of opinion in his own country sensitized him to the hardening of opinion in London, Paris, and Rome. Moreover, quite apart from being careful not to encourage the revolutionary Left, Wilson was worried about weakening governments, including the Polish and Rumanian governments, that carried the brunt of the containment of and the intervention in Russia.

In sum, a frontal attack on the victory-hardened Allies, which Socialists and Radicals on both sides of the Atlantic urged upon the President, was not to be undertaken lightly. The task and responsibility would have been staggering, the risk immense—the more so for a statesman and politician sworn to reason rather than passion, to agreement by consent rather than coercion, to reform rather than revolution. The issue is hardly whether or not Wilson was sincere about his principles and aims; nor is the issue one of the quality of his strategic and tactical skills as diplomatist and politician. Even assuming Wilson scored exceptionally high on all these counts, a prior question must

---

[6] Frederick Jackson Turner: "International Political Parties in a Durable League of Nations" (November 1918), in Ray Stannard Baker Papers, Firestone Library, Princeton University.

[7] "This principle of non-intervention was the principle which guided legitimist Europe after the Congress of Vienna, while in the struggle for liberation, international Communists all along advocated the energetic intervention in the affairs of the whole world." Karl Radek: *Ein offener Brief an Philipp Scheidemann* (*ca.* November 20, 1918; w.p.), 2–3.

be considered: how pertinent and consequential was Wilson's reformist project in the crisis setting of 1918–19?

Unlike Clemenceau, the President strained to understand this crisis in its world historical context. Both he and Lloyd George consistently rejected the conspiratorial view of the Russian Revolution, which they saw as a variant of the French Revolution in scale, ecumenical appeal, and duration.

Wilson's concern was less with the importance of the Revolution for Russia than for Europe and the world. He saw the example of the Revolution, embellished by stirring manifestoes, acting upon crisis-torn societies which in the prewar years had been rife with discontent and agitated by revolutionary parties and ideologies. According to Isaiah Bowman, the President told his advisers on the S.S. *George Washington* that the poison of Bolshevism was spreading because it was "a protest against the way in which the world had worked."[8] William Bullitt, who was present on this same occasion, recorded Wilson as saying that the only way he could "explain the susceptibility of the people of Europe to the poison of Bolshevism, was that their Governments had been run for wrong purposes." Wilson then added his prediction that unless the peace were made "on the highest principles of justice it would be swept away by the peoples of the world in less than a generation." In that event he intended "to run away and hide on the Island of Guam or somewhere else remote, for there would follow not mere conflict but cataclysm."[9] A bit later, when pleading with the Big Three for an accommodation with Lenin, he warned that "there was certainly a latent force behind Bolshevism which attracted as much sympathy as its more brutal aspects caused general disgust." Wilson attributed this sympathy to "a feeling of revolt throughout the world against large vested interests which influence the world both in the economic and in the political sphere."[1]

It was precisely because the Russian Revolution was "a menace to others" that Wilson was so reluctant to leave Russia to "settle her own affairs in her own way."[2] With the help and encouragement of his key advisers, notably of Herbert Hoover, Wilson spearheaded various Allied efforts to tame the Russian Revolution. In fact, these efforts came to be central to Wilson's overall peacemaking strategy.

Whereas the Entente Governments tended to advocate either direct or indirect military intervention—with America providing most of the

---

[8] Cited in Seymour: *Intimate Papers,* IV, 282.

[9] Bullitt's diary notes on the S.S. *George Washington,* entry of December 9, 1918, in Bullitt Papers.

[1] *F.R.,P.C.,1919,* III (January 16, 1919, a.m.), 583.

[2] In late December Wilson told a British official that "Russia should be left to settle her own affairs in her own way so long as she did not become a menace to others." Notes on interview with Wilson by Frank Worthington, Deputy Chief Censor, dated December 28, 1918, National Archives, Secret File, Document 811.001W/163.

funds, the material, and the food supplies—the American Delegation gave first priority to diplomatic, economic, and ideological intervention. Not that the Wilson Administration backed out of or cut back the armed intervention started in mid-1918. Still, by comparison it was particularly intent on exploring those avenues that might obviate military measures partially or altogether. Of course this nonmartial approach suited Wilson's view of the dynamics of the Russian Revolution, his diplomatic style, and America's foreign policy capabilities.

Rather than denounce the Bolshevik Revolution as either a sinister conspiracy or a vile crime, Wilson saw it as the natural and fitting culmination of lingering popular dissatisfactions with the tsarist regime, catalyzed by the strains of war and enthusiasm for the seductive promises of the Bolshevik ideology. Such dissatisfaction and ardor could not be conquered by force of arms, not least because a military onslaught threatened to restore the *ancien régime*. Clemenceau and, to a lesser extent, Lloyd George were not particularly bothered by the prospect of the Whites replacing Lenin, so that the irresolution of their intervention in the Russian Civil War was not a function of political scruples but of overstrained resources and anti-interventionist pressures. Wilson, however, refused to close his eyes to the ideological and political aftergrowth of the destruction of the Soviet regime. The qualified recognition of Alexander Kolchak, which was delayed until late May 1919, mirrored his desperate but unrealistic and self-deceiving attempt to transform the unmistakably counterrevolutionary intervention into a crusade for the democratization of Russia. That even his worst fears were justified was amply demonstrated once the Allied-sponsored overthrow of Béla Kun was followed by a White terror and by anti-Semitic pogroms.

On the intellectual plane the President understood that revolution and counterrevolution inevitably incited and needed each other. In terms of policy, however, he simply could not admit the impossibility of a moderate middle course. Like it or not, America was one of the senior partners in a coalition resolved to contain or destroy the Bolshevik Revolution. To achieve this objective the Allies needed the military services of Finland, Poland, Rumania, and Germany, even at the price of allowing conservative and reactionary forces in these countries to benefit from this anti-Bolshevik campaign.

It was to avoid paying this distasteful political price that the American delegates wanted to explore the use of nonmilitary methods of intervention. Their aim was to moderate and domesticate rather than destroy the revolutionary regime in Russia. In their judgment the ideological canons of Bolshevism and the lust for power of the Bolshevik leaders were not the primary moving force of the Soviet dictatorship. According to some American officials Lenin's iron rule at home and revolutionary agitation abroad were part of a *levée en masse* by a revolutionary government fighting for its life against internal insurgents and foreign invasion in a country bled white by war. Provided these mainsprings of revolutionary dictatorship were removed or reduced, the Soviet leaders could afford to relax their iron grip and agree to a united front of the Left for the reconstruction, modernization, and reform of Russia. The Allies could contribute to this relaxation of revolutionary discipline and terror not only by stopping their intervention and lifting the blockade but also by providing economic and technical assistance.

The Buckler-Litvinov conversations, the Prinkipo proposal, and the Bullitt Mission were so many efforts in this direction. All alike were opposed and sabotaged by the entire French Delegation, by key members of the American and British delegations, by antiappeasement forces in the Allied parliaments, by all but one of the Russian *émigré* groups in Paris, by the Whites in Russia, and by the governments of most of the new states along Russia's western borders. Some were motivated by power-political considerations and others by age-old national hatreds, but all alike called forth and embodied counterrevolutionary economic, social, and political forces. There was no corresponding reservoir of support for moderation. Wilson knew this; and so did Lenin.

Chances for a negotiated accommodation were never very good. The Big Four, including Wilson, insisted on military conditions that were designed to favor the Whites and their borderland allies and sought to extract debilitating political concessions in exchange for lifting the blockade and providing food. In turn, Lenin was careful not to play any of his spare trumps, notably critical and advanced military positions and control of the railways. Whereas strictly territorial issues might have been compromised, mutual distrust stemming from irreconcilable political, economic, and social persuasions stood in the way of an overall settlement—at a time that both sides still hoped for total victory. Lenin was not about to trust Wilson, whom he rightly suspected of being a prisoner—even if a reluctant prisoner—of the counterrevolution.

With the March-April crisis the Russian question once again became acute. The stand of the Right toward Bolshevism both inside and outside Russia stiffened still further in the face of rising labor unrest in the Allied countries, renewed Spartacist outbreaks in Germany, the establishment of a Soviet outpost in Bavaria, the triumph of Béla Kun in Hungary, and the explosive instability in Vienna. This rigidification was well under way when rumors of the Bullitt Mission incited the diehards to protest furiously against any dealings with Lenin and to urge stepped-up military measures.

Once again caught between the appeasers and the irreconcilables, Wilson abandoned a direct diplomatic approach in favor of an untried economic formula. The Nansen Plan for a commission of neutrals to feed Russia originated in the American Delegation. At first, in order to broaden its ideological appeal, the letter drafted by Hoover for Fridtjot Nansen's signature was supposed to be countersigned by Karl Hjalmar Branting. But the leader of the Second International preferred to stay in the background. Under the Nansen scheme the Russian Bolsheviks were asked to halt military operations "against our allies" on all fronts and to waive "political recognition or negotiation" in exchange for food and other essential supplies to be provided by a neutral relief agency. Obviously, the arrangements for the distribution in Russia of this "wholly non-political" relief would be decisive, primarily because their political implications were the crux of this proposal.

In fact, political rather than humanitarian purposes were at the heart of the Nansen Plan. This political design was forcefully sketched out by Hoover in a remarkable letter to President Wilson, dated March 28, 1919.[3]

> As the result of Bolshevik economic conceptions, the people of Russia are dying of hunger and disease at the rate of some hundreds of thousands monthly in a country that formerly supplied food to a large part of the world.

> I feel it is my duty to lay before you in just as few words as possible my views as to the American relation to Bolshevism and its manifestations. These views at least have the merit of being an analysis of information and thought gleaned from my own experience and the independent sources which I now have over the whole of Europe, through our widespread relief organization.

> It simply cannot be denied that this swinging of the social pendulum from the tyranny of the extreme right to the tyranny of the extreme left is based on a foundation of real social grievance. The tyranny of the reactionaries in Eastern and Central Europe for generations before the war, and the suffering of their common people is but a commonplace to every social student. This situation was thrown into bold relief by the war and the breakdown of those reactionary tyrannies. After fighting actually stopped on the various fronts the famine which followed has further emphasized the gulf between the lower and upper classes. The poor were starved and driven mad in the presence of extravagance and waste.

> It is to be noticed that the Bolshevik ascendancy or even their strong attempts so far are confined to areas of former reactionary tyranny. Their courses represent the not unnatural violence of a mass of ignorant humanity, who themselves have learned in grief of tyranny and violence over generations. Our people, who enjoy so great liberty and general comfort, cannot fail to sympathize to some degree with these blind gropings for better social condition. If

[3] The full text of this letter is in the House Papers, 10:37; excerpts are cited in Herbert Hoover: *The Ordeal of Woodrow Wilson* (New York: McGraw-Hill; 1958), 117–19.

former revolutions in ignorant masses are any guide, the pendulum will yet swing back to some moderate position when bitter experience has taught the economic and social follies of present obsessions. No greater fortune can come to the world than that these foolish ideas should have an opportunity somewhere of bankrupting themselves.

It is not necessary for any American to debate the utter foolishness of these economic tenets. We must all agree that our processes of production and distribution, the outgrowth of a hundred generations, in the stimulation to individual initiative, the large equality of opportunity and infinite development of mind and body, while not perfect, come about as near perfection as is possible from the mixture of avarice, ambition, altruism, intelligence, ignorance and education, of which the human animal is today composed. The Bolshevik's land of illusion is that he can perfect these human qualities by destroying the basic processes of production and distribution instead of devoting himself to securing a better application of the collective surplus.

Politically, the Bolsheviki most certainly represent a minority in every country where they are in control, and as such they constitute a tyranny that is the negation of democracy, for democracy as I see it must rest on the execution of the will of the majority expressed by free and unterrified suffrage. As a tyranny, the Bolshevik has resorted to terror, bloodshed and murder to a degree long since abandoned even amongst reactionary tyrannies. He has even to a greater degree relied upon criminal instinct to support his doctrines than even autocracy did. By enveloping into his doctrines the cry of the helpless and the downtrodden, he has embraced a large degree of emotionalism and has thereby given an impulse to his propaganda comparable only to the impulse of large spiritual movements. This propaganda, however, in my view will stir other populations only in ratio to their proportions of the suffering and ignorant and criminal. I feel myself, therefore, that the political danger of spread of Bolshevism by propaganda is a direct factor of the social and political development of the population which they attempt to impregnate. Where the gulf between the middle classes and the lower classes is large, and where the lower classes have been kept in ignorance and distress, this propaganda will be fatal and do violence to normal democratic development. For these reasons, I have no fear of it in the United States, and my fears as to other countries would be gauged by the above criterion. It is possible that the Soviet type of government might take hold in some other countries as a primitive form of democracy, but its virulence will be tempered by their previous degree of political subversion.

There remains in my mind one more point to be examined, that is as to whether the Bolshevik centers now stirred by great emotional hopes will not undertake large military crusades in an attempt to impose their doctrines on other defenseless people. This is a point on which my mind is divided with the evidence at hand, and it seems to me that the whole treatment of the problem must revolve on the determination of this one question. If this spirit is inherent in their doctrine, it appears to me that we must disregard all other questions and be prepared to fight, for exactly the same reasons that we entered the European War against Germany. If this is not the case, then it appears to me that from an American point of view we should not involve ourselves in what may be a ten year military entanglement in Europe. The American people cannot say that we are going to insist that any given population must work out its internal social problems according to our particular conception of democracy. In any event, I have the most serious doubt that outside forces entering upon such an enterprise can do other than infinite harm, for any great wave of emotion must ferment and spread under repression. In the swing of the social pendulum from the extreme left back toward the right, it will find the point of stabilization based on racial instincts that could never be established by outside intervention.

I think we have also to contemplate what would actually happen if we undertook military intervention in, say, a case like Hungary. We should probably be involved in years of police duty, and our first act would probably in the nature of things make us a party to reestablishing the reactionary classes in their economic domination over the lower classes. This is against our fundamental national spirit, and I doubt whether our soldiers under these circumstances could resist infection with Bolshevik ideas. It also requires consideration as to whether or not our people at home, on gradual enlightenment as to the social wrongs of the lower classes in these countries, would stand for our providing power by which such reactionaries held their position, and we would perchance be thrown in to an attempt as governors to work out some social reorganization of these countries. We thus become a mandatory with a vengeance. We become, in fact, one of four mandatories, each with a different political and social outlook, for it would necessarily be a joint Allied undertaking. Furthermore, in our present engagements with France, England and Italy, we become a junior in this partnership of four. It is therefore inevitable that in these matters where our views and principles are at variance with the European Allies we would find ourselves subordinated and even committed to policies against our convictions.

In all these lights, I have the following three suggestions:

First: We cannot even remotely recognize this murderous tyranny without stimulating actionist radicalism in every country in Europe and without transgressing on every National ideal of our own.

Second: That some Neutral of international reputation for probity and ability should be allowed to create a second Belgian Relief Commission for Russia. He should ask the Northern Neutrals who are especially interested both politically and financially in the restoration of better conditions in Russia, to give to him diplomatic, financial and transportation support; that he should open negotiations with the Allied governments on the ground of desire to enter upon the humane work of saving life, and ask the conditions upon which ships carrying food and other necessaries will be allowed to pass. He should be told that we will raise no obstructions and would even help in his humanitarian task if he gets assurances that the Bolsheviki will cease all militant action across certain defined boundaries and cease their subsidizing of disturbances abroad; under these conditions that he could raise money, ships and food, either from inside or outside Russia; that he must secure an agreement covering equitable distribution, and he might even demand that Germany help pay for this. This plan does not involve any recognition or relationship by the Allies of the Bolshevik murderers now in control any more than England recognized Germany in its deals with the Belgian Relief. It would appear to me that such a proposal would at least test out whether this is a militant force engrossed upon world domination. If such an arrangement could be accomplished it might at least give a period of rest along the frontiers of Europe and would give some hope of stabilization. Time can thus be taken to determine whether or not this whole system is a world danger, and whether the Russian people will not themselves swing back to moderation and themselves bankrupt these ideas. This plan, if successful, would save an immensity of helpless human life and would save our country from further entanglements which today threaten to pull us from our National ideals.

Third: I feel strongly the time has arrived for you again to reassert your spiritual leadership of democracy in the world as opposed to tyrannies of all kinds. Could you not take an early opportunity to analyze, as only you can, Bolshevism from its political, economic, humane and its criminal points of view, and, while yielding its aspirations, sympathetically to show its utter foolishness as a basis of economic development; show its true social ends; rap our own reactionaries for their destruction of social betterment and thereby their stimulation of Bolshevism; point, however, to the steady progress of real democracy in these roads of social betterment. I believe you would again align the hearts of the suffering for orderly progress against anarchy, not alone in Russia but in every Allied country.

If the militant features of Bolshevism were drawn in colors with their true parallel with Prussianism as an attempt at world domination that we do not stand for, it would check the fears that today haunt all men's minds.

In this letter Hoover brilliantly summarized the key tenets of the Wilsonian view of the Bolshevik problem: Russian Bolshevism was a condition to be cured rather than a conspiracy to be destroyed; there were considerable sources of Bolshevik contagion outside Russia; the spiritual appeals of the Bolshevik ideology were far from negligible; the reactionary consequences of a military crusade against Bolshevism could not be ignored; and a military truce combined with economic aid was most likely to redirect the revolutionary currents into reformist channels in Russia.

But the letter also struck some novel chords. Above all, Hoover made an insidious comparison of the "foolishness" of Bolshevik economic doctrines with the unequaled excellence of the American economic system. Moreover, he envisaged the possibility that doctrinally the Bolsheviks were sworn to export their economic and political system, if need be even by force of arms. Without abandoning the view that the Bolshevik system was primarily a product of historical conditions Hoover now stressed the doctrinal sources of Soviet conduct.

As a result, while Hoover's policy recommendations dovetailed with Wilson's drive to give priority to nonmilitary intervention, they also embodied a new departure. Accordingly, Wilson was urged to couple his economic intervention with an ideological counteroffensive. Hoover wanted the President to issue a manifesto criticizing the doctrine, promise, and practice of Bolshevism and setting forth the aims and methods of reformist and democratic capitalism. In other words, just as the recently completed crusade against the Central Powers had required and profited from the Fourteen Points, so this incipient crusade against the rival social-political system required an anti-Bolshevik manifesto.

Even though Wilson successfully insisted on certain political assurances as a precondition for recognizing Kolchak, he never went on to issue a full-blown manifesto proclaiming the objectives of the Big Powers' participation in armed containment and intervention. Perhaps he never did so because he could at best be halfhearted about an operation whose carriers and objectives were too counterrevolutionary for his own liking. The words and principles of a Wilsonian pronouncement would have been blatantly incompatible with the whole thrust of the enterprise, thus making it that much easier for Lenin and his champions to expose the hypocrisy of the democratic-reformist ideology. A declaration like that issued at Pillnitz against the French Revolution would have been more appropriate, but Foch or Churchill, rather than Wilson, would have had to formulate it.

It may well be that the democratization and moderation of the counterrevolutionary side in a civil war is a historical impossibility. In any case, Wilson lacked the courage, the political support, and the diplomatic leverage to force a credible effort for accommodation with Lenin; or, failing this, to make the operation essentially *defensive*. The intervention continued, with each participant's contribution determined by a variety of factors—among them power capabilities, domestic political pressures, national rivalries, and changing estimates of chances for the overthrow of the Bolshevik regime.

The military operations of this intervention impinged only occasionally on the politics and diplomacy of peacemaking. On the other hand, precisely because peacemaking and the containment of Bolshevism were so tightly interlocked the one could never be separated from the other. Once again it was Baker, the participant-historian of liberal persuasion, who faced up to this dilemma.

> The effect of the Russian problem on the Paris Conference . . . was profound: Paris cannot be understood without Moscow. Without ever being represented at Paris at all, the Bolsheviki and Bolshevism were powerful elements at every turn. Russia played a more vital part at Paris than Prussia. For the Prussian idea had been utterly defeated, while the Russian idea was still rising in power.[4]

The Revolution in Russia and the specter of revolution over liberated and defeated Europe left its mark on the entire settlement. Still according to Baker, the President could not risk breaking up the Conference because of "the need to hold the world steady, keep order and fight both extremes—militarism on the one hand and Bolshevism on the other."[5] This policy of caution benefited the counterrevolution more than it benefited the Revolution. Wilson wound up giving his consent to a diplomatic course that was decidedly right of center and not halfway between Foch and Lenin, as Baker implied.

Thorstein Veblen was the first to note that the compact to reduce Soviet Russia and contain Bolshevism "was not written into the text of the Treaty [but] may rather be said to have been the parchment upon which that text was written." In his view this was the only objective that the Big Four held in common. Veblen suggested, furthermore, that Wilson's "apparent defeat . . . was not so much a defeat, but rather a strategic alignment designed to compass what was indispensable, even at some cost to his own prestige—the main consideration being the defeat of Bolshevism at any cost—so that a well-considered view of the President's share in the deliberations of the Conclave would credit him with insight, courage, facility, and tenacity of purpose. . . ."[6]

In order to appreciate the world historical importance of the Paris Peace Conference, it is necessary to view it against the background of the extreme complexity of the international and domestic politics of 1918–19. This complexity was due to the convergence of the end of the Great War with the start of the Bolshevik Revolution in Russia, the collapse of political authority in Eastern and Central Europe, the threat of revolution throughout defeated Europe, and the right-wing upsurge inside the victor nations. These unanticipated and unintended con-

[4] Baker: *World Settlement*, II, 64.
[5] Ibid.
[6] See Veblen's review of Keynes: *The Economic Consequences of the Peace*, first published in the *Political Science Quarterly* (September 1920), and reprinted in Leon Ardzrooni (ed.): *Thorstein Veblen: Essays in Our Changing Order* (New York: Viking; 1934), 462–70.

sequences of the war produced conditions of national and international disequilibrium that rendered this peacemaking task more extensive and more intricate than any previously on record. Moreover, the interplay of national and international politics reached unequaled intensity. As a result, more than ever before, peacemakers had to be politicians in addition to being diplomatists. Also, the opportunities, purposes, and instruments for intervention in the internal affairs of other states assumed unparalleled proportions.

The debates and decisions of the Conference cannot be studied, therefore, as if these new conditions had not existed. The analytic framework of conventional diplomatic history simply must be enlarged to accommodate the complexities of international relations in an age of mass and crisis politics, in an age of international civil war. Furthermore, its scope must be broadened in order to show the impact of the dialectic between revolution and couterrevolution on the national and international level upon the processes of diplomacy. Thirdly, diplomatic history must abandon its national or bilateral perspective in favor of a multilateral, comparative, and transnational approach.

In any event, only a comprehensive diplomatic history can explicate the politics and diplomacy of peacemaking after the Great War. Without slighting the customary personal jealousies, national rivalries, and security dilemmas at the Paris conference table, it will then have in its purview the domestic politics in the participant nations, the specter of Bolshevism, and the intervention in Russia. Moreover, this updated diplomatic history will note that while the Peace Conference was in session in Paris, the charter meeting of the Third International was held in Moscow, the precursors of German Nazism fought Bolshevism through the Free Corps, Benito Mussolini scored his first fascist triumphs in Italy, and an awakening India provoked the British into the Amritsar massacre.

Part One

TOWARD
THE
ARMISTICE

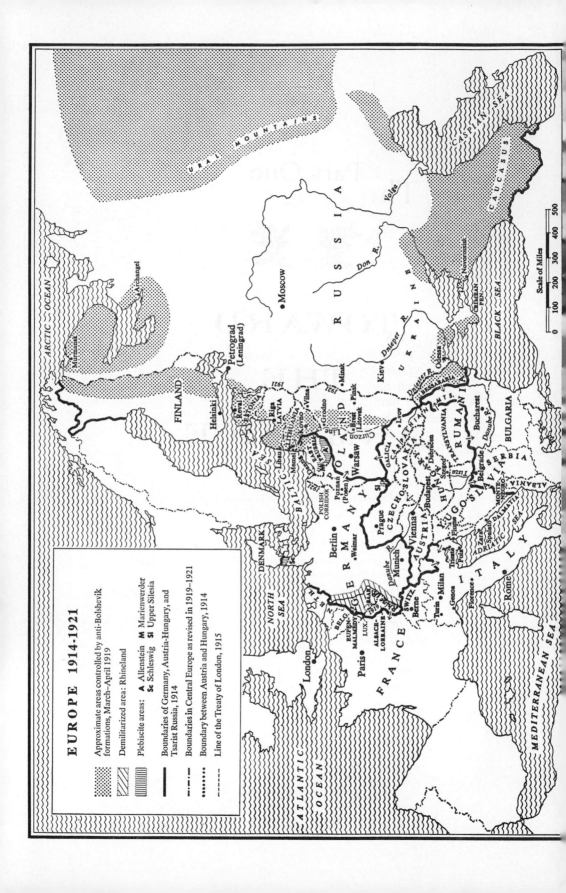

EUROPE 1914-1921

Approximate areas controlled by anti-Bolshevik formations, March–April 1919

Demilitarized area: Rhineland

Plebiscite areas: **A** Allenstein **M** Marienwerder **Sl** Upper Silesia
Sc Schleswig

Boundaries of Germany, Austria-Hungary, and Tsarist Russia, 1914

Boundaries in Central Europe as revised in 1919–1921

Boundary between Austria and Hungary, 1914

Line of the Treaty of London, 1915

Scale of Miles

0   100   200   300   400   500

ARCTIC OCEAN

URAL MOUNTAINS

CASPIAN SEA

CAUCASUS

R U S S I A

Volga

Don R.

Moscow

Archangel

Murmansk

Petrograd (Leningrad)

Dnieper

Minsk

Kiev

U K R A I N E

Odessa

CRIMEAN PEN.

Novorossisk

BLACK SEA

FINLAND

Helsinki

Reval

Libau

ESTONIA

Riga

LATVIA

Memel

LITHUANIA

Vilna

1921

Curzon Line

Grodno

Brest Litovsk

Pinsk

Dniester R.

BESSARABIA

CARPATHIAN MTS.

TRANSYLVANIA

R U M A N I A

Bucharest

Danube R.

BULGARIA

SERBIA

Belgrade

MONTE.

ALBANIA

DALMATIA

ADRIATIC SEA

Split

Fiume

Trieste

YUGOSLAVIA

Debrecen

Szeged

Tisza R.

H U N G A R Y

Budapest

AUSTRIA

Vienna

CZECHOSLOVAKIA

Prague

GALICIA

Lvov

P O L A N D

Warsaw

Poznan (Posen)

POLISH CORRIDOR

Sl

BALTIC SEA

PRUSSIA

DENMARK

NORTH SEA

Sc

G E R M A N Y

Berlin

Weimar

Danube

Munich

RHINE

EUPEN-MALMEDY

BELG.

LUX.

SAAR 1919

Sr

ALSACE-LORRAINE

Switz.

Berne

I T A L Y

Turin

Milan

Genoa

Florence

Rome

F R A N C E

Paris

London

ATLANTIC OCEAN

MEDITERRANEAN SEA

1

The Allied Left
in Retreat

AFTER JANUARY 1918 the effectiveness of Wilson's ideological appeals continued to be primarily contingent upon the course of the war. Allied military reverses were bound to feed the growth of Wilsonianism in the three Western nations while sapping its strength in the Central camp. On the other hand, any favorable turn in Allied and Associated military fortunes was destined to have the opposite effect: Wilsonianism would flourish in Central and East Central Europe at the expense of its sterilization throughout the Allied world. Meanwhile, Allied victories were likely to curtail the Bolshevik regime's disposition to persist in searching for an accommodation with Washington. Lenin expected the defeat of the Central Powers to reduce German pressure on Russia and to foster revolutionary conditions throughout Central and East Central Europe. This double reward would be partially offset, however, by the release of Allied troops and matériel for stepped-up intervention in the Russian Civil War. In any case, military developments and their political consequences determined the fate of Wilson's Fourteen Points and subsequent pronouncements. Diplomacy was relegated to playing an auxiliary role.

In preparation for discharging this adjuvant role, top officials in the Department of State set out to take the measure of political forces in both belligerent camps. In their judgment three major political divisions ran horizontally through the entire war-infested world rather than just vertically through each nation.

> The Imperialist favors the continuation of unrestricted competition between states. He aims at the aggrandizement of his native country without regard to the welfare of other countries. He is hostile to all endeavors to establish a supernational authority, such as a League of Nations. Von Tirpitz, Hertling, Radislavov, Sonnino, and Terauchi are typical Imperialists.

The Liberal is a nationalist; but a nationalist who insists that every nation has a right to be treated as an end in itself. He, therefore, hopes to see established a supernational authority as justiciar between peoples. President Wilson, Colonel House, Arthur Henderson, Albert Thomas, and Scheidemann are the world's leading Liberals.

The Social Revolutionary is a frank internationalist. He cares nothing about this war, but only about the class war which is to follow it. His vision of the future contains a world in which national lines are wiped out and the international proletariat rules. Typical Social Revolutionaries are Lenin, Trotsky, the *Avanti* group in Italy, the Spartacus group in Germany, the I.W.W. in the United States.

To facilitate the President's task of rallying support for his liberal program, U. S. ambasssadors and ministers were instructed to provide "a brief statement in regard to the men and parties in the world from whom he may expect support and those from whom he may be certain of opposition."[1]

Of course, as long as the outcome of the war continued to hang in the balance, there was more scope for diplomatic and political maneuver in support of the Wilsonian gospel in Allied than in enemy countries. But was the staff of the American embassies in London, Paris, and Rome inclined or equipped to provide balanced information about the restless Left? To be sure, W. H. Buckler was still at his post in Britain, but he had no counterpart in the other two nations. In any case, the State Department sent Ray Stannard Baker as Special Commissioner to England, France, and Italy both to survey and to contact this officially suspect segment of the political spectrum.[2] No doubt Baker was chosen largely because of his deservedly high reputation as one of

[1] Memorandum for Mr. Phillips, entitled "Instructions to Ambassadors and Ministers to report on the strength of forces of Imperialism, Liberalism, and Revolutionary Socialism in the countries to which they are accredited," June 13, 1918, in Bullitt Papers. For example, these instructions were cabled to Minister Garrett at The Hague on June 18, 1918, over Lansing's signature.

[2] Frank Polk to Ray Stannard Baker, February 15, 1918, in Baker Papers (General Correspondence), Box 2 of 18. "I spent nearly all of the year 1918 as a Special Commissioner of the State Department, visiting England, France, and Italy, and making a series of reports upon certain economic and political conditions in the Allied countries. These reports went primarily to the State Department and also to Colonel House . . . and some were transmitted direct to the President himself . . . [I] endeavored especially to see and understand the powerful undercurrents, the labour and liberal movements, at work in all these countries. I had also a close view of the [front line] war itself. . . . This experience I found invaluable in giving me a clear understanding of the backgrounds of the Peace Conference; the real foundations of military force and economic need upon which it rested; and the atmosphere of suffering, dread, hatred, newly aroused ambitions, in which, at Paris, the discussions took place. Too many of the critics in America of the Conference have been without an understanding of these underlying and precedent conditions." Baker: *Woodrow Wilson and World Settlement,* I, xxxi.

America's foremost journalists and muckrakers. In addition to having a superb reportorial instinct and a crisp style, he was finely attuned to the ideas and dispositions of the dissident Left, which he was instructed to seek out. Unlike the ambassadors and their regular staffs, whose contacts were confined "to the Old, the Privileged, and the Well Established," Baker was primarily interested in "the New, the Struggling, the Undeveloped, the Dispossessed." He saw it as his "principal job to examine and try to understand the great Radical and Liberal forces" which found no expression in America.[3]

Baker arrived in Britain in late February 1918. Within a few weeks he reported that he was "all but living" with Labour and Radical leaders and "with students of the labor movement." He conferred with Arthur Henderson, G. D. H. Cole, Graham Wallas, A. E. Zimmern, and Gilbert Murray.[4] His on-the-spot explorations confirmed some of the Inquiry's earlier conclusions: many Asquith Liberals, all the Radicals, and nearly the entire Labour movement stood with Wilson. Herbert Asquith and his supporters, accepting Wilson's program, would make "no demands for territory anywhere, either in Africa, Mesopotamia, or Palestine." Meanwhile, the *Memorandum on War Aims* adopted by the Inter-Allied Labour and Socialist Conference of February 20–4—"which, in confidence, was largely the work of Sidney Webb" and of which Baker enclosed a copy—had "unified to a remarkable degree the labor and liberal forces of Great Britain."[5] Baker was particularly heartened because "even Ramsay MacDonald had come around until he now stood practically upon the Wilson-War-Aims platform."[6] But unlike so many other American observers, Baker also stressed the dual objective of these composite forces of change: whereas externally they wanted "to bring about a League of Nations," internally they were striving for "control of the government by democratic elements, and the sweeping adoption of social reforms."[7]

It was on House's advice that in mid-July the Department of State instructed Baker to proceed to France and Italy "to make reports

---

[3] Baker to Polk, April 4 and October 26, 1918, in Baker Papers (Letters to the Department of State), Box 3 of 18.

[4] Baker to Polk, March 18 and April 4, 1918, in Baker Papers (Letters to the Department of State), Box 3 of 18. Presently, Baker received the following note from Buckler: "I have heard that you are investigating conditions in this country, and as there is a question relating to Labor on which I find it difficult to get information (for the private use of the State Department) I venture to ask if I may call on you and explain my difficulty." Buckler to Baker, April 28, 1918, in Baker Papers (General Correspondence), Box 2 of 18.

[5] For a discussion of this Conference and Memorandum see my *Political Origins of the New Diplomacy, 1917–1918*, 388–9.

[6] Baker to Polk, March 10 and 18, 1918, in Baker Papers (Letters to the Department of State), Box 3 of 18.

[7] Baker to Polk, April 4, 1918, in Baker Papers (Letters to the Department of State), Box 3 of 18.

similar to those he [had] been making in England."[8] In Paris, as in London, he found the "sincerest support for Wilson . . . among the radical and labor groups."[9] But of the three nations he visited none struck Baker as "more hopeful, so far as support for our program was concerned, than Italy." In his estimate "nowhere [else] was Mr. Wilson so felt, so instinctively understood." Actually, the Italian Left was too restless even for Baker's advanced tastes. The Maximalists, who even then were veering from Wilson to Lenin, had a firm grip on the powerful Socialist Party. In the event of a persisting military deadlock, accompanied by food shortages, there was "almost certain to be internal trouble." Only as long as "the Allies were winning . . . and talk of early peace was in the air, could the situation be nursed along."[1]

Indeed, Baker was so eager to see the *enragés* tamed, in Italy as well as in the two other Allied countries, that he was not willing to wait for military victory to chasten them; he also feared that the retribution of victory would be excessively harsh. He wanted the war cabinets, which stimulated Socialist militancy by their blatant subservience to conservative elements, to be prevailed upon to take Wilsonianism more seriously, while the fighting was still in progress.

As early as mid-April, Baker charged all the Allied leaders with being "realists" who wanted little beyond military victory and an "old-fashioned peace, with a scant effort to realize any of Mr. Wilson's ideals."[2] Once in France he reported that even more than in England "the Government and Conservative leaders supported Wilson more or less with their tongues in their cheeks, as a matter of policy." All they really wanted were America's "powerful armies and naval resources." But as for U. S. war aims, as formulated by the President, these they considered "more or less moonshine."[3] According to Baker, the "men who were in control" at best gave Wilson's aims "a kind of perfunctory lip-service, but the spirit was not in them." They were far more interested "in trade preferences and enlarged territory" than in the League of Nations. By August Baker could not help but notice that "every little turn of the tide toward military victory" brought forth "bare-faced expressions of what victory meant to these reactionary groups." What worried the muckraker-turned-diplomat was that this surfacing of the Old Diplomacy "made labor restless and increased its suspicion and

[8] Polk to Baker, July 13, 1918, and House to Baker, July 18, 1918, in Baker Papers (General Correspondence), Boxes 1 and 2 of 18.
[9] Baker (Paris) to Polk, July 27, 1918, in Baker Papers (Letters to the Department of State), Box 3 of 18.
[1] Baker (Rome) to Polk, September 28 and October 26, 1918, in Baker Papers (Letters to the Department of State), Box 3 of 18.
[2] Baker to Polk, April 11, 1918, in Baker Papers (Letters to the Department of State), Box 3 of 18.
[3] Baker (Paris) to Polk, July 27, 1918, in Baker Papers (Letters to the Department of State), Box 3 of 18.

hostility to the Governments,"[4] the more so because these governments also opposed labor's postwar domestic aspirations.

Quite mistakenly Baker assumed that in the impending "final death grapple between the old order and the new" the forces of stability would easily be overwhelmed by the forces of change. In his judgment the "reactionary government forces . . . were really rotten to the core" and lacking in both unity and vision. The labor and radical forces, for their part, were rapidly gaining in strength, *élan,* and determination, to the point that the "older leaders" were in danger of being surpassed by their militant rivals.[5] Needless to say, this resulting emasculation of the moderate forces and leaders of change jeopardized the prospects for a nonpunitive peace.

Baker urged that Washington support Socialists and Radicals in their two-front struggle against the hardened governments and the Left revolutionaries. He wanted the President to renew his ideological offensive in order to help Henderson and Jean Longuet hold the allegiance of the "doubtful labor elements," which were fast expanding. Of late, with Wilson content to let his views be "interpreted and twisted by the reactionary leaders . . . , the democratic groups which in the past gave him his only and sincere support" tended to question and doubt his resolve; there was no longer the "same enthusiastic approval of Wilson's position . . . as three or five months ago."[6] Baker even sensed a gnawing fear among British Labour and Radical leaders that notwithstanding Wilson, "the war spirit would run entirely away with America, and that America, coming freshly and enthusiastically into the war, would become so intent on a 'knock-out blow' that it would fail to seize opportunities" for a diplomatic settlement of the conflict.[7] In any case, particularly because Wilson could never hope for "whole-hearted support . . . from those at the moment in power" in the Allied countries, he should not allow the democratic forces to get away from him, as they were threatening to do.[8]

Baker became so desperate about the restlessness of the forces of movement in the face of America's apparent retreat from her idealistic position that he wrote to House directly.

[4] Baker to Polk, August 10, 1918, in Baker Papers (Letters to the Department of State), Box 3 of 18.
[5] Baker (London) to Polk, August 19 and 24, 1918, in Baker Papers (Letters to the Department of State), Box 3 of 18.
[6] Baker (London) to Polk, July 6 and August 10, 1918, in Baker Papers (Letters to the Department of State), Box 3 of 18.
[7] Baker (London) to Polk, July 8, 1918, in Baker Papers (Letters to the Department of State), Box 3 of 18. House conceded that as America "was getting up so much momentum . . . here and there the old commercial and imperialistic spirit" asserted itself. But he assured Baker that "the great body of our people were actuated by idealistic considerations." House to Baker, July 18, 1918, in Baker Papers (General Correspondence), Box 1 of 18.
[8] Baker (London) to Polk, August 10, 1918, in Baker Papers (Letters to the Department of State), Box 3 of 18.

When I first came here in March and for two or three months afterwards the whole labor and liberal group was strongly with us, but of late there have been many doubtful voices and a decided tendency to question our purposes, and to *wonder whether the American war spirit, which from this side seems to be rolling up into a tremendous volume, will take the world.* . . . Our true supporters here, the only group which believes sincerely in the Wilson program, is this labor and liberal group . . . [which] we ought never to let get away from us. Never was there such a need of constructive and idealistic leadership as now—nor of a unified political command. . . . [This] leadership must positively come from us—from Mr. Wilson. Mr. Wilson has touched the imagination of the world as no other leader has done or could do—but the most difficult part of the problem still remains ahead of us [italics mine].[9]

As the President maintained his silence Baker reported that radical leaders kept asking whether "Wilson really meant it" and whether they could "count on his following to put his program through"?[1]

These same concerns were reflected in the reports of Walter Lippmann, whose intelligence mission overlapped with Baker's. But in addition to taking soundings among popular elements he also conferred with high officials of the British Foreign Office, notably with Sir William Tyrrell and Sir Eustace Percy. He, too, noticed a "growing feeling that the old liberal leadership of the President had not been exercised sufficiently in the last few months." Like Baker, he was afraid that Wilson's silence would foster left-wing radicalism. But Lippmann was afraid that such radicalism would also rebound to the Right's advantage. He took the view that unless the President made a major address before the middle of October—"an address which would resound all over the world and was on par with his greatest speeches"—the impending general election in Britain could turn out to be "a very dangerous and a very ugly business." Following a conversation with Percy, Lippmann predicted accurately that with an improving military situation "the election might develop into a contest as to who could make the most violent statements."[2]

Lippmann's informants in the Foreign Office were so apprehensive about the diplomatic consequences of America's growing disregard for the political purposes of the war and about the bipolarization of domestic politics that Percy took the unusual step of preparing a personal statement for transmission to Colonel House.

America is resigning her place . . . as leader in democratic idealism. . . . The President's "war without stint" is a war in which

---

[9] Baker (London) to House, August 19, 1918, in House Papers, 2:7.
[1] Baker (Rome) to Polk, October 26, 1918, in Baker Papers (Letters to the Department of State), Box 3 of 18.
[2] Lippmann (London) to House, August 21, 1918, in House Papers, 9:17.

there is no hurry. . . . This war effort in the United States has stimulated American nationalism and makes America impatient of international ideals as if they were a form of pacifism. . . . America is saying . . . "let us have nothing that distracts our attention from the immediate task of the war."

[But] America cannot commend this appeal to us over here because the "immediate task of the war" is not to her, as to us, the task of securing an immediate conclusion of the war. . . . *We cannot damp down . . . America's determination to go on with the war as long as necessary. We cannot get over the colossal fact of America's conscious nationalism.* . . . In this dawn of her strength America cannot be expected to contemplate clearly a peaceful universal league including the enemy nation whom she so fervently hates.

. . . Out of an [inter-Allied] concentration of resources [during hostilities], a true league of nations can be evolved after the war. . . . *But if the President and the Government of the U.S. are to promote this policy, they must do so conscientiously and openly as the real path to a league of nations.* This policy will, I feel sure, lead public opinion in the Allied countries, and *take the sting out of vague labour movements* in favor of an interbelligerent socialist conference. *It will convince Allied labour that the Governments are really leading opinion in regard to the settlement of the world.* An essential part of it to this end will be a scheme which I can't see clearly at present, but which I am convinced is practicable, *for international arrangements for the protection of labour standards of living in all countries who are members of the Association of Nations* . . . [italics mine].[3]

This, then, was a semiofficial appeal by liberal conservatives or conservative liberals within the British government to House and Wilson to help them formulate a platform that would be attractive to the bulk of Labour and Radicals without being totally objectionable to the Tories, and that could form the basis for negotiations with the enemy.

At long last, on September 27, 1918, when inaugurating the Fourth Liberty Loan, Wilson forcefully reaffirmed his underlying peace principles. By then, however, the tide of battle had turned decisively in favor of the Allies and Austria-Hungary's first note requesting an armistice was a week old. This being so, Lloyd George, Clemenceau, and Orlando became still less inclined to yield to Wilson and to pacify the Left, while becoming doubly responsive to the Right.

As a result Baker concluded that it was a chief task of American statesmanship to supplement olympian pronouncements with other

[3] Statement by Sir Eustace Percy, transcribed and transmitted by Lippmann to House, August 21, 1918, in House Papers, 9:17. Lippmann noted that the feelings expressed by Percy "existed practically universally among the Liberals and Radicals from C. P. Scott down," but that he was "a good deal surprised to find how strong this feeling was among the men he had talked to in the Foreign Office."

methods for rallying the Radical and Socialist forces around Wilson. Incidentally, Baker consistently exaggerated the power of the Radical and Socialist Left, insisting that in the making of the peace the Left would make itself felt either constructively or destructively. He never allowed for the possibility that the non-Bolshevik Left might be checked by the superpatriots and crippled by sectarian conflicts.

Baker submitted two proposals to House upon the latter's arrival in Paris. He urged that the President come personally to Europe and get in touch with the leaders of the Radical and Socialist Left. Even if he "merely listened to them it would help vastly," though it would be better still if in conferences Wilson could convince them that he "was on the side of the people and intended to 'go through.'" At some later stage he might even have "to make, or threaten to make, an appeal direct to the people over the heads of the obstructors—as he did once in New Jersey." Baker's second suggestion was that Wilson "throw his support in favor of some form of international conference of workers, not necessarily Socialists, but all workers." Since the Socialists were in any case determined to hold such a conference, it might be advisable to sponsor it, possibly with the help of Samuel Gompers; and "the President himself might address this assembly and bring them to the support of his method." Meanwhile, even mere endorsement would add tremendously to Wilson's "prestige among all these classes, and it would *let off a lot of dangerous steam* in conferences and talk" [italics mine].[4]

Down to the Armistice, then, Baker worried less about the burgeoning growth of the Right than about the restlessness within the forces of movement which threatened to rebound to Lenin's advantage. In order to contain the defection of militant Socialists he wanted Wilson to reassure the Radical and Social Democratic Left that he stood by his Fourteen Points. Without this pressure for a nonpunitive peace the President would find it altogether impossible to shake the Big Three loose from their conservative and reactionary supporters.

Another method of bolstering the loyalty of the Allied forces of movement originated in the United States. Having effectively stimulated the patriotism, enthusiasm, and productivity of their own workers, America's labor leaders turned their attention to Europe. Whereas Baker went abroad to inquire how best to foster left-wing support for a Wilsonian diplomacy and peace, various American labor missions simply set out to "inspire the workers in Allied countries to the same single-minded devotion to prosecuting the War that characterized the American workingman."[5] To be sure, the Wilson Administration approved of these labor missions, but the prime movers were the Allied Governments. Especially in April and May 1918, when the German

[4] Baker (Paris) to House, November 1, 1918, in House Papers, 9:17.
[5] James T. Shotwell (ed.): *The Origins of the International Labor Organization* (New York: Columbia University Press; 1934), I, 99.

offensive was at its peak, they wanted to tame their own dissidents with the help of American labor spokesmen, whose war enthusiasm knew no bounds. In turn, the cabinets were prodded by the Social Patriots who were eagerly looking for reinforcements in their uphill struggle with the *minoritaires*.[6]

The first A.F. of L. mission, headed by James Wilson of the Patternmakers' League and composed of seven men and two women, visited Britain and France in April–May 1918.[7] To make sure that the U. S. Embassy in England would smooth the way for these delegates, Secretary Lansing assured Ambassador Walter Hines Page that they did not intend to "consider or discuss the policies or in any way interfere with the avowed purposes" of the American government or of any of the Allied Governments.[8]

On their rounds the members of the mission stressed emphatically that the war needed to be fought to a finish; that there could be no talk of peace until this victory had been won; and that it was heresy even to consider meeting with enemy Socialists in wartime. One American delegate even told an assembly of shop stewards that their job was "to beat the Hun first and settle their working differences afterwards." No effort was made to disguise the official auspices under which this mission had come to Britain. The delegates were welcomed at 10 Downing Street and Westminster; they spoke at mass meetings sponsored by the National War Aims Committee; and they attended a special dinner given by the Industrial League. Their hosts were George N. Barnes and G. H. Roberts, the two Labour Ministers, and even Havelock Wilson, the supreme Social Patriot—not the official leaders of the Labour movement.[9]

When they did meet with the Executive and Parliamentary Committee of the Party, James Wilson and his colleagues refused to endorse the February Memorandum on War Aims, claiming that the A.F. of L.'s own statement on war aims, adopted at its Buffalo Convention of 1917, was "inspired by similar principles." Evidently the British Labourites were more Wilsonian than their American interlocutors. There was agreement, however, that labor should ask to be represented at the Peace Conference and that a Labour Congress should be called to meet concurrently with this Peace Conference.[1] But this agreement was overshadowed by irreconcilable differences about the price to exact

[6] G. Paul Kellogg and Arthur Gleason: *British Labor and the War: Reconstructors for a New World* (New York: Boni and Liveright; 1919), 249–50.

[7] For the composition of this mission see Labour Party: *Report of the Eighteenth Annual Conference* (London, 1918), 7.

[8] Lansing to Page, April 2, 1918, cited in *F.R.,1918, Supplement 1*, I, 189.

[9] Kellogg and Gleason: *British Labor and the War*, 253.

[1] Labour Party: *Report of the Eighteenth Annual Conference*, 8–10; and Baker to Polk, April 30, 1918, in Baker Papers (Letters to the Department of State), Box 3 of 18.

for labor's continuing war enthusiasm and the question of holding an interbelligerent Socialist conference before the end of the war.

These two issues were but the occasion for the manifestation of fundamental ideological, political, and social divergences between American trade unionists and Allied Socialists. The former were syndical, nonpartisan, and pragmatic in outlook; the latter were Socialist, political, and ideological. Both Buckler and Baker realized that the gulf was too wide to be bridged, as was the gulf between Henderson and Havelock Wilson. While regretting this public display of discord in the Left, Buckler and Baker took some comfort from the fact that Camille Huysmans, Sidney Webb, and Henderson realized that "limitations, intellectual and otherwise, made it practically impossible for these American delegates to carry back to America an accurate report of the attitude toward war problems held by their European colleagues."[2]

But the British and the French cabinets cared little about the information these trade unionists might convey to America. They wanted labor endorsement for their policies, and this James Wilson seemed to provide, though with what degree of success is not clear. The American mission may have had a more favorable impact in France, where its stay was very brief, than in Britain, even though Buckler felt that its "intercourse with French Socialists did not tend towards harmony."[3] In any case, Ambassador William G. Sharp reported that "many members of the French Government, among them Mr. Clemenceau and Mr. Pichon, expressed to me their greatest satisfaction over the helpful influence which these delegates had exerted among the labor elements in France."[4] As for the *Temps* and the bulk of the press, after crediting the A.F. of L. with effectively blocking the resumption of relations with German Social Democracy, they predicted that hereafter the Second International's orientation would be decided in Washington rather than in Berlin.[5]

Eustace Percy was not nearly so sanguine about the outcome. Perhaps the American minutemen had only preached to the converted. Certainly "Sidney Webb's mind and the mind of the American Delegation simply did not meet at all." Not that Percy was particularly keen on Webb, who invariably reminded him of the prophet Jeremiah's exclamation that "my soul shall weep in secret places for their pride."[6] But he was worried, as were Buckler and Baker, that the American labor delegates' gospel of Social Patriotism was too crude, and hence ineffective, for war-weary workers who were about to enter their fifth year of effort, strain, and sacrifice.

[2] Buckler to House, June 29, 1918, in Buckler Papers.
[3] Buckler to House, June 18, 1918, in Buckler Papers.
[4] Sharp to Lansing, May 12, 1918, in *F.R.,1918, Supplement 1,* I, 230.
[5] *Le Temps,* July 8, 1918.
[6] Eustace Percy (Political Intelligence Department, Foreign Office) to William Bullitt, July 2, 1918, in Bullitt Papers.

Even so, the experiment was worth continuing, especially if Gompers himself could be prevailed upon to cross the Atlantic. Early in 1918 the President of the A.F. of L. had received many urgent requests to visit Europe from prominent Allied government and labor officials. The returning labor mission was asked to urge acceptance of these invitations strongly. Lord Northcliffe also pressed for his early visit.[7] At the same time Gompers himself came to the conclusion that the American labor situation was "in a fairly satisfactory condition . . . [and that] the virile courage and clearcut declarations of American labor stood out in sharp contrast to the hesitant attitude of labor in other countries." Under the circumstances "the service he could render by going to Europe would be more than he could at home."[8]

According to his own testimony Gompers resolved to go on a "Paul Revere mission"[9] to warn the great rank and file against the insidious influence of labor leaders whose outlook was political, international, pacifist, pro-German, and Socialist. Once in Europe he did not hesitate to tell an Inter-Allied Socialist and Labor Conference that Socialism holds nothing

> but unhappiness for the human race. It destroys personal initiative, wipes out national pride—and finally it plays into the hands of the autocrats. One has only to watch its ravages on the human soul— the soul without a country—to know that Socialism is the fad of fanatics, the sophistry of the so-called intelligentsia, and it has no place in the hearts of those who would secure and fight for freedom and preserve democracy.[1]

Gompers was determined to challenge and discredit the leadership of the Allied Socialist and labor movements. He considered each to be "dominated by some professor, some failure in professional life, who had got his fangs into the labor movement and usually poisoned and destroyed it."[2]

Not surprisingly, therefore, the impending visit by Gompers caused profound uneasiness in Allied labor circles, particularly since the British government and press hailed it as a timely antidote to pacifism in the labor movement. Rumors began to sweep London that Gompers was "coming to try to break up the Labour Party" and to head up an international organization to combat the renascent Second International, which was associated with Henderson and Longuet. Buckler informed House that according to Sidney Webb it was not desirable

---

[7] George L. Berry to House, August 2, 1918, in House Papers, 2:33. Berry was President of the International Printing Pressmen and had been a member of the James Wilson mission.

[8] Samuel Gompers: *Seventy Years of Life and Labor: An Autobiography* (New York: E. P. Dutton; 1925), II, 407–9.

[9] Gompers: *Seventy Years,* II, 411.

[1] Cited in ibid., II, 431.

[2] Cited in *The American Federationist,* December 1918, 1084–5.

that "any more American labor delegates preaching the doctrine of the 'knock-out-blow' and of complete non-intercourse with German Socialism" should come to Britain and France at this time. Similarly Baker advised the Colonel that to bring war-weary men "a message of interminable war, and for no clear democratic or socially constructive purpose, as Gompers would probably do, was not very promising." As it was, "older type labor leaders" like Barnes were finding it difficult to keep the upper hand in certain working-class districts, and Barnes was one of the men of whom the recent A.F. of L. delegation had so "highly approved." Baker even warned that the coming of Gompers was likely to accentuate labor unrest.[3] Inevitably Gompers would bolster the minority factions behind W. A. Appleton and Will Thorne against Henderson and C. W. Bowerman, who spoke for the vast majority of the Labour Party and the Trades Union Congress.[4]

Presently Eustace Percy and Colonel A. C. Murray, who had recently been on mission to Washington, summoned Buckler to notify him of their concern that Gompers's visit might stir up friction throughout the labor world; "the attitude of the press and indiscreet jingo utterances" might even contribute to changing the attitude of hitherto prowar labor elements.

> They both think, therefore, that it is of great importance *to keep the British Government in the background* and not to let British Labor suppose either that the Government or that the Northcliffe and Beaverbrook press is backing or pressing Mr. Gompers' views on the British Labour Party. They understand that if Mr. Barnes entertains Mr. Gompers he will do it as a representative of Labor and not as a member of the Government, though it is not clear that this distinction can be plainly marked. They say that the Northcliffe and Beaverbrook press had been privately warned not to indulge during Mr. Gompers' visit *in the expression of ecclesiastical approval* which they have used on several occasions recently . . . [italics mine].[5]

In turn, Gompers could help the situation by talking about plans "for the protection of labor standards of living" in the member nations of the future League. "If Gompers would only take up such a line as this . . . , he would produce a far more healthy revulsion of feeling in our Labour Party than by sticking to the tiresome issue about the Stockholm Conference."[6]

In spite of these behind-the-scenes trepidations among officials of

[3] Buckler to House, June 18, 1918, in Buckler Papers; Baker to House, August 19, 1918, in House Paper, 2:7; Baker to Polk, June 30 and August 24, 1918, in Baker Papers (Letters to the Department of State), Box 3 of 18.
[4] Cf. Page to Lansing (drafted by Buckler), August 20, 1918, cited in *F.R.,1918, Supplement 1,* I, 298–9.
[5] Buckler to House, August 24, 1918, in Buckler Papers.
[6] Statement by Sir Eustace Percy, transcribed and transmitted by Walter Lippmann to House, August 21, 1918, in House Papers, 9:17.

conservative liberal persuasion, when Gompers sailed for Liverpool on August 16, 1918, he was assumed to be answering an urgent summons from the Allied cabinets and to have the unqualified blessings of his own government. Actually Wilson appears to have been less enthusiastic than House about Gompers's venture abroad. The President found Gompers's vanity and arrogance altogether offensive, and he could not fathom his undisguised contempt for ideas and ideology. Even so, Wilson, who desperately needed Gompers's political backing, knew that Gompers had his mind set on the trip, that the Allies wanted him in their service, and that Colonel House had promoted the enterprise. Thus America's most prestigious labor leader embarked on a mission that would fire the war enthusiasm of Allied workingmen at the cost of simultaneously sapping the political and social forces favorable to a Wilsonian settlement. Incidentally, chances for a sane peace would have been improved considerably could Gompers have been prevailed upon to join forces with Henderson, Longuet, Giacinto Serrati, and Huysmans. But, needless to say, such a rapprochement was not within the realm of possibility.

Once in Europe Gompers and his fellow delegates[7] moved back and forth between meetings with high government officials, appearances before labor groups, and conferences with Labour leaders. The official visit in England began on August 30 when the British government demonstratively honored the mission with a luncheon at the Carleton Hotel. On this occasion George Henry Roberts, Secretary of the Norwich Typographical Association and Minister of Labour in the Cabinet, freely declared that "the contact of our guests with patriotic labour in this country will help us to defeat the efforts of those who would trick us into meeting with enemy subjects."[8] This luncheon as well as a dinner at Parliament House the following night were presided over by George Barnes, the Minister of Pensions. On both occasions Roberts and Barnes, in line with Eustace Percy's prescription, appeared in their Labour rather than their ministerial capacities. That the Cabinet prized the visit very highly was evident from the distinguished attendance at these and other official functions, which included Lloyd George, Balfour, Milner, Churchill, Robert Cecil, Austen Chamberlain, Lord Reading, Smuts, and Hughes. Moreover, Gompers not only sat "between Mr. Barnes and the Prime Minister" but also was taken to Buckingham Palace to be presented to the King and Queen. Later during this European trip, Gompers was also received by King Albert and by King Victor Emmanuel.[9]

In between these official occasions the American delegation at-

---

[7] The other members of the mission were Charles L. Baine, W. J. Bowen, John P. Frey, and Edgar Wallace. Guy H. Oster served as secretary.

[8] Cited in Kellogg and Gleason: *British Labor and the War,* 277.

[9] Gompers: *Seventy Years,* II, 416–17, 437, 447, 460; and Baker to House, September 1, 1918, in Baker Papers (Letters to the Department of State), Box 3 of 18.

tended a Trades Union Congress at Derby, a joint conference of the Parliamentary Committee and the Executive Committee of the Labour Party, and meetings of both the Edinburgh and the London Trades Councils. Gompers seized all these occasions to preach complete loyalty to the Cabinet, to proclaim a fight to the finish against German autocracy and militarism, to reiterate his refusal to meet with enemy Socialists during wartime, and to assert that the A.F. of L. alone was entitled to speak for American labor. When this last assertion was challenged he "replied that there was no such thing as an American Socialist Party but [only] a German adjunct in America of the German Socialist Party."[1]

In France and Italy the visit took a similar course. In Paris the official luncheon was attended by Clemenceau, Stephen Pichon, and André Tardieu. Gompers also conferred privately with Clemenceau, President Poincaré, and Marshal Joffre. Moreover, at the invitation of Paul Deschanel, the American labor leader addressed the Chamber of Deputies. On his labor rounds he attended a rally at which Alphonse Merrheim and other syndicalists—not Socialists—criticized the Entente's war aims and clamored for a Stockholm conference. Gompers claims that he listened to "their fantastic and irrational proposals as long as he could endure them and then tersely told them they were traitors to the cause of the people of France."[2] Before leaving France he spoke to Aristide Briand about his plan to reorganize the International of workers independent of political parties.[3]

In Italy the government gave a reception in the Capitol and a concert at the Augusteo; there were conferences with top officials; and cabinet members came to the railway station to publicize Gompers's departure from Rome for three major industrial centers. The mission proceeded to Turin, Milan, and Genoa, where antiwar sentiment was strongest. According to Ambassador Page, in these cities as in Rome, where antiwar Socialists tried to sabotage the mass labor rally to be addressed by Gompers, "there was a strong undercurrent against [the American delegates] among the Socialists who held that being pro-war was being anti-Socialist, since true Socialism was against all war." In spite of the total boycott by the Italian Socialist Party (ISP), the mission was reported to have "accomplished great good."[4]

In February Gompers had refused to attend the Inter-Allied Socialist and Labor Conference because the invitation had reached him at

[1] Gompers: *Seventy Years,* II, 417–21.
[2] Ibid., II, 440–6; and Sharp to Lansing, September 29, 1918, cited in *F.R., 1918, Supplement 1,* I, 330–1.
[3] Georges Suarez: *Briand: Sa Vie–Son Oeuvre* (Paris: Plon; 1940), IV, 387.
[4] Gompers: *Seventy Years,* II, 455–67; and *F.R.,1918, Supplement 1,* I, 378. A third A. F. of L. mission, again headed by James Wilson, visited Italy in September–October 1918. See A. F. of L.: *Report of the Proceedings of the 39th Annual Convention* (Atlantic City, June 9–23, 1919), 186–90.

the last minute and because the Henderson-Longuet axis appeared
certain of gaining the upper hand. The follow-up Inter-Allied Conference was scheduled to meet in London on September 17–20, 1918.
Since he was about to do battle against the independent-minded Socialists in Britain, France, and Italy, Gompers now considered accepting
an invitation to present his case in this transnational arena as well. But
before doing so he tried to drive a wedge between the trade unionists
and the Socialists. Accordingly, he wired C. W. Bowerman, W. A.
Appleton, and Léon Jouhaux—not Henderson—that the A.F. of L.
would be represented only provided the conference were restricted to
"*bona fide* Labor Representatives." This stratagem to exclude Socialists
failed, in that a cable signed by both Bowerman and Henderson notified
him that the Parliamentary Committee of the Trades Union Congress
(T.U.C.) and the Labour Party Executive had called an "inter-Allied
Conference of *bona fide* Labour Representatives including all Parties
[represented] at the inter-Allied Conference [of last] February, which
you were unable to attend."[5] Gompers yielded grudgingly.

When the conference convened on September 17 the moderate
elements were in a better position than seven months before. The five
A.F. of L. delegates, representing more than three million wage earners,
enlisted all of organized American labor in the ranks of Social Patriotism,[6] Gompers having bluntly refused to "sit in the same Congress
with delegates representing the American Socialist Party."[7] The official
Italian Socialist Party stayed away, in part to protest this exclusion of
American Socialists, thereby weakening the far left at the very time that
the A.F. of L. reinforced the far right.[8]

The question of an interbelligerent conference once again became
the touchstone of the deliberations. In February the Inter-Allied Socialist Conference had instructed the British delegation to communicate the
Memorandum on War Aims to the enemy Socialist parties with the
request that they declare themselves on it. By August the Bulgarian,
Hungarian, Austrian, and German parties, including the German Independents, had responded.[9] Whereas the first three accepted the Memo-

---

[5] This exchange of cables is cited in Labour Party: Minutes of the Executive Committee, 14, Minutes of August 8, 1918.

[6] "Albert Thomas is *persona grata* to Gompers, as they were in almost complete agreement at the [September] Conference." William E. Walling to Lansing, October 2,
1918, in Wilson Papers, II:150.

[7] Cited in Labour Party: Minutes of the Executive Committee, 14, Minutes of a joint
meeting on September 6, 1918, of the Parliamentary Committee of the T.U.C.
and the Executive Committee of the Labour Party, together with the delegation
of the A.F. of L.

[8] For the most comprehensive treatment of this Inter-Allied Socialist and Labour Conference see the contemporary report by Kellogg and Gleason: *British Labor and
the War*, 286–304.

[9] For the full text of these answers see Inter-Allied Labour and Socialist Conference:
*The Replies of the Socialist Parties of the Central Powers to the "Memorandum on
War Aims"* (London, 1918).

randum as a basis for discussion, the German Social Democrats, though willing to attend an interbelligerent meeting, were not prepared to do so. Even P. J. Troelstra, who had recently conferred with Philipp Scheidemann and was well disposed toward the Socialists of the Central Powers, "discovered, with manifest chagrin and disappointment, that in spite of four years of warfare the German Socialists were not animated by a new spirit." Henderson concluded, therefore, that "it would be both futile and harmful to make any attempt to organize an immediate international conference." His fear was that to do so would "provoke divisions within the several countries, and what was more important, [possibly provoke] a fatal split among some of the parties which had found such an encouraging measure of unity at the February Conference."[1]

Henderson summoned the September Conference to declare the SPD's (Sozialdemokratische Partei) reply "an obstacle" to the holding of an interbelligerent meeting; and, while reaffirming faith in the project, to appoint a commission which would seek to change the German attitude. This proposal was attacked from the left as well as from the right. Longuet, whose *minoritaires* were about to capture control of the SFIO (Section française de l'Internationale Ouvrière), unsuccessfully advocated an unconditional meeting with the German Socialists. Gompers was overwhelmingly rebuffed when he moved that delegates of Allied workingmen would "meet in conference with those only of the Central Powers who were in open revolt against their autocratic governors":[2] only the one Canadian and the four right-wing Italians sided with him. To make matters worse, over A.F. of L. abstention the Allied Socialists once again condemned the governments' intransigent passport policy,[3] with the warning that continuation of this policy was "bound to lead to an acceptance of the government's challenge by the organized labor movement . . . , the patience of the organized working people rapidly becoming exhausted by [such] continued affronts. . . ."[4]

Actually, the majority's radicalism was more apparent than real. To

---

[1] "For the Executive: Private and Confidential Memorandum by Arthur Henderson on Inter-Allied Conference Decisions, February 20–24, 1918," submitted and discussed on September 4, 1918, at joint meeting of the Parliamentary Committee of the T.U.C. and the Executive Committee of the Labour Party, and cited in Labour Party: Minutes of the Executive Committee, 14.

[2] For this motion as well as for the full text of most other resolutions and memoranda considered and voted by this Conference, see Labour Party: *Report of the Nineteenth Annual Conference* (Southport, 1919), 4–11.

[3] In August the British government again denied passports to Henderson and Bowerman. This time they had asked to go to Switzerland to discuss the enemy Socialists' replies to the Memorandum on War Aims with Troelstra, who had been refused admission to England. Page to Lansing, August 13, 1918, cited in *F.R., 1918, Supplement 1*, I, 297–8.

[4] Cited in Kellogg and Gleason: *British Labor and the War*, 303.

be sure, the fears of Baker, Buckler, and Percy were amply justified: by pressing the "tiresome" Stockholm issue, which had such burning symbolic and emotional overtones, Gompers antagonized even many of those who welcomed him as an ally against the internationalists. However, on two other major items on the agenda—war aims and intervention in Russia—the A.F. of L. exercised a moderating influence.

Shortly after his arrival in England Gompers was invited to prepare a comment on the Inter-Allied War Aims Memorandum for consideration at the September Conference.[5] Undoubtedly Henderson hoped against hope that Gompers would give his unqualified endorsement, thereby rallying the entire Allied and Associated Left around an advanced Wilsonian platform. But when Gompers presented his war-aims resolution he never even referred to the Memorandum which he found objectionable both because it dared criticize the Allied Governments and because it pressed for an interbelligerent conference. In more general terms, Gompers was not about to approve the platform with which the majority of British Labour and Continental Socialism was opposing him in the international politics of labor.

In his resolution, therefore, after pledging unqualified support for the war, Gompers preferred to call for the endorsement of Wilson's Fourteen Points. Moreover, as part of his campaign to ditch political Socialism in favor of bread-and-butter unionism, and in line with Percy's suggestion, he proposed that any future peace treaty include an economic and political bill of rights for wage earners. Such a charter would recognize that "the labor of a human being was not a commodity or article of commerce," stipulate that "the right of free association, free assemblage, free speech and free press shall not be abridged," and declare that "the basic workday in industry and commerce shall not exceed eight hours per day."[6]

Gompers's resolution was referred to a subcommittee on war aims which considered it in conjunction with the British delegation's report on the replies from the parties of the Central Powers. After rather hasty deliberations this committee presented for adoption a memorandum designed to blend the two, though in fact it was slanted in favor of Henderson's position. Accordingly, the conference was asked to welcome the confirmation that Wilson's Fourteen Points, presented by the A.F. of L., "gave to the proposals contained in the [February] Memorandum on War Aims"; to "accept these 14 propositions as a concise summary of the main principles which [that] Memorandum ex-

---

[5] Labour Party: Minutes of the Executive Committee, 14, Minutes of a joint meeting on September 6, 1918, of the Parliamentary Committee of the T.U.C. and the Executive Committee of the Labour Party, together with the delegation of the A.F. of L.
[6] The full text is cited in Kellogg and Gleason: *British Labor and the War*, 288–9; key passages are cited in Labour Party: *Report of the Nineteenth Annual Conference*, 4–5.

pounded in detail to the various questions to be dealt with"; and to urge the workers' organizations of the Allied nations to pressure their governments to "unequivocally . . . adopt these principles . . . in a Joint declaration of Allied Policy." The committee's draft-memorandum also "expressed sympathy" for the A.F. of L.'s bill of rights, but not without stressing that "most of these aspirations found expression in general terms" in the February Memorandum.[7]

After close to two days of debate this text was adopted by 57 against 10 votes of the extreme Left. For fear of encouraging the war cabinets and Gompers to feed on internal divisions, the British and French Independents abstained rather than oppose outright a pronouncement which was much too moderate for their taste. In turn, Gompers also abstained: he did not want to advertise his failure to sever the Social Patriots from the Henderson majority. Moreover, now that he had a foothold in the renascent International, he looked forward to exerting his moderating influence from within. Besides, the assembled delegates agreed that he should join Henderson, Albert Thomas, and Emile Vandervelde on the committee designated by the February Conference to lobby with the Allied and Associated Governments for the inclusion of labor representatives in the official peace delegations and to organize a "World Labour Congress" to meet at the same time and place as the official Peace Conference. Quite apart from having favored both objectives all along, Gompers must have welcomed this opportunity to join two steadfast Social Patriots in keeping a close check on Henderson.[8]

Before adjourning, the conference was called upon to consider a resolution on Russia, drafted by Vandervelde and sponsored by all major factions except the Americans—by Henderson, Longuet, Pierre Renaudel, Huysmans and Popovitch. The draft-text called for "an expression of deepest sympathy to the labour and socialist organizations of Russia," denounced the Treaty of Brest Litovsk for threatening the life of the Russian Revolution, and warned the Allied workers "against the tremendous dangers of a policy of intervention in Russia which, instead of supporting the efforts of democratic Russia, should favour the reactionary tendencies that aim at the reestablishment of the monarchy, and even, under the pretext of fighting Bolshevism, should serve the reaction against Socialism and Democracy."[9] In moving this resolution Henderson, on instructions from the Executive of the Labour Party, explained that it was not intended "to either approve or condemn Allied intervention, but [to] accept intervention as an accomplished

---

[7] For the full text of the committee's draft-memorandum see Labour Party: *Report of the Nineteenth Annual Conference*, 7–9.
[8] Cf. ibid., 9; and Kellogg and Gleason: *British Labor and the War, passim.*
  Gleason: *British Labor and the War, passim.*
[9] Cited in Kellogg and Gleason: *British Labor and the War*, 293.

fact," while warning Allied workers against possible counterrevolutionary consequences.[1]

The Independent Labour Party (ILP) and the French *minoritaires* found this equivocation on the issue of intervention altogether reprehensible: the conference was invited to pacify the opposition while at the same time sanctioning intervention. Even so, Longuet announced the withdrawal of his own resolution, which condemned intervention outright, in favor of the majority text. He claimed to do so on the understanding that the expression of sympathy to Russia's labor and socialist organizations included the Bolsheviks, who reluctantly had yielded to superior force at Brest Litovsk, and on the further understanding that the intervention stood condemned for violating the Socialist principle of self-determination. Vandervelde promptly served notice that if Longuet's interpretation were admitted he would have to repudiate his own resolution and shift his support to the American text.[2] According to this A.F. of L. motion the conference would ask the Allied Governments to vouch that armed intervention was aimed at "counteracting the sinister influence of the Central Powers upon the so-called Bolshevist Government," which was suppressing the freedoms of most Russian workers; and that no military success would ever be exploited to arrest "the march of the peoples of Russia towards true democracy."[3]

The two resolutions as well as the major factions were so far apart that the entire matter had to be returned to the committee which had reported out the original Vandervelde text. In committee Longuet held fast to his interpretation, thereby pushing Henderson into satisfying Vandervelde, who seemed on the brink of teaming up with Gompers. The amended version not only omitted all expressions of sympathy and all warnings against untoward consequences of intervention, but even avoided the word intervention altogether. In conformity with the sixth of Wilson's Fourteen Points the conference was urged to voice the opinion that the Allied effort "to assist the Russian people must be influenced only by a genuine desire to preserve liberty and democracy in an ordered and durable world peace in which the beneficent fruits of the Revolution shall be made permanently secure."[4] Since the plenary conference again was thrown into heated debate, the Henderson-Vandervelde group, by a narrow margin, secured cloture before having the amended resolution adopted by a substantial majority. Significantly, rather than vote against the resolution and thereby

---

[1] Resolution passed on September 18, 1918, at the meeting of the Executive Committee, cited in Labour Party: Minutes of the Executive Committee, 14.
[2] Kellogg and Gleason: *British Labor and the War*, 294.
[3] Cited in ibid., 293–4.
[4] For the full text of the final Russian resolution see Labour Party: *Report of the Nineteenth Annual Conference*, 10.

break with Henderson, Longuet abstained in explicit protest against the premature cloture.[5]

This September Conference demonstrated that Henderson, working in close harness with Huysmans and Branting, had become the pivotal figure in the campaign to rebuild the Second International. Ever since January he had entertained high hopes—unrealistically high hopes—of inveigling Gompers and, through him, three million organized American workers, into participating in this reconstruction. At a minimum Henderson wanted to head off an American drive for a rival trade-union international which could make serious inroads among right-wing Labourites, Socialists, and trade unionists. Such a defection would complicate his campaign to rally a sober centrist majority standing halfway between the declining and defensive Social Patriots and the growing and aggressive Independents and left syndicalists, whose mounting militancy was in part inspired by the Bolshevik Revolution. Henderson proposed to put this rejuvenated International squarely behind Woodrow Wilson. He banked on the President to put through a sensible peace, which, in turn, would help his own concerted efforts to build up the Labour Party. By the time the conference convened he was particularly eager to push this strategy. The first Austrian note, which had just reached the Allies, suggested that victory was in sight. Henderson expected Lloyd George to spring an early victory election. Labour was not ready to contain a "khaki" reaction, which would have dire consequences for the diplomatic settlement as well as for the course of domestic reconstruction. Only the International and Wilson could stem the anti-Labour tide.

Meanwhile, whereas the A.F. of L. was potentially the single most coherent pressure group supporting Wilson in America, abroad it actually undermined his position. In the international politics of Allied Socialism and labor, Gompers strengthened those leaders and forces which were least inclined really to oppose their own governments and to appease defeated Germany as well as revolutionary Russia. He thereby aggravated internal antagonisms which undermined the unity and effectiveness of the recuperating International on the eve of the Armistice. And just as Henderson was reluctant to break with Gompers, so Longuet and MacDonald were reluctant to separate themselves from Henderson. The net result was that the center faction which triumphed stood right rather than left of center in the Allied Socialist and labor movements. As the three Allied premiers headed toward armistice and peace negotiations with the Wilson Administration, they were not about to be excessively alarmed by this divided and temperate opposition to carthaginianism.

[5] Labour Party: *Report of the Nineteenth Annual Conference,* 10; and Kellogg and Gleason: *British Labor and the War,* 296.

2

The Victors and
the Armistice

GERMANY'S FIRST NOTE to Wilson, dated October 5, touched off a
fierce debate in the Allied camp between the advocates of a negotiated
armistice and those of unconditional surrender. Whenever a defeated
enemy asks for terms, the victors' military and civilian leaders have to
thrash out their divergent evaluations of the enemy's overall military
capabilities, of his army's current strategic and tactical position, and of
the probity of his intentions. But in this instance this debate within
government and high command was further complicated and inflamed
by party rivalries, which were spurred on by the expectation that the
free play of partisan politics was about to resume.

In fact, the Allied and Associated decision to grant an armistice
was as much a function of nonmilitary and nondiplomatic considerations as of Austria-Hungary's and Germany's decision to solicit it. In
taking these steps toward peace the governments of both camps experienced pressures and pursued objectives comparable to those that had
conditioned their steps toward war. In July–August 1914 the political
disequilibrium in the major European states had become an important
element in the causes of war;* in October–November 1918 this same
disequilibrium, vastly aggravated by the war itself, influenced the causes
of peace. Both then and now this political disequilibrium was the result
of intense party strife over key issues of national and international
politics.

Determined to take advantage of the war-generated mood of
national obstinacy to enlarge their influence and power, in the fall of
1918 the spokesmen of the forces of order in the victor nations
vigorously opposed a negotiated armistice. They mounted a strident

* See my essay "Domestic Causes of the First World War," in Leonard Krieger and
Fritz Stern (eds.): *The Responsibility of Power* (New York: Doubleday; 1967).

campaign for unconditional surrender with charges that Prince Max of Baden was a mere stooge of Ludendorff; that his notes were designed to entrap the Allies into a premature cessation of arms; that even the best Germans were bloodthirsty villains; and that unless the German armies were routed in pitched battle on German soil the Prussian militarists would never acknowledge that they had actually been defeated in the field. Besides, Germany alone was said to be responsible for the war, thereby putting herself beyond the pale of humanity and international law. Neither armistice nor peace treaty should be negotiated with an outlaw; both should be dictated. Rightists were out to reap maximum rather than optimum benefits of victory. They were unmindful of the political consequences of this policy of retribution for the defeated nations, or else they were sublimely confident that the victors could and should use military government to prevent revolution and to maintain acceptable and pliable successor regimes. Back home this stern policy enabled them to excite and enlist raw nationalist passions while at the same time redoubling their assault on the no-win and semipatriotic forces of movement, whose radicalism Rightists purposely exaggerated.

Whereas the forces of order zealously denounced diplomacy by negotiation, the opposing forces of movement championed it with matching fervor. Their equally stentorian campaign stressed the reality of political changes inside Germany, the sincerity of the armistice request, the fundamental decency of the average German, and the importance of not humiliating a fallen foe. Insisting that all the major European powers, and not just Germany, were responsible for the world catastrophe, Radicals and Leftists wanted all these partners in crime to sit around the conference table to negotiate first the armistice and then the peace. They were particularly alive to the impact that Allied policy was destined to have on political developments in Central and East Central Europe. Specifically, they asserted that while diplomacy by dictation would promote either revolution or reaction, diplomacy by negotiation would encourage and foster the cause of genuine reform. This policy of reconciliation served leaders of the Allied Left in their own struggle for power: they fired and utilized the idealistic sentiments unchained by the world crisis at the same time that they harnessed Wilson's prestige to their attack on the all-win and ultranationalist forces of order, whose imperialist and reactionary nature Leftists deliberately overdrew.

When soliciting the advice of their military chiefs the Allied and Associated statesmen took account of this pitched political battle, just as they kept a careful check on political developments in the crumbling Continental Empires. Needless to say, the generals differed among themselves about enemy capabilities and intentions as well as about those military conditions that, once satisfied, would leave the Allies in a position to secure their ultimate political objectives. Given all these cross-pressures—not to speak of the outburst of diplomatic rivalries among the victors in their moment of triumph—Germany's request for an armistice could not be met overnight.

In the United States consideration and debate of the German notes became caught up in the congressional elections of the fall of 1918. Whatever the ultimate motives and aims of the savage Republican attack on Wilson and the Democrats, the fact remains that the opposition unleashed it with an arraignment of the President's reply to Max von Baden's notes. In no time this derogation of Wilson's handling of these diplomatic exchanges was broadened into a full-scale attack on the Fourteen Points. In turn, this assault eventually contributed to Wilson's decision to issue an appeal to the voters urging them to reelect a Democratic Congress.[1]

Even in the preliminary stages of the election campaign, in the late summer of 1918, opposition leaders proclaimed that only a Republican Congress could insure complete victory abroad and sound reconstruction at home. The keynote was struck by Senator Lodge, whose broadsides against the President's peace program and strategy were identical with those of the most ardent bitter-enders in Britain, France, and Italy.

> The results which we must have can never be obtained by a negotiated peace. . . . As this war is utterly different from any war that the world has ever known, so must the peace which concludes it be utterly different from any peace which the world has ever known. It cannot be a peace of bargain, of give and take, and of arrangement. . . . The only peace for us is one that rests on hard physical facts, *the peace of unconditional surrender*. No peace that satisfies Germany in any degree can ever satisfy us. *It cannot be a negotiated peace. It must be a dictated peace*. . . . The victory bringing such a peace must be won inside, not outside, the German frontier. It must be won finally and thoroughly in German territory [italics mine].[2]

Even though President Wilson shared Senator Lodge's resolve to fight on to victory, he could never subscribe to his exclusive reliance on "physical facts" and on diplomacy by dictation.

Once the President entered into an exploratory dialogue with Prince Max, the Republicans sharpened and multiplied their sallies against the Administration's aims and methods for the transition from war to peace. Senator Miles Poindexter of Washington opened the major Senate debate which disclosed that the opposition was determined to criticize both the substance and presentation of Wilson's negotiations and notes. Poindexter began his address of October 7 with

---

[1] For Wilson's October 25 appeal to the electorate see pp. 123–7 below.
[2] *Congressional Record*, August 23, 1918, cols. 9394–5.

the customary warnings against German trickery. But before he was through he had questioned the President's constitutional authority to correspond with Max von Baden without the prior approval of the Foreign Relations Committee; he had reproved the President for failing to clear each step with Paris and London; and he had renewed the demand for unconditional surrender. His mistrust of Wilson was counterbalanced by his "faith that Clemenceau . . . , in some respects the greatest man that this emergency has produced, or that Lloyd George, the seer of Wales . . . , would yet be alert to protect their countries and ours from the results of any such unwise step." Poindexter was confident that the Big Three would applaud his defiant assertion that "there ought to be only one and not fourteen terms to an armistice, [namely] unconditional surrender," and that any other course would be comparable to what the "Bolsheviki of Russia perpetrated in a larger degree."[3] Senator Henry L. Myers of Montana elaborated on this anti-Bolshevik theme: since Eugene Debs, Emma Goldman, Alexander Berkman, the I.W.W., the anarchists, and the American Bolsheviki favored an armistice, it would be "wise for loyal people to oppose it."[4]

These were not isolated outbursts by irresponsible members of the opposition, since Lodge himself bluntly served notice that the "Republican Party stood for unconditional surrender and complete victory, just as Grant stood." Insisting that this objective could not be achieved by "clever discussion and exchanges of notes" he urged that only field commanders be authorized to deal with the enemy. Ferdinand Foch, Douglas Haig, and John J. Pershing would be sure to press for unconditional surrender as a prelude to the dictated instead of the negotiated peace, which the American people meant to have.[5] On October 14—hence the day after Max von Baden's note accepting Wilson's terms as a basis for negotiations reached America—the minority leader introduced a formal resolution stipulating that "there should be no further communication with the German Government upon the subject of an armistice or conditions of peace, except a demand for unconditional surrender."[6] Moreover, on October 20, the Republican

---

[3] *Congressional Record*, October 7, 1918, cols. 11155–8. In this same debate Lodge proclaimed that "an armistice now meant the loss of the war."

[4] *Congressional Record*, October 14, 1918, col. 11234. Theodore Roosevelt's daughter frankly admits that "we of the 'war-to-a-finish' party were fairly jumping up and down with suspicion and fury about what we considered the inconclusive character of Wilson's negotiations and notes. . . . After a second reading we found flaws; we never failed to find them. We were ingenious in our criticism—when it was not of content it was of presentation." Alice Roosevelt Longworth: *Crowded Hours: Reminiscences* (New York; Scribner's; 1933), 273.

[5] *Congressional Record*, October 10, 1918, cols. 11171–2. See Karl Schriftgiesser: *The Gentleman from Massachusetts: Henry Cabot Lodge* (Boston: Little, Brown; 1944), 296.

[6] Cited in *Congressional Record*, October 14, 1918, col. 11214. That same day Senator Frank B. Brandegee of Connecticut repeated that "any armistice at this time meant the losing of this war," and numerous other Republican Senators echoed this line.

Congressional Committee explicitly struck at the third of the Fourteen Points: whereas "free trade, absolute and complete, with all its tremendous ills" would result from continuing Democratic rule, a Republican House and Senate would prevent "a free tariff disaster."[7]

The Administration could hardly afford to ignore this frontal challenge. According to Senator Key Pittman, Democrat from Nevada, when the minority leader in the Senate "opposes the efforts of the President . . . his opposition becomes a matter of grave concern": should he become the majority leader he would be in a position to block the President's foreign policy. Pittman asked whether "a Republican United States Senate, under the leadership of Senator Lodge, [would] ratify treaties embracing the President's program"? He then supplemented this probing question with the highly partisan but not altogether inaccurate prediction that the coming elections inevitably would turn into a contest "between the policies of Woodrow Wilson and the policies of Senator Henry Cabot Lodge."[8]

Even though all three were Democrats of rabidly anti-German persuasion, Senators Henry F. Ashurst (Arizona), James A. Reed (Missouri) and Charles S. Thomas (Colorado) rose to defend the Administration. Ashurst claimed that if an uninformed stranger had "walked into the Senate galleries . . . he would [have been] led to believe that the President of the United States was on the verge of committing the most colossal blunder of all human history." Why these lamentations, these premonitions of disaster, and these anticipations of betrayal? Why, furthermore, did the Senators conceal their objections to the Fourteen Points "until this very grave hour"? Saddened that the Senate atmosphere was "supercharged with hostility towards the President," Ashurst voiced the hope that the caustic speeches by minority members were not made "for the purpose of securing any partisan advantage in the coming elections."[9]

Significantly, the Democrats themselves had grave doubts about the wisdom of Wilson's course in the face of Republican opposition. Either immediately before or after upholding the Administration's policy, the Arizona Senator requested a private interview in which he advised the President that "the Senate, the press, and the people" wanted him to demand "an unconditional surrender of the German armies." He even cautioned the President that he would be "destroyed" if he "signed away with his pen much of the advantage that our valorous soldiers had won with the sword." Wilson stood his ground: as far as his being destroyed was concerned, if it would serve his country "he was willing to go into a cellar and read poetry the remainder of [his] life." Meanwhile, did Ashurst think that the American people had forgotten

[7] Cited in *The Sun* (N.Y.), October 21, 1918.
[8] *Congressional Record,* October 10, 1918, col. 11167.
[9] *Congressional Record,* October 14, 1918, cols. 11229–31.

his Fourteen Points and his speeches of July 4 and September 27? When the Senator answered that they did not "remember the details," Wilson retorted, "well, I remember," adding that once "Germany fully meets all our terms we are through." Ashurst left "somewhat cheered," but not without telling Wilson that "his failure to demand unconditional surrender would give him leisure in which to read poetry, and that he would read it in a cellar to escape the cyclone of the people's wrath."[1]

Away from the Capitol, Republicans were even less restrained in their anti-Wilson campaign. Theodore Roosevelt in particular renewed his execration of the President's diplomacy. He agreed with Lodge that the Allies were after an unconditional surrender and a dictated peace to be secured "by the hammering of guns . . . [and not] to the accompaniment of the clicking of typewriters." Since the President lacked the tenacity and skill to achieve this objective, Roosevelt wanted the Senate to step in: he summoned it to take "affirmative action" not only against negotiations but also against "the adoption in their entirety of the fourteen points." The language of these Points and of Wilson's subsequent address was so vague and "thoroughly mischievous" as to be more likely to lead to the "conditional surrender of the United States" than to the unconditional surrender of Germany. No wonder, then, that the President's war aims were acceptable only to Germany and to "every pro-German and pacifist, and Socialist and anti-American so-called internationalist," while being offensive to all loyal Americans as well as to the Allies. Roosevelt urged the U.S. to begin acting more like an "ally" than an "associate" so that Germany should cease to count on Washington to "pose as the umpire between our faithful and loyal friends and our treacherous and brutal enemies." In sum, the ex-President wanted both houses of Congress formally to ask for Germany's unconditional surrender and to declare that America's peace terms remained to be formulated, to be discussed with the Allies, and to be accepted by the American people.[2]

In the *North American Review* George Harvey featured an equally unqualified disapprobation of Wilson. He, for one, saw no need for a peace conference. Once Germany had surrendered unconditionally and the Allied armies were well beyond the Rhine, the victors should simply pass sentence on the defeated criminals. Harvey clamored for "justice without discussion or debate, as inexorable as the wrath of God

---

[1] George F. Sparks (ed.): *A Many-Colored Toga; The Diary of Henry Fountain Ashurst* (Tucson: University of Arizona Press; 1962), 83–5.

[2] The full text of Roosevelt's October 24 telegram to Lodge is cited in *The Sun* (N.Y.), October 25, 1918. Even Taft, the other living ex-President, who was so much more reasonable and tempered than Roosevelt, criticized Wilson's handling of the pre-Armistice negotiations, in particular his failure to consult Clemenceau and Lloyd George from the very start. See Henry F. Pringle: *The Life and Times of William Howard Taft* (New York: Farrar and Rinehart; 1939), II, 910–11.

Germany had provoked." Moreover, he wanted the judges to exercise control over Germany "until the last taint of 'Kultur' was eliminated and the Blond beast was tanned and humanized."[3] Among the super-patriotic societies, the National Security League was the most enter-prising and effective champion of this policy of coercion, dictation, and retribution.[4]

The active supporters of Wilson's diplomatic policies were both less numerous and less vocal. Even in the Democratic ranks the victims of the anti-German hysteria were legion, in large measure because the Administration's own Committee on Public Information had done such an efficient propaganda job. Under George Creel's direction this com-mittee continued to characterize the war as a crusade of the forces of light against the forces of darkness, of freedom fighters against op-pressors, of civilians against militarists, and of the liberating culture of Athens against the repressive society of Sparta. With such images in the minds of soldiers and civilians, and of Republicans and Democrats, it was not particularly difficult to whip up popular emotions for a punitive and against a conciliatory treatment of the defeated enemy. Moreover, the loyalty campaign, executed with the help of the Justice Department, the Postmaster General, and self-appointed vigilantes, had fatally sapped the power, vitality, and prestige of the American forces of movement: the Socialists were pitifully weak and divided; the I.W.W. were persecuted relentlessly; and the Progressives were submerged in the hardened Democratic Party. As for the American Federation of Labor, it backed the Administration's domestic policies without, how-ever, endorsing or championing Wilson's diplomacy. In fact, Gompers, who was in Rome just then, "earnestly urged an unfavorable response" to Germany's armistice request.[5]

It would seem, then, that since January, when the Fourteen Points were issued, the domestic foundations of Wilsonianism had contracted still further. By October a self-confident and thriving Republican oppo-sition was vigorously assailing the President's policies; his dwindling and disconcerted supporters were forced to the defensive. To be sure, the President still could tap a vast reservoir of sympathy inside and beyond both the Democratic Party and Congress. But because of Creel's legacy and the Republican censure, it would be extremely hard to translate this reserve of sympathy into politically organized support.

At this juncture the Republicans were in a position to play politics with foreign policy: they proposed to use the armistice and peace issue to *advance* their political fortunes. The President could not afford this

---

[3] See Harvey's articles in *The North American Review* (October and November 1918), esp. 483–4, 493–5, 502–5, 641–9.
[4] See *The Sun* (N.Y.), October 15, 1918.
[5] Ambassador Thomas Nelson Page (Rome) to Lansing, October 7, 1918, National Archives, Document 763.72119/2066.

luxury. In his dual capacity of Chief Executive and World Statesman he was less concerned with turning his diplomacy to political account than with *maintaining* sufficient domestic support to implement it. Meanwhile, in formulating his foreign policy he could not place partisan concerns ahead of the requirements of international politics.

Throughout the pre-Armistice negotiations Wilson and his advisers never ceased to be troubled by the impact of American diplomacy on political stability in both Allied and enemy nations. Not only Colonel House but also Secretary of State Lansing espoused moderation in these diplomatic exchanges because of anxiety about the peacemongering forces of movement in England, France, and Italy. According to House, who was under the spell of Baker's reports, should Wilson place too many obstacles in the way of a reasonable armistice, Radicals, Labourites, and Socialists "would insist upon peace being made"; and should they be thwarted by bitter-enders, "strikes and possibly revolutions might be the result."[6]

Lansing had the same exaggerated estimate of the strength, unity, and resolve of the Allied Left. In a confidential letter he regretted that these internal conditions of America's cobelligerents could not be "publicly explained" to the American people. Since the latter were, as a whole, "the most bellicose, . . . [and wished] Germany crushed and peace made in Berlin," such an explanation might be useful in dealing "with this intense feeling, which approached fanaticism." Lansing went on to emphasize the complexity of "the many conditions and influences which had to be considered in dealing with the international situation." In addition to being watchful about internal developments in the United States and in the Allied nations, the President had to keep a close check on the unfolding German crisis.

> Furthermore, in Eastern Germany Bolshevism is raising its abominable head, and a Germany crushed might become a prey to that hideous movement. If it did, Europe might become a seething mass of anarchy. . . . We must take no chances on this war culminating in such a frightful catastrophe, beside which "the Terror" of 1792 would be a happy epoch. The horrors of Bolshevik Russia must not be repeated in other lands. The doctrine is spreading as it is. It is in all the nations of Europe and is (I say it with regret) gaining a foothold in this country.[7]

Judging by this and similar letters the Administration was fearful lest diplomacy by dictation foster Bolshevism abroad prior to feeding it at home. On the other hand, the Republicans charged that diplomacy by negotiation would advance Bolshevism at home before spreading it abroad.

[6] House Diary, October 24, 1918.
[7] Lansing to Edward N. Smith, October 12, 1918, in Lansing Papers, Vol. 39.

No doubt with these antithetical interpretations in mind, Lansing now wrote to Elihu Root, hoping to prevail on him to exert his sobering influence among his frenzied fellow Republicans. In this letter he explained that the central issue came down to "how far we should go in breaking down the present political organization of the Central Empires?". Whereas unabated military pressure might well strengthen the Right momentarily, it would soon clear the path for revolution.

> There are two great evils at work in the world today. Absolutism, the power of which is *waning,* and Bolshevism, the power of which is *increasing.* . . . The possibility of a proletarian despotism over Central Europe is terrible to contemplate. . . . How much encouragement should we give to radicalism in Germany in the effort to crush out Prussianism? [italics mine].[8]

In another letter Lansing told Wilson that he knew that the President shared his apprehensions about the threat to the structure of society in Central Europe, but was there "a solution," and, if so, where did it lie?[9]

As on so many other occasions *The New Republic* gave a most authentic and concise commentary on the official mind in Washington.

> The result of an exclusive policy of force would be to destroy the present coalition of parties in Germany and stimulate either a Junker or a Bolshevik revolution. Both of these alternatives would produce anarchy in Germany and throughout Middle Europe. . . . The Allies doubtless have it in their power to kill political moderation in Germany, just as they and Germany together killed it in Russia, but is it worth it? Will the civilization which they represent gain any advantage from offering the Germany people a choice between Junkerism and Bolshevism? . . . War dominated by a political purpose has saved civilization and Europe from Kaiserism. War released from political restraints may plunge it into Bolshevism. Peace will soon be necessary not only to consummate the victory over Kaiserism but to safeguard the world against its threatening antithesis.[1]

No doubt this was a vastly oversimplified analysis of the political alternatives in Central Europe: the horrors of Junkerism were overdrawn, its future viability was exaggerated, and the antithesis of Junkerism and Bolshevism was dubious at best. Nevertheless, here was an affirmation of the political purposes of war. And since the Administration placed these political purposes at the center of its war and peace strategy it was not about to close its eyes to the political consequences of defeat in the enemy camp.

[8] Lansing to Root, October 28, 1918, in Lansing Papers, Vol. 39. A copy of this letter went to Wilson.
[9] Lansing to Wilson, November 1, 1918, National Archives, Document 763.72119/2440.
[1] *The New Republic* (October 26, 1918), 358.

Wilson, House, and Lansing did not ponder the political scene in enemy Europe with stereotypes; nor were they ill-informed about developments there. Their information was in large measure based on dispatches from American diplomats in the neutral countries who, in turn, relied on special agents and on the enemy as well as neutral press. The data culled from these and other sources were then analyzed, evaluated, and summarized by the Central European specialists in the State Department. On this matter William Bullitt became particularly influential. He was responsible for daily, weekly, and special "Reports on Matters Relating to the Central Powers." Furthermore, at Lansing's request, between November 1 and 26 he prepared seven memoranda on "The Bolshevist Movement in Europe" and three on "The Bolshevist Movement in Germany." Bullitt's reports, which were consulted by important advisers and decision-makers, came to reflect the quality of the Administration's information and judgment about Central Europe during the pre-Armistice and pre-Conference negotiations.

Bullitt was called on to provide his superiors with an analysis of the political configuration as well as the aims, both domestic and foreign, of the government of Prince Max von Baden. On October 4 he characterized Prince Max as the "most prominent leader of the 'Delbrück group of moderate liberals' [who] in spite of his royal affiliations" was a sincere democrat and a genuine humanitarian and who throughout the war "consistently opposed the annexationists." His appointment, combined with the appointment of Scheidemann and Adolf Groeber, was likely to be hailed by "the Majority Socialists, Progressives, Centrists and at least half the National Liberals." Moreover, his government would enjoy the support of "all the leading papers of the Center and Left, [among them] the *Berliner Tageblatt . . . Frankfurter Zeitung, Hamburger Fremdenblatt, Münchener Neueste Nachrichten, Börsen Zeitung* and all the Majority Socialist papers."

As for program, in the domestic field Prince Max's government could be expected to give first priority to the reform of Prussia's electoral laws. Moreover, in Bullitt's estimate it was just barely possible that this government might also "make the Chancellor responsible to the Reichstag and the military authorities responsible to the Chancellor." But pending these reforms, in spite of the appointment of this quasi-liberal government, "the reins of power still remained in the hands of the Kaiser and the Military Authorities"; and the old power elite was standing by, ready to reclaim power as soon as Prince Max had "pulled the Imperial chariot out of the swamp into which it was now sinking."

Bullitt anticipated that in the diplomatic realm the new administration in Germany would agree to full freedom for Belgium; to complete autonomy for Alsace-Lorraine within the German Empire; to the "President's proposals in regard to the League of Nations, disarmament, removal of economic barriers and 'freedom of the seas' "; and to revisions of the treaties of Brest Litosk and Bucharest. In a parenthetical note Bullitt added that because of great fear of "the spread of Bolshevism throughout Europe" Prince Max was ready for a change in policy toward the Soviet government. Recently the new Chancellor had even "called upon all the Governments of the world to unite in opposing this spread" of Bolshevik doctrines.

In his policy advice the State Department official was of two minds. On the one hand he urged that no offer, however reasonable, be entertained until it was proffered by a "government controlled by the German people." On the other hand, should the Allies reject a moderate offer from the Max government, they might rally the German people around their own bitter-enders; they might also precipitate "a movement for immediate peace" in important segments of the Allied Left. In conclusion Bullitt suggested that "only the President had the insight and wisdom to decline the offer of peace which Prince Max would make and at the same time to preserve the unity of Allied labor."[2]

It is not known whether Wilson actually saw Bullitt's memorandum before drafting his notes of October 8 and 14. But whether he did or not, their text reveals that Wilson, like Bullitt, was less concerned with territorial provisions than with the political impact of his diplomacy on both Germany and the Allies. Certainly both notes were designed to force the pace of democratization in Germany; and the demand for an unqualified acceptance of the Fourteen and subsequent Points persuaded the Allied Left to trust Wilson not to exact exorbitant conditions.

The day following the second Wilson note, Bullitt submitted his second major report on the new German government. In this follow-up report, which was considerably longer, he was much more detailed, analytic, and critical.

Bullitt now appraised the Prince Max government to be a coalition of politicians and parties which had cooperated in successive political battles: first, in the fight against the resumption of unrestricted warfare; then, in the passage of the Reichstag Resolution of July 19, 1917; thereafter, through the inter-party committee, in the overthrow of Georg Michaelis; and last, in the replacement of Georg von Hertling by Prince Max. In foreign policy from 1915 onwards the leaders of the SPD, the Progressives, and the *Zentrum* "considered Russia, not England, the irreconcilable enemy of Germany," and they continued to do so to this day.

In spite of the developments of the Russian Revolution, the "moderates" have clung to their creed that Germany can only find

[2] "The appointment of Prince Max von Baden as Chancellor, and of Scheidemann and Groeber as Ministers without portfolio," Memorandum for Mr. Grew by William C. Bullitt, October 4, 1918, in Bullitt Papers.

salvation in democratic development and understanding with England and the United States. Ever since the appointment of Hertling they have striven to force the Government to make the sort of conciliatory peace offer which Prince Max of Baden made in his initial address to the Reichstag. And true to their policy of hostility to Russia, they have objected to the Government's butchery of the Russian Empire only *on the grounds that it was stupidly managed, and that it tended to make reconciliation with England and the United States more difficult.* They have fought loyally together for reform of the Prussian Electoral Laws. As a result of cooperation in all these political battles, they have come to know one another intimately and to form a close little camarilla.

This camarilla wanted "a friendly understanding with the Western Democracies as a protection against Russia"; and it was prepared to make concessions to England, France, and America in exchange for their consent to the "creation of a line of buffer states between Germany and Russia." While the coalition members differed about the degree of control Germany should exercise in these states, they were agreed on the importance of keeping Russia from acquiring a dominant position in this rimland. In pursuit of this overarching foreign policy objective the coalition would readily agree to an accommodation with regard to navigation in wartime, a League of Nations, free trade, independence and indemnity for Belgium, the return of French-speaking Lorraine to France, the creation of an independent Poland without Danzig or any other Prussian territory, and a colonial settlement in Central Africa.

In the sphere of domestic reform the consensus was not nearly so extensive. To be sure, the three major parties agreed on the urgent necessity for a universal franchise in Prussia and throughout Germany; all three were eager to establish civilian control over the military. But they parted company over "the degree of democracy which it was desirable to establish" in order to satisfy the Socialists at home and Wilson abroad. Whereas the Socialists insisted that the Chancellor be made unequivocally responsible to the Reichstag, the Centrists and Progressives, let alone the National Liberals, opposed such a fundamental break with the constitution of the Second Empire.[3]

This question of further democratization threatened to explode the pre-Armistice coalition. With the military situation beyond repair and with the double-edged pressure of Wilson and the Socialist movement, the plunge into constitutional reform became inevitable. Bullitt noted the coalition's "anxiety to convince the Entente of the genuine character of

3 "The Present German Government," Memorandum for Mr. Phillips by William C. Bullitt, October 15, 1918, in Bullitt Papers.

German reform." At the same time, with every passing day the "fear of a Bolshevist revolution" further accelerated Germany's political evolution. The *Vorwärts,* which dreaded "Bolshevism as much as reaction," was becoming "more and more fearful of revolutionary socialist outbreaks." Accordingly, the Majority Socialists, determined to contain the Independents and Spartacists, were pressing for additional constitutional reforms while counting on Wilson to support their efforts with measured armistice conditions.[4]

Meanwhile, Bullitt also had turned his attention to the study of "the Bolshevist Movement in Europe."[5] He and his superiors were nervous not only about the danger of a Bolshevik coup in Germany but also about the impact of such a coup on a Continent seething with unrest.

After noting that the Bolsheviks had "crushed all substantial opposition within the confines of Great Russia," Bullitt's first memorandum, dated November 2, 1918, provided a bold, impressionistic survey of this unrest: in the Baltic provinces, Poland, and the Ukraine, the withdrawal of German troops was likely to be followed by "an outbreak of Bolshevism"; in Bulgaria the newly established peasant Socialist Republic, under Alexander Stamboliski, "may or may not become Bolshevist in character"; Constantinople was on "the verge of starvation"; all the "western portions of the Dual Monarchy were threatened with anarchy"; Vienna was "threatened with famine . . . [and] harangued daily by Bolshevist orators many of whom were returned prisoners who had imbibed Bolshevism in Petrograd"; Bohemia was in grave danger of Bolshevism "not from Radical Socialism, but from famine"; Budapest had experienced serious riots; Liebknecht, Mehring, and other ultra-radicals were "inciting the German proletariat to immediate revolution"; propaganda agents of the Bolsheviks "with millions of dollars" were reported to be on their way to Italy and France; in Milan extremists were promoting a general strike; in France Longuet's "semi-Bolshevist" *minoritaires* had recently won control of the SFIO; and in South Wales the coal miners were preparing to strike on November 18.

Since none of these developments were in the American national interest, in the second half of his memorandum Bullitt turned to "methods of combating Bolshevism." In this policy-advising section his working assumption was that "economic disorganization and famine were the parents of Bolshevism." He warned, therefore, that if Central

---

4 "Weekly Report on Matters Relating to the Central Powers," No. 69 (November 2, 1918), No. 70 (November 9, 1918), and No. 71 (November 16, 1918), in House Papers, 26:111–13; and "Daily Report on the Central Powers," Nos. 5–6 (November 5 and 6, 1918), in House Papers, 26:96–7.

5 Bullitt's memoranda, which were dated November 2, 4, 5, 6, 8, 15, and 18, 1918, are in Bullitt Papers. The Secretary of State also instructed Phillips "to have Bullitt prepare all telegrams on Bolshevism." Lansing, Desk Diary, November 1, 1918.

Europe were "allowed to dissolve into economic chaos and to starve, no leaders on earth [could] prevent the establishment of a dictatorship of the proletariat with attendant pillage and murder."

Fortunately the U.S. had ample food supplies—the prime anti-Bolshevik vaccine—which the Wilson Administration should not hesitate to commandeer and use. Immediately following the surrender of Austria and Hungary the President should announce America's readiness to "alleviate the distress of the civilian population of the former Hapsburg Monarchy" by shipping food to Vienna and Bohemia "to be distributed by an American directorate" through the local Adler government and the Czech National Council. Should this be possible, *"the administrative agencies which controlled the food distribution would automatically obtain the greatest power over the proletariat and the American directors would control the Governments"* [italics mine].

Bullitt went on to specify the social forces, parties, and governments that were most likely to advance the cause of stability, democracy, and reform. In his judgment a careful differentiation between reformist and revolutionary Socialism was the key to effective anti-Bolshevik action. Since the reformists were the "bitterest" opponents of the Bolsheviks, the Bolshevik movement could most effectively be broken "by cooperation with the moderate socialist and labor leaders of Europe: Henderson, Webb, Albert Thomas, Renaudel, Scheidemann, David, Victor Adler, etc., etc." He recommended that the Administration "establish closer communication" with the "movement for social democracy" which was about to replace the "movement for political and national democracy." Whereas ever since the mid-eighteenth century the Continental nations had repressed this latter movement at the cost of recurrent revolutions, Britain had managed "to meet and compromise with radical elements in order to cut the ground from under the feet of anarchy." Bullitt looked to this British experience for guidance in the present effort to turn the movement for Social Democracy "into tranquil channels."[6]

In subsequent memoranda Bullitt gave a running digest of incoming information about major trouble spots as well as about the subversive activities of the Soviet government. According to his second memorandum *Vorwärts* was "growing more and more fearful" of revolutionary outbreaks in Germany; Pleasant A. Stovall, U. S. Minister in Berne, reported that in Budapest a Workers' and Soldiers' Council had been formed, foreshadowing "the beginning of a Bolshevist movement"; and Nelson Page warned that even though the strikes scheduled for Milan and Turin were called off on account of Italy's great military

6 "The Bolshevist Movement in Europe," November 2, 1918, by Bullitt, in Bullitt Papers.

victories, trouble could be expected in the future.[7] On November 6 Bullitt passed along Stovall's report of a "serious but not imminent" danger of Bolshevik outbreaks in Switzerland;[8] the request from the Austrian Legation in Berne "that American troops be sent to occupy Vienna to prevent Bolshevik uprisings"; an appeal by Prince Hohenlohe, of this same Austrian Legation, for immediate food supplies to "prevent the triumph of Bolshevism in Austria"; and a dispatch from the American Minister in Oslo that for fear of "internal trouble" the Norwegian government had refused to join the British and the French "in protecting the Baltic provinces against the spread of Bolshevism after the Germans withdraw."[9]

Two days later, in his third memorandum, Bullitt struck a note of particular urgency. He advised Lansing that on the strength of rapidly mounting evidence "immediate action by the United States and the Allies was necessary to prevent famine and economic disorganization from driving Austria and Hungary to Bolshevism." Stovall, who was an alarmist and a premature anti-Bolshevik, was Bullitt's main source of information about the ruined Dual Monarchy. He transmitted a request from the Swiss Political Department for Allied occupation of the Tyrol; offered the judgment that Bolshevism would triumph in Austria unless the Allies "provided food and forces to maintain order" throughout the population centers; and viewed Károlyi's cabinet as "extremely radical," just one step short of Bolshevism, against which he might not be able to hold his own. But more serious still were the latest dispatches about developments in Germany. Bullitt considered the Kiel mutiny to be an index "of the potential strength" of the Spartacist group which until the past few weeks had been "a negligible factor . . . [but then] gained adherents with the same rapidity which distinguished the growth of the Bolsheviki in Russia."[1]

Reports about Soviet Russia's activities compounded these dangers. A well-disciplined and -equipped Bolshevik army was said to be ready to "assist Bolshevik elements in neighboring countries"; Karl Radek was reported to be organizing an amply financed center for revolutionary subversion in Poland; Adolf Joffe, the Soviet Ambassador in Berlin, was the suspected mastermind of "the center of the Bolshevist world propaganda organization," authorized to transfer money for Bolshevik propaganda in Britain via Holland; and three to four hundred Bolshevik agents were alleged to have infiltrated Germany,

[7] "The Bolshevist Movement in Europe," November 5, 1918, by Bullitt, in Bullitt Papers.
[8] For the unrest in Switzerland see pp. 348–52 below.
[9] "The Bolshevist Movement in Europe," November 6, 1918, by Bullitt, in Bullitt Papers.
[1] "The Bolshevist Movement in Western Europe," November 8, 1918, by Bullitt, in Bullitt Papers.

some of them carrying arms and ammunition.[2] Even though Bullitt took some comfort from Joffe's last-minute expulsion from Germany,[3] he stressed that his removal would not disrupt "the Bolshevik propaganda organization for other European countries." According to the French Ambassador in Berne, there was "a central revolutionary staff" equipped with 52 million francs in Switzerland, which planned "to start Bolshevik revolutions at once in Germany, Hungary and Italy, and later in Switzerland."[4]

On the basis of all these reports, Bullitt—three days before the German Armistice—was convinced that Social Democracy was "inevitable" throughout Continental Europe. What was not clear was whether this development would be "orderly and peaceful, under the leadership of the moderate leaders of the working classes, or . . . disorderly and bloody under the dominance of the Bolsheviks." Although it was by no means certain that the U.S. and the Entente could "save Europe from a bath of Bolshevism," the effort had to be made.

Bullitt expanded, therefore, on his earlier proposal for fighting the Bolshevik menace. He now urged that Hoover be sent to Berne to "organize the provisioning of Tyrol, Vienna, and Bohemia," since there as elsewhere the "roots of Bolshevism could be cut only by food and restoration of economic life, and not by arms." Secondly, Colonel House should be asked to consider asking Lloyd George and Clemenceau to consult "the labor leaders and moderate socialists of their countries with a view to establishing a basis of cooperation against Bolshevism." Bullitt reinforced this second suggestion with the admonition that a "holy alliance" against Social Democracy of all varieties would push the moderate Socialists and the Bolsheviks into each others' arms, with class war and "the ultimate bloody triumph of Bolshevism" as a consequence.[5]

In England the debate over the Armistice was just as heated as in the United States. But whereas in America the irreconcilables were most prominent in the opposition party, in Britain they sat on the government's own back benches. Even so, largely through the *Morning Post* and the *Daily Mail* they not only stirred up the public at large but also exerted pressure on the archconservative wing of the Unionist party. As for the opposition—the Asquith Liberals, the Radicals, and Labour—it exercised a decidedly moderating influence.

As part of their campaign for unconditional surrender Britain's bitter-enders censured Wilson's exchanges with Max von Baden and denounced his overall peace program. By mid-October the American Embassy reported a "most remarkable change" in the public's attitude

[2] "Bolshevist Movement in Europe," November 4, 1918, by Bullitt, in Bullitt Papers.
[3] See pp. 236–7 below.
[4] "The Bolshevist Movement in Europe," November 6, 1918, by Bullitt, in Bullitt Papers.
[5] "The Bolshevist Movement in Western Europe," November 8, 1918, by Bullitt, in Bullitt Papers.

toward the Fourteen Points. When these were originally issued they had been hailed as "a brilliant statement" of Allied war aims. But now that their "achievement seemed possible" there were grave doubts about their sufficiency. In particular, there was rising criticism of the President's position on the freedom of the seas, the removal of trade barriers, the adjustment of colonial claims, the disposition of the Turkish Empire, and reparations. Also, Wilson was taken to task for not consulting his cobelligerents in the current negotiations.[6]

When the Prime Minister met with his closest associates to consider the first exchange between Berlin and Washington, he stressed that Britain "could not accept the principle of the freedom of seas included in the Fourteen Points"; Arthur James Balfour pressed for such additional terms as "ton-for-ton and punishment for the crimes of Germany in the War"; and Bonar Law broached the need for "a vast indemnity."

But rather than spend time on qualifications or enlargements of the President's Points, the assembled officials debated the prior question "as to whether it was desirable, at the present time, to have peace at all." Curiously enough, Lloyd George, who was an appeaser by temperament and outlook, took the hardest line of all, probably in order to test his colleagues' reaction to the intransigents. He wondered about the importance of "giving to the German people a real taste of war," which they would be spared if their armies were allowed to surrender while still on foreign territory.

> If peace were made now, the Allies would not have occupied a yard of German soil. While pointing out that historical comparisons were not always valuable, he compared the present situation to the Second Punic War. The Romans might have made peace by insisting on Carthage clearing out of Italy and Spain. The Romans, however, said that this was not enough, that they must actually invade Carthaginian territory and achieve victory on Carthaginian soil. History had shown that they were right. . . .
>
> The Prime Minister pointed out that, if peace were made now, in twenty years' time the Germans would say what Carthage had said about the First Punic War, namely, that they had made this mistake and that mistake, and that by better preparation and organization they would be able to bring about victory next time. . . . In a short time the Germans would say that these miserable democrats had taken charge and had become panic-stricken, and the military party would get in power again. The question arose as to whether we ought not to inflict an even more humiliating defeat on them.

This view found no support. General Sir Henry Wilson and Admiral Sir Rosslyn Wemyss, eager not to have the Germans put up "a great fight on their own frontier," insisted that from the military standpoint

---

[6] Irwin B. Laughlin (Chargé in Britain) to Lansing, October 15, 1918, in *F.R.,1918, Supplement 1*, I, 365–6.

they could "imagine no greater degradation than for the Armies to lay down their arms on foreign territory." As for Balfour, after cautioning against the public use of the "analogy which might be summed up in the words *'delenda est Carthago,'* " he argued that the "main test of victory was territory." Accordingly, to crush Prussian militarism it was less important to beat the enemy on his own soil than to force the Germans to give up territory, "such as Alsace-Lorraine, which they had held for 40 years; Posen and Silesia, which they had held for 130 years; to see her principal ally, Austria, smashed for ever; and to lose her Colonies." Even Bonar Law, let alone Churchill and Sir Alfred Milner, seemed to share this territorial perspective, so that the Prime Minister justifiably concluded that "all of them evidently were opposed to his idea that it was necessary, in order to inflict sufficient humiliation, to defeat the enemy on German soil."[7]

But the outcry for unconditional surrender continued at such a high pitch that the Cabinet could not ignore it. It fell to Milner to try to contravene the arguments of the bitter-enders. Ever since late 1917 the Secretary for War, not unlike Lord Lansdowne, had been frightened by the specter of revolution and full of forebodings about the suicidal political, social, and economic cost of the world war for all the belligerents. Now, in mid-October 1918, the campaign for unconditional surrender seemed to him to be furthering the polarization of British politics between the extremes of the Right and the Left, to the detriment of a sensible center; and to be fostering an unpredictable mixture of exasperation and revolution in the enemy nations. To check these trends, which would seriously complicate peacemaking, Milner advocated an armistice just as soon as Allied military supremacy was assured. He saw only drawbacks in the proposal that the Allied armies fight their way to Berlin.

It seems more than likely that Lloyd George was eager for Milner to speak his mind: on the eve of a general election, in which the Prime Minister courted maximum Unionist support, it was convenient to have a Conservative rather than a coalition Liberal challenge the intransigents. In any case, the journalist through whom Milner publicized his views was referred to him by Sir William Southerland, the Prime Minister's Political Secretary.[8]

In the controversial interview, which appeared on the front page of the (London) *Evening Standard* of October 17, Milner argued, as Wilson did, that "complete victory" would be achieved with the defeat and destruction of Prussian militarism and autocracy. Accordingly, the

---

[7] Draft Notes of a Conference held at Danny, Sussex, on Sunday, October 13, 1918 (2:30 p.m.), G.T. 5967, Cabinet 24/66.
[8] See *The History of the Times*, IV, Pt. I, 374–5; and A. M. Gollin: *Proconsul in Politics: A Study of Lord Milner in Opposition and in Power* (London: Anthony Blond; 1964), 568–9.

transformation of Germany's political system was the primary purpose of the war; the punishment of war criminals, reparations, and territorial readjustments were but secondary aims. He was confident that once Prussia's military machine was smashed, the average German would abandon his faith in the martial prowess of the Junker caste. But even assuming this lesson were not driven home, the German people would not be "converted by the fulminations of men, who in the same breath that they denounced the Hohenzollerns, also denounced the whole German nation, [and] represented them as monsters of iniquity." When told that the recent changes in Germany's political system were more apparent than real, Milner countered that the Allies should not be in "too great a hurry to denounce them as a sham." Neither should they attempt to dictate, from outside, drastic constitutional and personnel changes—these the Germans should be left to make on their own.

Of course, the armistice terms needed to specify "all that the military and naval experts considered necessary to put Germany completely into our hands." Milner strongly urged, however, that these terms include no "unnecessary or superfluous" items, otherwise the war might be prolonged for "another six weeks, possibly another six months." He was worried—especially since he overestimated Germany's ability to make a stand behind the Rhine—that a continuation of the war, with "the nerves of every nation in an almost indescribable degree of tension, might lead to unforeseen consequences." In particular he was afraid of disorder and despair conducive to the growth of Bolshevism.[9]

The interview prompted the advocates of the knockout blow to accuse Milner of being pro-German, of trying to save the Kaiser, and of playing into the hands of all compromisers. In no time this criticism reached such a hysterical pitch that Milner expected to be altogether "out of touch *with prevalent opinion*" by the time the peace was negotiated.[1] The course of the coupon election justified his worst fears; and even though he was eager for Wilson to come to Europe, he advised against his visiting England during the election campaign because anything he said "would be distorted by one side or the other for partisan effect." On Armistice Day, in a long conversation with Frank Cobb, Milner professed not to be excessively worried about Bolshevik inroads in Britain. But he continued to be apprehensive about the revolutionary movement in Germany. In order to help the new government maintain order and distribute food, he was prepared

[9] In addition to the text of Milner's interview in the (London) *Evening Standard*, October 17, 1918, see his letter to an unnamed friend, dated October 31, 1918, cited in *The History of the Times*, IV, Pt. I, 381–2, and Gollin: *Proconsul in Politics*, 570–1.

[1] *The History of the Times*, IV, Pt. I, 382. For a detailed discussion of the attack on Milner see Gollin: *Proconsul in Politics*, 571–4.

to modify the Armistice provisions with regard to locomotives, rolling stock, and the blockade.[2]

Lloyd George did not come to his War Minister's rescue. He kept aloof not so much because there was no love lost between himself and Milner, but because he was reluctant to alienate any important body of Unionists on the eve of the election—this notwithstanding his flamboyant boast that he was less afraid of revolution or Bolshevism than of reaction. Even so, in private he seems to have shared Milner's apprehensions about the political risks of needlessly protracting the war. Above all, he wanted to avoid another winter campaign.

Whereas Lloyd George eventually, after the Armistice, reconciled himself to the chauvinist hysteria so regretted by Milner, he never relented in his concern for the internal conditions in Germany. On November 11 he told the Cabinet that now it behooved England "to behave as a great nation and to do nothing which might arouse or harken a spirit of revenge later," the future depending "more on the way in which we behave after victory than upon the victory itself." Specifically, he urged that the enemy nations be provided with early food relief, not least in order to help them maintain themselves against anarchy.[3]

Churchill and Smuts were two other influential members of the inner circle who took this large view. In the prewar struggles over the budget and armaments, Lloyd George and Churchill had proved themselves to be political actors of similar temperaments, skills, and ambitions. Both now tolerated rather than counteracted the hysteria at home, while with regard to Germany their "mood was divided between anxiety for the future and a desire to help the fallen foe." On the eve of the Armistice Churchill stressed the importance of not destroying "the only police force available for maintaining order in Germany" and envisaged the build-up of the German Army "as it was important to get Germany on her legs again for fear of the spread of Bolshevism."[4] According to Churchill these same apprehensions reigned at the dinner table the night of the Armistice.

> The conversation ran on the great qualities of the German people, on the tremendous fight they had made against three-quarters of the world, on the impossibility of rebuilding Europe except with their aid. At that time we thought they were actually starving, and that under the twin pressures of defeat and famine the Teutonic peoples —already in revolution—might slide into the grisly gulf that had already devoured Russia. I suggested that we should immediately, pending further news, rush a dozen great ships crammed with

2 Frank Cobb to House, November 11, 1918, in House Papers, 4:1.
3 War Cabinet 500b, November 11, 1918 (a.m.), Cabinet 23/14; and Frank Cobb to House, November 11, 1918, in House Papers, 4:1.
4 War Cabinet 500a, November 10, 1918 (p.m.), Cabinet 23/14.

provisions into Hamburg. Although the armistice terms enforced the blockade till peace was signed, the Allies had promised to supply what was necessary, and the Prime Minister balanced the project with favoring eye.[5]

Judging by his own account Churchill, like so many other officials, contemplated the course of developments in Germany with the Russian parallel before his eyes.

The German revolution was the paroxysm of an incomparably stronger and more highly nerved organization [than the Russian revolution]. It passed across our anxious, satiated, jaded consciousness with no more attention than surviving troops just withdrawn into rest quarters after battle would pay to a distant cannonade. The story requires a book to tell. The interest is enhanced by comparison with what happened in Russia. So many of the conditions and episodes and their sequence are exactly reproduced. The nation is beaten in war, the Fleet and Army mutiny and dissolve, the Emperor is deposed, and Authority bankrupt is repudiated by all. Workmen's and soldiers' councils are set up, a Socialist Government is bustled into office; upon the famine-stricken homeland return millions of soldiers quivering from long-drawn torment, aching with defeat. The Police have disappeared; industry is at a standstill; the mob are hungry; it is winter. All the agencies which destroyed Russia are ready. They are organised; each individual knows his task; the whole procedure of Communist revolution is understood and scheduled. The Russian experiment stands as a model. In Karl Liebknecht, in Rosa Luxemburg, in Dittmann, in Kautsky and a score of others are the would-be Lenins and Trotskys of the Teutonic agony. Everything is tried and everything happens, but it does not happen the same way.[6]

Incidentally, because the Germans managed to keep their revolution in check Churchill credited them with conduct "important and helpful to them and to civilization."[7]

This same solicitude for the stability and future of Europe preyed deeply on the mind of Smuts, who had successfully practiced the politics of reconciliation in South Africa. With Russia as a sober reminder, he warned that "nations and states go to pieces under this awful pressure before their armies are finally beaten in the field." Should the war continue into 1919 there was "serious danger that the bad but more or less orderly political pre-War system of Europe may give place to a wild disorder of jarring and warring state fragments," and no League of Nations could prevent the "wild war-dance of these so-called free nations." In addition, unless there was a timely end to hostilities, reconciliation would be complicated by the "war fever

[5] Churchill: *Aftermath,* 20–1.
[6] Ibid., 199–200.
[7] Ibid., 199.

. . . [which was] beginning to rage in America, the temporary and evanescent chauvinism in this country, and the insensate spirit of revenge now apparently actuating France."[8]

Meanwhile an office in the New Scotland Yard was busy charting "The Progress of Bolshevism in Europe" much along the same line as Bullitt in the State Department. The first memorandum was submitted in early November 1918; the second one, in late January 1919. The latter reported that "to the persistent and ably conducted propaganda of the Bolsheviks was partly due the outbreak at Kiel, which precipitated the German request for an Armistice, and with the collapse of the German Empire the prospects of sweeping Europe with a wave of Bolshevism became brighter." Since the Germans took the risk of flooding themselves with Bolshevism provided "they could send it on its way westward," there now were "two separate sources of propaganda, Russian and German." After a rundown of the Russian government, the Red Army, the Terror, and the Bolshevik administration, the survey focused on Germany. The researcher conceded that it was "too early yet to form an opinion as to how far Bolshevism" would go, though he predicted that German diplomats would take advantage of the specter of Bolshevism to extract concessions from the Allies. This memorandum, which was read by A. J. B. (Arthur J. Balfour?), concluded with a country-by-country survey of conditions favorable to the growth of Bolshevism, care being taken not to exaggerate its dangers.[9]

Even if this particular document seems too *recherché,* another memorandum reveals that the Foreign Office was keeping as close and nervous a check on internal conditions in Germany as was the State Department. On November 20 it invited the American government's reaction to Wilhelm Solf's request that the Allies "let it be known that there would be no toleration of Bolshevism" and on his hope "that the moment there were signs that disorderly elements were getting the upper hand, [the Allies] would resume hostilities."[1] Lansing replied that since he and the President were about to proceed to Paris "it would seem best to determine there what measures may be agreed upon in regard to the Bolshevik menace in Germany."[2] The whole question of how to deal with Bolshevism in Russia, now that the war was over, was also left for consideration at the Peace Conference; meanwhile the

[8] "A Note on the Early Conclusion of Peace," October 24, 1918, by General Smuts, G. T. 6091, Cabinet 24/67. For excerpts see David Lloyd George: *War Memoirs,* 2 vols. (London: Odhams Press; 1938), II, 1973; and W. K. Hancock: *Smuts: The Sanguine Years, 1870–1919* (Cambridge University Press; 1962), 493–5.

[9] "The Progress of Bolshevism" (Secret), January 28, 1919, in House Papers, 31:207. The memorandum of early November 1918 is not in the House Papers, but it is referred to in the second memorandum which touches on 14 countries, including the United States.

[1] Barclay (British Chargé in Washington) to Lansing, November 20, 1918, in *F.R.,P.C., 1919,* II, 94–5.

[2] Lansing to Barclay, November 27, 1918, in ibid., 104.

British intervention in Russia was not only continued but actually stepped up.

In Britain the forces of movement favoring a negotiated rather than a dictated armistice and peace were infinitely stronger, better organized, and influential than in America. The entire Labour movement, except for Havelock Wilson's faction, was an active agent of moderation; and so were the Radicals. For the dissemination of their views these forces could count on two prestigious dailies, the *Manchester Guardian* and the *Daily News,* which hailed Milner's interview,[3] and on the weekly *Nation* and *Labour Leader.*

During the pre-Armistice negotiations the British Left made an eleventh-hour effort to oblige the War Cabinet to formally endorse Woodrow Wilson's Fourteen and subsequent Points. At the Inter-Allied Labour and Socialist Conference in September the Labour movement had rededicated itself to this end.[4] From early October to Armistice Day the *Daily News* incessantly goaded the Allied Governments to clarify their policies. In the face of their obstinate silence Philip Snowden in the *Labour Leader,* told Wilson that it was his duty to "deal as firmly with the Allied Governments" as he was dealing with the German government to secure an unqualified pledge to his program. By the end of October the "tone and temper and declarations of the British and Allied Press and of some notorious politicians" prompted him to exclaim: "would that we could be as certain of the defeat of Prussianism in the Entente Powers and in America" as in the Central camp.[5] Snowden shared Beatrice Webb's melancholic conclusion that "revenge and greed die hard when satisfaction seems at hand."[6]

But the Labour and Radical elements did not limit themselves to a press campaign. On six different occasions the government was asked in Commons whether the Allies had accepted Wilson's principles and objectives. Bonar Law, Robert Cecil, and Arthur Balfour took turns making equally evasive statements: there was constant communication with Washington; the government was anxious not to add to misapprehensions; it was "not desirable to discuss this matter now"; and the question of peace terms must "be left to the decision of the Government."[7] Meanwhile, Labour held a mass rally at Albert Hall in support of Wilson's policies and his exchanges with Prince Max;[8] and

---

[3] See *The History of the Times,* IV, Pt. I, 380.
[4] See pp. 47–50 below.
[5] *Labour Leader,* October 24 and 31, 1918; and Philip Viscount Snowden: *An Autobiography* (London: Ivor Nicholson and Watson; 1934), I, 487–8.
[6] Cole (ed.): *Beatrice Webb's Diaries,* 133, entry of October 13, 1918.
[7] *P.D.,110* (October 17, 21, 23, 24, 28, and November 18, 1918), cols. 283, 417–18, 768–9, 889–90, 919–20, 1069–79, 3190.
[8] This rally was held on November 3, 1918, with J. H. Thomas as principal speaker. The preceding day Horatio Bottomley, Havelock Wilson, and Lord Beresford

the Union of Democratic Control organized meetings in different parts of England. Moreover, the U.D.C. Executive once again assured the President of its support for his peace terms and vowed to resist all attempts "to enlarge these demands in a manner calculated to delay peace."[9]

No doubt the forces of change united around Wilson in preparation for an imminent election, in which they expected to be at a tremendous disadvantage. But certainly the Radicals, like important segments of the Labour and Socialist Left, were more immediately preoccupied with the perplexities of a lasting peace in general and of events in Germany in particular. For these Lib-Labs, as for the Allied officials who took the "big view," Central Europe appeared to be in a "race with chaos." In Germany the "train was laid for an explosion" such as had shaken Russia to her foundations. Immediately following the Kiel mutiny the *Daily News* prayed that military operations would end in time to forestall anarchy. Although on Armistice Day this Radical daily was encouraged by the "orderly and bloodless" course of the German Revolution, it also confessed that because of the Russian example satisfaction continued to be mingled with anxiety.[1] Germany being balanced "on a razor's edge between order and anarchy," the most momentous question, according to *The Nation,* was where her revolution would halt. The Allies should help it to a timely stop since "humanity and expediency alike demanded that Europe should not be allowed to lapse into chaos."[2]

Labourites and Socialists, for their part, were less engrossed in the hazards of permanent revolution than in the prospects for the growth of Socialism, in Germany and beyond.[3] And it comes as no surprise that Beatrice Webb was fascinated with Germany's "heroic struggle to reconstruct her political and social machinery," convinced that the "future of the civilized world depended on her success." In order to build this "well ordered socialist state," would the new government summon "from the depth of the German character a Will to Order" and mobilize Germany's science and public spirit much as "her militarist rulers had called out her Will to Power"?[4]

In October–November, then, there was considerable support for a favorable response to Prince Max's overture in the Cabinet, in Commons, in the political arena at large, and in the press. Moreover, the

---

addressed "an extreme anti-German" rally in that same hall. Laughlin to Lansing, November 6, 1918, in *F.R.,1918, Supplement 1,* I, 475.
[9] Cited in Laughlin to Lansing, October 2, 1918, in *F.R.,1918, Supplement 1,* I, 469–70.
[1] *Daily News* (London), November 7 and 11, 1918.
[2] *The Nation,* November 16, 1918.
[3] *Morning Post,* mid-October to late November, *passim.*
[4] Cole (ed.): *Beatrice Webb's Diaries,* 144, entry of January 14, 1919.

military were of the same mind. At G.H.Q. in Cambrai there was great confidence that Germany was in no position to fight on much longer, and the view gained ground that "you must have a Government, and not a revolution on which to impose terms."[5] When Lloyd George asked General Sir Henry Wilson whether he wanted a break-up and Bolshevism in Germany or an armistice, Wilson "unhesitatingly said 'armistice.'" Thus even the Chief of the Imperial General Staff reckoned that "the real danger now was not the Boches but Bolshevism."[6]

Finally, the Prime Minister and his top advisers were confident that Britain and the Empire would enter the Peace Conference with enviable advantages. As Lloyd George put it, England would go there "with the German Colonies, or most of them, in our hands; the German fleet in our grip, or at the bottom of the sea; the German mercantile marine handed over to us to make good our losses." To be sure, these were matters for negotiation; "but meanwhile we shall hold them," and as a solicitor he knew that "possession was nine-tenths of the law."[7]

In spite of all these forces, appraisals, and predispositions in favor of an unimpassioned diplomatic approach, which in fact became official policy, the British government did nothing to sell it to the public. Its failure to bolster Milner reinforced the impression that the Cabinet either was sympathetic to the supernationalists or decided not to challenge them for reasons of high politics, whether national or international. The first giant step toward a coupon election had been taken.

The British bitter-enders went on the offensive at exactly the same time as their American counterparts. They denounced Wilson's diplomatic principles, aims, and methods; they reviled Milner for being a latter-day Lansdowne; and they ominously insinuated that Lloyd George was in danger of falling under insidious pro-German and revolutionary Socialist influences.

By late October the American Embassy reported that whereas the "pacifist 'peace at once' party" was hardly heard, there was "a strong but numerically small party" calling for unconditional surrender.[8] These ultras—ill-defined to this very day—permeated the right wing of the Unionist Party, organized their own National Party, and disseminated their doctrine through the *Morning Post* and the *Daily Mail*. The articles and editorials in these two dailies clamored for the outright dictation of both armistice and peace terms. Nothing short of complete

[5] Geoffrey Dawson, who was visiting G.H.Q., to G. S. Freeman, October 18, 1918, cited in *The History of the Times*, IV, Pt. I, 372.

[6] Major General C. E. Callwell (ed.): *Sir Henry Wilson: His Life and Diaries*, 2 vols. (London: Cassell; 1927), II, 148, entry of November 10, 1918.

[7] Cited in Henry Wickham Steed: *Through Thirty Years, 1892–1922: A Personal Narrative*, 2 vols. (London: William Heinemann; 1924), II, 245.

[8] Laughlin to Lansing, October 29, 1918, in *F.R.,1918, Supplement 1*, I, 414.

defeat and unconditional surrender could "awaken the German people from its evil dreams and make the world safe for democracy." Englishmen were fighting "a foul and worse than bestial thing on which kindness and chivalry were worse than thrown away" and had better abide by the adage "once a German always a German, once a Prussian always a Prussian." Needless to say, reforms of the German government could never be trusted. The causes of war were "deeper than institutions and dynasties," they reached down into the German national character, which was cast for all time. Hence, "under whatever form of government, and whether Germany [be treated] indulgently or justly, the German people were and would remain the implacable enemies of this country."[9]

Brazenly the British irreconcilables went beyond the usual charge that first Prince Max and then Ebert were putting on a show of democratization for Wilson's benefit and to deceive the Allies into relaxing their war effort. It was beyond any German to be genuine in his peaceful and democratic professions. In sum, "justice on German lips was blasphemy," a peace of justice meant punishment, to be meted out after the criminal was arrested; and the only way to make Germany a safe neighbor was not by democratizing her but by "reducing her power." To achieve this reduction of power France should have a free hand to settle Germany's borders, while the Empire should retain the German colonies and collect her share of a debilitating reparations bill.[1]

What of the political consequences, inside Germany, of this Carthaginian diplomacy? Obviously, her leaders were deliberately exaggerating the Spartacist danger in order to frighten the Allies into making concessions. When the German Foreign Office asked for Allied food supplies to help maintain political stability, the *Morning Post* scornfully dismissed "Dr. Solf's Latest Moan."[2] At one and the same time the jingoists denounced Spartacism as Germany's own invention and welcomed it for crippling Germany by civil discord! Meanwhile, if the Allies were really concerned about Bolshevism they should apply themselves to destroying it in Russia, with the United States shouldering the bulk of this burden.[3]

This agitation for total and unconditional victory was also carried forward by the National Party. In the fall of 1917, when the first serious cracks, symbolized by Henderson's resignation from the Cabinet, appeared in the political truce, General Page Croft, M.P. for Christchurch, headed up a rebellion in the Unionist Party. He was exasperated

[9] *Daily Mail* (Paris), November 2 and 5, 1918; and *Morning Post*, November 4, 7, 8, 13, and 20, 1918.
[1] *Morning Post*, October 25, 1918.
[2] *Morning Post*, November 27, 1918.
[3] *Morning Post*, mid-October to late November, *passim*.

by political discord in wartime; he also wanted to put an end to industrial strikes, the sale of honors to war profiteers, and the laxity toward enemy aliens. Some twenty Tory M.P.'s and a dozen Tory peers blamed these afflictions on their own Unionist Party, which they felt truckled to Lloyd George who, in turn, was indicted for being excessively responsive to Labour and Liberal pressure.[4]

In protest Croft and a small cabal of supporters within and outside Parliament seceded from their parent organization to form the National Party. In its inaugural manifesto this National Party vowed to pursue "complete victory in the war and after the war"; to eradicate the German influence in Britain; to promote "class unity and confidence between employer and employed"; to safeguard national industry and agriculture; to further the unity of the Empire; to champion social policies designed to "ensure a contented, patriotic race"; and to press for postwar legislation to "eliminate waste in citizen life" and to safeguard the interests of ex-servicemen.[5] On the threshold of victory and elections this incipient party went on to stress that because the interests of labor, which were the "shuttlecock of party politicians," would be amply protected by M.P.'s elected by "a vast preponderance" of labor votes, it was industry that was most in need of a powerful voice. The New Nationalists proposed to provide the power and influence to promote England's economic interests by tariff protection, subsidies, and expansion of the consular services. As for the foreign policy platform, it now called for peace by dictation, retention of all German colonies, and complete restoration and reparation by Germany.[6]

But in addition to these programmatic aims there was a political rationale for this severance from the Unionist Party. The main tenets of this rationale suggest that the new National Party had close ideological affinities with such prewar mass movements from the Right as the Assembly of the Russian People in Russia, the Stoecker movement and the Pan-German League in Germany, the Christian Socialists in Vienna, the Ligue des Patriotes and the Action Française in France, and the Primrose League in England.

Here, then, was a glorification of the Throne; of "fundamental British traditions of freedom and self-government"; of the basic qualities of "courage, honesty, thoroughness and industry"; and of the "great and simple principles of life and politics" of the past. All of these were being corroded and undermined by the "cleverness, eloquence, skilful self-advertisement . . . and personal ambitions" of party poli-

[4] Cf. Brigadier-General the Lord Croft: *My Life of Strife* (London: Hutchinson; 1948), 129–30.
[5] The text of this manifesto was originally published in *The Times* (London), August 30, 1917, and, except for two paragraphs, is reprinted in Croft: *My Life of Strife,* 130–2.
[6] Sir Richard Cooper: *The Principles and Policy of the National Party* (London: n.p.; 1918), 13 and 16.

ticians who put class, sectional, and sectarian interests ahead of the nation. There was one chief obstacle to a truly national policy: "the worn out party system and its ruthless machines" which had developed into "an organized mockery of the nation." The New Nationalists proposed to free England "from the clutches of this octopus," but not by starting yet another party. Instead, they meant to launch a "movement" which would seek to "unite men and women of all parties" throughout the islands and the Empire who realized "that the old political associations were not merely inadequate for the work of national reconstruction, but were obviously in the way of it."[7]

In October 1918 Sir Richard Cooper, member for Walsall and Croft's closest associate, repeated this indictment of the party system.

It is impossible to put new wine into old bottles, and we therefore propose a new model which welcomes all patriotic men and women, whatever be their previous political conviction. . . . The Party System of Government brought this country to the verge of disaster: it is responsible for the early mismanagement of the war, for our unpreparedness for it, and for its consequent prolonged duration. It is this corrupt system that robbed us of the privileges of a Democratic Government. Until this evil is abolished there is little hope of National and Imperial progress.

Cooper realized that it was incongruous to "form a 'party' whose fundamental principle was to abolish the present party system." But the "founders of the new movement," being themselves members of Parliament, had to avoid any charge of hypocrisy. Besides, in Britain any movement working expressly for political purposes would anyway "be referred to as a 'party.' "[8]

In terms of leadership this incipient mass movement from the Right was peculiarly British. The founders and directors were of aristocratic rather than *petit-bourgeois* background; they were members of Parliament rather than political outsiders; they were landholders, military and naval officers, and businessmen rather than alienated intellectuals.[9] Otherwise, however, this projected mass movement from the

[7] See the manifesto cited in fn. 5, p. 79 above.
[8] Cooper: *National Party*, 6–7, 11.
[9] The charter manifesto appeared over the following signatures: Colonel Lord Ampthill, G.C.S.I., G.C.I.E.; Sir Charles Allom; Colonel Earl Bathurst, C.M.G.; Colonel Henry Bowles; Major Alan H. Burgoyne, M.P.; Brigadier-General T. C. Calley, C.B., M.V.O.; Lieutenant-Colonel The Hon. Douglas Carnegie, M.P.; W. Child Clark, Esq.; Sir Richard Cooper, Bt., M.P.; Brigadier-General H. Page Croft, C.M.G., M.P.; The Venerable Archdeacon Cunningham, D.D.; Major W. H. Drummond; Captain the Viscount Duncannon, M.P.; Lord Ebury; Francis Francis, Esq.; Lieutenant-Colonel Sir John Harrington, K.C.M.G., K.C.V.O., C.B.; The Hon. J. G. Jenkins; Lieutenant-Colonel Lord Leconfield; Lord Leith of Fyvie; Lieutenant-Colonel Sir Mervyn Manningham-Buller, Bt.; Admiral Sir Albert Hastings Markham, K.C.B.; George Miller, Esq.; Colonel Lord Montague of Beaulieu, C.S.I.; Colonel R. H. Rawson, M.P.; I. W. Raymond, Esq.; J. Mure Ritchie, Esq.; Lieutenant-Colonel Lord Stafford, D.S.O.

Right had much in common with those on the Continent. Ideologically there were jingoist incantations, racial allusions, antiparty declamations, and professions of common purpose; programmatically there were promises to social and economic interests requiring protection for their very survival; tactically there was reliance on blatant flattery of the national self, self-righteous exposure of corruption, and cunning exaggeration of the danger of the foreign enemy within.

Such emotional appeals were calculated to mobilize a mass vote with which to countervail the mass vote of the swelling Labour Party. The mass vote of the Right was expected to come from social and economic strata whose status, wealth, and income were threatened by rapid modernization and industrialization: old-fashioned craftsmen, unprogressive manufacturers and landowners, small shopkeepers, and tradesmen, low-level civil servants, and retired colonial officers and administrators. Even though the leaders called for the abolition of parties, they did not espouse any restriction of the franchise. On the contrary, in typical plebiscitary fashion they purposed to take advantage of the impending universal suffrage which would also give the vote to women, who might become particularly responsive to emotional appeals. They were confident that without renouncing their own elitist view of politics they could enlist the socially and economically immobile or backsliding strata which were panic-stricken by the onrushing flood of industrial modernity and labor.

The leaders of the National Party worked in close harmony with what remained of the Primrose League,[1] whose political formula was their guide. According to Ostrogorski that League was "a sentimental alliance between the masses and Toryism . . . appealing frankly to popular emotions and affections."[2] Moreover, the National Party as well as the Primrose League were activated by the same defensive political reflex so brilliantly diagnosed by Robert Michels. Both were controlled by "old groups of rulers" determined to preserve themselves by descending "during the elections, from their lofty seats, . . . to avail themselves of the same democratic and demagogic methods . . . employed by the youngest, the widest, and the most uncultured of our social classes, the proletariat." At the very least during election time "the conservative spirit of the old master-caste . . . [was] forced to assume a specious democratic mask."[3]

During the first year the high point of the National Party's campaign was a monster "Win the War" rally in Hyde Park: the crowd applauded the collection of over one million signatures on a petition

[1] See Croft: *My Life of Strife*, 141.
[2] Moisei Ostrogorski: *Democracy and the Organization of Political Parties* (London: Macmillan; 1902), I, 271.
[3] Robert Michels: *Political Parties: A Sociological Study of the Oligarchical Tendencies of Modern Democracy*, English trans. (Glencoe: Free Press; 1949), 4–5.

clamoring for the internment of enemy aliens before forming into a mammoth procession to Downing Street.[4] Lloyd George was likely to take notice only to the extent that Bonar Law and Sir George Younger, chairman of the Unionist organization, reacted by stiffening their conditions for cooperation in the impending election.

In any case, during the pre-Armistice negotiations the ultras were at least as noisy and influential as Lord Northcliffe, who then as later attracted attention because he flaunted his vanity, dared to tangle with Lloyd George, and advertised himself through the pages of his many newspapers. As expected, Northcliffe's position was inconsistent. Whereas he made no effort to temper the *Daily Mail*, *The Times*, under Dawson's editorship, followed a moderate course. Though it first called for unconditional surrender, *The Times* soon conceded that Wilson's exchanges with Prince Max "satisfied even the most exacting standards";[5] and, unlike the *Daily Mail* and the *Evening Standard*, *The Times* neither crucified Milner nor asked that the War Cabinet repudiate him. Admittedly, in a speech to American officers, Northcliffe swore that "any attempt by any British statesman to save the doomed tyranny, whether through timidity, or jealousy, or a feeble desire to avert Bolshevism in Germany, would bring down the strongest Government in Great Britain, and probably much else with it."[6] But it seems likely that Northcliffe's attack was less a function of his disagreement with the substance of Milner's views than of his resolve to force Lloyd George and Dawson to reckon with his influence: the Prime Minister was to appoint him one of the Peace Commissioners and to consult him concerning the upcoming elections, while Dawson, who was close to Milner, was to follow a less independent editorial policy.[7]

That the press magnate was testing his influence rather than joining the irreconcilables became evident on November 4, the day that all his papers prominently carried his "From War to Peace," a signed statement of his views on the future peace. In most essentials these coincided not only with government policy but also with the Wilsonian prescription.

Northcliffe cautioned the public that unlike the change from peace to war in 1914, which had been sudden and dramatic, the passage from war to peace would be "a slow and laborious process," both diplomatically and domestically. First there would be an armistice on

4 Croft: *My Life of Strife*, 139. The party also published *National Opinion*, whose circulation was very small; a wider audience was reached through the *Morning Post*, the *Globe*, and the *National Review*, which provided favorable coverage of its activities.

5 *The Times* (London), October 7 and 16, 1918.

6 Reported in the *Daily Mail*, October 23, 1918, and cited in *The History of the Times*, IV, Pt. I, 376, 387–8.

7 *The History of the Times*, IV, Pt. I, 376–8, 387–8, 393–4. Cf. Gollin: *Proconsul in Politics*, 572–6.

conditions "laid down by the military and naval leaders" which would make the resumption of hostilities impossible. This stipulation was in the spirit of Wilson's note of October 23 and not of the on-to-Berlin school. Germany's behavior in this first phase, which also required the cooperation of the victors and vanquished in the maintenance of order and the shift from military to civilian organization, would influence all subsequent proceedings.

Meanwhile, provided the Allies had adequate military guarantees, they could begin to tackle all major questions without waiting "to see whether the transformation of the German Government . . . was as genuine as it was presented to be," the more so since "the genius of Germany might evolve some form as good as, or even better than, existing institutions" elsewhere. Northcliffe again followed Wilson with regard to Belgium, Alsace-Lorraine, Italy's frontiers, the successor nations, the treaties of Brest Litovsk and Bucharest, the Polish question, and the Turkish Empire.

To be sure, he also strayed from the Wilsonian path. Germany was to "accept the full burden of material reconstruction, replacement and compensation," including compensation for civilian losses and injuries, in the invaded parts of France; she was to replace all damaged and destroyed merchant tonnage and pay compensation for the loss of life; and she would "in no case" recover her colonies. Even though with regard to reparations and colonies Northcliffe approximated the position of the ultras—and so did the Cabinet—he defied them by stipulating that violators of the "laws of war or of humanity" of *both* sides be tried as war criminals.

Similarly, he was out of step with the superpatriots concerning postwar reconstruction. In world politics Northcliffe envisaged a transition from the "old system of the balance of rival Powers" to the "League of Free Nations," with wartime inter-Allied agencies smoothing the way. Eventually disarmament, universally applied, would slowly develop the fabric of a new international system from which "the passions and fears of war" would be banished. At home Northcliffe saw the need for government action with regard to veterans, wages, housing, industrial relations, and pensions. In addition to requiring international cooperation, much of this social legislation would promote peace by absorbing tax revenues that would otherwise spark a new armaments race.

Radicals and Labourites were quick to notice that neither Northcliffe nor the magisterial *Times* was in league with the *Morning Post, Daily Mail, Nationalist Party,* and Horatio Bottomley. The *Daily News* considered it odd that of all people Northcliffe, who was still chief of the Department of Propaganda in Enemy Countries, should be the one to announce British endorsement of Wilson's terms.[8] Snowden ack-

[8] *Daily News*, November 5, 1918.

nowledged that Northcliffe's terms, "though exceptionable in some details, were on the whole not unreasonable."[9]

Northcliffe asked Lloyd George to put him in charge of peace propaganda until a final settlement was concluded, his "From War to Peace" to be the foundation for this effort.[1] But by publishing his quasi-official memorandum without the Prime Minister's clearance he presumed to speak with greater authority than he actually had. This publication, then, was designed as a test of his power and influence. As well as testing his influence, however, Northcliffe was momentarily alarmed by the rising specter of revolution abroad and at home. Snowden voiced the not unreasonable suspicion that since *The Times* continued to advocate the overthrow of the Bolshevik regime, Northcliffe's "new frame of mind towards Germany was prompted less by a generous impulse towards the German people than by fear of the advancing tide of social revolution in Europe."[2] This same general concern prompted Northcliffe to urge timely reforms as the best antidote to Labour radicalism in Britain.[3] But for Northcliffe's arrogant ambition Lloyd George, jealous of his own prerogatives, might have enlisted him to help restrain the irreconcilables who threatened to confound the Armistice, the election, and the peace. As it was, their personal feud rebounded to the benefit of the bitter-enders by weakening the coalition of appeasers vis-à-vis the Tories.

Of course, the German bid for terms also produced tempestuous debates in France. At first Prince Max's overture to Wilson was viewed with unconcealed suspicion and hostility by everyone except the Socialists. A highly placed U. S. official in Paris reported on good authority that the French government had asked the press "to adopt an uncompromising attitude": it meant to bolster the popular view that Berlin was resorting to diplomatic maneuvers to cover up military reverses and to placate political opposition.[4] The *Temps* charged that the Germans were invoking Wilson's principles only in order to trick the Allies into relaxing their military effort prematurely. According to *Figaro,* while Prince Max and Scheidemann were heading off a "movement of Soviets" in their own country, they were bent on encouraging soviets among the Allies as part of a plan to make them "put down their weapons five minutes too soon."[5]

On October 15 the *Temps* still argued that the Hohenzollerns had at best changed labels; that they needed a respite "to restore their

[9] *Labour Leader,* November 7, 1918.
[1] Northcliffe to Lloyd George, November 3, 1918, cited in *The History of the Times,* IV, Pt. I, 385-6.
[2] *Labour Leader,* November 7, 1918.
[3] See pp. 152-3 below.
[4] Frazier (Diplomatic Liaison Officer with Supreme War Council) to Lansing, October 8, 1918, in *F.R.,1918, Supplement 1,* I, 345.
[5] *Le Temps,* October 7, 1918; and *le Figaro,* October 5, 1918.

columns, their army, their people"; and that to treat with them was to restore their prestige and save them. But this edition had barely rolled off the presses when Herbette, the paper's chief editorialist, telephoned Ambassador Sharp to say that the next day the *Temps* would come out in support of Wilson's second reply to Prince Max, which had just reached Paris.[6] Presently Pertinax, who all along had been highly critical of the Fourteen Points, also had a change of heart: "the dialogue between Washington and Berlin was inordinately risky, . . . but things turned out better than one was entitled to hope."[7] That there was mounting support for negotiations was confirmed when the Radical Socialists as well as the *chambre*'s Army Commission swung behind Wilson.[8]

Clearly, after an initial flurry of disapprobation, French press and Parliamentary circles were less critical of Wilson's armistice diplomacy than were their British and American counterparts. For one thing, the French political scene was relatively calm, in that no election was in the offing. For another, the proximity of the battlefields, the staggering casualty figures, the devastation of the border provinces, and the economic and financial depletion made the French power elite particularly eager to avoid paying the extravagant cost of a final battle. Admittedly, Foch overestimated Germany's capacity to stall and wear down the advancing Allied armies; and generals and politicians alike were painfully aware of the large extent to which France's own military stamina was dependent on American power. Whatever the reasons, the military did not dissuade the civilians from exploring an agreement that would paralyze the enemy's residual military strength without destroying the organizational structure of his military establishment. At the same time, French military and Rightist circles confidently assumed that such an agreement would so cripple Germany that she could not withstand Carthaginian peace terms.

Realizing that the government's and the Right's ultimate objectives were predatory and punitive, the SFIO and the CGT once again tried to pressure Clemenceau into explicitly subscribing to Wilson's principles and aims. Especially now that Prince Max had accepted the Wilsonian platform and was prepared to discuss its application, the Allied Governments should be made to follow suit unequivocally and unambiguously. To this end a delegation of Socialists called on Clemenceau, but to no avail.[9] They then mounted a campaign in *Humanité* and the *Populaire* prior to interpellating the government in the chamber.[1] Speaking for the ex-*minoritaires* who had just wrested

[6] Sharp to Lansing, October 16, 1918, in *F.R.,1918, Supplement 1*, I, 364.
[7] *Echo de Paris*, November 7, 1918.
[8] *Le Populaire*, October 16, 1918.
[9] See the articles by Marcel Cachin and Paul Mistral in *l'Humanité*, October 25–6, 1918, and by Léon Jouhaux in *la Bataille*, October 24, 1918.
[1] See *l'Humanité* and *le Populaire*, October 27 to November 4, 1918.

control of the SFIO from the Social Patriots, Barthélemy Mayéras rose "to find out once and for all whether or not the Government of the French Republic was in agreement" with Wilson's aims and principles, particularly as they were formulated on January 8 and September 27. Pichon urged the deputies to postpone the matter *sine die,* insisting that such a discussion would harm the "national interest" by creating the impression that there were differences between Wilson and the Allies. With the approval of 406 deputies the government decisively turned back the Socialists, who mustered only 59 votes.[2]

Clemenceau could not have failed to notice this weakness and isolation, which was accentuated still further by factional discord within the Socialist camp. Albert Thomas and his closest associates among the Social Patriots, determined to dramatize their continuing battle with the ex-*minoritaires,* abstained from voting. Meanwhile Thomas became increasingly torn between distrust of the rising German Social Democracy and fear of a Spartacist breakthrough.

His rivals, the Longuists, obviously also distrusted the SPD, but their slogan was "down with Social Patriotism" on both sides of the Franco-German border. Rather than trust Scheidemann and Ebert, they relied on food shortages and war weariness to drive the German proletariat into the Independent and Spartacist ranks. In their judgment the "German revolution would either be social, or it would be a sham"; and should it take root the French *bourgeoisie* could not stop it at will. The new *majoritaires* indiscriminately cheered Wilson, Hugo Haase, and Liebknecht, all the time admitting that a truly revolutionary republic would hardly be to Wilson's taste.[3] Eventually, following President Wilson's note of November 5, advising Berlin that with two qualifications the Allies had accepted his program, the *Populaire* credulously acclaimed him for summarily squashing the secret treaties, the plans for the left bank of the Rhine, and the projects for an expedition to Russia.[4]

Once the officious, right-wing press endorsed the feasibility and expediency of reducing the enemy without a costly terminal battle, it focused almost exclusively on the direction, sufficiency, and consequences of the political transformation within Germany.

According to the *Temps,* if Germany's unity remained intact "all the so called liberal reforms would be a sham."[5] Systematically but discreetly all available pressures—economic, financial, and military—should be used to undermine Bismarck's proud but menacing edifice. To achieve this goal the *Temps* even was ready to tolerate, if not bolster, Spartacism. After all, Bolshevism was "the product of failure and

2 *JO* (November 5, 1918), 2878–9.
3 See *le Populaire,* October 18 to November 10, 1918, *passim.*
4 *Le Populaire,* November 8, 1918.
5 *Le Temps,* November 4, 1918.

defeat"; and victory would save France from this "mortal contagion," just as it had saved her from domination by Prussian militarism.[6]

But once Prince Max resigned in favor of Ebert and Scheidemann and the Emperor's crown was about to fall, the *Temps* showed signs of disorientation. Who would survive to represent Germany? Both the Reichstag and the Majority Socialists, having acclaimed the war and tolerated Field Marshal Erich Ludendorff, were being overtaken by events, perhaps leaving a shaky Duma to the mercy of an aggressive Soviet.

> We must be prepared to find ourselves faced with an unknown Germany. To be sure, she will no longer be a military force. But she will be a power just the same, one against which military guaranties and the classic policy of Richelieu might be inadequate. Armistice conditions can be imposed on an army, but they cannot be imposed on a propaganda. Whereas particularist tendencies could develop in a Germany where dynasties and privileges survived, none could survive, at least for the short run, in a Germany leveled out by the revolutionary steamroller.

> When Bolshevism triumphed in Russia, the German Government failed to understand the full import of the convulsion it expedientially promoted. It assumed that the war on the Eastern front could be terminated like any other war and that it could quietly reap the fruits of its victory. Germany's leaders did not see that to the military problem of winning the war and the political or economic problem of winning the peace a social problem had been added, which had to be tackled with entirely new methods. They paid dearly for this lack of vision.

Even though the *Temps* boldly contended that the Allies could avoid such shortsightedness, for the moment it was at a loss for specific policy advice.[7] Soon after the Armistice, however, when Spartacism threatened to overwhelm Berlin, this influential paper welcomed it as a specter with which to frighten Bavaria and the Rhineland, whose separatism was both anti-Prussian and anti-Bolshevik. Neither the *Echo de Paris* nor the *Journal des Débats,* two other dailies that were equally close to the Clemenceau administration, were prepared to tolerate a Red Prussia, however fleetingly, particularly as long as Russia remained in Bolshevik hands.[8]

Although Jacques Bainville's column appeared in the royalist and incipiently fascist *Action Française,* his writing was free of the venom with which Charles Maurras and Maurice Pujo dramatized the real and imaginary impotence, corruption, and obliquity of the Third Republic. Bainville agonized over France's security dilemma, at all times putting

[6] *Le Temps,* November 7, 1918.
[7] *Le Temps,* November 10, 1918.
[8] See pp. 303–4 below.

balance-of-power calculations ahead of ideological and political considerations. His was the voice of *raison d'état* which Richelieu would have recognized.

With Herbette, Pertinax, Capus, and Gauvain, he hastened to declare his trust in Wilson's handling of the pre-Armistice negotiations. Bainville hailed the President for planting a "keg of dynamite" under the foundations of the Second Empire with his "Socratic interrogation," and prayed that Wilson would ignite the charge even after the Germans had "simulated" a constitutional and parliamentary transformation. He entreated Wilson—the practical man, the historian, and the logician— to realize that constitutional reform without the dismantling of Bismarck's structure would result in a further centralization and concentration of the German-speaking peoples.[9]

Specifically, if in accordance with the principle of self-determination the Austro-Germans were left free to become part of the German nation-state, 40 million Frenchmen would have to face a bloc of 80 million Germans stretching from Hamburg to Vienna, and that at a time when there was no effective Russian counterweight. Admittedly, the existence of a German nationality could not be gainsaid; nor could anyone deny that it was "the most compact, the most homogeneous, and the best organized in Central Europe." Even so, under no circumstances should Germany receive German Austria as a reward for starting and losing the war. Besides, since there could be no question of "balkanizing and sovietizing" East Central Europe, Austria was needed to help organize that "mosaic" of small, weak, and antagonistic peoples, unfettered to either Berlin or Budapest. In sum, instead of making Allied opposition to the "federalization" of Austria-Hungary his "fifteenth point," Wilson should require Austria to make herself available for this very purpose.[1]

But Wilson stuck to his writ of dissolution, and on October 27 Vienna accepted it unconditionally. In the immediate circumstance Bainville welcomed the Austrian surrender for opening the southern gates to Germany: by exerting pressure on Bavaria, Württemberg, and Saxony the Allies now could hasten not only Germany's capitulation but also her dislocation. In the long run, however, the Allies, having secured the keys to the chaotic Austrian house, assumed the awesome responsibility for putting it in order. To be sure, they would have to look after the interests and claims of Italy, Rumania, and Serbia. But in addition to championing such special national interests, the Allies had to protect the interests of Europe as a whole.

> Europe's tranquility and welfare require, above all, that Austro-Germany cease to exist. Rather than reunite and weld together the Germanic peoples, they should be separated. Whatever remains of

[9] *L'Action Française,* October 16 and 25, 1918.
[1] *L'Action Française,* October 21, 24, and 26, 1918.

the skeleton of the Austrian state should be used to prevent the fusion of the various elements of the German race.

This skeleton could also serve to prevent Central Europe from crumbling into the same appalling confusion as Russia. Anarchy compounded by fierce ethnic squabbles was threatening to rise from the ruins of the only organization which, to date, has managed to regulate this chaos. . . . It is not the first time that Europe has faced this peril. Once before, in 1848, France and England recoiled in horror from the revolutions in Vienna and Budapest. It was then, after practicing the politics of nationality for ten years, that Palmerston exclaimed: "Austria is something worth saving."

Bainville wanted something of the Austrian mechanism saved, less to satisfy his own Catholic, monarchist, and social values than to lay the foundations for a new balance of power favorable to France.[2]

To achieve this overriding objective, the right of self-determination simply had to be denied to the Austro-Germans, and Germany needed to be consumed "by defeat, pest, and revolution." Once the Social Democrats were on the verge of assuming control in Berlin, Bainville exposed the danger of trusting a democratic but nationalist republic: "a vast Socialist state organized, like the trade unions, on the Prussian model, and a republican Germany where the nationalist spirit would promptly be revived, would only provide a few weeks of illusions." Whereas he dreaded revolution and anarchy in the Danubian basin and in Russia, he wished for them with "all his heart" in Germany. Unfortunately, at this particular juncture, anarchy was a "Slav rather than a Germanic disease." Bainville claimed that he could not discern any signs of serious and generalized Bolshevik disorders between the Rhine and the Elbe. In Germany almost as much as in France the mention of Bolshevism either stimulated a watchful fear or was considered a downright insult.[3]

But even assuming France and her Allies actually were confronted by a Soviet Germany, what then? Unlike Germany at the time of Brest Litovsk, the Allies, with all their enemies defeated, would be free to post reliable sentries. At the same time France, secure in her victory, should take advantage of the resulting "providential confusion," much as Richelieu and Oxenstierna had done in another era. With Berlin most likely to go Bolshevik, the anti-Prussians of western and southern Germany and the Poles in Silesia would try to break away, and France should conspire in these centrifugal movements.[4] Moreover, rather than sink scarce resources into faraway Russia to smother Bolshevism there, Paris should concentrate on building up Poland and Rumania as allies against both dissatisfied Germany and Russia.

[2] *L'Action Française,* October 29, 1918.
[3] *L'Action Française,* November 1, 1918.
[4] *L'Action Française,* November 10, 1918.

3

The Vanquished and
the Armistice

BOLSHEVISM in 1918, because of its novel and controversial nature, had a myriad of inchoate but passionate meanings and connotations. Inevitably each political actor's response to Bolshevism was a function of his particular class and status position, his political persuasion, and his attitudes toward the revolutions of 1789 and 1917. Some of the factors conditioning these reactions were common to men and women of similar standing and outlook throughout Europe and America; others were a function of particular national conditions and interests. Among these national variables the political consequences of victory and defeat were of exceptional import.

Under modern conditions of intense domestic conflicts both victory and defeat produce profound political consequences. Whereas victory furthers stability, order, and either conservatism or reaction, defeat generates instability, disorder, and either reform or revolution. Victory in war provides a welcome tonic for the forces of order and reaction; defeat in war presents a perilous opportunity to the forces of reform and revolution.

In the prewar years it was widely assumed that victory or defeat would significantly affect the struggle for power between the Right and the Left. Panic-stricken reactionaries—especially in Russia and Austria-Hungary—opposed war for fear that its strains would produce conditions favorable to revolution; self-confident conservatives tended to favor war in the hope that first the political truce and then victory would serve their partisan purposes; beleaguered liberals exercised extreme caution because, whatever the outcome, war could only further corrode their position vis-à-vis either the Right or the Left;

while most Socialists opposed war in spite of their conviction that defeat could blaze the trail to revolution.

The political consequences of defeat in war became increasingly evident in the sixty years preceding the world catastrophe. After the fall of Sebastopol in 1855 the Tsarist regime was forced to introduce the post-Crimean reforms, exemplified by the liberation of the serfs. Austria's defeat by Prussia in 1866 drove Imperial Vienna into the constitutional compromise with Hungary. The defeat of France in 1870–1 produced first the overthrow of the Second Empire, then the Commune, and eventually the precariously balanced Third Republic. China's defeat in the Sino-Japanese War of 1895 was followed by the Hundred Days Reform in 1898 and the subsequent Boxer Rebellion. Russia's defeat in the Russo-Japanese War generated the revolution of 1905–6 and the Octobrist reforms. Finally, in 1917, military defeat spurred the sequential March and November revolutions in Russia.

In October 1918, both inside and outside the three crumbling empires, statesmen and politicians anxiously faced the political consequences of the military defeat of Germany, Austria-Hungary, and Turkey. Would these consequences reach the scope and intensity of 1870–1, 1905–6, March 1917, or November 1917? Needless to say, the turn of events would be influenced by a wide range of factors: the extent of governmental chaos, army loyalty, flexibility of the ruling elites, food shortages, inflation, unemployment, perspicacity of reformist and revolutionary leaders, and Allied consideration for the successor regimes in the vanquished nations.

All interested parties had to take account of one additional component. Whereas the Commune of 1871 had been confined to Paris, and the revolutions of 1905 and 1917 to Russia, none of the impending insurgencies was likely to remain similarly insulated. Especially the course of the German Revolution seemed destined to be affected by the course of the Russian Revolution. Within and beyond Germany revolutionaries as well as counterrevolutionaries tended to see Prince Max as Prince Lvov, Ebert as Kerensky, and Liebknecht as Lenin. Some sought to avoid Kerensky's mistakes; others meant to match Lenin's achievements; and still others resolved to circumvent both reform and revolution in preparation for an early assault on the Soviet regime in Russia.

Not only revolutionaries and reformers were susceptible to the seductive promises and realities of Soviet Russia and Bolshevism. Neither German nor French Rightists were above contemplating the use of Russian Bolshevism and Prussian Spartacism to advance their national and class interests: the former excogitated a temporary alliance with Soviet Russia as part of a precipitate counterrevolutionary spasm against the Carthaginian victors and their treacherous respon-

dents within Germany; the latter furtively condoned Prussian Spartacism, confident that it would hasten the dissolution of the German
union and facilitate the expansion of French power, which in turn
would bolster France's forces of order.

From the beginning the governments of Prince Max and of Ebert
realized that they would have to fight on two fronts concurrently:
against Spartacism and decomposition at home and against a punitive
peace abroad. Inevitably domestic and foreign policy were intimately
related; in fact, they were cut of one cloth.

In order to check radicalism and disorder at home any provisional
government would have to provide food, employment, and credible
assurances of a decent peace. In turn, food, jobs, and peace were
contingent on the cooperation of the victors, whose help would be
difficult to enlist. On the one hand, the Allies were not likely to assist a
weak government which in order to survive might decree economic and
social reforms that the Allies considered too advanced; on the other
hand, there would be little, if any, inducement for the victors to grant a
Wilsonian peace should this government succeed in restoring and
maintaining order by sheer repression.

Max von Baden, Ebert, Haase, Solf, Erzberger, the German ambassadors in the neutral countries, Brockdorff-Rantzau, and Groener—
all correctly assumed that the Allies were anxious for Germany not to
go Bolshevik and not to come to a working arrangement with Soviet
Russia. They assumed, furthermore, that the Allies could be swayed to
make diplomatic concessions as an inducement for Germany not to
stray from the safe path.

However, the leaders of the New Germany differed about how best
to take advantage of this Allied fear of Bolshevism. Should they
exaggerate the strength of the Spartacists, the extent of Soviet-
supported subversion, the shortage of food, and unemployment? How
terrifying could they make the Bolshevik specter without risking a loss
in credibility? Should they renew diplomatic relations with Soviet
Russia? Alternately, should the German government offer to join the
Allies in their containment of and intervention in Bolshevik Russia?

All along it was difficult to decide which policy or combination of
policies was likely to yield the greatest dividends for the nascent
republican regime and for the German national interest. Some policy
makers urged that priority be given to domestic programs designed to
consolidate the new regime; others advocated the primacy of foreign
policy.

Count Ulrich Brockdorff-Rantzau refused to choose between these
two courses. Instead, he insisted that since "foreign and domestic
politics were practically inseparable he could not carry out foreign
policy successfully without domestic support." He explicitly called for
"the unqualified support" of the Provisional Government's authority;

the immediate summoning of the National Assembly; the early election of a Constituent Assembly; fiscal and financial rehabilitation; and the organization of a republican army.[1] Moreover, before finally accepting the post of Foreign Minister he stipulated that he be given a voice in the "solution of internal questions because . . . today more than ever the success of the Reich's foreign policy depends on internal developments."[2] But neither Brockdorff-Rantzau nor any of the other high elective or appointive officials stated or admitted the extent to which this primacy of foreign policy would or could be used to serve the internal political aims of the Weimar coalition.

Meanwhile, by October 22 Lenin indicated that he was fully prepared for this new turn in German policy. He noted that "finding the victors . . . extremely unaccommodating, [the Max von Baden government] was trying to frighten them with the specter of Bolshevism and to win their good graces by helping them against the Bolsheviks, against the proletarian revolution." Two weeks later he charged that the German government "was making every effort to achieve an alliance" with the Allies. He even claimed to know that the Germans had asked the Allies for permission to leave German troops in "Poland, the Ukraine, Esthonia, and Latvia" until such time as "pro-Entente armies of liberation appear on the scene to strangle the Bolsheviks."[3]

The German delegation at the Armistice negotiations in the forest of Compiègne knowingly and deliberately exploited the specter of Bolshevism. Erzberger, General Detlev von Winterfeldt, Count Alfred Oberndorff and Captain Vanselow repeatedly stressed that excessively severe armistice conditions would foster Bolshevism in Germany. Moreover, they warned that should Bolshevism sweep part or all of Germany, the victors themselves would no longer be safe.[4] Count Oberndorff told Weygand that intolerable terms would either lead "to a resolute fight to the finish or Bolshevism would triumph and turn the country into a chaos like Russia's. [Since] in case of . . . Bolshevism [France risked] the danger of contagion and the loss of German solvency for payment of reparations, [she] had a real interest in preventing the triumph of Bolshevism in Germany."[5]

Evidently Erzberger and his fellow plenipotentiaries needed no coaching. But just in case, on November 8, Foreign Minister Wilhelm

---

[1] GFM 2 (9105/5), H 233347–52, dated Copenhagen, December 9, 1918 (Brockdorff-Rantzau Nachlass).

[2] GFM 2 (9105/5), H 233332–7, dated Copenhagen, December 9, 1918.

[3] Lenin: *Collected Works* (New York: International Publishers; 1945), XXIII, 255, 273.

[4] Matthias Erzberger: *Erlebnisse im Weltkrieg* (Berlin: Deutsche Verlagsanstalt; 1920), 132–3; Maréchal Foch: *Mémoires* (Paris: Plon; 1931), II, 299–300; Commandant L'Hopital: *Foch, L'Armistice et la paix* (Paris: Plon; 1938), 87; Général Weygand: *Le 11 Novembre* (Paris: Flammarion; 1932), 61–3.

[5] Cited in Klaus Epstein: *Matthias Erzberger* (Princeton: Princeton University Press; 1959), 278.

Solf wired them that apparently the "fear of Bolshevism" was mounting and acting *friedensfördernd* in the Allied countries; that especially in Britain Joffe's expulsion had been welcomed; and that the German delegation "might be able to make use of this information in the armistice negotiations."[6]

But Foch simply contended that while Bolshevism was symptomatic of defeated nations, victor nations knew how to protect themselves against this peril. Similarly, Weygand was confident that "the victors had nothing to fear."[7] Obviously, Foch and Weygand endorsed Clemenceau's refusal—during the inter-Allied pre-Armistice negotiations—"to recognize that there was any danger of Bolshevism in France."[8] On that same occasion, unlike Colonel House and Lloyd George, Clemenceau and Sonnino denied any serious risk that the Wehrmacht's withdrawal from German-occupied Eastern Europe would court a Bolshevik influx into that strategically vital rimland. Clemenceau simply would not be "snared" by German propaganda, while Sonnino warned that the Bolshevik scare was part of an old German "trap" which the Allies had to avoid.[9]

On November 9 Clemenceau gave the following summary of Foch's minutes of his initial encounters with the German delegation:

> They have made no remark either as to the bridgeheads or as to the fleet. Their theme is to say that they will succumb to Bolshevism if we do not help them to resist it and that after them we ourselves will be invaded by the same scourge. They have asked that they be permitted to retire more slowly from the left bank of the Rhine saying that they required the means of forming an army to combat Bolshevikism and reestablish order. Foch replied to them that they could form this army on the right bank. They likewise objected that we were taking from them too many machine guns and that they would have none left to fire upon their fellow citizens. Foch replied to them that they would have their rifles left. They also asked what we wanted to do on the left bank of the Rhine. Foch replied to them that he did not know and that it was none of his business. Finally they asked to be reprovisioned by us, saying that they were going to die of hunger. Foch replied to them that it would suffice them to put their merchant marine into our programs and in this way they could be reprovisioned. They replied that they preferred to be given permits for their vessels. They complained that we were taking much too many locomotives, in view of the fact that theirs were

6 GFM 2 (4069/1), D 917041.
7 Foch: *Mémoires*, II, 295; L'Hopital: *Foch*, 87; Karl Friedrich Nowak: *Versailles* (New York: Payson and Clarke; 1929), 14–15.
8 Charles Seymour: *Intimate Papers of Colonel House*, IV, 119.
9 Gabriel Terrail [Mermeix, pseud.]: *Les Négociations secrètes et les quatres armistices* (Paris: Ollendorff; 1919), 233–4.

scattered everywhere. Foch replied to them that we were asking only what they had taken from us. They are very much depressed.[1]

Lloyd George quite justifiably looked upon Clemenceau's account as "characteristically terse and ruthless."[2]

Just the same, not even Foch was altogether immune to fears of the Bolshevik menace. In response to the Germans' repeated warnings of the political hazards of prolonging the blockade and starvation, under Article 26 the Allies now bound themselves to "contemplate the provisioning of Germany during the armistice as shall be found necessary." Likewise, frightened by Erzberger's admonition that the instant evacuation of occupied eastern territories either would enable the Red Army to move into the vacuum or would invite indigenous Bolshevik takeovers, Article 12 stipulated that this evacuation be held up until "the Allies think the moment suitable, having regard to the internal situation of these territories." Erzberger promptly claimed this delayed evacuation under Article 12 as his single greatest achievement in the Armistice negotiations. He and his advisers even boasted that they had "succeeded in establishing a common ground" with the enemy and that it had "fallen to the German delegation to stand up for the *allgemeinen Kultur-und-Menschheitsstandpunkt*."[3]

But the Allies themselves were far from indifferent to the possible spread of Bolshevism in these areas. Under Article 16 they reserved to themselves "free access to the territories evacuated by the Germans on their eastern frontier, either through Danzig or by the Vistula, in order to convey supplies to the populations of these territories or for the purpose of maintaining order." Furthermore, under Articles 25 and 29 the Allies secured complete control of both the Baltic and the Black Sea and the surrender of Russian warships captured by Germany.

Incidentally, the Armistice signed with Austria-Hungary on November 3 specified similar terms. Under Article 4 the Allied armies acquired the right "to occupy such strategic points in Austria-Hungary at such times as they may deem necessary to enable them to conduct military operations or *to maintain order* [italics mine]."[4] In the Armistice with Turkey the Allies were concerned with the strategic access to Russia rather than with internal order. In addition to assuring their access to the Black Sea they secured the right to occupy the forts of the Dardanelles and Bosphorus, as well as any strategic point "in the

---

[1] Cited in *F.R.,1918, Supplement 1*, I, 489–90.
[2] David Lloyd George: *War Memoirs*, II, 1983.
[3] GFM 2 (4069/1), D 916948–9 (Diary of the German Armistice Delegation at Compiègne); and *Stenographische Berichte der verfassunggebenden deutschen Nationalversammlung, 1919–1920* (Berlin, 1920), 527.
[4] *F.R.,P.C.,1919*, II, 176. "To maintain order! What does this mean? . . . We see with increasing clarity what reactionaries read into this very elastic phrase." Marcel Cachin in *l'Humanité*, November 6, 1918.

event of a situation arising which threatens the security of the Allies."
Under Clause 15 the Turks were forced to sanction the Allied occupation of both Batum and Baku.[5]

If the Provisional Government was to maintain order in politically
unstable Germany and to protect the eastern borderlands against the
advancing Red Army it needed the services of a loyal and efficient
army and police force. Adroitly the German delegates at Rethondes
urged that "it was to the advantage of everybody that the German
Army march back to Germany in orderly fashion; to do this the time
limit fixed for the evacuation had to be extended . . . not by allowing
merely additional days, but weeks."[6] Though it is not clear how the
Allies reacted to this line of argument, the fact remains that they did
nothing to interfere with the orderly withdrawal of the German army.
Moreover, the Germans were given an additional six days in which to
evacuate the right and left banks of the Rhine, an additional two weeks
for the surrender of 5,000 locomotives and 150,000 railway cars, and
an additional twenty days for the delivery of trucks. The victors also
agreed to have the enemy surrender 5,000 instead of 10,000 trucks,
25,000 instead of 30,000 machine guns, and 1,700 instead of 2,000
planes.[7]

In spite of these minimal concessions in the Armistice terms, the
negotiations in the Compiègne forest confirmed the leaders of the New
Germany in their estimate that Wilson rather than Foch, Clemenceau,
or even Lloyd George was their man. To be sure, they realized fully
that the event of victory had substantially reduced the President's
influence and power over his Allies. Even so, he would continue to be
Germany's trump card. Because of America's limited stakes in Western
Europe, Wilson could be expected to exert himself in favor of a
reasonable settlement. Moreover, because of his reformist persuasion
and temperament Wilson was likely to be particularly sensitive to
anarchy, famine, and revolution in Central Europe. And last, he alone
could muster the economic, financial, and shipping resources with
which not only to revictual Germany but also to temper France,
Britain, and Italy.

After receiving authorization to sign the Armistice—but before
actually signing it—Erzberger advised Berlin to impress on Wilson that
if famine and anarchy were to be avoided negotiations for a preliminary peace should start forthwith. Meanwhile, so as not to lose precious
time, the Allies should dispatch a commission to Germany which,

[5] *F.R.,1918, Supplement 1,* I, 441–2. The right-wing press in France welcomed these
provisions for facilitating the large-scale anti-Soviet military campaign in the
Ukraine, Kiev, and Odessa, which they favored. In turn, the Socialists denounced
these counterrevolutionary schemes. *Le Populaire,* November 3, 1918.
[6] Foch: *Mémoires,* II, 299–300.
[7] *F.R.,1918, Supplement 1,* I, 463–8, 494–8.

Erzberger was confident, would conclude that the rigorous application of the Armistice could result only in starvation.[8]

The following day Paul von Hintze, the Foreign Ministry's delegate at Supreme Headquarters, sent a still more urgent message: "Supreme Command considers it extremely important that President Wilson and all of America be filled with horror of the spread of Bolshevism in Germany. It suggests that to accomplish this the Foreign Ministry should utilize vigorously and with utmost speed all available channels to President Wilson and to America." That Berlin was on this same wavelength was clear from the marginal comment on this telegram by a high official in the Foreign Ministry: "Has already been taken care of and will continue to be forcefully pursued. By the way, from Wilson's speeches it appears that he himself is apprehensive of Bolshevism."[9]

Solf had lost no time in enlisting the German ambassadors in Switzerland, Denmark, and Holland in this same campaign. He instructed Romberg, Brockdorff-Rantzau, and Rosen to prevail on the governments to which they were accredited to apprise the Allies of their fear of political chaos and food shortages in Germany. Because of geographic proximity these neutral nations could claim to be particularly vulnerable should Bolshevism triumph in Germany. Apparently Solf and his ambassadors agreed to put special emphasis on the impending food shortages and their perilous consequences.[1]

By November 10 the American Legation in Berne reported a message by Solf to the Swiss Minister in Washington, for presentation to Lansing on the twelfth: "The German Government urgently requests the President of the United States to inform the German Chancellor Ebert by wireless, whether he may be assured that the Government of the United States is ready to send foodstuffs without delay *if public order is maintained in Germany* and an equitable distribution of food is guaranteed [italics mine]."[2] That very same day Lansing sent out the desired answer: "Accordingly the President now directs me to state that he is ready to consider favorably the supplying of foodstuffs to Germany and to take up the matter immediately with the Allied Governments, *provided he can be assured that public order is being and will continue to be maintained in Germany,* and that an equitable distribution of food can be clearly guaranteed [italics mine]."[3]

This exchange of cables promptly became an issue in domestic politics. The Spartacist *Rote Fahne,* insisting that Lansing's cable was

8 GFM 2 (4069/1), D 917051.
9 GFM 2 (4069/1), D 917243.
1 GFM 2 (4069/1), D 917062, D 917177, D 917244.
2 National Archives 862.48/34; *F.R.,P.C.,1919,* II, 629; Lansing, *Desk Diary,* November 12, 1918. In another message Solf urged the President to hasten the start of peace negotiations because of the "pressing danger of a famine." *F.R.,P.C.,1919,* II, 19.
3 *F.R.,P.C., 1919,* II, 629–30.

in reply to Ebert's, accused the Provisional Government of coaching President Wilson about the political conditions under which the Allies should supply food to Germany. In other words, the Spartacists upbraided Ebert for making political capital out of the food shortage and with using the Washington connection to buttress his own position. Whereas the government turned down an offer of Soviet wheat free of political strings, it solicited Western aid with strings attached.[4]

Actually the *Temps* was the first major European paper to see Ebert's move as part of a larger effort "to consolidate his government . . . vis-à-vis the dissident Socialists, and even vis-à-vis his USPD colleagues, with whom he was still forced to share power." First Prince Max had tried to use Wilson as umpire. Now, by addressing the President alone, rather than the Big Four, on a vital issue, Ebert sought "to transform the umpire into a champion of the German cause, the benefactor first into supplier, then into lender, and finally into partner." Obviously Ebert was not just after food supplies, otherwise he would not have proposed the political strings to Washington.[5]

Meanwhile Lansing's reassuring reply had been widely publicized and enthusiastically hailed on the front pages of all loyal German newspapers. In an unguarded moment both the *Frankfurter Zeitung* and the *Berliner Tageblatt* even reprinted the text of Solf's controversial cable of the tenth.[6] In spite of the publication of the document in the *Rote Fahne*, the *Temps,* the neutral press, and the two liberal German newspapers, the government availed itself of the *Vorwärts* to deny its authenticity, to characterize "the charge that Ebert had proposed any conditions to the Entente as a complete fabrication," and to dismiss it all as a typical "Spartacist swindle."[7]

In the meantime, in a message thanking Wilson, Solf reiterated that "the danger of anarchy could only be averted by the speediest grant of relief"; that it was essential to start negotiations leading "to the timely saving of our Fatherland through the magnanimous help of America"; and that "the matter might perhaps be put in the tried hands of Mr. Hoover."[8] Furthermore, the Foreign Minister sent personal representa-

---

[4] *Rote Fahne,* November 30, December 2, December 15, 1918. See also the Spartacist handbill "Wer schwingt die Hungerpeitsche?" in *Dokumente und Materialien zur Geschichte der deutschen Arbeiterbewegung,* 2nd Series (Berlin: Dietz; 1957), II, 523–5.

[5] *Le Temps,* November 16, 1918. Within two days the cabinet decided that to avoid antagonizing the Entente, future notes had best be addressed to all four Allies. See *Protokolle des Rats der Volksbeauftragten,* meeting of November 18, 1918, 5:30 p.m.

[6] *Berliner Tageblatt,* November 14, 1918 (p.m.), and *Frankfurter Zeitung,* November 15, 1918 (a.m.). Both papers had picked up the text from the wires of the Hollandsch Nieuws Bureau.

[7] *Vorwärts,* November 29 and December 1, 1918. The text of the denial in the *Vorwärts* of December 1, 1918, was prepared in the Foreign Ministry. See GFM 2 (4069/1), D 919214–17.

[8] *F.R.,P.C.,1919,* II, 18–19.

tives to Berne and Copenhagen to support the efforts of his ambassadors with first-hand reassurances that the Provisional Government was determined to maintain order, but that for this policy to succeed—which was also in the best interest of the Allies—it was "absolutely imperative" to hasten food supplies to Germany.[9]

During the weeks immediately following the Armistice, did the Provisional Government always initiate discussions or comments about the danger of Bolshevism in Germany, or were there occasions when the Allies took the initiative, either directly or indirectly?

In the Foreign Ministry, reports about Allied attitudes to Bolshevism from embassies in neutral countries were analyzed by Rudolf Nadolny, who incorporated them into his regular intelligence digests, which were submitted to all six *Volksbeauftragten*.[1] On one occasion the discussion of one of Von Romberg's reports by the cabinet prompted Barth to move, unsuccessfully, that "Social Democrats be appointed to run the embassies in Berne, The Hague, and Copenhagen."[2] By now Barth was suspicious of the concerted effort by Solf and his old-guard diplomats to play up or even encourage Allied opposition to revolution, to Workers' and Soldiers' Councils, and to resumption of relations with Soviet Russia. Barth might have been more suspicious still had he known that Solf had covertly notified the British Minister at The Hague that in case the Spartacists succeeded in securing Joffe's return "the situation would become critical" and that therefore the Allies should "let it be known that there would be no toleration of Bolshevism and it [was] earnestly hoped that the moment there were signs that disorderly elements were getting the upper hand they would resume hostilities."[3]

What, then, did German ambassadors report to Berlin? The major themes emerge clearly from one of Rosen's earliest dispatches from The Hague, dated November 13.

> American Embassy has had me informed confidentially that Entente is agreed that present and future concessions in food, armistice and peace terms will only be granted in case of continuance and existing composition of Ebert Cabinet. The Entente and America consider this socialist-bourgeois government under Ebert, which guarantees order and private property, as a pledge of goodwill for the settlement of pending issues and for peace negotiations.
>
> Should the Ebert Cabinet be forced to yield to Bolshevik demands, then the Entente would consider all heretofore promised concessions as invalid. Entente would have to cancel the Armistice and advance [into Germany]. Joffe's recall to Berlin might be the

[9] GFM 2 (4069/1), D 917488–9.
[1] GFM 2 (4069/1), D 917323–D 918134, *passim*.
[2] *Protokolle des Rats der Volksbeauftragten*, meeting of November 18, 1918, 5:30 p.m.
[3] *F.R.,P.C.,1919*, II, 94–5.

occasion for these steps. Entente could not assume responsibility for the life of Joffe and his followers.[4]

Early in the afternoon of November 16 Romberg wired two similar dispatches from Berne. He noted that according to the French press and the Swiss government the Allies would refuse to negotiate with a Bolshevik Germany and that judging by hints emanating from the U. S. and British embassies a Bolshevik regime would not satisfy Wilson's conditions for food. Romberg called on Berlin to launch a propaganda campaign abroad designed to reassure the Allies about the internal situation in Germany.[5]

During the following twenty-four hours Romberg reported that the French and American embassies would consider the return of Joffe to Berlin and the transit through Germany of Angelica Balabanov and other known Bolsheviks as evidence of German duplicity. He again urged his superiors to declare officially and publicly that relations with Moscow were not about to be resumed and that should any Bolsheviks travel through Germany, they would do so in a sealed car.[6] A week later Romberg sent word that immediately following the occupation of the Rhine bridgeheads the Allies were likely to demand that the Workers' and Soldiers' Councils be dissolved to make room for a legitimate government.[7]

From Copenhagen Brockdorff-Rantzau sent similar dispatches based on conversations with Erik Scavenius, former Danish Ambassador to Russia and now Foreign Minister, on statements attributed to Ulysses Grant-Smith, U. S. Chargé in Copenhagen, and on conferences with Abrahamson, the Vice-President of the British Red Cross.[8]

This information and counsel from the ambassadors were reinforced by admonitions from Hindenburg and from Germany's delegates on the Armistice Commission. On November 20 Field Marshal Paul von Hindenburg, fearful of any resumption of hostilities, advised the Foreign Ministry, Ebert, and Erzberger that he gathered from statements by Colonel House, British officials, and French newspapers that the enemy governments would conclude peace only with a government supported by the "majority of the people."[9] Along similar lines on

[4] GFM 2 (4069/1), D 917323-4. Rosen offered to send his informant, who was said to be personally acquainted with Haase and Bernstein, to Berlin.

[5] GFM 2 (4069/1), D 917462-4. The marginalia on this document read as follows: "for press and other uses . . . please advise the W.T.B. [Wolffsche Telegraphen Büro]."

[6] GFM 2 (4069/1), D 917940-95, D 917503-4, D 917552-4.

[7] GFM 2 (4069/1), D 918121.

[8] GFM 2 (4069/1), D 917602-3, D 917952, D 918133-4. On Brockdorff-Rantzau's telegram reporting Grant-Smith's statement, Solf made the following marginal notation: "To be placed before Mr. Ebert at once."

[9] GFM 2 (4069/1), D 917759. In their answer Ebert and Haase agreed that "we must do everything in order not to give the enemy any excuse for the resumption of hostilities." Ibid., D 917764.

November 22 Von Haniel, in a wire from Trier, pointed out that enemy spokesmen had confidentially hinted that the Allies "would not negotiate with the Workers' and Soldiers' Councils" (marginalia *gut*). By December 13 Erzberger flatly asserted that the Allies refused to recognize these Councils and recommended that this disapprobation be publicized.[1]

It seems no exaggeration to say that key agencies of the executive branch were actively engaged in the assessment, the use, and the abuse of Allied apprehensions about the danger of Bolshevism, anarchy, famine, and resumption of Soviet-German relations. In addition to Ebert and Solf, the participants in this diplomatic manipulation of the specter of Bolshevism were the Foreign Ministry, the Diplomatic Corps, the Armistice Commission, the Army, the War Press Office, the Censor, the Reichszentrale für Heimatdienst, and the Vaterländische Unterricht.

This semicoordinated campaign could only benefit the Provisional Government, and within this government the Majority Socialists as well as the imperial diplomatic and officer corps, to the detriment of the USPD, the Spartacists, and the Workers' and Soldiers' Councils. In brief, this constant play on Allied fears of Bolshevism served to strengthen the internal forces of the *status quo* against the forces of change, as the press realized from the very start.[2]

Beginning with the evening editions of November 11 the news, rumors, and evaluations of Entente and American attitudes toward the Provisional Government and Germany were front-page copy. "The Entente Opposed to a Bolshevik Germany" was the banner headline with which the first post-Armistice edition of the *Deutsche Zeitung* reported expressions of Allied anti-Bolshevism from The Hague. Within a week the *Deutsche Tageszeitung, Germania,* and the *Kreuzzeitung* also heralded the Entente's refusal to have any dealings with a Bolshevik Germany.[3] Incidentally, these dire forecasts in the right-wing press, as well as those in liberal, Socialist, and Catholic papers, tended to be based on the tendentious news releases of the Wolff Telegraph Service, prepared in the Foreign Ministry.

As of November 11 the *Berliner Tageblatt* kept stressing that since Wilson and the Allies refused to deal with any dictatorship—

[1] GFM 2 (4069/1), D 917911 and D 919162.
[2] Two Left-dissident participants attached considerable importance to this aspect of the German Revolution: Emil Barth: *Aus der Werkstatt der deutschen Revolution* (Berlin: Hoffmanns Verlag; 1919), *passim;* and Richard Müller: *Vom Kaiserreich zur Republik* (Vienna: Malik Verlag; 1925), II, *passim.* Since the Second World War East German scholars have been perhaps overly sensitive to the uses and abuses of the Bolshevik bogey. See especially Günter Rosenfeld: *Sowjetrussland und Deutschland, 1917–1922* (Berlin: Akademie-Verlag; 1960); and Albert Norden: *Zwischen Berlin und Moskau* (Berlin: Dietz Verlag; 1954).
[3] *Deutsche Zeitung,* November 11, 1918; and *Bulletin Périodique de la presse allemande,* No. 99 (November 12–21, 1918), 3.

whether of the Left or Right—the immediate election of a Constituent
Assembly was indispensable. The *Frankfurter Zeitung* made this same
plea, buttressed by the warning that if Germany were engulfed by chaos
the Allies would treat her as they were treating Russia. Both liberal
papers urged that while early elections were being prepared all the
forces favoring stability should pull together in the interest of securing
food and peace.[4]

It is still an open question whether Germany's food situation was
ever as desperate and acute as the government and its supporters made
it out to be.[5] Regardless, it now became fashionable to argue—both
inside and outside Germany—that whereas the Kerensky government
had fallen because of failure to win Allied approbation for a liberaliza-
tion of war aims or for Russia's withdrawal from the war,[6] the Ebert
government might fall because of its inability to procure food from the
Allies. Especially the parties and newspapers of the incipient Weimar
coalition emphasized the connective relationship of order, bread, and
peace—in that sequence. Accordingly, order was a prerequisite for
getting supplies from the Allies; the government needed food and raw
materials, the carrot rather than the stick, to solidify its position; and
the Allies, in particular Wilson, would only consider a stable but
moderate regime entitled to a place at the peace table and to membership in the League of Nations. Not surprisingly, between the Armistice
and the elections of mid-January the Weimar parties made their bid for
power with such slogans as "Without Order, No Bread"; "Disorder
Brings Famine"; "Peace Will Be Achieved Through Order"; and
"Bread, Order, and Peace Are Inseparable."[7]

Allied antagonism to revolutionary chaos and change helped to
settle three major issues of the German Revolution in favor of the
forces of order: the emasculation of the Workers' and Soldiers' Councils; the early election of the Constituent Assembly; and the decision
not to resume relations with the Soviet Untion. Needless to say, this use
of Allied pressure was but one of many factors working for the
consolidation of the Provisional Government.

Quite apart from the degree of order or disorder, what form of

---

[4] *Berliner Tageblatt,* November 11, 18, and 22, 1918; and *Frankfurter Zeitung,* November 13, 17, 23, and 28, 1918.

[5] As early as November 12 Romberg reported that the Allies assumed that Germany
had ample supplies until April. GFM 2 (4069/1), D 917244. Thereafter repeated
efforts were made to get Herbert Hoover or Alonzo Taylor to come to Germany
for an on-the-spot investigation. Incidentally, from November 1918 through April
1919 repeated promises rather than actual deliveries of food were politically
decisive. The visits of some of Hoover's men performed a similar stabilizing
function. See below, pp. 264 ff.

[6] See my *Political Origins of the New Diplomacy, 1917–1918,* 245–58.

[7] See *Revolutions-Urkunden-Sammlung* (Charlottenburg: Archiv-Dienst Englemann;
1919); and *Das politische Plakat* (Charlottenburg: Verlag "das Plakat"; 1919).

government would the Allies tolerate? This question produced a stormy debate on the eve of the first renewal of the Armistice on December 12 in Trier. The old Right as well as the new forces of order seemed intent on proving that the Allies would have no truck with the Provisional Government as presently constituted. Whereas the *Deutsche Zeitung* and, to a lesser extent, the *Berliner Tageblatt,* sought to avail themselves of this alleged diplomatic pressure to revive the old Reichstag and Bundesrat, the *Vorwärts* used it to extricate the Volksbeauftragten from the tutelage of the Executive Committee of the Workers' and Soldiers' Councils, to strengthen Ebert vis-à-vis Haase, and to move up the election of the Constituent Assembly.

According to the *Kölnische Zeitung* of December 10 the Allies were about to call for the dissolution of all Workers' and Soldiers' Councils; moreover "the Entente would refuse all negotiations not only with these Councils, but also with the present government which, given its one-sided Socialist composition, [could not] legitimately speak for the German people." This unauthenticated story was carried and commented upon by all the major dailies.

The *Deutsche Zeitung* seized this occasion to proclaim "the bankruptcy of the Revolution."

> The Revolution has led the German Reich into the abyss. . . . Nothing demonstrates the bankruptcy of the Revolution more clearly than the fact that the Entente does not recognize the present government. Well, Herr Scheidemann, who is the fool now? He who believed in a peace dictated by Germany, or he who chased the ridiculous phantasy of peace by mutual understanding? . . . It is beyond doubt that the present government is neither viable nor effective. It is equally beyond doubt that the enemy will refuse to negotiate with this small heap of hopeless old men. Furthermore it is certain that the occupation of Germany is merely a question of a few days.[8]

Ironically, many monarchists and reactionaries of ultranationalist persuasion were prepared to condone Allied military intervention which, though not likely to restore the *ancien régime,* would crush the Revolution.

The more moderate and responsible conservatives did not advocate such a drastic solution. They admitted that the debate about Allied intentions was part of the internal struggle for power which allowed for only two alternatives: either the Independents would break with the Spartacists or else they would break with the SPD, prepared to shoulder the full responsibility for the resulting radicalization of politics. Should they choose the second alternative, the Provisional Government would

[8] *Deutsche Zeitung,* December 12, 1918.

have to redouble its efforts to maintain order—which was all the Allies cared about. But in the last analysis "it was for internal reasons rather than out of external fear that this order was necessary."[9]

The *Berliner Tageblatt* set the pace in this campaign to use external pressures for domestic purposes. It was the first important daily to repeat—in heavy print—the report that the Allies were about to demand the dissolution of the Workers' and Soldiers' Councils. Moreover, on December 11 it reported that Foch had been ordered "to take measures against German anarchy"; that in both Britain and France pressure was building up against negotiations "in which representatives of the Workers' and Soldiers' Councils or of the revolutionary parties would participate"; and that the impending Allied ultimatum was inclining the cabinet to summon the Reichstag in the hope of both heading off foreign occupation and securing recognition.[1]

But the mouthpiece of the Majoritarians in the Provisional Government was most ouspoken and unscrupulous on this score of Allied pressure. In a banner headline clear across the front page, the *Vorwärts* warned of the "Approaching Invasion of Germany."

> It is almost certain that the Entente is . . . preparing a new ultimatum . . . to enforce the reestablishment of legitimate peace and order in Germany.
>
> According to the *Temps,* at the forthcoming Paris Conference the Allies will consider a note about the immediate disbanding of all Workers' and Soldiers' Councils. This note, to be dispatched after Wilson's arrival, sets a four-week time-limit for the restoration of the legitimate authorities. If this deadline is not met the Allies themselves will take charge of the struggle against Bolshevism in Germany.
>
> Moreover, there are further reports from London which support the credibility of this threat. . . . *The Times* writes that a Spartacist victory would be a summons to the Allies to invade Germany in order to reestablish order there.[2]

The *Vorwärts* itself conceded that whereas "the Right was taking advantage of these reports to agitate for a summoning of the Reichstag," the SPD would rather see the forthcoming national congress of Workers' and Soldiers' Councils overrule the USPD and move the national elections to an earlier date than February 16.[3]

Curiously enough, the *Frankfurter Zeitung* forcefully protested the irresponsible rumor-mongering of the *Tageblatt* and the *Vorwärts*. It

---

[9] *Deutsche Allgemeine Zeitung,* December 12, 1918 (p.m.).

[1] The morning and evening editions of the *Berliner Tageblatt,* December 11 and 12, 1918.

[2] *Vorwärts,* December 11, 1918 (a.m.).

[3] *Vorwärts,* December 11, 1918 (p.m.). This editorial also referred to the support for the reconvening of the Reichstag by the Centrist Konrad Adenauer, the Lord Mayor of Cologne.

intimated that the imputation of certain intentions to the Allies "might well be the outgrowth of interested phantasies"; lamented the spirit of the rising *Ordnungsfanatismus;* recalled the servility of the old Reichstag; praised the services rendered by the Councils during this transitional period; and expressed the hope that the national congress of Workers' and Soldiers' Councils would promote the unity of the Left and decide for prompt elections, thereby removing all excuses for Allied intervention, "should such [plans] really exist."[4] Within two days the paper's Geneva correspondent corroborated the suspicion that the intentions of the victors were being misrepresented deliberately: a careful check of the *Temps,* rather than yield any reference to an impending ultimatum, disclosed a certain French enthusiasm for disorderly conditions in Germany.[5]

The Independents, even though cautioning against politically inspired scares, never went to the extreme of altogether excluding the possibility of a counterrevolutionary intervention by the Entente.[6] Still further to the Left was voiced the opinion that although it was not "particularly surprising" that the bourgeois *Berliner Tageblatt* should circulate purposely misleading stories it was "scandalous" that the organ of the Majority Socialists should bend alleged Allied intentions to their own political purposes.[7]

In fact, the Armistice was renewed for a month without difficulty. Apparently Foch never even raised any questions about either the form or the composition of the Provisional Government. True, when Erzberger requested permission for the delegates of the Workers' and Soldiers' Council of Allied-occupied Kreuznach to travel to Berlin to attend their National Congress on December 16, Foch turned him down. But it was Erzberger who chose to construe this routine refusal as an Allied decision "not to recognize the Workers' and Soldiers' Councils." At Erzberger's suggestion, the government then proceeded to publicize widely this rebuff with a view to strengthening the hand of the moderates at the forthcoming Berlin Congress.[8]

But before this congress convened, the anti-republicans of the Right sought to take advantage of this campaign of intimidation to test their influence and power over the government, the SPD, the USPD, and the Councils. On December 12 the Centrist Konstantin Fehrenbach, President of the defunct Reichstag, served notice that he would convene this body at a place and time to be announced forthwith. He pretended to take this step, which he claimed Ebert should have taken,

---

4 *Frankfurter Zeitung,* December 12, 1918 (p.m.).
5 *Frankfurter Zeitung,* December 14, 1918 (a.m.).
6 *Freiheit,* December 11, 1919.
7 *Leipziger Volkszeitung,* December 11, 1918.
8 GFM 2 (4069/3), D 919162. It is not without significance that the *Vorwärts* never even pretended to protest Foch's refusal. See also *Frankfurter Zeitung, Deutsche Zeitung,* and *Deutsche Allgemeine Zeitung* of December 19, 1918.

because the Allies refused to recognize and negotiate with the present government. Professing that the Allies still acknowledged the legitimacy of the old Reichstag and the Bundesrat, Fehrenbach meant to invest this imperial legislature not only with the authority to select and confirm cabinets but also with framing the voting laws for the election of the projected Constituent Assembly.[9] Significantly, even the *Frankfurter Zeitung* and the *Berliner Tageblatt* cautiously endorsed Fehrenbach's scheme, suggesting that there might be no other way of getting peace, ending the blockade, securing food and raw materials, and liberating the Rhenish cities from enemy occupation.[1]

The Provisional Government instantly and scathingly denounced Fehrenbach. It declared once again that the Revolution had swept away the political institutions of the Second Empire, reaffirmed its own *Verhandlungsfähigkeit,* vouched that all Socialists would ignore Fehrenbach's call, and ominously inquired whether this "rump parliament" proposed to raise its own soldiers to fight those of the Republic. The government's unqualified censure killed the project. However, with the experience gained in manipulating the threat of revolution, the Social Democrats now proceeded to enlist the specter of reaction: they countered the "counterrevolutionary slogans summoning the defunct Reichstag with revolutionary slogans calling for the immediate election of the Constituent Assembly."[2] The so-called Fehrenbach plot enabled the Majoritarians to present their plea for immediate elections in a revolutionary guise at the forthcoming Berlin Congress of Workers' and Soldiers' Councils.

The issue of whether or not to convene a Constituent Assembly may well have been the single most revealing as well as most critical issue of the German Revolution. Center-right liberals proposed such an assembly as a moderating influence; the conservatives promptly appreciated the wisdom of this proposal; the Socialists also accepted it, squaring it with the Erfurt program and using it as a weapon against the *enragés;* most of the Independents agreed to it on condition that the Councils keep the upper hand until essential reforms were implemented; and, whenever their machinations were foiled, even the Fehrenbachs reconciled themselves to it. Only the Spartacists, the left-Independents, and the revolutionary Shop Stewards peremptorily rejected it in favor of a permanent council system.

Presently the timing of the elections became a hotly contested issue. Whereas the Independents wanted them delayed for a brief transitional period, their rivals wanted them held at the earliest practical date. This

9 *Vorwärts,* December 13, 1918 (a.m.).

1 *Frankfurter Zeitung,* December 13, 1918 (p.m.); and *Berliner Tageblatt,* December 13, 1918 (a.m.). Needless to say, the right-wing press gave unqualified support to Fehrenbach, in particular the *Kreuzzeitung,* the *Tägliche Rundschau,* and *Germania.*

2 *Vorwärts,* December 13, 1918 (a.m.).

question of timing sealed the schism between, on the one hand, the SPD and the right-Independents, and, on the other, the militants of the Left. Clearly, with the controversy reduced to what appeared to be a procedural squabble, those pressing for the earliest possible balloting were bound to draw Allied wishes and intentions into the balance.

To begin with, on the very eve of the Revolution Prince Max and his advisers quite suddenly decided that a Constituent National Assembly chosen by universal man and woman suffrage might be an effective antidote to mounting radicalism. On November 8, in a last-minute effort to circumvent the SPD's abdication ultimatum, the last Imperial Chancellor submitted the following proposal to the Kaiser:

> To enable the old Social Democratic Party to remain in the Government and to prevent the masses going over into the radical camp . . . His Majesty [should] at once declare his firm determination to abdicate as soon as the armistice negotiations have reached a point which permits of the issue of writs for the election of a Constituent National Assembly. Such an Assembly would have to determine the new forms of constitution . . . [and] regulate all the constitutional questions connected with the abdication.[3]

The next day, when the Kaiser's position became totally untenable, Prince Max thought that the time was ripe "to come out with the Abdication, with Ebert's Chancellorship, with the appeal to the people to determine its own Constitution in a Constituent National Assembly. . . . Perhaps we should then succeed in diverting the revolutionary energy into the lawful channels of an election campaign."[4] That same day, in the communiqué proclaiming the Kaiser's abdication, Prince Max flatly promised an Assembly; moreover, he secured Ebert's agreement "in principle to such a National Assembly" before yielding the chancellorship to him.[5]

Meanwhile, as of November 8 the liberal-bourgeois and conservative press eagerly threw its full weight behind the election compaign. When Theodor Wolff, the editor of the *Tageblatt,* finally conceded that the Kaiser had to go, he criticized the SPD's ultimatum for not instantly pressing for a Constituent Assembly "to settle the *Kaiserfrage* and to recast the constitution." Wolff, who was also one of the principal founders of the Democratic Party, envisaged such an Assembly as a "vital order-generating agency and a safety-valve for prevailing tensions." At last, in announcing Ebert's accession, he boasted that the Assembly would be convoked promptly, "just as we demanded it."[6]

For the *Frankfurter Zeitung,* also, the choice was now between National Assembly and Councils, Democracy and Bolshevism, Giron-

[3] Cited in *The Memoirs of Prince Max of Baden* (New York: Scribner's; 1928), II, 332.
[4] Ibid., II, 351.
[5] Ibid., II, 353, 355.
[6] *Berliner Tageblatt,* November 8–10, 1918, both morning and evening editions.

dism and Jacobinism. But having advocated genuine parliamentarism for decades the *Zeitung* considered itself best qualified to promote it now. Not without reason it begged all conservatives and Pan-Germans to restrain their eleventh-hour enthusiasm for representative institutions in order not to burden these with the suspicions with which they themselves were viewed.[7]

The SPD and USPD leaders were no less aware that the Constituent Assembly was in danger of being discredited by this fervent but opportunistic support in conservative and reactionary circles,[8] particularly since even the *Deutsche Zeitung* chose Armistice Day to concede that "in actual fact the National Assembly was *the only* chance to salvage something from this chaos and to facilitate the Anschluss of German Austria." Once the Provisional Government formally committed itself to elections, this Pan-German and monarchist organ reproached Ebert for not setting a firm polling day; and once this day was set for early February, it disapproved of this date for being too distant.[9] The National Liberals expressed their impatience in much the same terms.[1] Needless to say, by mid-December all the reconstituted, realigned, and relabeled reactionary, conservative, and liberal parties had issued manifestoes calling for instant elections and spelling out the programs—the thinly disguised counterrevolutionary programs—with which they proposed to fight these elections.[2]

Perhaps it was not without significance that prominent members of the intelligentsia lent their prestige to this broad-scale movement designed to curb the Revolution, to head off one-class rule, to salvage time-honored institutions, and to embrace the democratic institutions which promised to bring Germany food and preliminary peace. Among these scholars and intellectuals were such belated and reluctant converts from monarchism as Max Weber, Alfred Weber, Friedrich Meinecke, Ernst Troeltsch, and Hans Delbrück.[3] Moreover, those few independent spirits who had resisted the wartime jingoist hysteria now

[7] *Frankfurter Zeitung,* especially November 9, 11–12, and 21, 1918.

[8] *Vorwärts, passim; Freiheit,* November 27, 1918; Wilhelm Dittmann, in *Allgemeiner Kongress der Arbeiter und Soldatenräte Deutschlands, Dezember 16–21, 1918, Stenographische Berichte,* 23, col. 45.

[9] *Deutsche Zeitung,* November 11, 14, 18, and 23, 1918. See also *Berliner Lokalanzeiger, passim.*

[1] See their manifesto in the *Berliner Börsenzeitung,* November 13, 1918, cited in Kurt Ahnert (ed.): *Die Entwicklung der deutschen Revolution und das Kriegsende, Oktober 1–November 30, 1918* (Nürnberg: Burgverlag; 1918).

[2] See the comprehensive compilation of party and election manifestos of the DNVP, the Christian Democratic Peoples Party, DVP, and the German Democratic Party in Friedrich Purlitz (ed.): *Deutscher Geschichtskalender: Die deutsche Revolution* (Leipzig: Felix Meiner; 1919), I, 329 ff.

[3] Wolfgang J. Mommsen: *Max Weber und die deutsche Politik, 1890–1920* (Tübingen: Mohr; 1959), Ch. viii; Friedrich Meinecke: *Strassburg-Freiburg-Berlin, 1901–1919* (Stuttgart: Koehler; 1949), 258–9; Ernst Troeltsch: *Spektator-Briefe* (Tübingen: Mohr; 1924), 12; Annelise Thimme: *Hans Delbrück als Kritiker der wilhelminischen Epoche* (Düsseldorf: Droste; 1955), 142–9.

rallied around the revived Bund Neues Vaterland which as early as October 19, 1918, championed a National Assembly. The steering committee of this association included Albert Einstein, Wilhelm Herzog, Paul Cassirer, Alfred Fried, Käthe Kollwitz, Walter Schücking, and Heinrich Mann.[4]

This, then, was the domestic context in which the three major Socialist factions fought out the issue of Constituent Assembly *vs.* Workers' and Soldiers' Councils—while Wilson and Lenin exercised influence from abroad.

The SPD, supported by many of the unions, never intended the Revolution to go beyond the overthrow of the autocratic political institutions of the Second Empire. Once universal suffrage and full legislative control of the executive were effectuated—under a republic or a constitutional monarchy—the Social Democrats were willing to leave major economic and social reforms to the Reichstag in which they confidently expected to achieve and maintain a decisive majority. This program had the great merit not only of aligning Germany's political institutions with Western Europe's but also of appealing to Woodrow Wilson.

Whereas the moderate wing of the USPD fell in with this gradualist approach, the left-Independents, the Shop Stewards, and the Spartacists reversed the order. They would not trust any popularly elected assembly until after the bureaucracy was deimperialized, the Prussian army dissolved in favor of a people's militia, and key sectors of the economy were socialized. In these radical circles it was readily conceded that during a transitional period a proletarian dictatorship, in the guise of a provisional government accountable to the councils, would have to put through this vast and fundamental reconstruction.

These divergent strategies of the SPD, the temperate Independents, and the *enragés* clashed as early as November 9, when Germany's Socialist leaders thrashed out among themselves the terms on which to form a provisional government. In these hurried negotiations the executive of the SPD argued that the decision between a bourgeois and Socialist republic should be made by the electorate, speaking through a constituent assembly, and rejected out of hand even a transient class dictatorship as contrary to the democratic principles of Socialism. The SPD spokesmen contended, furthermore, that the bureaucracy would have to stay on at all levels of government so as not to endanger food distribution and essential services. For their part the USPD spokesmen wanted political power vested in workers' and soldiers' councils to be convened in a national congress, with "the question of the constituent

---

[4] Otto Lehmann-Russbüldt: *Der Kampf für den Weltfrieden, 1914–1927* (Berlin: Hansel; 1927), 80–3; and Romain Rolland: *Journal des Années de guerre, 1914–1919* (Paris: Albin Michel; 1952), 1683–5.

assembly postponed until after the new conditions created by the Revolution had been consolidated." Not only Ebert but also Haase dismissed Liebknecht's proposals that full power be given to peoples' commissars elected exclusively by the working population and soldiers.[5]

In the press of events the SPD and USPD agreed to share power in the *Rat der Volksbeauftragten* without resolving the question of the future relationship of this provisional cabinet to the Workers' and Soldiers' Councils, which had sprung up spontaneously and overnight. In their official declaration of November 12, however, they did promise that "further provisions" pertaining to the Constituent Assembly to be chosen by universal suffrage would follow, thereby hinting that the issue dividing the coalition partners was one of timing rather than of principle.[6]

Hereafter the radicals lacked the resolve, influence, and power to bring the discussion back to the more fundamental issue. In the leading Spartacist organ Rosa Luxemburg charged that "from the *Deutsche Tageszeitung* to . . . the *Freiheit,* from Reventlow . . . to Haase and Kautsky there was a unanimous call for the National Assembly and an equally unanimous dread of . . . power being in the hands of the working class"; scoffed at the idea that a social revolution could be consummated by "nice, quiet, and dignified discussions among the different social classes, followed by a roll-call vote"; alleged that the Assembly was designed to be "a bourgeois counter-weight to the Councils"; and denounced the champions of this Assembly for "deliberately or unconsciously reducing the Revolution to a level equivalent to a bourgeois revolution."[7] Karl Liebknecht censured the project with equal vigor at three outdoor rallies in Berlin.[8] And at a Workers' and Soldiers' Council meeting in the capital Richard Müller, the leader of the revolutionary Shop Stewards, issued the defiant but spurious threat that now that the Councils held power "the road to the Constituent Assembly would have to cut across his dead body."[9] To no avail.

The SPD used the conservative, liberal, and Allied pressures against the Councils and in favor of early elections to intimidate Haase, Dittmann, and even Barth. At the cabinet meeting at which Müller's ominous warning was discussed Ebert pointed up all the hazards of delay—"decomposition of the Reich . . . threatened general strike of locomotive engineers, collapse of the mark, and cancellation of foreign bank credit." When he presented his draft-project for a new electoral law to the cabinet, State Secretary Hugo Preuss intimated that technically it would be feasible to move the elections up from February 2,

[5] Purlitz: *Deutscher Geschichtskalender,* I, 38–42.
[6] Ibid., 50–1.
[7] *Rote Fahne,* November 18 and 20, 1918.
[8] *Dokumente und Materialien zur Geschichte der deutschen Arbeiterbewegung,* II, 444.
[9] Müller: *Vom Kaiserreich zur Republik,* II, esp. 84–5.

which he and his advisers originally had thought to be the earliest practical date. He and his advisers were then instructed to prepare for the contingency of an earlier polling date, since it "became increasingly evident that the hastening of the elections would be urgently needed not only for reasons of internal politics, but especially also for reasons of foreign policy (preliminary peace, economic aid)."[1]

But whereas Preuss and officials of the Interior Ministry pressed for, and Ebert endorsed, an election date of January 19, the Independents continued to hold out against a firm timetable just yet. Their arguments, which were practical rather than ideological, were not unlike those used unsuccessfully by the British Labour Party to block the precipitate khaki elections: the troops in the East and the war prisoners would be unable to vote; the decision should be left to the Congress of Councils; a premature election might occasion strikes by industrial workers and miners in Upper Silesia and Rhenish Westphalia, with catastrophic consequences for the rest of Germany, including Berlin; and the political parties needed time to present the issues to the vastly enlarged electorate.

Ebert countered that the "overwhelming majority of Germans demanded [a prompt] Constituent Assembly," but that as a concession to the Independents he was willing "to set the elections for February 2 instead of January 19, subject to confirmation by the All-German Congress of Workers' and Soldiers' Councils." Eventually, after Landsberg threatened that he and his colleagues would resign unless a fixed election day were announced within 24 hours, the Independents reluctantly settled for February 16.[2]

This date satisfied no one. The wave of disorders that swept through Berlin on December 6 encouraged reactionaries, conservatives, and liberals to charge that the deferment of elections sapped the Provisional Government's ability to maintain order at home and to impress the victors abroad. That very day rumors began to circulate that the SPD leaders themselves advocated elections for January 19.[3] According to Scheidemann the "Social Democrats decided that since the reckless Spartacist agitation was swelling disgust among ever more voters, the longer the elections were postponed, the less favorable the outcome."[4] But perhaps equally significant was the Majoritarians' fear that growing disorders would preclude elections altogether, estrange the bureaucracy and army, and affront the Allies, especially Wilson.

It is of particular significance that in this matter both Solf and Brockdorff-Rantzau exerted pressure on the Provisional Government,

---

[1] *Protokolle des Rats der Volksbeauftragten,* meetings of November 23 (a.m.) and November 26 (a.m.), 1918.

[2] *Protokolle des Rats der Volksbeauftragten,* meeting of November 29, 1918.

[3] *Berliner Tageblatt,* December 6, 1918 (p.m.).

[4] Philipp Scheidemann: *Memoiren eines Sozialdemokraten* (Dresden: Carl Reissner; 1928), II, 336.

notably on Ebert. In his letter of resignation Solf complained that "at the instigation of certain Cabinet members and for insufficient reasons" the election date "had been set a full month later than the earliest date designated by the Ministry of the Interior," and that this was decided "in spite of the fact that even if the National Assembly were convoked promptly freedom, peace, and imperial unity could barely be saved." Simultaneously Brockdorff-Rantzau's second condition for taking Solf's place was that these elections "still be held before February 16, 1919."[5]

By the time the National Congress of Workers' and Soldiers' Councils convened in Berlin on December 16 the SPD leaders were determined to try for the forward date of January 19 rather than February 16, the date agreed upon at the recent cabinet meeting. As it turned out, all factions and parties—whether left, right, or center—had vastly exaggerated the militancy of the leaders as well as of the rank and file of the local Workers' and Soldiers' Councils. The membership of this National Congress, composed of delegates chosen by councils throughout the nation and armed services, was overwhelmingly Majoritarian, moderate, and responsive to guidance by the same leadership which in August 1914 had advocated and concluded the political truce.

To be sure, as compared to 1914, the ranks of the radicals in the German Socialist and labor movement had grown significantly. War weariness, disillusionment over the defeat, food shortages, soaring prices, the Soviet Russian example, and Wilson's pressure had combined to foster various degrees of radicalism. However, much more would have been required for a total revolution to have had a real chance: the military defeat and economic breakdown would have had to be of considerably greater magnitude; the revolutionaries would have required a leader of Lenin's political sophistication, skill, and determination to take advantage of this breakdown; and the party apparatus of the *enragés* would have needed stricter organization and discipline.

To some small extent Soviet Russian guidance and aid might have compensated for these deficiencies. But on balance the Russian Revolution was likely to do more harm than good to the revolutionaries. "One reason why history rarely repeats itself among historically conscious people is that the *dramatis personae* are aware at the second performance of the *dénouement* of the first, and their action is affected by that knowledge."[6] Hence, even though the Spartacists meant to imitate the Russian Bolsheviks, their adversaries sought to avoid the blunders of their Russian counterparts. The German conservatives, liberals, army officers, and public officials rallied to Prince Max and Ebert instead of opposing them to the same degree to which Prince Lvov and

[5] GFM 2 (9105/5), H 233354–5 and H 233332–47. Both letters were written on December 9, 1918.
[6] E. H. Carr: *What Is History?* (New York: Knopf; 1962), 90.

Kerensky had been opposed. Moreover, the Allies were careful not to press Prince Max and Ebert as hard as they had pressed Prince Lvov and Kerensky.

As for the Social Democrats and the Independents, they were not about to be as tolerant of the Spartacists as the Mensheviks and Social Revolutionaries had been of the Bolsheviks. Starting in mid-October they deliberately mounted their pre-emptive offensive against all radicals. They knew what had happened to their Russian counterparts and were not willing to gamble on German Spartacists being any less ruthless than Russian Bolsheviks. This resolve to avoid repetition significantly fortified especially the Social Democratic leaders in the anti-Spartacist campaign for which they were predisposed by their ideology and tradition, equipped by their organization, and inspired by their nationalism.

For all these reasons the moderates easily dominated the proceedings of this Berlin Congress from the outset. Max Cohen-Reuss, of the reformist *Sozialistische Monatshefte,* presented the motion and argued the case in favor of moving up the elections to January 19 in a particularly dramatic, forceful, and effective manner.[7] In his speech Cohen-Reuss examined the Social Democrats' political fortunes in the light of the repelling Soviet Russian example and the deterrent threat of Allied intervention. Although he was enthusiastic about "the glorious Russian Revolution of the spring of 1917, . . . whose first demand was a Constituent Assembly," he execrated the subsequent Bolshevik Revolution for being anti-Marxist, dictatorial, and destructive. Eventually Scheidemann, the impatient politician, scornfully proclaimed that "in the present situation Karl Marx can be of no help to us."[8] But Max Cohen-Reuss, the *idéologue* chosen to debate the left-schismatics, could not dismiss the supreme law-giver quite so cavalierly. Instead, he argued that Marx had never prescribed a minority dictatorship, even for a transitional period; in fact, Marx had preached the very opposite of what the Bolsheviks were practicing in Russia. It was beside the point, therefore, to argue, as the USPD spokesmen did, that because the elections could not bring about a Socialist majority which would implement socialization measures, these should be rushed through by executive fiat. In any case, being committed to universal suffrage ever since Erfurt, "not more Socialism could be implemented than the majority of the people wanted." Meanwhile, the sooner these elections were held, the greater the majority. In brief, the Russian Bolsheviks, not the German Social Democrats, were violating the Marxist scriptures. Moreover, since the German middle classes were infinitely larger and

[7] The following discussion of Cohen-Reuss's address is based on the verbatim record in *Allgemeiner Kongress der Arbeiter und Soldatenräte Deutschlands, Dezember 16–21, 1918, Stenographische Berichte,* esp. 108–12, cols. 215–24.
[8] Ibid., 135, col. 269.

stronger than their Russian counterparts, it would be so much more difficult and risky to disfranchise them. Even more than in Russia, in Germany they were needed to keep production going.

In case of revolutionary excesses there was the additional danger of Allied intervention. Although the victors were not about to march in to restore the old order, they were even less likely to establish Socialism! Germany's first requirement was peace, and peace could not be secured without first restoring order and production and summoning the National Assembly.

> The Entente is ruled [by a coalition] of imperialist classes and anti-Bolshevik groups, including Socialists. In Russia the Entente uses military intervention against the Soviet dictatorship; and if it were not winter this dictatorship would probably be liquidated overnight. Politically informed persons could not possibly expect the Entente to polish off the Soviet dictatorship in Petersburg and Moscow in order to tolerate it here in Germany . . . especially since the Entente would find it so much more convenient and easier to impose its will on the German people. One would have to be blind not to assume that the Entente would oppose the establish-ment of a Soviet bloc stretching from Russia to the French border.
>
> Now some of the party colleagues who admit this still place their hopes in the peoples of the Entente. . . . But is it really all that simple to believe that peoples who have just scored a tremendous [military] victory could stage a revolution and then come to our rescue . . . ? It seems to me that . . . we cannot base our calcula-tions on this house of cards or sandheap. . . . Should it really come to a revolution in France and Italy—optimistically these might be the only two countries conceivably ripe for it—we would certainly get a less onerous peace. Nevertheless . . . what we need most urgently we will get from neither France nor Italy, but from England and America, who control the raw materials and the food of the entire world. And is there any one in this hall who believes that the most anti-Socialist nations in the world—England and America—will have a revolution? . . . Without aid from England and America, France and Italy would go under just like us.

This, then, was the tough-minded analysis of German Social Democ-racy's predicament on which Cohen-Reuss based his conclusion that the Workers' and Soldiers' Councils should efface themselves before the National Assembly and his motion that the elections should be ad-vanced to January 19.

Scheidemann placed his full authority and influence behind this brief. After conceding that the Councils had been a "transitional necessity," he held that since their usefulness was at an end, hereafter they could maintain themselves only with the help of machine guns. But German Social Democrats would refuse to become "Social Dictators," and they would seek to avoid Russian conditions, particularly since in

Germany so much more was worth preserving. The nation needed bread, peace, and jobs, and Scheidemann was firmly convinced that the Councils could provide none of these.[9]

Speaking for the pro-government Independents, Dittmann and Haase merely repeated the practical arguments for delaying elections which they had developed in the cabinet. By comparison, therefore, their speeches were timid, stale, and uninspiring. They admitted that neither in the cabinet nor at the congress was the issue any longer one of principle; only the timing of the elections remained in question. Here is Haase's plea:

> I beg you to resolutely resist all efforts to advance the election date. We want to bring mature, informed voters to the polls. The date could even be postponed; that would do no harm. I am confident that the masses will then be able to meet the great internal and external difficulties through those trusted organs which they have created. [Furthermore,] it would be possible to fill the young Republic with democratic and above all with Socialist content.[1]

It may have been fatal that Haase was either unwilling or unable to couch this plea in either Socialist, nationalist, or anti-Bolshevik rhetoric.

It was true, then, that by now the political objective of the official Independents had been reduced to holding out for the date of February 16; or perhaps they merely chose to test their strength vis-à-vis the SPD with an intrinsically trivial issue. Even if from the start the majority had not been pledged to support the SPD, the congress delegates might well have wondered whether a difference of four weeks over the timing of elections was really worth further divisions in the Socialist movement.

In any case, Cohen-Reuss's motion for January 19, which won 400 votes, was opposed by only (about) 50 delegates, apparently by the same 50 delegates who voted to postpone the election to March 16. Significantly Ernst Däumig's proposal to make a new Congress of Councils instead of a National Assembly the supreme source of sovereignty and legitimacy was supported by 98 against 344 delegates.[2] The fact that twice as many delegates rallied to this radical position was an indication that left-dissident Independents like Richard Müller and Ledebour had resolved to pressure Haase against making further concessions to Ebert. This same polarization between moderates and extremists was also promoted by the emasculation of the authority of the Central Committee of the Councils, by the Majoritarian composition of the new Central Committee, and by the dilatory treatment of the question of socialization.[3]

[9] Ibid., 125–6, cols. 269–72.
[1] Ibid., 128, col. 255–6.
[2] Ibid., 141, col. 282, 150, col. 300; and Purlitz: *Deutscher Geschichtskalender,* I, 244.
[3] Purlitz: *Deutscher Geschichtskalender,* I, 244–57.

In sum, this Congress of Councils ended in a smashing triumph for the SPD. The road to the National Assembly was clear and the domestication of the Councils was accomplished. But this victory was won at the cost of the radicalization of the USPD. By the turn of the year this radicalization was demonstrated in a new wave of disorders in Berlin, in the resignation of the Independents from the Provisional Government, and in the formation of the German Communist Party.[4]

Meanwhile, however, conservatives and liberals were ecstatic about the outcome of the congress. The *Deutsche Allgemeine Zeitung* praised it for its "practical work" and for removing this "peculiar parliament from the political scene." For the *Berliner Tageblatt* "the days of uncertainty were over"; the congress had not capitulated before radical pressures; and at home as well as abroad the decision to throttle the Councils and to advance the elections could have only salutary effects.[5]

Indeed, the Independent press had good reason to report that "the entire capitalist bourgeoisie was heaving a sigh of relief." With sarcasm it welcomed the return of "holy order" while bemoaning these dark days on which the Revolution "checkmated itself, or voluntarily gave away all its trumps." As for the Spartacists, they were still more violent in their denunciation of this inglorious "suicide."[6]

[4] For a systematic study of the prelude, course, and outcome of this Congress of Councils see Walter Tormin: *Zwischen Rätediktatur und sozialer Demokratie* (Düsseldorf: Droste Verlag; 1954), esp. Chs. 11–15; and Eberhard Kolb: *Die Arbeiterräte in der deutschen Innenpolitik, 1918–1919* (Düsseldorf: Droste Verlag; 1962).
[5] *Deutsche Allgemeine Zeitung* and *Berliner Tageblatt,* December 20, 1918.
[6] *Leipziger Volkszeitung* and *Rote Fahne,* December 20, 1918.

Part Two

POLITICAL
CONSEQUENCES
OF VICTORY

4

United States: Congressional Elections

AT FIRST GLANCE it would seem that whereas the November elections in America impaired the authority of Wilson, the December election in England enhanced the authority of Lloyd George. But closer examination discloses that both electoral contests were khaki elections which attested to the unprogressive political consequences of victory. In America and England similar right-wing political, economic, and social forces substantially increased their power in the state beyond the strength that they had mustered in the last prewar elections. Both Wilson and Lloyd George remained chief executives and became chief peace delegates; but in both capacities they had to contend with strong and unrelenting Rightist pressures.

For an understanding of peacemaking in 1918–19 a comparison of these American and British elections is more suggestive and meaningful than a comparison of the two congressional elections of 1918 and 1866. Admittedly, of all the off-year congressional elections, only these two can compete in historical importance with most or even all presidential elections. But the Republican Congress of 1918, unlike its forerunner of 1866, strikingly influenced the course not only of national but also of world history. The American and British elections of 1918 approximate each other in their course and outcome at home as well as in their impact abroad.

By mid-1918, with the off-year elections fast approaching, the political truce became severely strained.[1] This was the customary

[1] This discussion of the congressional election relies heavily on Seward W. Livermore: "The Sectional Issue in the 1918 Congressional Elections," in *Mississippi Valley Historical Review*, XXXV (June 1948), 29–60; Selig Adler: "The Congressional Election of 1918," in *The South Atlantic Quarterly*, XXXVI (1937), 447–65; and David Burner: "The Breakup of the Wilson Coalition of 1916," in *Mid-America*, Vol. XLV (January 1963), esp. 18–23.

season for the minority party not only to try to embarrass the Administration but also to test issues with which to defeat the party in power. When a revenue measure calling for new taxes to meet soaring war expenditures came before Congress, the Republicans obstructed it in order to advertise their opposition to levies on excess profits, high incomes, and luxuries. To surmount this partisan obstruction, Wilson went before a joint session of Congress on May 27 to urge that in the interest of the war effort politics continue to be "adjourned."[2] The Republicans yielded, but less out of spontaneous fidelity to the party truce than for studied fear of the political risks of undermining national unity in wartime.

The Old Guard, which had a firm hold on the Republican organization, was impatient to attack Wilson's wartime economic policies and controls as part of a more general assault on his prewar New Freedom. Admittedly, business leaders had assumed important posts in various war agencies, a development of which Wilson had warned in 1916. But leading Republicans, in addition to resenting the adventitious and circumscribed nature of this influence, were apprehensive that Wilson would use any political capital gained from diplomatic triumphs to renew his mandate for economic and social reform. After all, his foreign policy platform was in harmony with those of British Labour and the Second International, both of which seemed aggressively committed to building a new social order.

As long as victory was not in sight the Republicans were careful not to make an issue of Wilson's foreign policy, notably of his Fourteen Points, which had raised his prestige to new heights. However, especially in the East and North, they did denounce those Democrats who had opposed preparedness, while at the same time claiming credit for Republican diplomatic and military clear-sightedness as well as exemplary loyalty.

William H. Hays of Indiana, the new chairman of the Republican National Committee and chief election strategist, used these same patriotic themes to underpin his campaign against Southern domination of the Congress. Since so many Southern legislators had held out against preparedness and war, it was easy to impugn their patriotism while at the same time exposing their selfishness and greed. Both before and after America's entrance into war the Southern Democrats exercised disproportionate influence and power in large measure through their solid control of all key Senate and House committees. No occasion was lost to remind Speaker Champ Clark that in arguing against the draft he had affirmed that "in Missouri, conscripts and convicts were considered of the same class." The attack on Representative

---

[2] For the text of this address to Congress see Ray Stannard Baker and William E. Dodd (eds.): *The Public Papers of Woodrow Wilson*, 6 vols. (New York: Harper; 1925–7), V, 216–20.

Claude Kitchin of North Carolina, the unpopular chairman of the Ways and Means Committee, became particularly fierce. He, too, had resisted preparedness and war; and once at war, it became his avowed purpose to tax the warmongering interests north of the Mason-Dixon line to pay for the war they had wanted.

But Southern selfishness and greed were alleged to be particularly apparent in the cotton bloc's dictate that the price of cotton remain free even though wheat and other commodities be regulated. At the precise time that Wilson refused to revise the minimum price of wheat to above $2.20 a bushel, the Southern Democrats again fought off every attempt to either control cotton prices or to levy special taxes on soaring cotton profits.

The Republicans saw no chance of cutting into the Democratic vote in the Eastern industrial centers. Labor was prospering in the booming war economy, was encouraged by the progress in collective bargaining, and approved the Administration's tax and price control policies. Consequently Hays decided to fight a holding action in the East on an outright war and loyalty platform, while setting out to capitalize on the discontent of the wheat farmers in the Midwestern, Central, and Western states by firing their sectional resentment of Southern dominance in Washington. The objective was to capture the committee chairmanships that the Southerners controlled by virtue of their safe districts and seniority. In other words, since Kitchin could not be defeated in his Scotland Neck District, the only way to oust him from his critical chairmanship was by securing a Republican majority in Congress with the help of a dissatisfied electoral clientele outside the South. But the point to note is that should this strategy of enlisting the farmers succeed, the controlling Eastern business interests would benefit at least as much as the wheat farmers.

In the first phase of the campaign, then, Hays sought to generate popular enthusiasm for Republicanism by exposing the misdeeds of the small and avaricious Southern oligarchy, for the time being exonerating the President as its reluctant hostage. The Southern congressmen were charged with being eleventh-hour patriots, with dilatorily attending to essential war measures, and with serving narrow economic interests.

There was one other issue which was ideally suited for Hays's purposes. Whereas the majority of Eastern and Northern industrialists and businessmen passionately favored tariff protection, the agrarian South stood foursquare for free trade. More important, on this tariff issue Wilson was not a reticent prisoner of Southern congressmen. On the contrary, he zealously advocated free trade with the support of labor as well as of internationally oriented trading and banking interests. The President had pushed for the Underwood Tariff, and the third of his Fourteen Points called for "the removal, so far as possible, of all economic barriers and the establishment of an equality of trade conditions among all the nations consenting to the peace and associating themselves for its maintenance."

Hays proceeded to warn that a free-trade sellout could easily become a wedge for more far-reaching economic and social measures. Even though Wilson's Fourteen Points as a whole were spared Republican criticism until the fall of 1918, his third point was attacked instantly. This attack originated with the American Protective Tariff League, whose members were heavy contributors to the Republican campaign chest and whose tariff schedules were a guideline for the G.O.P. On January 17, 1918—immediately following the Fourteen Points address—this League's 33rd annual convention viewed "with disapproval and alarm that portion of the President's peace proposals which abandons the time-honored and always successful policy of Protection and the introduction in this country of the false and discredited policy of Free Trade, a policy which has been discarded by every civilized nation."[3] Thereafter the *American Economist,* the League's weekly organ, kept up a steady barrage against Wilson's trade policy and clamored for the election of a protectionist Congress. Needless to say, since ardent protectionism and fervent nationalism went hand in hand, the tariff advocates made use of autarkist arguments which clashed head on with the spirit and letter of Wilson's internationalism.

According to the *American Economist,* in "back of all the shouts for liberty and freedom is the bare, cold fact that this is an economic war, a war for national supremacy and security"; and Wilson intended to use the peace treaty "to saddle upon America a policy of Free-Trade or 'new-freedom.' " This being so, it was up to all patriotic Republicans to elect a "Protection majority in the Senate where such a treaty must be ratified [and a] Protection majority in the House to restore Protection in legislation." The League made no secret of the fact that it looked beyond blocking future tariff reductions to the repeal of the Underwood Tariff.[4]

In America, as in Britain, protectionist arguments tended to be cast in vote-catching anti-German slogans: "If you want to please the Kaiser, vote for a Free-Trade Congressman; if you want to offend the Kaiser and please the American workingman, vote for a Protective Tariff candidate." This solicitude for the welfare and employment of the workers was designed to give a popular, possibly even a populist, appeal to this campaign. In any event, "the real issue" of the election was whether America would be committed to free trade or protection after the war, and since "Republicans, generally speaking, were

[3] Cited in the *American Economist,* January 25, 1918, 37.
[4] *American Economist,* October 4, 1918, 190–1; and *Congressional Record,* October 14, 1918, 11232.

pledged to Protection," the *American Economist,* the Tariff League, and the *North American Review* urged the election of Republican candidates.[5]

That the Republican leadership was not insensitive to or did not discourage this campaign became clear during the pre-Armistice debates in Congress. During the first three weeks of October, the same Congressmen who advocated unconditional surrender singled out for criticism the third of Wilson's Fourteen Points more frequently than any of the others.[6] It may have been of some importance that Senator Lodge, who formulated the Congressional strategy, was a member of the Senate Finance Committee which had jurisdiction over tariff legislation. On October 20, the Republican Congressional Committee officially accused Wilson and the Democrats of being committed to a free-trade policy favorable to Germany: "free trade, absolute and complete, with all its tremendous ills, looms in the near future under a continuation of Democratic rule."[7] This line of attack became so salient that on October 23 Senator Gilbert M. Hitchcock of Nebraska, the mildly partisan chairman of the Senate Foreign Relations Committee, called Wilson's attention to the intensity with which the Republican National Committee and managers were "perverting this [free-trade] issue for the purpose of gaining control of Congress.[8]

By then the Republicans felt free to invigorate their sectional and tariff appeals with sharp thrusts at Wilson's overall diplomacy. On October 24 this penultimate phase of the election campaign culminated in Theodore Roosevelt's vitriolic censure of all of the President's major war aims pronouncement as well as of his exchange of notes with Prince Max.[9] This tirade, which was in the form of a telegram to Republican Senators, was merely the most offensive and provocative of a long series of partisan sallies. In self-defense, as of mid-October, Wilson was being urged to issue an appeal by Homer Cummings, Vice-Chairman of the Democratic National Committee; Albert Burleson, the Postmaster General; Representative Edward Pow, Chairman of the Rules Committee; and Joseph P. Tumulty, Secretary to the President.[1] It would seem, therefore, that Roosevelt precipitated rather than caused the launching of Wilson's controversial summons to the electorate to return a Democratic Congress so that he might continue to be "your unembarrassed spokesman in affairs at home and abroad." Meanwhile the Republican leaders, eager to blast the President for a blatantly partisan

---

[5] *American Economist,* October 4, 1918, 185, 191, 197; October 11, 1918, 204; October 18, 1918, 220; and October 25, 1918, 237.
[6] *Congressional Record,* October 1918, *passim.*
[7] Cited in *The Sun* (N.Y.), October 21, 1918.
[8] Hitchcock to Wilson, October 23, 1918, in Wilson Papers, II: 151.
[9] See p. 58 above.
[1] See Wilson Papers, *passim.*

maneuver, studiously avoided any discussion of T. R.'s savage broad-side.[2]

Unlike Cummings, Burleson, Pow, and Tumulty, who took a purely domestic view of the election contest,[3] Wilson was painfully aware that a Republican victory would complicate his search for a conciliatory peace. By October 14, when Wilson and his advisers drafted the reply to Prince Max's second note, the Republican campaign for uncondi-tional surrender was in high gear. Whereas Lansing urged that in drafting this reply the coming elections should be kept in mind, Colonel House, who was completely absorbed by the armistice negotiations, countered that elections should "not be considered in thinking of the settlement of this great world tragedy."[4]

Even though House proffered no advice on the advisability of issuing an appeal to the voters before he sailed for Europe, he con-sidered it a "political error" when news of it reached him on the high seas. After the event House felt that instead of calling for the election of a Democratic Congress the President should have asked for the election of candidates pledged to his war aims, "regardless of party." Meanwhile House waited for the results, confident that "if it turns out well, he [Wilson] will be acclaimed a bold and forceful leader; if it turns out badly, an opposite view will be taken."[5] Within a year, when the elec-tions and much else had turned out badly, House judged the appeal to have been "as great a political blunder as [Wilson] had made during his term of office." But in this one instance, the vainglorious but self-effacing Colonel had the candor to admit, at least to himself, that "may-be I did not myself appreciate, and I do not believe I did, the disaster to the President of an adverse majority in the Senate, [and wonder] if I laid sufficient stress upon the elections which were to be held during my absence."[6]

Perhaps the electoral fortunes of the Democrats would have been helped had Wilson rejected Prince Max's advances, though it is equally likely that the Republicans would have taken credit for a course so obviously alien to the President. Besides, Wilson could not afford to formulate his answers to Berlin exclusively in light of his domestic political requirements; he had to worry also about their impact on internal developments in the Allied as well as enemy nations.

The President was in a difficult quandary, not knowing how far to go in placating his opposition. He knew that the loss of congressional

[2] *The Sun* (N.Y.), October 26, 1918.
[3] "The time has not yet come for the unfolding of the details of the peace program. . . . It is a most unhappy time politically for any such considerations." Cum-mings to Wilson, October 22, 1918, in Wilson Papers, II: 151.
[4] House Diary, October 15, 1918.
[5] Ibid., October 25, 1918.
[6] Ibid., October 26, 1919.

support would weaken him for his impending encounter with the victory-hardened governments of Britain, France, and Italy, not least because it would throw Allied Wilsonians into disarray.

Wilson had good reason to claim, in his appeal, that a Republican victory would "be interpreted on the other side of the water as a repudiation of my leadership"; that it was "well understood there as well as here that the Republican leaders desire not so much to support the President as to control him"; and that "the peoples of the Allied countries with whom we are associated against Germany are quite familiar with the significance of elections." Paradoxically, the electorate was called upon to help perpetuate the congressional power of Democratic social and political forces which were no closer to Wilson's fundamental national and international purposes than was the Republican opposition.

Perhaps the President at one and the same time was excessively candid and obtuse. How many American voters could appreciate the rationale of underlining three times in one brief declaration the importance of strengthening his hand for negotiations with the *Allies?* Such an appeal had nothing in common with standard appeals for support of the Administration vis-à-vis the *enemy* in times of crisis. Few men and women on Main Street understood the message; but the Republican leaders understood it only too well. They maintained that the position taken by their party was exactly that of Lloyd George and Clemenceau, "whereas the opposition elements in these countries appear to be giving the most enthusiastic approval to the President's course."[7]

Not surprisingly the Republicans were delighted that Wilson himself had reconvened partisan politics.[8] With impunity they could attack the President, his supporters, and his policies during the last ten days of the campaign, which was a particularly crucial time for reaching the uncommitted and undecided voters. Four statements issued within three days of Wilson's appeal reveal the issues that the opposition pressed in the closing phase: a statement by Republican congressional leaders; a statement by Chairman Hays; a Senate address by Senator Philander C. Knox; and Roosevelt's speech in Carnegie Hall.

The congressional statement, drafted by Senators Lodge and Reed Smoot and Representatives Simeon Fess and Frederick Gillette, praised the legislative record of the Republicans as compared to the Democrats before itemizing what they would do in the event of victory. Accordingly, they vowed to replace Dent, Kitchin, and Clark; to maintain the

[7] *The Sun* (N.Y.), October 28, 1918.
[8] See Karl Schriftgiesser: *The Gentleman from Massachusetts: Henry Cabot Lodge* (Boston: Little, Brown; 1944), 297–8; Henry F. Pringle: *The Life and Times of William Howard Taft* (New York: Farrar and Rinehart; 1939), I, 913; Alice Roosevelt Longworth: *Crowded Hours: Reminiscences* (New York: Scribner's; 1933), 274–5.

regulation of wheat only provided the price of cotton be fixed simultaneously; to undertake the "economic preparation for the coming of peace"; to check waste; and to press the "War with greater vigor than ever before."

As for foreign policy, the congressional leaders affirmed that the Senate's role was "equal to that of the President in the consummation of peace by treaty." Once in control of the Senate they would first insist that the question of surrender be left to the generals and then press for terms to be "imposed" on the enemy. They proudly swore that the Republican Party stood for "unconditional surrender" and was "opposed to negotiations and discussions carried on in diplomatic notes addressed to the German Government."[9]

Hays also reiterated that the Republican Party was pledged to unconditional surrender and served notice that it would uphold the Allies "in whatever reparation they may exact for the frightful outrages inflicted upon them by the accursed Huns." In addition to this peripheral excursion into foreign policy, Hays berated the President for seeking "unconditional surrender to himself of the Republican Party, of the country, of the Allies—all to him, as the sole arbiter and master of the destinies of the world." While fighting autocracy abroad America could not tolerate autocracy at home.

Above all, however, Hays stressed that the nation's economic and social future hinged on the outcome of these elections. Taking advantage of Wilson's passing plea that he also be continued as the people's "unembarrassed spokesman in affairs at home," Hays painted a horrid picture of the domestic consequences of a Democratic victory. He alleged that the President wanted full power "to reconstruct in peace time the great industrial affairs of the nation in the same way, in unimpeded conformity with whatever *socialistic doctrines,* whatever unlimited government ownership notions, whatever hazy whims may happen to possess him at the time, but *first and above all with absolute commitment to free trade* with all the world, thus giving to Germany out of hand the fruits of a victory greater than she could win by fighting a hundred years [italics mine]." Hays vouched that a Republican Congress pledged to unconditional surrender and protection "will never assent to that."[1] Not surprisingly, the *American Economist* warned that Wilson's reconstruction program, which was endorsed by the British Labour Party, American Socialists, and Gompers (*sic!*), would culminate in "a surrender to Socialism."[2]

Senator Knox, in a speech confined to foreign affairs, declared that since wars were won "by bullets and blood, not by ink and eloquence,"

[9] The full text of this congressional statement is cited in *The Sun* (N.Y.), October 26, 1918.
[1] The full text of Chairman Hays's statement is cited in *The New York Times,* October 28, 1918.
[2] *American Economist,* November 1, 1918, 252–3.

the generals should be entrusted with the imposition of an armistice and of guarantees against Germany—"whether as an autocratic monarchy, a republic, or a democratic monarchy." Meanwhile, America, as "a naval power with a proud history and whose greatest power is the greatest sea power," should keep a completely free hand with regard to the international law of the sea, "mutually beneficial understandings" with the Allies, and tariff protection. As for the League of Nations, there would "be no room for a task of such problematical possibility" in the forthcoming peace negotiations. Knox did concede, however, that given the new interdependence of nations, there was need for a league for the "single purpose of enforcing the peace," though with minimal encroachments on national sovereignty.[3] Incidentally, even this guarded concession was not endorsed by Lodge, who two days later rejected *all* aspects of Wilson's search for a new international order.[4]

Theodore Roosevelt, for his part, gave full priority to the charge that Wilson was neither willing nor able to force Germany into unconditional surrender. With calculated scorn the ex-President told the unconditional surrender rally in Carnegie Hall that he had his "hands full keeping up with the President's notes . . . and that finding that Germany was one note behind, he [Wilson] did not think it fair to write another note to Germany, and so he wrote a note to America." In the course of his spirited address he celebrated "the triumph of the war spirit of America"; he renewed his demand that the Armistice "be obtained by machine guns and not typewriters"; he again called for the repudiation of the "mischievous" Fourteen Points which "had been greeted with enthusiasm by Germany and by all the pro-Germans on this side of the water, especially by the Germanized Socialists and by the Bolshevists of every grade"; and he declared that a Republican victory would assure the Allies and Germany alike that America was committed to unconditional surrender and to peace by dictation.[5]

Evidently the Republican leaders seized on the election appeal to discredit Wilson and his policies: they impugned his integrity as Chief Executive by portraying him as a narrow partisan; they deprecated his patriotism and courage by warning of his no-win and compromising foreign policy; and they disparaged his liberalism and Americanism by portraying him as a Socialist in domestic affairs.

This concerted assault forced the Democrats onto the defensive. The pressure was so strong that even the New York *World* wavered momentarily: the arguments of the appeal were compelling, perhaps, but it was inappropriate for the President to have made them.[6] Senator

---

[3] *Congressional Record,* October 28, 1918, 11486–8.
[4] *The New York Times,* October 21, 1918.
[5] See the reports of Roosevelt's speech in *The Sun* (N.Y.), October 28, 1918; and *The New York Times,* October 29, 1918.
[6] New York *World,* October 26, 1918.

Hitchcock had similar qualms, though he did insist that Wilson's hand had "practically been forced" by Republican attacks.[7]

Among his unqualified supporters the *Times* placed the blame squarely on the Republicans, notably on their readiness to promote the Roosevelt line.[8] According to the *New Republic* Wilson had no alternative "but to end a party truce which tied his hands but not those of his opponents." His appeal was a "courageous and salutary political utterance" which would encourage his supporters at home and abroad, who had felt abandoned during the last few months.[9]

But in the face of the Republicans' carefully orchestrated charge that the President had questioned their loyalty and patriotism, few influential organs managed to be as aggressively favorable to Wilson as the *Times* and the *New Republic*. Presently the Administration agreed to give battle on the enemy's grounds. Tumulty issued a public statement citing precedents for the President's partisan appeal and recalling Lincoln's injunction during the Civil War not to swap horses in midstream. Above all, the statement quoted profusely from the appeals for the election of a Republican Congress in 1898 by McKinley, Harrison, Roosevelt, Lodge, and Penrose. Even though the hostilities of the Spanish-American War had stopped by election time, President McKinley and leading Republicans nevertheless had claimed that a Republican Congress was necessary to enable the Peace Commissioners to secure a favorable peace.[1]

Roosevelt and the Republicans indignantly protested that the two situations were not at all comparable. Whereas today the Republican opposition stood for full victory, in 1898 the Democratic opposition had threatened to thwart it. As a result, the Republicans had felt obliged to call for support of their Administration which, after enforcing "unconditional surrender in Cuba, Puerto Rico and the Philippines . . . insisted upon the peace of overwhelming victory, no parleying having been held and no notes exchanged, and no conversation indulged in, and no Colonel Houses sent abroad until Manila and Santiago fell and the victory was an accomplished fact."[2]

Undeterred, the Democratic National Committee continued to justify the President's appeal with the precedent of 1898. In full-page newspaper advertisements on election day the Committee unequivocally stated that THE ISSUE IS LEADERSHIP! In other words, the Democrats accepted the challenge of openly matching Wilson's prestige and program with those of Lodge, Penrose, and Roosevelt. This advertisement declared that the Republican leaders, who were bidding for

[7] Quoted in *The Sun* (N.Y.), October 26, 1918.
[8] *The New York Times,* October 26, 1918.
[9] *New Republic,* November 2, 1918, 3–4.
[1] *The New York Times,* October 28 and 29, 1918.
[2] *The Sun* (N.Y.), October 28, 1918.

control of congressional committees, would "not approve a peace treaty based on the Wilson principles of peace"; that the choice was between "a peace of Liberalism and Justice, or a peace of Imperialism, Standpatism, and Militarism"; and that everybody wanted limitation of armaments and a League of Nations "except those who will profit by the Old Order." By electing a Democratic Congress the American voters would sustain the President who was "recognized everywhere as the true spokesman of Liberals and Progressives throughout the world."

Even though the Democratic leaders were far from confident about their own prospects, they were startled by the margin of the opposition's victory. From a minority of six in the Senate the Republicans raised themselves to a majority of two; in the House they transformed a minority of five into a majority of forty-five; and their popular vote exceeded that of the Democrats by roughly two million. Admittedly, the Republicans made greatest gains in the Central and Western states. Even so, the critical chairmanships were transferred from the agrarian South to the industrial North, especially to Massachusetts, New York, Pennsylvania, and Illinois.[3]

The Republicans, the Democrats, the Allies, and the enemy governments each advanced their own self-interested interpretation of the purport of these elections.

Prominent Republicans credited popular endorsement of their armistice and peace prescriptions for their triumph. According to Roosevelt, having made the fight on the issue of unconditional surrender, the Republicans now were committed to press for a victor's peace against both Kaiserism and Bolshevism.[4] They claimed to have received a mandate to insist that the Senate had the right not only to ratify the peace treaty but also to supervise the day-by-day preparations and negotiations. Certainly such was the intent of two Senate resolutions introduced by Albert Cummins (Iowa) and Senator Knox on December 2 and 3 respectively.[5] Moreover, on December 21, in a major foreign policy address in the Senate, Lodge reiterated that in addition to specifying that no treaty could be binding without the consent of the Senate, the Constitution gave the Senate the "clear right . . . to offer its advice, whether invited or unasked, at any stage of the negotiations."[6] Prominent Republicans purposely exaggerated the extent to which their victory signified a repudiation of Wilson's foreign policy, in part as an encouragement to their counterparts in the Allied nations. Confident that they had the votes with which to check

---

[3] In the House, Kitchin (N.C.) was succeeded by Joseph Forney (Mich.); S. Sherley (Ky.), by Gillette (Mass.); and Carter Glass (Va.), by Edwin Platt (N.Y.). In the Senate, Lodge (Mass.) became Chairman of the Foreign Relations Committee while Boies Penrose (Pa.) headed the Finance Committee.
[4] Roosevelt quoted in *The New York Times,* November 7, 1918.
[5] *Congressional Record,* December 2 and 3, 1918, 3, 23.
[6] *Congressional Record,* December 21, 1918, 723.

his reconstruction plans, they said less about the domestic consequences of their ascendancy.

Whereas the Republicans magnified the foreign policy intent and significance of the election results, the Democrats tended to minimize them. On the eve of critical diplomatic negotiations with the Allies, the President had every interest in publicly attributing the outcome to narrow sectional and political developments which would not impinge on his peace project. In private, however, Democratic leaders spoke otherwise. Senator Pittman (Nevada) told Wilson that the Republican leaders had "successfully deceived" the electorate with his "attitude towards peace with Germany," brazenly making the issue between unconditional surrender and a compromised peace.[7] Similarly, Creel endorsed the view that because of their "clean record of anti-Hun imperialist patriotism" the Republicans were able to appeal to the public's patriotism "against what looked like a demand for a partisan verdict for the Democrats." At the same time the Democratic campaign faltered because the supporters of Wilson's international policies had either been silenced or intimidated.[8]

In a multifactor analysis Homer Cummings pointed to the "lavish use of money" by the opposition, the strong Republican organization, the sectional issue, and resentment over Southern chairmanships in the Congress. But in addition there was the "surprisingly effective" misrepresentation of the President's attitude toward Germany "based upon the catchwords 'unconditional surrender' and 'no negotiated peace.'" In conclusion the Vice-Chairman of the Democratic National Committee noted that especially in Kentucky, Montana, and Idaho, but also in other states, the President's appeal helped rather than hurt the Democratic cause.[9]

This judgment that Wilson's appeal saved the Democrats from a worse defeat was widely shared by both independent and Democratic papers. The *Times, World,* and *Evening Post* blamed the reversal on the parochial politicians from the South, insisting that the President's own leadership, especially in foreign affairs, was unscathed by the outcome.[1]

Wilson himself corroborated this interpretation with his address to Congress on the eve of his departure for Paris. He practically ignored foreign policy in favor of domestic affairs. Moreover, his discussion of reconversion and reconstruction seems to have been calculated to placate those economic interests that had won out in the election. He advanced no general scheme of reconstruction; admitted that the government should only "mediate the process of change"; hailed the

[7] Pittmann to Wilson, November 6, 1918, in Wilson Papers, II: 155.
[8] Creel to Wilson, November 8, 1918, in Wilson Papers, II: 155.
[9] Cummings to Wilson, November 7, 1918, in Wilson Papers, II: 155.
[1] See the *Literary Digest,* November 16, 1918, 15.

removal of most wartime controls; indicated that even in 1919 taxes might be reduced; and asked Congress "for counsel" with regard to the railways. As for positive government interference during reconversion, he merely suggested that "a large floating residuum of unskilled labor" should be spared unemployment by the prompt resumption of public works and the reclamation of "arid, swamp, and cut-over lands."[2] On this occasion Wilson not only sought to divert the legislators' attention from foreign policy. He also hoped that his moderation in domestic affairs, which he came by so easily, might at some later date be negotiable for support of his peacemaking project.

Abroad, meanwhile, the Democratic defeat tended to be seen as a defeat for the President and his policies. Lloyd George claimed that it "lowered" his prestige and crippled his authority throughout the Conference . . . [and that] his occasional threats to appeal to American opinion . . . conveyed no real menace."[3] Even though *The Times* of London insisted that Wilson continued to speak with full authority for America, the paper nevertheless emphasized and welcomed the psychological importance of the elections. An editorial writer confidently predicted that the changes in Congress would "help to bring the President's ideals into still closer touch with opinion in America and in all Allied countries, [thereby] making for a stronger and a wiser peace." Before long the Washington correspondent of *The Times* reported that Lodge's attack on the Fourteen Points, delivered on the Senate floor on December 21, "was frankly addressed to the peoples and Governments of the Allied countries with the object of convincing them that the President's program had no support either of the American nation or of that branch of the Legislature before whom any treaty of peace must come for ratification."[4]

Meanwhile, even before the election the *Labour Leader* had warned that if President Wilson failed to win the support of his own people, the jingoists on both sides of the water would take courage, and chances for a reasonable and permanent peace would be seriously jeopardized.[5] Unfortunately those fears turned out to be fully justified and prompted H. N. Brailsford to these discouraging conclusions:

> That President Wilson will struggle manfully for a League of Nations peace I do not doubt. His power, however, is gone. Since the November elections he speaks no longer for the majority in the United States.
>
> The American propertied class is even less tolerant of Socialism

[2] For the full text of Wilson's speech see Baker and Dodd (ed.): *The Public Papers of Woodrow Wilson,* V, 308–23. Both *The New Republic* and *The Nation,* December 7, 1918, were sharply critical of his failure to spell out a comprehensive reconstruction program.

[3] David Lloyd George: *The Truth About the Peace Treaties,* I, 160.

[4] *The Times* (London), November 9 and December 23, 1918.

[5] *Labour Leader,* October 31 and November 7, 1918.

than its European cousin. The Republicans are bent upon a hard peace no less decidedly than our Coalition. They control the Senate, and the Senate, as the unhappy President knows, is capable of rejecting any Treaty which he negotiates. He will sit down with that knowledge at the conference table, and Mr. Lloyd George and M. Clemenceau will share his knowledge. He is an eloquent voice. The real power lies with Senator Lodge and Mr. Elihu Root. It will be prudent for us to make our calculations for the probable event that Mr. Wilson will fail to write his principles into the Treaty of Peace. He has nothing to bargain with. Our war lords no longer need his help.[6]

Even though wide segments of the Allied forces of movement accepted this analysis, only the more militant elements voiced it publicly. Hounded by jingoists as well as revolutionaries, obviously Allied Radicals, Social Patriots, and Independents had every reason to magnify the President's continuing prestige and power.

Of course, the same was true for the Germans, only more so. Since Wilson seemed to be their best and only protection against the vindictive Allies, even reactionaries and conservatives, let alone Socialists, wished him well. The *Deutsche Zeitung* nervously noted that should the Democrats lose, the Entente would simply push aside Wilson's Fourteen Points and wreak vengeance on Germany.[7] Of course, opportunistic Wilsonians like Hans Delbrück regretted the outcome of the elections,[8] while *Vorwärts* looked upon the Republican victory as evidence that "reaction was moving its headquarters from the East to the West."[9] But again, regardless of the sincerity or expediency of their professions of liberality, most German Wilsonians simply had to insist on the continuing if not rising power and influence of the American President. They needed him as he needed them.

[6] *The Herald*, December 28, 1918, 4.
[7] *Deutsche Zeitung*, November 6, 1918.
[8] *Preussische Jahrbücher*, January 1919, 147.
[9] *Vorwärts*, November 30, 1918.

5

Britain: Khaki Election

WHEREAS THE AMERICAN ELECTIONS became entangled with the heated debate over the Armistice, the British election coincided with the post-Armistice euphoria which instantly shaded into acute anxiety over the impending peace negotiations. In the United States the Right maintained that unconditional surrender was the key to military victory; in England it proclaimed that integral reparation and punishment of the Kaiser were essential for a lasting peace. In both campaigns the jingoists seized the offensive, exploiting war-generated nationalist and anti-Hun sentiments to enlist mass support for partisan political, economic, and foreign policy aims. In the United States the Republicans sought control of the Congress in order to dictate conservative economic and social policies at home and a tough peace abroad; in England the Unionists strove for an impregnable position in Commons in pursuit of identical objectives.

In terms of issues and interests the coupon election of 1918 resumed the electoral battles of 1910. In both years the contest revolved around socio-economic reforms, tax legislation, free trade, and Home Rule for Ireland. For all practical purposes, on all these issues the Liberals and Labourites tended to make common cause against the Unionists. But by the outbreak of war Britain's political system was being taxed by the "toryfication" of the Unionists and the "radicalization" of both Labour and the Irish Nationalists. These mutually reinforcing forces of reaction and revolution baffled and sapped the ruling Liberal Party. In the face of mounting revolutionary threats— whether real or imaginary—prominent Liberals looked to defensive cooperation with moderate Unionists on a platform of social imperialism, nonparty government, efficiency, and national preparedness. But because of die-hard pressures the coalition-inclined Unionist leaders hesitated to consummate such a drastic political realignment.

Similarly, the smaller Radical wing of the Liberal Party inclined to cooperation with moderate Labourites in quest of timely reforms calculated to undercut the Left, especially the extreme Left. But again, moderate Labourites became increasingly weary of Lib-Lab coopera-tion due to mounting militancy within their own movement.

The war merely heightened the discomfiture of this Liberal Party which owed its inflated influence and power to the altogether fortuitous circumstances surrounding the three prewar elections. The wartime political truce came as a godsend. Impelled by the exigencies of war, moderate Labourites and Unionists freed themselves from their respec-tive extremists in order to back first the Asquith and then the Lloyd George coalitions. By 1917, when the party truce became strained, it was clear that Lloyd George was more beholden to the Conservatives than to the Liberals. He had the near unanimous support of the Unionists, whose principal leaders also occupied critical Cabinet posts.

Henderson's resignation in August 1917 was in large measure a response to this conspicuous Unionist ascendancy. In particular the growing influence of die-hard Tories caused grave apprehension in the Labour movement.

Meanwhile the Liberal Party was in disarray. The Liberal MP's, who in 1916 bolted the parent party to support Lloyd George, had to be satisfied with a junior partnership in the Coalition. The other two thirds of the Liberal Parliamentary contingent floundered under the indifferent leadership of Asquith, who retained control of the National Liberal Federation. The few but prestigious Radicals continued to foresake the grand old party in favor of Labour. Unlike Lloyd George, Asquith distrusted and disliked the politics of the street. At a time that Labour captured the Wilsonian rhetoric and the Unionists monopolized patriotic appeals, his view, style, and program of politics remained rigidly pre-Midlothian.

Although in terms of issues and interests there were strong con-tinuities with prewar politics, the strategy and tactics of electioneering were changing. The war, Lenin, and Wilson were intensifying the ideological tenor of British politics; and the popular thrust of the war was hastening the transition to mass politics. The Representation of the People Act of 1918[1] provided for full manhood suffrage and met the suffragettes halfway by giving the vote to most women over thirty. Overnight two million men and six million women were added to the register.

This doubling of the electorate was likely to foster greater changes in the style of English politics than the great Reform Act of 1832. In the approaching election rival parties would have to fashion appeals with which to vie for the votes not only of seasoned political partici-

---

[1] See Charles Loch Mowat: *Britain Between the Wars, 1918–1940* (London: Methuen; 1955), 5–6; A. J. P. Taylor: *English History, 1914–1945* (New York: Oxford University Press; 1965), 115–16; L. C. B. Seaman: *Post-Victorian Britain, 1902–1951* (London: Methuen; 1966), 105–7.

pants from among the elites, the lower middle classes, and the artisans, but also of inexperienced servicemen, workers, peasants, and women. Birmingham's electorate jumped from 75,000 to 427,000. Of the close to two million voters in greater London, 800,000 were women and over 400,000 were soldiers and sailors.

With eight million new voters of untried party affiliations, a flood of fresh blood was rushing through the political system. These untutored voters would cast their ballots in new or redrawn constituencies, would come up against three-cornered contests, and would be further confused by the campaigns of such minor formations as the National Party and the National Democratic Party.

With the passage of franchise reform in mid-1918 all politicians, regardless of party, began to prepare for the next general election. Not only was this election overdue by some three years, but also the new voters and constituencies should be attended to at the earliest possible moment. Needless to say, the timing rested entirely with the Prime Minister, who could be expected to pick a date that, without damaging the national interest, would be favorable to his own political fortunes. Accordingly he was bound to wait until either the tide of battle had turned or the war had actually been won.[2]

A task force headed by F. E. Guest, the Chief Whip of the coalition Liberals, began to prepare the election as early as July 1918. It pressed Lloyd George to come to an agreement with the Conservatives with regard to a joint campaign program and to a guarantee of Conservative support for a core of coalition Liberals.[3] By August 21 Henderson spoke of "the strong probability that a general election would come before the end of the year."[4] He even claimed to know that the government would hold the election "about two months from now, at which the issue would be purely 'Khaki' and the victory would be carried through on the wave of enthusiasm produced by their present military successes."[5] Within a week the Organization and Election Sub-Committee of the Labour Party urged the Executive to convene a special National Conference to prepare for "the possibility of a General Election in November," which would be "a Khaki Election."[6] Similar calculations and plans crystallized in other political quarters, notwithstanding later expressions of indignation against the rushed election. Lloyd George himself noted the "obvious fear of an election on the part of Henderson and the Asquithians."[7]

---

[2] See Lord Riddell: *War Diary, 1914–1918* (London: Ivor Nicholson and Watson; 1933), 343–74, *passim,* entries from August through October 1918.
[3] Trevor Wilson: *The Downfall of the Liberal Party, 1914–1935* (London: Collins; 1966), 141–3.
[4] Labour Party: Minutes of the Executive Committee, 14, August 21, 1918.
[5] Buckler to House, August 24, 1918, in Buckler Papers.
[6] Labour Party: Minutes of the Executive Committee, 14, August 27, 1918 (a.m).
[7] Riddell: *War Diary, 1914–1918,* 349.

Even if only as an aside, Bonar Law admitted that it might be "extremely unfair that an election should be fought in the main on a Win-the-War policy, in which he [Asquith]—and the men who have acted like him—are to be opposed." The Deputy Premier was satisfied, however, that since these Liberals would obstruct Lloyd George in the future as they had in the recent Maurice Debate, he would be fully justified to take the field against them.[8]

With only about a hundred Liberal supporters in Commons and without a party organization of his own, Lloyd George had no choice but to make an electoral alliance. A popular front seemed excluded, not only because of the estrangement of Asquith and Lloyd George but also because Henderson would reject any such overture. But short of an outright partnership with the Unionists the Prime Minister might strike for a centrist fusion of moderate Conservatives and coalition Liberals. In any case, Bonar Law suspected that Lloyd George would like nothing better than to precipitate a split in the Unionist Party "as a result of which a majority would support him." Bonar Law and Sir George Younger prepared to head off this schism while at the same time pressing for a coalition in which Lloyd George, though at the head of the ticket, would do *their* rather than his own bidding.[9]

Even though on the tariff, Home Rule, and taxes their position was considerably to the right of the Prime Minister's, Bonar Law and Sir George were not unpliant Conservatives. Neither was of landed background, the former stemming from a family of bankers and iron merchants, the latter having risen as a successful Scottish brewer. As compared to the Tories in their midst, who pressed for reassurances on fiscal and tariff policies, they realized that "on the old lines" the Unionist Party would have no future. The war had aggravated economic and social problems which needed to be tackled with rational and modernizing, not atrophied, plans and methods. In the face of Labour's challenge, the two old parties should pull together because, according to Bonar Law, only a government "secure of support not of one section but of both" stood a chance of implementing essential reforms "in a way as little revolutionary as possible." Only Lloyd George could win a large popular following for a united front of moderation, though to do so his coalition partners would have to shed their reversionary image and platform. In other words, Bonar Law and George Younger proposed to enlist Lloyd George and his Liberals both to discipline their own "backwoodsmen" and to capture the votes with which to install a right-of-center administration. During the election there would be no enemies to the right, a strategic alignment which

---

[8] Bonar Law to Balfour, October 5, 1918, in Balfour Papers, 49693. Key excerpts are cited by Robert Blake: *The Unknown Prime Minister: The Life and Times of Andrew Bonar Law, 1858–1923* (London: Eyre and Spottiswoode; 1955), 384.

[9] Cf. Blake: *Unknown Prime Minister,* 384–5.

might at some future date be transmuted into a permanently fused party.[1]

All the time, Lloyd George was in a transparently weak bargaining position. Given his breach with Asquith and Henderson and without a "strong and well disciplined" machine of his own[2] he had only his own prestige to throw into the balance. Though he used that prestige to good advantage by extracting Unionist backing for the return of some 150 trustworthy Liberals,[3] he lacked the leverage to insist that die-hard influences be curbed among his coalition partners. Lloyd George entered the election contest as a reluctant hostage to Bonar Law, who himself was overcome by intractable elements.

Following prior consultations, on November 2 Lloyd George outlined the basis for a coalition election in a letter to Bonar Law which barely concealed this victory-driven rightist backlash.[4] It was agreed that "subject to the exigencies of the military situation," the general election would be held at the earliest possible moment with the object of explicitly inviting the country "to return candidates who undertake to support the present government not only to prosecute the war to its final end and negotiate the peace, but also to deal with the problems of reconstruction which must immediately arise directly an armistice is signed." In brief, loyalty to the war effort was to be converted into unqualified support for the government's entire domestic and foreign policy for five years to come.

Lloyd George proposed that this transformation be undertaken with a platform designed to "retain to the greatest extent possible the support" of Bonar Law's as well as of his own followers. The word *retain* was not without significance. The Conservatives, and more particularly the Tories, were on their guard against the erstwhile pro-Boer, the architect of the People's Budget, the strategist of the emasculation of the House of Lords, and the one time advocate of arms limitation. In the excitement of victory and with the National Party in the background, Lloyd George could hold them for the Coalition only provided he once again disowned his past. In language reminiscent of Disraeli he now declared his "fundamental object" to be the promotion of "the unity and development of the British Empire" and the consummation of "such conditions of living for the inhabitants of the British Isles as will secure plenty and opportunity to all." But to make doubly sure not to give offense, while at the same time keeping a free hand, he went on to assert that there was no need "to discuss in detail how this program is to be carried out."

[1] See Blake: *Unknown Prime Minister,* 385.
[2] David Lloyd George: *The Truth About the Peace Treaties,* I, 160–1.
[3] Trevor Wilson: "The Coupon and the British General Election of 1918," in *Journal of Modern History,* Vol. XXXVI, No. 1 (March 1964), 36.
[4] The full text of this policy statement of November 2 is cited in *The Times* (London), November 18, 1918.

Even so, Lloyd George proceeded to reveal the coalition strategy on which he and Bonar Law had agreed. In public he held out strident but innocuous promises of social and economic reforms, but in private he granted the Conservatives concessions with regard to tariffs, Home Rule, and the Welsh Church.

With regard to reforms, he fell back on a recent speech in Manchester in which he had discussed "the imperative need of improving the physical conditions of the citizens of this country through better housing, better wages and better working conditions." In Manchester, however, he did not add the social-imperialist rationale which he felt was required in this search for a united front with the Conservatives: "I lay emphasis on this because the well-being of all the people is the foundation upon which alone can be built the prosperity, the security, and the greatness both of the United Kingdom and of the Empire."

Having allayed their anxieties about his Socialist inclinations, Lloyd George moved on to court the Tories with concrete promises. Significantly, he discussed economic issues first. In line with his coalition project of 1910 he accepted "the policy of Imperial preference as defined in the resolutions of the Imperial Conference, to the effect that a preference will be given on existing duties and on any duties which may be subsequently imposed." Even though he resisted food taxes, he did not exclude "preference on any article, as for example, tea or coffee, on which for our own purposes we have imposed a duty"; also, he undertook to continue subsidies to landlords under the Corn Production Act. All in all the landed interests were assured that the "improved agricultural position" that had been reached during the war would be maintained as a matter of public policy. His assurances to the industrial interests were equally comforting. He vouched "that the key industries on which the life of the nation depends must be preserved" and that "security should be given against the unfair competition to which our industries have been in the past subjected by the dumping of goods below the actual cost of production."

Since so many Tory superpatriots and landowners were particularly sensitive to the Irish issue, Lloyd George could not avoid discussing it. He actually declared the Home Rule Act of 1914, which was on the Statute Book, to be open to revision; he also pledged never to press a "settlement which would involve the forcible coercion of Ulster," thereby abandoning a Liberal position of thirty years' standing. With regard to the less vital Welsh Disestablishment, he opposed its cancellation while at the same time promising to review the financial aspects of the Welsh Church Act. Incidentally, foreign policy was not even mentioned in this charter document, notwithstanding Lloyd George's claim that his primary aim for seeking a broad popular mandate was to strengthen his hand for the peace negotiations.

This letter of November 2, which the Prime Minister was reluctant to show to his Liberal friends,[5] was calculated to help Bonar Law and Sir George Younger secure the largest possible Unionist endorsement for a coalition campaign—and government. Within ten days and in agreement with the Conservative Ministers, Bonar Law read it to 600 prominent Conservatives, including M.P.'s and candidates, meeting under the auspices of the National Unionist Association. At this meeting at the Connaught Rooms, Bonar Law, Balfour, and Walter Long took turns expounding on the advantages of having had a Liberal in the Premiership during the war and of renewing the Coalition for the difficult period of reconstruction. Significantly Sir Edward Carson, unreconstructed Ulsterite and protectionist, rose to second the resolution "that this meeting, representative of all sections of Unionists, approves Bonar Law's statement of policy and expresses its perfect confidence" in his leadership.[6] The unanimous and enthusiastic passage of this resolution meant that the Unionists preferred the risk of cooperating with Lloyd George and his minority Liberals to the danger of leaving the Prime Minister to try an opening to the Left.

Ever since 1906, Conservatives were in a sizable minority in Commons. But from the very outbreak of war they expected the national emergency to further their political fortunes. In late 1918 "they believed that the events and passions of the war had been withering in their effects upon Liberal principles and ideals; they held that these had been stultified or proved visionary by all that had occurred; they knew that the quarrels between Mr. Lloyd George and Mr. Asquith had split the Liberal Party from end to end; and finally they knew that in the personal prestige of the Prime Minister they had an overwhelming advantage."[7] Trusting in their organizational vigor and confident in their exclusive copyright on flamboyant nationalism, the Conservatives did not hesitate to match their own strength and wits with Lloyd George's.

On November 12, the same day that the Unionists met at the Connaught Rooms, the Prime Minister met privately with 250 coalition Liberals at 10 Downing Street. Rather than reveal the text of his unfavorable "treaty" with Bonar Law, he made a forceful and eloquent address which was "Liberal from start to finish." After praising the patriotism of the Unionists the Prime Minister maintained that "the way to prevent the spread of the revolutionary spirit was to embark at once on large schemes of sound social progress"; elaborated on his reconstruction plans; and claimed to be "as much a Free Trader as ever," supporting his claim with a reference to the third of Wilson's Fourteen Points. He was consistent and explicit with regard to only one

[5] W. A. S. Hewins: *The Apologia of an Imperialist: Forty Years of Empire Policy* (London: Constable; 1929), II, 174–5.
[6] *Morning Post,* November 13, 1918.
[7] Churchill: *Aftermath,* 27.

major aspect of domestic policy: he conceded that "Liberal Home Rulers had very great difficulties in recommending their policy . . . after the way Ireland had behaved during the war." Instead of avoiding foreign policy altogether he envisaged a peace settlement "based on justice and not on revenge or avarice" and a League of Nations to maintain order among the new nations, to facilitate a reduction of armaments, and to eliminate conscription. Before adjourning, H. A. L. Fisher moved, Lord Leverhulme and Winston Churchill seconded, and the meeting unanimously passed a resolution authorizing Lloyd George to join forces with Bonar Law.[8]

But what about the Labour Party, which formally was still a member of the Coalition? In May 1918 the Labour Executive had first recommended that "the existence of the political truce should be no longer recognized." But at the Annual Conference in June and led by George N. Barnes, J. R. Clynes, and six other Labour Ministers, the forces favoring continuing cooperation with the government offered stiff resistance. Over the opposition of Robert Smillie, W. H. Watkins, Ben Turner, and Sylvia Pankhurst, Henderson finally yielded "that a skilled draftsman might have included in the recommendation the words 'as regards bye elections.' " Thus amended, the resolution was adopted by 1,704,000 against 951,000 votes,[9] thereby abrogating the political truce but leaving the Labour members in the government. Even though Labour's participation in the Coalition was continued, it was a foregone conclusion that with the end of hostilities Labour would reclaim its full freedom of action.

Henderson's overly optimistic progress report about his build-up of the party machine pointed in the same direction. Since the adoption of the new party constitution the previous February, he had worked full time at transforming the party from a loose confederation of trade union and Socialist organizations into a disciplined nationwide political organization of individual members acting through local branches. As of midyear the extension of the franchise gave an additional stimulus to his organizing drive. By then Henderson claimed to have 300 candidates in the field and predicted that by election time an additional 100 would enter the lists.[1]

Moreover, Labour set about providing its candidates with an elec-

---

[8] *Morning Post,* November 13, 1918; and *The Liberal Magazine,* December 1918, 578–80. After criticizing this speech for having been "shamelessly angled toward overcoming the doubts" of the audience, Trevor Wilson concedes that "a good many Coalition Liberals were deceived by the P.M. because . . . they wanted to be" and that on key issues they now stood closer to the Conservatives than to the Radical wing of their own party." *Downfall of Liberal Party,* 150–5.
[9] Labour Party: *Report of the Eighteenth Annual Conference* (London, 1918), 6, 31–3, 36–9; Buckler to House, July 2, 1918, in Buckler Papers; and Baker to Polk, June 30, 1918, in Baker Papers (Letters to the Department of State), Box 3 of 18.
[1] Buckler to House, July 2, 1918, in Buckler Papers.

toral program for their bid for power. Actually, Sidney Webb—member of the Executive, prominent Fabian, and guiding spirit of Labour's Research Department—completed a preliminary draft of this new program in late 1917; but it was left to the Conference of June 1918 to adopt, with only marginal dissent, the Executive's expanded but toned-down version of *Labour and the New Social Order*, which pledged a Socialist reconstruction of Britain.[2] This comprehensive domestic program supplemented Labour's foreign policy program, which was codified in the *Memorandum on War Aims*.

Even though Labour's principles and goals sounded radical—especially in 1918, when disingenuous critics denounced them for being Bolshevik-inspired—its methods were not at all revolutionary.[3] To be sure, the Fabians' stratagem of permeating the Liberal Party through its Radical faction was forever abandoned. But the newly charted road to power was equally democratic and parliamentary: "in order to help realize the new social order and to give legislative effect to the Labour policy on reconstruction, this conference emphasizes the necessity of having in Parliament and the country a vigorous, courageous, independent, and unfettered political party" of hand- and brain-workers. There was no mention of a one-party state; local and regional government was to be reinforced; and the abolition of the House of Lords was the most extreme constitutional change envisaged by Labour. The evolutionary rather than revolutionary impulse was also evident in the recurring insistence that society would be rebuilt with gradual and deliberate speed.

At the same time Labour did espouse a systematic and sweeping Socialist reconstruction and not just a "patchwork gerrymandering of the anarchic individualism and profiteering of the competitive capitalism of pre-war time." Its maximum program called for the nationalization of such key industries as railways and canals, electricity, coal, life insurance, and alcoholic drinks, and for extensive government controls in agriculture. As a start the government should retain and streamline its wartime ownerships and controls.

In both the Webb and the Executive version—but especially in the latter—the emphasis was on immediate and minimal goals. Accordingly Labour pressed for the *maintenance* of wartime wages, for cash and unemployment benefits for veterans, for the full restoration of civil liberties and collective bargaining, for the repeal and permanent abrogation of conscription, and for an emergency housing program.

But a set of intermediate goals, foreshadowing the welfare state,

2 G. D. H. Cole: *A History of the Labour Party from 1914* (London: Routledge; 1948), 53 ff.
3 The full text of *Labour and the New Social Order*, as adopted in June 1918, is printed in Paul U. Kellogg and Arthur Gleason: *British Labor and the War* (New York: Boni and Liveright; 1919), 395–412.

attracted particular attention. Labour wanted the work week reduced to 48 hours and comprehensive unemployment, health, and insurance benefits for all citizens. Moreover, future governments would assume the obligation to provide employment for all who wanted and were capable of work; they would "adopt a policy of deliberately and systematically preventing the occurrence of unemployment . . . [by arranging] the public works and the orders of National Departments and Local authorities in such a way as to maintain the aggregate demand for labour in the whole kingdom (including that of capitalist employers) approximately at a uniform level from year to year." Any slack would be taken up by the construction of public housing, schools, roads, and harbors and by afforestation and reclamation projects.

To pay for this bold design, as well as for the war, Labour proposed capital, inheritance, and surplus-profit levies; it also urged that indirect taxes be discarded in favor of a direct graduated income tax. The unqualified endorsement of free trade was also part of Labour's overarching concern for a more equitable distribution of the tax burden.

This, then, was the manifesto which raised such a stir both abroad and at home. While Russian Bolsheviks denounced *Labour and the New Social Order* as an updated version of the reformist Gotha program, American progressives hailed it as an inspiring blueprint for the future. The *New Republic* reprinted the complete text as a special supplement,[4] while Republicans attacked the document vigorously for its Socialist and collectivist aims. They also charged that since the Labour Party's *Memorandum on War Aims*—which the *New Republic* had reprinted in similar form—endorsed President Wilson's Fourteen Points, Labour's domestic platform betrayed the Socialist designs of all Wilsonians, including the President himself.

In Britain, meanwhile, the manifesto was widely looked upon as further evidence of Labour's new ideological momentum and of Henderson's on-going organizational drive. Politicians of all shades realized that Labour had opted for an irrevocable break with the Liberal Party. Even though the program was too mild for the shop stewards on the Clyde, the British Socialist Party, and the semirevolutionary faction of the ILP, it struck a responsive chord in most party members, trade unionists, reformist Socialists, and Fabians. The party was prepared for the election contest: it was led by an energetic Executive Committee; in close to half the constituencies there were local parties; 300 candidates were primed for the electoral battle; a coherent program provided guidance and inspiration; and party speakers appealed to voters with streamlined versions of Webb's gospel.

Even so, as early as late August, Henderson predicted that with

4 *The New Republic,* February 16, 1918, Vol. XIV, No. 172, Part Two.

an election held in a climate of imminent or actual victory the government would receive "overwhelming support" while most Labourites would be "wiped out."[5] Obviously Henderson would not admit his apprehensions in public. Instead he joined Asquith, who was equally fearful of a khaki election, in calling for a postponement. Labourites and Liberals argued that an immediate election would be unfair to the soldiers who, even assuming the ballots reached them, would be too uninformed to cast a thoughtful vote. Also, time was needed to debate the large issues of peace and reconstruction for the benefit of the new civilian voters and to establish party organizations in the redrawn and new constituencies.

Henderson, however, was driven beyond these unexceptional rationalizations; he warned against holding elections at a time when demobilization and reconversion would cause unemployment. Whereas Lenin would have capitalized on such conditions to drive on the revolution, Henderson urged that nothing be done "that would in the slightest degree encourage an emulation of this deplorable spirit that has characterized the life of Russia during the past few months." He was afraid that if Labour failed to get "its proportionate share of representation" in a snap khaki election those people who were "disposed to adopt revolutionary tactics" would be inclined to "take matters into their own hands." Should these dangers not deter Lloyd George from seeking a mandate to make peace, he should at least promise to go to the country again immediately upon the conclusion of peace in order to get an informed mandate for reconstruction. In Henderson's view, in a feverish nationalist atmosphere no government was "entitled to ask for a verdict of the country in order to enable them to make peace, and then to go along [for four years] and use the power thus given to deal with the great problems of reconstruction."[6]

Henderson knew that neither Lloyd George nor Bonar Law would be responsive to these threats and suggestions from the floor of the House of Commons. In fact, the decisive debates took place not in Commons but in the Executive Committee on November 7 and at an Emergency Conference on the General Election on November 14.

Not unexpectedly, the Executive Committee accepted MacDonald's motion to ask the Emergency Conference to leave the Coalition should the Prime Minister call an election. But that was in the morning of November 7. Later that same day the Parliamentary Labour Party, which was not nearly so pugnacious, vigorously opposed this drastic course which would force the Labour Ministers to choose between resigning from the government and leaving the party.[7]

[5] Buckler to House, August 24, 1918, in Buckler Papers.
[6] *PD*, 110 (November 7, 1919), cols. 2432–42.
[7] Labour Party: Minutes of the Executive Committee, 14, November 7, 1918 (a.m. and p.m.).

The Parliamentary Labour Party, under pressure from the Labour ministers, decided to wait until peace was actually signed between all the belligerents. That would mean accepting office in the new Government and continuing in office, at any rate for the many months that will elapse prior to signing the Treaty of Peace. If this policy be pursued, it seems extremely unlikely that the Labour ministers would carry out their present intention (which could always be reversed) of resigning from the Government on the formal conclusion of peace. Clynes came to the Executive determined to induce his colleagues to recommend this compromise to the Conference. Even Henderson wavered. Clynes threatened that all candidates who did not get the "Lloyd George Letter" would be swept into oblivion and that the Labour Party would be finally smashed.[8]

Anxious to maintain a maximum degree of party unity, Henderson strained to mediate between MacDonald and Clynes. But his efforts failed and the dispute had to be aired publicly at the Emergency Conference.

That conference had to decide whether Labour ought to withdraw from the Coalition upon the dissolution of Parliament or upon the signing of the peace treaty.[9] Clynes came foward to speak for the Parliamentary Labour Party and the Labour Ministers. Because by now Lloyd George had decided to call his election, the delegates scrutinized his speech for signs that an opening to the Left might, after all, be in the wind. But Clynes merely pleaded that unless Labour remained loyal to the P.M., it would be denied a seat on the peace delegation, and hence any voice in the making of the treaty, though he also urged Labour to influence construction from within the government. Here, then, was another plea for unity for the immediate job ahead, reinforced by admonitions from James Sexton, Tom Shaw, and Will Thorne about the electoral risks of a break with Lloyd George.

However, the sentiments of the meeting were with the anti-coalitionists from the very start. These had no difficulty recalling that in late 1916 Lloyd George had pledged Labour representation at the Peace Conference in exchange for support of the war, without any further strings. They simply refused to surrender as unconditionally to Lloyd George as the latter had surrendered to Bonar Law just a few days ago. Recent experience had proven the ineffectiveness of applying pressure from within the government. Especially with class conflicts coming to the surface over reconstruction policies, Labour should be in opposition instead of having its hands tied by coalition pledges and responsibilities.

[8] Cole (ed.): *Beatrice Webb's Diaries*, 135, entry of November 7, 1918.
[9] This discussion of the Emergency Conference on the General Election, held in Central Hall, Westminster, on November 14, 1918, is based on the report in the *Labour Leader*, November 21, 1918, 4.

G. B. Shaw made the most effective speech in support of the Executive's motion for a complete and immediate break. He charged that since the Prime Minister had capitulated to the Unionists on most vital issues he could not possibly satisfy any of Labour's demands. At best he would continue to make vague and innocuous pronouncements about the importance of timely social and economic reforms. As for the argument that Labour should stay on until after peace was signed, Shaw countered that the government could spin out the negotiations for two or three years. In conclusion he urged that Clynes be sent back to Lloyd George to tell him "Nothing doing!"

The delegates took this advice by overwhelmingly adopting the Executive resolution by 2,117,000 votes against 810,000. On this occasion the miners, the railwaymen, and the engineering workers— the core of the new unionists organized along industrial rather than craft lines—threw their full weight behind an independent political offensive, while especially the textile workers stood with the ministerialists.

Before adjourning, on MacDonald's motion the conference called for Labour representation on the British peace delegation and for an International Labour and Socialist Congress to meet concurrently with the official Peace Conference.

Whereas the election preparations of the Unionists and coalition Liberals took account of victory-induced nationalist impulses, those of the Labour movement were influenced by the revolutionary ferment on the Continent. Admittedly, not even MacDonald and Snowden wanted a Soviet republic for England. But they did want to foment and enlist popular unrest in support of a Wilsonian peace and of Labour reconstruction. Henderson sympathized with this approach, but unlike MacDonald, who continued to be a political enthusiast, he stood forth as a political operator and tactician. Henderson would let the enthusiasts generate electoral emotions which he would then translate into votes. He focused on the game of politics, as befitted the strategist of a party aspiring to opposition status in England. Moreover, once he had left the government in 1917, and given his own political skills, Henderson realized that his own political career was tied to the party he had set out to build.

Henderson was the victim of circumstance. As party organizer he must have been impressed with the Labour Ministers' arguments against going it alone. And yet he would no more place himself in the shadow of Barnes than he would let the enthusiasts run away with the rank and file. As for his efforts to maintain party unity, they were only partially successful. Even though Clynes, in line with the conference vote, dutifully resigned as Food Controller, G. N. Barnes, G. H.

Roberts, and G. J. Wardle stayed on as Ministers and prepared to run as coalition Labourites.[1]

Beatrice Webb quite aptly noted that "with placemen on the one hand, the professional rebels on the other, the Labour Party goes into the electoral battle a distracted, divided and depressed rabble of some three hundred nondescript candidates." While making the best of a bad situation Henderson doubted whether he would win his own seat and, if so, whether he would have any party to lead. In an equally discouraged mood Sidney Webb, his chief braintruster, predicted that Labour would be fortunate to capture sixty seats, which would all "be for massed Trade Union constituencies."[2]

Among the independent Liberals, meanwhile, there was mounting disorientation. Neither Lloyd George nor the Labour Party seemed interested in bargaining for their support. Like it or not, these Liberals were entirely forced back on their own withering resources, which consisted of nationally known leaders, time-tested electoral slogans, and prestigious newspapers.

Little is known about the advice Walter Runciman, John Simon, Herbert Samuel, and Reginald McKenna gave to Asquith. But apparently the ex-Premier refused "to fall in with a plan which emanated from his own supporters"—and which won favor with Lloyd George and Bonar Law—to join a three-cornered coalition in exchange for his becoming Lord Chancellor and bringing some of his associates along into the government.[3] At the same time Lloyd George rebuffed a deputation from Liberal constituencies which "urged him to fight in alliance, not with Bonar Law, but with Asquith."[4] Since both overtures came after rather than before the Lloyd George–Bonar Law pact was sealed, they were bound to miscarry.[5]

In private, Asquith hoped that the longer the election was deferred the greater the chances of healing the breach within his party. On public platforms, however, he denounced the indecent haste with which the public would be asked to make a thank offering to Lloyd George, protested that because there was no time to debate the issues, the soldiers and new voters especially would go into the election "blind-fold", and objected to having the electorate "draw a blank cheque" upon the next five years.[6] As the *Daily News* saw it, that blank cheque would be filled in by the Prime Minister in accordance with his obligations to Ulster Orangemen, Tory landowners, and protectionist

---

[1] Cole: *History of the Labour Party*, 44.
[2] Cole (ed.): *Beatrice Webb's Diaries*, 134–5.
[3] See Blake: *Unknown Prime Minister*, 386–7.
[4] Roy Jenkins: *Asquith: Portrait of a Man and an Era* (New York: Chilmark Press; 1964), 475–6.
[5] Cf. Lloyd George: *Truth*, I, 173–5.
[6] Asquith speaking in Glasgow on November 1, 1918, quoted in *Liberal Magazine*, November 1918, 530.

business interests,[7] who were simply using him as "bait upon their hook."[8]

With the Labour Party the rallying point for the forces of movement and committed to a comprehensive reform program, Asquith could no longer take an expediential left turn. He and Henderson agreed on nothing except an undisguised loathing for Lloyd George and a ritualistic dedication to free trade. The former Prime Minister never even tried to enlarge their common ground by going all out for Wilsonian aims in foreign policy.

Instead, the Asquithians sounded the alarm about an ominous, possibly revolutionary, political realignment: "the parties representing the classes, the vested interests, trade, finance, and so on, on one side, and Labour on the other," enraged by an indefensible election.[9] The Liberals, for their part, would uphold the traditional concept of party, according to which parties were not "mere machines for organizing votes and manipulating registers, and for getting or keeping seats, or place, or power, but . . . the vehicles and instrument of great and abiding principles." On formally launching their campaign Asquith proudly announced that opposition Liberals would go into the election as "Liberals without prefix or suffix," standing on the principles and the spirit of Liberalism. He commended this time-honored world view not as "a cut-and-dried syllabus of dogmas and precepts . . . [but] as a living faith, a spirit, an attitude of looking at things, . . . a form of political temperament and genius," ideally suited to adapt to changing times and conditions.[1]

That this rhetoric was hollow became transparent once Asquith laid out his program. His first point was free trade; the second, Home Rule for Ireland; the third, "the social side of the program"; and the fourth, the complete restoration of civil liberties.

The third point best revaled Asquith's bewilderment. In spite of his having written off the Tories, with regard to social questions he was no less elusive than Lloyd George.

> I will take the number of subjects seriatim, not that I can dwell upon them individually tonight: I have not time. But in regard to the relation of capital and labour, to the increased productivity of our primary industry, of land for public purposes, in its taxation and in the conditions of its occupation, the public interest should be always and everywhere paramount, to a comprehensive dealing in

[7] *Daily News,* November 10, 1918.
[8] *New Statesman,* November 23, 1918, 145, cited in Rixford Kinney Snyder: *The Tariff Problem in Great Britain, 1918–1923* (Stanford: Stanford University Press; 1944), 284.
[9] *Daily News,* November 15, 1918.
[1] The full text of Asquith's speech at Caxton Hall, London, November 18, 1918, is cited in *The Times* (London), November 19, 1918.

no pettifogging spirit with housing and public health and temperance (cheers), and to the making of adequate and at the same time elastic provision for the needs of our soldiers and sailors . . . in regard to all those points we have laid down principles and lines of settlement to which, so far as I know, no Liberal anywhere takes any exception, let alone expresses any dissent.[2]

The Leader of the Opposition made himself still less attractive to Radical and Labour opinion by not even mentioning the coming Peace Conference, leaving it to Sir John Simon to urge that Asquith be appointed a member of the British peace delegation![3] No wonder that before the election was over *The Times* characterized the slightly over 250 opposition Liberals as "little more than a stage army" incapable of offering a serious challenge and representing "all things to all men."[4]

It is against this background of developments in the Unionist, the Lloyd George, the Labour, and the Liberal camps that the khaki election evolved. Although until Dissolution on November 14 the peace issue remained in the background, by December 14—election day— this issue overshadowed all others. The contending parties raised questions relating to the treatment of Germany only very gradually, spurred on by the National Party and the Northcliffe press, especially the *Daily Mail*. These, in turn, were stirred up by the rising revolutionary danger in Central Europe, Wilson's imminent arrival on the Continent and in Britain, and the approaching peace negotiations.

When Lloyd George, Bonar Law, and Barnes inaugurated the coalition campaign on November 16, they sought to rivet the electorate's attention to domestic issues.[5] In fact, the Prime Minister flatly stated that "with regard to peace I have already spoken, and I am not going to dwell on it today, because I have so much other matter about which I want to say something." This other matter was the search for stability in times of revolutionary tensions abroad and at home.

At this moment the air of Europe is quivering with revolution. Two-thirds of Europe has been swept by its devastating deluge; the situation is full of perilous possibilities, and if the new Parliament . . . through the selfishness of interests—(cheers)—or the factions of partisans—(cheers)—if it fails, the institutions even of this country may follow those of many of the rest of Europe. This country has for generations set an example to the world of steadiness of government, of the power of adapting itself to new conditions. We cannot return to the old conditions. (Cheers.) War is like

---

[2] *The Times* (London), November 19, 1918.
[3] Asquith did want to go to Paris, but "Lloyd George was determined that . . . he should first pay the price of subordinating himself in the Government." Jenkins: *Asquith*, 476–7.
[4] *The Times* (London), December 12, 1918.
[5] The text of the three leaders' speeches is cited in *The Times* (London), November 18, 1919.

a ploughshare and a harrow. It has turned up and rent the soil of
Europe. You cannot go back. If you do not sow weeds will
grow. . . . If Parliament rises to the level of its great opportunities,
then the Empire and the Throne—(loud cheers) . . . will be
firmly established. . . .

Here, then, was a clarion call to reconstruct England in a spirit of
patriotism rather than partisanship, and under the unifying impact of
the all-purveying specter of revolution. The issues were vast and time
was pressing.

In these grave postwar conditions, as in wartime, the nation could
ill afford the luxury of party strife.

> Well, there are times when an Opposition is essential to good
> government, but those are the times when political events are so
> dull, so unexciting, that if it were not for party nobody would take
> the slightest interest in them. . . . In ordinary times but for party
> the people would take no interest in government. Now, those are the
> times for a strong Opposition. But when you have great, gigantic
> tasks that will affect not merely the structure of the Empire and the
> fate of the world, but which come home to every man in his own
> household and workshop, in the life and death of his children, you
> really do not want strong Opposition. (Cheers.) This is a time
> rather for the criticism of experts and not of parties. Opposition is
> organized fault-finding . . . [which] makes for delay. . . . What
> we want now is the criticism of the expert, testing, suggesting,
> improving, strengthening. . . .

Lloyd George pledged to place himself above parties, factions, and
interests to serve the public and national interest guided by a broad and
distinct consensus on fundamental principles, values, and purposes, as
well as on the order of their priorities.

Lloyd George felt no need to go beyond his programmatic statement of November 12. With aplomb he vouched to follow Disraeli's
prescription for "a minimum wage, for better housing, for shorter hours
and for making the health of the people a national concern"; and
Gladstone's prescription for "the settlement of Europe and the affairs of
the world, [with] regard for national liberty, national rights, whether
they are great or small."

On this same occasion Bonar Law also called for an end to party
politics, insisting that since "the nation is behind us we have the right to
have a House of Commons which is behind us too." To be effective in
peacemaking and reconstruction, the government would have to be
truly national, not factional. Bonar Law claimed only one of his
colleague's two mentors: Disraeli had first attracted him to politics and
he wholeheartedly subscribed to Disraeli's maxim that "unless the
Conservative Party was a national party it was nothing."

Unlike Lloyd George, the Unionist leader had the candor to admit that there was little difference between Conservative and national policies: "The thing we are for most—and it is really the conservative element in every nation—is to make the conditions of life of the vast majority of the people as good as it is possible to make them." Bonar Law's promises were minimal, and even these minimal promises were occasioned by the fear that England would head toward revolution if social and economic conditions became "intolerable."

It was a measure of the infeudation of the coalition Labourites in England—and of Social Patriots throughout Europe—that when it was Barnes's turn to speak, he boasted that since his two predecessors on the platform had "been converted to our point of view," he merely needed to say " 'Ditto' to all they had said." His only reason for breaking with the Labour Party was his firm conviction that he could serve the workers best from within a national government. Barnes appealed to Labour everywhere to do its duty in the difficult transition from war to peace production, "to eschew impatience and precipitancy, and to act and speak in such a manner as to help to get the country through what is going to be a very trying time."

It took another two weeks before, in response to a question at Netherton, George Barnes professed, "well, I am for hanging the Kaiser." The coalition Labourite was standing in the Gorbals Division of Glasgow, the heart of the red belt along the Clyde, against John MacLean, a self-avowed and notorious revolutionary. Actually, because MacLean was in jail for sedition and incitement to riot, William Gallacher, who was equally militant, stood in for him under the label of the British Socialist Party. Perhaps it was not all that surprising that when hard pressed by charges of treason to the workingclass, Barnes fell back on the appeals of jingoist nationalism.[6]

But of the three major parties, Labour was the first to make foreign policy an issue in the campaign. On November 14, in his summons to the ILP, Ramsay MacDonald gave first priority to the battle for "an equitable peace."[7] Two weeks later, the two opening paragraphs of the Labour Party's official capaign platform dealt with foreign affairs. The first paragraph advocated "a peace of reconciliation" fortified by an international labor charter, a League of Free Peoples, open diplomacy, and free trade. The second paragraph was an equally direct challenge to the right wing of the Coalition. Under the heading "Hands Off Democracy" Labour welcomed "the extension of liberty and democracy in Europe," warned the government "that intervention on the side of European reaction" would be disastrous, and demanded "the immediate withdrawal of the Allied forces from Russia." As if to

[6] *The Times* (London), November 28, 1918. While the local Unionist Association actively supported Barnes, the Liberal organization helped him by not running a candidate of its own.
[7] *Labour Leader,* November 14, 1918.

add insult to injury, before touching on social and economic issues, the Labour platform advocated self-determination for Ireland and India within "the British Commonwealth of Free Nations."[8]

Labour had sound reasons for giving priority to foreign policy: within the Labour movement the rival factions found it easier to agree on peace than on reconstruction goals; the Labour-sponsored Wilsonian platform was particularly attractive to Radicals; and the leaders assumed that the Wilsonian ideology had, in fact, caught the imagination of scores of citizens in all walks of life.

Besides, it appeared that the Coalition was trying to keep an entirely free hand for the Peace Conference. It would be risky to let Lloyd George fill in a blank check in foreign policy, now that he was bound "hand and foot to the Tory Party," whose ideals and aims paralleled those of the Republican Party—which had recently dealt such a devastating blow to Wilson. Many Labourites shared Philip Snowden's fear that "unless we get a democratic settlement of the war all idea of carrying great schemes of national reconstruction will have to be abandoned."[9]

Labour might have been better advised not to nettle the Coalition into a full-scale foreign policy debate. The political climate was not conducive to the display of moderation toward the beaten foe; and with questions of foreign policy under discussion, it would be that much easier for the Unionists to push their inflamed nationalism to the center of the stage.

Not that the die-hard Right waited until challenged by Labour. At first the *Morning Post,* which incidentally also opposed a hasty election, urged the Unionists to quit being prisoners of Lloyd George and the Liberals![1] But with the Dissolution the *Post* shifted to accusing coalition candidates of promising social and economic "pies in the sky" instead of focusing on peace terms which, though the overriding issue of the campaign, were omitted from all important electoral pronouncements. The Prime Minister and his associates had an obligation to alert the public to the precariousness of Britain's and the Empire's security; the continuing necessity for a high level of military and naval preparedness after the war; and the requirements of unflagging spiritual mobilization. Standing foursquare on this platform of well-founded realism the Coalition should ask for a vote of confidence to press England's national and imperial interests at the Peace Conference.[2]

In this view a tough peace would be the mainstay not only of British

---

[8] The full text of "Labour's Call to the People!" issued on November 27, 1918, is cited in Labour Party: *Report of the Nineteenth Annual Conference* (Southport, 1919), 185–6.

[9] *Labour Leader,* November 28 and December 5, 1918.

[1] *Morning Post,* November 4, 1918.

[2] *Morning Post,* November through mid-December, 1918, *passim.*

security, but also of domestic prosperity and reconstruction. The war effort had exhausted the nation and the Exchequer was heavily in debt at home and in America. Even so, the coalition candidates were promising new housing, improved transportation, higher wages, and better education, all of which would cost money. Especially since the *Morning Post* was hostile to drastic tax increases and reforms it held that only complete reparations and indemnities could pay the cost of war and reconstruction. Should Germany get away without paying for the war she had deliberately provoked, then England would "remain bowed beneath a weight of debt which will make reconstruction nearly impossible."[3]

The *Morning Post* had no patience with the misguided spirits who called for the Kaiser's scalp, charging them with seeking a "convenient scapegoat." Reparations, restoration, and indemnity—to cover the entire cost of the war—had the great merit of providing solid political and economic benefits as well as psychic and sentimental satisfaction. They appealed to the propertied classes which were anxious to escape higher taxes; they also appealed to the families and friends of the dead and wounded. In fact, the indemnities touched all voters in that they alone could keep down the overall tax burden. They would have the additional advantage of weakening Germany, not least by sapping her competitive position in international trade. But above all, with full indemnities a "country fit for heroes to live in" could be built without additional financial sacrifices by the classes and masses of England.[4]

Presently Northcliffe, whose flirtation with Wilsonianism was short-lived, joined the outcry for a stiff indemnity. No doubt he was still looking for a club with which to beat Lloyd George. But whatever his personal motivation, the fact remains that Northcliffe's prescriptions continued to be shaped by his fear of revolution. Specifically, he maintained that by truckling to "unteachable Tories," "British Junkers," and "reactionaries" Lloyd George had lost the freedom to "carry out such reforms as would prevent revolution."[5]

Northcliffe embraced a form of jingoist populism, catering to returning veterans and the unemployed with a combination of ideological opium and material bait through the pages of his *Daily Mail*. As of early December he asked his readers to vote only for candidates, regardless of party, who explicitly stood for eight points: (1) land and landbanks for discharged servicemen; (2) financial support for servicemen seeking to reopen business; (3) provision for new houses; (4) trial

[3] *Morning Post,* November through mid-December 1918, esp. November 28, 1918.
[4] *Morning Post,* November 27, 1918.
[5] *Daily Mail,* November 14, 1918; Reginald Pound and Geoffrey Harmsworth: *Northcliffe* (New York: Praeger; 1960), 679–81; *The History of the Times,* IV, Pt. I, 455–6.

of the Kaiser; (5) full indemnity and ton for ton; (6) expulsion of Huns; (7) exclusion of undesirables; and (8) reform of pension allowances.[6]

Northcliffe did not succeed in having *The Times* propagate this same platform, primarily because Geoffrey Dawson, the editor, would not turn against the leaders of the Coalition.[7] Nevertheless, *The Times* did join the clamor for complete indemnity. Perhaps at the suggestion of coalition headquarters *The Times* eventually asked "What is the Whole Bill?" and reported that whereas Home Rule and free-trade slogans were falling flat, Barnes's phrase about "hanging the Kaiser" and demands for Germany to pay the cost of the war were rousing electoral audiences.[8]

Before radio came into its own in the twenties and thirties the press continued to be the chief instrument of political information and propaganda. Needless to say, Northcliffe, Beaverbrook, and Riddell were the most inflential newspaper proprietors. But of equal if not greater importance was the editorial leadership given by Steed, Dawson, J. L. Garvin, A. G. Gardiner, H. W. Massingham, and C. P. Scott. At any rate, all politicians had a curious combination of faith in and fear of the press in this age of mass circulation and mass politics. Significantly, on the eve of the khaki election, Lloyd George sought to prevail upon faithful associates to purchase the *Daily Chronicle* for his own political use.[9]

Lloyd George's pre-election move would suggest that England's political class recognized that the press, both yellow and otherwise, was an instrument to be used and abused in the political struggle. Regardless of the personal motives—political, psychological, financial, or social—of either or both proprietor or editor, in the last analysis newspapers had as little or as much autonomous power as political parties. Their own institutional momentum need not be denied; nonetheless both were instruments rather than determinants of the political struggle.

Accordingly even though the press eventually became the most effective carrier of Carthaginianism, the thundering clamor to make the Germans pay and to hang the Kaiser did not originate in the business or editorial offices of Fleet Street.

By early November—hence, probably in full knowledge of the Lloyd George–Bonar Law compact—the National Party articulated a full-blown program of revengeful jingoism.[1] In addition to calling for

[6] *Daily Mail*, December 3, 1918.
[7] *The History of the Times*, IV, Pt. I, 446–50.
[8] *The Times* (London), December 7 and 9, 1918.
[9] Riddell: *War Diary, 1914–1918*, 352–3, 365.
[1] The National Party's "Fundamental Points of Policy" are cited in full in *Morning Post*, November 5, 1918.

unconditional capitulation, retention of all German colonies, and surrender of Germany's merchant fleet, these new nationalists swore that
Germany would "pay the costs of the war." These peace terms were
combined with a xenophobic design to purge England of every trace of
German influence, which these English superpatriots exaggerated as
effectively as the *Action Française* across the Channel or the National
Security League across the Atlantic. To cleanse and secure British
society, enemy aliens would be deported, enemy businessmen and
enterprises banned, German immigration blocked, naturalization requirements stiffened, and all foreign-born citizens or citizens of foreign
parentage barred from elective or appointive state office.

These Carthaginian-*cum*-xenophobic prescriptions were part of a
wider reactionary impulse. Guided by Tories of at best marginal
influence in the conservative but nevertheless modernizing political
class, the National Party charged the existing political institutions with
generating and responding to "secret funds," "the sale of honours," and
"financial abuses." These corruptions could only be overcome by
restoring "an effective Second Chamber" and, above all, by giving the
legislature "the power to institute inquiries." Accordingly, a Judicial
Committee of the Privy Council should investigate the conduct of
"minister, ex-minister, or official" at the request of "a definite number
of members of either or both Houses." The call, then, was not for the
abolition of the Parliamentary system as such, nor for the restriction of
the franchise. The aim was to reinvest the Upper House with some of its
lost power and glory while at the same time making the Lower House a
vehicle for populist-jingoist pressures.

The socio-economic program was further evidence that the
National Party was out to forge an alliance of obsolete elites with status-
anxious, nonproletarian masses. It catered to the former with "a scientific tariff according to the necessities of individual industries, including
agriculture," with "protection against dumping," and with "imperial
preference." To attract a mass following, the appeals of nationalism
were combined with vague promises of "adequate housing and measures for the improvement of health and the mitigation of infant mortal-
ity," qualified by the reminder that hard work was the essential prerequisite for social improvement.

Even though the social origins and economic interests of the leaders
and followers of this National Party remain unclear, its role in the
election of 1918 should not be overlooked. Under the leadership of
Brigadier-General Page Croft, M.P. for Bournemouth, and with the
help of the Tariff Reform League and the Empire Union, the party ran
twenty-six candidates, returned two, and polled 94,000 votes. Page
Croft himself was re-elected by the largest majority of any candidate
who stood without the coalition ticket.[2] Even though the Primrose

2 *The Times* (London), January 4, 1919.

League, the *Daily Mail,* and the *Morning Post* urged the election of coalition candidates, they were unashamed and open fellow-travelers of the National Party. The *Morning Post* flatly declared that whereas all three party machines were organized upon the prewar model and conspired to keep the issues on prewar lines, the National Party alone had the courage "to face the present and the future and to hammer out a creed from the hot metal of our recent experience." With obvious regret the editors conceded that the party was "too young, too small, and too ill-supported with means to have any chance of securing the support of the nation for its principles."[3]

Some of these avenging and jingoist ideas filtered into the Central Election Committee of the Coalition in London, which was run by the Unionists. Of the 364 Unionists and the 159 Liberals who received the coupon—the letter of endorsement signed by Lloyd George and Bonar Law—close to half were inexperienced in Parliamentary and national politics and less educated than the candidates standing for *re*election.[4] These newcomers to big-time politics were particularly prone to look to party headquarters for guidance.

From the outset candidates were reminded to keep the " 'big' point of view, the large issue, in the foreground." The electorate should be convinced that "no other Government could be trusted with Peace Negotiations [and that] the whole of the problems of Reconstruction must turn on the terms of Peace."[5]

The unfolding campaign literature told the voters that "without a real victory" there could be "no real Social Reform," that "victory in the field deserved victory at the polls," that they should "trust the men who won the war to make the peace," and that they were "about to decide what should be done with Germany."[6] But blatantly vindictive themes emerged only gradually. It was left to a summary election manifesto, late in the campaign, to promise the punishment of the Kaiser as well as of all Huns who had "ill-treated women, children, civilians, seamen, wounded, and prisoners." This leaflet also pledged the Coalition to make the Germans pay "the cost of the war and its destruction," to keep all Germans out of the country, and to safeguard British workers and industries against German dumping.[7]

---

[3] *Morning Post,* November through mid-December, 1918, *passim,* but esp. November 16 and 19, 1918.
[4] See J. M. McEwen: "The Coupon Election of 1918 and Unionist Members of Parliament," in *Journal of Modern History,* Vol. XXXIV, No. 3 (September 1962), 294–306, esp. 299–301; and Trevor Wilson: "The Coupon and British General Election of 1918," in *Journal of Modern History,* Vol. XXXVI, No. 1 (March 1964), 28–42.
[5] *General Election, 1918: Daily Notes for Speakers* (Private), No. 2.
[6] See National Unionist Association, Election Leaflets Nos. 1830–70.
[7] National Unionist Association, Election Leaflet No. 1874 ("The Policy of the Coalition Government"). Ironically, this statement opened with a passing reference to the League of Nations.

Similarly, the speeches of the coalition leaders became Carthaginian little by little. It was not until November 29 that Lloyd George, at Newcastle-on-Tyne, explicitly took up the indemnity issue. Speaking as lawyer, historian, and peacemaker he argued that in court the loser invariably assumed the cost of litigation; that in 1871 the Germans had made the French pay; and that now, too, Germany would have to "pay the costs of the war," though only "up to the limit of her capacity."[8] The *Morning Post* nodded approvingly for the first time.[9]

In this same address Lloyd George announced that he had appointed a blue-ribbon Committee of Experts "representing every shade of opinion" to determine this capacity. The membership of this committee hardly justified his claim of broad representation. For it consisted of Hughes of Australia, who yielded to no one in his rancor against Germany; W. A. S. Hewins, the Liberal Imperialist economist who joined Joseph Chamberlain's defection, resigned as director of the London School of Economics to head the staff of the Tariff Reform League, and was first suggested by Hughes; Lord Cunliffe, the Governor of the Bank of England who was Bonar Law's candidate and diligently fostered the indemnity illusion; Herbert Gibbs, a prominent City banker chosen by Hughes in consultation with Bonar Law; Walter Long, the lifelong Tory stalwart and Colonial Secretary; and Sir G. E. Foster, Canada's Finance Minister, who was the only member of moderate bent. Not only were all the *experts* of this committee of belligerently anti-Labour persuasion, but there were no moderate Unionist or Liberal *politicians* to counterbalance the influence of Long and Hughes. Could it be that Lloyd George's choice was a function of his decision to placate the men of the City and the jingoes who were in the ascendancy in the Conservative Party?[1]

On December 5, in a formal statement of coalition policy and aims, the Prime Minister intoned another three Right-populist themes: he joined in the new-fangled worship and acclaim of servicemen; he endorsed the prosecution of the Kaiser and his accomplices for wantonly planning and provoking the war; and he argued that because they had spied and plotted, enemy aliens had "forfeited any claim to remain" in England, where they took "the bread out of the mouths" of those whom they had sought to kill during the last four years. In closing, Lloyd George assured the electorate that "all the European Allies"—he did not mention England's American Associate!—had "accepted the prin-

[8] For the text of this speech see *The Times* (London), November 30, 1918.
[9] *Morning Post*, November 30, 1918.
[1] Imperial War Cabinet 38, November 26, 1918 (Noon), Cabinet 23/42 and 43. Cf. Lloyd George: *Truth*, I, 458–60; and Riddell: *Intimate Diary of the Peace Conference and After, 1918–1923* (London: Reynal and Hitchcock; 1934), 3, entry of November 30, 1918.

ciple that the Central Powers must pay the cost of the war up to the limit of their capacity."[2] Now that the Prime Minister was capitulating to the irresponsible fringe, *The Times* stepped up the pressure: rather than compute Germany's capacity to pay, which "is not our business," England should prepare, present, and collect the bill of expenses and damages.[3]

But Sir Eric Geddes, First Lord of the Admiralty, addressing a large rally at the Drill Hall in Cambridge on December 9, gave the most vivid but cold-blooded formulation of the indemnity issue.

> If I am returned Germany is going to pay restitution, reparation, and indemnity, and I have personally no doubt we will get every-thing out of her that you can squeeze out of a lemon and a bit more, but there are some things I would not take from Germany, because they would hurt our industries. I propose that every bit of German property, movable and immovable, in Allied and neutral countries, whether State property or the private property of Germans, should be surrendered to the Allies, and that Germany pay her precious citizens in her precious paper money. . . . I propose that not only all the gold Germany has got, but all the silver and jewels she has got shall be handed over. All her pictures and libraries and every-thing of that kind should be sold to the neutral and Allied world, and the proceeds given to pay the indemnity. I would strip Ger-many as she has stripped Belgium. (Cheers)[4]

The man who also coined the felicitous slogan that England would "squeeze the German lemon until the pips squeak!" was no parvenu: before the war he was an important railway executive, after the war he became chairman of the Dunlop Rubber Company and of Imperial Airways.[5] It was Geddes's venomous pronouncement which moved Beatrice Webb to write: "I feel physically sick when I read the frenzied appeals of the Coalition leaders—the Prime Minister, Winston Churchill and Geddes—to hang the Kaiser, ruin and humiliate the German people—even to deprive Germany of her art treasures and libraries. . . . It may be all election talk, but it is mean and brutal talk, degrading to the electorate."[6]

The blue-ribbon Committee, in its report of December 11, was the first to propose a concrete figure. It estimated the total cost of the war to the Allies to be roughly 24 billion pounds sterling; and recommended that the enemy powers be asked to make annual interest payments of 1.2 billion—in "cash, kind, securities, and by means of a funding

---

[2] The text of this statement is cited in *The Times* (London), December 6, 1918.
[3] *The Times* (London), December 7 and 9, 1918.
[4] *The Times* (London), December 10, 1918.
[5] Mowat: *Britain Between the Wars, 1918–1940,* 4.
[6] Cole (ed.): *Beatrice Webb's Diaries,* 139, entry of December 12, 1918.

loan"—for an indefinite number of years. Even though a Treasury committee, headed by John Maynard Keynes, estimated that two to three billion was the maximum Germany could pay and the Allies could absorb, the Prime Minister's task force felt no qualms about going the limit.

Lloyd George claims that both he and Bonar Law, who was Chancellor of the Exchequer, were "repelled and shocked by the extreme absurdity of this document [and this] wild and fantastic chimera," which he was careful not to publish. True enough, that same day, in a major speech at Bristol, Lloyd George once again stressed that Germany could only be asked "to pay to the utmost limit of her capacity" and warned against raising "false hopes" as well as against collecting the interest by having "sweated goods" dumped into Britain. But in this same penultimate election address, some 36 hours before the polls opened, Lloyd George watered down his own qualifications by assuring his audience that "the British Imperial Committee take a more favorable view of the capacity of Germany than do the officials of the Government Departments," that England had "an absolute right to demand the whole cost of the war from Germany," and that the "Committee appointed by the British Cabinet believe that it can be done." Needless to say, his audience in Bristol, the press, and the public at large took little notice of the reservations, preferring to fasten on to the golden prospect of 24 billion sanctified by the authority and prestige of an anonymous but prestigious and expert "Imperial Committee."[7]

In the second phase of the election, in addition to exploiting the pipedream of indemnities, the coalition leaders pressed the bogey of Bolshevism into service. The Prime Minister was bound to take advantage of the split in Labour. Again, he began on a mild note. He praised the coalition Labourites for patriotically and wisely upholding national unity while castigating the Labour Party for breaking the party truce for selfish partison reasons. With the progress of the campaign, however, the Labour movement came under increasingly severe fire for irresolute patriotism in wartime and reckless militancy in peacetime.

In pamphlets from the Central Election Committee every effort was made to portray Bolshevism and Socialism as synonymous. Russian "Bolshevism (or Socialism)," which owed its origin to a German conspiracy, was undisguised anarchy, robbery, and murder. Moreover, it banished religious weddings and funerals, confiscated church property, and made divorce "easy." Britons were told to take heed, since

[7] Lloyd George: *Truth,* I, 461–7. Cf. John Maynard Keynes: *The Economic Consequences of the Peace* (New York: Harcourt, Brace; 1920), 135–45.

"Bolshevist Socialism" would like to do for them what it had done for Russia. One of the anti-Socialist circulars advised the male voter to have it read by a woman member of his family and to then "act on her advice."[8]

A circular denouncing the ILP was particularly inflammatory. Although other electioneering materials were in black print, this particular item, impugning the ILP leaders for having "earned the praise and gratitude of our enemies," was printed in red. Other leaflets linked pacifism and pro-Germanism, charged that since MacDonald and Snowden had not helped win the war they could not help "win a strong peace," and questioned the loyalty of anyone seeking to resume relations with German Socialists.[9]

As late as December 5 Lloyd George himself was still relatively mild in references to Bolshevism, calling it "the poison of production" and the fomentor of class conflict, but without implicating the Labour Party.[1] But again, less than 24 hours before the polls opened Lloyd George, in a speech at Camberwell, gave his sanction to some of the wildest accusations disseminated by many of the coalition candidates throughout the campaign.

> The Labour Party is being run by the extreme pacifist, Bolshevist group [*sic!*]. . . . It was they who pulled Labour out of the Government. They pulled it out—why? What they really believed in was Bolshevism. Who are these men? They are the outstanding figures of that Party, I name one or two of them—Mr. Ramsay MacDonald, Mr. Snowden, and Mr. Smillie and others. . . . Supposing the Labour Party won. The moment they got in these are the men who would run the Government. That is exactly what happened in Russia.[2]

Meanwhile the Labour Party ran some 360 candidates, of whom 50 were sponsored by the ILP. The primitive condition of the Labour press handicapped the campaign from the very start. Both Lansbury's *Herald* and Snowden's *Labour Leader* were weeklies of limited circulation. Moreover, neither shared the Henderson-Webb outlook: whereas the *Herald* was of syndicalist and "guild socialist" persuasion, the *Leader* spoke for the pacifists in the ILP.

Curiously enough, Northcliffe rushed to the rescue, driven by his feud with Lloyd George and his fear of the consequences of denying Labour its day in court. As of December 3 the *Daily Mail*—both the home and the Continental edition—carried a daily "Labour" column,

---

[8] National Unionist Association, Election Leaflet No. 1846.
[9] National Unionist Association, Election Leaflets No. 1834–5, 1849, 1867.
[1] *The Times* (London), December 6, 1918.
[2] *The Times* (London), December 14, 1918.

made available "for the use of the Labour Party during the Election as they do not yet possess a daily newspaper." *Noblesse oblige.*

The final guest editorial in the *Daily Mail* branded the indemnity agitation as "humbug," designed to shift attention from the more fundamental question as to whether the war and reconstruction would be paid by "a levy on capital rather than crushing taxation upon the middle and working classes." Should vast indemnities nevertheless be imposed, their transfer would require the dumping of cheap German goods into Britain.[3] But on balance Labour's tone in this guest column was studiedly sober.

So was a series of widely distributed election leaflets, issued by the Labour Executive. Britain's allegedly radical party appealed to the electorate with the following titles: "Why Not Abolish the Poor Law?," "To the Man Who is Buying a House," "To the Woman in the Home," "Why All Who Believe in Education Should Vote Labour," "Why the Labour Party is Opposed to all Protective Customs Tariffs," "Why the Labour Party Supports the Nationalization of Mines and Railways," "Why Farm Workers Should Support the Labour Party," "Why Labour Supports a League of Nations," "Freedom is the Basis of the Labour Party's Policy," "What the Labour Party Means by Home Rule All Round," "To the Soldier, Serving and Discharged."[4] As compared to coalition appeals, this Labour propaganda lacked emotional invective and ideological verve; moreover, the "big point of view" and the "large issues" did not stand out.

In many ways the Radicals were more aggressive, possibly because they had longer experience in pressing big issues. The *Daily News* had a clear-cut "acid test: Who is on Wilson's side and who is against him?" In addition to applying this test each elector ought to realize that "a vote for the Coalition is a vote for Conscription." Whereas Labour's coordinated campaign against intervention in Russia did not begin until immediately after the election, the *Daily News* protested this intervention throughout the election without, however, condoning the class aspects of the Bolshevik regime. But rather than break with Asquith, who on the eve of the election joined the indemnity chorus, the *Daily News* urged independent Liberals and Henderson Labourites not to oppose each other: "In nine out of ten constituencies where a follower of Mr. Asquith is opposing a follower of Mr. Henderson the electors are asked to choose between two men standing in all essentials for the same principles." Here was a vastly exaggerated claim, since with few notable exceptions like Josiah Wedgwood, independent Liberals avoided coming out for Wilson's program. In private A. G. Gardiner, the editor of the *News,* admitted the gravity of the Lib-Lab plight and

---

[3] *Daily Mail,* December 12, 1918.
[4] Labour Party, Leaflets, New Series (for the General Election of 1918), Nos. 1–23.

confessed that he would have to "rely on the stiff jaw of one great man."[5]

The weekly *Nation* was less equivocal. Its readers were urged to "rally to Labour" because Labour stood uncompromisingly for Free Trade and the Open Door and because by "putting the case of Ireland and India in the forefront of its program the Labour Party [was] clearly affirming its position as the national party of progress and an inheritor of the Radical tradition in the sphere of nationalism and political democracy." Overoptimistically, the *Nation* gauged the drift among soldiers, intellectuals, and civil servants to be toward "Labour and those free Liberal candidates with a personality and program."[6]

The superpatriotic sweep exceeded the most optimistic predictions and justified the opposition's gloomiest apprehensions.[7] In addition to the 5.1 million votes, or 50 per cent of the popular vote, cast for coalition candidates as such, there were 200,000 votes for Havelock Wilson's coalition-financed National Democratic Party; 700,000 votes for noncouponed Unionists of pronounced Tory leanings; and 94,000 for Page Croft's National Party. The Unionists won 382 seats, or three fifths of the membership of the House. This immensely strengthened Conservative contingent could count on the loyal cooperation of 136 coalition Liberals, nine National Democrats, and two new Nationalists. Lloyd George retained his own seat in Carnarvon with a majority of 10,000 votes; Bonar Law and Churchill made an equally impressive race; and not one of Lloyd George's 40 ministerial colleagues was unsuccessful. Barnes defeated MacLean by a two-to-one majority, while three couponed candidates of the National Democratic Party easily won out over Ramsey MacDonald, Arthur Henderson, and Fred Jowett.

Of some 260 Members without previous Parliamentary experience, 168 sat on Unionist benches. And among these newcomers there was a particularly high proportion of businessmen as well as sons of businessmen and professionals. Accordingly, among Unionist M.P.'s those of landed background declined in favor of candidates standing on the Conservative ticket in provincial towns; the Unionists also cut heavily into Liberal strongholds in Scotland.

As Sir George Younger triumphantly reported to his Executive Committee, "The net result of the Election was that there were about 100 more Unionists than in the last Parliament."[8] Here were those

[5] *Daily News,* November through mid-December 1918, esp. November 27 and December 4, 1918; Irene Cooper Willis: *England's Holy War* (New York: Knopf; 1928), *passim;* Gardiner to Baker, December 13, 1918, in Baker Papers, Box 96.
[6] *Nation* (London), November through mid-December, 1918, esp. November 23 and December 14, 1918.
[7] This survey of the returns is based on *The Times* (London), December 30, 1918, and January 4, 1919; McEwen, "The Coupon Election of 1918," 294–306; Wilson, "The Coupon and the British General Election of 1918," 28–42.
[8] National Unionist Association: Minute Book of the Executive Committee, February 12, 1919.

"hard-faced men" who, according to Stanley Baldwin, looked "as if they had done very well out of the war."[9] While landed aristocrats regretted the commercialization and vulgarization of the Tory Party,[1] the *Morning Post* claimed "A Victory for Victory."

> Despite all that is said and feared about Bolshevism, Internationalism, Socialism, and all the other stinks of the political laboratory, the British people remain . . . national and patriotic in spirit. They have returned Mr. Lloyd George to power because they have had from him the most fervent expression of the national spirit. . . . They have been returned not by a faction, nor by a party, nor by a class, but by the nation.[2]

Indeed, with the help of nationalist and retributive appeals, Conservative social and economic forces massively improved on their prewar influence, power, and control. No doubt intransigent Tories would have preferred to exploit nationalist emotions for outright retrograde purposes. But since they did not want to "risk the return of a Revolutionary and Confiscatory Party which might cut the throat of society" they were prepared to use the Prime Minister as "a sort of safety razor, which might shave close but would not endanger life."[3] Under the circumstances they had to be satisfied with exerting pressure for a hard peace and against modernizing reforms from within the Coalition while basking in the glory of having unchained the jingoist ideology necessary for the containment of the forces of change.

As for the opposition, it survived in popular but not in Parliamentary terms, 1.3 million voting independent Liberal and 2.4 voting Labour. In Commons, however, the Asquithians were reduced to 26 Members. East Fife, which ever since 1886 had sent Asquith to Westminster, gave a margin of 2,000 votes to Sir Alexander Spirot, a relatively obscure Unionist, even though the coalition leaders had denied him the coupon "with self-conscious generosity."[4] Moreover, McKenna, Runciman, Samuel, Simon, and H. J. Tennant were wiped out, all except Simon in three-cornered contests; McKinnon Wood and Charles Hobhouse even forfeited their deposit of £150.00. Of the Opposition's front bench only three survived, and these three were of non-Cabinet rank. It fell to Sir Donald MacLean to lead the surviving Parliamentary skeleton, and he lacked the political prestige and debating skill to cover up his party's demise.

By virtue of having overtaken the Liberal Party in the electoral field, the Labour Party now became His Majesty's Opposition. But the new Parliamentary delegation was not only less militant but also less

---

[9] Quoted in Keynes: *Economic Consequences of Peace*, 145.
[1] See Lord Henry Bentinck: *Tory Democracy* (London: 1918), 2–3, cited by McEwen, "The Coupon Elections of 1918," 306.
[2] *Morning Post*, December 30, 1918.
[3] *Morning Post*, December 17, 1918.
[4] Jenkins: *Asquith*, 478–9.

experienced than either the Executive or the leaders of the Labour movement at large. Indeed, Sidney Webb's prediction had come true: of the 59 Labour M.P.'s, 49 came to Westminster from massive trade-union constituencies, the Miners' Federation alone sending forth 24 of them. Appropriately enough William Adamson, a Scottish miner, became Chairman of the Parliamentary Labour Party and thereby Leader of the Opposition. Thus at this critical juncture both the withering Liberal rump and the fledgling Labour Opposition were saddled with distinctly mediocre leadership.

But even with a first-rate Opposition Leader the Labour delegation could not have developed into an effective critic of domestic and foreign policy. Most of the trade unionists in the Parliamentary Party were rigidly national, anti-intellectual and anti-Socialist in their outlook, and therefore suspicious of the nationally prominent officers of the political movement. Whereas in terms of overall effectiveness in Commons, the defeat of Henderson, Webb, and Lansbury was particularly debilitating, from the point of view of foreign policy dissent, the total rout of the ILP was disastrous. Of the 50 Labour candidates who ran on the ILP ticket only three were successful, and all three—Ben Spoor, Neil Maclean, and William Graham—were new to Parliamentary, national, and Transport House politics. In addition to MacDonald the election banished F. W. Jowett, Philip Snowden, W. C. Anderson, Thomas Richardson, and H. B. Lees Smith. With the further defeat of Arthur Ponsonby and Charles Trevelyan, prominent converts from Radicalism to Independent Labour, the U.D.C. cabal in Commons was completely smashed. U.D.C. candidly confessed that its Parliamentary leaders had been "snowed under" by vast majorities, with "unfortunate [consequences] for the country."[5]

Under the circumstances Lloyd George's triumph turned out to be too complete. To paraphrase Keynes, having permitted the British electorate to be bamboozled, he found it difficult if not impossible to debamboozle it. Throughout the first half of 1919 the Prime Minister had to reckon with the consequences of an election which Balfour euphemistically referred to as "a very inconvenient necessity."[6] As House wrote to C. P. Scott, "the same mischief was done at the elections in both America and England: the reactionary forces were strengthened in such a way as to place difficulties in our path at every turn of the road."[7] In England the growling Conservatives exercised a veto over Lloyd George with regard not only to indemnities but also to social policy.

[5] *The U.D.C.*, January 1919, 290. Snowden was crushed by a majority of 16,802 votes, MacDonald by 14,223, Trevelyan by 7,629, and Ponsonby by 3,395.
[6] Balfour to House, December 13, 1913, House Papers, 2:10a.
[7] House to Scott, March 10, 1919, cited in J. L. Hammond: *C. P. Scott of the Manchester Guardian* (London: G. Bell; 1934), 260.

Churchill, meanwhile, in a letter to his constituents, placed the outcome of the election in a broader context.

The result of the election constitutes . . . a condemnation of tyranny, whether it takes the form of Kaiserism or of Bolshevism. Our path lies between these perils, which, from the one side in the shape of autocracy and from the other in the shape of anarchy, threaten and impede the onward march of peoples. The political experience and the sober virtues of the British nation have hitherto enabled us to beat down foes abroad and restrain folly at home. Here in this island we have found the way to preserve the continuity of our history without preventing progress: and the impressive majorities now being recorded in all parts of the country to the National Government are at once a vindication of British character and an example which may be of service to many struggling races in Europe.[8]

By February Churchill decided that the force of example could not by itself achieve a national union comparable to Britain's in Central and Eastern Europe. He therefore proposed to supplement it by large-scale military intervention in the Russian Civil War.

The outside world was fully alive to the importance of the general election. Washington received progress reports from the London Embassy.[9] Meanwhile, in Paris, Colonel House, who was indifferent to the American election, thought the general election was an opportunity "to nail the British government more securely to the President's program." To achieve this he arranged "to have questions put to the Government during the campaign to which they will have to reply specifically." Nothing further is known about the tenor of the questions which were asked, nor about the agents who asked them. However, House did send Frank Cobb of the New York *World* to England "to see the Liberal Leaders and editors together with the Laborites, to tell them what is at issue"; and Cobb kept House informed by daily letters.[1] In America, once the returns were in, the New York *Tribune* hailed the British electorate for backing "a victory of justice with reparation and sure barriers against another eruption of the Hun," just as the American voters recently had done.[2]

In France the right-wing press eagerly watched and approved the Coalition's campaign, while the Socialist organs cheered the Labour Party. The *Temps* expected Labour to win between 120 and 150 seats;

[8] Cited in *The Times* (London), December 30, 1918.
[9] See *F.R.,P.C.,1919*, I, 337–8, 409–11.
[1] House Diary, November 4 and 5, 1918; House to Cobb, November 11 and December 16, 1918, House Papers, 17:62; Cobb to House, November 11, 1918, House Papers, 4:1.
[2] *Tribune*, December 29, 1918.

the *Populaire* hoped for 200 or 225, insisting that the general election would give a good index of the Western European proletariat's *fin-de-guerre* mentality.[3]

The coalition victory encouraged the entire Right. The *Temps* celebrated Lloyd George's "triumph" in glowing terms, and so did Pertinax, who welcomed it as a good lesson for France. Defeatists, cowards, pacifists, and Bolsheviks were completely routed and sturdy patriots had achieved an impregnable position in Parliament.[4]

As for the Socialists, they were stunned by Labour's crushing debacle. To head off disheartenment the *Populaire* celebrated the 2.5 million votes for Labour candidates as a victory in defeat. But further to the Left the *Journal du Peuple* admitted that the outcome was "bad—worse than we thought"; it also noted that the nationalist impulse was so formidable that the Labour Party drifted into "national Socialism." Mayéras was equally disconcerted, in particular because the new Labour M.P.'s were not militants of strong internationalist persuasion, and because French Socialism was headed for a similar defeat in the first postwar election.[5]

There was even greater consternation in the enemy nations, whose governments placed their hopes—to avoid total disaster—in Wilson. But before the Peace Conference ever convened he suffered two setbacks—the first in America's congressional elections, the other in England's general election. Paul Lensch, Germany's Havelock Wilson, characterized Lloyd George's victory as a stinging rebuff to Germany's liberals and Socialists who invariably denounced the German Right for being the chief obstacle to diplomatic sanity. According to the *Deutsche Zeitung*, here was "another bitter lesson for those optimists who expected the German Revolution to make a favorable impression on the Allied peoples." Impelled by "Lloyd George's new caesarism," England was getting ready to drive a Draconian bargain.[6]

The coupon election continues to be a subject of controversy, and each major actor in the drama has his own scenarist. But from the peacemaking perspective, ephemeral speculations about the personal motives of Lloyd George, Bonar Law, Sir George Younger, and Arthur Henderson are of limited relevance. In England, as in America, the elections were destined to register the political consequences of victory in an era of mounting social and class tensions. Both elections witnessed the renewal of prewar party struggles under particularly trying and emotion-charged conditions. Only one new major issue came

[3] *Le Temps*, November 28 and December 14, 1918; *le Populaire*, November 13, 26, 29, 30, 1918; *l'Humanité*, December 11, 1918.
[4] *Le Temps*, *l'Echo de Paris*, and *le Matin*, December 29–30, 1918.
[5] *Le Populaire*, January 1, 1919; and *Journal du Peuple*, January 2, 6, 1919.
[6] *Die Neue Zeit*, January 17, 1919, 366–7; and *Deutsche Zeitung*, December 30, 1919.

before the voters, namely, the terms of peace. But even with regard to these peace terms the parties and factions squared off in accordance with previously held foreign policy principles and attitudes.

While the parties and issues were similar, the war had greatly accelerated both the realignment of political forces and the change in the conditions and instruments of electoral combat. In the Allied and Associated nations victory enabled the forces of order to seize the political offensive with jingoist, national-union, and Red-smear slogans. Even before the war, conservatives and reactionaries had used such slogans with growing success; after the war they caught on like fire. In both America and England the right-wing campaign turned into a calculated adaptation, for partisan purposes, of the ideology and methods of the wartime *bourrage du crâne*.

The leaders of the forces of movement were defenseless, in part because for the duration they themselves had also preached the patriotic gospel. With the end of the political truce they sought to free themselves from this ideological straightjacket. In the meantime, however, public opinion had been taught to favor unqualified jingoism over "me-too patriotism." The Lib-Labs themselves helped shape the climate of opinion in which social reform was more acceptable under national —reputedly national—than under partisan or class auspices. Moreover, in a frantic effort to prove their loyalty, they were wary of cooperation and identification with their own enthusiasts, internationalists, and revolutionaries, thereby denying themselves not so much numerical strength as ideological *élan*. In spite of this tactic of dissimulation, which was also a function of the perennial tug of war between moderates and extremists, the Lib-Labs continued to be fair game for slurs on loyalty and patriotism. Even before the war they had been the victims of these charges; but now these charges were doubly hysterical and damaging because they fed the new specter of Bolshevism.

In sum, as compared to the last prewar years, thanks to the nationalizing effect of successful war, the Right had considerably increased its prestige, influence, and power. The revolutionary developments in Eastern and Central Europe contributed to these gains by frightening otherwise moderate and sensible people into taking momentary refuge in super-patriotism. Surely this political consequence of victory had to affect the politics and diplomacy of peacemaking.

6

Wilson's Grand Tour

AT THE TIME of the Armistice Wilson resolved to go to Western Europe to take personal charge of America's peacemaking effort. Questionable personal motives may well have contributed to this decision. But even assuming Wilson went to Europe out of self-indulgent inclination or compulsion, those who were eager for him to stay home were similarly motivated. Certainly the Allied premiers never relished the prospect of standing in the American President's shadow. Nor were Lansing and House entirely altruistic when they recommended that the President visit Europe and participate in preliminary inter-Allied negotiations but that he not sit as a delegate in the Peace Conference.

Had Wilson remained in Washington he would almost certainly have been accused of staying on Mount Sinai with his Fourteen Tablets, of slowing down the Conference, of hampering the American Delegation, and of putting domestic politics ahead of foreign affairs. Without agreement on how a "wise" treaty would have looked, who can say whether House, Lansing, or Root would have done better? Could any one of these three have dealt more "successfully" with Clemenceau, Lloyd George, and Orlando, each of whom was determined to lead his own delegation? Perhaps so, provided a treaty acceptable to anti-Wilsonians be considered good and wise. Such a treaty might have been good for the Republicans, possibly even for the Democrats; but it would hardly have fostered a healthier international climate for the United States, for Europe, and for the world.

Moreover, by staying in Washington or by being in Paris without sitting as a delegate, Wilson would have become a choice rallying symbol and focus for dissatisfied delegations, suppliants, parties, and factions. The President himself recognized that by going to the seat of the Conference but remaining outside he would "be merely the center of a sort of sublimated lobby [and] all weak parties would resort to [him] and there would be exactly the same jealousy that was excited by

the Germans addressing themselves exclusively to me."[1] The governments of the defeated as well as of the successor nations, the Bolshevik
government, the opposition Socialists, and the Radicals all would have
petitioned or pressured Wilson. In turn, without direct involvement in
day-to-day negotiations and constant exposure to the arguments and
exigencies of the three premiers, the President would have been particularly responsive to such protestations. Since these protests, with few
exceptions, would have been directed against Carthaginian and counterrevolutionary policies, they would have stimulated the intransigence
of the forces of order on both sides of the Atlantic.

But quite apart from challenging the Right, a campaign to make
Wilson into a symbol-*cum*-agent of appeasement of the vanquished and
of Soviet Russia might have gone too far, even for the President. By
heading the U.S. Delegation, by being one of the Big Four, and by
chairing the League of Nations Committee, the President endowed the
Peace Conference with a progressive aura, with the result that the
Left-dissidents trusted the proceedings in Paris and Versailles, at least
temporarily. Had the President remained outside the Conference—either
in Paris or in Washington—restless Socialists, Labourites, and syndicalists especially might have defied the Conference from the very
beginning, instead of initiating defiance around May 1919. Wilson
loathed, feared, and resisted any premature polarization between Right
and Left. He was not about to ally himself with a radicalized Left, for
excesses on the Left invariably frightened him into closing ranks with
the Right. It was precisely to avoid this odious choice that he sought a
middle, reformist solution, both abroad and at home.

Fatally weakened by the outcome of the congressional elections,
the President looked for political support to Europe, where the nonrevolutionary Left was eager to follow his leadership. This marriage of
convenience promised to forestall the radicalization of that Left, while
at the same time strengthening the cause of moderation in Paris. A
partial but nevertheless distinct diplomatic victory in Europe might give
Wilson the strength and momentum to initiate a revival of the New
Freedom in Washington.

The Allied Governments and Rightists were as fearful of Wilson's
diplomatic triumph as were his American opponents, and for essentially similar reasons. They, too, were determined to make political
capital out of the hard-earned but exhilarating military victory. They
resorted to a time-honored strategy to contain the Left: especially in
order to satisfy its own extremists the Right claimed full credit for
preparedness, patriotism, loyalty, and bravery, while indiscriminately
accusing the Left of appeasement, internationalism, disloyalty, and
defeatism.

[1] *F.R.,P.C.,1919,* I, 134–5.

Clemenceau, Lloyd George, and Orlando were quite confident of their power and ability to curb or, possibly, fatally to mutilate the Left, provided the intervention of both Lenin and Wilson could be foiled. It was easy enough to thwart Lenin. Though many Socialist leaders were inspired by Soviet achievements and manifestoes, the Russian Bolsheviks were in no position to provide them assistance: they were too removed, both geographically and culturally; their instruments of subversion were embryonic; and their capacity for military and economic intervention was nil. Moreover, until peace was made, emergency laws enabled the belligerent governments to censor Bolshevik pronouncements, to keep out Soviet agents, and to jail suspected revolutionaries.

Potentially Wilson's intervention was considerably more dangerous than Lenin's. Wilson was an ally standing squarely in the Western tradition, not an undeclared enemy with alien cultural ties. Instruments of intervention were at his disposal, such as newspapers, parties, pressure and interest groups, and personal contacts. America had not only vast and ready economic and financial resources, but also ample tonnage with which to overcome geographic distance. The Allied Governments could neither censor Wilson's pronouncements, nor keep out his agents, nor arrest his fellow travelers.

When Wilson sailed for Europe the premiers, their supporters, and the jingoists understood that the President was coming not out of vanity but for imperative political reasons. They expected him to mount a campaign designed to subject the Allied Governments concurrently to external economic and internal political pressures. Should this twin flanking movement succeed, Wilson might circumscribe the diplomatic as well as the political wages of military victory: Lloyd George, Clemenceau, and Orlando might not only have to make concessions on the German colonies, the Saar, and the Dalmatian coast, but also on the nationalization of coal mines, the progressive income tax, and labor legislation.

Wilson's project was particularly disquieting because the Allied forces of movement eagerly rallied to the President, hoping to enlist him in their unequal struggle with the overbearing forces of order. Needless to say, Radicals throughout Allied and enemy Europe wholeheartedly endorsed Wilson's fundamental objectives as well as his methods for achieving them. But as Romain Rolland suggested, Wilson's real influence owed less to his following among the liberal middle classes of Europe—and Asia—than among the workers.

Whereas Wilson and the European Socialists were in broad agreement on most essential issues of international politics, they were at opposite poles on domestic issues, notably on the reconversion, reconstruction, and reform of the capitalist economy and society. Nevertheless, in spite of basic differences, Wilson and the Socialists sought each other out, all the time remaining on their guard. Wilson did not want to become a prisoner of the Socialists: they were too radical for his own taste and their support scared off liberal conservatives. The Socialists, for their part, did not want to become prisoners of Wilson, for he was excessively moderate for their own taste and was suspect particularly among the militants.

At first Wilson misjudged the European Socialists, exaggerating their strength, unity, and radicalism. As a result, he was extremely—excessively—cautious in his approaches to and relations with the Socialists. He wanted to use them to cow the premiers into moderation without, however, furthering the Socialists' power, self-confidence, and defiance. On the other hand, the Allied Socialists had no alternative but to remain loyal even to an overly cautious and compromising Wilson: Lenin was too far away, the Right and the incumbent governments were all powerful, the Socialist leaders were irresolute, and the immediate postwar crisis was considerably short of revolutionary in the victor nations.

This, then, was the political setting for President Wilson's European journey. Before the Conference opened he visited first France, then Britain, and last Italy. In all three countries he engaged in ceremonial rounds, preliminary diplomatic negotiations, and political soundings.

In France the Socialists had become increasingly pro-Wilsonian throughout 1918. This all but unanimous pro-Wilson sentiment was corroborated during and after the national congress of the SFIO in early October.[2] When the small Maximalist faction—led by Fernand Loriot and Paul Faure—urged the French proletariat to rely on its own strength instead of on Wilson, Mayéras countered that the party had to work with the President in spite of his never becoming a Socialist.[3] As of the Armistice the ex-*minoritaires,* who now controlled the party, as well as the CGT, consistently favored cooperation with Wilson at the same time that they reinstated the interdict against participation in bourgeois coalitions at home. Their Wilsonianism in foreign policy was combined with a reformist-revisionist rather than revolutionary domestic program.[4]

Even though the situation was far from revolutionary in post-Armistice France, undoubtedly there was an outburst of revolutionary élan in the labor movement. It was widely felt that the "signature of the peace would be the prelude to the thoroughgoing economic, political, and social transformations" for which Socialists had battled for so many decades.[5] The Socialists resumed their campaign for these trans-

[2] See my *Political Origins of the New Diplomacy, 1917–1918,* pp. 385–7.
[3] *L'Humanité,* October 7, 1918. See also *III*ème *Internationale,* November 9 and 20, 1918.
[4] For the official program of the CGT see *le Populaire,* November 26, 1918.
[5] See the text of the resolution adopted by the SFIO at its October congress in *l'Humanité,* October 11, 1918.

formations, inspired by the Bolshevik and German Revolutions and confident that the tragedy of the war as well as Wilson's pronouncements had confirmed their diagnosis of the causes of international conflict in this waning capitalist era.

The SFIO and CGT could use three tactics. They could propose reformist legislation in the *chambre* while preparing themselves for the next general elections. Since the Left was hopelessly outnumbered and outclassed within the *chambre* this approach was not promising. The outlook became altogether hopeless in late October when on the initiative of the Gauche Démocratique all anti-Socialist Republicans— left, center, and right—agreed to explore the basis for maintaining the *union sacrée* for the electoral and parliamentary struggles of the postwar era. Within a month the Entente Républicaine Démocratique was formed, the Gauche Démocratique (28 members) being joined by the Fédération Républicaine (32), the Républicains de Gauche (48), and the Gauche Radicale (56). This loose Parliamentary alliance of 164 deputies, under the presidency of François Arago, was the forerunner of the Bloc National Républicain which scored such a smashing victory in the elections of November 1919. Meanwhile this coalition stood on a program of traditional conservative republicanism. Moreover, it cooperated with the right wing of the Radical Socialists who, under Édouard Herriot's guidance, had just refused to join the Socialists in an appeal to Wilson. Even though this new political formation claimed to be equally opposed to the extremists of the Right and Left, its primary thrust was anti-Socialist. And the Socialists knew this.[6]

The second alternative was a direct-action campaign with recourse to public demonstrations, mass rallies, strikes, and, as a last resort, a general strike. But this alternative seemed equally unattractive to the Socialist leaders: the still powerful ex-*majoritaires* would never go along, the party was not geared for insurrection, and the repressive power of the victorious state could not be challenged lightly.

There was a third alternative, which involved a fusion of tactics. Why not use President Wilson's impending arrival in France to demonstrate and thus to increase the strength and solidarity of the French Left? With Wilson as their symbol the Socialist and syndicalist leaders hoped to hold the allegiance of all wavering Social Patriots and to test their influence among the non-Socialist segments of the forces of movement. It was Marcel Sembat of the centrist faction who first argued that the party could more effectively brace itself by specific deeds than through polemics. He wanted the SFIO and the CGT to make a start by organizing a huge reception for the President on the occasion of his arrival

[6] The organization of this coalition can be followed through *le Temps* of October 23, November 22, and December 25, 1918; its program is printed in *le Temps* of December 24, 1918. For the developments in the Radical Socialist Party see *l'Humanité*, October 28, 1918; and *le Populaire*, October 29 and 31, 1918.

in France. Could anyone "dream of a more beautiful occasion" to promote the unity of the party? This reception should be followed by rallies and manifestoes spelling out not only foreign policy objectives but also the whole range of political, economic, and social aims.[7] When Jean Longuet, the ex-*minoritaire* leader of the SFIO, endorsed this project he stretched its purpose to demand the end of intervention in Russia and a prompt meeting of the International.[8] All these demands were to be pressed inside and outside Parliament.

The architects of this campaign kept reassuring themselves, their followers, and their Maximalist critics that to support Wilson was not incompatible with being a Socialist. Without the backing of the French as well as the European proletariat Wilson could not accomplish his task. But in this cooperative venture "we will not be his auxiliaries: instead, he will be ours." Socialists could buttress Wilson in his labors at the Peace Conference without abdicating their class aspirations or abandoning their class action. Needless to say, Socialists would not follow him blindly, but they would support him against "the men of the left bank of the Rhine, of Syria, and of intervention in Russia," the more so because a good peace was the necessary precondition for domestic reforms.[9]

Accordingly the SFIO and the CGT planned a huge public demonstration at Brest, a roaring welcome along the streets of Paris, a mammoth cortege in front of Wilson's residence in the capital, public rallies throughout France, and a special "Wilson" edition of 150,000 copies of *Humanité*. A delegation consisting of Albert Thomas, Longuet, Adrien Pressemane, Jean Raffins-Dugens, Sembat, Alexandre Varenne, and Léon Jouhaux planned to go to Brest on December 13 to greet Wilson the moment he touched French soil; the following morning in Paris would become an "apotheosis" for the President. For all public demonstrations, but especially for the one in Paris, the SFIO and the CGT would take measures to avoid dangerous incidents or disorders.[1]

The special edition of *Humanité* carried testimonials from outstanding Frenchmen. Anatole France respectfully saluted the first citizen of the world; Charles Gide urged all democratic organizations to give Wilson the support he expected and deserved; Lucien Lévy-Bruhl assured the President that in addition to the masses, he could count on at least part of the intelligentsia, and that if Jean Jaurès were alive he would be Wilson's most enthusiastic champion; Romain Rolland, in spite of grave reservations, trusted Wilson to put a brake on the imperialist ambitions of the victor bourgeois governments; Léon Blum

[7] *L'Humanité*, December 6, 1918.
[8] *Le Populaire*, December 7, 1918; and *l'Humanité*, December 8, 1918.
[9] *Le Populaire*, December 5 and 6, 1918; and *Journal du Peuple*, December 14, 1918.
[1] *L'Humanité*, December 5 and 6, 1918.

thought this to be the moment to recall the ode in which Thomas Carlyle celebrated Dante because "if he had not spoken, many things would have remained unsaid—not dead, but living without a voice"; Victor Basch praised Wilson for having remained a man of peace while surrounded by the passions of war; and Maxime Leroy hailed him as a combination Marcus Aurelius and Montesquieu ordained to restore order in the world.[2]

This campaign gained so much momentum that even the Maximalist Committee for the Defense of International Socialism summoned its followers to join in. It felt called upon to insist, however, that these demonstrations should be given a proletarian and Socialist character; that an ideal rather than a man should be hailed; and that this ideal was international Socialism.[3]

Meanwhile other organizations also decided to mark Wilson's arrival by sending a delegation to call on the President, by issuing a special manifesto, or by holding a festive assembly. Notable among these organizations were the Ligue des Droits de l'Homme, the Coalition Républicaine, the Radical Socialist Party, the Veterans of the Commune, the Freemasons, and the Association of Men of Letters.

But only the Ligue des Droits de l'Homme and the Coalition Républicaine joined forces with the labor movement. They asked their followers to participate in the demonstrations in Paris and in mass meetings throughout the nation.[4] The Radicals merely sent a delegation to Brest with a manifesto honoring the man who was determined "to consummate the revolutions of 1787 and 1789"—to consummate the political rather than the social or economic gains of the French Revolution. The Radical manifesto also called for "restitutions, reparations, guarantees, and sanctions."[5]

This studiously guarded manifesto was symptomatic not only of the rising conservatism in the Radical camp but also of the misgivings with which the Right watched the Socialists develop their Wilson cult. The *Temps* accused the leaders of the 34,000 card-carrying members of the SFIO of conspiring to compensate for their intrinsic weakness: they were trying to swell their ranks by claiming that Wilson's ideas coincided with those of international Socialism, all the time forcing Wilson's vague gospel to suit their own needs. The Wilsonian peace formula was "but a pretext for creating a world wide movement of social revolution and for putting France on the road to Bolshevism." Both France and her guest would be embarrassed if a political party succeeded in "exploiting Wilson's visit for its own partisan purposes." The President should be the honored guest of the entire nation, which would celebrate

2 *L'Humanité*, December 14, 1918.
3 *Le Populaire*, December 13, 1918; and *Journal du Peuple*, November 13, 1918.
4 *Bulletin des Droits de l'Homme*, November–December 1918, 772-4.
5 *Bulletin du Parti Républicain Radical et Radical Socialiste*, December 14, 1918.

him for his material power—"we owed him half of our daily bread for an entire year"—and for his peace loving ideals. In brief, "it was neither out of naïveté nor for love of idle fancies that the people of Paris welcomed the ideal personified by President Wilson."[6]

Similarly Alfred Capus maintained that even though there was much for which to be grateful to Wilson and America, this gratitude had to stop short of requiring Frenchmen to neglect their own national interest. Unlike the Socialists, who wanted to "create a demi-god and impose a secular infallibility on France," *Figaro* refused to see any resemblance between Moses and Wilson or to accept the Fourteen Points as theological dogma.[7] As for Pertinax, he cautioned the Allies to maintain their diplomatic, military, and economic defenses while testing the new international society in the next quarter century.[8] After praising Wilson for his magnificent contribution "to the cause of our Western civilization," Charles Maurras forewarned him that the Socialists who opposed external war were "violent fomenters of internal war." In Maurras's eyes the President's lofty insight that the world needed a moral regeneration brought him to a vital crossroad.

> Wilson's campaign can follow the old, venerable, solidly built, and much travelled road of traditions, mores, cults, and all that which constitutes the spiritual fiber of the West—a slower but safer and more prudent route over which many new ideas can incorporate themselves solidly in the human spirit and will. . . . All *existing* elements should be enlisted in the construction of this better life. On the other hand, a new plan relying on *new materials* and placed on a new site requires a prior Bolshevik thrust which is exactly what horrifies President Wilson [italics mine].[9]

In sum, the *Temps, Figaro, Echo de Paris,* and *Action Française* subtly qualified their hostility to Wilson while at the same time blatantly exaggerating the revolutionary implications of the Socialists' Wilson cult.

Presently the usually well-informed William Martin reported growing official irritation with this Socialist drive to use Wilson for partisan ends; he also wondered whether the President was sufficiently aware of the danger of this campaign.[1] By December 7 André Tardieu had spoken to Colonel House about "the attempt of the Socialists to take Wilson under their wing." The following day Émile Hovelaque, a counselor to one of France's war missions to the U.S., "complained bitterly [to House] that the Government was doing everything to keep the President from receiving the welcome the French people desire to give him" and that it encouraged the publication of derogatory articles

[6] *Le Temps,* October 22, November 7, December 12 and 15, 1918.
[7] *Le Figaro,* November 16, December 3, 7, and 13, 1918.
[8] *Echo de Paris,* December 14, 1918.
[9] *L'Action Française,* December 7, 1918.
[1] *Journal de Genève,* December 5, 1918.

as well as of hostile statements by Wilson's opponents in America.[2]

At the last minute, on December 13, Clemenceau notified the SFIO and CGT leaders that they could proceed with their plans only provided they secured advance notice from the President that he would welcome their demonstration and receive their delegation. There were conflicting reports as to whether or not the Socialists ever formally asked the President for prior clearance.[3]

Meanwhile, however, in anticipation of official roadblocks and out of courtesy to Wilson, the Socialists had spoken with favorably disposed U.S. officials in Paris.[4] On December 5 Albert Thomas, Pierre Renaudel, and Marcel Cachin called to inform House and Auchincloss of their plan to send a delegation to Brest, to have a parade of 150,000 workmen in the capital, and to present a testimonial to the President. A few days later R. S. Baker informed House that he had "attended a joint meeting of the principal labor . . . and Socialist leaders of France . . . and had heard them work out their manifesto to President Wilson and discuss the visit to Brest." Incidentally, House had by then instructed Baker to tell French dissidents that in him they had "an ardent friend at court [but] that they should be moderate and should not go to excess in any direction, either in speech or action."[5]

William G. Sharp, the U.S. Ambassador to France, concurred that even though the French government was discouraging the enterprise, the President could not "refuse to accept the testimonial and to recognize the parade." Hence, Sharp and House decided that, subject to another talk with Clemenceau, the President "should receive the address and review the parade" after the state luncheon at the Élysée. On December 9, probably following this further talk, House cabled Wilson that "a committee of laboring men and Socialists headed by Albert Thomas . . . wished to present you with an address . . . and hold a monster parade in your favor. This is not definite but will probably take place."[6]

It is significant, however, that the President himself exercised extreme caution, since he inquired of House whether "it would not be possible, in some tactful way . . . to avoid the demonstration of laboring men and Socialists . . . [because he] feared embarrassment from any seeming identification with any single element, and recalled

[2] House Diary, December 7 and 8, 1918; and David Hunter Miller: *My Diary at the Conference of Paris*, I, 50.

[3] *Le Temps, l'Humanité,* and *le Populaire,* December 14–16, 1918; and R. S. Baker, Diary, Book XXI, 173–4, entry of December 14, 1918.

[4] In early November Albert Thomas had assured House that "all the sections of the Socialist Party, including the Radicals and the Extreme Left, cordially endorsed" Wilson's program. Memorandum on conversation between Albert Thomas and House, November 3, 1918, in House Papers, 29:23.

[5] House Diary, November 12 and December 5, 1918; Auchincloss Diary, December 5, 1918; R. S. Baker to House, December 12, 1918, in House Papers, 2:7.

[6] House Diary, December 7, 1918; and *F.R.,P.C.,1919,* I, 148–9.

the criticisms already made by those interested in opposing his principles with regard to the source of the popular support which he was
receiving." It is quite likely that Clemenceau intercepted this message
or had otherwise been informed of Wilson's wariness before he instructed the labor leaders to clear their plan with the President.[7]

In any case, in Brest the labor delegation was barred from the pier
and was kept from presenting its testimonial until the President was
about to step into his car at the railway station. The big demonstration
scheduled for Paris was canceled, even though the faithful were urged
to line up and cheer from the sidewalks between the Bois de Boulogne
and the Villa Murat. A second delegation, headed by Longuet, who
was fluent in English, was received by Wilson on the afternoon of his
arrival in the capital. Just before this delegation waited on the President, at the Place de Clichy a small band of militants unfurled a huge
red banner with the inscription *"Vive la paix Wilson,"* sang the International, and marched to the *grands boulevards,* where they were
dispersed by the police.[8]

On balance, in spite of government interference and minor disturb-
ances, the President received a roaring but orderly welcome in Paris.
R. S. Baker, still a journalist at heart, mingled with the crowd on the
Champs-Élysées.

> I could look all the way up toward the Arc de Triomphe, the
> broad avenue all clear, but the spaces on each side, the benches, the
> trees, the roofs all black with people. . . . From the talk all about
> me I felt that the People were genuinely and honestly sympa-
> thetic. . . . There were many working men and women in the
> crowd all about and many children. . . . Wilson with President
> Poincaré was in the first carriage. . . . He was loudly cheered. Mrs.
> Wilson's carriage was . . . smothered in flowers. . . . I walked
> rapidly down to the Place de la Concorde. . . . Here there were
> tremendous crowds and much enthusiasm. I am told that the
> reception was in every way larger and more enthusiastic than that
> accorded to any of the kings or generals who have been here. The
> crowds were certainly as great as on the day of the Armistice
> celebration. However, there was not just an abandon of joy. Cer-
> tainly the labor leaders must have put their million on the streets.
> . . . There has been no organized [labor] demonstration, but an
> enormous number of workmen and socialists were on the streets.
> The conservative parties here say that the Socialists are trying to use
> Wilson as a stick with which to beat Clemenceau and improve their
> own political condition. This is no doubt true: nevertheless they are
> the only groups who really believe in Wilson. . . . [The] great
> struggle is before us and as A. G. Gardiner of the *Daily News* wrote

[7] *F.R.,P.C.,1919,* I, 146–7.
[8] *Le Temps, l'Humanité,* and *le Populaire,* December 14–16, 1918.

me in a letter received this morning: "I know how grave things are, but I rely on the stiff jaw of one great man.[9]

This concluding note of pessimism was still more pronounced in one of Baker's reports to the State Department.

> The President had a wonderful reception here. . . . The masses are with him to a man, but he is going to have the struggle of his life with these ugly old forces of reaction—sly, greedy, and devilishly clever. What I fear, confidentially, is that he does not realize how powerful they are. . . . I would far rather see him fight to the end for his whole program and fail than to submit to a smeary peace.[1]

Clemenceau was both impressed and irritated by the spirited welcome to Wilson, which was in such stark contrast to the cordial indifference shown to other visiting dignitaries. On December 16, in advising London that he now favored the President's attendance at the Conference, he conceded that "if it became known that the President had expressed the wish to be present and had been refused the effect would be very bad, at any rate in France."[2] Admittedly, by now he had taken Wilson's measure and was satisfied that he could be managed in the privacy of the conference room, even if publicly Wilson continued to be a risk.

Clemenceau realized that the leftist Wilson cult was calculated to put additional steam behind the Socialist effort in the *chambre* to pressure him into committing himself to a Wilsonian program before the opening of the Conference. This campaign started on Armistice Day when the Socialists asked the *chambre,* unsuccessfully, to vote a special tribute to the President.[3] Two weeks later a delegation from the SFIO Parliamentary group, the Executive Committee of the party, and the Executive of the CGT called on Clemenceau to present the Wilsonian case, to request that the working class be represented on the peace delegation, and to secure permission to hold an international congress concurrently with the Peace Conference.[4]

The first formal interpellations followed on December 11. Cachin, Ernest Lafont, and Alexandre Blanc challenged the government to disclose the general outlines of its peace policy and to clarify the Russian policy of France and her allies. Pichon once again refused to be drawn into a foreign-policy debate, this time for fear that it would complicate current diplomatic negotiations, especially on the eve of Wilson's arrival. When he made the indefinite postponement of the

---

[9] Baker Diary, Book XXI, 167–76, entry of December 14, 1918.
[1] R. S. Baker to Frank Polk, December 18, 1918, in Baker Papers, Box 3.
[2] *F.R.,P.C.,1919,* I, 150.
[3] *JO,* November 11 and 22, 1918, 3003–9, 3064 ff.
[4] *Le Populaire,* November 24, 1918.

debate a question of confidence, he won easily by 342 against 108 votes.[5]

Thereupon Cachin served notice that official interference with their welcome of Wilson and the continuing refusal to discuss foreign policy left the Socialists no alternative but to force a debate in connection with the government's next budgetary request. Presently Henri Franklin-Bouillon, the right-wing Radical Socialist who was chairman of the Committee on Foreign Affairs, joined the protest. After disclaiming any sympathy for Socialist ideas he noted "with sadness that no other Parliament on earth was being kept in such absolute ignorance about the gravest issues of the day." The Ligue des Droits de l'Homme echoed this view.[6]

On December 27 the Clemenceau administration had to go to Parliament for 10 billion francs to cover civil and military expenditures for the first quarter of fiscal 1919. The Socialists were determined to make good their threat, notably because foreign policy, including French operations in Russia, significantly affected future expenditures. In an article entitled "Before the Debate" Cachin committed the Socialists to a comprehensive debate with a view to securing the government's unqualified assent to Wilson's peace program.[7]

Again Cachin was the lead-off speaker for the opposition. He argued that by subscribing to the spirit and letter of the Fourteen Points, France would implement the changes in diplomatic methods and objectives dictated by the revolutionary wave sweeping Europe from the Urals to the Rhine. In the course of his indictment Cachin declared his party opposed to the annexation of the left bank of the Rhine and of Syria and revealed that only the two Socialists on the Foreign Affairs Committee opposed the annexation of the Saar. He also called on the government to withdraw French troops from Odessa, Sebastopol, and other places in Russia, and to stop supporting General Denikin.[8]

Alexandre Blanc, the second Socialist speaker, confined himself to the Russian problem, questioning the constitutionality of making war on Russia without the approval of Parliament. He charged, furthermore, that the argument that the Allies were fighting not the Russian people but their unconstitutional rulers was reminiscent of the arguments used in 1792 and 1793 by the counterrevolutionary sovereigns and émigrés. Two days later even so moderate a Socialist as Alexandre-Marie Bracke spoke along similar lines.[9]

[5] JO, December 11, 1918, 3315–17.
[6] JO, December 11 and 29, 1918, 3317, 3710; l'Humanité, December 12–13, 1918; Bulletin des Droits de l'Homme, November 15–December 1, 1918, 797.
[7] L'Humanité, December 27, 1918; and JO, December 27 and 29, 1918, 3628, 3634, 3725.
[8] JO, December 27, 1918, 3628–32.
[9] JO, December 27 and 29, 1918, 3633–4, 3697–9.

Then it was Franklin-Bouillon's turn. Whereas the vast majority of the deputies listened to the Socialists with a mixture of condescension and hostility, punctuated by interruptions, they gave a respectful hearing to the prestigious Chairman of the Foreign Affairs Committee who was also a prominent leader of the largest party in the Palais Bourbon. At a recent meeting of the Executive Committee of his Radical Socialist Party Franklin-Bouillon had reaffirmed his allegiance to the realist school: he spoke of the danger of Austria joining Germany; he stressed the importance of barring Germany from Russia; he warned that France would be ruined for generations if she herself had to shoulder the cost of reconstruction and war; he claimed the frontiers of 1814, including the Saar; and he called for the demilitarization of the entire left bank of the Rhine and of a strip of at least 30 kilometers on the right bank of the Rhine.[1]

On December 29, this stolid pillar of the republican establishment began his speech with the complaint that France "was the only nation —I mean the only great democracy—which has not announced what has been called our 'war aims,' the government persisting in silence even following the conclusion of the Armistice." Of course, if France's Allies had remained equally silent, no harm would be done.

> But how can we feign to ignore that as of the day America entered this war and President Wilson . . . began to speak the methods of the old diplomacy simply had to be changed.
>
> Some people can disapprove of President Wilson's initiative; they can even see dangers in it. . . . But regardless whether one approves or condemns it, one cannot ignore it. This is the consequence of the Fourteen Points which, because all the Allies have accepted them, will be the basis for tomorrow's negotiations.
>
> Open diplomacy is replacing secret diplomacy; the diplomacy of peoples is supplanting cabinet diplomacy.
>
> This being so, what is the position of a nation like ours which alone remains silent about its aims? Whereas all it does is claim its rights, it leaves the impression of harboring unreasonable demands which it refuses to divulge. . . .

In sum, with regard to diplomatic method the government should publicly declare its peace aims; it should also appoint representatives of all the major parties—"from the extreme right to the extreme left"—to France's delegation to the Peace Conference.[2]

As for the objectives to be pursued in this Conference, Franklin-Bouillon, in the name of the vast majority of his committee, reiterated his position on Alsace-Lorraine, the Saar, both banks of the Rhine, and

[1] For the complete text of Franklin-Bouillon's speech of November 24, 1918, see *Bulletin du Parti Républicain Radical et Radical Socialiste*, December 14, 1918.
[2] *JO*, December 29, 1918, 3710–11.

Syria. With regard to each his proposals were in close harmony with the plans which were being elaborated in the Quai d'Orsay.[3]

He then turned to "the most agonizing problem," namely the Russian problem, for which neither the French nor the other Allied Governments had a coherent policy. A few days before, Pichon had informed the Committee on Foreign Affairs that France was about to cease all intervention; but yesterday, on the floor of the Chamber of Deputies, the Foreign Minister completely reversed himself.

Surely, as Russia's major prewar ally, France could not shirk her special responsibilities as well as rights. How, then, did the government envisage tomorrow's Russia? Between a unitary and a federated Russia, Franklin-Bouillon opted for a federal solution for a transitory period. He wanted Clemenceau to continue supporting the different anti-Bolshevik governments within Russia while also pursuing an energetic secessionist policy among the non-Russian peoples.

> Look at the map of the Baltic and the Black Sea. Without even mentioning Finland and Poland, the Estonians, the Latvians, the Lithuanians, and the Ukranians must be backed and organized. Herein lies both a solid rampart against Germany and the base from which to launch convergent action for the reconstitution of the real Russia. But these two policies must be carried out simultaneously . . . I flatly declare that we cannot not [*sic!*] intervene in Russia.

To implement this policy of dual intervention the French government should provide the anti-Bolshevik opposition inside and on the periphery of Russia with arms, cadres, volunteers, economic aid, and credits.

But—and this is significant—Franklin-Bouillon repeatedly emphasized that those Allies who had made the fewest sacrifices in the war and were economically more prosperous than France should contribute the bulk of this aid. He proposed, furthermore, that the Allies proudly proclaim their plan to the Russian people, together with the promise of land distribution with compensation and of a constituent assembly to decide Russia's political future.

Franklin-Bouillon concluded with a succinct summary of his Russian policy: "have a general plan; proclaim it boldly; simultaneously support the Russian as well as the peripheral elements; immediately establish, in addition to the base in Siberia, a base at Reval and Riga for the Baltic, and one at Odessa for the Black Sea; undertake intensive economic aid and moderate military action—very limited for France—that is the way to rally Russia's democratic masses and to save Russia." Certainly his overall position was much closer to the government's than to the Socialists'. In fact, Franklin-Bouillon was confident that Wilsonian or Socialist methods—in particular open diplomacy—could be put in the service of traditional and counterrevolutionary

[3] *JO*, December 29, 1918, 3711.

foreign policy. He had taken stock of the mood of Parliament as well as of the electorate at large.[4]

At this point the Socialists' Parliamentary maneuver backfired: Pichon came to the rostrum, but what he said was even less palatable to the Socialists than Franklin-Bouillon's exposé.

Turning to his loyal critics Pichon once again begged them to believe that his reluctance to reveal the details of his foreign policy was due exclusively to his not wanting to tip France's hand on the eve of critical negotiations. They should rest assured that the cabinet was ready for these negotiations with concrete proposals calculated to promote France's territorial, political, economic, and financial interests, within a framework of inter-Allied unity.

What were these interests? Even though the Clemenceau administration was as anti-annexationist as the Socialists, it was determined to redraw the Franco-German border in the general area of Alsace-Lorraine in "the light of history, law, justice . . . and France's security." France could not afford to trifle with her security because even though "Germany was defeated, she was not demolished." Her anarchist movements were superficial and the old military oligarchy retained considerable power. Without "full sanctions, reparations, and satisfactions" this victory could turn out to be a delusion. In any event, Germany would have to be territorially curtailed and fenced round, as well as internally reorganized. To achieve this goal the victors had the right to keep the Austro-Germans from joining Germany, even in violation of the self-determination gospel; and France would look to Czechoslovakia, Poland, and Yugoslavia to be "a particularly important support and a new guarantee of security."

As for Asia Minor, there France had historically and legally founded claims in "Syria, Lebanon, Cilicia, and Palestine," confirmed by the wartime Anglo-French agreements. At the Peace Conference every effort would be made to enlarge upon these concessions.

Conspicuously, Pichon, not unlike the other speakers in this debate, spent more time discussing the Russian problem than any other problem. Indignantly denying the charge that his government had no Russian policy, he vouched that France, with her Allies, would continue to protect her vital interests in Russia without, however, "intervening in the internal affairs of Russia and without applying pressure on any Russian to force him to choose any particular form of government" (*sic*).

France stood with her Allies in Murmansk, Archangel, and Siberia; the Allies were furnishing Kolchak and Denikin with matériel and munitions; French units had landed at Odessa; the British had sent a division to Batum; a warship was on the way to Novorossisk; General

[4] *JO,* December 29, 1918, 3712–13.

Berthelot was reorganizing the Rumanian army; and, in general, "all the forces on which we can count were being organized in Southern Russia in preparation for future action."

At this point in his speech Pichon sought to authenticate this "nonintervention" policy by reading Clemenceau's instructions to the commanding officers of the French forces involved in these operations. First a telegram dated December 13:

> The Allied plan is *not of an offensive character;* it merely seeks to deny the Bolsheviks access to these regions of the Ukraine, the Caucasus, and western Siberia whose economic resources they need in order to survive or in which Russian forces of order are organizing themselves.
>
> Hence, the first task is to *set up and maintain a defensive* front forward of these regions and in particular in eastern Russia. Should an offensive effort be necessary to destroy Bolshevism, it will subsequently have to be carried out by Russian forces. It is important that you impress the Russians with . . . [the fact] that the only purpose of our temporary protection is to permit them to organize themselves and to achieve a material superiority over their enemies.
>
> Your military action must therefore be based on a defensive plan and on an economical use of forces along a curtailed front until the Siberian army is organized and trained.

The broad outlines of this strategy were confirmed in a telegram dated December 21, which Pichon also read to the *chambre.*

> The Allied plan of action seeks to encircle Bolshevism economically while at the same time organizing the Russian forces of order. . . .
> The Allied Governments do not wish to intervene in the internal affairs of Russia. Our sole objective is to help Russia to come out of her anarchy and to reconstitute herself. For this we furnish material support and our technicians to the Russian forces of order.

Over turbulent exclamations from the Socialist benches, the Foreign Minister completed his outline of the government's grand strategy in Eastern Europe: through Odessa and through the southeastern confines of Rumania France planned to penetrate into the Ukraine, where she would replace the Germans by "sending military detachments, instructors and advisory missions and thus promote the creation of the Ukrainian army which is so indispensable to standing up to the Bolsheviks."

Not satisfied with covering himself with the authority of Clemenceau, he also invoked Allied sanction. Pichon claimed that there were "documents to prove beyond all doubt that French policy was in complete accord with Allied policy and that a different course could be pursued only by going it alone." Besides, a hands-off policy was out of the question as long as Russia was a *foyer de pestilence,* for she was endangering the rest of the world. No lasting peace was possible with Russia "torn by civil war and ruled by an odious, abominable government which was disseminating infamous propaganda."[5]

Without commending Clemenceau's Foreign Minister for his candor, Ernest Lafont, for the Socialists, expressed dismay that on the threshold of the Wilsonian era military victory should confer special rights over the vanquished (i.e., over Austria) and secret treaties should continue to be valid (i.e., for Syria). But the Russian problem was also at the center of Lafont's rebuttal. He criticized the government for teaming up with the leftovers of the *ancien régime* in Russia; he also warned that the Cabinet's *expéditions de petits paquets* could not be passed off as a policy of nonintervention which would cost no further French lives.

At this point Clemenceau interjected that even though the landings at Odessa would involve military engagements with possible casualties, these "could change nothing in the policy of the *cordon sanitaire* which Pichon had explained so masterfully."

Lafont was struck by the phrase *cordon sanitaire.* Though it had been used occasionally in the press, it had never been heard in the *chambre.*

> You yourself have just characterized with the new euphemism *cordon sanitaire* the policy which your Foreign Minister with greater frankness characterized as a blockade and as measures designed to starve that part of Russia which is controlled by the Bolsheviks. . . . Let us call things by their real name. It is a blockade. The press has used the word since a few days. The Foreign Minister earlier today made it his own. The plan is to intervene militarily along the periphery, together with [men of the old regime] in order more effectively to isolate Greater Russia from the rest of the world. . . . Will this [*cordon sanitaire*] mark the beginning of the League of Nations in this world? . . . Is this how this League will take its first steps in this world? Will it starve millions upon millions of people because you do not like their political regime? . . . The League of Nations, as you envisage it, will it be the new version of the Holy Alliance? Will it be assigned the task of restoring old forms of autocracy in those places of the world where these have been overthrown by natural popular movements? . . . By now you are so frightened . . . that even though you dare not go all the way, you nevertheless call for *une expédition d'ordre, une expédition de police, de pure police.* . . . As for us, we will not give one man or one *sou* for this reactionary police action across Europe, wherever it may be. . . . What is particularly disturbing to us . . . is that the same spirit which informs your Russian policy is being manifested

[5] *JO,* December 29, 1918, 3714–19.

in your policy in other parts of Europe, notably in the Polish question. . . .[6]

To add insult to injury, Renaudel, seconded by Albert Thomas, invested this fierce assault on Clemenceau's foreign policy with an amendment that truly angered the Prime Minister. These two very staunch and upright Social Patriots moved that the *chambre* vote appropriations for a single month instead of for a whole fiscal quarter, thereby threatening the government with a meddlesome foreign policy debate every month, especially for the duration of the Peace Conference.[7]

Finally, around midnight, Clemenceau, who had been on the government bench all along, chose to speak. But rather than go to the rostrum and as if to show his scorn for these proceedings, he addressed the *chambre* from his seat for three quarters of an hour. Before his speech—which was passionate, self-confident, uncompromising, and biting—he had surveyed the political horizon abroad and at home: he knew the results of the congressional elections in the U.S.; he had gauged Wilson's radicalism; he had just been informed of the outcome of the khaki election in Britain; he was calm about the Spartacist danger in Germany; he was encouraged by the SFIO's internal weaknesses and isolation; and he counted on Franklin-Bouillon not to make an expediential alliance with the Socialists. Furthermore, he knew that just then he had no serious rival: Paul Painlevé, Alexandre Ribot, René Viviani, Aristide Briand, and Albert Thomas were either discredited, politically isolated, or momentarily paralyzed by the vast popularity of the *père de la victoire*. And Joseph Caillaux was safely in jail.

Clemenceau first made it clear to Albert Thomas and others that it was the government's prerogative to accept or reject interpellations, and to pick its own time for such debates. He disdainfully denied that his government purposely kept Parliament in the dark and that of all the Allied leaders he alone had not spoken on war aims. In private as well as in public he had spoken whenever he was asked to do so. On the other hand, he should not be expected to rush to the rostrum whenever Lloyd George or Wilson delivered a speech. In what he was about to say he would exercise great caution, because he wanted to keep a free hand for negotiations and to spare future disillusionments.

What about diplomatic methods? The *vieux système* might well be in disrepute, but "in part [he] remained faithful to it." This system was rather "prosaic": nations organize their security by seeking good frontiers, maintaining armies, and upholding the balance of power. He would not forsake the alliance system which, if adequately bolstered before 1914, would have prevented the war. Now, at the Peace Conference, Clemenceau was determined to preserve the wartime alliance

[6] *JO,* December 29, 1918, 3720–4.
[7] *JO,* December 29, 1918, 3726, 3732, 3736.

for the postwar era: "for this entente I will make every necessary sacrifice." And with international guarantees "more difficult to establish in reality than in either speeches or books," for the time being France had no choice but to keep up her own defenses, while "gladly accepting whatever supplementary guarantees might be furnished."

When Bracke interjected that Clemenceau's words foreshadowed a rebirth of the Bismarckian system, the Tiger demurred: the balance-of-power system and process predated the Iron Chancellor, in that "since remote times peoples have been going at each other for the satisfaction of their appetites and of their selfish interests, [and] neither I nor you have made this history."

Clemenceau's Hobbesian outlook led him to take a very sober view of the coming Peace Conference. He expected each nation, whether large or small, to fight for its own interests; and so would France, even though for obvious reasons this was not the time to spell out the details of her program.

> . . . it is always easy to step onto a platform to deliver generalities which bind no one. . . . My main preoccupation . . . has been not to give rise to extravagant hopes for fear of later arousing too many disappointments. To make extravagant promises is bad politics because invariably one's concessions are insufficient. . . . [Moreover] even though I will press certain claims . . . I am not disposed to define these here . . . because I may have to sacrifice some of them to a higher interest . . .

So much for France's objectives.

But before closing this rather abstract and theoretical discourse Clemenceau still wanted to grapple with Wilson and the Socialists. By now he had repeatedly conferred with the President and the two had found much common ground. However, since America was so distant from Germany's borders it was only natural that Wilson did not share Clemenceau's preoccupations with the same intensity. Still, the President had a large, open, and exalted mind; he was "a man who inspired respect with the simplicity of his words and with the *noble candeur* of his spirit." Meanwhile, there were individuals who "for partisan reasons ascribed designs to Wilson which may not be his." If the Socialists were really interested in "infusing a new spirit into international relations" they should "start by displaying a new spirit in domestic affairs."[8]

For all practical purposes the debate was over. The Socialists still tried for a cutback in military appropriations, insisting that no funds be voted for the illegal expedition to Russia. Needless to say, this effort was easily defeated by 380 to 134.[9]

In the SFIO Parliamentary group, meanwhile, under the leadership

8 *JO,* December 29, 1918, 3732–4.
9 *JO,* December 29, 1918, 3736–7.

of Longuet, Cachin, and Sixte Quenin, some 25 to 30 deputies favored voting against the budget. But when the Social Patriots objected to this radical break with the government, Vincent Auriol and Lafont prevailed on the group to abstain in the interest of party unity.[1] As a result, whereas Renaudel's amendment to appropriate funds for one month only—which Clemenceau made into a question of confidence—was defeated by 386 to 88 votes, the government budget was approved by 414 to 6 votes.[2]

Clemenceau had every right to be proud and secure in this crushing victory, which he achieved without playing to the galleries. It never crossed his or Pichon's mind to pacify the Socialists. And even though Franklin-Bouillon received full satisfaction concerning France's Russian policy, on all other matters Clemenceau left him in the dark, confident that ultimately he would rally to the government. The *Temps* cheered the Tiger; Pertinax predicted that "today's realists would be tomorrow's genuine humanitarians"; and even Maurras applauded while once again calling the Socialists "perverted Frenchmen."[3] Clearly France had just had the equivalent of a congressional or khaki election. Three fourths of the deputies pulled together to check and isolate the restless but harmless Socialists. The forces of order feared these Socialists not so much for their actual strength as for their stubborn determination to ride Wilson's coattails, to force a hasty demobilization, to cut short the intervention in Russia, and to capitalize on the strains of reconversion and reconstruction.

For their part the Socialists were not at all sure that they had advanced their own and Wilson's cause. To be sure, they had smoked out the government. But Pichon's speech "foreshadowed the preparation for war rather than the organization of peace"; and his Russian policy was endowed with Allied and Associated sanction. Clemenceau, after "promising humanity a future of perpetual war," dismissed their hero rather cavalierly. While the Socialists wanted Wilson's *grandeur* and not his *candeur* praised, they charged that Clemenceau had dismissed him as *"un naïf, un innocent, une espèce de mouton."* What to do, except threaten further interpellations, at budget time?[4]

The speeches of Clemenceau and Pichon caused consternation among American officials in Europe, "the more so because the government immediately afterwards received an immense majority." Colonel House's reaction must have been widely shared.

It is about as bad an augury for the success of progressive principles at the Peace Conference as we could have. He has a

[1] *Le Populaire*, January 4, 1919.
[2] *JO*, December 29, 1918, 3736, 3792–6.
[3] *Le Temps, l'Echo de Paris,* and *l'Action Française,* December 30–31, 1918.
[4] *L'Humanité,* December 31, 1918; *JO,* January 16, 1919, 16–24; *le Temps,* January 18, 1919.

majority of practically four to one. Coming on the heels of the English elections, and taking into consideration the results of recent elections in the United States, the situation strategically could not be worse. It makes me feel how very fortunate it was that we got the American terms written into the German Armistice. Without that, I am afraid we would have but little chance of accomplishing the things we have so much at heart.

On his return from England on December 31 Wilson appeared to be equally disturbed by Clemenceau's speech.[5]

After a conversation with the President, House characterized this speech "as the greatest diplomatic blunder since the famous Sixtus letter"; implied that it might "cost France many millions that she might otherwise have had from us"; and advocated increasingly closer co-operation with England rather than France.[6] The Colonel begged the question whether Lloyd George and Balfour—who never expected Clemenceau to speak differently—were either free or willing to follow a moderate path.

Back in Washington Tumulty was moved to send his chief a dramatic cable:

> Clemenceau's speech demonstrates necessity for and wisdom of your trip and has set the stage for issue between balance of power and League of Nations. If America fails now, socialism rules the world and if international fair play under democracy cannot curb national ambitions, there is nothing left but socialism upon which Russia and Germany have already embarked. You can do nothing more serviceable than, without seeming to disagree with Clemenceau, drive home in your speeches the difference between two ideals, one the balance of power, . . . the other the concert of nations. . . . One has meant great standing armies with larger armaments and burdensome taxation, consequent unrest and bolshevism. If the statesmanship at Versailles cannot settle these things in spirit of justice, bolshevism will settle them in spirit of injustice. The world is ready for the issue. Clemenceau has given you a great chance; this country and whole world will sustain you. . . .[7]

Actually President Wilson would have preferred to start his European journey in England. Except for the naval and trade rivalry, there was a sound basis for Anglo-American diplomatic understanding. Moreover, in Britain the presidential party would have benefited from linguistic, cultural, religious, political, and personal affinities. But since the President could hardly have visited Britain in the midst of the election campaign, he landed in France.

[5] Henry White to Woodrow Wilson, December 31, 1918, in Wilson Papers, VIII A:6; and House Diary, December 29–31, 1918.

[6] House Diary, December 31, 1918, and January 1 and 4, 1919.

[7] Joseph P. Tumulty to Woodrow Wilson, December 31, 1918, in Wilson Papers, VIII A:6.

All along, however, the Wilson Administration was very much concerned about developments in England. To be sure, Wilson could continue to count on the faithful support of the Labour Party, the Independent Labour Party, the Trades Union Council, the Fabian Society, the Union of Democratic Control, and the left wing of the Liberal Party. But judging by the outcry over the pre-Armistice notes and by the tone of the election campaign the jingoists were making significant strides.

In late October Colonel House decided that Northcliffe and his newspaper empire might be enlisted to stem the onrushing Tory tide. Thus while having Cobb maintain contact with the forces of movement, which in any event would remain loyal to Wilson, House "hoped to use Northcliffe as a 'club' if necessary."[8]

At their first meeting on November 2 House asked Northcliffe to help him "in impressing my point of view upon Lloyd George," and apparently Northcliffe "offered the use of his publications."[9] It is impossible to determine whether or not this initial conversation influenced Northcliffe to publish his spectacular "From War to Peace";[1] but undoubtedly the moderate tone of this pronouncement encouraged the President's emissary to continue his probe. A few days later House and Northcliffe met again. House recorded that he was "endeavoring to work Northcliffe up to a liberal viewpoint and that [he had] a faint hope of succeeding; and that if he could get his powerful press back of the liberal movement it would be a triumph, since in the past it had been wholly reactionary."[2]

Whatever Northcliffe's motives and objectives may have been, the fact remains that for a while his press became extremely friendly to Wilson. *The Times* proclaimed that "we are all idealists now in international affairs, and we look to Wilson to help us to realize these ideals and to reconstruct out of this welter a better and fairer world." It welcomed the President's visit to Europe as an occasion for mutually beneficial exchanges about Wilson's program. And when the President touched French soil *The Times* "even on the morning of a General Election made no excuse for regarding the news of President Wilson's arrival in Europe as the chief event of the day."[3]

The enthusiasm of Wilson's reception in Paris encouraged House and Northcliffe to hasten the President's trip to Britain. "The reception Wilson received in Paris has changed the political sentiment, even in governmental circles, for the better, and we [i.e., House and Northcliffe] believe if he goes to England and gets such an endorsement from

[8] House Diary, October 28, 1918.
[9] House Diary, November 2, 1918.
[1] See pp. 82–4 above.
[2] House Diary, November 10, 1918.
[3] *The Times* (London), November 23 and December 14, 1918.

the English people, Lloyd George and his colleagues would not dare oppose his policies at the Peace Conference." With the President's approval House then told the British Ambassador that Wilson was prepared to visit England in late December. Needless to say, the British government promptly issued an invitation.[4]

Meanwhile the House-Northcliffe cooperation continued. *The Times* was granted an exclusive interview with the President, the text of the interview being carefully drafted by William Wiseman and Auchincloss and only slightly revised by Wilson himself. At Northcliffe's direction Wickham Steed wrote an accompanying editorial praising the President for his "modest, almost prayerful, earnestness"; asserting that no "just and lasting peace" was possible without a League of Nations; and predicting that Britain would give Wilson an even more rousing reception than had France.[5]

This interview was contrived by the moderates in the Lloyd George administration who were eager to forestall the political polarization that Wilson and his program were provoking in France. Certainly the friendly tone of the Northcliffe press cut into the hostility to Wilson that existed outside of Labour and Radical circles. In Britain, unlike in France, enlightened conservatives and inveterate liberals for quite some time had been trying to make their peace with Wilson's program, in particular with his vague League of Nations proposal.[6]

But House and Northcliffe, in planning the President's trip, sought to have it take him beyond official and dignified London. They arranged for the President to visit his mother's birthplace in Carlisle and to visit Manchester, both being planned "in order that he might pass through the principal industrial sections of England."[7]

On Wilson's arrival in France "the British Trades Union Congress and Labour Party, representing nearly five million workers, . . . enthusiastically associated themselves with their French comrades in extending a warm welcome to [him], the illustrious leader of World Democracy."[8] The British Left, however, did not mount a concerted welcome campaign: it was preoccupied with the election, Commons was not in session, and the Left lacked papers comparable to the *Humanité* and the *Populaire*. Moreover, Buckler told Henderson that dem-

---

[4] House Diary, December 17, 1918. See also Auchincloss Diary, December 18, 1918: "Northcliffe arrived in Paris yesterday and had a long interview with the Colonel. He is much impressed with the reception accorded the President in Paris, and has suggested the President go to England at once. This suggestion in all probability will be followed and I believe that the President will leave for England just before New Years."

[5] Auchincloss Diary, December 16–21, 1918; House Diary, December 18, 1918; *The Times* (London), December 21, 1918.

[6] See Henry R. Winkler: *The League of Nations Movement in Great Britain, 1914–1919* (New Brunswick: Rutgers University Press; 1952), Chs. v–vi.

[7] House Diary, December 28, 1918; and National Archives, Document 811.001W/6.

[8] Labour Party: *Report of the Nineteenth Annual Conference* (Southport, 1919), 21.

onstrations in support of the President "would embarrass him by offending the Governments with which he had to deal."[9] Hence, Labour greeted Wilson's arrival in London on December 26 with yet another manifesto hailing him for mobilizing "the forces of organized Democracy" and for "clarifying the vision and fortifying the will of the organized Democracy of Europe."[1]

Not that the British Left relented in its worship of Wilson. In private George Lansbury urged him to "stand firm" and, in case the Allies turned down his policy, to "appeal to the democracy of the world over the head of diplomats and statesmen."[2] Publicly, in *The Herald,* he warned Wilson not to allow himself to be "wangled," while assuring him that in the face of the rising forces of darkness he needed labor as labor needed him.[3]

The ILP's *Labour Leader* did not go all out for Wilson until the election returns laid bare Labour's weakness. Then Charles R. Buxton, shaken by the electoral outcome and by Clemenceau's speech, saw no alternative to strengthening Wilson's hand; Mrs. Philip Snowden appealed to women to support "the best of the bourgeois in his honest attempt to achieve the world's peace"; and Arthur Ponsonby prayerfully trusted that "President Wilson may prove sufficiently obstinate" to earn the faith that the peoples had to put in him.[4]

On the other hand the UDC anxiously looked forward to Wilson's visit. E. D. Morel flatly reiterated that "his policy is ours," while Josiah Wedgwood, addressing Wilson as "the fountainhead of all justice," commended himself "as your most devoted follower in the British House of Commons." Somewhat vaingloriously the UDC prophesied that if Wilson failed it would "be largely because the immense power of British Labour was not visibly demonstrated to be, and sufficiently exerted, upon his side."[5]

But instead of summoning the workers into the streets Morel and the Executive Committee once again asked Buckler to convey a message forewarning the President of the terrible dangers lurking ahead, notably the denial of self-determination to the Russians, exorbitant indemnities, territorial annexations, trade restrictions, and competitive naval armaments. Buckler immediately notified Morel that the President could not acknowledge this caveat because "in the present delicate situation a leader has to be careful in his relations with anyone who criticizes the people with whom he is compelled to deal." When the memorandum reached Wilson on the eve of his departure for England,

---

[9] Buckler to House, December 18, 1918, in Buckler Papers.
[1] Labour Party: *Report of the Nineteenth Annual Conference,* 22.
[2] Lansbury to House, December 18, 1918, in House Papers, 8:60.
[3] *The Herald,* December 14 and 24, 1918, and January 4, 11, and 18, 1918.
[4] *Labour Leader,* January 2, 1919.
[5] *The UDC,* November and December 1918, 277, 281–2; and Josiah Wedgwood to Woodrow Wilson, December 12, 1918, in Wilson Papers, VIII A:6.

his advisers saw nothing new in it, since the President hardly needed to be put on guard "against committing things he had no intention of perpetrating."[6]

On the eve of Wilson's arrival Oswald Garrison Villard, in Britain to report on the Left, was struck by the blind yet unmethodical adulation of Wilson.

> I found the Liberal and Labor friends I met wholly united on several points. I recorded that "they hate Lloyd George with a deadly hatred, feeling about his lack of principle as I do about Wilson's, only one hundred per cent more so. They all believe some kind of revolution inevitable here; the only difference is as to when it will come." Next, they were all clear in their minds that whether the war was lost or won would depend solely upon the Peace Conference. They unitedly placed all their hopes upon Woodrow Wilson, in whom they saw the savior of the world. They felt this so deeply that they resented any suggestion that he might prove unequal to the task. . . . I felt compelled to warn . . . [them] against having too much faith in Wilson and told them of some of the things he had tolerated or approved. . . . I stressed, of course, the value of his ideals and his admirable program but told them of his readiness to compromise. The applause when I sat down was merely dictated by politeness to a foreign guest.[7]

Indeed, the British forces of movement were solidly behind Wilson—partly out of genuine admiration, partly out of despair.

Wherever the President traveled in Britain—through the streets of London, Carlisle, or Manchester—his passage was like a triumphal procession. In London he received, among many other delegations,[8] a delegation from the Labour Party and the Trades Union Congress: on this occasion Henderson and Bowerman presented him with a testimonial. Moreover, even though Henderson was not invited to the gala dinner at Buckingham Palace, he did attend a luncheon at 10 Downing Street, together with the War Cabinet, Morley, Bryce, Grey, and Asquith.[9]

Labour's real day did not come until December 30. After a crowded and rousing welcome in the streets of Manchester, Wilson delivered an elevating but harmless address in Manchester's Free Trade

---

[6] E. D. Morel to W. H. Buckler, December 20, 1918; W. H. Buckler to E. D. Morel, December 21, 1918; Arthur Hugh Frazier to W. H. Buckler, December 24, 1918, in House Papers.

[7] Oswald Garrison Villard: *Fighting Years: Memoirs of a Liberal Editor* (New York: Harcourt; 1939), 373.

[8] Lords Parmoor and Buckmaster for the International League of Nations; Evelyn Wrench and Campbell Stewart for the English-Speaking Union; Lords Grey, Bryce, Asquith and Professor Gilbert Murray for the League of Nations Union; and Lord Gainford for the Society of Friends.

[9] *The Times* (London), December 27–28, 30, 1918.

Hall.[1] According to Massingham, his speech sounded "curiously syna-gogic—or perhaps it would be truer to say that it was not so much of the synagogue as of the hillside or the seashore." Though the audience included a few "Parliamentary candidates staggering under enormous majorities reaped in very different fields of thought," it responded passionately.[2] Villard, who was present, conceded that in all his "journalistic experience" he had never "attended a meeting so moving and so reverential, nor had he noted elsewhere such complete unanimity of sentiment or such a reverential spirit outside of a church."[3]

Wilson also took advantage of his escape from the official rounds in London to have a second meeting with C. P. Scott, the Liberal editor of the *Manchester Guardian*. A conference with Scott was not nearly as risky as a conference with an outright Labour or Radical dissenter; furthermore, Scott was an inveterate optimist. When the President "asked what bearing [Scott] thought the result of the elections might have on foreign policy, [he] thought very little," begging Wilson "not to regard the result of the election as a demonstration against the policy of a League of Nations." According to Scott, the President agreed with him "and said this was strictly analogous to what had happened in the recent congressional elections in America." In any case, not so much the British, but the French and Italian governments threatened to give trouble; and Wilson could always summon the public opinion of the world to his side.[4]

But all the cheering and reassurances could not change the election results which were announced toward the end of Wilson's visit. Furthermore, the President gave no *public* intimation that he might have to call on the peoples, especially on labor, to help him against even their own governments. In private he spoke along these lines to C. P. Scott; and in the privacy of a personal interview in Buckingham Palace he indicated that if he found "any tendency to grab [he would] make it known"—a tendency he had found among Italian statesmen. In this same interview Wilson confessed that he had come to Europe to do the little he could, but that he was under no delusion.[5]

Of course, like their counterparts across the Channel, the British forces of movement had no alternative but to continue venerating their idol. H. N. Brailsford alone had the insight and courage to expose the fallacies, dangers, and self-delusions of this continuing Wilson cult.

[1] For the text of this address see R. S. Baker and W. E. Dodd (eds.): *The Public Papers of Woodrow Wilson* (New York: Harper; 1925–7), V, 352–6.

[2] *Manchester Guardian*, December 31, 1918.

[3] Villard: *Fighting Years*, 381.

[4] Scott's memorandum on his conversation with Wilson is cited in J. L. Hammond: *C. P. Scott of the Manchester Guardian* (London: G. Bell; 1934), 249–50. See also C. P. Scott to Woodrow Wilson, December 31, 1918, in Wilson Papers, VIII A:6.

[5] Text of interview of Frank Worthington, Deputy Chief Censor, with President Wilson, December 28, 1918, National Archives, Secret File, Document 811.001W/163.

With the roar of cheers behind him and the hum of escorting planes in the air, President Wilson has come and gone. To some this visit will seem a triumph. To me it looks like an eclipse. . . . Since his great achievement in imposing the nominal adoption of the Fourteen Points upon the world, Mr. Wilson has been silent—silent through many speeches. Never has he spoken so often, never has he said so little. . . . He has sojourned in Paris, as it talked once more of the alienation or annexation of the Left Bank of the Rhine—and spoken no word of caution or protest. He has visited London fresh from electing the Coalition which is to hang the Kaiser and pile indemnities on the Germans, and hardly by a phrase or an allusion has he reminded us that there are two ways of conceiving the future peace. . . . He has moved with smiles and compliments among the men who are preparing a helot's future for the German nation, and neither by appeal nor by argument has he said a word to cool the fever of vengeance or abate the demands of greed. What he has done in private we do not know. Let us trust that he has battled stubbornly for the honest fulfillment, without additions, of the Fourteen Points. But in these battles he has fought disarmed. His power lies in his ability to evoke, by open speech, the latent sanity of mankind. That power he has suspended, while others have spoken. . . . In any event it is clear from Mr. Wilson's Manchester speech that he realizes that his ideal of justice is defeated. The settlement, he declares, is sure to contain unsatisfactory adjustments, which we must be prepared to revise at some future time [through the League of Nations].

That is a tempting line of refuge from pessimism. How easy it is to say that we are all heated today by passion: five or ten years hence we may be cool enough to realise that France ought not to have taken the Saar Valley, nor Italy to have annexed Avlona. Ten years hence it will be too late to alter these injustices. . . . Mr. Wilson is the world's greatest Liberal. Like all Liberals, he is destined to perpetual illusion, because he will not understand that a capitalist world will act after its kind.[6]

[6] *The Herald*, January 4, 1919.

7

Italy: Sonnino's Triumph

ITALY was Wilson's last stop before the opening of the Peace Conference. The announcement of his visit precipitated a ministerial crisis; his actual stay caused a great stir in Rome, Milan, Genoa, and Turin; and an unintended legacy of his trip was the making of Mussolini into one of Italy's most vocal anti-Wilsonians.

In all the victor nations the end of the war brought a revival of prewar politics. Italy was no exception. The men, parties, and factions that resumed their cooperation or struggles in 1918 were much the same as before, except that all had become energized by the experiences—both positive and negative—of war. Since Italian politics had been particularly turbulent before 1914, it was destined to be even more so in the postwar era.

On the eve of war Italy had experienced, in concentrated fashion, the emasculation of the moderate center which was so characteristic of prewar Europe, including Britain. Red Week and its aftermath demonstrated that the extremism of the Left and Right were feeding each other, to the detriment of the Giolittian moderators and manipulators. With increasing frequency political battles were fought in the piazza rather than in Parliament. Unlike Giovanni Giolitti, his successor Antonio Salandra had few qualms about repressing Leftists, cooperating with *traditional* Nationalists, and condoning *new* Rightists.

No doubt Mussolini and the direct-action syndicalists were tightening their hold on the Socialist Party. On the other hand, the fifty-man Socialist delegation in Parliament, led by Filippo Turati and Claudio Treves, remained solidly revisionist; and the expelled Reformist Socialists, led by Leonida Bissolati and Ivanoe Bonomi, were playing the political game. In other words, even though Red Week was due in large measure to the radicalization of the Left at critical local and regional points, it was not an expression of mounting unity and strength in the Socialist movement as a whole. Moreover, the failure of Red Week, which exposed the Left's schisms and irresolution, encouraged the government, the middle-class Nationalists, and the new Right to press their advantage.

As so often in history, the failure of this revolt strengthened intractable conservatives by frightening moderates into cooperating in or licensing pre-emptive counterrevolutionary ventures. During Red Week Salandra gave close to free reign to paramilitary jingoist gangs; and once the European war had broken out and Italy had withdrawn from the *Triplice,* Salandra looked for interventionist support to Gabriele D'Annunzio, Alceste De Ambris, Filippo Corridoni, and Roberto Farinacci.

In terms of the Italian political code Giolitti and Salandra were opposites. Attuned to progressive northern industrial capitalism, Giolitti knew that the continuing modernization of Italy would increase the size, influence, and power of the proletariat; and that traditional liberalism could not survive unless it were up-dated with an appealing social platform. In political terms this meant that he was prepared to forego right-wing support in search of cooperation with the Radicals, Reformist Socialists, and left Catholics. Above all he strained to prevent the alienation of labor from state and society by pushing timely but moderate political, economic, and social reforms.

Salandra, for his part, was much more of a traditional conservative with landed roots in southern Italy. His outlook was socially bourgeois, politically elitist, and economically opposed to welfare and labor legislation. Unlike Giolitti, he inclined to political collaboration with the Nationalists, rather than with the moderate Republicans and Socialists, in pursuit of a consolidation if not reification of an unreformed constitutional monarchy. When Salandra finally realized that the age of elitist politics was waning, he used inflated nationalist, not social reformist, slogans to build a mass following; and with these nationalist appeals he spun his ties to the Crown, the Nationalists, the conservatives, the irredentists, Mussolini, Luigi Albertini, the *petit-bourgeois* intelligentsia, and the status-seeking university students.

There was one other major difference between Giolitti and Salandra. From the Tripolitanian adventure of 1911 Giolitti had learned the high financial and political cost of war for a nation deficient in resources, retarded in economic development, and torn by party strife. Once it was clear, after the battle of the Marne, that the present war would not be over in a few short weeks or months, Giolitti was bound to advocate noninterference, especially since a discriminating neutralist policy promised substantial diplomatic as well as economic rewards.

Salandra, for his part, was much less hesitant to use war as an instrument of domestic and foreign policy because he either overlooked or minimized its perilous by-products. Both Salandra and Sonnino belonged to that school of European conservatives that was predisposed to risk war in the hope of bracing the *status quo* and the forces of order against the impatient forces of reform and revolution.

It is still difficult to assess the extent to which, in the spring of 1915, domestic politics influenced Salandra and the Crown to decide for intervention, while Giolitti endured in his neutralism, though political considerations certainly were neither excluded nor trivial.[1]

Of course Salandra and Sonnino looked to successful intervention on the Allied side to yield valuable territorial and diplomatic gains in Europe, the Near East, and Africa. In addition, however, they were eager to claim political credit for a successful and exalting patriotic war for sound conservatism, for fear that it might otherwise accrue to the democratic and progressive interventionists. They were confident that the new Right would back them up, using superpatriotic slogans to cut into the urban support of the liberalizing and reforming Republicans and Reformist Socialists.

At first Giolitti's 300-odd Parliamentary supporters held out against the extraparliamentary interventionist groundswell. But the moment these neutralists were slandered for being unpatriotic, disloyal, and Socialist they ceased to obstruct Salandra, especially since Giolitti failed or was unable to provide decisive leadership. Only the Socialists mobilized mass support for neutralism as part of their revolutionary struggle. But they were as reluctant to join forces with bourgeois anti-interventionism as the Giolittians were wary of a united front with them.

Not unexpectedly, once the nation was at war the political truce furthered the rightist design: the pro-Allied and pro-war Republicans, Reformist Socialists, and Giolittians obligingly took a back seat while the conservative Right and Center ran the show. Parliament went into near-perpetual recess, leaving the predominantly conservative Salandra Ministry to rule by decree. Needless to say, even though the administration tried to keep the terms of the Treaty of London secret, they soon were widely known; and little if anything was said about the war being a harbinger of democracy and reform by leaders who secretly continued to prefer the institutions of yesterday's to today's allies. Italians were summoned to make sacrifices for love of country, for *Italia*

[1] For Italy's entrance into the war and wartime politics see the following: Benedetto Croce: *A History of Italy, 1871–1915* (Oxford: Clarendon; 1929), Chs. xi–xii; Denis Mack Smith: *Italy* (Ann Arbor: University of Michigan Press; 1959), Chs. 34–7; Ivanoe Bonomi: *La Politica italiana da Porta Pia a Vittorio Veneto, 1870–1918* (Turin: Einaudi; 1944); Antonio Salandra: *Italy and the Great War: From Neutrality to Intervention* (London: Arnold; 1932); Edgar R. Rosen: "Italiens Kriegseintritt im Jahre 1915 als innenpolitisches Problem der Giolitti-Ära," in *Historische Zeitschrift*, Vol. 187, No. 1 (February 1959), 289–363; Rodolfo Mosca (ed.): *Vittorio Emanuele Orlando: Memorie, 1915–1919* (Milano: Rizzoli; 1960); W. Hilton-Young: *The Italian Left* (London: Longmans, Green; 1949), Ch. iii; Alberto Malatesta (ed.): *I Socialisti italiani durante la guerra* (Milan: A. Mondadori; 1926); Giorgio Pini and Duilio Susmel: *Mussolini, l'uomo e l'opera*, Vol. I (Florence: La Fenice; 1957); and Richard A. Webster: *The Cross and the Fasces* (Stanford: Stanford University Press, 1960), Chs. iii–iv.

irredenta, and for the glory of a renascent Roman *imperium* over the Adriatic and the southern Slavs. This people, which could not be aroused with horror stories of foreign invasion or submarine sinkings, was asked to swear by Salandra's and Sonnino's uninspiring *sacro egoismo.*

At first the Socialists, who in Parliament had voted against war, abided by Costantino Lazzari's injunction to adopt an attitude of "neither collaboration nor sabotage," thereby momentarily recapturing a welcome degree of unity. Gradually, however, the old fissures reappeared. Whereas the Maximalists and Internationalists actively fomented antidefensism and sent delegates to Zimmerwald and Kienthal, Turati and Treves became Italy's Social Patriots, except that unlike Henderson and Albert Thomas they remained outside the government.

By mid-1916 the strains of war, of which Giolitti had warned, began to tell. Salandra was succeeded by the ineffectual Paolo Boselli. To secure wider domestic support Bissolati was invited into the cabinet. In a bid for increased Allied aid Rome at long last declared war on Germany and tempered her anti-Slavism.

But it was only after the Russian Revolution, America's intervention, and the near-disaster at Caporetto that in Italy—not unlike in the other belligerent nations—the government became responsive to liberalizing pressures, both domestic and foreign. In October 1917 Orlando became Prime Minister. In spirit, purpose, and method Orlando was close to Giolitti, who continued to be ignored even after he endorsed the war loyally and publicly. Orlando advanced the Reformist Socialist Bissolati to Vice-Premier and appointed the Caillaux-like Francesco Nitti to be Minister of Finance.

Although the government acquired an altogether more democratic and social reformist coloration, Sonnino remained Foreign Minister. This conservative Nationalist first advocated joining the Central Powers and then briefly embraced an expedient neutralism before finally engineering intervention on the side of the Allies. Once at war he pursued a rigid anti-Slav policy, which he maintained even in the face of Bissolati's politico-diplomatic arguments and of General Armando Diaz's plea for military cooperation with the Slavs. At last Sonnino relented, but only under strong pressure from the Allied and Associated Governments. Especially once Orlando sided with the Slavophiles Sonnino could not prevent the meeting of the "Congress of Oppressed Nationalities of Austria-Hungary" in Rome from April 9 to 11, 1918.

By then the terms of the Treaty of London had been disclosed on the floor of Parliament, touching off a heated war-aims debate. All genuine Wilsonians—left Liberals, Radicals, Reform Socialists, official Socialists—asked the government to confine Italy's territorial claims to

Trent and Trieste, to seek a rapprochement with the Slavs of the Dual Monarchy, and to champion the revolt of the minority nationalities. Sonnino stood by in silent disapproval while the Rome Congress not only pledged Allied support for the emancipation of the subject peoples of Austria-Hungary but also endorsed the Torre-Trumbic letters conferring Italy's unofficial blessing on a united and independent Yugoslavia. Sonnino was outvoted again on September 8, 1918, when the cabinet, prodded by Bissolati, formally recognized "the movement of the Yugoslav peoples for the conquest of their independence and the[ir(?)] constitution into a free state to be in accordance with the principles for which the Allies are fighting and with the aims of a just and lasting peace."[2]

September 1918 marked the high point of the Wilsonian countermovement, which was directed against the thoroughly entrenched expansionists. In the *camera* the conservative and nationalist parties and factions, loosely fused into a *fascio di resistenza,* stood brazenly behind Sonnino; in the piazza the armed *Arditi,* wearing black shirts, campaigned against all *rinunciatari* who advocated the trimming of the Treaty of London or of any other territorial and colonial claims. During the war these impassioned interventionists indiscriminately blamed all military reverses, but especially Caporetto, on these neutralist, defeatist, and antinational *rinunciatari;* after the Armistice they claimed exclusive credit for Italy's intervention, for her armies' victories, and for the proper articulation of the nation's war aims.

The material and spiritual trophies of military victory were much more important to the Right in Italy than in the other victor nations. The interventionists, notably the right-interventionists, could not afford to forfeit the extravagant wages of victory for which they had asked Italians to make such great sacrifices, the more so because the anti-interventionists would feed on their humiliation. As it was, Italy, as compared to France, Britain, and the U.S., was edging toward an acute internal crisis: a huge public and foreign debt, severe inflation, and reconversion were about to compound her prewar distemper.

Instead of grappling with this domestic crisis, both the conventional and the new Right preferred to deflect attention from it with diplomatic chimeras. The acquisition or control of Trieste, Fiume, Dalmatia, Albania, the Dodecanese, southwestern Turkey, Armenia, and Djibouti promised to sustain an inflamed anti-Socialist nationalism while at the same time holding out such tangible satisfactions as space for surplus population, markets, raw materials (i.e., coal), and government jobs. Among the jingoist expansionists Mussolini alone also gradually advo-

[2] For the Congress of Rome and the September resolution see Victor S. Mamatey: *The United States and East Central Europe, 1914–1918* (Princeton: Princeton University Press; 1957), 239–49 and 313–15. See also Ivanoe Bonomi: *Leonida Bissolati e il movimento socialista in Italia* (Rome: Sestante; 1929), Ch. xvi, esp. 209.

cated far-reaching economic and social reforms, thereby creating his own brand of social imperialism.

The jingoists launched their offensive in the nationalist press during the pre-Armistice negotiations. At first this influential press distrusted Wilson's bilateral dealings with the Austro-Hungarian government; but soon even the *Perseveranza* and *Giornale d'Italia* grudgingly praised the President for his forceful response to Vienna's successive peace feelers. Simultaneously, with the fate of the Dual Monarchy irrevocably sealed, there arose the clamor that Italy was entitled to a privileged share of the Austrian succession.

The Treaty of London became the center of the controversy, this treaty being considered both sacred and void: the superpatriots wanted it strictly enforced at the same time that they declared it insufficient.

The break-up of Austria-Hungary and the collapse of Russia created an entirely new situation in the Adriatic and on the Dalmatian coast, one which the Treaty of London had not anticipated. According to the Sonninoite *Idea Nazionale*, "with the end of Austrian rule the chief obstacle to the free manifestation of the Dalmatians' Italian sentiments was removed." In the jingoist *Resto del Carlino* De Ritis insisted that "the Dalmatian isles and ports were a strictly necessary complement of the common frontier of Western Europe; [that] in all the culminating epochs of history the national and military unification of the Adriatic was a characteristic element of the political and moral solidarity of the European West; [and that therefore] in terms both of the completion of Italy's national unity and of Europe's strategic security the Dalmatian question was of universal importance." Just as the Trentino required the Brenner frontier, so Trieste required Fiume and the Dalmatian coast.[3]

The *Resto* was representative of the unreconstructed anti-Slav and antidemocratic press which cursed the stunting changes being advocated by Italian as well as foreign *rinunciatari*. Of course, the *Resto* extolled the Treaty of London as "the Great Charter of the Alliance." But it also swore that this treaty could not "sanction the total fulfillment of national unity" because in 1915, with Russia jealously safeguarding the rights of the south Slavs, Italy's diplomatists had been forced "to labor hard to secure the *minimum* claims for which we entered the war." Now that Russia was practically extinct Fiume need not, indeed, could not be left to the Slavs. In addition to Fiume the kindred *Perseveranza* claimed Spalato, the isles of Solta and Brazza, a protectorate over Albania, and compensation in Asia and Africa.[4]

Soon the entire irredentist and expansionist press rallied around

---

[3] *Idea Nazionale*, November 6–8, 1918, and *Resto del Carlino*, November 3 and 14, 1918, cited in *DR, APS* (November 20, 1918), 45.

[4] *Resto del Carlino*, November 6, 1918, and *Perseveranza*, November 9–10, 1918, cited in *DR, APS* (November 20 and 27, 1918), 45, 69.

Sonnino, who silently condoned its inflammatory editorials. The Italian expansionists of 1918–19 advanced the full gamut of self-contradictory arguments to support their ambitious claims. Depending on the claim, they would invoke the principle of self-determination, historical traditions, strategic necessities, balance-of-power considerations, or economic needs, all the time flattering the Italian self with anti-Yugoslav and anti-Allied diatribes.

Most of the chauvinist papers, which in 1914 had been Germanophile, did not pay lip service to the nationality principle until after Caporetto, and then reluctantly. But as soon as victory was won they combined their hymn to Greater Italy with ferocious anti-Slav propaganda. The Serbs, the Croats, and the Slovenes were portrayed as too primitive to form a modern nation, susceptible to infectious Bolshevism, and prone to imperialism. Austria-Hungary was defeated not by the nationality revolt, not with Yugoslav help, but by the Italian Army "in the magnificent Piave battle, in the battle that decided the fate of the whole European war." And to the victor belong the spoils, notwithstanding the professional Slavophiles. By December 10 the *Perseveranza* declared that "Italo-Slav relations were no longer merely concerned with territory [but that they had become] one of those problems of dignity, of prestige, and of sentiment, which passion often drives on to tragic solutions."[5] Internally, meanwhile, increasingly vicious attacks were leveled against leading advocates of Italo-Yugoslav cooperation, notably against Mola, Torre, Gallenga, Comandini, Bissolati, Di Cesaro, and Bonomi.

Even the Allies were subjected to the superpatriots' wrath. The British government was charged with backing the Yugoslavs under the insidious influence of Wickham Steed and the *New Europe* while also conspiring to monopolize the colonial booty at Italy's expense. As for the French, Sonnino's organ spoke quite bluntly to them.

> We chose, as between French and Germans, our Latin brothers at a moment tragically decisive for France; why be astonished if Italian opinion now expects a similar gesture on the part of the French in the bitter, hard, antipathetic struggle that has broken out in the Adriatic between us and the Slovenes and Croats . . . ? Can France doubt that Italy is likely to form in the Adriatic a much safer barrier than Yugoslavia against German expansion toward the Mediterranean basin?

The *Giornale d'Italia* proceeded to grant France the right "derived from history and victory, to systematize, as she feels best, her essential interests on the Rhine," leaving Italy an "analogous, even an identical right to settle in accordance with her own vital interests the question of the Adriatic." In any case, France should cease being squeamish, since

[5] See *DR, APS* (December 4, 1918, and January 1, 1919), 92–3, 168.

she herself proposed to violate the principle of self-determination with regard to German-Austria, the left bank of the Rhine, and the Saar.[6]

Even though these chauvinist organs were by no means representative of the entire Italian press, their furor could not be ignored. The British government's summary of the Italian press of December 8–20 concluded that the war aims controversy was beginning to have significant political repercussions.

> Never has the campaign against the Jugo-Slavs been more eager, never—despite the King's visit to Paris—have the indispensable anti-Slav conditions for an alliance with France been stated with greater emphasis in the so-called "Sonnino" papers. To what extent these represent public opinion is difficult to say. But, at all events, they must be rapidly creating a public opinion. For there is now next to no opposition. All papers condemn the excesses of the Slavs. The *Corriere della Sera,* with its vast circulation, still from time to time defends its past policy of reconciliation, but prints anti-Slav dispatches from its special correspondents. The *Secolo* (together with the weekly *Unità . . .*) seems to be the last important survival of that policy. The *Epoca*—which is described as Orlando's organ in statements which, though denied, are incessantly repeated—makes an appeal for reason, warns the public against its present obsession with the Jugo-Slavs, and tries to direct opinion to other important problems: colonies and war costs. The attitude of the *Giornale d'Italia*—again described as Sonnino's organ—has never been more violent. The anti-Slav Press has long been describing Italy's terms in the Treaty of London as limited by Russia, a thing of the past. It now begins a regular assault on the Italo-Slav "Pact of Rome" (which, however unofficial, was officially encouraged by Orlando), as "dictated by fear," after Caporetto.[7]

In any event, these papers provided Sonnino with a noisy claque for his project.

This press campaign received additional *éclat* from a huge victory celebration in Rome. Significantly the League of National Defense—the Fascio—summoned the mass meeting for November 20, the day that Parliament reconvened; and Salandra chose the Augusteo theater rather than the *camera* to attack the 1913 legislature for being "an old temple in which simony was increasingly practiced." Salandra was bidding for the leadership of all the Parliamentary parties and factions right of Center which had loyally supported his own conservative brand of interventionism; moreover, he hoped to win the allegiance of the extraparliamentary interventionists. Salandra was cheered by Alber-

[6] *Giornale d'Italia,* December 11 and 20, 1918, cited in *DR, APS* (January 1, 1919), 171–2; and *Perseveranza,* December 9 and 12, 1918, cited in Louis Hautecoeur: *L'Italie sous le ministère Orlando, 1917–1919* (Paris: Bossard; 1919), 160–1. Hautecoeur covers the anti-Allied aspects of the chauvinist campaign on 156–68.

[7] *DR, APS* (January 1, 1919), 167.

tini's *Corriere della Sera,* by Sonnino's *Giornale d'Italia,* and by Mussolini's *Popolo d'Italia.*[8]

In Parliament Orlando opened the debate with an impassioned but
vague address. Exclamations of *Viva Trento! Viva Trieste!* and *Viva
Fiume italiana!* rang out when he welcomed the "return" of Udine,
Trento, and Trieste to Italy; but his warm praise of Wilson's contribution to the victory evoked equally intense enthusiasm. Orlando said
little about his government's foreign and domestic policy, merely enjoining the *camera* to remember that the "war had been the greatest
political and social revolution of recorded history, surpassing even the
French Revolution."[9] As a show of Center-left solidarity vis-à-vis
Salandra and Sonnino, after this speech Giolitti conspicuously went
over to shake Orlando's hand. A scurrilous attack on the loyalty of the
democratic Left by Centurione, of the Fascio, stimulated another show
of unity, inclusive of the Socialists.

Turati, in his address, took a firm Wilsonian stand. He reaffirmed
that the Socialist Party endorsed Wilson's principles, called on Orlando
to honor his pledges to Yugoslavia, and warned that the westward-
sweeping revolution, which could not be shut out with a *cordon
sanitaire,* would never tolerate a victor's peace. Turati's domestic
precepts were altogether reformist.[1]

Claudio Treves was considerably more forthright and bellicose. He
defied Orlando and Sonnino to tell the nation whether or not
they were beholden to the Fascio. With the warning that "the
spirit of Zimmerwald was closer to Wilson than that of the Fascio," he
denounced those who would treat the Adriatic as a national lake and
escalate the intervention in Russia, which he likened to Brunswick's
counterrevolutionary campaign of 1792.[2] Actually, whereas in the
Socialist Party Turati and Treves were the pivot of moderation, in the
lower house they and their fifty followers constituted the far Left of the
political spectrum.

Immediately to the right and aligned with the reformist Italian
Socialist Union, the Democratic Entente took shape. Designed as a
prop for Orlando against both Sonnino and Turati, this new Parliamentary formation included 100 deputies from the Center-left. The
Entente's spokesman was the Radical Antonio Fradoletto, who presented an essentially Giolittian program, even though Giolitti and his
disciples remained isolated.[3]

Whereas the Right was not about to endanger a Cabinet in which

[8] *Bulletin périodique de la presse italienne,* No. 97 (December 10, 1918), 1–2.
[9] *Atti del Parlamento italiano: Camera dei deputati,* Discussioni, November 20, 1918,
    17240–5.
[1] *Camera,* November 21, 1918, 17263–74.
[2] *Camera,* November 27, 1918, 17764–6.
[3] *Secolo,* November 23, 1918, cited in *Bulletin périodique de la presse italienne,* No. 97
    (December 10, 1918), 2.

Sonnino had such a commanding position, the non-Socialist Left had no alternative but to bet on Orlando, Nitti, and Bissolati. As a result Orlando received an overwhelming vote of confidence without ever disclosing his true intentions. Only 33 Socialists cast negative votes.[4]

But in the Center and Center-left discontent was considerably sharper than this vote suggests. Gaetano Salvemini was one of the first non-Socialist critics to publicly challenge the Foreign Minister—who all these years had been "King, Pope and God of Italian foreign policy"— to clarify Italian aims in the Adriatic. Not that Salvemini wanted the Treaty of London abrogated. On the contrary, he proposed that America's endorsement be sought. To achieve this and to allay fears all around he wanted the Nationalists to stop "bellowing about *mare nostrum*" and the government to disclaim any intention of dominating the Adriatic strategically or economically at the expense of the Slavs. Salvemini, however, was not hopeful: Sonnino had "sworn never to do anything but what will render Italy hateful throughout the world" and he craved "to be suspected and he was succeeding marvellously well."[5]

The *Secolo* fully endorsed this criticism of Sonnino, taunting him for his failure to make provision for the disintegration of Austria-Hungary, the coalescence of Yugoslavia, and the future of Fiume. A Foreign Minister with such a record—who in 1914 had favored the Central Powers—was hardly the man to represent Italy at the Peace Conference without the balancing influence of Bissolati. The democratic forces had earned the right to have their own representative on the delegation: "by a superior discipline" these forces had "accepted Salandra, suffered Sonnino, supported the Boselli and Orlando ministries, sacrificing their own men and their own program." But now that the political truce was terminated their voices would again be heard.[6]

By mid-December the Italian Socialist Union (i.e., the Reformist Socialists), the Republican Party, the Democratic Entente, *Unità*, and *Secolo* became very restless. Not that the Foreign Minister had publicly endorsed or formulated the outcry against Yugoslavia and her Allied supporters; but the Reformist Socialist, Radical, and Republican Ministers had gauged Sonnino's position and influence in the cabinet and in the consulta. The democratic-liberal elements rallied behind Bissolati in the hope of prevailing on Nitti and Orlando to help contain the Foreign Minister and his conservative-national supporters. Their first overt step was the resignation of Gallenga, Chiesa, Comandini, and Dari, four Center-left cabinet ministers who decidedly shared Bissolati's foreign policy viewpoint and aimed at forcing a showdown

---

[4] *Camera,* November 27, 1918, 17782–4.
[5] Salvemini writing in *Unità,* November 16 and 23, 1918, cited in *DR, APS* (December 4, 1918), 94. See also Paolo Alatri: *Nitti, D'Annunzio e la questione adriatica, 1919–1920* (Milan: Feltrinelli; 1959), 20–5.
[6] *Secolo,* December 4 and 6, 1918, cited in *DR, APS* (December 18, 1918), 145.

between Bissolati and Sonnino on the eve of both Wilson's Italian visit and the Peace Conference.

This showdown came immediately after Orlando and Sonnino returned from accompanying the King on his state visit to Paris. Apparently, while in Paris they not only had reiterated to Wilson Italy's extensive Adriatic claims,[7] but also had assured the President that the entire cabinet endorsed these claims.[8] When Sonnino kept the upper hand at a cabinet meeting on December 27, Bissolati decided to resign, thereby opening a full-scale ministerial crisis.

Bissolati himself as well as the pro-Bissolati press stressed that dissension over foreign policy issues and not personal jealousies or political intrigues were at the bottom of the impasse. According to Bissolati the time had come for someone "to smash a window and let fresh air into the house"; he was no longer willing to remain in the cabinet "as a mere number"; Orlando would have to take account of his (Bissolati's) ideas.[9] In his letter of resignation the esteemed Reformist Socialist leader explicitly charged the cabinet with forsaking its motion of September 8 which had all but recognized Yugoslavia, insisting that on this question as on others "he found himself in profound disagreement with the prevailing foreign-policy direction."[1]

What, then, was his foreign policy alternative? Bissolati wanted to hold on to the Treaty of London to the extent of securing all of Istria for Italy. However, he advocated that all of Dalmatia except Zara and Fiume be freely yielded to the Yugoslavs before the Peace Conference, possibly with the stipulation that the eastern shoreline be demilitarized. Since the Greek islands in the southern Aegean were at best of limited economic and strategic value he urged that Italy not claim them. As for the Alpine frontier, he did not think that the Brenner line was absolutely essential; a line slightly to the north of Bolzano would be an adequate strategic position and would avoid bringing large numbers of German-Austrians under Italian rule.

These concrete proposals were part of a comprehensive diplomatic design. Bissolati accepted the nationality revolt and the birth of the successor states as irrevocable, he refused to exaggerate Yugoslavia's military threat to Italy, and he was keenly aware of Italy's incapacity to

---

[7] "I [Wilson] found the Italian statesmen quite incapable of taking a wide view of things. They demanded almost the whole of the Dalmatian Coast and practically all the islands of the Adriatic. They based their claim on the necessity for adequate defense." Record of conversation of President Wilson with Frank Worthington, Britain's Deputy Chief Censor, at Buckingham Palace, December 28, 1918, National Archives, Secret File, Document 811.001W/163.

[8] *Stampa*, December 28, 1918, cited in *Bulletin périodique de la presse italienne*, No. 100 (January 5, 1919), 4.

[9] Bissolati to Malagodi on December 28, 1918, in Olindo Malagodi: *Conversazioni della Guerra, 1914–1919* (Milano-Napoli: Riccardo Ricciardi; 1960), II, 463–5.

[1] The full text of this letter of resignation is cited in Leonida Bissolati (ed.): *La Politica estera dell'Italia dal 1897 al 1920* (Milan: Fratelli Treves; 1923), 393.

go it alone, given her high degree of economic and financial dependence. For all these reasons he looked to cooperation with Wilson while at the same time seeking an accommodation with Yugoslavia and Greece.

Cooperation with Wilson was at the heart of Bissolati's policy: Italy should avoid driving the Yugoslavs and Wilson into each other's arms while at the same time seeking a *quid pro quo* for being the only Allied power to fight with the President for his program. Bissolati not only wanted American support for Italy's territorial demands but also desperately needed economic aid in the form of reparations, loans, and credits.

The *Secolo* stepped forward as one of Bissolati's most outspoken champions, shielding the ex-Minister against fast-flying charges of Slavophilism and appeasement. Bissolati had "never denounced a single one of Italy's legitimate claims: he defends the Italianity of Trieste, of Fiume, of Zara [and] he combats every nationalistic aberration of the Yugoslavs." As for Sonnino, even if he himself was no extremist, by condoning the fiery jingoist press campaign he was losing his freedom. He now was caught up in the same "intoxication of victory" which in France and England had stimulated such very dangerous anti-Wilsonian tendencies. The *Messaggero* and the *Tribuna* also noted that what was happening in Italy paralleled developments in England and France.[2]

Indeed, the Italian jingoists drew inspiration from their British and French counterparts. The chauvinist press was full of favorable references to the course of the khaki election; and in the midst of the cabinet crisis Clemenceau's Parliamentary speech and triumph gave additional confidence to the intransigents. The *Giornale d'Italia* adjured all Italians to learn from the outcome of the British election and from Clemenceau's unyielding attitude. If the government meant to promote Italy's national interest it could not "play the St. Francis" at the forthcoming Peace Conference. The *Giornale* claimed that the entire cabinet agreed with Sonnino that now that Russia was out of the picture Italy had to strike for the Treaty of London plus Fiume. In brief, there was no need to choose between Dalmatia and Fiume; and Bissolati being seized by an "altruistic mania, it would be absurd to include him in the peace delegation."[3]

The jingoist *Resto del Carlino* also sought to drive home "Pichon's lesson." It would be intolerable for France to emerge from the Peace Conference with an enlarged empire and with improved frontiers while Italy was left in a weakened condition and with indefensible borders

[2] *Secolo*, December 28–30, 1918, *Messaggero*, December 30, 1918, and *Tribuna*, December 29, 1918, cited in *DR, APS* (January 15, 1919), 228.
[3] *Giornale d'Italia*, December 28–31, 1918, and January 1, 1919, cited in *DR, APS* (January 15, 1919), 227–8.

with Yugoslavia. As Pichon and Clemenceau so aptly said, each nation would press her own demands at the Conference. Though Italy had no German problem, she was obliged to protect herself against Yugoslav imperialism: "we should say that we have the right to prohibit the Danubian and Balkan peoples from uniting in a strong confederation just as France proposes to prevent the German-Austrians from joining Germany."[4]

Of course, with Wilson about to arrive in Rome, even the anti-Bissolati press was anxious not to offend the President or to advertise internal rifts. According to the *Giornale d'Italia* "the whole Cabinet unanimously favored, within the limits of the possible, the realization of Wilson's generous ideas, which find sympathy and agreement throughout the country, without distinction of parties and classes." The government of Italy, however, would join Britain and France in "tempering American ideals with European realities."[5]

But it was left to Mussolini to provide the classic reconciliation of Sonninoism and Wilsonianism. Were Bissolati and Sonnino in disagreement over the defense of Italy's interests in the Adriatic and in the Alps, or were they at loggerheads over the League of Nations, arbitration, and disarmament? Clemenceau was a Wilsonian, and yet he did not favor self-determination for Alsace-Lorraine; Lloyd George was a Wilsonian, and yet he did not propose to reduce or destroy the British navy or to return Gibraltar to Spain, Malta to Italy, or Cyprus to Greece; and the White House was Wilsonian, and yet there was no question of not completing America's huge naval program. "In principle we accept Wilson's program for the reorganization of the world; however we oppose anyone who in Wilson's or any one else's name wants to defraud Italy not of her war booty but of the vindication of her sacred rights in the Alps and on the seas."[6]

These last days of December and the first half of January were decisive for Mussolini's subsequent development. In particular, the results of the British election and the speeches of Pichon and Clemenceau confirmed him in his tentative estimate that under a chauvinist ideological cover the victor nations could and would check the advance of revolutionary Socialism. Mussolini hailed the "disastrous defeat of the British defeatists" with bubbling enthusiasm. In his judgment the outcome of the khaki election, in which universal suffrage was inaugurated, was "of the greatest political importance from the British, Euro-

4 *Resto del Carlino,* December 31, 1918, cited in *Bulletin périodique de la presse italienne,* No. 100 (January 5, 1919), 6.
5 See *DR, APS* (January 5, 1919), 227–8; and *Bulletin périodique de la presse italienne,* No. 100 (January 5, 1915), 5.
6 Mussolini writing in *Il Popolo d'Italia,* December 29, 1918, cited in Edoardo and Duilio Susmel (eds.): *Opera Omnia di Benito Mussolini* (Florence: La Fenice; 1953), XII, 88–90.

pean, and world perspective." In addition to repudiating Bolshevism, "that exclusively Asiatic phenomenon," the mass electorate spurned indolent Asquithism and extremist Labourism. The British people solidly rallied around the government and the men who had led them to victory and now proposed to "exploit" this victory in accordance with the politics of "democratic imperialism which in modern times had been the glory and privilege of the British race." Here was proof that the working masses of England were not "hypnotized by the Russian mirage," preferring to demonstrate their "harmony, order, and discipline through the ballot box." With the ranks closed behind him Lloyd George would enter the Peace Conference with enviable authority. Mussolini was confident that "if British-type coalitions took the field in this vibrant atmosphere of victory and with a clear program of immediate fulfillment in France and Italy, they would score a similar triumph."[7]

When he heard of the overwhelming vote of confidence for Clemenceau and Pichon, Mussolini hailed it as the second major plebiscite for a hard peace. Since France was not only determined "to maintain her position in Europe and the world but proposed to use her victory to strengthen this position," particularly along the Rhine, why should Italy refrain from pressing her claims in the Alps and the Adriatic? Similarly, since France would not hesitate to take territories of predominantly German population, why should Italy hesitate to take territories which at most contained half a million Germans or Slavs? And since neither France nor Britain intended to renounce their Mediterranean and colonial possessions or claims, why should "only Italy and Italy alone" adopt the trusting policy that had failed in 1878? Neither singly nor collectively were the Allies imperialist in any destructive sense. According to Mussolini, their imperialism was an expression of "the eternal and immutable law of life, . . . the need, the desire, and the will to expand in each individual, in each lively and energetic people." Moreover, contrary to common belief, imperialism need not be "aristocratic and military: it can be democratic, pacific, economic and spiritual." Under this definition Mussolini felt free to suggest that "in a certain sense President Wilson was the greatest and the most prosperous of all imperialists."[8]

In any case, the Italian government could no longer remain silent. It had the moral obligation and the political duty to speak as Lloyd George, Pichon, and Clemenceau had spoken: "The government must demonstrate that it has a compass and a goal. . . .The time has come to be specific, even geographically speaking." President Wilson's immi-

[7] *Il Popolo d'Italia*, December 31, 1918, cited in ibid., 96–9.
[8] *Il Popolo d'Italia*, January 1, 1919, cited in ibid., 100–3.

nent arrival in Rome presented Sonnino with a magnificent opportunity to articulate Italy's "minimum, absolutely inviolable" aims in Trieste, Fiume, and the Dalmatian littoral.[9]

The Presidential visit forced Orlando to hurry the settlement of the ministerial crisis. Rather than choose between Sonnino and Bissolati right then and there, the Prime Minister decided to temporize. After consulting Nitti, Bonomi, and Agostino Berenini he was able to make a show of liberalism without impairing Sonnino's position. Nitti continued as Minister of Finance. And in spite of their party's explicit interdict, the two prominent Reformist Socialists Bonomi and Berenini resolved to uphold Orlando, Bonomi accepting the post of Minister of Public Works. Eager to minimize the importance of Bissolati's departure, the Premier announced that the coalition government would continue to have the collaboration "of men of the same party as Bissolati."[1]

However, nobody was deceived, least of all Sonnino and his partisans, who were encouraged by the ease with which Italy's foremost Wilsonian was eased out of power. As for the leaders of the inchoate Wilsonian opposition, in public they hailed the liberality, unity, and strength of the Orlando-Nitti-Bonomi axis while in private conceding their weakness and redoubling their reliance on the American President.

Actually the Bissolati movement was much too embryonic and amorphous for Wilson to count on. Judging by Bonomi's action, Bissolati could not even vouch for the unity and steadfastness of his own Reformist Socialist Party. Similarly, Nitti refused to follow Bissolati's lead, postponing his own resignation in the hope of strengthening Orlando vis-à-vis Sonnino during Wilson's crucial visit. All along Nitti's conceit led him to overestimate the weight of his own threat of resignation while also hesitating to support a movement of which he was not the recognized leader.

Giolitti's continuing isolation was particularly fatal to the power and influence of the moderates. He continued to be criticized for his failure to go all out in his support of the war effort and the political truce. His rivals—and Nitti was among these—were constantly afraid that in any given political impasse he might once again outmaneuver them. As for Giolitti, he was not about to seek a rapprochement with Salvemini, Albertini, and Nitti who had failed to heed his warning that Italy was in no condition to fight a protracted war without sinking into a profound, possibly revolutionary, crisis. Now that this crisis was at hand Giolitti self-righteously reserved himself for the moment when he could emerge as savior and undisputed leader of a left-of-center coalition. Meanwhile his parliamentary followers floundered instead of

[9] *Il Popolo d'Italia*, January 2, 1919, cited in ibid., 104–6.
[1] *DR, APS* (January 15 and 22, 1919), 226–7, 252.

being harnessed to the Bissolati movement. Admittedly the editorials of the *Stampa* and the *Secolo* became increasingly pro-Wilson and pro-Bissolati; and presently so did Albertini's influential *Corriere della Sera* and Salvemini's prestigious *Unità*.[2] But this press campaign could not compensate for the lack of organized Parliamentary strength.

Perhaps if the Socialists had competed for the sponsorship of Wilson and Bissolati, the Reformist Socialists, the democratic Left, and the liberal Right would have pulled together. However, unlike in the other Western and Central European countries, in Italy the bulk of the Socialist Party never succumbed to the Wilsonian mystique.

To be sure, especially after the Fourteen Points address, Turati, Treves, and Giuseppe Emanuele Modigliani moved the moderate Parliamentary party constantly closer to a position comparable to that of the Labour Party, the SFIO, and the SPD.[3] And at the turn of the year Turati still seemed inclined to support Bissolati.[4]

But by advocating this course these Social Patriotic parliamentarians further isolated themselves from the Socialist and labor movement. Both the Italian Socialist Party (ISP) and the General Confederation of Labor (CGL) stuck to their antiwar rhetoric while unenthusiastically cooperating in the war effort. Starting in mid-1917 the Maximalist leaders, whose position was just short of revolutionary defeatism, capitalized on the example of the Russian Revolution, on war weariness, and on rising costs of living as they set out to radicalize the rank and file in preparation for a bid for power after the war. By early September 1918, when the national congress of the ISP finally was authorized to meet in Rome, the Maximalists had made a clean sweep: they scored 14,000 votes, leaving only 2,500 votes each to Turati's reformists on the right and Amadeo Bordiga's intransigents on the left.[5] Hereafter Constantino Lazzari, the Secretary of the ISP, and Giacinto Serrati, the Editor of *Avanti*—both of whom were in prison for seditious activities at the time of this Rome Congress—were firmly entrenched in key positions and their fellow Maximalists decisively dominated the party's executive committee.

As compared to the British Independents, the French ex-*minoritaires,* and the German Independents, the Italian Maximalists were weaker in the Parliamentary party, stronger in the party organization,

[2] Gaetano Salvemini: *Dal Patto di Londra alla Pace di Roma* (Turin: Piero Gobetti; 1925), 247–60.

[3] Leo Valiani: "Il Partito Socialista Italiano dal 1900 al 1918," *Rivista Storica Italiana,* Vol. LXXV, No. 2 (1963), 323–6.

[4] See Turati's article "Esiste il Parlamento?" in *Critica Sociale,* January 1–15, 1919, 1.

[5] Direzione del Partito Socialista Italiano: *Resoconto Stenografico del XV Congresso nazionale,* Rome, September 1–5, 1918 (Rome, 1919), *passim.* More easily accessible is the useful summary of the proceedings and the full text of the rival resolutions of this congress in Franco Pedone (ed.): *Il Partito Socialista Italiano nei suoi Congressi* (Milan: Edizioni Avanti!; 1963), III, 5–44.

more radical in their opposition to war, and more intensely under the Russian Bolshevik spell. Although Lazzari and Serrati lacked Lenin's and Trotsky's decisiveness, organizing skills, and self-confidence, on all major scores they compared favorably with MacDonald, Longuet, and Haase. Precisely because of their undisputed hold on the ISP, their widespread influence in the CGL, and the grudging support of the intransigents, the Maximalist leaders were not about to make ideological and programmatic concessions in order to forestall the secession of the Turatian Reformists. Besides, in Jaurèsian fashion, Turati would strain to the limit to avoid a formal schism, the more so since a schism would expose his faction's extraparliamentary weakness.

Potentially the Christian Socialists constituted a formidable political basis for the Bissolati movement. In the long run Don Luigi Sturzo, founder of the Catholic Popolare, hoped to provide a constructive social-reformist alternative to the counterrevolutionary Right and the revolutionary Left. But in Italy's fast-developing domestic crisis, with Maximalism an imminent threat, Sturzo put first things first: his Christian-Social gospel and party would help to check the Socialists even at the risk of giving uncongenial right-wing forces a temporary advantage. Significantly Sturzo explicity enlisted Wilsonianism in this holding operation.

> . . . While the representatives of the victorious nations are met to prepare the bases of a just and lasting peace, the political parties of every country must contribute to strengthen those tendencies and those principles which will serve to avert all peril of fresh war, to give a stable order to the nations, to actualize the ideals of social justice and improve social conditions of labor, to develop the spiritual and material energies of all countries, united in the solemn bond of the League of Nations.
>
> And as it is not just to compromise the benefits of the victory won by immense sacrifices for the defence of the rights of peoples and for the highest ideals of civilization, it is the duty of all healthy democracies, all popular governments, without exception, to find the real equilibrium of national rights, the supreme international interests, and the perennial motives of the peaceful progress of society.
>
> Therefore we uphold the political and moral programme, the patrimony of the Christian people, recorded in august words, and today defended by Wilson as a fundamental element in the future order of the world, and reject the imperialisms which create dominating nations and mature violent upheavals; therefore we demand that the League of Nations should recognize just national aspirations, hasten the coming of universal disarmament, abolish the secrecy of treaties, effect the freedom of the seas, uphold social legislation in international relations, equality of labor, religious liberty against all sectarian oppression, and that it should have the

strength to apply sanctions and the means to protect the weak peoples against the oppressive tendencies of the strong. . . .[6]

Bissolati and Wilson could hardly have hoped for a more sophisticated and sweeping endorsement of their cause. However, this appeal for the formation of the Popular Party—for which Sturzo had secured Vatican approval—was not issued until January 18, 1919. By then Wilson had come and gone, Nitti had resigned, and Sonnino was in Paris, confident that Orlando would give him free reign at the Peace Conference. Evidently Sturzo's summons came too late to help stem the anti-Bissolati tide. In fact, the failure of the Bissolati movement, in particular the refusal of the ISP enthusiastically to embrace Wilsonianism, may have prompted Sturzo to speed up the organization of his own party. Since the moderates were divided and leaderless in Parliament and lacked popular support in the country at large, Sturzo proceeded to build a mass party which would countervail the Socialists while at the same time helping to defeat Sonnino in the second round.[7]

Meanwhile U.S. officials watched the Italian political scene with considerable concern. Ambassador Nelson Page reported that "Bissolati's actual following in the country [was] not believed very large." R. S. Baker, who was in Italy once again to keep close contact with the "less articulate opinion of the democratic, liberal, and socialist forces," informed Colonel House "of the growth of a great imperialist spirit." Indeed, by the time he returned to Paris in mid-December he was "very much impressed and somewhat discouraged by the forces gathering in opposition to the President's policy." On the other hand, partly under the influence of Turati and Treves, Baker tended to exaggerate the unanimity and intensity of Socialist support for Wilson, though he quoted Massingham to the effect that, like Barnes in England, Bissolati "was a good man separated from his following." In any case, he urged the President to go to Italy in order to strengthen his following among Socialists and Radicals as well as among the electorate at large.[8]

Similarly, George Creel suggested that while in Italy Wilson "consent to receive a visit" from a Socialist delegation, headed by Turati, which was "not the extreme group." As for House, he insisted that even though Orlando and Sonnino were discouraging Wilson from going to

---

[6] The full text of this appeal is cited in Luigi Sturzo: *Italy and Fascismo* (London: Faber and Gwyer; 1926), 91–4.

[7] For the beginnings of the Popolari see Sturzo: *Italy and Fascismo, passim;* Giolio De Rossi: *Il primo anno di vita del Partito Popolare Italiano* (Rome: Ferrari; 1920); Gabriele de Rosa: *Storia del Partito Popolare* (Bari: Editori Laterza; 1958), Chs. i–ii; Edith Pratt Howard: *Il Partito Popolare Italiano* (Florence: La Nuova Italia; 1957), 102–89; and Webster: *The Cross and the Fasces,* Chs. iv–v.

[8] *F.R.,P.C.,1919,* I, 472; House to Baker, November 16, 1918, and Baker to House, November 22 and December 6, 1918, in House Papers, 17:17, 2:7; Baker to Woodrow Wilson, December 18, 1918, in Baker Papers, Box 3 of 18; Baker Diary, Book XXI, entry of December 14, 1918.

Milan and Turin, these were the "essential places" for him to visit. Since the President had his "greatest strength" in these big industrial centers they were "the only reason why [Wilson] should go to Italy at all."[9]

Wilson arrived in Rome on January 3. By then, thanks to the preliminary negotiations in Paris, he had taken the measure of the Orlando administration. He considered the Italian statesmen "quite incapable of taking a wide view of things," judging by their demand for "almost the whole of the Dalmatian coast and practically all the islands of the Adriatic." In his conversation with C. P. Scott in Manchester Woodrow Wilson had indicated that he expected Italy to be even more obstinate than France: Sonnino and Orlando were "obsessed" with the Eastern Adriatic and refused to discuss anything else.[1]

Since the President had few if any illusions about a Sonnino-dominated government and put little stock in official ceremonial functions, he was anxious to sound out the strength of his sympathizers. On the other hand, precisely because the events of the last few days had publicly dramatized the conflict within the cabinet, Sonnino and his supporters were determined to block Wilson from encouraging and mixing with the Bissolati movement.

Hence, when at the suggestion of John H. Hearley, the Acting Commissioner of the Committee on Public Information in Italy, the President planned to address a public meeting in Rome's Piazza Venezia inbetween his official rounds, he ran into insurmountable obstacles. Even a passing stop in this Piazza and an appearance on the balcony of the Quirinal were successfully forestalled by his hosts.[2]

Although in Rome it was easy and not at all exceptional for his hosts to confine Wilson's public exposure to formal receptions at the royal palace, the national legislature, and the Capitol—as well as to travel to and from these occasions—they could hardly control his private appointments. Consequently in the evening of January 4, shortly before leaving for Milan, Wilson met with Bissolati. No doubt the President deliberately sought out the controversial opposition leader in order to warn Sonnino that he might go over the govern-

[9] George Creel to Woodrow Wilson, December 24, 1918, and Colonel House to Wilson, December 25, 1919, in Wilson Papers, VIII A:5.

[1] Statement by President Wilson to Frank Worthington at Buckingham Palace, London, December 28, 1918, National Archives, Secret File, Document 811.001W/163; and C. P. Scott, memorandum on conversation with Wilson, December 29, 1918, cited in J. L. Hammond: *C. P. Scott of the Manchester Guardian* (London: G. Bell; 1934), 249. Even during the pre-Armistice negotiations Wilson concluded that Sonnino "belonged to the last century." National Archives, Document 763.72119/2312.

[2] George Creel: *The War, the World, and Wilson* (New York: Harper; 1920), 168–71; Florence C. Speranza (ed.): *The Diary of Gino Speranza: Italy, 1915–1919* (New York: Columbia University Press; 1941), II, 238–9; Admiral Cary T. Grayson to Joseph Tumulty, January 7, 1919, Wilson Papers, VIII A:8.

ment's head; Wilson also meant to give a boost to his Italian supporters. This consultation was the prelude to Wilson's abortive Fiume appeal of late April 1919.[3]

Besides producing calculated political effects the conference with Bissolati also served to clarify the President's mind about Italy's claims. Wilson wasted little time on either formalities or vague generalizations; he immediately turned to the crucial issues.

WILSON: And what is your opinion about Fiume?

BISSOLATI: Fiume should be a free city and a free port . . . under Italian protection.

WILSON: Do you believe that they would be able to support themselves as free cities, from an economic standpoint?

BISSOLATI: Yes, indeed. . . .

WILSON: You mean that Gorizia should be Italian?

BISSOLATI: Yes, but not Adelsberg, which is entirely Slav. The line should run close to Trieste.

WILSON: . . . What is that line further South?

BISSOLATI: That is an imaginary line in the water.

WILSON: Does it include the Islands?

BISSOLATI: Perhaps the exterior ones (Cherso and Lussino).

WILSON: . . . Sonnino . . . assured me that the Dalmatian coast and islands were a vital military necessity to Italy for defensive purposes. This I could not grasp, perhaps because of my somewhat old fashioned ideas.

BISSOLATI: Their military value is not so much for defensive as for offensive. . . . I believe in the immediate abandonment of all Italian pretentions to Dalmatia. I insisted upon this in the Council of Ministers, and it was because of this stand that I took, that I was obliged to resign from the Government. . . .[4]

The following day, in Milan, the President had a similar conversation with Luigi Albertini.[5] But in this Italian Manchester, Wilson above all made contact with those political elements which Baker, Creel, and House had commended to him.

To begin with, the Mayor of Milan, Emilio Caldara, was a Turatian

[3] Speranza (ed.): *Diary,* II, 237–8; and René Albrecht-Carrié: *Italy at the Paris Peace Conference* (New York: Columbia University Press; 1938), 84–5. On January 7 Ambassador Page sent the following urgent and excessively hopeful report to Wilson: "Bissolati's having seen the President has made a profound impression here. I had a conversation with Baron Sonnino late this afternoon which indicates, as possible, important changes [in] his position. Both he and Orlando, whom I had seen earlier in the day, were manifestly impressed and even anxious over this situation. . . . I think Sonnino is ready in view of recent manifestations to concede much more than ever before." *F.R.,P.C.,1919,* I, 473–4.

[4] The minutes of this conversation were taken by Lt. Lawrence G. White, approved by Bissolati, and sent by Ambassador Page to Wilson on January 7, 1919, Wilson Papers, VIII A:8.

[5] Speranza (ed.): *Diary,* II, 238. There may exist a record of this conversation; however, to date I have found none.

Socialist. He organized a reception at Palazzo Marino to which he invited, among others, representatives of the local Maximalist-controlled Socialist and trade union organizations. At first some of the leaders were inclined to vie with the interventionists for sponsorship of Wilson. Eventually, however, the executive committee of the local party turned down the invitation and in effect called for a boycott of all events and demonstrations connected with Wilson's visit.[6]

Not only Caldara but also many rank-and-file members and sympathizers of the ISP ignored the party directives. January 5 was a triumphant day for the President in the streets of Milan, at City Hall, and on the Piazza della Scala. While Albertini and Mussolini joined invited guests in La Scala at a gala dinner, followed by scenes from the second act of *Aida,* "in the square below, [which was] crammed with people . . . there was no end of '*Viva Wilson.*' " Likewise in Genoa and Turin, where Wilson made brief stops on his way back to Paris, many workers seemed to join in the reception. Nevertheless contemporary reports by U.S. observers that the Maximalist leaders had been hard pressed to prevent their followers from defecting to Wilson were considerably exaggerated.[7]

As in France and Britain very few anti-Wilsonian voices openly and vociferously disturbed the general exaltation with which the President was greeted along the streets, in the piazzas, and through the press. Both during and immediately following the visit discordant notes could only be found in the *Resto del Carlino* and the *Idea Nazionale.* These papers kept reiterating that Italians had not died for a vague ideology; that they would insist on both Dalmatia and the League of Nations; and that they expected their government to act in the spirit of the recent congressional elections in the U.S., the khaki election in Britain, and Clemenceau's pronouncement in France.[8]

The liberal Right, the democratic Left, and the Socialists realized that the uncompromising foreign policy views expressed in these few papers rather than Wilson's widely cheered conciliatory diplomacy continued to guide the cabinet. The *Corriere della Sera* warned of disaster if the right of the victors and the strongest dominated the coming peace negotiations: the European nations would start on a new cycle in their struggle for power and in their arms competition; "America, disillusioned, would disinterest herself in Europe"; and the League of Nations would fail because it could not be "imagined without the participation of the United States." The *Stampa* also cautioned

6 *Avanti,* January 2–4, 1919.
7 G. A. Borgese: *Goliath: The March of Fascism* (New York: Viking; 1938), 139–40; Speranza (ed.): *Diary,* II, 239; Page to Ammission, January 11, 1919, in *F.R.,P.C., 1919,* I, 153–4.
8 *Resto del Carlino,* January 4–8, 1919, and *Idea Nazionale,* January 3–8, 1919, cited in *DR, APS* (January 22, 1919), 250–1, and *Bulletin périodique de la presse italienne,* No. 101 (January 23, 1919), 3–5.

against a return to the prewar concert of Europe at a time when Europe was no longer a closed field and ceased to dominate the world, either in arms or in ideas.[9]

Once Wilson had left, it was up to Bissolati himself to carry forward the campaign for a foreign policy that would serve Italy's national interest as well as the President's broader design for a new world order. There was little time before the Peace Conference would open in Paris. It would be easier to prevail upon Orlando to restrain Sonnino at the outset than to do so once the Conference was well under way.

At this juncture the Italian League for the Society of Nations scheduled meetings in important cities throughout the peninsula with a view to explaining and spreading the Wilsonian program. On January 12 Guglielmo Ferrero spoke in Florence, Giuseppe Canepa in Turin, Giretti in Genoa, and Salvemini in Pisa. Bissolati chose to present the first full-scale exposition of his policy under this society's auspices in a lead-off address at La Scala in Milan in the evening of January 11.

But forty-eight hours before this appointed day the Italian press flared up over an extensive interview which Bissolati had granted on December 29 to the Rome correspondent of the *Morning Post,* but which this British counterpart of the *Resto del Carlino* published only on January 6. Instantly the ex-Minister was variously denounced for explaining himself in a foreign newspaper before doing so at home, for harming Italy by divulging internal conflicts to the external world, and for choosing a jingoist paper as his platform.

In this interview Bissolati outlined the full range of his disagreements with Sonnino: whereas he favored the closest possible application of the nationality principle, the Foreign Minister, stubbornly wedded to the London Treaty, was prepared to violate this principle in Dalmatia, in the Dodecanese, and in Southern Tyrol. Bissolati wanted to avoid irredentism in Italy as well as among Italy's neighbors. Hence he advocated giving Dalmatia to Yugoslavia on condition that Fiume —which Sonnino could not claim under the Treaty of London—become a free port under Italian rule and that Italy keep all of Istria. Unlike Sonnino he wanted good relations with Yugoslavia whose birth was an accomplished fact. Similarly he wanted to develop friendly relations with Greece by not claiming the essentially barren thirteen islands in the southern Aegean and with Germany by not claiming the German-speaking Tyrol north of Bolzano. Moreover, Bissolati warned Sonnino of the risk of incurring a serious diplomatic defeat at the Peace Conference, since Wilson, who was not bound by the secret London Treaty, was not likely to countenance annexationist claims.

The jingoist and nationalist press hastened to mount a full-fledged

[9] See *DR, APS* (January 22, 1919), 251.

attack on this interview. Bissolati was accused of promoting the harmful myth of Italy's and Sonnino's imperialism instead of denouncing the imperialism of Britain, France, and Yugoslavia. Notwithstanding the trimmers who proposed to make rewards and concessions to all countries except their own, Italy considered the Treaty of London sacred. As for Fiume, this port was so obviously Italian that it could never be separated from mother Italy.

Even though Albertini approved the spirit of the interview which contradicted Orlando's recent rationalization of the cabinet crisis, the *Corriere della Sera* also wondered about Bissolati's views on the imperialism of the other Allies. Furthermore, the *Corriere* had concrete reservations about his territorial program: the Alpine border should be at the Brenner in order to secure a natural strategic frontier; Dalmatia should go to the Slavs except that Italy should retain Zara and the Dalmatian isles and Yugoslavia should demilitarize the entire coastline; and in the Aegean, Italy should retain Rhodes and be compensated for renouncing the other Dodecanese islands. In spite of these reservations the *Corriere* enthusiastically hailed Bissolati and joined all men of good will in the hope that the impending Milan speech would further clarify the ex-Minister's proposals.[1]

And, in fact, Bissolati prepared a closely reasoned statement for the widely advertised meeting at La Scala. Even though hostile superpatriots prevented him from delivering most of this speech it still deserves notice as the most comprehensive Italian war-aims declaration in the era of the Great War.[2]

In this declaration Bissolati set his concrete territorial program in a broad Wilsonian context, combined it with a projection of Italian diplomatic strategy and tactics, and refined it in the light of the friendly criticism of his *Morning Post* interview.

Accordingly, he insisted that Italy entered the war on the side of the Allies not for loot but out of indignation over the German-Magyar assault on Serbia, the violation of Belgium, and the invasion of France. Italy successfully participated in a crusade to rid the world of repressive and imperialist regimes, to liberate oppressed nationalities, and to create a new international community with the help of a League of Nations.

To be sure, the key provisions of the Treaty of London were sacred: Trentino, Gorizia, Trieste, and Istria would return to Italy without discussion. However, since the U.S. and other nations were not party to this treaty they were bound to question some of the other provisions which to them as well as to him seemed contrary to Wilson-

---

[1] This summary of the press reaction to the interview in the *Morning Post* is based on DR, APS (January 22, 1919), 252–3; and *Bulletin périodique de la presse italienne,* No. 101 (January 6, 1919), 6.

[2] For the full text see Bissolati: *La Politica estera dell'Italia,* 394–414.

ian ideals as well as to Italy's national interest. Even if the League were not established and Europe temporarily returned to the prewar international system, Italy should not press excessive territorial claims. The nation simply could not afford to make enemies of Yugoslavia, Greece, and Germany except at the cost of occupying vis-à-vis France and Britain the same subordinate position which Italy had occupied in the prewar *Triplice*. Furthermore, especially Italy, as the least wealthy of the Great Powers, had every interest in minimizing those international tensions which stimulate expensive arms races. For all these reasons Bissolati advocated that Italy become "Wilson's most trusted ally at the Conference and the vanguard of the Wilsonian movement in Europe." Above all, Italy should not fall prey to those exaggerated egotisms which victory had unchained in England and France and which threatened to paralyze Wilson's labors.

This, then, was the point at which Bissolati took into account the friendly critics of his *Morning Post* interview. He spoke of imperialist pressures in the Allied nations, but without using these as an excuse or justification for Italian annexations. Instead, he urged that all nations come to the Conference prepared to make mutual concessions and that out of enlightened self-interest Italy show the way with spontaneous concessions to Greece, German Austria, and Yugoslavia.

Athens should be turned into an ally in the southern Adriatic and the Balkans by voluntarily placing the Dodecanese at the disposal of the Conference for restitution to Greece. Even though he did not accept Albertini's claim to Rhodes or compensation, Bissolati hoped that these and similar concessions would earn rewards for Italy. He stressed once again that these islands were unmistakably Greek, economically unattractive, and—in view of Turkey's collapse—strategically obsolete.

As for the Alpine frontier, Bissolati conceded that strategically the Brenner line of the London Treaty was better than the Upper Adige-Eisach line. However, he preferred the good over the perfect frontier, especially since the latter would create a dangerous German irredentism in the Southern Tyrol.

Because the territorial problems of the eastern Adriatic were most hotly disputed Bissolati clarified his position on Dalmatia at great length and with deliberate precision. He reiterated once again that the birth of Yugoslavia was irrevocable; he renewed his plea that Italy voluntarily rather than under diplomatic pressure abandon the Treaty of London wherever it violated the nationality principle; and he reiterated Italy's claim to control of Fiume. But he now also explicitly envisaged an Italian presence in Zara, Pola, Valona, and the off-shore islands as well as the demilitarization of the entire coast. Under such a settlement Dalmatia would become a defensive rather than offensive outpost for Yugoslavia, whereas if Italy controlled all the Dalmatian islands, ports, and territories these would be considered offensive rather than defensive strong points.

No doubt Bissolati had a vastly exaggerated estimate of Wilson's strength in the U.S. and in Allied councils, seriously underestimating the political pressures opposed to "the diplomacy of voluntary concessions" in the Allied as well as in the new nations. As a former cabinet minister he might have been more realistic about the difficulties of taming the post-Armistice Sonninos; and as an ex-Socialist he might have increased the credibility and appeal of his position by at least touching on domestic reforms and on Allied policy toward Bolshevik Russia.

But these and other shortcomings cannot detract from the vision, practicality, and sincerity of Bissolati's program. In retrospect the Scala address can be characterized as his political testament;[3] at the time, however, it was a political act requiring courage, conviction, and self-sacrifice. Bissolati had few illusions about his active and organized support in the cabinet, in Parliament, and in the country at large. He knew that his modulated proposals could not compete successfully with the inflammatory appeals of the intransigent annexationists or the Socialist anti-interventionists. No doubt he trusted excessively in reason and in reasoned rather than emotive persuasion; he also remained wedded to the political methods and institutions which were so congenial to the power elite of the democratic Left and the liberal Right. The *Secolo* expressed this elite's ineffectual code by urging Orlando to give Sonnino the full responsibility of power and to send him "to the Peace Conference with ideas acclaimed by ignorant crowds, but to leave to us the right to disapprove and to discuss."[4]

The superpatriots, for their part, were not about to limit themselves either to cool analysis and free discussion or to the use of traditional political tactics. In the wake of the *Morning Post* interview the anti-Bissolati campaign was in high gear: the *Resto* and the *Idea* continued to heap abuse on all trimmers; on January 10 Mussolini published a poisonous article under the title "Il Nuovo 'Parecchio' Di Bissolati"; and overnight the walls of Milan were covered with jingoist posters excoriating the scheduled Scala meeting.

In his article Mussolini denounced all Bissolatians as fanatical Slavophiles and *rinunciatari*. Bissolati himself was charged with sabotaging Italy's legitimate national interests in Dalmatia and in the Alto Adige, with surrendering rather than negotiating, and with being driven to this *parecchio*—sell-out—by political fear. Italy had just "decided the fate of the world" and there was no reason for Italians to fear this victory and to act like "poor little children." All Yugoslavs were as intransigent and expansionist as Trumbic, but there was less reason for

<hr />

[3] Bonomi: *Leonida Bissolati e il movimento socialistà in Italia*, 221.
[4] Cited in *DR, APS* (January 29, 1919), 274.

Italians to capitulate to the Slavs than there was for the French to yield
to more than 70 million Germans. Four years ago Bissolati had favored
the violent battle against Giolitti's *parecchio;* who would have
thought, asked Mussolini, that after this prodigious victory the ex-
Minister and ex-soldier would present "a scarcely corrected and barely
revised edition of the Giolitti-Bülow masterpiece?" Indeed, why should
the Wilsonians in France call for the blockade of Germany and claim
the Rhine frontier while Wilsonians in Italy proposed to "fraternize"
with the Slavs and to renounce the Adriatic?[5]

Mussolini was about to pay his second visit within the week to
Milan's world-renowned opera house. On Sunday evening he had
attended the gala event in honor of Wilson as a taciturn journalist; this
Saturday night he attended the League of Nations rally at the Scala as
an obstreperous political agitator.[6] Mussolini and the futurist poet
Filippo Marinetti were most prominent among the rabid interventionists and annexationists who came determined to interrupt this rally
with hostile demonstrations. As it was, because of the crescendo of the
jingoist campaign, trouble was expected. And Mussolini and his co-
adjutors were well placed to stage their disturbance since they had
managed to secure tickets—from whom is still unclear—entitling them
to pack strategically located subscription boxes.

Even before Bissolati was introduced, the tumult began; and within
an hour it engulfed the hall. With difficulty Bissolati managed to deliver
the first part of his address in which he discussed the League of Nations.
The moment he touched on the controversial territorial questions,
pandemonium broke loose. The superpatriots in the audience shouted
insults; unfurled streamers; threw thousands of tracts from the galleries;
and manhandled pro-Bissolatians, including decorated and wounded
soldiers. Efforts to restore order by a battle-scarred Lieutenant
Facchinetti, by General Gramantieri, and by the Catholic leader Paolo
Cappa, were of no avail.

Borgese, the then foreign editor of the *Corriere della Sera*, described the scene in particularly vivid terms.

> For a few minutes Bissolati was allowed to go on, seemingly
> undisturbed by the confused murmur of the hall. Then at a given
> moment, as if an invisible baton had given the sign, the infernal
> symphony began. Squeaks, shrieks, whistles, grumbles, nearly hu-
> man, and all the thinkable counterfeits of the wild pack's howling,
> made up the bulk of the sound wave; but a human, nay, a patriotic
> cry became distinguishable now and then and ruled the inarticulate

[5] *Il Popolo d'Italia,* January 10 and 11, 1919, cited in Susmel (eds.): *Opera Omnia,*
XII, 125–30.
[6] For this rally at La Scala and its aftermath see Borgese: *Goliath,* 140–43; G. A.
Chiurco: *Storia della Rivoluzione fascista* (Florence: Vallecchi; 1929), I, 83–4;
DR, *APS* (January 29, 1919), 273; *Bulletin périodique de la presse italienne,*
No. 102 (February 2–3, 1919), 1–4.

mass with the rhythm of a brutal march. They said: "Croati no! Croati no!" meaning that they wanted no friendship with Croats or Yugoslavs; and they meant too that Bissolati was a Croat.

He withstood the trial and multiplied the resources of his voice. Some protests in his favor—too human, indeed, to prevail over the beastly symphony—arose from other sections of the theatre. . . . [But] now suddenly Bissolati recognized Mussolini in the chorus: that unmistakable voice, dishearteningly wooden, peremptorily insistent, like the clacking of castanets.

He turned his head to the friends who were nearest to him and said in a low voice: "Quell'uomo, no!"—"I will not fight with that man!"

From that moment on he read his pages only as a formality, to himself. No applause was audible at the end. The crowd, part triumphant, part impotently disgusted, cleared the theatre.[7]

Later that night several of these triumphant proto-Fascist agitators and troopers proceeded to smash office windows at the *Corriere della Sera* and at the *Secolo*.

During the following week—which witnessed another cabinet crisis in Rome, the formal opening of the Peace Conference at Versailles, and the assassination of Karl Liebknecht and Rosa Luxemburg in Berlin—Mussolini pressed on with his campaign. Whereas the *Corriere* sought to dismiss Saturday night's events as the work of "a few trivial political adventurers,"[8] under the caption *Liquidarzione* the editor of *Il Popolo* hailed it as the well-deserved obliteration of defeatism in Milan and as a resounding plebiscite in support of the Italian national interest.[9]

Mussolini rejected the argument of bourgeois democracy that unless the Allied and the Italian governments made a Wilsonian peace Leninism would win the day; and so did Antonio Gramsci. But while Gramsci exposed Wilsonianism as a bourgeois fraud designed to ward off the Socialist revolution,[1] Mussolini, for his part, proclaimed that the renunciation of Dalmatia and Alto Adige would be the greatest boon to Leninism. In any case Bissolati represented "nothing and no one in Italy." The former Minister was *liquidato* and on the eve of the Peace Conference the discredited *rinunciatari* simply would not be allowed to "use of specter of Bolshevism to blackmail the nation" into overthrowing Sonnino. Italy needed a strong peace in addition to a trans-

[7] Borgese: *Goliath*, 143.
[8] Cited in Chiurco: *Storia della Rivoluzione fascista*, I, 83. Because of this insult Mussolini challenged the *Corriere*'s Director to a duel!
[9] Cited in Susmel (eds.): *Opera Omnia*, XII, 134–6. By April 1921 Mussolini referred to the Scala incident as Fascism's *prima battaglia*. Ibid., XVI, 240.
[1] In a heavily censored article Gramsci criticized Canepa who, at the Turin rally of the League for the Society of Nations, had offered Wilson as an alternative to Lenin. See *Opera di Antonio Gramsci*, Vol. IX, *L'Ordine Nuovo: 1919–1920* (Rome: Einaudi; 1954), 204–6.

formation of national life that would start with immediate economic and social benefits for the proletariat of the trenches.[2]

In fact, as he wrote to Gabriele D'Annunzio, this "fundamental renovation of national life" required that Italy's victory not be "mutilated."[3] Mussolini and D'Annunzio now joined forces. They endorsed a counterrally initiated by various patriotic leagues and committees for Dalmatia, Fiume, Trentino, and Trieste, as well as by the *fascio parlamentare.* This rally was held at La Scala on January 17. Those attending heard pro-Dalmatian and pro-Fiume speeches by Mussolini, Massimo Rocca, and self-styled delegates from Fiume and Dalmatia, and cheered when a group of Arditi used force to expel an editor of the *Corriere* who from a third-row seat had "permitted himself an exclamation." Meanwhile Socialists had gathered on the Scala side of the Galeria Vittorio Emmanuele; eventually there were scuffles between them and the interventionists which required action by the police and left one hundred casualties.[4]

Being detained in Venice, D'Annunzio was unable to attend in person. However, it was as a champion of this counterdemonstration at La Scala that on January 15 he published his "Open Letter to the Dalmatians." Even though heretofore he had published his political articles in the *Corriere,* the content and style of this letter would have been out of place in Albertini's stolid organ. Whereas Bissolati had just issued his political testament, D'Annunzio issued an appeal which—in addition to being impassioned and dramatic—was premonitory of a new politics. It belonged in *Il Popolo d'Italia;* and that is where it appeared.

> . . . Victorious Italy, still in arms, ought [at the time of the victory of Veneto] to have said to her rivals: Behold my sacrifice. Do you wish to weigh it? . . . Behold my victory. Do you wish to measure it? But it transcends your measure, as it transcends the old pact. Whether this to-day is valid or invalid does not matter to me. It has been absorbed by my right. And behold my right, for which I have fought alone, for which I have suffered alone, for which all alone I have entirely remade my forces and my courage thrice.
>
> This victorious Italy ought to have said, clearly, steady in her discipline, compact in her will, concise in her affirmations: "My frontier on the east is marked by the Monte Valebiti and by the Dinaric Alps, which continue the Julian Alps. All that band of countries . . . belongs to me. . . ."
>
> Instead we witness a wretched spectacle. We seem almost op-

[2] *Il Popolo d'Italia,* January 12–18, 1919, cited in Susmel (eds.): *Opera Omnia,* XII, 134–55.

[3] Giorgio Pini and Duilio Susmel: *Mussolini: L'Uomo e l'Opera* (Florence: La Fenice; 1953), I, 378.

[4] Ibid., I, 380; and Chiurco: *Storia,* I, 83–6.

pressed by our triumph. We beg for the smile of the arbiter. We celebrate the thirty-two teeth of that indecipherable smile. We place in the arms of a gracious guest the she wolf of Rome stamped in massive gold. . . . The people of the *revanche,* drunk with victory, again fly all their plumes in the wind, tune up all their fanfares, quicken their pace in order to surpass the most resolute and speedy—and we step aside to let them pass. The people of the five meals, its bloody work hardly ended, reopens its jaws to devour as much as it can—and we pull our belts a few holes tighter around our sobriety. The people of the star spangled banner do not hide that they have brought off the very best and biggest of their deals, *sub specie* of the eternal ideals—and we already allow strangers to disturb the sources of our new wealth.

And what peace will in the end be imposed on us, poor little ones of Christ? A Gallic peace? A British peace? A star spangled peace? Then, no! Enough. Victorious Italy—the most victorious of all the nations—victorious over herself and over the enemy—will have on the Alps and over her sea the Pax Romana, the sole peace that is fitting. If necessary we will meet the new plot in the fashion of the Arditi, a grenade in each hand and a knife between our teeth.[5]

The ultrainterventionists of 1914–15 all along had been destined to become the ultra-annexationists of the post-Armistice period. Then as now these proto-Fascists were an amorphous group; their own Parliamentary strength was nil; their active patrons among Italy's political and military elites were few; and their followers had to be counted in the hundreds rather than in the thousands or ten thousands.

Nevertheless, on both occasions their influence was far from negligible. The screeching and fanatical tone of their jingoist pronouncements together with their paramilitary demonstrations and skirmishes gave them their extraparliamentary romance and influence in Italy's crisis-torn society. Their effective power, however, was not their own, nor was it of their own making. Traditional right-wing conservatives, nationalists, royalists, and generals legitimized these new Rightists by repudiating neither their program nor their tactics. The old Right was so obsessed with its uphill struggle against the Center-left and the Left that it welcomed the informal, unsolicited, and seemingly compliant succor even of these new revolutionaries of the Right. There was no alliance or coalition but a predisposition to take advantage of each other's assets; they certainly did not deny or disavow each other. Besides, the two Rights—the old and the new—had many sentiments, values, and objectives in common: both were antirational, antiparliamentary, antiparty, antipacifist, anti-Socialist, and passionately nationalist. As always, however, they had a much wider area of agreement with regard to the ills of the existing state and society than with regard to the shape of the future society and the means to reach it.

[5] Cited in *DR, APS* (January 29, 1919), 275.

Obviously this handful of proto-Fascists could not stand comparison with the legions of Socialists. Notwithstanding debilitating internal squabbles, at the turn of the year—hence, before the *Popolari* mushroomed—the Socialist and trade-union formations had no rival in organization and numbers. There were more than 60,000 dues-paying party members; 670 city, state, or regional party organizations; 450,000 members of the CGL; some 100 newspapers and periodicals; 883,409 electors (in the last prewar elections); 400 Socialist-controlled communal councils; and some 45 deputies in the *camera*.

But in spite of, or probably because of, this massive strength and influence, the ISP, unlike the feeble revolutionaries of the Right, was completely isolated. Not only the entire Right but also the Center and the non-Socialist Left constantly exaggerated the radicalism of the ISP, proclaimed their own anti-Socialism, and out-of-hand precluded any collaboration. In other words, whereas the weakness of the nascent Fascists commended them as a useful tool to the Right, the strength of the Socialists frightened the Center and non-Socialist Left into repudiating and quarantining them. Granted, the Maximalists did everything in their power to restrain Turati from exploring the basis for a united front. However, the liberal Right and the democratic Left were equally reluctant to make concessions to the Socialists. In their eyes the revolutionaries were a greater danger than the counterrevolutionaries and they estimated that they had the strength to fight both simultaneously. Besides, Sonnino and his cabal were certain to destroy themselves with their own arrogance and mistakes in both foreign and domestic policy.

The second post-Armistice ministerial crisis marked another advance for Rightists of varying hues. Nitti had tendered his resignation to Orlando during the second day of Wilson's visit in Rome; but Orlando did not accept it until January 15. By then the nationalists and conservatives, encouraged by the collapse of the Bissolati movement, were pressuring Orlando to remove him from the cabinet. They successfully played on the Prime Minister's not totally unfounded fear that while attending the Conference in Paris Nitti would seek to supplant him in Rome—much as Orlando had intrigued against Boselli.

The Right found Nitti objectionable on two counts: in domestic affairs he was a Giolittian reformer while in foreign policy he was a Bissolatian compromiser.

As Minister of the Treasury and as a financial expert, he was desperate about Italy's economic exhaustion at a time when the nation had to shoulder the heavy cost of reconversion, reconstruction, social reform, and the public debt. His awareness of the seriousness of the fast-developing economic and social crisis as well as his Radical predispositions inclined him to press not only for excess profit and personal income taxes and further obligatory loans, but also for a sharp cut-back in military expenditures and close cooperation with the Allies, especially with Wilson. In other words, even in his Treasury capacity Nitti advocated policies which were incompatible with Sonnino's project.

Significantly, Orlando seems never to have considered rallying the moderates in the cabinet against Sonnino and his supporters. By standing firm with Nitti, Bonomi, and Berenini he might have had a fighting chance. By so doing he might have encouraged Bissolati and Turati to get together, prodded the Democratic Entente to become bolder, and seduced the Giolittians to follow his lead. Would Sonnino really have resigned? And, if so, could Orlando have carried on, or would he have had to give way to either Nitti or Giolitti?

In any event, the Prime Minister acted in mid-January as he had acted two weeks earlier. He undertook another cabinet reshuffle which he again claimed to be insignificant. In fact, the departure of Nitti merely compounded the concessions to the Right which Orlando had initiated with Bissolati's resignation.

How, then, did Orlando paper over this newest defection? Just as Bonomi was pulled into the cabinet to "replace" Bissolati, so now Luigi Facta, one of Giolitti's close but ineffectual friends, replaced Nitti. As part of this same effort to hold the Center-left Orlando also appointed Fradeletto, the leader of the Democratic Entente, to be Minister of Liberated Areas; he also retained Bonomi and Berenini in their posts.

However, these moderates were more than offset by other appointments. To begin with, instead of giving the Treasury to Facta—who became Minister of Justice—Orlando gave it to Bonaldo Stringher. An apolitical expert who for eighteen years was manager of the Bank of Italy, Stringher was not likely to take politically unsettling initiatives. In addition to putting the Treasury in safe hands Orlando made three appointments which left no further doubt about his own orientation. Two members of the Parliamentary Fascio entered the cabinet: Vincenzo Riccio became Minister of Agriculture and Giuseppe Girardini became Minister of Pensions. Furthermore Orlando drew Enrico Caviglia and Giuseppe De Nava from the Center-right to take over the War and Transport ministries.

Quite clearly, in terms of domestic policy, the cabinet had become more conservative. This shift to the Right immediately made itself felt in foreign policy. Not only was Sonnino's hold on the Foreign Office tightened still further, but also Orlando completed the Italian Delegation to the Paris Peace Conference by appointing Salandra and Salvatore Barzilai. Both of them were outright annexationists: whereas Salandra stood squarely in the conservative camp, Barzilai was a fiery Mazzinian irredentist. Certainly both could safely be relied upon to work in close harness with Sonnino. This crowning blow prompted the

Corriere to ask how Orlando could remain head of a cabinet "whose foreign policy corresponded neither to his ideas nor to his methods?" Since the Sonnino forces had triumphed and forced out Bissolati and Nitti "logic would . . . [demand] the resignation of Orlando and the formation of a Cabinet presided over by Sonnino."[6]

But neither logic nor politics justified such a demand. To begin with, the new cabinet fairly accurately reflected the balance of power and opinion of the parties and factions in the *camera*. Under the spell of victory the openings to the Left which dated from the crisis period of the war were bound to be closed, as they were also being closed in the other victor nations. The Italian Right and Center-right was in the offensive mood in large measure because it was apprehensive—and justifiably so—that under a vastly expanded franchise the first postwar elections would give the forces of movement a sweeping majority. This was the time to act decisively since the liberal Right and the democratic Left continued to be fatally fractured and leaderless as well as subject to intimidation by the patriotic upsurge and the specter of Bolshevism.

Just as Lloyd George accommodated himself to Bonar Law and the forces supporting him, so Orlando for the time being made his peace with Sonnino and his champions. His method of accommodation was a function of Italy's political system. In Britain the two-party system and collective cabinet responsibility argued in favor of early recourse to the ballot. In Italy, however, the brittle multiparty system and the long-standing practice of *trasformismo* encouraged Orlando to make the cabinet reshuffles in which he excelled. Probably Clemenceau, operating in a similar multiparty setting, would have acted likewise if Malvy, Caillaux, and Albert Thomas had not been successfully removed in late 1917.

Only Woodrow Wilson stood out against the predominant legislative mood and pressures, but he did so in a political system in which the Executive is enjoined to give strong leadership in foreign affairs and in a nation in which his appeals over the heads of elected representatives were not about to benefit a dangerous revolutionary party. Since Orlando did not propose to renounce power he had only two choices: take account of the Parliamentary majority and cooperate with Sonnino, or rely on a Parliamentary minority while appealing for extraparliamentary support. Even assuming Serrati had offered the help of the ISP—which was not in the cards—Orlando was not about to ask for it. As in England, in Italy the war had accelerated the emasculation of the moderate Center which alone could have sustained those Wilsonian policies which may have been as close to Orlando's as to Lloyd

[6] *Corriere della Sera,* January 19, 1919, cited in *DR, APS* (February 5, 1919), 297.

George's heart. In early 1919 the choice was not between Wilson and Lenin; it was between cooperation with Sonnino and encouragement of Serrati. Under these circumstances Orlando never hesitated, just as in similar circumstances Lloyd George, Clemenceau, or even Wilson would never have hesitated. Sonnino was his man; rather, Orlando became Sonnino's alter ego.

Part Three

CONTAINMENT

8

German Revolution: Between Washington and Moscow

EVEN IN HER DEFEAT and revolutionary turmoil Germany continued to be the classic *Land der Mitte*. Whatever the internal developments in Eastern Europe and Russia, because of her geographic location Germany could not do without an eastern policy as part of her overall foreign policy. The metamorphosis of the two eastern empires changed the form without changing the substance of Germany's foreign policy objectives in Eastern Europe. Similarly, the wielding of the specter of Bolshevism in Eastern Europe as well as within Germany merely added a new variant to the time-honored diplomatic strategy of exploiting the rivalries of the European powers for Germany's benefit. Perhaps the most significant variant consisted in the intense interplay between the struggle for power within Germany and the exploitation of these rivalries for Germany's national interest. This interaction had been in evidence even during the Bismarckian era; since 1917, however, it had become so intense that it assumed qualitatively new dimensions.

An unsigned memorandum dated November 5, 1918, and entitled "Program for Our Eastern Policy" characterized the agonizing reappraisal under way in the German Foreign Ministry. This memorandum held that until recently Germany's eastern policy had been guided by two principles: maintenance of relations with the Soviet government in order to keep the eastern front from flaring up; and encouragement of the formation of border states to promote "our security and Russia's weakening."

But with the end of hostilities German-Soviet relations were due for a change. The Bolsheviks being fatally weakened at home and abroad, they could be of no further use to Germany. In addition, their propaganda was now "extremely dangerous for us and they compromise us, who are considered their patrons, with the future Russia and with the entire world." Germany simply had to move away from these Bolsheviks; and the best way to do this was to break relations with them as promptly as possible.

With regard to Germany's *Randstaatenpolitik,* however, this position paper recommended modifications rather than a totally new course. Changes were necessary because Germany "no longer had the power to hold effectively the border states" and because both Wilson and the Provisional Government were pledged to a revision of the Treaty of Brest Litovsk.

> But this [commitment] should not prevent us from supporting these border states . . . *as far as possible* politically and *as long as possible* militarily. . . . Should the Entente force us to leave this area, we would have no choice but to evacuate. In that case, however, the Ukraine and the other forces joining her in her opposition to Bolshevism must receive from us whatever means of self-defense we can spare. . . . The same applies to Lithuania and the Baltikum. . . .
>
> In the context of the majority program, Wilson's points, and the Entente's anticipated demands our eastern policy can continue to pursue the decentralization [*i.e.,* decomposition] of Russia with the aid of the nationality principle while at the same time creating for ourselves as far as possible political sympathies and economic opportunities throughout the entire eastern territories [italics mine].

To achieve these broad aims diplomatic relations should be severed and, as far as possible, German troops should be left in all the occupied border territories except in the Caucasus and in Poland, where less direct influence should be applied.[1]

Groener was in complete agreement with this strategy. On November 16 he advised the Eastern Command that "a rapid evacuation of the eastern territories, especially of the Ukraine and the Baltic territories, was not at all in the national and economic interest of Germany." It would be of great economic value if Germany could manage to keep troops in the Ukraine "even after the conclusion of peace." Accordingly, reliable units should be withdrawn only to the extent that they were needed to protect railway lines in Poland and for the Heimatschutz. Groener also authorized the organization of volunteer units in the East.[2]

Throughout the eight months from the Armistice through the Peace Conference the Foreign Ministry stuck to these aims, estimates, and tactics.[3] In terms of material power there was much to fear as well as to expect from the Entente. In addition to having the military power to

[1] GFM 6, 102/54.
[2] Text cited in Emil Barth: *Aus der Werkstatt der deutschen Revolution* (Berlin: A. Hoffmann's Verlag; 1919), 75.
[3] This profile of the Foreign Ministry's evaluation of the Russian problem is based on the following documents: GFM, E 4097H/1:D 924954–64, D 925069–78; GFM 2, 9105/8:H 235124–32, H 235207–12, H 235177–85.

enforce compliance with the Armistice the victors were in a position to supply or to withhold vital foodstuffs, raw materials, and credits; to grant or to deny a reasonable peace; to admit or to exclude Germany from the League of Nations.

As for Soviet Russia, she was militarily weak and overextended. Economically she could offer no immediate help; for the long run Germany could rely on geography and experience to help her resume the economic penetration of Russia in competition with the Allies. Meanwhile, there loomed the serious threat of Soviet propaganda aggravating unrest in Germany.

All things considered, it seemed by far more expedient to pursue an active foreign and military policy in the East than in the West. This eastern focus commended itself for a number of additional reasons: the collapse of the two eastern empires had left a vacuum in an area of comparative logistical disadvantage for the war-weary Allies; the same Allies were anxious for help in keeping Bolshevism out of the rimland; and so were powerful elements in the nascent successor states.

During the Armistice negotiations it became clear that the Allies were as anxious to enlist enemy support for debarring Bolshevism from the rimland as the Germans were anxious to provide it.[4] Article 12 of the Armistice brought welcome Allied sanction for Germany's modified *Randstaatenpolitik* in the area stretching from the Baltic Sea to the Black Sea. Continuing occupation—or delayed evacuation—would keep Bolshevism and Russia out while keeping Germany in.

Not all territories of this area were equally favorable to a continuing German presence. At the southern end of the belt, in the Caucasus, naval power gave the British great leverage. Similarly, at the northern end, in the *Baltikum,* British naval power was expected to enforce a German withdrawal once Soviet Russia was contained there, though these successor Baltic states were considered good prospects for future economic and political penetration.

Even though these two flanking positions were recognized to be of paramount strategic and economic importance, the German Foreign Ministry never doubted that Poland held the key to Eastern Europe. Quite clearly, for as long as Russia was quarantined Poland was bound to develop into France's major stronghold in Eastern Europe. Once firmly established a large Poland would serve a dual anti-German function: in coalition with France Poland would be a serious military counterbalance while simultaneously constituting a barrier to the renewal of German economic and political influence in Russia.

The Allies, in particular the French, could be expected to champion Polish claims on Germany, Lithuania, and the Ukraine in order to raise as powerful as possible an ally in Eastern Europe. In turn, Germany

4 See p. 95 above.

would have to give top priority to keeping Poland down to size, using her remaining power and influence to encourage and support not only Lithuania but also the Ukraine in their nation-building enterprises. In the process of limiting Poland Berlin would thereby acquire two valuable allies.

But why not check Poland by establishing a working relationship with Soviet Russia? It would seem that in the last analysis the Foreign Ministry—under Max von Baden as well as under the Scheidemann administration—decided against such a rapprochement for domestic rather than diplomatic reasons.

A resumption of relations with Soviet Russia would serve the Bolshevik cause in Germany as well as in parts of the rimland: the Moscow regime would gain in prestige; Soviet diplomatic and political agents would find it easier to disseminate their propaganda; it would be difficult to keep German Spartacists and Radek in jail. On the whole the government's campaign against Spartacism might be seriously crippled.

To be sure, Lenin might promise to desist from fomenting the revolution in Central Europe, as he had promised under Article 2 in the Treaty of Brest Litovsk. But what reasons were there for trusting Lenin to keep a promise to Friedrich Ebert that he had broken with the Kaiser, especially since he despised the Majority Socialists with a bitter passion? The German Foreign Ministry was convinced that because the Bolsheviks embraced their immanent principles with religious fervor, they would inexorably export the revolution to all countries and by all means. At this particular juncture, however, Germany was exceptionally vulnerable because of both her geographical proximity to the revolutionary center and her prostrate condition. Moreover, since the Bolsheviks, by their own admission, looked upon Germany as the key to the world revolution, they could be expected to make a particularly determined effort there. In other words, as long as political conditions in Germany remained "in the balance," the political risks of cooperating with Moscow outweighed any possible diplomatic gains.[5]

Once Allied attitudes were taken into account these risks were still greater, since the victors would view any rapprochement with Moscow with great suspicion, if not with overt hostility. They might refuse to negotiate with a government doing business with the regime against which they were mounting a broad-scale intervention; and they would certainly impose a hard rather than a lenient peace. Furthermore, should the blockade be continued, the prospects for short-run stability would be jeopardized while long-run economic reconstruction would be hampered by Germany's exclusion from the Western financial and trading community.

[5] Of course, theoretically the policy of diplomatic cooperation with Moscow and repression of Spartacism at home was possible.

No wonder the domestic as well as the diplomatic cost of cooperation with Soviet Russia appeared altogether exorbitant to the majority parties and the Foreign Ministry. Presently they refused to take up diplomatic relations with Russia, rejected her offers of economic aid, discriminately barred fraternal delegations and newspaper reporters, arrested Radek, denounced the Bolshevik conspiracy, and fought against Russian and indigenous Bolsheviks in the East European rimland.

But before studying these policy strokes it should be emphasized that they were part of a comprehensive diplomatic strategy, outlined by Brockdorff-Rantzau himself at the first cabinet session to deal with foreign policy after the election results were tallied.[6] On this occasion the new Foreign Minister reverted to fundamentals. With stark realism he insisted that for the foreseeable future the foundations of German foreign policy would be extremely shaky, due to economic disorganization, military weakness, and political instability. A nation-state in this spent condition could only fall back on moral suasion, in this instance "on international law and on the moral claims of a numerically consequential people." However, not only was international law ill-defined, but also the German people's moral claims were being gainsaid. Only Wilson and the Allied Socialists could be expected to protest this denial of German rights, but probably to no avail.

But notwithstanding her very limited power capability, Germany had to engage in international politics for both external and internal reasons. Perhaps in these revolutionary times Germany could make a virtue out of necessity: "an effort must be made to convince our enemies that Germany's economic breakdown and political impotence are contrary to their own interests, and that in actual fact we have common interests. The appropriate method to reach this goal is to flaunt the danger of Bolshevism." According to Brockdorff-Rantzau, America and England especially were afraid of Bolshevism in Russia, in Central Europe, and throughout the Western world. With the Allied Governments attaching such great economic and political significance to reparations, they should be made to realize that a prolonged economic crisis would most likely pave the way for Bolshevism in Germany and that a Bolshevik Germany neither would nor could pay reparations.

Granted, in the foreseeable future the Allies did not want German military and naval power to be a threat. However, army contingents

---

[6] GFM 2, 9105/8:H 234798–802. Brockdorff-Rantzau's memo is dated Berlin, January 21, 1919, and carries the title "Next Assignments of German Foreign Policy"; the marginalia reads "my program, tentative, drafted in haste, communicated to departments before reproduction." This analysis will also draw on a memorandum of that same day, likewise drafted by Brockdorff-Rantzau and read by him to General Groener after the conclusion of the plenary meeting of the cabinet. GFM 2, 9105/6:H 233876–80.

were being reduced to such a low point that they would be hard put to maintain internal order, thus also endangering the "political interests of Germany's *Western* enemies." Actually the Allies should have a greater interest in a peaceful and orderly Germany, in a Germany capable and willing to protect herself, than in "an impotent Germany, in a Germany which is the playground for political agitation and for revolutionary unrest."

Having outlined this minimal and torpid role, Brockdorff-Rantzau proceeded to formulate Germany's maximum and activist role in the dawning era of international civil war:

> Above all, however, the Western Powers need a Central European Power which is capable of barring Bolshevism from Western Europe. In case the Western Powers consider establishing a front against Bolshevism along the Rhine [they should realize] that Bolshevism would soon jump over this trench and penetrate into the Entente nations. These nations would be much better protected if this front against Bolshevism were organized along the Vistula and the Memel. Provided order is maintained in Germany, the character of the German people is the [best] guarantee that the spark of radical Bolshevik theory and practice will not reach the West.

In a paragraph that was crossed out (but is clearly legible) the Foreign Minister carried his argument one step further: until such time as Germany regains sufficient military strength "American and British troops would have to cooperate with German troops in the defense of the border against this *Socialismus Asiaticus.*"[7]

Apparently Brockdorff-Rantzau thought that defensive containment could easily strangle the Leninist regime. He proposed to interest the Allies in Germany's cooperation by convincing them that it would be to their common advantage to hurry along the economic recovery of Russia: "it was only natural that yesterday's enemies should cooperate in the restoration of Russia" in order to secure dividends for France, profits for Britain and America, and salaries and wages for Germany. Here were the taproots for the settlement of reparations and war debts.

Just as British and American troops would be needed to man the anti-Bolshevik front, so American capital would be essential for the reconstruction of the German economy. Because of America's recent forced-draft financial and industrial growth, which enabled her to "play the leading role in the world," she in particular would welcome this reconstruction as a means to perpetuate prosperity. By using U.S. capital in the reconstruction of the German economy, Germany would make a start "in bringing America, in her own interest, over to our side."

[7] It is impossible to tell whether this paragraph was crossed out before, during, or after the cabinet meeting.

Brockdorff-Rantzau concluded his exposé with a crisp summary of the steps to be taken in pursuit of an understanding with the Western Powers: offer a "common fight against Bolshevism on the far side of Germany's eastern borders, but only in the form of a defense"; demand "a reasonable and fair peace" as a means of keeping Germany "economically and politically viable"; and propose an agreement for the common economic reconstruction of Russia.

This summary suggests that Brockdorff-Rantzau saw little chance of breaking up the Allied coalition and of Wilson's exercising a moderating influence, now that the Allies could dispense with him and the congressional elections had weakened him. Rather than try to play the victors off against each other Germany would seek to foster and join a community of anti-Bolshevik powers, hoping to extract diplomatic concessions in return for joining an anti-Bolshevik crusade.

The relations and contacts between the Provisional Government in Berlin and the Leninist regime in Moscow developed within this broad diplomatic and political framework. It is hardly surprising, therefore, that quite apart from the Social Democrats' long-standing anti-Bolshevism and anti-Slavism the Provisional Government was likely to be unfavorably disposed to Soviet overtures.

Since Ebert, Scheidemann, and Landsberg were such thoroughbred nationalists and realists they might have checked their passionate anti-Bolshevism temporarily for the purpose of reducing Germany's diplomatic impotence with Soviet Russian material aid. However, whereas Soviet Russia was bursting with ideological energy that threatened to magnify rather than check Germany's diplomatically debilitating domestic disorders, she was unable to match this ideological power with promises of food, raw materials, credits, and military aid.

Lenin, who had no illusions about the Majoritarians, was keenly aware of the importance of supplementing ideological with material aid. By early October, with the revolution in Germany increasingly imminent, he anticipated that Soviet Russia would offer the German revolutionaries wheat and military aid at considerable sacrifice to herself. Lenin urged that the Soviets multiply their efforts to store up grain stocks "to help the German workers, should they be hard pressed in their struggle for emancipation"; and he indicated that whereas heretofore his goal had been "an army of one million men by the spring" under the new circumstances "we [will] need an army of three million."[8]

But the day after the German Revolution, when this policy was implemented and publicized, Soviet Russia reduced her promise to two trainloads of grain—a total of 50 cars, each containing 1,000 prud of

8 V. Lenin: *Collected Works* (New York: International Publishers; 1945), XXIII, 229–30.

wheat or other foodstuff.[9] To be sure, the modest scope of this offer was concealed with the assurance that these trains were ready to roll immediately and with the promise that others would follow. Moreover, in addition to dispatching the two trains to Kovno within a few days, Chicherin prepared to send Grigori Zinoviev to Berlin for the purpose of organizing grain imports from Russia.[1]

Apparently not only the Majoritarians but also Haase, Dittmann, and Barth were skeptical of Soviet Russia's capacity to give more than token aid. As a result, "the paltry two trainloads from Moscow were weighed against the prospects of transatlantic abundance; it would have been quixotic to accept the Soviet pittance at the risk of antagonizing Washington and the western allies."[2] By November 17 the cabinet decided against accepting the offer. Haase advised Moscow that the cabinet was in a position to pass up this "most generous and appreciated offer": the Provisional Government had just approached President Wilson and "there now were prospects of food supplies reaching us from overseas."[3] Whereas until today Wilson's conditional promise of food of November 12 had served the Provisional Government's internal policies, on this occasion it influenced the government's diplomatic response.

Needless to say, this question of whether or not to accept food shipments was subsidiary to the fundamental question as to whether or not Germany ought to resume diplomatic relations with the Soviet government. These relations had been suspended rather than broken just three days before the German Revolution.

In early October 1918 the conservative press had launched a violent campaign against the Soviet Embassy in Berlin. With considerable justification this Embassy was portrayed as a center of subversion from which Joffe, the Ambassador, distributed money, disseminated propaganda, and directed Bolshevik agitators and organizers. At first the Majoritarians denounced these accusations as part of a last-ditch counterrevolutionary stand. But then, as of early November, they joined this attack primarily because now that power was within their reach they were anxious to prevent any aid from flowing to the Sparta-

---

9 See GFM 6, 102/54 for Chicherin's telegram to Haase.
1 Text of Chicherin's long distance conversation with Oskar Cohen on November 12, 1918; of Radek's conversation with Soldiers' Council of Kovno on November 11, 1918; of telegram of German Workers' and Soldiers' Council in Moscow to Councils in Berlin, Kiel, and Munich on November 14, 1918; and of Chicherin's conversation with Haase on November 16, 1918, in GFM 6, 102/54 and 55. See also Günter Rosenfeld: *Sowjetrussland und Deutschland, 1917–1922* (Berlin: Akademie-Verlag; 1960), 144. On November 17, 1918, the *Freiheit* claimed that the two trains were "but a beginning of [Soviet] aid."
2 E. H. Carr: *The Bolshevik Revolution, 1917–1923* (London: Macmillan; 1953), III, 98.
3 Text of Haase's conversation with Rotkegel, spokesman for the Moscow German Workers' and Soldiers' Council, November 17, 1918, in GFM 131.

cists and the left-Independents. As for the Prince Max government, it was not only determined to check the growth of radicalism, but it also sought to impress Wilson and the Allies with Germany's opposition to that variety of revolution against which the Allies themselves were intervening in Russia.

It was on November 4 that a case carried by a Soviet Russian courier broke open "according to plan" on a platform of the Silesian Railway Station in Berlin.[4] The police officers who happened to be near the scene discovered a mass of German-language propaganda broadsheets which they claimed had been printed in and imported from Russia. The Max von Baden government had chosen this stratagem to expose publicly the subversive activities of the Soviet Embassy and to establish a basis for the suspension of diplomatic relations.

On November 5 Solf asked for the mutual withdrawal of all diplomatic personnel until such time as the Soviet government guaranteed not to intervene in Germany's internal affairs and effectively carried out the promised punishment of the assassins who had killed Ambassador Mirbach on July 6, 1918. In the meantime Germany's affairs in Russia would be handled by Hauschild, the Consul General in Moscow, and Breiter, the Consul General in Petrograd.[5] On November 6, at the very moment when the Kiel revolt began to reverberate throughout Germany, Joffe and his staff reluctantly left Berlin for the Russian border.

The *Frankfurter Zeitung* hailed this expulsion with the assertion that while the German people of course contested the Entente's right to prescribe internal reforms for Germany, it resolutely rejected Moscow's much more dangerous propaganda. Without even bothering to discriminate among different varieties of intervention the *Vorwärts* insisted that Germany did not want Russian-like conditions because, in spite of the fact that Russia was a predominantly agricultural nation, under the Bolshevik regime people were starving to death. There could be no doubt of the German proletariat's commitment to Socialism; but it vigorously rejected the Russian variety of "Socialismus Asiaticus." In conclusion the *Vorwärts* charged that whereas the SPD and the USPD wanted an early peace, the Spartacists wanted to continue the war until state and society were in total decomposition.[6]

In Moscow, meanwhile, Lenin realized that the old order in Germany had been forewarned against the revolutionary consequences of total defeat. He immediately pinpointed his Ambassador's expulsion as part of a larger scheme to win favor with the Allies: Germany expelled Joffe "with the idea that by doing them a service they might be more

---

[4] *The Memoirs of Prince Max of Baden* (New York: Scribner's; 1928), II, 289. See also Carr: *Bolshevik Revolution*, III, 94, esp. n. 5.
[5] For the text of this note see Lenin: *Collected Works*, XXIII, 270–2.
[6] *Frankfurter Zeitung* and *Vorwärts*, November 6, 1918.

generous to her; as though to say 'we too are playing the hangman against your enemies, the Bolsheviks'."[7] In fact, Lenin used Joffe's expulsion as evidence for his increasingly frequent warnings that with the end of the war the Soviet regime would be opposed by a formidable united anti-Bolshevik front.

It seems most doubtful, indeed, that Lenin and Chicherin ever really expected the new Provisional Government to call Joffe back to Berlin unconditionally. After all, Scheidemann, as an influential member of Max von Baden's government, had played a major role in his expulsion; and Scheidemann, his SPD colleagues, and the officials of the Foreign Ministry saw no reason to reverse themselves. Moreover, Lenin realized that just as Kerensky had refused to break with the Allies, so Ebert, who was equally determined to strengthen the Allied tie, would not risk a rapprochement with Moscow. Nevertheless, precisely because Lenin was so fearful of complete encirclement he simply had to explore every avenue, however unpromising. In order to recapture the mood and tempo of this new round in German-Soviet relations it should be remembered that whereas the Ebert regime expected to be able to fall back on the Allies, the Soviet regime had no alternate port of call. This threat of complete isolation and encirclement accounts for the fact that at one moment the Bolsheviks seemed to importune the hostile and dangerously efficient Social Democrats while at the next moment they threatened them. Of course Lenin and Chicherin all along calculated that at a minimum their spurned diplomatic overtures would discredit the Majoritarians in the eyes of all genuine revolutionaries.

As of November 10 Chicherin pressed for the resumption of diplomatic relations while the Provisional Government pursued a deliberately noncommittal course.[8] On November 14 Joffe sent Haase a telegram from Borisov in the hope that instead of leaving this border town for Moscow he might return to Berlin. In this telegram he inquired whether diplomatic relations existed between the Provisional Government and Soviet Russia, or whether the former insisted on the same two conditions as the defunct imperial regime. Haase simply replied that diplomatic relations existed—which was technically correct —without referring to the demand that the Soviet Ambassador desist from intervention and that the Soviet government make amends for Mirbach's assassination.

On November 14 two additional telegrams were sent from Moscow and Berlin respectively. From Moscow Chicherin addressed the Workers' and Soldiers' Councils of Berlin, Kiel, and Munich with a list

---

[7] Lenin: *Collected Works*, XXIII, 273, 284.
[8] The following extended discussion of telegrams, radio messages, and teletype conversations between Berlin and Moscow during the weeks following the German Revolution is based on GFM 6, 102/54–8, *passim;* and GFM 131, *passim.*

of complaints: the Soviet government's inquiries were not being answered by the Provisional Government; the wheat shipments were in danger of being held up at Kovno; and Joffe continued to be stuck in Borisov instead of being invited back to Berlin. The wire asked the German Councils to redouble their pressure for prompt cooperation between Moscow and Berlin. Meanwhile Ebert and Haase protested to Chicherin about the irregular manner in which the German Workers' and Soldiers' Council in Moscow, speaking for German war prisoners in Russia, had taken over the German Consulate. In particular they protested the arrest of the German consular personnel and refused to recognize the Moscow Council as their diplomatic agent. In reply Chicherin claimed that he could not interfere with the German Workers' and Soldiers' Council in Moscow, that he refused to do business with the representatives of the Hohenzollerns, and that he was waiting for the readmission of Joffe.

Chicherin sent messages to the Workers' and Soldiers' Councils in Germany urging them to intensify their pressure on the Provisional Government in favor of German-Soviet cooperation. Furthermore, he and Radek capitalized on all those resolutions by German Workers' and Soldiers' Councils which called for a prompt resumption of relations with Moscow. It is also true that on November 11 the Soviet government had sent a fiery and incendiary appeal to the German Councils.

> . . . The Scheidemänner together with the Erzbergers will sell you to capitalism. In the Armistice they will agree with the British and French capitalists that you surrender your arms. Soldiers and sailors, do not surrender your weapons. . . . With these weapons effective power must be seized and a Workers', Soldiers', and Sailors' Government, headed by Liebknecht, must be formed. Do not let yourselves be talked into a National Assembly. . . .[9]

The Majoritarians, the Foreign Ministry, and the Supreme Command pointed to these and similar messages and appeals as irrefutable evidence of the Soviet government's aggressive revolutionary activities and intentions. In fact, they deliberately exaggerated and distorted them for their own political purposes.

The incendiary nature of the appeal of November 11 need not be denied in order to substantiate this charge of exaggeration and distortion. Actually, this violent appeal seems to have been drafted before November 9; and it appears to have been the only one of its kind for the entire month of November. Furthermore, even this blatant call to arms was part of a larger message which reflected the Soviet government's *defensive* rather than offensive concerns.

[9] This message is also cited in *Dokumente und Materialien zur Geschichte der deutschen Arbeiterbewegung*, II, 360.

The struggle for peace and freedom must be combined with the struggle for bread. In the Ukraine, the Don, and the Kuban of Russia there is enough bread for both us and you. For this reason the British Government is racing to reach Southern Russia through the Black Sea in order to help Generals Denikin, Krasnov, and Skoropadsky snatch the workers' bread away. Our Red Army fights courageously against the bands of workers' enemies which are also being supported by your generals and the Government of Scheidemänner. If you want bread, you must act quickly before the British snap it away. The German . . . Councils must immediately issue orders by wireless and through emissaries to the German soldiers in the Ukraine . . . while the Red Army attacks these bands from the North. . . .[1]

Germany's power elite, including the SPD leaders, never conceded—either privately or publicly—that the Leninist regime had legitimate defensive concerns in the face of mounting external intervention. And yet, in Moscow's communications to the Provisional Government and to the Councils, defensive themes overshadowed all others.

By November 14 Chicherin called for diplomatic relations in order to forestall clashes between Russian or local Bolsheviks and German armies in German-occupied Eastern Europe, including German-occupied Russia. The following day Radek advocated German-Russian cooperation in the liquidation of the White Guards—in Poland, Lithuania, Latvia, and the Ukraine—which he claimed were equally dangerous for both revolutions. Moreover, he urged the three Independent members of the cabinet not to permit Germany's military commanders in the eastern territories to carry out their own counterrevolutionary policies. Only toward the end of his telegram did Radek propose to send French, British, and American comrades to agitate among Allied war prisoners in Germany, possibly to stimulate opposition to intervention in Russia among them. As a last resort he warned that should Berlin fail to answer within twenty-four hours "we will use our own ways of contacting German workers and soldiers in the interest of the Russian and German revolutions—which are identical."

But the one and only official long distance conversation provides further evidence that the Soviets were more concerned with defending themselves against external intervention in the Russian Civil War than with offensively carrying or spreading the Bolshevik Revolution to Germany and Western Europe. This was the very revealing conversation of November 16 among Chicherin and Radek at one end of the teletype and Haase at the other.

After declaring that he had tried unsuccessfully to reach Haase for five days Chicherin gravely noted that the lack of regular contacts had already caused serious harm. If the German government immediately

[1] Ibid., II, 361.

had returned Russia's Black Sea fleet and guaranteed the use of the Ukrainian railways, by now the Soviet government would be in a better position to ward off the impending landing on and occupation of the Black Sea coast. Not only was the Ukrainian government ready to welcome Allied naval units in Odessa and Novorossisk, but also the Entente, at the Jassy Conference, was making preparations for a major drive through the Ukraine. In their deliberations at Jassy the Allies and the Whites counted the German troops as partners. And, in fact, the German government was acting as if it had an agreement with the Allies to keep German troops in place until reliable anti-Bolshevik units could relieve them.

According to Chicherin there was still time to do something about this southern front.

> We cannot sit here quietly and wait for the British to organize a counterrevolution in the south which would be aimed not only against us but also against the German Revolution. Even Ebert should be able to understand this, given the logic of his own situation. We cannot wait; the ground has been prepared in the Ukraine. However, if we advance without prior agreement with the Germans, bloody clashes are bound to take place. . . . Your troops should be instructed to receive ours as friends. . . . We cannot leave our friends in the lurch. As a basis for the counterrevolutionary movement the strongholds of the White Guards are of utmost danger to both us and you. . . . [You should] see to the disarmament of the White Guards and [you should] dismiss your commanders in the Ukraine.

Later in this same conversation Chicherin stressed that the situation in the Baltic Sea was even more acute than in the Black Sea, asking Berlin to defer clearing the Baltic Sea of mines in order to retard the British advance. Also, would the Provisional Government sell Russia the German ships anchored at Reval? Should this be impossible, could it issue instructions that the Russian fleet be given a friendly reception in that port? But above all, it was absolutely vital that the defense of Petrograd be organized not in the eastern extremities of the Gulf of Finland but much further to the west.

In this conversation Chicherin seemed primarily concerned with pre-empting Allied and German moves designed to intervene in Russia, to support the Whites in the Civil War, and to contain the Revolution by denying the Soviets control of former Russian territories. Needless to say, should Lenin and Chicherin succeed in this pre-emptive strategy they would not only stabilize the Revolution in Russia but also acquire the necessary strength to intervene in support of revolutionary movements abroad. Nevertheless, at this juncture the Soviet regime was first and foremost set on taking defensive measures against a very real and sizable onslaught.

To be sure, Chicherin also spoke of other matters. He repeated that Moscow was anxious to send its own commissioners to the Russian war prisoners in Germany; he requested the Provisional Government to instruct the Soldiers' Council at Kovno to clear the two food trains; and he announced that the Soviet executive was about to send several "prominent" comrades to Berlin as well as several "French and British agitators to agitate among war prisoners and on the Western front." But since Joffe continued to be stranded at Borisov under "humiliating conditions," Chicherin gave first priority to the Ambassador's immediate return to Berlin. Or did the Provisional Government "take the same position as the defunct German government about the diplomatic break with Russia"? In conclusion Chicherin inquired whether Haase had received his numerous telegrams and radio messages, as an aside warning against the machinations of the "*Geheimräte* and other officials" of the old regime.

Then it was Haase's turn to outline the Provisional Government's position. He sought to create a friendly atmosphere by "deeply regretting" that thus far there had been no contact between them, by acknowledging receipt of Chicherin's telegrams, and by claiming credit for having initiated today's conversation.

> I fully understand your position. [But] I ask you and your friends to consider our internal and external situation. Under no circumstances will our troops want to fight any more. All over the Soldiers' Councils urgently demand a prompt peace. They would oppose whoever caused the Armistice to be broken. . . . The condition of our troops is such that no power can succeed in arousing them for military action. As a result your questions about mines in the Baltic Sea and the sale of ships answer themselves. . . . [Similarly] the proposal to send French and British agitators . . . is rejected out of hand [because] any *such efforts would signify the resumption of hostilities with the Entente and would undermine imports of urgently needed foodstuffs.* . . .

On the other hand, Haase promised to inform the cabinet about the obstruction of the food trains by the Soldiers' Council at Kovno "in order that necessary instructions be issued." He also indicated that the cabinet would make a decision about diplomatic relations as soon as the conditions surrounding the takeover of the general consulates was cleared up. Meanwhile "you of course know my position [and] I shall speak with Joffe this very day."

Instead of Chicherin, it was Radek who countered Haase's well-intentioned but essentially negative statement. As compared to both Chicherin and Haase he was much more direct and forceful without, however, playing the radical revolutionary.

> We fully understand the difficulties of Germany's situation and Comrade Chicherin *has not proposed any common military hostili-*

ties against the Entente to you; he has not even protested against the
German Government disposing of war ships which . . . are ours.
What concerns us is that the revolutionary German Government did
not even consider it necessary to inform us—officially or confidentially—of those Armistice provisions which are aimed against the
workers of Russia. [Since for this information] we have had to rely
on irregularly intercepted radiotelegrams *we request above all communication of those Armistice terms which touch on Russia.*

Chicherin's proposals take account of the German soldiers' war
weariness. All we ask is that the German Government should
instruct the military authorities in the Ukraine and in the occupied
territories not to resist those future military operations which will
not be aimed against the German Army. *If the German troops are in
no condition to fight against the Entente they should be equally
incapable of fighting us.* The German Government only needs to
confidentially impress this on the field commanders and to use
trusted commissioners to make sure that individual commanders
should not display greater belligerency toward us than toward the
Entente. . . .

We now emphatically request that you advise us within 12 hours
whether the German Government is prepared to permit responsible
Polish, Lithuanian, Latvian, and Ukrainian comrades to return to
their native countries and whether it is prepared to instruct the
occupation authorities to promptly break up the headquarters of the
White Guards, to permit the formation of workers' councils and to
deal with these councils concerning the safe withdrawal of German
troops and local administration until such time as this withdrawal is
technically feasible.

We fully understand that this cannot be done overnight. . . . *But
we cannot simply wait until the White Guards attack us from
German-occupied territories or until German soldiers who are completely abandoned to counterrevolutionary officers prepare a blood-
bath for those comrades who believe that the German Revolution
liberated them as well.*

Again, the emphasis fell on the East European rimland: whereas the
Soviet regime desperately sought to dismantle or prevent the establishment of counterrevolutionary strongholds, the Ebert-Solf regime was
equally determined to maintain Germany's outposts. Furthermore, the
policies of both regimes were bound to have important external as well
as internal consequences.

Only at this point did Radek's response turn heavily ideological. In
pressing for Joffe's return to Berlin he indignantly rejected the notion
that it should be contingent on whether or not "we observe the full
ceremonial toward William's servants." Moreover, he requested permission for Rakovsky and Bukharin to travel to Vienna and transit
rights for Soviet couriers to Switzerland. He also asked that he be given
the opportunity to speak with Liebknecht and Rosa Luxemburg.

But even Radek thought of expressing the hope that once Germany met these requests *"the Allies will not cut off your bread."* As for the British and French agitators, he wished to remind Haase that Article Two of the Treaty of Brest Litovsk had prohibited but not prevented the Soviet government from spreading revolutionary propaganda among the Germans. On the other hand, "we cannot force anyone to accept the assistance which we wish to extend to the German, French, and British people, if the German revolutionary government flatly rejects it."

Before signing off Radek expressed his belief that in spite of "all the differences separating the Russian Communist government from the Scheidemann as well as the [Haase] parties," the two could and should cooperate in order to "spare the German soldiers and the [local] populations of the occupied territories grief and misery.", Insisting that "in situations requiring quick and energetic actions" the Bolsheviks were not in the habit of waiting, Radek warned that if the German government persisted in its evasion "we will be forced to do on our own initiative and responsibility whatever the situation demands."

Radek's revolutionary forays failed to intimidate Haase, who hastened to remind his interlocutors that he was not in charge of the Foreign Ministry and that he was only one of a six-member executive. He promised that on the basis of this conversation he would immediately raise all these issues with his colleagues and that in these deliberations he would be guided by his "long-standing and fundamental principles." He revealed that even though the Independents had been in the government for only five days, diplomatic relations with Russia and the evacuation of the occupied territories had been discussed "immediately and repeatedly." Meanwhile "I recommend that you personally intervene" to ease the conditions of the staff of the Consulate General in Moscow and that "you promptly wire information" about the personnel of the Consulate General in Petrograd.

Significantly Chicherin closed this unique exchange between two equally illegitimate governments with the assurance that the personnel of both consulates was safe and that in response to Berlin's telegram of November 14 his government had decided to transport this personnel to Germany. In fact, that same day, either before or after this long-distance conversation, four telegrams[2] advised Berlin that preparations for the departure of this diplomatic personnel were in full swing and that therefore the road should be clear for Joffe's return as well as for the appointment of a German Ambassador to Moscow.

Now the scene shifted back to Berlin, where Haase immediately reported his conversation to the cabinet. Eventually, late in the afternoon of November 18, the six Volksbeauftragten discussed the state of German-Soviet relations in the light of Germany's relations with the

2 Rotkegel to Haase, Chicherin to Kautsky, Chicherin to Haase, Chicherin to Solf.

Allies and of domestic developments. Eduard David, Karl Kautsky, and Rudolf Nadolny were present and took part in the discussion.[3]

> *Haase* proposed that [we] proceed in a dilatory fashion. *Reports from* the embassies in the Hague, Berne, and Stockholm were introduced. According to these reports the Entente is prepared to make concessions with regard to peace terms and food supplies to the present bourgeois-socialist republic provided and as long as the government keeps its present composition under Ebert's leadership; but in case of growing Bolshevism she would immediately intervene by every means. Even the return of Joffe would be enough to change the outlook for peace. *Landsberg and Nadolny* called attention to the wireless messages in which the Soviet government abuses the German government and incites the workers to overthrow it,[4] and to other wireless messages which celebrate the solidarity of the German Revolution and the Russian Soviet Republic. *Kautsky* agreed with Haase: the decision should be postponed. The Soviet government would not survive much longer; it would be finished in a few weeks . . . [therefore one] should negotiate and gain time. Should Joffe, after 8 or 14 days, accept the condition not to carry out agitation among British and French prisoners of war [in Germany], his return might then perhaps be possible. *Haase* requested that news dispatches and embassy reports should be kept strictly apart. Many of the press reports claim to emanate from American or authoritative sources; however, only two statements by American representatives in Berne, one by the British Ambassador in the Hague, and one by the British Ambassador in Finland are well-founded. *Barth* reported that Liebknecht and Rosa Luxembourg also agreed with a dilatory treatment. Even the left-dissident circles must yield to unalterable facts. In Germany no one would consider using terroristic acts or Bolshevik methods as long as the counter-revolutionaries do not launch a violent offensive. It was entirely up to the counterrevolution whether the Revolution would proceed peacefully or by terror. Adolf Müller had reported that the Entente had positively informed Switzerland that if Switzerland did not remove the Bolsheviks, the Entente would clean up. The same held true for Denmark. . . . *Haase:* should it be the goal of anti-Bolshevik activity to unite all states for a common fight against the Socialist Revolution, we could not lend ourselves to this. (*David:* very true!) The French and British Socialists were also unanimously opposed to the dispatch of troops to Russia. It would be irresponsible to sacrifice even one drop of German blood for this. *Ebert* reported that a Danish comrade had urgently warned him that the

---

[3] *Protokolle des Rats der Volksbeauftragten,* meeting of November 18, 1918, 5:30 p.m. Cf. Philipp Scheidemann: *Der Zusammenbruch* (Berlin: Verlag für Sozialwissenschaft; 1921), 224–5; Friedrich Ebert: *Schriften, Aufzeichnungen, Reden* (Dresden: Reissner Verlag; 1926), 103–4; Barth: *Aus der Werkstatt,* 68–75.

[4] This was a reference to the Soviet appeal of November 11, 1918, cited p. 239 above, and which was published in the *Rote Fahne* on November 18, 1918, the day of this cabinet meeting.

Bolsheviks were also about to be expelled from Denmark. Their fall was imminent. In Ebert's judgment the Government's principal task was to conclude peace. Whatever interfered with peace had to be set aside. *Nadolny* warned that the declaration of sympathy for Russia adopted by the Workers' and Soldiers' Councils at the Busch Circus was being used against [the Government]; the Executive Committee [of the Councils] also had to declare itself on foreign affairs. *Barth:* I kept this Executive Committee informed of our policy on Russian affairs. Thus far this policy has been approved without opposition. *Kautsky:* We want to live in peace and friendship with the entire world, including the Russian Republic. No one could take offense with this point of view.

Before adjourning, this meeting unanimously resolved to send a telegram to Moscow, the intent of which could only have been to implement a "dilatory" policy. This telegram,[5] sent on November 21 and signed by Solf and Kautsky, declared that the Provisional Government had carefully considered the questions raised in the conversation with Haase and in various telegrams. At the outset it wanted to protest against the appeal of November 11 which interfered in Germany's internal affairs. Since this appeal called for the establishment of another government, would Moscow please indicate whether or not it recognized the present government? In any case, preconditions for the re-establishment of diplomatic relations were unequivocal recognition of the Provisional Government in Berlin and a pledge by the Soviet government to refrain "from exerting influence on the German people to set up another government." Moreover, Berlin required a clarification about the removal of the consulates general as well as the immediate return of the consular personnel.

Clearly, the cabinet would have set the same conditions even if the Soviet appeal of November 11 had never been issued. This appeal merely provided a convenient occasion for shifting the Berlin-Moscow dialogue entirely away from substantive issues to questions of diplomatic method and form. Above all, the telegram avoided any reference to the occupied territories; and Haase had not brought these to the fore in the cabinet session—in spite of the fact that in late September even the SPD had committed itself to the immediate evacuation of the occupied territories.[6] Obviously, Solf and Nadolny had every interest in not stirring up an international or domestic debate about the rimland. Likewise, the Eastern Command was urgently pressing the government not to have any dealings whatever with Moscow. Though fearful that Soviet propaganda would cause serious unrest in the occupied territories, it considered this unrest to "be a decidedly lesser

[5] For the full text see Scheidemann: *Der Zusammenbruch,* 225–7.
[6] *Protokoll der gemeinsamen Sitzung des Parteiausschusses und der Reichstagsfraktion,* September 23, 1918 (unpublished manuscript in International Institute for Social History, Amsterdam), 37.

evil than taking the Bolshevik bait." Both the Tenth Army and the units around Kiev were prepared to use every means to counteract Bolshevik propaganda; even the Soldiers' Councils could be trusted to cooperate for this purpose.[7]

Whereas the Foreign Ministry and the Army kept their expert eyes on the eastern territories, the Volksbeauftragten focused their political attention on Allied reactions. According to Scheidemann, "closer relations, let alone an alliance [with Russia], were unthinkable [because] they would have made our position . . . untenable vis-à-vis the Entente." In full accord with its Independent members the Provisional Government avoided "any relations which in any way would have been misconstrued or could have aroused suspicion." No question of principle was ever involved: "this Russian policy suited our needs and it was therefore the only correct one."[8]

Even so, Lenin and Chicherin had to keep trying. Before receiving Berlin's telegram Chicherin, anxious to oblige Haase, advised Solf that Hauschild and Breiter, together with their consular staffs, were on their way to the border. Two days later, on November 23, the exchange took place there: Joffe and his party returned to Moscow while the German diplomatic contingent crossed over to the German side, thus fulfilling one of Berlin's two preconditions.

Then, on November 26, Chicherin sought to remove the last remaining hurdle. He assured Solf—not Haase, Oscar Cohn, the Councils, or Liebknecht—"that his repeated proposals to reestablish diplomatic relations presumed recognition." The Russian government approved of the principle that the Berlin government was based on the Workers' and Soldiers' Councils.[9] Moreover, whatever it might think of the membership of the Provisional Government, the Soviet government always recognized "existing conditions as well as the government which effectively exercised power." In brief, "the recognition of the present German government was not in question." In so far as influencing public opinion was concerned, Chicherin thought it preferable that the two governments not place any restrictions on each other. Nevertheless, if such a mutual self-denial was "an essential prerequisite for the establishment of normal relations" the Russian government was "prepared to accept even this condition." What if the German government had taken this "bait"? No doubt the course of the Russian Civil War, the intervention, and the German Revolution would have determined whether or not it was in Lenin's interest to keep such a promise. In any

---

[7] Obost I to Foreign Ministry, November 16, 1918, in GFM 131.

[8] Scheidemann: *Der Zusammenbruch,* 227.

[9] In their telegram Solf and Kautsky claimed to speak for "the German People's Government in agreement with the Executive Committee of the German Workers' and Soldiers' Councils." Until the Constituent National Assembly met in Weimar in February 1919, these Councils claimed to be the source of the Provisional Government's legitimacy.

event, apparently the German government never responded to Chicherin's latest dispatch.

At this very moment Chicherin's direct appeals to German workers to apply pressure for the reestablishment of relations elicited a concrete response. On November 29 the Executive Committee of the Workers' and Soldiers' Councils of Greater Berlin, which was organizing the All-German Congress of Councils for December 16, voted to ask the Provisional Government to allow a Soviet delegation to attend this Congress. Not unexpectedly the government was equally if not more opposed to internal than to external pressure.

The Foreign Ministry hastened to sound out the Soldiers' Councils on the eastern front, knowing full well that these Councils were led by officers and soldiers loyal to Germany's mission in the East. As expected, on December 2 Ambassador Berchem reported from Kiev that the local Soldiers' Council would go on record against the admission of a Soviet delegation. The Executive Committee of the Central Council of the eastern front at Kovno had already done so.

> The Eastern Armies energetically fight against Bolshevism. . . . Our soldiers who are in position along the Great Russian front are being fallen upon and attacked by Bolshevik hordes and often suffer bitter losses. What would be the justification for allowing the representation in Berlin of that Government which we consider the greatest threat for Germany's Socialist future? . . . [We have] decided to issue strict orders to all the military commands as well as to all Soldiers' Councils of the entire Eastern front to refuse transit to the Russian delegation . . . and ask that you thoroughly justify this attitude with the anti-Bolshevik tendencies of the Eastern Armies with which you are familiar. In view of the overall situation in Berlin the agitators from Moscow represent a tremendous danger in spite of their small number.

Judging by these instantaneous and clear-cut reactions Obost could safely rely on these Councils to fight the battle against Bolshevism without too much prompting from on high.

It was a high-powered Soviet delegation which reached the frontier-post of Dvinsk on December 7, in that it was led by Bukharin, Joffe, Radek, and Rakovsky. The Soviet leaders must have had altogether unrealistic estimates of the mood and politics of the Soldiers' Councils on the eastern front. Furthermore, did they really expect the Provisional Government to reverse itself under external Soviet and internal radical pressure and admit, in addition to Joffe, three prominent and seasoned revolutionary leaders?

Anyway, since the delegation, instead of crossing the border surreptitiously, presented itself to the Dvinsk Soldiers' Council, this Council dutifully wired Berlin for instructions. This wire reached the cabinet not only after the Foreign Ministry and Army had pressed their views but also in the wake of the first bloody street fighting in the German capital. Over Barth's opposition the cabinet instructed both Dvinsk and Kovno not to admit the delegation: the Soviet representatives should be politely asked to "desist from entering on account of the situation in Germany."[1] By December 12 the Soviet delegates started their return trip to Moscow via Minsk.

Only Radek left the Russian party at Minsk and clandestinely made his way to Berlin. However, he did not reach the German capital until shortly after the conclusion of the All-German Congress of Councils. This congress decisively rejected a resolution criticizing the government for turning back the Soviet delegation and calling for the prompt establishment of friendly relations with revolutionary Russia; instead, it trusted the government to use its own best judgment with regard to German-Soviet relations.[2]

Radek, for his part, attended the founding congress of the Communist Party of Germany which met in Berlin from December 30 through January 1. By then the German capital had experienced its second and more serious wave of street fighting, which precipitated the resignation of the Independents from the government. Also, the Foreign Ministry was warning the new all-SPD government about the dangers of leaving Radek at large. In a rather imperious memorandum the Foreign Ministry asserted that since he was Russia's propaganda chief, Radek had to be considered an official of the Soviet government; besides, he was in Germany without visa or permission. The memo repeated the unsubstantiated charge, first formulated by Solf on December 21, that Radek's declared program was to unleash civil war in Germany and "to combine with the German workers to fight the Entente along the Rhine, at the latest this coming spring." In addition to threatening internal peace Radek was about "to ensnare [Germany] in renewed entanglements with the Entente which in any case will assume that Radek's visit could not take place without the government's knowledge and permission." Since this "was a matter of far-reaching political importance" the Foreign Ministry could not act on its own. But it counseled the cabinet to order the immediate arrest and deportation of Radek, to establish a reliable border control along Germany's eastern frontier, and to prevail on the press to protest clearly and violently the presence of Bolshevik representatives. Four days later, on January 3, 1919, Erzberger asked General Detlev von Winterfeldt to find out whether the "Entente would

---

[1] *Protokolle des Rats der Volksbeauftragten,* meeting of December 9, 1918, a.m. On December 11, 1918, the *Vorwärts* claimed that the admission would have seriously threatened "internal conditions and above all the conclusion of peace."

[2] *Allgemeiner Kongress der Arbeiter-und-Soldatenräte Deutschlands, am 16. bis 21. Dezember 1918: Stenographische Berichte* (Berlin 1918), 25, 183.

welcome Radek's and Joffe's surrender [to the Allies], possibly at Spa."[3]

All this time, in spite of continually clearer indications that neither official nor unofficial relations could be established, Chicherin continued to badger Solf, Haase, and the Councils with telegrams assailing German activities in the occupied territories. First, he warned of German-Russian clashes; then, as the Red Army advanced, he reported bloody incidents in Reval, Pskov, Minsk, Gomel, and Kiev. Above all, he urgently protested the cooperation of German units with White Guards in the Baltikum and with White Guards and Petlyura in the Ukraine. In those places where German units were forced to retreat they actually carried off with them non-German grain inventories, rolling stock, and hospital equipment; in some places they wantonly destroyed communication and transportation equipment.

No doubt Chicherin vastly exaggerated pro-Bolshevik sentiment and support in the occupied territories. On the other hand, he rightly assumed that there was no third alternative: these territories would be either a revolutionary or counterrevolutionary stronghold in the protracting civil war and the soaring intervention. His admonition that the Reichswehr's military and political activities in the rimland would also harm the German Revolution was prescient; his diplomatic remonstrance that these activities would have damaging consequences for German-Russian relations was pathetically ineffective. While Berlin was resigned to settling with the Entente for the status quo in the West, in the East Germany was determined to use every means to save what could be saved. Since domestic pressures were not forcing a change in Germany's eastern policy, only Allied pressure or the Red Army could do so.

However, Berlin tried to get these opposing forces to cancel out each other. This became evident when the Red Army occupied Narva and Pskov in late November; Minsk in mid-December; and Riga, Mitau and Kharkov in early January. Each Soviet advance galvanized the Allies into reminding the Germans of Article 12 in the Armistice.

On December 9 and in nine subsequent notes the Allies maintained that under this article Germany had an obligation to keep order—*i.e.*, to fight the Bolsheviks—in German-occupied Russian territories and that German troops could not withdraw without Allied permission. Repeatedly these representations to the German Armistice Commission were combined with the accusation that Germany was

---

[3] See GFM 6, 38, for Solf's open broadcast addressed to the Soviet government; for Chicherin's reply to this broadcast; for the Foreign Ministry's memorandum of December 31, 1918; and for Haniel's wire advising the Foreign Ministry of Erzberger's request. For Radek's subsequent arrest and Allied interest in it see pp. 506–8 below.

actually encouraging the expansion of Bolshevism in the Baltic provinces and in the Ukraine.[4]

The Germans firmly rejected this interpretation. They emphasized that whereas the Allies had originally called for the immediate evacuation of these territories, it was the German delegation at Compiègne which had suggested that German troops mount the guard temporarily. "We were authorized to do this. However, Germany did not thereby incur an obligation toward the Allies to maintain peace and order." In successive notes of December 10 and January 9 Von Winterfeldt explained that the Allies had only lately shifted to the view that "German troops had to remain in the East and had to participate in the fight against the Bolsheviks." The German Supreme Command simply could not share this view.

Germany had volunteered to perform this service, and she could perform it only to a degree commensurate with her own power and resources. There were a host of reasons for the retreats in the Crimea, Finland, the Baltic provinces, and the Ukraine: the army was exhausted; the soldiers on the eastern front were of advanced age and were war weary; there was a shortage of competent officers; certain units refused to fight against the Bolsheviks; and Polish activities in Posen called for a redeployment of German forces.

Once the Foreign Ministry and the Army had evidence that the Allies were seriously worried about Bolshevism in Eastern Europe, they had every interest in exaggerating Germany's military weakness there. Accordingly, Foch was advised that "the eastern armies no longer constituted an adequate defense" for these territories. At best volunteers might be enlisted not to prevent but to slow down the retreat before the mounting pressure of the Red Army. However, should the Allies be interested in protecting this rimland, they themselves would have to be more helpful. Specifically, German troops at Odessa should not have to surrender weapons, ammunition, and provisons if they were expected to put up a good fight in the Ukraine. Moreover, the Allies should see to it that the Poles check their designs on German, Lithuanian, and Ukrainian territories. Meanwhile, just in case, on January 14 Erzberger agreed with the Supreme Command that "should the Allies ask for the establishment of a common front against Bolshevism I could sign such an agreement."[5]

On the eve of the opening of the Paris Peace Conference in mid-January 1919 German-Soviet relations were at a complete impasse.

[4] GFM 2, 4069/5:D920621–3, 4069/4:D919760–1. See also *Vorwärts*, December 31, 1918; and *le Temps*, January 13, 1919.

[5] GFM 2, 4069/3:D919027–9, E4097H/1:924943–52; *Protokolle des Rats der Volksbeauftragten*, meeting of December 27, 1918, 10:45 a.m.; *FR, P.C.,1919*, II, 65; *Rote Fahne*, January 3 and 4, 1919; Matthias Erzberger: *Erlebnisse im Weltkrieg* (Stuttgart/Berlin: Deutsche Verlagsanstalt; 1920), 350.

Lenin and Chicherin were fast abandoning whatever little hope they may have had about internal pressures—not necessarily a revolution—in Germany causing a favorable change in Berlin's policy in Eastern Europe. On the other hand, Ebert and Brockdorff-Rantzau prepared to continue their policy of maintaining Germany's hold on large parts of Eastern Europe and of securing other Allied concessions by fighting Bolshevism in the East and at home while at the same time intimidating the Entente with an exaggerated Bolshevik specter.

In early 1918 Otto Bauer had registered a protest about the anti-Bolshevism of Central European Socialists which was still valid a year later. In a moving letter to Kautsky he had maintained that since the European proletariat had failed to help the Bolsheviks, no outsider had the right to ask Lenin and Trotsky to sacrifice their revolution to other interests. They had no alternative but to defend themselves, if necessary even by dictatorial means. Meanwhile European Socialists had the responsibility at least to take a sympathetic attitude toward the Russian Bolsheviks. In Bauer's judgment the prevailing hostility to the Soviet regime among Central European Socialists stemmed from an "exclusive concern with foreign [*i.e.,* Allied] reactions, an expeditious peace, and the content of the peace treaty . . . without regard for the internal consequences of this policy." Socialist leaders could hardly hope to fire the revolutionary ardor of the workers if through their anti-Soviet policy they *"machen ihnen die Revolution mies."*[6]

[6] Otto Bauer to Karl Kautsky, January 4, 1918, in Kautsky Papers (in International Institute for Social History, Amsterdam), 503.

9

The Allies and the German Revolution

EVEN THOUGH a revolutionary era was waning when Europe's statesmen set about making and keeping the post-Napoleonic peace, they remained sensitive to the interconnection of stability in international and domestic affairs. The victors feared that a punitive peace would weaken the returning king in favor of extremists of either the ultra-royalist Right or the revolutionary Left in France, while also complicating the transition from war to peace in the Allied nations. By granting their beaten foe a moderate peace they hoped to help Louis XVIII complete the legitimate and conservative restoration which they considered an essential prerequisite for European tranquillity and security. Not only the new balance of international power but also the victors' conservative domestic equilibrium required that France be admitted to the Vienna Congress, that she be given a conciliatory peace, and that she be integrated into the Concert of Powers.[1]

Similar considerations preyed on the minds of most Allied statesmen and their advisers at the end of the Great War. But whereas compared to their predecessors of a century ago they had a considerably more sophisticated, reasoned, and systematic insight into the relationship of international and domestic politics, they soon discovered that a policy of twofold restoration was infinitely harder to implement in 1918–19 than in 1814–15. In 1918–19 the defeat of the Central Powers coincided with the opening rather than the closing of an era of turmoil and violence: revolutionaries and counterrevolutionaries were preparing for battle; the foundations of the existing order were badly shaken, especially in the defeated nations; and excitable electorates, meddlesome mass media, and the interdependence of national economies confounded the search for internal as well as international quietude.

[1] See H. G. Schenk: *The Aftermath of the Napoleonic Wars* (London: Kegan Paul; 1947).

This turbulent atmosphere and environment conspicuously affected Allied reactions to the German Revolution. Even those who refused to be alarmed by the mounting chaos in Central Europe acknowledged that the course of events in Germany would significantly influence both the short- and the long-run developments throughout the Continent. In 1814–15 the victors had helped consolidate the Bourbon Restoration in defeated France in pursuit of a new balance of power and as a prophylaxis against the recurrence of an abated revolutionary fever; in 1918–19 the Anglo-Americans supported and the French tolerated the Ebert regime first and foremost as a hedge against the rising ecumenical Bolshevik Revolution in Germany, in Eastern Europe, and in Russia. From the pre-Armistice negotiations through the opening of the Peace Conference this concern for containing the Revolution east of the Rhine tended to take precedence over the settlement of diplomatic scores.[2]

How did the Allied and Associated Powers go about keeping an up-to-date fever chart of German developments? What were their diagnoses of the causes and the nature of Spartacism? How did they propose to strengthen Ebert vis-à-vis Liebknecht?

To stay abreast of latest developments in Central Europe both the foreign offices and the military commands prepared daily and weekly reports based on information gleaned from the Allied, neutral, and enemy press and from regular agents in enemy and neutral countries. Moreover, Allied embassies and consulates in Holland, Switzerland, and the three Scandinavian countries filed regular dispatches based on information provided by the neutral governments as well as by regular and special German agents. Equally important intelligence came from the delegations to the Permanent Armistice Commission, from special civilian and military agents sent into enemy territories, and from enterprising newspaper correspondents.

As expected, these reports were not without bias. The officials who drafted them shared an all-pervasive anti-Spartacist consensus, disagreeing only about the nature and seriousness of the Spartacist threat and the best way to fight it. Those who were most agitated about Bolshevism in Germany and elsewhere were particularly prone to credit every alarmist story, whatever its source, to recommend compliance with the supplications of the Provisional Governments, and to minimize the political price paid by Ebert for the support of the armed forces, the bureaucracy, the corporate elite, and those in the occupied eastern territories who were determined to maintain Germany's presence there.

Recent events in Russia continued to be the touchstone for the study of the German scene. On November 12 William Bullitt noted that Liebknecht and Mehring aspired "to play the same role that Lenin and

[2] For the pre-Armistice negotiations see Ch. 2 above.

Trotsky had played in Russia, and were counting on the shortage of food, the disorganization of transport, and disorderly demobilization to throw the country into chaos and to bring about the dictatorship of the proletariat which they desired."[3] Within two weeks Bullitt developed this analogy at considerably greater length.

> The parallel between the course of the Revolution in Germany and the course of the Revolution in Russia is obvious. As the Government of Prince Lvov represented the progressive bourgeoisie of Russia, so the Government of Prince Max represented the progressive bourgeoisie of Germany. As Kerensky represented the moderate democratic socialists of Russia, so Ebert represents the moderate democratic socialists of Germany. As Lenin represents the anti-democratic proletarian dictatorship in Russia, so Liebknecht represents the anti-democratic proletarian dictatorship in Germany. Kerensky fell and Lenin succeeded him, partly, to be sure, because of Kerensky's own mistakes, but partly because the Allies and the United States did not take his appeals for material and spiritual aid at anything like their face value.[4]

Possibly under the influence of Bullitt another State Department analyst concluded that the issue was "whether the proletariat would be guided by the more moderate Socialists or would follow the path indicated by the Russian Bolsheviki and carry through a complete and violent social revolution."[5] The American Section of the Permanent Armistice Commission supported this analogic diagnosis with a report that German General Staff officers "had described in some detail the development of the present political and military crisis in Germany and its similarity and relationship with the breakup of the Russian Empire."[6]

The American observers, however, recognized that the Russian and German situations were not identical. Among the dissimilarities was the unwavering loyalty of the Reichswehr to the Provisional Government. According to the State Department, "the world and Germany were fortunate in that Hindenburg had shown himself loyal to the duty of . . . preserving [his soldiers'] discipline in time of revolution as in the day of battle." Whereas the soldiers had "favored the revolution actively" they were now opposing the establishment of a Spartacist regime by undermining the Soldiers' and Workers' Councils. These estimates were confirmed by Major General Rhodes who reported that in spite of internal difficulties the Germans would succeed in repatriating their

[3] Daily Report on the Central Powers, No. 10, November 12, 1918, in House Papers, 26:101.
[4] For the full text of Bullitt's memorandum of November 25, 1918, see *F.R.,P.C.,1919*, II, 98–101.
[5] Department of State, Weekly Report on Matters Relating to the Central Powers, November 16, 1918, in House Papers, 26:113.
[6] Major General C. D. Rhodes, Chief, American Section of the P.A.C., to Commanding General, A.E.F., November 19, 1918, in House Papers, 26:70a.

armies in an orderly fashion and that therefore "the extremity of total anarchy . . . does not appear imminent."[7]

Eventually *The New Republic* provided a summary contrast of German and Russian conditions which is likely to have coincided with official estimates. As compared to Russia, Germany was a "small, compact country," with an "older civilization" and with "firmer traditions." Moreover, being industrially advanced, Germany had "a more complex and integrated national economy, . . . more cities, and . . . a more elastic and effective system of communication both for goods and ideas." As for the German people, they lived closer together; spoke the same language; were of one race; were more disciplined as well as better trained in self-government; and were more nationally self-conscious. "Germany, in short, was a more highly unified, integrated, capitalized, industrialized, intelligent, and disciplined community than Russia and was less easily thrown out of gear."

In *The New Republic's* judgment all "these forces of cohesion" favored the Provisional Government whose primary interest was not social revolution but the preservation of national unity, to be achieved by providing food, employment, and a lenient peace. But Ebert could not succeed without Allied help, since the decisive "factors of food, work and peace . . . were partly within Allied control." With Russia under Bolshevik control and with Eastern Europe "on the verge of famine" the Allies could not afford the loss of "pivotal" Germany.[8]

This appeal for Allied support came from many quarters. Major General Rhodes recommended that even though the Armistice should be strictly enforced, the Allies should stop short of the point where "further pressure might bring about total disruption of [Germany's] political system, and hence would contribute to the state of Anarchy which we as well as Germany are anxious to avoid." By December 3 the Allied Armistice Commissioners informed their German counterparts that since it was not desirable to "leave large cities without sufficient troops for police purposes, and in contemplation of the fact that no German troops may remain in evacuated territory beyond the dates laid down by the Armistice Agreement, the commands of the Allied Armies have received orders to take the necessary measures to bring about the required occupation of important centers for the maintenance of order, on receipt of a specific request from the German Command which is opposite them. Also that with respect to the city of Cologne, in regard to which a definite request for Allied troops had been made, the British Army would immediately take the necessary steps to insure the maintenance of order in that city."[9]

[7] Memoranda by Department of State and report from Major General Rhodes in House Papers, 26:105, 26:113, and 26:70a.
[8] *The New Republic,* December 21, 1918, 213–14.
[9] Major General Rhodes to Commanding General, A.E.F., November 24 and December 3, 1918, House Papers, 26:70a, 26:70c.

This notification was in response to repeated German representations at Spa and elsewhere. Again and again enemy spokesmen claimed that by enforcing their tight timetable for evacuation and for surrender of transport material the Allies were endangering the orderly return of the German armies, the morale of all law enforcement agencies, and the delivery of food supplies to urban centers. Given the close economic tie between the left bank of the Rhine and the rest of Germany modifications were required, otherwise the country would "inevitably advance toward more or less Bolshevik conditions." Should there be no alleviations, "all efforts of Germany to oppose anarchy, effect orderly demobilization, and insure the feeding of the population would prove unavailing"; in the near future Bolshevik conditions would develop which would "find their reaction in the adjoining Entente and neutral countries." Solf protested that in violation of Wilson's promises, this Armistice was "not a bridge leading to peace but the prosecution of war by other means" which would deliver Germany to "anarchy and chaos."[1]

In addition to these requests not to construe the Armistice too rigidly, the Allies were inundated with appeals and recommendations for economic and political aid designed to help stem the rising tide of Spartacism. On November 14 the U. S. Embassy in Switzerland recommended that the "Entente inform Germany that peace will be signed only with representatives of a Constituent Assembly." On November 20 the British Chargé in Washington advised Lansing that Solf wished the Entente Powers to let it be known that they would not tolerate Bolshevism in Germany, even if this meant resuming hostilities. The following day the U. S. Vice-Consul in Zurich learned "from a most reliable source in Berlin" that the German government would welcome a threatening Allied demand for an end of all Spartacist activities, for a "binding declaration" promising a constituent assembly, and for prompt elections. That same day Ulysses Grant-Smith, the U. S. Chargé in Denmark, relayed the advice of a reliable neutral diplomat in Berlin that "the most important thing the Entente can do is of course to send food . . . ; another very important thing would be that President Wilson puts it as clearly as possible before the German nation that he wants general elections." Grant-Smith endorsed both suggestions, insisting that the "forces of real democracy" would benefit from an early showdown.

On November 23, Grant-Smith cabled his impressions of a conversation with two German emissaries and a neutral diplomat. Again the Allies were asked to make a conditional promise of food relief and to come out for a constituent assembly, being careful, however, not to exclude "a socialist republic democratically based." In both cables Grant-Smith stressed that of all the Allied leaders the President's

[1] *The Times* (London), November 19, 1918; and *F.R.,P.C.,1919*, II, 30–1, 40–4.

influence alone would carry weight. Meanwhile, the two German emissaries also urged the Allies to send agents to investigate conditions first-hand.

Within three days the U. S. Chargé in Copenhagen—where Brockdorff-Rantzau was still stationed—wired that in a confidential talk with a reliable reporter Scheidemann had declared that "opposition to the Constituent Assembly—[by which] the Government must stand or fall—would disappear if Wilson were to say that peace could be made only with the Constituent Assembly or Government supported by it"; and that the Allies should "announce loudly that food was coming to a democratic Germany, followed quickly by at least a few shiploads," while also trying to "delay the fulfillment of the Armistice terms especially regarding the delivery of the railroad equipment so that it can be used in transporting coal and food."[2]

This regular flow of indirect interpellations conditioned Washington in particular to heed the direct appeals by Ebert and Solf. On November 12 Ebert asked Wilson to promise foodstuffs on condition that the German government maintain order and distribute the aid equitably.[3] Bullitt promptly endorsed this request with the additional report that according to one of the Chancellor's agents Ebert believed that unless he could announce "in the immediate future a reassuring statement regarding food supply, the present government . . . would be overthrown and anarchy would prevail."[4] No sooner had Washington obliged with a promise of food[5] than Solf returned to the charge: since only timely relief could save "our Fatherland" from famine and anarchy, he adjured Wilson to send Hoover to meet with German plenipotentiaries at The Hague and to receive a German commission in America, while also asking the Allies to send a mission to Berlin "to establish the facts."[6]

By November 25 Bullitt urgently advised Lansing that during the past week Germany "had moved along the road to Bolshevism" with great speed: Spartacism was particularly strong in Prussia and the major seaports; the Spartacists were reported to be in control of Kiel, Bremen, and Düsseldorf; in Berlin Liebknecht's meetings were becoming increasingly popular; and the militant Executive Committee of the Workers' and Soldiers' Councils was opposed to an early summons of a Constituent Assembly. Moreover, Russian Bolsheviks were supplying Liebknecht—"who on November 21 formally announced that he was a Bolshevik"—with "unlimited funds and materials for the dissemination

[2] F.R.,P.C.,1919, II, 28–30, 94–5, 98–8, 103, 107–8, 692, 640–1.
[3] For a discussion from the German side of Ebert's request see pp. 97–8 above.
[4] Daily Report on the Central Powers, No. 10, November 12, 1918, in House Papers, 26:101.
[5] See p. 97 above.
[6] F.R.,P.C.,1919, II, 640–1; and National Archives, Document 862.00/315.

of propaganda." Unless Ebert received prompt economic as well as political support he would be swept away by a Liebknecht-Mehring dictatorship.

> . . . There is need for amelioration of certain conditions of the armistice, there is need for immediate supervision by Mr. Hoover of food distribution, and there is also need for the right word at the right time from President Wilson. In order that the right word may be said at the right time it is necessary to establish at once the closest unofficial relations with the Ebert Government.
>
> The gravity of the situation cannot be overemphasized. Unless we support the Ebert Government a little more strongly than the Russian Bolsheviki are supporting the Spartacus group, Germany will become Bolshevist. Austria and Hungary will follow Germany's example. And the remainder of Europe will not long escape infection.[7]

Lansing rushed Bullitt's diagnosis to Wilson with the recommendation that since it dealt with "the most critical question" of the hour it should "be acted upon without delay."[8]

Still that same day, November 25, House was instructed to ask the Allies whether they would join in a statement notifying the German authorities that "there could be no official dealings with them . . . in connection with the final settlement of peace until a constituent assembly had been brought together."

The French rejected this suggestion out of hand: such pressure would counteract the federalist and autonomous tendencies so favorable to the reorganization of Germany and Europe. Besides, Paris claimed to object to "direct intervention in the internal policy of another country [since] this in itself was contrary to the practices of great democracies which profess an absolute respect for the internal life of other states."[9] Perhaps Washington anticipated this refusal. On November 27 Lansing notified the British government, which shared Washington's concern, that in view of the fact that Wilson and he were about to leave for Paris "it would seem best to determine there what measures may be agreed upon in regard to the Bolshevik menace in Germany."[1]

According to Bullitt the encounter in Germany was part of a larger struggle, less between "Socialism and Capitalism . . . [than] between

---

[7] *F.R.,P.C.,1919*, II, 99–101.

[8] Ibid., II, 98–9.

[9] Ibid., II, 102–4. Quite early French military intelligence predicted that the German Revolution would proceed peacefully "thanks to the support of the Provisional Government by the bureaucracy, the military authorities, and all the political parties." Propositions de l'État Major de l'Armée, 2ème Bureau A, November 23, 1918, Klotz Papers, File 4.

[1] *F.R.,P.C.,1919*, II, 94, 104.

democratic, moderate Socialism and anti-democratic Bolshevik Socialism." In the event the U.S. had a special responsibility to strengthen
the "democratic, anti-Bolshevik forces" by clarifying their own position.
He called on Wilson to make it plain that whereas America did not
"object" to the establishment of a Socialist government in Russia and
did not "care" whether Russia became a "centralized republic or a
loose confederation of Soviets," she did object strongly "to government
by murder and mass terror and to the exclusion from the franchise of
large portions of the population." Moreover, in answering a recent
Soviet overture, Washington should make it clear that until the "class
dictatorship" gave way to a government "established on lines of
essential democracy" no U. S. government could supply economic aid.
In Bullitt's view, such a reply to Lenin would strengthen "moderate
Socialism" in its struggle with "anti-democratic Bolshevik Socialism"
not only in Russia but throughout Europe.[2]

Secretary Lansing was even more horrified by and hostile to Bolshevism than his subordinate. He freely confessed that instead of
thinking about "indemnities or anything of that sort" he worried about
this new peril. "Bolshevism must be suppressed. It is the worse form of
anarchism. . . . Bolshevism is worse than any autocracy, a greater
enemy to individual liberty. . . . America is sound to the core, but
Europe is not." And Bolshevism being "the madness of famished men,"
Lansing considered food the "great cure" to be provided even to enemy
Germany. But unlike Bullitt, Lansing had serious reservations about
teaming up with moderate Socialists to fight radical Bolshevism, emphasizing the "danger of compromise with any form of radicalism and
the unwisdom of giving special recognition to a particular class of
society."[3] This caveat points to disagreements in the Administration,
not about fighting Bolshevism as such, but about the European political
and social forces with which America should work as she was about to
throw her economic and ideological aid into the fray.

This concern with Bolshevism in general and in the Central Powers
in particular was not confined to government circles. The newspapers
abounded with references to the Red peril, very often to justify continuing intervention in Russia.[4] On November 23 *The Literary Digest*
summarized the week's press under the heading "Bolshevism Threatening the World." The editors introduced their survey in unequivocal
terms: "A shudder runs through the Western nations as they watch the

[2] Memorandum for Lansing, "The Bolshevist Movement in Europe," November 15,
1919, in Bullitt Papers.

[3] Lansing to Ch. L. Parmelee, November 13, 1918, Lansing to R. S. Hungerford, November 14, 1918, and Lansing to E. N. Smith, November 14, 1918, in Lansing
Papers, Vol. 40; and Lansing to Wilson, November 9, 1918, in Wilson Papers,
11:155.

[4] See Walter Lippmann and Charles Merz: "A Test of the News," A Supplement to
The New Republic, August 4, 1920, *passim*.

millions of Central Europe plunge from autocracy, to anarchy, and our publicists begin to ask if we must fight again against the new foe."[5]

In the Philadelphia *Public Ledger* former President Taft warned that with Bolshevism sweeping westward American armies might have to go set Russia straight and to help the Austrian people "regain the self-control denied them by the bloody hands of anarchy and mob rule." Because Bolshevism was not only "anti-democratic and autocratic, but also aggressive," the New York *Globe* worried about a combined Russo-German offensive scuttling the future peace. According to Frank Simonds, in the New York *Tribune,* "if the recent course of events in Germany be not promptly changed, nothing seems more certain than that we shall at no distant time find ourselves facing eastward over the Rhine upon a vast seething mass of anarchy, extending from the Rhine to the Siberian wastes and including within its limits the 300,000,000 people of Russia, Germany, and Austria." In Simond's view, after conquering Russia and Germany and invading Austria-Hungary and Bulgaria, German Socialism would subvert the Western democracies. "A new war of ideas has begun between Central Europe and the Western nations. It may lead to a new war before the old war has finally been liquidated. . . . To national war international class war may now succeed, will now succeed, if Germany and Russia can bring it about." As a conservative Simonds never bothered to distinguish between the moderate Socialists in Germany and the revolutionary Bolsheviks in Russia. Still, he was in step with important segments of the press which suspected the conniving Germans of masterminding the Bolshevist movement.

But how to fight this new evil? The *Wall Street Journal* bluntly asked Americans to "recognize the fact that hunger breeds anarchy, and that the most effective weapon against Bolshevism is a loaf of bread." This prescription was endorsed by the New York *Tribune,* the Chicago *Daily News* and the Boston *Globe*. But the New York *Evening Sun* opposed "buying off anarchy with subsidies of meat and grain"; the Florida *Times-Union* speculated whether starvation might not only breed but also kill Bolshevism; and the New York *Herald* wondered whether "bullets would not be more effective than bread against the spread of Bolshevism." For the new isolationists William Lockwood proclaimed that the American people had not gone to war "for an opportunity to enter into [a] world-wide system of communism under which we are to divide up our wealth with the world's poverty"; America's "separate Destiny" would not tolerate the surrender of American "ideals and interests to those of other lands" or the sacrifice of America's "peculiar advantages."

But the idea of fighting Bolshevism with food gradually pressed to

---

[5] *The Literary Digest,* November 23, 1918, 9. The following survey of the press is based on this digest, 9–11.

the fore. It was Lansing who proposed to Wilson that Hoover, who by now was in Paris, be sent to Berlin "to get in touch with the actual situation, both political and economic." As soon as the President agreed, the State Department broached the idea to Edgar Rickard, the Acting Food Administrator. Rickard suggested that since his agency was being "flooded with protests . . . with regard to the plans for feeding Germany," Hoover's visit would "merely increase this trouble by giving great publicity to it." On the other hand Alonzo Taylor and Vernon Kellogg, "both of whom knew Germany and spoke German fluently, could go in without any publicity at all." Lansing was agreeable and instructed House to discuss this modified proposal with Hoover as well as the Allies. Again there were difficulties with the Allies, except that this time the British objected to a purely American initiative. This objection was symptomatic of the broader conflict that developed between Hoover and Allied representatives over the auspices —American or inter-Allied—under which relief and economic aid should be distributed in liberated as well as enemy Europe.[6] In this instance Hoover decided to send the two agents into Germany anyway, while recommending that "for amity's sake" Lansing inform London of this decision.[7]

Hoover acted so boldly because he knew the President's mind about the use of food for intended political purposes. Before Hoover sailed for Europe on November 16 the two had repeatedly exchanged views about the magnitude of U.S., as compared to Allied, food surpluses, shipping space, and financial resources, about the overarching national objectives to be secured with this readily available material power, and about the desirable degree of inter-Allied cooperation.

Moreover, on November 11, in announcing the signing of the Armistice to the American people, the President had vowed that hereafter America would "assist by example, by sober and friendly counsel, and by material aid in the establishment of just democracy throughout the world."[8] That same day he went to Capitol Hill not only to advise Congress of the Armistice but also to speak at great length about the diplomatic-*cum*-political uses of economic power and surplus. In spite of the adverse election results and to the dismay of all blind anti-Germans, he refused to strike a self-righteous, belligerent, and victorious note, even in this climactic moment. Instead, he spoke of the "humane temper and intention" of the victors; he singled out the article of the Armistice (Article 26) which promised food supplies

[6] See pp. 273–8 below.
[7] *F.R.,P.C.,1919*, II, 101–5. See also Frank M. Surface and Raymond L. Bland: *American Food in the World War and Reconstruction Period* (Stanford: Stanford University Press; 1931), 189.
[8] *F.R.,P.C.,1919*, I, 1.

to the beaten foe; and he announced that steps were being taken to organize relief.

The President then proceeded to state the larger purposes of these policies. To judge by his rhetoric, Wilson tried to recapture the broad vision and to restate the political strategy that had given his peace-without-victory speech and his Fourteen Points address those rare but unmistakable qualities of statesmanship and ideology.

> . . . the great and hazardous tasks of political reconstruction . . . now face [the Central Empires]. . . . *Hunger does not breed reform; it breeds madness* and all the ugly distempers that make an ordered life impossible.
>
> For with the fall of the ancient Governments, which rested like an incubus on the peoples of the Central Empires, *has come political change not merely, but revolution,* and revolution which seems as yet to assume no final and ordered form, but to run from one fluid change to another, until thoughtful men are forced to ask themselves, with what governments and of what sort are we about to deal in the making of the covenants of peace? With what authority will they meet us, and with what assurance that their authority will abide and sustain securely the international arrangements into which we are about to enter? There is here matter for no small anxiety and misgiving. When peace is made, upon whose promises and engagements besides our own is it to rest?
>
> Let us be perfectly frank with ourselves and admit that these questions cannot be satisfactorily answered now or at once. But the moral is not that there is little hope of an early answer that will suffice. It is only that we must be patient and helpful and mindful above all of the great hope and confidence that lie at the heart of what is taking place. *Excesses accomplish nothing. Unhappy Russia has furnished abundant recent proof of that.* Disorder immediately defeats itself. If excesses should occur, if disorder should for a time raise its head, a sober second thought will follow and a day of constructive action, *if we help and do not hinder.*
>
> The present and all that it holds belongs to the nations and the peoples who *preserve their self-control and the orderly processes of their Governments;* the future to those who prove themselves the true friends of mankind. To conquer with arms is to make only a temporary conquest; to conquer the world by earning its esteem is to make permanent conquest. I am confident that the nations that have learned the discipline of freedom and that have settled with self-possession to its ordered practice are now about to make conquest of the world by the sheer power of example and of friendly helpfulness.
>
> The peoples who have but just come out from under the yoke of arbitrary government and who are now coming at last into their freedom will never find the treasures of liberty they are in search of

if they look for them by the light of the torch. They will find that every pathway that is stained with the blood of their own brothers leads to the wilderness, not to the seat of their hope. They are now face to face with their initial test. We must hold the light steady until they find themselves. And in the meantime, if it be possible, we must establish a peace that will justly define their place among the nations, remove all fear of their neighbors and of their former masters, and enable them to live in security and contentment when they have set their own affairs in order. I, for one, do not doubt their purpose or their capacity. *There are some happy signs that they know and will choose the way of self-control and peaceful accommodation. If they do, we shall put our aid at their disposal in every way that we can.* If they do not, we must await with patience and sympathy the awakening and recovery that will assuredly come at last [italics mine].[9]

Compared to their offensive stance in 1917 and early 1918, Wilsonians all over were now on the defensive against radicalism: in the victor nations against the militant Right, and in Central Europe against the militant Left. Wilson's latest pronouncement was too subtle and indirect to be of use to his supporters in their pitched political and ideological strife with the rising forces of counterrevolution and revolution.

The day following this speech the Administration issued an important amplification. In acceding to Ebert's request that America "promise foodstuffs provided public order be maintained," Secretary Lansing explicitly referred to the President's address to Congress,[1] thereby translating Wilson's abstract design into concrete policy. Now that the Majority Socialists in Germany and Austria could claim conditional access to American food reserves, their chief slogan *"ohne Ordnung kein Brot"* became credible.

German Austria, and more particularly Vienna, were in dire and pressing need of food. By late October Pleasant A. Stovall, the U. S. Minister to Switzerland, reported that Bolshevism was raising its head to an alarming degree, that starvation was imminent in the urban centers, and that unless Allied supplies and soldiers were rushed to these centers the returning soldiers might help put over a revolution.[2]

After the Armistice these warnings became increasingly frantic. The diplomatic representatives of the neutral nations in Vienna, headed by the Papal Nuncio, notified the Allied and Associated Governments that "a revolution was on the point of breaking out in Vienna," and urged them to intervene in accordance with Paragraph 4 of the Armistice. In their judgment "the occupation by the Allied forces of Vienna

9 For the full text of this Presidential address see Ray Stannard Baker and William E. Dodd (eds.): *The Public Papers of Woodrow Wilson* (New York: Harper; 1925–7), V, 294–302.
1 *F.R.,P.C.,1919*, II, 629–30.
2 *F.R.,1918, Supplement 1*, I, 419, 446, 472–4.

as a strategic base should immediately put a stop to the sinister movement which may menace, as in Russia, the foundation of Society." Also, the Austrian government and the neutral nations called on the Allies to ease the blockade in accordance with Article 5 of the Armistice, the capital being in desperate need of both coal and food.[3]

Wilson's response was instantaneous. On November 5 he appealed to the erstwhile member-nations of Austria-Hungary "to see to it that the momentous changes now being brought about were carried through with order, with moderation [and] with mercy as well as firmness."[4] His linking of order and food for Germany had an immediate impact in Austria. All Austrian moderates insisted that since their country was in infinitely greater need of supplies than Germany order simply had to be maintained.[5] By November 21, possibly in imitation of Berlin, the Provisional Government of Austria supported its earlier requests for food and coal with both a threat and a promise. The victors were told that although the country was caught up in "dangerous social and political disturbances," in accordance with Allied wishes the government would take "all possible measures to maintain internal order and peace, and to prevent a catastrophe."[6]

Three days later, on November 24, Woodrow Wilson promised food on condition that order and peace be maintained. Eventually Otto Bauer concluded that whereas "Wilson's [pre-Armistice] note of October 18 had unchained the national revolution, his note of November 24 demanded the termination of the social revolution." In Bauer's view the German-Austrian proletariat could have kept the internal bourgeoisie in check, but it lacked the power to stand up to "the bourgeoisie of the Western Powers which presently stepped forward as the protector of the bourgeois order in German Austria." The coal and food shortages put the new Austrian government completely "at Hoover's mercy," notably because of continuing conflicts with Czechoslovakia and Yugoslavia. As a result Austrian Social Democracy faced a dual assignment: to take advantage of the end-of-war crisis to advance the Socialist cause, while at the same time avoiding revolutionary excesses of civil war which would precipitate Allied-sponsored "famine, invasion, and counterrevolution."

Bauer insisted, furthermore, that whereas in Austria and Hungary the Socialists had emerged in pivotal positions, in Czechoslovakia, Poland, and Yugoslavia the bourgeoisie was the primary carrier of the national revolution. As a result, particularly with the German Revolution stopped in its tracks, German Austria was surrounded by ideologically hostile regimes. It seemed, almost, as if the Entente had broken the

[3] *F.R.,P.C.,1919*, II, 188–91, 649, 654, 676.
[4] *F.R.,1918, Supplement 1*, I, 470.
[5] *Neue Freie Presse*, November 13, 16, and 20, 1918.
[6] *F.R.,P.C.,1919*, II, 633.

dominance of the Hohenzollerns and Habsburgs only in order to install "the rule of the Western European bourgeoisie over all Western and Central Europe. . . . As long as Western bourgeois democracy faced the Habsburgs and the Hohenzollerns, it was revolutionary; but the moment it was confronted by the proletarian revolution it turned counterrevolutionary."[7]

Lenin did not miss the significance of this new departure in Allied, especially in U.S., policy. From now on Wilson's dangerously deceptive and seductive slogans would have the additional lure of instantly available economic and financial aid. Lenin put it more crudely, in that he charged that with "a simple weapon—the noose of famine," Wilson's agents were "throttling revolution," "playing the gendarme," and "issuing ultimatums."[8] He made a sober estimate of the scope of the food crisis on the Continent as well as the size of food surpluses in America, the more so because he respected the immutable realities, the expert calculus, and the decisive use of power. Therefore, rather than scorn or disdain Wilson, he sought to understand his operational code in order to fight him more effectively.

According to Hoover, throughout 1918 the U. S. Food Administration prepared for one of two alternatives: "either the continuation of the war until the new harvest of 1919 or, if the war ended, the famine which would inevitably follow."[9] Now that the war was over America had a surplus of 18 to 20 million tons of food for export in 1919 as compared to six million tons in an average prewar year. The greatest surpluses were in breadstuffs, animal feeds, pork products, animal and vegetable oils, and sugar.[1] On the eve of the Armistice Hoover advised the President that in the coming year the U.S. would provide 50 to 60 per cent of the outside world's food imports. The value in prices of that time was likely to be about three billion dollars; and easily more than two billion dollars' worth of food would go abroad on credit or as charity.[2]

In Europe, meanwhile, food was desperately short, shipping and railway transport were tight, and the public treasuries were empty. The situation was least critical in the rural areas where the European peasants and villagers still provided for their own needs. "The problem

[7] Otto Bauer: *Die Oesterreichische Revolution* (Vienna: Wiener Volksbuchhandlung; 1923), 114–21, 126–7.

[8] V. Lenin: *Collected Works* (New York: International Publishers; 1945), XXIII, 329–30.

[9] Herbert Hoover: *The Ordeal of Woodrow Wilson* (New York: McGraw-Hill; 1958), 88–9.

[1] Since American companies controlled the Cuban sugar crop it counted as part of U.S. surplus.

[2] S. L. Bane and R. H. Lutz (eds.): *The Blockade of Germany After the Armistice, 1918–1919* (Stanford: Stanford University Press; 1942), 5–7; and Bane and Lutz (eds.): *Organization of American Relief in Europe, 1918–1919* (Stanford: Stanford University Press; 1943), 9–10, 49.

thus narrowed itself to the support of the cities and large towns pending restoration of order and the establishment of confidence in future supplies—and the cities were the centers of anarchistic infection." Hoover estimated that out of a total population of 420,000,000 approximately half, or 200,000,000, would require relief or aid of varying scope. In decreasing order of need he listed the urban populations in the liberated, the enemy, the neutral, and the Allied nations. Provided the American surplus of breadstuffs was made available, the bread picture would be more than satisfactory. On the other hand Hoover envisaged a critical shortage in fats, the deficiency amounting to 35 per cent.[3]

As of October Hoover and the men around him began to weigh systematically the opportunities and perils of American surpluses and European shortages for the Wilson Administration's foreign and domestic policy. By the time food shipments started—about sixty cargoes were loaded by late November and another eighty by the end of the year[4] —there was little talk of the purely humanitarian and altruistic motivations or aims for relief, aid, and credits. Instead, political purposes of the highest and basest order were subsumed under reasons of state: food would help prevent and contain Bolshevism and anarchy in Central and Eastern Europe; aid and relief programs would help avert the collapse of agricultural and commodity prices in the U.S.; the use of economic power would promote American economic interests vis-à-vis those of the other Allies; and prompt relief and reconstruction would speed the return of unfettered capitalism. Humanitarian impulses and Hoover's personal ambitions ran a poor second to these basic political and economic goals.

It is noteworthy that all these objectives of American economic aid were clearly perceived from the very outset. Admittedly Hoover had the most precocious, integrated, and operational conception of the politics and diplomacy of foreign aid. But he merely articulated and synthesized ideas and programs that just then crystallized in influential segments of the American power elite. Furthermore, once Wilson was satisfied that Hoover's ambition and vanity did not impair his loyalty to the Administration, he gave free reign to the Director General of Relief to implement this foreign aid program with his unexcelled zeal, knowledge, and executive skill.

Gradually Hoover's own pronouncements and operations became the best indicator of the overall direction of U. S. policy. On November 12 he made an initial policy statement at a special meeting of Federal Food Administrators—who probably expected to be discharged.

[3] Bane and Lutz (eds.): *Blockade of Germany*, 6–7, 16–17, and *Organization of American Relief*, 9–13, 66.
[4] Bane and Lutz (eds.): *Organization of American Relief*, 2–3.

At this moment Germany has not alone sucked the food and animals from all those masses of people she has dominated and left them starving, but she has left behind her a total wreckage of social institutions and this mass of people is now confronted with engulfment in absolute anarchy. If we value our own safety and the social organization of the world, if we value the preservation of civilization itself, we cannot sit idly by and see the growth of this cancer in the world's vitals. Famine is the mother of anarchy. From the inability of governments to secure food for their people, grows revolution and chaos. From an ability to supply their people, grows stability of government and the defeat of anarchy. Did we put it on no higher plane than our interests in the protection of our institutions, we must bestir ourselves in solution of this problem. There are millions of people now liberated from the German yoke for whose interests we have fought and bled for the last eighteen months. We dare not neglect any measure which enables them to return to health, to self-support and to their national life. This is the broad outlook of some kind of Food Administration during the next twelve months. As to what the detailed structure of our organization may be, to effect these ends, or even its actual name, can be developed from time to time to suit necessity. It will be months until formal peace, in the meantime the organization must remain intact if we are to serve the high purposes that I have outlined. And after that we can decide our courses upon the basis of our national duty.[5]

Shortly thereafter Hoover outlined the political appeals with which to mobilize public support for this new assignment: "From a political point of view the urgent necessity of setting up supplies need not be placed on a higher plane than . . . to [stem] the tide of Bolshevism, . . . [that] no peace can be hoped for amongst unstable states, . . . [that it is necessary] to secure stability of government even amongst the enemy if we are to collect [our debts], . . . [that] if our [occupation] troops are forced into states reeking with anarchy, we will have actual loss of life . . . [that] if Bolshevism continues to spread, it will sooner or later attack our own institutions and we shall be put to no mean expense and loss of life in its repression."[6] There then followed "An Appeal to World Conscience" to be read in churches on Sunday, December 1, and at club meetings during the week of December 1 to 7. According to this invocation, America had to fight starvation, to preserve newly liberated nations, and to prevent in other parts of Europe "such debacle as has taken place in Russia."[7]

These pronouncements by Hoover and the press bureau of the Food Administration were but mild precursors. The anti-Bolshevik arguments for foreign aid reached a peak in January 1919 when the

[5] Cited in ibid., 45–6.
[6] Ibid., 52–3.
[7] Ibid., 66–7.

President requested $100,000.000 to finance the relief of liberated areas, thereby affording the Congress the opportunity to debate, amend, and eventually pass the nation's first major appropriation for foreign aid in peacetime.

Because congressional opposition to this appropriation was so stubborn, Hoover, the American Peace Delegation, and the President sent from Paris appeals urging passage of this measure. In all these appeals the specter of Bolshevism loomed large.

Again Hoover set the pace. He argued that "the outstanding factor in the physical, moral, and political salvation of the liberated peoples, [is] credits." Having sacrificed many lives in the cause of democracy the American people

> have now to learn the practical value of this new factor of credits. It is not a mysterious thing, but it does require a calm and shrewd financial leadership. This we have, inside and outside of Congress. If its interest is awakened in time, the United States can finish its job splendidly and can banish the specter of Bolshevism, which today attempts to lure the distressed peoples into such hopeless misery and anarchy as now afflicts Russia.[8]

In another message, after invoking the need for credits to help dispose of large surpluses, Hoover once again claimed that only "strong liberal relief" could "stem the tide of Bolshevism without the expenditure of lives and vast sums on military action."[9]

The American Peace Commissioners used this same rhetoric in a wire to the Secretary of the Treasury. Warning of "the progress toward communism" and of the very real "peril to Western Europe if Bolshevism prevails in Central Europe," they held that American credits could contribute to the reestablishment of "sane governments capable of resisting the advance of Bolshevism from Russia and thus [form] a bulwark to protect the West from coming into open conflict with the elements which frankly declare themselves enemies of all existing governments." In a separate cable the Commissioners asked Frank Polk to impress Congress with the necessity "to feed even Germany in order to prevent starvation and anarchy"; Congress was only being asked to appropriate $100,000,000 to use food "for this humanitarian and expedient undertaking."[1]

Since the opposition of the Republicans was particularly fierce, Henry White, the Republican member on the Peace Commission, either was asked or felt compelled to go on record. In an alarmist cable to Senator Lodge he sought to frighten the Republican leaders into curbing their hostility to Wilson and to new expenditures in order to deliver on their self-proclaimed anti-Bolshevism.

[8] Ibid., 145.
[9] *F.R.,P.C.,1919*, II, 704–5.
[1] Ibid., 698, 706–7.

. . . the condition which . . . now dominates the entire European situation above all else [is the] steady westward advance of Bolshevism. It now completely controls Russia and Poland [*sic!*] and is spreading through Germany. Only effective barrier now apparently possible against it is food relief, as Bolshevism thrives only on starvation and disorder. . . . Confidentially Paderewski has sent us a most urgent appeal for assistance in Poland where conditions he says are desperate. I consider it therefore of utmost importance that President's request . . . be granted at once. Impossible to inaugurate Peace Conference under proper auspices without previous adequate provision to cope with situation. . . . It is too late I fear to stop Bolshevism in Russia and Poland, but there is still hope of making Germany, Rumania, and certain other areas effective barriers. . . . I cannot too strongly impress upon you urgency of meeting situation herein described.[2]

Apparently not all the Peace Commissioners were convinced of the wisdom of using such anti-Bolshevik tirades. In any case, they closed all their cables with the injunction that these only be shown in strictest confidence to key political leaders. As late as January 10 the President himself still confessed that he saw "no great advantage to be derived from words and public statements in the matter of Bolshevism."[3]

The following day, however, Wilson sent this cable to Senator Thomas S. Martin, Chairman of the Senate Appropriations Committee, and Representative Swagar Sherley, Chairman of the House Appropriations Committee:

I cannot too earnestly or solemnly urge upon the Congress the appropriation for which Mr. Hoover has asked for the administration of food relief. Food relief is now the key to the whole European situation and to the solution of peace. Bolshevism is steadily advancing westward, has overwhelmed Poland, and is poisoning Germany. It cannot be stopped by force, but it can be stopped by food, and all the leaders with whom I am in conference agree that concerted action in this matter is of immediate and vital importance. The money will not be spent for food for Germany itself, because Germany can buy its food, but it will be spent for financing the movement of food to our real friends in Poland and to the people of the liberated units of the Austro-Hungarian Empire, and to our associates in the Balkans. I beg that you will present this matter with all possible urgency and force to the Congress. I cannot see how we can find definite powers with whom to conclude peace unless this means of stemming the tide of anarchism be employed.[4]

Tumulty, who acted as intermediary, asked Martin and Sherley to treat the presidential message confidentially for the time being. In turn

---

[2] Ibid., 711–12.
[3] Wilson to Lansing, January 10, 1919, in Wilson Papers, VIII A:9.
[4] Cited in Bane and Lutz (eds.): *Organization of American Relief,* 176–7.

Tumulty rushed to inform the President of his own doubts about "the wisdom" of publicizing it: "I am afraid of the effect on country of recognition in your message of the rising tide of Bolshevism." In reply, after conceding that in principle it was "inadvisable" to publish these views, Wilson stressed that the appropriation was so "absolutely necessary" that the Administration "would be justified in publishing the message if it was necessary for its passage."[5]

Without waiting for this answer the Democratic leaders on their own decided to push the anti-Bolshevik argument. Representative Sherley read the President's cable as well as the other messages from Paris on the House floor on January 13 and the day following Tumulty claimed that "on the strength" of Wilson's cable the House had passed the appropriation by the sizable margin of 242 to 73, with 114 not voting. Senator Martin followed suit on the Senate floor and the upper house gave its assent by 53 to 18 on January 24.[6]

Meanwhile, in the appropriations debate in Washington and in the nation at large the Bolshevik issue had crowded all other considerations into second place. Congressional supporters merely rehearsed the arguments provided by Wilson, Hoover, and the American Commission; and the press followed suit. The New York *Tribune* called for "a good-barrage against the spread of Bolshevism"; the Chicago *Daily News* saw "hunger as the most potent ally of Bolshevism"; and the Boston *Globe* welcomed the prospect of "the League of Nations [beginning] with a soup-kitchen."[7]

Even the opposition had to dispose of these arguments before citing other reasons for blocking the credits. Senator Lawrence Sherman, Republican from Illinois, declared that there was "only one cure for Bolshevism, and that was military force"; Senator Miles Poindexter, Republican from Washington, argued that Bolshevism could "not be stopped with food, but only with force"; Senator Henry Myers, Democrat from Montana, refused to be browbeaten by highwaymen who threatened that "unless you feed us we will turn Bolshevik and set the world on fire"; and Senator Thomas Hardwick, Democrat from Georgia, maintained that since at home Wobblies and Bolsheviks were being shot and jailed there was no reason "to employ different methods" toward Bolsheviks in Europe. Similarly, the New York *Herald* was skeptical that Bolsheviks could be bribed to be good and wondered "whether bullets would not be more effective than bread against the spread of Bolshevism"; and the New York *Sun* questioned

[5] Tumulty to Wilson, January 11, 1919, and Wilson to Tumulty, January 14, 1919, in Wilson Papers, VIII A:9, 11.

[6] *Congressional Record,* 65th Congress, 3rd Session, House, January 13–14, 1919, *passim;* and Senate, January 18, 20–1, and 24, 1919, *passim;* and Tumulty to Wilson, January 14 and 24, 1919, in Wilson Papers, VIII A:11, 14.

[7] Cited in *The Literary Digest,* January 25, 1919, 12–13.

the American people's readiness "to favor buying off anarchy with subsidies of meat and grain."[8]

Of course, the advocates of aid in particular used—whether deliberately or unconsciously—the anti-Bolshevik rhetoric to cover up more material interests. Organized pressure in favor of this appropriation and other aid activities was applied by industries which with the sudden end of the war were left with large inventories. The dollar-a-year men, the advisers, the suppliers, and the bankers working for, with, or through the Food Administration, the Grain Corporation, the Wheat Export Company, the Sugar Equalization Board, the War Industries Board, and the War Trade Board constituted an influential lobby or pressure group. Eventually Senator William Borah, Republican from Idaho, charged that the supplication for aid had not originated in Europe but with the packers in Chicago. In reply Senator Gilbert Hitchcock, Democrat from Nebraska, candidly confessed that economic commitments and interests could not be ignored: "If Hoover told the packers they were under obligation to buy these hogs at this [fixed] price until March, he is under obligation . . . to see that they get a fair price for their product." Even Borah could not completely disregard the reminder of the senior Senator from Nebraska that it "was just as important to keep our word to the packers as it would be to keep our word to the farmers or anybody else."[9]

For quite some time Hoover dreaded the collapse of American farm and commodity prices which, in turn, could set off a general economic crisis. An end of Allied purchases of pork, grain, condensed milk, and sugar would be fatal, especially if purchases by the neutral nations continued to be restricted and the blockade of the enemy countries was maintained. The situation was most critical in pork and pork products, of which there was a surplus of 400 million pounds. When Britain, France, and Italy canceled wheat and pork orders placed before the Armistice Hoover told Wilson that unless this situation was remedied "we shall have a debacle in the American markets . . . and we shall not only be precipitated into a financial crisis but shall betray the American farmer." He even excluded price concessions, since the support prices were "the very minimum on which our American producers can come out whole."[1]

Hoover advised the President to apply pressure on the Allies to honor past commitments, to lift all restrictions on exports to neutrals,

---

[8] *Congressional Record,* 65th Congress, 3rd Session, Senate, January 18, 20, 21, 1919, 1665–6, 1759, 1792, 1805; and *The Literary Digest,* January 25, 1919, 12.
[9] *Congressional Record,* 65th Congress, 3rd Session, January 22–3, 1919, 1869, 1911.
[1] *F.R.,P.C.,1919,* II, 775, 703, 713–14; and House Diary, December 3, 1918. "Hoover explained, first, that the food situation in Germany was the key to the political situation [and] secondly, that there was a very grave commercial difficulty with regard to pork products" of which he had a surplus of 70,000 tons and whose prices the British desired to break. Cecil Diary, January 7, 1919.

and to ease the blockade on Germany; and on the Congress to provide credits. Allies and Congress alike were treated to subtle threats. The Allies were told that in order for peace negotiations to "open auspiciously it was essential to have the better feeding of the liberated, neutral and enemy territories . . . in actual progress"; they were also reminded that future loan and war-debt negotiations might well be influenced by their position concerning food surpluses. In a similar vein, Congress was told that it was "urgently necessary to dispose of our food supplies in order to . . . protect the producers from disaster and the consequent chaotic results" and that to do this the aid bill simply had to be passed. Obviously, while the urgency of stabilizing the market should not be minimized, it was "most fortunate that we have this surplus which is necessary to save human lives and to stem the tide of Bolshevism in Europe."[2]

In spite of the Treasury's objection to the maintenance of high prices and to foreign loans designed for this purpose the emergency aid was passed, new loans were extended to the Allies, and the Allies reinstated their contracts; moreover, the restrictions on the neutrals were lifted, and even the blockade of Germany gave way.[3] By early May 1919 Hoover exulted that soon surpluses of pork, cereal flour, rye, wheat, and possibly even of rice and beans would be "cleaned up . . . beautifully," thereby leaving the situation "very much more comfortable" than anticipated in January.[4] Actually the $100 million appropriation paid for only about 5 per cent of the total relief operation in 1919, the balance being covered by the Food Administration, Treasury loans, cash sales, and credit transactions.

U. S. foreign aid was multipurpose: it helped stem the Bolshevik tide in Central and Eastern Europe; it placated and served interests at home; and it facilitated the reconversion of the American economy to peace conditions. But there was a fourth function of equally great magnitude. As America's military and naval power began to count for less with the Allies, her economic and financial resources counted for correspondingly more. Allied as well as American leaders expected these resources to assume considerable political weight in the impending peace negotiations. Whereas the Allies sought to curtail the thrust of this untried instrument of power, the Americans prepared to harness it for their own national purposes.

During the immediate postwar crisis the Allies proposed to limit the political impact of U. S. economic and financial power by channeling it through existing inter-Allied organizations. Created to expedite the war

---

[2] *F.R.,P.C.,1919*, II, 688–9, 697, 714–15, 705–7; and McCormick Diary, January 11, 1919.

[3] See Bane and Lutz (eds.): *Organization of American Relief*, 209–20; and *F.R.,P.C., 1919*, II, 705.

[4] Cited in Bane and Lutz (eds.): *Organization of American Relief*, 470–1.

effort against the Central Powers, these organizations made decisions by unanimous vote. Since Britain, France, and Italy were likely to stand together, the U.S. would have to either accept their dictates or face risky stalemates. Their proposal to perpetuate these wartime agencies for the relief and reconstruction period was only in part anti-Wilsonian. The Big Three were not only fearful that the President would use economic blackmail to impose a Wilsonian peace; they also were anxious about America's rise to world power irrespective of the party or President in control in Washington.

At first the Allies wanted the inter-Allied Maritime Transport Council to become the general coordinating agency for economic relations among Allies as well as with the neutral, liberated, and enemy nations; and the inter-Allied Food Council to assume the critical assignment of distributing surpluses for aid purposes. A second plan, drafted in the hope of meeting American objections, envisaged a new inter-Allied Economic Council whose decisions would be binding on the U. S. Food Administrator, its executive, and its administrative mandatory.[5]

In brief, in full awareness of their (hopefully) temporary economic, financial, and shipping debility, the Allies pressed for a continuing economic pool in order to exercise some measure of control over the flow of U. S. aid. At a minimum they wanted to share in the prestige and influence, both immediate and long-run, resulting from the use of American resources in the relief and reconstruction of Europe; and they sought to protect their deteriorating commercial, shipping, and financial position in international trade.

It appears that Hoover was the first U. S. official to suspect Allied motives, to appreciate America's economic predominance, to articulate the reasons for maximum national control, and to sway Wilson in favor of making American resources an instrument of self-reliant national power.

On October 24 Hoover informed the President that his "instinct" was entirely hostile to agreements entangling the United States in the acceptance of Allied "views and, practically, in the acceptance of their distribution of our supplies." American food, raw materials, tonnage, and credits being "dominant," Washington should "maintain a complete independence." By going it alone America could use her economic power "to confer favors," "to restore government and order in Russia," to secure rapid return transport for U. S. troops, to influence reconstruction, and to insure the supply of those raw materials in short supply at home.[6]

---

5 Bane and Lutz (eds.): *Organization of American Relief*, 26; *F.R.,1918, Supplement 1,* I, 612–16; *F.R.,P.C.,1919,* II, 657–61. Cf. F. S. Marston: *The Peace Conference of 1919* (London: Oxford University Press; 1944), 104–5.
6 Cited in Bane and Lutz (eds.): *Organization of American Relief*, 26–7.

Within two weeks Wilson gave his approval to a momentous policy directive which Hoover drafted after conferring with the President. This directive was for the guidance of Joseph C. Cotton, the Food Administration's representative in London, which was the economic nerve center of the alliance.

> For your general advice this Government will not agree to any programme that even looks like inter-Allied control of our economic resources after peace. After peace over one-half of the whole export food supplies of the world will come from the United States and for the buyers of these supplies to sit in majority in dictation to us as to prices and distribution is wholly inconceivable. The same applies to raw materials. Our only hope to securing justice in distribution, proper appreciation abroad of the effort we make to assist foreign nations, and proper return for the service that we will perform will revolve around complete independence of commitment to joint action on our part. . . . Above all the extension of the functions and life of Inter-Allied Food and Maritime Councils, either now or after peace, [should] be prevented. . . . We must continue to act with entire independence in our commercial relations with all neutrals and Belgian Relief. . . .

In forwarding a copy of this ukase to House, the Secretary of State stressed that it would "not be communicated" to the Allies, that the Department "entirely" approved it, and that Hoover was about to leave for London, Paris, and Vienna.[7]

On Armistice Day Hoover urged the President to define the Administration's "principles in these matters" for the Allies and for the guidance of U. S. agents in Europe. He recommended that Wilson announce that America considered herself the "trustee of our surplus production of all kinds for the benefit of the most necessitous and the most deserving"; that no cooperative arrangements looking "to the control of our exports after peace" would be entered into; and that the functions of the wartime inter-Allied councils would not be extended into the postwar period. Even though these guidelines were communicated only to American officials in Europe, Washington announced formally that Hoover would leave on November 16 to negotiate with the Allies about the organization of relief and economic aid.[8]

Hoover, for his part, was not inclined to compromise with the Allies, especially once Wilson endorsed his narrow national approach, which he pressed with religious fervor. Even Frank Polk begged Hoover "not to start a fight with the British by attempting to take the lead and [by] ignoring existing organizations"; and Vance McCormick

[7] Cited in Bane and Lutz (eds.): *Blockade of Germany,* 10–11; and *F.R.,1918, Supplement 1,* I, 616–17.

[8] Bane and Lutz (eds.): *Blockade of Germany,* 11–15, and *Organization of American Relief,* 36–7.

urged the President to impress Hoover with the importance of working with the Allies. To no avail.[9]

Hoover sailed for Europe, convinced that it was hopeless to "deal with the problem through the second class minds and jealousies" of the inter-Allied councils; that the food world now required "a Commander in Chief [like] Foch" who would be responsible to the Peace Conference rather than to "the pinheads of bureaucratic Europe." Needless to say, this commander in chief should be an American because the U.S. was "the disinterested nation . . . [furnishing] the bulk of the supplies [and capable of increasing] its supplies by call from its own citizen as commander." Hoover's advisers and assistants on this mission were not likely to restrain him. Among them were Norman Davis of the Treasury, Hugh Gibson of the State Department, Robert A. Taft, and Lewis Strauss. Edward N. Hurley, the Chairman of the Shipping Board, sailed at the same time as Hoover; and Hurley had "about as much use for the Allied Maritime Transport Council as the devil has for holy water."[1]

Hoover, Hurley, and Davis arrived in London on November 21 and in Paris on the twenty-sixth, where they pressed Hoover's scheme relentlessly. By the twenty-seventh Colonel House, fully won over to their course, asked Wilson to instruct him to push that course with the Supreme War Council.

> Owing to *the political necessity of American control* over American resources and the greater coordination and efficiency to be obtained thereby, I am sure that you will agree with me that the office of Director General of Relief must be held initially by the United States Food Administrator and in case of necessity by such a successor as may be nominated by me. I would suggest, however, that the policies of the Director General should be determined by the Supreme War Council to whom he should have to report, it being our united policies in these matters *not only to save life but also to stabilize Governments* [italics mine].

The President instantly complied, "on the assumption that Mr. Hoover agrees. [*sic!*]"[2] Thus reinforced, Hoover, Hurley, and Davis stepped up the pressure. In a move designed to disconcert the Allies, they asked them to specify what they proposed to contribute in food, clothing, raw materials, shipping, and finance to the relief and rehabilitation of Europe.[3]

[9] Polk Diary, November 14 and 20, 1918.
[1] Bane and Lutz (eds.): *Organization of American Relief,* 49–50; Hoover: *Ordeal of Woodrow Wilson,* 93; Gordon Auchincloss to Vance McCormick, November 28, 1918, in House Papers, 29:147.
[2] Cited in *F.R.,P.C.,1919,* II, 636–9, 643. See also Hoover: *Ordeal of Woodrow Wilson,* 96–9.
[3] Bane and Lutz (eds.): *Organization of American Relief,* 72.

On December 12 Lord Reading, Etienne Clémentel, and Silvio Crespi presented a compromise scheme which was totally unacceptable to the Americans. According to the Hoover task force, their plan "would subordinate and jeopardize prevention of starvation until complete agreement of all four governments on every point—political, financial, transportation, and source of supply, instead of mere agreement on general policy as proposed by the President." There were "situations in Europe requiring attention within days, perhaps within hours," and yet the Allies would make it impossible to act with "the rapidity necessary to prevent starvation and anarchy."[4] Moreover, should American producers be delivered into "the hands of an organization in which we have only a one fourth voice" the Administration would find it difficult to enlist the "support and imagination" of the American people for this program. Hoover and Davis charged that instead of appreciating that the U.S. was animated by "political factors of deep meaning" the Allies begrudged the enormous credit which would "accrue to the United States if this relief work were done promptly and efficiently by Hoover and his aides."[5]

Given this impasse Hoover advised the President, who was in Paris by now, that pending agreement with the Allies, the U.S. should relieve critical situations by independent actions. Once again Wilson complied promptly, instructing the U. S. Food Administration to take the required emergency action. He also invited the Allies to cooperate in this interim measure designed "to help stem the tide of disorder rapidly sweeping westward," while renewing his plea that they join in carrying on relief work "with the maximum of efficiency under a single leadership chosen from the country whose resources will inevitably have to be drawn on almost exclusively for this work."[6] Finally, on December 23, the British and the French gave way: they agreed to the American plan, except that a special council composed of two delegates of each of the Big Four instead of the Supreme War Council would act as overall coordinating agency.[7]

The new Supreme Council of Supply and Relief held its first session on January 11. But the formation of this council represented an empty Allied victory, since from the start this council and its working committees were closely watched by the Supreme War Council and the Big Four. Moreover, even though they suspected Hoover of wanting to be "food dictator," the Allies acquiesced in his appointment as Director

---

[4] For the text of the Allied counterproposal and of the critical memorandum by Hoover, Davis, and Cotton, see *F.R.,P.C.,1919,* II, 657–61.
[5] House Diary, December 12, 1918, and Hoover to Rickard, December 16, 1918, cited in *F.R.,P.C.,1919,* II, 666.
[6] Ibid., 665–7, 672, 675–6; and Bane and Lutz (eds.): *Organization of American Relief,* 91.
[7] *F.R.,P.C.,1919,* II, 689, 691.

General of Relief.[8] Hereafter the Allies managed to assert themselves in one area only: they delayed the lifting of the blockade of the neutral as well as enemy nations, even though Hoover arranged to have it circumvented. Retrospectively Hoover boasted that since America was "doing 95% of the whole job," he considered "all the 'discussions' and all the committees' meetings . . . more mental exercise than reality . . . [and that he] did not take the 'discussions' seriously enough to even battle as to who was 'Chairman' of these committees."[9]

Admittedly, no direct food shipments from the Allied and Associated Powers reached Germany before March 25, 1919. But relief and rehabilitation were not completely paralyzed during the five months that the victors wrangled among themselves and with Germany. In the broad perspective of the raging civil war in Central and Eastern Europe—instead of in the narrow perspective of Germany's plight during the post-Armistice blockade—the wholesale promise and the substantial fulfillment of American aid played a crucial stabilizing or counterrevolutionary role between November 1918 and April 1919. Even the Ebert regime benefited handsomely from these pledges, from the salutary effect of actual food deliveries to adjacent liberated nations and to Vienna, and from supplies which trickled into Germany from surrounding neutrals. In other words, because the sinews of economic aid were located in and controlled by the United States, because powerful American interests and their spokesmen favored prompt action, and because the Allies were unable to impose a rigid blockade on liberated and neutral Europe—for all these reasons Wilson and Hoover were able to proceed with their emergency holding operation.

Significantly Hoover told the President on November 9 that in his view "pending the rehabilitation of trade, . . . the next four or five months" would be the critical period, also in the battle against Bolshevism and rank anarchy in Europe.[1] Time was of the essence. Within three days the President approved Hoover's emergency program. The War Department was asked to purchase and ship food supplies to European ports for reconsignment or storage; also, the surplus inventories of the Quartermaster in Europe were made available for distribution. Simultaneously the Shipping Board, the Belgian Relief Commission, and the Grain Corporation were pressed into service. Hoover assured the President that provided shipping were made available 350,000 to 400,000 tons of food could be started on their way to Europe in the

---

[8] See Bane and Lutz (eds.): *Blockade of Germany*, 32–3, for minutes of the inaugural session at which this Council's name, objectives, and methods were formally recorded. It was Lord Derby who told House that "except for Hoover himself there would be no difficulty about the food administration." House confided to his diary that there was "some reason in [Derby's] assertion, for that is Hoover's besetting fault." House Diary, December 27, 1918.

[9] Hoover cited in Bane and Lutz (eds.): *Organization of American Relief*, 4.

[1] Ibid., 36.

second half of November. Whereas slightly more than half of this tonnage went to French and Southern European ports for redistribution or consignment, the balance was sent to British ports for redirection to Northern Europe.[2]

According to reliable estimates, 58 or 59 cargo ships were loaded before the end of November, 79 in December, 15 in January, 33 in February, and 50 in March. A total of 70,732 tons arrived in Europe in January, 90,310 in February, and 172,906 in March. There was a time between December and the lifting of the blockade in late March when "over 1,200,000,000 pounds of fat and 100,000,000 bushels of wheat were stored . . . in Copenhagen, Amsterdam, Rotterdam and Antwerp." Supplies were also stored in Trieste and in Constantinople.[3]

In the meantime special or permanent missions were sent into most countries to estimate relief requirements, to survey transportation, and to make financial arrangements. On December 28 Hoover reported that

> Colonel McIntosh has already arrived in Trieste. Colonel Atwood and staff leave tonight for Ragusa en route to Belgrade, leaving representatives at Cattaro and other points. Doctor Vernon Kellogg, Colonel Grove and Hugh Gibson leave Berne tonight by special train for Warsaw by way of Vienna to take charge of relief measures which it is hoped to develop for Poland. A commission representing the American and . . . [Allied] Governments under chairmanship of Doctor Alonzo Taylor with the assistance of Captain Gregory are leaving tonight for Vienna in response to representations as to the dangerous situation which has developed in that city. . . .[4]

On the basis of reports from these and similar missions, relief programs were drawn up and then modified to suit changing conditions.

Still in January it was estimated that for February 557,399 metric tons of food would be required; the estimate for March was 321,333 tons. Austria, Czechoslovakia, Poland, Rumania, and Yugoslavia were considered particularly critical areas to be supplied with foodstuff from the storage and forwarding ports. On February 2 Hoover announced that 10,000 tons were being unloaded in the Bay of Cattaro for the Montenegrins; 70,000 tons were moving toward or unloading in Trieste for the Serbs, Bosnians, and Czechs; 30,000 tons were about to arrive in Constanza for the Rumanians; 40,000 tons were in transit

---

[2] Ibid., 35, 37, 43; and *F.R.,P.C.,1919*, II, 630.

[3] Bane and Lutz (eds.): *Organization of American Relief*, 2–4, 221; Herbert Hoover: *Memoirs* (New York: Macmillan; 1953), 333; Surface and Bland: *American Food*, 282–5, 318–19.

[4] Cited in Bane and Lutz (eds.): *Organization of American Relief*, 127. For Hugh Gibson's summary of his observations during his travels in the territories of the former Austro-Hungarian Empire in January 1919 see *F.R.,P.C.,1919*, XII, 228–39; a report by Alonzo Taylor is cited in David F. Strong: *Austria, October 1918–March 1919* (New York: Columbia University Press; 1939), 256–62.

from Rotterdam to Danzig for the Poles; and another 20,000 tons were being held in Rotterdam for the Finns. Great Britain and Italy were also helping out: the British sent 10,000 tons to the Serbians, a considerably smaller shipment to Vienna, and some 12,000 to 15,000 tons to the Rumanians; the Italians supplied the Austrians with 10,000 tons.[5]

Because of the collapse of the Austro-Hungarian common market the rump German-Austrian Republic faced an exceptionally grave food and fuel emergency. In particular Vienna "lived from hand to mouth, never with more than two or three weeks' minimum allowance of food in sight and often much less." In mid-December Hoover estimated that whereas the German situation would not become acute for two or three months, in Austria it was " a question of hours rather than days." Within a few days Hoover's delgates as well as Allied officials began talks with an Austrian delegation in Berne and an inter-Allied commission began to work out of Vienna.

Since Austria was an enemy country the U. S. Treasury was not authorized to make loans even though Austria and the city of Vienna were able and willing to put up collateral. But eventually, quite apart from Austrian cash purchases and an allocation of five million dollars from President Wilson's National Security and Defense Fund, an arrangement was made under which the Allies, who shared Hoover's anxiety about Vienna, received a Treasury loan to be used to purchase American supplies for Austria. Furthermore, the Director General of Relief used his influence, power, and facilities to rush food as well as coal to Vienna from neighboring Czechoslovakia, Yugoslavia, and Switzerland.

In late December the Viennese population was told that the first Allied food train of 60 freight cars had crossed into Austria at Buchs and that the second train would follow in a few days. By the end of February 24,000 tons of grain had reached Vienna from the Allies alone.[6]

The importance of this large-scale prophylactic action around Germany should not be minimized. But whereas neighboring countries received actual help before and immediately after the opening of the Peace Conference, for the time being Germany herself had to be satisfied with promises. Perhaps this delay of relief and aid was due not only to political and diplomatic obstacles. To be sure, political opposition to relief and aid for enemy Germany was fierce throughout the victor nations, French diplomats and generals being particularly hostile. It

[5] Surface and Bland: *American Food*, 31–4; Bane and Lutz (eds.): *Organization of American Relief*, 143, 220–1; *F.R.,P.C.,1919*, II, 644. For obvious reasons Hoover always exaggerated the performance of the American Relief Administration.
[6] *F.R.,P.C.,1919*, II, 666–7, 683–5, 694; Bane and Lutz (eds.): *Organization of American Relief*, 105–6, 128, and *Blockade of Germany*, 51–5; Surface and Bland, *American Food*, 153–6, 310–11, 414 ff.; *Neue Freie Presse*, December 27–30, 1918. See also Strong: *Austria, passim*, esp. 250–6, 264–71.

may well be, however, that because Germany, unlike Austria, was never really on the brink of disaster the urgency for action was not nearly so great.

Although the Provisonal Government never stopped wailing about the danger of starvation, it was in no particular rush to mortgage its merchant fleet and gold in order to get the blockade eased or lifted. This reluctance tended to substantiate Allied calculations that Germany's food crisis would not come to a head until some time in March or April. Incidentally, it was of the greatest significance that all this time food stocks earmarked for Germany were being stocked in American and European ports. As a result, once the March-April crisis of the Peace Conference developed and the blockade was lifted, food and other supplies were able to reach Germany on very short order.

Meanwhile, before the Peace Conference opened the Allies sent political agents into Central Europe, including Germany, to study the situation firsthand and to give a semblance of support to the new governments. In other words, Hoover's men were not the only ones to visit enemy and liberated Europe, possibly because they were inclined to exaggerate the imminence of the economic crisis.

The first British missions went into Germany on December 12. In a "Memorandum on the Prospects for Order and Ordered Government" the British agents agreed that much would depend on the economic situation. But they also cautioned against magnifying the danger of Bolshevism, particularly since they expected the Provisonal Government to apply its superior force against the Spartacists.[7] A separate report on economic conditions was not particularly disquieting; nor were the reports by two subsequent British missions in January.[8]

Almost simultaneously the American government dispatched the Coolidge Mission to the territories of the former Austro-Hungarian Empire and the Dresel Mission to Germany, to report on political conditions. To facilitate the work of both missions the U. S. Minister in Switzerland was "authorized to enter into appropriate negotiations with the Governments of Germany and Austria-Hungary." Archibald C. Coolidge was instructed to plan for a lengthy stay, to set up headquarters in Vienna, to send agents to major cities, and to furnish the American Peace Commission with frequent and quick, "even if imperfect," information.[9]

The Dresel Mission stayed in Germany only ten days, from December 27 through January 5; and while there Ellis Loring Dresel and his assistant, Franklin Day, visited only Munich and Berlin. But there they

---

[7] G.T. 6551, Cabinet 24/72/1–2, also cited in *F.R.,P.C.,1919*, II, 126–9.
[8] *Reports by British Officers on the Economic Conditions Prevailing in Germany, December 1918 to March 1919*, Command Paper 52, London, H.M.S.O., 1919.
[9] *F.R.,P.C.,1919*, II, 218–19. For a more detailed treatment of the Coolidge Mission, see Chs. 15, 16, 21, and 24 below, *passim*.

had interviews with, among others, Professor Lujo Brentano, Count
Max Montgelas, Kurt Eisner, Erhard Auer, Theodor Wolff, Solf,
Walter Rauthenau, Hugo Preuss, Scheidemann, Brockdorff-Rantzau,
Ebert, Maximilian Harden, Max Warburg, and Gustav Noske. Not one
of these respondents pleaded for immediate food shipments. Rathenau
and others estimated that there was enough food until around March 1;
moreover, they felt confident that Spartacism could and would be
stopped. Instead, the victors were urged to contribute to the fight
against Spartacism by declaring emphatically that only a stable and
democratically based government could expect food and peace from
the Allies. Noske and a few others even claimed that the shortage of
coal and industrial raw materials, owing to lack of rolling stock, was
more pressing than the food supply.

Dresel expected the "moderate element ultimately to remain in the
ascendant," partly because he considered Noske's appointment a sign
"that a determined effort would be made to keep the anarchists under
control." He concluded, furthermore, that there was "no danger of
actual starvation for a number of months to come," that estimates for
the exhaustion of all stocks varied from March 1 to June 15, and that
probably the date of mid-June was "substantially correct." He did
warn, however, that malnutrition was evident, especially among children in Berlin and Munich. Dresel closed his report with four recommendations: a commission of political observers should be stationed in
Germany; an economic commission should also be sent there, possibly
authorized to make preliminary arrangements for consignments of fat;
the coal situation should immediately be studied; and, above all, the
political statement, which was constantly being solicited, should be
issued "at the earliest possible moment."[1]

On balance Dresel's report must have had a calming effect on the
American Delegation on the very eve of the Paris Peace Conference and
of the second renewal of the Armistice in Trier.[2] It certainly was no
basis or summons for instant and drastic action, especially since Wilson
and Hoover had already implemented Dresel's most urgent recommendation by their recent pronouncements and actions. The other recommendations were easily and promptly acted upon: on January 26 the
Gherhardi Mission left for Germany for a two-month stay to report on
political developments; on January 30 Doctors Taylor and Kellogg went

[1] For the appointment, itinerary, and objectives of the Dresel Mission see National
Archives, Documents 184.013/2–12. The Mission's interim as well as final re-
ports and recommendations are printed in F.R.,P.C.,1919, II, 130–72.
[2] The Dresel report was submitted to the President for his "special attention." Wilson
Papers, VIII A:10. After an oral presentation before the American Peace Com-
missioners, the Secretary of State concluded that Dresel "believed the Majority
Socialists would succeed in handling the situation and would grow stronger."
Lansing Diary, January 9, 1919.

to investigate food conditions; and on January 17, at Trier, the Germans were permitted the monthly import of 70,000 tons of fats and 200,000 tons of breadstuffs on condition that they place their mercantile fleet at the Allies' disposal.[3]

---

[3] *F.R.,P.C.,1919,* XII, 1; Bane and Lutz (eds.): *Blockade of Germany,* 35–41; *F.R.,P.C.,1919,* III, 521–3, 611.

10

The Allies and the Russian Revolution

NEITHER the Versailles Treaty nor the "suburban" treaties settled the Russian problem. It does not follow, however, that the Paris Peace Conference failed to deal with it. In fact, individually and collectively the Big Four spent more time and energy on the Russian question than on any other major issue.

The Russian question was tackled both directly and indirectly. Decisions were made about Russian representation, intervention and the Civil War, the blockade, and the secession of western borderlands. These decisions significantly affected not only the course of the Civil War in Russia but also the territorial settlement in Eastern and East Central Europe as well as in the Balkans.

Even compared with the German question, the Russian question was exceptionally complex and vast. The Russian government's legitimacy was denied by Russian counterrevolutionaries at home and abroad, as well as by the Big Four. Not unlike in the Austro-Hungarian and Turkish Empires, restless nationalities were breaking loose, except that geographically, numerically, and politically the surviving core of the Russian nation was infinitely greater than its Austrian or Turkish counterpart. Whatever the outcome of the Civil War and the loss of territory Russia, like Germany, was not about to be reduced to the rank of a minor successor state.

Both the victors and the losers were constantly aware of this *sine qua non* of international politics which remained one of the chief determinants of the balance of power. For a variety of reasons the French—but also their partners—opposed the admission of Bolshevik Russia to the new (anti-German) Concert of Europe. But their insistence on an overextended Poland and Rumania was motivated by the same fears and hopes which before the war had led them to put such a high premium on the Franco-Russian alliance.

Since Germany was a defeated enemy the victors had both a legal and moral right to sit in judgment over her, within the controversial limits of the pre-Armistice agreement. But Russia could not be dealt with in such cavalier fashion. To be sure, Clemenceau kept arguing that Bolshevik Russia had betrayed her Allies and broken Russia's legal engagements by signing the treacherous separate peace at Brest Litovsk. Nevertheless, even he could not expunge certain memories from the public mind: Russia had been a principal ally, she had made a crucial military contribution between 1914 and 1917, she had made greater human sacrifices than all the Allies combined, and she had taken part in the preliminary distribution of spoils. Even without Socialist opposition and general exhaustion the Big Four could not easily have ordered a full-scale invasion of Russia for the purpose of overthrowing the Bolshevik regime.

Russia was neither ally nor enemy. During the Conference an outcast regime ruled in Moscow; and this regime was feared not because it ruled just then over a powerful nation but because it was the carrier of highly contagious ideas. Simultaneously the Whites and the seceding nationalities enlisted Allied help in their incongruous yet highly effective struggle against the Bolsheviks.

Actually the Big Four never ceased to consider Bolshevik rule abortive and therefore transitory, if not evanescent. All along they were confident that with the help of their direct and indirect intervention a sane Russia would re-emerge forthwith. Not that they were clear or agreed about possible and desirable alternatives to Bolshevism in Russia. But no matter. A tsarist autocracy, a constitutional monarchy, a bourgeois republic, or a social democratic regime—each in its own way could be expected to reclaim Russia's imperial heritage. A tsarist regime would ask for the Straits; the monarchists would be likely to press for a return to the *status quo ante* in both Asia and Europe as well as for a unitary state allowing minimal autonomy for the Russian Poles; republicans would hold out for equally extensive borders with minor "federalist" concessions for the most obstreperous nationalities; the Social Democrats promised to be least "imperial" and "unitary," though they could least afford to preside over the liquidation of the Russian Empire.

To be sure, in order to achieve the overthrow of the Bolshevik regime the Allied and Associated Powers were prepared to compensate their dependent allies in the counterrevolution with territories which had formerly belonged to Imperial Russia. As a reward for contributing to the struggle against Lenin the anti-Bolshevik and anti-Russian governments of Rumania, Poland, the three nascent Baltic states, and Finland received Allied sanction for the annexation of Russian territories or for secession from mother Russia. But these were *ad hoc* compensations—post-Armistice promissory notes—subject to renegotiation in the event the counterrevolution succeeded.

Whatever the foreign policy goals of the major Russian factions may have been, without reversing the foreign policy setbacks of the Bolsheviks no restoration regime was likely to survive very long. Not that the Allies would have to bolster such a regime by granting all the territorial and financial compensations to which Russia was entitled as a victor and as a signatory of the secret treaties. Still, they would have had to withdraw or reduce aid to the nascent border states and Rumania which were battling Russia. With the re-entry of a legitimate, nonrevolutionary, and nonproselytizing Russian government the Allies were likely to favor Russia over Poland; especially France would rather throw dissatisfied Poland than dissatisfied Russia into Germany's arms.

In the five articles dealing with Russia (Articles 12, 13, 14, 15, 16) the Armistice gave an excellent preview of the victors' dilemma: they were determined to remove German power and influence from the Eastern borderlands, but they were equally determined to prevent them from falling to the Russian Bolsheviks. Accordingly the Allies insisted on the cancellation of the Brest Litovsk treaty while at the same time stipulating that "all German Troops at present in territories which before the war formed part of Russia must . . . return to the frontiers of Germany as soon as the Allies shall think the moment suitable, having regard to the internal situation of these territories."

Clearly, this second provision hardly would have been necessary if the Tsarist or Kerensky government had still been in power. In that event Russian troops as a matter of course would have relieved the retreating German armies in these territories. Furthermore, the Armistice would have specified the quick repatriation of some two million Russian prisoners from the Central Powers instead of making the disposition of these prisoners contingent on the will of the Western victors.

Evidently the Allies were not carried away by the exaltation of their victory over the Central Powers. They were not about to abandon the counterrevolutionary purpose which all along had been a significant aspect of the predominantly anti-German thrust of their intervention in Russia. Presently the rationale for this intervention changed: the Allies claimed to be obliged to protect the Czech legions, other pro-Entente military and political formations, and valuable Allied stores. But their underlying purpose was the overthrow of the Bolshevik government which was accused of both past and present misdeeds. Among past sins were the separate peace, canceled debts, and the expropriation of Allied property. But the continuing terror overnight became the basic publicly avowed rationale for intervention. That this terror was primarily a product of continuing civil war and intervention was never admitted.

Of course, given the new circumstances the Allies had to review their strategy and tactics of intervention. Meanwhile, until this review was completed within each Allied government as well as within inter-Allied councils the situation needed to be steadied. In the Armistice, therefore, the Allies enlisted German aid to deny access to the border-lands to the Bolsheviks pending the decision whether these borderlands would be used as a defensive *cordon sanitaire* or as a staging ground for offensive military operations. Similarly, the Bolsheviks were to be denied the use of Russian prisoners pending a decision whether these would be kept in German camps or integrated into the White armies.

In any case, neither inter-Allied agreements nor any of Wilson's pronouncements underwrote the independence of Finland, the three Baltic states, the Ukraine, the Caucasus, or Armenia. The relations between the Russian government and these component nationalities were as much a subject to *domestic* jurisdiction as relations between the British government and the Irish separatists. The Lvov and Kerensky governments had promised unfettered independence to the Poles. But the Finns had merely received an assurance of autonomy, just as Lloyd George had maintained the promise of Home Rule for Ireland. In neither instance were these fully sovereign governments of Russia and England bound by international agreements to undertake what were essentially internal reforms. In brief, whereas the Central Powers had harbored blatant annexationist designs on Russia's peripheral terri-tories, prior to the February Revolution it would never even have occurred to the Allies to ask or press Russia to promise or grant independence to any of her nationalities. Quite the contrary was the case, judging by the Doumergue convention.

Only in the case of Poland was this Doumergue convention super-seded by the Fourteen Points, it being an irony of fate that Wilson rather than Clemenceau should have been the first to advocate a fully independent Poland. Whereas initially Wilson championed the Poles because of his belief in self-determination and in response to pressures of the Polish-American community, Clemenceau embraced their cause almost exclusively for reasons of power politics. Given Clemenceau's preoccupations he increasingly tended to favor those Poles who wanted to annex territories with large Lithuanian, Ukrainian, and German minorities.

It goes without saying that the Finns, Estonians, Latvians, Lithu-anians, Ukrainians, and Poles were not merely puppets of the Allies. Their nationalist leaders anyhow were bound to carry forward their age-old struggle against Russian domination, especially now that the danger of German annexation or domination had receded. They sought auton-omy or independence not from the Bolsheviks but from Greater Russia. In pursuit of this goal they were determined to capitalize on Russia's exhaustion in the war. Had Russia been strong when Germany was defeated the prospects of these nationalities would have been dim, indeed. As it was, the Russian collapse and the Bolshevik Revolution served their purposes quite nicely. Not only did the Russian government—at this stage the Bolshevik government—lack the power to reimpose rigid Great Russian control, but also the Western Allies were prepared to assist them in their independence struggle. This is not to deny the fiery anti-Bolshevism of these nationalists; but their anti-Bolshevism was essentially superimposed on a chronic anti-Russianism which had very deep historical, cultural, religious, economic, and class roots.

Though in principle committed to self-determination, the Bolsheviks refused to welcome or sanction secessions, both as Russians jealous of their national patrimony and as revolutionaries apprehensive about counterrevolutionary control or influences in the strategically important rimland. They realized, of course, that the same weaknesses which had forced them to sign at Brest Litovsk would now compel them to make concessions—however reluctantly—along Russia's western borders. Since they were not invited to the Paris Peace Conference these adjustments could only be made bilaterally, either by force of arms or by negotiation.

The Russian *émigrés* were equally opposed to contracting Russia's borders. Needless to say, they encouraged the Allies, who hardly needed encouragement, not even to consider asking the Bolsheviks to represent Russia at the Peace Conference. They were confident that the Bolsheviks would soon be overthrown through the combined efforts of the Whites and the Allies, aided by the congenial political incapacity of the upstart Bolsheviks and by rising popular revulsion against their tyranny.

While waiting for this inevitable and swift overthrow, the *émigrés* proposed to make interim arrangements for the representation of Russian interests. They specifically denied the Allies the right to act on Russia's behalf when the French recommended the establishment of a special inter-Allied caretaker committee. Instead, they advocated the admission—either as delegates or as consultants—of leading personalities from the defunct Tsarist regime, the late Provisional Governments, and the various opposition governments in Russia.

The initiative was taken by prominent members of the diplomatic corps, particularly by Boris A. Bakhmetev and V. A. Maklakov, the defunct Provisional Government's ambassadors to Washington and Paris respectively.[1] As early as December 1917 many of the Russian ambassadors to the Allied and neutral countries had met to organize a Conference of Ambassadors which was to look after Russia's interests in the

---

[1] For these organizing efforts see Boris A. Bakhmetev, Oral History Project, Columbia University, No. 89, III, 400 ff.; a seven-page letter by V. A. Maklakov to H. H. Fischer, March 31, 1934, in the Hoover War Library on War, Revolution, and Peace; Polk Diary, *passim*.

Allied world. This conference, with headquarters in Paris, now turned its attention to the problem of Russian representation at the Peace Conference.

Maklakov and his colleagues argued that as long as the Bolshevik government was not recognized, Russia's ambassadors and envoys were her only legal representatives abroad. Simultaneously they realized that as long as the territorial governments in Russia's northwest and south and in Siberia were divided among themselves, these, too, would fail to be recognized; their division would also leave the Conference of Ambassadors without a directing principal and without firm roots within Russia. With the unification of the White governments in Russia not feasible on short notice, for the time being the ambassadors had to settle for co-opting delegates from all three regions into their group.

They were equally anxious to demonstrate their "liberality." Many of the diplomats abroad held their appointments from the Tsar; and by now, within Russia, both Kolchak's and Denikin's governments were quasi-dictatorial and quasi-reactionary. To be at all effective the delegation would also have to be representative of Russia's liberal tradition and of her February Revolution. Especially President Wilson, but also large segments of politicians and opinion on both sides of the Atlantic, recognized the legitimacy of Russia's February Revolution as enthusiastically as they recognized Germany's November Revolution. Therefore Bakhmetev urged Prince G. E. Lvov to come along to Paris, while Maklakov cabled an urgent invitation to Nicolas Chaikovsky at Archangel.[2]

By early January the ambassadorial organizers of this embryonic Russian Political Conference were well on the way to forging a broad anti-Bolshevik front: this conference was to encompass "the camp of Old pre-revolutionary Russia, and the camp of the New Russia which accepted the February Revolution of 1917." Since at this time no one could tell which of these two camps would emerge on top after the overthrow of the Bolsheviks, both had to be represented, if only in order to impress world opinion with the conference's democratic pluralism.[3]

[2] Polk Diary, November 9 and December 4, 1918; Bakhmetev: Oral History Project, Columbia University, No. 89, III, 403; *F.R.,P.C.,1919*, I, 272; Poole (Archangel) to House, December 16, 1918, National Archives, Documents 183.9 Russia/5. Bakhmetev and Lvov, both of whom were in America, reached Paris by about December 20; Chaikovsky got there by mid-January. Shortly after the Armistice Chaikovsky had made the following statement: "There can be no place for Bolshevik usurpers at the international peace congress because peaceful relations between nations are incompatible with the policy of violence on which Bolshevik power is based. Such a policy can only lead to civil war and inevitably leads to war with neighboring nations. . . . That is why there can be no true end to the war without final liquidation of Bolshevism." Cited in *F.R.,Russia,1918*, II, 570–1.
[3] Maklakov to Fischer, March 31, 1934, 3, in the Hoover Library.

At the close of these organizational sessions Bakhmetev hastened to assure Lansing "of the unity of view of different Russian factions, from moderate conservatives to national socialists, with respect to Russia's international situation." He claimed that this *union sacrée,* as well as the connection "with all the centers of national movement in Russia," entitled the conference to a hearing and boded well for its effectiveness.[4]

As the membership and the organization of the Political Conference finally took shape this concern for blending into the overall political atmosphere in Paris was confirmed. But not unlike the Allied delegations, the Russian Conference became considerably more liberal in appearance than in reality. Accordingly Prince Lvov, the President of the First Provisional Government, became the chairman, and Chaikovsky, the veteran Socialist and ex-leader of the Northern Government, became one of the chief public spokesmen. Together with Maklakov, who was a prominent Cadet, they acted and signed for the conference. But with Serge Sazonov the fourth member of this steering group, it was no secret that the reins of power were firmly in altogether more conservative, traditional, and expert hands. In particular, under his guidance the leading members of Imperial Russia's diplomatic corps assumed a dominant position.

It was perfectly natural that Sazonov—the Tsar's last great Foreign Minister—should have emerged as a key figure. His authority was broadly based: he was Kolchak's Foreign Minister; he was both Kolchak's and Denikin's delegate in Paris; and he was presumed still to have excellent connections with Poincaré and the Quai d'Orsay. Moreover, in this conference he had the cooperation of such seasoned tsarist diplomats as Alexander Izvolski, the Foreign Minister who had been a chief architect of the Triple Entente, and Michael de Giers, the Ambassador to Italy.

Upon his arrival in Paris in mid-January Sazonov declared that even though the Whites required their help the Entente troops could soon return home, since "one blow would be enough to overthrow the Bolshevik regime." As for the post-Bolshevik government, there was no need to worry: "we are all men of good will, patriots of all political persuasions, as is evident from the fact that Savinkov[5] and Chaikovsky are associated with us."[6]

The French Left refused to be taken in and instantly characterized Sazonov's new role as "a pure and simple scandal." Nicholas II's ex-diplomat reminded the Allied Left of secret treaties, Russian imperial-

---

[4] *F.R.,P.C.,1919,* I, 274-5.
[5] Boris Savinkov, the dashing ex-terrorist who served as Vice-Minister of War under Kerensky, was very popular in the Allied Socialist movements, especially among anarcho-syndicalists.
[6] Sazonov's interview with Claude Anet in *le Petit Parisien,* January 20, 1919.

ism in the Balkans, designs on Constantinople and the Straits, and Russian subjugation of the Poles and other peoples.[7]

The influence of the Russian diplomatic corps was also felt in the central administrative organ of the Political Conference. Bakhmetev was chosen to be chairman of its political commission. He was responsible for the drafting of documents as well as for the day-to-day activities.

> I think I [Bakhmetev] was chosen [because] I represented a possible link between the right and the left. I was in very good relations with the right. . . . I did not know at all what would be the attitude towards me on the part of Sazonov, de Giers, and all the old diplomacy. . . . A few days . . . we rather [tested] each other. Then, somehow, the ice melted, and both Sazonov and de Giers gave me their absolute support. . . . At no time [did they object] to the things which were proposed by this Political Directory . . . [in which] I had two extremely brilliant and effective collaborators. . . . These were two men who [had been] high officials in the old ministry under Sazonov—the secretary of the department, Baron M. F. Schilling, and M. Basily [a high official in the Russian Embassy in Paris]. . . .[8]

The chairmen and members of the other commissions were equally inclined to cooperate with the imperial experts.[9]

The declaration of principles of the Russian Political Conference "worked out with the approval of the Omsk and Ekaterinodar authorities," held few surprises.[1] It goes without saying that a return to the *ancien régime* was firmly excluded. Instead the conference promised that as soon as the White governments in Russia had organized their armies and suppressed anarchy they would summon a legally and freely elected constituent assembly to shape "new forms of public life."

Though this was not the time for concrete programs, general guidelines for reconstruction were agreed to by all Russians: popular sovereignty; religious and legal equality; careers and education open to talent; rapid economic development through the encouragement of "private initiative" and foreign investment; labor legislation; agrarian reform; and administrative decentralization.

The declaration also promised a new "policy toward the border nationalities." After the February Revolution Russia had "proclaimed the independence of Poland, abolished all restrictions on Finland's

---

[7] *L'Humanité*, January 16 and 19, 1919.

[8] Bakhmetev: Oral History Project, Columbia University, No. 89, III, 413–15.

[9] Generals Stcherbatchev and Golovin of the Military and Naval Commission; Arthur Rafalovich of the Financial and Economic Commission; S. Tretiakov of the Commission for the Care of Civilian Populations in Russian Territories Liberated from the Bolsheviks.

[1] Transmitted by Bakhmetev to Lansing on January 29, 1919, National Archives, Document 183.9 Russia/22.

constitution, reconsidered Finland's ties to Russia, and raised the question of autonomy for the Baltic and other peoples." Whereas the Bolsheviks had interrupted this process, tomorrow's Russia would resume it, resolved to "destroy the very roots of artificial and unhealthy separatism." In order to prevent national power from constantly being undermined, a mutually beneficial organic unity would be fashioned between the state and the nationalities within time-tested institutions of "federalism or autonomy."

Successive position papers on the major territorial problems paid little heed to these noble but vague precepts. Also, they simply ignored the Bolsheviks as if they were but a passing nuisance. Russia's eternal interests needed to be reaffirmed; and the diplomatic corps was in Paris to reaffirm them.

Above all, the eastern frontiers of Poland could not be allowed to exceed the limits of Congress Poland. Any attempt to restore Poland's prepartition eastern borders had to be rejected in the name of self-determination as well as of international stability. The aspirations of White Russia, Eastern Galicia, and Lithuania would be fatally thwarted by Polish annexation. Moreover, Russia's vital economic and strategic interests would be seriously injured. Not least important, Poland would suffer by aggrandizing herself at Russia's expense: she would be saddled with severe internal conflicts and with a hostile Russian neighbor unwilling to help her against Germany.

The hard core of the argument was cast in terms of unadulterated power politics.

> The renewal of ancient conflicts between Russia and Poland would necessarily neutralize the power of both states, so that neither one could serve as a counterweight against Germany. . . . A Great Poland could not possibly become a substitute for Great Russia as a pillar of the European equilibrium. Since Poland's population would forever remain numerically inferior to Russia's she could not aspire to such a role. In spite of Russia's momentary military weakness her vast manpower reservoir constituted a firm basis for recovery. Poland would be one of Germany's weakest neighbors; and therefore Poland was bound to be one of the first victims of a humiliated, ulcerated, and avidly vengeful Germany. . . . Would Poland be able effectively to countervail Germany's ambitions and threats? . . . In the future the stability and peace of Europe would require a strong Russia in full control of adequate means of defense.[2]

The Political Conference advanced equally strong arguments for the retention of Russia's Baltic provinces. It expressed surprise that the Allies were contemplating a dismemberment of Russia which paralleled Germany's fondest imperialist dreams. Granted, the Allies were moti-

[2] Conférence Politique Russe: *Considérations sur les Frontières orientales de la Pologne* (Paris, 1919), 5–8.

vated by high principles of self-determination and by the search for a buffer zone between Russia and Germany. But they should also remember that the Baltic peoples were no more entitled to independence than Ireland, India, and Morocco. No doubt the Baltic peoples had legitimate grievances against centralist and autocratic Russia. But the New Russia would allow them to use their own language and develop their own culture. The Allies should also remember that the Baltic peoples would never have the capacity to stand up to both Russia and Germany simultaneously; and should they ever opt for cooperation with Berlin the ambitious annexationist dream of Brest Litovsk would be fulfilled.

Further north Russia had vital interests that could not be sacrificed to Finland's bid for independence. Even assuming this bid were ever satisfied, Russia's security interests would have to be safeguarded. Finland's geographic location was of such critical strategic importance to Russia that Finland could not be left free to enter into an alliance with a power hostile to Russia.

In sum, Russia could not consent to Finland's pursuing an independent foreign policy; and for reasons of security Russia needed a controlling voice in the Gulf of Finland. Otherwise not only Russia would suffer. France would be left isolated in Europe if Russia were denied an adequate military frontier in the north.[3]

On the surface it appears as if this Russian Political Conference "represented a rather liberal-conservative attitude and was neither reactionary nor extremely left."[4] Moreover, even though Sazonov played a key role, the conference seems never to have been completely subordinated to Kolchak.[5]

But in fact the center of gravity was decidedly on the Right. Kerensky and other *émigré* leaders of the non-Bolshevik Left were severely critical of the domination of the conference by conservatives, if not reactionaries. They realized that Sazonov's readiness to liberalize Russia's rule of her western minorities was essentially expediential: it was calculated to secure especially American and British support for the overthrow of the Bolsheviks. Neither Wilson nor Lloyd George, each for his own reasons, was likely to support Kolchak and Denikin as long as these White leaders aspired to no more than a restoration of tsarism. The democratic Left kept warning Wilson of the danger of intervention in favor of reaction: with the slogan "neither Kolchak nor Lenin" they urged the President to intervene on behalf of Russian democracy, of Russian Social Democracy.[6] Wilson's and Lloyd

---

[3] Conférence Politique Russe: *Quelques Considérations sur la question des provinces baltiques et de la Grande Pologne* (Paris, 1919), 3–8, and *Quelques Considérations sur le problème finlandais* (Paris, 1919), 9–11.
[4] Bakhmetev: Oral History Project, Columbia University, No. 89, III, 411.
[5] Maklakov to H. H. Fischer, March 31, 1934, 5, in the Hoover Library.
[6] See the *Bulletin de la Ligue Républicaine Russe,* the organ of this *émigré* democratic Left, *passim.*

George's reluctance to recognize Kolchak without prior guarantees of democracy soon became apparent.[7]

Meanwhile, there were *ultras* in Paris who accused the Russian Conference of making excessive concessions to the Left. These *ultra émigrés* rejected the Wilsonian and republican-federalist formulas as incitement to the border nationalities against the Russian people and state, warned against the hazards of displacing the center of the European system toward the Atlantic, and swore unconditional allegiance to Kolchak. In their judgment only a new Franco-Russian alliance could provide the Continent with security, stability, and peace; and this alliance required that Russia instantly recover her "full territorial integrity, unitary internal order, and Great Power dignity."[8]

This extreme position might well have expressed the real purposes of Kolchak, and even of Sazonov. But it was hardly the suitable platform with which to claim the right of representation for the Russian Political Conference, to thwart the admission of delegates from the border peoples to the Peace Conference, and to secure maximum Allied aid for Kolchak and Denikin.

It was an open secret that even the French were torn between favoring the rebirth of a Great Russia and encouraging a new order in the rimland. Under ideal circumstances Clemenceau and his advisers would have liked nothing better than the quick restoration of a large, stable, and conservative Russia. Furthermore, cooperation with Denikin and Kolchak in the overthrow of the Bolsheviks certainly would have been more congenial to Clemenceau than to Lloyd George and Wilson.

However, starting in October 1918, Clemenceau had to define France's policy in Eastern Europe in the light of pressing priorities and of limited capabilities for energetic unilateral action. With the military collapse of the Central Powers the German armies began their withdrawal from the Ukraine. Hereafter first priority was assigned to keeping the Bolsheviks out of this emerging power vacuum as well as out of other parts of the rimland. The time, space, and resources gained with this holding operation could subsequently be used to overthrow the Bolshevik regime.

But who could step into this breach? There was France's Eastern Army, but it was doubtful that it could move into Southern Russia with sufficient speed and strength to establish an effective *cordon sanitaire*. In the absence of French strength there were three essentially incompatible partners available for this operation: the Germans, the Ukrainian nationalists, and the Poles. The Armistice enjoined the Germans momentarily to mount the guard. Meanwhile, the Ukrainians and the Poles—whose hostility for Russia-*cum*-Bolshevism was as great as their

---

[7] See Ch. 23 below.
[8] See *La Russie Nouvelle*, the organ of these *ultras, passim.*

mutual enmity—should be provided with military and economic aid. In brief, in order to contain Bolshevism Clemenceau was prepared to sanction and abet the decomposition of Russia.

As for giving material aid to the Ukrainians and the Poles, the French were not nearly as well placed as the British and the Americans. France's manpower was drained; her northeastern industrial basin was in ruins; her war debts were staggering; and her armaments arsenal was depleted. Given this near-fatal hemorrhage of national power Clemenceau had to look elsewhere for resources to be brought to bear in Eastern Europe. Of course, he would seek to enlist such resources without compromising his bid for a dominant diplomatic role in that unsettled part of the Continent.

Thus Clemenceau, no less than Foch, was eager to contribute French military and technical cadres for intervention in and along the periphery of Russia. However, he hoped to convince the British, and more particularly the Americans, to provide the finances and the supplies; and he looked to the Whites, the Rumanians, the Ukrainians, the Poles, and even the Greeks to provide the necessary manpower.

Actually there were sound reasons for concentrating on the southern and central sectors rather than on the northern sector of Russia's European borders. France's Eastern Army was nearby to offer guidance and support; French officers and agents were in close touch with Denikin; and the Rumanian and Polish governments as well as the Ukrainian separatists were eager to participate in the containment of Bolshevism in the hope of extending their borders at Russia's expense. Of course, the French would also have to mediate the territorial disputes between and among their new allies.

Moreover, to the extent to which the primary instrumental aim was to prevent the Russian carriers of Bolshevism from advancing westward, the French could argue convincingly that the southern and central sectors were particularly vital. In addition to being fair-sized and cohesive nations, Rumania and Poland were the strategic gateway to East Central and Central Europe where military defeat had left an explosive legacy of political instability, economic disorganization, and national rivalries. Preferably the Dnieper should become the defensive rampart; at worst the Bug or the Dniester to the east of the Carpathians. This was an assignment for land armies, though naval units would deliver supplies to Black Sea ports for shipment inland.

Not that the French considered the Baltic and the Crimea altogether unimportant. However, even assuming the Soviets captured both areas, given their total lack of seapower they would still have to take the land route to Central Europe. Hence, provided Poland and Rumania were adequately fortified the Soviets would continue to be locked in.

Evidently Clemenceau as well as Foch underestimated the feasibility of delivering fatal blows to the seats of Soviet power in Petrograd and Moscow through and with the help of Finland and the three nascent Baltic states. In this regard the French were in considerable measure prisoners of their suspicions of England. They were reluctant to yield first place to Britain, which had the naval power required for control of the Baltic and the Black Sea and for support of Judenich and Denikin. In case of a successful British-supported and -directed overthrow of Lenin England might well steal the march on France. The Baltic countries, including Finland, might become a British sphere of influence; and in the extreme south the British might dominate the Caucasus which in addition to having vast oil reserves was an important key to the disputed Near East.

By October 27, 1918, Clemenceau sent urgent instructions to General Franchet d'Esperey, the Commander in Chief of the Eastern Army, which was composed primarily of French and British troops and whose headquarters were in Salonica. The General was told to start dividing his attention between the fading struggle with the Central Powers and the coming assault on Russian Bolshevism. He was to prepare a plan for the "economic encirclement" of Bolshevism as well as for inter-Allied military intervention in Southern Russia. This military intervention would be a "function of the possibilities opened up to us following our intervention in Rumania and of the imminent capitulation of Turkey which will enable us to reach the region around Odessa via the Black Sea." Of course, the French government still had to secure the agreement of the Allied and Associated Governments. In the meantime, however, so as not to squander valuable time, Franchet d'Esperey should work up his plans in consultation with General Berthelot, the Commander of Allied forces on the Rumanian front.[9]

Almost simultaneously Franchet d'Esperey as well as the Quai d'Orsay received urgent requests for material and financial aid from Denikin. These requests were endorsed by delegates from all major Russian counterrevolutionary factions—ranging from Mensheviks to Monarchists—who met with Allied representatives in Jassy November 17–24, 1918.[1]

Even before this Jassy Conference closed, the French had promised Denikin assistance in the form of arms, ammunition, and provisions. Moreover, on November 16 Berthelot had indicated that 12 French and Greek divisions were being prepared for Southern Russia. And, in fact, on November 23 an Allied naval squadron arrived at Novorossisk;

---

[9] For the text of these instructions see Jean Xydias: *L'Intervention française en Russie, 1918–1919* (Paris: Editions de France; 1927), 113–15.

[1] Louis Fischer: *The Soviets in World Affairs*, 2 vols. (2nd ed., Princeton: Princeton University Press; 1951), I, 152–4. Miliukov not only advocated the dispatch of 150,000 Allied troops; he even favored the use of German units.

four days later agents of the French and British governments set up shop in Ekatrinodar, the headquarters of Denikin's Volunteer Army.[2]

These initial steps were part of Clemenceau's broader design. This design started to take shape by mid-November when the Premier instructed his Foreign Minister promptly to define and settle the principles, the form, and the pattern of inter-Allied intervention in Southern Russia.

> 1. As for principle, can the Allies engage in open or latent hostility with Bolshevism by giving the Ukraine the support required to maintain order and to Denikin the assistance necessary for his progress?
>
> 2. In what form should this support be given? Should it be exclusively in the form of material aid, should instructors and cadres also be provided, or should our full forces be committed in the Caucasus, the Don, and the Ukraine?
>
> 3. As for the pattern of execution, the clauses of the Franco-British convention of December 23, 1917 with regard to Allied action in Southern Russia no longer fit the new situation.

Clemenceau told Pichon that the Americans, Italians, Rumanians, and Greeks should be invited to take part; and that in case military units were used, these should be chosen in the light of the actual distribution of Allied forces (in the East, Mesopotamia, Syria) as well as of transport facilities.

At this point Clemenceau proceeded to suggest a modification of the Anglo-French convention of December 1917. Since in Southern Russia the principal and immediately available forces were French, the supreme command should be entrusted to the French not only in the Ukraine, but also in the Don where General Denikin, the successor of General Alekseev, had already organized his armies with the 100 million francs which the French government had placed at the latter's disposal. In the Caucasus and in Armenia the inter-Allied command should be taken over by the British for the same reasons and under the same conditions. According to the original convention Britain had been assigned the Cossack territories.

Once his policy was set, Pichon should brief General Berthelot who would direct the operations in Rumania and Southern Russia. Simultaneously Franchet d'Esperey should be given instructions with regard to "the resources to be placed at Berthelot's disposal" and the assistance to be furnished forthwith to General Denikin. Needless to say, this assistance to Denikin should have an inter-Allied character. This same inter-Allied posture should be maintained in the event of the transfer of

[2] A. Zaïontchkovsky, A. Anders, et al.: *Les Alliés contre la Russie avant, pendant et après la guerre mondiale* (Paris: André Delpeuch; [1926?]), 250–1.

units from the Allied forces in Syria via the Straits and Batum.[3] Within the next few days Clemenceau reinforced these general instructions to Pichon with the concrete assurance that a division was ready to embark for Odessa and that two other divisions were "available to take the place of German troops in Kiev and to prevent the Ukraine from falling into Bolshevik hands."[4]

Pichon asked F. A. Kammerer, the third-ranking permanent official of the Quai d'Orsay and its leading expert on Russian affairs, to draft the requested policy memorandum. Judging by his preliminary working notes Kammerer had little patience for questions of principle: since the Allies were fighting the Bolsheviks it was immaterial whether these hostilities were labeled latent or open. There was a job to be done: the Germans should be asked to evacuate the Ukraine at the earliest possible moment, of course without permitting the Bolsheviks to fill the vacuum. Hence, the Allies had to expedite the organization of the Ukrainian army; they should also send in some of their own units. Meanwhile, "a *cordon sanitaire* against the Bolsheviks had to be maintained in front of the Ukraine until the Ukrainians themselves could go over to the offensive in the spring." At the same time Denikin's request for assistance could easily be met since he needed primarily material aid, cadres, and instructors. As for the Franco-British convention, even though it required renegotiation, it was no obstacle to the immediate start of this intervention.[5]

It took Kammerer until November 26 to complete the final draft of the policy paper which Pichon promptly transmitted to Clemenceau. In this paper the Foreign Minister and his staff demonstrated that they fully shared the Premier's fundamental assumptions about the Russian problem.

> Like you I [Pichon] judge the reestablishment of order in Russia as one of the essential factors for the peace of Europe: it is necessary in order not only to protect France's immense financial interests in Russia but also to put an end to the agitation and the incendiary propaganda of the Maximalists in Europe. Their power consists in . . . their being able to dispose of Russia's vast financial resources.
>
> . . . We must act fast, all the time limiting our risks and taking account of the new conditions which the Armistice has created in France, i.e., the mounting demand for partial demobilization and the faltering morale of our troops.
>
> The Archangel expedition is blocked and a campaign in the Gulf of Finland cannot be envisaged because of the insoluble problem of

[3] Clemenceau to Pichon, November 15, 1918, Quai d'Orsay, File Z 619–11 (14.318BS/3).
[4] Pichon to Clemenceau, November 26, 1918, Quai d'Orsay, File Z 619–11 (4594).
[5] Kammerer's notes on Clemenceau's letter to Pichon (14.318BS/3), November 16, 1918, Quai d'Orsay, File Z 619–11.

feeding Petrograd. Moreover, the dispatch of Polish regiments to Poland involves almost insuperable political difficulties.

Only the Ukraine remains. It can easily be reached either through Bessarabia or through Odessa; a few cadres could easily reconstitute a Ukrainian army to be sent against the Bolsheviks; and the arrival of our divisions would be welcomed enthusiastically and would encourage the Ukraine to be concerned with Russia [rather than with Poland].

The execution of this plan, which coincides with the guide lines you have given me, involves coordination with the armed forces of Britain and even of Rumania, though these must be used with caution. The prompt arrival of our troops in the Ukraine will secure order in the Donetz basin.

A second theater of operations, which the convention assigns to British troops, encompasses the Don and the Kuban . . . where Denikin's forces must be supplied, armed, and equipped through Salonica and Odessa. There you will have to establish liaison between British and French troops. It should be easy to come to an agreement, given England's interest in the Caucasus and Persia and given the importance of Baku's oil resources. . . .

If this double action in the Ukraine, on the Don and in the Kuban leads to an agreement with the British—which is probable—the defeat of the Bolsheviks would be further hastened by the establishment of a bank authorized to issue a Russian franc. . . . This franc would be used by the Allied armies to finance their requirements . . . and to rapidly kill the ruble, the Bolsheviks' principal weapon.

It is up to you to evaluate the extent to which, from the military point of view, this limited plan is realizable. . . .[6]

By the time this memorandum reached Clemenceau, the Premier had received advice from other quarters. In his answer to Clemenceau's preliminary instructions of October 27, Franchet d'Esperey voiced the field commanders' skepticism about France's capability for direct *military* intervention.

My troops are inadequate for an advance into this vast frozen land, especially in winter. At best I could hold Odessa and neighboring ports. But I must tell you that whereas during the war our troops accepted their prolonged stay in the East in a spirit of patriotic resignation and as much as they joyfully entered into Hungary in preparation for their triumphal march into Germany, operations or occupations in the Ukraine and Russia would generate discontent and might lead to troublesome incidents.[7]

Similar warnings about the war-weariness and the precarious morale of the French units in the *Armée d'Orient* came from General d'Anselme.[8]

6 Pichon to Clemenceau, November 26, 1918, Quai d'Orsay, File Z 619–11 (4595).
7 Cited in Xydias: *L'Intervention française en Russie*, 115.
8 Ibid., 345–8; and various cables from mid-November through mid-December 1918, Quai d'Orsay, File Z 619–11.

But these same officials who recommended caution in the commitment of French manpower advocated intervention by all other means. The moment they heard that the British were planning a show of naval strength in the Black Sea, the dispatch of a military mission to Denikin, and the occupation of Batum and Baku, their plea for French action became particularly urgent. Clemenceau responded by sending various military missions to Denikin as well as to the Ukraine and by ordering munitions and supplies to be shipped to Denikin through British-held Novorossisk. As for troops, Clemenceau and the French High Command considered committing three French and three Greek divisions, the bulk to be drawn from the Eastern Army; they also envisaged the use of Rumanian units and the replenishment of France's contingents in the Eastern Army with Indo-Chinese and African troops.[9] For the time being France could spare little except instructors for the Siberian front.[1]

These dispositions reveal that even though Clemenceau was determined to use French power to contain Bolshevism and to deny Britain a monopoly in Southern Russia, he was not anxious to mount a large-scale direct intervention with French infantry. He stuck to this policy in spite of repeated calls for Allied troops from Saint-Aulaire and Denikin, General Janin and Kolchak, as well as from many of the *émigrés*.

Eventually, on December 13, Clemenceau sent a cable to General Janin at Vladivostok explaining his overall plan in Russia as well as his reticence to commit sizeable land forces.

> The inter-Allied plan is not of an offensive character; it merely seeks to deny the Bolsheviks access to those regions of the Ukraine, the Caucasus, and Western Siberia whose economic resources they need in order to survive and in which the Russian elements of order are being organized.
>
> Hence, the primary aim is to establish and maintain a *defensive* front forward of these regions and in particular of eastern [?] Russia. Should an offensive effort be required to crush Bolshevism it will subsequently have to be carried out by the Russian forces themselves. It is essential that you impress on the Russians that the sole purpose of our temporary protection is to permit them to organize themselves and to acquire material superiority over their enemies.
>
> Your military operations must therefore be based on a defensive plan and on an economical use of resources along a curtailed front until the Siberian army is organized and trained [italics mine].[2]

[9] Pichon to Clemenceau, November 26, 1918, and Clemenceau to Pichon, November 30, 1918, in Quai d'Orsay, File Z 619–11.
[1] Clemenceau to General Janin, December 13, 1918, Quai d'Orsay, File Z 619–11 (15.176).
[2] Cited by Pichon in *JO* (December 29, 1918), 3717.

Should economic strangulation fail, the Whites and the Ukrainians might at some later date have to take the offensive against the Bolsheviks. Meanwhile, however, most of the available resources, including limited Allied manpower, would be used to contain Bolshevism, especially in Southern Russia.

Accordingly, on December 17 the first units of France's 56th Infantry Division went ashore in Odessa. Most of these soldiers were Senegalese and Algerian. Soon they were joined by Polish and Greek units. Under the command of General d'Anselme this well-equipped inter-Allied but French-run force spread out to key points along the Ukrainian coast of the Black Sea. By February 1919 it reached a total strength of 12,000 (including 3,500 Poles and 2,000 Greeks). All along an Anglo-French fleet of more than 20 warships and numerous transports plied the waters in the immediate vicinity. Moreover, before the end of December 1918 the French also put several thousand colonial troops and one battalion of Greek soldiers into the Crimea.

On December 22 Clemenceau was in a position to give a still more explicit outline of his strategy and purpose in another cable to Janin, with copies to Pichon and Foch. He repeated that no troops would be available for Siberia. But he revealed that bases were being set up on the shores of the Black Sea, in particular at Odessa, Nicolaev, and Sevastopol; and that at a later date, as detachments became available, troops would move inland in the direction of Kiev and Kharkov. Simultaneously, the Russian elements of order would receive material aid and technicians. In this connection the liaison with Denikin's army was particularly important. According to Denikin's agent at Salonica, the White General agreed with these plans. He, too, realized that this slow and gradual strategy was dictated by manpower and transportation difficulties.

All along the Allies should remember their minimum and instrumental objectives: "the simultaneous economic encirclement of Bolshevism and the organization of the Russian elements of order." According to Clemenceau, since the Allies did not intend to "interfere in the internal affairs of Russia," there was no need to "issue a declaration of war against the Bolsheviks." After all, France's sole and ultimate aim was to "help Russia overcome anarchy and restore herself."[3]

France's chiefs of mission in Archangel and Vladivostok, as well as her ambassadors in Washington, London and Rome, were impatient with Clemenceau's refusal to launch a frontal assault. On December 29, in the midst of the foreign policy debate in the Chamber, Pichon set out to disarm these critics with a detailed outline of and justification for limited, circumspect, and indirect intervention.

[3] Clemenceau to General Janin, December 22, 1918, Quai d'Orsay, File Z 619–9 (15.462BS/3).

I have no illusions about the present worth of the Russian contingents which the Russian generals are trying to organize in different parts of Russia.

Neither am I unaware of the ebb-and-flow of Soviet power, the ingratiating fury of its propaganda, and the gathering strength of its military organization, though I do not attribute to this disease of the Slav spirit a mysterious and universal power. The French Government is in a better position than you to make up-to-date evaluations of the practical feasibility for Allied action, the various obstacles to simplistic solutions (such as complete intervention or absolute abstention), the changing situation, and the relative importance of the great problems which one after another will have to be settled.

Neither America, nor England, nor Japan, each for different reasons, is anxious to launch a large scale intervention in Russia which in both time and space threatens to involve us well beyond our available resources and fundamental objectives. Because France made the heaviest sacrifices during the war she is in no position to take such a course by herself: public opinion and parliament would refuse to follow the Government if it got involved in an hazardous undertaking.

This is not to say that we are disinterested in the Russian problem; *but we limit our action to our capabilities.* At all points we keep a watchful eye and we act.

In the Baltic French ships are joining the British squadron.

In the North, at Murmansk and Archangel, our soldiers stand next to British and Allied contingents.

From Vladivostok to Omsk General Janin, assisted by General Stefanik, leads and organizes Russian, Czech, and Allied troops: the brilliant success of the Siberian troops at Perm demonstrates that it is not unreasonable to expect an energetic Government like Admiral Kolchak's to organize, in a short time, a national army which could be the core for Russia's self-recovery.

In the West, we are seeing to the return of the Polish legions to Danzig as well as to their provisioning with *American* aid.

French, Greek, and Rumanian divisions, under the command of General Berthelot, are getting ready to take up positions from Kiev to Odessa and Sevastopol, where landings have already been made.

Military missions and Allied contingents, principally British units, are on their way to the Caucasus and to Denikin's army via Novorossisk.

At all points arms, munitions, matériel, provisions, and cadres are being furnished to Russian troops by the French, the British, and the Americans.

This prudent but concerted and coherent intervention represents the maximum effort which the Allies can sensibly afford at this moment, though this effort will be supplemented by economic and financial measures designed to destroy the ruble which the Bolsheviks issue in a constant stream.

No doubt it is more seductive to imagine the thundering march of an army of 200,000 men equipped with all modern instruments, supported by powerful logistics and economic aid, and certain of sweeping away a Red Army which, though numerous, lacks real cohesion and is incapable of warding off organized troops.

But such a policy is a function of the imagination rather than of a careful assessment of realities. It cannot stand critical analysis [italics mine].[4]

Clemenceau and his Foreign Minister settled for this policy of limited intervention after a careful scrutiny of French capabilities, an informed estimate of British and American intentions, and a measured appraisal of the combat readiness of the Whites, Ukrainians, Poles, and Rumanians. Their evaluation of Soviet capabilities and objectives was considerably less studied: on the one hand Clemenceau argued that the Soviet regime was so weak that it could easily be suffocated with a strict defensive quarantine; on the other hand he had to dramatize and exaggerate the Bolshevik threat in order to both launch and legitimize even his minimal containment policy.

This issue of Soviet intentions was aired in open press and Parliamentary debates rather than in confidential consultations within the executive branch of the government. Whereas Clemenceau was at pains to reassure the belligerently anti-Bolshevik Right that his defensive policy was more than adequate, he had to frighten the anti-interventionist Left into suffering or supporting it.

A high-pitched debate in the press prepared the ground for the major Parliamentary debate of December 27–29, 1918. Not insignificantly the foreign policy expert of the rabidly anti-Bolshevik *Action Française* was no enthusiast for intervention. Among French Rightists Jacques Bainville was unique in that he argued that France lacked the money, material, and manpower for effective intervention. He urged that instead of running the risks of military and diplomatic overextension France should take the initiative in quarantining and blockading—in starving—the Bolsheviks into submission.[5]

Editorialists in the *Temps,* Pertinax in *Echo de Paris,* and Alfred Capus in *Figaro* were not nearly so circumspect, though they, too, were painfully aware of France's impotence. As compared with Bainville they were less reluctant to press Britain and America into active service.

The Center and Center-right were particularly adept at conjuring up an altogether terrifying German-Bolshevik conspiracy. To begin with, they held, Bolshevism was merely the latest version of the Pan-German bid for dominance in Eastern Europe. As long as Bolshevism

---

[4] Pichon to Archangel, Washington, London, Rome, Berne, Vladivostok, December 29, 1918, Quai d'Orsay, File Z 619–9 (1029, 4403, 7789, 5012, 2750, 177).

[5] *L'Action Française,* November 1918–January 1919, *passim.*

survived in Russia and Germany was politically unstable, Berlin would be in the driver's seat. Ebert had the option of either working with or against Lenin. Should Germany defy the Allies by going Spartacist, the world Bolshevik movement, in addition to gaining immense prestige, would come under German control. Alternately, under cover of anti-Bolshevism Ebert could move into the East European vacuum while at the same time re-establishing a unitary and militarist *Obrigkeitsstaat*.

This being the case the Peace Conference should begin by tackling the Eastern question; the German question then would take care of itself. It would not do, however, to set up a *cordon sanitaire,* such a negative policy being immoral, ineffective, and illusory. What was needed was a positive policy, with Poland as pivot. According to the *Temps,* since the Baltic was the key to the Russian question, the Allies should, in addition to girding Poland by rushing Haller's divisions to Danzig, open up the Kiel Canal and encourage anti-Russian separatism in Estonia, Latvia, and Lithuania. Intervention in the Ukraine was also advocated, but not nearly so forcefully. The *Temps* made a particular point of reminding Clemenceau that barbed wire, bullets, and food would be ineffective unless they were tied to an ideological program. The anti-Bolshevik crusade should be fought under the flag of nationalism and peasant proprietorship.[6]

Pertinax was equally insistent that the Eastern question be given first priority. He argued that even during the war Allied strategy and diplomacy had neglected Eastern Europe; in the postwar world this neglect could be still more costly. Unlike the *Temps* Pertinax urged that Odessa and Kiev be made the staging area for intervention. But, above all, time was of the essence: the Allies should start their crusade before their fighting spirit was slackened, their military establishments dismantled, and their war economies reconverted.[7]

These and similar strategic proposals were not nearly as important and conspicuous as the strident anti-Bolshevik tirades with which they were editorially interlaced. Even though the leading conservative and reactionary papers failed to agree on any one set of counterrevolutionary measures, their consensus about overriding aims was complete: the immediate containment of the Leninist regime in preparation for its early overthrow at minimal cost. By the time the Peace Conference convened, the *Temps* and its sister papers had substantially contributed to creating the impression at home and abroad that France was seething with extreme and aggressive anti-Bolshevism.

Meanwhile the Socialists had launched their anti-interventionist campaign. On November 5 the Executive Committee of the SFIO called on its members to make the first anniversary of the Bolshevik

---

[6] *Le Temps,* November 1918–January 1919, especially December 6, 10, 12, 13, 26, 27, 1918, and January 7 and 15, 1919.
[7] *L'Echo de Paris,* November 1918–January 1919, *passim.*

Revolution an occasion for protesting the Allied intervention in Russia. A week later this same committee denounced all plans designed to stifle revolution, whether in Russia, Germany, or the territories of Austria-Hungary. Finally, on December 24, the SFIO explicitly called for the withdrawal of Allied but especially French troops from Russia and for the end of the blockade. The following day the CGT threw its full weight behind this campaign.[8]

These formal party and trade-union pronouncements merely punctuated the running protests in the *Humanité* and *Populaire*. In their pages Socialist leaders repeatedly exposed the counterrevolutionary implications of Articles 12 and 16 in the Armistice, while also expressing their anger over the slow pace of demobilization. They claimed that this slow pace was a function of Clemenceau's need for troops for his projected interventions, which were reminiscent of the Sainte-Alliance. To dramatize the government's refusal to set a timetable for demobilization on December 20 the nine Socialists resigned from the Chamber's Army Commission, and threats of street demonstrations followed.[9]

Not that the SFIO was united in its opposition to intervention. To be sure, Longuet and Loriot were at the head of the anti-interventionist campaign. But Longuet and his associates combined their opposition to intervention with disclaimers of sympathy for Bolshevism, simply claiming that according to the Wilsonian gospel the Russian people should be left to choose their own form of government. On the other hand, Loriot and Paul Faure, rather than hide Bolshevik excesses, contended that it was absurd to expect the Bolsheviks to respect civil liberties at a time when they were besieged by enemies at home and abroad.[1]

Still, whereas Longuet and Loriot, for different reasons and without mutual consultation, opposed intervention, Albert Thomas advocated it. Thomas claimed that Wilson's pre-Armistice diplomacy had brought down the curtain on the age of nonintervention. He looked to the Allies to rid both Russia and the world of Bolshevism in the name and interest of the League of Nations. Hopefully their intervention would pave the way not only for a democratic regime in Russia but also for a new deal for Russia's oppressed nationalities.[2] Cachin sought to rally the interventionist Social Patriots and the anti-interventionists around the demand that the government announce its aims in Eastern Europe to both the Russian and the French people.[3]

---

[8] *L'Humanité* and *le Populaire*, November 7–8, 13–14, and December 25–27, 1918.
[9] *L'Humanité* and *le Populaire*, November–December 1918.
[1] *Le Populaire*, November 15 and 27, and December 12, 13, and 20, 1918.
[2] B. W. Schaper: *Albert Thomas: Trente ans de réformisme social* (Assen: Van Gorcum; 1959), 188.
[3] *L'Humanité*, November 16, 1918.

In the great foreign policy debate of December 27–29, 1918,[4] Cachin made the Russian question a touchstone of the government's peacemaking policy. As part of the SFIO's drive to smoke out Pichon and Clemenceau he and other prominent Socialist deputies pressed for a public declaration of French intentions in Russia. Cachin, Moutet, and Lafont—the three moderate Socialists who in April 1917 had gone to Russia to bolster the Provisional Government—insisted that Clemenceau must not go to war against Russia without Parliamentary sanction, otherwise he would be violating the constitution; and warned him not to circumvent Parliament with informal police operations, for the Socialists would censure these as well. Lafont feared the worst because the cabinet's Russian policy was being formulated by Philip Berthelot and Kammerer who, in turn, were surrounded by Russian émigrés, Polish imperialists, and French reactionaries.[5]

This Socialist campaign against intervention in Russia was not altogether ineffective. Starting with their November 26 memorandum Kammerer and Pichon took account of rising pressures for demobilization and faltering army morale. Similarly, in their note of December 29 they pointed to "public opinion and Parliament" as obstacles to large-scale intervention. At the minimum, Clemenceau used the Socialist protests and threats as a convenient political justification for not going beyond the limited commitment dictated by France's depleted military power and by her intricate diplomatic position.

But the Parliamentary debate also reassured Clemenceau that the Center and Center-right fully backed him. Franklin-Bouillon, the president of the Commission on Foreign Affairs, spoke for this dominant bloc in the Chamber. He argued that because France alone had been intimately tied to Russia before the war, she had a special obligation toward that unhappy country.

Franklin-Bouillon regretfully conceded that during a transitional period France had no alternative but to support the seceding nationalities. In order to defeat the Bolsheviks and remove the Germans from the rimland, not only Finland and Poland had to be supported, but also Estonia, Latvia, Lithuania, and Ukrainia. In addition to providing strategic territories and infantry legions for the anti-Bolshevik crusade, these nascent states were the natural generators of the nationalist ideology so necessary to the enterprise. On the other hand, in order to undermine the Russian people's allegiance to the Bolsheviks, the former needed to be convinced that the intervention was not designed to deprive them of the liberties they had won during the February–

---

[4] For the origin, course, and outcome of this debate, see pp. 177–86 above.

[5] *JO* (December 27 and 29, 1918), pp. 3631, 3633, 3720–3. When Lafont attacked Kammerer's memoranda, Pichon indignantly interrupted him to say that the Foreign Minister and not subordinate officials in the Quai d'Orsay were responsible for French foreign policy.

March Revolution. As for Allied matériel and manpower, the bulk would have to come from Britain and America. To the extent to which France proposed to supply troops, these should be special volunteers to be compensated with high pay and special privileges.

In his summary Franklin-Bouillon demonstrated once again that even though Clemenceau neither consulted nor informed him about foreign policy developments, he never strayed far from the official path.

> Have an overall plan. Proclaim it publicly. Act in conjunction with Russian elements as well as with border nationalities. In addition to the Siberian base immediately establish bases at Reval and Riga for the Baltic and at Odessa for the Black Sea. Start an intensive economic program and supplement it with limited military action, with France making only a very marginal contribution. This is the program with which both to rally the democratic masses of Russia and to save Russia. But time is of essence: Poland and the Ukraine are already seriously threatened, and tomorrow may be too late.

Clemenceau and his advisers could not have asked for more.[6]

Since Franklin-Bouillon spoke for the vast majority of the Chamber, Clemenceau felt that the time had come to unveil the policy which had taken shape during the last few weeks. Pichon was asked to speak for the government. He gave the broad outlines of current and projected military operations, military as well as economic aid, and technical assistance. The deputies—as well as the French nation, the Allies, and the Russians—were told about French activities in the North, in Siberia, in Odessa, in Rumania, and in the Ukraine. Pichon even read the two cables in which Clemenceau had explained his design to General Janin on December 13 and 22.[7] Of course Pichon also claimed that France was acting in complete accord and harmony with her Allies.

Whereas the Foreign Minister meant to impress the interventionists with the fact that the government had a comprehensive policy whose implementation was well under way, he felt that he had either to cajole or to intimidate the skeptics and anti-interventionists in order to neutralize their opposition to bold action.

> We do not intervene in the internal affairs of Russia. We will not pressure a single Russian to force him to choose any particular form of government.
>
> We are merely *defending ourselves by protecting our vital interests* in a country to which we have bonds of considerable importance. . . . In a country in which French nationals are incarcerated, tortured, and threatened with death *we are compelled to intervene* [italics mine].

[6] *JO* (December 29, 1918), 3712–13.
[7] See pp. 300–1 above.

Furthermore, the Bolshevik regime was a serious threat to Europe and the world. It ruled "exclusively" by terror; thousands of innocent victims were being summarily executed; tens of thousands were being thrown into prison. As long as this "center of pestilence" survived no lasting peace was possible: this "odious, abominable regime was spreading infamous propaganda" abroad, constantly threatening Europe with a renewal of war.[8]

In Britain the Russian question received equally urgent and sustained attention in the government as well as in the daily press, the parties, and Commons. Whereas France was predisposed in favor of restoring a large though conservative Russia as a counterweight to Germany, Britain was bound to prefer a reduced Russia. For decades the Foreign Office had devoted itself to checking this sprawling land empire: in 1856 Britain had gone to war and in 1878 she had risked war, while all the time mounting the guard along Russia's frontier with Persia, Afghanistan, and Tibet. It was the rapid eastward spread of German power and influence that had brought about the Anglo-Russian accommodation in Persia, Afghanistan, and Tibet in 1907; and only the stalemate of the war induced Britain reluctantly to consent to Russia's annexation of the Straits and of Constantinople.

From the point of view of this traditional Anglo-Russian rivalry in the Balkans, the Near East, and the Middle East, England could only welcome Russia's collapse. Britain was conveniently released from the wartime secret treaties; she could stake out her claims to the Turkish legacy without worrying about Russia's claims or her collusion with France; and she was freed from pressures along the northwest frontier as she faced the unrest in postwar India. Some superrealists were not satisfied with these benefits of an endogenous nature. They wanted England to take advantage of Russia's plight to roll back her borders, especially in the Caucasus, Finland, and the Baltic provinces. Of course, whereas certain old Foreign Office hands pushed self-determination for border minorities primarily in order to bring them under British influence, latter-day Gladstonians and a large array of Wilsonians advocated it primarily in obedience to their high principles, thereby unintentionally providing the government with a welcome ideological cover. Indeed, many Wilsonians throughout the world found it difficult to reconcile their opposition to intervention in Russia with their advocacy of self-determination for the border peoples.

In any event, Britain was able to plan and implement her intervention so much more coherently than France precisely because the rollback of Russia was perfectly compatible with English security and economic interests. Clemenceau never ceased wondering whether a powerful Russia might not be essential as a counterweight to Germany.

[8] *JO* (December 29, 1918), 3716–18.

He was hesitant, therefore, to promote the breakup of Russia and he was indecisive in his policy toward the mutually embattled Lithuanians, Poles, Ukrainians, and Denikin Whites. Immediately after the Armistice it was Clemenceau's hope that the Allies might be able to overthrow the Bolsheviks without serious territorial amputations of imperial Russia; he only gradually conceded that such amputations were equally essential to the containment and overthrow of Bolshevism.

Lloyd George had no such dilemma. England did not much hesitate to recognize Finland and the three Baltic states and to encourage separatism in Transcaucasia. Especially with Germany thoroughly defeated, London was considerably less worried than Paris about the future threat of a resurgent Germany, so that the renewal of Anglo-Russian rivalry became a more immediate concern. As long as the Bolsheviks survived, their country should be reduced in size and weakened. But from the British point of view "no one could wish that Russia's boundaries should be the same as before"—in Finland, the Baltic nations, Transcaucasia, and Turkestan.[9]

By October 18 Balfour alerted the Cabinet that an Armistice with Germany would bring Britain face to face with "a serious state of things in Russia." Though the wartime motives and justifications for intervention would disappear, England could not withdraw her forces from European and Asiatic Russia without suffering "a serious loss of prestige and letting down her friends." After Austen Chamberlain, sensitive to Washington's caution, pressed for talks with Paris and Smuts stressed that "Bolshevism was a danger to the whole world," the Cabinet instructed the Foreign Office, in consultation with the Chief of the Imperial General Staff and the First Sea Lord, to prepare a paper "on the subject of our present and future military policy in Russia."[1]

In a preliminary note Robert Cecil urged that after the Armistice Britain support "with money and arms as far as we can any [viable] Government in Siberia" while also helping to "set on its legs a national Government in each of the Baltic States and, if we can reach it, in Poland also."[2] On November 1 the Foreign Secretary followed with a terse and concise position paper. In his introduction Balfour argued that Britain would refuse to dissipate her forces "over the huge expanse of Russia"; that the Russians would have to "choose their own form of government"; and that England had "no desire to intervene" in their domestic affairs. It did not follow, however, that England could "disinterest herself wholly from Russian affairs." In particular, the Allied and Associated Powers, including Britain, owed a moral obligation to

[9] Balfour quoted in Notes of an Allied Conversation held in the Cabinet Room, 10 Downing Street, on December 3, 1918 (a.m.), appendix to Imperial War Cabinet 41, Cabinet 23/42.
[1] War Cabinet 489, October 18, 1918 (noon).
[2] Robert Cecil to War Cabinet, October 20, 1918, G.T. 6050.

those anti-Bolshevik forces which never relented in the fight against the Central Powers. Above all, they had to help the Czechs, who were their Allies. In addition, the Allies were "responsible for the existence of the new anti-Bolshevik administrations in the south-east corner of Russia in Europe, in Siberia, in Trans-Caucasia and Trans-Caspia [and] in the territories adjacent to the White Sea and the Arctic Ocean." This being the case, they had to support them. But how far should they go in this direction?

> How far we can [support them], and how such a policy will ultimately develop, we cannot yet say. It must largely depend upon the course taken by *the associated Powers who have far larger resources at their disposal than ourselves*. For us no alternative is open at present than to use such troops as we possess to the best advantage; where we have no troops, to supply arms and money; and in the case of the Baltic provinces, to protect as far as we can the nascent nationalities by the help of *our fleet*. Such a policy must necessarily seem halting and imperfect to those who on the spot are resisting the invasion of militant Bolshevism, but it is *all that we can accomplish or ought* in existing circumstances to attempt [italics mine].[3]

Since France and Italy were even worse off than England Balfour was inclined to make the scope of Allied, particularly of British, intervention contingent on the effort that the U.S. and the Dominions were prepared to put forth.

But General Sir Henry Wilson weighed in with the most detailed analysis and projection. In his judgment, one of the chief wartime justifications for intervention remained valid: to prevent Germany from acquiring a preponderant influence in Russian affairs, an objective which could "almost be described as the 'war after the war.' " With Bolshevism "a danger to the world" which had to be fought, the Allies had to prevent the Germans from "deriving benefit . . . from combating Bolshevism" in the form of absorbing the border states. In addition, it was "contrary to British principles" to abandon friends, so that these states should be given "a fair chance" to defend themselves. There was also the problem of extricating British troops from Russia. According to General Wilson, only those at Archangel presented some difficulty, though he was confident that the "Bolshevists would be only too pleased to assist us" to bring them out over land while the White Sea was icebound.

As for "continued or more efficient intervention," there were two major alternatives.

---

[3] "Notes on our Policy in Russia," November 1, 1918, Appendix to War Cabinet 511, November 29, 1918 (p.m.). This document is cited in Churchill: *Aftermath*, 166–7, but mistakenly dated November 29.

(a) *The first is to create a ring of States all round Bolshevik Russia, the object being to prevent Bolshevism from spreading;* to deprive it of supplies and power of expansion, and to reduce it to absolute exhaustion. This would entail incidentally the starvation of large numbers of people, and would require the occupation by Allied troops of the Border States for an indefinite period, i.e. until non-Bolshevik Russia was obviously going up, whilst Bolshevik Russia was going down. . . . A proposal for creating a chain of States and for garrisoning them has been considered, but it must again be pointed out that the period of occupation under such a scheme would be of unknown duration. From a purely military point of view such a plan is indefensible, for it is one of passive resistance and of complete surrender of the initiative to the Bolsheviks. It involves the dispersal of forces in small packets over an enormous area, none strong enough to effect anything, whilst the Bolsheviks from their central position can concentrate against any one, and each will be a source of anxiety. . . .

(b) *The second alternative is to grasp the nettle firmly by taking active military measures with a view to crushing Bolshevism definitely at the earliest possible date.* This is the quicker and more certain plan of checkmating possible German expansion, since the Border States would once more come into the orbit of a united Russia, the only Power that can permanently check German expansion eastwards; but there are great difficulties in the way of such action,

General Wilson excluded the first alternative primarily because not only the British but also the French and the American public would not tolerate the recruitment of garrisons against an enemy with whom they had "no particular quarrel." As for the second plan, even though it constituted "the only certain method of dealing a fatal blow to Bolshevism within a definite time," it presented grave political and military difficulties. Politically it would be difficult to marshal public support while also running counter to American views, thereby weakening England's position at the Peace Conference. Militarily Russia presented such formidable problems of climate and space that the campaign could not be finished "until the summer of 1919."

This being the case, the only available course was "to do all we can in the way of material help to give our friends a fair start, and then to withdraw . . . from *European* Russia" by the time peace was signed, while seeking the "establishment of a firm Russian Government in Siberia." On Russia's western front the Chief of Britain's Imperial General Staff, not unlike Foch, considered Poland to be "the most important State," whose army should be reinforced with Haller's corps, with liberated Polish war prisoners, and with arms and ammunition. In the Ukraine, where the retreating Germans would leave a dangerous vacuum, Britain should "support stable elements with money, stores and ammunition once the Black Sea was opened, whilst Rumania should occupy Bessarabia, and so form a barrier on the west." Pending a political settlement of Lithuania, Latvia, and Estonia, the Allies should supply their provisional governments with arms as well as "afford them such moral support from the Baltic coast as *naval conditions* permit." On the northern front Britain should seek to effect a "settlement between Finns and Karelians" while also holding Archangel through the winter. In sum, England "should take immediate advantage of the opening of the Baltic to provide our friends with warlike stores, and of the opening of the Black Sea to occupy such ports on its eastern shores as may be necessary in order to extend a hand to those elements in the Caucasus which tend to make a stable Russian Government [italics mine]."[4]

On November 13, at the Foreign Office, Balfour presided over a special conference to consider Britain's Russian policy, attended by Milner, Cecil, Lord Hardinge, Sir George Clark, the Directors of Military and Naval Intelligence, and Major General Radcliffe, the Director of Military Operations. With General Wilson's memorandum before him, the Foreign Secretary reiterated the principle that Britain could not "embark on an anti-Bolshevik crusade in Russia," primarily because "the people of this country would not consent to such a crusade." Balfour's second principle was not nearly so modest: "the border States of Western Russia from the Baltic to the Black Sea" were to be backed up, support to "follow on recognition." After a short discussion and with only Cecil warning against excessive promises to the frail Baltic governments, this conference recommended that Britain remain at Murmansk and Archangel, "recognize the Omsk Directorate as a *de facto* Government," maintain her Siberian expedition, select officers to assist the Czechs in Western Siberia, occupy the Baku-Batum railway, give material aid to Denikin, supply the Baltic states with military material, take over Krasnovodsk, and seek to amend the Anglo-French Convention of December 1917 to extend the British sphere "to include the country between the Don and the Volga."[5]

The recommendations of this special Foreign Office conference were before the War Cabinet when Balfour broached the Russian-*cum*-Bolshevik question on November 14. He once again unfolded his peripheral strategy, insisting that Britain could not allow the western and southeastern border states "to be overwhelmed by Central Russia and incorporated into Central Russia, as these states contained popula-

4 "Memorandum on Our Present and Future Military Policy in Russia," by General Sir Henry Wilson, G. T. 6311.
5 Minutes of the Proceedings of a Conference held at the Foreign Office on November 13, 1918 (3:30 p.m.), Appendix to War Cabinet 502, November 14, 1918 (noon).

tions of different race, language, and religion, and were, on the whole, more civilized and cultivated than the Great Russians." Compared to the Foreign Secretary, Milner and Curzon in particular were inclined to assign higher priority for aid to southern, southeastern, and Siberian Russia than to the Baltic provinces, these being areas "which most closely affected the interests of the British Empire."[6] Just as naturally Cecil urged that Britain and her Allies should make it known to revolutionary, defeated, and neutral Europe that they proposed to "use their control over the food supplies of the world to assist the forces of order against disorder," and he arranged to publicize this resolve through an answer to a Private Notice Question in Commons. The War Cabinet having ratified the "decisions of the Foreign Office Conference," the Prime Minister called attention to the importance of generating public support for these policies of containment and counterrevolution. With Bonar Law suggesting that the government "get the press of the country to take up the question of Bolshevik excesses more fully," the Foreign Office was charged with collecting relevant materials about "the behavior of the Bolshevik Government . . . with a view to full and speedy publication."[7]

Within a few days, when Arthur Ponsonby, Colonel Wedgwood, and other dissenters asked critical questions about the failure to withdraw British troops from Russia, Balfour and Cecil justified continuing intervention with undisguised anti-Bolshevik rhetoric. The Foreign Secretary maintained that the Soviet government deliberately exterminated "by starvation, murder, and wholesale execution . . . all parties which do not support their regime." His Undersecretary, Cecil, spoke of the "outrageous proceedings of the so-called Government in Russia" whose great offenses against humanity included the killing "without justification of one of our naval officers in Petrograd who was doing his duty—protecting the Embassy from entry by unauthorized persons [*sic!*]."[8]

But it was left to Lord Milner, the Secretary of State for War, to

---

[6] It took four months for a high British official to question this assumption: "I know that a certain section of the Government considers that the Caucasus is one of the gates to India, treating, I suppose, the Caspian, Transcaucasia, and Afghanistan merely as a kind of private avenue leading to the actual Indian frontier. Even if this somewhat fantastic theory be accepted, may we not enquire what conceivable hostile Power is likely to attempt to invade India at this stage of the world's history?" Robert Cecil to Lloyd George, March 9, 1919, Robert Cecil Papers, 510706.

[7] War Cabinet 502, November 14, 1918 (noon). "In pursuance of the Cabinet Instructions I saw Sir George Riddell about the anti-Bolshevist campaign. He told me . . . to get together all the facts on the subject . . . and he would arrange for the facts to be distributed to the more important popular papers. . . ." Robert Cecil to Lloyd George, November 20, 1918, G.T. 6330.

[8] *PD, 110* (November 18, 1918), cols. 3175, 3259–64. When an M.P. interjected that Britain no longer had an Embassy in Petrograd, Lord Cecil impatiently countered that this observation was "perfectly irrelevant."

issue the most stirring justification for staying on in Russia. He emphasized, above all, the moral obligation to assist those elements that had
helped the Allies fight Germany but had never relented in their anti-
Bolshevism.

> If the Allies were all to scramble out of Russia at once, the result
> would almost certainly be that the *barbarism,* which at present
> reigns in a part only of that country, would spread over the whole of
> it, including the vast regions of Northern and Central Asia, which
> were included in the dominions of the Tsars. The ultimate conse-
> quences of such a disaster cannot be foreseen. But they would
> assuredly involve a far greater strain on the resources of the British
> Empire than our present commitments [italics mine].[9]

In October Milner had used an interview to urge an early Armistice to
prevent Bolshevism in Central Europe;[1] now he wrote an open letter
advocating limited intervention to prevent Bolshevism from spreading
to the confines of Britain's Asian Empire.

Not that Lloyd George had no qualms and hesitations about this
policy of intervention. Politically and practically he balked at Britain's
undertaking "the protection of the inhabitants of any part of Russia
against Bolshevism," invoking the parallel of the French Revolution,
when Britain had intervened in favor of minorities in the Vendée and at
Toulon with unfortunate consequences. He also warned that "if it was a
point of honor now that we should not withdraw our troops," the same
argument might still be valid a year or even four years later. Obsessed
by the difficulty of finding sufficient troops for Britain's numerous
requirements and worried about Labour opposition, at a minimum he
wanted to withdraw some 14,000 men from Northern Russia, but
Balfour, Curzon, and Milner would not let him.[2] Milner best summarized the position of these advocates of active containment. Unlike
Churchill, who called for an offensive by "large forces . . . abun-
dantly supplied with mechanical appliances," Milner opposed aggressive action.

> He did not wish the fire to spread; he wished to confine it to the
> area it had already ravaged. [Though he was prepared to withdraw
> from Archangel] he did not want to see the spread of Bolshevism to
> the Don and Turkestan. Bolshevism was, at the present moment, the
> greatest danger of the civilized world; he did not wish to attack its
> adherents, lest this should provide them with sympathy; but he
> wished to hold the marches. He would come to terms with the

9 *The Times* (London), December 19, 1918.
1 See pp. 70–2 above.
2 War Cabinet 511, December 10, 1918 (noon); and Imperial War Cabinet 45, December 23, 1918 (p.m.).

Bolsheviks if they agreed to remain within their own boundaries. He would not agree, for instance, to their conquering Siberia.

Milner advanced this disingenuously defensive argument in support of a request for infantry contingents to go to the Caucasus, insisting that he "would rather not occupy Germany at all" than deny British troops to countries in which "they secured order."[3]

Evidently Lloyd George, isolated in his own Cabinet, went along with a host of allegedly prophylactic measures without bothering about inter-Allied consultations. The first British naval squadron entered the Black Sea as early as November 16; and on November 23, the same day that an Anglo-French squadron unloaded equipment at Novoros-sisk for shipment to Denikin, the first British troops went ashore at Batum. Even before these troops started their advance toward Tiflis another British force had landed in Baku following the withdrawal of Turkish troops. Hereafter these two units proceeded to occupy the 400-mile railway which linked Batum and Baku, the Black Sea and the Caspian Sea. The immediate aim of this occupation was not to establish a base for a vast military *offensive* against the Soviet regime or to exploit the oil fields of Transcaucasia. Instead, it was designed to close the ring around the Bolsheviks by denying them access not only to strategic ports through which the Allies planned to ship aid to the Whites but also to desperately needed resources. In brief, through this operation Britain made an essential contribution to the *cordon sanitaire* which was meant to strangle the Bolsheviks, thus saving the Allies the military, political, economic, and diplomatic strains of a larger direct and offensive intervention. Also, for the time being the British held an area from which they meant to exclude first the French and then the Russians.

The British contribution to the *cordon sanitaire* was nearly equally vital along Russia's northwestern borders. By early December units of the Royal Navy steamed into the Baltic Sea. On their way to the entrance of the Gulf of Finland the Sixth Light Cruiser Squadron made brief symbolic calls at Memel, Libau, and Riga. Eventually, on December 12, it dropped anchor just outside the harbor of Reval.

Estonia was in grave danger. Not only had the Germans retreated too rapidly—out of spite and in order to concentrate on the defense of Baltic territories closer to home—but they had also made off with military equipment and rolling stock. When the British fleet arrived, close to half the country was under Bolshevik control and an internal Bolshevik revolt was brewing in the city of Reval. The heavily besieged troops of the Provisional Government, headed by Premier Konstantin Päts, desperately needed equipment as well as a boost in morale.

The British provided both. The task force supplied the 10,000-odd

3 Imperial War Cabinet 45, December 23, 1918 (p.m.).

Estonian soldiers with considerable quantities of war materials, especially with small arms. This show of force combined with actual rather than promised assistance had a profound psychological impact. But more assistance was to come. On December 14 the British warships carried out a heavy bombardment which contributed both the fire power and the *élan* to intimidate the rebels within the city and to rout the opposing Bolshevik troops east of the city. Hereafter the British also ferried Finnish volunteers across the Gulf of Finland to reinforce the Estonian front. Reval was saved.[4]

Latvia was under similar pressure. Whereas Britain and France gave *de facto* recognition to the Provisional Government of Estonia in March 1918, they did not confer it on the Provisional Government of Latvia until Armistice Day. A week later Kārlis Ulmanis, the president of the Peasant League, emerged as the Premier of an essentially conservative cabinet. In a desperate struggle to save Riga from the approaching Red Army as well as from internal mutiny Ulmanis asked August Winnig, the German High Commissioner in the Baltic, for assistance. Simultaneously the British pressed the German government to help hold Latvia and Western Lithuania in accordance with Article 12 of the Armistice.

Winnig was both unwilling and unable to make a major effort just then. Presently, on or about December 23, a naval task force of the Sixth Light Cruiser Squadron pulled into Riga. Instantly E. S. Alexander-Sinclair, the commanding Rear Admiral, was besieged with requests for help, notably for troops to join in the battle. But the officer refused, his instructions being "to land arms and give naval support, if required, but not to land men unless circumstances made it urgently imperative to do so." However, he did unload 5,000 out of 20,000 rifles, which were used to train men "on the shore, alongside one of his ships," and he ordered a British detachment to make a symbolic parade through the city. Finally, on December 27, when the Latvian troops mutinied against Ulmanis, the H.M.S. *Ceres* opened fire from the sea while German infantry units moved in from land. But it was too late. Riga fell on January 3, 1919, under the combined assault of local Bolsheviks and the Red Army.[5]

Augustinas Voldemaras, the Lithuanian Premier, appealed to the

---

[4] Stanley W. Page: *The Formation of the Baltic States* (Cambridge: Harvard University Press; 1959), 125–8.
[5] Imperial War Cabinet 48, December 31, 1918 (a.m.); Page: *Formation of the Baltic States,* 115–20; Alfred Bilmanis: *A History of Latvia* (Princeton: Princeton University Press; 1951) 305–14. To avoid involvement in intervention on a larger scale as well as damage from ice and from the obliteration of navigation marks through the mine fields, the Sixth Squadron was ordered to withdraw from Riga and Reval. One ship was left at Libau, which was free of both ice and Bolshevik trouble.

Allies in the same desperate terms as had Päts and Ulmanis. The Red Army was fast approaching Vilna. Whereas the Allies were unable to reach so far inland, the Germans retreated in "violation" of the Armistice. Furthermore, the bitter Lithuanian-Polish rivalry over Vilna sapped the anti-Bolshevik effort of the Lithuanian forces and precluded a joint military campaign with Polish units. Not surprisingly Vilna fell to the Red Army on January 5.[6]

With the fall of Riga and Vilna—which coincided with the Red Army's capture of Kharkov and advance toward Kiev—both the Allies and the Germans became seriously alarmed. Whether the weakness of the Latvian and Lithuanian armies or the strength of the Bolshevik army primarily accounted for this advance, it had to be halted.

Trotsky and Lenin broadened the defense perimeter around Petrograd by pushing out toward Kovno and Kiev. Meanwhile, provided the Royal Navy did not develop Estonia and Southeastern Finland into a forward operational base, it could contribute little to the campaign against Bolshevism, especially since Lenin was not likely to challenge British seapower in the Baltic Sea!

The Red Army could only be stopped and thrown back on land with infantry. Eager to assume responsibility for the defense against Bolshevism in the Baltic yet unwilling to engage land forces in Latvia and Lithuania, the British Cabinet had no alternative but to press the Germans into service. Significantly, the Allied resolve to compel the Germans to implement Article 12 of the Armistice coincided with the fall of Riga and Vilna. In turn, with the fall of these cities and the threat to Kovno, the German government began to fear for East Prussia, particularly since in late December and early January the Spartacist disorders still worried Ebert. As for Ulmanis and Voldemaras, they, too, were sufficiently frightened to consider compensating the Germans for helping stem the Bolshevik tide.

Enter the Free Corps, which was a by-product of the specter of Bolshevism. Since the Allies found it impolitic to raise volunteers to fight the Reds, they asked the Germans to do so. While the Germans provided the freedom fighters, the Latvians and Lithuanians paid for their services and equipment. In addition to legitimizing this enterprise with Article XII, the Allies also helped it through their financial and material assistance to the provisional governments of the nascent Baltic states.

Not that the German government, Winnig, the volunteers, and the German Balts were innocent of political, economic, and territorial ambitions in the Baltic provinces. But why should they have been more selfless than all the other anti-Bolshevik freedom fighters? The Poles,

[6] Alfred Erich Senn: *The Emergence of Modern Lithuania* (New York: Columbia University Press; 1959), 55–71.

the Rumanians, and even the nascent Baltic nations expected generous compensation for their service in the anti-Bolshevik crusade. Surely, the price paid was not excessive by contemporary standards. The Provisional Government of Latvia promised "Latvian citizenship, upon their request, to all voluntarily enlisted alien [German] members of the Latvian defense forces after they have participated in the struggle for the liberation of the territory of the Latvian State from the Bolsheviks for at least four weeks."[7] But whereas in Latvia the German volunteers gained citizenship and the right to settle, in Lithuania they simply fought for "four marks per day."[8]

True enough, General von der Goltz, the Chief of all the Free Corps in the Baltic provinces, looked upon anti-Bolshevism as a welcome and convenient smokescreen for Germany to recoup in the East what she would lose in the West and overseas.[9] Ernst von Salomon "never took the slogan 'Fight Bolshevism' seriously," but conceded that "the West's fear of Bolshevism made our war in Courland possible."[1] Perhaps it should be added that within Germany the specter of Spartacism was exploited to equally good advantage by reactionaries, conservatives, militarists, and proto-Nazis.

Whatever the motives of individual volunteers—personal gain, adventure, idealistic nationalism, anti-Bolshevism—the *Freikorps'* Baltic expedition was inseparable from the all-European confrontation between revolution and counterrevolution. Britain's encouragement was a function of Allied fear of Bolshevism. If the French seemed to drag their feet, they did so not because they were any less afraid of Bolshevism but because they distrusted the Germans, were jealous of British influence in the Baltic, and sided with Poland against Lithuania. In any case, Great Britain's sanction was decisive since England was responsible for the Baltic sector of the anti-Bolshevik front. Hereafter the Red Army was kept out of Kovno and never crossed the Niemen River.

In the meantime Woodrow Wilson had visited England. During his conversations with the President, Lloyd George received confirmation that Wilson, being "very much opposed to armed intervention," was not about to underwrite a major effort in Russia. Wilson considered the U.S. presence in Archangel, Murmansk, and Siberia with very mixed feelings. Lloyd George gathered that he was inclined to look for an early occasion to withdraw from Northern Russia; and U.S.–Japanese relations were likely to determine his attitude with regard to Siberia. In any event, the President wanted to probe the intentions of the Soviets—

---

[7] Cited in Bilmanis: *History of Latvia*, 313.
[8] Senn: *Emergence of Modern Lithuania*, 77.
[9] General Rudiger Graf von der Goltz: *Meine Sendung in Finland und im Baltikum* (Leipzig: Koehler; 1920), *passim*.
[1] See Robert G. L. Waite: *Vanguard of Nazism: The Free Corps Movement in Postwar Germany, 1918–1923* (Cambridge: Harvard University Press; 1952), 98–107.

by contacting Litvinov[2]—before setting his course concerning both intervention and Russian representation at the Peace Conference.[3]

It was against this background of Wilson's reticence and the completion of the ring around Bolshevik Russia that at the turn of the year the War Cabinet settled down to a detailed examination of Britain's future policy toward Lenin. The impending start of the Peace Conference in Paris also forced the issue in London.

The Prime Minister introduced the discussion with an argument for limited, indirect intervention. Lloyd George estimated that the Bolsheviks "were badly equipped and badly organized and that most trained officers were with their opponents." As a result, all the Allies needed to do to promote "peace between the warring sections" was to equip the Whites and the Czech Legion sufficiently well "to hold their own" against the Red Army. In sum, Lloyd George wanted to steer a middle course. He opposed full-fledged intervention because the Allies "were not prepared to undertake this task" and for fear that it would rally the Russian people around the Soviet regime. On the other hand, he opposed immediate withdrawal because it would mean the defeat of the Whites and the victory of Lenin. His middle course was based on the facile assumption that should the Allied-supported White armies fail to topple Lenin they could easily force him into a compromise. Lloyd George never seems to have faced the question whether in the Russian Civil War, as in other civil wars, both sides might be equally committed to unconditional surrender.[4]

Both Sir Robert Borden and George Barnes shared the Prime Minister's caution. Rather than offer Canadian troops for a vast military campaign, Sir Robert wanted the Allies "to induce the Governments of the various States in Russia to send representatives to Paris." There the Allied and Associated nations could apply pressure "to bring about conditions of stable government under the power and influence of the League of Nations."[5]

Barnes endorsed Borden's proposal for the transmogrification of the Bolshevik regime.

> It was clear that we could not fight Bolshevism in Russia except on a large scale. It was no use merely poking with sticks into the kennel to infuriate the dog. He would be in favor of getting all sections of Russians, including the Bolsheviks, to meet, at the instance of the Peace Conference, with a view to adjusting their own differences. If this failed, then intervention might be justified, though he considered that it should be limited to economic pressure. He did

2 See pp. 422–6 below.
3 David Lloyd George: *The Truth About the Peace Treaties,* I, 188–9.
4 Lloyd George: *Truth,* I, 316–19.
5 Ibid., 199–200.

not consider that we could suppress Bolshevism forcibly without American help.

As Labour's self-styled spokesman, Barnes's views carried considerable weight. He and his cabinet colleagues could not have been immune to the rising popular clamor for immediate demobilization, the end of conscription, and rapid withdrawal from Russia.[6]

Lord Cecil and Lord Milner tried to tighten up Borden's scheme with the suggestion "that all parties in Russia should be told to stand fast where they were till the Peace Conference was over." But then Cecil added the proviso that during this truce of God the Allies give material and financial assistance to the Whites and continue the blockade, and that the Imperial War Cabinet prepare to help those countries that were threatened by Russian Bolshevik invasion. Milner endorsed these modifications of Borden's proposal, wryly noting that if the Bolsheviks agreed to these terms "they would, in fact, have begun to cease being Bolsheviks."[7]

But in the Cabinet Winston Churchill was the most outspoken and persistent advocate of direct military intervention.

He was in favor of joint action by the five great Powers, or, if America refused to act, by the rest. The intervention should be collective, and not by one Power only, and with joint contingents. He was all for negotiation, with the object of securing a satisfactory settlement without fighting. But he considered that there was no chance of securing such a settlement unless it was known that we had the power and the will to enforce our views. What we should say to the Russians was that if they were ready to come together we would help them: and that if they refused, we would use force to restore the situation and set up a democratic Government. In his view, Bolshevism in Russia represented a mere fraction of the population, and would be exposed and swept away by a General Election held under Allied auspices. A decision on this question was urgent. It was the only part of the war which was still going on, and if we ignored it we should come away from the Peace Conference rejoicing in a victory which was no victory, and a peace which was no peace: and in a few months we should find ourselves compelled to gather our armies again, and summon the Conference anew in order to deal with the situation.[8]

Churchill wanted to negotiate or dictate from a position of military strength. He was unclear, however, about the shape of post-Bolshevik Russia, underestimated Lenin's popular support, and oversimplified the problem of holding general elections under foreign bayonets.

In any event, Churchill's "realism" found few supporters. Even

6 Ibid., 325.
7 Ibid., 200, 329.
8 Ibid., 325–6.

Lord Curzon took exception: although he kept insisting that Britain stay on in the Caucasus, he had grave doubts about England's capacity for direct intervention. To be sure, with Cecil and Milner he was inclined to favor a policy of active coercion, but all three stopped short of endorsing Churchill's summons to unilateral military intervention. Significantly both Bonar Law and Balfour also sided with the circumspect rather than the extreme interventionists.[9]

In the light of this inconclusive debate the Prime Minister now formulated "the views which he was in favor of putting forward to President Wilson and M. Clemenceau in Paris." On this momentous occasion Lloyd George did not touch on the military and naval actions which were well under way in Transcaucasia and the Baltic. Only at the insistence of others did he admit that Britain would continue to support "in any manner *short of military intervention* . . . any existing Government with which we [have] been cooperating" and which was subject to "*external* aggression by the Bolsheviks [italics mine]."[1]

This rededication to the *cordon sanitaire* came at the end of a long statement in which Lloyd George argued that the risks, costs, and complications of offensive military measures were altogether forbidding. His statement was exceptionally incisive and informed; it also had sound historical perspective. In sum, the Prime Minister presented another of his statesmanlike impromptu briefs.

> He was definitely opposed to military intervention in any shape. In the first place, it appeared to him a tremendously serious undertaking. The Germans, who had occupied only a relatively small part of Russia, within striking distance of Petrograd and with practically nothing in front of them, had found themselves unable, either to go to Petrograd or to save the situation in the west, while all the time they and the Austrians had something like a million men stuck in that morass, the greater part of whom they had not even yet succeeded in disentangling. In our case the Allies were on the mere fringe of Russia with less than 100,000 troops. The Bolsheviks had raised their forces to 300,000, which might exceed 1,000,000 by March, and had greatly improved their organisation. Where were we to find the troops with which to march into the heart of Russia and occupy the country? We already had to find troops for Germany, Palestine, Mesopotamia, and the Caucasus. He asked what contribution Australia, Canada, or South Africa were prepared to furnish to the task of conquering and keeping down Russia? No British troops could be found for the purpose without conscription, and if Parliament endorsed conscription for that purpose he doubted whether the troops would go. Our citizen army were prepared to go anywhere for liberty, but they could not be convinced that the suppression of Bolshevism was a war for liberty.

[9] Ibid., 323–4, 329–30.
[1] Ibid., 330.

A further reason which weighed with him was the danger that military intervention would only strengthen the very force which we set out to destroy. It was impossible to ignore the parallel of the French Revolution. There, too, there had been horrors as bad as, or worse than, those of the Bolsheviks, perpetrated by a small fraction, which had secured the control of France. There, too, we were invited to help. Toulon and La Vendée corresponded to Riga and the Ukraine. But the very fact that we intervened enabled Danton to rally French patriotism and make the terror a military instrument. When the Revolution was followed by a military dictatorship we were worse off. France became organised as a great military machine imbued with a passionate hatred against us.

Were we prepared to face a revolutionary war against a population of over 100,000,000, associating ourselves in this intervention with allies like the Japanese, against whom feeling in Russia was so passionately strong? He knew of no authority on the strength of which we could be justified in hypothecating our resources and our manhood in the belief that the Russians would regard us as deliverers. For Russia to emancipate herself from Bolshevism would be a redemption, but the attempt to emancipate her by foreign armies might prove a disaster to Europe as well as to Russia. The one sure method of establishing the power of Bolshevism in Russia was to attempt to suppress it by foreign troops. To send our soldiers to shoot down the Bolsheviks would be to create more Bolsheviks there. The best thing was to let Bolshevism fail of itself, as it might and probably would if it did not represent Russian sentiment. That would serve as a deterrent for similar experiments elsewhere, just as the failure of similar movements to establish Communism in 1848 had had a salutary effect in Europe.

In conclusion, he hoped that the Cabinet would agree to support him in refusing to countenance any military intervention, and in inviting the representatives of all sections of Russia to appear before the Peace Conference, as Sir Robert Borden had suggested, with a view to their composing their differences.[2]

It would seem that momentarily Lloyd George was once again under the spell of Wilson and Labour. Only a few weeks before he himself had contributed to the anti-Bolshevik hysteria; and a few days ago the outcome of the khaki election had been announced. Possibly because he feared the pressure of the "hard men" Lloyd George hastened to put the brakes on them. The khaki Commons was likely to cheer on Balfour, Curzon, Milner and Cecil, possibly even Churchill. Not that he was about to break with them, since in his new Cabinet Curzon become Lord President of the Council, Milner Colonial Secretary, Cecil a prominent member of the peace delegation, and Churchill Secretary of State for War and Air. Nevertheless, he did have to slow

2 Ibid., 327–9.

them down, particularly since the reactionary and conservative press was stepping up its anti-Bolshevik campaign.

As expected, the *Morning Post* continued to take the lead. With Russia a "plague-spot" all of Europe was in danger of infection and a real peace settlement was impossible. The Allies laid themselves open to criticism "not because they have intervened in Russia but because they have not intervened effectually." The time had come to support "our friends" in Russia with all "those modern weapons in which the Bolsheviks are deficient." Moreover, the League of Nations should organize a police force: it need not be great in size, and perhaps it should be composed of volunteers. These weapons and this inter-Allied *Freikorps* simply had to supplement Wilson's plan to stop Bolshevism with food. "If force alone cannot stop Bolshevism, neither can it be stopped without force since, after all, Lenin and Trotsky are not exactly kittens to be choked with cream."[3]

The stately *Times* and the closely affiliated Continental *Daily Mail* were equally convinced that the Allies could not leave "the broad territories of Russia a scene of wholesale massacre and loot." The Allies had to go to Southern Russia to save "what yet remained of civilization there." By December 18 the *Daily Mail,* in a banner headline, reported that the Bolsheviks were planning to have an ARMY OF THREE MILLION BY MARCH. How could this mounting flood be contained?

Of course neither paper had any sympathy with the view that intervention was wrong. On the other hand, Britain and France were in no condition to intervene on a large scale. The best they could do was to establish a *cordon sanitaire*. "If America, who has large interests in Russia, should desire to use her comparatively fresh forces in crushing Bolshevism nobody is likely to object except the Bolsheviks, but for the Allies in Europe it is a different matter." Quite apart from their military and financial weakness they were subject to overwhelming pressure "against armed intervention in the form of an expeditionary force."[4]

Still, this was no time for complacency.

> Of all the problems before the Peace Conference, none is quite so urgent as that of our relations with the new Imperialism of the Russian Bolshevists. . . . The present Russian Government . . . is the most Imperialistically minded Government in Europe. Just as the Germans before the War used to plead fear of "encirclement" as an excuse for indulgence of their ambitions, the Russian Bolshevists, realizing that isolation means the end of their tyranny, have begun an actively aggressive campaign outside their own borders with the object of extending the frontiers of Russia, of establishing communication with their German sympathizers, and of making as

[3] *Morning Post,* December 21 and 31, 1918, and January 15, 1919.
[4] *Daily Mail* (Paris), December 27, 1918, and January 2, 1919.

many converts as possible to their own political views. We do not
share the exaggerated fears of an extension of Bolshevism to
England, but its extension into the borderlands between Russia and
Germany is a very serious danger. . . . We shall merely have
exchanged German imperialism for Bolshevism; and the last state
will be worse than the first, for whereas German imperialism, at any
rate in peace time, did not seek to subvert the political order, this
subversion is the whole object of the new Russian Imperialism. All
the protests against interfering in the internal affairs of Russia are
beside the mark. . . .

There is no question now of landing the army of a million men
which some are talking about; even the question of intervention in
Russia proper may stand over for the present. But the defensive
measure necessary to protect the border States against Bolshevist
aggression cannot safely be postponed without the risk of the
gravest injury to our Polish friends and without the certain penalty
of finding our problem exaggerated out of all recognition by our
neglect. There are enough men in Poland to do all that is required.
All that they want is organization and the materials of war, and this
they should have at once without delay. . . .

Furthermore, in addition to giving aid and support to the anti-Bolsheviks in Southern Russia, the Royal Navy would secure the Black Sea,
the Caspian, and the Baltic. "Deprived of access to the sea Bolshevism
will soon wither and there need be no question of the employment of
large numbers of British troops in extensive land operations."[5]

The *New Europe* was another influential interventionist organ. In it
Bernard Pares asserted that Russia was far too big to be left out of the
settlement; that the East European and Balkan barrier between Russia
and Germany was valueless without a pro-Allied Russia; and that the
Allies had no alternative to going to Russia themselves to get rid of
Bolshevism which was nothing but an orgy of "riot and murder" and
whose power was "in machine guns and nothing else."[6]

Both Masaryk and Beneš encouraged this view that prompt intervention was needed to restore a reliable Russia. At the same time they
offered the services of the Czech Legion, maintained that because of
her central geographic location Bohemia was the ideal staging area for
intervention in Budapest, Vienna, Rumania, and Poland, and insisted
that since Hungary was in particularly grave danger of falling to
Bolshevism the Czechs had to occupy all of Slovakia.[7]

According to the *New Europe* the days of the principle of nonintervention were over; and since the fate of Russia was the key to the peace

[5] *The Times* (London), January 4 and 13, 1919.
[6] *The New Europe*, November 28, 1918, 147–51.
[7] *Le Matin*, November 5, 1918; *l'Action Française*, December 7 and 10, 1918; *la Nation Tchèque*, Nos. 10–11, November 15–December 1, 1918.

and tranquility of Europe the success or failure of the new international order depended on prompt intervention for the consecration of the March Revolution of 1917. Should the Allies fail to challenge the Bolsheviks before the fall of Vilna and Riga they might have to do so after the fall of Warsaw, Berlin, and Budapest. But in spite of attaching such overarching importance to intervention, even the *New Europe* had to admit that "after four years of war only *volunteer armies* could be employed."[8]

The entire Right as well as the *New Europe* were clamoring for the use of every conceivable instrument of intervention short of big infantry units. They impatiently rejected the suggestion that negotiations be tried. Nor were they in the least bit bothered by the central contradiction in the interventionists' argument: on the one hand the Bolsheviks were portrayed as brutal but anarchist rebels lacking in popular support and organizing ability, and therefore on the verge of collapse; on the other hand their power was said to be awesome and ready to sweep all of Europe before it.

The pervasive disinclination to dispatch big military expeditions developed in response to the fast-growing "Hands Off Russia" campaign of the forces of movement. By December 12 the *New Statesman* declared that "the time had come to break the self-imposed silence which we have observed with respect to the British government's attitude toward Russia."[9] Six days thereafter the Executive Committee of the Labour Party resolved "that a letter be addressed to the Prime Minister asking for a statement of Government policy on Russian Intervention."[1] In this letter Henderson and Bowerman, who signed for the Parliamentary Committee of the Trades Union Congress, asked for assurance against interference and for a promise that British armed forces would be "withdrawn at the earliest possible moment."[2] In the absence of an answer the Labour Party sent a second letter to Lloyd George on January 3; it also asked Lord Milner to "receive a deputation to discuss the policy of Allied Intervention."[3]

But since there was no official reply to these and other "private" communications, the Labour Party took the issue to the floor of the House of Commons. Like the ex-*majoritaires* in France, Adamson, J. H. Thomas, and Clynes made a point of loudly proclaiming their own anti-Bolshevism; unlike their French colleagues, however, they stub-

---

[8] *The New Europe,* January 16, 1919, 2–4.
[9] Cited in Stephen R. Graubard: *British Labour and the Russian Revolution, 1917–1924* (Cambridge: Harvard University Press; 1956), 64.
[1] Labour Party: Minutes of the Executive Committee, 15, December 18, 1918.
[2] For the text of this letter see Labour Party: *Report of the Nineteenth Annual Conference* (Southport, 1919), 25; and G.T. 6604, Cabinet 24/73.
[3] Labour Party: Minutes of the Executive Committee, 16, January 3, 1919; and Labour Party: *Report of the Nineteenth Annual Conference,* 25–6.

bornly held that the Red Terror was no valid excuse or pretext for intervention.[4]

In considerable measure, at least, these private and Parliamentary remonstrances were a response to the anti-interventionist protest of the internationalists in the party, the trade unions, and the UDC. It was almost as if these wartime dissenters saw a connection between the jingoists' attack on them—which had just resulted in their annihilation in the khaki election—and the victor governments' attack on the Soviets. Through the *Labour Leader* the ILP agitated for the "Recall of Our Soldiers from Russia!" because the intervention was designed to restore tsarism and violated self-determination. The ILP also sought to set the record straight: the Bolsheviks were not Jews and criminals; they did not keep themselves in power by terror alone; and the Russian masses were not eager for Allied intervention.[5]

Through the *Herald* George Lansbury carried on what may well have been the most effective propaganda to "Bring the Boys Home From Russia!" It was Lansbury who first publicized the post-Armistice unrest in the army which was of such great concern to the government and which sparked disquieting rumors in political circles.

The first mutiny at Shoreham on November 13 was followed by mutinies and disorders on both sides of the Channel. By the time Lloyd George appointed Churchill to the War Office during the first days of January "the temper of the Army and the problem of demobilization caused increasing anxiety"; and within a week, upon assuming his new post, Churchill was "confronted with conditions of critical emergency."[6] Perhaps the Prime Minister put Churchill in the War Office not only because he needed an expert hand there but also in the hope of blunting Churchill's enthusiasm for military intervention in Russia by exposing him firsthand to the difficulty of holding a conscript army which wanted immediate demobilization above all else.[7]

After the turn of the year the military unrest became particularly serious in key embarkation centers in England as well as in British army camps in the Pas de Calais. On January 3, by prearrangement, the men refused to report for reveille at Folkstone. This mutiny was triggered by impatience with discipline after the war's end; dissatisfaction with food; antagonism between officers and men; and restlessness inspired by revolutionary developments on the Continent. The rebels' immediate goal was to stop transports from taking troops from

[4] Graubard: *British Labour and the Russian Revolution, 1917–1924*, 67–70.

[5] *Labour Leader*, January 23, 1919.

[6] T. H. Wintringham: *Mutiny: Being a Survey of Mutinies from Spartacus to Invergordan* (London: Stanley Nott; 1936), 312; and Churchill: *Aftermath*, 41.

[7] The Prime Minister offered Churchill either the Admirality or the War Ministry. He opted for the former, but then he was asked to take the War Office. See Churchill: *Aftermath*, 40–1.

Folkstone to France; their broader objective was to force the government to speed up demobilization.

The following day some 10,000 soldiers marched through the streets of Folkstone; a mass meeting was held; a Soldiers' Union was formed; and the mutineers chose their spokesmen, "every one, be it noted, a Trade Unionist." These developments were sufficiently serious for Field Marshal Sir William Robertson to come down from London personally to direct his officers' negotiations with these spokesmen. Aside from promising to "forget the incident," the officers agreed that all men with jobs would immediately be demobilized while those with prospects of employment would receive a week's leave to nail down their jobs. By Saturday night, January 4, the camp at Folkstone had emptied "and the latest to leave were the leaders of the movement, who watched their last comrades go free before they went free themselves."

News of these events rapidly spread to other embarkation and staging points: 7,000 men demonstrated at Shoreham, 1,500 at Shortlands, and 4,000 at Dover. Incidents of insubordination also occurred at Sydenham, Grove Park, Kempton Park, Park Royal, Aldershot, Maidstone, Chatham, Bristol, and Fairlop.

In London, meanwhile, 400 men scheduled for departure to Salonica refused to entrain. Moreover, on January 7, some 1,500 soldiers, belonging to the Army Service Corps at Park Royal, assembled first at Whitehall and then in Downing Street, and asked for an interview with the Prime Minister. While Lloyd George "was quite prepared to see the delegates or the soldiers in a body," his colleagues took turns restraining him. Milner doubted the wisdom of such a confrontation, fearful that this precedent would foster "the tendency to indiscipline and disorder." Likewise, General Wilson disliked the idea of the Prime Minister conferring with delegates of soldiers who "had disregarded their officers," the more so since the "soldiers' delegation bore a dangerous resemblance to a Soviet." Besides, the practice might spread, there being reports of simmering unrest in military camps around Boulogne, Calais, and Dunkirk and on ships in Libau, Archangel, and Murmansk. Finally, it was decided that General Robertson would meet the soldiers' delegates to inform them that though their alleged grievances would be promptly investigated, these should be voiced through proper channels, while the Premier would issue a statement on demobilization the following day.[8]

That these grievances centered around bad food, unreasonable hours of duty, and general impatience with demobilization was quite clear. But some of the men also appear to have feared that the delay in their demobilization was due to their being marked for service in

[8] War Cabinet 514, January 8, 1919 (a.m.). See also the article "The Great Mutiny," by *The Herald's* special correspondent at Folkstone, in *The Herald,* January 11, 1919; Wintringham, *Mutiny,* 313–18; Churchill: *Aftermath,* 42.

Russia. In any case, no less an authority than General Wilson, in commenting on "the signs of unrest in the Army at home," told the Cabinet that "it was notorious that the prospect of being sent to Russia was immensely unpopular," the result being that "it was impossible for us to reinforce our troops in North Russia and Siberia."[9]

This unrest continued into late January and the first half of February. "In a single week more than thirty cases of insubordination . . . were reported from different centers" in England. Both in early January and later the local military authorities in most cases restored discipline by persuasion and promises of speedy demobilization. "Although the situation was very threatening in many places, almost the only spot where there was actual and serious rioting was at Luton, where owing to the weakness of the civic authorities, the Town Hall was burnt by the mob." Starting January 27 "regular mutiny broke out at Calais," the ringleaders being members of Ordnance and Mechanical Transport detachments who were "closely associated with political Trade Unionism." Since about three or four thousand armed men almost completely took over Calais, two divisions had to be recalled from forward positions to help restore order and discipline. Nearly simultaneously rioting broke out in Glasgow and Belfast and rear-line army units were called on to assist the civil authorities in restoring the situation.[1]

Whatever the causes of this incipient mutiny it was bound to be exploited by the opponents of intervention. At the end of its report on the mutiny *The Herald* asked "whether English troops were to risk death by cold and starvation in Russia; whether it was intended that they should engage in a war against the Russian Revolution; and whether Russia shall not be left to evolve her own destiny, without the shedding of more British blood?" Since except for the projected intervention in Russia there was no reason for not bringing home the boys and demobilizing them, "the cure for army unrest" was self-evident.[2] Presently Beatrice Webb suspected that "the incipient revolt of the armies" was about to become a chief moderating influence in Paris. She thought she could hear Lloyd George explain to Clemenceau: "My dear friend, our soldiers won't go to Russia, not even to Berlin: that is the plain fact. And don't rely on Wilson. He himself is obsessed by his great dream of self-determination: his people have only one settled intention—to get back to lucrative business. Unless your armies are ready to conquer Russia and police the world we must have a peace which will be in fact a peace of consent."[3]

Had Wilson come to Europe determined to mount a frontal assault

9 War Cabinet 515, January 10, 1919 (a.m.).
1 Churchill: *Aftermath*, 50–1; and War Cabinet 523, January 31, 1919 (p.m.).
2 *The Herald*, January 11 and 18, 1918.
3 Cole (ed.): *Beatrice Webb's Diaries*, 143, entry of January 14, 1919.

on Bolshevik Russia both Clemenceau and Lloyd George—let alone Sonnino—more than likely would have followed his lead. Even if Wilson had not assigned additional troops to intervention, he himself could easily have provided the anti-Bolshevik crusade with an inspiring ideology which would have neutralized the opposition of the European Left, while his country had the necessary reserves of material, food, and money with which to equip the crusaders. In fact, however, with the defeat of Germany, the President's earlier indecision about intervention was reinforced. This indecision, which stemmed from many sources, inclined Wilson to abide by existing commitments rather than immediately to execute either a complete withdrawal or a resolute offensive.

Very much like Lloyd George, he had a grudging admiration for the Russian Revolution despite its betrayal by the Bolsheviks. He was in full sympathy with the political transformation intended by the two successive Provisional Governments, but he took strong exception to the subsequent use of violence in pursuit of forced-draft economic and social changes. Even though he wanted to get rid of the Bolsheviks, he was hesitant to do so by teaming up with reactionary forces in Russia as well as outside. He half hoped that the Bolsheviks would oblige him by removing themselves and thus save him the embarrassment of removing them by coercion. At the same time Wilson no doubt expected that a little coercion would go a long way not only because he considered the Bolshevik leaders incompetent fanatics but also because he could not conceive of the Russian people supporting this treacherously tyrannical regime. There were even tactical reasons for preferring limited and indirect coercion: it would make it more difficult for the Bolsheviks to pose as champions of the Russian national interest against foreign aggressors.

Of course, beyond these personal perspectives there were political factors, both international and national, that fostered the President's disinclination to step up intervention. As compared to France, and even as compared to Britain, the U.S. had a markedly limited stake in Russia. From the point of view of American military security Russia's future size or power were of small concern: after all, as long as America continued to be essentially a naval power and Russia a land power, security concerns could not claim first priority. In this regard Washington's major objective was to exclude Japan from Eastern Siberia rather than to project American influence into this area, an objective of consequence in the U. S.–Japanese rivalry in China. Significantly, the Secretary of War, Newton D. Baker, urged Wilson to "simply order our forces home by the first boat," primarily because he feared that otherwise America might be "rudely awakened some day to a realization that Japan has gone in under our wing and so completely mastered the country that she cannot be either induced out or forced out by any action either of the Russians or of the Allies."[4] Subsequently not only Baker but also General March repeatedly called the President's attention to the growing restlessness of American soldiers in Russia, especially in Siberia.[5]

From the diplomatic point of view American objectives were equally limited. Whereas France and Britain hankered for a return to their respective prewar arrangements with Russia, the U.S. was ready to settle for a Russia hostile to new violations of the Open Door in China. Not that Washington attached no importance to the safety and welfare of the new states of Eastern and East Central Europe, which at a minimum required Russian benevolence. But Washington tended to focus on Russia's Pacific role, France on her European role, and England on her Middle Eastern role.

Economically the United States' stake was no less marginal. As compared to France and England, private loans and investments as well as government loans to Russia were small, and so was the level of trade. To be sure, future trade and investment opportunities could not be discounted. However, business opportunities in China rather than in Russia excited American politicians, traders, and bankers. There was no significant Russian trade lobby.[6] Likewise, the Russian-American community which might have exerted pressure for intervention was small and dispersed. Whatever organized pressure there was came from Polish-Americans whose dream of a reborn Great Poland could only be fulfilled at Russia's cost.

There were, then, few if any readily definable and significant military, business, or ethnic groups pressing for large-scale intervention.[7] On the other hand, the defiantly anti-interventionist groups were small and ineffectual as compared to their counterparts in Britain, France, and Italy. The American Socialist Party had a relatively small membership and following and it had only very tenuous connections with organized labor. Even though its membership dropped only from 83,138 in 1916 to 74,519 in 1918, the Socialist Party had been fatally weakened by the war. "The party's press was impotent, many leaders were in prison or on their way there, internal strife was more intense than it had ever been before, relations with organized labor

[4] Newton D. Baker to Woodrow Wilson, November 27, 1918, Baker Papers, Box 8.
[5] Wilson Papers, VIII A: 7, 8, and 9, *passim*.
[6] For comparative figures of French, British, and American war loans as well as prewar government and private loans and investments see Leo Pasvolsky and Harold G. Moulton: *Russian Debts and Russian Reconstruction* (New York: McGraw-Hill; 1924), esp. 21, 181–2.
[7] G. Leonid I. Strakhovsky: *American Opinion about Russia, 1917–1920* (Toronto: University of Toronto Press; 1961); Frederick L. Schuman: *American Policy Toward Russia Since 1917* (New York: International Publishers; 1928); William A. Williams: *American-Russian Relations, 1791–1947* (New York: Rinehart; 1952).

were more strained than before the war, and the hostility of large segments of the public was greater than ever." Moreover, since the Western element of the party had been decimated, the left wing of the Socialist movement was now on the East Coast. Only this left wing vigorously opposed all forms of intervention; and within this left wing the Slavic-Jewish federations provided the bulk of the membership. During the incipient Red Scare, the ethnic, religious, and language composition of these federations made it particularly easy for the superpatriots to smear radical Socialists as un-American.[8]

Precisely because the A.F. of L. was so loyal and Carthaginian and the Socialist Party so enfeebled and besieged—and without congressional representation—the few Radical dissenters who were anti-interventionist were hopelessly isolated and inefficacious. Moreover, whereas all but a few Allied Radicals—and Socialists—continued to trust in Wilson, American Radical dissenters had long since broken with him. Bourne and Villard, the one antiwar and the other prowar, could only cry in the wilderness.[9]

The most effective anti-interventionist voices were raised by Progressive Republicans in Congress. On December 12, 1918, Hiram Johnson (Republican, California) introduced the first resolution requesting information concerning U.S. policy in Russia. In introducing this precatory resolution, which was referred to the Foreign Relations Committee, he confessed that "some of us" would have made this inquiry a few months before, except that "we considered it inappropriate and indiscreet" while the war was still in progress. But now that the war was over and Germany was defeated this self-imposed silence had to be broken. American boys continued to fight in Russia; and yet, neither had Congress declared war nor had the country been told what the boys were fighting for.

The Russian situation was being discussed in England and France. Furthermore, British and French labor dared discuss it. "The only place in all the world where there has been poverty of discussion or fear of discussion was in the United States of America." On December 30 Johnson came back to this charge: he told the Senate that through Milner and Pichon the British and French governments, unlike the Wilson Administration, had at least responded—"whether honestly or not"—to insistent popular clamor for information.

Meanwhile he attacked Creel's continuing portrayal of the Bolsheviks as German agents. How could this indictment be sustained since in

[8] David A. Shannon: *The Socialist Party of America* (New York: Macmillan; 1955), 121–3; Theodore Draper: *The Roots of American Communism* (New York: Viking; 1957), *passim;* John Higham; *Strangers in the Land* (New York: Atheneum; 1963), 224 ff.
[9] Cf. Christopher Lasch: *The American Liberals and the Russian Revolution* (New York: Columbia University Press; 1962), *passim.*

the Armistice the Germans were instructed to keep the Bolsheviks out of enemy-occupied Russian territories? Johnson, and subsequently Borah—both having been contacted by Raymond Robins—repeatedly asked whether it was not true that before as well as after signing the treaty of Brest Litovsk the Soviets had made repeated overtures to American officials in Russia?

In any case, even though the military intervention was originally launched as part of the military campaign against the Central Powers, now that these were defeated it need not be continued. "Or are we now engaged in destroying Bolshevism? If we are, what have we decided shall take its place? Are we again to put the Romanovs upon the throne? Do we seek a dictator for this starved land?" If these were the Allies' purposes, then the implications were vast, indeed. There was a concealed danger that this intervention in Russia was merely the prelude to "war against revolution in all countries, whether enemy or ally." Should the League of Nations be formed upon this motive it would quickly "degenerate into a Holy Alliance." Instead, the U.S. had a particular obligation to steer a safe course between the "Scylla of Bolshevism . . . and the Charybdis of Reaction."[1]

Robert M. LaFollette (Republican, Wisconsin) endorsed all of Johnson's arguments. He, too, insisted that an explanation was due in plain and direct language. Not only was Germany defeated, but the pretext that the Bolsheviks were German agents could not hold: "I cannot accept as sufficient the Sisson Papers over which the slime of chicane and falsification and fraud and forgery is plainly manifest."

As for the argument that intervention was necessary to disarm the Red terror, it was equally unconvincing. Terror was the by-product of every revolution in history. "The bloodier the revolution the stronger the evidence that unspeakable oppression preceded it. The law of action and reaction is the same, not only in physics, but also in the affairs of men." Besides, America had no legal right to be there; even if the Russian government was bad by her standards, it was not for America to overthrow it; and if Bolshevism was what the Russian people really wanted they should have it. In passing LaFollette reminded the Senate that instead of setting the world straight it should remember that "we have enough to do at home."[2]

William E. Borah (Republican, Idaho) was the third major stalwart of the opposition to Wilson's Russian policy. He conceded the legitimacy of having gone to Russia as a war measure; he even conceded that U.S. troops should remain to protect both the Czechs and Allied stores—but no longer. The aim should be to bring out both

[1] *Congressional Record,* 65th Congress, 3rd Session, Senate, December 12 and 30, 1918, 342–5, 864.
[2] *Congressional Record,* 65th Congress, 3rd Session, Senate, January 7, 1919, 1101–3.

troops and stores in the shortest possible time. Beyond this Borah took the position that "the Russian people have the same right to establish a Socialist state as we have to establish a Republic."[3]

It should be noted that since there were no Socialists in the Senate, Johnson, LaFollette, and Borah were by far the most extreme critics in the upper chamber. But even they did not call for immediate withdrawal. At this time their initiative was parallel to that of the moderate Left in the Allied Parliaments: they asked for a public clarification of policy, protested offensive rather than defensive moves in Russia, and urged that American soldiers be withdrawn from Russia "as soon as practicable."[4] As long as their resolutions rallied only marginal congressional and press[5] support they had at best a cautionary, possibly a dissuasive, effect.

Actually the forces inclined to favor different degrees and forms of intervention were gaining ascendancy over the recalcitrants. The entire issue arose after the congressional elections had ushered in the post-Armistice hardening of opinion, the upsurge of both conservative and jingoist nationalism. There was little inclination, inside as well as outside Congress, to be soft on Bolshevism, either at home or abroad. The issue was not drawn between intervention and nonintervention, but between direct and indirect intervention, and between unilateral and inter-Allied intervention.

At one extreme of the spectrum were those Senators who proposed that primarily military means be used. Senator Charles E. Townsend (Republican, Michigan) wanted more U. S. soldiers put into Russia at once. Likewise, in order to take "this hideous monstrosity by the throat and strangle it forever" Senator Charles S. Thomas (Democrat, Colorado) advocated reinforcements for "our gallant men" in Russia. His complaint was that the Allies and America were pursuing the "worst possible policy" by sending insufficient forces there. Significantly, both Townsend and Thomas voted against the $100 million "anti-Bolshevik" food bill.[6]

Then there were Senators who asked for all or nothing. Both William S. Kenyon (Republican, Iowa) and William F. Kirby (Democrat, Arkansas) insisted that if United States troops had to be in Russia they should be there in sufficient force to do the job, otherwise they

---

[3] *Congressional Record,* 65th Congress, 3rd Session, Senate, January 9, 1919, 1161–3.
[4] Because Johnson's precatory resolution was bottled up in the Foreign Relations Committee, after a month had gone by he introduced another resolution, this one calling for withdrawal "as soon as practicable." See *Congressional Record,* 65th Congress, 3rd Session, Senate, January 13, 1919, 1313.
[5] See *The Nation, The Call* (New York), *The New Republic,* and *The Literary Digest,* November 1918 through January 1919, *passim.*
[6] *Congressional Record,* 65th Congress, 3rd Session, Senate, January 3, 14, and 24, 1919, 987, 1392, 1996.

should be withdrawn. But whereas Kenyon not only preferred with-drawing them but also voted against the food bill, Kirby was inclined to send the required reinforcements while voting for bread as well.[7]

Evidently the question of intervention could not be reduced to a partisan issue, otherwise Henry Cabot Lodge (Republican, Massa-chusetts) would have done so. Although Lodge tended to criticize Wilson's indecision and charged the Administration with doing too little and too late, broadly speaking he was in the President's corner. He, too, was convinced of the absolute evil of Bolshevism, looked for an effective mixture of military, economic, and ideological interven-tion, and strained to stay in step with the Allies.

For Lodge the Bolsheviks were "a band of anthropoid apes." Quite apart from their inefficiency, these *Untermenschen* used murder and massacre to undermine their nation and to destroy "property and all the instruments of industry." According to Lodge, if this anarchy were "permitted to spread through Western Civilization, that Civilization would fall."

As a first step the Allies should aid Yugoslavia, Czechoslovakia, Poland, Lithuania, and the other peripheral states. At the same time they should busy themselves with cleaning up the contagious mess in Russia.

> We cannot shirk the Russian question. . . . Of the problems bequeathed by the war . . . that of Russia is probably the most difficult. . . . The restoration of Russia is essential not only to the peace but to the economic life of the world. . . . We have troops now in the northern part of Western Russia, and other troops in Vladivostok. Unfortunately they are so few in number that it is greatly to be feared that they are wholly inadequate for the work they may have to do. Nevertheless they are there and must be sustained and very probably increased. . . .

In addition to leaning toward sending more troops Lodge threw his full weight behind the food bill.[8]

Undoubtedly Lodge was disposed to support Johnson's effort to force the Administration into discussing its Russian policy, into getting the advice and consent of the Senate. However, except for this tactical accord, they remained poles apart. In direct contrast to the progressive anti-imperialist from California, the conservative nationalist from Massachusetts wanted the United States to intensify its overall anti-Soviet effort.

Beyond this specific discord these unholy allies differed con-textually. Johnson's nascent isolationism was less a policy of hermetic seclusion than a policy of nonentanglement and unilateralism. The

[7] *Congressional Record,* 65th Congress, 3rd Session, Senate, January 7 and 24, 1919, 1104 and 1996.
[8] *Congressional Record,* 65th Congress, 3rd Session, Senate, December 21, 1918, 725–6.

proto-isolationists above all wanted to keep the U.S. out of the vise of alliances or leagues with essentially conservative and imperialist powers. Their nonentanglement was designed not only to spare Americans involvement in the dangerous and costly machinations of power politics, but also to neutralize the antiprogressive political, social, and economic consequences of dynamic *Weltpolitik*. Not that they craved either to compromise U. S. security or to slow down America's rise to world power. They merely concluded that since unilateral intervention —with Associate rather than Allied status—had worked in 1917–18, aided by this recent demonstration of U. S. might it was likely to work even better in the future. Meanwhile American economic influence could continue to spread into the four corners of the world; and the triumph of social-economic reform and political liberty at home would exert a useful influence abroad.

Not surprisingly, progressive nationalists, alongside anti-imperialist liberals, were opposed to the use of force in the fight against Bolshevism in Russia as well as to the Red Hunt in the fight against radicalism in America. To the extent that they admitted the legitimacy of U. S. participation in the battle against Bolshevism abroad, they tended to sanction the use of bread rather than bullets. Similarly, at home they advocated timely reforms and guaranteed civil liberties as the best antidote to radicalism. The progressive nationalists were suspicious of Wilson because they believed that in domestic affairs he had long since sold out to corporate conservatism and given a free hand to the persecution of aliens and dissenters, and in foreign affairs he was about to involve America in an attendant Holy Alliance.

Lodge was driven by diametrically opposite fears as well as objectives. He and his conservative nationalist cabal suspected Wilson of preparing a vast political maneuver aimed at restoring his own reformist and liberal image and policies at home.[9] They knew that the President chafed under the corporate and business interests that during the war had tightened their hold on the Administration and the Democratic Party. Moreover, they knew that even though Wilson had no sympathy for the Wobblies, he was ill at ease about those repressive procedures of Attorney General Gregory and Postmaster General Burleson which flagrantly infringed on civil liberties. Now that the war emergency was over he might be expected to be less inclined to leave his witch-hunting officials a free hand. In fact, Lodge probably exaggerated—either unintentionally or with malice—Wilson's urge to recover his reformist and libertarian posture. Moreover, quite apart from the fact that Wilson's first-term reforms had not been all that radical, at this time the liberal and progressive critics of the Administration's wartime domestic policies were in disarray.

In any case, Lodge was not willing to take a chance on the Presi-

[9] See pp. 56–7, 121–7 above.

dent's cooperating with the democratic Left in Europe to secure a Wilsonian peace, a League, and a *modus vivendi* with Bolshevik Russia, since this foreign policy achievement could provide the basis and momentum for a reformist crusade at home. However, in pitting his conservative nationalism against Wilson's progressive internationalism, Lodge embraced neither isolationism nor unilateralism. On the contrary, he was anxious to cooperate with Allied conservative nationalists who were equally apprehensive about the double-edged Wilsonian offensive. They, too, realized that Wilson and the democratic Left had to be defeated in the diplomatic realm in order to head off a later but related upsurge in home affairs.

Compared to leading isolationists Lodge was considerably more sophisticated about the "international" dimensions of domestic politics in this new revolutionary age. Most budding isolationists as well as many anti-imperialist liberals assumed that their program could flourish in America even if conservatism ran rampant in the major European nations, *provided* the U.S. remained free of formal alliances. But Lodge, for his part, realized that the triumph of conservatism in America was contingent on the triumph of conservatism in Europe, that neither was viable without the other.

In brief, Lodge's thirst for personal glory, his pursuit of partisan advantage, and his realism in foreign policy cannot by themselves account for his campaign to press Wilson into continuing unconditional cooperation with the Allies.

> Nothing can be accomplished unless we work in complete harmony with those who are associated with us in the war against the Central Powers. I know very well that technically we had no treaty of alliance with the Allies . . . but technicalities are of no consequence in the presence of facts. . . . To attempt in any way to separate us from our Allies now or to prevent perfect unity of action is as harmful as such efforts were when we were fighting in northern France and on the plains of Flanders. To encourage or even to permit any serious differences to arise between the United States and Great Britain, or with France, or Italy, or Belgium, would be a world calamity of the worst kind. . . . We cannot . . . leave the work half done. We are as much bound, not merely by interest and every consideration for a safe future but by honor and self-respect to see that the terms of peace are carried out. . . . We cannot halt or turn back now. We must do our share to carry out the peace as we have done our share to win the war of which the peace is an integral part.[1]

Would Lodge have urged this course of cooperation if the Allies had come out for a Wilsonian peace and progressive domestic reforms? In this event the roles of the progressive isolationists and the conservative

[1] *Congressional Record,* 65th Congress, 3rd Session, Senate, December 21, 1918, 725.

nationalists might well have been reversed! The *North American Review* might quickly have abandoned the position that the Allies were "entitled to a voice superior to our own in the Peace Conference."[2]

With regard to Russian policy, as with regard to German policy, the Republicans tended to criticize Wilson for being out of step with the Allies. In the Senate Lodge and Miles Poindexter (Republican, Washington) kept hammering away at this point.[3] Outside Congress even Taft contended that force was the only means to stamp out Bolshevism at its source, and that this crucial aim could not be achieved unless America contributed to a combined Allied force.[4] Also, influential newspapers implied that the inadequacies of Allied intervention were in large measure due to the President's indecision.[5]

Indeed, not only the Congress was kept in the dark. The Allies also repeatedly tried to elicit the President's views on Russia and the Bolshevik regime. But Wilson kept his own counsel; he insisted that since he was about to leave for Europe he would rather defer comment until after consultation with the Allied Premiers.[6] Like Lodge he attached supreme importance to maintaining a united front with the Allies; unlike him he was determined not to let *them* set the pace.

Once in Paris and London it quickly became evident that the President was reluctant to see military intervention stepped up, that he wanted to explore and test Soviet intentions, that he advocated the use of Allied pressure to produce a compromise among the conflicting factions in the Russian Civil War, and that if all else failed he was likely to go along only with indirect and nonmilitary intervention.

All this time, while steeped in inter-Allied negotiations, he was kept informed about the debate back home. On January 11 Polk, who favored tough measures, sent a cable advising the American Peace Delegation (Ammission) that whereas some Senators were demanding the withdrawal of troops, others were simply asking for information. Polk claimed to be "disturbed over [this] situation," estimated that any government sending additional troops would obviously encounter "great difficulty," and suggested that provided arrangements could be made to protect the local Russians, the expedition to Archangel—but not the one to Siberia—should be withdrawn. Above all, however, he thought it essential that the Administration define its "attitude towards the Bolsheviki"; that the Associated Governments combined state how far they were "prepared and able to go in supporting elements of law and order"; and that Wilson advise the State Department "what funds

2 December 1918, 813.

3 *Congressional Record,* 65th Congress, 3rd Session, Senate, January 9, 1919, 1, 168.

4 Theodore Marburg and Horace E. Flack (eds.): *Taft Papers on the League of Nations* (New York: Macmillan; 1920), 158, 177, 183–4.

5 See *The New York Times,* December 17 and 22, 1918; and *The Literary Digest,* January 11, 1919, 14.

6 *F.R.,1918,Russia,* II, 569–70, 572, 574; and *F.R.,1919,Russia,* 3.

for military supplies [he had] in mind from which this government could supply financial aid."[7]

Polk assumed that Wilson and Lansing agreed on the importance of holding on to the Siberian railways both in order to maintain America's position in relation to the Japanese and to keep open a vital line of communication to European Russia. But given the increasingly critical and inquisitive Congress, how would the Administration raise the large sums of money needed to implement the Stevens Railway Plan?

> There is no question but that the Republicans are trying to force an extra session, and leading Democrats seem to feel that the extra session is inevitable. If successful, Republicans through control of various committees, will make attacks on every phase of policy of Administration in Russia. We are committed now to a plan for operation of railways in Siberia. . . . In view of the attitude of Congress on the Food Bill, I [Polk] should doubt the possibility of securing money for this purpose by an appropriation. . . .[8]

Even though Polk kept emphasizing the unrelenting progressive Republican protest he was first and foremost worried about the dominant conservative Republicans exploiting this protest for their own anti-Wilsonian purposes.

The Administration had to avoid a full-fledged debate of the Russian question in the midst of the Prinkipo exploration, especially since in such a debate Wilson would once again have to frighten the economy-minded Congress with the specter of Bolshevism. More important still was the Administration's reluctance to risk a test of strength with the Republicans during this early phase of the Peace Conference. The outcome of the November elections had dealt a severe blow to Wilson's prestige on the eve of this Conference. The President could not afford to advertise the growing rift between the legislative and the executive branches: a reduced congressional majority, let alone a defeat, would fatally impair Wilson's position in Paris.

Hence Polk was instructed to discuss the different aspects of the Siberian situation only in *secret hearings* before the most appropriate congressional committees. In these hearings he was to emphasize the strategic importance of the Trans-Siberian Railway; the "potential value of this railroad as a means of developing American commerce particularly from the West coast of the United States to Russia"; and the need to counter Japan's control of the Chinese Eastern Railway as well as her military and commercial activities in Siberia. In closing his instructions to Polk the Secretary of State indicated that the Ammission

---

[7] *F.R.,1919,Russia*, 323–5; and Lansing to Wilson, January 15, 1919, Wilson Papers, VIII A:11.
[8] Polk to Lansing, January 24, 1919, cited in *F.R.,1919,Russia*, 245.

wanted to use this request for funds as an experiment in taking Congress "more into confidence on such matters."[9]

But Polk promptly advised against this experiment.

> It would be very inadvisable for me to go to Congress at this time with any plan, one, of acquiring money to be expended abroad, or two, having anything to do with Russia. In regard to the first objection, having just been through the fight to obtain the money for the $100,000,000 fund for feeding Europe, I am convinced that I would not be given any consideration whatever, in view of the fact that our plans in regard to the railroad . . . are so absolutely indefinite. In the Committee on Appropriations the whole fight made on the Food Bill by the opponents and the criticism made even by our friends was that they did not have enough information. . . . I am advised by everyone that an attempt to get any agreement from committee would be hopeless.
>
> In regard to the second objection, the first question to be asked would be what is the Russian policy. If no answer could be given, the reasons for not being able to give an answer would have no weight. . . . Any attempt to commit Congress to a definite policy in the Siberian railroad, which is only a part of the whole Russian problem, would be hopeless unless some definite information could be given on the whole subject. The Vice President said that if the Russian question were thrown into Congress at this time, it would probably jeopardize all the appropriation bills. In view of the unanimous opinion of all who have been consulted, I think it would be wiser for me not to approach them for money for this purpose. . . .

The President had no alternative but to withdraw his earlier instructions. The congressional committees were circumvented. He authorized Polk to notify the Japanese that the United States accepted the railway plan subject to further discussion with regard to financial arrangements. Meanwhile Wilson proposed to pay the U. S. railway corps in Siberia out of his Presidential fund and out of the fund for National Security and Defense.[1]

These unsettling political developments in Washington merely reinforced Wilson in his predisposition to seek an accommodation with Lenin before even considering tough and costly measures. It was after consulting with Wilson and in the light of the Bolshevik advance in the Baltic region that on January 2 the British government formally submitted Borden's proposal to the Allies. The Soviet government, Kolchak, Denikin, Chaikovsky, and the "Governments of ex-Russian States" were to be asked "to abstain from further aggressions, hostilities, and reprisals . . . [as a precondition for being invited] to

[9] *F.R.,1919,Russia*, 246–8.
[1] Ibid., 248–50, 262.

send representatives to Paris to discuss with the Great Powers conditions for a permanent settlement."[2]

Even though this conciliatory scheme took account of Robert Cecil's safeguards, the French government hastened to nip it in the bud. Disingenuously, Pichon praised the proposal's "generous spirit of universal reconciliation." The Bolshevik regime, however, was based exclusively on the "lowest passions, anarchist oppression, and the negation of every principle of public and private law." Should the Allies have either "the weakness or the imprudence" to deal with this regime they would immeasurably promote the spread of Bolshevism of which they were likely to be the first victims. In any case, the French government *"ne praticera [sic!] pas avec le crime."* Instead, the Allies had to go on furnishing arms, money, and even military support to the anti-Reds. By so doing and by treating this regime as an enemy it would soon collapse, especially since it was incapable of organizing procurement, transportation, order, and credit. In the meantime, all Russian factions, except the Bolsheviks, could appear before the Allies and present their claims. Whereas Sonnino sided unequivocally with Pichon, the Japanese government did so less categorically.[3]

Lloyd George reported that the French government dissented from the British proposal, "adopted a very strong line," and "wished to fight Bolshevism."[4] This French veto coincided with Foch's first representations in favor of a stepped-up Allied military effort in Eastern Europe. On January 2 he sounded out General Bliss about "the chance of sending [70,000] American troops to Poland and elsewhere to stem the tide of the Russian Red Terror."[5] The American General was not at all receptive. To begin with, Bliss was a Wilsonian in that he did not think that Bolshevik ideas could be killed with bullets. He had no recipe for ridding Russia of Bolshevism, and he even seemed insensitive to the dangers for the rimland. With transatlantic detachment Bliss argued that all that was required to establish a "natural barrier between western Europe and Russian Bolshevism" was to feed Germany to "a

---

[2] For the text of this draft-proposal which Balfour sent to the French, U.S., Italian, and Japanese governments see Wilson Papers, VIII A:7; and *F.R.,1919,Russia,* 2–3.

[3] Pichon's reply caused a sensation in France, since the Socialists somehow obtained it, published it, and denounced it fiercely. See *l'Humanité,* January 11–18, 1919. The complete text of this reply is cited in Gabriel Terrail [Mermeix, pseud.]: *Le Combat des trois* (Paris: Ollendorff; 1922), 276–8. Mermeix mistakenly dates this document December 5 instead of January 5. See also *F.R.,1919,Russia,* 6–7, 15.

[4] British Empire Delegation 1, January 13, 1919 (a.m.). The Premier chose this occasion to summarize British policy: "(a) Non-interference with the internal affairs of the Bolshevik area; (b) Assistance to the countries under Allied protection against invasion by troops from without, but no interference as between two political parties within such countries; (c) As to the Ukraine, the Don, and Siberia, any assistance, financial or material, that might be possible, excluding troops."

[5] Bliss Diary, January 2, 1919, in Bliss Papers, Box 65.

reasonable extent and build up there a strong democratic government
. . . provided we do not wait until it is too late."

But quite apart from not sharing Foch's confidence in the efficacy
of force, Bliss also worried about the danger of U. S. overextension.

> The British and the French positively assert that they cannot send
> any troops, that their people are too tired and that they will not fight
> any longer. Therefore, if we do not act wisely, a situation may be
> created that will require us to assume this enormous burden or see
> the civilization of western Europe greatly imperiled. . . . [More-
> over] if Germany becomes Bolshevik and joins hands with all of
> Eastern and Central Europe, an attempted permanent occupation of
> Germany by the French may prove a great disaster. This is espe-
> cially true because of the seething ferment of discontent in Italy,
> France, and England. It may be that a Bolshevik Germany would
> pull them all down in her own ruin.

Certainly until mid-January, when the German elections finally reassured the Allies, Bliss assigned first priority to Germany's stabilization.[6]

Foch also turned to Colonel House, possibly in the hope that he
might be more sensitive to the importance of keeping Bolshevism out of
the rimland. On this occasion Foch was more specific: he wanted
an inter-Allied force, primarily composed of American troops, to guard
the Danzig-Thorn railway (as they were about to guard the Trans-
Siberian?) over which Polish troops now in France and Italy could be
brought in to strengthen Poland.[7]

Apparently House and Bliss were equally opposed to the deployment of United States manpower in the East. With their attention still
riveted on Germany they held that provisions rather than soldiers were
the appropriate instrument of control. In the afternoon of January 7
the three other American Peace Commissioners, including the President, rallied to the Bliss-House position.[8]

The next day Colonel House pressed these views on both Clemenceau and Orlando.

> I had a heart to heart talk with Clemenceau about Bolshevism in
> Russia and its westward march. I made him confess [sic!] that
> military intervention was impossible. I did not go into the remedy as
> I did not care to get into an argument with him about feeding the
> Central Powers, but I thought that since we were agreed that
> military intervention was impossible, then we should exert all the
> wisdom possible in order to devise some plan by which this critical
> and dangerous situation might be met. He assented.
> Later in the afternoon, when Orlando called, I gave him very

[6] Bliss Diary, January 6–7, 1919, in Bliss Papers, Box 65.
[7] Minutes of a meeting between House and Foch, January 7, 1919, in House Papers,
   29:26.
[8] Bliss Diary, January 7, 1919, in Bliss Papers, Box 65.

much the same kind of talk, and he, too, agreed with my conclusion.[9]

As on so many other occasions House exaggerated the significance of Clemenceau's agreement with his own rather vague proposals. Clemenceau was not on the verge of yielding to either Wilson or Foch.

He was much more likely to continue pressing his *cordon sanitaire* policy, which enjoyed solid support in the British government. When Foch's scheme to send troops to Poland came before the Cabinet, only Churchill chose to speak for it. The new War Minister thought it "quite impossible" for England to "stand aside and let Poland go to pieces." In addition to voicing his confidence that volunteers could be raised for service in the East, he suggested that it "might be advisable to let Germany know that if she were prepared to organize her Eastern front against the ingress of Bolshevism, the Allied Governments would raise no objections." For Churchill, unlike for Foch, "it was a matter for serious consideration" whether the Allies should not "bolster up the Central Powers, if necessary, in order to stem the tide of Bolshevism." But the Cabinet decided to ignore both Foch and Churchill in favor of reaffirming its policy of "walling off a fire in a mine" by giving every aid short of troops to "existing governments with which Britain was cooperating" and which were threatened by "external aggression."[1]

Thus when the Peace Conference opened on January 12 Allied policy was still in an impasse. Both Wilson and Lloyd George stood by the Borden scheme, while Clemenceau and Sonnino persisted in their refusal to have any dealings whatever with Lenin. The only tangible result of the preliminary soundings was the unmistakable confirmation that for a host of reasons Wilson and America were not ready to underwrite a major anti-Bolshevik offensive.

In his diary Colonel House recorded a personal reflection which may well help account for the continuing impasse.

> I have partially succeeded in frightening not only the President but [also] the English, French, and Italians regarding what might be termed "the Russian peril." Personally, I really do believe there is not as much danger as I make to them. If I had the imperialistic views that some of these people have who are at the heads of their governments, I would not confess that military intervention was an impossibility, because I believe that it could be successfully accomplished if gone about properly. A voluntary and a mercenary army of very small proportions, equipped with artillery and tanks, would in my opinion do the work.

Perhaps there were prominent officials in all the major delegations and general staffs—and not only among the French—who shared this

---

[9] House Diary, January 8, 1918.
[1] War Cabinet 515, January 10, 1919 (a.m.).

outlook. Foch, Churchill, the *émigrés,* Dmowski, and Brătianu benefited from this lingering expectation. Churchill for quite a while
assumed "that twenty or thirty thousand resolute, comprehending, well-
armed Europeans could, without any serious difficulty or loss, have
made their way very swiftly along any of the great railroads which
converged on Moscow; and have brought to the hard ordeal of battle
any force that stood against them." But apparently he and the other
superrealists, as well as Lenin, needed quite a while before they realized
"that twenty or thirty thousand resolute men did not exist or could not
be brought together."[2]

Meanwhile, even before the Peace Conference opened, the Allied
and Associated Powers singly or in collaboration had taken the necessary steps to complete the naval and military encirclement and the
economic blockade of Soviet Russia. Above all, especially with the
Freikorps closing the breach in Latvia and Lithuania, the road to
Central and East Central Europe was barred. This *cordon sanitaire* was
effective in spite of rivalries among the counterrevolutionary powers
and the lack of an effective offensive striking force. At best this
quarantine—combined with the aid without which the Whites could
not last—would choke the Soviet regime by denying it basic supplies of
food and fuel. At worst the Allies gained a breathing spell during which
they could help stabilize Central and East Central Europe while at the
same time deciding and preparing their next moves.

[2] Churchill: *Aftermath,* 243.

Part Four

MARKING TIME

11

Location, Delegations, Agenda, Intelligence

THE CONSTELLATION of political forces in the Allied and Associated nations was more decisive for the course and outcome of the Paris Peace Conference than the personalities, negotiating skills, and historical culture of the members of the major delegations. Similarly, the near-anomie throughout Central and Eastern Europe rather than deficiencies or mistakes in the planning, organization, and running of the Conference shaped the erratic pace and agenda of the negotiations.

Even the decision to hold the Conference in highly excitable Paris bears the marks of these revolutionary conditions. From the beginning the French government was anxious to be host to the Congress that would correct the injustices of 1871 and other years. The Belgian government also put in a bid since a congress held in Brussels would dramatize Germany's most recent violations of international law.

But both Colonel House and President Wilson demurred. House feared that in case of sharp differences "between one of the Allies and the French it might be embarrassing." Wilson was altogether opposed to meeting under French auspices; as an alternative he proposed a neutral site relatively free of French, British, and German influence, preferably in Lausanne. In early November House easily persuaded the Allied Premiers, including Clemenceau, to hold the Conference in Switzerland, in either Geneva or Lausanne.[1]

Before the choice between these two cities was made, however, President Wilson had second thoughts. On November 7 he cabled House that Versailles might after all be "the best place" since in France "friendly influences and authorities were in control" while Switzerland was "saturated with every poisonous element and open to every hostile

[1] *F.R.,P.C.,1919*, I, 119–20; and Callwell (ed.): *Henry Wilson*, II, 144, entry of October 28, 1919.

influence in Europe."[2] What was the nature of these "hostile" influences which prompted Wilson to now prefer the heady atmosphere of victorious Paris?

At the very time that House was meeting with the Allied Premiers in the French capital, the specter of Bolshevism gripped Switzerland. The immediate occasion for this panic was the announcement by the Swiss Social Democratic Party that on November 7 it would hold mass rallies throughout the nation to celebrate the first anniversary of the Bolshevik Revolution.

Led by Robert Grimm and Fritz Platten, the Socialist Party was particularly strong and radical in German Switzerland; geographically these central and northern cantons were dangerously close to Germany, which, as of October 1918, hovered on the brink of revolution. In 1915 and 1916 the Swiss authorities—federal as well as cantonal—reluctantly had tolerated the revolutionary conclaves in the villages of Zimmerwald and Kienthal, both of which were in the Canton of Berne; in 1917 they had breathed a deep sigh of relief when successive convoys of Russian revolutionaries, including Lenin's famous sealed train, finally left Zurich for Russia. Now, in November 1918, Zurich was again in the center of the stage because its municipal and cantonal authorities urged the federal government to participate in precautionary measures against the scheduled Socialist rally in the Fraumünsterplatz.

But even prior to this official initiative, the very influential *Journal de Genève* began to publish articles and editorials warning that the coming Socialist rallies were part of a dangerous Bolshevik conspiracy. Significantly, the Socialist Party was considerably weaker and less radical in Suisse Romande, the home of the *Journal,* and in the Tessino, than in German Switzerland; moreover, the editors of this paper were enthusiastically pro-Allied and pro-Wilson.

Nonetheless these Swiss Wilsonians asserted that although German imperialism had been dissipated, a new imperialism—namely Bolshevik imperialism—now threatened all of Europe.

> But we in Switzerland do not want to serve as a staging area for the apostles of European subversion. . . . We can no longer close our eyes and ignore the direction in which the Swiss lieutenants of the Bolshevik dictatorship are taking us. Especially now that the thunder of revolution growls in the East we must more than ever be on our guard.

The editors were the first to reveal on good authority that the federal authorities were not only alive to the danger but were taking certain precautionary measures.

Once the full scope of these measures was officially announced, the

---

[2] Cited in *F.R.,P.C.,1919,* I, p. 121.

Journal took the lead in blaming foreign and native agents of the German-Bolshevik conspiracy for Switzerland's turmoil. In April 1917 the Swiss authorities had obliged the German government by turning Lenin loose; a year and a half later a defeated and ungrateful Germany threatened to become the handmaiden of the Russian-based Bolshevik conspiracy.

> Switzerland, however, refuses to consider Bolshevism as an elusive and terrifying specter; she is determined to take by the scruff of the neck all individuals, made of flesh and bones, who champion Bolshevism; and she will teach them the unmistakable lesson that no foreign doctrine can supplant [Swiss] liberties.[3]

It seems doubtful indeed that in late October, when the rallies of November 7 were publicly summoned, the Socialist leaders were planning either a general strike or a revolution. Certainly, if such had been their original intention, they would not have proceeded so openly. On the other hand, Grimm and his colleagues may have had a contingency plan in case the rallies succeeded beyond even their own optimistic expectations. Furthermore, they were bound to draw last-minute inspiration, courage, and daring from the collapse of the Austro-Hungarian and the Wilhelmine empires, which was completed only after they had issued their original summons. In any event, alerted by the Russian experience of 1917, the Swiss government was inclined to prepare for the worst.

On October 31 the Zurich authorities advised the Federal Council that without the help of federal troops the municipal and cantonal police could not master an organized putsch. Thus far there was "no imminent danger of a revolutionary movement breaking out in Zurich." Nevertheless, in case the situation should change quite suddenly, the necessary precautions had to be taken immediately. These preparations should be hastened since, in the event of serious revolutionary developments in Germany, "these could easily have an impact on Switzerland, in particular on the tense conditions in Zurich."[4]

This civilian estimate was promptly seconded by General Wille of the Swiss General Staff. After an on-the-spot investigation on November 2–3, Wille confirmed to his superiors in Berne that barring developments "beyond our borders no putsch or disorders were expected in Zurich, at least not before mid-November." But he also endorsed the Zurich government's request for advance authority to use local contingents of the Federal Army.

> All in all everyone lives in fear of a sudden and totally unexpected [*sic!*] proclamation of a general strike. . . . All the necessary

---

[3] *Journal de Genève,* November 4–12, 1918.
[4] Cited in Jacob Ruchti: *Geschichte der Schweiz während des Weltkrieges, 1914–1919* (Berne: Paul Haupt; 1928), I, 432.

preparations have been made thanks to the effective organizing talent and discipline of the central leadership, the workers' councils in the factories, and the soldiers' councils.

. . . Under these circumstances I must also believe in the possibility of a sudden, unexpected outbreak of revolution, *especially since during the last two years I have repeatedly told the Federal Council of my conviction that at the Zimmerwald and Kienthal congresses it had been decided to begin the overthrow of Europe's political order in Switzerland.* . . . The present moment is particularly propitious: the authorities have done nothing at all to prevent the violent overthrow of our political institutions. . . . For humanity it is much more important to *prevent* crimes than to smash criminals while committing their deeds or to hang them after the event [italics mine].

In conclusion General Wille requested the immediate disposition and deployment of troops, specifying that these should consist of four cavalry brigades which would be particularly suited for street fighting and least infected by "Bolshevism and soldiers' councils."[5]

The local and cantonal governments now banned the Socialist rally. But instead of canceling it altogether, the Socialist leaders merely postponed the rally to November 10. General Wille's reaction to this move was to urge Berne that "the assignment of the four brigades be decided tomorrow, November 5, and deployed by Saturday, November 9." In the afternoon of the fifth, after an additional request to the Zurich authorities for protection, the Federal Council decided to act: it now dispatched four infantry regiments in addition to the four cavalry brigades.[6]

In the official proclamation announcing these extraordinary measures, the Council declared that an ever-increasing anxiety had seized Zurich, the nation's most populous urban center. The government of that city had asked for troops to reassure the public and to prevent possible disorders. A few newspapers and groups were threatening to transplant Russia's revolutionary and anarchist experiment to Switzerland; simultaneously, shady foreign characters were sowing hatred and exploiting the shortages and high prices due to the war. Since these subversive elements would not hesitate to use violence, the federal government had to take precautions, especially since "the government's task was to *prevent rather than to repress disorders;* and public opinion quite rightly would never tolerate a policy of either improvidence or weakness [italics mine]." Having thus justified preventive repression, the Council admitted the need for extensive political and social reforms, though it warned that in Switzerland social reform and revolution would forever remain irreconcilable.[7]

[5] Ibid., 433–4.
[6] Ibid., 434–5.
[7] The full text of this communiqué is cited in *Journal de Genève,* November 9, 1919.

The Socialist leaders, meanwhile, were confronted with a hard choice: to cancel their widely publicized demonstrations and lose prestige and faith with friend and foe alike; or to let it come to a test of strength even at the risk of eventually beating a hasty retreat. Actually the two alternatives were equally unattractive. If the leaders opted for the test of strength they did so largely out of spontaneous enthusiasm and reckless defiance; they acted neither out of rational calculation nor in accordance with carefully planned revolutionary strategy, tactics, and goals.

No doubt the Socialists feigned excessive innocence with their claim that they never intended more than a resounding testimonial to the Russian Revolution. On the other hand, there may well have been a considerable measure of truth in their charge that the government's preventive troop concentration in and around Zurich was a conscious and deliberate challenge, if not a provocation.

In any case, Grimm, Platten, Schneider, and Müller built their case on this indictment of the established order. The Swiss working class simply could not tolerate this pre-emptive counterrevolutionary measure. Hence, the Olten Action Committee, functioning as executive and coordinating organ, called a twenty-four-hour general strike for November 9 to protest "against the military and bourgeois dictatorship." This strike, which coincided with the German Revolution, was only partly successful. Whereas economic life came to a near standstill in the major cities of German Switzerland, the strike movement had at best a moderate following in most of French and Italian Switzerland. Moreover, throughout Switzerland public communications, including railway transport, continued to function.[8]

The enterprise came off without serious disorders and neither police nor army interfered. The proscribed rally which had been postponed to November 10 was no more successful. On that day a delegation of the Olten Committee sought and was granted an interview with the Federal Council. The delegation threatened to renew the strike for an indefinite period unless the authorities withdrew the troops from Zurich and authorized the mass meeting on the Fraumünsterplatz. In addition, the delegation gave notice that even without this permission the mass meeting would take place at three o'clock in the afternoon. The Council, emboldened by the massed troops and the partial failure of Saturday's strike, refused what it rightly considered an ultimatum and ordered the troops to break up the meeting which had started at 3:00 p.m., as scheduled. The thick crowd dispersed after about 500 shots had been fired in the air and three demonstrators and one soldier had been wounded.

The strike was to resume at midnight on November 11. Under Grimm's chairmanship the Olten Committee hastily formulated an

[8] Ruchti: *Schweiz während des Weltkrieges,* I, 436–7.

incoherent minimum program designed to attract democratic and liberal support—or, at any rate, to win the sympathy of the non-Socialist forces of movement—and to lay the basis for renewed negotiations with the Council. This program called for immediate elections of a new National Council on the basis of proportional representation; the enfranchisement of women; the obligation to work; the forty-eight-hour week; democratization of the army; fair food rationing and distribution; old age and sickness insurance; state monopoly of imports and exports; and the extinction of the national debt by levies on the property owning classes.[9]

Again the government not only stood firm but summoned additional troops, and again the strike had the same limited effectiveness. Nor did any of the troops go over to the strikers. Of circa 400,000 strikers only about 100,000 participated freely and with enthusiasm. No help came from beyond the borders. Quite the contrary, the threat of Allied intervention hung over the country, and so did the threat of an American food quarantine.

Eventually, the Olten Committee called off the strike on its third day, November 14. It justified this humiliating capitulation with the assertion that the nonparticipation of the railway workers had undermined the movement and that the proletariat did not have at their disposal weapons comparable to those of the armed forces. With revolutionary pride the Committee rejected all the concessions which the National Council had granted under pressure. These concessions included a promise of extensive social reforms, the expansion of the Socialist membership in the National Council, an increase in the number of Federal Councilmen, and a promise that a new electoral law would be voted in December. Once the strike was over, it was widely felt that even though the Socialists' minimum program had been presented under inadmissible conditions, certain parts of that program would simply have to be carried out in order to remove long-standing discontents which the war and the revolutions in Eastern and Central Europe had aggravated still further.[1]

The U. S. Legation in Berne kept Washington informed about this unrest. In particular James C. McNally, the Vice-Consul in Zurich, sent regular reports via Berne. He reported the original summons for the rallies of November 7; the first general strike in "protest against mobilization of additional units of army taken in anticipation of Bolshevik difficulties"; the resumption of the strike on November 11; and the fact that Switzerland was "teeming with Bolshevik sentiments, that leading bankers were fearful of Switzerland's future, and that Russian agitators as well as the abnormal cost of food" were responsible. On November 12 the Swiss Minister called on Lansing to explain "the

9 Ibid., 438–40.
1 *Journal de Genève*, November 13–27, 1918.

strike in Switzerland and the troops sent to Zurich." The following day McNally reported Bolshevik attempts to "control water supply [and] electric light, to burn hotels, etc."; he estimated that unless the army remained loyal, "revolution [was] imminent." Finally, on November 15 Washington received the comforting news that the "firm attitude of the Federal Council and the defection of railway men etc. had defeated the Platten Committee."[2]

Meanwhile, however, Lansing and Polk had supported the President's judgment that the Peace Conference should meet in Versailles instead of in Switzerland. The Secretary of State cabled to House that because the "headquarters of Bolsheviks and other revolutionaries" were in Switzerland the President could not go there. Similarly, the Assistant Secretary of State informed the Colonel that the Department was "seriously concerned over revolutionary committees in Switzerland . . . [and that it feared] it would be difficult to protect lives of peace delegates as we could not take in our own armed forces."[3]

Paris and London also watched developments in Switzerland with great care. During the first week of November the French Ambassador made "strong representations to the Swiss Government regarding their weakness and timidity vis-à-vis of the Bolshevik movement and activities . . . [and] provided documentary proof of sums being spent by Bolsheviks in Switzerland on propaganda and regarding their activities generally." With the support of his British colleague he pressed for the expulsion of Bolsheviks from Switzerland even after the Federal Council adopted its precautionary military measures.[4]

In any case, the Allied Premiers did not need this worry about revolutionary conditions across the Alps to welcome Colonel House's reversal enthusiastically. Clemenceau's original proposal to meet in Versailles and Paris was unanimously adopted: the Congress would convene in Versailles while the preliminary inter-Allied Conference would meet in Paris. Curiously enough, this is an instance in which the peacemakers acted too quickly rather than too slowly. Had they waited with their decision until after the defeat of the Olten Committee, French Switzerland might have become host to the Peace Conference before becoming the permanent site for the League of Nations.

It never occurred to Wilson to suggest that the Conference meet in the United States. The atmosphere in Washington would not have been any more Wilsonian than in Paris. But perhaps a Conference and Peace

---

[2] National Archives, Documents 854.5045/3, 854.5045/5–7, 854.00/32–5; and Lansing, Desk Diary, entry of November 12, 1918.

[3] Both cables are cited in Auchincloss Diary, November 9–10, 1918.

[4] Sir H. Rumbold (British Ambassador in Berne) to Foreign Office, November 7, 1918, and Robert Cecil to Rumbold, November 11, 1918, in Cecil Papers, 51094. Before endorsing the expulsion demand Cecil checked with Lloyd George, "thinking he might have some objection on old liberal grounds about the Right of Asylum." He found, however, that the Premier was "very anti-Bolshevik and quite in favor" of this representation. Cecil to Balfour, November 11, 1918, in Cecil Papers, 51094.

of Washington would dramatically and effectively have aroused the American people "to their new obligations" and helped them "understand their new relationship to foreign policy problems." With uncanny prescience *The New Republic* predicted that "the time may come when European statesmen will regret their neglect of this opportunity of attaching the American people more firmly to the existing but experimental European allegiance. European statesmen still need the help of the new world in order to restore the balance in the old."[5]

So much for the site of the Conference. What about the composition and quality of the principal delegations? In an era of mass politics the chief executives could hardly stress expertise to the detriment of political requirements.

Of necessity, especially in the absence of clear-cut pre-Conference agreements, the chief executives had to select themselves, thereby quite properly raising the Conference to the summit level. The Big Four would not only have to make on-the-spot decisions, but once having made such diplomatic decisions—which invariably involve compromises—they then had to muster political support for them. Diplomacy without politics belonged to an earlier age. Lloyd George, Clemenceau, and Orlando never considered not heading their own delegations; nor were they criticized for taking their participation for granted by contemporary political opponents or by retrospective pundits and historians.

Wilson, however, was not so fortunate; hostile and friendly critics attacked him right from the start. And yet it would seem that his decision to head the U. S. delegation was not at all exceptionable. He, too, was chief executive. Like the Allied Premiers, he could not conceive of turning the assignment over to the foreign ministers. In appointing House he would not only have fatally undercut his Secretary of State, but he would also have had to side-step time-honored institutions and channels of government. It was one thing to use Colonel House as a special emissary to streamline inter-Allied cooperation and to negotiate well-defined bilateral agreements in wartime; it was quite another to appoint such an emissary to represent the nation and the Administration in the solemn, multilateral, and open-ended peace negotiations at the summit level.

Besides, however attractive it may have been for Wilson to remain as a sort of final arbiter in the White House, this alternative was not really open to him. No doubt the President genuinely believed that at this point the United States was pursuing less selfish aims than the Allies; but he did not preach a self-righteous and unhistorical exceptionalism which would entitle America to special and preferred treatment. Why should the Allied chief executives be asked to sit around the negotiating table with a presidential emissary who would constantly

5 *The New Republic,* November 23, 1918, 82.

ask for time to refer matters to his superior? Of course, while the war lasted and the Allies were anxious to maximize American power by keeping Wilson at his Washington command post, they were both ready and eager to accept a special envoy. But now that the war was over and American aid was so much less essential and urgent they would agree to such an arrangement only provided, and as long as, they benefited from it.

On the political side, it is likely that if the President had stayed in Washington, he would have been accused of doing so for narrow partisan reasons, of lacking the courage and skill to confront personally the Allied leaders, and of leaving the initiative and advantage to the grabbing Europeans. Certainly Wilson hoped to raise his political stock at home by performing forcefully and successfully at the Peace Conference; this improved standing would then help secure the advice and consent of the Senate.

Considerations of political and legislative support heavily influenced each of the Big Four in the selection of his subordinate delegates. Lloyd George took into account the fact that his majority was "a Coalition of political parties—mostly Conservative, but with a substantial Liberal contingent and a faithful remnant of Labour members representing a very large Labour and Trade Union vote cast for us at the Election." Lloyd George went as head of government and as leader of a broad spectrum of Liberal opinion; Bonar Law represented "the largest party amongst [the Government's] supporters"; so did Foreign Secretary Balfour, who was also indispensable "by virtue of his office, his experience, and his fine intelligence"; and Barnes, the Labour leader, was selected because he was "a distinguished representative of his class." The fifth delegate was chosen on a rotating basis from among the Dominion Prime Ministers.[6]

Granted, the Coalition had a staggering majority in Commons. Within that majority, however, the hard-faced Tories were bound to keep pressuring Lloyd George and even Bonar Law to pursue intransigently an England-first policy. Just the same, Lloyd George did not select one of their spokesmen to come along to Paris; nor did he appoint Northcliffe in the hope of neutralizing his own "Lodge." In an extreme emergency Lloyd George could always threaten to call on the Labour and Liberal M.P.'s to help countervail Tory back-benchers.

Clemenceau's problem was somewhat more complicated. The all-popular and influential Marshal Foch was the hero and self-appointed spokesman of the extreme anti-German and anti-Bolshevik factions. Even Clemenceau could hardly afford not to make the Commander in Chief of the Allied Armies one of France's five plenipotentiaries. Foch eventually pressed policies that were much too extreme for Clemen-

[6] David Lloyd George: *The Truth About the Peace Treaties,* I, 209.

ceau, even though the latter used these proposals to frighten Lloyd George and Wilson into concessions. Still, it was preferable to have Foch plot from within rather than from outside the delegation and government. As for Pichon, Klotz, and Tardieu, they were representative of the political truce of victory and served Clemenceau faithfully. The Premier felt no need to court labor with a major seat; he merely made Léon Jouhaux a technical adviser on labor questions. And very much like Lloyd George, who sent the liberal conservative Robert Cecil into the League of Nations Commission, Clemenceau gave Léon Bourgeois this assignment. He was confident that Bourgeois would stubbornly hold out for a League which would either be a pliant instrument of national policy or, failing that, an innocuous debating society.

The make-up of the Italian Delegation reflected the ascendancy of Sonnino's supporters since the Armistice. Like his British colleague, Orlando went to Paris not only as head of government; while there he also continued to be the hope of all Italian Wilsonians who refused to believe that Orlando had *really* abandoned them in favor of Sonnino. In fact the Premier became a hardy champion of his Foreign Minister's policy, in part, perhaps, because Sonnino had no political ambitions of his own. The other three plenipotentiary delegates—G. F. Salvago Raggi, Antonio Salandra, and Salvatore Barzilai—were destined to remain in the background because, given Italy's limited interests, there was not enough work to go around. All three, however, had strong roots in the Center-right and were of Sonninoan persuasion. Still, there was that ritualistic bow to the moderate Left: Giuseppe Canepa, the Reformist Socialist, and Giovanni Longinotti, the Social Catholic, were on the delegation as advisers on labor questions, though they were scarcely noticed in either Paris or Rome.

This same concern with the politics rather than the diplomacy of peacemaking was also evident in the Wilson Administration. As compared to the Allied Premiers, however, the American President was considerably more reluctant to conciliate the political opposition which espoused a hard peace. Not that Wilson was altogether unyielding. To be sure, he went against the advice of Colonel House and others in refusing to appoint Elihu Root as the Republican spokesman on the Peace Commission. Since Wilson was convinced that Root was "hopelessly reactionary," he thought that the appointment would shock his "progressive" supporters at home, including American labor, while "discouraging every liberal element in the world."[7] At the time, the President may have been justified in his fear that, coming so soon after the setback of the congressional elections, Root's appointment might further erode the political basis, both national and international, for a peace of reconciliation.

[7] *F.R.,P.C.,1919*, I, 131, 171–2; House Diary, December 1, 1918, and October 26, 1919; Philip C. Jessup: *Elihu Root* (New York: Dodd, Mead; 1938), II, 379–80.

Wilson was confronted with the selection of a representative and influential—and yet loyal—member of the opposition party at a time when in America bipartisanship in and the primacy of foreign policy were still in their infancy. Perhaps Taft would have been a sound choice, especially given his prominent contribution to the League to Enforce Peace; yet his unsteady course during the November election made Wilson rather reticent. In any event, the President appointed Henry White, whose political influence and power in the party were modest even though he enjoyed the respect of the Republican leadership. Indeed, it would seem that there were few, if any, candidates for this novel and delicate post who would have been acceptable to both Wilson and Lodge.

At the same time that the President eliminated Root for fear of antagonizing the liberal elements, he also decided against William Jennings Bryan. Wilson claimed that he had full confidence in the principles of his former Secretary of State and "in his influence at the Conference." But Bryan was "soft-hearted" in a very "hard-hearted" world, a world that was "a bit abnormal in its acute sensibilities," in which public opinion was "excited and superheated and suspicious." As a result Wilson did not "dare" appoint him: "a very large and influential body of our public opinion" would unjustly assume that Bryan "would be too easy and would pursue some utopian scheme."[8]

In spite of a concerted campaign to have Samuel Gompers selected as one of the five Peace Commissioners,[9] the President also passed him over. In this instance Wilson again is likely to have had a dual political purpose: at home he did not want to incite antiunion and anti-Socialist sentiments, while abroad he was careful not to arouse the suspicion of the leaders of the Second International. Thus, he informed his Secretary of Labor as well as the Secretary of the A.F. of L. that the peace delegates should not represent "special classes or interests . . . but the country as a whole." But rather than alienate Gompers completely he eventually invited him to come to Paris in an advisory capacity. Gompers was to serve the U. S. Delegation as Jouhaux and Canepa were serving theirs. Wilson, moreover, hoped to prevail on the President of the A.F. of L. to overcome his active opposition to the proposed meeting of the Second International; this opposition threatened to weaken seriously the Socialists' campaign in support of a moderate peace treaty.[1]

Even in the selection of his Peace Commissioners Woodrow Wilson was a man of the middle, the statesman and politician who realized the importance of steadying national and world opinion if a sound peace

[8] Woodrow Wilson to Secretary of the Navy Daniels, November 16, 1918, and to Senator Henry L. Myers, November 20, 1918, cited in *F.R.,P.C.,1919,* I, 159, 163.
[9] Starting November 14 the White House was deluged with wires and letters from union leaders throughout the nation. See Wilson Papers, VI:187.
[1] *F.R.,P.C.,1919,* I, 168, 173, 178. See pp. 381–2, 384–6 below.

were to be achieved. This laudable but untimely concern rather than the banal wish not to share the limelight with other prominent political figures was at the bottom of Wilson's decision against Root, Bryan, and Gompers. This same concern had a positive side as well in that it guided Wilson in his selection of Secretary of State Lansing, Colonel House, General Tasker H. Bliss, and Henry White.

It is evident, then, that political factors significantly influenced the Allied chief executives in their choice of peace delegates. Under contemporary political and social conditions this selection could hardly have been based on kinship or patronage. But what about foreign policy skill and expertise? Were they sacrificed to the bitch goddess of politics?

To begin with, the Allied chief executives were not as ignorant of international politics as legend would have it. The fact that Wilson, Lloyd George, Clemenceau, and Orlando were eminent politicians rather than diplomats before they became heads of government was an advantage rather than a detriment to them in their peacemaking task. Party politics and power politics are not antithetical. Quite the contrary: experience in the domestic politics of modernized societies and in two- or multi-party systems is an excellent school for aspiring practitioners of international politics. In both spheres power is calculated, compromises are made, objectives and capabilities are meshed, and prestige is jealousy guarded. Needless to say, as a result of their prior political experience, politician-statesmen have a particularly sharp but essential sensitivity to the requirements of legislative and party sanction for diplomatic agreements.

The Big Four may not have been seasoned experts in the geography, ethnography, strategy, economy, and political history of East Central Europe and the Balkans. Except for a few experts, who had intimate knowledge of the disputed areas between Czechoslovakia and Poland or Hungary and Rumania? Certainly neither the foreign ministers nor Colonel House were any better informed than their superiors; and, incidentally, they were ill-informed not because they owed their jobs to petty graft or political patronage but because detailed knowledge about Teschen and Transylvania quite rightly was not a prerequisite for their appointment. After all, chief executives and foreign ministers of major powers should above all have an overall view of and an insight into the processes of international politics rather than a thorough knowledge of a few select geographic areas. In each particular case this overall view and this insight must then be combined with detailed information provided by expert advisers. Whereas the President and the Premiers had to be generalists, the experts had to be specialists—and their functions were not interchangeable.

Agreement among the Allied and Associated Governments was easily reached on such matters as the location of the Conference, which was to be held in Paris, and the size of the delegations, to be limited to five plenipotentiary delegates for each major power. In the selection of delegates as well, the chief executives were guided by roughly similar political considerations; almost as if by prior accord the Premiers and the President did not compete with each other in the search for strictly diplomatic expertise among the principal negotiators.

But the moment the victors settled down to a discussion of fundamental procedural questions, serious disagreements began to be evident. During the second half of November the French precipitated the first really substantive exchanges with three versions of a policy paper designed to fix both the underlying principles and the agenda for the Peace Conference.

In the first two versions, which hardly differed, the experts of the Quai d'Orsay, guided by the precedents established by the congresses of 1814–15, 1856, and 1878, urged that the forthcoming Conference should begin with a proclamation of guiding principles. These should be three in number: (1) the right of self-determination by free and secret vote combined with guarantees for minorities; (2) mutual renunciation of the secret treaties (in order to avoid giving Constantinople to Russia); and (3) inviolability of the August 1914 metropolitan and colonial frontiers of the Allies (designed to exclude all but enemy colonies from the peace negotiations).[2]

Notwithstanding the apparent clarity and directness of these three points this document was internally inconsistent. It recommended the second principle—mutual renunciation of secret treaties—with the dual assertion that it was in complete accord with President Wilson's ideas and that it would conveniently absolve the Allies of all imperialist suspicions.

Elsewhere in this prospectus, however, the Fourteen Points were cavalierly dismissed for being excessively vague. In spite of their acceptance, with two reservations, during the pre-Armistice negotiations, Wilson's Points were to be abandoned in favor of the Allied Note of January 10, 1917. That note had been sent in response to Wilson's invitation to the statesmen of both sides to spell out their war aims; it predated America's entry into war, the Russian Revolution, and the ideological upsurge of the conflict; and it disingenuously proclaimed that Allied war aims would "only be set forth in detail, with all the compensations and equitable indemnities for harm suffered, at the moment of negotiation."[3] Indeed, this Allied Note was likely to leave the peacemakers complete flexibility, if not license. In conclusion Paris

---

[2] The full text is cited in David Hunter Miller: *My Diary at the Conference of Paris,* II, 4–16.

[3] For the full text of the January 10 Note see G. Lowes Dickinson (ed.): *Documents and Statements Relating to Peace Proposals and War Aims* (London: Allen and Unwin; 1919), 10–13.

now suggested that the peacemakers complete the settlement of territorial, military, and reparations terms before proceeding to the discussion of the League of Nations.[4]

D. H. Miller instantly and succinctly summarized America's objections. The Allied declaration of January 1917 had never been agreed to by the U.S. On the other hand, on November 5, 1918, following interAllied agreement in Paris, Wilson had informed the German government that subject to two qualifications the Allies "declared their willingness to make peace" on the terms and principles laid down in the Fourteen Points address and in subsequent addresses.[5]

In the third and official version of the document, which reached Washington on November 29, the French government returned to the attack. Except for the Quai d'Orsay's cryptic guiding principles, the Conference lacked a fixed basis for negotiation.

> Neither the four armistices signed with Bulgaria, Austria-Hungary, Turkey and Germany, nor the answer of the Allies of January 10, 1917 . . . nor the President's fourteen propositions . . . can furnish a concrete basis for the labors of the Congress.

But there was a way out. The Allied and Associated Powers should begin with "the settlement of the war properly so-called" by organizing the new states; disposing of the territorial questions, including the neutralization of territories "for protection purposes"; fixing indemnities, including reparations for war damage, "restitution, reconstruction, compensation in kind, reimbursement of expenses unlawfully imposed"; and securing "the recognition by Germany of the responsibility and premeditation of her rulers justifying the measures of penalization and precaution taken against her." Once these and similar questions arising out of the war were settled, the Conference could examine the organization of the Society of Nations.[6]

Wilson could have accepted this plan only at the risk of denying himself at the outset. Even the suggestion to cancel all secret treaties was now watered down: by late November the Quai d'Orsay merely called for "the suspension of all previous special agreements arrived at by some of the Allies only, with a view to the fullest freedom of the examination by the Congress." Perhaps Wilson nevertheless should have tried to pressure the Allies into a full cancellation of their wartime agreements in exchange for his acceptance of the French plan. Quite apart from the fact that Italy represented an insurmountable obstacle, this would have been a steep price to pay. Not only would the discussion of the League of Nations have been postponed until after the

---

[4] Cf. F. S. Marston: *The Peace Conference of 1919: Organization and Procedure* (London: Oxford; 1944), 36–8.
[5] D. H. Miller's memo is cited in *F.R.,P.C.,1919*, I, 359.
[6] This document is cited in Baker: *Woodrow Wilson and World Settlement*, III, 56–63.

settlement of the war, but this prior settlement would have proceeded unrestrained by the principles, aims, and methods of the New Diplomacy. In fact, under these procedures the Allies could easily have afforded to dispense with the secret treaties; they could have relied on their negotiations to provide mutual compensations similar to those of the treaties.

In addition to denying himself as well as foregoing his creative effort of the past year, Wilson would have undermined his own diplomatic and political position. Throughout Europe his supporters would have been thrown into disarray. In the defeated nations his peremptory infraction of the pre-Armistice agreement would have encouraged and strengthened the extreme Left; in the victor nations his effortless abandonment of the New Diplomacy would have eroded still further the moderates who were so heavily besieged both on their right and their left; and Lenin would have had a field day. In turn, this impairment of Wilson's constituency could only have sapped his bargaining position with the Allied Premiers. Hence, he would have entered the negotiations—the secret negotiations—bereft of his ideological and moral suasion as well as of his political sanction.

It would seem, then, that Wilson's decision to oppose the French plan was not an outgrowth of his infatuation with the League of Nations idea. To be sure, he was determined to make the League an integral part of the treaty and therefore insisted that consideration of the League could not wait until after the immediate bread-and-butter issues had been settled. Much more was involved, however. The President meant to serve notice that he had only just begun to fight for his grand design. He would fight to secure a negotiated peace on the basis of his principles. While engaged in this arduous diplomatic struggle— whose ultimate objective was the reconstruction, reform, and stability of the international order as well as of the major national societies— Wilson had to try to keep the world steady. In pursuit of this immediate and instrumental objective Wilson had to prevent further chaos in Eastern and Central Europe while at the same time preventing the obliteration of his own supporters in the Allied countries.

That such was his project was evident as of January 12 when the Council of Ten[7] held its first session. On this occasion Marshal Foch urged that the Polish legions in France be rushed home to help stabilize Poland's new frontiers and government, especially against the westward-moving Bolshevik menace; he also urged that Russian prisoners in Germany be enrolled in the counterrevolution. Immediately Wilson made it clear that he doubted that this Bolshevik advance "could be checked by arms at all." With Lloyd George's endorsement he insisted that before taking military measures the Allies should agree on a

[7] For the organization, composition, functions, and procedures of the Council of Ten see Marston: *Peace Conference of 1919,* Chs. v and vi.

general policy to check Bolshevism "as a social and political danger."[8]

The following afternoon the Supreme War Council had one of its periodic wrangles over the payment for food supplies to be shipped to hard-pressed Germany. Even though Wilson agreed that the Associated Governments should not have to shoulder the financial burden he issued a stern warning.

> . . . Any further delay in this matter might be fatal, as it meant the dissolution of order and government. . . . So long as hunger continued to gnaw, the foundations of government would continue to crumble. Therefore, food should be supplied immediately, not only to our friends, but also to those parts of the world where it was to our interest to maintain a stable Government. . . . [The Allies] were faced with the great problems of Bolshevism and the forces of dissolution which now threatened society. . . . The want of food would lead to a crash in Germany.[9]

On this particular occasion the President's warning had little, if any, effect; nevertheless it revealed his concern for the social and political rather than for the strictly diplomatic and military aspects of peacemaking.

Later that afternoon, at a meeting of the Council of Ten, this same concern led him to oppose a new version of France's November plan. Clemenceau had instructed André Tardieu to prepare a revised and vastly enlarged plan of procedure.[1] In this new Tardieu Plan the French Delegation at long last conceded that the Conference would settle the war and chart a new organization of international relations along the principles set forth by Wilson in various speeches as well as in his final pre-Armistice note to Germany. Tardieu furthermore clarified the relationship between the "Peace Preliminaries" and the "Final Peace Treaty," between the "Powers with General Interests" (the Great Powers) and the "Powers with Particular Interests" (the Small Powers), and between the meetings of the Allied and Associated plenipotentiaries and the sessions of the technical committees.

All the plenipotentiaries, including Wilson, seemed to welcome these procedural clarifications. The President, however, was disturbed by the other section in the Tardieu Plan which outlined the sequence in which the major problems and issues would be taken up. Quite apart from being very unclear about the place of the League of Nations, the French agenda gave top priority to the territorial settlement with Germany. The Russian problem was given last place; it was to be postponed until after the settlement not only of the German problem but also of the Central European, Oriental, and Balkan questions.

---

[8] *F.R.,P.C.,1919*, III, 471–3, 496–7.
[9] Ibid., 516.
[1] André Tardieu: *La Paix* (Paris: Payot; 1921), 97. For the full text of this plan see *F.R.,P.C.,1919*, I, 386–96.

In Wilson's judgment the Russian question "called for immediate decision." Apparently this sense of urgency about Russia was an integral part of Wilson's anxiety about the perilous disorder and instability throughout defeated Europe east of the Rhine. Accordingly he insisted that the peacemakers had "to remove quicksand before they could begin to walk, . . . [that] the order of discussion should be settled from time to time, [and that] a list of subjects to be discussed could be prepared, but not the order of sequence."[2] In brief, the Big Four could not afford to tie themselves to a rigid agenda; they needed maximum flexibility in order to be able to help establish the political and economic preconditions for their peacemaking labors.

Both Lloyd George and Clemenceau now agreed to leave the agenda flexible while instructing all the delegations, including those of the Small Powers, to prepare their dossiers. But whereas the Big Four also agreed to continue meeting in private—in the Council of Ten—in order to exchange views, Clemenceau wanted an immediate inaugural session of the entire Peace Conference of nonenemy nations. The French Premier maintained that such a session was needed in order to satisfy public opinion, to issue mandates to all the delegates but especially to the Council of Ten, and to charter Committees of the Conference as a whole. Since Wilson seemed to be holding out for a postponement of this plenary session Clemenceau sought to placate him with the assurance that "nothing of importance need be discussed."[3]

And, indeed, the inaugural session of the Plenary Peace Conference, held on January 18 in the Peace Rooms of the Quai d'Orsay, was all pomp and ceremony combined with a legitimization of the dominant role of the Powers with General Interests. But within a week Clemenceau's design emerged in clear outline: whereas the Council of Ten (i.e., the Conference of the Great Powers) would continue to attend to vital territorial, military, and colonial questions, five commissions of the Plenary Conference simultaneously would examine questions of less crucial importance.[4]

Except for the technical Commission of International Control of Ports, Waterways, and Railways, the Commissions of the Plenary Conference received highly ideological assignments. In line with the Quai d'Orsay's master plan Clemenceau sought to relegate consideration of the new international order to an obscure and ineffectual League of Nations Commission. Wilson foiled this plan by first appointing himself American delegate on this Commission and then becoming its elected Chairman; thus Wilson endowed it with prestige, power, and newsworthiness. It was on this occasion that Wilson earnestly but unconvincingly proclaimed that "select classes of mankind [were] no

[2] *F.R.,P.C.,1919*, III, 536.
[3] Ibid., 536–7.
[4] Ibid., 677–83; and Marston: *Peace Conference of 1919*, 70, 90.

longer the governors of mankind, [that] the fortunes of mankind [were] now in the hands of the plain peoples of the whole world," and that unless these peoples were satisfied no peace settlement could last.[5]

Unintentionally Clemenceau enabled Wilson to dramatize the League issue, especially since the Commission was scheduled to submit the completed draft-Covenant to a solemn and widely publicized meeting of the Plenary Conference. The Commission on International Labor Legislation, which was the only other Commission to report to the Plenary Conference, performed the same function of giving heart to the Wilsonians and Socialists—both Allied and enemy—who suspected the Old Diplomacy practiced by the formidable and remote Conference of Great Powers. Eventually, once France was plagued by strikes, even Clemenceau was anxious that the I.L.O. Convention "should be adopted by the Plenary Conference as an earnest of an attempt to better conditions of the working classes . . . [and] to produce a good effect on workers in France."[6]

Whereas the League and Labor Commissions pacified the Left, the Commissions on War Guilt and on Reparations satisfied the Right. In political rather than diplomatic terms, however, the bow to the Left was more effective and important, in large measure because at this stage the Right hardly needed to be reassured.[7]

Now the Big Four were free to devote themselves to vital and material matters. Even though they had decided not to adopt a fixed agenda, they still had to start somewhere. On January 23 Lloyd George argued that "European questions were so complicated that it would take a long time for such people as the Czecho-Slovaks and Poles to set forth a reasoned case." He proposed, therefore, that since "Oriental questions and Colonial questions were less involved," the Council of Ten should tackle them first. Whereas Clemenceau immediately agreed "to begin with the colonial questions," Sonnino's approval was not nearly so enthusiastic.

As for Wilson, he once again responded by voicing his concern for conditions east of the Rhine.

> . . . The world's unrest arose from the unsettled condition of Europe, not from the state of affairs in the East [i.e., the Orient], or in the Colonies, and that the postponement of these questions would only increase the pressure on the Delegates of the Peace Conference. He would therefore prefer to set in process immediately all that was required to hasten a solution of European questions. He

[5] F.R.,P.C.,1919, III, 177 ff., esp. 180.
[6] Lloyd George speaking at British Empire Delegation 17, April 3, 1919 (p.m.).
[7] Cf. Marston: Peace Conference of 1919, 75: "It will be at once apparent that, of the five subjects, two (the League and International Labour) were connected with the future international order, and were therefore very suitable for reference to the Conference as a whole, and two (Reparations and War Guilt), it may be suggested, were given prominence in order to satisfy public opinion."

entirely approved of utilizing intervals for the discussion of less important matters.

At this particular session Wilson did not specify what concrete steps could be taken in Europe; he merely agreed to a discussion of colonial questions which he as well as Lloyd George judged to be of secondary importance.[8]

But this was the fourteenth session of the Council of Ten. Even though the first thirteen meetings had been primarily taken up with procedural and organizational matters, ten of them had made time for a discussion of substantive issues. And among these the Russian-*cum*-Bolshevik issue had been given top priority. Whereas Clemenceau and Foch wanted the Conference to strengthen Poland as a rampart against the advance of Bolshevism, Lloyd George and Wilson pressed for a prior effort at negotiation with the rival factions of the Russian Civil War. All three of them were agreed, however, that developments in Russia and in the borderlands between Russia and Germany were bound to impinge heavily on their peacemaking enterprise.

Significantly, nearly the entire five sessions preceding the decision to take up the colonial issue had been devoted to the Russian question; and at the last of these five meetings the Big Four had issued the Prinkipo invitation. In this invitation, which was drafted by Wilson, the Powers declared that they were "keenly alive to the fact that Europe and the world [could not] be at peace if Russia [was] not." The representatives of the warring factions in Russia, including delegates of the Bolshevik government, were asked to meet with representatives of the Allied and Associated Powers; they were requested to reply promptly and were expected at Princes Island in the Sea of Marmora "by the 15 February, 1919."[9]

Surely, it is not unreasonable to suggest that notwithstanding all its flaws, this Prinkipo proposal was designed to help reduce the unrest of Europe. More than likely, the Big Four now decided to proceed with the relatively uninvolved and ready colonial questions while waiting for replies to their invitation. At the same time they notified "all the delegations representing Powers with territorial claims to send to the Secretariat their written statements within 10 days."[1]

Under the circumstances it was sound diplomacy and politics to postpone discussion of the complex and touchy territorial questions in Eastern and Central Europe. Quite apart from the fact that most dossiers were incomplete, it was prudent and correct to mark time until it was clear whether or not Russia—who continued to be a major power in spite of her present weakness and fragmentation—would be

[8] *F.R.,P.C.,1919*, III, 700.
[9] Ibid., 469 ff. For detailed treatment of the Russian problem at the Conference up to and including the Prinkipo proposal see Ch. 10 above.
[1] *F.R.,P.C.,1919*, III, 700.

represented at the Conference. Moreover, the Directing Powers needed additional time to study and steady conditions in Eastern and Central Europe. Given the premises of the victors, it was hardly a waste of time to counteract disorder and Bolshevism there.[2]

Even the French momentarily ceased to insist that the Big Four settle Germany's borders before considering any other issues or taking other actions. It was Foch who with Clemenceau's entire approval kept coming back to the need to stabilize conditions in Poland, a nation whose course would profoundly affect not only the German settlement but also the troubled situation in Russia and the rimland. According to Tardieu there was much more to peacemaking than the drawing of frontiers, the fixing of reparations, and the distribution of colonies.

> . . . the [principal] peace negotiators had to devote part of their time to the current administration of Europe and the world. . . . Many of the situations were intimately related to peacemaking and benefited from being treated by those who were responsible for the peace. Europe was alive, but her life was difficult both materially and morally. These difficulties could not wait. Relief measures had to be taken without delay and political as well as national conflicts called for decisions. Special organizations watched these situations: the Armistice Commission in Spa and the Supreme Economic Council. These had to be guided and given instructions. This took up time, but it also gained some. What would have happened if [the Big Four] had not done this? What would have happened if famine had been allowed to decimate Poland and Germany; if the various threats of revolution in Hungary, Bavaria, and elsewhere had not been closely followed? For that matter, there was no choice. By ignoring these realities in order to focus exclusively on peacemaking the peace would have been delayed and jeopardized. Let the theoreticians deplore this "supergovernment," but in Paris in 1919 it was a necessity.[3]

Indeed, not only Wilson but all the principal peacemakers realized that they had to take a hand in steadying Europe. They had it in their power to grant or to refuse economic aid, political recognition, and diplomatic concessions to the shaky governments of Central and Eastern Europe. This is not to say that Europe was as clay in their hands. In

---

[2] Most interpretations have missed, ignored, or distorted this relationship between the decision to begin with colonial questions and the concern with Russia as well as the specter of Bolshevism. Cf. Baker: *World Settlement*, I, 252–4; Paul Birdsall: *Versailles Twenty Years After* (New York: Reynal and Hitchcock; 1941), 58–60; Wilhelm Ziegler: *Versailles: Die Geschichte eines missglückten Friedens* (Hamburg: Hanseatische Verlagsanstalt; 1933), 53–4; Augusto Torre: *Versailles: Storia della conferenza della pace* (Milano: Instituto per gli Studi di Politica Internazionale; 1940), 148–50; Thomas A. Bailey: *Woodrow Wilson and the Lost Peace* (New York: Macmillan; 1944), 163–5; Marston: *Peace Conference of 1919*, 99–101; Seth P. Tillman: *Anglo-American Relations at the Paris Peace Conference of 1919* (Princeton: Princeton University Press; 1961), 76.

[3] Tardieu: *La Paix*, 118–19.

all the states, both old and new, there were governments whose fortunes were only in part at the mercy of decisions in Paris; for the rest their fortunes were shaped by indigenous political, economic, and military developments. In other words, just as the governments and policies of the victor powers were shaped by the interplay of domestic and international politics, so were those of the defeated and new nations.

Still, whereas the collapse of the government of one of these nations could not shake the victor governments, the decisions of the latter could have a critical influence on the former. The supergovernment in Paris had it in its power decisively to facilitate or complicate the task of the governments of Scheidemann, Renner, Károlyi, Masaryk, Pilsudski, Brătianu, and Pasić.

Of course, this supergovernment was embryonic at best. The same conflicts of interest which marked the peace negotiations proper also affected such executive decisions as the feeding of the defeated nations, the drawing of cease-fire lines between hostile successor nations, and the supply of arms to rival suppliants. Moreover, in case of anticipated or actual disagreements, each associated power was at liberty and had the means to act alone in its own national interest.

In fact, each individual power gathered the information that was requisite for action. There was ample expert information about the political and human geography of Central and Eastern Europe. What was needed was up-to-date political intelligence which could serve as a basis for emergency executive measures.

Diplomatic relations with the defeated nations and Soviet Russia were still broken; with the new nations they either did not exist as yet or else they had been so recently established that there had been no time to exchange diplomatic and consular missions. Hence the powers had only inadequate information about rapidly changing conditions: they read partisan newspapers of Poland and Czechoslovakia, listened to the biased pleas of supplicant delegates and lobbyists, and studied the political reports of agents who were trained, hired, and experienced to spy on military rather than on political movements.

As compared to Britain and France, the U.S. was at a particular disadvantage. America's intelligence network in Central and Eastern Europe was nonexistent; few American newspapermen could claim experience in this area; and business contacts were equally sparse.

Soon after his arrival in Europe, Colonel House complained that U. S. officials had no "dependable information concerning political and economic conditions in the following countries: Poland, Bohemia, Ukraine, Austria, Serbia (including Yugo-Slavia), Hungary, Bulgaria, Albania, and Turkey." Most of their information consisted of reports furnished by interested British, French, and Italian agencies. There was a desperate need for "accurate and unbiased information"; it should be secured by American agents reporting from these countries "through

American eyes." By November 15 House received Wilson's and Lansing's approval for the organization of a network of agents throughout Central and Eastern Europe, a courier service, and a political intelligence section in the American Delegation to the Peace Conference. Most agents were to be selected from U. S. military and naval personnel in Europe and, even though they would not be formally accredited to their stations, "so far as possible the governments in the localities to which they are sent will be requested to give them assistance in the conduct of their work." Needless to say, they would not wear their uniforms. And from the beginning House proposed to confer with Hoover since it was his hope that these agents could "work in close cooperation" with relief agencies.[4]

Presently House and his advisers planned to explore an even more direct use of Hoover and his projected operation. House requested permission to ask the relief tsar "to lay the basis for a political intelligence system during his visit to the Central Powers." Hugh Gibson was to accompany Hoover. He was to remain in Vienna as Hoover's assistant, to set up headquarters within the relief headquarters, to supervise agents, and to travel about on instructions from Paris. General Nolan and Colonel Van Deman agreed with Joseph Grew, Gibson, and Auchincloss that military and naval personnel could serve in civilian clothing and that each agent should be "provided with a document from Hoover designating him as a member of the United States Food Administration, or whatever relief organization may be established."[5]

Presumably after checking with the President, Lansing cabled his approval of this plan. In turn, on November 27, in a conference with House, Herbert Hoover expressed his "entire accord" and agreed to "designate as members of the United States Food Administration any men whom I [House] may assign for work in the field."[6]

Because of inter-Allied disagreements over relief policies and organization, the implementation of this plan was temporarily delayed, along with Hoover's larger project.[7] But by December 24 Lewis Strauss, one of Hoover's top assistants, informed the Ammission that, among others, Hugh Gibson and Vernon Kellogg had left for Prague, Alonzo Taylor and T. T. C. Gregory for Vienna, and J. W. McIntosh for Trieste.[8]

Meanwhile the American Commissioners started to send out officers in civilian clothing. These agents were responsible to the Ammission directly rather than to the State Department; and they

[4] F.R.,P.C.,1919, I, 194–5.
[5] Ibid., 199–201.
[6] Ibid., 201, 203.
[7] See pp. 273–8 above.
[8] National Archives, Document 184.01/3.

secured advance clearance from the enemy and new governments into whose territories they were now dispatched.[9]

These field agents went on different types of missions. On December 17 Ellis Loring Dresel was instructed to proceed to Germany to investigate political conditions there. He returned to Paris by January 5 and personally reported his findings to the Ammission.[1] There were other such temporary and on-the-spot investigating missions: the Field Mission to Munich; the Gherardi, Second Dresel, and Conger Missions to Germany; the Lord Mission to Poland; and the Bullitt Mission to Russia.

But there were also missions of a more permanent nature. The Coolidge Mission to the territories of the former Austro-Hungarian Empire was the most notable of these. It was appointed by the American Delegation on December 27 and it set up headquarters in Vienna. Its agents circulated throughout Central and Eastern Europe and remained in the field until mid-May 1919 when the State Department's Halstead Mission took over.[2] Colonel Greene's Mission to the Baltic and Colonel Rigg's Mission to Southern Russia belonged to this same category.

But what was the assignment of all these political missions? The reports and memoranda from the field agents supplemented the information that was available from other sources in Paris. The Intelligence Section of the American Delegation in particular used these materials in the preparation of daily intelligence digests about political, economic, and military developments for the Commissioners.[3] Furthermore, apart from helping in their evaluation, the technical experts also took account of this welcome data in their work.

Since Professor Coolidge's "studied and well balanced conclusions did not lend themselves readily to telegraphic language" they were incorporated into long reports which couriers took to Paris. Before long, however, the mission in Vienna had to conciliate the delegation with "a daily telegraphic summary of current events."[4]

In addition to insisting on brief and frequent reports the principals in Paris also wanted evaluation and advice. Allen Dulles requested that the Coolidge Mission should "clearly distinguish between what is told

9 *F.R.,P.C.,1919*, I, 206; and National Archives, Document 184.01/6.
1 For detailed treatment of the first Dresel Mission see pp. 281–2 above.
2 For detailed treatment of the Coolidge Mission see Chs. 15, 16, 21, and 24 below, *passim*.
3 William C. Bullitt prepared this daily digest, and he was particularly alarmed about conditions in Central and Eastern Europe. Until he left on his mission to Russia he gave Lansing almost daily briefings in which he kept warning of the Bolshevik danger. Lansing also saw his nephew Allen Dulles who was involved in this political intelligence work as well and who was equally alarmist. Incidentally, by February 14 Lansing recorded that Dulles gave him "a lot of advice on how to run things [but that] his judgment was not very sound." Lansing Diary, *passim*.
4 Walter Goodwin Davis Diary, entry of February 6, 1919.

you and your valuation and criticism" and that wherever possible it should "make definite and precise recommendations of lines of policy which it would be desirable for America and the Entente to follow."[5]

In Paris, then, the information, evaluations, and recommendations of the various missions became a basis for policy formulation. But these missions also served a political function in their different out-posts. Since they requested advance clearance, their hosts considered them as informal diplomatic missions. Especially for the enemy govern-ments in Berlin, Vienna, and Budapest, they were a rare and highly valued link to the outside world. Renner, Károlyi, and Scheidemann looked upon the members of these missions as friendly counsels at the victors' court: Coolidge or Dresel would plead their cause for economic aid, recognition, and moderation with both Wilson and Hoover.

National and local authorities, moreover, were very sensitive to intimations and suggestions emanating directly or indirectly from the American missions. In fact, since they considered Coolidge a political agent, they assumed that his values, judgments, and objectives were an expression of American if not inter-Allied wishes and intentions. And, indeed, the American Delegation fully intended its agents to influence these authorities by their presence as well as with their advice.

Unfortunately U. S. officials never issued detailed instructions to their missions. They simply assumed that there was a pervading anti-Bolshevik consensus among U. S. civilian and military officials in Europe. But these officials did not have concise and informed notions of Bolshevism, but on the contrary, quite vague and confused ones. For almost all of them Bolshevism was a dictatorial form of government thriving on political rivalries, famine, economic chaos, and national disillusionment, and almost all of them believed in a combination of economic aid, Wilsonian peace, and democratic rule as the only effec-tive prophylaxis.

To be sure, the Allied and Associated Governments pursued con-flicting objectives, for instance in Poland. It would seem, however, that they, too, shared a minimum consensus: they were opposed to Bolshe-vism, anarchy, and disorder. Hence, the British and the French delega-tions also sent missions to Germany, Austria, Poland, the Baltic provinces, and different parts of Russia.

In late January the Council of Ten decided to send an inter-Allied Commission to Poland. The instructions issued on this occasion reflect the combination of aims which the U. S. and Allied missions, separately and collectively, pursued in Central and Eastern Europe.

According to these instructions the Commissioners were to convey "as early as possible" information about the situation in Poland. Al-though the "military and food questions were the most urgent, . . . reports on the political and social conditions" were also desperately

[5] Allen Dulles to Walter G. Davis, February 3, 1919, in Walter G. Davis Papers.

needed. In addition, the Warsaw government should be warned "against adopting a policy of an aggressive character" toward her new and old neighbors, especially against Czechoslovakia and Germany. Simultaneously, the inter-Allied Commission was to inquire how far the Polish government possessed "the means to maintain order within their existing territory and of preserving it from external aggression" from Bolshevik or any other forces.

The Commissioners were asked to recommend measures necessary to provide the government with the material supplies required for the battle against domestic and foreign enemies. With regard to food the Commissioners "should cooperate with the Mission about to be dispatched to Poland by the Supreme Council of Supply and Relief."[6]

A draft version of these instructions which had "proved to be too long"[7] was still more explicit. In this discarded version the Commission was instructed to "collect all information on the general feeling, the real strength of parties, their tendencies, and their influence on the present government." But again inquest was to be combined with action. The Commissioners were encouraged to "give pressing advice of union to the different groups."

According to another section of this longer version, their principal object was to study the "exact situation" with regard to the immediate Bolshevik danger due to external action, internal disintegration, and "intense propaganda by Bolshevik agents and publications." The Commission was asked to recommend the aid measures that should be taken in the interest of both Poland and Europe. At the same time, it should be made understood that help given to Poland "should in no way whatever tend towards aggression or conquest, nor be diverted from its essential aim, which is to insure the existence of the new State forming in itself a protection against anarchy coming from the East."[8]

Even without the extra complication of the dual specter of Bolshevism and Soviet Russia, the situation in the territories of the defeated Empires would have posed unparalleled problems for the peacemakers in Paris. East of the Rhine, but especially in the successor nations, governments were new and weak, party struggles were intense, minority tensions were acute, and frontiers were militantly contested.

Surely it was not the delay in reaching diplomatic decisions that caused these struggles, confusions, and uncertainties. On the contrary, the unexpected chaos in Central and Eastern Europe stood in the way of a quick settlement. In fact, this chaos was the second major surprise of the war, the first one having been the escalation from a short and limited war into a long and unlimited war of universal and revolutionary proportions.

---

[6] *F.R.,P.C.,1919,* I, 818–22, 838–40.
[7] Ibid., 772.
[8] Stray British draft-proposal in the House Collection.

A Statistical Committee of the sort that had rendered such useful services at the Congress of Vienna could not instantly have provided the political intelligence required for lasting decisions. It is even doubtful that in January–February 1919 it could have provided the technical information about nationality, religion, economics, and strategy necessary for the major territorial settlements. With few exceptions even the new governments themselves were in no position to present carefully worked out claims. By the end of the original ten-day period provided for the submission of territorial claims, "no documents [were] received by the Secretariat General, except a part of the Greek case and a report by the Czecho-Slovak Delegates."[9] And it is most unlikely that all the claimants purposely delayed presenting their case in order first to improve their bargaining position by taking possession of contested territories.

In any case, the Big Four were agreed that they had to secure political intelligence and to stabilize governments. Moreover, they were in a genuine quandary about Russia: they agreed to bar the Bolshevik government without resolving the issue of Russian representation. It was in the hope of coming to grips with these fundamental political realities that they sent out their missions, organized the Supreme Economic Council, and issued the Prinkipo invitation. They could have dispensed with these improvised procedures only on condition that their "super-government" had been sufficiently united, powerful, and organized to enforce quick and often arbitrary decisions throughout Europe.

[9] *F.R.,P.C.,1919*, III, 840.

12

The Stillborn
Berne Conference

EVEN DURING THE WAR prominent Allied Socialists repeatedly tried to prove to themselves as well as to their opponents that reports of the death of the Second International in early August 1914 had been vastly exaggerated. This effort took the form of several inter-Allied Socialist conferences and of the striking but miscarried Stockholm project.[1] Quite naturally with the end of the war the Socialists energetically renewed their campaign on behalf of their International.

The last full-scale Congress of the Second International had been held in Basel in late November 1912. Fearful that the limited and localized Balkan tensions might touch off an unlimited and general conflict this congress—which originally had been scheduled to meet in Vienna in 1913—met to consider the international situation and proposals for antiwar action. Victor Adler, August Bebel, Jaurès, Keir Hardie, and George Plekhanov jointly drafted the ringing antiwar resolution which monopolized the attention of the delegates. This resolution was a superb synthesis of the International's recent pronouncements and fundamental theses on international politics. Because of insurmountable disagreements among the national delegations, however, the text failed to prescribe specific, coordinated, and direct antiwar action for Europe's Socialist parties. It merely reiterated the oft-repeated warning that a general war inevitably would hasten the overthrow of the established political and economic order while trusting this specter of revolution to frighten the cabinets into a peaceful course.

Whereas the Balkan crisis had precipitated that Basel Congress, the crisis of July 1914 prompted an emergency session of the International's Bureau in Brussels. Again some of the outstanding giants of European Socialism faced up to the danger of war; and once again they

[1] See my *Political Origins of the New Diplomacy, 1917–18, passim.*

restricted themselves to rousing but ineffectual antiwar protests and warnings. This time the groundswell of officially stimulated nationalism throughout Europe further reinforced their endemic inability to agree on common political action rather than rhetoric.

The Socialists were unable to prevent the outbreak of war or to bring about a negotiated peace in 1917; but their warnings of the revolutionary consequences of a general war turned out to be prophetic. In all fairness it should be noted that their warnings and predictions never singled out the nation that would be the first to be caught up in this revolutionary vortex; nor did they anticipate synchronized and equally extreme revolutionary developments throughout Europe. On balance, the Socialists realistically assessed the revolutionary consequences of total war which Europe's diplomats and politicians tended to ignore or minimize—at considerable risk and cost to themselves. In any case, protracted total war produced total revolution in defeated Russia and partial revolution in the defeated Central Powers. These revolutions made many Socialists justly proud of the perspicacity of their historical vision while also firing their political ardor.

But as compared to the prewar years the Second International now faced new and heightened obstacles to effective common action. The war had exacerbated national feelings, loyalties, and animosities among Socialists; as a result of the German and Austrian revolutions the International now comprised prominent Socialists who simultaneously were high officials in all-Socialist governments; the Bolshevik Revolution had intensified the ideological and programmatic rift among revolutionaries, revisionists, and reformists; and the projected Third International pointed toward a serious schism.

At this particular juncture, then, the Socialist front had advanced substantially beyond its prewar line without, however, promoting the unity of the Second International. Perhaps the centrifugal pressures could more readily have been checked—but even this is doubtful—if in the meantime the International had not been denied the counsel and guidance of its most respected and seasoned prewar leaders. Fritz Adler, Longuet, Henderson, and Axelrod could not hope to exercise the same wide-ranging moral, intellectual, and political influence as the late Victor Adler, Jaurès, Keir Hardie, and Plekhanov. Moreover, Kautsky never really achieved a commanding position, in part because of his rather lame censure of the murder of Karl Liebknecht and Rosa Luxemburg and his undisguised hostility to the Bolshevik Revolution. And the assassination of Kurt Eisner soon eroded the moral, humanitarian, and internationlist foundations of European Socialism still further. Certainly the sober and steadying influence of Branting and Huysmans could not compensate for these losses.

Simultaneously Lenin, Trotsky, Zinoviev, and Chicherin emerged as inspiring revolutionary leaders of all-European stature who proposed to bury instead of rebuild the Second International. They loomed so large because they had staged the first successful proletarian revolution, were courageously battling against concerted external intervention, and kept issuing seductive ideological manifestoes. For many Socialists even the brutalities and repressions of the Bolshevik Revolution failed to cancel out these appeals.

Before August 1914 the Second International had been first and foremost concerned with preventing the outbreak of general war; following the Armistice this International set out to secure a good— a Wilsonian—peace.

The initiative was taken by the same Allied Socialists who in 1917 had endorsed Wilson and promoted the Stockholm project. In particular Henderson took the lead; Longuet enthusiastically seconded him. As for the Allied Social Patriots, they renewed their opposition to meeting with enemy Socialists until after peace was signed, and Gompers backed up their position. Eventually Albert Thomas reluctantly agreed to participate, but only after extracting significant concessions.

From the outset it was clear that the Berne Congress would be multipurpose for Allied and Central Socialists alike. This Congress would not only serve to revive the International and to exert pressure on the Peace Conference; it would also become an instrument of party politics, factional struggles, and national rivalries.

Throughout the war Allied Socialists and trade unionists remained determined to have a voice at the future Peace Conference. They kept advancing two proposals designed to achieve this objective: that at least one of each nation's principal peace plenipotentiaries be a labor delegate and that an International Labor and Socialist Conference be held concurrently with the Peace Conference.

The demand for representation on the peace delegations was not met. The Labour Party refused to recognize Barnes as its spokesman; Gompers and Jouhaux were given subordinate posts; and Italian Socialism received no satisfaction whatever.

This rebuff did not take Henderson and Huysmans by surprise. As of early October 1918 they realized that with military victory and with unflagging reliance on Gompers the cabinets would become increasingly unyielding.

> The organized working class movement will encounter great difficulties if it asks for admission to the Diplomatic Conference. The Governments will reply, with some show of reason, that the representatives of States and not of Classes are responsible for negotiating peace. Moreover, the leaders of the Governments have not yet made any definite promises in this connection. If I am correctly informed Mr. Lloyd George . . . has limited himself to saying that

he would consult Labour representatives. He might therefore merely consult one of his Labour Ministers and his pledge would be fulfilled. . . . Mr. Clemenceau feels himself bound by no promise. . . .

Whatever happens . . . the TUC and the LP ought to put the following questions to the British Government. 1. Will representatives of the organized British working class movement be admitted to the Diplomatic Conference? 2. If not, will a Labour Minister be a member of the British delegation? 3. In any case, would the Labour organizations be authorized to appoint experts who would be consulted as military and naval experts are consulted (especially on labor questions like wages, hours, conditions)?[2]

These questions actually seem to have been put to Lloyd George, since in addition to appointing Barnes he consulted leading Labourites as experts. Eventually Henderson claimed that his own consultation in Paris—while passing through on his way to Berne—had been "in response to a summons he had received in his individual capacity to advise the British Section of the Allied Commission charged with the formulation of the International Labor Charter, and at which consultations the Parliamentary Committee of the TUC had been represented by Messrs. Stuart-Bunning, Shirkie, and Bowerman."[3]

Given this meager Socialist representation on the peace delegations, the Internationalists prepared to put all their energy into the drive for a concurrent Socialist Conference. But even according to Huysmans a conference "sitting at the same time as the Diplomatic Conference and at the same place" should only be called provided the governments did not oppose it.[4] Throughout 1917–18 the cabinets had checked the Internationalists by simply refusing passports. Would the Allied and Associated Governments continue to withhold passports from their own Socialists while at the same time denying entry permits to enemy Socialists?

Since Henderson and Longuet were not inclined to defy their own governments they hastened to get official sanction. In early November, during the same interview in which Lloyd George advised the Labour leaders of his "intention to include a Labour Member of the Government" in the British Peace Delegation, he asked that they submit a memorandum on the concurrent conference for his consideration.[5]

This memorandum was presented to the Prime Minister on Armi-

[2] Memorandum by Huysmans submitted by Henderson to the Executive Committee of the Labour Party for discussion on October 16, 1918 (a.m.), in Labour Party: Minutes of the Executive Committee, 14.

[3] Joint Meeting of the Executive Committee of the Labour Party and the Parliamentary Party, June 4, 1919 (a.m.), Labour Party: Minutes of the Executive Committee, 17.

[4] Labour Party: Minutes of the Executive Committee, 14, October 16, 1918 (a.m.).

[5] Report on interview with the Prime Minister to the meeting of the Executive Committee, November 7, 1918 (p.m.), in Labour Party: Minutes of the Executive Committee, 15.

stice Day. In it Henderson and his colleagues presented their case in the most moderate and cooperative light, going out of their way to emphasize that the proposal for a concurrent conference was originated by the A.F. of L. in 1914. Only "in the second stage" did the A.F. of L. and the Allied Labor and Socialist Movement reach common agreement on this proposal, notably at their inter-Allied Conference in September 1918.

> A resolution welcomed the declaration by the A.F. of L. of the fundamental principles to be included in the Peace Treaty, as being in substantial agreement with those applied in detail in the Memorandum on War Aims of the Inter-Allied Labour and Socialist Conference of February 1918, and also with the 14 propositions of President Wilson. The resolution further declared, on the suggestion of the A.F. of L., that "a world Labour Peace Congress should be held at the same time and place as the Peace Conference that will formulate the peace treaty closing the war." The Conference also agreed to add Mr. Gompers to the Special Commission of Messrs. Henderson, Vandervelde, and Thomas constituted at the previous Inter-Allied Conference [to organize this concurrent Congress].
> . . .
> It has been felt on all occasions [that such a Conference] . . . would create an atmosphere which would tend to the reduction of difficulties among the diplomatists themselves. . . . The presence of Labour representatives amongst the plenipotentiaries together with a concurrent conference, would mark the responsibilities of Allied Labour in the highest degree.
> Further, an international minimum standard of Labour conditions is of great importance to highly industrialized countries . . . and Prince Max of Baden has observed that this question will be raised at the Peace Conference by the Plenipotentiaries of the German Government. If agreement on this question could be obtained amongst the official representatives of organized Labour during the preliminary stages of negotiations the world Labour Conference would prove to be of invaluable assistance to the Commission which may have to elaborate these aspects of the peace treaty. . . .

Having presented such a reasonable case, the memo concluded with the assumption that British Labour's right to attend a conference "at any time and place . . . would not be challenged."[6]

At first glance it looks as if for tactical reasons organized labor was hiding behind both Wilson and Gompers. In fact, this offer of dutiful service once again demonstrated that the British as well as the other

---

[6] *Memorandum on the World Labour and Socialist Peace Conference to be held During the Peace Negotiations: Presented to the Prime Minister on behalf of the Parliamentary Committee of the T.U.C. and the National Executive of the L.P.*, November 11, 1918, G.T. 6384, Cabinet 24/70; and Labour Party Archives, Correspondence, 1918–20, file Peace Conference and International Meetings.

Internationalists were not champions of civil disobedience or sub-version. In their judgment a Wilsonian peace was the essential pre-condition for the advance of democratic Socialism throughout Europe. Nominally they were Centrists. In practice, however, they were anxious to break with the Maximalists in the hope of achieving a closer working relationship with the Social Patriots, with Gompers, and with the Wilsonians outside the Socialist and labor camp. Especially the Social Patriots and Gompers should be won to a revival of the Second Inter-national; in addition to giving the appearance of substantial power, such a comprehensive and safe International would be difficult to arraign for being radical, Bolshevik, and pro-German.

A deputation from the SFIO and the CGT also waited on Clemen-ceau to inquire whether an international congress, which would in-clude German Socialists, could be held at the same time and place as the Peace Conference, or, barring this, whether if held elsewhere, the necessary passports would be issued. Although the French Premier excluded a conference in Paris, for fear of "undesirable public demon-strations," he promised not to offer any obstacles to holding it outside France, subject to Allied approval. He saw no harm to Germans attending such a conference, confident that their attendance was not likely to increase their prestige. Besides, he was eager to "avoid the hostility which would be caused by the refusal of passports."[7]

This request for a concurrent congress was on the agenda of the inter-Allied conversations held at 10 Downing Street on December 3, prior to Wilson's arrival. Barnes, who introduced the subject, thought that the governments had "to choose between two evils: if they permitted the Conference, it would attract to it all sorts of doctrinaires and extremists; if they refused permission, agitation against the Gov-ernment would be fomented in each country." Only Hughes and Sonnino spoke out against the request, stressing the danger of giving labor "any greater privileges than . . . any other sectional interest." To meet this objection, Balfour suggested that other interests be granted the same privilege. In any case, Lloyd George having readily conceded Clemenceau's point that French "public opinion would not tolerate" a conference in Paris attended by Germans, the Allied Governments agreed that they would "place no obstacles in the way of an international labor, religious, or any other conference being held, provided that, until Peace was signed, it was held in a neutral country."[8]

Barnes promptly notified Henderson of this decision, though with the request that he consider it "confidential and unofficial" until it was cleared with Wilson. Incidentally, Lloyd George agreed that Barnes

[7] Clemenceau quoted in Notes of an Allied Conversation held in the Cabinet Room, 10, Downing Street, on December 3, 1918 (a.m.), Imperial War Cabinet 41.
[8] Notes of an Allied Conversation held in the Cabinet Room, 10, Downing Street, on December 3, 1918 (a.m.), Imperial War Cabinet 41.

inform Henderson "on the quiet so that as much time as possible might be given you [Henderson] to make the necessary arrangements."[9]

Even though this compromise decision was encouraging Henderson was not pleased with it. He anticipated serious difficulties with Albert Thomas and Gompers, both of whom were likely to stick to the letter of the September resolution and insist on meeting in Paris, thereby scuttling the entire project. Henderson also worried about the reaction of Vandervelde, the fourth member of the organizing committee; he would hold out for Paris since he expected to be sent there as one of Belgium's principal plenipotentiaries.[1]

Given the hardening of public opinion in the Allied nations the Premiers' decision could not be reversed unless President Wilson firmly sided with the Internationalists. But Wilson's attitude was hesitant and unclear. While on the S.S. *George Washington* he reserved his "judgment as to restricting the labor conference to a neutral country where hostile influences are more likely to have free access."[2] Presumably this was a reference to the same "hostile influences" which four weeks before had caused Wilson to abandon Switzerland as a site for the Peace Conference. Presently Acting Secretary of State Polk warned against holding the conference in a neutral country "as there would be a chance of its being captured by the extremists and Bolsheviks."[3]

In the meantime Gompers applied concerted pressure not only to have the concurrent conference held in Paris but also to have attendance restricted to Allied and Associated delegations. Wilson must have realized that a rump conference dominated by Allied Social Patriots and Gompers was not likely to advance his cause. But he also appreciated the risks and difficulties of pressing for a full-scale conference in the French capital.

As a result he had no alternative to reluctantly suffering the neutral site, especially since he, even more than Lloyd George, was anxious to have the continuing support of all sober-minded Internationalists. On December 18 Gompers was advised that in Wilson's view the conference "might very properly be held in Paris or in any other place at any time . . . [and] that the leaders should feel entirely free to do what they conceived best." Another remonstrance from Gompers from across the Atlantic failed to change Wilson's mind. The President defended his new course for being "wise, prudent, and expedient" in spite of the risk that should the Socialists be "forced to sit

[9] George Barnes to Arthur Henderson, December 4, 1918, Labour Party Archives, file Materials on Berne.

[1] W. H. Buckler to Arthur Hugh Frazier, December 17, 1918, Buckler Papers; and Vandervelde to Henderson, December 13, 1918, in Labour Party Archives, Correspondence 1918–20, file Peace Conference and International Meetings.

[2] Lansing to House, December 8, 1918, National Archives, Document 763.72119; and *F.R.,P.C.,1919*, I, 341–3.

[3] Ibid., 539–40.

in a neutral country their discussions and conclusions [would] certainly be dominated by dangerous radical elements."[4]

As soon as it was apparent that Wilson concurred in the Premiers' decision Henderson contacted his three colleagues on the organizing committee. On December 19 he informed Vandervelde, Albert Thomas, and Gompers that the concurrent conference could not be held in Paris, but that there would be no obstacles in the way of meeting in a neutral country. Simultaneously he advised L.-O. Frossard that under these circumstances "duly appointed delegates ought not to have any difficulties about passports." And, in fact, by January 1, 1919, Sir Eric Drummond, Foreign Secretary Balfour's private secretary, assured Henderson that the Passport Office and the Military Permit Office had been instructed to issue his papers. When some of his colleagues feared that their papers might be delayed Henderson promptly asked Barnes to take the necessary "steps to ensure that the officers responsible are acquainted with the attitude of the Government in this matter." Clemenceau also kept his promise to authorize passports.[5]

The British organizers took it for granted that Switzerland was the neutral country in which to assemble, with a preference for French Switzerland which was pro-Allied and where Socialism was relatively weak and moderate. And in French Switzerland they favored Lausanne over Geneva: the former had the advantage of being on the direct railway line to Paris, while Calvin's city suffered from its "reputation of being the center of Bolshevik influences."[6]

After Henderson turned to the Foreign Office for help in obtaining the Swiss government's permission, the British Minister in Berne was instructed to press for an early decision. It seems that spokesmen for French Switzerland balked at having the conference in either Geneva or Lausanne. Confident that the Olten Committee was successfully squashed, the Federal Council finally designated Berne as the authorized site. In the meantime both the Swiss government and Branting had been in touch with Gustav Müller, President of the Swiss Socialist Party and mayor (Stadtpräsident) of Berne. Following the Olten fiasco, in which he had played an active part, Müller was anxious to disassociate himself from Platten and Grimm. On February 2 he resigned

---

[4] Ibid., 539–41; and Wilson to Lansing, December 24, 1918, Wilson Papers, VIII A:5.
[5] Henderson to Vandervelde, Thomas, and Frossard, all on December 19, 1918, and Henderson to Barnes, January 7, 1919, Labour Party Archives, Correspondence 1918–20, file Peace Conference and International Meetings; Eric Drummond to Henderson, January 1, 1918, Labour Party Archives, file Materials on Berne; Henderson to Gompers, December 19, 1918, cited in American Federation of Labor: *Report of Proceedings of the 39th Annual Convention, Atlantic City, June 1919*, 13–14; Pierre Renaudel: *L'Internationale à Berne* (Paris: Grasset; 1919), 8.
[6] Henderson to Branting and Vandervelde, December 19, 1918, Labour Party Archives, Correspondence 1918–20, file Peace Conference and International Meetings.

as President and split with the Zimmerwaldian majority. This resignation followed a special congress of the Swiss Socialist Party which by a vote of 238 to 147 decided against participation in the renegade Berne Conference.[7]

In still another *démarche* Henderson requested the Executive of the International to authorize the organizing committee of the Inter-Allied Labor and Socialist Conference to issue official invitations for the tenth congress of the Second International to be held in Berne. Branting promptly gave this authorization; and Huysmans, the Secretary of the International Socialist Bureau, continued to give Henderson his whole-hearted cooperation.

All along Henderson was first and foremost determined to woo Gompers, to reassure the Social Patriots, and to satisfy the cabinets.

He was particularly eager to attract Gompers to Berne. He recommended, therefore, that the conference be "described as an International *Labour* and Socialist Conference, in order to meet the prejudices of the A.F. of L. [italics mine]." Henderson barred the American Socialist Party which, though anathema to Gompers, had been represented at the February and September conferences.

> In my view it is more important for the prestige of the Conference in English speaking countries that the A.F. of L. should be represented. We desire to sustain the demand for a Wilson Peace. The American Socialists opposed the intervention of America which alone has made a Wilson Peace and even the victory of the Allies possible. We must appreciate the intensity of the bitterness which marks the relations between the Trades Union and the Socialist Movement in America [on foreign and domestic questions].

Moreover the British labor leader advocated the organization of an international trade union congress to meet alongside this "Labour and Socialist Conference."[8]

But Henderson was no more successful than Woodrow Wilson: the American labor leader stubbornly persisted in his opposition. In fact, while Lenin endangered the unity of the world Socialist movement with his summons for a Third International, Gompers threatened it with his plan for a new, purely trade union international. Meanwhile, after his arrival in London on January 17 and in Paris on the twenty-fourth, Gompers kept telling Allied Socialists and syndicalists that he would refuse to meet with enemy delegates; that he would have no truck with

---

[7] Branting to Henderson, January 10, 1919, F.O. 608/237; Eric Drummond to Henderson, January 1, 1919, Labour Party Archives, file Materials on Berne; Renaudel, *L'Internationale à Berne*, 8–13; *Berner Tageblatt* and *Berner Tagewacht*, January 10–February 5, 1919; *Journal de Genève*, January 11, 1919.

[8] Henderson to Vandervelde and to Frossard, December 19, 1918, Labour Party Archives, Correspondence 1918–20, file Peace Conference and International Meetings.

political Socialists of any nationality; and that to "protect deliberations from a Bolshevik stampede" any labor conference would have to be held in Paris. Gompers ruled the upcoming Berne Conference to be "irregular in conception"; the A.F. of L. had achieved its political independence in the U.S. and it was not about to surrender it to the Socialists in Europe. Significantly, his protestations precipitated the resignation of Will Thorne and Charles W. Bowerman from the British delegation recently appointed by Henderson.[9]

Gompers may well have acted with the encouragement of the Allied Governments. As of late November these displayed a strong interest in having Gompers return to Europe. At first Gompers estimated that Paris and London were so anxious to have his services that they would pay for them with active support of his schismatic drive. But once the Premiers had made their decision to allow a conference in a neutral country their hands were tied. In any case, Gompers went to Paris without formal assurances, probably hoping to reverse this decision by personal intervention. His effort came to nothing. Instead, in addition to being appointed American representative on the Labor Commission, on February 1 Gompers was elected Chairman of this Commission. Apart from satisfying his *amour-propre* this chairmanship was designed to help the cause of economic over political trade unionism.[1]

In the meantime, however, the Allied Premiers may have been quite as anxious as Wilson to prevail on Gompers to go to Berne. Certainly without official sanction or encouragement Albert Thomas, who was "altogether skeptical" about the enterprise,[2] would not have endorsed it. Furthermore, Thomas and other Allied Social Patriots now decided that by attending they could give the conference a pronounced anti-German as well as anti-Bolshevik twist. With Gompers at their side the Social Patriots could have dominated the conference completely.

As it was Albert Thomas and Renaudel set stiff conditions for their attendance.[3] Henderson, Huysmans, and Branting practically assured them in advance that the Berne Conference would begin with a debate on war responsibility and guilt. The French ex-*majoritaires* were determined to put the German *majoritaires* into the dock in order to compel them to confess and expiate their sins publicly, a procedure which

[9] Samuel Gompers: *Seventy Years of Life and Labor* (New York: Dutton; 1925), II, 474–85; American Federation of Labor: *Report of Proceedings of the 39th Annual Convention*, 14–19; *American Federationist*, March and April 1919, *passim*.
[1] Gompers: *Seventy Years*, II, 478–9; Lansing to Wilson, November 29, 1918, Wilson Papers, II:157; Polk Diary, December 6, 1918; Buckler to Frazier, December 18, 1918, Buckler Papers.
[2] Albert Thomas to Henderson, December 25, 1918, Labour Party Archives, Correspondence 1918–20, file Peace Conference and International Meetings.
[3] See the article signed and published by Thomas and Renaudel on the eve of the Berne Conference in *l'Humanité*, February 4, 1919.

threatened to break up or denature the conference. But Thomas was ready to pay this price. He was less concerned with international working-class unity and a Wilsonian peace than with his two-front offensive against the ex-*minoritaires* in France and the Centrists in the Second International.

Moreover, this stirring up of nationalist passions was related to another precondition—which, incidentally, was equally welcome to Gompers. The rejection of the Marxist interpretation of the causes of the war in favor of the bourgeois war-guilt thesis was to be part of a frontal assault on Bolshevism. The French Social Patriots made it clear that they would ask the Berne Conference to condemn and repudiate Bolshevik methods and tactics explicitly. Henderson more readily met this condition than that of assigning war guilt. Anti-Bolshevism had the great merit of appealing to Majoritarians and Centrists on *both* banks of the Rhine while at the same time reassuring the Premiers, Wilson, and Gompers. With obvious satisfaction Henderson declared that "neither the Russian Bolsheviks nor the German Spartacists would be represented [and that] the strongest hostility to the Berne Conference came from Continental Bolsheviks."[4] Neither the Hendersonites nor the Majoritarians any longer combined their anti-Bolshevik pronouncements with fierce protests against the counterrevolutionary intervention in Russia.

This hostile posture merely reinforced all Zimmerwaldians and Kienthalians in their contempt, hatred, and enmity for all Socialists who had turned defensist during the war and who after the Armistice were unwilling to resume the class struggle. Even assuming they had been invited, the Russian Bolsheviks and the German Spartacists would have stayed away. Similarly the Maximalist-controlled Swiss, Italian, Yugoslav, and Rumanian Socialist parties decided to boycott Berne.

This wholesale boycott by the extreme Left was proportionately more significant than the recoil of the A.F. of L. and the Belgian Socialist Party. Especially once Henderson had made vital concessions to the Social Patriots in pursuit of the broadest possible backing for a Wilson peace the Centrists—the carriers of the stunted Stockholm proposal—were on the defensive.

Before the Berne Conference ever opened it was apparent that under the leadership of the French ex-*majoritaires* and under the pretext of condemning Bolshevism the Social Patriots of all nations planned a basic overhaul of the Second International. Whereas before the war the International at least paid lip service to the class struggle and to the revolutionary seizure of power, in the post-Armistice world there would be no such pretense. Admittedly, reactionaries and conservatives continued to condemn Henderson, Thomas, and the immi-

---

[4] Statement by Henderson cited in *Daily News,* January 21, 1919.

nent Berne Conference for being cat's paws for the Bolsheviks. But the cabinets knew better. They issued passports and George Lansbury "received more attention and genuine help in Paris in [his] difficult task of getting to Berne than [he] believed could have been possible." Especially since the risks were so minimal the Premiers decided to be kind; and "kindness always disarms."[5] Besides, the Socialists were to be given leave to demonstrate their disunity, failure of nerve, and weakness to the world. At long last the Allied Premiers had learned the lesson of Stockholm.

But while the Allied Governments meant to neutralize the International the U. S. Delegation sought to use this "safe" International to promote a Wilsonian peace settlement. This purpose was manifest in late January. It was then that the delegation made last-minute efforts to convince Gompers to go to Berne and, having failed in these efforts, decided to send an unofficial observer to the Swiss capital.

William H. Buckler was one of the advocates of this course. As early as January 1 the President and Colonel House thought that after returning from his exploratory meeting with Litvinov in Stockholm Buckler might go to Berne.[6] He was a logical choice for this assignment, having close relations with Henderson, MacDonald, and the British Radicals.[7] Moreover, as guide for the A.F. of L. delegation on its European travels in September–October 1918 he had come to know and respect Gompers. As Henry White's half-brother he had the additional advantage of political respectability.

Buckler was one of many U. S. officials who urged Gompers "to go to Berne and act with Branting and with the Germans in opposing Bolshevism and supporting the 14 Points."[8] Buckler sympathized with Henderson's view that "the present British Cabinet was governed by reactionary influences and was conspiring with similar forces dominant in France and Italy to neutralize so far as possible the President's ideal of a clean peace." Without the help of International labor Wilson would have to be prepared for a "western replica of the Brest Litovsk Treaty . . . [and] for a world . . . made safe for hypocrisy."[9] Now that it was clear that the concurrent conference could not be held in Paris, Buckler probably nursed the hope that provided he could get Gompers to Berne he might be able to mediate between him and Henderson.

Buckler continued to be high on the Second International after his

[5] George Lansbury writing in *The Herald,* February 8, 1919.
[6] House Diary, January 1, 1919. For Buckler's mission to Stockholm see pp. 424–6 below.
[7] See my *Political Origins of the New Diplomacy,* 335–8.
[8] William H. Buckler to Georgina Buckler, February 1, 1919, Buckler Papers.
[9] He sympathetically reported this view of British progressives after confidential conversations with Henderson and G. Fitzmaurice. Buckler to House, December 18, 1918, Buckler Papers. Buckler suggested "that this note be destroyed, so that [his informants] be not compromised, if the note should go astray."

meeting with Litvinov in Copenhagen; William C. Bullitt was of this same school prior to his meeting with Lenin in Moscow. Even after the comforting outcome of the German elections Bullitt continued to be obsessed by the specter of Bolshevism over Europe. In his judgment a Wilsonian peace alone could prevent the explosive polarization between the extreme Right and Left and the unsettling rapprochement of the outcast and dissatisfied Russia and Germany.

January 27 was the day that Gompers met with the American Commissioners, including the President.[1] That very day, in the wake of this confrontation in which Gompers made no secret of his distaste for the Berne Conference but still reserved his position, Bullitt drafted a most suggestive and revealing policy memorandum on "the International Labor and Socialist Conference."

> Mr. Gompers and his companions formally asked this morning for advice as to the course they should pursue in regard to the International Labor and Socialist Conference which is to take place at Berne next Monday. They are to call on the President for a reply at 6 o'clock tomorrow evening.
>
> It is possible for the President to decline to advise them in regard to their conduct; but if he does give them a direct reply, it will influence vitally the relations between our government and the labor movement of Europe.
>
> I therefore respectfully submit for your consideration the following facts and conclusions:
>
> 1. It is impossible for Mr. Gompers to split the trades union movement and the political labor movement of Europe. The leaders of these movements are working in perfect accord and all of them regard Mr. Gompers without sympathy.
>
> 2. It is undesirable for us to urge Mr. Gompers to follow a course of disruption.
>
> Today the President has an enormous prestige with European labor. His proposal in regard to Russia and his address on the League of Nations completed his hold on the leaders of the labor movement. (For example, Cachin said in my presence to a company of people that the Russian decision had given him the first happy moment he had had since the war broke out; and Lansbury today said that when he heard the President at the Quai d'Orsay on Saturday he was so stirred that he wept and could hardly keep from cheering.)
>
> The leaders of French and British Labor plan at Berne to draw up resolutions on three things: (a) League of Nations (b) Territorial settlements (c) International Labor legislation. *They intend to follow definitely the lines the President has laid down. It is possible, therefore, to steer the conference at Berne so that it will be an enormous support to the President in his work here.*

1 Lansing Diary, January 27, 1919; House Diary, January 27, 1919; Bliss Diary, January 27, 1919, Bliss Papers, vol. 65.

3. It is respectfully suggested, therefore, that the President should advise Mr. Gompers to go to Berne in a spirit of cooperation and not of hostility: That the President should explain to Mr. Gompers the broad outline of his policy in regard to Germany, Russia and the League of Nations: That the President should advise Mr. Gompers to use his efforts to obtain the passage of resolutions at Berne of the same sort as the terms for which we are working in Paris.

In addition it seems most essential to send to Berne either Buckler or some one else who is well acquainted with the European Labor leaders to report to us on their projects and to guide them along the lines we wish them to follow.

4. Finally, it seems most unfortunate that at this moment when all the Governments of Europe have given passports to their socialists and labor leaders for the conference at Berne, the Government of the United States should refuse passports to the delegates of the Socialist Party of the United States. The press reports that this has been done. It seems distinctly worth while to reverse this decision [italics in the original].[2]

As was his custom Bullitt exaggerated the unity of Europe's Socialist and labor movement, his sympathy for the Internationalists—the Centrists—blinding him to the Social Patriots' ascendancy. Moreover, Bullitt underestimated the ideological, political, and financial potency of Gompers's stance. Even so, his insight was sharp.

But the President—who may or may not have seen this memorandum—did not follow Bullitt's advice. Gompers claimed that when he saw Wilson on the twenty-eighth the President was "in full accord" with his decision not to go to Berne; he also reported that the President denied rumors about a break between them over this issue.[3]

It is more likely that the President "declined to advise" Gompers. He hoped all along that since his own wishes were no secret, the President of the A.F. of L. would take them into account. Wilson expected that the wisdom of Buckler's and Bullitt's position would be as apparent to Gompers as it was to himself as well as to House, Bliss, and White. But such was not the case. Instead, Gompers asserted that "even if W. C. Bullitt or any other person correctly represented the view of the American Commissioners . . . that [view] was in opposition not only to our views but to our entire course [and] that if these men represented American labor, there was no further use for the A.F. of L. commission to remain in Paris."[4]

Once Gompers had irrevocably refused to go to Berne, the American Commissioners had to take other steps to keep in touch with

2 William C. Bullitt to Colonel House, January 27, 1919, House Papers as well as Bullitt Papers.
3 Gompers: *Seventy Years*, II, 484-5.
4 Ibid., 483.

developments there. On January 29 Bullitt himself was "directed to proceed to Berne and to remain at Berne until the business for which you are being sent is completed."[5] The Commissioners could have sent Buckler or even a neophyte in the politics of international labor. But they chose Bullitt in the hope of convincing Henderson that they did not endorse Gompers. Moreover, as compared to Buckler, who was primarily familiar with British Labour politics, Bullitt was well informed about labor politics in England as well as throughout Continental Europe, largely by virtue of his assignments first in the State Department and then in the Peace Commission. Ideologically he was a frightened Radical who looked to the International to help Wilson defeat both Lenin and Clemenceau. And, significantly, in Berne Bullitt shared a hotel room with Norman Angell who was there to report the Conference for Northcliffe's *Times*.[6]

The Commissioners also acted on Bullitt's recommendation to allow American Socialists to go to Berne. They validated the passports of Frank Bohn and Charles Edward Russell after Lansing assured them that Russell was "a reliable and loyal American" and that since Bohn was traveling with Russell he could also be trusted. But as in the case of Bullitt, "any action on the premises should be informal and verbal."[7]

The International Labor and Socialist Conference finally opened at 3:00 on February 3 in the auditorium of the Volkshaus in Berne. Twenty-six nations were represented by 97 delegates. The German and Austrian delegates occupied the front rows. All the other delegations separated them from the French delegates, who arrived last. This physical separation was symbolic of profound antagonisms among Socialists of enemy camps, but especially between French and German Social Patriots. Henderson tried to reduce hostilities and tensions between them. But between Hermann Müller, Hermann Molkenbuhr, and Otto Wels on the one hand and Albert Thomas, Pierre Renaudel, and Edgar Milhaud on the other, this distrust never subsided.

Genuine enthusiasm for international reconciliation could only be found among Centrists of all shades. Those furthest to the left were most inclined to combine the search for international reconciliation with outright sympathy for the Soviet experiment, violent opposition to Allied intervention in Russia, and extensive social and economic reforms. The signatures on a collective postcard to Romain Rolland from Berne revealed the full range of this Centrist coalition: Amédée Dunois, Raoul Verfeuil, Jean Longuet, Louise Kautsky, Kurt Eisner, Ramsay MacDonald, Ethel Snowden, Paul Faure, A. Forel, W.

[5] Memorandum from Joseph C. Grew, Secretary of the Ammission, to William C. Bullitt, January 29, 1919, Bullitt Papers.
[6] Sir Norman Angell: *After All* (London: Hamish Hamilton; 1951), 231.
[7] *F.R.,P.C., 1919*, XI, 4.

Herzog, K. Kautsky, Friedrich Adler, Marcel Cachin, Charles Rappoport, Ernst Toller.[8]

By virtue of his election as President of the Conference Hjalmar Branting had the difficult job of delivering the keynote address.[9] With a view to establishing a favorable atmosphere for the proceedings he sought to pacify nationalist and ideological passions without, however, hiding his own sympathy for a position halfway between Albert Thomas and Henderson.

In the spirit of Albert Thomas, Branting insisted that the conference would have to assess the International's failure to prevent war in 1914 by honestly and publicly fixing responsibilities. He furthermore left little doubt that he, too, favored an explicit denunciation of Bolshevism. Branting claimed that the delegates at Berne would know how to protect genuine Socialism from those who were perverting its name in the interest of an antidemocratic dictatorship of the proletariat.

These two points, which respectively opened and closed his address, did not cement the unity of the assembly; however, the central part of Branting's inaugural speech, which was inspired by Henderson, came close to producing such an effect. Not unexpectedly the Wilsonian flag was unfurled for this purpose.

Branting credited Wilson with trying to engineer a revolution in the minds of capitalist statesmen and politicians and claimed that the peace ideas, which informed his ideological offensive, coincided with the Socialist platform. Since the Allied statesmen in Paris were determined to thwart Wilson, the organizers of this conference were impressed with the importance of rallying the working class around him. In France, Britain, and Italy the workers had already demonstrated their sympathy for the President.

> However, if the working class wanted to effectively influence and, if necessary, at the decisive moment launch a special action in support of the Wilsonian effort and to influence decision-making in Paris, this working class first had to rediscover its own unity. It had to lay the basis for common action. . . . The Stockholm effort having failed . . . this Berne Conference now was organized for this purpose. Paris having become the rallying center for the ruling classes, Berne should become the rallying center for the working class. Berne had to mark the start of concerted working class action against any attempt designed to prevent the fulfillment of the Wilsonian program. . . .

[8] Romain Rolland: *Journal des années de guerre, 1914–1919* (Paris: Albin Michel; 1952), 1720. Some of these signatories were unofficial observers. For a complete list of official delegates see Labour Party: *Report of the Nineteenth Annual Conference* (Southport, 1919), 214, or Renaudel: *L'Internationale à Berne*, 24–6.
[9] For the major portions of Branting's address see Renaudel: *L'Internationale à Berne*, 30–5.

Of course, the Berne Conference would develop this program in a Socialist direction. In particular, the working class would press for a universal and popular, against a victors' and government, League of Nations; it would also press for the inclusion in the treaty of a Magna Carta of Labor.

Branting's address was an apt preview of the agenda. Prepared by the Henderson task force, this agenda crystallized around these five topics, in this sequence: (1) War Responsibilities; (2) League of Nations; (3) Territorial Questions; (4) International Labor Charter; and (5) Democracy vs. Dictatorship. Similarly, the audience reaction to Branting's address pointed to the major areas of both consensus and disagreement. The second and the fourth topics promised the most unified response while topics one and five threatened to be particularly divisive.

Albert Thomas managed to be the first delegate to get the floor (by prearrangement?) in order to move priority for the discussion of the war responsibilities of the Socialist parties.[1] Actually, he was not in the least interested in a dispassionate discussion or study of the issues involved, being determined to indict the German Imperial Government as well as the German Majoritarians with bitter passion and unqualified hostility. He tore into the Majoritarians for their empty and deceptive assurances in late July and early August 1914; for their passive approval of the Treaty of Brest Litovsk and the related Hindenburg offensive of March 1918; and for their refusal to concede the right of plebiscite to Alsace-Lorraine in their answer to the Stockholm questionnaire.

Pierre Renaudel supported this indictment with a reading of the minutes of Hermann Müller's eleventh-hour meeting with French Socialists in Paris on August 1, 1914. According to these unverified minutes Müller unequivocally affirmed that rather than vote war credits the SPD would "either vote against these credits or abstain unanimously." But when the time came the Social Democrats endorsed not only war credits but also the invasion of Belgium. After reproving Liebknecht for turning Bolshevik, Renaudel attributed his defection to revulsion against the SPD; he also told the German Majoritarians that Liebknecht's blood was on their conscience. In conclusion he asserted that the International had to make a choice not between French and

[1] This analysis of the proceedings is based on a variety of sources: Renaudel: *L'Internationale à Berne, passim; Official Bulletin of the International Labor and Socialist Conference,* published by the Press Committee of this Conference, Nos. 1–8; and the press (in particular *Berner Tagewacht, le Temps, l'Humanité,* and *le Populaire*). Unless otherwise specified excerpts from speeches are from Renaudel's book which is the single most complete and accessible source; excerpts from the resolutions are from the English version in Labour Party: *Report of the Nineteenth Annual Conference,* 196–204.

German Socialists but between German "*majoritaires* and *minoritaires*." Thomas and Renaudel left no doubt that for them this examination of responsibilities was the *sine qua non* for this conference.[2]

How would the accused defend and justify themselves? Unlike the plaintiffs, they were represented by men of limited stature and authority. Whereas Albert Thomas and Renaudel were free to come to Berne, Ebert and Scheidemann, their German counterparts, were tied down in Berlin. No doubt it would have been difficult for one or both to leave Germany in the face of continuing political unrest and in the midst of preparations for the opening of the National Assembly in Weimar. On the other hand, since Germany had most to gain from organized International opposition to a dictated peace, perhaps either Ebert or Scheidemann should have appeared briefly in Berne in his dual capacity as leader of the German Revolution and as government leader faithfully upholding the pre-Armistice agreement.

In any case, it was left to Wels and Müller to answer for the Majoritarians. Theirs was a stiff assignment. Wels received at best grudging credit for his role in the repression of Spartacist disorders in Berlin in early December 1918; especially the French Social Patriots but also the German *minoritaires* suspected his jingoist and militarist inclinations. As for Müller, he had just been accused of calculated duplicity. In addition they had to speak for both party and government.

Otto Wels was the first German to speak.[3] In the interest of united action in the future he would have preferred not to engage in quarrelsome recriminations about the past. The Majoritarians had the distinction of having staged a democratic revolution, an achievement which entitled them to the confidence of this conference.

Nevertheless, Wels could not ignore the indictment. His defendant's brief held no surprises. He argued that no SPD leaders had sat in the Imperial Government in July–August 1914; that at the time Germany was threatened by the Russian peril; and that a call for a general strike would not have been followed. Moreover, after war had broken out they never approved their government's methods of fighting it, the Majoritarians remaining firmly committed to the reconstitution and reparation of Belgium.

Wels also tried to go over to the offensive. He claimed that while his government had instructed Kautsky fearlessly to study the causes of war in the Foreign Ministry archives, as yet the Allies had taken no such step. Furthermore, since the Allies had pressed Russia to stay in the war they had to take their share of the blame for the victory of Bolshevism in Russia and for Brest Litovsk.

---

[2] *Le Temps, le Petit Parisien,* and *le Figaro,* February 5, 1919.
[3] Renaudel does not cover the speeches of Wels and Müller. See *le Temps, le Petit Parisien,* and *le Figaro,* February 5, 1919.

Hermann Müller also denied Germany's unilateral guilt. He called for the establishment of an impartial neutral commission to study the question of responsibilities. As for his own behavior on and after August 1, 1914, Müller unconvincingly claimed that by the time of his return from Paris to Berlin the threat of Russian mobilization had changed the situation drastically.[4] In closing he warned of the disruptive consequences of a condemnation of the SPD.

Now that the Social Patriots from opposite sides of the Rhine had gone at each other it was the turn of first the German and then the Allied Centrists.

Kurt Eisner's speech early during the second day of the conference was courageous, idealistic, and moving. By not sparing the SPD and its spokesmen he angered the latter; simultaneously he became the hero of the Allied Social Patriots who completely failed to appreciate and understand the humanitarian spirit and impulse of his diagnosis. In agreement with Thomas, Eisner felt that the question of responsibilities had to be faced, otherwise mutual confidence could not be restored in the International. But he wanted it left to each individual and national faction to own up to whatever the errors of omission and commission may have been.

> We must expose the lies and follies of this epoch. Clarity and truth must triumph. But today it is not easy to speak. We are a defeated people. A year ago I would have been ready to attack violently and without pity. Today, however, after the defeat, it is all too easy to attack. . . . The Revolution came too late not to be suspect abroad. However, it responds to the profound aspirations of the people and even during the war numerous Socialists went to prison for opposing militarism.
>
> The outside world has not understood the German Revolution and the profound changes it has wrought . . . as proven by the recent elections. . . . These elections favored the group which broke the politics of war. . . .
>
> If the German Government was not guilty why, then, did we make the Revolution? In effect, Wels' speech was animated by the old spirit. But altogether wrong conclusions could be drawn from it. Actually we were all deceived in August 1914. . . . In 1914 I was also convinced that tsarism was the great danger. But the first German White Book opened my eyes. . . . The Majoritarians do not have to come here as penitents, but they ought to admit that for four and a half years they were victims of error and of lies. . . .
> Today it is an established fact that the war was wanted by a small horde of mad Prussian militarists in league with big armaments makers, politicians dreaming of world conquest, capitalists and princes. . . .

[4] Upon his return to Germany Müller repeatedly declared that accusers of the SPD had no understanding whatever of Russia's position in 1914.

In the afternoon of February 4 Kautsky continued in a similar vein. He, too, maintained that the German people had been duped in 1914. But as compared to Eisner he was much more direct in his assault on the Majoritarians. He reproached Scheidemann, David, and others for having actively shielded the government whenever it was criticized; he also insisted that whoever approved the treaties of Brest Litovsk and Bucharest but refused Alsace-Lorraine the right of self-expression was not entitled to speak today. On the other hand, the *minoritaires* who had protested these policies had earned the right to demand that the German people be treated equitably. At a minimum the Allies should immediately provide food and other supplies, otherwise a recrudescence of Spartacism could not be avoided.[5]

After George H. Stuart-Bunning complained that Thomas's motion threatened to undermine the proletariat's pressure and influence on Paris, Jean Longuet delivered one of the most compelling and applauded speeches of the entire conference.[6] Longuet was in a position to speak with particular authority. Unlike Eisner and Kautsky he was a Centrist from the victor camp, he was leader of the ex-minority which now dominated the French Socialist movement, and he was not hampered by responsibilities to a heavily besieged all-Socialist government.

Longuet endorsed his German colleagues' criticism of the SPD. Whatever the Russian danger may have been it did not justify the violation of Belgium's neutrality; the Majoritarians failed to protest against the abuses of the civil population of northern France and of submarine warfare; and no SPD voices were raised against Brest Litovsk. Eisner and Kautsky, however, had leveled these charges with greater force and courage than he could ever have mustered since they were, in fact, criticizing their own country.

Longuet found it impossible to dodge Eisner's summons for "clarity and truth." Without in any way denying, excusing, or minimizing the disproportionately large responsibility of the German Majoritarians, he confessed that Socialists of other nations had their share of sins: "In varying degrees Socialists throughout the world succumbed to the chauvinist storm . . . ; all over there was an anguished preoccupation with national defense . . . ; and just as this preoccupation degenerated . . . in nationalism the preoccupation with *union sacrée* degenerated in governmentalism and ministerialism."

Against this general background Longuet then spoke of the wartime neglect of internationalism in France and of the French Independents' campaign against their ex-*majoritaire* colleagues who had opposed Stockholm and practiced uncritical ministerialism. To be sure, it might be useful to fix responsibilities, as Thomas requested. However, was Thomas justified in going on to ask for the exclusion of the SPD? If

[5] *Le Temps,* February 6, 1919.
[6] For the text of Longuet's speech see *le Populaire,* February 13, 1919.

such a proposal were made "there would have to be other exclusions as well, in many other parts of Europe."[7] There could be no question of excluding between 11 and 12 million German Socialists who, according to Eisner and Kautsky, had just scored a genuine democratic and Socialist advance.

By the end of the second day this debate moved from the floor of the conference to a special commission[8] so that other business might be transacted simultaneously. This commission, still under the threat of a French Majoritarian walkout, after one night and a full day agreed on a compromise resolution which the conference then voted unanimously, except for one negative vote[9] and Thomas's own abstention.[1]

Eisner presented the original draft for this resolution; Wels considered it excessively stringent. But Wels could be counted upon to cooperate in the search for compromise, since his government was eager to launch a unified pro-Wilson conference in which German delegates would play a leading role. He eventually accepted Branting's proposal that the Berne Conference acknowledge that the question of the "*immediate* responsibility for the war had been clarified by the discussion and by the declaration of the German Majority affirming the revolutionary spirit of the New Germany"; it was left to a future conference to pass judgment on the underlying *historical* responsibilities. Henderson's proposal to include a reference to the "declaration made by the German delegates during the [concurrent] debate on the League of Nations" helped Wels to accede to this watered-down but nevertheless formal imputation of unilateral guilt.

A commission to draft a resolution on the League of Nations had started its sittings even before the conference convened;[2] and the plenary discussion had begun while the commission on responsibilities

---

[7] At this point Renaudel belligerently interrupted to ask whom Longuet had in mind and to protest against vague insinuations. Longuet ignored Renaudel's interruption. *Le Temps*, February 6, 1919. In his own account Renaudel mentions Longuet's speech only in passing and only hints at this incident. See Renaudel: *L'Internationale à Berne*, 48.

[8] Membership of this commission: Branting, Emanuel Buchinger (Hungary), Renaudel, Longuet, Wels, Eisner, Henderson, Stuart-Bunning, Anton Němecz (Czechoslovakia), Wilhelm Ellenbogen (Austria).

[9] The lone dissentient was Edgar Milhaud. Professor of Political Economy at the University of Geneva and author of many books on the foreign policy of Socialism, Milhaud was a French citizen, an intimate friend of both Renaudel and Thomas, a fervent Wilsonian, and one of the four ex-*majoritaires* on the French delegation. I had the privilege of studying under Milhaud in Geneva; I also cherish the memory of numerous instructive and spirited conversations in his home.

[1] *Le Temps*, February 8, 1919. Thomas claimed that he did not vote against the compromise resolution because the debates had awakened the conscience of the German Majoritarians and because the International would continue the battle for international peace and justice for which French soldiers had fought and died.

[2] Membership of this commission: F. M. Wibaut (Netherlands), Kautsky, Müller, J. H. Thomas, Ethel Snowden, Ellenbogen, Němecz, Juan B. Justo (Argentina), Janko Sakasov (Bulgaria), Cachin, Milhaud, Nina Bang (Sweden).

was still hammering out its compromise. Now that Thomas's steep hurdle had been cleared the League became a welcome meeting ground for delegates whose tempers by now were frayed and short. The discussion was free of acrimony, sober, and swift. Of course, the debate was this smooth largely because the delegates deliberated about basic but vague principles and functions rather than about specific methods of implementation.

Moreover, as this debate proceeded it became perfectly evident that otherwise antagonistic delegates were united in their resolve to influence Paris. They were encouraged by the establishment of a League of Nations Commission by the Plenary Peace Conference; by Wilson's address on that solemn occasion; and by his accession to the presidency of that Commission. Somehow they deluded themselves that the adoption of a workable covenant and the imposition of a Carthaginian peace were mutually incompatible.

Accordingly, the Berne resolution prescribed a "real peace of justice" as an essential foundation for the League of Nations. It was Ramsay MacDonald who argued that with a peace comparable to the peace of 1871 there could be a League "on paper but not in fact." He even warned that, in case the Conference sanctioned territorial annexations and violations of self-determination, a Government League might become a powerful instrument for the preservation of an unjust and explosive status quo, a new version of the Sainte Alliance.

As a protection against this contingency MacDonald urged the delegates to pay close attention to the basis and membership of the League.

> The Governments in Paris are said to have accepted the principle of a League of Nations. I view this declaration skeptically. Therefore our resolution must be unequivocal. In a separate paragraph it must emphasize the need to base the League not on Governments but on parliaments representing the entire nation. . . . We want a League of Nations and not a league of ministers and diplomatists.

Cachin and even Milhaud supported MacDonald. With typical revisionist and reformist confidence they trusted in universal suffrage and Parliamentary representation. The League of Nations should consist of delegations from national Parliaments in which all major parties and factions would be represented, thereby guaranteeing the Socialists a voice in the deliberations of the international or supernational parliament while they were still in a hopeless minority in their respective national legislatures.

The delegates heeded this advice. In their resolution they specified that "representation in the central organ of the League should be, not by delegates of the executive branches of the governments of the constituent States, but by delegates from the parliaments representing all parties therein, thus ensuring not an alliance of cabinets or governments, but a union of peoples."

But additional safeguards would be needed. To prevent a victors' League all nations, including the defeated, should be part of the League of Nations from the start; and in order not to perpetuate a Concert of Powers in which the Great Powers or the Powers with General Interests would be dominant all independent nations, regardless of size, "should have equal rights and equal duties." As for those peoples who had not yet achieved independence, "they should be placed under the protection of the League and be encouraged and assisted to fit themselves for membership."

The major aim of this League would be to prevent wars by eliminating the conditions leading to international tensions, conflicts, and arms races. In pursuit of such a goal the League should abolish standing armies; eventually "bring about complete disarmament"; mediate and arbitrate disputes through an International Court; banish economic war by controlling tariffs, promoting free trade, and supporting the "open door" in colonies; control the "production and distribution of foodstuffs and raw materials throughout the world"; and administer a Labor charter.

To enforce its decisions the League should have the use of those armed forces which would remain until complete disarmament was achieved. Moreover, it would have "at its disposal means of economic pressure."

This resolution was adopted unanimously and enthusiastically around noon on Thursday, February 6. Certainly many of its provisions were unacceptable to the men of the Old Diplomacy; some even were objectionable to those of the New. However, Berne's extremism and innovation were of Radical rather than Socialist vintage: peace of reconciliation, popular representation, pacifism, arbitration, free trade, open door, and labor legislation. Only the international controls of food and raw materials carried collectivist overtones; and these controls were conceived—in terms of Fabian efficiency—as an extension of wartime institutions into the postwar world.

Nevertheless the resolution claimed the League as a "Socialist ideal," charging non-Socialists with embracing it only in this moment of postwar crisis. Once this crisis had been weathered, non-Socialists would abandon it and "the capitalist rivalry between States" would become acute again. Berne did not summon the workers to transform the states internally in order to make them solid pillars of the League; it merely asked that workers prepare themselves once again to restrain the aggressive propensities of these capitalist states. Hereafter, in addition to acting through the Second International, the proletariat would also act through its minority representation in an international parliament.

Meanwhile, with a view to securing the "peace of justice" which was the essential underpinning for this League, the Berne Conference had to tackle the complex territorial questions raised by the war. The leaders of the International realized only too well that the method and content of their settlement would be decisive for the future course of international politics.

Ever since 1870–1, when Marx and Engels issued such a penetrating diagnosis of the causes and consequences of the annexation of Alsace-Lorraine in violation of France's awakened national self-consciousness, Socialists had incessantly warned against further annexations. More important even than any legal and moral wrong involved, such violations of national feelings—whether for reasons of economic gain, prestige, or security—unleash a clamor for *revanche,* facilitate the exploitation of jingoist sentiments by interested factions, stimulate the arms race, and precipitate the formation of hostile alliances.

In 1919 the danger of further violations was particularly great. The war had whipped up the nationalist passions of victor, defeated, and nascent nations alike. Governments were enlisting these passions for a vast variety of diplomatic and political aims. Even in Berne, let alone in Paris, this intoxication was evident among French, German, Hungarian, Czech, and Yugoslav delegates. Moreover, the national awakening in the non-Western world had to be taken into account.

The leaders in Berne realized the primacy of these national and territorial questions, the obstacles to their equitable and lasting settlement, and the limited contribution the International could make in this controversial sphere. In fact, as in the case of the League of Nations, they could only hope to reinforce Wilson's resolve to uphold his principles.

That such was their strategy became evident at the very outset of the debate which started Thursday afternoon. Longuet proclaimed that in the face of these burning national passions and hatreds the International would play a mediating role. The International would seek to convince opposing nationalites "of the limits of their respective claims" while at the same time supporting the efforts of "the President of the bourgeois U. S. Republic, who represented a higher stage of humanity than the bourgeois governments of Europe." Should Paris nevertheless come up with peace treaties pregnant with new wars, the International would pronounce them null and void.

In presenting the report of the commission on territorial questions Paul Mistral admitted that at Paris territorial and national questions would inevitably take precedence over economic questions.

> The annexation of Alsace-Lorraine had created and maintained a gulf between France and Germany. Those who today ask for similar

annexations are men of short vision who want to ignore the facts and lessons of recent history in the Balkan Wars, the treaty of Brest-Litovsk, the treaty of Bucharest, the struggle for independence throughout Eastern Europe.

Among the leading statesmen only Wilson had "a broad vision." He, too, was a fervent advocate of the right of self-determination as the sole basis for a durable peace within the unsettling confines of the capitalist system.

Once again it was decided to limit the resolution to general principles while airing specific applications in debate. This resolution was divided into two parts. In the first part the conference set forth the guidelines for the settlement of territorial and nationality questions: self-determination, plebiscite or referendum under League auspices, protection of minorities guaranteed by the League, and League-sponsored economic cooperation between new states.

In the second part the resolution summarized the Socialist critique of the Old Diplomacy. It explicitly rejected "the right of the victor to the spoils of war," the validity of wartime secret treaties, the drawing of frontiers in the light of strategic or economic necessities, and the policy of "*faits accomplis.*"

Probably at the behest of their government and with a view to securing equal treatment in both Berne and Paris, the German Majoritarians moved that the future of Alsace-Lorraine be decided by plebiscite under League supervision. Recalling that after 1871 he had joined Bebel in protesting the annexation, Molkenbuhr and his colleagues made their demand on the basis of Wilson's Fourteen Points and the principles of the International, to which they subscribed.

Though Kautsky criticized his Majoritarian countrymen for their eleventh-hour conversion to the Wilsonian gospel, he nevertheless supported this call for a free plebiscite. In spite of the fact that an overwhelming vote in favor of France was a foregone conclusion, a crucial purpose would be served: future Pan-Germans would never be able to argue that Alsace-Lorraine belonged to Germany and that the Allies had been afraid to consult the local population. But Renaudel demurred, insisting that such a procedure would advance the cause of chauvinism in France. He did vouch, however, that French Socialists were as determined as ever to oppose designs on the Saar and the left bank of the Rhine. Reluctantly the German delegates withdrew their special motion and put their hope in the general principles of the Berne resolution.

Many other territorial issues came before the conference and the commission, but none received such prominent attention. The German delegates came to an agreement on the Aaland Islands and on

Schleswig with their Swedish and Danish colleagues. Similarly, the Georgian and Armenian delegates agreed to settle their border by plebiscite.

On the other hand, the Czechs were in an altogether uncompromising mood in their discussions with the Hungarians as well as with the Austrians. In this instance even Kautsky, who was of Czech birth, failed to make a dent: he wisely but unsuccessfully urged the Socialists of the new nations to champion the just claims of their peoples without, however, embracing their hatreds and their desire for vengeance.[3]

As compared to the peacemakers in the French capital the delegates in Berne, largely at the initiative of British Labour, took an advanced position on colonial issues. Significantly, the single longest paragraph of the territorial resolution was: "Protection of the populations of dependencies, protectorates, and colonies to be assured by the League of Nations, which should take steps to prepare the native populations as rapidly as possible for the exercise of the rights of full self-determination, through the founding of schools, grants of local autonomy, by the freedom of the press, the right of holding meetings and of forming associations, together with other political rights." In a separate declaration the British delegation advocated Home Rule for India and Egypt as well as self-determination for Cyprus following the formation of the League of Nations.[4]

The International Labor Charter was the fourth item on the agenda. Of the five major resolutions voted by the Berne Conference the resolution on international labor legislation was the most comprehensive and practical; it also left a substantial imprint on the labor charter in the Versailles peace treaty.

And yet this resolution consumed least time and generated fewest disagreements. Delegates of all nations and factions spontaneously agreed that until such time as the capitalist system was completely abolished the evils of this system should and could be "considerably mitigated both by the resistance of organized workers and by the intervention of the State." In pursuit of this immediate and transitional goal the Berne Conference updated and internationalized the second part of the Erfurt program. The fact that the final goals and fundamental principles of Socialism were barely mentioned was further proof that reformism continued to outdistance revisionism, let alone Leninism.

Actually the text of this resolution was drafted at the Trade Union Conference which was meeting concurrently in the same building as the Labor and Socialist Conference.

Jouhaux was the principal driving force behind this parallel conference which Gompers might have joined provided the President of the

[3] *L'Humanité*, February 9, 1919.
[4] See Labour Party: *Report of the Nineteenth Annual Conference*, 205.

French CGT had cut all relations with political labor. This Jouhaux refused to do, and organized American labor stayed away. As a convinced Wilsonian Jouhaux was determined to marshal trade union support not only for a labor charter but also for the League of Nations.[5]

Jan Oudegeest, the secretary of the provisional Bureau of the Trade Union International in Amsterdam, repeatedly argued that this syndical conference was not authorized to discuss the League or other political issues; and his position was endorsed by the German, Austrian, and Scandinavian delegates. But Albert Bourderon and Alphonse Merrheim, as well as Stuart-Bunning, the British delegate, joined forces with Jouhaux. All three were impatient with procedural niceties. Especially Merrheim stressed that unless President Wilson were actively supported the syndical International might not even survive.[6] Eventually Jouhaux had his way. The syndical conference adopted a resolution calling for the establishment of a League along the lines suggested by the political conference in the other hall of Berne's *Volkshaus*. The resolution also warned that under the present social system the working class would have to use its concerted international power to keep the League from becoming an instrument of bourgeois reaction and repression.[7] For the time being the nonpolitical trade unionists who longed for cooperation with Gompers were checked and Jouhaux's Wilsonian affirmation was spread on the record.

Jouhaux's conference now drafted as well as debated, and the twin conferences unanimously passed, the Resolution on International Labor Legislation. Its chief concern was "the unfair competition of backward countries which endangered labor and industry in the more advanced States." In other words, whereas the Socialists and trade unionists proposed to press for social and economic reforms in national legislatures through the League's "permanent labor commission," they would bring about the "adjustment of national differences"—presumably with a view to raising conditions in the less developed nations to the higher levels of the most advanced industrial countries.

But the prescriptions for labor legislation also exceeded the reformist proposals of the Erfurt program in both scope and specificity. The Berne resolution called for free and compulsory primary education as well as for free and universally accessible higher education. Under the age of 15 children were not to be employed in industrial occupations; between 15 and 18 they would work a maximum of six hours a day while being "allowed time off to attend classes." Similarly woman labor was to be carefully regulated and equal pay would be paid to each

[5] Bernard Georges and Denise Tintant: *Léon Jouhaux: Cinquante ans de syndicalisme* (Paris: Presses Universitaires; 1962), I, 255–9.

[6] *L'Humanité*, February 10, 1919.

[7] For the text of this resolution see Renaudel: *L'Internationale à Berne*, 83–4.

sex for equal work. Other sections dealt with the regulation of home work, the rights of immigrant labor, the regulation of emigration and immigration, and social insurance by the state.

The heart of the resolution, however, was in the sections dealing with hours of work, the right to organize, minimum wages, and unemployment. Above all, here was a clear-cut and unqualified demand for the eight-hour day and the forty-eight-hour week; "for the right of combination and association in all countries"; for mixed wage boards to fix "legal minimum rates of wages . . . to provide a proper standard of living"; and for "a system of unemployment insurance." Incidentally, whereas employers and employees were to be equally represented on the national wage boards, only representatives of organized labor and governments would sit in the annual conference of the League's permanent labor commission.

The Bolshevik-*cum*-Russian issue was the last item on the agenda. It was at least as divisive for the International as was the question of responsibilities; in all likelihood it was even more so since it exposed divisions along ideological rather than national lines. And whereas Wilsonianism helped bridge the gap between the French and the Germans on the question of responsibility, it was less serviceable in the confrontation between active anti-Bolsheviks and passive sympathizers with the new Soviet regime.

Even before the Berne Conference convened Albert Thomas and Renaudel had urged that this conference formally "repudiate the methods and tactics of Bolshevism." They characterized Lenin's professionally prepared seizure and consolidation of power through the dictatorship of the proletariat as a "caricature of Marxism"; and they warned that since the Bolsheviks were propagating their methods throughout Europe, the world, and the Socialist movement the Berne Conference had to combine its disavowal of Bolshevism with a reaffirmation of democratic Socialism.[8]

Thomas launched his attack in the same address in which he indicted the German Majoritarians. He accused the Russian Bolsheviks of violating the International's most hallowed canons. The prewar International did not preclude recourse to revolutionary violence in given situations; nor did it forget that the Socialist party was a party of revolution and total transformation. On the other hand, the International did discourage "agitation and subversion"; it condemned the revolutionary efforts of those who "refused to take account of the requirements either of economic evolution or of national sentiments"; and it denounced the champions of the dictatorship of the proletariat for advocating "nothing but a caricature of both Marxism and Socialism." In this address Thomas moved that since the future of Socialism

8 *L'Humanité,* February 4, 1919.

was seriously threatened "by the new trends of so-called Bolshevism" Berne's agenda should provide for a consideration of "the role of democracy in the establishment of the Socialist order."

P. J. Troelstra was the first to oppose Thomas. Not that he either approved or even sympathized with Bolshevism. He felt, however, that the delegates should not engage in acrimonious debates which would weaken the International at a moment when only maximum unity and pressure could make an impression on the proceedings in Paris.[9]

Longuet seconded Troelstra's plea. He protested against the proposed summary exclusion and condemnation of the Bolshevik movement. Longuet first wanted more information about Russian Bolshevik methods, tactics, and practices. But above all he suspected the motives of the sponsors of this *a priori* censure: they belonged to the "extreme right" of the Socialist movement which throughout the war had sabotaged the work of the International.[1] With the support of Troelstra, Adler, Eisner, and some 30 other delegates, Longuet sought to keep this controversial Bolshevik issue off the agenda as well as off the floor.

But since Thomas had the majority of delegates as well as both Branting and Henderson on his side this preliminary debate was now moved from the public plenary session to a closed special commission.[2] There the delegates spoke even more freely and their search for compromise encountered insuperable difficulties.

Renaudel introduced a rather startling resolution. In line with Marxist dogma his resolution reaffirmed the "legitimacy" of revolutionary action in the face of the "*violences* of bourgeois and capitalist domination"; it also tied the triumph of Socialism to the development of capitalism, clearly implying that not all nations were equally ripe for the jump. But should the revolutionary situation outrun economic development (as a result of war?) a premature Socialist regime was nevertheless bound to establish and stabilize itself "through the use of democratic institutions whose ultimate foundation was the universal franchise." Renaudel left no doubt that he wanted the Russian Bolsheviks promptly to dismantle their dictatorship.

Simultaneously Renaudel cautioned Central and Western European Socialists against the perils of grasping opportunity. Whereas Lenin urged and expected Socialists to take full advantage of the postwar crisis, Renaudel warned against its pitfalls. Capitalism was disoriented; inventories were destroyed; famine threatened; and scarce resources had to be allocated for the reconstruction of war-ravaged territories. All these factors of uncertainty and instability required a

[9] *Le Temps,* February 6, 1919.
[1] *Le Populaire,* February 13, 1919.
[2] The complete membership of this commission is not known. However, the following delegates are known to have served on it: Branting, MacDonald, Longuet, Renaudel, Axelrod, Bienstock, Sukhomlin, Adler, Eisner, Wels.

careful "calculus of the relationship of forces between the proletariat's offensive capabilities and the bourgeoisie's power of resistance." Needless to say, this great caution was an outgrowth of conditions in France as well as of French reluctance to characterize the changes in Central Europe as revolutionary.

Wels could not endorse this denial of the German Revolution, though he eagerly joined and even surpassed Renaudel in his democratic professions. In the name of the German Majoritarians he called on the conference to declare "parliamentarism the immutable basis of all Socialist politics"; and to condemn "any infringements—whether imperialist or Bolshevik—by any Government of the rights and liberties of each people and individual." The German roots of Wels's proposal were as evident as the French roots of Renaudel's.

Neither Renaudel nor Wels even bothered to balance their anti-Bolshevism with a protest against external intervention in the Russian Civil War. This was left to Ramsay MacDonald. In addition to indiscriminately praising the Russian, German, and Austro-Hungarian revolutions he protested against all forms of intervention. Moreover, at the suggestion of the Russian Mensheviks and Social Revolutionaries MacDonald called on the International to establish a commission to go to Russia "to study events . . . and the theoretical principles on which these were based." In separate resolutions Branting and Eisner made similar proposals. But unlike Branting the Bavarian leader continued to share Adler's and Longuet's preference for keeping these issues private.

By a vote of five to two, with two abstentions, the members of the commission now instructed Branting to draft a compromise resolution for submission to the plenary conference. Both the vote and the choice of Branting indicated that the declared anti-Bolsheviks were winning the day. The President of the Berne Conference realized all along that his draft of the majority resolution on "Democracy and Dictatorship" would be decisive for the future life of the Second International.

This resolution began by carefully distinguishing between two separate phases of the Socialist revolution. Branting unequivocally hailed the "great *political* revolutions" in Russia, Austria-Hungary, and Germany. This opening paragraph neither condoned nor criticized the use of violence in the first, political phase.

The International should make it quite clear, however, that the use of violence would not be legitimate in the second, social phase. Branting asked the Berne Conference to urge that "democratic and republican institutions" be used to "bring about the great *Socialist* transformation." All previous congresses of the International had adhered "to the principles of Democracy." The Berne Conference merely renewed this determination of the working classes to carry on "the class struggle" with time-honored democratic means: "freedom of speech and press, right of assembly, universal suffrage, government responsible to Parliament, and right of association."

It followed that only socializations adopted by democratic processes would be considered legitimate. Specifically, the conference was asked to reject all reforms that failed to command "the support of the majority of the people."

Surprisingly Branting's resolution contained no outright protest against intervention in Russia. It merely proposed that the International censure the governments for "using Bolshevism as a bogey" while at the same time cautioning the workers that "counterrevolutionary forces were already at work everywhere."

Possibly Branting meant to compensate for this omission by refraining from an outright denunciation of Bolshevism. Formally the issue was shelved: a study mission would go to Russia and the question of Bolshevism would be placed on the agenda of the next conference.

But this formal postponement could not hide the fact that this proposed rededication to civil liberties, universal suffrage, and Parliamentarism was designed to be an implicit, if not explicit, anti-Bolshevik manifesto. Branting meant to legitimize the revived International. He sought to give it a platform with which to fend off the corrosive appeals of the schismatic Third International and to explore further cooperation with advanced Radicalism, notably with Wilson.

Of course, Social Patriots and reformists enthusiastically pushed and supported this policy. More significant, however, was the spirited public endorsement of Branting's resolution by leading Internationalists, Independents, and Revisionists—by MacDonald, Henderson, Kautsky, and Bernstein. All four resolved to articulate the International's democratic heritage, thereby also cleansing Socialism of the last vestiges of *revolutionary* Marxism.

MacDonald proclaimed that the "reign of minorities" could only be a brief phase in a revolution whose aim should be the "conquest of liberty and the establishment of a democratic regime." He conceded that it was too early to pass judgment on Bolshevism. Meanwhile, however, the Berne Conference had to reaffirm the proletariat's conviction that "democracy, liberty, popular control, and above all popular representation in Parliament had to remain the basis of human society."

Similarly Henderson asserted that "Socialism without democracy was nonsense." Naturally, Henderson was less reticent to judge Bolshevik Russia: "I was there at the time of the Revolution and thus was able to determine that Bolshevism is nothing but oppression, violence, and terror." His primary concern was the reestablishment of the International and its effective influence on international politics. To achieve this twin aim it was necessary to "clearly choose between the purely destructive character of Russian Bolshevism and the constructive character of genuine Socialism."

In addition to condemning the Soviets' dictatorial rule Kautsky charged that Bolshevism compared unfavorably with capitalism in the production of goods and services: Bolshevism was ruining industry, disorganizing the proletariat, and chasing the urban proletariat back to the fields. Its only positive effect was "the establishment of a new militarism." In order to hold and increase its ranks the International simply had to adopt an "unambiguous and plain" attitude toward the Soviets.

Bernstein, who arrived in Berne just in time for this public debate on February 9 and 10, took an equally unequivocal position.

> The Bolshevik problem is a question of life or death for Germany. The Bolsheviks are the real counterrevolutionaries in Russia; they will kill the revolution. Their interpretation of the Marxist theories of the dictatorship of the proletariat is altogether false. All they have created is an army led by tsarist officers and trained to repress the will of the people. Theirs is a reign of corruption, a shameless corruption which they seek to spread to other countries. Germany has had the experience: Bolshevism leads straight to the decadence of mankind.

Whereas the British and German Centrists joined the Majoritarians in their unrestrained and unqualified hostility to Bolshevism, the French and Austrian Centrists refused to fall in line. Longuet and Adler had theoretical, tactical, and partisan objections, many of which they aired in a separate resolution.

They objected, above all, to the sweeping affirmations about Socialism's democratic postulates, practices, and restraints. Even assuming these were tailor-made for Western Europe they were not likely to be universally applicable. The methods of political conquest and Socialist transformation were bound to vary with the nature and degree of political, economic, and intellectual development in different countries, areas, and continents. Longuet and Adler rejected the universal claims of Branting's resolution as well as of Lenin's *State and Revolution*.

Furthermore, at this juncture they were reluctant to press a "premature judgment on the Bolsheviks' political methods." Such a course would tend to foster the growth of an irreparable schism with Lenin, to put the Second International entirely in the hands of the same men "who passively or actively hindered international action for four and a half years," and to encourage the bourgeois governments and parties in their anti-Socialist offensive.

The minority at Berne also proposed to send a commission into Russia. Simultaneously, however, and in partial imitation of the Paris Peace Conference, it hoped to invite representatives of all Socialist sides of the Russian Civil War to present their case. In order both to make this invitation attractive to Lenin and to reduce their own isolation in the International the minority Centrists needed a platform from which to attract the kindred but missing Italian, Rumanian, Serb, and Swiss Socialist parties.

This isolation of the minority Centrists was exposed in broad daylight in the late afternoon of February 10, just before the Berne Conference closed with the singing of the *International*. The Chair announced the results of an informal canvass. The overwhelming majority of delegates and delegations sided with Branting. Only the Norwegian, Spanish, Greek, and Dutch delegations lined up with the French ex-*minoritaires* and half the German-Austrians in support of the Adler-Longuet resolution.[3]

With a view to supervising the implementation of its resolutions as well as the preparation of a full-scale congress of the International, the conference chartered a Permanent Commission composed of two representatives from each delegation. This commission met in the evening of February 10, before the delegates left Berne. It set up an Executive Committee in which Branting, Henderson, and Huysmans were co-equals. In turn this Executive Committee, reinforced by Renaudel, Longuet, MacDonald, and Stuart-Bunning, was instructed to proceed to Paris to present and explain the Berne resolutions to the peacemakers. Moreover, this same delegation was to act as a watchdog committee and lobby in Paris. And last, the commission appointed an eight-man delegation to investigate political and economic developments in Russia.

Quite clearly, Paris rather than Moscow had top priority. The watchdog committee rushed to the French capital in the hope of catching Wilson before his departure for the U.S. on February 14.[4] Even though this interview never materialized, on February 16 the committee met with Clemenceau who, as President of the Peace Conference, accepted copies of the Berne resolutions and suggested that the committee contact the appropriate commissions in Paris.[5] On February 21 this watchdog committee had a similar meeting with Lloyd George, who was accompanied by Lord Curzon.[6]

A failure to secure passports for Berne's delegation to Russia was the first and clearest concrete index of official resistance to Socialist

---

[3] The spokesmen of the French *Comité pour la Reprise des relations internationales* were the only ones to refer to Bolshevism as "a liberation effort by the workers and peasants of Russia" and to call on the conference to come out flatly in opposition to further intervention and in favor of the immediate withdrawal of Allied troops. Their resolution rallied no supporters beyond the four sponsors (Frossard, Verfeuil, Paul Faure, and Loriot).

[4] *Le Populaire, l'Humanité,* and *le Temps,* February 12, 1919.

[5] *L'Humanité,* February 17, 1919; and *le Temps,* February 18, 1919.

[6] Labour Party: *Report of the Nineteenth Annual Conference,* 17.

representations and pressures.[7] Henderson could not understand why the Allied Governments "refused passports to the anti-Bolshevik Socialists whom the Berne Conference proposed to send to Russia."[8] Perhaps these governments would have been more amenable provided prominent Social Patriots could have dominated the Berne delegation. Instead, the mission to Russia was to be composed of Longuet or Paul Faure for France, Kautsky or Rudolf Hilferding for Germany, Adler or Bauer for Austria, and MacDonald for Britain. For totally different reasons these Centrists were equally distasteful to Lenin. Nevertheless the Soviet government announced that it would welcome them and facilitate their inquiry.[9] Needless to say, the Centrists were not about to imitate Radek and sneak across borders illegally. They were not revolutionaries; they preferred to wait patiently for Wilson's influence to get them their passports. But they waited in vain.

Just then the Big Three were not susceptible to intimidation. After the January elections Germany seemed calm; in the Allied nations the Left was on the defensive; and Wilson was not to return to Paris until the very eve of the March–April crisis. Moreover, they had taken the measure of the Berne Conference: Socialist leaders had respectfully requested interviews with them, loyally applied for passports, fiercely denounced Bolshevism, and only mildly protested against continuing intervention in Russia.

Even Wilson and the American officials in Paris concluded that Henderson would continue to stand by, ready to do the President's bidding. On his return to Paris Bullitt presented a reassuring diagnosis of Berne.

> The Conference was composed of the moderate Socialist elements of 26 countries. There was not one Bolshevist in attendance, and numerous speakers condemned the antidemocratic standpoint of the Bolsheviki. Indeed, during the five days I sat in the conference hall I heard not one word of "revolution."
>
> The entire conference showed an almost pathetic confidence in President Wilson. Speaker after speaker praised the President and insisted that the masses of Europe must stand behind him in his fight for the League of Nations.

Bullitt merely warned that unless there was some provision for popular representation in the League the Socialist and labor leaders would oppose the Covenant.[1] Although leading Socialists and syndicalists

[7] Labour Party: Minutes of the Executive Committee, 16, March 12, 1919; and *le Populaire*, March 14–18, 1919.

[8] W. H. Buckler to Colonel House, March 29, 1919, House Papers, 29:32.

[9] *Le Populaire*, February 23, 1919; and Bergen of the German Foreign Ministry to Kautsky, March 5, 1919, Kautsky Papers (D II/253).

[1] Memorandum for Colonel House, February 9, 1919, Bullitt Papers. This memo as well as the text of the Berne resolution of the League of Nations and an Ammission Bulletin summarizing the other resolutions are printed in David Hunter Miller: *My Diary at the Conference of Paris*, V, 240, and XVII, 52–4, 114–15.

publicly expressed their disillusionment with the draft-Covenant published on February 14,[2] they were no more likely to break with Wilson
over an abortive League than with his three colleagues over the
passports. In private Henderson actually conceded that "even in its
present shape the League was an enormous asset to civilization." He
did advocate, however, that Germany be admitted "as soon as possible
in order to link her up with the Entente and to prevent her from lapsing
toward Russia."[3]

Indeed, the Big Four and their advisers drew a deep breath now
that the Berne Conference had confirmed the moderate temper and
internal fragility of the Second International, its distrust of the German
Majority, and its readiness to participate in the struggle against Bolshevism. According to Sir Horace Rumbold, the British Minister in Berne,
the Bolshevik issue rather than the question of cooperation with Germany was "the rock" on which the International would "eventually
split." In the meantime, of course, Lloyd George and Clemenceau continued to be concerned about the Socialists' unabated Wilson cult,
though they must have been reassured by the decision of Berne's
Permanent Commission to proclaim May Day 1919 an occasion for
demonstrations in favor of the League of Nations.[4]

From the diplomatic point of view the Allied Premiers also made
significant gains. Certainly French apprehensions that the German
Majoritarians would turn the International into an instrument of their
national power were laid to rest. Before the war the German Social
Democrats had been the single most influential national party in the
International; at Berne British Labour assumed the pivotal position. The
Germans themselves were the first to recognize this shift. From the very
start they agreed with Henderson that only Anglo-German cooperation
could check the disruptive offensive of Albert Thomas and Gompers
from the right flank and Lenin's schismatic attack from the left flank.

Kautsky in particular kept insisting that without British Labour there
could be no International, that the services of this Internaional were
essential for the survival of the fledgling Social Democratic Weimar
Republic, and that the future of Weimar was inseparable from the
future of German Social Democracy in particular and of world Socialism in general.

> British Socialism will achieve more than German Socialism; it will
> have an impact on the entire world. We can only benefit from this
> development. Socialism in Russia and Germany is economically so

---

[2] Austin Van Der Slice: *International Labor, Diplomacy, and Peace 1914–1919*
(Philadelphia: University of Pennsylvania Press; 1941), 358–9.

[3] W. H. Buckler to Colonel House, March 29, 1919, House Papers, 29:32.

[4] Sir Horace Rumbold to Foreign Office, February 8, 1919, and to Balfour, February
13, 1919, F.O. 608/237; P. J. Troelstra: *Politische Aufgaben der Sozialistichen
Internationale* (Lucerne, 1919), 24; *l'Humanité*, April 12, 1919; *le Populaire*,
April 29, 1919.

bankrupt that it will not be able to develop on its own steam. We are urgently dependent on British and American aid. We have every interest that this aid should come to us from a Socialist England and an America permeated with Socialism.[5]

Whatever the errors in this diagnosis, Kautsky was right in his assertion that as compared to 1914, the center of gravity in the world Socialist movement was no longer in Germany. There now were two centers, one in Russia and the other in England. And, of course, Kautsky was one of the leading advocates of a Western rather than an Eastern orientation.[6]

Meanwhile Bolsheviks within and outside Russia were appalled and infuriated, but not surprised, by the moderate thrust of this effort to resuscitate the Second International. Before, during, and after Berne they denounced the Centrists—let alone the Social Patriots—for believing in Wilson instead of Marx, for promoting the League of Nations instead of the International, and for condoning Allied intervention instead of the Bolshevik Revolution.

Admittedly, the schism in the International between the *enragés* who rallied to Zimmerwald and the Socialists—both Centrist and Majoritarian—who rallied to Stockholm had profound prewar and wartime roots. Throughout the war, moreover, Lenin and Zinoviev repeatedly called for the organization of a new International, the leaders of the Second International having betrayed the working class by actively endorsing or silently condoning the war efforts of their respective governments. After the Armistice the Bolsheviks were encouraged to strike out on their own by the postwar unrest, notably throughout *defeated* Europe, which they meant to exploit. Also, the foundation of the German Communist Party in late December 1918, at the height of this unrest, seemed to prefigure a chain of kindred Bolshevik parties throughout the Continent and beyond.[7]

It was on January 24, 1919, that the Soviet radio invited all genuine revolutionary groups to designate representatives to meet at a time and place to be specified to form a new International.[8] But this conference did not convene until March 2, its organization and first sessions proceeded without publicity, and few prominent delegates of revolutionary groups outside Russia attended.

Obviously, Lenin proceeded with great caution. Above all, as long

---

[5] Unabhängige Sozialdemokratische Partei Deutschlands: *Protokoll über die Verhandlungen des ausserordentlichen Parteitages in Berlin,* March 2–6, 1919, 127–8.

[6] Karl Kautsky: *Vergangenheit und Zukunft der Internationale* (Vienna: Verlag der Wiener Buchhandlung; 1920), 81, 85–6.

[7] This discussion of the background to the inaugural meeting of the Third International relies heavily on James W. Hulse: *The Forming of the Communist International* (Stanford: Stanford University Press; 1964), Chs. 1–2.

[8] For the text of this summons as well as of other relevant documents see *Der I und II Kongress der Kommunistischen Internationale* (Berlin: Dietz Verlag; 1959).

as the Buckler-Litvinov conversations and the Prinkipo proposal[9] held out any chance of accommodation with the Allies, he refrained from taking revolutionary steps that would further heighten hostility and suspicion. But accommodation became increasingly unlikely. The breach in Soviet–German relations was punctuated by the assassination of Karl Liebknecht and Rosa Luxemburg, while the Allies proceeded to step up their assistance to the Whites, the Poles, and the Rumanians.

In the last analysis, however, "the leaders of the Second International provided the Bolsheviks with the strongest provocation to action."[1] The Berne Conference, and more particularly its anti-Bolshevik stance, confirmed their worst prejudices, suspicions, and fears. European Socialism was fast becoming an integral part of the bourgeois, capitalist, and counterrevolutionary amalgam which, frightened by Bolshevism, proposed to fight it. Even before the full text of the speeches and resolutions reached Moscow, *Pravda* denounced the Berne "lackeys" and "social obscurantists" for hiding behind the League of Nations as they enlisted the renascent Second International in the counterrevolutionary cause: "One feeling unites them: a furious hatred for Bolsheviks. One slogan unites them: the slogan of war against the Bolsheviks. The first words of the Yellow International were 'Fight the Bolsheviks!' "[2]

[9] See Ch. 13 below.
[1] Hulse: *Forming of the Communist International*, 9.
[2] *Pravda*, February 6, 1919, cited in ibid., 13.

13

Russia: The Buckler Mission
and Prinkipo Summons

THE PARIS PEACE CONFERENCE opened on January 12, when the Big Four held their first formal meeting. Heretofore only two or three of the Allied and Associated Chief Executives had met at any one time and place. But as of this Sunday afternoon the Chief Executives of the five "Powers with General Interests"—Japan joined on January 13—convened as a continuing Conference of Great Powers which became the combined executive and steering committee of the plenary Versailles Peace Congress.

When the military and naval experts were in attendance, this Conference, minus Japan, sat as the Supreme War Council. At all other times it sat as the Council of Ten, each Chief Executive being seconded by his Foreign Minister and surrounded by a host of advisers. On March 24 this Council of Ten was reduced to a Council of Four—the Chief Executives. Japan was excluded from this inner sanctum largely because the crisis which precipitated the establishment of this more efficacious decision-making organ was essentially European.

During the first phase of the Peace Conference—which ran from January 12 through March 24—the victors repeatedly began their sessions as meetings of the Supreme War Council; then, following the withdrawal of the military, they continued as the Council of Ten. The nineteen times that the Supreme War Council met, the military and naval advisers were in attendance either because they were summoned or because they themselves requested a hearing. They gave expert advice concerning extensions of the Armistice; proposals for tightening the *cordon sanitaire;* projects for military intervention; efforts to stop hostilities between small nations; and military and naval aspects of the peace treaty.

Even though these critical situations could not be adjusted without the threat or deployment of military and naval power, each military response was largely a function of overarching diplomatic and political considerations. The generals and admirals were subordinate to the statesmen. In those few instances in which the military did force the hand of the Conference, one of the Big Four rather than the Conference as a whole either failed to curb his own generals or else attempted to confront his fellow peacemakers with a *fait accompli.*

Throughout the Peace Conference economic power was used in much the same fashion and for similar purposes as was military power. Given the fluid situation between the Rhine and the Urals these two forms of power were equally essential instruments of control. Occasionally Foch was a few steps ahead of the Conference by virtue of his paramount position in the Supreme Command and his firm control of French troops. Similarly, occasionally Hoover set the pace because of his dominant role in the Supreme Economic Council and his ready access to American relief and aid. In the last analysis, however, the Conference of Chief Executives—first the Council of Ten and then the Council of Four—decided all vital matters of military and economic policy, regardless of organizational and procedural prescriptions.

On January 12 the Supreme War Council and the Council of Ten met at 2:30 and 4:00 p.m., respectively, in the Foreign Minister's conference room at the Quai d'Orsay. Whereas the former considered the second renewal of the Armistice with Germany, the latter turned to organizational and procedural questions. It was symptomatic of the entire Peace Conference that the specter of Bolshevism significantly impinged on the deliberations of both opening sessions.

Needless to say, every time the Armistice came up for monthly renewal Marshal Foch pressed the victor governments to inflict additional controls and humiliations on Germany. Presently Foch discovered that this coercion of Germany was perfectly compatible with the containment of Russian Bolshevism. His attention riveted on Poland, he insisted that a strong Poland could serve not only as a check to Germany but also as the linchpin of the anti-Bolshevik bulwark.

Undaunted by his recent rebuffs from Bliss and House, Marshal Foch now brought his plan for a quick build-up of this "land without frontiers" before the Big Four. On this occasion he argued, in a memorandum circulated on the eve of this meeting, that a vigorous Polish army was the key to political stability in Eastern Europe. To achieve this goal, under Article XVI Germany should be forced to recognize explicitly Allied access rights by sea to Danzig and by rail and river from Danzig to Thorn, so that an occupying force of two inter-Allied divisions could then be deployed along the Danzig-Thorn railway. "To prove the disinterestedness of this occupation," Foch proposed that these troops be under U.S. command and that America provide one entire division, each of the other Allies providing only one regiment. Once this transportation route was firmly secured Poland's valued organized and equipped divisions—formed by General Haller with Polish prisoners captured by the Allies—could be transferred from France and Italy.[1]

President Wilson instantly intervened to say that this proposal could not be considered in isolation. He feigned not to notice that it had an anti-German thrust. Instead he contended that the scheme "formed part of the much larger question of checking the advance of Bolshevism westward." In Wilson's mind there was considerable doubt "as to whether this advance could be checked by arms at all." At any rate, he thought it unwise to resort to military measures before the Conference had agreed on a general policy of checking Bolshevism "as a social and political danger." Lloyd George also urged that the "general policy towards Bolshevism" should first be discussed, Foch's proposal being subsidiary to it.

In the face of this opposition Clemenceau yielded rather readily, especially once Lloyd George reassured him that since "all the powers required were covered by Article XVI" there was no need to beat the impending deadline for the Armistice renewal. Obviously the Council of Ten rather than the Supreme War Council was the proper forum for the formulation of a general policy toward Bolshevism.

But before the military advisers withdrew the Council considered another memorandum which left no doubt about either Foch's or the Big Four's fear of Bolshevism. In this second memorandum Foch discussed both the possible dangers and uses of the 1,200,000 Russian war prisoners detained in German camps. At a minimum, the Allies should prevent the Red Army from drawing reinforcements from this manpower pool. At the same time they should win these Russians for the anti-Bolshevik cause by improving their "material and moral condition." Eventually some of these prisoners could be recruited for service in parts of Russia that were free of Soviet control.

> The only provinces towards which transports of prisoners might be prepared are, therefore, on the first hand Poland, on the other Southern Russia, and we must be content with forwarding towards these areas cases not suspect of Bolshevism and able there to reinforce parties faithful to our cause.

To implement this policy Foch urged the Allies to seek German agreement for the establishment of a special inter-Allied commission in Berlin.

Although Foch's Danzig-Thorn project was postponed, his recommendation concerning these Russian prisoners was promptly ratified. Lloyd George and Balfour freely conceded that should the Allies

[1] For the text of Foch's *aide-mémoire* see *F.R.,P.C.,1919*, III, 477–9.

"decide to fight Bolshevism" this manpower would constitute one of the "available" means and methods. As for Wilson, he himself suggested that Foch be "asked to formulate a clause giving the Allies the right to lay down to which parts of Russia Russians should be sent."[2]

Soon after the three generals—Foch, Bliss, and Henry Wilson— withdrew, the Council of Ten came up against the Bolshevik issue in a discussion of Russian representation. Not one of the Ten ever suggested that the Leninist regime be invited to send a delegation to represent Russia in the Conference. Pichon flatly held that the Conference need recognize neither the Bolshevik nor the Omsk government. Instead, while denying Russia representation as a state, the Conference should "unofficially" hear the views of distinguished *émigrés* such as Sazonov and Prince Lvov.

Both Lloyd George and Wilson were fearful that by granting these *émigrés* a hearing the Conference would create the impression that the Allies considered them representatives of Russia. Lloyd George argued, furthermore, that the question of Russian representation could not be divorced from the Allies' overall Russian policy.

> The Allies [were] . . . in a fix for the reason that they had no definite policy in Russia. They ought to decide whether to withdraw their troops or to reinforce them. Unless reinforced, they were of no use whatsoever. He had nothing to say against [such people as Prince Lvov except] that they represented every opinion except the prevalent opinion in Russia. . . . He feared the fact that it [Bolshevism] was prevalent must be accepted. The peasants accepted Bolshevism for the same reason as the peasants had accepted it in the French Revolution, namely, that it gave them land. The Bolsheviks were the *de facto* Government. . . . We recognized the Don Government, the Archangel Government, and the Omsk Government, although none of them were good, but we refused to recognize the Bolshevists. To say that we ourselves should pick the representatives of a great people was contrary to every principle for which we had fought. It was possible that the Bolshevists did not represent Russia. But certainly Prince Lvov did not, neither did Savinkov. . . . The British Government made exactly the same mistake when they said that the *émigrés* represented France. This led them into a war which lasted about twenty-five years. The Russian peasants probably felt towards Trotsky much as the French peasants did towards Robespierre. This question must now be settled. He hoped that the Allies would not separate and announce that they had made perpetual peace when Siberia, which formed about half Asia, and Russia, which formed about half Europe, were still at war. He, himself, would make proposals in due course, but, in the meantime, he wished to protest against an attempt to select representatives for some hundred million people.

2 Ibid., 479–81, 472–3.

Nevertheless, Lloyd George and Wilson agreed that during this interim, spokesmen of the Russian Political Conference could be "interviewed personally or asked to supply memoranda."[3]

On January 13 the assembled statesmen had to turn their attention once again to the Armistice whose monthly extension came due on the sixteenth. At this second session of the Supreme War Council the specter of Bolshevism made its appearance in connection with financial and economic clauses. In addition to the top military and naval officers, the chief economic advisers were in attendance, notably Étienne Clémentel, Louis-Lucien Klotz, Louis Loucheur, Hoover, and Hurley.

On Klotz's initiative the Allies considered what steps should be taken to put Germany's gold reserves and printing presses for money in a safe place. Convinced that money was one of the chief instruments of Bolshevik subversion, Bonar Law wanted the Allies "to prevent the gold and presses from falling into the hands of the Spartacus group." Both Bonar Law and Wilson were confident that Ebert would welcome an Allied demand that it take the necessary safeguards, though the Conference agreed that no such clause should be inserted in the new Armistice "except at the wish of the German Government."[4] Although Ebert hardly needed to be pushed in such matters, neither he nor Erzberger welcomed *overt* Allied pressure on the very eve of the German elections.

At this same session of the Supreme War Council the Big Ten themselves, rather than the second echelon, inaugurated the tortuous, divisive, and endless squabble about the feeding of Germany. All were agreed that both the letter and the spirit of the Armistice required that food be supplied. But sharp differences arose over how much and on what conditions German merchant shipping should be put at the disposal of the Allied and Associated Powers for this purpose. Also, the differences over German payment for these emergency supplies became close to insurmountable.

At the time the Germans had a merchant marine of nearly 3 million tons which had been kept in mothballs all through the war. Given the post-Armistice shipping shortage, this tonnage was bound to be tapped in one way or another. The Germans had only one fear: that once these ships were part of the Allied shipping pool they would be attached for reparations. From the very start, therefore, Erzberger demanded that these ships, while serving in this pool, should continue both to fly the German flag and to be operated by German crews.

In any case, the British and the French were equally determined to recruit this idle tonnage. Balfour reported that Lord Reading, Britain's representative on the Inter-Allied Relief Commission, wanted the Allies to propose a bargain to the Germans instead of putting new conditions

[3] Ibid., 490–1, 533.
[4] Ibid., 509–10, 543.

into the Armistice. "If you want food you must hand over your ships. . . . In this way *the weapon of food would still be left in our hands.* . . . A certain quantity of food would be handed over to them in return for the use of a certain number of ships [italics mine]." Reading and Hoover had a limited and well-defined objective: to get food to Germany without diverting scarce Allied tonnage from other pressing purposes.

Bonar Law and Clemenceau were not so easily satisfied. While the former wanted "the balance of shipping beyond the tonnage required for Germany's food supplies to be used for the payment of food supplied," the latter urged that the Germans be forced "to give up these ships temporarily for the good of Europe . . . , since the whole of Europe had to be fed."

The hard school easily won the day. The Ten agreed that without delay Germany should have to turn over her entire merchant marine, this fleet to be "put to sea flying a flag or flags of the Allied nations." Wilson, Hoover, and Reading had to be satisfied with the promise that only in case of a stubborn German refusal would the acceptance of this injunction be made a condition for the renewal of the Armistice.[5]

Although these requisitioned ships were expected to yield considerable returns, the question of payment for food supplies had to be faced squarely. The British simply refused to have this cost of food added to the German bill primarily because the French and the Belgians were entitled to the largest share of reparations. Bonar Law maintained that "a necessity" like food should be paid for in cash, gold, or German securities held abroad. But the French were just as stubborn. Klotz would not allow the Germans to take food money from funds owed as reparations to the Allies, particularly to France and Belgium. This was a financial rather than a food question, and France could not agree that the cost of food supplies should receive priority over Germany's previous debts.

In the face of this stalemate, aggravated by the shipping controversy, President Wilson became impatient and irritable, especially since the aid bill for 100 million dollars had not yet been passed in Washington. The Allied Food Council had recommended that at the earliest possible moment Germany should be allowed to import 200,000 tons of breadstuffs and 70,000 tons of pork products.

> President Wilson expressed the view that any further delay in this matter might be fatal. They were discussing an absolute and immediate necessity. So long as hunger continued to gnaw, the foundations of government would continue to crumble. Therefore, food should be supplied immediately, not only to our friends, but also to those parts of the world where it was to our interest to maintain a

[5] Ibid., 512–15, 521–2.

stable Government. He thought they were bound to accept the concerted counsel of a number of men who had been devoting the whole of their time and thought to this question. He trusted the French Finance Department would withdraw their objection, as they were faced with the great problems of Bolshevism and the forces of dissolution which now threatened society. . . . President Wilson urged that, unless a solution for the immediate situation could be found, none of these debts would be paid. The want of food would lead to a crash in Germany. The great point, however, was this— that the Associated Governments have no money to pay for these supplies; therefore Germany must pay for them. But if they were not paid for and supplied immediately there would be no Germany to pay anything.

With the British and American delegations presenting a common front on this issue, the French grudgingly acquiesced to giving the new debt priority for two months. In return, the Conference consented to prepare an overall priority list to go into effect at the end of that period.[6]

During the negotiations at Trier the German Financial Delegation and Erzberger dutifully took note of Allied wishes about safeguarding the gold reserves and the money presses. Erzberger also willingly agreed to the formation of an Allied commission to care for Russian prisoners. However, Erzberger flatly refused to surrender the merchant fleet unconditionally. At last, in Clause 8 of the Armistice renewal, he won a pledge that the handing over of the fleet "in no wise" prejudged its final disposition. The Allies also agreed to fix and pay "suitable compensation" for the use of the vessels and to admit a German representative to the Inter-Allied Maritime Transport Council.[7] It was to take another two months before this shipping agreement began to be implemented. This delay was grist for the mill of those who all along had accused the Germans of vastly and deliberately exaggerating the danger of starvation.[8]

Having disposed of the Armistice renewal, the Conference needed only two additional sessions to reach agreement on procedural matters, including publicity and official languages. Then, before the afternoon

---

[6] Ibid., 515–17, 528–9.

[7] For these Armistice negotiations see Edmund Marhefka (ed.): *Der Waffenstillstand: Das Dokumentenmaterial der Waffenstillstandsverhandlungen* (Berlin: Deutsche Verlagsgesellschaft für Politik und Geschichte; 1928), I, 125, 158–9, 179–81; and Norman Davis to Woodrow Wilson, January 22, 1919, Wilson Papers. The text of the Armistice renewal is in *F.R.,P.C.,1919*, II, 11–15. Epstein suggests that since the Allies in any case planned to demand the ships it would have been preferable "to lose them as a *quid pro quo* for urgently needed foodstuffs in January than to lose them for nothing in July." However, Allied intentions were not that evident and set at the time and such a "surrender" would have been incompatible with the diplomatic style and strategy of both Erzberger and Brockdorff-Rantzau. Klaus Epstein: *Matthias Erzberger and the Dilemma of German Democracy* (Princeton: Princeton University Press; 1959), 293–4.

[8] Epstein: *Matthias Erzberger*, 294.

session of January 15 adjourned, Lloyd George suggested that the following morning the Council of Ten should turn to the Russian question. The British Prime Minister called on all delegations to come prepared with memoranda summarizing their intelligence about conditions in both European and Asian Russia, "with special reference to the Bolsheviki."[9] Hence, even though the Conference was convened to settle the fate of the defeated powers, the German question was not the first substantive issue on the agenda of the Paris Peace Conference: instead "it was mutually agreed that the strongest most pressing question and the one to be considered first by the representatives of the Five Great Powers was the Russian situation, with particular reference to the Bolsheviki question."[1]

In preparation for these deliberations both Lloyd George and Wilson specifically commissioned their experts to provide them with careful estimates. The General Staff presented the Prime Minister with an "Appreciation of the Internal Situation in Russia";[2] and R. H. Lord of the Inquiry submitted a memorandum on "The Present Situation of the Bolshevists in Russia" to the President.[3]

According to the British General Staff the Bolsheviks' "internal political position remained strong"; their "prospects in Soviet Russia itself were good"; they were "sparing no effort to hasten" a second revolution in Germany; and by spring the Soviet government should be able to put in the field approximately half a million men "from the Baltic to the Black Sea." At the same time the Bolsheviks realized that their opportunities in neutral countries had already been "very seriously curtailed" and that the front opposing them was gaining in strength. There were indications that they wanted negotiations with the Allies so as to have a breathing space.

In his report R. H. Lord distinguished the political, military, and economic aspects of Bolshevik strength. Politically the Bolshevik government "seemed weaker than formerly," except that "the fear of foreign intervention and of an accompanying counterrevolution was

---

[9] While one set of minutes reports that Clemenceau moved the discussion of the Russian problem, the other mentions Lloyd George. Since on the twelfth the British Prime Minister had indicated that he "would make proposals in due course," it is more than likely that he took the initiative. *F.R.,P.C.,1919,* III, 564, 577.

[1] Lansing to Polk, January 22, 1919 (very secret and personal), National Archives, Document 763.72119/3472.

[2] General Staff, War Office, "Appreciation of the Internal Situation in Russia," January 12, 1919 (marked Secret and For Use at Peace Conference), in Wilson Papers, VIII A: 10.

[3] The Director of the Inquiry forwarded the memorandum with this covering letter: "Dear Mr. President: Mr. Leland Harrison has informed us of your request for the accompanying memorandum and map on the Bolsheviki, prepared by Dr. R. H. Lord, specialist on Russia in this section, to be in your hands *by ten this morning* [italics mine]." Mezes to Wilson, January 16, 1919, Wilson Papers, VIII A: 11.

rallying many elements" around the regime. Militarily the Bolsheviks were shifting "their chief efforts to, and winning success in, the Baltic Provinces, Lithuania and the Ukraine," while recent operations had gone against them on the eastern, southeastern, and northern fronts. Economically their situation was "more critical than at any previous time." As for their present and prospective military strength, the Red Army had 286,000 men in the field (16,000 in the north; 120,000, east; 115,000, south; and 35,000, west); an additional 300,000 were "under mobilization orders."[4]

These findings reinforced rather than weakened the inclination of Lloyd George and Wilson to take some diplomatic soundings before considering further military measures. Apparently the Bolsheviks were not about to collapse; nor was the Red Army about to sweep into Eastern Europe. Should the Borden plan succeed, the Bolsheviks would be making concessions. Meanwhile the risks of failure were marginal since the ring around the Bolsheviks was already nearly complete and the balance between them and their enemies was not likely to shift in Lenin's favor in a matter of weeks. Quite the contrary.

In other words, these intelligence estimates, however incomplete and haphazard they may have been, provided a realistic underpinning for the men of the "newer progressivism [who were] concerned more with the conditions than with the forms" of the Russian Revolution. The Anglo-American Chief Executives "viewed the upheaval with tolerance," blaming both the Revolution and its excesses on the misdeeds of the *ancien régime* and ascribing Russia's defeat to the "ineptitude and corruption" of the tsarist ruling classes. According to Lloyd George, theirs was the attitude of "the Fox Whigs towards the French Revolution," while Clemenceau, who "forgave all the terrors of the French Revolution, . . . judged harshly the violence and horrors perpetrated in the Russian Revolution, although the provocation was if anything greater."[5]

Lloyd George claims that except for the opposition in the Council of Ten as well as in London and Washington he and Wilson "would have dealt with the Soviets as the *de facto* Government of Russia."[6] He does not make clear, however, whether he would have dealt with the Bolshevik regime to the extent of asking it to represent Russia at the Conference. No matter, because the domestic opposition was widespread and vocal. Furthermore, within the Conference opposition was not limited to Clemenceau, Pichon, and Sonnino. In the British Delegation Bonar Law was inclined to oppose the implementation of the Borden plan.

[4] In a "Confidential Statement on Russian Conditions" dated January 21, 1919, and issued for the information of the press, Ray Stannard Baker gave much the same picture, including the estimate that the Red Army had about 300,000 men under arms. Baker Papers, Box 17 of 18.

[5] David Lloyd George: *The Truth About the Peace Treaties*, I, 330–1.

[6] Ibid., 331.

"He told Lloyd George that the Conservative Party in England felt strongly on the subject of Bolshevism, and that if he pressed this issue with Clemenceau it would . . . 'break your Government.' "[7]

In this context, then, on January 16 Lloyd George formally renewed the British proposal which the French had indignantly spurned barely ten days ago. In fact, at the outset he sought to correct Pichon's misconceptions about Balfour's *aide-mémoire* of January 2.

> It had never been suggested that the Bolshevik Government should be recognized to the extent of offering them a seat at the Peace Conference. It was only proposed that a truce among the various warring factions in Russia should be suggested. When this truce had been made, representatives of the various Governments should be invited to come to Paris to explain their position and receive from the Allies, if possible, some suggestions for the accommodation of their differences.

The British government made this proposal in order to gather more facts with which to form "a correct judgment."

Meanwhile the Allies had to proceed on the basis of incomplete information. But according to their information, "hopes that the Bolshevik Government would collapse had certainly been disappointed." Lloyd George then "quoted a report from the British Military Authorities in Russia . . . to the effect that the Bolshevik Government was stronger now than it had been some months previously." In particular the peasants were fearful of counterrevolution, even in the Ukraine.

As Lloyd George saw it the Allies had to choose from among three alternative policies towards Russia.

> (i) We could say that Bolshevism was a movement as dangerous to civilization as German militarism had been, and that we must therefore destroy it. Did anyone seriously put forward this policy? Was anyone prepared to carry it out? He believed that no one could be found to do so. The Germans, at the time when they needed every available man to reinforce their attack on the Western front, had been forced to keep about a million men to garrison a few provinces of Russia which were a mere fringe of the whole country; and, moreover, at that moment Bolshevism was weak and disorganized. Now it was strong and had a formidable army. Was anyone of the Western Allies prepared to send a million men into Russia? He doubted whether a thousand would be willing to go. All reports tended to show that the Allied troops in Siberia and in Northern Russia were most unwilling to continue the campaign and determined to return to their homes. To set Russia in order by force was

[7] Sir William Wiseman, Diary (Paris, January 17, 1919), in House Papers, 90:40. According to Wiseman the Prime Minister "flared up at once and said that 'if that is the case the Government had better be broken.' " Wiseman himself "did not think Bonar was very tactful; he seemed to be holding the whip over the P.M."

a task which he for one would not undertake on behalf of Great Britain, and he questioned whether any other Power would undertake it.

(ii) The second policy was a policy of insulation, the policy known as "cordon sanitaire." This policy meant the siege of Bolshevik Russia, that is to say, the Russia that had no corn, but a large famished population. These people were dying by thousands, if not by hundreds of thousands, of famine. Petrograd had been reduced from the proportions of a great city to those of a moderate town. Our blockade of Russia would lead to the killing, not of the ruffians enlisted by the Bolsheviks, but of the ordinary population, with whom we wish to be friends. This was a policy which, if only on grounds of humanity, we could not support. It might be suggested that the continuance of this policy in Russia would lead to the overthrow of the Bolsheviks; but who in Russia was able to overthrow them? General Knox[8] reported that the Czecho-Slovaks were tainted with Bolshevism and could not be trusted, neither could the Russian troops of Kolchak. He had just seen a map revealing the area held by Denikin. He occupied with an effective force of perhaps 40,000 men what might be described as a little backyard near the Black Sea. Denikin was said to have recognized Kolchak, but he was quite unable to get into touch with him, as an immense Bolshevik area intervened between them. Kolchak, moreover, appeared to pursue the revival of the old regime in Russia; hence the lukewarmness of the Czecho-Slovaks in his cause. They were unwilling to fight in order to set up another Tzarist regime. So also were the British. This would not be helping to create a new world.

(iii) The only other way he could think of was the plan he had proposed—that of asking representatives of the various Russian Governments to meet in Paris after a truce among themselves. The name of M. Sazonoff had been mentioned as representing the Government at Omsk. M. Sazonoff had been long out of Great Russia. It was questionable whether he knew anything of the conditions at Omsk. He was a strong partisan, and might as well be consulted on the present temper of Russia as the *New York Tribune* on the opinions of Mr. Wilson. We could not leave Paris at the conclusion of the Peace Conference congratulating ourselves on having made a better world, if at that moment half of Europe and half of Asia were in flames. It had been alleged that if Bolshevik emissaries came to France and England they would proselytise the French and British peoples. It was possible that Bolshevism might gain ground in these countries, but it would not be as a consequence of the visit of a few Russian emissaries. He himself had no fears on this score. Moreover, conditions could be imposed on the delegates, and if they failed to observe them they could be sent back to Russia. With this threat over them it was most likely that they would avoid giving offense as they would be anxious to explain their case.[9]

8 Major General Alfred W. F. Knox, in command of the British forces in Siberia.
9 *F.R.,P.C.,1919,* III, 581–3, 589–93.

There was little for President Wilson to add to this exhaustive and compelling exposé and argument. He merely insisted that his British colleague's information "corresponded exactly" with his own. In particular, his own experts also emphasized that the fear of foreign aggression and of counterrevolution was rallying the people of Russia around the Bolshevik regime. Furthermore, in Russia as elsewhere, there was "a latent force behind Bolshevism which attracted as much sympathy as its more brutal aspects caused general disgust." But Wilson stipulated a precondition for coexistence which to date Lloyd George had only entertained in cabinet discussions: the Bolsheviks would have to stay out of or withdraw from the Baltic countries, notably "Lithuania, Poland, Finland, etc." Provided they refrained from such invasions and from reprisals he was in favor of bringing representatives of all the Russian factions before the Great Powers. Certainly of all the proposals, the British proposal alone was likely to lead somewhere.[1]

Meanwhile, Lloyd George and Wilson had initiated preliminary and secret but nevertheless semiofficial soundings of Soviet intentions. As recently as October 24 Chicherin had sent a sardonic, tactless, and incendiary message to Wilson. In this open letter he had accused the President of posing as an evangelist of peace and good will toward Russia while directing a hostile intervention in Archangel and Siberia.[2] Soon hereafter, however, the Bolshevik government began to modulate its propagandistic diplomacy. The Soviet leaders could not exclude the possibility that the Allies would use the resources freed by the defeat of Germany to mount a concerted counterrevolutionary offensive. At a minimum they could be expected to make some of these resources available to the Whites, whose survival hinged on this external support. Whereas a policy of revolutionary bluster might precipitate a frontal assault, a peace offensive could either forestall or blunt it by fostering dissension between, on the one hand, the advocates of direct military intervention and, on the other, the proponents of indirect measures or even of accommodation.

The first Soviet feelers reached the Allied and Associated Governments through the Norwegian Legation in Petrograd. On November 3 Chicherin verbally indicated that the Bolshevik government was ready to make concessions to the Entente powers and that in order "to arrive at an understanding" he was particularly eager to have the opportunity "to enter into negotiations with the United States."[3] Three days later he

---

[1] Ibid., 584–5, 592–3.

[2] For the full text of this note see *F.R.,1918,Supplement 1,* I, 488–55, or Jane Degras (ed.): *Soviet Documents on Foreign Policy, 1917–1924* (London: Oxford University Press; 1951), 112–20.

[3] *F.R.,1918,Supplement 1,* I, 471. On November 7, 1918, Lansing sent the following reply to the U.S. Legation in Christiana: "Department prefers to make no answer to message of Bolshevik Minister for Foreign Affairs and is not prepared to negotiate with Bolshevik authorities." National Archives, Document 763.72119/2491.

sent identical notes to the five principal powers offering to take up negotiations with a view to liquidating all hostilities. Chicherin asked that he be informed "when and where representatives from both sides [could] meet," insisting that it was of "no consequence to the Russian Soviet Government what place may be chosen for such negotiations."[4] On November 8 the All-Russian Extraordinary Congress of Soviets publicly endorsed these offers of conciliation and negotiation.[5] But the principal Allies chose to ignore these overtures.

The Soviet government decided, therefore, to send Maxim Litvinov to Stockholm to promote this peace policy through every available channel. He arrived there in the evening of November 30; the following morning he sought out Arthur Ransome, the understanding but far from Communist special correspondent of the Radical *Daily News*. According to Ransome, Litvinov's "official appointment was that of Commercial Attaché for Scandinavia, but in reality he was empowered to enter into negotiations."[6]

On December 23, following a series of informal probes, Litvinov, now signing as "Plenipotentiary of the Russian Federative Republic of Soviets," addressed an official letter to the American, British, French, and Italian Ministers in Stockholm. He informed them that he had "been authorized by the Soviet Government to enter into preliminary peace negotiations [to settle] all the outstanding questions which may give rise to a continuation of hostilities."[7]

The next day, Christmas Eve, he repeated this offer in a special appeal to President Wilson, whose "sense of justice and impartiality" he singled out for praise. In this appeal he stressed, above all, that "the accused side had never been allowed to put fully their case and to answer the charges made against them." Litvinov assured Wilson that the "so-called 'Red Terror'—which was grossly exaggerated and misrepresented abroad—was not the cause but the direct result and outcome of Allied intervention." Continued or stepped-up intervention could only lead to the further radicalization of opposing extremes. Should the interventionists prevail, Russia would be subjected to a dreadful White Terror, military dictatorship, tsarist restoration, and economic paralysis. In any case, the Soviet regime was "prepared to go to any length of concessions . . . if they can secure thereby conditions enabling them to work out peacefully their social schemes."[8]

Both Lloyd George and Wilson were very much disposed to follow up the Soviet overtures. On December 23 the Imperial War Cabinet weighed Litvinov's repeated efforts to spell out a basis for negotiations.

4 *F.R.,1918,Supplement 1*, I, 484.
5 Degras (ed.): *Soviet Documents*, 123.
6 *Daily News*, December 3, 1918.
7 *F.R.,1919,Russia*, 1–3.
8 Degras (ed.): *Soviet Documents*, 129–32.

R. H. Clive, the First Secretary of the British Embassy in Stockholm, was instructed "to obtain, in writing, from Litvinov his proposals for an understanding with the British Government."[9] Clive had started informal negotiations when the Anglo-American Chiefs discussed the Russian question during the President's visit in London. Though Wilson showed no "keenness on the idea that Russia should be represented at the Conference" he suggested that the Allies ask Mr. Litvinov "formally and definitely what his proposals were."[1] But before Britain's informal inquiry could be transformed into an official inter-Allied *démarche*, Paris and Rome had to be consulted. The French promptly entered their objections.[2]

Apparently Clive's informal inquiry took the form of a letter, dated December 30, by Dr. Ludwig Meyer, Judge of Christiana's Supreme Court, asking the Soviet government to specify the terms on which it would be prepared to settle. As a preface to his reply of January 10 Litvinov not unreasonably asserted that since the Allies were the "attacking party" it was really their turn to formulate terms instead of persistently ignoring Soviet overtures.

Even so, Litvinov gladly proceeded to unfold his government's views. To begin with, the Soviets were "willing to give the Allies' friends the necessary guarantees for their safety and an amnesty for past offences." Also, since the end of foreign intervention would bring the end of the Civil War, the restrictions on civil liberties could be considerably relaxed during the transitional phase. With regard to Poland, the Ukraine, and other parts of the former Russian Empire, the Soviet government would "abstain from any violation of the rights of these provinces to self-determination" provided other foreign powers refrained from intervening in "the party or class strife in these provinces." Furthermore, in addition to reconsidering some of the recent decrees affecting Russia's financial obligations toward other nations, the Soviet government would "desist from carrying on any propaganda in the Allied countries which could be construed as interference with their internal affairs." Finally, Litvinov closed with a disarmingly naïve yet forceful summary of Lenin's demands: the Allies should "discontinue all direct or indirect military operations against Soviet Russia, all direct or indirect material assistance to Russian or other forces operating against the Soviet government, and also every kind of economic warfare and boycott."[3]

[9] Imperial War Cabinet 45, December 23, 1918 (p.m.).
[1] Imperial War Cabinet 47, December 30, 1918 (p.m.).
[2] Affaires Etrangères to French Embassy in London, January 2, 1919, Quai d'Orsay, File Z 619–5; and British Empire Delegation 1, January 13, 1919 (a.m.).
[3] *The Herald*, February 22, 1919. In this same letter Litvinov referred to his recent appeal to President Wilson; he also indicated that he had outlined Soviet peace terms in a conversation with Dr. Ludwig Meyer on December 25. There is good reason to believe that the general outlines of these terms had reached the Allied

The President, for his part, brought Litvinov's inquiries before the American Peace Commissioners immediately upon his return from London to Paris. After a meeting of nearly an hour on New Year's Day, the U. S. Delegation "agreed to send W. H. Buckler to Copenhagen [i.e., Stockholm] to listen to what the representatives of the present Soviet government of Russia have to say in their own behalf."[4] Buckler was promptly summoned to Paris from London in order to receive his instructions. By January 8 the United States Embassy in London was informed by telephone "that it was the desire of the President that Mr. Buckler proceed at the earliest possible moment to Stockholm in conformity with the instructions given him during his recent visit to Paris," and that, if possible, Buckler should return to Lausanne by January 20.[5]

In a rather remarkable letter to his Secretary of State, Woodrow Wilson indicated that he had more than just a casual interest in this exploratory mission.

> I must say that I still see no great advantage to be derived from words and public statements in the matter of Bolshevism. What I am at present keenly interested in is in finding the interior of their minds, and I hope that you have been able to get hold of Buckley [sic][6] and get him started to the interviews which we discussed the other day and *which I regard as of capital importance.*
>
> The real thing with which to stop Bolshevism is food [italics mine].

Lansing promptly reported that Buckler was expected to arrive in Stockholm on January 13.[7]

Buckler had three conferences with Litvinov: from 9 to 10:30 p.m. on January 14; from 3:30 to 6:00 p.m. on the fifteenth; and from 12:15 to 4:00 p.m. on the sixteenth. Arthur Ransome was present throughout the entire third session and also spent some time alone with Buckler. The U. S. agent made careful notes of the substance of these

---

capitals by the end of the year. It should be noted that at this very same time Chicherin was also still pushing for an accommodation with the Ebert regime. See pp. 238–50 above.

[4] House Diary, January 1, 1919.

[5] Lansing Diary, January 3 and 7, 1919; and *F.R.,1919,Russia,* 4.

[6] Wilson misnamed his envoy Buckley and Secretary Lansing spoke of him first as Butler and then also as Buckley. Lansing Diary, January 3 and 7, 1919. Needless to say, Henry White knew the correct name of his half-brother; and so did House, who since mid-1917 had been in close contact with the special counselor in the London Embassy. "I took occasion to express my high regard for Buckler and the work which he had been doing since the beginning of the war." House Diary, January 1, 1919.

[7] Wilson to Lansing, January 10, 1919, and Lansing to Wilson, January 13, 1919, in Wilson Papers, VIII A:9 and 10.

talks; in turn, Litvinov "read and initialed [these notes] as a sign that they accurately represented his view."[8]

According to these notes, Buckler explained at the very start of their confidential conversations that he "was merely a private telephone through which Litvinov could supplement his telegram of December 24, but that he had no authority to make proposals of any kind." Not surprisingly the Soviet plenipotentiary readily agreed to proceed with what became a monologue rather than a dialogue.

Litvinov first sought to explicate his government's changing attitude toward the President. Immediately following the November Revolution they had been encouraged and impressed by Wilson's pronouncements. But then came the intervention as well as the Sisson forgeries. Smarting under these hostile acts the Soviet government recently issued a "propagandist and discourteous" note, which it now regarded "as a mistake." The Christmas Eve appeal was designed to "make it plain to the U.S. that the Soviet government was genuinely anxious for real and permanent peace."

However, even though the Soviet government was prepared to make concessions on every point, it was not about to surrender.

> They wish to ascertain whether the total destruction of the Bolshevik party is an aim of the Allies and of the United States—if so, the present struggle must continue—or whether the Allies and the United States really desire peace and [have the] willingness to compromise. If they *do*—which L. fears is not the case—they can easily have it. . . . [For the Soviets] the ending of the present war and the economic restoration of Russia were objects so desirable that they justified some compromise, on mere financial and industrial matters, such as was made under German pressure at Brest-Litovsk.

Litvinov suggested that delegates from both sides could work out the details for such a compromise. The Soviet delegates would be most conciliatory since apart from wanting peace the regime realized that it required technical assistance as well as "foreign machinery and manufactured imports."

Significantly, however, Litvinov did not hesitate to tackle more delicate political issues.

> If peace were once made Russian propaganda would no longer menace the countries not sharing the Bolshevik doctrines. The war declared by the Allies has called forth this revolutionary propa-

---

[8] Notes by W. H. Buckler of conversations with Mr. Litvinov in Stockholm, January 14 to 16, 1919, handwritten copy in Buckler Papers; typed copy in House Papers, 31:205. This typed copy is part of an enlarged report submitted in Paris on January 29, 1919, which also included a summary of Buckler's conversation with Ransome as well as a copy of Litvinov's letter of January 10 to Ludwig Meyer.

ganda as a measure of retaliation, just as it has produced violence and terror in other forms; but these will all cease as soon as the war stops.

It simply was not true that his government maintained "a sort of secret Salvation Army for spreading the Bolshevik gospel." To be sure, propaganda had been used against Imperial Germany, Soviet Russia's foremost enemy. But during his eight months in England as his government's representative, Litvinov had conducted "no political propaganda." And the Soviets knew only too well that "no amount of propaganda could produce" revolutionary conditions in Western countries not ripe for revolution.

Furthermore, the government would extend an amnesty "to those who had taken part in attacks upon Russia." Since such persons were few in number "they might be permitted to leave Russia for foreign countries."[9] As for Poland, Finland, and the Ukraine, the Soviets were prepared to grant them full rights of self-determination. "So long, however, as foreign powers support the capitalist classes in those countries, the Russians feel justified in supporting the laboring classes."

In their third and last meeting Litvinov returned to what he considered the very crux of the situation: "the only real question was whether the Allies and the United States would allow the Soviet government to exist, [and that] if they would, an agreement would not be difficult to reach." For special emphasis Litvinov ominously claimed that "even persons friendly to the old system realized that there would be danger of starvation and anarchy if the present machine, however imperfect, were overthrown by force." It was on this last point that Ransome expanded in his talk with Buckler.

Actually, Ransome thought that even without active military intervention Soviet power could, in time, be broken, provided the Allies continued their blockade and their material aid to the Whites.

> But assuming this to be feasible, he pointed out that intervention could not thereupon cease. . . . The Allies would then have smashed the only [effective] government . . . and would be faced with a Russia seething with anarchy and requiring to be policed. No government there could exist without strong military support. . . . The effort of policing Russia—in addition, perhaps, to policing parts of Germany and Austria—would produce in Allied countries and in the United States those very conditions of strain and discontent which favor the growth of Bolshevism. Ransome and L. both said that this fact was fully realized by a large class of Bolshevists, who oppose any compromise with the Allies and long for more

9 Around mid-January Chicherin addressed an open radio telegram to Washington assuring Senator Hitchcock that the safety of the Czechs could be guaranteed by mutual agreement. See *F.R.,1919,Russia,* 8–9.

strenuous Allied intervention. . . . A continuance of intervention by the Allies would, in Ransome's opinion, play into the hand of these extremists. On the other hand . . . the more statesmanlike and intelligent Bolsheviks, like Lenin, Chicherin, Vorovsky and L. himself preferred to reach that millennium by slower stages, and, provided their Soviet form of government would be preserved, favor an understanding with the Allies.

Buckler was sufficiently impressed with Ransome's views to recommend his being summoned to Paris.[1]

All this time the Russian question never ceased to occupy the Peace Conference in Paris. In an effort to counteract the Anglo-American appeasers, Pichon and Sonnino insisted that the Council of Ten give a hearing to the anti-Bolshevik side.[2] Accordingly, Joseph Noulens, the former French Ambassador to Russia, was invited to testify on January 20; and the following day, the Council interrogated M. de Scavenius, the former Danish Minister in Petrograd. Both were passionately anti-Bolshevik, emphasized the peril hanging over Europe, vacillated between magnifying either the strength or the fragility of the Red regime, and advocated the dispatch of additional Allied military contingents.[3]

It was a few minutes after the Council dismissed de Scavenius that Woodrow Wilson, who except for one question[4] had not participated in the questioning of the ex-Ambassadors, claimed the floor. He had just been handed Buckler's telegraphic summary of his interviews in Stockholm, which he now proceeded to read to the meeting. Before adjourning, it was decided to take up Buckler's report at the afternoon session.[5]

That afternoon the conciliators once again tried to surmount the opposition of the intransigents. Fortified by Buckler's report Wilson and Lloyd George pressed ahead with the Borden plan.[6] Before coming to this session, they agreed that Wilson would propose a modification of the British plan, perhaps in order to serve notice that they would retreat no further.

Clemenceau had stubbornly refused to have the Bolsheviks in the French capital. According to both Lloyd George and Balfour he

---

[1] However, once the Prinkipo invitation had gone out, Ransome's presence in Paris was no longer required. Also, British officials were leery of "his well-known Bolshevik sympathies." W. H. Buckler to Georgina Buckler, January 22, 29, and 30, 1919, Buckler Papers; and *F.R.,1919,Russia*, 38.

[2] *F.R.,P.C.,1919*, III, 583–4, 593.

[3] Ibid., 623–42.

[4] "President Wilson enquired whether it must be understood that all but the intellectual minority were with the Bolsheviks. Mr. Noulens said that what he wished to convey was that all the well-to-do classes, including the richer peasants and working men, were against the Bolsheviks." Ibid., 624.

[5] For the text of this telegraphic report see *F.R.,P.C.,1919*, III, 643–6.

[6] It is an exaggeration to say that "the Buckler meeting with Litvinov was what eventually swung [this] meeting in favor of Prinkipo." See *The Bullitt Mission to Russia: Testimony Before the Committee on Foreign Relations of the United States Senate of William C. Bullitt* (New York: Huebsch; 1919), 6.

claimed that "Ministers and members of the Chamber were unanimously opposed to the Bolsheviks coming here and . . . that if the Conference forced that course upon him, he would have to resign." To circumvent this obstacle the American and British delegates proposed that the various Russian groups should be asked to send their delegates to Salonica or Lemnos instead of to Paris. Under this revised plan, in addition to being kept from Clemenceau's doorsteps, the Bolshevik emissaries could reach the new meeting place by sea, "without passing through other countries." (No need for sealed trains!) As a further inducement Lloyd George offered that pending negotiations the withdrawal of English and Imperial forces "would be temporarily withheld" and that "as regards any steps . . . to protect against invasion any independent state about to be set up, we should be prepared to cooperate."[7]

The Tiger yielded both because under these conditions the meeting in the Eastern Mediterranean would not be incompatible with the *cordon sanitaire* and because he was determined that there "should not be even the appearance of disagreement" among the victors.

Consequently it fell to Sonnino to speak for the irreconcilables. He argued that all Russian groups, except the Bolsheviks, were represented in Paris; and that men like Sazonov were ready to testify right then and there. Since the Allies were fighting the Bolsheviks, they were "enemies" and should not be heard.

> He would point out that, for Italy, and probably for France also, as M. Clemenceau had stated, it was in reality a question of self-defense. He thought that even a partial recognition of the Bolsheviks would strengthen their position, and, speaking for himself, he thought that Bolshevism was already a serious danger in his country.

Accordingly, rather than treat with the Bolsheviks, the Allies should assist all the anti-Bolshevik groups to form an effective striking force, "provided they pledged themselves not to serve the forces of reaction."

When Sonnino proposed that in addition to supplying arms, food, and money the Allies should send soldiers, Lloyd George asked a very practical question, one that he had previously put to the British Empire Delegation: Where would these troops come from?

> Lloyd George said the British Empire now had some 15,000 to 20,000 men in Russia. M. de Scavenius had estimated that some 150,000 additional men would be required, in order to keep the anti-Bolshevik Governments from dissolution. And General Franchet d'Esperey also insisted on the necessity of Allied assistance. Now Canada had decided to withdraw her troops, because the Canadian

7 British Empire Delegation 2, January 20, 1919 (p.m.); and Lloyd George: *Truth*, I, 346, 353-4.

soldiers would not agree to stay and fight against the Russians. Similar trouble had also occurred amongst the other Allied troops. And he felt certain that, if the British tried to send any more troops there, there would be mutiny.

M. Sonnino suggested that volunteers might be called for.

Mr. Lloyd George, continuing, said that it would be impossible to raise 150,000 men in that way. He asked, however, what contribution America, Italy, and France would make towards the raising of this army.

President Wilson and M. Clemenceau each said none.

Mr. Orlando agreed that Italy could make no further contributions.

At this point Orlando, who had just returned from settling the cabinet crisis stemming from Nitti's resignation, interceded. He could do no less than agree with Sonnino and Clemenceau that Bolshevism "constituted a grave danger to all Europe," particularly to his own country.

> Italy was now passing through a period of depression, due to war weariness. But Bolsheviks could never triumph there, unless they found a favorable medium, such as might be produced either by profound patriotic disappointment in their expectations as to the rewards of the war, or by an economic crisis. Either might lead to revolution, which was equivalent to Bolshevism.

But since Italy was in no position to provide more soldiers (Orlando had to keep one eye on the Italian Left and the other on the Adriatic) he rallied to the modified British plan. To make it unanimous Baron Makino also gave his assent.[8]

Indeed, the Conference opted for this compromise solution in large measure because just then the Allies lacked the military power for a direct challenge to the Reds. Even the most ardent interventionists doubted the reliability of the Whites and the Big Four were agreed that they could not raise the additional 150,000 troops which would be required for an offensive.[9]

Wilson was asked to draft the note of invitation. He was the natural choice for this delicate assignment: he had moved the amended proposal and he alone could present it to the world as an act of good will and conciliation.

> The single object the representatives of the Associated Powers have in mind in their discussions of the course they should pursue with regard to Russia has been to help the Russian people, not to hinder them, or to interfere in any manner with their right to settle their own affairs in their own way. . . . *They recognize the abso-*

8 *F.R.,P.C.,1919*, III, 647–53, 663–8.
9 Lansing to Polk, January 27, 1919, in *F.R.,1919,Russia*, 35.

*lute right of the Russian people to direct their own affairs without
dictation or direction of any kind from outside.* They do not wish to
exploit or make use of Russia in any way. *They recognize the
revolution without reservation, and will in no way, and in no
circumstances, aid or give countenance to any attempt at a counterrevolution* [italics mine].[1]

Wilson rightly claimed that the Conference could not ignore Russia's
Civil War because "Europe and the world cannot be at peace if Russia is
not."

The powers had a dual purpose: (1) to promote agreement among
the opposing factions in the Civil War, to be followed by (2) the
reintegration of Russia into the community of nations. Unfortunately
even the sponsors of this scheme were not agreed on the best method to
achieve the first aim. Whereas Lloyd George thought that the Allies
should press for acceptance by all groups of a constituent assembly,
Wilson wanted the Allies to restrict themselves to providing their good
offices of mediation and conciliation.[2] His draft, therefore, had to be
vague and ambiguous.

Who was to be invited? Surely, this was not only a highly sensitive
but also a very complex issue. In an effort to avoid further controversy
this part of Wilson's text had to be equally open-ended.

> The Associated Powers invite every organized group that is now
> exercising, or attempting to exercise, political authority or military
> control anywhere in Siberia, or within the boundaries of European
> Russia as they stood before the war just concluded (except in
> Finland) to send . . . three representatives for each group.

This formulation was designed to accommodate two categories of opponents in the Civil War.

The first category consisted of rival political governments in Russia,
in particular the Bolshevik regime and the governments organized to
fight it. Among the latter, the governments of Omsk, Ekaterinodar, and
Archangel stood out and there might yet be others. But since the Social
Revolutionaries, Mensheviks, and even Cadets were not prominently
represented in any of these governments, perhaps their spokesmen
should be admitted as well.

The second category was even less clear-cut in that it included all
the nationalities of the Russian Empire that had established governments of their own. The independence of Poland and Finland alone
could be taken for granted, and both were expressly exempt from this
all-Russian gathering, even though their borders remained to be settled.
But with the criterion for inclusion being neither *de facto* nor *de jure*
recognition, at a minimum the list of nascent nation states would

---

[1] For the text of the invitation see *F.R.,P.C.,1919*, III, 676–7.
[2] Cf. ibid., 652.

include Estonia, Latvia, Lithuania, the Ukraine, Georgia, Armenia, and Azerbaijan. But were there others? And was it all that clear as to who should be admitted to speak for the Ukraine?[3]

One way of circumventing these enormous difficulties was to draft the invitation in ambiguous terms. Another was to transmit it publicly—by radio and press—rather than in the form of individual notes. This subterfuge enabled the Allies to avoid recognizing not only the Bolsheviks but also all the other parties. Significantly even the smallest anti-Bolshevik group was allocated the same number of seats—three—as the Soviet regime, which controlled the bulk of Russia and Russians.

As it turned out this obstacle of identifying and admitting the groups was not nearly as insurmountable as the explicitly stated preconditions for the conference. All groups were invited only

> provided . . . there is a truce amongst the parties invited, and all armed forces anywhere sent or directed against any people outside the boundaries of European Russia as they stood before the war, or against Finland, or against any people or territory whose autonomous action is in contemplation in the fourteen articles upon which the present negotiations are based, shall be meanwhile withdrawn, and aggressive military action cease.

Inevitably a truce is considerably more complicated to arrange and supervise in internal than in external war. In this instance these natural difficulties were vastly compounded by the demand for withdrawal which applied only to the Bolsheviks and not to their enemies. In other words, the Reds were asked to withdraw from the Baltic provinces and to stay out of the Ukraine and the Caucasus, which could feed and supply them. As for the Allies, they proposed to maintain their military and naval bases in Russia, to continue their assistance to all anti-Bolshevik groups, and to keep up the blockade.

In any event, representatives of all Russian groups were expected to meet representatives of the principal powers by February 15 on the Princes Islands in the Sea of Marmora. Why Wilson chose Prinkipo over Salonica or Lemnos is still open to conjecture. One set of detractors complained that Bolsheviks should not be invited to a vacation island full of fine hotels and endowed with a splendid view of the coastline of Europe and Asia; others thought it most inappropriate to put anyone but Bolsheviks on an island whose Byzantine convents once had housed prisoners whose heads were shaved and whose eyes were gouged out. However, still others half-complimented Wilson for his choice: nearby was another small island to which, before the war, the

---

[3] Cf. R. H. Lord's memorandum on "Representation of Russian Governments at the Conference," January 20, 1919, National Archives, Document 183.9 Russia/16, and "Outline of Tentative Report and Recommendations Prepared by the Intelligence Section in Accordance with Instructions for President and the Plenipotentiaries," January 21, 1919, 15 ff., House Papers, 29:20, and Wilson Papers.

Young Turks had relegated thousands of *pariah* dogs from Constantinople either ravenously to devour each other or simply to starve. At a minimum, all the opponents of Prinkipo gave full credit to Clemenceau for having made the best of a bad situation, for having kept Radek-type revolutionaries out of Paris or some other tension-ridden capital of Western or Northern Europe.

No sooner was the invitation released to the press and flashed over the wireless in the form of a press communiqué than the opponents of the scheme set out to sabotage it. The range of opposition was wide and varied, and while part of it was spontaneous, another part was premeditated. The Russian Political Conference rushed to announce that it would never sit down with the Bolsheviks; its principals inside Russia instantly followed suit, probably with the encouragement of local Allied officials. In the Allied nations the Prinkipo proposal not only galvanized the Right into furious public protests but also prompted the interventionists in the foreign offices and war offices to sabotage it from within their administrations.

As this storm of opposition rose about them, the Big Four did relatively little to counteract it. That Pichon should have used the full resources of the Quai d'Orsay to encourage the *émigrés*, the Whites, and the nationalities to thwart Prinkipo was hardly surprising. But even Wilson and Lloyd George failed to apply pressure for acceptance of the summons among the anti-Bolshevik Russian groups. Had these groups been put on notice that future aid would be contingent on participation in this exploratory round table they might well have thought twice before refusing.[4]

Using the right-wing press to particularly good advantage, the "official" *émigrés* in Paris defiantly declared that they would under no circumstances have any truck with their treacherous enemies. The very evening of the announcement Sazonov told Pertinax that he personally would boycott Prinkipo, confident that Kolchak and Denikin fully endorsed his stand. In an interview with a correspondent of the *Matin* he was altogether categorical: "Never, and under no circumstances, will I go to Prinkipo. How dare the [Conference] even propose it? The Allies are quite wrong in assuming that in Russia political parties are fighting over a political principle or idea. What is face to face is anarchy and civilization, crime and the right to live. On one side are the murderers, on the other their victims."[5] Simultaneously Sazonov and Lvov authorized the correspondent of the *Daily Telegraph* to announce that the governments of Omsk, Ekaterinodar,

[4] Cf. E. J. Dillon: *The Inside Story of the Peace Conference* (New York: Harper; 1920), 355–60; and Sisley Huddleston: *Peacemaking at Paris* (London: Unwin; 1919), 54.
[5] *Echo de Paris*, January 23, 1919; *le Matin*, January 24, 1919; *l'Action Française* and *Journal des Débats*, January 25–26, 1919.

and Archangel would never designate delegates to meet with "the assassins of our brothers and the gravediggers of our fatherland."[6]

The "unofficial" *émigré* organizations balked with equal vehemence. In a widely disseminated memorandum to Clemenceau in his capacity as President of the Peace Conference, they accused the Big Four of abetting a band of criminals who after usurping power with the help of German gold had betrayed the Allies during the war. Men of "courage and honor" could never accept a truce which would leave the Red terror intact. Besides, the *pourparlers* in the Sea of Marmora could not possibly "reconcile the irreconcilable."[7] With the same haste Miliukov told Reuters in London that the only way to solve the Russian problem was to overthrow the Bolsheviks,[8] all liberal-minded Russians being agreed that this could be achieved provided the military effort be guided by a strong "directory." The time to argue about political reforms and self-determination was after rather than before the reestablishment of order.[9]

Meanwhile word filtered out of Russia that the White governments felt perplexed, betrayed, and discouraged. According to one report the Omsk government, though "unquestionably opposed," might consider sending delegates in order to "comply with the wishes of the Allies." But elsewhere in Siberia a survey of opinion by E. L. Harris, the U. S. Consul General at Irkutsk, was not nearly so optimistic. In an effort to head off a refusal Polk cabled Lansing that since the call for Prinkipo threatened to destroy the morale of the Whites perhaps the Allies should first recognize the Omsk government. At a minimum "some statement" should be made to reassure Kolchak and Denikin, in spite of the fact that "Kolchak was probably a reactionary." In reply Polk and Harris were told that recognition "might follow but could not precede" Prinkipo.[1]

The Provisional Government at Archangel was equally shocked at being dealt with "on the same basis as the Bolsheviks." Only a few Social Revolutionaries and Social Democrats—now out of the government—considered going to Prinkipo, determined to expose its futility. Rather than work for acceptance DeWitt C. Poole, the American Chargé, protested his government's appeasement by submitting his resignation. Needless to say, he was urgently—and successfully—prevailed upon to stay on "in order to prevent grave, and perhaps disastrous effects upon the morale of American troops" in the Archangel

---

[6] Cited in *le Temps,* January 26, 1919. The correspondent himself reports this incident in Dillon: *Inside Story,* 358.

[7] This protest was signed, among others, by the Ligue des Russes fidèles à la patrie et aux alliances and by the Leagues for the Regeneration of Russia (in Cooperation with the Allies) in Paris, in Switzerland, and in Rome.

[8] *Le Temps,* January 26, 1919.

[9] Paul Miliukov writing in *The New Europe,* February 13, 1919, 109–12.

[1] *F.R.,1919,Russia,* 38–9, 44–6, 68, 71.

district.[2] Like Poole, the French and British agents in Ekaterinodar did not exert themselves to win Denikin to Prinkipo.

Finally, on February 12, "the unified governments of Siberia, Archangel, and Southern Russia" sent a formal note to the Peace Conference. Over the signatures of Sazonov and Chaikovsky they turned down the invitation, claiming that "between the Bolsheviks and the national Russian groups no conciliation was possible" and that by accepting all Russian patriots as well as the Allies would suffer "irreparable moral harm."[3] By this time the Allies had already been rebuffed by the delegation of the Georgian Republic in Paris; by Syderenko speaking for the Ukrainian Republic; and by Brătianu speaking for Bessarabia, which he claimed had "willingly" seceded from Russia to join Rumania.[4]

In the midst of this widespread boycott some of the American and British advocates of Prinkipo became seriously concerned. Buckler had just returned to Paris. Accompanied by Bullitt and on instructions of the American Peace Commissioners he went to see Philip Kerr, the Prime Minister's private secretary, to report on his talks with Litvinov and to test British intentions. Kerr and his visitors agreed that British and American troops should be withdrawn as soon as possible from Archangel—in mid-year, following the spring thaw—where the situation was deteriorating rapidly; they also agreed that their governments should meet the representatives of the Soviet government "even if no other Russian representatives should accept the recent Peace Conference invitation."[5]

The French did not share this view. To be sure, Clemenceau appointed two representatives to Prinkipo: M. Conty, Ambassador in Copenhagen, and General Rampont. In this regard he was in step with his Allies. Wilson appointed George D. Herron and William Allen White; Lloyd George asked Sir Robert Borden to represent Britain and the Empire; and Orlando designated Marchese della Pietro Torretta, former Ambassador to Russia.

But except for this formality, the French dragged their feet. Their closely censored press kept up a fiercely hostile barrage, and the Quai d'Orsay used promises of continued aid to backstop the intransigence of

---

[2] Ibid., 35–8, 42–3, 47, 51–2.

[3] Ibid., 53–4.

[4] Ibid., 49, 70; and *F.R.,P.C.,1919*, III, 733.

[5] *F.R.,P.C.,1919*, XI, 5–6, 9–10, 14; *F.R.,1919,Russia*, 38; Buckler to Georgina Buckler, January 31, 1919, Buckler Papers. Bullitt advised House that "it seemed dignified and honorable at this moment to inform the Archangel Government that since it cannot agree to the Allied proposal . . . we shall decline to support it further with arms, but will make provisions for the safety of all Russians who are willing to remain at Archangel." Bullitt to House, January 30, 1919, in *Bullitt Mission to Russia*, 17.

the Ukrainian and other anti-Soviet governments.[6] Presently Herron reported from Geneva that judging by conferences with visitors from all parts of the East "everywhere French officials have been urging all parties and nationalities to refuse to participate in Prinkipo."[7]

Even so, there were also some positive responses. The governments of Estonia, Latvia, and Lithuania, quite apart from being on the brink of disaster, were beyond French influence. All three nascent Baltic republics sent conditional acceptances: they would go to Prinkipo to conclude peace with Russia under the auspices of the Allied Powers, provided their independence was recognized and admittance was granted them to the Peace Conference. In other words, they looked to Prinkipo to help secure the same status of independence that Poland and Finland had secured without such negotiations.[8]

Of course, from the very outset there was particularly intense speculation and curiosity about the Soviet response. Would Lenin accept this proposal? And, if so, since it was loaded in favor of his enemies, for what purpose? Even among the Big Ten there were conflicting guesses: Sonnino thought that Bolsheviks would welcome the summons, Lansing very much doubted it. Whatever his response, Lenin was certain to be vilified.

Since October it had been apparent that Lenin gave first priority to delaying or preventing a combined assault by the capitalist states. Certainly by late January, when even the Soviets realized that Germany was not about to go Bolshevik, he was in a defensive rather than in an offensive frame of mind. As a supreme realist his minimum and immediate goal was a breathing spell. This time could then be used to consolidate the Bolshevik regime while fostering dissension among its enemies.

Actually Lenin and Trotsky were not worried about the winter season. They knew that the Red Army could continue its advances until the end of winter; but as of spring, with the weather more propitious for offensive military operations, the Allies and their satellites could be expected to strike. In other words Lenin was prepared to forego a limited advance now in the hope of forestalling a large-scale assault in April. He may well have estimated that such a military attack might cost him considerably more than the concessions he would have to agree to over the conference table.

Besides, having launched the peace offensive, the Bolsheviks could hardly ignore its first breakthrough. The Prinkipo summons confirmed Lenin and Chicherin in a diplomatic course designed to take advantage

---

[6] *Bullitt Mission*, 32.

[7] George Herron to Hugh Wilson, January 12, 1919, and George Herron to Colonel House, February 13, 1919, in House Papers, 31:218, 7:15.

[8] *F.R.,1919,Russia*, 50, 53, 72–3.

of the rift between Wilson and Clemenceau; they also meant to capitalize on opposition to intervention among the Allied peoples. In any case, however disadvantageous the terms of this invitation, the Bolsheviks could not spurn it without fatally damaging their own peace offensive: their enemies would find it that much easier to question the sincerity of their peace professions and to hold them responsible for continuing war and bloodshed.

Even so, given the highly unfavorable terms of the invitation, Lenin could hardly appear overly eager for fear that his eagerness would be mistaken for weakness. As it turned out, once he did accept, Alfred Capus and others declared that Lenin was hurrying to Prinkipo because he was doomed without immediate Allied recognition.[9] In any case, on January 24 he advised Trotsky that he would have "to go to Wilson" and that in order to improve his bargaining position for this second Brest Litovsk he should quickly seize a few more cities.[1] Incidentally, the Red Army occupied Kiev on February 4.

Simultaneously Chicherin prepared the diplomatic groundwork. Unlike all the other Russian groups the Bolsheviks had no established lines of communication to the Allies through which to secure additional information about Prinkipo. Chicherin sent a radiotelegram to V. V. Vorovsky, who was in Stockholm with Litvinov. But since Buckler had returned to Paris[2] and given the tight deadline, this channel might prove ineffective. Therefore Chicherin sent a copy of his radiotelegram to Jean Longuet, editor of the *Populaire,* leader of the *minoritaire*-dominated SFIO, and son-in-law of Karl Marx.

The French censor dutifully kept Chicherin's note from its addressee; but for some mysterious reason it was printed in the *Temps.*[3] Needless to say, this open message to a prominent Socialist leader was singled out as evidence of Lenin's subversive methods and intentions, even though the Allies themselves refused all contact with Moscow on the ground that it might be misinterpreted as recognition of the regime. Apparently the Reds were expected to send an unqualified "we accept" over the radio, without asking any questions.[4]

Instead, Chicherin had the presumption to ask for confirmation of

---

[9] *Le Figaro,* February 6 and 7, 1919.
[1] Lenin sent a wire saying "I am sorry but you will have to go to Wilson." Apparently Trotsky refused this diplomatic assignment, but did step up his military operations. Isaac Deutscher: *The Prophet Armed: Trotsky, 1879–1921* (New York: Oxford; 1954), 429.
[2] Buckler had suggested that perhaps he should stay on in Copenhagen or Stockholm to keep the "telephone" lines open, but he was recalled to Paris. See *F.R.,P.C.,1919,* III, 645–6.
[3] *Le Populaire,* January 27, 1919; and *le Temps,* January 26, 1919.
[4] See Chicherin to Wilson, Moscow, January 29, 1919, in Wilson Papers, VIII A:15. Only the President was willing—unsuccessfully—to have the Council of Ten contact Chicherin in order "to take away the excuse that they had received no invitation." *F.R.,P.C.,1919,* III, 835–6.

the authenticity of the radioed invitation, to suggest a relocation of the conference, and to seek clarification of the proposed truce-*cum*-withdrawal. To make matters worse, he implied that the Soviets were prepared to negotiate from strength.

As for authenticity, Chicherin claimed—not without irony—that the Prinkipo announcement was so *invraisemblable* that pending further information the Soviets might actually have to consider it an "unfounded rumor." Still, should the invitation be authentic, they would give it serious consideration.

The choice of Prinkipo added to their doubt about the authenticity of the Allied announcement. This isolated island held nothing but one-sided disadvantages for the Soviets. It was ideal for highly secret negotiations, with news managed and controlled by the sponsors, with no chance for publicizing the Bolshevik case, and with great obstacles to referring to Moscow for instructions.

But above all the purpose seemed rather unorthodox. The Allies proposed to act as mediators among opposing Russian groups even though they themselves were supporting all anti-Bolsheviks and made no offer to pull back their own troops from Russia. Worse still, the Allies called for a truce and withdrawal by the Bolsheviks at a time when the Red Army was advancing and local Bolshevik revolutions, unaided by this Red Army, were taking place in different parts of the Ukraine.

Longuet promptly requested an appointment with Pichon. On January 31 he and four colleagues—Mistral, Valière, Paul Faure, and Frossard—met with the Foreign Minister. They asked that after checking with the Allied Governments he might provide them with answers to the following questions for transmission to Chicherin: Were the Allies disposed to withdraw their troops, lift the blockade, and cease aid to the anti-Bolshevik groups as a prelude to Prinkipo? Did the invitation apply only to nationalities seeking self-determination or did it also apply to political enemies? Could the conference be held in a Scandinavian country or in Holland? Naturally Pichon refused to answer any of these questions; he even denied Longuet permission to communicate with Chicherin by telegram. But Longuet managed to get around this ban. Via New York he gave Chicherin the questions asked of the Quai d'Orsay, informed him of Pichon's refusal to answer, and reported that while the Whites would boycott Prinkipo the Baltic republics were likely to be there to claim their independence.[5]

Certainly Lenin and Chicherin would not have spurned the invitation if the Whites had accepted. But given the latters' angry warmongering, the Bolsheviks' willingness to talk promised to pay particularly handsome propaganda dividends.

[5] *Le Populaire*, January 31 and February 1–4, 1919.

Thus on February 4, no doubt after consultation with Lenin,[6] the People's Commissar for Foreign Affairs announced his government's readiness "to enter into immediate negotiations on Princes Islands or in any other place with all the Allied Powers jointly or with individual Powers among their number or with any Russian political groups, as the Allied Powers may wish."[7] But Chicherin's acceptance came at the end of a note in which he defined the attitude of the Soviet government "with utmost clarity and frankness."

In fact, this note merely elaborated on the proposals outlined in the letter to Ludwig Meyer and in the Litvinov-Buckler conversations. Chicherin reiterated that in spite of a steadily improving "military and internal" situation the Soviets were eager to "make weighty concessions" in order to secure a cessation of hostilities. But they were determined to stop short of endangering their own regime.

> Since the capacity for resistance of the enemies which Soviet Russia has to fight depends entirely on the aid which they receive from the Allied Powers, and since these are, therefore, its only real adversaries, it is precisely to them that the Russian Soviet Government addresses its statement concerning . . . [its] concessions.
> . . .

Perhaps this vital truth should not have been stated so bluntly. The Allies, in particular Wilson, did not like to be told that they were participants rather than referees in Russia's Civil War. Nor did they want to admit publicly what they admitted among themselves, namely that except for Allied help, the future of the anti-Bolshevik cause in Russia was not very bright.

Chicherin's note divided the negotiable issues into three groups: economic, territorial, and political. In the economic area the Soviet government was prepared to negotiate about the extent of its financial obligations arising from the Russian loans; about guaranteeing "the payment of interest on these loans by a certain amount of raw materials"; and about granting "mining, timber, and other concessions" to the Allied Powers.

As for the territorial issues, Chicherin declared that his government did not "intend to insist on excluding from these negotiations all consideration of the annexation of Russian territories by the Allied Powers." Here Chicherin insolently implied that the Allies had ambitions not unlike those of the Germans at Brest Litovsk. Actually he was not worried about Allied claims on Russian territories; he did not even worry about the secession of border nationalities. His real concern was the future relationship of the Allies to these nascent states along

[6] For a recent Soviet interpretation of Prinkipo see B. E. Stein: *Die russische Frage auf der pariser Friedenskonferenz, 1919–1920* (Leipzig: Koehler & Amelang; 1953), Ch. iv.
[7] For the text of Chicherin's reply see Degras (ed.): *Soviet Documents*, 137–9.

Russia's borders. For Chicherin insisted that "the maintenance in any part of the territory of the former Russian Empire, with the exception of Poland and Finland, of armed forces of the Entente or of forces which are maintained by the Allied Governments or receive financial, technical, military or any other kind of support from them, should also be classified as annexation." In this connection the surprise is not that the Soviets were reluctant to yield the capitalist nations a sphere of influence along her European borders but that they so readily agreed to a Western-supported build-up of Poland and Finland.

Lastly, Chicherin announced that the Soviet government would even consider including "in the general agreement with the Allied Powers an undertaking not to interfere in their internal affairs, observing, however, that it cannot limit the freedom of the revolutionary press."

Chicherin's statement was an easy target. The Soviets failed to meet the essential condition: instead of unconditionally and unilaterally withdrawing and announcing a cease fire, they reserved these vital points for negotiation. Moreover, by seemingly offering money and territory they laid themselves open to the charge that they were trying to ensnare the Allies in undignified horse-trading. But above all, they shifted the accent from Allied-supervised negotiations among the various "indigenous" parties in the Russian Civil War to direct negotiations between the Soviet government and the Paris Peace Conference.

The Russian Political Conference pounced on this fundamental shift, particularly since Soviet-Allied discussions might conceivably take place despite the Whites' boycott. The conference pointed out that Chicherin proposed to make peace with the Allies even though these, far from seeking such a peace, were exclusively concerned with the return of internal order in Russia. In fact, Chicherin's proposition was a "literal replica of the policy which the Bolsheviks had followed at Brest Litovsk." The *émigrés,* speaking for themselves and their principals, protested the Bolsheviks' offer to grant concessions of state property to the Allies; denounced their readiness to cede Russian territories to the Allies as they had ceded them yesterday to Germany; and exposed the Bolshevik attempt to deceive public opinion by promising to pay debts which until recently they had refused to recognize. In sum, with these tactics the Bolsheviks were pursuing one—and only one—goal: "to preserve in Russia a center from which to spread Bolshevik agitation abroad, just as in spite of their promises to Germany they had continued this agitation after the peace of Brest Litovsk."[8]

That flaming revolutionary ideologists in Russia thought along these lines is undeniable. Just then Zinoviev told the Petrograd Soviet

[8] Cited in *le Temps,* February 9, 1919.

that revolutionary Russia could consent to an onerous peace with the Allies since in the last analysis, as the experience of Brest Litovsk had shown, it would be to the Soviets' advantage. "The piece of paper on which this accord will be written could be torn up as easily as the one of Brest."[9] The Bolsheviks had at least as great a need as the Big Ten to reassure various constituencies that compromise was not equivalent to sellout.[1]

In the last analysis the breakdown of Prinkipo was less diplomatic than political. To be sure, neither Lenin nor Sazonov complied with the terms of the invitation. But this failure was due to the fact that the issues between them were not negotiable. More important still, domestic political pressures tied both Wilson's and Lloyd George's hands, assuming they themselves had wished to compel first Pichon and then Sazonov to meet Lenin halfway.

Throughout Europe as well as America the Prinkipo invitation triggered off a new round of public recriminations between the Right and the Left, the interventionists and the anti-interventionists. The debate became so heated primarily because the issue was said to involve much more than just Allied policy toward Soviet Russia: at the Conference the anti-Wilsonians were in danger of losing the first major round to the Wilsonians. Both sides contributed to making the invitation appear considerably more radical than it really was—the Right by denouncing it as a sellout to Bolshevism, the Left by praising it as the beginning of the end of intervention.

In France the Right was livid with rage. Only Jacques Bainville expressed his opposition in measured tones. He argued that in the event of intervention in international politics there could be no all-European or universal perspective, each major power pursuing its own national interests. Canning had consulted Britain's political, economic, and commercial interests when, in 1823, he kept the Sainte Alliance out of Latin America; Lloyd George and Wilson would obey the same canons of international politics by keeping the nascent League out of Russia in 1919.[2]

All the other great editorialists of the Right were in a much less philosophic mood. Pertinax relied on the Whites to see to it that Prinkipo be stillborn and insisted that even if the Allies could not send more troops they should urgently build up the Polish dike. Certainly this was a time for action, not words: "ideology, ignorance, and electoral considerations" simply could no longer be tolerated.[3]

[9] Reported in *Odesski Listok*, February 23, 1919, cited in *Bulletin Périodique de la presse russe*, No. 76 (February 1–16, 1919), April 12, 1919, 2.
[1] Though Lloyd George denounced the offer of financial and territorial concessions as a bribe, he also acknowledged that "all that was for consumption in Russia, and we knew that." *P.D., 112* (February 12, 1919), col. 197.
[2] *L'Action Française*, January 22 and 29, 1919.
[3] *Echo de Paris*, January 23, 1919.

Claude Anet proclaimed that if the Allies really wanted further information a large conclave was the last way to get it. The Bolsheviks could hardly be trusted to provide honest and reliable information about their regime; and to get at their aims, both national and international, the Allies needed merely read the Maximalists' endless theoretical and propaganda tracts. If, then, the Allies were not out to document themselves they could only have one other aim: to make peace among the belligerents of the Russian Civil War. Did they *really* expect Kolchak and Denikin to sit around a common table with Lenin and Trotsky? The failure of this enterprise was a foregone conclusion. Since even Wilson knew this, could it be that he needed to demonstrate the impossibility of reconciliation before then launching an offensive? After all, he had not intervened in the European war until after he had demonstrated the impossibility of reconciling the opposing camps.[4]

August Gauvain in the *Journal des Débats,* Alfred Capus in *Figaro,* and Herbette in the *Temps* were equally hostile. Moreover, they and their colleagues once again denounced the Socialists for trying to make political capital out of a decision that was not in the national interest of France.

And, in fact, the Socialists did have a field day. Wilson remained the same; he continued to speak the language they expected of him. "Once again the philosopher had come out of his ivory tower, and none of the Allies dared oppose him." Even though they were grateful to Lloyd George for his support, it was Wilson who saved France from a new war in the East, just as he had saved her in 1917–18. To be sure, he failed to have the Bolshevik regime recognized as the sole legitimate government of Russia. However, he scored two important points: unofficial recognition and the postponement of military intervention.[5] It goes without saying that the Socialists pleaded with the Bolsheviks to trust Wilson's proposal. But even if the police had not interfered with their public demonstrations against intervention,[6] the SFIO lacked the power and influence effectively to countervail the Quai d'Orsay and its noisy claque in Parliament and in the press.

In Italy *Avanti* juxtaposed Pichon's recent proclamation that France would not "compromise with crime" to the Prinkipo invitation, crediting the change to the fact that the "Soviets were stronger than the Entente." Even Treves thought there was no alternative to inviting the Bolsheviks to Paris. But such extreme views were overshadowed by

---

[4] *Le Petit Parisien,* January 24, 1919. All along Anet wrote violently anti-Bolshevik articles under such titles as "The Bolshevik Epidemic" or "The Bolshevik Contagion." Finally, toward mid-February, he left for Warsaw to report on Bolshevism from what he considered the front line.

[5] *L'Humanité* and *le Populaire,* January 23–25, 1919.

[6] *Le Populaire,* February 1, 1919.

more modest assessments. Orlando's *Epoca,* the *Secolo,* the *Messagero,* and the *Tempo* not only hoped the Soviets would accept but also hailed the invitation as "Wilson's first victory." All these left-liberal papers could not have hoped for a better omen at the very start of the Peace Conference. On the other hand, the more sedate and conservative *Corriere della Sera* and *Tribuna* were considerably less enthusiastic about this "strange compromise." O. Malagodi felt that a skeptical Conference had only reluctantly supported Wilson, who tended to consider Bolshevism as a Russian instead of as a universal phenomenon. He trusted that the Conference would soon recognize the peril for what it really was and either "destroy or isolate" it.

However, in Italy also, the fiercest reservations were voiced by the extreme Right. Rather than simply oppose Prinkipo, the *Giornale d'Italia* redefined its purpose: the Bolsheviks would be forced to choose between accepting a democratic government and facing instant destruction. The editors thought they recognized Wilson's style and procedures; he had once before posed as an impartial arbiter! Similarly, the *Idea Nazionale* and the *Resto del Carlino* claimed that under the compromise invitation the Russians were summoned before an Allied tribunal. Thus the principle of intervention in Russian affairs was firmly established. As yet the Allies were not intervening militarily; but they had started a diplomatic intervention which could become the prelude to military intervention.[7]

In Britain the Left was as ineffective as in France and Italy: it, too, could only threaten trouble in case further troops were sent, and it, too, lacked the strength to force a withdrawal from Russia. The *Daily News,* the *Manchester Guardian,* the *Labour Leader,* and *Common Cause* rallied behind Lloyd George, half hoping that the Prime Minister was, after all, making a common front with Wilson against both Clemenceau and the hard-faced men in Parliament. In Commons Wedgwood demonstratively congratulated Lloyd George for backing up Wilson and putting the Tiger on notice "that public opinion in this country is absolutely and fundamentally opposed to any further intervention in Russia."[8]

These words of praise were drowned out by fierce censure in the *Morning Post,* the *Daily Mail,* and *The Times.* Much more than Allied-Russian policy was at stake. The Prinkipo proposal was the first overt act of the Peace Conference. By offering to deal with criminals more guilty and brutal than the Germans it dealt a fatal blow to its own moral stature as well as to the League of Nations.[9]

Above all the influential *Times* gradually turned against Lloyd

[7] *Bulletin Périodique de la presse italienne,* No. 103, February 9–10, 1919 (January 19 to February 1, 1919), 2–3.

[8] *P.D.,112* (February 12, 1919), cols. 98–9.

[9] *Morning Post* and *Daily Mail* (Paris), January 24 to February 6, 1919.

George. At first it praised his wisdom of letting Wilson act as sponsor of Prinkipo, and *The Times* thought that if the Bolsheviks met "the other representatives of Russia and the Allies succeeded in . . . ascertaining the will of the Russian people, then the suicide of Bolshevism was assured." On the other hand, should the Bolsheviks refuse to honor the summons they would reveal themselves as enemies of the human race and "whatever steps the Conference may find it desirable to take in order to vindicate its authority could be taken without misgiving and with the assurance that it had popular sympathy behind it."[1]

But then Wickham Steed's influence began to tell. He traced the origins of the Prinkipo invitation to a recent suggestion by a "Jewish writer" in the *Manchester Guardian;* and he held that dealings with Lenin could only stimulate the growth of Bolshevism in Central Europe. Steed charged that the decision had been taken "without any adequate preparation or study"; that neither Sazonov nor the seceding nationalities had been consulted; and that the European situation was so critical that "firm decisions and quick actions" rather than further deliberations were needed.[2]

As on so many other occasions Steed was in intimate contact with the leaders of the successor states. Among these Dr. Karel Kramár, the first Czech Prime Minister and head of the Czech Delegation to the Peace Conference, was one of the first to be up in arms.

> We have 50,000 Czechoslovak troops in Siberia who saved the situation there for the Allies and whom we have, with difficulty, persuaded not to come home at once. This quasi-recognition of the Bolsheviks without our opinion having been asked may upset the whole position. It [Prinkipo] is an unpardonable piece of light-mindedness.[3]

These East Central European circles disseminated their indignation through the pages of the *New Europe,* whose headquarters were in England. According to them Prinkipo was a "poor joke," an insult to all loyal Russians, equivalent to recognition and encouragement of Bolshevism, and the "negation of the principles expounded in the 14 Points." The editor of the *New Europe* claimed to have been prepared for this amateur diplomacy since he knew "something of the secret wires which connect the three great international forces—the Jewish bankers, the Ultramontanes, and a certain wing of the Marxists." The worst mistakes could have been avoided if only the Allies had consulted the *émigré* leaders—from Lvov to Sazonov—as well as spokesmen of "those border nations which are our loyal allies and which will have to

---

[1] January 23 and 24, 1919.
[2] Wickham Steed: *Through Thirty Years,* II, 270; and *The History of the Times,* IV, Pt. I, 465–7.
[3] Cited by Steed: *Thirty Years,* II, 271.

bear the brunt of Bolshevism."[4] Through Steed these voices made themselves heard to a broad British public.

On February 11 anti-Prinkipo spokesmen launched a frontal assault in Commons. Although he was extreme in his views Brigadier General Page Croft seemed to speak for the House when he claimed that "any candidate at the election would agree that the defeat of Bolshevism and Pacifism were the only things that people really cared about at the polls."[5] Anyway, Lloyd George felt that he had to defend and justify his Russian policy.

This was a stiff assignment indeed. He spoke after Lenin's answer and Sazonov's refusal were known but before the Council of Ten had considered them. Lloyd George set out to pacify his right-wing critics without, however, completely yielding to their pressure. He assured the House that there had never been any "proposal to recognize the Bolsheviks." Moreover, he confirmed that the Allies had been giving more than just moral comfort to the Whites.

> We have given them substantial support. They have had financial support. It may be right or it may be wrong, but the Allies have done it. They have had support in ammunition and in guns. Pretty much the whole of their equipment—at least a good deal of it—has been supplied by the Allies. . . . That has been the position up to the present moment. I do not want to go too far, because this is a question which will be under discussion, no doubt, in the next two or three days in Paris, and I do not wish to interfere in the least with the progress of those discussions. . . . Everybody agrees that you cannot intervene . . . [since nothing] short of a big expeditionary force . . . would be of any use. . . . The next proposal is "support of the other Powers." What does that mean? Are you to confine it to munitions? Or are you to send men? America will send neither men, money, nor material, and therefore it practically falls upon France and ourselves. Has anyone calculated the cost?

In closing the Prime Minister expressed the hope that Commons realized the immense difficulty of this Russian problem and urged Members to "turn their minds occasionally from the newspapers . . . just to read up the story of the French Revolution."[6]

Instead of providing strong leadership, Lloyd George vacillated and hedged. In addition to parrying press and Parliamentary critics, he had to fend off Churchill in the Cabinet. Worried by the recent advances of the Red Army, on February 12 the War Minister asked for a stepped-up anti-Bolshevik effort, in preparation for a major push in the spring. The Prime Minister countered that to mount a successful drive, it "was

[4] *The New Europe,* January 13, 1919, 49–52, and February 6, 1919, 73–5.
[5] *P.D.,112* (February 11, 1919), col. 86.
[6] *P.D.,112* (February 12, 1919), cols. 193–8.

necessary to have a million men advancing from Odessa and through Poland," and that material support to the Russian Whites would be of no use unless "at least 150,000 men" were sent along. In any case, since the Russian question would come up in Paris on the fourteenth and should be "decided before President Wilson left for America," he wanted the War Office to prepare a paper "in time for discussion on the next day." That paper should consider four alternatives: intervention, evacuation, a middle policy of material aid to the anti-Bolshevik governments of Russia, and defense of "all those States which depended upon the Great Powers for their protection."[7]

General Wilson dutifully submitted a one-page memo outlining general principles, along with the explanation that for lack of time he could not work out a detailed scheme. The Chief of Staff categorically rejected "the employment of large Allied forces for an offensive campaign in Russia" as being "impracticable . . . under present conditions." He was equally opposed to the other extreme of complete withdrawal of men and matériel. Such an evacuation would "bring complete disaster on all the forces of law and order," proportionately enhancing the Bolshevik forces; the moral effect would be "tantamount to disowning the anti-Bolshevik course." Specifically, such new states as "Estonia, Poland, and Georgia" would be completely overrun and submerged. What Wilson proposed was open "recognition and material support" to raise the morale and the fighting capacity of all anti-Bolsheviks.

> If supplies, equipment, and munitions, together with a comparatively small number of tanks and aeroplanes, manned by volunteer specialists, are sent it will at least enable the Bolsheviks to be held and confined within their present limits. This means their ultimate collapse, since Bolshevism, which can produce nothing, can exist only by extending its system of organized rapine into fresh territory.

Some of this military assistance would go to embryo states—notably Estonia and Poland—which would assist in an "offensive-defensive on the Northern and Western fronts." But the "main offensive efforts" would be undertaken by "Kolchak's Army from the Urals and by Denikin's forces from the region of the Black Sea." In closing General Wilson promised an early estimate of "the numbers available for the various fronts."[8]

The Cabinet met at noon on the thirteenth to consider General Wilson's paper, which turned out to be excessively vague. Not surprisingly, Churchill readily jumped into the breach. After conceding that "unless the Russian forces could be made into an effective army"

---

[7] War Cabinet 531, February 12, 1919 (a.m.).
[8] "Allied Policy in Russia: Memo by the Chief of the Imperial General Staff," February 13, 1919, G.T. 6805, Cabinet 24/75.

the proposed "offensive-defensive" would be impossible, he stressed that it was up to the Allies to animate their wavering minds.

> The Russian morale depended upon the Allies having a decided policy and carrying it out energetically. . . . He would ask the General Staff to say what was the maximum to be attained, within the limits prescribed, *upon the basis that we declared war by a united declaration in Paris.* . . . The Paper would indicate the possibilities in the various theaters of war, consider the question of the approaches to British India. . . . [Moreover] he would make a plain proposition to the U.S., that if they were not prepared to come in and do their share they should have no right to stop the Omsk Government from coming to terms with the Japanese [italics mine].

Edwin Montagu promptly asked Churchill how he would reconcile all-out assistance to the Russians with the proviso that this assistance be kept within limits. Since the scheme presumed a declaration of war, and assuming that even "with material aid and a limited number of troops" from the Allies the Russians were unsuccessful, "what limit could we place upon the reinforcements we should have to send? Would it not prove necessary to send conscripts to support the volunteers?"

Churchill stood his ground without flinching, even after General Wilson interjected that "he could not submit a paper based on such nebulous material." Churchill replied that the General Staff could measure the "prospects of success" should the Allies decide to send out "a message of defiance to the Bolsheviks" specifying the material support "they were prepared to give to the anti-Bolsheviks." In any event, it seemed to Churchill that the "choice was between a forlorne hope . . . and certain disaster."[9]

Since Churchill was the most rabid interventionist in this inner circle, it seems surprising indeed that Lloyd George should have chosen this particular minister to represent him in the Council of Ten on the Russian question. While the Prime Minister eventually claimed that Churchill "very adroitly seized the opportunity created by the absence of President Wilson and myself to go over to Paris," the fact remains that he was sent there by his chief. Moreover, Churchill was instructed to reach the French capital in time to attend a meeting of the Council of Ten at which Wilson would still be present. At that meeting, in the evening of February 14, Churchill, in Balfour's presence, claimed that "in view of the imminent departure of President Wilson the Cabinet had asked him to go over and obtain some decision as to the policy" on Prinkipo. Had Lloyd George intended to continue the search for accommodation he would have instructed the considerably less belli-cose Balfour accordingly; he certainly would not have given *plein pouvoir* to his War Minister whom he subsequently accused of throw-

[9] War Cabinet 532A, February 13, 1919 (noon).

ing "the whole of his dynamic energy and genius into organizing an armed intervention."[1]

On the eve of his trip to Washington to open the 66th Congress Wilson alone refused to abandon the search. With Lloyd George's momentary defection Wilson was isolated in the Council of Ten. At the same time the Congress was turning against him at home.

The Prinkipo proposal received the same mixed reception in America as in all the other Alllied nations. Of course, the liberal press was overjoyed, and so were most Administration papers.[2] Even Villard sent back word that Prinkipo was "an act so cheering, wise, and right-minded as to call for the highest praise to Wilson."[3] But there was little comfort in this editorial approval.

In the short run, Wilson was first and foremost concerned with developments on Capitol Hill. There the Prinkipo invitation produced altogether unhappy results. Hiram Johnson pressed his resolution for withdrawal of troops from Russia with the argument that the proposal proved Wilson's continuing indecision which, in the last analysis, favored the present half-hearted intervention.[4] At the same time, in the House, a number of Congressmen from Midwestern states—most of the American soldiers in Russia were from Wisconsin, Michigan, and Cook County, Illinois—renewed their campaign for withdrawal.[5]

This congressional campaign for withdrawal received public support at a mass rally held on February 2 at the Poli Theater in Washington, just a few blocks from the Capitol. In the presence of several Representatives—at least three—this rally first listened to sympathetic accounts of Soviet Russia by Albert Rhys Williams and Miss Louise Bryant before then recording its opposition to all forms of intervention.[6]

This rally became grist for the mill of the superpatriots and their associates who were in the midst of their offensive against American radicalism of all shades. They seized upon it to prove that the Bolshevik conspiracy was about to attack the vitals of the federal government. Their cause received another boost the very next day: it was on February 3 that the general strike in Seattle was publicly proclaimed. The following day the Senate, by unanimous consent, empowered the Overman Judiciary Subcommittee to investigate Bolshevik propaganda

---

[1] Lloyd George: *Truth*, I, 367–8; *F.R.,P.C.,1919*, III, 1041–2; Churchill: *Aftermath*, 172–3.

[2] *Literary Digest*, February 8, 1919, 16–17. See also Christopher Lasch: *The American Liberals and the Russian Revolution* (New York: Columbia University Press; 1962), 179, 255.

[3] *The Nation* (February 1, 1919), 166.

[4] *Congressional Record*, 65th Congress, 3rd Session, Senate, January 29, 1919, 2261–6.

[5] *Congressional Record*, 65th Congress, 3rd Session, House, February 1, 1919, 2543, as well as 672, 843, 864.

[6] *Congressional Record*, 65th Congress, 3rd Session, Senate, February 3 and 4, 1919, 2606–7, 2650–8.

and subversion.[7] Hereafter the issue of intervention became increasingly enmeshed with the surging Red Scare. With few exceptions the same senators who encouraged or condoned Red-baiting at home tended to advocate a tough policy toward Soviet Russia. At a minimum they could be relied upon not to favor withdrawal or accommodation.

Presently even Johnson and Borah began to shield themselves from the charge of pro-Bolshevism. Especially Borah now argued that the best way to check "Bolshevism, anarchism, and IWW-ism" was not by intervention but by "preaching Americanism from every rostrum . . ., by a rebaptism of national pride . . ., by working out more just and humane laws, by effectuating a more equitable distribution of our prosperity, and by filling with greater national interest our whole social life."[8]

To be sure, Senators Lodge and Sherman now made common cause with Johnson and Borah in that they voted in favor of Johnson's resolutions (Nos. 411 and 444) calling for withdrawal of troops. On February 7 the vote went against Johnson by only five votes; a week later, on February 14, there was a tie and Vice-President Thomas Marshall had to cast his vote in order to have the motion tabled.[9]

But Lodge and Sherman were not voting in favor of an accommodation with Bolshevik Russia. Lodge reluctantly agreed that it might not be a proper function for America to intervene in Russia for the establishment of an acceptable government. But he quite emphatically objected to the Soviets "invading the territory of people like the Esthonians, Livonians, and Lithuanians . . . and to their interference with those governments and with Poland." In fact, he even declared that "those people should have our support." Lodge came fairly close to defining Wilson's own purposes and yet for partisan reasons he voted with Johnson. As for Senator Sherman, his motivation was equally partisan. He wanted to get at Wilson by condemning the military intervention in northern Russia as an act of executive usurpation: it was as "complete an assumption of dictatorial power as that of Napoleon when he was First Consul and seized the reins of authority."[1]

Certainly the overwhelming majority of Senators in the closing session of the 65th Congress and the opening session of the 66th was not in favor of being soft on Bolshevism either at home or abroad. More likely than not the Senate favored a policy of active and tough—not just passive—containment of Soviet Bolshevism just short of in-

---

[7] *Congressional Record,* 65th Congress, 3rd Session, Senate, February 4, 1919, 2654; and Robert K. Murray: *Red Scare: A Study in National Hysteria, 1919–1920* (Minneapolis: University of Minnesota Press; 1955), 58–64, 94–5.
[8] *Congressional Record,* 65th Congress, 3rd Session, Senate, February 4, 1919, 2655–6.
[9] *Congressional Record,* 65th Congress, 3rd Session, February 7 and 14, 1919, 2878, 3342.
[1] *Congressional Record,* 65th Congress, 3rd Session, February 13 and 14, 1919, 3263, 3338–9.

creased *direct military* intervention. Significantly, beleaguered by the Republican majority, in which the progressives played a subordinate role at best, Woodrow Wilson found himself forced into company with Senators King, Thomas, Myers, and Overman—the foremost Red-baiters. And among the three Republicans who voted with his Democratic supporters to defeat Johnson's resolution (No. 444) was Senator Porter J. McCumber from North Dakota. McCumber called for an army of "one hundred or two hundred or five hundred thousand if necessary to put an end to the rule of Lenin and Trotsky." He supported this clarion call to arms with the rhetorical question as to why America should deport and jail Wobblies at home but hesitate to "lay her hands upon these brutes in Russia?"[2]

Wilson set out for Washington in the hope of mending his political fences. But before leaving he firmly vetoed the Churchill-Foch proposals. At the same time he gave Bullitt the green light to steal away secretly to Russia to sound out Lenin. Thus Wilson demonstrated that he had the determination and power to prevent a major military assault. However, he lacked the courage and insight as well as the political and diplomatic support for a policy of positive accommodation with the Soviets. Above all, he was not prepared to break with the Allies, though it may well be that he underestimated their dependence on the United States. In any event, the Russian question remained in limbo while Wilson was away from Paris.

[2] *Congressional Record*, 65th Congress, 3rd Session, February 14 and March 3, 1919, 3337, 4882.

14

Russia: The Bullitt Mission

STARTING in mid-February the pressures of domestic politics pulled the first team back from the Peace Conference. Lloyd George had to go to London to attend to rising labor unrest, the mineworkers having announced a strike which threatened to paralyze the British economy. Orlando repaired home for similar reasons, Italian labor being caught in an inflationary spiral and suffering from mounting unemployment at the very time that the jingoist agitation for Fiume went into high gear. At Tumulty's insistence Wilson made a quick trip to Washington to check the Republican rebellion in Congress by pleading for bipartisanship in foreign policy and by appealing directly to the electorate. Meanwhile the high cost of living caused increasing uneasiness in France and an assassin's bullet briefly immobilized Clemenceau.

For nearly a month the second team occupied the seats of the mighty. With rising labor unrest the premiers were bound to think twice before deploying additional Allied troops for counterrevolutionary purposes. But the exodus of Lloyd George, Orlando, and Wilson left the field to politicians and generals who were conservative—even reactionary—rather than liberal in their attitude to Bolshevism at home and abroad. Compared to Lloyd George and Clemenceau, Balfour and Pichon found it considerably more difficult to restrain Churchill, Henry Wilson, and Foch. As for Sonnino, he enthusiastically encouraged the military's plea for bold and resolute action. The American Delegation alone remained faithful to the Prinkipo course since General Bliss embraced it with at least as much conviction as Colonel House.

This changing of the guard in Paris coincided with the expiration of the Prinkipo deadline. Churchill rushed to the French capital to force a discussion of the Russian question just before President Wilson's departure. He unequivocally declared that his Prime Minister wished to know whether "the Allied policy which had led to the . . . Prinkipo [proposal] was to be pursued or, if not, what policy was to be substituted for it." The British Secretary of State for War and Air thought that "if only the Bolsheviks were to attend the Conference . . . little good would come of it." Besides, by their dilatory policy the Allies were undermining the morale and effectiveness of the Allied soldiers and pro-Allied Russians who all this time had been fighting the anti-Bolshevik battle. Churchill warned that the withdrawal of Allied troops would result in "the destruction of all non-Bolshevik armies in Russia and . . . would be equivalent to pulling out the linch-pin from the whole machine." Forced to concede that "none of the Allies could send conscript troops to Russia," he proposed to compensate for this politically conditioned default by furnishing "volunteers, technical experts, arms, munitions, tanks, aeroplanes."

At this February 14 meeting of the Supreme War Council Churchill surprised even Clemenceau, who felt that a "matter of such importance could not be settled at a short and unexpected meeting." But while Clemenceau expected to be available in Paris for future sessions, it was 7:00 p.m. and Wilson was about to board a train for Brest.

The President could not leave in good conscience without at least expressing "his personal thoughts on the subject." In his judgment the Allied and Associated troops were not doing any good in Russia in large measure because the local White armies were not particularly effective. Certainly "not one of the Allies was prepared to reinforce its [inadequate] troops." Concerning the proposal to send volunteers and supplies, the President was skeptical. Whereas volunteers "probably could not be had," in many areas supplies "would certainly be assisting reactionaries." The Allies were in a "cruel dilemma." Sooner or later they would have to withdraw their troops; and he himself inclined to do so now. But he would leave it to the Council to discuss Churchill's proposal, prepared to "cast in his lot with the rest."

In the meantime, however, the Allies still needed the clear information about the Bolsheviks which Prinkipo was designed to provide. "As far as he was concerned he would be quite content that informal American representatives should meet representatives of the Bolsheviks" for this purpose. Indeed, since the Russian governments refused to come to Prinkipo perhaps the Allies should "imitate Mohammed, and go to them."[1]

Wilson was still temporizing. On this occasion he gave his sanction to contingency planning to be prepared while he tested the political mood in America and an American emissary—Bullitt—tested Lenin's intentions.

The following day, February 15, the Council settled down to a comprehensive consideration of Churchill's proposal. Rather than open the discussion himself, Churchill, by prearrangement with Clemenceau,

---

[1] *F.R.,P.C.,1919*, III, 1041–4. Lloyd George "was averse to going to Prinkipo to meet the Bolsheviks alone." Cabinet 532A, February 13, 1919 (noon).

agreed that General Alby, the French Chief of Staff, should present a detailed summary of the military situation in Russia. According to Alby the Red Army had benefited from Allied indecision during the past two months. On the northern front the situation "continued to be rather disquieting." On the western front the situation presented a mixed picture. General Mannerheim claimed that he could "easily take Petrograd unassisted [provided] the Allies were prepared to support him and to provision the city." In Estonia Russian and Finnish volunteers had helped to throw back the Bolsheviks. However, "in Courland and Lithuania the Bolsheviks, having taken Riga, Dvinsk, and Vilna, were marching on Kovno and Grodno and approaching the German frontier." The Germans seemed to be assisting them both there and further south, where the Bolsheviks had taken Pinsk and were advancing toward Brest Litovsk.

On the southern front the Ukraine was in particularly grave danger. Kiev, Kharkov, and Ekaterinoslav had fallen; most of the Ukrainian Directorate's troops either were dispersed or had gone over to the Bolsheviks; and the Directorate itself was on the verge of taking refuge in Galicia. Moreover, a large section of the Donets basin was lost, and General Krasnov's troops were falling back on Rostov. Even though Denikin's volunteer army had held its own in the northern Caucasus, it now had to buttress Krasnov's threatened left wing. The Bolsheviks had about 180,000 to 200,000 troops along this entire southern front, but the Allies could easily bring up about 100,000 men from the eastern army,[2] and Rumania could provide another 100,000 from men now idle in Bessarabia and Rumania.

On the eastern front the news was all bad. Following Kolchak's capture of Perm, the Reds had resumed their offensive. General Janin was worried because the training, morale, and even the officers of the Siberian forces were defective, and the Czechs had long since ceased to be at their peak.

In brief, except in Estonia, the Red Army was advancing at all points. This advance not only boosted its morale but also threatened to provide the Soviet regime with critical food supplies from the Ukraine and raw materials from the Donets. The Red troops had superior numbers and equipment, improved organization and discipline, and "systematic propaganda . . . which everywhere preceded military action."

Next to these sources of strength, however, there were "irremediable sources of weakness." The Red Army lacked competent officers of all ranks, was handicapped by primitive communications, and was short of such modern equipment as heavy artillery and aircraft. The policy conclusion was almost self-evident.

[2] Two French divisions from Rumania, two Greek divisions from Salonika, one Italian division from Bulgaria, and one English division from Salonika.

Thus the Red Army owes its success to the fact that, up to the present, it has never encountered adversaries superior to it as regards either numbers, supplies, or morale.

Being better officered and equipped, even though numerically inferior, regular Allied troops would easily defeat it. Such a success could be won at very slight cost, provided that powerful technical means (such as armoured cars and bombing aeroplanes) were employed, which equipment the Bolsheviki entirely lack and the action of which their unequal morale could make it impossible for them to withstand [italics mine].[3]

Against this background Churchill insisted that the Council of Ten bring the entire Russian question to a head in order to avoid irreparable damage to the position of the Allied and friendly armies. Either the Allies should force immediately a negotiated end of the civil war in Russia or they should be free "for such action as they might wish to take."

The former aim could be achieved by giving the Bolsheviks an ultimatum for compliance with the unconditional requirement for Prinkipo:

Unless within 10 days from the 15th instant the Bolshevik forces on all fronts have ceased to attack and have withdrawn a distance of not less than 5 miles from the present position of their adversaries' outpost lines, the Princes Island proposal will be deemed to have lapsed. If, however, within 5 days a [satisfactory] wireless notification is received . . . a similar request will be addressed by the Allies to the forces confronting them.

Simultaneously, rather than waste the days consumed in this diplomatic probe, an Allied Council for Russian Affairs should immediately be set up: "this Council should have political, economic, and military sections, with executive powers within limits to be laid down by the present Conference."

But above all the military section should be organized at once. Then, if Prinkipo failed, the Council would be "in possession of a definite war scheme, together with an appreciation of the situation and an estimate of the chances of being able to carry through to success the suggested plans."

Before concluding his opening statement Churchill implored the Council to realize that until 1914 Russia had been the "counterpoise of Europe." Should the Allies abandon her to her fate, within five to ten years Germany would become "the supreme influence in Russia," thereby laying the foundations for a renewed disruption of the European equilibrium. "In his opinion Russia was the key to the whole

---

[3] *F.R.,P.C.,1919,* IV, 10–13.

situation, and unless she formed a living part of Europe, unless she became a living partner in the League of Nations and a friend of the Allied Powers, there would be neither peace nor victory."

Although Sonnino, Clemenceau, and Makino enthusiastically endorsed Churchill's military proposal, they took strong exception to giving the Bolsheviks another crack at Prinkipo. The original invitation had been a mistake: it had impaired the morale of the Whites and enhanced the prestige of the Bolsheviks. Moreover, the Reds had defiantly insulted the Allies with their bribes. In any case, they had been given their chance and a second invitation would merely compound the damage.

But House and Balfour, resolved to resist Churchill, asked for time to consult their respective principals. Both confessed that although they had never expected much of Prinkipo, the scheme had its propaganda advantages. House spoke of the need "to finesse the situation"; Balfour wanted a message sent to compel the Bolsheviks "either to cease hostilities or to refuse negotiations . . . [thereby] putting them on the horns of a dilemma while at the same time placing the Allies in a better position in regard to public opinion." Finally, at Balfour's suggestion, the Conference adjourned both questions—the renewal of the Prinkipo summons and the Council for Russian Affairs—unil Monday afternoon, February 17.[4]

The weekend up to and through mid-day Monday saw feverish consultations between American and British officials, within the American and British delegations, and between Philip Kerr in Paris and Lloyd George in London.

On Sunday Auchincloss met with Sir William Wiseman and Sir William Tyrrell. He and House also met with Branting, MacDonald, and Henderson who, fresh from Berne, persuaded them that to win the confidence of the Russian masses the Allies had to come out in favor of peasant proprietorship. On the basis of these informal conversations Auchincloss and Wiseman elaborated the following plan:

1. Don't say negotiations are broken off.
2. Issue statement saying Bolsheviks have not complied with conditions for meeting and have misinterpreted the Allies' note.
3. Allies will now make another statement to clear the issues.
4. What we will do if they come:
   a. don't want to interfere in Russia.
   b. foreign loans, concessions, etc. are not our only interests in Russia.
   c. in favor of peasants having land.
   d. want to be of service to Russia.
5. What we will do if they do not come:
   a. conclude Russia does not want to join world peace.

4 Ibid., 14–21.

    b. will protect neighboring states from their *terroristic* armies.
      i. by sending forces to these states.
      ii. by drawing an economic cordon around Russia.[5]

With one modification and one addition these guidelines were accepted by the four U. S. plenipotentiaries in the morning of February 17. Lansing advocated dropping the threat of "sending forces" in favor of protection "by every means in our power." And House added that if the Bolsheviks met the Allies halfway by ceasing hostilities prior to any discussions, the Allies "would be glad to help them with food and raw materials."[6]

    Having fixed their position on the first item—the note renewing the Prinkipo summons—the American Commissioners turned to Churchill's proposal for a Russian council. They had asked General Bliss to come prepared with a memorandum outlining their attitude toward "the creation of a military committee to prepare a plan of operations against Russia." In his memorandum Bliss argued that the U.S. would not participate "in a new war of unknown extent and duration until the present war was ended by a declared and settled peace." If peace were concluded at once the American people might recognize that as long as Russia was in turmoil that peace was not secure. At the same time the "resumption of a state of peace elsewhere in Europe may, directly or indirectly, go a long way of itself in removing or diminishing the menace of Bolshevism."[7] Bliss successfully urged that at the very outset of the discussion of the military committee in the Council of Ten the American Delegation "should make it clear that whatever the Allies and other Associated Powers may do, there was every reason to believe that the United States would not take part" in military actions.[8]

    Concurrent with the American Commission, the British Empire Delegation met to prepare for Monday afternoon's session of the Council of Ten. Since Balfour was the ranking British official in Paris he carried a particularly heavy responsibility. The difficulties of framing a Russian policy being so enormous, he collected his own thoughts in a special memorandum. From the privacy of his study the outlook seemed altogether bleak to Balfour. The morale of the Allied troops was "not really satisfactory on any of the fronts;" even with the Allies providing disciplined nuclei and aid "the Russian levies had been small . . . and had not fought well;" and the Red Army was "growing in numbers and improving in discipline." Consequently, unless the Bolsheviks collapsed under their own weight, by summer they would be

[5] Auchincloss Diary, February 16, 1919.
[6] Auchincloss Diary, February 17, 1919; House Diary, February 17, 1919; Lansing Diary, February 17, 1919; *F.R.,P.C.,1919*, XI, 42–3.
[7] Ibid., 44.
[8] Bliss to House, February 17, 1919, in Bliss Papers, Box 69; and *F.R.,P.C.,1919*, XI, 45.

in a position "to make a formidable, perhaps overwhelming attack on any front they may select," the more so because the Allies were in no position to send reinforcements "on an important scale." Moreover, in addition to these military difficulties, the White Russians, who were putting up such a poor fight and admitted their absolute dependence on external aid, refused to be guided by Allied advice. They not only declined to go to Prinkipo but Sazonov and his colleagues also held out for the restoration of Russia's prewar boundaries. In exasperation Balfour confessed to himself that "should we decide to leave Russia to her fate, it will not be for these gentlemen to criticize our action."[9] Of course, Balfour realized that "the obvious conclusion from these premises" was the withdrawal of Allied troops "as soon as weather conditions permit." However, "this conclusion, though natural, was wrong," primarily because it would "discourage our friends and enormously encourage the Bolsheviks," rendering their triumph certain. Moreover, if the Bolsheviks were "relieved from all anxieties on their southern, eastern, and southeastern fronts, they could devote their whole energies to the west," where their successes would have even more disastrous consequences than in other directions.[1]

No wonder that when opening the February 17 meeting of the British Empire Delegation the Foreign Secretary freely confessed that the situation "was illogical, confused, and embarrassing" and that it would be difficult to discover a policy "which would be at once logical, militarily feasible, and acceptable to public opinion at home." He thereupon yielded the floor to Churchill who, after rejecting the alternative of an anti-Bolshevik crusade by 1,000,000 to 1,500,000 men, urged that the Allies help the Russians save themselves by providing their armies with "money, arms, and equipment, and by encouraging volunteers from among [their] own citizens, officers, and men to guide these armies and provide the necessary technical experience." Specifically, he proposed that the Allies institute "a Military Commission which would be given a week to ten days to determine . . . whether, within these limits, some active policy towards Russia was feasible and likely to be effective." Should this scheme not be feasible, Russia would have to be abandoned by the Western powers, with the consequence that Japan and Germany would find a free field. The "ultimate result" might well be "a predatory confederation stretching from the Rhine to Yokohama menacing the vital interests of the British Empire in India and elsewhere, menacing indeed the future of the world." In conclusion Churchill claimed that he had "pressed these views on the Cabinet in London [and] had been sent over here to see if some plan could be worked out." Even though Robert Borden insisted that the Canadian troops would have to be recalled from Siberia in the early spring and

9 "Memorandum on the Russian Situation," February 15, 1919, Balfour Papers, 49751.
1 "The Russian Situation," February 26, 1919, Balfour Papers, 49751.

soon thereafter from the north, the delegation agreed that in the afternoon, at the Council of Ten, "the British Representatives should press . . . for the institution of the Military Commission proposed by Mr. Churchill."[2]

This outcome was at odds with the Prime Minister's latest instructions, which may or may not have reached the delegation before or during its deliberations. Over the weekend both Churchill and Philip Kerr had contacted Lloyd George. Churchill had sent him the draft-text of the ultimatum as well as an outline of his companion proposal.

> In anticipation of the Soviet Government refusing to accept Allied terms and continuing hostilities, it is suggested that suitable machinery should be set up forthwith to consider practical possibilities of joint military action by the Associated Powers acting in conjunction with the independent border states and pro-Ally Governments in Russia. . . . This commission would make it its business, among other things, to examine competent representatives of Russia, Finland, Esthonia, Poland and other border States, in order to form an estimate of the actual military support which these States and Governments are in a position to supply, and to prepare a plan for the utilization of the joint resources . . . [to be ready] within whatever time limit is set in the ultimatum. . . .[3]

Although the Prime Minister approved the draft-ultimatum he was worried about the projected military commitment. He claimed that before leaving for Paris his War Minister merely envisaged "to send expert details who volunteer to go to Russia together with any equipment we can spare." In his view it was up to Kolchak, Denikin, and Krasnov to raise the forces required for the salvation of Russia.[4]

Meanwhile Kerr had sent a truly alarming report in the name of that section of the British Delegation which, in opposition to Churchill, worked in close harness with the American Delegation. Apparently Kerr portrayed Churchill's double-barreled proposal as the newest rallying ground for all advocates of concerted armed intervention. The miners just having voted to strike, Lloyd George was deeply troubled by the spreading labor unrest.[5] He was also sensitive to America's reluctance to endorse and finance the enterprise. Consequently he sent a strong telegram designed to restrain Churchill.

> If Russia is really anti-Bolshevik then a supply of equipment would enable it to redeem itself. If Russia is pro-Bolshevik not

2 British Empire Delegation 8, February 17, 1919 (noon).
3 Cited in Churchill: *Aftermath*, 173–4.
4 Ibid., 174–7.
5 "Lloyd George: Winston is in Paris. He wants to conduct a war against the Bolsheviks. That would cause a revolution! Our people would not permit it." Riddell: *Intimate Diary of the Peace Conference*, 21, entry of February 16, 1919.

merely is it none of our business to intervene with its internal affairs; it would be positively mischievous [and] it would strengthen and consolidate Bolshevik opinion. I beg you not to commit this country to what would be a purely mad enterprise out of hatred of Bolshevik principles. An expensive war of aggression against Russia is a way to strengthen Bolshevism in Russia and create it at home. We cannot afford the burden. Chamberlain tells me we can hardly make both ends meet on a peace basis even at the present crushing rate of taxation and if we are committed to a war against a continent like Russia it is the direct road to bankruptcy and Bolshevism in these islands.

The French are not safe guides in this matter. . . . I urge you therefore not to pay too much heed to their incitement. . . .

I also want you to bear in mind the very grave labor position in this country. Were it known that you had gone over to Paris to prepare a plan of war against the Bolsheviks it would do more to incense labor than anything I can think of; and what is still worse it would throw into the arms of the extremists a very large number of thinking people who now abhor their methods.

I sincerely hope you will stand by your first proposal subject to the comments which I have passed upon them. Please show these telegrams to the Foreign Secretary.[6]

Much to the dismay of both Churchill and Henry Wilson the Prime Minister asked Kerr to show his instructions not only to Balfour but also to Colonel House. Kerr did so at 2:30 p.m., a half hour before the Council convened. Consequently Balfour and House entered the afternoon session jointly resolved to stop the activists.[7]

Curiously enough, the minutes of this afternoon session of February 17 are brief to the point of dissimulation. They simply record that "a discussion on the policy to be pursued in Russia ensued, and after an exchange of views, it was decided to postpone the resumption until later in the week."[8]

In fact, the discussion was so "acrimonious" that it was omitted from the *procès verbal*. Evidently Churchill stuck to his demand that the Russian question be referred to a military committee and that this decision be publicized in the press. Whereas Clemenceau and Sonnino supported him, first House and then Balfour objected strenuously. When House indicated that America would send neither troops nor matériel Clemenceau exploded and made a rather "offensive speech": he even implied that the other Allies "would discuss Russia without America." But then Balfour "took up the cudgels," thus checkmating

---

[6] David Lloyd George: *The Truth About the Peace Treaties*, I, 371–2. Significantly Churchill does not refer to or reproduce this telegram in *Aftermath*.

[7] House Diary, February 17, 1919; Auchincloss Diary, February 17, 1919; Lloyd George: *Truth*, I, 374.

[8] *F.R.,P.C.,1919*, IV, 28.

the militants. Eventually the Tiger apologized for his outburst to both House and Balfour. No formal resolution was taken and it was expressly agreed that there should be no press release of any kind. Instead, the military advisers were instructed to study informally those aspects that came into their sphere of expertise; but rather than submit a joint report each adviser was to report to his own delegation. Pending these informal studies, even the message to the Bolsheviks was to be held up. The mercurial Henry Wilson denounced this evasion as "the greatest depth of impotence he had ever seen the Frocks fall to."[9]

There are no minutes of the informal meeting of the military advisers on February 18. Bliss went there to read his memorandum and to reiterate that "from a military point of view it would be a piece of criminal folly to start another war on the other side of Germany until the present war had finished." He emphasized that instead of making policy the military should restrict themselves to implementing policies adopted by the Big Ten.[1]

But the French generals were anything but hesitant to set the pace. In the wake of Churchill's original proposal, on the seventeenth the *État Major* submitted a full-blown plan to the Quai d'Orsay. According to this plan Bolshevism should be closed in on all fronts: in Poland, in the Ukraine, in the Crimea, and even in eastern Prussia—though an official at the Quai d'Orsay crossed out the last-named area! With a view to finishing off Bolshevism before the onset of the winter of 1919–20, the pro-Allied Russian armies should be reinforced with interned prisoners, with matériel, and with a unified command. And as a first and immediate step the Allies should support Yudenich, who was to take Petrograd, also making plans to feed that city after liberation. Still on the seventeenth, Clemenceau advised Pichon that the Allies simply had to coordinate their efforts: that England should see to the material support of Finland and the Baltic countries, that France should act through Poland, and that for prestige purposes France should send information and propaganda missions to all nations participating in this enterprise.[2]

As part of the informal consultations among the military advisers, on February 18 Marshal Foch sent a lengthy memorandum to Sir Henry Wilson. In this memo he asserted that this was the time to dictate final peace terms to Germany: the German government needed peace in order to consolidate its own position and it lacked the military strength to resist Allied demands. But above all, once these conditions

---

[9] This debate has been reconstructed on the basis of the House Diary, February 17, 1919; Callwell (ed.): *Henry Wilson*, II, 170, entry of February 17, 1919; Auchincloss Diary, February 17 and 19, 1919; Lloyd George: *Truth*, I, 374.

[1] *F.R.,P.C.,1919*, XI, 49.

[2] "Projet de l'État-Major," February 17, 1919, and Clemenceau to Pichon, February 17, 1919, in Quai d'Orsay, File Z619–9.

had been imposed on Germany the Allies would be free to "turn their attention to the Russian problem." Colonel House reported to President Wilson, who was then on the high seas, that

> the Marshal thinks the Allies may lose the War if they fail to arrive at a satisfactory solution of the Russian question, either by Germany settling it in her own interests, or by the spread of anarchy. He favors the solution of helping all the anti-Bolshevik elements in Russia, and all the neighbors of Russia who are resisting Bolshevik encroachments. He would go so far as to accept German cooperation after the signing of his preliminary treaty of peace, and thinks it might be very valuable.[3]

Hereafter this argument about the need to dispose of the German question in order to deal decisively with the Russian question was repeatedly advanced by Clemenceau, Pichon, and Tardieu as they sought to force a harsh preliminary peace on Germany prior to Wilson's return.[4]

Within a week General Wilson submitted his own plan for "future military operations in Russia." He attached first priority to guaranteeing the borders of Finland, Estonia, Latvia, Lithuania, Poland, and Rumania. Once the boundaries of these six states were definitely fixed, "the Bolsheviks should be given peremptory orders to withdraw beyond their frontiers." In case "direct military intervention" were required, Finland should be the responsibility of America; Estonia, Latvia, and Lithuania also of America, or failing America, of England; and Poland and Rumania of France and Italy. For the other fronts General Wilson recommended in the north, withdrawal, probably starting in June; in Siberia, continued material aid and substitution of 1,000 to 2,000 volunteer instructors and experts for the withdrawal of two British divisions; in Denikin's theater, continued supply of military stores, "including tanks, aeroplanes, armored cars, guns, machine guns, etc., with personnel up to a total of 1,000–2,000, all volunteers, necessary to instruct the Russians in their use;" and in Trans-Caspia, two divisions to "hold the Batum-Tiflis-Baku line and the adjoining country" as long as Britain continued to support Denikin and Kolchak, or until relieved by other Allies. General Wilson made a special point of recommending that both Denikin and Kolchak be notified that British troops would not be used "on the actual fighting front" but would confine themselves to covering "Denikin's rear and flanks by holding the country south of the Caucasus and the Black Sea and the Caspian Sea."[5]

[3] House to Wilson, February 19, 1919, cited in Charles Seymour: *Intimate Papers of Colonel House*, III, 332–4.
[4] *F.R.,P.C.,1919*, IV, 87–95.
[5] "Note for the Cabinet on Future Military Operations in Russia," February 24, 1919, G.T. 6885, Cabinet 24/75. These proposals had Churchill's full concurrence.

Although Foch's renewed representations to hasten General Haller's divisions to Danzig went far beyond General Wilson's project, they were not incompatible with it. On February 24 and 25 Foch told the Council of Ten that without a strong Poland the *cordon sanitaire* could not be effective, and that these divisions had to be sent for the purpose of "constituting Poland." Actually, so as to expedite matters, the Allies should straightaway fix not only Germany's western borders but also her eastern frontiers. And this eastern frontier should run "to the West of the Thorn-Danzig railway . . . thereby freeing the port and the railway lines of all German control." Again, he claimed that his overriding aim was to release energy for the anti-Bolshevik crusade.

. . . Since the Armistice . . . the Allies had been marking time in the West, and they had lost ground in the East. Consequently, the situation on the Western Front should forthwith be settled so that all the resources in men and material thus set free could be made available for the solution of the Eastern problem.

In Russia at the present moment Bolshevism and complete anarchy reigned, and sooner or later these Russian questions must be solved, otherwise the fruits of victory would be lost, either through the cementing of an alliance between Germany and Russia, or through the spread of Bolshevism in Germany. . . . [The] Preliminaries of Peace must be signed, and that could be done with Germany alone in a fortnight's time. . . . In other words, his plan would be to settle all the important outstanding questions on the Western side in order to enable the Allies to use the resources thus made available for the solution of the Eastern questions.

The difficulties which the Allies had to face in Russia were due not only to the enormous distances . . . but also to the nature of the enemy that had to be dealt with. The enemy might be badly organized, but he was scattered over an enormous territory, acting like a violent virus. Now to fight against such an enemy . . . troops need not be strongly organized or of superior quality. The necessary conditions would be fulfilled by the employment of such armies as might be raised locally in the countries of Eastern Europe. For instance, the Polish troops would be quite able to face the Russians, provided the former were strengthened by the supply of modern appliances and engines of war. But great numbers were required, which could be obtained by mobilizing the Finns, Poles, Czechs, Rumanians, and Greeks, as well as the Russian pro-Ally elements still available.

These young troops [should be] placed under a unique [i.e., unified] command. . . . If [all] this were done, 1919 would see the end of Bolshevism, just as 1918 had seen the end of Prussianism. But in order to attain that objective, just as the Allies had a base on the Western front, the Rhine, which enabled them to impose their will on Germany, so would it be necessary to constitute a similar base on the Eastern side, consisting of a chain of independent states—the Finns, the Estonians, the Poles, the Czechs, and the Greeks. The constitution of such a base would enable the Allies to impose their demands on the Bolsheviks.[6]

No doubt an immediate preliminary peace with Germany would above all else have secured France's vital objectives in terms of borders, reparations, and German disarmament. Moreover, it is quite likely that Foch used the appeals of anti-Bolshevism to marshal support for an order of priority in peacemaking that obviously was to France's advantage. Still, the plea for an immediate punitive peace cannot be divorced from the broader anti-Bolshevik projects of Foch and Churchill, and even of Clemenceau. From Lenin's point of view it made little difference whether Foch proposed to eliminate Bolshevism in order to make Russia and Eastern Europe into a reliable anti-German bastion or whether he sought its overthrow for ideological or moral reasons. Certainly Bliss instantly realized that Foch wanted a quick peace with Germany in order to wage war on Russia.[7]

In spite of the agreement not to publicize these debates and disagreements, the right-wing press in Paris—prodded by official leaks and with the censor's blessings—launched a fierce interventionist campaign. As early as February 16 Pertinax was championing Winston Churchill's cause. The *Temps* followed suit on the seventeenth. Herbette renewed his charge that without a trustworthy Russia even a disarmed Germany would remain an unmitigated threat to Europe. The infamous Soviets would forever by ready to join the Germans in taking Poland, Lithuania, and the Baltic countries in a cross fire. Furthermore, the Germans would spread their influence by working the sugar mills of the Ukraine, the factories of the Donets, and the grain elevators along the Volga. In brief, the League of Nations and the Bolshevik regime could not coexist; without the occupation of Petrograd the Allies could not secure a lasting peace.[8]

In *Figaro* Gabriel Hanotaux and Raymond Recouly took the same general line. As a matter of course France would assist the build-up of a greater Serbia, a greater Rumania, a greater Poland, and a greater Czechoslovakia. Even so, these new and still fragile nations could never develop into an adequate counterweight to 80 million Germans. France had need of her Russian ally and the Western Powers should rush guns, artillery, tanks, planes, and military cadres to the border peoples and the pro-Allied Russians. Moreover, the Russian prisoners in Germany should be put into the field, fully equipped. Inasmuch as the German and Russian questions were so thoroughly interwoven the settlement of one without the other made little sense.[9]

[6] *F.R.,P.C.,1919*, IV, 104–7, 120–4.
[7] Bliss Diary, February 26, 1919, Bliss Papers, Box 65.
[8] *Echo de Paris*, February 16–24, 1919; and *le Temps*, February 17 and 20, 1919.
[9] *Le Figaro*, February 17–28, 1919.

It was perfectly clear that even though "Churchill's project was dead"[1] interventionist pressures, plots, and appeals continued unabated. As a result those American and British officials who opposed direct military intervention but favored active containment threw themselves into elaborate consultations in the hope of working out an acceptable course. They wanted to attempt another Prinkipo project, one modified along the lines elaborated by Auchincloss and Wiseman.

These informal explorations began with a conversation between Colonel House and Philip Kerr, who dutifully reported to Lloyd George. In turn, the British Prime Minister sent over an outline of his views. He reiterated that while the Allies would send no troops to Russia they stood ready to continue supplying material assistance to all anti-Bolshevik governments that had the will and capacity to put up a fight. As for Poland, Finland, and the other states to be "carved out" of Russia, they should receive moral, material, and, "if necessary, full military support." Should the Allies place Estonia, Lithuania, and Latvia in the same category as Poland, these Baltic nations should also be included in the defensive perimeter.[2]

On being informed that Lloyd George planned another approach to the Bolsheviks on the basis of these terms. Balfour thought that this time the Allies should first consult with the pro-Ally Russians. Hence, Kerr prepared a draft-message to be sent to "Kolchak, Denikin, and other pro-Ally forces in Russia." In this message they were told that another offer of negotiations was about to be made to the Bolsheviks provided the latter were willing to "make peace on terms which would free the Governments and territories now opposed to them from the danger of military aggression."

Balfour and Kerr proposed to send along with this message to the pro-Ally Russians a draft of a message to be beamed to the Bolsheviks. According to this second message the Allies were prepared to make peace with Soviet Russia on the following conditions:

1. Hostilities to cease on all fronts.
2. All *de facto* Governments to remain in full control of the territories which they at present occupy.
3. Railways and ports necessary to transportation between Soviet Russia and the Sea to be subject to the same regulations as international railways and ports in the rest of Europe.
4. Allied subjects to be given free right of entry and full security to enable them to enter Soviet Russia and go about their business there provided they do not interfere with politics.

---

[1] Ammission to Wilson, February 23, 1919, in *F.R.,1919,Russia,* 73. See also *F.R.,P.C., 1919,* XI, 66–7.

[2] Kerr to House, February 21, 1919, in House Papers, 31:209. The text of the Prime Minister's letter to Kerr, which Kerr quoted to House, is cited in Lloyd George: *Truth,* I, 375–7.

5. Amnesty to all political prisoners on both sides; full liberty for all Russians who have fought with the Allies.
6. Trade relations to be restored between Soviet Russia and the outside world under conditions which, while respecting the sovereignty of Soviet Russia, ensure that Allied supplies are made available on equal terms to all classes of the Russian people.
7. All other questions connected with Russia's debt to the Allies and so forth to be considered independently after peace has been established.
8. All Allied troops to be withdrawn from Russia as soon as Russian armies above quota to be defined have been demobilized and their surplus arms surrendered or destroyed.[3]

These, then, were the broad outlines of policy on which the British and American delegations were agreed. In anticipation of a reconsideration of the Prinkipo course by the Conference some of the American experts provided their Commissioners with additional supporting data. They carefully mapped out the steps to be taken, got up a complete collection of pertinent documents, and prepared a Wilsonian draft-declaration on Russian policy to be issued by the Council of Ten.[4] According to Bullitt this renewal of the Prinkipo project was never brought before the Council of Ten because of the attempt on Clemenceau's life. Lloyd George, who had been scheduled to return to Paris on February 24 to join with House in putting it over, decided to remain in London for another week because "as long as Clemenceau was wounded . . . he was boss of the roost and anything he desired to veto would be immediately wiped out."[5]

Still according to Bullitt, his own mission was a direct result of this turn of events.

> Therefore, it was decided that I should go at once to Russia to attempt to obtain from the Soviet Government an exact statement of the terms on which they were ready to stop fighting. I was ordered if possible to obtain that statement and have it back in Paris before the President returned to Paris from the United States. The plan was to make a proposal to the Soviet Government which would certainly be accepted.[6]

And, indeed, Bullitt was in the center of the informal Anglo-American consultations. He saw both House and Kerr repeatedly between Febru-

[3] Both draft-messages are attached to the Kerr letter cited in the preceding footnote.
[4] See "Notes on the Russian Situation," "A Declaration of Policy Issued in the Name of the Allied and Associated Governments," and "Draft Message for the Bolsheviks and All Groups in Russia," in House Papers, 31:209. The authors of these position and advisory papers are not known. See also the unusually suggestive position paper on "Policy of Allies toward Russia" which Samuel E. Morison, of the Russian Division of the Inquiry, sent to Isaiah Bowman on February 24, 1919, in House Papers.
[5] *Bullitt Mission,* 33–4.
[6] Ibid., 34.

ary 18 and 21, and he was familiar with the conditions on which the second Prinkipo proposal was to be predicated.[7]

Even so, it would seem that neither the origin nor the purpose of the Bullitt Mission was quite as Bullitt portrayed them.

To begin with, the idea of sending a mission of inquiry into Russia was not at all new. Northcliffe suggested it to Auchincloss in early January, and when Auchincloss, in House's name, proposed it to the President a few days later, Wilson said that the approach was also in his mind.[8] On January 19 House discussed the matter at considerable length with Bullitt. They concluded that missions of the Allied Governments should enter Russia together but should report separately to their respective principals; noted that Lloyd George inclined toward appointing General Smuts to head a British mission; and agreed that among Americans Judge Learned Hand, Raymond Fosdick, and William Allen White were best equipped for this assignment, possibly with Albert Rhys Williams as an adjunct because "of his personal connections in Great Russia." In a memorandum summarizing this conversation House was reminded not to forget "Bullitt as general bootblack" for the American mission.[9]

This idea of sending in missions was abandoned in favor of the Prinkipo proposal. But once Prinkipo turned out to be stillborn the idea was revived in the American Delegation. At the Council of Ten Woodrow Wilson spoke of imitating Mohammed and going to the Bolsheviks to secure information, but it is not known whether he ordered a mission before he left Paris. Lincoln Steffens suggested to House that a "secret sounding commission" be sent in to see that the Bolsheviks "understand what you are up to and to make sure that they will come in the desired state of mind to an official meeting."[1] By February 16 House and Lansing conferred about a mission; according to the Secretary of State, he "talked with House about sending Bullitt to Russia to cure him of Bolshevism."[2] Eventually House claimed that Lansing rather than he had "first upheld Bullitt's expedition."[3] In any case, Lansing and House made the decision to send Bullitt on his journey without consulting the other American Commissioners.[4]

[7] Ibid., 34–8; and E. L. Woodward and Rohan Butler (eds.): *Documents on British Foreign Policy, 1919–1939*, 1st Series (H.M.S.O., 1949), III, 425–6.
[8] Auchincloss Diary, January 9 and 13, 1919.
[9] Bullitt to House, January 19, 1919, Bullitt Papers. Bliss thought that in case the Borden plan failed, an inter-Allied commission should go into Russia with prior consent of the Bolshevik government. Bliss Diary, January 19, 1919, in Bliss Papers, Box 65.
[1] *The Autobiography of Lincoln Steffens* (New York: Harcourt Brace; 1931), 790.
[2] Lansing Diary, February 16, 1919.
[3] Charles Seymour, Memorandum on Conversation with Colonel House, March 17, 1920, in House Papers, 32:139.
[4] Henry White and Tasker H. Bliss to Joseph C. Grew, November 19, 1919, National Archives, Document 184.022/29.

It was on February 18—hence after the defeat of Churchill's proposal but before the attempted assassination of Clemenceau—that Bullitt was "directed to proceed to Russia for the purpose of studying conditions, political and economic, therein, for the benefit of the American Commissioners."[5] Between February 18 and 22, when he started his journey, Bullitt engrossed himself deeply in the informal Anglo-American consultations. He also secured a copy of the terms for settlement with the Bolsheviks that Kerr had drafted on the basis of conversations with Balfour and of Lloyd George's letter.[6] Whether or not Bullitt was instructed to show these terms to Lenin is an altogether different matter.

During these same four days the Bullitt party was organized. Captain Walter W. Pettit, of Military Intelligence, was designated to be Bullitt's assistant. Since December Pettit had been attached to the Russian Division of the Inquiry. He had traveled and lived in Russia, spoke and wrote the language, had an "excellent grasp" of the Russian situation, and was an ex-social worker.[7] A certain R. E. Lynch, of the U. S. Navy, was assigned to serve in a secretarial capacity. And Lincoln Steffens—rather than Albert Rhys Williams—was to travel along in a purely personal capacity, thereby giving the mission what was thought to be a useful "radical" cachet.[8]

Bullitt and his party arrived in London on the twenty-third. There, in the strictest of confidence, he informed the British government of the purpose and character of his mission, and also made arrangements for a ship of the Royal Navy to take his companions and him to Oslo. They spent the first few days of March in Stockholm establishing contact with the Bolshevik government in order to obtain permission to proceed to Petrograd and Moscow. By March 8 the party arrived in Petrograd accompanied by an unofficial representative of the Soviets. On the ninth Bullitt had his first substantive conversation with Chicherin and Litvinov. Thus even before he continued to Moscow for his conference with Lenin, he was able to cable back to Paris that "the Soviet Government was disposed to be reasonable" and that he expected to transmit "an exact detailed statement of the position of the Soviet Government on all points" by the end of the week.[9]

---

[5] Lansing to Bullitt, February 18, 1919, cited in *Bullitt Mission*, 4; and *F.R.,1919,Russia*, 74.
[6] *Bullitt Mission*, 35–7.
[7] Grew to General Churchill, February 21, 1919, Bullitt Papers; and R. H. Lord to Grew, March 18, 1919, National Archives, Document 184.02202/8.
[8] Ammission to U.S. Embassy in London, February 21, 1919, National Archives, Document 184.022/3. According to Steffens, "knowing that I was regarded as a friend of Russia, [House] wanted me to go unofficially as a friend of Bullitt, capable of official repudiation." *Autobiography of Lincoln Steffens*, 791.
[9] *Bullitt Mission*, 47–8; *F.R.,1919,Russia*, 74–7; National Archives, Documents 184.022/5–11; Ira Morris (Stockholm) to House, March 6 and 11, 1919, in House Papers, 10:48; *Autobiography of Lincoln Steffens*, 791.

The Ammission, Bullitt, and Lenin were equally anxious to avoid publicity at this early and critical stage. On the other hand, the risks in keeping the Allied Governments in the dark were all too great. Of course, the British, except for the Foreign Office, were in on the secret, but the French and the Italians had to be told. Some time between March 10 and 15 Lansing appears to have advised Pichon and Sonnino that Bullitt was in Petrograd and Moscow—with his blessings but in an unofficial capacity—for the sole purpose of gathering what he hoped would be valuable information.[1] However, even assuming the French and Italian authorities had never been formally advised, it is most unlikely that their alert intelligence services would have failed them in this one instance.

In Moscow, meanwhile, Lenin and Chicherin continued to be eager for Allied overtures in spite of the not insignificant successes of the Red Armies. The Soviet leaders were still guided by the same objectives, calculations, and apprehensions that had prompted all their post-Armistice peace feelers. They fully expected their enemies to intensify military operations with the first spring thaw. According to Chicherin, if no agreement were reached "the policy of blockade would be pressed with vigor [and the Allies] would send tanks, etc., to Denikin, Kolchak, Petlura, Paderewski, etc."[2] The Soviets were desperately eager to stave off this assault. Lenin was the master realist. For him it was sound politics rather than Bolshevik dogma to retreat one step in order subsequently to advance two steps. He was ready to pay an exorbitant price for the space and time required to consolidate the Soviet regime. Needless to say, Lenin was not about to sacrifice voluntarily half of Russia; it was up to the Allies to "impose" their terms, much as the Germans had imposed theirs at Brest Litovsk. War or peace, and whatever the degree of national and political humiliation, the Revolution would preserve its moral posture and propaganda advantage.

Since the international civil war was bound to continue during any truce, the Soviet regime—which was short on military and economic power—had to husband these moral and propaganda resources. Lenin realized that once the lines between revolutionary Russia and the League were drawn, a frontal attack on adjacent states would be out of the question; and for quite some time the Soviets would lack economic surplus for political action beyond their borders. He would have to wait for the capitalist world, and with it the surrounding states, to be shaken by severe internal crises. Meanwhile, he could at best foster these crises by ideological warfare.

[1] *F.R.,1919,Russia,* 76; National Archives, Documents 184.022/5 and /18; Lansing to Pichon, March 15, 1919, Bliss Papers, Box 69.
[2] Chicherin to Rakovsky, March 13, 1919, cited in Louis Fischer: *The Soviets in World Affairs,* 2 vols. (2nd edn., Princeton: Princeton University Press; 1951), I, 171.

Bullitt was no *sympathisant* or fellow-traveler. He had a reformer's instincts. The Berne Conference had just reinforced his faith in the Wilson-Labour program for the reconstruction of Europe. Especially since he himself was no Socialist, he fastened on to the foreign policy aspects of this program. This much he had in common with Arthur Henderson: they both knew that if the direct interventionists had their way with regard to Russia they would also dictate the rest of the peace treaty along Carthaginian lines, with the concomitant result of either enthroning reaction or provoking revolution. On the other hand, a *modus vivendi* with Lenin was compatible with key tenets of the Wilsonian formula: the Russian people was entitled to choose its own form of government and the minority peoples were entitled to self-determination. Back of this plan was the unspoken assumption that indirect intervention would continue. The League would protect the states carved out of the former Russian Empire against aggression while economic power would be used to de-revolutionize the Leninist regime and to strengthen its neighbors.

Lenin, Chicherin, and Litvinov took it for granted that whatever the scope of his mission Bullitt did not need to be convinced that they were not about either to surrender or to turn themselves into Wilsonian democrats. Obviously neither side wanted a truce—or peace—for the sake of a truce or to avoid further bloodshed. Whereas Lenin estimated that a truce would facilitate the survival of the Russian Revolution, Bullitt advocated it as an effective instrument of containment. In brief, provided the Bolsheviks suspended their revolutionary expansionism and the Allies suspended their counterrevolutionary rollback, there was room for negotiation.

Consequently the Bolshevik leaders spoke frankly with Bullitt. He found them "full of a sense of Russia's *need* for peace, and therefore disposed to be most conciliatory." He soon realized that although the Soviet regime was not bursting with strength, it would neither yield nor collapse. In his judgment the economic situation was by all odds the single greatest weakness, on account of the blockade in part, but above all because of the breakdown of the transportation—particularly of the railway—system. But even in this connection he warned that "starvation would drive Russia to the left [toward the left Social Revolutionaries and anarchy], not to the right."

Except for these tragic economic conditions the Bolsheviks seemed to be leading from strength. Not only was the Red Army growing rapidly, but internally there were no serious disorders. As a result of foreign intervention the Mensheviks and the right Social Revolutionaries were rallying around the government; the Cadets were in exile or in disarray; and the left Social Revolutionaries, who were even more prone to violence than the Bolsheviks, were a small fanatical group without popular following. Bullitt could see no alternative to the Soviet regime and he advised Paris of his "conviction that the Soviet Government was the only constructive force in Russia today."[3]

Bullitt's conversations with Chicherin, Litvinov, and Lenin were not recorded. The most reliable source to go by is the draft agreement which they handed to Bullitt for submission to the Peace Conference. Judging by its wording the American emissary must have given a copy of Kerr's eight-point proposal to his Soviet interlocutors. According to Steffens "on the train to London Bullitt showed penciled on a sheet of paper the seven [?] items which . . . Kerr . . . had given him as the terms for the Bolsheviki to agree to."[4] Even Lenin's preliminary outline for the agreement closely followed the form and terms of Kerr's tentative proposal. Of course, Lenin made some additions and changed the priority of certain points. But above all, with regard to all major military, political, and economic terms he insisted on mutual agreement and complete reciprocity.[5]

The final draft agreement—prepared by Litvinov and approved by Lenin[6]—stipulated that "hostilities cease on all fronts" for the duration of peace negotiations; that "all existing *de facto* Governments . . . on the territory of the former Russian Empire and Finland remain in full control of the territories" they occupy at the time of armistice and mutually undertake not to overthrow each other's government by force; that the economic blockade be lifted and trade relations reestablished with the assurance that Allied supplies "be made available on equal terms to all classes of the Russian people"; that the Soviet government have the unhindered transit and use of all railways and ports of the former Russian Empire and Finland; that citizens and officials of both sides have the right of free entry into each others' countries "provided they do not interfere in the domestic politics" of host countries; that a general amnesty be declared and prisoners of war be repatriated; that all Allied troops "be withdrawn from Russia and military assistance cease to be given to anti-Soviet Governments . . . immediately after signing of this agreement"; that all armies be reduced to peacetime levels simultaneously under inspection and control; and that *de facto* governments "all recognize their responsibility" for the Tsarist debts and agree to repay them.[7]

Lenin certainly offered staggering territorial concessions, even as compared to Brest Litovsk: the vast areas controlled by the North Russian government, by Kolchak, and by Denikin; large parts of the Baltic provinces, White Russia, and the Ukraine; Bessarabia; and

---

[3] See Bullitt's telegrams, posted from Helsingfors, in *F.R.,1919,Russia,* 76–84.

[4] *Autobiography of Lincoln Steffens,* 791.

[5] V. I. Lenin: *Collected Works* (New York: International Publishers; 1945), XXIII, 533–4.

[6] Fischer: *Soviets in World Affairs,* I, 171.

[7] For the final and complete text see *Bullitt Mission,* 39–44, or *F.R.,1919,Russia,* 78–80, or Jane Degras (ed.): *Soviet Documents on Foreign Policy,* 147–50.

Transcaucasia. Had an armistice been signed then and there the Soviet regime would have been confined to an area centered around Moscow and enclosed by a circle running from Vilna through Riga, Petrograd, Vologda, Kazan, Samara, Saratov, Kharkov, Kiev, and Minsk.

In exchange, however, Lenin would have secured certain advantages as well. To be sure, the Allies still would not evacuate their troops and stop their aid to the anti-Soviet governments until after peace was signed. But now there was a *quid pro quo:* the Red Army would not have to withdraw from its most advanced positions in the Baltic provinces and the northern Ukraine as a precondition for negotiations. Quite apart from avoiding the humiliation of such a one-sided and unconditional withdrawal Riga, Vilna, Minsk, and Kiev were valuable not only as military outposts but also as diplomatic pawns. Moreover, Finland, Poland, and even Germany would be committed to a cessation of all hostile activities. And last, the timetable reveals that Lenin was determined not to throw away his temporary military advantage: the armistice was to be for only two weeks, subject to prolongation; the conference was to begin within at most a week after this armistice went into effect; and the Soviet government bound itself to accept the projected terms provided the Allies offered them no later than April 10.

Bullitt left Moscow on March 14. Even though he did not get back to Paris until the evening of the twenty-fifth, his telegram with the full text of the Soviet proposal reached the American Delegation on the eighteenth. That was four days after Wilson's return to Paris and four days before the Conference was shaken by reports that Béla Kun had supplanted Károlyi in Budapest.

From the beginning even the American Commissioners were in disagreement among themselves. Lansing and White were inclined to refuse Lenin's latest offer, while House was in favor of exploring it.[8] House promptly sent a telegram to Bullitt, hoping to intercept him in Stockholm. In this wire House conveyed "our warmest congratulations and wishes"; but above all he wanted to tell Bullitt that if he did not have "the proposals in writing . . . it was essential for action here to secure them in official form."[9] And even though the Commissioners at first agreed that Pettit should remain in Petrograd and establish a courier service to Helsingfors, on March 22 they reversed themselves and ordered Pettit to withdraw from Russia immediately.[1]

This ephemeral link to Lenin was broken even before Bullitt had a

[8] Lansing Diary, March 19, 1919.
[9] Ammission to U.S. Legation in Stockholm (for Bullitt), March 19, 1919, Bullitt Papers. Due to an administrative mix-up this telegram never went out; House gave a copy to Bullitt after his return to Paris. *Bullitt Mission,* 46.
[1] *F.R.,P.C.,1919,* XI, 125, 128–9; Grew to Alexander Kirk, March 21, 1919, Lansing Papers, Vol. 42; *F.R.,1919,Russia,* 85, 95–6.

chance to argue his case. No sooner had he reached Paris late on the twenty-fifth than he went into a long conference with Colonel House.

> Bullitt got back tonight from Russia. His story is interesting and at least I can see a way out of that vexatious problem, that is, if we can get action by the Prime Minister and the President. I cautioned Bullitt against telling all he told me. Russia, according to him, is orderly but starving, and if relations are not opened with the outside world, anarchy will be prevalent, for the man without bread will steal and murder for it. That part of his story, I told him, must be for my ears alone. Most of the Allies, I regret to chronicle, would just as soon have the people starve as not. They were willing to allow the people of the Central Empires to starve, and they are just as willing to have Russia go the same way. *It is fear that will bring about a Russian settlement, not pity.* Most of the world seems to have lost its sense of compassion [italics mine].[2]

The following morning and most of the afternoon Bullitt presented his case to Lansing, White, and Bliss. Apparently he did not frighten them sufficiently, since Lansing felt he painted a rather rosy picture, "slid over the terrible conditions, laid most everything on disorganized transportation," and even praised Lenin. Eventually Bullitt made the exaggerated claim that it was the sense of these discussions "that it was highly desirable to attempt to bring about peace on that [Lenin–Kerr] basis."[3]

In the meantime Bullitt had already called on Kerr to give him copies of his report as well as of the Soviet proposal, and to arrange for a breakfast meeting with Lloyd George for March 26.[4] General Smuts, Maurice Hankey, and Philip Kerr were present early that morning. Even though Lloyd George agreed with Smuts that the proposal should be considered very seriously, he maintained that public opinion, as expressed in the inflammatory *Daily Mail,* continued to tie his hands. Since his own reports about conditions in Russia coincided with Bullitt's, Lloyd George considered sending in "somebody who was known to the whole world as a complete conservative in order to have the whole world believe that the report he brings out is not simply the utterance of a radical." For this assignment he thought of Lord Lansdowne, who once before, in November 1917, had cleared the atmosphere for sensible talk;[5] but he was fearful lest this assignment "kill"

---

[2] House Diary, March 25, 1919.

[3] Lansing Diary, March 26, 1919; and *Bullitt Mission,* 65. Apparently there are no minutes of these particular sessions of the Daily Meetings of the [American] Commissioners Plenipotentiary. See *F.R.,P.C.,1919,* XI, 132–3.

[4] Woodward and Butler (eds.): *Documents on British Foreign Policy, 1919–1939,* 1st Series, III, 426. Even from Helsingfors Bullitt had asked House to show these materials to Kerr. *F.R.,1919,Russia,* 84.

[5] See my *Political Origins of the New Diplomacy, 1917–1918,* 282–7.

Lansdowne politically. Lloyd George also eliminated Robert Cecil, who was needed for work on the Covenant, and Smuts, who was about to leave for Budapest.[6] In any case, a British mission never materialized not because the proper envoy could not be located but because Lloyd George lacked the courage and political support to defy Wickham Steed, *The Times,* the *Daily Mail,* Churchill, and the unyielding Conservative majority in Commons.[7] On the other hand, had Woodrow Wilson given a strong lead, Lloyd George would certainly have been considerably less responsive to these pressures.

The same hour that Bullitt was breakfasting in Lloyd George's apartment Colonel House tried out his scare tactics, at the same time groping toward a compromise plan. In an extended conversation he told Orlando that an American agent just back from Russia had found Lenin eager for an accommodation on the basis of existing boundary lines and on the further condition of mutual restraints on propaganda. However, should the Allies refuse to treat, the Bolsheviks were ready to throw 1.2 million armed men against their enemies. House also conjured up his favorite specter: there was the added danger that sooner or later the Germans would link up with the Russians and "everything east of the Rhine would then be arrayed against the Western Powers." Consequently, with the Allies unable and unwilling to send an adequate military expedition, they would be wise to seek a settlement *pour éviter le pire.* To achieve this they need not even meet the Bolsheviks on Prinkipo or anywhere else. They should simply "draw up a treaty in Paris, practically our own terms . . . and send this treaty to Moscow for their signature, promising to sign it ourselves in the event it was agreed upon there." Of course, Orlando was game.[8]

Later that same day House turned to Gordon Auchincloss and David Hunter Miller—not to Bullitt—to make a draft of a treaty to be sent to Lenin. Both Auchincloss and Miller were conservative rather than reformist anti-Bolsheviks, were opposed to a settlement, and found Lenin's armistice terms "most unfavorable to us." Nevertheless, though they made no secret of their own views, House asked them to work out "an armistice drawn up to suit ourselves."[9]

Auchincloss was also a member of the cabal which now advocated that in view of the famine in Russia the Allies—in particular the U.S.—manipulate both the promise and denial of relief for political purposes. In brief, the Bolsheviks should be told that unless they signed an

6 *Bullitt Mission,* p. 66.
7 Cf. Wickham Steed: *Through Thirty Years,* II, 301–7; *P.D.,114* (April 2, 1919), cols. 1327–30, 1334; *The New Europe,* April 10, 1919, 293 ff.; *Daily Herald,* April 10, 1919; *Pall Mall Gazette,* April 12, 1919.
8 House Diary, March 26, 1919; and Minutes of a Conversation Between Orlando and House, March 26, 1919, signed by A. Hugh Frazier, House Papers, 29:31.
9 David Hunter Miller: *My Diary at the Conference of Paris,* I, 206; and Auchincloss Diary, March 26, 1919.

armistice and with it a relief agreement on Allied terms, the blockade would continue. Simultaneously a propaganda campaign should be launched to convince the peoples of Europe, including Russia, that the Bolsheviks alone were responsible for the starvation because of their callous refusal to agree to perfectly selfless and innocuous terms.

Vance McCormick, Chairman of the War Trade Board, and Herbert Hoover began to formulate this plan around March 1. At the former's suggestion Oscar Straus, the Paris representative of the League to Enforce Peace, invited both these champions of economic warfare to come to dinner on March 4, together with Bakhmetev and Sazonov. At this dinner McCormick proposed his "scheme for economic relief of Russia by joint Allied and neutral action, to be distributed under proper military protection." Within two weeks Fridtjof Nansen called on McCormick. Apparently the Russian *émigrés* in Paris "were trying to get him to head an international movement to help Russia get arms and munitions and one hundred million dollars to down Bolshevism." McCormick thought he talked sensibly; and by late March he was convinced that Nansen "was the man to start a satisfactory neutral relief to aid Russia without recognizing the Bolshevik Government." After a talk with Bullitt, whom he considered "quite pro-Bolshevik," McCormick was confirmed in his impression "that the Bolsheviks were on their last legs and were ready to trade."[1]

President Wilson was also beginning to think along relief lines. His concern for Russia was unabated, although he continued to be confused about which course to follow. On March 24, he opened the first meeting of the Big Four with the warning that there now "was a veritable race between peace and anarchy." The following day, while discussing the Hungarian crisis, Wilson inclined to leave the Bolsheviks to stew in their own juice in Russia, while taking all necessary steps to prevent Bolshevism from triumphing elsewhere. On the twenty-sixth he joined Lloyd George in warning that an excessively hard peace would throw Germany into Bolshevism.[2]

The fact that Wilson did not receive Bullitt was not a sign of lack of interest or urgency. After all, Bullitt was not one of his close advisers. In all likelihood Wilson saw Bullitt's telegrams as they came in from Helsingfors; and to have asked for a written rather than an oral report, with Lenin's proposal attached, was neither bad nor even unexceptional procedure. In January Wilson had made good use of Buckler's report without either meeting him or getting his name straight![3]

[1] Vance McCormick Diary, March 4, 18, 29, and April 6, 1919; and Auchincloss Diary, March 7, 1919.

[2] Paul Mantoux: *Les Délibérations du conseil des quatre*, I, 13, 20, 28.

[3] *Bullitt Mission*, 48–65. Bullitt's report for the President was undated; it seems to have been written between March 26 and 28; and the original, bearing Bullitt's signature, is in Wilson Papers, VIII A:31.

To be sure, on March 26, after telephoning the President, House complained that "as usual he found that his 'one track mind' was against taking up this [Russian] question at present."[4] The following morning, however, they actively discussed the question. According to House's own testimony, it was Wilson who suggested that he "talk to Hoover and [Henry M.] Robinson of the Shipping Board and see whether we could get ships and food to Russia in the event we wished to do so." Now that Hungary had gone Bolshevik, Vienna seemed on the brink, and Bavaria was in turmoil, Wilson and Hoover wanted 500,000 instead of 300,000 tons to supply Europe with food. In spite of the shipping shortage, that afternoon Hoover was "strongly in favor of sending food into Russia provided the Russians kept their military forces from interfering" with their neighbors.

> He feels that as soon as the fighting stops the Bolshevik army will disintegrate and the distribution of food to the people of Russia will make them less eager to continue their policy of agitation. . . . Hoover suggested further that we get Nansen or some neutral to start an organization for the relief of Russia, presumably similar to the American Relief for Belgium.

It would not be easy to devise a neutral organization geared to act as an intermediary between the Allies and the Bolsheviks. But the effort was worth making because "this plan could be carried through without French cooperation" and because something had to be done to prevent the Bolshevik forces "from sweeping over all of Europe."[5]

On March 26—the same day that House thought that Wilson was otherwise preoccupied—the President asked Hoover for "a memorandum on [his] information and opinion on the Soviet problem."[6] Within forty-eight hours Hoover formulated a spirited policy paper which synthesized many of the ideas which had circulated over the past few weeks and which formally proposed the establishment of a neutral relief commission.

> As the result of Bolshevik economic conceptions, the people of Russia are dying of hunger and disease at the rate of some hundreds of thousands monthly in a country that formerly supplied food to a large part of the world.
> I feel it is my duty to lay before you in just as few words as possible my views as to the American relation to Bolshevism and its manifestations. These views at least have the merit of being an analysis of information and thought gleaned from my own experience and the independent sources which I now have over the whole of Europe, through our widespread relief organization.

4 House Diary, March 26, 1919. Cf. *Bullitt Mission,* 73.
5 House Diary, March 27, 1919; and Auchincloss Diary, March 27 and 28, 1919.
6 Herbert Hoover: *The Ordeal of Woodrow Wilson* (New York: McGraw-Hill; 1958), 117.

It simply cannot be denied that this swinging of the social pendulum from the tyranny of the extreme right to the tyranny of the extreme left is based on a foundation of real social grievance. The tyranny of the reactionaries in Eastern and Central Europe for generations before the war, and the suffering of their common people is but a commonplace to every social student. This situation was thrown into bold relief by the war and the breakdown of these reactionary tyrannies. After fighting actually stopped on the various fronts the famine which followed has further emphasized the gulf between the lower and upper classes. The poor were starved and driven mad in the presence of extravagance and waste.

It is to be noticed that the Bolshevik ascendancy or even their strong attempts so far are confined to areas of former reactionary tyranny. Their courses represent the not unnatural violence of a mass of ignorant humanity, who themselves have learned in grief of tyranny and violence over generations. Our people, who enjoy so great liberty and general comfort, cannot fail to sympathize to some degree with these blind gropings for better social condition. If former revolutions in ignorant masses are any guide, the pendulum will yet swing back to some moderate position when bitter experience has taught the economic and social follies of present obsessions. No greater fortune can come to the world than that these foolish ideas should have an opportunity somewhere of bankrupting themselves.

It is not necessary for any American to debate the utter foolishness of these economic tenets. We must all agree that our processes of production and distribution, the outgrowth of a hundred generations, in the stimulation to individual initiative, the large equality of opportunity and infinite development of mind and body, while not perfect, come about as near perfection as is possible from the mixture of avarice, ambition, altruism, intelligence, ignorance and education, of which the human animal is today composed. The Bolshevik's land of illusion is that he can perfect these human qualities by destroying the basic processes of production and distribution instead of devoting himself to securing a better application of the collective surplus.

Politically, the Bolsheviki most certainly represent a minority in every country where they are in control, and as such they constitute a tyranny that is the negation of democracy, for democracy as I see it must rest on the execution of the will of the majority expressed by free and unterrified suffrage. As a tyranny, the Bolshevik has resorted to terror, bloodshed and murder to a degree long since abandoned even amongst reactionary tyrannies.

He has even to a greater degree relied upon criminal instinct to support his doctrines than even autocracy did. By enveloping into his doctrines the cry of the helpless and the downtrodden, he has embraced a large degree of emotionalism and has thereby given an impulse to his propaganda comparable only to the impulse of large spiritual movements. This propaganda, however, in my view will stir other populations only in ratio to their proportions of the suffering and ignorant and criminal. I feel myself, therefore, that the political danger of spread of Bolshevism by propaganda is a direct factor of the social and political development of the population which they attempt to impregnate. Where the gulf between the middle classes and the lower classes is large, and where the lower classes have been kept in ignorance and distress, this propaganda will be fatal and do violence to normal democratic development. For these reasons, I have no fear of it in the United States, and my fears as to other countries would be gauged by the above criterion. It is possible that the Soviet type of government might take hold in some other countries as a primitive form of democracy, but its virulence will be tempered by their previous degree of political subversion.

There remains in my mind one more point to be examined, that is as to whether the Bolshevik centers now stirred by great emotional hopes will not undertake large military crusades in an attempt to impose their doctrines on other defenseless people. This is a point on which my mind is divided with the evidence at hand, and it seems to me that the whole treatment of the problem must revolve on the determination of this one question. If this spirit is inherent in their doctrine, it appears to me that we must disregard all other questions and be prepared to fight, for exactly the same reasons that we entered the European War against Germany. If this is not the case, then it appears to me that from an American point of view we should not involve ourselves in what may be a ten year military entanglement in Europe. The American people cannot say that we are going to insist that any given population must work out its internal social problems according to our particular conception of democracy. In any event, I have the most serious doubt that outside forces entering upon such an enterprise can do other than infinite harm, for any great wave of emotion must ferment and spread under repression. In the swing of the social pendulum from the extreme left back toward the right, it will find the point of stabilization based on racial instincts that could never be established by outside intervention.

I think we have also to contemplate what would actually happen if we undertook military intervention in, say, a case like Hungary. We should probably be involved in years of police duty, and our first act would probably in the nature of things make us a party to reestablishing the reactionary classes in their economic domination over the lower classes. This is against our fundamental national spirit, and I doubt whether our soldiers under these circumstances could resist infection with Bolshevik ideas. It also requires consideration as to whether or not our people at home, on gradual enlightenment as to the social wrongs of the lower classes in these countries, would stand for our providing power by which such reactionaries held their position, and we would perchance be thrown into an attempt as governors to work out some social reorganization of these countries. We thus become a mandatory with a vengeance. We become, in fact, one of four mandatories, each with a different political and social outlook, for it would necessarily be a joint Allied undertaking. Furthermore, in our present engagements with France, England and Italy, we become a junior in this partnership of four. It is therefore inevitable that in these matters where our views and principles are at variance with the European Allies we would find ourselves subordinated and even committed to policies against our convictions.

In all these lights, I have the following three suggestions:

First: We cannot even remotely recognize this murderous tyranny without stimulating actionist radicalism in every country in Europe and without transgressing on every National ideal of our own.

Second: That some Neutral of international reputation for probity and ability should be allowed to create a second Belgian Relief Commission for Russia. He should ask the Northern Neutrals who are especially interested both politically and financially in the restoration of better conditions in Russia, to give to him diplomatic, financial and transportation support; that he should open negotiations with the Allied governments on the ground of desire to enter upon the humane work of saving life, and ask the conditions upon which ships carrying food and other necessaries will be allowed to pass. He should be told that we will raise no obstructions and would even help in his humanitarian task if he gets assurances that the Bolsheviki will cease all militant action across certain defined boundaries and cease their subsidizing of disturbances abroad; under these conditions that he could raise money, ships and food, either from inside or outside Russia; that he must secure an agreement covering equitable distribution, and he might even demand that Germany help pay for this. This plan does not involve any recognition or relationship by the Allies of the Bolshevik murderers now in control any more than England recognized Germany in its deals with the Belgian Relief. It would appear to me that such a proposal would at least test out whether this is a militant force engrossed upon world domination. If such an arrangement could be accomplished it might at least give a period of rest along the frontiers of Europe and would give some hope of stabilization. Time can thus be taken to determine whether or not this whole system is a world danger, and whether the Russian people will not themselves swing back to moderation and themselves bankrupt these ideas. This plan, if successful, would save an immensity of helpless human life and would save our country from further entanglements which today threaten to pull us from our National ideals.

Third: I feel strongly the time has arrived for you again to reassert your spiritual leadership of democracy in the world as opposed to tyrannies of all kinds. Could you not take an early opportunity to analyze, as only you can, Bolshevism from its political, economic, humane and its criminal points of view, and, while yielding its aspirations, sympathetically to show its utter foolishness as a basis of economic development; show its true social ends; rap our own reactionaries for their destruction of social betterment and thereby their stimulation of Bolshevism; point, however, to the steady progress of real democracy in these roads of social betterment. I believe you would again align the hearts of the suffering for orderly progress against anarchy, not alone in Russia but in every Allied country.

If the militant features of Bolshevism were drawn in colors with their true parallel with Prussianism as an attempt at world domination that we do not stand for, it would check the fears that today haunt all men's minds.[7]

While the President considered this proposal, House and Auchincloss continued to work closely with Hoover. At their suggestion Hoover thought of associating Branting with Nansen in this venture.[8] But Branting and Bullitt alike were beginning to be shunted aside. Presently Buckler gained the impression that Hoover was "talking like the *Daily Mirror* on the conquest of Bolshevism by food"; he found it "extraordinary to hear a man talking calmly of feeding a whole continent, as if it were an everyday job"; and he concluded that instead of Bullitt's peace proposal Hoover's plan for food relief plus armistice might go through.[9] Indeed, Wilson, no less than House and Lloyd George, was fearful of Wickham Steed, especially after Tumulty cabled him from Washington that "the proposed recognition of Lenin had caused consternation here."[1]

Paradoxically the March–April crisis[2] strengthened rather than weakened the opponents of an accommodation with Lenin. For the first time since the German elections the specter of Bolshevism was once again haunting Central and East Central Europe. This threat was doubly serious because in the Allied nations it coincided with an upsurge of labor unrest and renewed protests against intervention in Russia. In response to this twofold challenge reactionaries and conservatives—who, as always, vastly exaggerated the danger and imminence of revolution—would not tolerate conciliation, however much Wilson, Lloyd George, and Orlando might have favored it. Above all, since the Right embraced the conspiratorial view of history and revolution, it would not tolerate any appeasement of the Bolshevik regime, the core and embodiment of the contemporary conspiracy. Caught between a strong and established Right and an impatient but fledgling Left, and themselves baffled and frightened by events, Wilson and Lloyd George lost their nerve. They inclined to placating the Right

[7] House Papers, 10:37.
[8] Auchincloss Diary, March 29 and 31, 1919; and House Diary, March 29, 1919.
[9] Buckler to Georgina Buckler, April 3 and 4, 1919, Buckler Papers.
[1] Steed: *Thirty Years*, II, 302–5; House Diary, March 27–8, 1919; Auchincloss Diary, March 27–28, 1919; Tumulty to Wilson, April 2, 1919, Wilson Papers, VIII A:31.
[2] For a detailed discussion of this March–April crisis see Chs. 17–19 below.

without, however, surrendering to it completely. In brief, concerning the Russian question, they abandoned the Kerr-Bullitt plan in favor of the Nansen plan.

The letter which Nansen addressed to each of the Big Four on April 3 actually was drafted by Hoover. In this letter Hoover had Nansen pose as a noncommitted neutral who out of pure humanitarianism wanted to organize the provisioning of Russia "where hundreds of thousands of people were dying monthly from sheer starvation and disease." He proposed the establishment of a commission of neutrals "upon the lines of the Belgian Relief Administration," and expressed the view that "the existing authorities in Russia" could not refuse "the intervention of such a commission of wholly nonpolitical order, devoted solely to the humanitarian purpose of saving life." Nansen inquired about the conditions under which the Big Four would approve such a scheme and the extent to which they would support it with money, shipping, food, and medical supplies.[3]

That same day Colonel House instructed Auchincloss and David Hunter Miller—two confirmed advocates of relief with armistice but without a reciprocal political settlement—to prepare an answer to Nansen's (i.e., Hoover's!) letter. In their draft-reply they agreed that conditions in Russia were "shocking to humanity." They also declared that the Allied Governments were ready to cooperate with a neutral commission "without thought of political, military or financial advantage" and with no other aim than "the humanitarian purpose of saving life." Provided the *de facto* governments of Russia were as willing as the Allies to give relief, no political obstacles would stand in the way.

Of course, subject to the supervision of the commission, the distribution of supplies "should be solely under the control of the people of Russia." In order to maximize the speed and benefits of relief, however, "the control of transportation in Russia . . . should be placed wholly" under the commission. Furthermore, Nansen's proposal could not be considered unless there were a "cessation of hostilities by Russian troops [and] a cessation of all hostilities on the Russian fronts."[4]

Auchincloss took this draft first to House and then to Hoover, and both thought it was splendid. At the Colonel's request he also showed it to Hankey and Kerr, who reacted sympathetically. Only Bullitt was not pleased, though Auchincloss "did not expect him to be."[5]

Bullitt was severely critical of the spirit and rhetoric, to say nothing of the substance, of this draft-reply. He forewarned Auchincloss that

[3] *The Memoirs of Herbert Hoover, 1874–1920* (New York: Macmillan; 1951), 414–16; and Hoover: *Ordeal of Woodrow Wilson*, 120–1. The text of Nansen's letter is also cited in *F.R.,1919,Russia*, 102, and Miller: *My Diary*, VII, 428–9.
[4] The full text of this draft is cited in *F.R.,1919,Russia*, 103. It was based on a preliminary but wordier note written by Miller alone. See Miller: *My Diary*, VII, 430–2.
[5] Auchincloss Diary, April 3 and 4, 1919.

two of his terms were "obviously unfair" and altogether unacceptable to Lenin. To ask the Soviet government to give the commission control of Russia's transportation system was equivalent to asking the Soviet government "to put its head in the lion's mouth." Lenin was equally unlikely to settle for a unilateral cessation of hostilities: the proposal made no mention of the hostilities by Allied troops, did not envisage their withdrawal, and said nothing about stopping Allied aid to the Whites and the seceding nationalities. What better proof for Trotsky's thesis "that any armistice would simply be used by the Allies as a period in which to supply" modern equipment to the anti-Soviet governments?[6]

At House's request Bullitt submitted his own draft for a reply to Nansen in which he combined the armistice-*cum*-relief proposal with the Kerr-Lenin peace plan. Accordingly, during the two-week armistice, representatives of the Allies and all the *de facto* Russian governments would meet at Kristiana (Oslo) to end the civil war, reestablish international relations, and arrange for the provisioning of Russia. The "equitable distribution of supplies and utilization of transport facilities would be agreed upon by the Conference on consultation with representatives of those neutral States which are prepared to assume the responsibility for the provisioning of Russia."[7]

But since House had long since deserted Bullitt for Auchincloss and Hoover, he never even considered this counterproposal. Instead, he authorized Bullitt to make minor revisions of the Miller-Auchincloss text in line with his earlier two-point criticism. Thus Bullitt stipulated that Russia's transport problem would be solved with the "assistance, advice, and supervision" of the neutral commission and that the cessation of hostilities would, of course, "involve a complete suspension of the transfer of troops and military material of all sorts *to* and within" the territories of the former Russian Empire.[8] Auchincloss felt that these changes "would make it impossible to send the Polish Divisions to Poland (a matter we have been working for for three months and which Foch just yesterday arranged), would not require adequate control over the Russian railways for the movement of food," and would fail to win French and British endorsement.[9]

In the afternoon of April 6 the American Commissioners held a meeting at Woodrow Wilson's bedside to resolve the Russian question. By then the President had studied all the pertinent documents—the Kerr-Lenin plan, Bullitt's report, Hoover's memorandum, the Nansen inquiry, and the various draft-replies to Nansen. He was also fully

[6] Bullitt to Auchincloss, April 4, 1919, cited in *Bullitt Mission*, 83; and Miller: *My Diary*, VII, 435–6.
[7] Cited in *F.R.,1919,Russia*, 104–6. Cf. *Bullitt Mission*, 79.
[8] Ibid., 84–7; and Miller: *My Diary*, VII, 440–1.
[9] Auchincloss Diary, April 6, 1919.

briefed about the political storm which was raging on both sides of the Atlantic, Lloyd George's surrender to Wickham Steed, and Clemenceau's bitter resistance to dealing with Lenin. After discussion the President formally decided for the Nansen plan; and among the draft-replies he opted for the Auchincloss-Miller text, softened by Bullitt's twin amendments.[1] Lenin's offer was left to expire, and Bullitt's subsequent request that an extension be sought to permit the Nansen plan to be considered by the Big Four was summarily rejected. There was to be no connection whatever between the Bullitt Mission and the Nansen plan.[2]

The Big Three remained to be won over. Before Wilson brought the draft-reply to the Council on April 9 House and his assistants had rallied Lloyd George and Orlando. Wilson had also authorized a further change to the effect that the Russian authorities would have to bear the full cost of relief. Even though Clemenceau reluctantly consented, he alone delayed signing the final text.[3]

Finally, on April 16, Clemenceau signed, thereby clearing the way for the Council to send a joint reply to Nansen. House had been forced to work on the Tiger for a full week. Once he had succeeded the Colonel thought

> The reason I get along with Clemenceau better than the President . . . is that in talking of such matters as the Russian question, the President talks to him as he would to me, while I never think of using the same argument with Clemenceau as I use with the President. One is an idealist, the other a practical old line statesman. When I told him about Russia and the good it would do France and the rest of us to open it up, he saw at once and was willing. If I had told him it was to save life in Russia and to make things easier there, it would have had no effect.[4]

In fact, it is much more likely that Clemenceau stalled until House had secured Wilson's approval for the fifteen-year occupation of the Rhineland. It was only after House brought him this offering that Clemenceau called off the hate-Wilson campaign in the kept press and signed the Nansen document.[5] Having signed it he extracted the additional promise that the Americans, in particular Hoover, would have no "direct dealings with the Bolsheviks."[6]

[1] House Diary, April 5–6, 1919; Lansing Diary, April 5–6, 1919; Lansing Diary, April 5–6, 1919; Auchincloss Diary, April 6, 1919; Buckler to Georgina Buckler, April 7, 1919, Buckler Papers.
[2] *Bullitt Mission*, 90–2; Pettit to Bullitt, April 5, 1919, House Papers, 10:48; Herter to Bullitt, April 10, 1919, Bullitt Papers; *F.R.,P.C.,1919*, XI, 148.
[3] Miller: *My Diary*, VII, 442–3; Mantoux: *Délibérations*, I, 207; House Diary, April 6 and 14, 1919.
[4] House Diary, April 14, 1919.
[5] House Diary, April 15–17, 1919. Cf. Seymour: *Intimate Papers*, IV, 406–9.
[6] Auchincloss Diary, April 16, 1919.

Clemenceau and Pichon need not have worried about Hoover who, quite independently, was violently hostile to direct dealings. The day after the Big Four issued their answer to Nansen, the Food Tsar nearly took a step which—intentionally or unintentionally—threatened to transform an unacceptable proposal into an outright provocation to Lenin.

In accordance with his letter of March 28, Hoover felt that the offer of relief should be coupled with a solemn anti-Bolshevik manifesto. When neither the President nor the Council issued this manifesto, he himself felt called upon to do so. Consequently on April 18 Hoover gave out an intemperate statement "attacking the tyranny, cruelty, and incapacity of the Soviet regime, together with the cynical admission of the expectation that the relief enterprise just approved would do this regime more harm than good." In line with House's arguments to Clemenceau he added, furthermore, that "many social observers believe that Bolshevism will die out much more quickly in the world if its real character is illuminated and made visible so that all may read, than if it is cooped up in a dark room."[7]

The moment House heard that Hoover was about to take this initiative he asked him to delay until they could discuss it the following morning.

> It [the statement] is the most foolish thing I have known Hoover to do yet, although I am somewhat accustomed to an occasional "brainstorm" from him. We have been for several weeks trying to get the Russian matter in the shape that it now is and he has helped me as much as anyone. Just as soon, however, as we have it signed by the President and the three Prime Ministers Hoover gives out a statement which would absolutely destroy any chance of its success. Whether his action is because of his inordinate desire for publicity I do not know.[8]

When he met with House he yielded and agreed not to release his statement. By that afternoon, however, Hoover had changed his mind again. He had just been informed that French sources were insinuating that by pressing on with the Nansen scheme, over French opposition, he and the U. S. Delegation were supporting Bolshevism.

> I have no objection to making any personal sacrifice necessary to obtain large political objectives. I do not, however, think it is fair to the American officials or to the American people that we should not define precisely where we stand on Bolshevism. While I regard the *parlor operators who are coquetting* with this fire with contempt I realize that we stand to further the forces of disorder in the United

[7] Ray Stannard Baker: "Manuscript Material with Notes from the Peace Conference Records Regarding the Russian Problem as Presented at Paris," 32–3, in Baker Papers, Box 18, Folder 2.
[8] House Diary, April 19, 1919.

States if we stand still. . . . It is possible that the whole Mission will be driven into making a *defensive* statement within the next three days, whereas if I make an *offensive* statement now we will never have to do so. Even if this is not the case, unless we disarm the parlor operators we will have to answer for a stimulus to this clap trap over the next twelve months [italics mine].[9]

House instantly went into consultation with the President and the Commissioners, "and they were unanimous in the opinion that it was a childish thing to do." By invoking their sanction the Colonel just barely prevailed on Hoover to hold his fire for the time being.[1]

In January Wilson had hoped in vain that the food bill could pass Congress without recourse to anti-Bolshevik rhetoric. Now this same issue was raised at the Peace Conference. But whereas Wilson could momentarily silence Hoover and ignore his own Russian experts,[2] the right-wing critics whom Hoover sought to pacify were altogether more truculent. At this precise moment they became particularly belligerent because of favorable military developments in Russia.

On April 6 the French fleet mutinied at Odessa and the Allies evacuated this all-important Black Sea base. But this upset, which was deliberately played down, was overshadowed by Kolchak's capture of Ufa on March 14 and his advance to within 35 miles of Samara during the following four weeks. Furthermore, the Poles were advancing on a broad front (of some 150 miles) and occupied Vilna on April 19, while the Rumanians were beginning to recover lost ground from the Hungarian Bolsheviks.

By April 25 the London *Times* carried an editorial on "The Progress in Russia." The opponents of Prinkipo now denounced the Nansen scheme as yet another ill-concealed and dangerous conspiracy of appeasement. Kolchak's advances enabled them to argue that this was hardly the time to provide Lenin with food, however indirectly. The right-wing press was up in arms; the Finnish government insisted that it was "particularly undesirable that food should be supplied just at the present moment when the Bolsheviks were being so vigorously pressed by their enemies on every side"; and the Russian Political Conference declared that food supplies had to be kept out of the hands of Bolshevik authorities and that the struggle for liberation "must not for any reason be halted."[3]

In no time the brightening prospects of the civil war in Russia and the attendant pro-interventionist outcry left their imprint on the Ameri-

---

[9] Hoover to House, April 19, 1919 (p.m.), House Papers, 7:68.
[1] House Diary, April 19, 1919.
[2] The Russian Section of the Ammission called on Wilson to issue a declaration like the one that had lead to the German Armistice. Memorandum on Russian Policy, March 31, 1919, Wilson Papers, VIII A:30.
[3] *The Times* (London), *Daily Mail* (Paris), *le Temps, le Figaro, Echo de Paris, Journal des Débats,* April–May, 1919, *passim;* and *F.R.,1919,Russia,* 109–10.

cans and the British, let alone on the French. Since Kolchak was getting "stronger every day," as early as April 21 Polk again urged the recognition of the Omsk government. "If we recognize Omsk, will it be breaking faith in regard to [the Nansen proposal]? Lenin will not agree to stop fighting for food unless we get the anti-Bolsheviks to stop also. This is hard on Kolchak as he is winning now." McCormick resolved to put this question to Wilson, all the time hoping that the Nansen scheme could be delayed "as things are moving pretty fast with Kolchak and I think some further thought should be given to recognizing the Omsk Government."[4]

Presently not only Sir Henry Wilson and Churchill but also Lloyd George was carried away by talk of the imminent fall of the Soviet government. Following his disavowal of Bullitt on May 7 he estimated that the time had come for the Big Four to take stock.

> The situation in Russia has changed in a most remarkable fashion: we are witnessing a real collapse of Bolshevism, to such a point that the British Cabinet asks us for an immediate decision with regard to our Russian policy. According to my information, Kolchak's forces are about to link up with those at Archangel; it is also possible that he will shortly arrive in Moscow and set up a new government there.

These advances were so spectacular that Chaikovsky as well as Paderewski urgently petitioned the Allies to force the Whites—Kolchak and Denikin—to declare formally that their aims were neither reactionary nor militarist.[5]

In view of this hardening attitude toward Lenin in the Anglo–American camp, Clemenceau and Pichon took courage. They kept the Nansen project in the balance by once again blocking communications with Moscow. The Norwegian explorer, who was in Paris, filed a telegram to Lenin conveying the reply he had just received from the Allies. But the French telegraph and radio systems refused to transmit it. After a week he complained to Bullitt who, in turn, reported to Herter that Nansen was "at his wits' end because of this red-tape delay."[6]

That was one of Bullitt's last official acts. Just a few days before he had written to Pettit, who was still in Stockholm, that the Nansen proposal was "the total result of our efforts, and I am rather ashamed of it." With biting sarcasm he expressed the hope that Nansen would "finally acquire the Nobel Prize" for his efforts! As for himself, he was dead tired and he needed a week's rest in Italy; but he had "not yet

4 McCormick Diary, April 21 and 24, 1919, 72, 74.
5 Mantoux: Délibérations, I (May 7, 1919, 11:00 a.m.), 505–6.
6 Bullitt to Herter, April 24, 1919, Bullitt Papers.

decided whether to resign altogether, or simply to take leave of absence."[7] Just then the group around House came close to making this decision for him. Auchincloss thought that "we ought to get rid of Bullitt [because] he has been stirring up everyone with a lot of silly talk about Russia and the Bolsheviks and his loose talk is doing us more harm than good."[8]

With Bullitt off on vacation, Buckler was left to look after Nansen's scheme. Progress continued to be slow. The subterfuge of translating the message to Lenin into Norwegian and sending it by Norwegian cypher failed; and the suggestion to send Pettit to Petrograd with it was vetoed because Wilson had promised Clemenceau not to have any direct contacts with the Soviet government. At long last Hoover sent Nansen's dispatch to his food office in Holland with instructions to have it transmitted over the Dutch radio station. The Soviets acknowledged receiving it on May 4.[9]

Chicherin's answer was dated May 7; it reached Copenhagen by wireless on the fourteenth; and it was in Paris by the following morning. Whereas in mid-May Paris was still jubilant and overconfident about Kolchak's advances—wishful thinking and counterrevolutionary cunning contributed to vast exaggerations of these advances, notably in the press—Lenin knew that the spring offensive toward the Volga and Moscow had been halted. In late April the Red Army, now swollen to close to 1.5 million by the call-up of trade unionists, struck hard at Kolchak's overextended left flank, and soon thereafter the White troops were beating a disorderly retreat toward the Urals and Siberia. And at this time Denikin's summer offensive from the south toward Moscow had not yet started.[1]

The Soviet leaders, therefore, were as cool and collected in their response to Nansen as they had been in their responses to Buckler, Prinkipo, and Bullitt. After thanking Nansen for his interest and

[7] Bullitt to Pettit, April 18, 1919, Bullitt Papers.
[8] Auchincloss Diary, April 23, 1919. For Bullitt's resignation see pp. 800–1 below.
[9] Buckler to Herter, April 25, 1919, Morris (Stockholm) to Bullitt, April 26, 1919, Haynes (Helsingfors) to Ammission, May 3, 1919, and Bullitt to Morris, May 6, 1919, Bullitt Papers; Buckler to Georgina Buckler, April 25, 1919, Buckler Papers; Hoover: *Memoirs*, 417–18.
[1] "Three major campaigns formed the climaxes of the civil war in 1919: Kolchak's offensive . . . in the spring . . . ; Denikin's advance . . . in the summer; and Yudenich's attempt to capture Petrograd, in the summer. Had all these offensives converged simultaneously on the centers of Soviet power, the counter-revolution might have won. But the White Guards operated on 'external lines'; and they were separated from each other by thousands of miles. Each White Army grew up independently and at a different pace; and the commander of each was eager to win laurels exclusively for himself. The Red Army, on the contrary, benefitted from operating on 'internal lines' . . . and its operations were eventually planned and its resources controlled from a single center." Isaac Deutscher: *The Prophet Armed: Trotsky, 1879–1921* (New York: Oxford; 1954), 432–3.

compassion for Russia's suffering and privations Chicherin blamed these on the blockade of the Allied and "so-called Neutral" powers, and on the attacks by the White Guards which were made possible by Allied aid. Actually, in order to stop bloodshed the Soviet government had recently agreed to go to Prinkipo; it had also responded favorably "to overtures made by one of the Great Powers." In both instances the Soviets had been amenable in spite of the "extremely unfavorable conditions proposed to us."

With complete justification Chicherin insisted that not the Soviets but rather their enemies were responsible for the impasse.

> The Prinkipo Conference was frustrated not by us but by . . . the protégés of the Associated Powers, the counter-revolutionary governments of Kolchak, Denikin, and the others. These are the tools with the help of which the Entente Governments are making war upon us. . . . Kolchak from the east, Denikin from the south, the Rumanian [feudals], the Polish and Finnish most reactionary militarists, the German Barons and Esthonian White Guards from the west and Russian White Guard bands from the north, these are the enemies whom the Entente Governments [move] against Soviet Russia. . . .

These enemies were essentially reactionary: Kolchak and Denikin were tsarist, monarchist, and autocratic, and wherever they advanced the land which the peasants had seized was taken from them, while workers were subjected to a White terror. As for the Polish legions and Petlura's troops, they were perpetrating "massacres of Jews which by far surpass the most horrible misdeeds of the Black Hundreds." The Associated Governments were supporting these so-called freedom fighters with "war materials, foodstuffs, financial help, military commanders, and political advisers and on the north and east fronts sent their own troops to help them."

Chicherin pointed out that in their note the Allies were misusing Nansen's humanitarian intentions for their own political purposes. Certainly the "cessation of hostilities and of transfer of troops and material" was a highly political matter. The Soviets could discuss this cessation only "if we discuss the whole problem of our relations to our adversaries, that is, in the first place, to the Associated Governments." At any rate, there could be no question of making concessions on these issues which were so fundamental "for our existence under the disguise of a presumably humanitarian work."

On the other hand, the Soviets gratefully welcomed the nonpolitical part of the proposal. Chicherin promised to give Nansen "every possibility of controlling the realization [of his] humanitarian scheme" and agreed to cover the complete cost of relief. He asked Nansen to name the time and place where Soviet delegates could meet the leaders of "your commission" to discuss the details, including the disentanglement of the political and nonpolitical parts of the proposal.[2]

As long as the civil war raged in Russia there could be no nonpolitical relief to either side. To begin with, all the trumps were in the hands of the counterrevolution. At this juncture not only was there no revolutionary ally for Lenin to call on for aid, but even nations which for reasons of power politics might have considered helping the Russian Revolution were in no position to do so. All the food and medical supplies were controlled by the Allies. Lenin knew this and he never expected Hoover to accept his counterproposal which would have transferred scarce supplies—needed elsewhere—from the Allied camp into the Soviet perimeter, thereby strengthening his regime.

But since Nansen was unschooled in the politics and diplomacy of counterrevolution, he did not immediately realize that this counterproposal would be altogether unacceptable to his principal. Hence, he advised Hoover that he "intended to meet Lenin's delegates perhaps [in] Stockholm but [would] be glad to hear Hoover's opinion as soon as possible."[3]

By return telegram Hoover advised Nansen that until the entire matter "had been given further consideration by the Governments here we consider it extremely inadvisable to arrange any meeting with Bolshevik representatives."[4] Needless to say, while reviewing the entire Russian question once again the powers proposed to continue sending military and other aid—except troops—to all the anti-Bolshevik armies on the same generous scale as during the past half year. In turn the Soviets had to recognize that their peace offensive had failed. The world was divided into two hostile camps.

> What first appeared as a civil war waged on Russian territory between the Red Army and armies of the 'white' generals now took on the shape of a war between the revolutionary Soviet regime and the principal Powers of the capitalist world; and against these Powers 'political warfare' in the form of propaganda for world revolution was the most effective weapon in the Soviet armory.[5]

[2] The full text of Chicherin's reply is in *F.R.,1919,Russia*, 111–15.
[3] Ibid., 115.
[4] Ibid., 115–17.
[5] E. H. Carr: *The Bolshevik Revolution, 1917–1923* (London: Macmillan; 1953), III, 115. Also see Arthur Ransome: *Six Weeks in Russia in 1919* (London: Allen and Unwin; 1919), 147.

15

Storm Signals

ALL THE TIME that the Allied statesmen and their advisers testily searched for mutually acceptable terms for a German settlement, they kept a careful check on internal developments in Germany and Central Europe. Between the Rhine and the eastern Mediterranean in the West and the Pripet Marshes and the western shores of the Black Sea in the East the foundations of government continued to be unstable. In retrospect the chances of a collapse of order and authority may appear to have been quite small; at the time, however, the specter of revolution was ever-present. The demonstration effect of the Bolshevik Revolution and the exploits of the Red Army served to make this specter particularly credible and frightening.

Not surprisingly there was little if any apprehension about political and economic instability precipitating a right-wing coup or reaction. Only a few voices, mainly in the rightist and jingoist press, were obsessed by the long-term dangers of Ebert's reliance on Field Marshal Hindenburg and Hugo Stinnes.

The *Temps,* the *Action Française,* and the *Morning Post* yielded to no one in their anti-Bolshevism abroad or at home without, however, allowing it to dull their anti-Prussianism.

Even before the January elections Herbette kept warning that in the face of severe internal disturbances the high command of the SPD would rely increasingly on the military, political, and economic cadres of Imperial Germany and that this cooperation would proceed under the cover of violent nationalist slogans. The *Temps* was ambivalent about the restoration of order in Berlin on the eve of the elections.

When the first Bolshevik insurrection failed in Petrograd, its leaders survived and its shock troops remained armed. In Berlin Liebknecht and Luxemburg were killed after their arrest, and the suburbs are being disarmed. This difference in treatment clearly demonstrates that the Scheidemann-Hindenburg coalition has no intention of experiencing Kerensky's fate.

When the election returns revealed that the SPD lacked a majority—even if it should get together with the USPD—the *Temps* predicted the continuing ascendancy of those political forces which had changed their party labels without changing their principles, objectives, and methods. In fact, the Republic threatened to best the Empire: the modernization and centralization of state and society, combined with the accession of Austria, might be the crowning of Bismarck's edifice.[1]

Jacques Bainville issued similar caveats. Judging by the orderliness and the outcome of the elections, in less than three months Germany had recovered from her military defeat and political turmoil. The exile of the Kaiser and the democratization of the franchise could not veil the overriding continuities in leadership, institutions, and foreign policy.

> Our vision of European affairs has been warped by our obsession with Bolshevism. Under cover of this *grande peur,* Germany has reorganized herself. She has used the specter of Bolshevism to divert attention from her own affairs while at the same time ridding herself of this poison. History will be scandalized to record that the Paris Bourse went up in response to the reestablishment of order in Berlin and rose still higher when the elections revealed that Germany was back in the saddle [italics mine].

After all, it was obvious that Scheidemann and Brockdorff-Rantzau meant to advance Germany's national interest by capitalizing on Wilsonian principles, by bidding for the support of international Socialism, by flaunting the specter of Spartacism, and by threatening an arrangement with Lenin.[2]

The *Morning Post* was cast in the same incongruous position of protesting the crackdown on Spartacists in the Ruhr which it wanted applied to the shop stewards on the Clyde. In a bid for Allied indulgence, "Big Bertha" had thrown a quick fit of hysteria, which ended with the murder of Liebknecht and Luxemburg. Judging by the elections, "Big Bertha was herself again." Except for the USPD, which counted for little, the parties of the new Reichstag—all but one hiding behind new popular labels—either supported or were supported by the solidly entrenched power elite of the defunct Empire. Indeed, the new and the old Germany were "much the same," William II being used as a "lightning conductor" with which to run the Allied wrath "harmlessly into the ground." Not that Spartacism in Germany should be ignored. But the way to throttle it was to squash Bolshevism in Russia. Spartacism could not triumph or survive in a Germany sandwiched between a stable Eastern Europe and a West duly reinvigorated by a victor's peace.[3]

[1] *Le Temps,* January 16, 18, and 25, 1919.
[2] *L'Action Française,* January 31, 1919.
[3] *Morning Post,* January 22, 1919.

During the first half of 1919 the Big Four welcomed rather than feared this creeping restoration. Not order and stability but disorder and instability caused them anguish. With few exceptions Allied officials and observers countenanced whatever support the old cadres were giving to the unstable governments and economies of Germany, Austria, and Hungary. Rather than worry about the German army thwarting Allied efforts to impose harsh peace conditions, the victors hoped that the governments of Berlin, Vienna, and Budapest would marshal sufficient military strength to prevent or suppress left-wing uprisings. Perhaps if the borderlands had not separated Germany from the Red Army the Allies might even have encouraged Berlin to rearm right then and there. Under the circumstances, however, they could build up the armies of Poland, Rumania, and Czechoslovakia to fight Europe's, including Germany's, external war against the westward advance of Bolshevism.

Meanwhile the Big Four relied on Friedrich Ebert, Karl Renner, and Count Michael Károlyi to organize their own *internal* security forces. Taken as a whole the Paris Conference was prepared to condone the excesses of the Free Corps, political assassinations, and the end of social reform in pursuit of the stabilization of these regimes. Moreover, the Allies assisted this process with economic and political aid.

Not that the Allies had a monopoly on intervention in these smoldering civil wars. The Soviets were also in the field, though their capacity for intervention was severely limited. In addition to lacking the military power to break through the *cordon sanitaire,* they were in no position to hold out credible economic and diplomatic bribes. Lenin had little to work with: a flood of propaganda, a few sacks of gold, a platoon of political agents, and fallout from Allied mistakes and disagreements. To make matters worse, the Communist parties in Central Europe were embryonic at best, their leadership being totally untutored.

The Allies had substantially greater leverage. They had surplus food and raw materials as well as the power to grant or deny acceptable peace terms, so that they intervened with economic and diplomatic rather than military instruments. Whereas the moderation of the blockade and of peace terms promised to consolidate the enemy governments, their stiffening was likely to benefit the radicals of both the Right and the Left, particularly the latter. Unlike Lenin, the Big Four could rely on powerful respondents throughout defeated Europe: the established governments and the entire spectrum of anti-Bolshevik parties.

In 1919 the blockade had a variety of functions. The most conventional was that of helping coerce the enemy to comply with military and diplomatic terms. At first sight, with Germany's armies in disarray, it appeared as if little coercion would be required. But because the quick pace of demobilization also sapped and relaxed the Allied armies another form of pressure was needed. It was Marshal Foch who insisted that from the military point of view the blockade could not be dispensed with. In his judgment "the blockade, the severity of which [could] be increased or diminished according to changing circumstances, [would] remain the best and swiftest means for enforcing the Armistice agreement and, in a general way, for compelling Germany to bow to our wishes."[4] There were also cruder expressions of this same view. Both the *Morning Post* and Charles Maurras declared that the blockade was "the vise" with which the Germans could "be squeezed" into accepting Allied terms.[5]

But even these military-*cum*-diplomatic uses had vast political implications. The denial of food and raw materials weakened the enemy governments by increasing social and political unrest, notably in urban and industrial centers. Whereas the Allies fully intended to use the blockade to overthrow Lenin—and Béla Kun—such was not their intention with Ebert, Renner, and Károlyi. On the contrary, they meant to fortify them against their Left-radical opponents.

In the short run Wilson and Lloyd George gave first priority to relaxing the blockade in pursuit of political stability in Central Europe. But since Clemenceau did not share their intense alarm about the Spartacist danger, he resisted giving precedence to short-run political concerns over long-range diplomatic objectives.

Ray Stannard Baker sensed that the Paris Peace Conference had inaugurated a new era in the "use of economic power for political ends," and that the blockade should be viewed as just one aspect of economic warfare.

> This new problem, which year by year is destined to become a more significant factor in all international relationships, concerns the use of the enormous power arising from control of the economic necessaries of life—food, coal, and other raw materials—for determining the destinies of nations, in short, the use of the "economic weapon." It was only in its crude beginnings at Paris; but the world will have a fuller taste of it in the future.[6]

This instrument of control was so suitable and effective even in 1919 because of the convergence of three historical conditions: the war had wrought unprecedented economic exhaustion in Central Europe; politically, the urban and industrial centers of this area were peculiarly vulnerable to major economic dislocations; and as of 1917 the Bolshe-

---

[4] Foch to Pichon, February 3, 1919, cited in Suda L. Bane and Ralph H. Lutz (eds.): *The Blockade of Germany After the Armistice, 1918–1919* (Stanford: Stanford University Press; 1942), 92.

[5] *Morning Post,* January 22, 1919, cited in ibid., 707; and *l'Action Française,* February 24, 1919.

[6] Baker: *Woodrow Wilson and World Settlement,* II, 349–50, 352.

vik Revolution acted as a catalytic agent on the political tensions in these centers.

Throughout East-Central Europe the major urban and mining centers bore careful watching. These alone registered the unsettling political consequences of semistarvation, unemployment, crippled transportation, shortages of coal and raw materials, soaring inflation, intense national rivalries, and the peasants' reluctance to sell their produce for inflated paper currencies. The political organizers and the social carriers of the resulting disorders were primarily urban; in terms of class and status they came from the proletariat, the *petite-bourgeoisie,* and the intelligentsia. To the extent, then, to which these spasmodic conditions contributed to social and individual anomie they did so in major cities rather than in villages and provincial towns.

In the major German cities as well as in Vienna and Budapest the crisis was compounded by national humiliation, loss of *grandeur,* and despair about the future. Furthermore, even though the pre-Armistice revolutions were largely revolutions from above, the new governments were dependent on shaken bureaucracies and on praetorian guards of questionable loyalty.

On the other hand in Poland, Czechoslovakia, and Yugoslavia the fledgling governments benefited from the euphoria of liberation, the challenge of nation-building, and Allied military, economic, and political aid. Indeed, as compared to old—but defeated and truncated—Austria and Hungary these three fledgling states were much more likely to maintain political stability. Even or possibly especially the fierce border conflicts between the new and the old nations, as well as among the new nations themselves, served to promote this consolidation.

The Big Four had powerful instruments of control at their disposal. Thanks to America's economic miracle, they disposed of considerable stocks of food and raw materials. Furthermore, they devised an efficient shipping and distribution system while also making arrangements for financing.

> The control of food, fuel, clothing, and the raw materials of industry, is the key to world politics today. Those who command the bulk of the supply of these indispensable things, and command it along lines of strict centralization, have the *whip hand* over the rest of the world. It places them in possession of a form of pressure more far-reaching, more adaptable, more easily and swiftly applied, than any of the great world conquerors have ever wielded, a pressure of which Napoleon's unrealized conception of a Continental blockade was merely a vague hint or a clumsy sketch. . . .
>
> What gives economic suasion this tremendous efficacy is, of course, the fact that the world is now more closely bound together than ever before. All countries are dependent upon one another to a degree hitherto unknown. The dependence varies according to the

stage of development which a particular country has reached. . . .
It takes time to grasp all the implications of a power so unprecedented in its range [italics mine].

The Allies used this power—to deny or allocate essential supplies—in
their dealings with Russia, the successor states, and the defeated
nations.[7]

It is doubtful that without fear of the *political* consequences of food
shortages and unemployment the blockade of Germany would have
been relaxed in mid-March. Even after the reassuring outcome of the
mid-January elections American and British officials continued to
monitor all signs of political and industrial instability.

On his return from his hasty trip to Germany, Dresel and other high
American officials convinced the Commissioners to station a quasi-
permanent mission there. This new mission, headed by Captain W. R.
Gherardi, U.S.N., was instructed to keep Ammission posted about
political conditions.

The Gherardi Mission left Paris on January 26. Eleven of its fourteen members were officers in uniform. With Brockdorff-Rantzau's approval headquarters were set up in Berlin, while Dr. H. H. Field and
First Lieutenant George Howe were stationed in Munich and the others,
using Berlin as home base, went on special assignments to "places requiring special attention," such as Dresden, Leipzig, Frankfurt a/M, and
Hamburg. Simultaneously Alonzo Taylor and Vernon Kellogg, on their
way to East-Central Europe, visited Germany to investigate food and
economic conditions. Even though they continued to be under Hoover's
direction they were instructed to maintain contact with Gherardi.[8]

The Gherardi Mission neither received nor required detailed instructions. All concerned took it for granted that above all the mission
was expected to gather and evaluate information about the smoldering
civil war in Germany. Furthermore, Gherardi assumed that he was
expected to make recommendations about how the Allies might best
help Scheidemann stabilize his government.

Accordingly, on February 2, in this first substantive dispatch,
Gherardi reported that the government's situation was critical "because
of active resistance in Bremen, Düsseldorf, and Eisenach, where
Spartacists were in control"; that the Free Corps sent to Bremen were
of "doubtful qualifications"; and that although Berlin appeared to be
quiet there were "considerable apprehensions" about renewed Spartacist outbreaks. In conclusion he intoned a recommendation which by
now was second nature with all reformists, especially in official American and British circles: only the prompt lifting of the blockade on

---

[7] Charles Roden Buxton: "Economic Suasion: The New Weapon," in *Labour Leader*,
January 30, 1919, 7.
[8] R. Tyler, Capt. U.S.A., to Joseph C. Grew, January 20, 1919, National Archives,
Document 184.012/9; and *F.R.,P.C.,1919*, XII, 1.

food and certain raw materials could "enable the present government to hold the situation and to suppress the danger of further disorganization."[9]

Thereafter, during the first three weeks of February, Gherardi sent detailed and accurate reports about the third wave of Spartacist and left-Independent disorders. On February 4 he warned that the uprisings in Bremen and Hamburg foreshadowed nation-wide antigovernment demonstrations to confound the opening of the Constituent Assembly in Weimar on the sixth. That day he wired that there was a design not only in the timing but also in the targets.

> The Spartacist movement at present is strongest in Düsseldorf, Hamburg, Bremen, Kiel, and Brunswick. These towns, with the exception of the latter, are of the greatest importance to the Government, as they control the routes by which food might enter Germany; Hamburg and Bremen representing the most feasible seaports and Düsseldorf controlling the big railways crossing the Rhine.

He emphasized that all forcible opposition would continue to come from the Left.[1]

When the Independents flatly refused to join the SPD in a Weimar coalition Gherardi became particularly alarmed. By themselves the Spartacists could not paralyze the nation; but this addition of a second network of opposition was ominous. Even though these dissident Independents were "as yet a small minority," they were likely to attract "people dissatisfied with the results obtained by the Government." Above all, the radical wing of the USPD was practically indistinguishable from the Spartacists in both aim and method. As a precaution Gherardi decided to send Franklin Day to Weimar to speak with Haase, the leader of the "moderate section."[2]

By the time Day returned to Berlin on the twenty-first Gustav Noske and the Free Corps had reestablished government control over Hamburg, Bremen, and Düsseldorf. Day notified Paris that these key centers and Berlin would be spared new flare-ups provided the food situation deteriorated no further. Following his interview with Haase this American agent warned that the USPD was still "flirting with Bolshevism"; that wherever Spartacists "created disturbance they could count on the support of the Independents"; and that "wherever such support was not given the Independents, at least by their neutrality, obstructed the Government's efforts to reestablish order."[3]

Not that Day blindly chastized the USPD. From the very outset

9 Ibid., 2.
1 Ibid., 4–5.
2 Ibid., 7–8.
3 Ibid., 29–30.

both Gherardi and Day were critical of the SPD's excessive solicitude for the bourgeoisie, the bureaucracy, and the army. In their effort to maintain themselves in power Ebert and Scheidemann banked on the Democratic Party and the Catholic Center as well as on the moderate wing of the USPD. However, "opinion appears to be that they are compromising themselves to secure the support from the right much more than from the left and in doing so they are bringing into political strength men and ideas whose liberalism is tinged with reactionary tendencies." Gherardi was uncomfortable because with Brockdorff-Rantzau at the Foreign Office "no change had occurred and no democratic spirit existed except as circumstances dictate for the moment."[4]

As early as February 4 Gherardi bluntly confessed that "the Ebert-Scheidemann Government with its attendant influences was not a great change from the old bureaucratic system." At the same time, however, he also conceded that there stood "between them and straight Bolshevism no class or party from which a government could be drawn which would have the confidence of even a small part of the people."[5]

Even so, with every passing day the mission became increasingly touchy about the political cost of anti-Bolshevism. Immediately following the SPD's pact with the Democratic Party Gherardi detected "a decided change in tone." He considered this Democratic Party to be composed of old-time politicians—Friedrich von Payer, Friedrich Naumann, Bernhard Dernburg, and reputedly Count Johann von Bernstorff—who were determined "to incite resistance to any acceptance of probable Allied terms." On instructions from Paris a member of the mission—Major Arnold Whitridge—checked this assessment against that of General Dupont, the head of the French Military Mission in Berlin. According to Dupont, whereas in December some responsible Germans had actually asked the Allies to occupy Berlin to save the capital from Spartacism, by now *"ils sont devenus beaucoup plus fiers,"* the new government "growing more and more reactionary."[6]

Franklin Day's visit to Weimar merely reinforced these impressions. He was disturbed because the new government was making excessive concessions to the bourgeois parties.

> The Ebert-Scheidemann Government is reluctant to change even certain externals such as the terms "Reichsverfassung" which the Independents proposed should be "Verfassung der Republik," and to acknowledge boldly the republican and socialist character of the state. . . .
> The National Assembly in its *transactions,* as well as in its *personnel,* differs but little from the Reichstag. The *tone* of the speeches by all members of the Assembly from the extreme right to

[4] Ibid., 3–4.
[5] Ibid., 4.
[6] Ibid., 12–13, 15.

the Majority Socialists has changed but little; they are not aware of Germany's defeat. . . . Although monarchical sentiment is confined to the extreme right, the Democracy of the Democratic Party is not so wholly different from the Liberalism which created the idea of "Mitteleuropa". . . . The Elections to the National Assembly "were elections dictated by the fear of Spartacus." The influence of the Majority Socialists who represent a slightly better political idea than the ancient Liberals, is stronger than their representation shows; they lost much ground to the bourgeois parties at the election because of panic. Whatever the faults of the Majority Socialists may be, they at least possess the energy to govern practically which the German Democrats lack entirely. As long as it however does not have the absolute majority, the Ebert-Scheide-mann group is forced to ally itself with the Democrats and to support a phrasey Nationalism out of keeping both with the internal and external situation. *It is not impossible that this support of such a Nationalism is also due to a fear of Bolshevism and a hope that it may crystallize the forces of order* [italics mine].

But whereas Allied jingoists distrusted this return to order for foreboding a full-scale restoration, Day perceived it as a dangerous catalyst for the radicalization of the Left. He reported that even Theodor Wolff admitted that the Independents were benefiting from "the tendency of the Majority Socialists to become more and more conservative."[7]

By the time Day filed this report about his findings in Weimar the mission, which he now headed, was being phased out. During his absence from Berlin the German government had uncovered a plot against Gherardi's life, allegedly by "Russian and Bolshevik elements." In any case, Gherardi rushed to Paris where on February 17 he conferred with his superiors. On his advice it was decided to recall the military members of the mission; to leave Day, a civilian, in Berlin, possibly under the supervision of an older man; and occasionally to send "traveling commissions of experts" to collect firsthand information, to be brought back to Paris immediately and in person. Incidentally, the military members did not return straight to Paris. On their way back, "by arrangement with the [German] Foreign Office," they spent about two weeks studying local conditions in various cities: Major Blaney and Captain Peirce went to Cassel, Frankfurt a/M, and Mannheim; Major Whitridge and Lieutenant Dewald to Munich, where they conferred with Field; and Captain Black and Lieutenant Stonestreet to Breslau.[8] In early March they reported to Paris that in both Cassel and Frankfurt starvation, the death rate, and unemployment were rising rapidly; that in Breslau and Upper Silesia the food and employment

[7] Ibid., 30–1.
[8] *F.R.,P.C.,1919*, XI, 46–9; and *F.R.,P.C.,1919*, XII, 27–8, 37–8.

situation was critical; and that serious disturbances could not be averted unless supplies reached there quickly.[9]

Presently Gherardi was relieved of his political assignment. But before resuming service at sea he submitted a summary of his findings and recommendations. In this summary he emphasized the Pan-German background and ambitions of the Democratic Party, whose influence was ascendant in the government; he stressed that there had been "no change in viewpoint" in the power elite; he noted a "spirit of complaint and whining"; he scorned Brockdorff-Rantzau as well as his cousin and adviser Bernstorff for failing to "realize that times had changed from those when German influence was powerful in the world"; and he predicted that the German Delegation would play the Bolshevik card in the forthcoming peace negotiations.

Gherardi was prepared to look the other way because in the last analysis the struggle was "between democracy and Bolshevism." Should the Ebert-Scheidemann government collapse Germany would be left "in a state of anarchy which would enable the Bolshevik movement to take possession, and Bolshevism was as possible for a disorganized Germany as it was for a disorganized Russia." For the immediate future the government's survival was contingent on economic conditions rather than diplomatic prospects. Alonzo Taylor and Vernon Kellogg, as well as a British commission, shared Gherardi's judgment that without prompt and substantial imports even the present inadequate food rations would have to be "greatly reduced by the end of March." The remedy was self-evident: to avoid the fatal political consequences of creeping undernourishment and unemployment, the Allies should instantly relax the blockade.[1]

As head of the "German desk" Dresel processed and evaluated all the dispatches from the mission, including Gherardi's summary report. Even though he readily agreed that Bolshevism was a serious danger and that the lifting of the blockade was the appropriate prophylaxis, he balked at any criticism of the German regime. In commenting on Gherardi's memorandum Dresel contended that "the mental attitude of the people towards the rights and wrongs of the war, and the question whether Bolshevism is being used as a slogan to get good terms, are not the all-important things at the present moment." This was no time to be squeamish; the perils of the moment were so great that the Allies had to give every possible support "to the good elements which exist."[2]

Dresel was equally impatient with a memorandum filed by Professor R. J. Kerner after his return to Paris from two months with the Coolidge Mission. Kerner characterized Germany as "a republic with-

[9] Ibid., 47, 52–62.
[1] Ibid., 33–6.
[2] Dresel to Grew, March 4, 1919, National Archives, Document 184.01202/59.

out republicans," the old bureaucracy still being in power and innumerable Germans being convinced that they had been misled rather than defeated. The German people were being urged to choose between two projects: "one is that of preparation of *revanche* . . . , the other is Bolshevism, i.e. to Bolshevize Central Europe and then overwhelm the rest." Kerner recommended that Germany—as well as Austria and Magyaria—be given economic aid only in return "for their adoption of a policy which will frankly admit their defeat, . . . publicly disavow the idea of *revanche,* and which will disavow and discontinue their participation in Bolshevik propaganda whose purpose is to wreck the new states."[3]

Dresel could not have disagreed more. He claimed as his own a view expressed elsewhere: that the war had taught the Germans an unforgettable lesson and that "the curious Germans who believed otherwise had been reduced to an infinitesimal faction." In any event, this was a time for *unconditional* aid.[4] Since the last week of February saw the start of a new wave of disorders, strikes, and insurrections this advice was about to be heeded.

A few days following Gherardi's departure from Berlin the government regained control and reestablished order in the coastal ports; the greatly feared general strike in the Ruhr was forestalled by a combination of cajolery and force; and key cities like Düsseldorff and Essen were made safe for local coalitions of SPD and Democratic politicians.

But no sooner had these flames been dampened than others promptly flared up. On February 21 Kurt Eisner was assassinated in Munich; beginning February 24 a widespread strike movement crippled the industrial and mining centers of central Germany, notably of Saxony and Thuringia; Weimar was caught in the center of this unrest; and starting March 3 and for a full ten days Berlin was in the grip of a general strike. In turn, Noske and the Free Corps had their finest days.

The two ranking civilians of the Gherardi Mission were left to evaluate these dramatic and fast-moving events, Day from Berlin, H. H. Field from Munich.

Not surprisingly Day's dispatches became altogether alarmist, to the point that they completely disregarded the continuing decline of democratic and reformist elements and impulses in the government.

Even before March 3, when the Workers' Council of greater Berlin called the general strike in the capital, Day characterized the situation as extremely grave. He considered Eisner's murder the prelude to the establishment of a Soviet in Munich and the signal for "outbreaks of radical movements in many parts of Germany." Even though Haase and Barth opposed another premature test of strength with Noske, the

---

[3] *F.R.,P.C.,1919,* XII, 352–5.
[4] Ibid., 355.

left-Independents, over whom they were fast losing influence, could not be restrained while the Spartacists exploited the situation for their own ends. According to Day the strike movement was well planned and in Berlin it was "generally believed to be the *prelude to a second revolution.*" How would the government react? And what about the Allies? "While radical labor agitation [was] not Bolshevik in its immediate aspects" it had strong affinities with Spartacism and would keep thriving on rising unemployment and food shortages. Once again the prescription was self-evident: "I venture to state that the opportunity to work and a betterment in food conditions alone can prevent what seems today to be an impending catastrophe [italics mine]."[5]

Franklin Day supplemented this official dispatch of February 27 with a personal letter to Dresel, following a long talk with Colonel Arthur Conger. Since the Armistice this intelligence officer, who was a seasoned expert on German affairs, had been watching the political and military situation for General Pershing; he also saw something of General Groener.[6] Day was so convinced of the urgency and seriousness of the situation that he decided to cover his own observations with the authority of an older and more seasoned expert.

> Conger agrees with me that we *stand before the danger of a second revolution here.* It is his belief that measures must be taken to get some economic aid here as the situation is becoming daily worse. Our couriers from Munich barely got through. . . . There are strikes everywhere and all of Central Germany will soon be striking. . . . The Independents are making every effort to start another revolution and I fear we are before its advent. *It will be a real revolution.* That would not matter and *I would not object to the Independents if they had not flirted with the Bolsheviks so. Once they start the Spartacists will get arms and power and the devil may break loose.* The Independents are of course the only ones who appreciate the question of guilt and they count on this to strengthen themselves with the Entente. I think we could not support them. They are unscrupulous and do not hesitate to use every means from arms to perjury and breaking faith to further the world revolution which they so desire. *They are not Bolsheviks but once radicalism begins it will be hard to stop.* I have talked all this over with Conger and he quite agrees.
>
> Of course you know how hard it is to make any political prognosis nowadays, but *things do seem here to be before the breaking point.* If the food and economic situation becomes much worse then trouble will really begin. These opinions do not come from the

[5] Ibid., 41–3.
[6] Klaus Epstein: *Matthias Erzberger and the Dilemma of German Democracy* (Princeton: Princeton University Press; 1959), 305–6; and Gordon A. Craig: *The Politics of the Prussian Army, 1640–1945* (New York: Oxford; 1956), 364–5.

Foreign Office which has offered to give me opinions on the situation from the political point of view and whom I do not trust. I personally do not think we should play with fire too much. The calm of the last weeks was a calm before the storm. It may not become a storm but we all here think it is going to be a real storm this time. It would be funny and a relief if I were wrong but I feel bound to give you my opinion [italics mine].[7]

Wherever he turned he detected signs of growing radicalization; and he repeatedly predicted that because of the effectiveness of the USPD agitation the government had no alternative but to announce some dramatic changes in policy.[8] On March 4 Day advised Paris of the partially effective general strike in Berlin: "it is impossible to say what the outcome of this strike will be, [but] the tension is such that a small riot could easily develop into a revolution."[9]

Field's analysis of the Bavarian turmoil was equally alarming. Before the fatal assassination he met no one who approved of Eisner. "A tremendous outbreak of antisemitism" intensified this disapproval, the Jews being blamed "for everything."[1] Immediately following Eisner's murder Field reassured Paris that "the attack on Eisner formed no part of a reactionary conspiracy but was the result of a personal conviction that to save the country Eisner had to be removed." Actually Erhard Auer, the Majoritarian Socialist Minister who was wounded alongside Eisner, sent Field a message to this effect from his hospital bed.[2]

But whatever the immediate cause and whoever the assassin, Eisner's death and martyrdom opened a Pandora's box. The Majoritarian leaders, without whom order could not be maintained, suffered a disastrous loss of prestige, self-confidence, and popular appeal. In their panic they made overtures to the Independents, but in view of feverish Spartacist agitation a united front was difficult to achieve. Indeed, Field was grim in his prognosis.

> The outlook is extremely dark. I expect to see a bolshevist reign installed in the near future. . . . The number of unemployed is growing rapidly. The finances of the state are desperate. A railway strike is threatened. The food situation is said to be also much worse than the masses know.
>
> Concomitant with the appearance of this second revolution there is a strange outburst of particularism. The appearance of Prussian

---

[7] Day to Dresel, February 27, 1919, National Archives, Document 184.01202/70. Copy of this letter in House Papers, 5:13.
[8] *F.R.,P.C.,1919*, XII, 41–7.
[9] Ibid., 50.
[1] Ibid., 14.
[2] Ibid., 43.

troops would be the signal for the flaring up of old hatred of the most extreme violence. . . .

In bourgeois circles and in certain revisionist majority socialist circles one can hear the view expressed that Entente occupation would be the best solution. . . .

The persons working for the cause of order seem frequently to believe that their hands would be greatly strengthened, if it were only possible for them to point to certain pronouncements of policy on our part, such as the declaration that we never would consent to treat with a government installed on bolshevik principles.

The present uprising can certainly not be called a food revolt. Nevertheless, many persons point out to me that the supply of food would go far to save the situation. Personally, I do not believe that any revulsion of feeling could be secured through the mere sending in of food. . . . On the other hand, it is very likely that the want of food is prominent among the remoter causes of the present unrest, partly as a direct cause of discontent, partly as a physiological factor in undermining the mental balance of the population. . . .[3]

In one respect, at least, Field's analysis and advice were exceptionally sophisticated. For him food was not the sole key to either the cause or the treatment of unrest. In a subsequent memorandum he offered a succinct summary of his multifaceted counterinsurgency prescription: "help against starvation (food supply), help against unemployment (raw materials), moral help (pronouncements against minority dictatorships, etc.), and help against disorders (in the last instance military occupation)."[4]

No doubt the dispatches from the Gherardi Mission were checked against information from other reliable Allied and Associated sources. But the dispatches themselves reached and influenced the Commissioners and their advisers. On March 5 Day's reports were the basis for a summary cable in which Ammission advised Polk that the German masses were becoming more radical; that the situation in Munich was chaotic; that a catastrophe might engulf Berlin; that alone the immediate dispatch of food and raw materials could "remedy Bolshevist tendencies and unemployment"; and that the Conference was considering such action.[5] Simultaneously House registered his concern, blaming the Conference for deliberately running the risk of thrusting Germany into Bolshevism. He claimed to have urged the Entente Governments repeatedly to send food "and yet they have sat complacently here and blocked every move the Americans tried to make to remedy this distressing and dangerous condition."[6] Similarly, Vance McCormick noted that "cables all show a state of revolution"; that the Allies were

[3] Ibid., 38–41.
[4] Ibid., 72.
[5] Ibid., 51.
[6] House Diary, March 3, 1919.

"living on top of a volcano"; and that without immediate relief the Allies would face "another revolution in Germany and Bolshevism."[7] Finally, because "the situation was so acute and critical and conditions so chaotic" the Commissioners recalled both Day and Field for fear that they be caught in compromising or even "dangerous situations."[8]

The findings and recommendations of the Gherardi Mission—and of Conger—corroborated those of other firsthand observers: Kellogg and Taylor of Hoover's staff; fourteen officers of a British Mission of Enquiry; F. C. Tiarks, a Director of the Bank of England and Commercial Adviser to the British Army of Occupation; and General H. C. O. Plumer, Commander of the British Army of the Rhine.

From Berlin on February 11, Alonzo Taylor filed a preliminary estimate of Germany's food requirements for the half year starting in the spring and until the next harvest. According to his stark message, on paper the average daily food ration could be raised to 2,450 calories provided Germany received monthly shipments of 320,000 tons of flour and 100,000 tons of mixed pork products for six months; 10,000 tons each of condensed milk and of vegetable oils for four months; and permission to resume limited trading and fishing in the North Sea.[9]

Once back in Paris, on February 22, Kellogg and Taylor submitted a report based on personal observations, government statistics, and conferences with officials and experts in the German capital. Their own inquiries, supported by data supplied by food officials "in cities exceeding 30,000 inhabitants," convinced them that as of approximately May 1 "the machinery of distribution would be unable to supply large sections of the German industrial population with foodstuffs." While food shipments, as suggested in Taylor's preliminary wire, could help maintain order, lack of employment and working class disappointment with the revolution, in addition to hunger, were generating disorder. Hoover passed on these estimates first to the Ammission and then to the Supreme Economic Council, dramatizing their urgency with yet another warning that there would be a "total breakdown in the whole social system unless the food situation in Germany were instantly remedied."[1]

---

[7] McCormick Diaries, March 5, 1919, 49.
[8] National Archives, Documents 184.014/16B and 18 (Ammission to Day, February 26 and March 10, 1919), and 184.012/50 (Ammission to Polk, March 21, 1919).
[9] Taylor to Hoover (via Gherardi), February 11, 1919, National Archives, Document 184.01202/34.
[1] F.R.,P.C.,1919, X, 15–16, 23–5; and Bane and Lutz (eds.): Blockade of Germany, 130–1. "Dr. Taylor just back from Germany. . . . He says the present government of Germany the same old crowd with Kaiser gone. People unreconstructed yet he is not hopeless about proper leaders [?] getting control, as he thinks present government on very thin ice. Many leading men think Germany now in Kerensky period of Russia and Bolshevism bound to come. I doubt it. Too many people own their own property. Very different from Russia." McCormick Diaries, February 19, 1919, 44.

The fourteen British officers who surveyed Germany were split up into teams of two to investigate conditions in Berlin, Munich, Hamburg, Hanover, Leipzig, Dresden, Magdeburg, and Cassel between January 12 and February 12, 1919.[2] In a joint report to their superiors, after praising Noske's accomplishments, they conceded that the prospects were anything but reassuring. In Berlin alone unemployment was increasing by 5,000 daily, with concurrent jumps in the cost of living. In mid-February the number of unemployed reached over 200,000 in Berlin, 72,000 in Hamburg, 32,000 in Munich, and 22,000 in Leipzig. The causes were many: rapid demobilization, slow reconversion, shortage of coal, hesitancy of entrepreneurs, high wages, and malnutrition. Staples were in such short supply that "the mass of the population was living on rations which, whilst maintaining life, were insufficient to nourish the body adequately." According to the Central Food Office in Berlin, making due allowance for local variations, breadstuffs would be exhausted around early April, potatoes in late May, and fats the end of March. In brief, unemployment was the most dangerous festering sore, especially in "the large industrial centers," hunger running a close second as the "chief predisposing cause of Bolshevism." All the officers were agreed that only the prompt shipment of supplies, especially of fats, could prevent new troubles.[3]

Sir John Field Beal, second-ranking British representative first on the Council of Supply and Relief and then on the Supreme Economic Council, was now altogether in Hoover's camp. He had carefully weighed the evidence from British and American observers; he even noted that in the judgment of Dr. Frederick Ferriers, Chief Executive Officer of the International Red Cross, "the approach of famine was nearer than was understood by the Entente agents who had gone into Germany, and that the approach of starvation must result in Bolshevism." Late March or early April would see the beginning of shortages in select cities. The situation was one of utmost urgency and without Allied action, within the next few weeks Germany would "probably be overtaken by economic and political disaster, with consequences which may spread to Allied countries."[4] William Wiseman now cabled to Lord Reading that judging by reliable reports Germany "was much nearer collapse than was generally realized." Suddenly the Supreme Economic Council was "confronted by a tremendous task" which was only beginning to be "realized by political leaders."[5]

---

[2] Among these officers Captain E. W. Tennent was a director of a firm trading in metals and chemicals; Captain C. W. Bell an employee of an important Indian trading firm; and Captain W. Stewart Roddie a Treasury official.

[3] *F.R.,P.C.,1919*, X, 19–22. This report was made available to the press and the Continental edition of the *Daily Mail* carried the entire text. See also *Reports by British Officers on the Economic Conditions Prevailing in Germany, December 1918–March 1919*, Cmd. 52, London, 1919.

[4] *F.R.,P.C.,1919*, X, 16–19.

[5] Wiseman to Reading, March 2, 1919, Wiseman Papers, 90:29.

The assassination of Eisner and the general strike in Berlin seemed to justify even the worst fears. By this time the British government was every bit as determined to get the blockade relaxed—over French obstruction—as the American government.[6] Of course, Labourites and Radicals all along advocated this course,[7] but many of the hardfaced men remained to be convinced. Since Churchill had their respect, he went to Commons to muster support: "to delay indefinitely would be to run a grave risk of having nobody with whom to settle, and of having another great area of the world sink into Bolshevik anarchy." And this was the third time during the World War and world crisis that the Marquess of Lansdowne sounded the warning that Europe was "rapidly approaching a catastrophe which might prove to be one of the most disastrous that had ever occurred in the civilized world."[8] Before too long official circles noted that "public opinion was rapidly coming around to the necessity of feeding Germany."[9]

No doubt elements other than this crescendo of alarm went into the decision to loosen the blockade in mid-March. The principal delegates and their advisers were moved variously by humanitarian concern for women and children, Christian charity for fellow men in distress, Labour and Radical protests, and the pressures from certain interest groups and their political spokesmen. Especially with the American Delegation the pressing availability of vast food surpluses, some of them perishable, counted heavily.

By mid-January all these influences had led to the removal of the blockade from the liberated countries of East-Central Europe. The agreements between the American Relief Administration and the recipient governments formally stipulated the purposes of aid: "supplies and foodstuffs [were being provided] in order to prevent starvation . . . and to assist . . . in the maintenance of order and to stop the spread of anarchy from other countries."[1]

The fact remains, however, that Germany, unlike Vienna,[2] continued to be blockaded, except for small quantities of food which were filtered in through the surrounding neutral nations.[3] To be sure, as of mid-January the Council of Ten was agreed that Germany needed food

---

6 "This morning the P.M. sent for me, and I joined him sitting with Arthur [Balfour], Henry Wilson, Austen Chamberlain, and Hankey. We discussed the economic situation and the necessity of feeding Germany. He seemed in a very good frame of mind, recognizing to the full the necessity of keeping Germany from revolution." Cecil Diary, March 6, 1919.

7 See the fiery editorial "The Greatest Crime of the War" in the *Labour Leader*, March 6, 1919, 8.

8 Cited in Bane and Lutz (eds.): *Blockade of Germany*, 720–2.

9 Murray to Reading, March 11, 1919, Wiseman Papers, 90:29.

1 Cited in Bane and Lutz (eds.): *Organization of American Relief*, 293.

2 See pp. 590–1, 732–3 below.

3 See Bane and Lutz (eds.): *Blockade of Germany*, 45, 49–50, 75–8, 119; and *F.R.,P.C.,1919*, X, 7.

supplies to tide her over until the next harvest; and that in the first instance she should receive 200,000 tons of breadstuffs and cereals and 70,000 tons of pork products. On January 16 Article 8 of the second renewal of the Armistice stipulated that, provided Germany placed her passenger and cargo fleet at the disposal of the Allies, these supplies would be forthcoming. Even the French reluctantly agreed to this scheme, with the reservation, however, that the question of financing these imports be settled first.[4]

At the Spa Conference of February 6–8 the Allied and the German delegates readily agreed that the transfer of the German merchant fleet, the shipment of food, and the financing of supplies were part of one and the same transaction. But a detailed agreement was not easily worked out.

Before transferring their fleet the Germans wanted an ironclad assurance that the Allies would supply all their food requirements until the next harvest. Understandably they balked at handing over their *entire* fleet in exchange for *partial* revictualling, for fear that each new installment would cost them additional concessions.[5]

As for the French, they objected on two scores. First, they were opposed to a guarantee which would emasculate the blockade as an effective instrument of intimidation and pressure. Secondly, the French continued to veto the Anglo-American financial scheme under which Germany would pay for these imports with securities and gold otherwise earmarked for reparations.

At the second Spa Conference, on March 4–5, the German delegates, after checking with Berlin, left no doubt that even though they were anxious to "dispose of the food question by the transfer of their shipping" they would insist that the Allies guarantee "a definite program of food supplies . . . up to the next harvest."[6]

By this time the German government could afford to take a somewhat stronger stand. Brockdorff-Rantzau knew that the current disorders in central Germany, Munich, and Berlin were having a "softening" effect on the Allies. They provided credibility for Berlin's prophecy that a vast Bolshevik wave was about to sweep over Europe. On February 15, in Trier, Edler von Braun, the Under Secretary of State in the Food Ministry, cautioned the Allies that unless the package deal were promptly consummated "the collapse of Germany before Bolshevism and the innundation of Europe by Bolshevism could not be prevented."[7] Three weeks later, at Spa, Richard Merton, one of the four principal German delegates, issued a similar warning to James A.

4 See Bane and Lutz (eds.): *Blockade of Germany,* 35–43; and *F.R.,P.C.,1919,* III, 515–17, 521–3, 611.
5 Bane and Lutz (eds.): *Blockade of Germany,* 83–95, 103–10.
6 *F.R.,P.C.,1919,* IV, 266–7.
7 Cited in *F.R.,P.C.,1919,* XI, 108–9. See also John Maynard Keynes: *Two Memoirs* (London: Hart Davis; 1949), 39.

Logan and E. F. Wise, his American and British counterparts.[8] Simultaneously Brockdorff-Rantzau himself told Major General Sir Richard Ewart, Chairman of the Inter-Allied Commission and British Red Cross representative in Berlin, that the situation was extremely serious and that if Bolshevism won out in Germany it would soon thereafter engulf the Allies. When Ewart saw Brockdorff-Rantzau a second time to tell him that his views had been conveyed to Paris, the Foreign Minister elaborated on his earlier warning. He predicted that if driven to desperation a nation of 70 million would turn Bolshevik rather than commit suicide. To be sure, German Bolshevism would be "less brutal" than the Russian variety; but this relative mildness would make it so much more "contagious" beyond Germany's borders.[9]

In the meantime the Allied reaction to Karl Radek's arrest was most heartening. After frantic efforts to locate Radek in Vienna, Munich, and Hamburg, he was finally spotted and taken into custody in Berlin on February 12. In announcing his arrest over the Nauen Radio on the fourteenth the government claimed that he had been caught with highly incriminating documents on his person. According to these documents Soviet Russia was planning to invade Germany in the spring, the invasion to coincide with Spartacist uprisings. The documents also were said to contain a blueprint for the infiltration of subversives into France and Britain.[1]

The following day Chicherin issued an indignant and scathing denial in Moscow, dismissing the Nauen broadcast as "an absurd fairy tale" and an "infamous and disgusting manoeuvre." He furthermore accused the "counterrevolutionary" Ebert-Scheidemann regime of trying to frighten the German people with the lie that revolutionary uprisings in Germany "would bring a Russian invasion."

Within a week the Allies were heard from. At Spa Lieutenant General Haking, Chief of the British Armistice Commission, took aside General Hammerstein, his German opposite, to inquire informally whether he would entertain an inquiry about the Radek matter. On receiving an affirmative response Haking handed him the following note.

> The British Government has directed me to obtain from your Government the original documents found in the possession of

[8] See Bane and Lutz (eds.): *Blockade of Germany*, 185–6.
[9] Memorandum on conversation with General Ewart by Brockdorff-Rantzau, March 19, 1919, GFM H234072–76; and Minutes of a conversation between Brockdorff-Rantzau and Groener in Berlin, April 4, 1919, GFM H234106–121.
[1] Telegrams and memoranda dealing with the Radek case are now available on microfilm in GFM 6:38, Public Record Office. In this discussion all citations will be from the documents in this microfilm file. For a summary treatment of Radek's arrest and official Allied reactions see Otto-Ernst Schüddekopf: *Karl Radek in Berlin: Ein Kapitel deutsch-russischer Beziehungen im Jahre 1919* (Sonderdruck aus dem *Archiv für Sozialgeschichte*, II, Hannover: 1962), esp. 103–7.

Radek and the other conspirators arrested about the same time, and hand them to me as early as possible for transmission to the British Government.

Haking assured Hammerstein that this exchange of information would be to the advantage of both parties; that prompt compliance would "be an evidence of good faith on the part of the German government on their repeated assurances that they were opposed to Bolshevist intrigues"; and that this was a test of Berlin's readiness to cooperate in the containment of Bolshevism. He also wanted the names of British Bolsheviks. In conclusion Haking indicated that General Nudant was advised of this *démarche,* but that he preferred to handle it on a personal basis with Hammerstein.[2] The British officer was so anxious for a reply from Berlin that he repeated his inquiry within less than 48 hours.[3]

Within those same forty-eight hours the Foreign Ministry completed its reply. First there was considerable embarrassment, since contrary to exaggerated press reports precious little, if anything, had been found on Radek. In fact, the find was so meager that it was worse than unconvincing: it might actually "increase Allied distrust."

Nevertheless, it was decided to try to capitalize on the British inquiry. Hammerstein was instructed to assure Haking that the German government gladly would give the British access not only to all the captured documents but also to other materials testifying to the dangers of Bolshevism and to the government's order-keeping measures. On the basis of Berlin's information and experience the strength of Bolshevism could "not be exaggerated" and the government was of the opinion "that this threat, which was hanging over all *Kulturnationen,* could be met effectively only by the common action of all governments." At any rate, there was so much to show that it would be difficult to collect the data for transmission to Haking. Instead, Hammerstein suggested that the British send one or more agents to Berlin for an on-the-spot investigation.[4]

Curiously enough, a French agent was the first to arrive in Berlin for a look at the Radek cache. For the first three days, and until General Nudant interceded, Captain Desruaulx was given the runaround.[5] But starting March 15 he spent two very full and instructive days. Needless to say, the Radek dossiers turned out to be very thin, in particular because they "contained nothing concrete about Radek's connections in France and Britain"; the notes on Radek's interrogations in Berlin were equally disappointing. However, the Foreign

---

2 Haniel to Brockdorff-Rantzau, Erzberger, OHL, and War Ministry, February 23, 1919.
3 Haniel to Foreign Ministry, February 25, 1919.
4 Foreign Ministry to Haniel, February 25, 1919.
5 Haniel to Brockdorff-Rantzau, March 13, 1919.

Ministry arranged for Desruaulx to have a meeting with Eduard Stadtler, the organizer of the *Anti-Bolschewisten Liga,* and "Stadtler gave him a short but impressive briefing." He spoke about the danger of Bolshevism and its international implications, as well as about the need for common action. After listening to other "experts" in this new field of anti-Bolshevism, during the afternoon of March 17, a German officer took Desruaulx for an automobile ride to show him the battle scars of the most recent street fighting in the capital. The Captain left for Paris that night. Even though he was persuaded that the Germans' anti-Bolshevism was genuine and active, he told his hosts that a common anti-Bolshevik effort would have to wait until after peace was signed.[6]

The following day, March 18, a three-man British team arrived: Major Bertie, Captain Harding, and Captain Brandt. In the telegram announcing their arrival Haniel recommended that they be given the same treatment as Desruaulx; he also expressed the hope that these visits might be the beginning of "an international action against the Bolshevik movement."[7]

An experienced Foreign Office official by the name of Thermann took charge of the British officers. He tried to give them "a clear picture of Bolshevism in Germany and of the extreme seriousness of the situation; [he] also tried to brief them on the ways and means of fighting Bolshevism. . . . They were informed about the legal, military, political, and spiritual campaign against Bolshevism in Germany." At one point, in a meeting with an official of the Ministry of Justice, the British officers suggested that in certain Allied quarters the German Right continued to be suspected of exploiting Bolshevism for its own purposes. The official's retort was swift: it was altogether ridiculous to believe the fable that a reactionary imperial party was promoting Bolshevism in order eventually to commend itself as the last savior of the established order. Like their French predecessor, the three Englishmen were duly impressed. In compliance with an urgent summons they returned to Paris in late March; Brandt and Harding, however, were back in Berlin on April 18 to establish a permanent vigil.[8]

No wonder the German delegates at the second Spa Conference stood their ground. When Logan, head of the U. S. Delegation, returned to Paris he ventured to give his personal estimate of the deadlocked negotiations. Bound by rigid instructions the Allied delegates had dealt with their opposites at Spa as if there were no rioting or

---

[6] Foreign Ministry Memorandum, no date.

[7] Haniel to Brockdorff-Rantzau, March 15, 1919.

[8] Haniel to Brockdorff-Rantzau, March 15, 1919; Foreign Ministry to Haniel, March 19, 1919; Memorandum by Thermann, no date; Memorandum by Dr. Weismann of the Ministry of Justice, April 1, 1919.

shooting in the streets of Berlin. Instead of advertising food as a weapon against Bolshevism, the Allies continued to give the appearance of seeking "an unfair exchange of foodstuffs for ships." Quite rightly the Allies should resist being frightened by the "shaking of the red flag." On the other hand, without return to a normal economic life order could not be restored in Germany. Furthermore "the continued success of our efforts to combat Bolshevism by the supply of foodstuff to the Polish . . . and Czechoslovakian people, and other outlying states, was dependent to a large extent on the maintenance of good order in Germany."[9] Impressed by the convergence of views in the dispatches of Day, Field, Logan and others[1] all the top American officials—the Four Commissioners (Wilson was still away), Dresel, Hoover, McCormick, Davis—agreed that this dangerous deadlock had to be broken forthwith.[2]

Since this deadlock stemmed from disagreement over fundamental policy issues it could not be broken by the second-echelon Supreme Economic Council. It had to go to the Council of Ten, where it was thrashed out on March 7–8. However, the full economic high command was on hand for these momentous sessions: for the U.S. Herbert Hoover, Norman Davis, Bernard Baruch, Oscar Straus, Thomas Lamont, Vance McCormick, and Henry Robinson; for Britain Robert Cecil, John Maynard Keynes, and William Beveridge; for France Albert Clémentel, Louis-Lucien Klotz, and Louis Loucheur; and for Italy Signor Silvio Crespi.

As Chairman of the Supreme Economic Council Cecil was asked to introduce the discussion.[3] He reported that his council had met to consider the stalemate and that there was agreement that ever since January 16 Germany was legally bound to yield her ships. At the same time, under Article 26 of the original Armistice the Allies had an obligation "to provision Germany . . . as shall be found necessary." In arguing that it was in the "general interest" to meet this obligation, Cecil stressed "the obligation of humanity and the grave danger of Germany drifting into Bolshevism unless food were sent into Germany."[4]

At this point Cecil submitted a draft proposal which, except for two

[9] Cited in Bane and Lutz (eds.): *Blockade of Germany*, 188.
[1] See, e.g., the *Press Review* (Issued by 2nd Section, General Staff, G.H.Q.A.E.F.) No. 389, March 14, 1919, Enemy Press: German.
[2] *F.R.,P.C.,1919*, XI, 99–110.
[3] This account of the proceedings of the Council of Ten on March 7 and 8, 1919, is based on *F.R.,P.C.,1919*, IV, 253–4, 274–93.
[4] "Lord Robert Cecil had taken a deliberately prosaic line and had almost said that, while of course the obligations of humanity and the fear of Bolshevism were at the back of all our heads, he recognized that it would not be in the best of taste to rub such points in too crudely." Keynes: *Two Memoirs*, 56.

points, had been unanimously approved by the Supreme Economic Council. Actually, the Big Ten were being asked to endorse the Anglo-American plan. In exchange for her merchant fleet Germany would receive immediate delivery of the agreed-upon 270,000 tons, together with explicit permission to import up to 370,000 tons of food monthly (300,000 tons of breadstuffs and 70,000 tons of fats) until September 1. Germany would pay for the supplies with visible and invisible exports, credits from neutral nations, the sale of foreign holdings, and advances against such collaterals as foreign investments and gold.

As expected, first in the Supreme Economic Council and now in the Council of Ten the French were adamant, insisting the Germans should only be fed a month at a time, otherwise the Allies would cripple their one remaining sanction. Furthermore, they should pay for their imports with exports of raw materials as well as with commercial credits from neutral or Allied nations. Only once all other credit sources were exhausted should the Allies consider siphoning off resources needed for reparations and indemnities.

In an effort to break this renewed filibuster—Clémentel, Loucheur, Klotz, and Clemenceau took turns in hammering away at the same two points—first Hoover and then Lloyd George flaunted the specter of Bolshevism.

Hoover was not likely to make any concessions, not even when reminded that Germany's "few pieces of gold and few securities" were about to be given away to those who had surpluses rather than to those who had suffered the greatest damages during the war. He knew that neither Congress nor Wall Street would make a loan or a gift to feed Germany. All this time tremendous inventories were building up in Rotterdam and other Continental ports while the situation in Central Europe continued to disintegrate.

Hoover spoke as Wilson might have spoken, had he been back from Washington. The President's absence from the council chamber was in large measure compensated for by the awe-inspiring presence of the Ammission's chief economic and financial experts. Indeed, the Food Tsar compelled the assembled delegates to listen with care.

> Some time about the 1st May next, food would become so scarce in all [German] towns of 50,000 inhabitants and more, that starvation would stare the people in the face, and that would constitute a very grave danger for the whole Government of the country. That was the substance of the reports received from the most trustworthy sources in Germany. Therefore, unless the Allies were willing to run the risk of supplying certain quantities of food to Germany, in return for the possible surrender of her merchantships, thus enabling her to maintain a stable Government, *the efforts of the representatives now sitting in the Council Chamber would be washed out to nothing within the next sixty days* [italics mine].

Instead of discussing the substantive issues Hoover simply warned, raged, and threatened.

Lloyd George adopted pretty much the same Cassandra-like tone.

He urged with all his might that steps should at once be taken to revictual Germany. The honour of the Allies was involved. Under the terms of the armistice the Allies did imply that they meant to let food into Germany. The Germans had accepted our armistice conditions, which were sufficiently severe, and they had complied with the majority of those conditions. But so far, not a single ton of food had been sent into Germany. The fishing fleet had even been prevented from going out to catch a few herrings. The Allies were now on top, but the memories of starvation might one day turn against them. The Germans were being allowed to starve whilst at the same time hundreds of thousands of tons of food were lying at Rotterdam, waiting to be taken up the Waterways into Germany. These incidents constituted far more formidable weapons for use against the Allies than any of the armaments it was sought to limit. The Allies were sowing hatred for the future; they were piling up agony, not for the Germans, but for themselves. . . . British Officers who had been in Germany said that Bolshevism was being created, and the determining factor was going to be food. As long as the people were starving they would listen to the argument of the Spartacists, and the Allies by their action were simply encouraging elements of disruption and anarchism. It was like stirring up an influenza puddle, just next door to one's self. The condition of Russia was well-known, and it might be possible to look on at a muddle which had there been created. But, now, if Germany went, and Spain: who would feel safe? As long as order was maintained in Germany, a breakwater would exist between the countries of the Allies and the waters of Revolution beyond. But once the break-water was swept away, he could not speak for France, but trembled for his own country. The situation was particularly serious in Munich. Bavaria, which once had been thought to represent the most solid and conservative part of Germany, had already gone. . . . Mean-while the Conference continued to haggle. Six weeks ago the same arguments about gold and foreign securities had been raised, and it had then been decided that Germany should be given food. He begged the Conference to re-affirm that decision in the most un-equivocal terms, unless this people were fed, if as a result of a process of starvation enforced by the Allies, the people of Germany were allowed to run riot, a state of revolution among the working classes of all countries would ensue with which it would be impos-sible to cope.

For the special benefit of Foch and his sort the Prime Minister revealed that according to General Plumer British soldiers would refuse to continue the occupation if "children were allowed to wander about the streets, half starving." Lloyd George interrupted his own speech to read a wire from Plumer—sent from Cologne on March 8 at 2:45 p.m.—which was handed to him at the conference table. In this wire Plumer emphasized the "imminent danger . . . of the great activity by subversive and disorderly elements" due to the food crisis and requested that the date for the arrival of the first supplies be fixed for "no later than March 16." This military testimony produced the intended dramatic effect, especially since the Prime Minister's colleagues did not know that he had arranged for this wire through the good offices of Tiarks and Riddell.[5]

Clemenceau nevertheless stood his ground. He readily conceded that Germany had to be fed "as soon as possible." According to French reports, however, bad distribution rather than outright shortages were responsible for food hardships and the Germans should be able to remedy this situation without outside help. In other words, the crisis was not all that immediate, otherwise instead of withholding their fleet the Germans would instantly surrender it to meet their most pressing requirements. No, the "Germans were using Bolshevism as a bogey"; they were trying to "blackmail" the Allies with a view to discovering the overall pliancy of their diplomacy. On January 16 in Article 8 the Germans had agreed to surrender their fleet; their failure to comply constituted a flagrant legal breech as well as an undisguised defiance.

In an effort to pacify the French Premier Lloyd George himself proposed and the Council agreed that prior to discussing the provisioning of Germany with her delegates in Brussels, the latter would have to "formally acknowledge and undertake to execute" the obligations of Article 8.

The chief hurdle still lay ahead. Klotz doggedly opposed the draft provisions for the financing of German imports. He argued that if German gold and securities were pledged for this purpose, no funds would remain for reparations. At best their use should be contemplated at the end of one or two months, should it turn out that the Germans were really incapable of producing the quantities of coal and raw materials exports necessary to cover their food purchases. For the interim Klotz agreed to an expenditure of 450 million francs, but he insisted that he could not approve 2 billion francs—the cost of the Anglo-American program—without endangering the reparations and finances of France.

This intransigence aroused the British Prime Minister into one of the angriest outbursts at the Conference, couched in the form of a fierce personal attack on Clemenceau's Minister of Finance. Lloyd George reminded Klotz that on January 13, at Klotz's own insistence, the Ten had agreed to reconsider the question of financing at the end of two months. Now that these two months were up, instead of being ready to

[5] Riddell: *Intimate Diary of the Peace Conference*, 29–30.

move forward Klotz was defending his uncompromising stand with the same old arguments. In his pique Lloyd George used a time-honored diplomatic stratagem: he feigned to censure Klotz for misrepresenting the true position of his government. Turning to Clemenceau, he appealed to him "to put a stop to these obstructive tactics, otherwise Mr. Klotz would rank with Lenin and Trotsky among those who had spread Bolshevism in Europe." With this Hectorean charge Lloyd George rested his case. According to Keynes—who was present—in the tense moments that followed "all around the room you could see each one grinning and whispering to his neighbor 'Klotzky.' "[6]

Even Colonel House, who a few days ago had failed to move Clemenceau,[7] now declared that although it pained him "to take sides against France," the American delegates could go no further to meet French wishes. Signor Crespi also fell in line. "Italy, who was sadly in need of coal," was prepared to accept the financial plan which provided that German gold could be pledged as collateral, but it could not be sold outright except by agreement among the Associated Powers that all other means of payment were inadequate.

France now stood alone. Was this the time and issue for a veto, with all the risks such a veto involved? Nothing could be gained by yet another delay, since France's position was not likely to improve with Wilson's return! Furthermore, what if during such a delay a Spartacist wave nevertheless swept over Germany? And last, given France's need for economic aid for herself and her new allies in Eastern Europe, would it be wise to break with Hoover, Cecil, and their entourage?

The French Delegation decided to retreat to a position that must have been prearranged. Significantly it fell to Loucheur, the Minister of Reconstruction, to expound the compromise formula, which was also designed to keep up appearances. As a prominent industrialist and financier[8] Loucheur understood and was respected by his Anglo-American opposites. He admitted that because of the present emergency a credit for considerably more than 450 million francs was urgently needed. The Allies were about to commit themselves for some 2 billion francs. He suggested that as a compromise the Conference immediately open a credit for half this sum; at a later date further credits could always be opened as the need arose. By simply passing over all the controversial points Loucheur brought France into step with her Allies. With minor changes the Big Ten now accepted the

[6] Keynes: *Two Memoirs*, 61. Following this session of March 8 Lloyd George told Riddell that he had made "a violent attack on Klotz . . . in which he said that if a Bolshevik state were formed in Germany, three statues would be erected— one to Lenin, one to Trotzky, and the third to Klotz. Klotz made no reply." Riddell: *Intimate Diary*, 30. Also see Louis-Lucien Klotz: *De la Guerre à la paix* (Paris: Payot; 1924), 112–13.
[7] *F.R.,P.C.,1919*, XI, 94.
[8] See Louis Loucheur: *Carnets Secrets, 1908–1932* (Brussels: Brepols; 1962), 5–12.

entire draft-proposal which Cecil had presented in the name of the majority of the Supreme Economic Council, a proposal that went far to meet the demands which the Germans had formulated at Spa.

The road was clear for the Brussels Agreement. It was easily negotiated with the German delegates in the Belgian capital on March 13–14, 1919. The Germans themselves immediately realized that as compared to a week ago in Spa the tone of the negotiations had considerably improved. Of course, there were compelling domestic reasons for signing. However, the foreign policy rationale was every bit as prominent. Now that the Allies were so accommodating the German delegates were anxious to meet them halfway, the more so since they were intent to create a favorable atmosphere for the impending peace negotiations.[9]

The Germans promptly began the delivery of their ships and made their first payment on March 22. Simultaneously Hoover diverted several cargoes to German ports; the SS *West Colfax,* carrying 6,600 tons of wheat flour, docked in Hamburg on March 25.[1] This first ship was designed to symbolize and foreshadow the new material and moral support for the Ebert-Scheidemann regime. Time being of the essence, Hoover did not wait for some 700,000 tons of German cargo ships to cross the Atlantic to the U.S. and Canada to load up and return with food. Instead, he drew on American and British stocks in Europe; he also loaded approximately 200,000 tons of American shipping in U.S. ports. By the end of May Germany had been supplied with some 380,000 tons of foodstuffs.[2]

Had the Allies waited too long? Would Germany manage to avoid that second revolution? Beatrice Webb saw "the clouds in the east grow steadily darker and the flood of anarchy and barbarism [seemed to her] to get steadily nearer." Caught between these darkening Continental clouds and the upsurge of labor unrest in Britain she wondered "when the crash would come."[3] In Germany it was a "race against time and Spartacism."[4] Even the *Temps, Figaro, Action Française,* and the *Daily Mail* conceded that Germany was hovering on the verge of disaster. However, these papers continued to proclaim that without resolute action in Eastern Europe and Russia the situation was beyond repair. Not the shortage of food in Germany but Allied indecision with regard to Soviet Russia, Poland's western frontiers, and Haller's divisions was at the root of the rapidly approaching crisis. Of course, reparations and Germany's western frontiers should also be settled

[9] Lersner to Brockdorff-Rantzau, Brussels, March 15, 1919, GFM H234766–7.
[1] American Relief Administration: *Bulletin,* No. 19 (July 25, 1919), 14–15.
[2] Hoover to Dresel, April 15, 1919, cited in Bane and Lutz (eds.): *Blockade of Germany,* 368–9; and *F.R.,P.C.,* 1919, X, 277, 427–9.
[3] Cole (ed.): *Beatrice Webb's Diaries,* 153, entry of March 12, 1919.
[4] *The Nation,* March 15, 1919.

without further delay. Would the Allies "wait to get clear ideas and to act upon them until some 'unforeseen' complication gave them and their work a terrible jolt—without forewarning?"[5]

These apprehensions also rose to the surface in official circles. After speaking with Robert Lord, who had just returned from Poland, Ray Stannard Baker was inclined to agree with Bliss "that only the first out of our 30 years war have been passed!" Starting around March 18 the Press Secretary of the American Delegation registered a decided change in mood and outlook.

> (March 18) The great and crucial point of the conference is arriving with corresponding feverishness of opinion. At the same time the world is near collapse. We hear that the industrial situation in England is acute, with huge strikes threatened. A Dutch editor told me yesterday that the situation in Holland is bad. It is so all over the world. Peace must be swift if it [is to] beat anarchy. As the pressure intensifies, the work centers in fewer and fewer hands, smaller conferences, quieter decisions—inside understandings that the painful documentary historian will never get and never evaluate properly. Today the Three met for a long conference at the Crillon —Wilson, Lloyd George, and Clemenceau. . . .
>
> (March 20) An undeniable tone of pessimism prevails here. It seems to be a race of peace with anarchy. Very bad news from Germany (dined tonight with Villard, just back from there). The industrial situation in England is acute and from America we hear of bitter attacks on Wilson and the League of Nations. . . .
>
> (March 21) More pessimism. The Committee of Ten and the War Council talked for hours on the Polish question and got nowhere. Colonel House continues to be optimistic and predicts a speedy settlement, but a great wave of criticism is now arising all over the world and most of it specifically directed at President Wilson. In the meantime Bolshevism spreads and an enormous industrial and social unrest. . . .
>
> (March 22) . . . the air is full of nervous tension. While these men talk the world is falling apart. . . .[6]

Secretary of State Lansing was equally worried. He spoke at length with Villard, who painted "a very black picture, feared it was too late to check Bolshevism in Germany, thought it could have been done in December, and said the Germans would refuse to sign too harsh a peace." Since Lansing urged Villard to tell his alarming story to Bliss and White it is more than likely that he shared this diagnosis.[7]

An equally somber mood settled over the British Delegation. Like his American opposite Lord Riddell characterized the situation as "a

---

[5] *Daily Mail* (Paris), March 21, 1919.
[6] Baker Diary, Book XXII, March 17–21, 1919, 84–93.
[7] Lansing Diary, March 21, 1919; and Oswald G. Villard: *Fighting Years* (New York: Harcourt Brace; 1939), 444–5.

race between peace and anarchy."[8] Lloyd George, Balfour, and their principal advisers despaired of finding a common ground with the French on indemnities and especially on the Rhine frontier.[9] They were worried lest this continuing stalemate favor the forces of disorder throughout Central and Eastern Europe, in spite of the ongoing food transfusions. Also, they worried about Brockdorff-Rantzau opting for a "second" Brest Litovsk, backstopped by cooperation with Leninist Russia.

In the British Delegation there was a rising awareness that in the future Eastern Europe was bound to become Germany's primary theater for diplomatic activity. It was there that frontiers were uncertain, governments were untried, and armies were embryonic. To be sure, regardless of developments in Russia the Allies were committed to building up buffer states in the eastern marshes. Still, here were welcome troubled waters for Germany to fish in. Not only would Poland be weak and strategically inaccessible to her Western mentors but she would also be at loggerheads with Russia, Lithuania, and Czechoslovakia.

This likelihood of a future German *Drang nach Osten* did not escape Allied notice. While the right-wing press simply issued shrill and dire warnings, Balfour considered this drive in the context of the Anglo-French dispute over Germany's western borders. On March 18, in another of his classic diplomatic think pieces, the Foreign Secretary cautioned the French not to be narrowly obsessed with the Rhine. Balfour readily conceded the precariousness of France's security: Germany would have nearly twice France's population; she would eventually seek revenge; arms limitation would be a precarious experiment; and the League might be impotent. Still, he was skeptical whether control of the Left Bank could act as an effective shield.

> I desire to point out that, in the first place, if there is a renewal of German world politics, *it is towards the East rather than towards the West that her ambitions* will *probably be directed.* Her great successes in the War were Eastern successes; and her great failures were Western failures; and, so far as anybody can forecast the fate of Europe, it would seem that in the West the forces that will in the future make for effective defense are far stronger than in 1914.
>
> On the other hand, the collapse of Russia, and the substitution of a number of small and jealous states, will increase the opportunities for German diplomatic intrigue, and diminish the resisting power of the anti-German forces in the East.
>
> I conceive, therefore, that if international relations and methods are, as the French assume, going to remain in the future what they

[8] Riddell: *Intimate Diary*, 37, entry of March 21, 1919.
[9] See ibid., 36; and Lord Hankey: *The Supreme Control at the Paris Peace Conference, 1919* (London: George Allen and Unwin; 1963), 100.

have been in the past; and if what civilization has to fear is the renewal without substantial modification of German ambition, *it is in the East rather than in the West that the storm will first break;* and no attempt to guard against the danger of the future can be deemed other than narrow and incomplete which concentrates its whole attention upon bridge-heads and strategic frontiers upon the Rhine and the Treaty of 1814, and draws all its inspiration from Generals and Statesmen absorbed in the military memories of 1870 and 1914.

If Germany is going to be a great armed camp, filled with a population about twice as great as that of any State in Europe [excluding Russia!]; and if she is going again to pursue a policy of world domination, it will no doubt tax all the statesmanship of the rest of the world to prevent a repetition of the calamities from which we have been suffering. But the only radical cure for this is a change in the international system of the world—a change which French statesmen are doing nothing to promote and the very possibility of which many of them regard with ill-concealed derision. They may be right; but if they are, it is quite certain that *no manipulation of the Rhine frontier is going to make France anything more than a second-rate Power, trembling at the nod of its great neighbors in the East, and depending from day to day on the changes and chances of shifting diplomacy and uncertain alliances* [italics mine].[1]

Of course, Clemenceau and Foch were not suggesting that only Germany's western frontiers be manipulated. They fully intended to manipulate her eastern frontiers as well. Moreover, they proposed to guarantee these frontiers with a network of diplomatic and military alliances. As a seasoned statesman of the old school Balfour could not entirely suppress his sympathy for this conventional search for security. And perhaps he would not have had even fleeting doubts, provided that in the East France could have relied on Russia instead of on so many untried successor states. In that event Foch and Clemenceau would have been less stringent with Germany; in turn Britain would have been less reluctant to enter a tight security system. Whereas Britain shied back from joining France in keeping down a bitterly *dissatisfied* Germany and in upholding an artificially *inflated* Poland, she was inclined to help her to contain a *defeated* Germany and a little Poland.

So that Clemenceau should stop pressing for a separate Rhineland Lloyd George successfully prevailed on Wilson to join in offering France an Anglo-American guarantee against German invasion in the West. Even though Clemenceau readily dropped his demand for the separation of the Rhineland he insisted that the proffered guarantee be coupled with extensive physical pledges: occupation up to the Rhine and including the bridgeheads; permanent demilitarization on both

---

[1] Cited in Blanche E. C. Dugdale: *Arthur James Balfour* (London: Hutchinson; 1936), II, 204–5.

banks of the river; and permanent Allied inspection to ensure the enforcement of these provisions.[2]

Since Lloyd George and Wilson found Clemenceau's counterproposal unacceptable, a new round of time-consuming negotiations was about to start. While Balfour, in his memorandum of March 18, picked up the diplomatic thread, the Prime Minister and his closest advisers took time out to review Britain's overall diplomatic project and objectives in the light of the Anglo-French impasse and the all-European crisis.

What cannot be overlooked is that this review, which culminated in the remarkable Fontainebleau Memorandum of March 25, got under way *before* Paris was shaken by Béla Kun's takeover in Budapest. Henry Wilson initiated it on March 18 by engaging Philip Kerr and Maurice Hankey in wide-ranging discussions. The following day, in a memorandum to the Prime Minister, Hankey expressed his uneasiness about the course of the negotiations: "Philip Kerr has several times pointed out to you and to me that, while every exaction on Germany was justified on its merits, the accumulation of these would put Germany in an utterly impossible position."[3]

Hankey went on to outline his own views which, though at variance with Henry Wilson's, coincided with Kerr's. He himself has provided a summary of this memorandum, including one crucial excerpt.

> My general view was that in the coming years Bolshevism was the greatest danger to Europe. Already it had gripped most of Russia and was spreading to neighboring countries from the Baltic to the Black Sea and Mediterranean. These countries were too weak to resist and too divided to combine. Germany and Austria were the only countries capable of providing a line of resistance unless the Peace Treaties were so drastic as to deprive them of the power to do so. After describing the situation in detail I urged the adoption of the following principles as a basis of the German Treaty:
>
> First: The enormity of their crimes must be brought home to the German people.
>
> Second: Means ought to be found for providing them with the physical force for resisting Bolshevism.
>
> Third: We ought to try and build up the self-respect of the German people so that they may resist the approach of Bolshevism and believe in their own civilization rather than in that which comes from Russia.
>
> Those principles were followed by many detailed suggestions, including an assurance that the disarmament of Germany was part of the disarmament of the world; that Germany should in due course be permitted to become a probationary member of the League of

2 André Tardieu: *La Paix* (Paris: Payot; 1921), 197–200.
3 Cited in Hankey: *Supreme Control at Paris*, 97.

Nations; and that vindictiveness should have no place in the Peace Treaty.[4]

This position paper prompted Lloyd George, on March 21, to ask a few of his key advisers to retire with him to Fontainebleau for the weekend of March 22–24 in order to reassess England's and the Empire's position. There remains some question as to who was actually in the party. That Henry Wilson, Kerr, and Hankey were present at Fontainebleau is certain. However, contrary to Lloyd George's testimony,[5] Smuts was not along.[6] On the other hand, Edwin Montagu may well have been there.[7]

In any event, judging by the membership of this special task force Lloyd George was contemplating an appeal to liberal-conservative and Wilsonian sentiment even at the risk of straining relations with the right-Unionists and Clemenceau. No doubt Henry Wilson shared his colleagues' fear of Bolshevism in Germany and of German-Soviet cooperation. However, he alone, in Foch-like fashion, advocated exorcising this dual threat by forceful action in Russia and Eastern Europe, while maintaining his sympathy for French claims along the Rhine. All the others, including the P.M., now reflected the growing opinion which, intimidated by the specter of Bolshevism, tended "toward a fairly moderate treatment of Germany, in order not to crush her morally, the idea [being] that a reasonably strong German state was a healthy thing for Europe."[8]

In brief, Lloyd George chose this moment for one of his sudden and disconcerting turnabouts. He acted under the influence of the surging crisis in East-Central Europe, the persistent labor unrest in Britain (especially the threatening miners' strike), and the reduction of the

---

[4] Ibid., 98. This summary rather than the full text is reproduced because Robin Hankey, Lord Hankey's son, advised this author on April 11, 1964, that his father's papers were still closed. However, a copy of this memorandum is preserved in the Smuts Papers, and Hancock gives the following summary: "[It emphasized] the potential expansionist force of Bolshevism and the flimsiness of the 'line of outposts' immediately confronting it—that is to say, the chain of new States or would-be States strung out along the western borders of Russia. If the outposts were weak, what barrier lay behind them? The Habsburg Empire, for all its faults, had once been an effective barrier but it no longer existed. Only the German barrier remained. What folly, therefore, to pursue towards Germany a policy which would leave her helpless in face of Bolshevist attack and political subversion or, alternatively, draw her in desperation to make common cause with the Bolshevists. For Germany was just as well placed, the memorandum insisted, to become 'the head and brain of Bolshevism' as the barrier against its westward expansion." W. K. Hancock: *Smuts: The Sanguine Years, 1870–1919* (Cambridge University Press; 1962), 514.

[5] Lloyd George: *Truth*, I, 403–4.

[6] Hancock: *Smuts*, p. 514.

[7] Callwell (ed.): *Henry Wilson*, II, 175. See Riddell: *Intimate Diary*, 38, for the untenable claim that the party consisted of the Prime Minister, Henry Wilson, Cunliffe, Keynes, and Kerr.

[8] Wiseman to Reading, March 21, 1919, Wiseman Paper, 90:29.

coalition majority from 5,000 to 2,000 in the recent by-election in West Leyton.[9] He went off for the weekend "to think out the possibility of drastic changes which would give the whole peace settlement a more inspiring appearance and one more in sympathy with the progressive forces making themselves felt all over the world."[1]

[9] These results were announced on March 14. An earlier by-election at Birkenhead had foreshadowed this trend.

[1] Wiseman to Reading, March 23, 1919, Wiseman Papers, 90:29.

16

The Rise of Béla Kun

THE TREATY OF TRIANON, delineating Hungary's borders, was not completed until a full year after the signing of the Treaty of Versailles. Even so, the Hungarian question constantly impinged on the debates in Paris, particularly once Béla Kun had started his 133-day rule.

At first the German problem entirely overshadowed the territorial issues stemming from Hungary's defeat. Germany was the ogre of the vanquished nations, and in the West she had a common border—to be redrawn—with the Continent's principal victor. As for Hungary, especially following her eleventh-hour secession from the Dual Monarchy, she faced her judges as a secondary foe, while all her border disputes involved minor powers, notably Rumania, Yugoslavia, Czechoslovakia, and Austria.

Suddenly, midway in the Conference, Hungary ceased to be a second-rank defeated power with a low claim on the attention of the Big Four. The moment Hungary turned into the world's second citadel of Bolshevism—a revolutionary outpost in the heart of East-Central Europe—she moved to the very center of their concern.

To be sure, the boundaries with her four neighbors remained to be drawn. Meanwhile, however, the peacemakers had to decide whether to recognize, contain, or overthrow this defiant revolutionary regime. In turn, this essentially ideological and political decision complicated the Hungarian settlement.

Even before the drastic overturn in Budapest, Hungary and her rivals buttressed their appeals to the Big Four with anti-Bolshevik protestations. Accordingly, Károlyi forewarned the Allies that they could yield to Rumania's and Czechoslovakia's extreme territorial demands only at the grave risk of enthroning Bolshevism in Hungary. At the same time Brătianu denounced Károlyi for encouraging Bolshevism, claimed that the incorporation of all of Transylvania was needed to maintain order in Rumania, and implied that territorial rewards were the price for Rumanian participation in the containment or overthrow of Russian and Hungarian Bolshevism. Similarly, Beneš and Kramář not only kept reminding the Big Four of the Czech Legion's dutiful service in Russia but also commended Czechoslovakia as a vital bastion of political and economic stability in Bolshevik-infested Central Europe.

With Béla Kun triumphant in Budapest, the rhetoric of anti-Bolshevism became doubly strident and plausible. Not that either Rumania and Czechoslovakia needed this newest Bolshevik break-through to frighten the Allies into granting their claims, the territorial commissions having long since recommended generous awards for these fellow victors. Still, the scare helped convince the Big Four to ratify these recommendations; and eventually it also inclined them to reward Austria with Burgenland for not going over to Bolshevism.

Throughout the 133 days the Council of Four, the Council of Ten, the military advisers, the blockade agencies, and the national delega-tions wrestled with the question of intervention. As in the case of Russia, the Big Four shied back from direct and large scale military intervention with their own armies, and for much the same reasons. But except for this self-restriction, they initiated, approved, or condoned every other form of direct or indirect intervention. They denied diplo-matic recognition, maintained the blockade, sanctioned and assisted the armed interference by Rumanian and Czech troops, and conspired with *émigrés* as well as with anti-Kun factions within Hungary.

Admittedly, Paris never elaborated and implemented a coherent plan for the strangulation of the Hungarian Soviet. On this issue, as on most others, the Big Four were far from unanimous. Their differences, however, were not over intervention as such. Within a broad anti-Bolshevik consensus they merely differed about the strategy, tactics, and scope of intervention. Certainly neither Wilson nor Lloyd George, let alone Clemenceau, ever contemplated helping Béla Kun consolidate his regime. They meant to drive him out not because he was diplomatically unaccommodating but because they considered Soviet Hungary, pres-ently coached and prospectively supported by Soviet Russia, a danger-ous center for the political subversion of East-Central Europe.

As for Béla Kun, from the beginning he realized that the survival of his regime hinged on Soviet Russian aid, the spread of the revolution in Central Europe, and paralyzing dissensions among the counterrevolu-tionary powers. At the same time, just as the Big Four followed an inconsistent interventionist course, so Béla Kun pursued a changeable line of revolutionary action. For tactical reasons the Allies prevailed on the Rumanians not to cross the Tisza River, while Béla Kun ordered the withdrawal of his troops from those areas of Slovakia occupied during the May offensive against the Czechs.

The immediate background of these events lies in October–Novem-ber 1918, when military defeat undermined the existing government, economy, and society not only in Imperial Germany but also throughout Austria-Hungary. In a last-minute effort to preserve the established order, enlightened members of the ruling power elite in both halves of the Dual Monarchy adopted the foreign policy platform of the Liberal, Radical, and Socialist opposition. On October 24 they contrived to have Count Julius Andrassy supersede Count Stephen Burián as Foreign Minister, with instructions to secure a separate, negotiated settlement. Within five days, and as part of this same policy of preservation, the Emperor summoned Count John Hadik to replace Alexander Wekerle as Minister President of Hungary. Both Andrassy and Hadik wrongly assumed that even in the face of external defeat and internal chaos they could steady the ship of state and prop up the social order without a substantial opening to the democratic and Socialist Left.

Meanwhile, however, on October 25 a National Council was constituted under the presidency of Count Michael Károlyi, the Hungarian Max von Baden. This makeshift assembly was composed of self-appointed delegates from Károlyi's Independence Party, the Radical Party, and the Social Democratic Party. By proclaiming that hereafter cabinets were responsible to this rump assembly, Károlyi and his supporters proposed to challenge the legitimacy of the aristocrat-dominated Parliament.

The program of the National Council called for a new deal at home and abroad. Internally it prescribed the complete independence of Hungary; universal suffrage; representative government; civil liberties; amnesty for political prisoners; and comprehensive land reforms. Externally it advocated an immediate separate peace or armistice; self-determination for the non-Magyar peoples, which hopefully would opt to remain within a democratic Hungarian confederation; the recognition of "Ukrainia," Poland, Czechoslovakia, Yugoslavia, and German Austria; and the annulment of the Treaties of Brest Litovsk and Bucharest.[1] The Social Democratic Party was by far the largest and best organized of the three parties which rallied around this program, the National Council, and Károlyi.

The domestic as well as the foreign situation continued to deteriorate at breakneck speed, with chaos threatening on both the home and the fighting front. The Socialists became increasingly exacting, and stepped up their pressure; the national minorities prepared to throw off agelong Magyar oppression; and following Bulgaria's surrender, the army was in disarray.

Consequently even the diehards of Hungary's political class, not to mention Hadik, now conceded that only Károlyi and his program could head off a total collapse of the *ancien régime* and the fatal

[1] Michael Károlyi: *Gegen eine ganze Welt: Mein Kampf um den Frieden* (Munich: Verlag für Kulturpolitik; 1924), 458–60.

dismemberment of the nation. Because the Socialists momentarily trusted him, Károlyi was in a position to restrain the urban workers, intellectuals, and journalists, as well as the impoverished and abused peasantry. Moreover, with the help of the Socialists and of Radicals like Oscar Jászi, he stood a chance of mending the battered allegiance of the Slovak, Rumanian, and Serbian minorities. Most important, because of his abiding and well-known sympathy and contacts with the Western democracies, Károlyi was the most promising channel to the Allies, particularly to Wilson.

On October 31 Károlyi was asked to form a cabinet after he and Sigismund Kunfi, the moderate spokesman of the Social Democrats, assured Hadik and Archduke Joseph that they could maintain order. In this pursuit, and in response to Socialist demonstrations in Budapest and certain provincial cities, the new cabinet swore an oath to the National Council rather than to the Habsburgs. This bloodless dismissal of the monarchy was completed by November 16, when the first Republic was proclaimed without waiting for the sanction of a constituent assembly.[2]

With the expedient but disingenuous encouragement of yesterday's political masters, Károlyi embraced the republican cause for reasons as much of domestic politics as of foreign policy. Even though the Social Democrats held only two posts in the new cabinet—Kunfi was Minister of Education and Ernest Garami Minister of Industry—they were the dominant political force in the government. The Socialists owed this disproportionate influence to their unrivaled party organization and discipline in an otherwise "party-less" political system as well as to their close ties with the trade unions. Since they held the key to political order and economic production, Károlyi had to do their bidding.

Except for a small faction, currently reinforced by returning prisoners of war from Russia, the Hungarian Social Democratic Party was anything but revolutionary, its leaders being reformist and revisionist in domestic affairs and Wilsonian in international politics. Furthermore, before and following the Armistice they gave first priority to the achievement of a Parliamentary republic and a peace of self-determination, leaving wide-ranging economic and social reforms for the future.[3]

Incidentally, in those climactic pre-Armistice weeks, outside observers tended to exaggerate vastly the radicalism and militancy of

2 Cf. Von Fürstenberg to Foreign Ministry, October 31 and November 2, 1918, GFM (92/I/26) 25497, 25667.
3 On taking office Kunfi is said to have made the following statement: "As a convinced Social Democrat, I find it difficult to say that we do not want to employ the methods of class hatred and class warfare. And we ask that everyone support us in the great task ahead by turning off class interests and by pushing denominational considerations into the background." Cited in Béla Szántó: *Klassenkämpfe und die Diktatur des Proletariats in Ungarn* (Vienna: Verlagsgenossenschaft "Neue Erde"; 1920), 21.

these Socialists. The Russian lesson was all too recent and Hungary's "revolution from above," which preceded Germany's and Austria's, had all the marks of a dangerous experiment. There was widespread fear that the well-meaning Károlyi would unintentionally deliver his country to Bolshevism.

The German Ambassador in Vienna reported to Berlin that according to a reliable informant, who had just come from Budapest, "a second Russia" was inevitable. In a similar vein, Germany's Consul General in the Hungarian capital, Count von Fürstenberg, warned that the Károlyi government was likely "to be swept away during the next few days." Fürstenberg even made arrangements to entrust the protection of German interests to the Dutch Consul in anticipation either of Allied occupation or of a Bolshevik take-over.[4]

The American Legation in Switzerland sent equally alarming estimates to Washington. In Pleasant A. Stovall's judgment Károlyi's Cabinet was so radical that another step "to the left could mean the acceptance of Bolshevism." He doubted that further concessions to the Socialists would enable Károlyi "to hold his own against the Bolshevik movement."[5]

In any case, the Hungarian Socialists themselves were sworn to a moderate course; and their minimum and priority program was not overly offensive to Károlyi and his non-Socialist supporters. Even though non-Socialists would have preferred a constitutional monarchy, they were satisfied that, far from being a cowardly concession to revolutionary pressures, their acceptance of the republic was in the best national interest.

Károlyi's primary objective was to secure a moderate peace by enlisting Wilson and the European forces of movement against the Carthaginians of France, Britain, and the surrounding states. Hence, he eventually favored a republican regime in order to convince Wilson that Hungary's transition to democracy was as thorough and reliable as that of Germany, Austria, and the successor states.[6]

Max von Baden, Ebert, and Renner were never their own foreign ministers. In the new Germany, Solf, Erzberger, and Brockdorff-Rantzau were the chief diplomatic spokesmen; in the new Austria, Bauer occupied the Foreign Office. This division of functions and responsibilities provided valuable flexibility at home and at the conference table.

[4] Wedel to Foreign Ministry, November 2, 1918; Von Fürstenberg to Foreign Ministry, November 3, 1918; Foreign Ministry to Fürstenberg, November 4, 1918; Schubert (O.H.L.) to Foreign Ministry, November 3, 1918, in GFM (92/I/26) 25774, 46749, 25892, 46883.

[5] Stovall to Department of State, November 5, 1918, cited in Daily Report on the Central Powers, No. 8, November 8, 1918, in House Papers, 26:99.

[6] Michael Károlyi: *Memoirs: Faith Without Illusion* (New York: Dutton; 1957), 125–9, 138–9, 142–3.

Such a division never materialized in the new Hungary. Károlyi acted as President of the National Council, Prime Minister,[7] Foreign Minister, and President of the Republic—all rolled into one. Since he considered a prompt and auspicious diplomatic opening to the Entente and Wilson essential to his bid for stability and reform, he applied the bulk of his attention and energy to foreign affairs, thereby also staking all his personal, political, and symbolic power, influence, and prestige.

Károlyi himself headed the delegation that traveled to Belgrade to secure a modification of the Padua Armistice. This Armistice had been signed on November 3 by the Austro-Hungarian General Staff, with no representative present to speak or sign for the new, independent Hungary. In seeking out General Franchet d'Esperey, the Allied Commander in Chief for the Southeastern theater, Károlyi hoped to elicit a gesture of goodwill and sympathy for himself and his regime; favorable occupation terms; and assurances for the integrity of Hungary's borders.

But unlike Károlyi, the French General was not disposed to forget that Hungary was a defeated enemy suing for terms, at a time when French armies might still have to fight their way to Berlin. As an old-time soldier, Franchet d'Esperey accepted the political, social, and religious values of France's conservative military caste, so that he distrusted the Wilsonian perspective on the politics of military surrender under conditions of intense internal chaos and conflict.

To be sure, he treated Károlyi correctly.[8] He readily conceded that during the war the Allies had learned to appreciate the Count as "an honest man" and urged Hungarians to rally around him, "since he was the only man who could alleviate their lot." But other members of the Hungarian delegation did not fare so well. When the Chairman of the Hungarian Soldiers' Council, a young army captain, was introduced to Franchet d'Esperey, the General turned to Károlyi and scornfully exclaimed *"Comment, vous êtes déjà tombé si bas!"*[9] And on being introduced to Baron Louis de Hatvany, a delegate of Jewish faith, he could not conceal his anti-Semitism.[1]

In the interest of his mission Károlyi chose to ignore these humiliating and arrogant asides. But he, too, was dismayed when on referring

7 On January 11, 1919, Dyonis Berinkey became Prime Minister, but he never ceased to be overshadowed by Károlyi.
8 Unless otherwise indicated, this discussion of the Belgrade meeting is based on Károlyi: *Memoirs*, 132–5.
9 See also Dr. Stefan Koerfer: *Die Folgen des Weltkrieges in Ungarn* (Vienna: Verlag von Moritz Perles; 1919), 43.
1 Subsequently Wilhelm Böhm, Károlyi's future Defense Minister and later Commander in Chief of the Red Army, told a *Times* (London) reporter that after asking a member of the delegation to a window in order to look him over closely, Franchet d'Esperey insolently remarked "Ah!, I see, you must be a Jew by your nose." C. B. E. Ashmead-Bartlett: *The Tragedy of Central Europe* (London: Thornton Butterworth; 1923), 113.

in his opening statement "to Wilson and his democratic principles, the general waved his hand contemptuously." Evidently Károlyi's good name counted for little. Franchet d'Esperey refused to guarantee that French, Italian, or U. S. troops—rather than Rumanian, Czech, or Serb units—would move into those regions that were earmarked for Allied occupation. Nor would he agree to prevail on the Czechs and Poles to let in coal from Germany[2] or to ask the Allies to resume diplomatic relations so as "to give [the Hungarian] Government their moral support [thereby enabling it] to cope with its difficult task." Only when Károlyi threatened to resign did Franchet d'Esperey omit Clause 17 which, among other things, stipulated that only in case of internal disorders (which in this case neighbor states could instigate at will) were the Allies entitled to take over the administration of the affected areas.

On the whole, though, the Belgrade Convention was a purely military instrument.[3] Even though the various demarcation lines had political implications, they were not designed as political boundaries, and therefore were bound to leave a legacy of conflicts. Only the Serbs were well served, Franchet d'Esperey having consulted them in advance. On the other hand, the Rumano-Hungarian line was unsatisfactory to both sides, while the Czech-Hungarian demarcation remained unsettled.

By reserving themselves the right to enlarge the various occupation zones, the Allies—unintentionally—invited Hungary's neighbors to extend their zones to approximate their territorial claims. No sooner had the National Council in Budapest ratified the Armistice Convention on November 13 than the Rumanians advanced in Transylvania from the line of the Maros River, laid down in the Belgrade Armistice, to some few miles short of the line stipulated in the secret Treaty of Bucharest of 1916. The Czechs occupied most of Slovakia, including districts south of the Ipoly River and north of the Danube, whose population was overwhelmingly Magyar. Even the Yugoslavs decided to improve on their excellent positions by crossing the Drava River and proceeding to north of Pécs, along the way taking possession of Hungary's last remaining anthracite coal mines.[4]

Having failed in his first diplomatic foray, Károlyi appealed directly to Wilson. In his message of November 16, 1918, he advised the President that his government relied "on the generosity of the Western democracies"; that the revolution had swept away autocratic institu-

---

[2] According to Baron Hatvany, when Károlyi insisted that without coal Hungary would go Bolshevik, Franchet d'Esperey snapped back: "I am about to go to Russia. It will be swept away. There is no more Bolshevism." Cited in Arpad Szelpal: *Les 133 jours de Béla Kun* (Paris: Fayard; 1959), 31.

[3] For the text of this military convention see *F.R.,P.C.,1919*, II, 183–5.

[4] Francis Deák: *Hungary at the Paris Peace Conference: The Diplomatic History of the Treaty of Trianon* (New York: Columbia University Press; 1942), 10–14.

tions and politicians and entrusted power to long-time democrats who were committed to the Fourteen Points; that because of frontier encroachments and economic boycott Hungary's society and economy were moving toward an abyss; and that Wilson should support the Hungarian Republic in its "severe struggle against dissolution and against the menace of anarchy."[5] Within ten days he sent a second note, this one designed also to flatter, impress, implore, and threaten Wilson's three Allies. He cautioned that because the occupations by the three neighboring armies were endangering the orderly distribution of food and because the shortage of coal was dislocating economic life, it was "more and more difficult to maintain the new democratic order." Károlyi proposed to send diplomatic missions to the Allies to discuss the "means of averting or at least provisionally alleviating . . . the peril of anarchy . . . sweeping upon the Hungarian Republic."[6]

In spite of these and numerous other protests and admonitions neither Wilson nor the three Premiers did anything to halt or undo these transgressions by Hungary's neighbors. Actually the Károlyi administration was not primarily concerned about the constant extensions of the Armistice lines as such. Its chief grievance was that throughout their occupation zones the Rumanians and the Czechs especially, less so the Yugoslavs, acted in full sovereignty, thus usurping and prejudging the decisions of the Peace Conference.[7]

Evidently, particularly Károlyi, but many of his supporters as well, had vastly overestimated his personal standing with the Allies as a lever to secure favorable territorial limits for the new Hungary.[8] Quite early, in late December, the Austrian envoy in Budapest expressed dismay at "the naïveté with which the Károlyi Cabinet believed [itself] able to turn a lost war into a political victory."[9] Indeed, Károlyi's failure to extract as much as a gesture or sign of encouragement from the Allies, notably from Wilson, fatally contributed to the instability of his government which simultaneously was beset by staggering domestic problems.

Even without these foreign policy reverses the government's cohesion would have been sorely tried. Károlyi had no political base of his own. In the old Parliament fewer than 25 deputies had rallied to his Independence Party, which was a parliamentary formation without organized popular support. Besides, his followers were considerably less progressive than he, many of them having turned away only recently from Count Albert Apponyi's stolid Conservative Party. Simi-

[5] *F.R.,P.C.,1919*, II, 193–5.
[6] Ibid., 204–5.
[7] See the first of a series of reports by Professor Archibald C. Coolidge, who visited Budapest from January 15–20, 1919, in *F.R.,P.C.,1919*, XII, 372–4.
[8] See Alfred D. Low: "The Soviet Hungarian Republic and the Paris Peace Conference," in *Transactions of the American Philosophical Society*, New Series, Vol. 53, Pt. 10 (1963), 42.
[9] Cited in Low: "Soviet Hungarian Republic," 41.

larly, the equally fragile Radical Party was torn between the capitalist recruits from Count Stephen Tisza's entourage and the advanced democratic faction which was largely composed of intellectuals of Jewish faith.

These two parties were not only internally divided and structurally ephemeral. Under the influence of their conservative wings both balked at Károlyi's heavy reliance on the Social Democrats, the third and by far most powerful member of the government coalition. As of mid-December Martin Lovàszy, prominent Independent and Minister of Education, charged that the Social Democrats were falling under the spell of Bolshevik revolutionaries and that the Allies were rebuffing Károlyi because his government was too radical. Hence, Lovàszy spearheaded a campaign to forge an alliance of all non-Socialist parties, which would form a purely bourgeois cabinet headed by either Károlyi or himself.[1]

Károlyi's Independents and the tiny Republican Party readily fused to become the new Republican Independence Party. But the other parties and factions to the right of the government found it impossible to agree on common goals and methods. Notwithstanding their fear of the Left, the landlord-dominated Smallholders' Party, the confessional and monarchical Christian Socialists, and the agrarian '48-Social Democrats continued to go their separate ways.

In sum, Lovàszy's alliance never got off the ground. As a result, and since he spurned the overtures of outright counterrevolutionaries like Julius Gömbös, Károlyi could not afford a break with the Socialists. In protest, at the turn of the year, Count Theodore Batthyányi (Minister of Interior), Albert Bartha (Minister of Defense), and finally Lovàszy himself—all three members of Károlyi's Party—resigned from the cabinet.

These defections reinforced the very trend they were designed to protest, if not reverse, in that Károlyi was forced to lean still more heavily on his Social Democratic colleagues. Ironically, just then the Socialists were preparing to drive a hard bargain: they had a pronounced sense of their unrivaled organizational and numerical strength, which owed much to the burgeoning trade unions;[2] they were subject to mounting pressures from their own radical wing; and they were resolved to checkmate Lovàszy's campaign. Since they considered this campaign to be part of an ill-disguised counterrevolutionary

---

[1] Von Fürstenberg to Foreign Ministry, December 20, 23, and 30, 1918, in G.F.M. (92/I/26) 54287 and 54531; and *Pester Lloyd*, January 7, 1919, *Arg Est*, January 8, 1919, and *Az Ujsag*, January 10, 1919, cited in *Bulletin Périodique de la presse hongroise*, No. 30, April 13, 1919 (December 1, 1918 through March 20, 1919), I, 4.

[2] The trade union membership rose from 215,000 in January 1918 to 721,000 in December 1918; and to above one million by February 1919. Wilhelm Böhm: *Im Kreuzfeuer zweier Revolutionen* (Munich: Verlag für Kulturpolitik; 1924), 100.

maneuver, Kunfi served notice that any attempt to set up an exclusively bourgeois government would precipitate civil war.

Actually, when Lovàszy's resignation brought the lingering cabinet crisis to a head, the Socialist movement was torn between three uneven factions: an insignificant minority calling for complete withdrawal from the coalition; a formidable majority advocating the formation of an all-Socialist cabinet; and a strong minority pressing for continuing in the government coalition on condition that the Socialists' representation and influence be increased.

The Executive Committee of the Workers' Council met on January 8, 1919, to settle on one of these three courses.[3] For the smallest and most moderate faction Garami argued that the Socialist Party lacked the trained cadres and disciplined members with which either to exercise a larger share of power or to rule alone. He urged, therefore, that the Socialists withdraw from all levels of government for the purpose of devoting themselves to educating the inflated but untutored rank and file, which was being incited by Bolshevik agitators. Meanwhile, the party should pledge its support to the cabinet, conditional on the government's "protecting the achievements of the revolution and suppressing the counterrevolution, whether from the Left or the Right."

Alexander Garbai, as chief spokesman for the majority and the official party apparatus, warned of the risks of continuing in the coalition: the Socialists would not be able to control the new military establishment; the old bureaucracy would continue in power; and the socialization of the economy would be indefinitely postponed. He, for one, would rather "die in a counterrevolutionary struggle with the bourgeoisie than in a struggle in which the proletariat would be on both sides of the barricades." And he was confident that a Social Democratic government could easily contain the Bolsheviks, should they decide to act up. Böhm sided with Garbai because, in his judgment, only "an all-Socialist government, based on Socialist and labor organizations as well as on the army, would be in a position to check the Communist agitation or at least maintain order until after the election of the National Assembly."

Speaking for the middle position, Kunfi maintained that withdrawal from the government could only benefit the counterrevolution. As for a proletarian dictatorship, it would not be viable both because the provinces would cut off the food supplies to the cities, especially to Budapest, and the surrounding foreign armies would advance to crush the regime. As a third alternative Kunfi favored increasing the Party's influence in the coalition, while also building the preconditions for a Socialist regime through organizational and agitational work. Jacob Weltner, the editor of the main party organ, *Népszava,* endorsed this

---

[3] This discussion of the Executive Committee meeting is based on Böhm: *Im Kreuz-feuer,* 179–89.

proposal, while stressing that since all difficulties were due to Bolshevik propaganda and agitation among the new party members "we should use calumny against calumny, terror against terror, revolvers or machine guns against revolvers or machine guns."

By a vote of 169 to 100 the Workers' Council (Soviet) supported Garbai's motion for an all-Socialist government. But given the sizable minority, Garbai promptly withdrew his motion for fear of fostering a party schism. The next vote went 147 against 83 in favor of Kunfi's position. In response to Böhm's entreaty, 78 of the opponents, all of them metal workers, changed their vote, thereby isolating five Communists in solitary defiance. These same five Communists voted against the otherwise unanimously adopted resolution that, in addition to the two current cabinet posts, the Socialists take over the Ministry of Defense and the Ministry of Interior—the crucial ministries for "the suppression of the counterrevolution, whether from the Left or the Right."

Károlyi's Independent and Radical cabinet colleagues vigorously objected to this escalation of Socialist power, particularly because of the critical nature of the two ministerial strongholds.[4] At their insistence Károlyi made a counterproposal which, however, was too generous for their liking: the Socialists would get the Ministry of War; the Interior would go to Vincent Nagy, a thoroughly reliable Independent, to be assisted by a Social Democratic state secretary; and a fourth but less sensitive portfolio would also be allocated to the Left. When the majority of the Socialist Party's Executive rejected this compromise, on January 17 Károlyi took the unusual step of going before it in a desperate effort to break the deadlock. In an emotion-charged and tearful plea he expressed his apprehension that a Socialist withdrawal would precipitate a total collapse. Eventually, after once again threatening his own resignation, he persuaded the majority that continuing participation was vital in terms of both domestic and foreign affairs, and that they had to cooperate on conditions acceptable to the rest of the coalition.

On January 18 the new government finally was announced. In addition to Garami and Kunfi, who kept their posts, Böhm took over the Defense Ministry from the Independent Count Alexander Festetics;[5] and Julius Peidl became Minister of Labor and Welfare. According to the *Pester Lloyd,* these appointments demonstrated that the balance in the cabinet continued to shift in favor of the Socialists.[6]

Needless to say, this settlement of the cabinet crisis did not remove either the conditions or the issues that were tearing asunder the Hungarian state and society. Due to the Rumanian, Czech, and Yugoslav

[4] *Pester Lloyd,* January 9, 1919, cited in *Bulletin Périodique de la presse hongroise,* No. 30, 4.
[5] Károlyi's brother-in-law and prosperous landowner.
[6] January 18, 1919, cited in ibid., 4.

occupation of the wealthiest industrial and mineral-bearing provinces, the economy of the Magyar heartland was completely dislocated. The dominant agricultural sector caused least concern, except that the poor peasantry and the agricultural workers pressed the revolutionary government to implement the promised land reforms. On the other hand, the shortage of raw materials, the loss of traditional markets, the continuing blockade, and the disruption of internal commerce created havoc in the industrial sector. It was in that sector that unemployment rose to alarming proportions, further aggravated by the Socialist-sponsored, forced-draft military demobilization: by mid-December 1,200,000 men were released and two weeks later the entire demobilization was completed. Simultaneously the modest unemployment allocations were straining the exchequer; and the shortage of manufactures, which the peasants wanted in exchange for their produce, drove prices up.

Even a unified and strong government would have been stymied by this grave economic situation, which was so largely a function of Hungary's hopelessly constrained international position. To make matters worse, not only the cabinet but also the three coalition parties themselves were unable to agree on fundamental policies, with the notable exception that in foreign policy one and all were wistful Wilsonians. Károlyi advocated Stolypin-like agrarian reforms for the purpose of giving his regime a solid peasant underpinning. But his landed and bourgeois-capitalist supporters were not alone in blocking him. In Russia Lenin had successfully confiscated and distributed the land for essentially political reasons, but in Hungary both the bulk of the Social Democrats and the Communists resisted this course. They did so because in their view the parceling out of large estates would cut productivity, increase the influence of the counterrevolutionary peasantry, and complicate nationalization and collectivization in the future.

With proper party support it would have been within the power of an undivided cabinet to mitigate agrarian discontent. With regard to labor ferment, however, this would have been possible to a much lesser extent, primarily because developments in the industrial sector were so totally contingent on the diplomatic situation, in which the government was particularly helpless. Neither the Big Four nor the neighboring countries were prepared to lift the blockade or to provide loans. Moreover, in the unlikely event that the coalition government should nationalize key industries, the Allies in all likelihood would tighten the noose still further.

The government, then, was hopelessly paralyzed, leaving ample scope for revolutionary agitation. The Communists could hardly have been expected not to seize their opportunity.

Béla Kun had arrived in Budapest on November 17; he and other war prisoners recently returned from Moscow constituted the Bolshevik nucleus. In Russia these Hungarians had become faithful converts to and students of Leninist principles, strategies, and tactics. On November 25 the disciplined Hungarian Communist Party was charted, together with *Vörös Ujsag,* its press organ. In close cooperation with some of his prisoner colleagues from Russia and with a group of alienated, mostly Jewish, bourgeois intellectuals, Béla Kun began his propaganda work among the demobilized soldiers and officers, the unemployed, the fresh party and trade union recruits, and the poor farm laborers.[7] According to Böhm, from the very start the Communists deliberately stirred up "the *Lumpenproletariat* against the proletariat, the unorganized and politically unconscious masses against the organized and class conscious workers, and the unemployed and disabled veterans against the employed."[8]

Following time-honored revolutionary practice, the Bolsheviks denounced the government and its supporters with simple, straightforward slogans while at the same time holding out quick and easy panaceas for complex problems. They also placed themselves at the head of every popular demonstration, strike, or insurgence which the government or the Social Democrats either opposed or ignored, all the while striving to radicalize those that had other sponsors. Special teams of Red activists were formed to carry forward this work.

In no time Bolshevik militants were prominently mixed up and identified with every kind of disturbance: on December 12, with a demonstration by some 6,000 officers and men of the Budapest garrison clamoring for the dismissal of Colonel Bartha, the Minister of War, in favor of a civilian; on December 17, with a similar demonstration, supported by the local Soviet, in Szeged, calling for the dismissal of the official in charge of food distribution; after the turn of the year, with the gas and armaments workers in the capital demanding a special holiday bonus; on January 5, with a riot by mine and steelworkers in Salgotarjan, an industrial town shortly to be occupied by the Czechs; on February 1, with a rent strike in Budapest; on February 12, with a demonstration in Budapest by demobilized non-coms for 5,400 crowns of separation pay; on February 17, with the interruption of a sumptuous marriage in the main ballroom of one of Budapest's most elegant hotels; on February 20, with the seizure of estates by the poor peasants of Gödöllö and Kerepes; and throughout January and February with the take-over of large factories by the workers employed in them.[9]

Through these and many other disorders the Bolsheviks dramatized their support for higher wages for workers, greater benefits for the

7 Szántó: *Klassenkämpfe,* 23.
8 Böhm: *Im Kreuzfeuer,* 108.
9 Szelpal: *Les 133 jours,* 51–2, 62–4; and *Pester Lloyd,* January 6, 9, and 11, 1919, and *Népszava,* January 29, 1919, cited in *Bulletin Périodique de la presse hongroise,* No. 30, 2.

unemployed, indemnities for veterans, low rent and cheap food for poor city dwellers, and land for the peasants. In crisis-torn Hungary demands of this nature were no surprise. Although the Bolsheviks undoubtedly instigated some of this clamor, their major contribution consisted of fitting these bread-and-butter demands into a coherent ideological context; of discrediting the government and the Social Democrats for not meeting transparently minimum demands; of providing dedicated leaders; and of helping generate an atmosphere of excitement and distrust through *Vörös Ujsag,* party pamphets, fliers, posters, and mass meetings. All along they charged the order-seeking Károlyi administration, including the Social Democrats, with doing the bidding of the counterrevolution.

As happens so often, pro-government spokesmen and dailies artificially exalted the status and influence of the Bolsheviks by blaming them for every protest and disturbance. Worse still, they vastly exaggerated the scope of Bolshevik agitation and influence in order to justify their own call for the resolute repression of mischief-makers and for the halt of reformist concessions to the nonrevolutionary Left.

At the time of the cabinet reshuffle the Independents and Radicals asked for bolder anti-Bolshevik measures in exchange for the Socialists' enlarged share of government power. Moreover, by late January 1919 this request was urgently endorsed by the Police Chief of Budapest and by the Commander of the National Guard.[1] Allied agents pressed along similar lines. "A blunt-minded member of a visiting mission, headed by Hugh Gibson, urged Károlyi to jail all Bolshevik agitators; while Sir Thomas Cunningham, who claimed to speak for the Big Three and for whom every striking laborer was a Bolshevik . . . threatened dire things if Bolshevism were not immediately stamped out."[2] Even prominent Socialists, notably Garbai and Joseph Pogány, advocated recourse to repressive measures of the Noske variety.

Nevertheless, in spite of their fierce hostility to the Bolsheviks, most Social Democrats were reluctant to curb them by police measures. Some objected to using *ancien-régime* methods against political opponents; others hesitated for fear of precipitating civil war; still others would not throw away the scare value of radicalism in dealings with the bourgeoisie; and all alike trembled at the prospect that the inherited army and police might emerge as a White guard bidding for control of the Revolution. As of now Minister of War Böhm devoted himself to organizing a reliable public force on the model of the Austrian *Volkswehr.*[3]

[1] Szelpal: *Les 133 jours,* 65–6.
[2] Memorandum by Hugh Gibson to Secretary Lansing, *circa* February 1, 1919, cited in *F.R.,P.C.,1919,* XII, 233; Walter G. Davis Diary, entry of February 13, 1919; *F.R.,P.C.,1919,* XI, 65.
[3] Böhm: *Im Kreuzfeuer,* Ch. xxiv.

Even so, on January 28 the Workers' Council voted to expel all Communists from its ranks; on February 3 the Socialist Ministers gave their assent to the foreclosing of *Vörös Ujzag;* and on February 9 the Congress of the Social Democratic Party resolved to oust Bolsheviks from both the party and the trade unions.[4] During these two months the authorities also carefully watched the Austrian border for Bolshevik agents and money, and the Russian Red Cross Mission was asked to return home.

These and similar measures gave considerable comfort to Allied observers. On February 10 Charles M. Storey, whom Coolidge had posted permanently in Budapest, sent his chief an optimistic report on "Bolshevism in Hungary."

> Bolshevism is such a bugbear to the Hungarians that it has been very difficult to ascertain the true proportion of the movement. . . . However, we are beginning to be convinced that at present there is little or no danger of a Bolshevik uprising. . . . A raid was made upon the offices of the *Vörös Ujsag* by the police . . . [so that] its publication has ceased. . . . Lack of paper as well as of money also interfered with Kun's activities. . . . Furthermore unemployment does not seem to be so widespread in Budapest as at first believed. . . . [Kun's activities] among the unemployed . . have been counterbalanced by the Government supporting them out of the public purse . . . and by the Social Democratic Party's bitter opposition to Bolshevism. . . . Károlyi told me . . . that he had received word secretly that Lenin had become dissatisfied with Kun's progress and had decided to recall him. . . .
> It is our opinion that [these actions] will put an end to effective Bolshevik activity for the present. . . .

Significantly, however, Storey concluded this dispatch with an ominous caveat. In his judgment, the lack of coal, of clothing, and eventually of food, as well as rising prices, might create a situation "in which Bolshevism may rapidly spread . . . unless by the end of March some alleviation is forthcoming."[5]

Apparently Storey failed to take into account that in response to the government's and the Socialist Party's restraints, however half-hearted, the Bolsheviks would step up their agitation. Hereafter they set out to destroy rather than infiltrate and subvert the rival Social Democratic movement. Their language became more abusive and they multiplied their financial outlays.

On February 20 Budapest was shaken by the single most serious disturbance to date. Wrought up by the enduring economic crisis, a

---

[4] Cf. Böhm: *Im Kreuzfeuer,* 190–5; and Wilhelm Nemény: *133 Tage Bolschewisten-herrschaft* (Berlin: Kulturliga; 1920), 8.
[5] Full text of Storey's report is cited in *F.R.,P.C.,1919,* XII, 392–3.

mass of unemployed workers congregated in the center of the city. Some of their leaders who spoke on this occasion limited themselves to calling on the government to raise unemployment benefits and lower food prices. Others, however, combined such unexceptional demands with a summons to the workers to arm themselves, followed by the injunction to march in formation to the headquarters of the *Vörös Ujsag*. On arriving there Béla Vagó, Tibor Számuely, and Béla Kun incited the crowd still further. Vagó, who had been the spokesman of the Communist faction in the Workers' Council, lambasted the *Népszava;* again called on the workers to procure arms for themselves; and summoned them to a mass meeting in front of Parliament for the following afternoon to protest the Socialist Ministers' defense of the existing social and economic order and their betrayal of Socialist principles.[6] Béla Kun's harangue was equally extreme: "Social Democracy is our enemy No. 1. We must destroy it in order to clear the road which will lead us to Communism. . . . Down with the Social Democrats! Down with the *Népszava*, that lackey of the bourgeoisie."[7]

Thereupon, and apparently at the spontaneous suggestion of an unidentified member of the crowd, a band of armed men marched to the headquarters of *Népszava*, the Hungarian *Vorwärts*, which by now were ringed and occupied by policemen and workers' guards. Who fired the first shot remains a mystery. At any rate, there was a heavy exchange of fire, the security forces using machine guns. Nonetheless, when the shooting was over, there were seven dead policemen; and among eighty wounded the vast majority also belonged to the constabulary.

Kunfi not yet having returned from the Berne Conference, it was left to the other three Socialist Ministers to assess the situation before meeting with their cabinet colleagues. Determined to set a stiff example, Böhm demanded harsh punishment not only for those workers who participated in the actual shooting, but also for whoever incited the crowd to violent action. The Minister of Defense and the leader of the radical wing of the Socialist Party seized this occasion to check the acquisition of weapons by workers and veterans, the appeals to class struggle and violence, and the drift into civil war. Peidl readily rallied to this view and, with less enthusiasm, so did Garami.[8]

The cabinet was only too relieved that at long last the Social Democrats were seeing the light. It was on their recommendation that Béla Kun, his closest associates, and the leaders of the discharged but armed veterans—a total of 69 activists—were rounded up that very

---

[6] Speech as reported in *Népszava*, February 21, 1919, cited in Böhm: *Im Kreuzfeuer*, 196–7.
[7] Cited in Szelpal: *Les 133 jours*, 70.
[8] Böhm: *Im Kreuzfeuer*, 197.

night and thrown into jail.[9] Following these arrests the offices of *Vörös Ujsag* were thoroughly searched. According to the German envoy, on the premises the police found Bolshevik agents of German, Russian, and Czech nationality. There and elsewhere during their searches they also uncovered evidence that the Bolshevik Party had 10,000 members in Budapest and 25,000 members in the provinces, and had spent about 1.5 million crowns of Soviet Russian origin over the last three months. Von Fürstenberg commented that the assault on *Népszava* had been so badly prepared that the entire episode suggested Russian Bolshevik pressure for instant action in return for continuing financial aid.[1]

Due to these arrests the Bolshevik demonstration which had been scheduled for Friday morning was never held. Instead, led by the metal workers, with whom Böhm was particularly influential, 250,000 working men marched past the *Népszava* offices on their way to the square in front of Parliament, where they staged a mass rally in support of the government. On this occasion, to the cheers of the crowd, Socialist speakers rededicated themselves to the defense of the revolution against the extremists of the Left and Right.

Böhm and his colleagues expected that in exchange for sanctioning the repression of Bolshevik radicalism, the non-Social cabinet members would agree to measures against the counterrevolution of the Right. But this expectation was never fulfilled. As compared to the Bolsheviks, the counterrevolutionaries—landowners, capitalists, officers, churchmen, and bureaucrats—were temporarily quiescent. Their strongholds were in the provinces, and they agitated by private word of mouth rather than mass rallies.[2] In any case, the Károlyi administration refused to initiate legal proceedings against or careful surveillance of known right-wing enemies of the "revolution from above."

By not following up the repression of Bolshevism with a demonstrative vigil over the Right, the cabinet aroused distrust in many segments of the Socialist movement. This apprehension was heightened by reports about the brutality to which Béla Kun was subjected in prison.

It so happened that only a low wall separated the jail from the police barracks. Early Friday morning a group of armed policemen, incensed by the previous day's killing of their colleagues, scaled this wall and compelled the prison director to show them his star prisoner. In a fit of fury they suddenly seized Béla Kun and proceeded to beat and kick him until he bled profusely and was unconscious. Finally, the director and the guards, reinforced by the jail physician and the police prefect, extricated Kun and carried him to the infirmary.

[9] Károlyi: *Memoirs*, 148. According to the Defense Minister, this action was recommended by Dietz, the Commandant of the capital's security forces, and unanimously approved by the cabinet. Cf. Böhm: *Im Kreuzfeuer*, 198.
[1] Von Fürstenberg to Foreign Ministry, March 16, 1919, G.F.M. (92/I/27) 9294.
[2] Von Fürstenberg to Foreign Ministry, February 23, 1919.

The non-Socialist press reported this incident in sensational terms.[3] By overdramatizing the brutality of the assault by a large number of police agents on a single, helpless prisoner these papers unintentionally generated popular sympathy for the victim. Moreover, this entire episode corroborated earlier charges, even in democratic newspapers, that the Budapest police force continued to be run and staffed by men of the *ancien régime*, men who were reactionary, antilabor, and anti-Semitic.[4] Almost overnight Béla Kun became a celebrated martyr for that growing segment of public opinion that now also clamored for a thorough purge of the police force.

Meanwhile Lenin expressed his displeasure by arresting three members—all three Social Democrats—of the Hungarian mission which was in Moscow to negotiate the repatriation of some 100,000 war captives. This combined internal and external pressure brought about the release of 29 of the 60 prisoners, while Béla Kun and those who remained in jail with him were classified and treated as political prisoners.

Bolshevism was not squashed by this arrest of 40 key activists, by the intensified scrutiny of the party at large, and by the continuing suppression of the Communist press. Perhaps these measures would have been more effective if Hungary's internal and external situation could have been stabilized or improved. But such was not to be the case; conditions actually got worse. At home, the rifts in both the coalition parties and the cabinet perpetuated the stalemate in land reform; the industrial crisis, aggravated by the blockade, enlarged the ranks of the unemployed; the oversupply of labor depressed wages; mounting shortages of essential manufactures pushed prices ever higher; and a fear of food shortages began to seize the major cities.

The cabinet was too divided, its resources were too scanty, and its overarching project was too ambiguous to contain this internal crisis. In the diplomatic realm, notwithstanding broad cabinet agreement, the outlook was equally grim. The neighboring countries persisted in relentlessly expanding their territorial and political controls at the expense of Hungary. The Rumanians and Czechs ignored with impunity the half-hearted commands of the Big Four; and the Hungarian army was in no condition to restrain the interlopers. Nonetheless Károlyi stuck to the extravagant hope that by performing a spectacular foreign policy feat he could unify the government and bridge over internal tensions.

While he probed for this unlikely diplomatic breakthrough, his hold on the cabinet continued to slip. In particular, the vital center which he

---

[3] See the report in *Arz Est*, cited in Böhm: *Im Kreuzfeuer*, 201–2.
[4] *Pester Lloyd*, February 7, 1919, cited in *Bulletin Périodique de la presse hongroise*, No. 30, 3.

tried desperately to maintain was being eroded by the radicalization of both the Left and the Right.

On the Left, ever more Social Democrats became restless with the government's uncertainty, division, and ineffectiveness in the domestic crisis. The four Socialist cabinet members had an increasingly difficult time convincing their party and trade union colleagues that the coalition ought to be continued. All alike blamed the desperate economic conditions on the refusal of the bourgeois ministers, parties, and interests to consent to essential reforms. Moreover, in the face of the hostile territorial encroachments, the plea that domestic moderation and order were preconditions for coal imports and just boundaries wore very thin.

All along the Bolsheviks stimulated and intensified rather than caused this excitability. It may well be that Béla Kun had prepared a second team of leaders for the event that the first team should be arrested, looking to the example of Liebknecht and Luxemburg. But even had he not done so the crisis would have bred both cadres and followers. In addition, some leaders had escaped the police roundup; 29 were released from jail; and Soviet-trained war prisoners and money continued to arrive from Russia. Also, on March 19 Colonel Vix told two members of the Coolidge Mission in Budapest that there were "about 1,000 Russians more or less in Hungary . . . , and that he had made efforts to deport these from time to time, but that the French authorities no longer would receive them in Odessa, and if they were expelled to Ukrainia, they would simply increase the Bolshevik population in that country and were likely to slip back to Hungary again, and that the other countries refused to receive them."[5] Whatever the extent of Soviet Russian help, the crisis provided wide scope for Bolshevik agitation and organization.

The Bolsheviks pressed their propaganda offensive among the unemployed, the army, the poor and landless peasants, and the disgruntled veterans. In their speeches at public rallies they more than ever held the cabinet and the Social Democrats accountable for the plight of the poor, for the neglect of their grievances, and for blocking the road to the Socialist paradise. The Bolsheviks also garnered tremendous psychological advantages from their incessant protest against the arrest of their leaders by a presumably revolutionary government, in which Social Democrats held key positions. Since the domestic situation continued to deteriorate, the Bolsheviks found an ever-widening audience within the Socialist and trade union movements.

These inroads made a particularly strong impression on the leaders of the majority faction, whose resolution in favor of an all-Socialist government had been defeated. Ever since the last cabinet crisis the

[5] P. L. Goodwin to A. C. Coolidge, March 19, 1919, National Archives, Document 184.01102/254.

rebel faction had grown in size, revolutionary fervor, and self-confidence. Joseph Pogány, the most prominent and fiery spokesman of these impatient ultraradicals within the Social Democratic Party, applied constantly stronger pressure on the four Socialist cabinet ministers.

By early March these ministers had agreed with Károlyi to fix the elections for a national assembly for April 13. Kunfi and Böhm—not to speak of Garami and Peidl—were prepared to trust the fortunes of the Socialist cause to the ballot box. They were confident that the party would win a comfortable majority, thanks to its unrivaled organizational structure and its proven ability to mobilize opinion.

Pogány, however, was not in the mood to take chances. He expected many enemies of the revolution to rally behind the banners of a middle course in an expediential election alliance. Moreover, because the Bolsheviks had taken such a strong stand, one that attracted many hotheaded Socialists to join them in disrupting the election meetings of other parties, he felt called upon to prove his own revolutionary fervor. In mid-March he insisted, therefore, that he and his colleagues would refuse to summon their followers to participate in a free and open election campaign unless Károlyi and the bourgeois parties guaranteed the Socialists more than 50 per cent of the seats, regardless of the outcome. He ominously threatened that if this guarantee were not forthcoming, and in the event that the Socialists failed to receive a majority, he and his followers would forcefully overthrow the new assembly.[6]

At the same time, Ignatius Bogár, the pro-Bolshevik leader of the typographers' union, visited Béla Kun in jail to examine the preconditions for uniting all genuinely revolutionary elements of the Socialist and trade union movements. At the end of their discussion Bogár asked Kun to draft a program to be used as a basis for further talks.

Béla Kun obliged, and his draft-platform was ready on March 11.[7] As expected, it was bitterly uncompromising in tone and content. He violently opposed participation in and support of bourgeois governments, placing his faith in the growth of workers' organizations which would act as agencies for the various workers', soldiers', and peasants' councils. In his view the Hungarian Revolution was about to pass from "its general and national phase into the era of . . . social revolution"; and it would do so not as a bourgeois republic, but as "a transitional centralized republic, composed of councils representing the propertyless workers and peasants." He also wanted all army and police formations disbanded, their place to be taken by a "class army of the armed proletariat."

First among the measures to be adopted by a revolutionary government was the confiscation of large landholdings, which were not to be

[6] Böhm: *Im Kreuzfeuer,* 248–51; and Szántó: *Klassenkämpfe,* 43.
[7] For the full text see ibid., 43–8.

carved up into small plots. In addition, he called for the socialization of the banks, confiscation of all bank deposits and balances, nationalization of large manufactures and the entire transport industry, government monopolization of wholesale and foreign trade, separation of church and state, the immediate implementation of social security measures, and the use of schools to educate youth for Socialism.

In foreign policy Béla Kun was equally extreme, advocating an immediate break with the policy of "territorial integrity and defense." In his view, this policy was merely designed to promote class cooperation, as was the incessant claim that the procurement of coal and food was dependent on good relations with the Allies. The liberation of the Hungarian proletariat would be achieved not through bidding for American food, nor through the exchange of munitions for coal with the counterrevolutionary governments of Poland and the Ukraine, but rather through an alliance with the revolutionary proletariat of Russia, Germany, Latvia, and the Ukraine. In any event, the proletariat would fight a revolutionary war against predatory neighbors only after state power was safely in its own hands and on condition that "no new national oppressions be created."

In brief, between March 10 and 20, Hungary's domestic crisis came to a boil. While Pogány pressed the Socialist Ministers, Bogár carried on negotiations with Béla Kun that envisaged violent insurrection. At the same time the iron, metal, printer and typesetter unions, as well as entire army units, were going over to the Bolsheviks, while in the provinces peasants were seizing the estates of landlords. On March 18, the printers and typesetters went on an indefinite strike, creating a complete paralysis of the press. On the nineteenth in Budapest, the unemployed staged another demonstration during which the Welfare Ministry was stormed; that same day reserve officers held a protest rally in front of the Ministry of Defense. On the twentieth Böhm received word that the Communist Party, following a mass meeting at Csepel, had decided to liberate Béla Kun on Sunday, March 23.[8]

Foreign observers in Budapest soon realized the seriousness of the situation. On March 16 Von Fürstenberg wired Berlin his reluctant conclusion that "this unhappy land was helplessly drifting into Bolshevism," adding that if Spartacism won the upper hand in Germany, Hungary's course would be altogether inevitable. Unfortunately, in official circles, particularly among Social Democrats, there was much criticism of the Ebert regime's forceful repression of the Spartacist movement. According to Von Fürstenberg, the Károlyi administration kept moving further to the left in an effort to blunt the agitation of the Communists. Whereas the German government considered Bolshevism the greater danger, the Hungarian government never ceased being apprehensive about its right-wing opposition. These contrasting atti-

[8] Böhm: *Im Kreuzfeuer*, 266; and Szántó: *Klassenkämpfe*, 49–50, 54–9.

tudes had significant foreign policy consequences. Berlin flaunted the specter of Spartacism, especially once it ceased to be an imminent threat, in the hope of frightening the Allies into moderation. Károlyi, for his part, deemphasized it so as not to give grasping neighbors an excuse for pre-emptive intervention, which the Allies would be likely to condone in the event of Communist ascendancy.[9]

On March 20 the German Consul reported that in the last few days "the signs of inner decomposition and dissolution had multiplied to such an alarming extent that before long there would be, in all probability, new outbreaks and the country would sink into anarchy." The loss of influence of the Socialist leaders over the rank and file was particularly striking. Von Fürstenberg anticipated that in a climate of terror and intimidation the Social Democrats would win a sweeping majority in the elections. He put little stock in those elections since "governmental institutions were developing along the Russian pattern at breakneck speed." No doubt the Socialists had it in their power to destroy the old social order, but would they be able to construct a Socialist society? Meanwhile, in the unlikely event that the Social Democrats should be beaten at the polls, civil war was inevitable. To guard against this, rather than run a slate of its own, the Radical party urged its followers to vote for Socialist candidates.[1]

On March 21 the German military attaché sent an equally alarming dispatch, insisting that a Soviet government was just around the corner. Since Károlyi and his colleagues had dismantled the Hungarian army, a military counterstrike from within was out of the question. As for the French Military Mission, it followed a rather puzzling course. At the same time that it "promoted Bolshevism" by enforcing the blockade and by encouraging territorial occupations, it threatened the government "with the advance of neighboring armies in case disorders should increase." In the final analysis, a "minority could [easily] restore order, but such a minority did not exist." The morning of the twenty-third Oberst von Massow, in a postscript, informed Berlin of the Bolshevik take-over, Károlyi's resignation, the break with the Entente, and the opening to Russian Bolshevism.[2]

In mid-March Lieutenant P. L. Goodwin, of the Coolidge Mission, was ordered to report personally to the Ammission. On March 18, before leaving for Paris, he and Captain Nicholas Roosevelt met with Károlyi, several other members of the government, and Colonel Vix. On the basis of this conference he filed the following dispatch.

In Budapest the elections are to be held on April 13th, and the election campaigns are being made throughout the country, espe-

[9] Von Fürstenberg to Foreign Ministry, March 16, 1919, GFM (92/I/27) 9292.
[1] Von Fürstenberg to Foreign Ministry, March 20, 1919, GFM (92/I/27) 9292.
[2] Oberst von Massow to War Ministry, March 23, 1919, in GFM.

cially by the Social Democrat Party. This is the only party which is really well organized at the present time, and it maintains its strength by means of a sort of terrorism over the whole population.

At one time the Social Democrats were allied with the Radical and Karolyi parties. They have gotten rid of these and have even prevented the Karolyi party from holding public meetings. The group of Bourgeois parties has been regularly interfered with, and its meetings interrupted by the Social Democrats. There are no prospects of a fair election, as a sort of terror exists, which is frankly recognized by the President. He claims that the Social Democrats will have a small majority, about 55%, in the coming Parliament, and that this will be sufficient to satisfy them and allow them to carry out their programme. If they do not get the majority, but this result is unlikely, the Social Democrat party has threatened to seize the government by force. . . .

The government at the present moment is very weak. There is a tendency to force out all members of the Cabinet who are not Social Democrats. During the campaign in the country, ministers not Social Democrats have been prevented from making speeches. I should not be surprised to hear of the resignation of all ministers who are not Social Democrats before the first of April. Their position is becoming impossible very quickly. In this case, Karolyi would be in an even weaker position than he is at present, and in spite of the opinion of many people that he has a large vote in the population of Hungary, I do not think that he is strong enough to do anything at all against the Social Democrats. The month of April is going to see one of two things; either the complete triumph of the Social Democrat party by means of a majority of 60% in the new Parliament, and a complete Social Democrat government, or a defeat of the Social Democrats by a small amount, and a fight between town and country. Under these last conditions, there would be a state of anarchy similar to what has existed in Germany at times, unless foreign troops were brought in to maintain order and give a chance for fair elections. It appears that some English representatives here have made inquiries as to the number of foreign troops needed to maintain quiet, and the number of 30,000 has been given as sufficient. If Budapest were well controlled by foreign troops, the rest of the country could be held by a very small number.[3]

The signs that Hungary was in the grip of a prerevolutionary crisis were unmistakable by the time foreign policy developments intensified this crisis still further. On March 19 Colonel Vix, the Chief of the French Mission, asked the Chiefs of the three other Allied Missions to meet him at his headquarters at nine o'clock the following morning, prior to making a collective *démarche* with the Hungarian government. Captain Nicholas Roosevelt, the ranking member of the Budapest

---

[3] Goodwin to Coolidge, March 19, 1919, National Archives, Document 184.01102/254.

branch of the Coolidge Mission, arrived fifteen minutes early in order to "explain to him again that [he] was not empowered to take any action of a diplomatic or military nature." Though Vix readily conceded that Roosevelt had no official diplomatic or military status, he pointed out that the note about to be presented by the mission chiefs to Károlyi incorporated a decision taken by the Allied Powers at the Paris Peace Conference, with which Roosevelt was connected. This being the case, Vix was anxious that the Hungarian government, on being advised of this decision, "have ocular proof of [Allied unity] in the persons of the representatives of the French, British, Italian and American Governments." Having failed to reach Coolidge by phone for instructions, and at the urging of the British and Italian representatives, Roosevelt decided to go along.[4]

The four Allied representatives arrived at Károlyi's office some time between 10:00 and 11:00 a.m. As spokesman for this imposing delegation and as "dean" of the Allied Missions, Vix handed him the note which dealt with a new demarcation line in Translylvania and the establishment of a neutral zone. Károlyi did not have to read through the entire document to realize its full portent. Before going any further he had his War Minister summoned, so as to have the benefit of his advice. Thereupon Vix suggested that Minister President Berinkey might also be called in. Both arrived on rather short notice, Böhm interrupting work on plans to forestall or check the Bolshevik uprising announced for Sunday, the twenty-third.[5]

All three were equally dismayed by the demands of the note, whose origin went back exactly one month. On February 21 Tardieu, the Chairman of the Committee on Rumanian Affairs, had reported to the Council of Ten that in retaliation for "acts of cruelty . . . Rumanian troops had moved forward with the intention of occupying the whole of [Transylvania] up to the line fixed by the Treaty of 1916." Even though the Rumanians had not reached that line as yet, because of the undefined nature of the Hungarian-Rumanian frontiers, there was danger of the opposing armies becoming embroiled in serious conflicts. Tardieu proposed, therefore, that each side be assigned an extreme line beyond which they would not be permitted to advance; and that a neutral zone be established between these two lines, "to be occupied by Allied troops with a view to preventing the spread of Bolshevism, which was prevalent in Hungary."[6]

The matter was referred to the Military Representatives of the Supreme War Council. After taking testimony from Rumanian and

---

[4] Roosevelt to Coolidge, "Presentation to President Karolyi of Peace Conference Decision Regarding Evacuation of Transylvania," March 20, 1919, cited in *F.R.,P.C., 1919*, XII, 413–14.

[5] Ibid., 414; and Böhm: *Im Kreuzfeuer*, 266.

[6] *F.R.,P.C.,1919*, IV, 59–60.

French officials, they reported back on February 26. Their recommendation was that Rumanian troops be allowed to advance to the line Arad-Nagy Várad-Nagy Károly-Szatmár Nemett, some 45 miles beyond the armistice line but short of the frontiers promised by the Treaty of Bucharest. The military advisers also proposed that Hungarian troops withdraw some 31 miles west of the treaty line of 1916, this neutral zone to be governed by Hungarian civil administrators but policed by two Allied infantry battalions and one cavalry regiment, with "the mission of maintaining order and tranquility." The Council of Ten accepted these recommendations.[7]

While the Hungarians were kept in the dark about this decision, the Rumanians were kept fully informed. Even though these lines favored Bucharest, Brătianu was determined to press his maximum demands, which went even beyond the generous awards of the secret treaty. He decided, therefore, to encroach on the neutral zone, which was purely Magyar territory, before the lines should be finally frozen.[8]

It was on this morning of March 20, with a delay of close to four weeks, that through the Vix note the Hungarian government was finally advised of the new lines and the neutral zone in Transylvania. The timing of this presentation remains a mystery. Since Hungary fell into the French sphere, it was left to French military authorities to communicate the decision, Vix acting under the direction of General de Lobbit, the French Commander at Belgrade. Later on in the Peace Conference, General Bliss expressed his suspicion that the pro-Rumanian arrangements were part of Foch's ambitious project to fight Bolshevism throughout Eastern Europe.[9] On February 25, as well as on March 17, when Foch came before the Peace Conference to press for a vast military campaign against Russian Bolshevism, he assigned a central role to the Rumanians. Both times his project was turned down. On March 17, however, the Big Four decided to continue *indirect* intervention, heavily relying on Rumania and Poland to provide the major share of manpower and the fortified territorial bases from which to operate.[1] To implement this policy they decided to supply Rumania with the necessary material, food and clothing. The French were eager to compensate Brătianu for his services with a faithful execution of the Treaty of Bucharest.

In February and March Foch repeatedly warned of the danger of a breakthrough by the Red Army between Lvov and Czernowicz, which would be fatal for all of Southeastern Europe. No doubt Hungary was the weakest defensive as well as offensive link of the military and political chain this side of the Carpathians. Judging by Lieutenant

[7] Ibid., 145–6.
[8] Sherman D. Spector: *Rumania at the Paris Peace Conference* (New York: Bookman Associates; 1962), 109–11.
[9] See Baker: *Woodrow Wilson and World Settlement*, III, 238–48.
[1] See *F.R.,P.C.,1919*, IV, 121–5, 379–83.

Goodwin's report on the conversations predating the note, Colonel Vix was worried about this gap, as were so many other French officers.

He feels that the Bolshevik army is extremely strong, even rating it as high as 2,000,000 men, extremely well trained and equipped, and that it will be very difficult to resist it. The only places where there is any good chance of resistance is in Poland, where efforts are being made to stop the advance, and in Roumania, where plans are being made to prepare against this advance. This leaves an open door between Roumania and Czechoslovakia for the Bolshevists to come in if they care to. With the Czechs and Roumanians at loggerheads with the Hungarians at every point, Hungary will be unable to withstand Bolshevism as well.[2]

Especially following the decision of March 17 to bank so heavily on Poland and Rumania, the time had come to implement the decision of February 26 to establish a neutral zone. Hungary was about to be convulsed by internal disturbances or else subjected to a victory of militant Social Democrats in the elections on April 13. In either case, the *cordon sanitaire* would be weakened and Rumania and Poland would have to worry about rearward pressures. By a timely enforcement of the decision of the Peace Conference this setback could be avoided: Rumania's military and political position would be strengthened; the Rumanian and Czech armies could close the strategic gap by linking forces at Csap; and should the Hungarians be intractable, the Allies would have a ready excuse for the military occupation of the entire country.

Whatever the reasons, the note was presented as a thirty-hour ultimatum, the withdrawal of Hungarian troops to begin within five hours. Significantly, after reading through the entire document, Károlyi instantly commented on the absence of a demarcation line in the north: "this clearly showed that Hungary was to be dismembered [and] . . . that the Peace Conference had decided to allow Czechoslovakia and Rumania to share the Ruthenian country, and to have a common border." As for the neutral zone, it was apparent that, taking the Armistice as a base line, the Rumanians would advance some 100 kilometers into Magyar territory while the Hungarians were expected to withdraw twice that distance. Besides, given Rumania's endless infractions of the Belgrade Convention, Károlyi made it clear that even Allied guarantees could not induce him, his colleagues, or the public at large to trust Bucharest's promise not to overstep fixed lines in the future. Notwithstanding assurances that the new demarcation lines would not prejudice the final distribution of territories, these military borders were in danger of being transformed into political frontiers, and Vix could only deny it half-heartedly. In the last analysis, however,

[2] Goodwin to Coolidge, March 19, 1919, National Archives, Document 184.01102/254.

the three Hungarian leaders were first and foremost concerned with the internal political aspects of this development. Károlyi kept stressing that the note was a matter of the greatest internal political importance; that the "political consequences could only be revolution"; and that neither his own government nor any other government would last a day if it signed such a humiliating agreement.[3]

So as to leave no doubt about the nature of such a revolution, Böhm interjected that if the note were accepted "the Communist Party would jump in a few days from a few thousand to 200,000 or more"; and that the resignation of the cabinet would bring anarchy and revolution. Vix promptly replied, in German, *"das ist mir ganz egal"* ("I couldn't care less") either about the growth of Bolshevism, the consequences of resignation, or the composition of a new government. In sum, Vix denied that the issue was political; it was simply a question of "acting upon a decision already taken in Paris." Should the ultimatum not be accepted by 6:00 p.m. on March 21, the Entente Missions would immediately leave the country.[4]

During their consultations with the cabinet and with party leaders, both Károlyi and Böhm emphasized that in response to their inquiries Vix had declared that the demarcation lines were intended to be provisional political boundaries and not revised armistice lines.[5] Angered by Rumania's consistently aggressive behavior, and since the note did not explicitly rule out further spoliations, both the politicians and the public-at-large were inclined to believe the worst.

Eventually Károlyi as well as Béla Kun justified his rejection with references to this verbally expressed interpretation of the note rather than with the written text as such. Colonel Vix at once published a statement formally denying ever having declared that Hungary's political borders were involved. According to Vix's official rectification, when Károlyi referred to past violations of the Belgrade Convention, he merely expostulated that Hungary was being asked to accept not a modification of the Armistice but a new decision of the Peace Conference. In turn Károlyi, in an unyielding rejoinder, charged Vix with having declared explicitly that this new line should not be confused with earlier armistice and strategic demarcations, "since it had been decided upon not by soldiers but by the politicians of the Peace Conference, who were concerned with provisional boundaries."[6]

[3] Roosevelt to Coolidge, March 20, 1919, in *F.R.,P.C.,1919*, XII, 414–16.
[4] Roosevelt to Coolidge, March 20, 1919, in ibid., 415–16; and Böhm: *Im Kreuzfeuer*, 267–8.
[5] See Károlyi: "Die Geschichte meiner Abdankung," in *Arbeiter-Zeitung* (Vienna), July 25, 1919, cited in Szántó: *Klassenkämpfe*, 50–2.
[6] Böhm: *Im Kreuzfeuer*, 267; and Roosevelt to Coolidge, March 20, 1919, *F.R.,P.C., 1919*, XII, 416. The full text of Vix's rectification of March 23 and of Károlyi's rejoinder of the twenty-sixth are cited in *Bulletin Périodique de la presse hongroise*, No. 31, May 1, 1919 (March 21 to April 11, 1919), 2.

Captain Roosevelt forwarded the text of these charges and counter-charges to Paris in a covering note in which he recorded his own recollection that "Vix did once remark, in an off-handed manner, that he supposed the decision . . . had some political significance. Yet it was apparent from the conversation that followed that the point at issue was the creation and occupation of a neutral zone, and Vix refused to discuss the political aspects of this question." Perhaps under the shock of recent developments Károlyi had "misunderstood Colonel Vix's attitude to serve his own purposes."[7] In a parallel dispatch Von Fürstenberg reported that political circles assumed that Károlyi "either completely invented the alleged verbal demand or at least deliberately falsified it in order to prepare himself and his government for a decent exit to justify temporarily the new overturn, and to reconcile the bourgeoisie with it." His impression was that Károlyi "had deliberately twisted Vix's oral communication," an impression confirmed by French officials.[8]

These contemporary evaluations were not far off the mark. When Károlyi met with his cabinet during the afternoon of March 20, he confessed that the Allied note, as interpreted by Vix, vividly demonstrated the failure of his Western orientation, based on Wilson's policy.[9] Since the bourgeois parties were the main champions of this bankrupt policy in the coalition cabinet, their moral credit was depleted. Hereafter only an all-Socialist government could salvage the situation. The Socialists had for months been the real power; they alone could check the Communists; and only they could mobilize the sympathy and support of the Socialist International for the Hungarian cause. In Károlyi's judgment the entire bourgeoisie would gladly back "such an all-Socialist government, dedicated to the defense of the nation against predatory imperialists and to the maintenance of public order." Of course, the new administration would have to come to an agreement with the Communists to make sure that internal disorders would not hamper the life-and-death struggle against the external enemies. But free of their non-Socialist associates and policies, the Socialists should be in a strong position to strike a favorable bargain with their Bolshevik rivals. Meanwhile, Károlyi proposed to stay on as President of this all-Socialist government, leaving the supreme direction to a Socialist premier.

Böhm was the second Minister to speak. He entirely endorsed Károlyi's view that in the face of impending external encroachments

---

[7] By now Roosevelt was back in Vienna, while Coolidge was on a hurried visit to Paris. Hence, in Coolidge's absence, Roosevelt wrote and signed this covering letter on March 31, 1919. See National Archives, Document 184.01102/291.

[8] Von Fürstenberg to Foreign Ministry, March 30, 1919.

[9] This discussion of the cabinet meeting of March 20, 1919, p.m., is based on Károlyi: "Die Geschichte meiner Abdankung," *Arbeiter-Zeitung* (Vienna), July 25, 1919, cited in Szántó: *Klassenkämpfe,* 50–2; and Böhm: *Im Kreuzfeuer,* 271–3.

and internal civil war, there was no alternative to rejecting the ultimatum and forming an all-Socialist government, backstopped by an agreement with the Communists.

Kunfi, the third speaker, demurred, though he agreed that the note was altogether unacceptable. He urged that Vix and the Allies be put on notice that if they persisted in their ultimatum, the coalition would resign in favor of an all-Socialist government. This admonition should be reinforced with the additional warning that in no time such a government would have to come to some arrangement with Bolshevism. Kunfi wanted the bourgeois Ministers and their parties to issue this official warning publicly, over the air waves, in order to exert maximum moral pressure on the Allied Governments.[1]

Garami objected to Kunfi's proposal. Quite apart from the fact that the Allies had ignored all earlier warnings, by now Hungary's internal crisis was so acute that a coalition regime was no longer viable. In quick succession, then, all the bourgeois Ministers zealously pressed for the immediate acceptance of the Károlyi-Böhm proposal, for the resignation of the incumbent government, for Károlyi's retention of the Presidency, for the appointment of an all-Socialist cabinet on the morrow, and for this new cabinet to reject the Vix note.

Rather than adopt this policy then and there, the cabinet Ministers recessed until 5:00 the following afternoon, March 21, in order to take counsel with political and military leaders. Károlyi won enthusiastic support from prominent politicians of all bourgeois parties, all of whom were anxious to shift the blame for the coming catastrophe to other shoulders. As War Minister, Böhm satisfied himself that the officers and men of the Szekler Division—the army's best-equipped and best-disciplined 5,000-man unit—were vigorously opposed to yielding to the Allies, even at the cost of turning the government over to Socialists and Communists.[2]

But the really crucial consultations took place among the Socialist leaders, who had to decide whether or not to assume sole responsibility under such highly inauspicious developments at home and abroad. Their deliberations took place in an atmosphere of mounting tensions in the capital. The ongoing newspaper strike encouraged the spread of disquieting rumors about the Vix note; there were mass meetings in favor of Béla Kun's release; 30,000 metallurgists as well as the Buda-

---

[1] On March 22, 1919, in a cable from Constantinople, General Franchet d'Esperey advised Paris that "representatives of bourgeois parties had proposed to Vix an alliance with the Entente against Russian Bolshevism on condition that the existing demarcation lines be maintained and that the Allies send 15,000 men to Budapest to enable the government of order to survive; or, in case of an Entente refusal, they would make an alliance with Bolshevism." Dossier Klotz, No. 20.

[2] Böhm: *Im Kreuzfeuer*, 269–70. General Josef Breit eventually conceded that "not a single high officer came forward to rally the troops in an effort to prevent the Bolshevik take-over." Cited in Szelpal: *Les 133 jours*, 97.

pest garrison went over to the Communists; the Soldiers' Council decided to support the Bolsheviks; and the Bolsheviks began to occupy public buildings in various parts of the city. Moreover, the imminent government crisis encouraged the Bolsheviks to prepare an even bigger push for Sunday than originally planned.

The Socialist party's Administrative Commission convened in the morning of March 21, the radical trade unionists Eugene Landler, Pogány, and Eugene Varga having been invited to participate. Böhm presented and spoke in support of the cabinet's policy proposal.[3] Needless to say, an all-Socialist government could afford the acceptance of the note even less than a coalition regime. But since this defiance of the Entente was likely to lead to war, the precondition for this whole enterprise was an agreement with the Communist Party in order to put a clamp on civil disorders. In sum, the issue was not between acceptance or nonacceptance, but between revolution and counterrevolution.

Only three voices were raised in opposition to assuming full power and the attendant search for compromise with the Communists, all three from the right wing of the party. Manó Buchinger wanted the coalition to continue in power while accepting the Allied ultimatum under protest. For their part, Garami and Peidl doubted that the bourgeois Ministers could be had for this enterprise. But rather than form a united front, the Social Democrats, who were losing control over the masses, should ask the Communists to rule by themselves. Having taught the Entente a good lesson, the Communist take-over, after turning into a fiasco, would return the experienced Social Democrats to power. In any event, except for these three moderates, this enlarged commission—ranging from Kunfi and Weltner to Garbai and Pogány—endorsed Károlyi's proposal, as outlined by Böhm. No one ever introduced a formal motion to form an all-Socialist government without Communist support, "since under the present circumstances all alike were convinced of the futility of any such effort."

Even early in this session Landler, the Left-radical lawyer, was asked to go to the city jail for a preliminary talk with Béla Kun. He soon reported that the Bolshevik leader was willing to discuss a compromise with a Socialist delegation. Before adjourning shortly after 1:00 p.m., the commission instructed Weltner, Pogány, Landler, Kunfi, and Josef Haubrich to begin these negotiations immediately.

In the press of time this delegation never received detailed guidelines. Upon arriving in the prison around 3:00 p.m. Weltner informed Béla Kun that provided they could come to an agreement an all-Socialist government would be formed.[4] The entire discussion was over in half an hour. Weltner and Kunfi were so rushed that without ever

---

[3] For the most complete coverage of this session see Böhm: *Im Kreuzfeuer*, 271, 273–7.
[4] For a three-paragraph report by a Communist participant in this rather unusual conference see Szántó: *Klassenkämpfe*, 53–4.

examining any Communist statement of purpose, specifically Béla Kun's letter to Bogár of March 11, they declared themselves familiar with the Bolshevik platform.[5] They accepted that platform as a basis for unifying the two parties which would then set up a Soviet government, affiliate with the Third International, and reject the Allied note.

Béla Kun eagerly seized this unexpected opportunity, unaware or in disregard of Rosa Luxemburg's recent injunction that the Spartacists should "not accept power for the mere reason that all other parties failed."[6] After all, though still in jail, he was now in the driver's seat, the agreement being the product of capitulation rather than negotiation. Accordingly, the two parties merged to form the Hungarian Socialist Party. The leaders of both defunct parties agreed to cooperate within the new party as well as with the new government, within the framework of a dictatorship of the proletariat. The revolutionary regime would postpone *sine die* the scheduled elections for the National Assembly, would organize a people's army without delay, and would make a close alliance with Soviet Russia "to safeguard the proletarian regime against the imperialism of the Entente."[7]

That same March 21, at 3:30 p.m., the Socialist Party Executive met to consider the action recommended by the Administrative Commission.[8] Garbai had barely completed his outline of the radical reorientation in Socialist policy when the delegation of five arrived from the prison to announce that an agreement had been signed with Béla Kun. By now excitement had already reached such a pitch, in the streets of the capital as well as in the meeting hall, that few bothered to inquire about the terms of this accommodation. Against the lonely dissent of Otto Róth, the executive endorsed the Károlyi-Böhm project, including cooperation with the Communists.

For the Socialists one last hurdle remained to be cleared. The Workers' Council was scheduled to meet at 7:00 in the evening to ratify this endorsement. Once again Garbai, in his lead statement, denounced the Allies for throttling the Hungarian Republic.

> We were convinced that the Entente would bring about a just peace but Vix's *ukase* changes all that. In Paris they are bent on an imperialist peace, and they want to separate us from the Danube. . . . From the West we can expect nothing but a dictated peace, which forces us to abandon free elections. . . . There is no alternative to the acceptance of a new form of dictatorship. The Entente

---

[5] Whereas Szántó:*Klassenkämpfe*, 54, claims that during his morning visit Landler had informed Béla Kun that the Social Democrats were prepared to accept the Bogár platform, Böhm: *Im Kreuzfeuer*, 286–7, explicitly denies this.

[6] Cited in Franz Borkenau: *The Communist International* (London: Faber; 1938), 119.

[7] The full text of this agreement is cited in Szántó: *Klassenkämpfe*, 54–5; and Böhm: *Im Kreuzfeuer*, 278.

[8] See ibid., 278–9.

has driven us into adopting a new course which will secure for us from the East what the West has denied us. . . . The armies of Russia's proletarian masses are advancing. We will form an all-Socialist Government and proclaim the dictatorship of the proletariat. . . . We will go into battle with new means and methods. . . . •

When in his conclusion Garbai appealed for the ratification of the agreement signed with Béla Kun, he insisted that cooperation between Social Democrats and Communists was essential for success.[9] After Alexius Bolgár had made a similar plea in the name of the Communists, the Workers' Council approved the new course and instructed the leaders of the new party to set up an all-proletarian government.

Meanwhile the cabinet had reconvened at 5:00 p.m. Even though all of the Socialist Ministers were on hand, they did not inform their non-Socialist colleagues either about developments in their party or about the compact with Béla Kun. Instead, Böhm and Kunfi successfully pressed for Kun's immediate release from prison, implying that this step was the essential precondition for an accommodation with the Bolsheviks. The remainder of this cabinet session was taken up with trivial issues, Károlyi delaying the appointment of the all-Socialist cabinet until after the Workers' Council had approved his plan. The cabinet adjourned at 6:00 p.m., the hour that the ultimatum expired and that Károlyi informed Vix of his government's decision to resign rather than carry out the decision of the Peace Conference.[1] Adjournment at 6:00 p.m. also enabled Böhm and Kunfi to attend the meeting of the Workers' Council. Before taking leave, Károlyi called Kunfi aside to tell him that "in the event of a new Socialist Government, [he] would appoint him Premier"; he also asked that Kunfi notify him of the Council's decision any time that night, no matter how late. Kunfi, who himself had been to prison earlier that afternoon, still kept quiet both about the negotiations with Béla Kun and the terms of the agreement.[2]

While Károlyi waited for the Council's decision, the Socialist and Communist leaders conferred about the composition of the new government at the headquarters of the Social Democratic Party. Shortly after 9:00 p.m. Béla Kun arrived. He was in a surprisingly conciliatory frame of mind. There was "general agreement that the government would be made up of Social Democrats, except for the post of Foreign Minister, which would be occupied by a Communist, notably by Béla Kun, in order to give a tangible demonstration of our turn toward Soviet Russia."[3] Since both Garami and Weltner refused to

[9] This speech is reconstructed from non-overlapping excerpts cited in Böhm: *Im Kreuzfeuer*, 296–7; and Szántó: *Klassenkämpfe*, 55–6.

[1] Cited in Deák: *Hungary at the Paris Peace Conference*, 409–10.

[2] Károlyi: *Memoirs*, 154–5; and "Die Geschichte meiner Abdankung," in *Arbeiter-Zeitung* (Vienna), July 25, 1919, cited in Szántó: *Klassenkämpfe*, 52–3.

[3] Böhm: *Im Kreuzfeuer*, 291–2.

serve, cabinet members had to be chosen from the radical wing of the expiring Socialist Party. Accordingly, it was decided to make Garbai Prime Minister, Landler Minister of Interior, Varga Minister of Finance, Kunfi Minister of Education, Pogány Minister of War, and Böhm Minister for Socialization.

At this point Béla Kun's lieutenants began to balk. They objected to Károlyi staying on as President of the Republic. Determined to break with the past, they demanded that Károlyi resign, that the new government be known as a Soviet Republic, that the ministers be called Peoples' Commissars, and that the cabinet become the Council of the People's Commissars. Again because of their loss of influence over the rank and file, the Social Democrats reluctantly accepted these changes, which were a flagrant departure from the Károlyi-Böhm plan. They also agreed that the principal Communist leaders serve as deputy commissars and members of the government. Thus Tibor Számuely became Deputy Commissar of War and Georg Lukács Deputy Commissar of Education.

The time had come to inform Károlyi of this radical turn; he also had to be asked for his resignation. This unpleasant mission fell to Kunfi, the most moderate member of the new team, who went to the Royal Palace around 2:00 a.m., March 22. With downcast eyes he told Károlyi that the Workers' Council had voted for a dictatorship of the proletariat, consonant with the decision to rely on Soviet Russia. The President was furious and felt that the Social Democrats had betrayed him. Nonetheless, Kunfi begged him to sign the following proclamation in the interest of forestalling bloody civil strife.

> The Government has resigned in circumstances requiring a change in policy. Ordered production can only be guaranteed if the proletariat takes full power. In addition to mounting economic anarchy, the foreign situation has reached a critical point. The Paris Peace Conference has secretly decided on the military occupation of almost all of Hungary. The Entente Mission has declared that as of today the demarcation line must be considered as a political boundary.
>
> The evident purpose of further territorial occupations is to make Hungary into a military base from which to advance against the armies of Soviet Russia along Rumania's borders. The territories taken from us will be used to reward the Rumanian and Czech troops with which the Soviet armies are to be crushed.
>
> In the face of this Peace Conference decision, I, the Provisional President of the Hungarian People's Republic, appeal to the world proletariat for assistance and transfer all power to the proletariat of the Hungarian people.[4]

[4] For the full text see *Pester Lloyd,* March 22, 1919, cited in *Bulletin Périodique de la la presse hongroise,* No. 31, 2.

But Károlyi bluntly refused to sign this document, forcing Kunfi to return to political headquarters for consultations. Within an hour he was back in Károlyi's office, accompanied by either Pogány or Paul Kéri, the pro-Bolshevik journalist, or both. The President still would not yield. Even with the sound of occasional gunfire in the distance and the warning that rising militancy among workers and soldiers created a highly explosive situation in the capital, he stood his ground.[5] Even so the procalamation was published over his name in *Népszava* shortly after dawn on March 22. In the interest of the national cause, at that time Károlyi did not protest this illegal use of his name.[6]

More than that, when Vix denounced the distortions in this proclamation, the former Premier rushed to its defense. He thereby created the impression that in protest against Allied demands he himself had handed over power to the new, Communist-dominated Hungarian Socialist Party and that he himself had legitimized the peaceful transformation of Hungary's Provisional Republic into Europe's second Dictatorship of the Proletariat.

Béla Kun further reinforced the impression that this bloodless revolution was a product of wounded national pride. Admittedly, he did not ignore the internal economic and political causes for the triumph of the Soviet regime, as so many contemporary observers and retrospective historians have done. Instead, he gave equal emphasis to diplomatic factors, in particular to their interplay with domestic events. On this score his first official proclamation as People's Commissar for Foreign Affairs was altogether clear.

> Hungary's Proletarian Government was an outgrowth of two forces: one was the resolve of the industrial workers, the landless peasants, and the soldiers no longer to endure the yoke of capitalism; the other was the imperialism of the Entente, which intends to rob Hungary of her food supplies, raw materials, and other vital resources by mutilating her territories. The Hungarian people responded to the Entente's ultimatum to immediately and permanently hand over their country to the Rumanian oligarchy with the establishment of the Dictatorship of the Proletariat.[7]

Almost simultaneously, in addressing his first mass rally following his release from jail, he credited "Wilson's deceitful and perfidious peace program" for bringing about working class unity.[8]

---

[5] Károlyi: *Memoirs*, 155; Böhm: *Im Kreuzfeuer*, 281; E. Szatmari: *Im roten Buda-pest*, 3–4; Szelpal: *Les 133 jours*, 92–6.

[6] Károlyi did so later, in his *Memoirs*, 155.

[7] The full text of this proclamation of March 23, 1919, is cited in Baron Albert Kaas and Fedor De Lazarovics: *Bolshevism in Hungary: The Béla Kun Period* (London: Grant Richards; 1931), 327–8. The part of the text here quoted is cited in Böhm; *Im Kreuzfeuer*, 298.

[8] Speech of March 22, 1919, cited in Béla Kun: *La République hongroise des conseils* (Budapest: Editions Cornive; 1962), 112.

The typesetters and printers having resumed work in the early hours of March 22, the non-Socialist press was able to register its views. The major dailies unanimously supported Károlyi's stand, throwing all the blame for the overturn on the Allies. The *Pester Lloyd* flatly declared that "the creation of the Soviet Republic was the reply of the Hungarian proletariat to the reckless, booty-seeking imperialism of the Entente and her satellites." This paper attributed the economic crisis to the loss of the wealthiest provinces and charged that the proposed Rumanian line crudely violated Wilson's principles. "The answer to the peace of violence which the Conference of Paris seeks to dictate is the Red flood which, starting from Russia, now will spread from Hungary toward the West." In *Vitág* Louis Biró insisted that Hungary would have "signed her own death warrant by accepting the ultimatum which clearly proved the bankruptcy of bourgeois policy to every one." By establishing a Soviet Republic, by appealing to Europe's proletariat, and by turning to Russia, "Budapest was sounding the alarm in Paris, Vienna, Prague, Munich and Berlin."[9] In this same inflamed nationalist spirit, Thomas Kobor, the editorialist of the conservative *Az Ujság* claimed that Hungarians had "set their own house on fire in order to set fire to the whole world." The bourgeois *Az Est* seemed proud that Budapest "was shaking up the world," notably Paris, and that together with the Russian giant, "the courageous and vigorous Hungarian proletariat was at the forefront of progress."[1] All these papers and editorials refrained from commenting on internal developments, preferring to justify the revolution in purely nationalist terms.[2]

Under the cover of this ultranationalist braggadocio, the Council of Peoples' Commissars, in which Béla Kun was the real power, declared martial law, appealed for law and order, and called for maximum economic effort. At the same time, on March 22, its first session, the Council decreed a host of revolutionary measures: the abolition of titles and privileges; the separation of church and state; the preparation of elections of Workers', Soldiers', and Peasants' Councils; the establishment of a revolutionary tribunal; and the speedy draft of proposals for the socialization of factories, apartment houses, and latifundia. The Council also announced that it would make an alliance with Soviet Russia; that it placed Hungary under the protection of the Red Army; and that it was resolved to defend the Soviet regime "to the last drop of blood."[3]

[9] *Pester Lloyd* and *Vitág, March 22, 1919,* cited in *Bulletin Périodique de la presse hongroise,* No. 31, 2–3.
[1] Cited in Szelpal: *Les 133 jours,* 105, 115.
[2] Presently the non-Socialist press was gagged.
[3] *Népszava,* March 23, 1919, cited in *Bulletin Périodique de la presse hongroise,* No. 31, 3.

Part Five

THE PEACE CONFERENCE SHAKEN

17

The Hungarian Jolt

THE INTERNAL POLITICS of the victor and defeated nations never ceased to infringe on the diplomatic labors of the Big Four. Throughout Europe and, to a lesser degree, in America, similar underlying conditions gave rise to unsettling and urgent political issues and pressures.

Soon after the exaltation over the Armistice subsided it became glaringly obvious that instead of settling major and divisive domestic issues, the war had actually exacerbated them. Especially now that a Socialist Revolution had swept Russia and threatened to sweep other countries, economic and social questions claimed first priority. Before the war, when the national capitalist economies were prosperous though unstable, the forces of order had remained adamant in the face of labor's insistent and organized agitation for the forty-eight-hour week, collective bargaining, welfare legislation, and tax reform. In 1919 reactionaries and conservatives threatened to become still more unyielding. In addition to denouncing even reformist labor and Socialist leaders for harboring Leninists projects, they claimed that the war had exhausted the exchequers and that the economies could not afford new overheads for social programs. They further stated that graduated income taxes would discourage innovative entrepreneurs from renewing and modernizing their plants, and that higher wages would impair the nation's competitive position in international trade.

On the other hand, labor and Socialist leaders were determined to cash in on the promises made to them when they accepted the political truce; there simply could be no question of returning to prewar conditions. They angrily refused to enter a second political truce, this one to be dictated by the harsh exigencies of recovery and reconstruction. Even the Social Patriots could not afford to advertise their moderation because they, too, were subject to radical pressures. The entire Left was energized by the example of Russia, the flood of new—and primarily young—recruits into the Socialist parties and trade unions, and the expansion of the franchise. At this same time the strains of reconversion gave a tangible stimulus to the impatience and clamor of labor: in the post-Armistice year the wage earners were hardest hit by the rising cost of living and by unemployment due to rapid demobilization, cancellation of war contracts, and shortages of raw materials. Not least important was the political isolation of organized labor and the Socialist parties, now that the specter of Bolshevism was frightening the radical bourgeoisie into the camp of the forces of order.

Because the Right dominated the legislative chambers as well as the press, the militants of the Left favored compensating for their Parliamentary weakness by having recourse to such extraparliamentary tactics as mass demonstrations, strikes, and, in the extreme, mutinies.

Especially in the victor nations the Right made effective use of its Parliamentary strength. Wilson was concerned about the opposition of Lodge rather than La Follette. He also realized that should Clemenceau or Lloyd George be overthrown, more intransigent premiers would replace them. In Italy, meanwhile, he hoped to use Bissolati and Turati to pressure Orlando into standing up to Sonnino and his supporters.

At any rate, each of the Big Four took time out to face his legislature at least once in efforts to quiet the seething right-wing rebellion; and not only Lloyd George but also Wilson, Clemenceau, and Orlando were each served with a summons signed by forbidding groups of defiant right-wing parliamentarians enjoining them to impose a harsh peace. Significantly, most of the same lawmakers who advocated a Carthaginian peace also were champions of the domestic *status quo;* only their reactionary and proto-fascist allies wanted domestic changes which were unacceptable to traditional conservatives. For the time being, however, conservative nationalists furtively welcomed the support of these jingoists in the battle for the stiff peace which they proposed to exploit in the interest of maintaining and consolidating the existing power structure. The campaign against the League Covenant in the U. S. Senate was designed permanently to arrest the New Freedom; the campaign for exorbitant reparations in Britain and France was calculated to obviate the need for tax and social reform; and the campaign for the annexation of Dalmatia in Italy was meant to help the Right explode the Socialist contention that Italian blood had been shed in vain.

With varying degrees of enthusiasm and disingenuousness the Big Four used the existence of these concerted right-wing pressures to justify selfish national demands: Wilson held out for the Monroe Doctrine rider, Lloyd George for astronomical indemnities, Clemenceau for a 15-year lease on the Saar, and Orlando for Fiume. Furthermore, the Russian policy of all four, but especially of Wilson and Lloyd George, was influenced by the anti-Bolshevik rampage of their right-wing critics.

The Socialists and trade unionists also made themselves heard and felt. Their Parliamentary leaders persistently raised questions, initiated debates, introduced resolutions, and moved votes of no confidence. However, such Parliamentary maneuvers invariably backfired; for these debates and votes merely dramatized their Parliamentary weakness, isolation, and impotence. Whereas La Follette, Wedgwood, Cachin, and Turati succeeded in registering their Wilsonian and reformist dissent, Lodge, Kennedy Jones, Franklin-Bouillon, and Salandra— supported by the jingoist fringe—moved in to marshal impressive votes for resolutions which either upheld the government or called on it to hold out for "twenty-four shillings to the pound" in peace negotiations and in vital domestic affairs.

Not that the Socialist representations were totally useless. By flaying the government and the Right in the hostile legislative halls the elected deputies not only publicized the Left-dissident cause but also slowed down the rise of the militant Socialist and labor leaders outside Parliament. Moreover, with regard to Allied intervention in the Russian Civil War this Parliamentary agitation had a decidedly restraining though not deterrent influence. Especially in Commons and in the *chambre* the dissenters exposed and dramatized the mutinies, warned of future military disobedience, protested the expense of the intervention, and castigated the Allies for making common cause with reaction in Russia as well as in the border states.

But even this Parliamentary critique of intervention would have been considerably less effective had it not been vigorously reinforced by extraparliamentary action. In fact, the deputies repeatedly and belatedly echoed the protests and exposés of the militant spokesmen of the parties, the unions, and the left-wing press. Without strikes and mass demonstrations and without lingering threats of coordinated direct action in the form of a general strike the Allied Governments and Parliaments would have expanded the intervention in Russia and would have refused the forty-eight-hour week. Presently, most of the leaders —in Parliament, in party councils, and in the unions—recognized that foreign and domestic policy could not be divorced from one another. They rightly estimated that substantive reforms were contingent on a Wilsonian peace and on the survival of the Russian Revolution. Should the superpatriots have their way at the Peace Conference and in Russia, they would use the political capital gained with this foreign policy triumph to get out of whatever reforms they had agreed to in the interest of maximum war production and under the duress of post-Armistice labor unrest.

Not surprisingly, therefore, the political overtones of the strikes of 1919 became increasingly pronounced. As of late March work stoppages—whether on the factory, municipal, regional, or national level— ceased to be narrowly or primarily industrial. In addition to demanding the forty-eight-hour week without a cut in take-home pay, the workers struck or threatened to strike for a Wilsonian peace, against intervention in Russia, and for basic structural changes. Eventually, by late May, the Allied Socialist and trade union leaders—and by no means only the Zimmerwaldians among them—decided that only a simultaneous general strike in Britain, France, and Italy could advance their political-*cum*-industrial cause. The abortive general strike of July 21–22, 1919, to protest the continuing intervention in Russia, was the outcome.

In their own countries the Big Four were more responsive to and intimidated by the Right than the Left. In viewing the defeated nations, however, they were worried about the danger of Bolshevik-type revolutions rather than about right-wing coups. In private even Clemenceau, Pichon, and Foch conceded that at this particular juncture in Central and Eastern Europe Bolshevism was a greater threat than Prussian militarism. Of course, as compared to Wilson and Lloyd George, they were much more resistant to blackmail: they calculated that without contact with Soviet Russia—which the *cordon sanitaire* precluded—the Spartacists could not take over; thus they were not easily frightened into giving either food or a lenient peace.

Still, when Károlyi turned over power to Béla Kun *all* the delegations were equally stunned and terrified. Whatever the ultimate diplomatic and military purposes of Colonel Vix's *démarche* may have been, neither Clemenceau nor Foch could have wished or anticipated this turn of events. Even though there were internal causes—political, economic, social, and military—for the Bolshevik ascendancy in Budapest, these were overshadowed by the external slights to Károlyi's liberal regime and to the Magyars' inflamed national arrogance. While the Big Four, *pour décourager les autres,* readily agreed to take every necessary measure first to isolate and then to crush Béla Kun, they continued to differ about the most effective way to prevent similar defiances elsewhere.

Until March 22 Allied realists considered Wilson unduly alarmist whenever he warned that the imposition of oppressive peace terms on the unstable governments and unsettled social and economic conditions of the defeated nations could produce catastrophic results. Hereafter such warnings could no longer be dismissed quite so lightly, particularly since the volcanic eruption in Hungary was followed by serious tremors elsewhere. There were authentic reports of an imminent collapse in Vienna; a Soviet-type republic was proclaimed in Bavaria; strikes broke out in the Ruhr, in Hamburg, and in Saxony; the sailors of the French squadron at Odessa mutinied, thus hastening the evacuation of this strategic Black Sea port; and the Red Army stayed Kolchak's advance and continued to push ahead in the Ukraine. To make matters worse, these worrisome developments in the defeated empires coincided with the upsurge of labor unrest in Britain, France, and Italy.

For the Wilsonian cause this convergence may have been fatal. At first it seemed that the President could only benefit from a renaissance of the Left in the Allied nations and from the panic which the Hungarian *coup de tête* produced in Paris. Certainly Lloyd George's Fontainebleau memorandum pointed in this direction. But the Right was quick to realize that leniency in Paris would merely encourage and fortify the Left in its direct-action campaign—that success would breed success.

Hence, the forced-draft campaign by the right-wing press, Parliamentary majorities, and satellite pressure groups to commit the three Allied Premiers to a Carthaginian peace was as much designed to contain the reformist Left at home as to root out the Revolution in Russia and Hungary. The 300-odd Unionist members of Parliament not only challenged Lloyd George to keep his election promises with regard to indemnities and to streamline the operations against the Soviets; they were equally vocal in their insistence that the domestic demands of the miners, the T.U.C., and the Triple Alliance be rejected.

An additional consequence of this panic among the *traditional* Right was the encouragement of the *new* Right: in America the Red Hunt and the Centralia Massacre; in Britian the condoning of Brigadier General Page Croft and of the Amritsar Massacre; in France the shrill voice of the *Action Française;* in Italy the formal organization and the paramilitary sorties of Mussolini's Fascist anti-party party; and in Germany the ready reliance on the *Freikorps* to clean up the Ruhr and Bavaria, with Hitler an interested observer of the bloody liberation of Munich in early May 1919. Simultaneously, the intervention in Russia was capped with the recognition of Kolchak while General Mannerheim, Admiral Horthy, Dmowski, and Brătianu became increasingly welcome allies in the anti-Bolshevik freedom fight.

This uneven and uncoordinated drift toward conservatism, reaction, counterrevolution and proto-fascism resulted in the ruin of Wilsonianism and the erosion of moderate Socialism. Among Socialists and trade unionists, and notably among the young post-Armistice recruits, an apostasy of momentous dimension and significance set in. It now appeared that Lenin's indictment of Wilson and Wilsonianism was not altogether without merit: however reluctantly, the President was one of the chief movers of the counterrevolutionary enterprise. Next to his role in the intervention and his consent to British, French, and Rumanian grabs, his ordering of the *George Washington* to Brest was at best a well-intentioned gesture. As for the Fiume appeal, he delayed it until after the cardinal British and French claims had been satisfied, thereby leaving the impression that he was trying to recover his virginity at Italy's expense. Furthermore, he did not return to his wartime and pre-Armistice diplomatic tactics until after the peak of the March-April crisis, in part for fear of excessively endangering the stability of the Allied Governments.

By late April not only in Italy but all over Europe many Independent Socialists were fast abandoning Wilson and the Berne International. Not that they were anxious or ready to join the Third International which had just been launched in Moscow in early March. But they felt that they had been duped. They now reached the conclusion that to get a new world order the internationally organized proletariat would have to harness its own strength rather than second the efforts of the radical bourgeoisie. By breaking with Wilson, the Social Patriots, and Berne they meant to compete with Lenin for the allegiance of the rapidly growing ranks of disillusioned, impatient, and angry Socialists and syndicalists. Even now, for the leaders of the left-ILP, the left-SFIO, the left-ISP, and the left-USPD, the choice was no longer between the Second and the Second-and-a-Half Internationals but between the Second-and-a-Half and the Third.

In any case, Wilson could no more trust these insurgent Socialists than they could trust him. Hereafter he erred on the side of caution, while the Socialist insurgents erred on the side of radicalism. In late April Wilson did not covet the support of Serrati, Lazzari, and Nenni; in turn, they were even more hostile to the President now than they had been at the time of his January visit. And even Bissolati and Turati, who by this time were cut off from the Socialist movement, refused to answer Wilson's appeal.

The March–April crisis marked another important milestone in the emasculation of the moderate, democratic, and reformist vital center which had begun during the prewar decade. Bolshevism and Fascism were crystallizing in terms of one another; they became the polar forms of the political and ideological response to the fast-developing world crisis. In this spreading national and international civil war, the fear of revolution was driving conservatives and bourgeois liberals into expediential cooperation with outright reactionaries as well as with the new Right. These political and social carriers of counterrevolution could rely on the military, police, and legal establishments to do their bidding.

As for the Bolsheviks, in March–June 1919 they were almost completely isolated. To be sure, fear of counterrevolution and reaction, both real and contrived, brought them recruits from among the left-Independents, the anarcho-syndicalists, the regular trade unionists, and the disaffected intellectuals. But until these new converts were solidly *encadré* they constituted a psychological tonic for Bolshevik morale rather than effective revolutionary shocktroops. Nor were there any fellow travelers in positions of authority in the capitalist world, and there was no Comintern. The best Lenin and Béla Kun could hope for were developments largely beyond their own control: intensified diplomatic rivalries among the Allied Powers; neutralism or *rapprochement* with the Soviet camp by the hard-pressed vanquished powers and by such dissatisfied victors as Italy and China; and a breakdown of major capitalist economies under the strains of reconversion, reconstruction, war debts, and labor unrest. Still, the Bolsheviks' immediate prospects were grim, and Lenin knew it.

THE SAME Saturday afternoon that Lloyd George and his senior advisers arrived in Fontainebleau for their weekend powwow the first disquieting telegrams about the revolt in Budapest reached Paris. The gravity of the Hungarian turmoil was recognized instantly.

That very day, March 22, Secretary Lansing sent an "urgent memorandum" to the President.

> Your attention is called to the two telegrams quoted below which have just been received from Professor Coolidge of the American Mission in Vienna.
> 'March 21. Budapest telephones [that] newspapers [are] not coming out; [the] rebellion [is] apparently getting [the] upper hand. Board [is] sitting. Károlyi said to have left.
> 'March 21, 10 P.M. Károlyi Government [has] resigned. Böhm, Kunfi, Pogány, Béla Kuhn [are] now in power. No fighting so far reported. General mobilization has been ordered.'
> Of the four men mentioned in the second telegram the first two are the leading and more radical Social Democrats in the Hungarian Cabinet; the third is the leader of the Soldiers' Councils of Hungary; and the fourth, Béla Kuhn, is the Bolshevik leader who was imprisoned by order of the Government in the latter part of February.[1]

For the next week or so Lansing plied Wilson with telegrams about Hungary from Vienna, Budapest, and Berne; he also provided him with analyses of the Hungarian events and their ramifications by American officials in Paris.[2]

Unfortunately the President nowhere recorded his immediate reaction in writing, interview, or speech. But all around him American officials registered their profound concern. Colonel House was altogether discouraged.

[1] Lansing to Wilson, March 22, 1919, Wilson Papers, VIII A:27. For the original of the two telegrams see National Archives, Documents 184.01102/250–251.

[2] Lansing to Wilson, March 24, 1919, Wilson Papers, VIII:27; Lansing to Wilson, March 27, 1919, National Archives, Document 184.01102/254 and 274; *F.R.,P.C., 1919*, XII, 416–19, 424.

From the look of things the crisis will soon be here. I hear rumblings of discontent every day. The people want peace. Bolshevism is gaining ground everywhere. Hungary has just succumbed. We are sitting upon an open powder magazine, and some day a spark may ignite it.

I feel, too, that the President's prestige is trembling in the balance. . . . He is taking terrible chances by frittering away his time and opportunity. If the world were not in such a fluid state I should not object to matters going as deliberately as they have been going; but under present conditions, I cannot but feel that we are gambling each day with the situation. . . .

. . . The world is crumbling about us. . . . Hungary went over to Bolshevism yesterday, and other states are tottering while we sit here trying to satisfy the greed and fears of certain of our Allies.

House rushed to the President on the twenty-fourth. For nearly an hour he urged him to force the Conference out of its "rut," since unless peace were made promptly "no one excepting ourselves [could be found] to sign." He claimed to have "advised a showdown" with the Big Three on reparations, French security, and Italian borders. He also claimed to have recommended that the Big Four meet in continuous executive session, without their retinue, until these questions were settled.[3]

On this occasion, as on so many others, House was both vain and inconsistent. He now felt that all would be well if only he still had the "authority to decide questions on his own initiative as he did while the President was away."[4] He even boasted to Baker that he "could make peace in a week, . . . [possibly] in an hour."[5] House chose to forget, however, that only a few weeks earlier he himself had given an altogether less simplistic diagnosis. Then he still credited Wilson with a "full and detached understanding of the situation," even though he regretted that he lacked a "certain executive quality which in some measure unfitted him for this supreme task." Nevertheless, of those in high authority, the President stood out. Except for Balfour, Smuts, and Cecil, who lacked either initiative or authority, or both, House considered the others to be "largely controlled by prejudice and selfishness" and unable to "see beyond national boundaries."

Moreover, House conceded that this selfishness was politically conditioned. Not only was the American Delegation being hamstrung by Congress; the other delegations were equally subject to right-wing Parliamentary pressures. And finally, until early March House contemplated Wilson's hesitancy in the context of the simmering civil war: "if the President should exert his influence among the liberal and laboring classes, he might possibly overthrow the Governments in Great

[3] House Diary, March 22 and 24, 1919.
[4] House Diary, March 22, 1919.
[5] Baker Diary, Book XXII, March 30 and April 3, 1919, 113 and 132.

Britain, France, and Italy, but if he did he would still have to reckon with our own people and he might bring the whole world into chaos."[6]

Now that this chaos was closing in on the Conference House blamed it all on the indecision of the first negotiating team, although by his own admission the causes were altogether more complex. This "bright, lively little man [remained] optimistic in the presence of tragic events" only because he overestimated his own as well as Wilson's capacity to regulate them. More and more House impressed Baker as a "dilettante—the lover of the game." As an adviser without "profound responsibility" House had little at stake. He was accumulating "experiences to put in his diary"; he loved to move among the mighty; he excelled at conciliating opposing views and interests; but in the end he was plagued by the "fault of his virtue" in that he "conciliated over the border of minor disagreements into the solid flesh of principle."[7]

Of course, in the presence of his fellow Commissioners, the Colonel sought to disguise his self-assurance. Lansing, who looked upon the Hungarian explosion as proof that the "volcano was beginning to erupt," sought out not only House but also White and Bliss; and all three shared his view that the situation was "critical."[8]

For Bliss the situation was becoming "blacker and blacker" by the day. Bolshevism was "the last despairing cry of people who had lost all faith in their government," and they were driven to it by the absence of "honesty and common sense" among politicians "over here."[9] The turbulence in Eastern Europe was so pervasive that the Conference had to spend more time on "Russia, Poland, Czechoslovakia, Rumania, and now Hungary than on peace terms with Germany."[1] Before long Bliss even worried about revolution in France, Italy, and England, in part blaming Soviet propaganda. The Allies could not postpone much longer the decision between treating or fighting with Lenin.[2]

General Bliss, however, was dead set against military intervention, either in Russia or in Hungary. In addition to denouncing the neutral zone in Transylvania as "absolutely unjust," he accused the French of deliberately creating a situation that would give them an excuse to break the Armistice and drag America into a vast inter-Allied crusade against Bolshevism, first in Hungary and then beyond. "If we join the other Associated Powers in attempting the military coercion of Hungary aided by Russia, we shall be committing ourselves to a war of enormous magnitude, and of indefinite duration; one which will have to be financed entirely by us; and one in which, because of the war-

[6] House Diary, March 3, 1919.
[7] Baker Diary, Book XXII, April 3, 1919, 131.
[8] Lansing Diary, March 23, 1919.
[9] Bliss to Mrs. Bliss, March 25, 1919, in Bliss Papers, Box 66.
[1] Bliss to Newton D. Baker, April 3, 1919, Bliss Papers, Box 75.
[2] Bliss to Mrs. Bliss, April 17, 1919, Bliss Papers, Box 66.

weariness of the people of our allies, we may find ourselves standing alone."[3] Bliss kept insisting that once America directly or indirectly—through aid to Poland and Rumania—extended the military intervention started in Archangel, she would in all likelihood be committed to "a long series of wars for the purpose of throttling the revolutionary movement in Europe." And Bliss, for one, questioned not so much the expense in money and men as the wisdom of "combating these new forces of revolution." Evidently even Wilson's military adviser looked upon economic relief as the proper instrument of control.[4]

And, of course, so did Hoover, especially since he knew that whatever the immediate circumstances of the Hungarian and other rebellions, these were built "on a foundation of real social grievance." The common people of Eastern and Central Europe, who until the recent collapse had been ruled by reactionary tyrannies, were particularly susceptible to the wild promises of the authoritarian Left. Certainly there could be no question of recognizing the "murderous tyrannies" of Russia and Hungary. Nor should America participate in a joint military intervention which would promote reaction throughout Europe. Instead Hoover proposed a neutral relief commission to extend aid, especially to Russia, provided the Bolsheviks guarantee to "cease all militant action across certain defined boundaries and cease their subsidizing of disturbances abroad." Such a proposal would not only test the intentions of the Soviets, but it would also "give a period of rest along the frontiers of Europe and would give some hope of stabilization."

Simultaneously Hoover urged the President to consider reopening his ideological offensive. Wilson should take an early opportunity "to analyze . . . Bolshevism from its political, economic, humane, and its criminal points of view, and, while yielding its aspirations, sympathetically show its utter foolishness as a basis of economic development; show its true social ends; rap our own reactionaries for their destruction of social betterment and thereby their stimulation of Bolshevism; point, however, to the steady program of real democracy in these roads of social betterment."[5] Hoover persuaded his chief that, pending consideration of these measures, U. S. shipping authorities should be instructed to furnish all the requested tonnage for relief in the month of April. This was "a service second only to the mission of our Army in

---

[3] Bliss to Wilson, March 28, 1919, cited in Baker: *Woodrow Wilson and World Settlement*, III, 238–45. For the minutes of the meeting of March 27, at which the American Commissioners asked Bliss to draft a memo to Wilson even though he put them on notice that "it would be red hot," see *F.R.,P.C.,1919*, XI, 134–5. See also Lansing Diary, March 27–28, 1919; and House Diary, March 28, 1919.

[4] Bliss to Wilson, March 26, 1919, Bliss Papers, Box 70.

[5] Hoover to Wilson, March 28, 1919, House Papers, 10:37.

Europe," and the failure to deliver would have incalculable conse-quences.[6]

Among the lower echelons in the American Delegation the mood became every bit as gloomy, leading to an outpouring of diagnoses of and cures for the fast-spreading disease. When Buckler was asked to be U. S. Minister in Warsaw, he balked and asked for certain assurances. Before "climbing the Polish pyre" he felt that he was entitled to know whether his government and the Allies were still determined to force an unacceptable peace on Germany, whether the "drift" in Russian policy would continue, and whether "the French policy of creating the largest Poland possible, as a supposed bulwark against Russia," would still be followed. In his judgment this French policy would surround Poland with aggrieved nationalities which, like Hungary, were likely to go Bolshevik. Eventually Buckler decided that since he could not be an "effective exponent" of this policy, either Lord, Coolidge, or Dresel had best be considered for this assignment.[7]

A conversation with Cachin reinforced Buckler in his reticence. According to Cachin, Károlyi's fall was precipitated by the affronting and narrow-minded actions of local French generals who claimed to act for the Conference.

> In Cachin's opinion the Hungarian explosion proves the futility of arresting Bolshevism by a *cordon sanitaire*. The only sure way to arrest it is to stick to the Wilsonian principles and not allow them to be compromised by French militarism. "Either Wilson or Lenin" is a perfectly true motto.

In a separate statement, which the Commissioners sent on to Wilson, Cachin stressed that the President, who until recently had personified "popular idealism," was becoming increasingly "impotent in the midst of imperialist diplomacy." As a result popular interest was shifting away rapidly from the Conference and "being drawn to the East of Europe." The French Socialist leader hoped that should Wilson act decisively, the day might still be saved and "Liberalism might come through well-ordered channels rather than through class upheavals." The adoption of a liberal Russian policy would be the necessary first step, to be followed by a moderate peace with Germany.[8]

Immediately after his return from Moscow, Bullitt rallied to the

[6] Wilson to Newton Baker and Hurley, March 24, 1919, cited in Suda L. Bane and Ralph H. Lutz (eds.): *The Blockade of Germany After the Armistice, 1918–1919* (Stanford: Stanford University Press; 1942), 291.

[7] Buckler to House (personal), March 27 and 29, 1919, Buckler Papers. "Buckler in a letter which does not please me at all, wishes his name withdrawn as Minister to Poland." House Diary, March 29, 1919.

[8] "Memorandum on Conversation between Buckler and Cachin," March 28, 1919, Buckler Papers; and U. S. Commissioners to Wilson, March 28, 1919, Wilson Papers, VIII A:29. Judging by the marginalia on this latter document, the President read it.

Buckler-Cachin thesis. In a brash letter he bluntly told the President that now that the Magyars and the Bavarians had followed the Russian example he was "face to face with a European Revolution." Bullitt lost all sense of proportion: under the shock of recent events he thought it likely that even the Rumanians and Albanians would overthrow their governments and establish "varieties of Communism." But along with such extravagant forecasts, which were designed to jolt the President, Bullitt formulated a passionate but arresting summary of the reformist response to the heightened perils.

> For the past year the peoples of Europe have been seeking a better way to live for the common good of all. They have found no guidance in Paris. They are turning towards Moscow. To dismiss this groping of the peoples for better lives—this European Revolution—with the word 'Bolshevism,' is to misunderstand it as completely as Lord North misunderstood the American Revolution. The peoples turn towards Moscow; but the impulses which drive them are remote from theoretic communism. . . . Six months ago all the peoples of Europe expected you to fulfill their hopes. They believe now that you cannot. They turn, therefore, to Lenin. . . .

A *modus vivendi* with the Russian and European Revolution was the essential prerequisite for a sound peace. There was still time to guide this Revolution "into peaceful and constructive channels" by cooperating with the "constructive and kind" elements of the Revolution, by feeding instead of starving people, and by making peace instead of mounting interventions. On the other hand, blockade and intervention would inevitably drive the Revolution "in self defense, to terror and massacres, as intervention drove the French Revolution more than a century ago and the Russian Revolution last year."[9]

Of all the *hommes de bonne volonté* in the American Delegation, Ray Stannard Baker was the most intensely loyal to the President. He shared Wilson's *Weltanschauung*. Rather than attribute the current impasse to the failings of one or all of the Big Four, he tended to be cowed by the magnitude of this historic moment. Not that he discounted the importance of great men, but he sensed that their powers of control were severely limited. Nor was he uncritical of Wilson. Baker was repeatedly impatient with his chief's reluctance to launch a new ideological offensive. Still, for his Press Secretary, Wilson was "the great serious man of the Conference—gray, grim, and lonely." No, he did not love him—"but beyond any other man I admire and respect him; *he is real;* he is the only great man here." No doubt Clemenceau was serious and honest, but for "smaller causes, immediate gains, selfish ends." Lloyd George, too, was serious, though he "lives for the moment . . . and seizes any compromise," always ready to sacrifice "future

[9] Bullitt to Wilson, April 6, 1919, Bullitt Papers.

benefit for present gain." As for Orlando, he had neither "depth nor vision" and was inclined to play "little games of politics while the world was afire."[1]

Because he was in Wilson's corner and saw both House and him so regularly, Baker's day-by-day reactions came close to being those of the official Wilsonian mind and persuasion. He repeatedly taunted House, Lansing, and Bliss for being such inveterate diarists; and once he realized that their diaries would become the source for their "ponderous memoirs" he confessed, in jest, that he "would rather read Lenin's."[2] But all along he kept his own diary. Particularly during the March–April crisis he made nearly daily entries. In these he unwittingly caught that uncomfortable mixture of frustration, fear, and hope that characterized the charged atmosphere in the Wilsonian camp.[3]

> March 23. Great anxiety here lest the peace be delayed until the whole world is aflame with anarchy. Yesterday we had news of the Hungarian revolution, with the accession to power of the Bolsheviks; Egypt is in rebellion and the British industrial situation is acute. . . . I had tea with . . . Nansen . . . and Villard. Interesting talk, and mostly pessimistic regarding the present situation.
>
> March 27. What whirling days! . . . Wilson very impatient with the slow progress of the deliberations. Says Clemenceau is the chief obstacle. . . . In the meantime Lenin and Bolshevism loom ever higher. Bullitt is back from Russia and I have had a long talk with him; there is an increasing tendency toward trying to deal with Lenin.
>
> March 29. Still pessimistic—everyone pessimistic. I took a walk with Colonel House. . . . He now begins to be worried; blames the "Four" for not getting down to business. . . . I urged the necessity of a plain statement of fact from the President and an appeal to the people of the world on broad grounds. . . . We discussed Bullitt's report from Russia . . . but could get no authority to put it out. The Colonel advised me to take it down to the President to see if he would release it for publication, which I did this evening, without result. It is dangerous, unless we have taken up the policy of dealing with the Bolsheviks. No progress of any consequence today. Lenin looms always on the horizon to the East.
>
> March 31. . . . I talked with the President about the feeling everywhere of the danger of the situation. "I know it," he said. I told him also that he was being blamed on all sides for the delay. "I know that too," he said. I then suggested cautiously that sooner or later he would have to show what the reasons really were for the delay. "If I were to do that," he said, "it would immediately break

---

[1] Baker Diary, Book XXII, April 3, 1919, 135–6.

[2] Baker Diary, Book XXII, April 1, 1919, 119.

[3] Baker's *Woodrow Wilson and World Settlement* cannot be understood, appreciated, and criticized without taking account of his diary, from which he quotes only few and brief—and occasionally edited—excerpts.

up the Peace Conference—and we cannot risk it yet." . . . As I walked back . . . Ramsay MacDonald and Jean Longuet . . . joined me. . . . Longuet says the workmen of Paris are considering a 24-hour strike of protest. They were both blue about the outlook. . . .

April 2. I found the President tonight again much discouraged. . . . I suggested that the time might come soon when he would have to speak out. The other day when I made a similar proposal he said: "That would break up the Peace Conference. . . ." But tonight it was plain that he had been thinking of the possible necessity of making such a move. "If I speak out," he said, "I should have to tell the truth and place the blame exactly where it belongs—upon the French."

"The downfall of a government in France," I said, "is not as serious a matter as it would be in England." I told him I had heard that Clemenceau had already been conferring with Poincaré about his possible resignation—and had even talked with Barthou, who is said to be his choice as his successor. "A new premier would probably be no better than Clemenceau," he said. . . . I spoke of the feeling of unrest in the world; and of the blame that was everywhere being charged, unjustly, against him. "I know that," he said. "I know that." He paused. "But we have got to make peace on the principles laid down and accepted, or not make it at all." In the meantime there are reports of new revolts in Germany and spreading unrest in Hungary. Where are we going? . . .

April 3. To cap the climax the President fell ill today. . . . He had a severe cold with fever. . . . The Four jump about from question to question and decide nothing. There is unlimited greedy bargaining, especially by the French and Italians, only the President growing grayer and grimmer all the time, standing upon principles of justice and right. He will probably be beaten. I only hope he goes down fighting for his own principles and does not yield. It will be better for him and for the principles—for the world—in the long run. . . . Indeed, Orlando's government will probably fall unless they get Fiume. . . . The worst of all the imperialists are the weaker newer nations. . . .

April 4. If it were not for the feeling that peace *must be made,* that the Peace Conference *cannot be allowed to fail,* I should say that everything was going to smash. The President was in bed all day, the Italians are threatening to go home. News comes from North Russia that the Bolsheviks are pressing the Allied troops there and threatening their extermination.

The Four met today with Colonel House taking the President's place. The Colonel prefers to work with Clemenceau rather than Lloyd George. He told me today that Lloyd George said to him, "You and I do not agree as well as the President and I agree." The Colonel is still optimistic! The other members of the commission, Secretary Lansing and Mr. White, know next to nothing of what is going on. . . .

The Colonel would make peace quickly by giving the greedy ones all they want! The Colonel sides with the group which desires a swift peace on any terms, the President struggles almost alone to secure some constructive and idealistic result out of the general ruin. If these old leaders only knew it, Wilson is the only strong bulwark[4] left of the old order; he would save it (the present democratic system)[5] by making it just, decent, honest. What they are doing with their greedy demands and selfish interest, is to give new arguments, new force to Lenin and his extreme policy of decentralization and horizontal internationalism. They can't see this—and plunge on to their doom.[6]

Wilson is the supreme champion of the old order, the old nationalism, and would save it. He does not even *see* the new social revolution as a reality. Colonel House sees it and would, as usual, conciliate it. So does Lloyd George see it! and would temporize with it. So does Clemenceau see it—and would fight it. . . .

April 5. . . . There is some slight evidence today that peace will be made because peace must be made—a peace written on paper and signed by a few old men none of whom will believe in what he is doing—but it will solve nothing, decide nothing. Wilson is still in bed. Colonel House is still chirping hopefully . . . while Bavaria is setting up a Soviet Republic. . . . The only hope left for this Conference is that Wilson will come out with a last terrific blast for his principles and their *specific application* and go down in the ruin—I fear he won't. And that is complete failure. For what good will be a League of Nations unless the settlements upon which it rests are just? A League the only purpose of which is to guarantee "grabs" of land by France, Italy, Poland, etc., etc. is doomed to speedy failure. I have been here mostly because I saw a chance to help along the reconstructive movement, with the organization of a L. of N. to keep the peace of the world. It now looks as though the League would be so weak, its foundations so insecure, that I could not myself support it. It will make very little difference *now* what peace is signed, for nothing essential will be settled. . . .

---

4 Editing by Baker (probably at different time from first writing): line drawn through "bulwark," though he may not have intended to delete this word, and above is written "against"; above left is written "Leninism."

5 Parenthetical phrase written above line and probably part of later writing.

6 Compare this last paragraph with the version of this same paragraph in Baker: *World Settlement,* II, 47: "The Colonel would make peace quickly by giving the greedy ones all they want! He sides with those who desire a swift peace on any terms: the President struggles almost alone to secure some constructive result out of the general ruin. If these old leaders only knew it, Wilson is the only strong bulwark left in the world against a wild Bolshevism on the one hand and a wilder militarism on the other. He would save the present democratic political system in the world by making it just, decent, efficient—by proving that it can solve the real problems so clearly seen by the extremists. But what these old leaders are doing, with their greedy demands and selfish interests, is to give new arguments to Lenin and new force to Foch. They can't see this—and plunge on to their doom."

In this edited version Baker creates the impression that Wilson was equally opposed to Bolshevism and militarism, to Lenin and Foch.

April 7. This has been a great day and we are now upon the very crisis of events. . . . This morning Admiral Grayson sent me word that the President had ordered the George Washington to sail immediately for Brest. . . . I went up to see Mr. Wilson at 6:30, the first time since he fell ill. . . . What he said put new courage into me. He is going to fight, and fight to the end. . . . When I talk with Colonel House . . . I am half persuaded that he can win peace—a peace that doesn't much matter—but when I talk with this man—this tremendous, grim, rock-like man, I think he can die for faith, that he can bring down the world around him before giving over his convictions. . . . The President said: "What about this difference between Lansing and House?" I said, "They do not agree at all as to the present situation in the Conference. Colonel House is strongly optimistic, Mr. Lansing is pessimistic." The President said, "Mr. Lansing is much nearer right." . . . Wilson will get *something* out of it, but will disappoint most of the world now dreaming of ideal results and doubtful whether Wilsonism or Bolshevism is the remedy. . . .

April 9. . . . A desperate effort is being made to separate Wilson and Lloyd George. Northcliffe and his press are attacking George bitterly for his "kindness" to the Germans and his effort to work with the Russians. . . . It is a struggle between Northcliffe and Wilson for Lloyd George—who has no soul. Italy is falling apart. I doubt whether peace arrives before anarchy after all. All the forces are working against Wilson. . . .

April 10. . . . The President is evidently being required to give ground for the political exigencies of Lloyd George and Clemenceau. It is either that or invite at once the explosion of the world. News today indicates that Italy is tottering into the abyss; and word from Germany gives little hope that the Germans will sign the treaty when they really get it. . . .

April 12. . . . The fundamental mistake in this whole conference has been its *secrecy*. If the President's point about "open covenants *openly arrived at*" had been rigidly adhered to, governments would have fallen, but the world would have escaped much of its present difficulty. And yet it could not be, for it would have destroyed the old order which Wilson and all the others are bent upon saving. It would have let in the revolution! It was a pillar which could not be broken without bringing down the whole house. Nothing much counts any more. A treaty may be made, but it probably never will be signed and if signed it will have little meaning. We are plunging irresistibly into an unknown world full of danger. . . . That stern man upon the hill . . . *will break,* not because men oppose him, but because the whole flood of events of the world are against him. It grows clear every day that the old order, the old world is sick unto death—and there is no saving it. All I can see in the future for a long time are suffering, anarchy, the black darkness of unrestrained passions. How the world needs a new evangel! How it needs a teaching of simplicity, honesty, and loving kindness. Nothing else in the least matters! Who shall declare it? . . .

April 14. . . . Though he has been forced to compromise much, he has succeeded in forcing enough of his ideas in the Conference to antagonize everybody. The treaty will satisfy nobody, and the President will be the man most blamed. . . .

April 17. . . . The treaty-making is drawing to a close unsatisfactorily. They are hurrying to get it done before the world falls apart. Weyl said to me today: "The Fourteen Points have been thrown overboard." "Like the Ten Commandments and the Golden Rule," I said. The world is suffering from disillusionment. It is difficult to apply ideal moral principles to specific cases; yet the principles remain and are everlasting true. It is Wilson's great service that he announced them, not that he could not apply them. . . .[7]

Bliss, Hoover, Buckler, Bullitt, and Baker all agreed that the Allies should respond to the Hungarian revolution and the attendant March–April crisis with relief measures and with diplomatic and ideological counterthrusts. Other U. S. advisers, however, recommended that such measures should be mixed with and supplemented by military action.

One such adviser was Captain Nicholas Roosevelt of the Coolidge Mission. He left Budapest 36 hours after the explosion and was in Paris by March 26. In his view a broad spectrum of political and social elements conspired to use "Bolshevism for essentially . . . national ends."[8] The main significance of the Hungarian revolution was that the first important decision of the Conference was "met by open defiance"; and Germany was bound to be next unless the Allies took timely action. The Czech and Rumanian armies should not be asked to advance, for fear that they would further arouse Magyar nationalism and because their military establishments were not yet quite up to the job. Roosevelt wondered whether the Allies should consider moving in with their own troops, in spite of the certainty of Hungarian resistance. As a last resort the blockade was "a practical weapon" readily at hand, though it would not become effective until two months hence, when the food situation would become "desperate."[9]

Professor Philip Marshall Brown, the second-ranking member of the Coolidge Mission, who stayed at his Hungarian post throughout Béla Kun's 133 days, also characterized the revolution as a national protest. He wired that since the mass of the people were not even remotely Socialist and since the Soviets were too far off to assist local radicals, by prudent action the Allies could still "prevent Hungary from

---

[7] Baker Diary, Book XXII, March 23 to April 17, 1919, 104–80.
[8] Lansing to Wilson, March 27, 1919, National Archives, Document 184.01102/254.
[9] Captain Nicholas Roosevelt to the Ammission, March 26, 1919, cited in *F.R.,P.C.,* *1919*, XII, 416–19.

becoming completely Bolshevik." Personally he preferred a conciliatory course spearheaded by an assurance that the Peace Conference
"had no intention of mutilating Hungary or of breaking her up without
due regard for the wishes of the people." Still, should the new regime
seize complete and effective control, Paris might consider military
intervention "by British and American troops combined with conciliatory assurances."[1] On March 29 Brown was convinced that "the mass
of the Hungarians would welcome friendly intervention, if not too long
delayed." He even indicated that since there was not likely to be serious
armed resistance not more than 30,000 troops would be needed.[2]

These estimates by men with firsthand experience were put side by
side with position papers drafted by technical advisers stationed in
Paris. Professor Robert J. Kerner, one of the junior experts on Eastern
Europe, had the distinction of being the only one to attribute more
importance to the internal than to the external causes of the Hungarian
turmoil. In his view, set forth on March 24, the occupation of additional Hungarian territory was only the ostensible cause. The real cause
was the fear of the Social Democrats, especially the radicals among
them, that they would fail to get an absolute majority in the coming
elections. Among contributing internal causes he also cited peasant
unrest over land reform as well as Károlyi's undue mildness toward
"Bolshevik agitators, editors, press agents and politicians." The extreme
Left was left free to graft reformist appeals onto the surging popular
shock over territorial violations.

In his recommendations Kerner was altogether unequivocal: the
Conference should order immediate and effective military occupation
by Entente—preferably not Italian—troops combined with equally
prompt relief measures. Without such action first Hungary and then
Austria would soon be in the grip of Bolshevism; in German Austria it
was "merely a question of time"; and inevitably Czechoslovakia and
Poland would be "isolated and soon overwhelmed."[3]

Since coming to Paris from the Berne Legation Allen W. Dulles
had been preparing current intelligence reports on the countries of the
defunct Austro-Hungarian Empire, especially on German Austria.[4]

---

[1] Ibid., 419–21, 424.
[2] Roosevelt (now back in Vienna) to Coolidge (still in Paris), March 30, 1919, National Archives, Document 184.01102/286.
[3] Memorandum entitled "The Question in Hungary" by R. J. Kerner, March 24, 1919,
House Papers. Kerner was pro-Slav, especially pro-Czech.
[4] The U.S. Minister in Berne, who was Dulles's superior in his first diplomatic post,
cabled the following advice: "Prompt military intervention in Hungary will save
Europe from Bolshevism. Every day's delay according to my best advice will aid
the enemy. Prestige of Peace Conference at stake. Small force of Americans or
British would settle the trouble, if used at once. Military occupation of Vienna
and Berlin may be spared by firm action now." In his view Bolshevism at home and
abroad were one, and the war would not be finished "until this Hydra of
Bolshevism was put down." Pleasant A. Stovall to Wilson, March 27, 1919,
Wilson Papers, VIII A:29; and Stovall to House, April 9, 1919, House Papers.

Convinced of the vital importance of preserving Vienna, Dulles was particularly shaken by the emergency in Vienna's sister city. There seemed to be but limited time in which to save the situation. Dulles was impatient with scholarly studies of the remote and immediate causes of the Hungarian crisis, preferring to make recommendations for countervailing action.[5]

1. Measures should be taken to isolate the Hungarian Revolution from Russia and prevent its spread to neighboring countries.
   a. The Czechs and Rumanians should be allowed to occupy the passes of the Carpathian Mountains and the railway connecting Czechoslovakia with Rumania, south of these passes.
   b. The Servians or the French should be permitted to occupy a strip of territory to connect the Slovene territory with the Danube near Pressburg, now held by the Czechs.
   c. The Czechs should be granted the necessary railway connections along their present line of occupation in Slovakia.
2. Measures should be taken to endeavor to control the situation in Budapest.
   a. A number of small gunboats or monitors might be sent to Budapest. It is understood that the British have a gunboat there at present. More could probably be sent from the Black Sea.
   b. Food supplies should be sent to Hungary under the condition that ordered distribution is assured. In any case a trial shipment should be sent as proof of good faith in this matter. . . .[6]
   c. If possible a statement of policy regarding Hungary should be made. Tell the Hungarians the truth about the dismemberment of their country but give them some hope of economic and food assistance and fair treatment with the boundaries which are granted them, as well as speedy peace if an organized government is established.
3. Measures should be taken to prevent a repetition of the mistakes which have brought about the present situation in Hungary.
   a. Faulty coordination between Paris and Entente representatives in Austria-Hungary is to some extent responsible for Hungary's revolution. To prevent similar mistakes the Inter-Allied Commission, which should be the final Allied authority in Austria and Hungary, should be sent to Vienna. This Commission should act on instructions from Paris. This would tend to eliminate the ill-advised initiatives of various Entente military officials.
   b. Foodstuffs should be hastened to Austria and Bohemia in every possible way. . . .

[5] "The Present Situation in Hungary: Action Recommended by A. W. Dulles," March 24, 1919, sent that same day with a covering letter by Lansing (Dulles's uncle) to Wilson, Wilson Papers, VIII A:27.

[6] A 25-car train of food supplies went through to Budapest in early April. *The Memoirs of Herbert Hoover* (New York: Macmillan; 1951), 398.

c. Every effort should be made to have a treaty ready for Austria and Hungary at the same time as for Germany.

Within a week Dulles stressed that the new demarcation line simply *had* to be enforced, though the Budapest regime should be assured that this line was provisional. Moreover food should no longer be promised in exchange for "organized government"; what was wanted was "responsible government." When all was said and done, the Hungarian defiance should not go unchallenged, otherwise the peoples of Eastern Europe would continue to lose "confidence and respect" for the Conference and turn to Russia. Paris should break its silence; the world needed "a declaration from Wilson to restore confidence in his principles."[7]

Except for Roosevelt, Brown, Kerner, and Dulles, whose influence was marginal, American officials did not call for military measures against Béla Kun; and those few who did spontaneously fitted such measures into the prevailing Wilsonian consensus.

In fact, the Hungarian revolt stimulated renewed respect for Wilson's overall peacemaking project. Except at great risk the victors could not afford to drive the enemy to desperation with punitive peace terms and coercive economic measures. Furthermore, however legitimate France's security needs, these could not, by themselves, dictate Allied policy along the Rhine, in Eastern Europe, and in Russia. The prescription was self-evident: stern but just peace terms, relief in furtherance of governmental stability throughout Central-Eastern Europe, and containment of Bolshevik regimes by all means short of direct military intervention.

With few exceptions—notably Hughes, who still meant to hang the Kaiser—the principal members of the British Delegation approached this outlook even before March 22; Béla Kun merely helped to complete their conversion. By now Lloyd George knew the high cost of giving first priority to Anglo-French harmony. In pursuit of British security he was anxious for France to improve her overall power position vis-à-vis Germany. He shied back, however, from being party to a territorial settlement which would endow the Continent with an explosive legacy of festering national rivalries and irredenta, especially in Eastern Europe. The British became increasingly skeptical of Foch's sublime confidence that the new buffer states in the rimland could counterbalance both Soviet Russia and Germany.

In the short run London was fretful about Bolshevism engulfing the rimland before these states could be set up; for the long pull there was a nagging realization that the artificial inflation of Poland, Czechoslovakia, and Rumania was bound to provoke the Germans and Magyars to take their revenge.

[7] Dulles to the Peace Commissioners, April 1, 1919, House Papers.

With the Hungarian revolt the short-run foreboding became dominant. What if Austria and Germany went the same way? Then all of Europe east of the Rhine would sink into anarchy compounded by Bolshevism; there would be a German-Russian *rapprochement;* and given her power and technology Germany could be expected to become the senior partner in this alignment, with control over Eastern Europe.

In this moment of panic Lloyd George and his immediate entourage—Balfour, Kerr, and Hankey—resolved to make certain that Germany should not be driven into Bolshevism or an alliance with Soviet Russia. This prudential policy also envisaged bolstering Germany for possible future service against Bolshevism in Eastern Europe.

Needless to say, neither Lloyd George nor most of his Unionist supporters would ever have contemplated a break with Clemenceau. Nonetheless, he calmly faced mounting strains with the Tiger since he knew himself to be covered by Wilson and by Labour.

This, then, was the context in which, during that nervous weekend, the Prime Minister and his aides reappraised the accomplishments, disagreements, and prospects of the Conference. Upon arriving in Fontainebleau the party took in the sights, thereby deliberately creating the deceptive impression that they had come for a rest. But soon all four repaired to the Premier's sittingroom. Lloyd George left no doubt that he was after a searching and fundamental inquiry; and he proposed to have a go at it by asking each of the participants to assume a role for the purpose of these deliberations. In this role-playing exercise Henry Wilson gave both the German and the French point of view, while Hankey spoke for the average Englishman. Eventually Lloyd George presented his own conclusions, with Kerr all along acting as secretary.[8]

Of the four, Henry Wilson alone blamed the President for the drift into disaster,[9] wanted Germany squeezed, and clamored for a tough anti-Soviet course. But even he grudgingly acknowledged the hazards of crushing Germany. During the proceedings he assumed the role of a *boche,* arguing that rather than sign oppressive peace terms he would "turn to Russia, and in the course of time help that distracted country to recover law and order, and then make an alliance."[1] Once General Wilson concurred with the "Frocks" in this limited respect, the caveat against incensing and alienating Germany was certain to become the major thrust of the Fontainebleau memorandum.

In origin and purpose this memorandum[2] was of the same lineage

8 Lord Hankey: *The Supreme Control at the Paris Peace Conference* (London: Allen and Unwin; 1963), 100–1.

9 Riddell: *Intimate Diary of the Peace Conference,* 38.

1 Wilson's own diary entry cited in Callwell (ed.): *Henry Wilson,* II, 176.

2 "Some Considerations for the Peace Conference Before They Finally Draft Their Terms," *Memorandum Circulated by the Prime Minister on March 25, 1919,* Cmd. 1614, London, 1922. Close to the full text is cited, but mistakenly attributed to Bliss, in Baker: *World Settlement,* III, 449–57; and, except for a few rather

as Lloyd George's address to the Trades Union Congress on January 5, 1918 and Wilson's Fourteen Points address three days later.[3] Both then and now Lenin's appeals had to be counteracted; Russo-German cooperation had to be headed off; enemy Socialists and Liberals had to be encouraged; the Allied Left had to be conciliated; and French diplomacy had to be restrained.

Of course there were important differences. Whereas in early 1918 the Anglo-Americans sought to undermine the Imperial regimes, a year later they were anxious to stabilize the successors to those regimes. Similarly, whereas then they were inclined to maximize the nationalist rebellion in Eastern Europe, now they sought to dampen the zeal of the successor states. Lastly, in January 1918 Wilson in particular meant to encourage the Soviets to stand up to Germany; in March 1919 the Allies needed to restrain Berlin from flirting with Moscow. Nevertheless, both diplomatic initiatives had a common motif: timely moderation designed to offset the advance of mutually invigorating revolution and reaction.

There was a difference in form as well. The January initiatives took the form of public pronouncements calculated to appeal directly to enemy and Allied peoples as well as governments. The Fontainebleau memorandum was an official document for distribution only to the Big Four and their chief advisers. Not that this position paper's general outline long remained a well-guarded secret; in due course Lloyd George himself did his best to publicize his latest conversion. But since, unlike a year before, in 1919 the British Right was in ascendance and on the offensive, the Prime Minister instantly was pressured to stick by his extravagant election promises.[4] Intimidated by the Allied Right and reluctant to make empty promises to the enemy regimes, the British Prime Minister and the President were equally hesitant to make an open appeal without prior agreement among the Big Four. Had this agreement materialized, both statesmen most likely would have gone on to issue public manifestoes couched in the accustomed liberal-reformist rhetoric. As it was, this rhetoric even permeated the document with which, behind closed doors, Lloyd George meant to convince Clemenceau that his German policy was worse than sterile, that it was ruinous.

Clemenceau being the primary audience, the British *mémoire* pointedly opened with a reminder that the peace of 1871 had failed to provide Germany with long-term security precisely because France had been left to smolder over the loss of the twin provinces. "Injustice,

significant omissions, in David Lloyd George: *The Truth About the Peace Treaties*, I, 404–16. Kerr prepared an original draft of this memorandum for discussion and minor revisions by the entire Fontainebleau party. Hankey: *Supreme Control at Paris*, 101.

[3] See my *Political Origins of the New Diplomacy, 1917–1918*, Chs. 8, 9.

[4] See pp. 623–32 below.

arrogance, displayed in the hour of triumph, will never be forgotten or forgiven."

For this reason Lloyd George declared himself "strongly averse" to transferring more Germans and Magyars to be ruled by other nations "than could possibly be helped." He was afraid that the proposal of the Polish Commission to "place 2,100,000 Germans, under the control of a people which is of a different religion and which has never proved its capacity for stable self-government throughout its history . . . [would] lead sooner or later to a new war in the East of Europe." In his judgment, then, the nationality principle should have precedence over "considerations of strategy or economics or communications." In the West the Rhenish provinces should not be detached but demilitarized, and France should either get the frontier of 1814 or the present Alsace-Lorraine frontier "with the use of the coal mines in the Saar Valley for a period of ten years."

As for reparations, the amount chargeable unquestionably exceeded Germany's capacity to pay. The Allies should agree, therefore, that the enemy "should pay an annual sum for a stated number of years," with 50 per cent going to France, 30 per cent to the British Empire, and 20 per cent to others. But in the interest of appeasement "the duration for the payments of reparation ought to disappear if possible with the generation which made the war."

Lloyd George was not exclusively or even primarily concerned about the long-term diplomatic and military consequences of inequities in the treaty. What influenced him, by his own admission, was the imminent and impending convergence of the enemy's exasperation with the revolutionary spirit. While he punctuated his long-term concerns with analogic references to 1871, he dramatized the imminent revolutionary danger by stressing the dissimilarities between 1815 and 1919. At the time of the Congress of Vienna the revolutionary spirit had spent itself, but during the current Paris Peace Conference the reverse was true.

> The revolution is still in its infancy. The extreme figures of the Terror are still in command in Russia. The whole of Europe is filled with the spirit of revolution. There is a deep sense not only of discontent, but of anger and revolt, amongst the workmen against pre-war conditions. The whole existing order in its political, social and economic aspects is questioned by the masses of the population from one end of Europe to the other. In some countries, like Germany and Russia, the unrest takes the form of open rebellion; in others, like France, Great Britain and Italy, it takes the shape of strikes and of general disinclination to settle down to work—symptoms which are just as much concerned with the desire for political and social change as with wage demands.
> Much of this unrest is healthy. We shall never make a lasting

peace by attempting to restore the conditions of 1914.[5] But there is a danger that we may throw the masses of the population throughout Europe into the arms of the extremists whose only idea for regenerating mankind is to destroy utterly the whole existing fabric of society. These men have triumphed in Russia. They have done so at a terrible price. Hundreds of thousands of the population have perished. The railways, the roads, the towns, the whole structural organisation of Russia has been almost destroyed, but somehow or other they seem to have managed to keep their hold upon the masses of the Russian people, and what is much more significant, they have succeeded in creating a large army which is apparently well directed and well disciplined, and is, as to a great part of it prepared to die for its ideals. In another year Russia, inspired by a new enthusiasm, may have recovered from her passion for peace and have at her command the only army eager to fight, because it is the only army that believes that it has any cause to fight for.

The greatest danger that I see in the present situation is that Germany may throw in her lot with Bolshevism and place her resources, her brains, her vast organising power at the disposal of the revolutionary fanatics whose dream it is to conquer the world for Bolshevism by force of arms. This danger is no mere chimera. The present Government in Germany is weak; it has no prestige; its authority is challenged; it lingers merely because there is no alternative but the spartacists, and Germany is not ready for spartacism as yet. But the argument which the spartacists are using with great effect at this very time is that they alone can save Germany from the intolerable conditions which have been bequeathed her by the war. They offer to free the German people from indebtedness to the Allies and indebtedness to their own richer classes. . . .

If Germany goes over to the spartacists it is inevitable that she should throw in her lot with the Russian Bolshevists. Once that happens all Eastern Europe will be swept into the orbit of the Bolshevik revolution and within a year we may witness the spectacle of nearly three hundred million people organised into a vast red army under German instructors and German generals equipped with German cannon and German machine guns and prepared for a renewal of the attack on Western Europe. This is a prospect which no one can face with equanimity. Yet the news which came from Hungary yesterday shows only too clearly that this danger is no fantasy. And what are the reasons alleged for this decision? They are mainly the belief that large numbers of Magyars are to be handed over to the control of others.[6] If we are wise, we shall offer to Germany a peace, which, while just, will be preferable for all sensible men to the alternative of Bolshevism. I would, therefore, put it in the forefront of the peace that once she accepts our terms, especially reparation, we will open to her the raw materials and markets of the world on equal terms with ourselves, and will do

[5] The remainder of this paragraph is omitted in Lloyd George: *Truth*, I, 407.
[6] Up to this sentence this paragraph is omitted in Lloyd George: *Truth*, I, 408.

everything possible to enable the German people to get upon their legs again. We cannot both cripple her and expect her to pay.

Finally, we must offer terms which a responsible Government in Germany can expect to be able to carry out. If we present terms to Germany which are unjust, or excessively onerous, no responsible Government will sign them;[7] certainly the present weak administration will not. If it did, I am told that it would be swept away within 24 hours. Yet if we can find nobody in Germany who will put his hand to a peace treaty, what will be the position? A large army of occupation for an indefinite period is out of the question. Germany would not mind it. A very large number of people in that country would welcome it as it would be the only hope of preserving the existing order of things. The objection would not come from Germany, but from our own countries. Neither the British Empire nor America would agree to occupy Germany. France by itself could not bear the burden of occupation. We should therefore be driven back on the policy of blockading the country. *That would inevitably mean spartacism from the Urals to the Rhine, with its inevitable consequence of a huge red army attempting to cross the Rhine. . . .*

From every point of view, therefore, it seems to me that we ought to endeavour to draw up a peace settlement as if we were impartial arbiters, forgetful of the passions of the war. This settlement ought to have three ends in view. First of all it must do justice to the Allies by taking into account Germany's responsibility for the origin of the war and for the way in which it was fought. Secondly, it must be a settlement which a responsible German Government can sign in the belief that it can fulfill the obligations it incurs. Thirdly, it must be a settlement which will contain in itself no provocations for future wars, and which will constitute an alternative to Bolshevism, because it will commend itself to all reasonable opinion as a fair settlement of the European problem [italics mine].

Even Brockdorff-Rantzau could not have improved on this attempt to frighten the Conference with the twin specter of Bolshevism and of a German-Russian bloc. Indeed, it was this fear which drove Lloyd George to press for terms which would induce Germany "both to sign and to resist Bolshevism." In addition to granting her a fair territorial settlement in Europe and a tolerable reparations bill, Germany should be assured that her disarmament would be the first step toward general disarmament and that she would qualify for admission to the League.

Meanwhile France would receive assurances for this transitional period of trial. Until the League had proven itself as an effective collective security agency "the British Empire and the United States ought to give to France a guarantee against the possibility of a new German aggression"; and the victors should maintain considerable land and naval forces.

[7] The remainder of this paragraph is omitted in Lloyd George: *Truth*, I, 408.

But even in this section in which Lloyd George sought to reassure France, he was unable to point to a continuing German danger without at the same time keeping his eye on the Bolshevik menace. Accordingly, it was the British Prime Minister, and not Lenin, who spoke of the League of Nations as a shield against "imperialist empires or imperialist Bolshevists." Likewise, the victors had to maintain considerable military establishments not only until Germany had demonstrated her renunciation of imperialist ambitions but also until "Germany had settled down . . . and until Russia had given proof that she [did] not intend to embark upon a military crusade against her neighbors."

In his conclusion Lloyd George went one step further: he stressed that the Allies were faced with direct military invasion as well as with indirect subversion. Bolshevik imperialism not only threatened Russia's immediate neighbors, but also threatened "the whole of Asia and was as near to America as it was to France." Neither the armies of neighboring countries nor the security forces of the League could intervene in the internal wars of sovereign states. In any event, Lloyd George declared that it was "idle to think that the Peace Conference [could] separate, however sound a peace it may have arranged with Germany, if it [left] Russia as it is today." He did not indicate whether, if need be, he favored the use of military force to overthrow Lenin, though this solution was not explicitly excluded. He simply wanted to remind his colleagues of the importance of dealing with the Russian problem "as soon as possible."

Quite independently General Smuts reached the same general conclusions as the Fontainebleau party.[8] On March 26, in a forceful letter to Lloyd George, he pleaded for a reversal of the Carthaginian course on which the Conference seemed embarked. In view of the Continent's mounting instability, the Allies could not "destroy Germany without destroying Europe"; nor could they save "Europe without the cooperation of Germany." A resentful Germany would seek vengeance among the new Eastern states which were being enlarged at her expense. Particularly with Russia in momentary eclipse, Germany would survive as "the dominant factor" holding the key to Europe's peace or ruin. Because of her defeat and disarmament Germany could not become a military danger "in this generation." In the meantime, by appeasing her now, the Allies might turn her "into a bulwark against the oncoming Bolshevism of Eastern Europe."[9]

Once the Big Four convened, on March 27–28, to take stock of the new situation, it was apparent that Clemenceau and Orlando would continue to block a policy of appeasement. But the roots of this

8 W. K. Hancock: *Smuts: The Sanguine Years, 1870–1919* (Cambridge: Cambridge University Press; 1962), 514–15.
9 This letter is discussed, together with excerpts, in Hancock: *Smuts,* 510–12.

obstruction were not exclusively diplomatic; they were also deeply embedded in the domestic politics of all the Allies.

Lord Robert Cecil was one of the few officials to face squarely the political obstacles to appeasement. In a fiery letter to Colonel House he mentained that the central dilemma of the Conference was that there were no peace terms which could satisfy the national aspirations of the Allies while at the same time giving the enemy a chance to recover. Needless to say, he agreed that a ruthless treatment of Germany might produce fatal consequences for the entire Continent. On the other hand, he felt duty bound to point out that moderate terms would "bitterly disappoint all the Allied countries," possibly to such an extent that some or all of the cabinets would fall. Sir Robert characterized the dilemma in a telling formula.

> If we seek to impose hard terms on the enemy, we shall almost inevitably produce Bolshevism in the enemy countries, but temporarily at any rate we shall satisfy . . . and prevent anarchy in the Allied countries. If, on the other hand, we seek to impose moderate, liberal terms of peace, we may now be too late to save the enemy countries from Bolshevism, and we may, through disappointment, produce Bolshevism among the Allies. . . . [In other words] ought we to ruin the enemy countries in an attempt to save ourselves, or ought we to take a very grave risk of ruining ourselves in an attempt to save the enemy countries?

Nevertheless, a solution had to be found, and he suggested that the President alone could take the Conference off the horns of this dilemma.

What Cecil proposed was daring and imaginative. But whereas his proposal took full account of the enormous domestic pressures in the Allied nations, it was rather naïve about internal developments in the U.S. He wanted Wilson to present the Council of Four with a draft treaty based strictly on the Fourteen Points and to insist that unless it was accepted promptly he would have to return home immediately. Inevitably France and Italy would protest the territorial terms, and Britain would object to the reparations clauses. To make it possible for the Allied leaders to give up some of their claims, which were politically and economically conditioned, the President should offer them compensation. In effect he should say

> We will give to you what you most need to prevent anarchy and to re-establish normal conditions. We will give you relief from your most crushing financial burdens. We will agree to postpone the payment of your War Loans to us, if you will do the same thing among yourselves. Your present loans shall be converted into a new obligation, without interest, which you can pay us when you are in a position to do so. But if we do this, you must understand that the

peace is to be an American peace—that is, my interpretation of the fourteen points.

Although he conceded that such a proposal would cut away only "half the difficulties," Cecil strongly implied that Rightist intransigence was determined by economic factors: forthwith the British would become reasonable about reparations, the French would be relieved of their "great financial nightmare," the Italians would be saved from absolute bankruptcy, and territorial issues would "fade into their proper insignificance."

In conclusion Cecil—who had already been discouraged by Bernard Baruch—admitted that the American people might balk at making additional sacrifices. He was confident, however, that once they realized that Europe was "exhausted, nervous, and angry," that U. S. trade would suffer if Europe were plunged into anarchy, and that it "lay in their power to save" the Continent, Americans would not "hesitate to make a far bigger sacrifice than this."[1]

By the time this official though unpublicized Anglo-American response to the Hungarian revolution and its portents was formally brought to the Council of Four, the entire European press was up in arms. Until mid-April there was a pitched panic, especially in right-wing papers. Enraged by the prospect of leniency towards the enemy, the advance of Bolshevism toward Central Europe, signs of a second Prinkipo, and a Leftist upsurge at home, editorialists freely dispensed vicious denunciations, dire warnings, and reckless panaceas.

Appropriately enough, the French press was particularly vitriolic. The leading Parisian dailies succeeded in enveloping the Conference in an atmosphere of bitter recriminations, mutual suspicion, and impending doom. These violent attacks on every real or imaginary step toward moderation suited Clemenceau. That he encouraged this onslaught was no secret; but in all likelihood he could not have prevented, dampened, or stopped it. With or without guidance or restraint by the official censor the France-First papers espoused official views almost by reflex. Even when they seemed to favor Foch over Clemenceau they rightly assumed that the Premier saw merit in their exaggerations.

The *Temps* was shaken because the Allies were on the point of closing the breach between Poland and Rumania when Hungary decided to go Bolshevik.[2] A quick glance at the map indicated that Hungary was situated not only in the rear of the line at which Bolshevism was to be halted, but also in the midst of France's new client states. Since all these states had significant Magyar minorities, they were threatened by dangerous fifth columns. Moreover, should the Hungarian Bolsheviks link up with those of Russia and the Ukraine,

[1] Lord Robert Cecil to Colonel House, April 5, 1919, House Papers.
[2] *Le Temps*, March 24, 1919.

would Poland be able to hold Lemberg? In sum, "lightning had struck in the center of a powder magazine." And what about Vienna and Berlin, which were threatening to go the same way? Under present circumstances it was nothing short of prudent to "expect the worst and to prepare for it." Without delay the foundations of peace should be laid, with particular attention to the frontiers of Germany and the territorial demands of Italy, Czechoslovakia, Poland, Yugoslavia, and Rumania. Once these foundations were firmly set the rest of the peace structure could go up. In particular, since the chaos was invading Europe from the East, the Conference had to set a Russian policy.[3]

Suddenly, however, the *Temps* asked that the order of priority be reversed: the Russian problem should be taken up first, as Wilson had done in the Fourteen Points! Russia simply could not be left to Lenin, otherwise all of Eastern Europe would be in danger and before long the Allies would have to mobilize again. At the time of Prinkipo, Bolshevism was still safely isolated in Russia, but now, with a branch in Budapest, it threatened to lay siege to Europe. Any dealings with Lenin would raise Bolshevism's prestige while sapping the morale of the new states which had to be made into solid "bulwarks of civilization and pillars of the new order."[4]

Pertinax shared this view that with the Hungarian revolution the "door to the heart of Europe was wide open to Bolshevism" and that instead of temporizing the Conference should face up to the danger.[5] In this same vein August Gauvain tended to be grateful to Károlyi for bringing matters to a head. He self-righteously told his readers that if the Allies had sent an expedition to southern Russia, as he had suggested, the Reds would long since have been driven out of eastern Poland and the Ukraine, leaving the Hungarian revolution a matter of small consequence. But now that the damage was done the Allies should immediately reinforce the sparse contingents around Odessa and organize volunteer units for service wherever they might be needed. These volunteer corps—these *Freikorps*—could do double duty, since following the present emergency they would become the nucleus of the League of Nation's security force. In the meantime they would help the Poles put the Germans in their place; take part in driving the Red Guards back from the Baltic provinces; go on to liberate Petrograd; and clean up the Ukraine.[6]

In the *Figaro* Raymond Recouly took the more orthodox view that the Hungarian revolution was sheer blackmail, the Red specter being the chosen weapon and Germany being the thinly disguised mastermind. Should Budapest get away with this dress rehearsal Berlin would

[3] *Le Temps,* March 25, 1919.
[4] *Le Temps,* March 27 and 29, 1919.
[5] *Echo de Paris,* March 25, 1919.
[6] *Journal des Débats,* March 25–26, 1919.

immediately follow suit. There were but few Bolsheviks in Hungary, the capital being nearly half Jewish and the rest a nation of peasants. This was a nationalist revolt behind a Bolshevik smoke screen. Fortunately Hungary was surrounded by nations who were even more anxious than the major powers themselves to crush this overt rebellion of the vanquished against the victors. Without further time-consuming palaver Foch should be placed in command of a punitive expedition, also because those few Bolsheviks who had pushed themselves into sensitive posts should not be given the opportunity to entrench themselves.[7]

Gabriel Hanotaux and Joseph Reinach, also in the *Figaro,* were in complete agreement with Recouly, except that they suspected Germany of a vast conspiracy to take over Eastern Europe under the cover of Bolshevism—not unlike Germany's erstwhile introduction of Bolshevism into Russia in her own national interest. At a minimum Poland and Rumania—"the Thermopylae of Western Civilization"—should immediately be built up for the defense of the strategically vital rimland. In this conservative Catholic daily, Alfred Capus, the Director, alone confessed to being unclear about Bolshevism. For him it was "a product of national defeat and ruin rather than a spontaneous and inevitable product of modern society." Even so, many aspects of the Bolshevik phenomenon remained unknown, and it was this ignorance and not the reality of Bolshevism that caused him much anxiety. What view of Bolshevism did the Allies and the French government take? And what was their policy toward Russia?[8]

For Bainville the delays at the Conference combined with the senseless dislocation of Austria-Hungary—both of which he constantly denounced—were taking their expected toll. The defeated nations were beginning to team up with revolutionary Russia strictly for reasons of foreign policy: the Magyars, encouraged by the Germans, were inviting "a barbarian invasion" which without further harm to their internal regime promised to reverse the balance of forces between the victors and the losers. Even though at this juncture he also banked heavily on the new satellites of Eastern Europe to control the fire, he insisted that in the last analysis Béla Kun and Lenin could not be put in their place unless Ebert and Brockdorff-Rantzau were first brought to heel. Bainville once again warned that the system of small states could not possibly plug the hole in the anti-German barrier left by the simultaneous disappearance of Russia and Austria-Hungary.[9]

Except for the charge of German complicity, the British press stressed the same themes as the French press, *The Times* combining most of them in its first leader on the Hungarian revolt.

[7] *Le Figaro,* March 23–26 and 29, 1919.
[8] *Le Figaro,* March 25 and 28, and April 2 and 7, 1919.
[9] *L'Action Française,* March 24 and 26, and April 5, 1919.

The Bolshevik revolution in Budapest and the Hungarian offer of an alliance with Russia . . . ought to clear the thunderous air in Paris. For the issue now is . . . whether the Conference is to have the authority to impose any settlement at all in Eastern Europe. . . .

Hungary lies well on the western side of the sanitary cordon against Bolshevism, and by the terms of the Armistice she indubitably submitted to the authority of Paris. Her offer of an alliance to Russia is therefore an act of rebellion, and the acceptance of the offer by Russia an act of trespass. The Paris Conference cannot acquiesce in the detachment of this territory from its jurisdiction. . . . If nothing were done it would be an invitation to Germany to follow suit. . . . Clearly it is an occasion for vigorous action. . . . Germany is not in a [military] position to oppose . . . the [Allied decision to build up the buffer of states] between the Central Powers and Russia. . . . But over Russia we exercise no curb. Our Army in the North is on the defensive. Odessa we are evacuating. Russia will respect the decisions of the Conference when we show that we are both able and willing to support our policy by force. . . . We must have the strategy of our policy. On the Western front we have it; on the Eastern front it has still to be created.

The paper considered the establishment of the Council of Four and the decision to speed Haller's troops to Danzig as signs of a "healthy reaction."

But *The Times* continued to be most concerned about the hazards of a German-Russian axis. The Allies, and not Germany, should liberate Russia from Bolshevism, which was fighting the Conference "by waging war against States which they proposed to set up . . . and by unscrupulous propaganda." Bolshevism was motivated by an active spirit of aggression, every convinced Bolshevik being an apostle and proselytizer vowed to spread the system to the entire world. "Between the Red League of Lenin and the ideals of the League of Nations there was a chasm which no compromise could bridge." There was "no need to march armies from end to end of Russia." But the Whites and the new states without delay should be provided with arms, ammunitions, and supplies, and volunteer forces should be raised.[1]

Because his beloved new Slavic nations were particularly imperiled Wickham Steed took the Magyar rebellion as a personal affront. In the Paris edition of the *Daily Mail* he vented his rage on Wilson whom he held "directly responsible for the nervous inertia" of the Conference. The "jolt," which had long been predicted, should cut short "long-drawn cogitations" and result in swift and firm local treatment. Unless handled "without gloves" the Budapest convulsion would certainly be followed "by other unforeseen complications at Vienna, and possibly throughout Germany." The riposte should be a "combination of bread

[1] *The Times* (London), March 25–31 and April 3, 1919.

and the sword," the latter in the form of airplanes dropping bombs on the Hungarian capital. This call to arms against Béla Kun was part of Steed's renewed agitation against an accommodation with Lenin which was so widely rumored following Bullitt's return.[2] Steed prophesied that the Conference would drift "on to the rocks" unless the President tailored his principles to fit Clemenceau's practical demands.[3]

The *Morning Post* wanted to give Clemenceau the supreme direction of Allied diplomacy in order to counter the Hungarian "try on" and, further, to wrest security and reparations from the enemy at once. Not only the League of Nations but also the principle of self-determination were "contraptions" invented by the Germans and naïvely taken up by Wilson and Lloyd George, the same "old women in Paris whom it was possible to deceive and frighten" with Bolshevism.[4]

The enemy press, which was closely monitored in Paris, played into the hands of Allied irreconcilables by fulfilling their worst prophecies. The *Berliner Tageblatt* and the *Vorwärts* without hesitation accused the Allies, notably the French, of strangling Hungary. They put the world on notice that Germany would also take drastic steps should the peace terms violate Wilson's principles. Having brought about the overthrow of both Kerensky and Károlyi with their reckless diplomacy, the Allies should not need a third lesson. Of course, Bolshevism was the very last resort, and the Weimar regime's anti-Bolshevism was a matter of record. Nevertheless, "if a just peace could not be had the most unjust of all wars, namely civil war, would be kindled in all the capitals of the world."[5]

The Austrian press shuddered because overnight "Bolshevism had become Vienna's neighbor." Heretofore it had been a "half Asian affair" and, as compared to Budapest, Moscow was relatively inacces-

[2] *Daily Mail* (Paris), March 23–28, 1919. House had long prided himself on a close working relationship with Steed. Especially throughout the first half of March, while Wilson was absent, he claimed to have outlined, instigated, or inspired numerous editorials and articles for the Northcliffe press (*Times* and *Daily Mail*). Through Steed, whom he saw frequently, House had this press at his "disposal. . . [and] frightened, persuaded and coerced" Lloyd George. Now, however, he and Wiseman were "disturbed by . . . [his] editorials . . . on the Russian question. . . . Wiseman advised giving Steed 'the cold shoulder' for a few days. Instead of that, I sent for him and had it out with him. I told him he was not playing the game and he ought not to have written editorials concerning so important a matter without first consulting me. . . ." House Diary, March 4, 6, 11, 15, 16, and 28, 1919. Actually, House got on with Steed only as long as he inclined to share the journalist's essentially Clemencist views. By April 1, 1919, House complained to Steed that the President "was being influenced more and more by Lloyd George who was showing the *Manchester Guardian* to him and was persuading him that only by a pro-Bolshevik and semi-pro-German policy could a disaster be avoided in England." Wickham Steed: *Through Thirty Years*, II, 310.

[3] *Daily Mail* (Paris), April 4, 1919.

[4] "The Need for a Generalissimo," editorial in the *Morning Post*, March 25, 1919.

[5] *Berliner Tageblatt* and *Vorwärts*, March 23–26, 1919.

sible. The *Neue Freie Presse* appealed to Paris to stop its suicidal incendiarism before it was too late.

> Because of the Peace Conference's mistakes Vienna has accidentally become the crossroads where Paris and Moscow meet, where Lenin fights the West. . . . The conquest of Vienna is to open his way to the West, to Italy and France and perhaps also to England. . . . Vienna has become a social battlefield. The Russians stand before her walls, just as the Turks once did. . . .

For the present this city of two million subsisted on American food trains; their stoppage would be tantamount to a death sentence. Yet this critical circumstance cut two ways: whereas the Allies were disinclined to risk the political consequences of starvation, the Social Democrats or their radical critics were reluctant to gamble with two million lives.[6]

The Social Democratic Administration and the *Arbeiter Zeitung* could not altogether conceal their admiration for their Hungarian opposites. Pressured by Italy and Czechoslovakia, Otto Bauer and Friedrich Adler sympathized with this rebellion, this "dictatorship of desperation." However, they decided at once that they could neither follow this act of courage nor respond to Béla Kun's appeal for help.

> We are in an even worse situation than our Hungarian brothers. To be sure, we could displace our own bourgeoisie as easily and rapidly as they did; a few battalions of *Volkswehr* could see to that. But compared to the Magyar proletariat we are altogether more dependent on the Entente. . . . Because of their food reserves the Hungarians can survive the withdrawal of the Allied missions from Budapest. We could not survive. We have no flour of our own and are at the mercy of Allied supplies. Should Allied food trains be withheld we would be without bread. The Hungarians ask us to break with Paris in order to take up with Moscow; but Moscow is far off, the Soviet armies are still thousands of kilometers away, and Poland and the Ukraine make up a formidable obstacle. We are slaves of Paris because only Paris can supply us with bread. . . . We have food reserves for less than two weeks. . . . No illusions! We could master our own bourgeoisie with great ease; but the Allied bourgeoisie keeps us in chains which we cannot afford to break, thereby holding its protective hand over the local bourgeois classes.[7]

Neither Hoover nor Lenin could find fault with this self-assessment. The Allied Right, however, cursed Vienna's heartless and calculating expediency.

Editorials in the neutral press contributed to the all-European

6 *Neue Freie Presse*, March 22–23, 1919.
7 *Arbeiter Zeitung*, March 22–24, 1919.

panic. In the *Journal de Genève,* William Martin characterized the second Hungarian revolution as "history's very last solemn warning to the peoples of the West." As compared to her neighbors Hungary still had a tolerable food situation, so that this was not a hunger strike but a protest against the direction, pace, and uncertainty of the Conference. As a Swiss, Martin could authoritatively warn Paris that the separation of Southern Tyrol might provoke a catastrophe in precariously balanced Vienna. After four months the peacemakers were confronted with *"une formidable entreprise de chantage mondial."* The Rumanian dam was in danger of breaking, the Ukraine was all but gone, and the Red Army would be difficult to stop once it reached the southern slopes of the Carpathians. This extreme emergency called for extreme measures. With a view to "teaching a terrible lesson" to all neighboring peoples the Hungarian revolution should be "drowned in blood." And the Allies should take note that behind the fragile dyke of small Central European nations only Germany could "protect the West against Bolshevism." Should Germany fall, the Russians would advance from the Danube to the Rhine.[8]

Impassioned Socialists and Radicals were of two minds. Had they been certain that the Budapest revolution was not "the first act of a European tragedy," they would have cheered.[9] Under the circumstances, however, the Left-opposition press simply declared that Paris deserved this backlash of the blockade, of the refusal to deal sensibly with Lenin, and of the subservience to the Right and their spokesmen in the Conference. Whatever cheering there was stemmed from the prayerful hope that this panic would stimulate Wilson and Lloyd George to vigorous, wise, and united action. Even then there were ill-concealed doubts about Wilson's inclination or readiness to act. According to the *New Republic* a "very bold strike might still save Europe," but unless Wilson hurried "the depth of his fall would be measured only by the heights of the aspirations he had proclaimed."[1]

Clemenceau, Sonnino, and the Allied Right were determined to exploit Wilson's hesitations as well as the rivalries among his supporters. They also realized that with all the forces of movement—now including Lloyd George—once again rallying around the President, the next round of negotiations would be decisive. Unless they stood their ground now, the moderates might sweep the Conference as well as the cabinets. Half regretfully the *New Europe* acknowledged that the "men who were most firmly resolved to apply to the territorial settlement the principles to which the Allies stood pledged were those who seemed most disposed towards a compromise with the forces of subversion and

8 *Journal de Genève,* March 25 and 29, 1919.
9 *The Nation* (London), March 29, 1919, 771–2.
1 *The New Republic,* March 29, 1919, 257–8, and April 5, 1919, 288, 291.

anarchy which threatened them from the East, while those whose Eastern policy was most logical were bent upon sheer reaction."[2]

Even prior to the Hungarian crisis many of the delegates sensed that the Council of Ten had became unwieldy and that this top executive organ of the Conference needed to be overhauled.[3] This vast assembly was not geared for closely reasoned, brisk, give-and-take negotiations. Above all, because of the large membership of each delegation, it was well-nigh impossible to protect the confidential nature of the deliberations.

With the Conference about to enter its most crucial and delicate stage these procedures needed to be streamlined. The very same day that Lloyd George decided to spend a weekend taking stock, he complained bitterly at the Council of Ten about recent leakages to the press.[4] Unless the privacy of debates could be guaranteed the Prime Minister would find it difficult to launch a basic reappraisal and confrontation. He repeatedly urged the President and the two other Premiers to consider meeting in private, under eight eyes only. Indeed, it would seem that Lloyd George quite as much as Colonel House lobbied for the transformation of the cumbersome, dilatory, and ajar Council of Ten into what both hoped would be a more streamlined, purposeful, and impermeable Council of Four.[5]

On the afternoon of March 24 President Wilson formally proposed that the Big Four discuss the "most difficult and urgent questions" among themselves. He introduced his proposal with the admonition that they were up against "a veritable race between peace and anarchy, and that the peoples were beginning to be impatient." Lloyd George, who had just returned from Fontainebleau, eagerly seconded this motion. He stressed the urgency of the moment with the plea that "if necessary" the chiefs should meet twice daily and that the new regimen should start the following morning. Clemenceau readily went along in as much as he was assured that the Four would immediately turn their attention to reparations, French security, Italy's borders, and the status of Austria.[6]

During the next week, however, the new Council could not restrict its agenda to these conventional and tractable diplomatic issues. Neoteric and unruly situations constantly clamored for the Council's time, attention, and executive decisions: the Hungarian revolution, the impending withdrawal from Odessa, the reinforcement of Rumania, the

---

[2] *The New Europe,* April 3, 265.

[3] See F. S. Marston: *The Peace Conference of 1919* (New York: Oxford University Press; 1944), 109–10, 161–3.

[4] The French press had detailed information about the P.M.'s opposition to the recommendations of the Polish Commission, and attacked him for it. *F.R.,P.C., 1919,* IV, 444–7.

[5] Hankey: *Supreme Control at Paris,* 407.

[6] Paul Mantoux: *Les Délibérations du conseil des quatre,* I, 13.

transfer of Haller's troops to Poland, and the Polish-Ukrainian conflict over eastern Galicia.[7] Actually both types of issues became pawns in the grand review which the Anglo-Americans initiated without advance notice to the two Latin delegations. The Fontainebleau memorandum and Clemenceau's unyielding rebuttal set the general framework for this confrontation.

Lloyd George circulated his memorandum to his three colleagues on March 25; two days later he asked Clemenceau whether he had received and studied it.[8] The French Premier sought to avoid or delay a head-on collision for fear of exacerbating their differences in the heat of debate. He indicated, therefore, that he planned to return a written answer after the document had been translated for President Poincaré.

President Wilson, however, refused to be put off. With persistence he inquired whether in principle Clemenceau agreed that it was essential to treat Germany with moderation and fairness so as not to give her cause for *revanche*. For the future Wilson was less afraid of "wars caused by secret government plots than of conflicts stemming from popular dissatisfaction." To mark the point, Lloyd George hastily interjected that even in 1814–15, when Europe's condition had been considerably less explosive, Wellington and Castlereagh had convinced Blücher that a solid France was indispensable for European civilization and order.

Clemenceau felt obliged to give his reaction right then and there, without benefit of a position paper, which was not completed until the thirty-first.

He began by agreeing in a rather mechanical fashion that the Allies should not abuse their victory lest they provoke a nationalist outburst. Moreover, he wanted it understood that among the victors there were no differences about principles but only about specific applications.

With these formalities out of the way, Clemenceau plunged into a heated attack on appeasement. In his judgment Lloyd George was unduly scared by enemy threats. Doubtless the Germans would rage, would contest every point, and would threaten to refuse their signature. Furthermore, they "would capitalize on incidents like the one which just occurred in Budapest and which could occur in Vienna tomorrow." And yet, though such dangers could not be ignored, they should not be exaggerated.

The central fact was still that the Allies had won a costly war and were entitled to the "fruits of victory." Granted, the Allies should not be unjust to the Germans. But the Germans, including the Social

[7] On April 1, 1919, Wilson emphasized that "peace with Germany would not automatically remove all other causes of difficulty" and that the nationality conflicts in Central Europe were "an inexhaustible source of disorder and war." Mantoux: *Délibérations,* I, 113.

[8] The following discussion of the debates of March 27, 1919 (a.m.) is based on ibid., 41–8.

Democrats, made no distinction between just and unjust peace terms, preferring to dispute all of them indiscriminately.

As for France's security claims, these were bound to be more complex than those of the two naval powers, which in addition to certain natural advantages would benefit from the destruction of Germany's fleet. In pursuit of a new balance of power strategic considerations could not be ignored in the Polish settlement, and seven million Austrians could not be allowed to accede to Germany.

In conclusion, Clemenceau warned of the danger of sparing the vanquished at the expense of the victors. True enough, the Allies had good reason to avoid stirring up Bolshevism in Germany. On the other hand, if in Britain and France popular expectations about peace terms were disappointed, there could be serious trouble. If it came to a choice between revolutionary disturbances in the enemy or Allied camp he thought it preferable that these not take place in any of the Entente nations.

The closing statement infuriated Lloyd George, who refused to equate left- and right-wing pressures. The revolutionary threat originated on the Left and not on the Right, and he claimed extensive firsthand experience in fighting this threat in Britain. Precisely because he countered Bolshevism not by force but by trying to satisfy "the legitimate aspirations which generate it," such powerful labor leaders as Robert Smillie, of the Miners Federation, were coming around to helping the government prevent internal conflicts. As for foreign policy, oppressive rather than lenient peace terms were likely to provoke a Bolshevik explosion in England.

> The British worker does not want to weigh down the German people with excessive claims. Unlimited hatred of the German is much more common among the upper classes. . . . Should our terms appear unduly moderate, I will have great difficulties in Parliament, but these will not come from the lower classes.

Not that the proletariat was insensitive to France's security dilemma. In fact, only yesterday George Lansbury, "one of our most notorious pacifists," had assured him that he would support a reinsurance guarantee as part of a just settlement.

He could not, however, share Clemenceau's faith in the advice of military experts. Lloyd George very much "admired and liked Marshal Foch," but he also thought that "in political questions he was a child." In 1871 Moltke had sold Bismarck on the doctrine of the strategic frontier; and Disraeli had justified the occupation of Afghanistan with this same doctrine. Surely, in both cases the sequel had been less than spectacular, and the Big Four should not want to be guided by this same military metaphysics.

Another general had just written him, and this one did not share

Foch's views. General Smuts was worried about putting two million Germans under Polish jurisdiction.[9] Was Clemenceau prepared to send troops to restrain Germany from supporting a revolt by this *irredenta?* Lloyd George doubted very much that at some future date U.S. and British public opinion would sanction military measures to uphold an unjust arrangement in such a distant outpost. Besides, Germany was being cut down to size. She was about to lose her colonies, her fleet, six to seven million citizens, and a large proportion of her natural resources. Moreover "militarily she was being reduced to the level of Greece while her naval status would become comparable to that of the Argentine Republic." To top it all, Germany would be compelled to pay stiff reparations.

The Allies had to guard themselves against adding the "drop of water which might cause the pitcher to overflow." Lloyd George was fearful that this loss of two million Germans to Poland might be that fatal "drop." Turning to Clemenceau he asked point-blank: "in 1871, which did France resent more, the loss of Alsace-Lorraine or the obligation to pay a 5 million indemnity?" He did not stop for Clemenceau's answer, claiming to know it in advance. Instead, in another melodramatic flourish Lloyd George recalled that during his first visit to Paris he had been struck by the Strasbourg monument draped in black. Even Clemenceau nodded agreement when Lloyd George insisted that the Allies should not give Germany cause to "erect such monuments in her cities." But the Tiger demurred as soon as the P.M. advocated that Danzig be turned into a free port.

In his written reply of the thirty-first, drafted by Tardieu, Clemenceau refuted the Fontainebleau paper more systematically.[1] Not unreasonably he accused Lloyd George, the chief executive of the largest overseas empire, of being outrageously Europe-centered in his brief. Germany had aspired to world power and the war had been a world conflict. Without worrying about stimulating resentments in Germany, the victors were dealing fatal blows to her *Weltpolitik:* she was scheduled to lose all her colonies and navy, as well as large segments of her merchant marine and foreign markets.

Assuming a good case could be made for appeasing Germany, why attenuate territorial conditions in Europe without making colonial, naval, and commercial concessions. Whereas the naval powers expected to obtain permanent relief, the Continental nations were asked

---

[9] Toward the close of this session Lloyd George read the full text of Smuts's letter discussed p. 584 above.

[1] André Tardieu: *La Paix* (Paris: Payot; 1921), 129–32; and Clemenceau to Wilson, March 31, 1919, Wilson Papers, VIII A:30. According to Lloyd George, Tardieu's original draft was so "irreconcilable in its tone" that Clemenceau threw it over and composed a more tempered version. See Lloyd George: *Truth,* I, 416–20, also for a translation of the full text of the document for which Tardieu claims credit but which the P.M. attributes to Clemenceau.

to be satisfied with "partial and temporary" solutions in Poland, Czechoslovakia, and the Saar, as well as with regard to the security guarantee.

Next he turned to the ever-present specter of revolution. Resentment of territorial conditions could also further Bolshevism outside Germany, notably in Poland and Bohemia. Should violence be done to their sense of nationality, "Bolshevism would find these two peoples an easy prey, and the only barrier which at the present moment separated Russian from German Bolshevism would be shattered." The resulting anarchy would lead to the control of the rimland by either a Bolshevik or a reactionary Germany. Moreover, the Allied peoples themselves had to feel that the peace was just and equitable. Otherwise "national disappointment" might stimulate Bolshevism not only in Central Europe but elsewhere as well.

Clemenceau's written rebuttal was not discussed in the Council of Four. Instead Lloyd George also gave his answer in writing. The tone of his reply was sarcastic, even mischievous, since he had decided that "on the whole it was better not to take [Clemenceau's memo] too seriously."[2] He taunted Clemenceau by excusing himself for harboring the illusion that France attached importance to her rich German African colonies, to Syria, to priority in indemnity payments, to the return of Alsace-Lorraine, to her share of merchant and naval booty, and to a joint Anglo-American guarantee. No doubt he was wrong: "what France really cared for was that the Danzig Germans should be handed over to the Poles." He regretted his error and for good measure withdrew his Saar proposals because Clemenceau treated them "as a further proof of British selfishness."[3]

All the time that they were caught up in this wide-ranging policy debate the Big Four pored over the fast-changing situation in Eastern Europe. They knew that each executive decision would affect the course as well as the outcome of the general debate.

The deteriorating military situation around Odessa was the first executive problem to come before the Council of Four on its opening day.[4] Generals Berthelot and Franchet d'Esperey were advising Paris that this Allied beachhead on the Black Sea was threatened with famine, in large measure because of the Red Army's advance into the granary of the southern Ukraine. They urgently requested 30,000 tons of wheat and the same tonnage of coal monthly for the purpose of counteracting unrest among the one million local population. Furthermore, in a telegram that morning, Franchet d'Esperey asked that Polish troops from Italy be sent to reinforce the 25,000-strong inter-Allied

[2] Lloyd George to Wilson, April 2, 1919, Wilson Papers, VIII A:31.
[3] Lloyd George: *Truth,* I, 420–2.
[4] The following discussion of the debates of March 25, 1919 (p.m.) is based on Mantoux: *Délibérations,* I, 18–23.

expeditionary force. General Alby, Chief of the French General Staff, who was summoned to appear before the Four, revealed that Italy was disposed to send 7,000 of these Poles right away.

It made little sense to look at Odessa in isolation, and Clemenceau was anxious to expand the inquiry. Accordingly, General Alby was asked to report on the situation in Rumania, since in view of the crisis in Budapest and in Odessa that country was now of pivotal importance. On the basis of telegrams from the two senior French generals in the area Alby estimated that the Rumanians could field about ten divisions along the Dniester on condition that the Conference equipped them; with the additional support of two Allied divisions an imposing military instrument could be forged.

With a map spread before them Lloyd George and Wilson demurred. The Prime Minister reminded Clemenceau and his military adviser that under existing agreements France was responsible for this sector of the Russian front, while Britain looked after the sector under Denikin's command. Consequently it was up to France to first spell out what aid and manpower she herself could furnish before then specifying what she wanted her Allies to contribute.

America was not a party to this agreement, and so Wilson raised a broader question. Since judging by these telegrams the population in and around Odessa tended to be hostile to the Allies, why maintain this heavily beleaguered beachhead at all? This hostility "confirms me in my policy, which is to leave Russia to the Bolsheviks—they will stew in their own juice until circumstances make the Russians wiser—and to restrict ourselves to preventing Bolshevism from invading other parts of Europe."

Lloyd George instantly noticed that Wilson's advocacy of containment was compatible with the reinforcement of Rumania, which he favored, though on a more modest scale than the French. He proposed, therefore, that the Allies establish their defensive barrier in Rumania, if necessary abandoning Odessa. Probably by pre-arrangement the P.M. called in Major General Thwaites, Director of British Army Intelligence, and Lieutenant Colonel F. H. Kisch, his Russian expert, to inquire what would happen if Odessa fell.

THWAITES: The Bolsheviks will immediately attack Rumania.

LLOYD GEORGE: Which is preferable, to defend Odessa or to concentrate our forces in Rumania?

KISCH: According to an experienced source the occupation of Odessa by the Bolsheviks will create the impression in Russia that they scored a great victory over the Allies. Thus this development would be important from the point of view of morale; but that would be the only important reason for holding Odessa.

LLOYD GEORGE: If a choice had to be made between sending food and equipment to Odessa or Rumania, which would you chose?

THWAITES: If forced to choose, of the two Rumania is more important.

The Big Four also summoned Foch. He, too, was asked where to concentrate limited resources. Foch was not the man to put in a command performance. Rather than choose dutifully between Odessa and Rumania, he seized this opportunity to challenge the statesmen, bluntly telling them that the answer "depended on the intentions" of the Conference. Clemenceau deftly interrupted to say that it was really a question of "finding out what we *can* do."

Undeterred, Foch spread out a map showing the military and political situation between the Black Sea and the Baltic and proceeded to outline yet another variant of the ambitious plan which he had unsuccessfully unfolded twice before, on February 25 and on March 17. Needless to say, this third time he took full account and advantage of the recent upset in Budapest.

FOCH: At this moment the Bolshevik peril stretches southward and toward Hungary; it will continue to spread as long as it is not checked; it must be stopped at Odessa and Lemberg [Lvov]. The Bolshevik breakthrough toward Hungary is to be expected at this second point. Hence the door at Lemberg must be shut and we must hold fast at Odessa. Are the [Allied] Governments aware of the importance of linking these operations and to what extent will they participate in them? The Allied forces in this region are negligible; the Rumanian army is easiest at hand, though it needs rebuilding. Is an overall solution wanted? Without a unified plan no matter how many breaches we close there will always be new ones.

CLEMENCEAU: How do you visualize the build up of an uninterrupted barrier?

FOCH: It must be constructed out of the reorganized Polish and Rumanian armies, and by holding the Odessa sector.

CLEMENCEAU: What is the importance of Odessa as such?

FOCH: Odessa has no importance, except for morale purposes.

LLOYD GEORGE: What if for purposes of aid you had to choose between Odessa and Rumania?

FOCH: I would try to hold the two as long as possible. . . . What the Allies must do [above all], is to appoint a general [independent of Franchet d'Esperey] to go to Rumania to take command of the Rumanian army, to direct the defense of the entire Rumanian front, and to try and effect a link-up with the Poles.

LLOYD GEORGE: Can the Rumanians defend their front by themselves?

FOCH: They have 12 divisions which, to be sure, need equipment and shoes. With proper aid they could raise between 16 and 18 divisions. . . .

LLOYD GEORGE: . . . I am convinced that no resources should be wasted in trying to hold our precarious and hopeless position in

Odessa. We must withdraw the 25,000 men from around that city to Rumania and ship the 30,000 tons requested for Odessa to Rumania as well.

FOCH: To abandon Odessa is to abandon Southern Russia; but, to speak the truth, since Southern Russia has already been lost it cannot be lost a second time.

CLEMENCEAU: [Britain] would divert 100,000 sets of clothing from Denikin to Rumania.

FOCH: Whatever is sent to Denikin is lost in any case. I do not attach great importance to Denikin's armies because these cannot exist by themselves. Such armies must be supported by government, laws, and control of the country. A government without army is actually preferable to an army without government. That is why I say to you: bank on Rumania, because there you have not only an army but also a government and a people.

Before recessing Foch was asked to prepare a plan which could serve as a basis for final decision, while Lloyd George confirmed his readiness to divert supplies from Denikin to Constantsa.

Within 48 hours Foch was back with his plan all worked out.[5] In a brief prologue he stressed that with Hungary overwhelmed by Bolshevism there existed a "redoubtable menace" immediately to the rear of the *cordon sanitaire*. Particularly if Vienna fell, the road to Western Europe would be wide open. In view of the enormity and urgency of this danger the following measures were indicated: (1) the Polish and Rumanian armies should be strengthened, the former by the transport of Haller's divisions to Danzig, the latter by every conceivable kind of aid; (2) the breach at Lemberg should be closed in order to secure a continuous front; (3) a new and independent command should be organized for this entire front; (4) the "blaze in Hungary" should be extinguished so as to purify the "rear areas"; and (5) Vienna should be occupied by Allied troops under U.S. command "to protect communications against the Bolshevik peril."

President Wilson objected at once. This plan[6] went considerably beyond the withdrawal from Odessa and the reinforcement of Rumania on which the Conference seemed to have settled two days ago. Specifically, he could not agree to "close the breach at Lemberg," since he was not prepared to side with the Poles against the Ukrainians in the contest over this city. Secondly, the junction of Polish and Rumanian forces seemed designed as a first step toward direct military intervention in Russia, to which he was opposed. And last, he could not sanction the occupation of Vienna, not least because the Armistice would not allow

---

[5] Except when otherwise indicated the following discussion of the debates of March 27, 1919 (p.m.) is based on Mantoux: *Délibérations,* I, 52–7.

[6] For the full text, dated March 27, 1919 and in English translation, see Wilson Papers, VIII A:29. An altogether inadequate ten-line précis is given in Mantoux: *Délibérations,* I, 52.

it. Why not simply "reinforce the Rumanian citadel" without preparing for offensive action?

With similar scepticism Lloyd George asked Foch whether he wanted this continuous dam because the Bolsheviks posed a military threat or because he expected trouble of another sort?

Foch fell back on his favorite imagery. The only protection against an epidemic was a *cordon sanitaire* consisting of "one *douanier* every two hundred meters" to prevent individuals from crossing the line. Should there be the additional threat of a military breakthrough, a stronger barrier would be needed. Admittedly, he wanted "a barrier against both dangers," but this was not equivalent to preparing an offensive capability.

With the Danubian basin at the center of this debate the Italians broke their silence. Orlando reported that according to the Italian High Commissioner in Vienna the situation in Budapest could still be saved by sending Allied troops, on condition that there were no Czechs, Rumanians, or Poles among them. Moreover, whereas some moderates in Vienna had inquired whether Italian troops could occupy the city, others thought that two American regiments could easily do the job. When General Diaz was consulted he asked that if Vienna were to be occupied—as he hoped it would be—this assignment should fall to Italian soldiers.

The Anglo-American military advisers still had to be heard. Somewhat disingenuously Henry Wilson suggested that it was up to the "Frocks" and not to the generals to decide whether or not to take military action against Bolshevism. However, should the Council opt for military action then Foch's plan was "all right for a beginning." Above all, further delays should be avoided. Bolshevism's victory in Budapest had already lengthened the Allied front by 500 kilometers, and should Vienna fall during the coming week an additional 1,000 kilometers would have to be covered. As if to leave no doubt about where he stood, Henry Wilson "pointed out that if military action was not the answer to Bolshevism, then, if Vienna and Berlin went Bolshevist, military action would be quite unable to enforce terms of peace."[7]

As usual, General Bliss was out of step with all the other military men. He began by lamenting the vague use of the words "Bolshevik" and "Bolshevism." Before resorting to military force to fight the dreaded peril the Big Four should first be clear about its nature. Were they preparing themselves to fight *Russians* who threatened to carry Bolshevism into Europe on bayonets? Or were they battling the *idea* of Bolshevism which was striking roots in areas convulsed by devastation, national rivalries, social conflicts, and disillusionment? Agreed, the *cordon sanitaire* could stop an onrushing army. On the other hand, "the progress of an idea, whether good or bad," could not be checked by a

---

[7] Mantoux: *Délibérations,* I, 54; and General Wilson's diary entry of March 27, 1919, cited in Callwell (ed.): *Henry Wilson,* II, 177.

"line of bayonets." It might, however, be contained by promptly drawing boundaries, thereby removing one source of agitation, and by lifting the blockade and getting the world back to work.[8]

Partly to counteract Bliss's testimony Marshal Foch entered one last plea, insisting that the occupation of Vienna was absolutely essential to safeguard Allied communications with Bohemia, Poland, and Rumania. Finally, he reiterated that his overall plan provided for a defensive barrier and not an offensive platform against Bolshevism, but that behind this barrier *"on pourra faire les nettoyages nécessaires."*

President Wilson was the first to speak once the military advisers had withdrawn.

> We are back with the familiar question as to whether it is possible to organize armed resistance against Bolshevism. . . . The word "Bolshevism" covers a host of things. In my judgment, to try and stop a revolutionary movement with field armies is like using a broom to stop a vast flood. . . . The only [effective] way to act against Bolshevism is to destroy its causes. But this is a tall order since we are not altogether clear about these causes. In any event . . . [let us] fix the frontiers and open all the doors to commerce.
>
> As for the occupation of Vienna by U.S. troops, it is out of the question. . . . I have constantly opposed the reopening of an eastern front, and it is this which is proposed to us once again. We wanted the limited question of [aid to Rumania] examined. . . . Instead we are presented with a plan which envisages the establishment of a continuous front from the Baltic to the Black Sea. We are advised to "cleanse Hungary," namely to crush Hungarian Bolshevism. As long as this Bolshevism remains within its own borders it does not concern us. . . .

There was little for Lloyd George to add, except to endorse Wilson's opposition to a march on Budapest with the jocular observation that actually few nations needed a revolution as badly as Hungary! Both Clemenceau and Orlando had no choice but to yield. Foch was instructed to confine his measures to the evacuation of Odessa, the reinforcement of the Rumanian army, and the diversion of supplies from Denikin to Brătianu. Within two days the Big Four decided to send an emissary to Budapest to hold out an olive branch to Béla Kun. This emissary was instructed to assure the revolutionary regime that even though the zone would be enforced, the Conference could be trusted to make its final disposition on the basis of Wilsonian principles.

The Fontainebleau spirit had scored a passing and circumscribed triumph: Foch's grand design was checkmated, Smuts was chosen to be the emissary to Budapest, and Lloyd George was elected to draft Smuts's instructions.

Yet Foch did not come away altogether empty-handed. The build-up of Rumania was authorized. No one, not even Wilson and Lloyd

8 Mantoux: *Délibérations,* I, 54–5; and "Memorandum on Address to Council of Four," March 27, 1919, in Bliss Papers, Box 71.

George at the height of their Fontainebleau apprehensions, ever questioned Rumania's critical role in the containment of Bolshevism in both Russia and Hungary. And Brătianu knew only too well that his enormous territorial claims in Transylvania and Bessarabia could be satisfied only by magnifying the offensive military propensities of Bolshevism, by urging military intervention, and by putting his troops at the disposal of the counterrevolution.[9]

Not only Rumania but also Poland was anxious to cooperate with Foch. The negative decision about the Lemberg gap did not deter Foch from pushing the build-up of the Polish citadel. Perhaps the junction could be achieved by combat instead of by diplomatic ukase. In any case, Foch was determined to get on with the dispatch of Haller's units. The Germans rightly suspected the French and the Poles of seeking to create a *fait accompli* in Danzig. Therefore they refused to have some 70,000 to 80,000 troops pass through this Baltic port. They did agree, however, to have them disembark in other ports—Stettin, Koenigsberg, Memel, and Libau—or cross Germany by rail from the Rhine bridgeheads.[1]

In trying to wear down German objections to the transfer, Lloyd George and Wilson explicitly assured Berlin that Haller's divisions would not be used along Poland's western borders; they were earmarked to maintain internal order and to reinforce the front against Bolshevism along Poland's eastern borders.[2] At the same time the Allies—not the Poles—tried their best to assure the Ukrainians that these troops, which finally started on their journey in mid-April, would not be used against them in the battle over Eastern Galicia, but would be used to fight the Red Army.[3]

In any case, Clemenceau and Foch were confident that regardless of how Haller's units arrived and where they were assigned, they would make a notable contribution to Poland's overall military strength. The Quai d'Orsay tended to give Warsaw *carte blanche* to strike out in all directions—against Germany, Bolshevik Russia, the Ukraine, and Lithuania. Of course, in pursuit of territorial expansion Dmowski and Pilsudski, like Brătianu, incessantly and successfully played on the Bolshevik fears of the Allies. Whenever the Lithuanians or the Ukrainians protested Poland's aggressions not only the French but also the British and the Americans hesitated to censure Warsaw or to cut off material and moral support. The Conference considered Poland the linchpin of the *cordon sanitaire*, and Warsaw could name its price.

9 Sherman D. Spector: *Rumania at the Paris Peace Conference* (New York: Bookman Associates; 1962), *passim.*
1 For the proceedings of March 24, 27, 29–30, 1919, see *F.R.,P.C.,1919* IV, 472–3; Mantoux: *Délibérations,* I, 51–2; *F.R.,P.C.,1919,* V, 15–18.
2 Mantoux: *Délibérations,* I, 76–8 (March 29, 1919).
3 David Hunter Miller: *My Diary at the Conference of Paris,* X, 328, 336–9, 345–6, 354–7, 364–7, 376–7, 388–9.

18

Intrusion of Politics: Britain

ENGLAND'S DOMESTIC SITUATION was far from quiescent during the first
three months of 1919. The government was plagued by serious labor
unrest in the form of strikes and strike threats. Significantly, the peak of
this unrest came in March, which was also a month of great turmoil in
Central and Eastern Europe. Lloyd George was caught between these
coincident upsurges, and as a reformer he proposed to appease both
with timely concessions. In this sense the Sankey Report and the
Fontainebleau Memorandum were cut of the same cloth.

Compared to the Continental belligerents, Britain emerged unscathed from the war. Apart from the long-term cost of the huge
foreign and national debt, the economy was sound. There was no
industrial devastation and the inflation was moderate, the workingclass
cost of living having risen by only 120 per cent in the course of the
war.[1] Moreover, because the Irish rebellion did not flare up until late
1919, there were no acute border or nationality conflicts. Precisely
because England, with her resplendent Empire essentially unimpaired,
gave the appearance of being such a solid social fortress, her domestic
unrest threatened to have an unsettling effect on the rest of Europe.[2]

Perhaps the first three months following the khaki election would
not have become quite so agitated if the Unionists had not swept
Commons so thoroughly. For four years organized labor, restrained by
patriotic appeals, had deferred pressing its claims. But now that the
political truce had expired, pent-up feelings and demands simply refused to be dampened or put off any longer. And yet the new khaki
Parliament held out little, if any, hope for forward-looking legislation.
Not surprisingly, therefore, labor reached out for the strike weapon,
and militant trade-unionists rather than accommodating party leaders
set the pace.

[1] A. W. Kirkaldy (ed.): *British Finance During and After the War, 1914–21* (London:
Pitman; 1921), 245.
[2] See *le Temps*, March 1, 1919; and *Journal de Genève*, March 23, 1919.

These labor leaders pursued two sets of goals. Immediately following the Armistice they mounted a campaign designed to alleviate the hardships of demobilization, reconversion, and inflation. In addition they renewed their campaign for those reforms that they had moved to the center of the political stage on the eve of the war. In practice these immediate and long-range objectives were never separated: the reduction of the work week to forty-eight or forty hours promised to absorb demobilized workers while at the same time consummating a time-honored workingclass platform. Moreover, the drive as a whole was invigorated by the psychological impact of the Soviet experiment on the more restless spirits among the leaders as well as among the rank and file.

During those first three months of 1919 optimism about placing ex-servicemen in jobs did not run high, particularly since as a result of restlessness and dissatisfaction—and even mutinies—in the armed forces, demobilization was speeded up. It took until spring to get reconversion into high gear, to resume foreign trade, and to start bringing down the cost of living. Meanwhile overtime pay dried up and employers sought to take advantage of the soft labor market not only to cut hourly wages but also to break or weaken the unions.

Unemployment was highest in cities like Birmingham, Glasgow, and Sheffield, where war industries were concentrated. In the engineering trades unemployment reached 14 per cent; because the blockade remained in force the employment picture was discouraging in port cities, especially among the traditionally underpaid, overworked, and excitable dockworkers.

The government pushed through remedial measures. For the transition employers were enjoined from reducing hourly wages. Also, demobilized servicemen were given special unemployment donations. In mid-March there were 990,000 workers on relief. Of these 495,000 were women. Among the men 165,000 were veterans and 227,000 discharged defense workers.[3]

Even if relief donations had been more than a mere pittance these measures could not have counteracted the swelling ferment in the labor world. Lloyd George quite rightly singled out the deep-seated fear of recurring unemployment as a fundamental cause of unrest, adding that only workmen who before the war had passed "through cycles of unemployment knew its terror." The Prime Minister also conceded that since economic conditions during the war had been better than at any time "during our lifetime" people were dubious about the economy's capacity to sustain this prosperity in peacetime.[4] Indeed, fear of backsliding into prewar conditions stimulated unrest and demands for

---

[3] See the statement by the Parliamentary Secretary to the Ministry of Labor in *PD, 113* (March 19, 1919), cols. 2190 ff.

[4] *PD, 112* (February 11, 1919), col. 72.

structural reforms quite as much as the enthusiasm for a new millennium.

Discontent was further quickened by the strident reaction in important segments of the Unionist Party, the press, the entrepreneurial classes, and the government. In particular, labor was incensed by the right-wing agitation for stepped-up intervention in Russia, suspecting that successful counterrevolution abroad precluded reform at home.

In the labor movement the response to these postwar anxieties and hopes was highly differentiated. The Labour Party and the ILP were still in disarray as a result of their defeat at the polls; both were torn by sharp disagreements over fundamental questions of foreign and domestic policy; and only the moderate elements were represented in the Parliamentary Party. In his maiden speech as Leader of His Majesty's Opposition, William Adamson made a point of reassuring the House that he was the leader of a "party of constitutionalists . . . [which would] not give encouragement either to revolution or to unofficial action in the labor movement."[5]

This assurance was given at the end of worrisome strikes in Belfast and Glasgow where shop stewards and others had lost none of their militancy. Even though the Labour Party and Trades Union Executive disavowed these "unauthorized" strikes, they elicited sympathy among the leaders of the Triple Alliance of Miners, Railwaymen, and Transport Workers, whose cooperation continued to improve during and immediately following the war. Alliance leaders secretly sympathized less because they approved the aims and tactics of the rebellious leaders, who villified them for their moderation, than out of shock at the intransigence and harsh reaction of the employers and the government. In the last analysis, however, these internecine arguments and conflicts in the labor movement partly canceled out the very considerable increase in membership of the party, the ILP, and the unions during the first quarter of 1919.

The industrial crisis started in the second half of January.[6] In Belfast 40,000 shipbuilding and engineering workers, unable to pry their employers loose from the 54-hour week, went on strike. In their drive for the forty-four-hour workweek they were joined instantly by the relatively small number of gas, electricity, and other public utility workers. As a result industry and public transport came to a complete standstill. For the first time in British history a great industrial center was on the verge of a general strike.[7]

---

[5] PD, 112 (February 11, 1919), cols. 60–1.
[6] "The outlook during the past fortnight has become rather dark. Strikes have been taking place all over the country . . . [for] the 47-hour week." Fortnightly Report on Revolutionary Organizations in the U.K. and Morale Abroad, No. 31 (January 28, 1919), GT 6713, Cabinet 24/74.
[7] Manchester Guardian and Daily News, January 29, 1919.

In the Clyde district, also, the leaders of the engineering and shipyard workers pressed for a forty-hour week, without reduction in take-home pay, for some three weeks before giving the strike signal. They claimed that they demanded the shorter week in order to absorb the 30,000 unemployed workers who had registered with the Glasgow Labour Exchanges by January 25. According to Neil MacLean, M.P. for Glasgow, "the workers knew from past and bitter experience what a large unemployed army meant to them, and they were determined to forestall any advantage being gained over them by the employers."[8]

Some 40,000 workers struck on January 27; within two days 100,000 were out. Under the leadership of William Gallacher, David Kirkwood, and Emanuel Shinwell large but orderly demonstrations were held in the center of Glasgow on Monday the twenty-seventh and Wednesday the twenty-ninth. During the second day of demonstrations an 11-man deputation waited on the Lord Provost. The delegates asked the Provost to inform the Prime Minister "that they wished the government to intervene with the employers in order to secure a reduction of the working hours to forty per week, without reduction in wages, so as to provide work for those who had been demobilized and were without employment." They also indicated that they would delay considering other methods until Friday, by which time the Provost promised to have a reply from London.

In its semiofficial reply the government refused to intervene, except to maintain law and order. It called on the public not to take an exaggerated view of the disturbances; emphasized that the number of strikers was very small compared with the total working population; and insisted that the chief point of the strikes was that "they were concerned not with getting better conditions, but were revolts against the authority of the men's unions." Three of the eleven spokesmen had no official connection with the trade unions and, as "everybody knew, there were certain men in this country who wanted a complete revolution of our social system, and who were endeavoring to make use of any unrest to help forward their views."[9]

Having decided on this rejoinder, which was disseminated through the press, the Cabinet turned to a consideration of the possible impact of the strikes in Glasgow and Belfast on the unrest seething in other parts of the country. In many cities, including in the capital, workers were rallying behind the forty-hour movement; strike talk was in the air, notably among 200,000 engineering workers in the London district. Also, the Miners' Federation was up in arms because the government seemed inclined to reject offhand its demand—presented on January 9—for full unemployment maintenance, a 30 per cent wage increase, the

[8] *Labour Leader,* February 13, 1919, 4.
[9] The Provost's telegram to London and the government's reply are cited in *Daily News* and *Morning Post,* January 31, 1919.

six-hour day, and nationalization of mines. In Hamilton, a suburb of Glasgow, even usually disciplined miners "paraded the streets, blocked the tram service, waved red flags, and sang the 'International.'" Local militants seemed in a mood to defy national trade union officials.[1]

On January 28 Sir Robert Horne, the Minister of Labour, still reassured the Cabinet that there was no need to be "unduly alarmist about the situation" and that a press campaign "laying stress on the unauthorized character of the strikes" would go far to steady the situation.[2] By the thirtieth, however, the government was no longer quite so sanguine that propaganda and caveats were all that was needed. Bonar Law "thought it vital for the War Cabinet to be satisfied that there was a sufficient force in Glasgow to prevent disorder and to protect those volunteers and others who would be made available to take over the operation of the generating stations and municipal services." He, for one, was "certain that if the movement in Glasgow grew, it would spread all over the country." Even though Churchill, the War Minister, cautioned against "exaggerating the seriousness of the disturbances," England having gone through equally dangerous strikes before the war and "the disaffected being in a minority," he agreed that precautionary measures were indicated. With the concurrence of Austen Chamberlain he stressed the importance of not showing the fist "in advance of public opinion." Churchill conceded that "there would have to be a conflict in order to clear the air." But the government should wait to take action until there was "plenty of provocation . . . and some glaring excess had been committed." Under those conditions, and after showing forbearance, the nation would rally and the troops "could be used more effectively." In any case, the Cabinet decided to post John Lamb, Assistant Under-Secretary of the Scottish Office, in Glasgow; to instruct the Lord Advocate to examine the "legal grounds for the arrest of ringleaders"; and to notify the Lord Provost and Sheriff of Lanarkshire to maintain electric light, to keep "the military in readiness to give their services when requested by civil authorities," and to take "firm, but not provocative action . . . to put down disorder."[3]

At noon the next day—Friday, January 31—a huge crowd assembled in George Square, in front of Glasgow's Municipal Building, waiting for their deputation to come out with London's answer.

> After some time a continuous roar was heard from the square, and when the windows were opened the crowd could be seen running from the square and the police using their baton on them.
> The deputation demanded to see the Lord Provost at once. He was still engaged. They denounced the batoning of the people in the square as a breach of faith, and left the building.

[1] *Manchester Guardian*, January 31, 1919.
[2] War Cabinet 521, January 28, 1919 (p.m.).
[3] War Cabinet 522, January 30, 1919 (p.m.).

As soon as he got outside Kirkwood was batonned down by a sergeant of police and carried unconscious into the Chambers. Gallacher had already been clubbed down from the place where he was speaking and was at the moment having his broken head dressed. . . . The Riot Act was read. . . . On appeals to the authorities Kirkwood and Gallacher were allowed to speak from the balcony and advised the crowd to march from the square to the Glasgow Green. This was done, but on the way further trouble broke out between the police and the strikers, the most sanguinary conflict of the day taking place just outside the Green. . . .

In the early hours of Saturday Councilor Shinwell was arrested at his home, the charge being incitement to riot, and since then several of the Strike Committee have been arrested on a similar charge. . . .

It looks as if the authorities were desirous of provoking a conflict. Late that night thousands of troops were rushed into the town. Machine guns are dominating the square and public places, rolls of barbed wire are in the municipal buildings, and several tanks are kept in readiness in the principal meat market. Glasgow is an armed camp; it has its army of occupation. . . . Meantime Kirkwood, Gallacher, Hopkins, Shinwell, and others are in prison, and have been refused bail. . . .[4]

The Cabinet did, indeed, take an extremely serious view of these events when it met that Friday afternoon. In the opinion of Robert Munro, Secretary for Scotland, it was "more clear than ever that it was a misnomer to call the situation in Glasgow a strike—it was a Bolshevist rising." Estimating "the malcontents at 10,000," he considered the outbreak to be of "limited dimension in number if not in effect" and was confident that "public opinion would support the Government in quelling any disorder." Major General C. F. Romer, of the War Office, promptly reported that "the necessary orders had been given to the G.O.C., Scotland, with regard to the movement of troops" and that about 12,000 men "could be put into Glasgow at short notice." As an additional precaution the Deputy Chief of the Imperial General Staff arranged for "6 tanks and 100 motor lorries with drivers to go north by rail that night."[5]

Hedged in by the firmness of the government, the obstinacy of the employers, the hostility of the press, and the disavowal by the trade union executives at the center the Clyde revolt collapsed by February 11.[6]

In many Labour circles the government was charged with merely

---

[4] "Prussianism in Glasgow," by Neil MacLean, M.P. (for the Govan Division of Glasgow, who was a participant observer) in *Labour Leader*, February 13, 1919, 4.
[5] War Cabinet 523, January 31, 1919 (p.m.).
[6] Of all the activists only Gallacher and Shinwell were given brief jail sentences for inciting to riot.

professing nonintervention but in actual fact abetting a strike-breaking counteraction. Certainly the "occupation" of Glasgow pointed in this direction. And so did such other maneuvers as the threat to arrest the strike committees of Belfast and Glasgow, the invocation of the Defense of the Realm Act, and the intimation that conscript soldiers would operate public utilities including the railways and the London subways. The *Herald* proclaimed that if "public services were so important that the government must maintain them at the cost of strike-breaking, then these services should be in the ownership of the public."[7]

Within the government the view gained ground that the strike in Glasgow was part of a studied revolutionary plot, particularly once the tubes and the buses were struck in London and the electricians threatened to go out as well. According to the Fortnightly Report on Revolutionary Organizations drafted by Basil H. Thomson and circulated to the Cabinet by the Home Secretary, "the plan of the revolutionary minority was to use the Clyde as the touchstone for a general strike and, if it proved successful, to bring out the engineers and the railways all over the country, to seize the food, and to achieve a revolution." Thomson claimed to know that during the disorders of Friday, January 31, "the intention was to seize the Municipal buildings in Glasgow."[8] Even before the flare-up in Belfast and Glasgow Curzon "was alarmed by the fact that no concerted action was being taken by the various Departments with regard to combating the spread of Bolshevism" in England. He proposed that instead of continuing to work "entirely on their own . . . a Minister without portfolio should be placed in charge of coordinating the activities of the different Departments."[9]

Curzon's suggestion, about which the Home Secretary was instructed to report to the War Cabinet, looked less alarmist in the light of current developments. While the idea of a Minister for anti-revolutionary activities was discarded, on February 4 the Cabinet accepted Curzon's alternate proposal to establish a permanent Committee "to take in hand not only the preparations and organization necessary to meet a strike, but also publicity and propaganda." On this same occasion, when it was also agreed that the army should be used to maintain order and, in extreme situations, to man essential services and industrial operations, Churchill reassured his colleagues that judging by the "great steadiness" of the troops in dealing with recent disturbances "the Government could depend on the loyalty of the Army."[1]

[7] February 15, 1919, p. 12.
[8] Report on Pacifism and Revolutionary Organizations in the U.K. and Morale Abroad, No. 31, January 28, 1919, G.T. 6713, Cabinet 24/74.
[9] War Cabinet 518, January 22, 1919 (noon).
[1] War Cabinet 525, February 4, 1919 (a.m.), Cabinet 23/9.

The newly appointed Industrial Unrest Committee[2] established subcommittees to deal with public utility services, protection, transport, communications, electric works, and the organization of road transport, while the Cabinet authorized the expenditure of "such sums as might be necessary to defray the cost of propaganda" by the Labour Department. Once this first strike wave was over, the Committee prepared for the eventuality of a strike by the Triple Alliance, formulated a "scheme of coal priority" for the event of a coal strike, and in conjunction with the general staff of the Home Forces decided on "the priority of services to be protected by the military."[3]

Meanwhile, since all these preparations and contingency plans were kept from public view, the Right suspected the government of lacking the resolve to meet the challenge. Consonant with the conspiratorial view of labor protests and strikes, it insisted that to minimize unemployment by the shorter work week was but the "nominal object . . . and one of those plausible pretexts." In truth the strikers in Belfast and Glasgow were "the unconscious instruments of a planned campaign, drawn up by 'intellectuals' in the background, who desire to emulate Lenin and Trotsky and the 'Spartacus' leaders in Germany." Here was an "attempt to open up the class war," and let no one suppose that "any sort of conciliation would put an end to the trouble."[4] Of course, the *Morning Post* simply blamed it all on a small band of revolutionaries, especially foreigners, and among these Jews from Eastern Europe were most dangerous![5]

All this time Lloyd George nervously watched this unrest from Paris.[6] Early in the second week of February he became particularly concerned about the unabated pressure from the miners, supported by

[2] Membership: the Home Secretary (Chairman), the President of the Board of Trade, the Minister of Labour, the Secretary for Scotland, and Representatives of the Admiralty and War Office.

[3] Explanatory Note to War Cabinet, Industrial Unrest Committee, Cabinet 27/59, and War Cabinet 528, February 6, 1919 (p.m.), Cabinet 23/9.

[4] *The Times* (London), February 1, 1919. Apparently this was the editorial which prompted Northcliffe to complain to Dawson, who was soon to be replaced by Steed as editor, that such one-sided interpretations did not take account of the social and economic roots of the unrest, including malpractices of employers. Whatever his personal and political reasons for this complaint, it was largely justified. *The History of the Times*, IV, Pt. I, 471-6. Obligingly, future editorials spoke of "the mischief done by the grudging and mean employer who tries to get around the terms of some agreement involving concessions that he does not like." *The Times* (London), February 14, 1919.

[5] *Morning Post*, February 1 and 5, 1919.

[6] The Prime Minister "referred . . . to the labour situation . . . and gave me the idea that he viewed the future with grave apprehension. . . . His elder daughter spoke of bringing her baby to London. He objected and said there might be riots and that the child had better stay where she was." Riddell: *Intimate Diary of the Peace Conference*, 21, February 8, 1919. "The Labour situation at home seems dangerous. There have been grave riots on the Clyde." Harold Nicolson: *Peacemaking 1919*, 257, February 4, 1919.

the entire Triple Alliance. The Clyde rebellion had been relatively easy to master, since the Trades Union Executive remained loyal to the government.[7] But it was altogether more risky to apply the same stern measures in a dispute with the miners who occupied such a central position in the T.U.C. Their refusal to go to the pits could paralyze the entire economy.

Sir Robert Horne, the Minister of Labour, with the encouragement of other Cabinet ministers, was disposed to be uncompromising. On February 10, he informed the miners' representatives that whereas the government—which still operated the mines—was prepared to grant a cost-of-living increment of one shilling daily, it could not meet the greater part of their demobilization claims. As for the broader questions of wages, hours, and nationalization, a committee of inquiry could be set up to look into them. Robert Smillie indicated that this counterproposal fell woefully short of his union's demands, but that he would nevertheless submit it to the Special Miners' Conference scheduled to meet in Southport on February 12 and 13. Since a month before, at a preliminary Miners' Conference, many of the delegates had been in a considerably more militant mood than their leaders, it was generally expected that the government would be rebuffed and strike action initiated.[8]

Lloyd George hurried to London on the tenth. That was the day that Commons convened to hear and to debate the King's Speech inaugurating the new Parliament. Soon after the Prime Minister rose to speak it was clear, however, that he had not rushed back either for ceremony or in order to present a systematic outline of his administration's domestic and foreign policy.

Lloyd George frankly conceded that these domestic disturbances were complicating peacemaking in Paris.

> Every morning before I went to the Peace Conference I had messages from London about a strike, and when I returned in the evening about another strike. . . . I do not mind saying it, I think it would have been to the advantage of the Peace Conference had I been able to remain there a few days longer.

Little was said about foreign affairs.

Nearly his entire address was devoted to a discussion of Britain's social unrest.[9] What he said was disorganized, diffuse, and repetitive. His associates had barely briefed him and word that the Clyde move-

---

[7] "Bonar Law thought that the Trade Union organization was the only thing between us and anarchy, and if the Trade Union organization was against us the position would be hopeless." War Cabinet 525, February 4, 1919 (a.m.).

[8] G. D. H. Cole: *Labour in the Coalmining Industry, 1914–1921* (Oxford: Clarendon; 1923), 70–2; and R. Page Arnot: *The Miners: Years of Struggle* (London: Allen and Unwin; 1953), 185.

[9] *PD, 112* (February 11, 1919), cols. 67–81.

ment had finally collapsed reached him only then. Moreover, he had to restrain the militants on both sides of the House and control the issues. Encouraged by the Clyde victory certain High Tories expected him to simply threaten more baton charges. On the other hand, Labour and trade union leaders impatiently awaited the announcement of constructive measures to head off further troubles. No wonder that during this speech, in which he improvised and straddled, Lloyd George felt, as he looked in front of him, that he was addressing a trade union congress and, when he turned around, that he was speaking to a chamber of commerce.[1]

In an effort to placate left-Liberal, Radical, and Labour opinion— as well as from personal conviction—Lloyd George began by stressing the genuine and legitimate causes and fears behind the unrest. But this conciliatory part of his speech was unconvincing. Without elaborating he merely promised to soon introduce bills "to deal with housing, with health, with the development and the transport of the country, the revival of rural life, with land settlement for soldiers and others, and with reclamation and afforestation." Even the moderate Labour M.P.'s were outraged. William Brace and J. H. Thomas promptly but unsuccessfully moved an amendment regretting "the absence of any mention of definite proposals for dealing with the present causes of industrial unrest and for securing, as regards wages and working hours, conditions of labour that will establish a higher standard of life and social well-being for the people."[2]

Lloyd George was more convincing when he turned to satisfy the "hard men," possibly because he wanted to lull them into leaving him a free hand. They were pleased to hear him say that labor disturbances were undermining the confidence of businessmen who were "essential to setting the wheels of industry and commerce going"; and that reducing hours without reducing wages would drive up the cost of British products, thereby endangering the vital export trade. Finally, the wage question was a national question, since no one could "consider individual trades without reference to their bearing on other trades." Miners take note.

Although Lloyd George acknowledged that there was room for negotiation, he did not bother to elaborate on guiding principles or terms. Instead, he defiantly declared that there would be no dealings with men who were seeking to destroy both trade unionism and the state, or who threatened to tie up vital industries.

> Any demand which is pressed forward with a view not to obtaining fair conditions, but with ulterior motives—to hold up and to overthrow the existing order and to destroy Government, relying not

---

[1] Riddell: *Intimate Diary*, 22, February 16, 1919.
[2] *PD, 112* (February 13, 1919), cols. 325–406. The amendment was defeated 311 to 59.

upon the justice of the claim, but the brute force which is behind it, then may I say as to that, in all solemnity, on behalf of the Government, we are determined to fight Prussianism in the industrial world as we fought it on the Continent of Europe with the whole might of the nation. . . . I am prepared to say with full knowledge that no section of the community, however powerful it may be, can or will be allowed to hold up the whole nation. . . .

The coalition Unionists were heartened by this forceful language. On the eve of the Miners' Conference "their" leader flung the gauntlet not only at Gallacher, who had already been defeated, but also at Robert Smillie.

If anything, this blunt threat galvanized the miners, who were now on notice that the government was preparing for a trial of strength. At their conference of February 12 and 13 they voted unanimously to reject Horne's counteroffer.[3] With equal enthusiasm the delegates voted that the entire membership of the Miners' Federation should be polled to determine whether or not to strike on March 15 if the government refused to meet their conditions (30 per cent wage boost, six-hour day, full maintenance, and nationalization). The Miners' Executive made no pretense of neutrality and the ballot was to be completed by February 22.

Horne wrote to Smillie in a last-ditch effort to head off this poll, but to no avail. The government, the Unionists, and the press then proceeded to agitate against the miners, above all soliciting public support with the warning that increased coal prices would ruin the nation.[4] Finally, on February 21—the day before the strike ballot was completed—Lloyd George invited the Miners' Executive to 10 Downing Street.

The Prime Minister now asked Smillie to postpone the strike deadline from mid-March to the thirty-first so as to enable a Royal Commission to make a thorough investigation and to put forth preliminary recommendations. At first Smillie demurred, but eventually he agreed to submit the P.M.'s request, which remained to be refined, to a special Miners' Conference scheduled for February 26.

On the twenty-fourth Lloyd George himself went to Westminster to

3 Except when otherwise indicated this discussion of the miners' crisis is based on Cole: *Coalmining Industry*, 70–90; and Arnot: *The Miners*, 182–202.

4 At this precise moment the Executive Committee of the Unionists instructed the speakers subcommittee to see "if any propaganda could be carried out to counteract industrial unrest." Within a month this subcommittee resolved "that it [was] absolutely vital to the interests of this country that a propaganda campaign should be undertaken by the Government to allay the present industrial unrest, and that they are prepared to give such assistance as the Government may think necessary." Still a month later a Unionist committee "was being formed in the House of Commons to coordinate the anti-Bolshevik propaganda . . . and conferred with various bodies reported to be conducting similar propaganda." National Unionist Association, Minute Book of the Executive Committee, February 12, March 11, and April 8, 1919.

move "a Bill to constitute a Commission to inquire into the position of and conditions prevailing in the Coal Industry."[5] In other words, this particular commission was to be chartered by Act of Parliament rather than by executive order. The Labour M.P.'s, in close consultation with Smillie, seized this opportunity to extract a guarantee against further delays. They suspected Lloyd George of playing for time: he probably wanted to build up coal inventories, to hold out until milder weather would cut coal consumption, and to prepare countermeasures.[6]

The Labourites stubbornly refused to agree to March 31 as the date for completion of the interim report even after the Prime Minister asked them not to "throw the whole of the industries of this country into confusion and disaster for the sake of 16 days."[7] At last the opposing parties settled on March 20, five days after the strike deadline.[8]

But Lloyd George did not come down until after additional pressure had been applied. When the results of the strike ballot were tabulated on February 24 they turned out to be even more dramatic than anticipated. Out of 720,246 votes, 615,164 were for the work stoppage and only 105,082 against, a decision of nearly six to one in favor of continued militancy. Moreover, J. H. Thomas ominously announced that in all likelihood the miners could count on support from other trades.

> No speeches of any kind will get over the fact . . . that the Miners' Federation have a mandate . . . to cease work unless their demands are conceded. . . . But it would be deceiving the House . . . if I did not also make it perfectly clear that there are other complications. The transport workers have definitely rejected the latest offer made to them. They have definitely refused . . . to allow the offer of 48 hours to go to arbitration and my own union [Railwaymen] are at the moment in negotiation. Tomorrow the Triple Alliance . . . meets to determine their action. No one can minimize the seriousness of the situation.
>
> I frankly recognize that the issue is this: If we have on the one hand a strike of these three great bodies, it will not only paralyze industry and may not only easily ruin the country, but even if we succeed by a strike we shall have defeated the State, and that is, after all, a very serious thing which I do not minimize for a moment. On the other hand, if we lose there may easily be a period of reaction and oppression for many years to come.[9]

[5] *PD,112* (February 24, 1919), col. 1441.
[6] *The Herald,* March 1, 1919. As early as February 10 the Industrial Unrest Committee began to build up stocks of coal by cutting down on exports, the Prime Minister agreeing that "it was important to have available every possible ounce of coal." War Cabinet 530, February 10, 1919 (a.m.).
[7] *PD,112* (February 24, 1919), col. 1449.
[8] *PD,112* (February 25, 1919), cols. 1705-7.
[9] *PD,112* (February 24, 1919), col. 1492.

And, in fact, when the leaders of the Triple Alliance met they vowed not to settle any industry-wide disputes without prior consultation and agreement among themselves. They decided, furthermore, not to participate in the National Industrial Conference, which was suggested by the National Alliance and had the full support of the Federation of British Industries. Opening on February 27 accompanied by great publicity, this joint conclave of employers and workers was supposed to formulate proposals for dealing with current industrial disorders. Even though Arthur Henderson lent his name and prestige to this enterprise, Smillie, Thomas, and Bevin boycotted it from the very start.[1]

On February 26 the Miners' Conference accepted the executive's recommendation to participate in a Royal Commission on condition that Labour be given adequate representation.[2] It also postponed the strike deadline to March 22, thereby leaving itself two days to weigh the interim report promised for the twentieth.

Labour secured fully half of the representation on the tripartite Coal Industry Commission. The Miners' Federation itself appointed Robert Smillie, Herbert Smith, Frank Hodges, and Sir Leo Chiozza Money; and by agreement with the government Sidney Webb and R. H. Tawney also were appointed to speak for the Labour side.[3] During the two weeks—March 4 to 17—that the commission held public hearings these six prominent men of the Left acted as if theirs was a mandate to put the capitalist system on trial. In their role of self-styled prosecutors they mercilessly exposed the inequities in the mining industry in particular and in capitalist enterprise in general. They asked for a stiff sentence: nationalization of the mines in addition to drastically improved conditions. For the entire labor world these widely publicized hearings turned into a shared catharsis, while the government gambled on them to act as a safety valve for pent up pressures and emotions.

Smillie and Webb captured the headlines and successfully kept the three coal-owners' representatives on the defensive. As expected, the management side was loath to admit to any of the charges of profiteering, labor exploitation, and technological obsolescence. It was left to the Chairman and the three government members of the Royal Commission to act as buffers and mediators, as best they could.

That Lloyd George was determined to appease the miners at the expense of the owners was never in doubt. Justice Sir John Sankey, the Chairman, was sympathetic to the cause of social reform and responsive to the Prime Minister's signals. Moreover, by appointing Arthur Balfour to be the ranking government spokesman, the P.M. kept open

[1] Eventually Henderson admitted that the recalcitrants had been right not to trust the Lloyd George government. See Mary Agnes Hamilton: *Arthur Henderson* (London: Heinemann; 1938), 211–15.
[2] Cole (ed.): *Beatrice Webb's Diaries,* 152, entry of February 28, 1919.
[3] See ibid., 147–52, entries of February 22 and 28, 1919.

to himself a channel of authoritative and direct intervention. All signs pointed to a compromise solution.

Not that the government was all that confident that the miners would accept an offer considerably short of their fourfold demand. To hedge against the possibility of a refusal the Ministry of Labour and the Home Office worked to split the Triple Alliance by trying to reach an accommodation with either the transport or the railway workers.

Moreover, the Home Army needed to be readied for the contingency of a deadlock. But notwithstanding Churchill's recent reassurances, could it be relied on to put down disorders stemming from industrial disputes? In any case, to make sure of the loyalty of the army for what could easily become a serious test of strength the War Office decided to check into the dispositions and feelings of the Home Forces.

All commanding Generals and Station Commanders were instructed to answer the following comprehensive circulars.[4]

Secret and Urgent. (Form Number).

(1) I am directed to request that until further notice, you will furnish information on the headings hereunder as regards the troops in your Area, and that you will arrange for a report to reach this Office *without fail* not later than first post each Thursday morning.

    (a) Will troops in various areas respond to orders for assistance to preserve the public peace;

    (b) Will they assist in strike breaking;

    (c) Will they parade for draft to overseas, especially to Russia;

    (d) What has been the effect of Army Order XIV of 1919 on the men; do they consider the policy of dividing the Army into the classes of demobilisables and non-demobilisables a sound one, and, if so, do they think that the line of cleavage has been equitably fixed; is there any dissatisfaction with either the principles or the details of that order; and, if so, what are your recommendations?

    (e) Any other information or suggestions.

(2) You will please give your own views for the information of the General Officer Commanding _____.

(3) You will, of course, understand that any material change in a situation and any cases of disorder or indiscipline are to be reported at once.

(4) The above is to be circulated to all Officers Commanding Stations, Formations, and units in the Area under your command,

---

4 Somehow the *Daily Herald* obtained these secret circulars and published them on May 13, 1919. When the next army estimates came before the House, Adamson read out these circulars and asked the War Secretary for a full explanation, touching off a heated debate. *PD, 116* (May 29, 1919), cols. 1470–1570.

and to save time you will please instruct Officers Commanding Stations to forward reports under the headings given above direct to these Headquarters attaching any report from an Officer Commanding Formation or Unit which is of importance. They will quote the above _____ number and mark the reports "Secret and Urgent."

(5) I am to add that the above is required with a view to the establishment of an efficient Intelligence Service, whereby the Army Council can keep its finger on the pulse of the troops, and that the information desired is required for the information of the Secretary of State.

(Sgd.) _____

For _____ Command.

1919.

To Station Commander, _____, No. _____ Area _____.

Will you please let me have the following information for the C.M.A. _____ Area as speedily as possible with regard to the Units on the Station under your command:—

(a) Whether there is any growth of Trade Unionism among them;

(b) The effect outside Trade Unions have on them;

(c) Whether any agitation from internal or external sources is affecting them;

(d) Whether any soldiers' councils have been formed;

(e) Whether any demobilisation troubles are occurring, and if so (i) what troops are demonstrating, (ii) the numbers involved, (iii) what their grievances are, (iv) what has been done.

(Sgd) _____

These circulars, which were meant to be kept secret, offer telling proof of the interplay of social unrest at home and the Russian Revolution abroad, certainly in the official mind.

Adamson, Wedgwood, Clynes, and MacLean berated the government for this distrust of trade unionists and for the contemplated use of military force in domestic affairs.[5] Churchill, for his part, tried his best to minimize the documents' political significance, characterizing them as routine military instructions drafted at a time of mutinies, strikes, and strike threats.

> There was a threatened railway strike, and the actual strike . . . all over the tube railways in London. There was a threatened strike of the electricians. . . . There were serious riots in Glasgow, which

[5] *PD, 116* (May 29, 1919), cols. 1470–7, 1498–1510, 1534–41. For a survey of reactions of prominent labor leaders see *Daily Herald,* May 14, 1919.

required the presence of a large number of troops. There was the threatened strike of the Triple Alliance. . . .

Given these circumstances the military authorities had the duty to find out "exactly what their troops would do, and also to know what their troops would not do." Naturally, the workmen had an "absolute right" to use their bargaining power. However, should vital services—light, water, electricity, transport, food distribution—affecting the "health, life and safety of large cities" be endangered, the state had an obligation to intervene. There was no question of strike-breaking; it was a matter of protecting the general public and welfare.

Churchill disclosed that the replies strongly confirmed that troops could be "relied on to assist the civil power to preserve the public peace and to protect persons and property." As for strike-breaking, most reports deprecated the use of troops for that purpose, the general feeling being "that it would not be fair to ask troops to do what they themselves would consider 'blackleg' work." Churchill went on to reassure the House that only volunteers were sent to Russia, the replies confirming that "troops would parade for drafts overseas, with the exception of Russia."[6]

Evidently the Home Army was not on the verge of mutiny. Even so, there was need for considerable caution. In all likelihood the qualified replies reinforced Lloyd George's inclination to be cautious not only with further direct armed intervention in Russia but also in his test of strength with the Triple Alliance.

The outcome of a by-election had this same effect. The West Leyton Division, a London suburb, went to the polls on March 1; but the results were not announced until the fourteenth. In the khaki election a coalition Unionist had carried this Division by 11,000 against 5,300 votes for A. E. Newbould, an Asquith Liberal. Now Newbould won by a majority of 2,000 votes against J. F. Mason, a High Tory who ran with the P.M.'s endorsement, in spite of having opposed his budget in 1909.[7] These returns were a portent; another came three weeks earlier, in a Liverpool Division, when the coalition majority had been whittled down from 6,000 to 1,400 by a Labour candidate. Lloyd George, who was back in Paris by now, eagerly seized on these straw votes to create more elbow room for himself and the coalition Liberals. He persuaded Bonar Law that it was imperative not to allow the intransigent Tories to obstruct essential industrial, social, and land reforms.[8]

[6] *PD, 116* (May 29, 1919), cols. 1510–18.

[7] *The Times* (London), March 15, 1919; and *Liberal Magazine,* April 1919, 137.

[8] Riddell: *Intimate Diary,* 38–3, entries of March 15 and 16, 1919. West Leyton was a middle- rather than working-class constituency which was the first to register its "suspicion that the people had been 'sold' into the hands of the strong reactionary element in the Government." *The Times* (London), March 15, 1919.

For Lloyd George the week of March 16 was critical at home and abroad. Whereas in domestic affairs Tory obstinacy threatened to bring about a break with organized labor, at the Peace Conference French intransigence aggravated instability in Central and Eastern Europe.

The Prime Minister was torn. The Cabinet wanted him in London, while the peacemakers wanted him in Paris. At home he was wanted to direct the final stage of the campaign to settle the explosive industrial crisis: the Sankey Report was due on March 20, the executives of the Triple Alliance were scheduled to meet on the twenty-first, and the miners' strike notice called for a decision by the twenty-second. On this occasion *The Times* spoke for the entire Establishment, including the government.

> Such is the program for the week, and it is unnecessary to empha-
> size the gravity of the crisis. Next week the nation and all its
> activities may be paralyzed. . . . We do not say that there will be a
> strike, but it is possible, if not probable, and it ought to be
> unthinkable. . . .

Lloyd George summoned Bonar Law to Paris for a strategy session.[9] After his return to London he stayed in close touch with the chief. He advised him that in Commons he proposed to accept the interim Sankey Report and to promise a report on nationalization within two months or so. But he also proposed to serve notice that since "miners and railwaymen are servants not of employers, but of the State . . . a strike would be against the State and that the State must win and must use all its power for that purpose, otherwise it would be the end of Government in this country." Should there nevertheless be a strike, he would seek legislative authorization for the government to confiscate strike funds and to arrest strike leaders. And in the event that Lloyd George's absence came under fire, he would say that he had his "full authority . . . to act in that way and shall so act."[1]

Presumably Lloyd George reasoned that the Conservative Leader, himself a businessman, would find it easier than he to sell the Sankey Report to the coalition Unionists; and in case of trouble he could always rush home dramatically to break a stalemate.

In any case, the P.M. chose to stay on in Paris to confront the High Tories of the Peace Conference, leaving it to Bonar Law to brave their counterparts in the Cabinet and in Commons. He was getting ready to start a concerted drive for a moderate and quick peace, also in the hope that "the Peace Conference would react on Labour."[2] On March 19, at Lloyd George's request, Wilson, Clemenceau, and Orlando sent him a letter, which was widely disseminated in England, requesting that he

[9] Bonar Law was in Paris on March 15–16, 1919.
[1] War Cabinet 548, March 20, 1919 (p.m.); and Robert Blake: *The Unknown Prime Minister* (London: Eyre and Spottiswoode; 1955), 413.
[2] Riddell: *Intimate Diary*, 36, entry of March 19, 1919.

stay on in Paris, a letter Clemenceau might not have signed quite so readily had he suspected the impending Fontainebleau offensive. In Britain this letter provoked the charge that the Prime Minister was trying "to play the old game of patriotism and the supremacy of foreign affairs."[3]

The Report of the Royal Commission was ready on March 20, the agreed date. Rather, three reports were ready, since the commission was hopelessly split: a Labour Report, a Management Report, and the Sankey Report signed by the Chairman and the three Government members. This last report steered a middle course between the other two. It recommended a reduction of the work day from eight to seven hours, with the six-hour day to follow in 1921, "subject to the economic position of the industry" at that time. It also proposed a wage increase of two shillings per day and the levy of one pence per ton (*circa* one million pounds per year) to be "applied to improve the housing and amenities of each particular colliery district." As for nationalization, it was to be the subject of a later report. Meanwhile, however, the government made a commitment by endorsing a key passage in the interim report: "Even upon the evidence already given, the present system of ownership and working in the coal industry stands condemned and some other system must be substituted for it, either nationalization or a method of unification by national purchase and/or by joint control."[4]

In the evening of March 20, following careful deliberation in the Cabinet, Bonar Law went to the House to announce that the government was ready to accept the Sankey Report "in the spirit as well as in the letter." He left no room for further concessions to the miners, except to fix the date for the nationalization report for mid-June. Quite the contrary. The Leader of the House backed up his concessions with the same tough language that Lloyd George had used on February 11.

> I wish to say that the Government has shown a desire to go to the utmost limits, to take the greatest risks. . . . But this, if the strike comes, will not be like an ordinary strike. . . . In the case both of the railways and the coal mines, the employers under present conditions are the State. It would, if it comes, be a strike against the community. . . . If such a strike comes the Government—and no Government could do otherwise—will use all the resources of the State without the smallest hesitation. . . . We shall use . . . all the resources of the State to win and to win quickly. This is not a threat. . . .[5]

But that is precisely what it was intended to be, and the Miners' Executive and Federation took it as such.

[3] Cole (ed.): *Beatrice Webb's Diaries, 155*, entry of March 20, 1919.
[4] Cited in Cole: *Coalmining Industry*, 86–7; and Arnot: *The Miners, 199–201*.
[5] *PD, 113* (March 20, 1919), cols. 2346–8.

Once again the unions deliberated in an atmosphere of intimidation. Apparently only the railwaymen were inclined to hold out for better terms, though they, too, yielded once the miners indicated that they would not assist them with funds in case of a strike. The Miners' Conference met on the twenty-first and instructed the Executive to make one last effort to extract additional concessions. Even though Smillie tried, he knew from the start that he would get nowhere. On March 26 he moved that the conference take another ballot of the entire membership to determine whether or not to accept the government's terms, each blank to be accompanied by a separate statement drafted by the Executive and urging an affirmative vote.

This second ballot was taken on April 9–10, a few days after the National Industrial Conference, with great fanfare, proposed that the maximum work week be fixed at 48 hours. Five days later the returns revealed that Lloyd George's improvised strategy had worked: 693,084 against 76,992 favored accepting Sankey's package. Ninety per cent of the membership voted, and the proportion for acceptance was nine to one. The strike notice was finally canceled on April 16.

Without a doubt Lloyd George was the victor. He had adroitly used both the carrot and the stick to keep labor in line during the great unrest of the first quarter of 1919. The carrot took the form of the interim Sankey concessions and the sweeping recommendations of the National Industrial Conference; the stick was the twice-repeated threat to call out armed soldiers either to suppress disorders or to operate vital industries, this threat owing its credibility to the Glasgow operation.

Even if at the height of the crisis the leaders of the Triple Alliance had known of the War Office's anxiety about the reliability of the Home Army they would not have been any less prudent. They were not revolutionaries bent on mounting barricades. They never as much as dreamt of staging a frontal assault either on the state or on capitalism. Smillie, Thomas, and Henderson were a mix of Eduard Bernstein, Samuel Gompers, and Woodrow Wilson, eager to settle for a partial fulfillment of their immediate, short-run demands. They were so little alienated from British society and politics that they quite naturally trusted Lloyd George's promise to push on with structural reforms in the course of postwar reconstruction. They never even asked themselves what would compel the Prime Minister to keep his word now that they were blunting their own strike weapon and Labour was still without adequate leverage in Commons.

Whereas until the end of March the forces of movement kept the Cabinet on the defensive, thereafter the forces of order seized the initiative. They were moved to action by Lloyd George's appeasement at home and abroad.

Domestically, even though the Sankey Report did not come close to meeting labor's demands, it conceded more than the Right considered either necessary or desirable; and it set a dangerous precedent. Above all, the Right was determined to contain reforms of wages and hours and to block structural changes of the sort contemplated for the second installment of the Coal Commission's Report. Lloyd George needed to be reminded that the Unionists were dominant in the Coalition, that they were not willing to dance to his reformist tunes, and that they meant to exercise the power—the disproportionate power—that they had extorted through the khaki election. And this was the time to speak up, because even granting the limited gains of the Triple Alliance, it had backed down as readily as the Unionists had predicted, thereby betraying its powerlessness and failure of nerve. J. H. Thomas anticipated this Tory response with his warning that if the industrial-action campaign failed, "there may easily be a period of reaction and oppression for many years."[6]

But Lloyd George's projected appeasement in foreign affairs also incited the jingoists and Conservatives. Reports of his switch to moderation toward both Germany and the Soviets stirred vitriolic Parliamentary debates and precipitated minatory telegrams. March 31 was a memorable day: the *Westminster Gazette* published an interview revealing the gist of the Fontainebleau thesis and the *Daily Herald* announced that the Conference was about to deal with Lenin on the basis of proposals brought back by Bullitt.

The P.M. himself leaked this information through friendly papers in the hope of building popular support for his new course. However, as fate would have it, this effort backfired. In the wake of the industrial crisis labor lacked the unity, strength, and enthusiasm effectively to push political action on his behalf. On the other hand, the coalition Unionists were vigorous and primed to take advantage of labor's disarray. Lloyd George's own right flank quickly resolved to use the news leaks as a pretext to open a concerted offensive against him.

All along the intransigents of the Coalition kept reminding the Prime Minister of his election pledges, notably of his pledge to demand the full cost of the war from Germany. Increasingly antagonistic questions were raised in Commons, by Lieutenant Colonel W. Guinness on February 13 and March 13,[7] and by Lieutenant Colonel Claude Lowther on March 17.

Lowther was a firebrand on this issue. Aroused by sinister rumors that the government was on the verge of an "economic *volte face*," he wanted to be assured that they had not "departed from the Prime Minister's electioneering pledge . . . that the whole of this war bill" would be presented. Even if Germany was in no position to begin pay-

---

6 See p. 615 above.
7 *PD, 112* (February 13, 1919), col. 265; and *PD, 113* (March 13, 1919), col. 1463.

ments at once, her assets should be hypothecated for at least 25 years. Lowther proclaimed that some 400 Members "were returned and pledged up to their eyes" on the question of indemnity.[8]

With Lloyd George in Paris it was left to Bonar Law to placate those of his own party members who were out for blood. He repeatedly took the line that British delegates on the Reparations Commission were under instructions to extract from Germany the largest amount she was *capable* of paying. Yet Lowther and his cabal of Colonels and Generals—Guinness, Martin Archer-Shee, H. C. Surtees, John Norton-Griffiths, and C. E. Yate—refused to take into account Germany's *capacity* to pay. They simply demanded that she be billed for the whole cost of the war, a position endorsed by the Federation of British Industries. His patience sorely tried, Bonar Law eventually retorted that although the victors could assert their right to the full cost, it was not the policy of the government "to make a demand which we know Germany in no circumstances can pay."[9]

Even the chief had never made such a forceful statement. In fact, perhaps Lowther should be excused for his calculated exaggerations because the Prime Minister himself had done nothing to counteract the extravagant expectations which had been built up during the general election.[1] On the contrary, his selection of economic advisers revealed that he was reluctant to show his hand. Whatever Bonar Law's influence may have been, it was Lloyd George who appointed Hughes, Cunliffe, and Sumner to the Reparations Commission. Although he subsequently feigned to have been astonished by their megalomania[2] he knew their real disposition from the very start. Only when these three threatened to trap him in a position which was unacceptable to the U.S. and to Germany, did he turn to more liberally inclined advisers like Keynes, Cecil, or Montagu. Whereas Cunliffe estimated that Germany could pay between 45 and 120 billion dollars over an unspecified number of years, Keynes leaned toward 10 to 15 billion payable over 25 to 30 years.[3]

In the absence of an expert consensus, Lloyd George's own economic sense as well as his political instincts made him opt for Keynes

[8] *PD, 113* (March 17, 1919), cols. 1870–2, 1878.
[9] Ibid., cols. 1875–8; and "Peace Aims" by the Federation of British Industries, February 18, 1919, G.T. 6854, Cabinet 24/75.
[1] "It seems that we are demanding indemnities, having undertaken last November to the Americans only to insist upon reparations. This is of course in consequence of the Prime Minister's election pledges, which he was practically forced to give, but the situation is awkward. . . ." Cecil Diary, February 15, 1919.
[2] David Lloyd George, *The Truth About the Peace Treaties,* I, 473–4.
[3] Baker: *Woodrow Wilson and World Settlement,* II, 280–1, 288. See also Paul Mantoux: *Les Délibérations du conseil des quatre,* I (March 26, 1919, a.m.; March 31, 1919, a.m.), 31, 86.

and Cecil, whose concern for the transfer problem he also shared. He nevertheless retained the *ultras* in their sensitive posts. After his return from London in early March he admitted to House that "he knew that Germany could not pay anything like the indemnity which the British and the French demanded." Even so, for political reasons he wanted the treaty to stipulate a large sum, "even if Germany could never pay it, or even if it had to be reduced later."[4] Within a few days not only Lloyd George but also Clemenceau claimed that their hands were tied by the expectations of their constituents.[5]

When Bonar Law came to Paris in mid-March to discuss the industrial crisis with Lloyd George, he took time out to deal with the reparations impasse. Apparently he proposed to Norman Davis that the Allies ask for 50 billion dollars from Germany, but that they accept payment in marks and privately intimate that she would not be expected to pay the full amount.[6] The American experts were unreceptive to this subterfuge. Nevertheless, Lloyd George returned to the attack. The very morning preceding his seclusion in Fontainebleau he told Lamont and Davis that even though he agreed with them as well as with Montagu and Keynes that 25 billion was the maximum Germany could pay, Cunliffe continued to hold out for 55 billion. He urged the Americans to convert Cunliffe and his colleagues to their view because he was afraid that he would "be crucified at home if his original experts were not also brought down to reasonable figures."[7]

There then followed the Fontainebleau memorandum in which Lloyd George steered clear of figures altogether, except to demand that the British Empire be awarded 30 per cent of any amount collected from Germany. Accordingly, he argued that Germany lacked the capacity to ever pay the full bill; that she should pay "an annual sum for a stated number of years"; and that, if possible, these years should end "with the generation which had made the War."

When on March 26 the Big Four touched on reparations in their general reappraisal, Lloyd George seemed somewhat braver.[8] He answered Loucheur's statement that if it were not for solemn promises to the electorate he would accept the American figures in exceptionally forceful language.

> It will be as difficult for me as for Mr. Clemenceau to dispel the current illusions about reparations. 400 Members of Parliament have sworn to extract from Germany every last penny she owes; I

[4] House Diary, March 6, 1919.
[5] Ibid., March 10, 1919.
[6] Ibid., March 16, 1919.
[7] Ibid., March 24, 1919.
[8] This discussion of the debate of March 26, 1919, is based on Mantoux: *Délibérations,*
  I, 26–30.

shall have to face them. But our duty is to serve our country for the best. If I am overthrown because I have not done the impossible, my successor, whoever he will be, can do no better, and if he makes extravagant promises without keeping them, within a year he will be declared crazy and we will be vindicated.

It is my conviction that the Germans will not sign the terms which are being envisaged. In their place I would not sign them. Germany will go over to Bolshevism. Europe will remain mobilized, our industries will be paralyzed, our states will go bankrupt and we can be held responsible for not having known how to make peace. We must decide to act with wisdom, regardless of what your opposition and ours think.

Wilson hastened to express his admiration "for the spirit" of these words: "there was nothing more honorable than to be chased from power for standing up for what is right."

The President went on to corroborate Lloyd George's arguments. The financial problem had to be looked at in political terms. Crushing economic penalties, say for 35 years, might throw Germany into Bolshevism. It was his belief that no Parliament on earth would dare oppose reasonable financial arrangements, provided the Big Four "took the trouble to explain them."

As a compromise Loucheur, Klotz, and Clemenceau proposed that the Conference proclaim its right to war damages; fix the "maximum and minimum amounts of the yearly annuities without designating a total figure"; and chart a commission—hopefully dominated by France —to work out this final figure. Whereas Clemenceau thought that public opinion would buy this solution Wilson held that it would reject it for leaving this vital question of the *number* of annuities, and hence of the total and final bill, unsettled.

Quick to withdraw from sacrificing his office to "what was right," Lloyd George saw the kinship between his own reparations guidelines, formulated at Fontainebleau, and those of the French Delegation. He welcomed the Klotz-Loucheur formula for promising to help the governments evade debates in their respective legislatures, where the irreconcilables set the tone.[9] He reiterated that "from the point of view of British domestic politics it was essential not to abandon the claim on the whole cost of the War while at the same time avowing that circumstances compelled the Allies to limit themselves to more moderate demands."[1]

But not only the British and French chiefs had to reckon with their conservative and jingoist constituencies. Wilson, also, was handicapped. Just as the British Prime Minister suspected that Keynes rather than Cunliffe was closest to the mark, so the American President sensed

[9] Mantoux: *Délibérations,* I (March 28, 1919, a.m.), 61.
[1] Mantoux: *Délibérations,* I (March 29, 1919), 83.

the intimate connection between Allied war debts owed to the U.S. and enemy reparations due to the Allies. As of December 1918 the British government intimated that an across-the-board cancellation of inter-Allied war debts would simplify the explosive reparations issue by enabling the Allies to reduce their claims on Germany. It would also hasten the financial rehabilitation of Europe and the world. But from the start, and without ever relenting, Wilson's economic advisers, the Treasury, and the business and financial communities—not to speak of Congress—voiced their implacable opposition to any review of these debts. Even though in private Wilson's experts must have pinpointed the connection between reparations and war debts as clearly as Cecil and Keynes, in committee they adamantly controverted it.[2] In any case, Lloyd George was the foremost victim of this politically conditioned American obstruction, since it closed off his last escape hatch.

At this point the offensive against appeasement was launched and, together with Bolshevism, reparations became one of the principal subjects for controversy by opposing loyalties.

It all started with an otherwise innocuous interview, attributed to a "High British Authority," in the *Westminster Gazette* of March 31. Moderation was the keystone of this article written by Sisley Huddleston, the Paris correspondent of this Asquithian daily. The article bristled with phrases that were the stock in trade of Wilsonians:

> ". . . there must be no *casus belli* left to Germany. . . . There must be no German irredenta . . . and Germany must receive no deadly wound in Poland. . . . We want a sane peace. . . . We have to face realities and prepare a practical treaty . . . whether it disappoints Allied peoples or not. . . . You cannot go on stripping Germany bare. . . . We must be moderate. . . . We shall, however, get something, and I think it will be something worth having, but certainly the question of indemnities, in the sense of going beyond the mere repairing of material damage, is not even posed. . . . Consider what would happen if we were not moderate. . . . A large occupation army for over thirty years . . . who is going to pay for this occupation? Where is the army coming from? . . . Are we going to keep up conscription for an indefinite period? . . . Certainly there will be some disappointments, but this is inevitable.[3]

Actually, Lloyd George and his principal advisers had made repeated efforts to have this moderation thesis disseminated, but the British pressmen in Paris were so brainwashed that they failed to pick

[2] See Lloyd George: *The Truth About Reparations and War Debts* (London: Heinemann; 1932), 100–6; and Bernard M. Baruch: *The Making of the Reparation and Economic Sections of the Treaty* (New York: Harper; 1920), 45–54.
[3] Cited in Sisley Huddleston: *Peace-Making at Paris* (London: Fisher Unwin; 1919), 149–53; *Morning Post*, April 19, 1919; *PD, 114* (April 2, 1919), cols. 1312–13.

up the cue at semiofficial briefings. Huddleston caught it only because he himself advocated a peace of reconciliation. The *Morning Post,* however, was irate. In a fit of self-righteousness it claimed that judging by internal evidence the anonymous High Authority quoted in the article was none other than the Prime Minister himself![4] Such was, indeed, the case. Lloyd George had given one of his many off-the-record interviews, which, in the midst of delicate diplomatic negotiations, normally were treated with discretion. Yet on this particular occasion this jingoist paper managed to attribute—intentionally or unintentionally—sinister intentions where there were none. The *Morning Post*'s own correspondent was present at the briefing, though unlike Huddleston he never saw the actual text of the Fontainebleau memorandum. In other words, the *Post* knew the official source but claimed to have identified it only by dexterous textual analysis. Anyway, its purpose was achieved: Lloyd George stood accused of going soft on both Germans and Bolsheviks behind the back of Parliament and the nation.[5]

Not surprisingly Lieutenant Colonel Claude Lowther eagerly took this indictment to the House of Commons.[6] He moved adjournment for the purpose of forcibly reminding the government of their sworn duty to the House, the country, and the man on the street to exact the uttermost farthing from the vanquished. He was fearful that the peace delegates were being swayed from their true course by nefarious influences. Notable among these were "international financiers . . . [and] professional moneygetters" whose greed for profit was compounded by other sins. These insidious profiteers were "anti-English Englishmen" who preferred to change their names—which were "often biblical"—and who as "far as Motherland and patriotism are concerned were pariahs."[7]

[4] *Morning Post,* April 1–2, 1919.
[5] For this episode see Huddleston: *Peace-Making at Paris,* 142–3, 155. When the full text of the Fountainebleau memorandum was first published three years later, Huddleston explicitly disclosed that "the bulk of my article—written a few days after the Lloyd George document was drawn up, and based upon the document whose very phrases are employed—came from the mouth of Mr. Lloyd George himself. Since now he desires it to be known that these were his views in 1919, he cannot complain of my confirmation . . . that it was no subordinate, but Mr. Lloyd George himself, who revealed in 1919 the secret of Mr. Lloyd George. He said these things to all who cared to listen and to understand, but few there were who chose to understand." *The Times* (London), April 3, 1922.
[6] In *Peace-Making at Paris,* 138 and 144, Huddleston states that Lowther was one of the politicians who at this time was urged by Northcliffe to take a stand before it was too late. There is no evidence to support this contention, except the P.M.'s insinuations, which cannot be trusted. Incidentally, Lowther needed no such prodding, having made himself heard in February and March. Moreover, even at the end of the Boer War he had advocated hypothecating the natural resources of the Transvaal in order to recover the cost of that war. See Ronald B. McCallum: *Public Opinion and the Last Peace* (London: Oxford; 1944), 45.
[7] *PD, 114* (April 2, 1919), cols. 1304–6.

Lowther considered both America and Wilson, though Anglo-Saxon and Protestant, to be equally subversive influences. It was high time to stop placating America and to resist the sway of "the higher philanthropy of that great philosopher President Wilson . . . who is also to bear with such perfect equanimity and such splendid fortitude the financial embarrassments of every country but his own."[8]

Lowther now repeated that even though Germany might be crippled momentarily, she was accountable for the whole cost of the war, and that "whatever we let her off at short of 20*s*. in the pound should be regarded as an act of grace on our part." As it was the British taxpayer and Exchequer were overburdened and overextended. Without full reparations and indemnities the situation would become worse still, since now the state was obligated to pay pensions and soldiers' benefits, to aid agriculture, and to subsidize "certain tottering industries." For Lowther, as for any Mercantilist-*cum*-Malthusian, the choice was simple: "if one of the two countries have to be in that intolerable financial position for 50 years, I pray God that that country may be Germany and not England." Of course, his trust in the power of prayer was short-lived; he believed in superior military power to coerce the recalcitrant Germans. Lowther left no doubt that he expected the Allies to prepare "a peace by dictation, and not a peace by negotiation."[9]

After Commander Sir Edward Nicholl (Cornwall, Penryn, and Falmouth) served notice that if the Prime Minister failed to "exact the uttermost amount of the bill" he [Nicholl] would resign his seat in Westminster, William Kennedy Jones (Hornsey, London) claimed the floor. It was he who explicitly based his charge that Paris was "dallying with the new idea of being moderate" on the Huddleston interview; he also played on the *Morning Post*'s contrived identification of the high and distinguished authority.[1] Kennedy Jones was outraged by the intimation, in the interview, that indemnities beyond the repair of material damages would be passed over. He yielded to no one in his certainty that Germany had the capacity to pay both kinds of damages —the full bill even beyond Cunliffe's estimates—and refused to be intimidated by the threat that an overburdened Germany would go Bolshevik. "What about Britain if the peace settlement fails to redeem the pledges of the Government; and leaves Britain with a depleted Treasury, staggering under the load of taxation twice as heavy as Germany?" Instead of constantly worrying about what Germany could tolerate, it would be more pertinent to inquire how much Britain could not bear.[2]

[8] Ibid., col. 1307.
[9] Ibid., cols. 1308–9.
[1] Ibid., cols. 1312–13.
[2] Ibid., cols. 1315–18.

Kennedy Jones and his colleagues did not worry about higher taxes as such. What concerned them was the political and social struggle attendant upon new tax legislation, with labor pressing for graduated and direct income levies. This connection between the social conflict at home and peacemaking in Paris was hinted at by Augustine Hailwood (Manchester, Ardwick), who reprimanded the government for "trying to appease the country by Socialist legislation" instead of with a stiff reparations bill.[3]

The Leader of the House did not really know how to go about quelling this mushrooming rebellion. Bonar Law was truly caught in the middle in that his own position was half-way between Lowther and Clemenceau on the one hand and the "Fontainebleau" Lloyd George on the other. He once again reminded Commons that even in the general election he and Lloyd George had stressed that there were limits to Germany's capacity to pay. He furthermore protested the constant slurs on Wilson, because Britain was determined to maintain close relations not only with France but also with America. Bonar Law was a quiet speaker; his answers were measured. His sober style was inappropriate for this emotion-charged session.

Finally, in anguish, Bonar Law made a disarming declaration which dramatized his own alienation from the metapolitics of his own backbenchers: "I have had the feeling that I am more out of sympathy with Members who support the Government on this subject [of reparations and indemnities] than on any other which has been raised. . . . *Our feelings and sentiments* on this subject are just as strong as those of any honorable Member who has spoken, and if we cannot come to the same conclusion it is simply because *our minds* will not allow us" [italics mine].[4] In a cable to Lloyd George in Paris he confessed that he just finished having a "bad time about indemnities." He knew he had convinced no one and that "probably nine out of ten of the Unionist Members at least were very disgusted."[5]

In no time both Lloyd George and Bonar Law discovered that this assessment was none too pessimistic. Dissatisfied with their Leader's statement the diehards cast about for another way of applying pressure on the P.M. in Paris. Either on his own or with coaching from Northcliffe, his former associate, Kennedy Jones conceived the idea of a minatory telegram to be signed by as many M.P.'s as possible and to be addressed to Lloyd George with maximum publicity.[6] Within twenty-four hours a task force of eight Members secured over 200 signatures for the wire that reached Paris on April 8.

[3] Ibid., col. 1333.
[4] Ibid., cols. 1333–4.
[5] Bonar Law to Lloyd George, April 3, 1919, cited in Blake: *The Unknown Prime Minister*, 407. See also Mantoux: *Délibérations*, I (April 5, 1919, a.m.), 152.
[6] Cf. Wickham Steed: *Through Thirty Years*, II, 320–1.

The greatest anxiety exists throughout the country at the persistent reports from Paris that the British delegates instead of formulating the complete financial claim of the Empire are merely considering what amount can be exacted from the enemy. This anxiety has been deepened by the statement of the Leader of the House on Wednesday last.

Our constituents have always expected—and still expect—that the first action of the Peace Delegates would be, as you repeatedly stated in your election speeches, to present the Bill in full, to make Germany acknowledge the debts and then to discuss ways and means of obtaining payment.

Although we have the utmost confidence in your intention to fulfill your pledges to the country, may we, as we have to meet innumerable inquiries from our constituents, have your assurance that you have in no way departed from your original intention.

During the following 48 hours the number of signers reached 370.[7]

On April 9 Bonar Law flew to Paris for urgent consultations with Lloyd George. Determined that this rebellion should not go unchallenged, they agreed to serve notice that they were "prepared at any moment to submit to the judgment of Parliament and, if necessary, of the country our efforts loyally to redeem our promises." They parted company, however, over the definition of these promises. Lloyd George looked for some way of signifying that he was not simply a dutiful delegate of the Unionist wing of the Coalition. He was anxious not to separate himself completely from the forces of reform without whose support his appeasement at home and abroad could never get off the ground. In a first draft of a reply, therefore, Lloyd George specified that he and his colleagues meant "to stand faithfully by all the pledges we gave to the constituencies in respect of *the peace terms and of the social program.*" Bonar Law, however, argued that the reference to electioneering pledges on social problems—which had remained vague, indeed—"would be unnecessarily provocative in the state of his party's mind at that moment." It was of more than passing symbolic significance that in this opening round of the right-wing counteraction the Prime Minister deferred, however reluctantly, to his coalition partner. For in his reply of April 9 he simply promised to stand by *"all the pledges* [italics mine]."[8]

---

[7] The eight initiators were Major Sir Edward F. Coates (Lewisham, West); Major Sir Edward A. Goulding (Worcester); Mr. Angus V. Hambro (Dorset, South); Mr. Percy A. Hurd (Somerset, Frome); Mr. W. Kennedy Jones (Hornsey, London); Mr. James R. Lonsdale (Armagh, Middletown); Lieutenant Colonel Claude Lowther (Lancashire, Lonsdale); and Lieutenant-Colonel W. E. G. A. Weigall (Lincolnshire, Horncastle). See the dispatch of the Parliamentary Correspondent of *The Times* (London), April 9, 1919. The text of the telegram is also cited in Lloyd George: *Truth,* I, p. 563.

[8] Both the preliminary and the final draft of this reply are cited in Lloyd George: *Truth,* I, 563–5. The wire was telephoned to one of the Prime Minister's private

While in Paris, Bonar Law also met with the British Delegation to discuss the indemnity issue. Except for Hughes, the entire delegation, including Cunliffe, supported Lloyd George's proposal that Britain seek a compromise which would include "pensions and separation allowances as well as all kinds of material damages, prisoners of war, etc." The Australian Premier alone held out for the "complete cost of the war," claiming that otherwise the Empire would be cheated. Bonar Law, fresh from London, conceded that "if he had to say to the House of Commons that he had abandoned the principle of the costs of the war, the position would be hopeless." Admittedly, the main advantage of Hughes's plan "was that it met the unbalanced view of the extremists in Great Britain." But the Unionist Leader thought that he could neutralize this extremist fringe if he could say that the Germans had been told "we think you ought to pay the whole costs and you must recognize this . . . [but] recognizing that you cannot pay the whole, you must pay on the categories that have been proposed." Even this concession failed to appease Hughes who "did not care two straws for what the U.S. said or did."[9]

The French Right also was on a campaign to force Clemenceau to give explicit assurances to Parliament. Raoul Péret, the Chairman of the Budget Committee, insisted that without information about the reparations settlement it was impossible to draft new tax legislation. Of course Péret as well as Franklin-Bouillon, the Chairman of the Foreign Affairs Committee, were pressing for the full bill. With Clemenceau refusing to come before the *chambre* the Right drew inspiration from the British Unionists. On April 10 a large group of senators sent a manifesto parallel to that of the 370, which was subsequently endorsed by 300 members of the Lower House. These French parliamentarians insisted that "the full cost of the war be charged to the enemy" and that the enemy be held accountable for "the reparation of damage to persons as well as to property."[1]

Moderates on both sides of the Channel were dismayed. The *Nation* charged that while Europe "hung, as by its eyelids, on the verge of complete anarchy, a band of distressed electioneers would give it a

---

secretaries who delivered it to Kennedy Jones. *The Times* (London), April 10, 1919. There is a curious entry in Riddell: *Intimate Diary*, 50, April 11, 1919: "L[loyd] G[eorge]: Kennedy Jones acted badly. The message he sent to me was not really in accordance with his instructions. B[onar] L[aw]: But the message was signed by four excellent men in addition to Kennedy Jones. He then went over the names, and without arguing the point clearly showed that he attached grave importance to the message. He went on to urge L. G. to return to England for a few days."

[9] Under such a plan a grand total of 11 billion pounds would have been collected over 50 years, with 5.1 billion going to France and 2.2 billion to the Empire. British Empire Delegation, 19A, April 11, 1919 (a.m.).

[1] Cited in *Daily Mail* (Paris) and *Le Matin*, April 11, 1919. See below, pp. 650 ff.

push into the abyss." The *Daily Express* characterized the wire as an outright "blackmailing message." Even Asquith declared that he had "no fancy for the [new] fashion of bombarding plenipotentiaries with a succession of minatory round robins from the lobbies of the House."[2]

In France it was left to the Socialist press to ring the alarm. According to the *Populaire,* in both Britain and France the Right was waking up to the danger of being cheated out of the fruits of victory and the two manifestoes were a function of a pronounced fear of mounting social unrest.[3]

Throughout the late winter and the early spring the British government's policy towards Soviet Russia also came under heavy attack. Left-wing criticism took the form of party and trade union protests against armed intervention. Most labor manifestoes combined these protests with demands for economic and social reforms. Of course, the role of the Labour and Radical press was decisive: it publicized these protests and independently stimulated disquiet over intervention. The entire cause benefitted immensely from the dissidents' success in fusing the anti-interventionist campaign with the emotion-laden drive against the extension of conscription. The Left argued convincingly that were it not for current and projected counterrevolutionary operations the end of conscription could be hastened.

Judging by the mutinies of early January and the Home Army circulars of February–March, this left-wing campaign was not altogether ineffectual. Although Labour lacked the strength to compel a withdrawal from the Russian Civil War, it wielded sufficient influence to deter the government from sharply increasing the number of British troops. Eventually the government yielded to this inflammatory protest against the use of further conscripts and issued a call for volunteers either to help maintain or to cover the withdrawal of its garrisons in Russia. Meanwhile economic, military, and technical aid to the Whites and to anti-Bolshevik border governments continued on a substantial scale.

The clamor for the intensification of British intervention, like the clamor for indemnities, was organized by the diehards. No member of the inner Cabinet even inclined to side with Lowther and Kennedy Jones on reparations. With regard to intervention, however, the diehards knew that in Churchill they had a spokesman at court.

On March 3, after affirming that in the future Britain's military establishment should never again become the same inadequate skeleton it had been before the war, Churchill reassured the House that the government had no intention of shirking its duty in Russia. British

2 *The Nation* (London), April 12, 1919, 33; *Daily Express,* April 10, 1919; and *The Times* (London), April 12, 1919.
3 *Le Populaire,* April 12–13, 1919.

troops in ice-locked Archangel and Murmansk—scheduled to stay on until late summer—would be "properly supported . . . and sustained with reinforcements necessary to their safety." In the extreme south, Britain had an army of "a moderate . . . but certain size"; the Batum-Baku railway was occupied "in some force"; a fleet of armed vessels of the Royal Navy controlled the Caspian; and Denikin's army—"the best of all the Russian armies now fighting against the Bolsheviks"—was being supplied with arms, ammunition, equipment, and military advisers. Naturally, "no special British interests of any sort were being served, not even in the Caucasus."

According to the War Minister, England was merely doing her share in the containment of Bolshevism sponsored by the Peace Conference in Paris. All the Allies were "in it to a certain extent, and all were in it with extreme reluctance." However unpleasant, the job needed to be done. It was one of the "most absurd conceptions" to suppose that a durable peace could be signed with "the greater part of Europe and Asia weltering in chaos and anarchy." By mounting this containment, which needed to be streamlined, the Allies were simply discharging a duty to the League of Nations which had to face up to this grave problem from the very start. The League was "on its trial," and His Majesty's Government, for one, were "not only lip-servers of the League of Nations idea."[4]

Sir Donald MacLean, the Independent Liberal leader, protested against the proposed strengthening of Britain's presence in Russia "by men, munitions, and money," stressing that throughout the country and in the army nothing was "causing graver unrest and anxiety" than this Russian policy. Lieutenant Colonel Guinness and Horatio Bottomley, however, were heartened by Churchill's report.[5]

On March 25 Churchill gave a second *tour d'horizon* of the situation in Russia. This time he started with the Baltic, where in addition to giving aid, especially to Estonia, Britain had ceased to obstruct the operations of Von der Goltz's forces, which were moving towards Windau and Riga. No doubt it was "a disadvantage to somewhat increase German influence in this district." But it was worth this price: Von der Goltz was saving the Baltic provinces from being ravaged by Bolshevik terror.

Further south, as a result of the revolution in Budapest and the pressure on Odessa, Rumania was in particularly acute danger. In advance of the debates in Paris Churchill expressed the "hope and trust

---

[4] *PD, 113* (March 3, 1919), cols. 80–6, 179–82. "Winston was in a rather bad temper having had his head washed, I suspect, by the P.M. for making rather an indiscreet speech in the House of Commons. Moreover, he is mad to intervene in Russia and destroy Bolshevism—a foolish proposal, at any rate at this time of day. . . ." Cecil Diary, March 9, 1919.

[5] *PD, 113* (March 3, 1919), cols. 88–102.

that energetic efforts would be made to succour Rumania, which [had become] the great buttress of our fortunes in that part of the world against the advancing tide of Bolshevik anarchy and terror." Meanwhile Britain was continuing her broad-scale support to both Denikin and Kolchak, except that no additional British troops were being involved.[6]

Since there were no signs of a cutback in intervention, Sidney Arnold (Yorkshire, West Riding, Penistone) and Vernon Hartshorn (Glamorgan, Ogmore) decided to move an amendment to the pending Service Bill precluding service by conscripts in Russia, except for those already there.[7] They argued that unless the government gave this formal guarantee, opposition to the temporary extension of conscription would continue rising.

Churchill was determined to stand his ground. He was perfectly agreeable to explaining once again "that it was not the intention of the Government to use this Bill for the purpose of *raising great armies* of conscripts" for service in *"the heart* of Russia." But he could not accept any formal limitations on the use of the army, which had to remain "free to go anywhere and to do anything." Twice he reiterated that he did not contemplate using these forces "during this year of anxiety" in either the Russian or the industrial sphere (italics mine).[8]

Colonel Wedgwood was quick to point out that the informal guarantee tendered by Churchill was deliberately limited. Since the Minister only committed the government not to send *large* conscript armies, he probably envisaged the dispatch of small units. Furthermore, by merely excluding service in the *heart* of Russia, he reserved his position on armed military support to the border states.[9] That the Left opposition was hopelessly isolated in Commons was evident when the restrictive amendment was defeated by 281 against 48 votes.[1]

Even so, Churchill was on his guard. In early April, instead of sending conscripts to reinforce the British garrisons in northern Russia, Churchill raised 4,000 volunteers for this purpose.[2] At the same time, in an effort to legitimize continuing intervention against the Red pestilence, the government issued a propaganda broadside. In an official 88-page White Book it gave a lurid exposé of the atrocities perpetrated by the Soviet regime, based on reports to the Foreign Office from British officials and citizens who had recently come out of Russia. This publication bristled with inflammatory captions: Insanity, Massacre and Infant Nationalization; Nationalization of Women and Chil-

[6] *PD, 114* (March 25, 1919), cols. 370–4.
[7] *PD, 114* (March 26, 1919), cols. 473–7, 489.
[8] Ibid., cols. 483–8.
[9] Ibid., cols 489–92.
[1] Ibid., cols. 493–4.
[2] *The Times* (London), April 4 and 9, 1919.

dren; Bolshevik Torture and Brutality; Pillage and Torture; and Bolshevik Orgies.[3]

At this juncture the *Daily Herald* carried two dispatches from George Lansbury in Paris about the return of an American mission from Russia with a reasonable offer from Lenin.[4] On April 2, in the midst of the indemnity debate, Lieutenant Colonel Sir Samuel Hoare (Chelsea) inquired whether the British government had been advised of this mission and whether it was true that Lenin's offer was "meeting with a favorable reception with certain highly placed persons in Paris?" Having been given advance notice of this question, Bonar Law took the precaution of telephoning the Prime Minister in Paris. Hence, he now replied with full authority and without qualification that he had "today telephoned to the Prime Minister, that he also knew nothing about it" and that therefore he did not think it necessary "to say more on that subject."[5]

But of course this denial could not squash the fast-flying rumors about the Bullitt Mission, Lenin's offer, and the excited discussion of this offer in Anglo-American circles.[6] In no time the advocates of intervention resumed their assault. A. Clement Edwards (East Ham, South) moved adjournment in order to discuss "something which is alleged to be taking place at the Peace Conference." Notwithstanding the Leader's statement he knew "without fear of contradiction" that Bullitt and Steffens had been to Russia; had conferred with top Bolshevik leaders, including Lenin; and had returned with proposals which provided for the recognition of the Bolshevik government. Edwards warned that "the vast majority" of the House of Commons would repudiate "the plenipotentiaries who recognized a regime whose wicked cruelty" had just been exposed in an official White Book.

> If there is to be formal recognition in response to these overtures . . . what are you going to say if Bolshevism lifts its ugly head in this country! [An Hon. Member: "It is doing it now!"] . . . If you are going to give formal recognition to it in Russia as a sort of short way out of the difficulty, you are simply going to bring anarchy, revolution and red ruin on the whole of the civilized communities of the world.

[3] *Bolshevism in Russia or Revolutionary Socialism in Practice,* Cmd. 8, London, April 1919. "Yesterday it was announced that more troops were to be sent to Russia. This morning the Government produced a White Paper of 88 pages on Bolshevik atrocities. The connection is not difficult to see." *Daily Herald,* April 4, 1919.
[4] *Daily Herald,* March 31 and April 1, 1919. Lansbury seems to have seen Lloyd George as well as House and Wilson on more than one occasion.
[5] *PD, 114* (April 2, 1919), cols. 1327–30, 1334.
[6] "Mr. Bonar Law's denial . . . has caused a lot of surprise here. For in Paris it is an open secret that Bullett [sic] and Lincoln Steffens brought back . . . not, indeed, a draft treaty, but a message of the terms which the Soviet Government would accept as a basis of negotiations if they were proposed." Lansbury writing in *Daily Herald,* April 3, 1919. Within ten days Lansbury reported the actual terms of the Lenin-Bullitt proposal.

Instead of temporizing with the "pestilential evil of Bolshevism," the Allies should "stamp it out at all costs." As a first step they should help General Yudenich capture and hold Petrograd by providing the food and supplies he was asking for.[7]

Edward's motion was seconded by Brigadier General Henry Page Croft, who was as alarmed now as he had been at the time of Prinkipo. In his view the "achievements of Bolshevism in Russia . . . made the achievements of . . . the Huns in the war pale into insignificance." Should the Allies recognize Lenin, "the forces of disorder" in Britain would receive a major boost; and the "moral force of the Government in dealing with the Bolshevik peril . . . would be tremendously weakened." No, the Conference could have no truck with murderers and villains. Page Croft suggested that "this House could send a message this evening to the Prime Minister in Paris" so as to strengthen his hands and enable him to say "to any tempter . . . that this country will not betray the whole of history and her faith."[8]

Lieutenant Colonel Guinness was even fiercer than Page Croft. For him, as for so many rabid anti-Bolsheviks, the White Paper was a godsend. He declared that he would "far rather have a German Emperor ruling in England than international Socialism under the auspices of Bronstein, alias *Trotsky.*" At least the German Emperor had women and children murdered by bullets or shells; the Bolsheviks, for their part, called on "Chinese executioners to saw asunder their victims and to gouge out their eyes before they finally put them out of their misery." Almost in the same breath he urged that with the help of the blockade Bolshevism should be allowed to burn itself out, even though such a policy was both "slow and cruel." It was only because they were starving that the Bolsheviks were making their present overtures. Of course, Guinness had no objection to feeding Russia on condition that "you send an army . . . to see that the food goes to those people who are starving." Meanwhile, he endorsed the suggestion to send another telegram to the Prime Minister.[9]

But the peak of this debate was not reached until Horatio Bottomley was heard from. On this occasion he did not even stop short of Red-baiting Lloyd George: he claimed to need "a lot of convincing" that the Prime Minister of England was not a Bolshevik and that he had no sympathy with them. He insinuated that Lloyd George was under the spell not only of Lenin but also of Wilson.

> If pressure was being brought upon the Peace Conference to entertain these [Bullitt] proposals, it was coming from some wild, airy, idealistic element in the Conference which, under the guise of great ideals and altruism . . . was keeping a keen eye all the time

[7] *PD, 114* (April 9, 1919), cols. 2141–50.
[8] Ibid., cols. 2150–4.
[9] Ibid., cols. 2154–2159.

upon the material benefits which will go to those countries farthest away from Europe when the trouble comes. . . . I say that if President Wilson is a party to that or if he is for one moment sympathetically considering such a suggestion, the sooner he goes back to America and takes the opinion of the American people, whom he does not represent today, the better for the peace of the world.

Bottomley sided with those who were first and foremost concerned about the domestic consequences of diplomatic relations with Lenin. Rather than caution Lloyd George in a telegram, he called on Members to express their determination to go even so far "as to oppose this Government, and, if need be, . . . [to] resign our seats, and go back to our constituencies, rather than have any part in recognizing this Bolshevik regime."[1]

Both Wedgwood[2] and J. H. Thomas could always be relied on to jump to the defense of Wilson. In the face of this onslaught they tried to stand up for the Prime Minister without, however, making much of an impression.[3]

With Bonar Law on his flying visit to Paris to confer on the indemnity issue, Mr. Edward Shortt, the Home Secretary, spoke for the government. Given his office it was perhaps natural that he should begin by touching on certain domestic aspects of Bolshevism. After complementing the House for not harboring "a single Bolshevik sympathizer" at a time when Bolsheviks were active throughout the nation, he gave reassurance that the undercover agents who were feeding on the current industrial unrest were being tracked down and "carefully watched." He wanted the House to know that "every single day that passes I sign a certain number of orders getting rid of some of them" by deportation or arrest.

Having matched his own anxiety about internal subversion with Bottomley's, the Home Secretary moved on to the heart of the question. Yes, two American gentlemen had recently returned from Russia; but he did not know whether or not they brought back definitive proposals from Lenin. On the basis of his latest information from Paris he could say with certainty that there were no such proposals before the British Delegation. Just the same, Shortt promised "to convey to the P.M. the undoubted fact that the unanimous feeling of the House was in favor of this Resolution" urging the government not to appease Lenin.[4]

Even though Edwards then withdrew his motion[5] the diehards

---

[1] PD, 114 (April 9, 1918), cols. 2161–6.
[2] Some ten days before Wedgwood had unsuccessfully asked for debate of a motion calling for the withdrawal of troops and the blockade from Russia at the earliest possible moment. PD, 114 (March 31, 1919), col. 855.
[3] PD, 114 (April 9, 1919), cols. 2154, 2167–70.
[4] Ibid., cols. 2173–77.
[5] Ibid., col. 2182.

resolved to go forward with the wire first proposed by Page Croft. That evening this telegram went out, asking the Prime Minister to decline to agree to any recognition of the Bolshevik government. This second minatory memorial in less than forty-eight hours gathered over 200 signatures in a matter of five hours.[6]

To what extent should Lloyd George have permitted himself to be influenced by this pressure from the majority of the House? As he contemplated whether or not to persist in his appeasement course he must have wished that the victory of the Unionist wing of his Coalition had been less complete in the last general election.

Of course, Lloyd George could still look for support outside Parliament. With the peak of the industrial crisis passed, Labour began to turn its attention to foreign policy issues, in part to cover up its less-than-spectacular gains in the domestic field. Also, a campaign against intervention in Russia promised to generate useful ideological energy and to provide a convenient rallying point. And last, even though the labor leaders, almost to a man, were anti-Bolshevik, they realized that the overthrow of the Soviet regime would inevitably encourage the British Right to press its counteraction still further. The fear of this counteraction motivated them quite as much as self-confidence in their own strength and cause.

Whatever the reasons, labor's campaign against intervention got its real start during the first half of April. On the first of the month the Labour Party's Advisory Committee on International Questions urged the Executive Committee to press for the immediate raising of the blockade of, and the conclusion of peace with, Soviet Russia.[7] Three days later Smillie startled the Joint National Labour Conference, which convened in London's Central Hall to support a Wilsonian peace. In the name of the Miners' Federation he asked this conference to call upon the government to take steps immediately "to withdraw all British troops from Russia; to raise the blockade; to withdraw the Bill now before Parliament for the conscription of men for further military service; and forthwith to release all conscientious objectors." Significantly, Ben Turner and Robert Williams rose to second and support this resolution, which was unanimously adopted. But Smillie, fresh from his recent confrontation, knew that the government would not be cowed by paper resolutions, however impressive the list of signatories. It would respond only to votes in Commons or to industrial action. Hence both he and the Executive of the Labour Party approached

---

[6] *The Times* (London), April 10, 1919.

[7] Labour Party, Advisory Committee on International Questions, Minutes and Agenda, 1918–20, meeting of April 1, 1919. Present for this meeting: J. L. Stocks; A. E. Zimmern; G. D. H. Cole; D. Burns; Pethick-Lawrence; C. P. Buxton; L. S. Woolf, and Mrs. Cole. The resolution also called for an inquiry into the government's relations with capitalist companies in Russia and for permission for the British Cooperative Movement to open up trade with its Soviet counterpart.

the Parliamentary Committee of the Trades Union Congress with the suggestion that the political and the trade union leaders meet to agree on measures for the implementation of the miners' resolution.[8] At the same time the *Daily Herald* proclaimed that "resolutions and protests were not enough"; asked "what will Labour *do, not say?";* and enjoined its readers to "Act, Don't Talk!"[9]

On April 16 the Miners' Federation and the Triple Alliance met in Southport to wrap up the first round of industrial unrest. After formally accepting the Sankey compromise and withdrawing the strike notice, the Miners' Conference by acclamation approved Smillie's omnibus resolution on Russia, conscription, and the blockade. It also instructed its executive to put the matter before the Triple Alliance that evening. In turn, the executive of the Triple Alliance resolved to ask the Trades Union Congress to convene, at the earliest possible date, a special national conference of the trade union movement "to decide what action, if any, should be taken in order to compel the Government to comply with any, or all, of the terms" of Smillie's resolution.[1]

In other words, having exhausted the strike threat with some measure of success in the industrial field, the leaders of the Triple Alliance proceeded to advocate its use for political ends. The Parliamentary Committee of the T.U.C., however, was firmly controlled by moderate trade unionists who vigorously and successfully thwarted concerted industrial action in support of such unmistakably political demands as the withdrawal from Russia.[2]

This opening phase of the "Hands Off Russia" campaign coincided with another by-election, this one in Central Hull on March 29. In this Yorkshire port, which was still depressed by the blockade, the Unionists suffered their most dramatic upset. Their candidate, Sir Eustace Percy, was roundly defeated by Lieutenant Commander J. M. Kenworthy, a courageous and fiercely independent Asquith Liberal who criticized government policy root and branch. Kenworthy explicitly came out against conscription, intervention in Russia, the blockade, a hard peace with Germany, coercion in Ireland and tariffs. As an act of solidarity, Newbould, the recent victor in West Leyton, came to give him a helping hand.

The political world was stunned to learn, on April 10, that for the first time in its history Central Hull had elected a Liberal. Admittedly, the margin of Kenworthy's victory was a slim 917 votes. But the startling fact was that in the khaki election a coalition Unionist—Sir Mark Sykes—had carried this division with a majority of 10,371 votes,

8 *Daily Herald,* April 5, 1919.
9 *Daily Herald,* April 8 and 9, 1919.
1 *Daily Herald,* April 17, 1919.
2 See Alan Bullock: *The Life and Times of Ernest Bevin* (London: Heinemann; 1960), I, 103–5.

so that in less than four months the Unionist vote had shrunk by 6,106 votes while that of the Independent Liberals had jumped by 5,182. Such a quick and far-reaching reversal was unprecedented in recent by-elections. Perhaps if this defeat had stood by itself it might have been considered a freak; in the event, however, it came on the heels of Liverpool and West Leyton.[3]

Immediately following the declaration of the poll Kenworthy claimed it as a victory for "a clean and just peace" and as a warning to Lloyd George not to allow himself "to be bullied" by the 370 reactionaries who had signed the indemnity telegram.[4] According to the *Daily Herald* Kenworthy "went out wholeheartedly for a Wilson peace —and the people of Hull went after him." For the *Labour Leader* "Liverpool was the black cloud, West Leyton the thunder clap, and Central Hull the deluge."[5]

But was this exultation justified? *The Times* and the *Daily Mail* ascribed the upset to rising popular impatience with the government's vacillating and irresolute policies in Paris as well as at home. Actually, since there was no Labour candidate in the field,[6] the voters could express their protest against the ins only by voting for Kenworthy. Perhaps, then, Central Hull was not so much a vote for Kenworthy, whose ideas were considerably more advanced than those of Asquith and his followers, as simply a typical reaction against a government whose achievements were incommensurate with popular needs and expectations.

That the Independent Liberals were not radical dissenters was amply confirmed on April 11, when Sir Walter Runciman gave a dinner for Asquith and Sir Donald MacLean at the Connought Rooms. Kenworthy had hurried to London in time to transform this testimonial dinner into a victory celebration. On this occasion Asquith gave a speech full of empty phrases and stilted shibboleths, and almost completely free of criticism of the government. "Even those of us who hoped for a vigorous support for the Liberalism of President Wilson, against French reaction, who object to the starving of the women and children of Eastern and Central Europe, who loathe the idea of Churchill's new war against the social revolution abroad, there was in Mr. Asquith's speech no word of hope." It was this fatuous speech which drove Colonel Josiah Wedgwood finally to sever even his nominal tie with the Liberal Party and to formally join the ILP.[7]

---

[3] For the fullest coverage and analysis of this by-election see *The Times* (London), April 12, 1919.
[4] Cited in *The Times* (London), April 12, 1919.
[5] *Daily Herald*, April 12, 1919; and *Labour Leader*, April 17, 1919.
[6] Presently the Labour Executive decided to contest future by-elections; and an ILP candidate ran unsuccessfully in Central Abardeen on April 16. Labour Party: Minutes of the Executive Committee, April 2, 1919.
[7] For Wedgwood's letter to the Secretary of the ILP see *Daily Mail*, April 17, 1919.

But even assuming Wedgwood's disaffection and Labour's in-cipient "Hands Off Russia" campaign exemplified an upswelling popular revolt against Lowtherism, this revolt was still too embryonic, possibly even too ephemeral, for Lloyd George to build upon.

The Prime Minister was under strong pressure from Bonar Law and other cabinet colleagues to hurry back to London in order personally and publicly to confront his Unionist detractors in Commons. Before leaving Paris he told Wilson, Clemenceau, and Orlando, half in jest, that in case the House refused him a vote of confidence they would have to resume negotiations with either Lord Northcliffe or Horatio Bottomley.[8]

On the occasion of his arrival in England an editorial in *The Times* conveniently summarized the three major issues on which the Unionists were waiting to be reassured: Russia, reparations, and French security. Of these three they attached greatest importance to Russia. This leading article was particularly significant: it was Steed's first piece after taking over the editorship from Dawson.[9] The *Daily Mail* and the *Morning Post* gave Lloyd George similar instructions, except that theirs were insultingly peremptory. According to Lloyd George himself, it was in London that he "found that the unrest was not confined to the question of Reparations, but that it had been worked up because of the time occupied by the Conference in making peace, and more particularly because of my attitude towards the Bolshevik Government in Russia."[1]

On April 16, in the House, the Prime Minister led off with a justification for the allegedly slow pace of the peace negotiations.[2] He argued that given the scope of the peacemaking assignment it was astounding that the negotiations progressed as rapidly as they did. In fact, the only reason why the Big Four could afford such a quick pace was because should they make any serious mistakes they could rely on the League of Nations to readjust and correct them in the future. Thus rather than wasting time, as the self-styled realists charged, the drafting of the Covenant was acually saving some.

If the Big Four were rushing their labors it was primarily because throughout Central and Eastern Europe there was a close race between peace and anarchy.

> In many lands the foundations of society [were] crumbling into
> dust. . . . The gaunt specter of hunger was stalking [about]. . . .
> The Central Powers and Russia were lying prostrate, broken, and all
> these movements of Spartacists and Bolsheviks, and revolutionaries
> in each of these countries were more like the convulsions of a

---

[8] Mantoux: *Délibérations*, I (April 11, 1919, a.m.), 223–4.
[9] *The Times* (London), April 16, 1919; and *The History of the Times*, IV, Pt I, 499.
[1] Lloyd George: *Truth*, I, 564–5, 568.
[2] For the full text of this speech see *PD*, *114* (April 16, 1919), cols. 2936–56; for substantial excerpts see Lloyd George: *Truth*, I, 565–76.

broken-backed creature, crushed in a savage conflict. It was in these conditions and with these materials that [the Big Four] were making peace. . . .

At the same time, the collapse of three old empires left a legacy of mutually antagonistic small states whose borders were extremely difficult to fix. Lloyd George, for one, did not mind confessing that he had never heard of Teschen, clearly implying that if he were less ignorant of such places the pace of negotiations could be quickened.

Next Lloyd George turned to Russia, which unfortunately had ceased to exist as one nation subject to one central authority.

> Russia is just like a volcano; it is still in fierce eruption, and the best you can do is to provide security for those who are dwelling on its remotest and most accessible slopes, and arrest the devastating flow of lava, so that it shall not scorch other lands.

From the beginning, then, the Prime Minister publicly reaffirmed his commitment to containment. At the same time he assured the House that recognition was out of the question and that it had "never been discussed."

On the other hand, there were compelling reasons for not intervening. Of overarching importance was the fundamental and age-old principle of British foreign policy "never to interfere in the internal affairs of another country, however badly governed, . . . to impose any form of government."

In addition there were important practical considerations. History showed that Russia was "very easy to invade but very difficult to conquer, and easy to get into but very hard to get out of." Direct armed intervention would require a gigantic military campaign, for which no one was prepared to provide the troops. And assuming Russia were conquered, an occupation army would have to stay on at an exorbitant cost, which would hasten England's bankruptcy.

Of course, Britain and her Allies could not abandon Denikin and Kolchak, who had been their faithful allies during the war. By supplying them with material and financial aid—not with men—Britain was not departing from the principle of nonintervention. She was merely helping Russia's own sons redeem their country.

Simultaneously the "flow of lava" was being arrested by a *cordon sanitaire* stretching from the Baltic to the Black Sea. The Allies recognized their obligation to defend their Allies, notably the new states, along Russia's periphery against attack; they were also supplying "the necessary equipment to set up a real barrier against invasion by force of arms."

As for the matter of a mission, "men of all nationalities" were going to and coming from Russia all the time. Even though the British Delegation had had "no approaches of any sort," he had heard reports that others had received proposals which they assumed to be authentic. In particular, "some young American" was said to have returned with "communications." However, apparently even President Wilson did not attach any value to these, otherwise he "would have brought them before the Conference, and he certainly did not do so."[3]

Judging by the time he devoted to the Russian question, Lloyd George, in agreement with *The Times,* considered it more critical than the indemnity issue, with which he concluded his reply. After a perfunctory assurance that he stood by all his election pledges, he made a meek attempt to show that these were compatible with appeasement. Accordingly England wanted "a just and stern but not a vindictive peace, so as not to create a legitimate sense of wrong . . ., excite national pride needlessly . . . [and] soil this triumph of right by indulging in the angry passions of the moment." Yet the Prime Minister did not go beyond these broad generalizations. Neither did he so much as allude to the interview in the *Westminster Gazette.*

Instead of taking the House Members into his confidence by sharing with them the apprehensions which weighed on his mind, he chose to divert them with a savage assault on the purported instigator of the telegram of 370. No, he did not object to the telegram as such. But he did take the strongest exception to the "reliable source" that provided the information which had prompted it. Shifting his eyes back and forth between Kennedy Jones and Lowther he claimed that through his own sources of information he had learned the identity of that reliable source.[4] It was the same source that last November had issued model peace terms. Whereas at the time, rather than refer to indemnities or the Kaiser's trial, it had advocated support for Wilson,[5] now it "must have everything . . . and hysterically attacks all those great ideals." Moreover, whereas a few weeks before that same source had charged the government with trying to frighten the working classes with the Bolshevik bogey, today Bolshevism ceased to be a mere bogey and was "a monster . . . [which] I am doing my best to dress up as an angel."

---

[3] Technically Lloyd George gave a correct account: the British Delegation had not *officially* received proposals of any sort, and President Wilson did not put Lenin's offer to Bullitt before the Conference. On the other hand, the Prime Minister covered up Britain's role in the preparation and transport of the Bullitt Mission as well as his breakfast with Bullitt after the latter's return to Paris. See pp. 471–2 above.

[4] Since international wires were still subject to government control, Lloyd George may have been advised of the exchange of telegrams between Northcliffe and Kennedy Jones preceding the minatory manifesto of 370. It remains an open question whether this intelligence supported the accusation that Northcliffe had initiated this exchange and instigated the remonstrance. Needless to say, Kennedy Jones and Lowther hid behind the *Westminster Gazette* interview without acknowledging any contact with Northcliffe. Cf. *PD, 114* (April 16, 1919), cols. 2951, 3004–5; Steed: *Thirty Years,* II, 320–1; Huddleston: *Peace-Making at Paris,* 137–8.

[5] See pp. 82–4 above.

No, that source was anything but "reliable," it was "here today, jumping there tomorrow, and there the next day." Lloyd George, for one, preferred to rely on a "grasshopper." Much damage was being done to the cause of Allied unity by the "diseased vanity" by which the *Times* had become "merely a three penny edition of the *Daily Mail.*"

This dramatic assault on Northcliffe, combined with the reassurance that Russian Bolshevism was being contained actively, disarmed the Parliamentary rebels. In the ensuing debate nothing further was said about indemnities. Especially Kennedy Jones and Lowther were put on the defensive. As for Edwards, Hoare, and Guinness, they could no longer rant about the danger of recognizing Lenin. All Edwards could do was to renew his plea for material aid for the drive on Petrograd, while the other two now shifted to clamoring for the recognition of Kolchak.[6]

Not surprisingly, the left opposition took comfort from the P.M.'s spectacular foray against the *ultras*. To be sure, Adamson and Wedgwood still criticized the government's Russian policy, in particular the recent dispatch of reinforcements to northern Russia. Otherwise, however, they as well as Kenworthy closed ranks around the Prime Minister, Kenworthy in the hope of bolstering his own inclination to cooperate with Wilson, if need be at the price of separating himself from the Lowther wing of his own Coalition.[7]

In the press the reaction to the Prime Minister's speech was considerably less restrained and polite.[8] The best *The Times* could say was that as a result of the telegram Lloyd George might begin "to play a straight game in Paris." On balance, however, Commons had been treated to an apologia of "half-truths and palliatives, *suppressio veri* and *suggestio falsi*, false analogies and cheap rhetorical effects." No one had ever called for a huge army to conquer Russia, and if the P.M. were really serious about containment, why discourage the Poles by denying them Danzig? As for Teschen, "every body had heard of it who knew the later history of Maria Theresa, Frederick II, and Catherine II, and who knew the origin of Russian influence in Germany, or who knew the beginnings of the French Revolutionary War." The *Daily Mail* also credited the 370 for putting Lloyd George on the carpet while at the same time charging him with maligning the Northcliffe press in order to avoid giving solid information. With biting sarcasm the *Morning Post* asked why Lloyd George denied that the Allies were intervening in Russia's internal affairs when, in fact, they were intervening all over the place? Along with *The Times,* this organ of superpatriotism urged that the territorial demands of Poland and

---

[6] *PD,114* (April 16, 1919), cols. 2960–1, 2986, 2996.

[7] Ibid., cols. 2956–60, 2971–84, 2989–93.

[8] Whereas the Parliamentary "Opposition collapsed utterly . . . the disaffected press did not entirely cease to grumble." Lloyd George: *Truth*, I, 576–7.

Czechoslovakia be satisfied as an encouragement in their battle against Bolshevism. Curiously enough, not one of these three hostile papers as much as mentioned indemnities.[9]

Even the *Daily News,* in the opposite camp, concurred that except for denouncing Northcliffe's mob appeals, Lloyd George had "told them nothing at all." Similarly, the *Labour Leader* condemned the "soap-box oration" which misled the nation by avoiding issues, raising irrelevant matters, and slaying imaginary dragons. The Prime Minister had merely won "a temporary triumph and postponed the day of reckoning." Only the *Daily Herald* was a trifle more charitable. Claiming to read between the lines, it suggested that Lloyd George knew what was right but was hesitant to implement his program. This being the case, it was up to Labour to apply pressure by "vote, resolution, action" to compel the Prime Minister to act in line with his innermost convictions.[1]

---

[9] *The Times* (London), April 17, 1919; *Daily Mail* (London), April 17, 1919; *Morning Post,* April 19, 1919.

[1] *Daily News,* April 17, 1919; *Labour Leader,* April 24, 1919; *Daily Herald,* April 18, 1919.

19

Intrusion of
Politics: France

CLEMENCEAU himself made the shocking admission that in many ways
France had won only a Pyrrhic victory. He conjectured that in a
relatively short time defeated Germany would be in a substantially
stronger and healthier condition than victor France—demographically,
industrially, commercially, and financially. Even in the short run Germany had the edge. Her factories were intact, ready to resume production; and her war debt was internal rather than external, and therefore
relatively easy to liquidate by fiscal and monetary manipulation.[1]

Especially those politicians and generals whose faith in the old
diplomacy and the balancing of power had not been shaken engaged in
this conventional but crude capability analysis. To a man the French
Delegation assumed that unless Germany were dealt with severely
France's decline as a major power could not be arrested. Whereas
Germany's sinews of power, including her unity and central location,
remained essentially unimpaired, the erosion of French power was
compounded by the disappearance of the vital Russian counterpoise.

Of the Western Allies France paid by far the highest price for
victory in men, in property damage, and in financial outlay. Out of
close to 8.5 million metropolitan Frenchmen called to the colors, 1.3
made the supreme sacrifice. An addition 2.8 million were more or less
severely wounded, and of these 600,000 were permanently disabled.
During the war the birth rate was cut in half; and on account of the
high casualty rate among young men the recovery of the birth rate was
likely to be slow.

It was fatal that both the battlefields and the occupied territories
were located in the nation's most highly industrialized basins. As a

1 Interview with an Associated Press correspondent, cited in *l'Action Française*,
    February 10, 1919.

result some 230,000 private and industrial structures were completely razed; 350,000 were partially destroyed; and 6,000 kilometers of railway were laid waste. In agriculture there was a savage loss of animal stock: one million horses, 2.5 million head of cattle, and 7 million sheep. Not surprisingly, compared to 1913 (100 per cent), in 1919 industrial production stood at 60 per cent and agricultural output at 70 per cent.

Actual physical damage was estimated to fall somewhere between 130 and 160 billion gold francs. In addition, France lost her very considerable loans to and investments in Russia. Moreover, she had to liquidate gold stocks and foreign securities and contract vast inter-Allied loans in order to finance essential imports. Internally, meanwhile, the war was financed by defense bonds and inflation, not by taxes. While internal and external borrowing combined amounted to 300 billion gold francs, by 1918 the wholesale price index (1913:100) had risen to 353.

The chief obstacles to sound war financing were political and administrative. The conservative *sénat* and *chambre* were reluctant and slow to vote essential income and surplus profit taxes, and once a modest income tax was passed in late July 1917, it was loosely enforced. In 1918 revenue covered only one eighth of the total budget.

In 1919 government expenditures barely receded due to new obligations and programs: pension payments for war widows and next of kin, disability pay for the wounded, separation allowances for veterans, reconstruction of liberated areas, reparations for the *sinistrés,* wheat subsidies, and interest payments on the national and foreign debt. Even so, for obvious political reasons, tax reform was postponed until after the national elections, which were delayed until November 1919.

As a result during the first year of peace the budgetary disequilibrium worsened, the wholesale price index climbed to 423, and the foreign exchange value of the franc was cut in half.[2] This economic and fiscal crisis was at the root of labor unrest as well as of the campaign for *"réparation intégrale."*

The high cost of living combined with the fear of unemployment contributed substantially to the radicalization of the French Left in the spring and summer of 1919. Between October 1918 and mid-April 1919 the membership of the SFIO rose from 34,000 to 57,150; by the end of the year it reached 133,000. The big surge in the CGT came in

[2] This sketch of the cost, financing, and economic legacy of the French war effort is based on Charles Gide and William Oualid: *Le Bilan de la guerre pour la France* (Paris: Presses Universitaires; 1931), *passim;* Georges Lachapelle: *Les Finances de la III*ème *République* (Paris: Flammarion; 1937), 90–5; William F. Ogburn and William Jaffé: *The Economic Development of Post-War France: A Survey of Production* (New York: Columbia University Press; 1929), 93–5; Robert M. Haig: *The Public Finances of Post-War France* (New York: Columbia University Press; 1929), 23–50; Germain Martin: *Les Finances publiques de la France et la fortune privée, 1914–1925* (Paris: Payot; 1925), 133–5, 322–3.

the spring, and by midyear the 1.5-million mark was in sight. Most of the recruits were youthful, either discharged young veterans or boys of draft age.

But the *élan* of the Left was not a function of this injection of youth as such. This ferment was a composite of revulsion against the horrors of war, antimilitarism, antijingoism, distrust of Social Patriotism, disappointment with the fruits of victory, enthusiasm for the Russian Revolution, and pro-Wilsonianism.

Naturally enough, moderates like Renaudel and Jouhaux continued to lose ground. Even the ex-*minoritaires* were subjected to constant pressure from the far Left to keep proving their militancy in both word and action. Although this extreme Left was hopelessly outnumbered, Longuet and Merrheim were at all times responsive to the revolutionary pronouncements of Fernand Loriot and Pierre Monatte.[3]

By not taking any effective measures to check runaway inflation[4] and by not even bothering to promise social and economic reforms for the postwar era both the government and the Right helped to spur the Socialist and labor rebellion.[5] This confrontation between Right and Left soon centered around the tax issue.

Precisely because the Clemenceau administration put off submitting a budget in order to avoid the tax issue, it had to ask Parliament periodically for piecemeal appropriations. And every time it made such a request both the left Radical Socialists and the Socialists exploited the occasion to try and force the cabinet to unfold its fiscal and economic intentions. In turn Clemenceau steadfastly thwarted these efforts out of regard for the Center and Right which clamored for both the fiscal *status quo* and a Draconian peace, in particular for extortionate reparations.

Whenever the government was challenged to formulate and unveil its economic and financial policies the Minister of Finance countered with a stock phrase which soon became a popular slogan: *"l'Allemagne payera."* All the time Klotz wanted it understood that German reparations were the key to rehabilitation, reconstruction, and, in time, social reforms. As of early December he declared that instead of preparing a budget he would devote himself to drawing up a list of restitutions and reparations to be exacted from the enemy. "If, thereafter, it should become evident that new taxes were absolutely necessary and that the

---

[3] For the most thoroughly documented analysis of this radicalization see Annie Kriegel: *Aux Origines du parti communiste français, 1914–1920,* 2 vols. (Paris: Mouton; 1964), *passim.* Less complete data and interpretations can be gleaned from Edouard Dolléans: *Histoire du Mouvement ouvrier,* II, 1871–1920 (Paris: Armand Colin; 1953), 283–6; and Paul Louis: *Histoire du Socialisme en France* (5th ed., Paris: Marcel Rivière; 1950), 355–7.

[4] *JO,* February 11–14 and 19, 1919, 509–20, 549–62, 585–95, 623–33, 717–39.

[5] See the special issue which *l'Humanité* devoted to the campaign against *la vie chère* on March 2, 1919.

French people had to tax itself further either by direct or indirect taxes," he would then introduce appropriate legislation. Meanwhile, however, he refused to "reverse the order of precedence" between reparations and taxes.[6]

Whereas the Right fanatically approved this order of priorities, the Left refused to be taken in. Even the Radical Socialist members of the Budget Commission insisted that quite apart from the cost of the war, the yearly postwar budget would level out in the neighborhood of 18 billion francs, or nearly three times the prewar figure. Surely the existing tax structure could not carry this increased load; nor could reparations close this large gap. The Radical Socialists urged Clemenceau and Klotz to give consideration to new taxes and additional inter-Allied loans while at the same time completing the bill to be presented to Germany.[7] As for the Socialists, they were considerably more radical with their demand that the government stop deceiving itself as well as the public. In order to balance the budget, even without providing for essential social reforms, exceptional—if not revolutionary—fiscal measures were mandatory. It was Marcel Sembat, of the very moderate center faction in the SFIO, who first prescribed a 25 per cent capital levy. And it was he who repeatedly warned in the Budget Commission that, judging by past history, an economic crisis could be set off by a breakdown in the fiscal structure, and that mounting deficits combined with tax entanglements were known to have played a singularly decisive role in past revolutionary situations.[8]

Straightway the *Temps* upbraided the Socialists for letting Germany off lightly in the hope of capitalizing on France's economic hemorrhage for their own party purposes.[9] Léon Daudet used this same argument, of course with considerably greater heat:

> As royalists and men of order, but above all as patriots, we want Germany to pay because we want neither a revolution nor Bolshevism in France. Sembat and his friends want France instead of Germany to pay because they want . . . a social revolution, either Bolshevik or para-Bolshevik, which, this time, would cause the end of France and of civilization.

His intimate collaborator, Charles Maurras, even made a virtue of necessity: this dire need to collect two to three billion francs from the enemy promised to foster the recovery of France's battered moral unity. "Let necessity be blessed" and Frenchmen should not have to pay "one *sou* more" than before the criminal attack in 1914.[1]

On February 18, Klotz testified before a joint meeting of the

[6] *JO*, December 3, 1918, 3236.
[7] *L'Humanité*, February 7, 1919; and *Journal des Débats*, February 15 and 20, 1919.
[8] Marcel Sembat writing in *l'Humanité*, February 7 and 13, 1919.
[9] *Le Temps*, February 14, 1919.
[1] *L'Acton Française*, February 9 and 18–19, 1919.

Budget and Finance Commissions. He once again swore to demand the full cost from Germany; he also committed the government to an attempt to secure priority payment for certain French claims. This time, however, he expanded somewhat on the relationship of reparations and taxes. He still vowed only to collect from the taxpayer that which would be indispensable to balance the budget. Klotz also assured the deputies that he did not plan to increase the income tax, primarily because it had been raised during the war! But then he dropped a bombshell: to help cover the deficit the government expected to ask for a "capital levy whose payment would be spaced out over a good many years."[2] He did not elaborate either on the base or the rate of this proposed levy.

Both Parliament and the press instantly were up in arms. The *sénat* was altogether scandalized. In the *chambre* even most of the Radical Socialists balked. Although they were inclined to concede the need for additional tax revenue they meant to raise it through indirect consumer taxes and not through direct levies on either income or capital.[3] Alfred Capus was distressed because now that the blood tax had been paid, a money tax was in the offing; and he urged Klotz to reduce "the capitalists' shivers" by at least outlining his intentions in greater detail. Meanwhile he should remember that France's claims on Germany could serve as collateral for big foreign loans.[4]

Within ten days the Budget Commission, under the chairmanship of the temperate Radical Socialist Raoul Péret, formally commented on Klotz's testimony. According to an official communiqué, its members unanimously agreed that even under the best of circumstances the budget could not be balanced without additional taxes. But since a capital levy was not the answer, the government should at once examine and propose other sources of revenue. Meanwhile, in order to check the dangerous price spiral the paper presses should be slowed down. Furthermore, the government should seek Allied credits on the basis of France's reparations claims, to be fixed at the earliest possible moment.[5] With the enthusiastic endorsement of *Figaro* and the *Temps* the Finance and the Foreign Affairs Commissions of the Senate were not nearly so accommodating. In a terse announcement they not only rejected the capital levy; they also insisted that consideration of new taxes be deferred until after Germany's debt was established, stressing the urgency of securing an immediate and sizeable down payment.[6]

On March 7 the *chambre* plunged into its first full-scale financial

2 Cited in *le Figaro*, February 19, 1919.
3 See L. Marcellin: *Politique et Politiciens d'après guerre* (Paris: Renaissance du Livre; 1922 [?]), 75, entry of February 27, 1919.
4 *Le Figaro*, February 19 and 25, 1919.
5 The full text of this communiqué is cited in *le Temps*, March 1, 1919.
6 For the text of the Senate communiqué as well as for editorial comment see *le Figaro*, March 1, 1919; and *le Temps*, March 2, 1919.

debate. Speaking for the Budget and Finance Commissions, Péret reiterated some of the major points of his recent communiqué. He began by confessing that he was deeply troubled about the inflation, urging that unless the government promptly arranged for inter-Allied loans the monetary inflation would get out of hand. With regard to the capital levy, he reiterated that in addition to being confiscatory it discouraged enterprise and investment. But rather than develop an acceptable tax program Péret spoke vaguely about a financial and economic League of Nations whose first act would be to float loans, Germany's debt to the Allies to serve as collateral. On this score he seemed to speak for the Radical Socialist Party which had just discovered a new panacea: rather than face up to the tax problem, its spokesmen pointed to fresh inter-Allied loans as the road to both immediate and long-term salvation.[7]

Then it was the turn of the SFIO's foremost expert on public finance, Vincent Auriol, to deliver a hard-hitting attack on the cabinet's do-nothing attitude. At the outset he agreed that France had suffered more than Germany and that Germany *"doit réparer ces dévastations intégralement."* But since even the government conceded that it would be some time before substantial payments could be collected, there was need for interim arrangements. Surely deficit financing and defense bonds were not the answer. As for Allied loans to be hypothecated on reparations, the exchequer was already burdened with both the principal and the interest charges of the gigantic wartime loans. And last, Klotz's talk about new taxes was unconvincing because to this day he had failed to enforce the collection of those taxes which were on the books, notably the surplus profit and income taxes.

According to Auriol, when all was said and done the Minister of Finance continued to bank exclusively on German reparations. Klotz knew only too well that in 1919 the deficit would amount to eight to ten billion. And yet he made believe that "in addition to paying reparations, Germany could balance our budget and pay our bonds." To stubbornly fall back on these reparations was "worse than madness, it was *un bluff misérable."*

Come what may, the 18 billion budget could not be covered without an active tax policy. The surplus profit and income taxes needed to be streamlined and enforced; and a capital levy was unavoidable. In conclusion Auriol emphasized that this budget of 18 billion did not even provide for those essential social reforms which could not be put off much longer. Nor did it provide for the large military establishment that would be needed should the League be stillborn. In that event, with due allowance for the rapidly spiraling cost

[7] *JO*, March 7 and 12, 1057–62, 1135–42; *Bulletin du Parti Républicain Radical et Radical Socialiste,* March 8, 1919; Marcellin: *Politique et Politiciens d'après guerre,* 77, entry of March 8, 1919.

of modern armaments, another eight to ten billion would have to be added.[8]

In his answer Klotz refused to make any concession; he also avoided any reference to his earlier capital-levy proposal.

> I have the duty to tell you in plain language—because it is the policy of the entire Government—that no financial sacrifice will be asked from this nation before the basis of the enemy's indebtedness has been established. . . . At this time the Government concentrates all its attention and vigilance . . . on our claims against the enemy. . . . Our country is entitled to *une réparation intégrale*.

Klotz called for a straightforward vote of confidence after claiming credit, without giving particulars, for initiating a project to establish a financial section in the League.[9]

For the Socialists, Lafont censured the Minister for again deceiving the public for purely electoral purposes, while Péret pleaded that at a minimum he should concede that at some future date the government might have to turn to the French taxpayer.[1] To no avail. The votes were tallied and 243 deputies loyally upheld the government. Only 108 negative votes were cast, of which 89 were Socialist. Even Péret dared go no further than abstain, in company with a substantial faction of Radical Socialists.[2] Incidentally, many of them abstained less because they differed with the government than because Clemenceau and his administration treated them so cavalierly.[3]

The right-wing press still was not satisfied. The *Temps* took Péret to task for not being more explicit and more forthright in his repudiation of the capital levy. By merely mentioning it, Klotz had shaken the capital market; the financial community denounced it as a concession to the theory of class conflict and as evidence of creeping Socialism. Besides, *in extremis* German and not French capital should be confiscated. Klotz, for his part, was guilty of not making it crystal clear that nothing further would be asked of the French taxpayer. The principle of the enemy's absolute responsibility for the full cost of the war had to be asserted once and for all. And last, as an exponent of fiscal soundness, the *Temps* asked the government to balance the budget by cutting public expenditures, though for the moment it preferred the "gout" of inflation to the "amputation" of capital levies.[4] Alfred Capus also warned that unless France received concrete proof "of the fertility of victory" she would be confronted with the most "tragic economic

---

[8] *JO*, March 7, 1919, 1062–71. See also Frossard's editorial in *le Populaire*, March 10, 1919.
[9] *JO*, March 13, 1919, 1161–7.
[1] Ibid., 1173–4.
[2] Ibid., 1174.
[3] Cf. E. Beau de Loménie: *Les Responsabilités des dynasties bourgeoises* (Paris: Editions Denoël; 1947), III, 127–8.
[4] *Le Temps*, March 9, 13, and 15, 1919.

and financial difficulties." Foreign loans and French enterprise, without vast reparations, could not head off this crisis.[5]

Not surprisingly the *Action Française* was least satisfied with the course and outcome of this debate. Péret as well as Klotz failed to recognize the war for what it really had been: a monumental people's war and not a conventional war among states. As a result both focused on material damages to the exclusion of "the personal losses" suffered by the soldiers, which should be compensated in the form of the *part du combattant*. At the same time yesterday's defeatists and today's Bolsheviks were savagely attacking the just and inspiring aphorism that *le boche doit et peut tout payer* as part of their campaign to undermine popular faith in the "fertility and richness of victory." They, too, realized that the destiny of France was "rigorously, directly, and immediately dependent on the political, economic, and financial exploitation of her military triumph."[6]

If anything, this conservative and jingoist criticism encouraged Klotz to persist in his provisional and makeshift fiscal course. Since the first quarter of 1919 was due to expire on March 31, the government needed legislative approval for the regular budget for the second quarter and also for the much larger extraordinary budget for military and emergency expenditures for those same three months. But even though the Clemenceau administration came prepared with a careful itemization of anticipated expenditures, it gave no breakdown of the contribution to revenue of taxes, reparations, and loans. Klotz continued to rely on the Center-Right majority to rubber stamp his provisional and partial budgets.

For effect the Socialists bitterly complained that the government deliberately left only three or four days for debate at the end of each trimester. In fact, they eagerly seized this opportunity to mount carefully prepared interpellations. Stirred by the coup in Budapest and by reports of impending disaster in Odessa, Cachin gave advance notice that this time the SFIO intended to hammer away at the government's counterrevolutionary interventions in Eastern Europe.[7]

On March 24, the appointed day, Cachin once again offered his excuses for complicating these budgetary debates, much as he had done the previous December when the Socialists had forced a broad-gaged foreign policy debate.[8] This time they proposed to focus on French policy towards Russia, which to them was the essential issue of the hour.

Cachin led off with the legalistic reprimand that the government had embroiled France in a state of war with the Soviet government without

[5] *Le Figaro,* March 10, 1919.
[6] *L'Action Française,* March 10, 1919.
[7] *L'Humanité,* March 20 and 22, 1919.
[8] See pp. 177–86 above.

either consulting Parliament or declaring war. There were French troops in Russia and the government was mobilizing the border peoples and supporting the Whites with large-scale material and financial aid. This intervention was doubly reprehensible because under the false banner of liberty it advanced the cause of reactionary generals, forces, and regimes.

In spite of the investment of great effort and resources, the counter-revolutionary crusade was in grave difficulties, notably on the southern front, where the Red Army was sweeping ahead. At the same time, there was growing restlessness in the Allied expeditionary corps. Cachin disclosed that according to reliable letters from Odessa, there had been some recent incidents of disobedience among French troops. As a result the government was hesitant to use regular army personnel for reinforcement or replacement. Instead, with the appropriations here requested, Clemenceau proposed to send paid volunteers recruited from the Eastern Army and from the fifth Colonial Division in Lyon. He was also pressuring some 60,000 Russian troops in France to "volunteer" for service with Denikin.

Over violent outcries on the right side of the *chambre* Cachin not only declared that under the circumstances the soldiers in Odessa were justified in disobeying orders but also appealed to the soldiers of France "not to volunteer for service in M. Pichon's counterrevolutionary army."

After charging Pichon—who was present—with having scuttled Prinkipo, thereby putting himself "at the head of this international reaction," Cachin brashly called for a complete reversal of policy. "In the shadow of yesterday's events in Budapest" he wanted the government to call off intervention, to lift the blockade, and to recognize the Soviet regime.[9]

Lafont and Mayéras, who seconded this indictment, were particularly indignant about France's co-conspirators. In the Ukraine French generals were siding with Denikin, with large landowners, and with centralists against Socialist and left-Democratic federalists. Throughout the Baltic provinces and in Poland the anti-Bolshevik campaign stimulated the growth of reaction. Even Germanophiles like General Mannerheim, who had just visited Paris, were being encouraged, while the German government was ordered not to release Russian prisoners unless they volunteered for service with the Whites.

Another climactic moment came when Mayéras reminded the deputies of Article 9 of the basic law of July 16, 1875, prohibiting the President of the Republic from declaring war without the prior consent of both houses. In response to noisy protests from right-wing benches he then added insult to injury by invoking Article 35 of the Declaration of the Rights of Man of June 24, 1793, which legitimized rebellion in special circumstances. The uproar on the Right persisted until Paul

9 *JO*, March 24, 1919, 1405–12.

Deschanel, the President of the *chambre,* admonished Mayéras against issuing appeals for insurrection from the parliamentary platform.[1]

When calm was finally restored, Franklin-Bouillon rose to censure Pichon for not taking the Foreign Affairs Commission into his confidence. Needless to say, he was in complete disagreement with the Socialists on the Russian issue. He merely took this occasion to plead for information, also about the pending German settlement. In particular, he put the Foreign Minister on notice that his Commission, which would have to ratify the finished treaty, "was first and foremost concerned about the financial clauses."[2]

On March 26 Clemenceau sat by approvingly as Pichon passed over Franklin-Bouillon's broader inquiry in favor of giving battle on the Russian-Bolshevik issue. Both of them were confident that on this narrower issue the entire Center and Right would close ranks behind the government against the Socialists. They hoped that this tactic would enable them to string along those diehards who had a fixation on reparations and pressed the government to be totally inflexible.

According to Pichon, to bar the expansion of the Bolshevik scourge was not at all equivalent to declaring war on Russia. While others, inspired by Bolsheviks, fostered insurrection and congratulated soldiers for mutinous activities, the government was fighting for law and order.

For the remainder of his address Pichon forgot all about the Socialists. He preferred to concentrate on the arduous task of appeasing those Radical Socialists who felt that France was doing too much and those Rightists who had the opposite complaint. He did so with a survey of the military situation which proved that France's Allies were doing more than their share, and that their combined effort was substantial indeed.

First, in the north, the Allies had intervened at Chaikovsky's request. At this time, of the 35,000 Allied and Russian troops in Murmansk and Archangel, only about 2,500 were French. In Archangel alone Britain had 13,000 men and America 5,000.[3] Around Murmansk the situation was slightly on the upgrade, thanks to the increasing effectiveness of Finland's effort, while on the Archangel front the Red Army had forced the Allies to retreat northward by some 80 kilometers. However, the port was safe by a margin of another 100 kilometers.

In the Siberian theater Kolchak was improving his position militarily as well as politically. His forces had just taken Ufa and were driving ahead toward Samara. In addition to 92,000 Russian troops, there were 118,000 Allied soldiers on that front. Notwithstanding the

[1] *JO,* March 24–25, 1919, 1413–19, 1446–9.
[2] *JO, March* 25, 1919, 1448–52.
[3] Plus about 1,350 Italians, 2,000 Serbs, and 11,800 Russians.

fact that a French officer, General Janin, was in command, there were only 760 Frenchmen among them. The largest contingents were provided by the Czechs (55,000), the Japanese (28,000), the Poles (12,000), and the Americans (7,500). Yugoslavia, Rumania, and Canada each had 4,000 men, Italy and Britain 2,000 and 1,600 respectively.

France's major effort was concentrated on the southern front, in accordance with the Anglo-British accord of December 1917. For the moment, the military picture was not excessively encouraging. On March 10 Kherson had to be evacuated; four days thereafter Nicolaev fell. In Odessa conditions were precarious primarily because of the difficulties of provisioning an urban center of 800,000 souls; but reinforcements were on the way to help stem the tide. Inevitably the Ukraine was feeling the impact of these reverses. At any rate, the bulk of the Allied forces was in position around Odessa, notably four French regiments, three Greek regiments, and a very complete Rumanian regiment.

Pichon wanted the French contribution to the Allied presence in the East to be viewed in proper perspective. Admittedly, there were 140,000 Frenchmen in the field, but so were 200,000 Greeks, 190,000 Rumanians, 140,000 Britons, 140,000 Serbs, and 40,000 Italians.

The Russian question, then, was an inter-Allied question, to be decided not by any one government, but within the framework of the Peace Conference. It touched on a host of exceptionally complex diplomatic issues, notably the future status of the Ukraine and of the Baltic provinces. The fate of both the Ukraine and Lithuania was intimately involved with that of Poland, while the claims of Latvia and Estonia impinged on Russia's access to the sea.

Rather than divulge where he stood on any of these diplomatic problems he simply reiterated that there could be no accommodation with the Bolsheviks, who could not be trusted. Even as Lenin and Trotsky had agreed to come to Prinkipo, they had issued their summons for the first congress of the Third International. This congress had met in early March to fire incendiary broadsides not only against the Peace Conference and the Allied Governments, but also against the Berne International. The Allies had no alternative but to maintain their *cordon sanitaire* against the expansion of this revolutionary peril. But to avoid unnecessary anxiety and hostility, Pichon, not unlike Churchill, concluded with the disingenuous assurance that there "was no question of penetrating into the interior of Russia, or of sending a large expeditionary force."[4]

This pledge actually helped keep most of the Radical Socialists in line, for they protested against *"toute expédition militaire en Russie"* without, however, taking a stand against the strangulation of the

[4] *JO*, March 26, 1919, 1475–80.

Revolution by other means.[5] Jean Bon, Frederic Brunet, and Louis Deshayes, who rejected this subterfuge, were hopelessly isolated in their party.[6]

The Socialists, of course, were incensed. They were particularly outraged by Pichon's studied effort to create the impression that the Allies were in broad agreement on the Russian question. Longuet accused Pichon of deliberately concealing that his government was the chief initiator and architect of this anti-Bolshevik campaign. The honor of Wilson—still their hero—was at stake. But rather than cast Wilson as an outright opponent of active containment, the Socialists claimed that the *politique de sainte-alliance* was "running up against the lofty preoccupations" of the American President and the "more prudent policy" of the British Prime Minister.[7]

Furthermore, they furiously rejected the implication that the *cordon sanitaire* was a purely defensive instrument and that no additional troops would be needed to hold the line. Whereas Pichon told them that there were 140,000 men in the *armée de l'orient*, the pending extraordinary budget provided for the support of 170,000.[8]

On March 29 Renaudel moved that the appropriation for troops in the East be reduced by ten million francs. In justification of this token cutback he stressed the recent bankruptcy of the *cordon sanitaire* in Budapest and the Ukraine and forced Louis Abrami, the Deputy Minister of War, to admit that there had been new cases of indiscipline in Odessa as well as in the north. This arch-moderate also warned that if the government persisted in this policy of counterrevolutionary intervention—which was a central link in its overall foreign and domestic policy—it would lose the support of those Socialists, who, with Wilson, were the best rampart against Bolshevism.[9]

The government was dead set against Renaudel's amendment, less because of the amount involved than for the intended defiance. Abrami repeated that France had comparatively few soldiers in Russia, that these were there by virtue of international agreements, and that they were under explicit instructions not to interfere in Russia's internal affairs! After Longuet interjected that this was no time for bad jokes, Abrami stated that Clemenceau had authorized him to say that he was opposed "to sending an expedition to Russia" and that "not one additional man would be sent to Russia."

While Longuet, Cachin, and Alexandre Bracke broke in to demand

---

[5] The text of the resolution adopted by the Radical Socialist group is cited in *le Petit Parisien,* March 28, 1919; and in *JO,* March 29, 1919, 1617, 1625.

[6] *JO,* March 26 and 29, 1919, 1481–2, 1624–9; and *Bulletin du Parti Républicain Radical et Radical Socialiste,* May 10, 1919.

[7] *Le Populaire,* March 28, 1919.

[8] Cachin writing in *l'Humanité,* March 29, 1919.

[9] *JO,* March 29, 1919, 1617–23.

the immediate withdrawal of the men there now, Antoine Borel, a dissident Radical Socialist, inquired whether those who were coming home to be demobilized would be replaced. Abrami answered this question with a flat "no!," adding that a first contingent had already been withdrawn from the north. On the other hand the government and the Allies were duty-bound not to abandon Rumania, Poland, and the Baltic provinces. Henceforth these and other border states would receive maximum moral and material aid, including arms, money, clothing, equipment, and supplies of all sorts.[1]

The Socialists eagerly exploited the obvious discrepancies between Abrami and Pichon. They pointed out that whereas the former promised that no further troops would be sent to Russia, only three days ago Pichon had spoken of reinforcements for Odessa. When the Foreign Minister explained that at the time these were already on their way to relieve other units, Lafont retorted that Abrami pledged unqualified withdrawals, without replacements. In this same vein Maurice Violette noted that under Abrami's policy all French soldiers should be out of Russia before long. Pichon heatedly denied the accuracy of this interpretation and left no doubt whatever that French troops would stay on.[2]

With the fiscal trimester running out Pichon pressed for an early vote, confident that his Parliamentary strategy was working. True enough, the extreme Right harped on the need for full and gigantic reparations, but never without assuring the Clemenceau administration of their support.[3] And even though Franklin-Bouillon registered his dissatisfaction with Pichon's accounting to the *chambre,* he was not about to join the Socialists in opposition.[4]

Renaudel's amendment was easily defeated by 350 to 121 votes. Nonetheless, on this limited Russian issue the Socialists were united and they were joined by a small band of Radical Socialists among whom Bon, Brunet, Deshayes, and Jobert were most prominent. On the budget installments as a whole, however, the ranks of the opposition faltered. Only 39 Socialists voted against the civilian credits, and 71 against the military and exceptional ones. Moreover, on both, Bon and Franklin-Bouillon only abstained. In the final analysis Clemenceau and Pichon scored as impressive a majority now as the previous December.[5]

This latest demonstration of Socialist impotence encouraged the Center and Right to intensify their pressure on the government. In

[1] Ibid., 1624–5.

[2] Ibid., 1625–6.

[3] See the statements by Edouard de Curières de Castelnau, Jean Ybarnégaray, and César Ginoux-Defermont in *JO,* March 28, 1919, 1567.

[4] *JO,* March 29, 1919, 1627–9.

[5] *JO,* March 28 and 29, 1919, 1575, 1654, 1655; *le Temps,* March 31, 1919; *l'Humanité,* March 31, 1919.

imitation of the British M.P.'s, on April 10 the *sénat* issued a manifesto signed by all the members present that day.[6] The key paragraph reaffirmed that they expected "in particular, the exaction from the enemy of full restitution, the reparation of damage done to persons and to property, that the full cost of the war shall be charged to the enemy, and that an exemplary penal sentence shall be imposed on the responsible authors of the greatest crime in history."[7] The following day some 300 members of the lower House signed a motion associating themselves with this manifesto. They declared themselves "bent on affirming the complete unity of both Houses with a view to strengthening the French representatives at the Peace Conference in their legitimate claims."[8]

Simultaneously Péret wrote to Clemenceau for concrete details about his reparations policy. He reiterated that without information about the amount of reparations and methods of payment his Commission could not balance the budget or estimate what new charges might have to be levied. Clemenceau was warned not to persist in the dangerous subterfuge of hiding behind Article VIII of the Constitution of 1875.[9] In any case, Péret served notice that the Commission expected the government to "steadfastly uphold the right of victorious France to reparations for damages and the full cost of the war." When the Premier peremptorily rebuffed Péret in an acrid eight-line letter Piou, a veteran right-wing member of the Commission, argued for a further and stronger manifesto.[1]

On April 13 a delegation of the Radical Socialist group in the *chambre* had a one-hour interview with Clemenceau. René Renoult, the chairman of the Parliamentary group and leader of this delegation, was an avowed advocate of a stiff peace. Although Renoult and his 11 colleagues were vague about border issues and the disarmament of Germany, they were considerably less so when it came to reparations. They impressed on Clemenceau that the enemy should provide France with all her coal needs, notably through French ownership of the Saar mines, and that France should seek "the integral reparation of damage done to all persons and things, including the payment of all war pensions."[2] Again Clemenceau dodged specific questions, leaving

[6] "Lloyd George has received a petition signed by 400 members. . . . Our senators and representatives will follow their example." Marcellin: *Politique et Politiciens d'après guerre*, 84, entry of April 10, 1919.

[7] The full text is cited in *le Matin*, April 11, 1919.

[8] The full text is cited in Marcellin: *Politique et Politiciens d'après guerre*, 86, entry of April 12, 1919.

[9] Article VIII: "The President of the Republic shall negotiate and ratify treaties. He shall inform the Chambers of them as soon as it is compatible with the interests and safety of the State to do so."

[1] *Le Matin* and *le Temps*, April 11, 1919.

[2] *L'Humanité*, April 14, 1919.

Radical Socialist delegates with general promises which failed to satisfy the party's Executive Committee.[3]

Meanwhile the press suspected that his obstinate silence was a cover for dangerous appeasement. Clemenceau stood accused of preparing to present Parliament with an unpleasant but irreversible *fait accompli*. The *Temps* was indignant because reparations, which were of greatest interest to France, were about to be discussed in Commons, but not in the *chambre*. The constitution did not intend to deny elected representatives the right to "either control or influence" the peace treaty, leaving them only the choice between unqualified acceptance and rejection.[4] At a minimum, the principal Parliamentary commissions—Budget, Finance, Foreign Affairs—should be advised and consulted.[5] According to Auguste Gauvain, while not only Clemenceau but all four peacemakers acted as if they were engaged in a dishonorable enterprise which had best remain hidden, in fact they had "nothing to hide." They should come down from Sinai to renew contact with and draw strength from the people they were sworn to serve. Significantly, Gauvain also considered the Parliamentary commissions the proper forum, no doubt because these were in reliable hands and avoided dangerous public debates by meeting behind closed doors![6]

The time had come for Socialists to wonder about the wisdom of spearheading Parliamentary protests which kept turning against them. Not only the French Parliament was dominated by a khaki-like majority; so were the Parliaments in Italy, Britain, and even America. And the manifesto of 370, the remonstrance of the *sénat*, and the minatory pronouncements by Lodge all went to prove that the Right was engaged in a concerted drive to impose a harsh victor's peace.[7]

Still, Socialists and dissident Radicals were reluctant to give up on the *chambre* which, in spite of all the odds, was their best propaganda channel. Perhaps with a view to keeping Clemenceau and Pichon from giving secret testimony to one of the conservative-dominated commissions, they decided to force the issue to the floor. On April 16, the very day that Lloyd George was to address Commons, André Lebey formally interpellated Pichon "on the means the President of the Council proposed to use to inform Parliament of the terms of Peace." To every one's surprise, Clemenceau's alter ego instantly agreed to speak on this particular and well-defined question. But they were quickly dismayed by the brevity and pungency of his statement: "it was a matter of confidence in the negotiators, that is to say in the Government," which was constitutionally bound to submit the final treaty for ratification.[8]

[3] *Bulletin du Parti Républicain Radical et Radical Socialiste,* May 10, 1919.
[4] *Le Temps,* April 11–12, 1919.
[5] *L'Intransigeant,* April 11 and 14, 1919.
[6] *JO,* April 12 and 14, 1919.
[7] *Le Populaire* and *l'Humanité,* April 12–13, 1919.
[8] *JO,* April 16, 1919, 1997–8.

All efforts to entrap Pichon into a substantive debate failed. Franklin-Bouillon then tried to get the interpellation held over until the following day, by which time the text of Lloyd George's address would have reached Paris. But even this postponement was unacceptable, Pichon insisting on a vote of confidence on the procedural constitutional issue right then and there. A motion for a one-day deferment was defeated 334 to 166 votes; and a motion to go into secret session— reminiscent of the *comité secret* of early June 1917—lost by the same margin. At last Pichon won his vote of confidence 345 to 121, the Center-left falling into line to give the government a three-to-one margin.[9]

All this time the radicalization of the Left continued apace. Restlessness swept the CGT, which made the eight-hour day its chief rallying symbol and objective. On December 15, 1918, the National Committee proclaimed that this demand had top priority. Quick to recognize the legitimacy and popularity of this plank, the Social Patriots especially rallied to the cause; in their uphill battle for reformism they did not want it pre-empted by the extremists of the industrial and political movement.[1] In late January Renaudel, Albert Thomas, Voilin, and Lauche moved that the *chambre* pass a law establishing the eight-hour day and the forty-eight-hour week in both industry and commerce.[2] This proposal was referred to the Labor Commission for study and advice. By mid-February the Executive Committtee of the CGT became impatient with the slow pace of this Commission's labors, insisting that now that other nations adopted or were about to adopt the eight-hour day, the argument about the loss of competitive advantages was falling to the ground.[3]

Within a month this impatience reached new heights, no doubt partly under the stimulus of labor unrest in England. On March 23–24 the CGT's National Committee explicitly condemned any further delays. The time for discussion had passed; time-consuming studies could no longer be tolerated. In order to impose the shortened work day the following unions declared themselves ready to stand together: railwaymen, merchant seamen, dockers, metalworkers, construction workers, and transport workers. Furthermore, the CGT notified all concerned that it was preparing "a first demonstration of power and determination" for May 1, a demonstration meant as a solemn "warning."[4]

[9] *JO,* April 16, 1919, 1998–2011. The following day the Socialists unsuccessfully interpellated the government about continuing troop shipments to Russia and about "the maximum reparations that France could hope for." *JO,* April 17–18, 1919, 2047, 2060, 2078–9.

[1] See *l'Humanité* and *le Populaire,* December 15–31, 1918.

[2] *JO,* January 28, 1919, 245; and B. W. Schaper: *Albert Thomas* (Assen: Van Gorcum; 1959), 194.

[3] *L'Humanité,* February 21, 1919.

[4] *L'Humanité,* March 25–26, 1919; and Dolléans: *Histoire du Mouvement ouvrier,* II, 299.

This unambiguous warning caused a sensation. The CGT was upbraided for initiating "the new British method," which had just extracted concessions which amounted to a "profound upheaval in the industrial life of Great Britain." Was this French imitation of English tactics but a prelude to coordinated all-European strikes?[5]

There also were signs of mounting excitement in the SFIO. A special congress was scheduled for April 20–23. In preparation, the three major factions feverishly jockeyed for position. The ex-*minoritaires* dominated the Socialist press, tightened their hold on local organizations, and spearheaded the assaults on Pichon in the *chambre*. The lines appeared to be drawn between Longuet and Loriot rather than between Longuet and Renaudel.

In the midst of this internecine struggle and on the last day of the Parliamentary debate of March 24–29 a jury acquitted Raoul Villain, the young deranged nationalist who had assassinated Jean Jaurès on July 31, 1914. The entire Left denounced this verdict as a cruel injustice, a deliberate provocation, and a *geste de guerre civile*. Villain's exculpation was particularly galling because it stood in such crying contrast to another sentence handed down two weeks earlier: a swift and unanimous court-martial gave the death penalty to Émile Cottin, the 22-year-old who had unsuccessfully tried to assassinate Clemenceau just a few weeks before. The Socialists promptly charged that whereas the unsuccessful assassin drew the supreme penalty, the successful one was absolved. This defiance to the party—in the form of a mutilation of the revered memory of Jaurés—could not go unchallenged.[6]

One of the two defense lawyers proposed that the Left organize a giant protest march on the following Sunday, April 6.[7] Since the arrival of Woodrow Wilson in mid-December, the Left had had no grand occasion to measure and display its popular following in the capital. As a result the leaders of the SFIO and the CGT eagerly seized this magnificent opportunity to call the workers into the streets, though they displayed caution in choosing a Sunday afternoon.[8]

The response exceeded even the most optimistic expectations, some 300,000 persons answering the summons on such short notice. The *Temps* could no longer mock the SFIO as the party of 34,000! Ten times that number marched in perfect discipline, singing the "International." The militants who urged that this was the time to risk a test were vindicated and encouraged.[9]

[5] *Le Temps*, March 29, 1919.
[6] See *l'Humanité, le Populaire, la Bataille*, and *Journal du Peuple*, March 30 to April 2, 1919; and Maurice Garçon: *Histoire de la Justice sous la IIIᵉ République* (Paris: Arthème Fayard; 1957), III, 144–50.
[7] Jean Paul-Boncour: *Entre Deux guerres: Souvenirs sur la IIIᵉ République* (Paris: Plon; 1945), II, 14–15.
[8] *L'Humanité*, April 4–6, 1919.
[9] *L'Humanité* and *le Populaire*, April 7–9, 1919.

Within two days Marcel Cachin claimed an initial success for the demonstration threatened for May 1, punctuated by Sunday's mass *défilé*. On instructions from the Premier, M. Colliard, the Minister of Labor, introduced an eight-hour law in the *chambre*. On April 11 Briand and others moved an amendment to the effect that the reduction in hours should not be a "determinate cause" for salary cuts, and on the thirteenth the Executive Committee of the Radical Socialist Party unanimously voted to support the bill.[1]

Certain of the Center-left, Colliard pressed for speedy action. He announced that the administration wanted to give the eight-hour day to the working class "without strike, and industrial peace, and under conditions which safeguard production." Since labor expected prompt results and not long speeches, he asked both Houses to pass the once-amended bill without further changes or delay. On April 17 the *chambre* passed the bill unanimously; and within a week even the *sénat* followed suit without a dissenting voice.[2] Simultaneously Alphonse Merrheim concluded the first eight-hour day contract between the unionized metalworkers and the Union of Metallurgical Industries, consisting of industries engaged in mechanical, naval, electric, and metal production.[3]

There would seem to be little doubt that passage of the law was expedited by current pressures and considerations: the CGT's thinly veiled strike threat, the expediency of strengthening the moderates on the eve of the special SFIO congress, and the need to drive a wedge between the industrial and political segments of the labor movement. Clemenceau preferred appeasing labor pre-emptively to being stampeded into concessions by strikes or organized protests.[4] As for the Left, with the exception of the extreme faction, it considered the bill a promising first step, even from the point of view of reformist syndicalism and Socialism. This preface to the total transformation of society came on the very eve of May Day and thus had the virtue of proving the new-found strength of the proletariat.[5] Although Pierre Monatte agreed that the government wanted to dampen the revolutionary crisis, he suggested that the eight-hour law was a gift or a by-product of the Russian Revolution rather than "the fruit of our effort."[6]

At the special congress of the SFIO the passage of this law was

---

[1] L'Humanité, April 9, 1919; Bonnefous: *Histoire Politique de la IIIᵉ République*, III, 30–1; *Bulletin du Parti Républicain Radical et Radical-Socialiste*, May 10, 1919.
[2] *JO*, April 16–18, 1919, 2018–20, 2029–42, 2048–60; and Bernard Georges and Denise Tintant: *Léon Jouhaux* (Paris: Presses Universitaires; 1962), 354 ff.
[3] *L'Humanité*, April 19, 1919.
[4] See Général Mordacq: *Le Ministère Clemenceau: Journal d'un témoin* (Paris: Plon; 1930), III, 251. Mordacq opposed the law.
[5] *Le Populaire*, April 20, 1919.
[6] Georges and Tintant: *Léon Jouhaux*, 358, n. 2; and Dolléans: *Histoire du Mouvement ouvrier*, II, 316–17.

hailed as evidence that it paid to pursue immediate, piecemeal reforms instead of exclusively preparing the ground for wholesale revolution.[7] In the discussion of the party's platform for the coming elections, Loriot argued against dampening the revolutionary situation, since all reforms within the capitalist system were a sham. In any case, the polls were not the proper focus for revolutionary activism. All the party needed was a general statement of maximum purposes combined with a streamlined organization.

Léon Blum, who contributed substantially to the draft proposal, could not have disagreed more. He warned against confusing revolution with insurrection. Revolution, in the sense of a transformation of property relations, could be brought about by peaceful and legal methods, implemented by a transitional proletarian dictatorship which would be needed longer in retarded societies like Russia than in advanced societies of the West. Politics being the key to this amphibious transformation, the Socialists were advocates of universal suffrage, proportional representation, and unicameralism. In the end the rhythm of economic and social reforms would be a function of the degree of Socialist power and influence in Parliament.

Longuet also spoke for the electoral platform. In his judgment it reflected the recent radicalization of the Left and formed the basis for unity in the Socialist movement. It was an effective weapon and rallying ground for a prerevolutionary situation.

Even though Verfeuil was most sympathetic to Loriot's *politique du pire,* he, too, had to admit that the revolution was not around the corner. "We drag behind us the chain and ball of victory which poisons our nation. As long as this poison of victory is not eradicated it will be difficult to launch a successful revolutionary action. There will be a waiting period." The *Temps* gleefully hailed this unexpected confirmation that victory had "immunized the nation and society against revolution, disorder and anarchy."[8] Verfeuil, reluctant to share Loriot's scorn for reforms, offered a compromise resolution.

But Verfeuil and Loriot mustered only 296 and 245 votes respectively. The other 1,394 delegates rallied around Blum's draft platform, thereby confirming the party's determination to fight the next national elections with a conventional program for immediate reforms. At Bracke's urging the congress stipulated that no candidate could run on the party ticket without explicitly adhering to this program. It also precluded local coalitions with non-Socialist parties.

[7] The following discussion of the April congress is based on the minutes published in *l'Humanité* and *le Populaire,* April 21–24, 1919; and Parti Socialiste: *17ème Congrès National tenu à Strasbourg 25–29 février 1920: Compte rendu sténographique* (Paris, 1920), 11–14 and *passim.*
[8] *Le Temps,* April 24, 1919.

The ex-*majoritaires* endorsed these election plans without major mental reservations. However, their efforts to have them take the place of a statement of general principles and maximum objectives were thoroughly defeated. This statement was repugnant to them because of its fundamental criticism of Social Patriotism. It flatly declared that the class struggle demanded the "systematic and symbolic refusal" of credits and the refusal to participate in coalition cabinets or electoral races, at the risk of expulsion from the party. In his fury, Renaudel not only proclaimed that he and his colleagues would never apologize for anything they had done during the war, but also impugned Longuet's integrity by questioning the sources of the financial support of the *Populaire,* the hard-hitting daily of the ex-*minoritaires*.

These smear tactics did not work. Having tied the Social Patriots to the party with the electoral program, Longuet and his colleagues refused to pacify them any further. Longuet, Blanc, Frossard, and Faure were in search of a double-purpose formula: should it fail to overcome Loriot's intransigence it would nevertheless signify that the party had opted for a distinct leftward orientation. In the final vote Longuet won by 962 over 232 for Loriot. Significantly Renaudel and Blum, afraid that an impasse might rebound to Loriot's advantage, abstained instead of casting 789 negative votes.

In the field of foreign affairs the same fissures were in evidence. Without so much as a debate the congress denounced the Peace Conference for violating and abandoning the Fourteen Points and for transforming the League into an instrument of material exploitation and popular repression. It also arraigned the imperialist designs of the Clemenceau government as well as those of the Parliamentary majority.

Once the congress turned to the question of international affiliation, the debate became as heated as it had been over the general statement of principles. The ex-*majoritaires* argued for unconditional loyalty to the Second International. Mayéras and Renaudel denied the existence of a genuine Third International, Lenin having summoned it only in the interest of Soviet Russian diplomacy. Besides, since the Bolsheviks refused to come to Berne while agreeing to meet bourgeois representatives at Prinkipo, why should French Socialists go to Moscow? Longuet, however, held out for conditional allegiance. He would not join the Third, in part because it was a small sectarian faction as compared to the vast Second International, which he meant to reconstruct. This Second International needed the same leftward reorientation which the party had just voted for itself. Accordingly, the SFIO wanted the leaders as well as the national sections of the Berne International purged in accordance with the new statement of general principles. Needless to say, Loriot took the position that the Second was beyond repair, all Bolsheviks having sworn never to return to it. He

asked, therefore, that the SFIO at once join the Third unconditionally. Again the ex-*minoritaires* won the day, this time with 894
votes for Longuet's motion, against 757 for Mayéras', and 270 for
Loriot's.

Though unity was maintained, it was precarious at best. The
Maximalists now played the role which the ex-*minoritaires* had played
until October 1918, and Longuet was loath to break with them. He was
equally determined not to become the prisoner of the Social Patriots
who seemed to be fashioning close bonds with Blum's alluring centrist
faction. To be sure, the Longuists kept control of the party. But they
were buffeted by increasingly irreconcilable forces to their right and
left, just as in the CGT Merrheim had to steer a perilous middle
course between Jouhaux and Monatte.

Meanwhile the government and the Right took comfort from this
debilitating factionalism. The *Temps* suggested that just as the International had collapsed at the outbreak of war, so the SFIO was
faltering at the outbreak of peace. The congress offered the spectacle of
a party "more than ever divided against itself, floundering in inco-
herence, and powerless to adopt policies suited to the demands of the
hour."[9]

As May Day approached both the labor movement and the government prepared for a test of strength. The initiative came from the
Executive Committee of the CGT, which decided that passage of the
eight-hour law should not be allowed to lull the workers into complacency. In and of itself the bill was but a declaration of principle. It
remained to be implemented and enforced through uphill labor-
management negotiations.[1] On April 18, on the eve of these negotiations, the CGT executive called for a general work stoppage on May 1,
hoping thereby to improve labor's bargaining power. This same work
stoppage, however, was also intended to register organized labor's
political demands for total demobilization, peace without annexation,
and the end of intervention in Russia.[2]

The government had hoped that the eight-hour bill would momentarily placate the syndicalist leaders and see the Peace Conference
through the traditionally uneventful celebration of May Day in Paris.
But this was not to be. The last labor demonstration in Paris had been
called on short notice and for Sunday afternoon, when holiday strollers
were expected to swell the protest. This twenty-four-hour general strike
was scheduled for Thursday, a working day, and there were two weeks
in which to plan it. Clearly, the Left was becoming more daring and

[9] *Le Temps,* April 25, 1919.
[1] Georges and Tintant: *Léon Jouhaux,* 356–7.
[2] This strike summons is printed in *l'Humanité,* April 19, 1919; and *le Populaire,* April
20, 1919.

defiant. Supposing this second demonstration in less than four weeks succeeded in an orderly fashion, would a third and possibly larger one be equally harmless? Perhaps the government should make a cautionary show of force now, when both the CGT and SFIO were severely torn internally, rather than later, when both would be better united.

In any event, soon after the strike summons was issued the government began to deploy troops around Paris as well as around all other major industrial centers. These troops were moved into position during the night and were instructed to keep out of sight.[3]

These measures could not be kept secret. By April 24 Cachin sought to interpellate the government about them. But the *chambre* recessed until May 6 after Pams, the Minister of Interior, bluntly declared that the government could not agree to give advance information about precautionary measures "designed to maintain public order in all eventualities."[4]

This protest was continued by the labor press, the SFIO, and the CGT. All alike emphasized that not only the CGT executive but all the large union organizations were determined that this work stoppage should take place *avec le calme et la dignité que confère la puissance* and in strict discipline. Why, then, this distrust of the workers? This exceptional display of power and these troop concentrations could have no purpose other than intimidation—except possibly provocation. But the proletariat was in no mood to be bullied. According to Cachin it would go right on mounting "the most powerful general mobilization of workers" the French bourgeoisie had ever seen both in celebration of the eight-hour day and as a demonstration of labor's resolve radically to change the regime.[5]

The government's unyielding attitude played into the hands of extremists, who were particularly influential in the Seine. On the twenty-sixth the executive of the federation of unions of this *département* formally protested the troop concentrations.[6] Two days later the delegates of 63 of the 117 member unions in the Seine, impatient with the CGT executive's excessive prudence, voted to combine the work stoppage with massive street demonstrations. Even though Clemenceau promptly prohibited these demonstrations, the federation nevertheless went ahead, encouraged by the Left-*minoritaire* Socialists in their *département*.[7]

Both Jouhaux and Marcel Laurent, the Deputy Secretary General of the CGT, refused to be pushed into this head-on confrontation,

[3] *L'Humanité*, April 21–24, 1919; and Mordacq: *Le Ministère Clemenceau*, III, 250.
[4] *JO*, April 24, 1919, 2183–4.
[5] *L'Humanité*, April 25–26, 1919.
[6] *L'Humanité*, April 27, 1919.
[7] Dolléans: *Histoire du Mouvement ouvrier*, II, 299–300; and *l'Humanité*, April 30–May 1, 1919.

particularly once the government had made its position clear.[8] Unfortunately, however, their original summons had spoken of the work stoppage as a *démonstration* without specifically either precluding or encouraging the organization of attendant mass demonstrations; and by now such demonstrations were scheduled for Paris and other cities. At this late date Laurent could neither disown nor cancel them. The best he could do was to counsel caution and discipline. He did so in a last-minute appeal in which he did not disassociate the central leadership from the projected undertaking.

It is difficult to imagine the feverish activity of our syndicates in even the most remote corners of France. Never before were such precise and extensive measures taken. And these preparations which are marked by unbounding enthusiasm resemble the extraordinary bustle which preceded important offensives during the late War.

Nevertheless, properly speaking, we are not preparing an attack. Our operation will be a vast reconnaissance and an affirmation of our forces with the purpose of notifying the enemy that he will have to yield ground.

The barrage of fire will last only one day in order to permit the observers of the opposite side to assess our strength.

I know that this is a reversal of tactical principles; however, we have nothing to gain from an ambush. [I repeat that] the demonstration will take place *avec le calme et la dignité que confère la puissance* and in order to exhibit clearly what organized labor can do when it is disciplined. Work will resume on May 2. . . .

Some restless spirits and others who are impatient for the execution of total plans are distressed because we have confined ourselves to such a limited demonstration. . . . To have recommended calmness is apparently equivalent to not being revolutionary! Is it necessary to point out the deplorable nature and the limited effectiveness of street disorders? Must we fall in with those who admire the revolutions of Central and Eastern Europe only because they produced so much bloodshed?

Let us beware of being bewitched and let us eliminate from our minds this obsession to imitate. It is childish to pretend that these situations are identical.

The Permanent Administrative Committee of the SFIO reinforced this appeal for restraint with a manifesto urging all workers "to follow strictly the instructions given them by the CGT."[9]

On Thursday the work stoppage was complete throughout Paris and the suburbs.[1] But while in the morning the streets were deserted, in the afternoon this ominous calm was broken, in spite of heavy rains.

[8] Georges and Tintant: *Léon Jouhaux*, 362.
[9] Both appeals are printed in *l'Humanité*, April 30–May 1, 1919.
[1] This account of May Day is based on *le Temps* and *le Figaro*, May 2–4, 1919.

The *Union des Syndicats de la Seine* had scheduled a mass meeting at the Place de la Concorde for 3:00 p.m., and the workers were expected to converge on this focal point from all parts of the capital and the *banlieue*.

By 1:00 p.m. the police, the *garde républicaine,* and regular troops were deployed in the heart of Paris with instructions to seal off the Concorde. Police barriers went up at key points, notably at the rue Royale, the Madeleine, the Esplanade des Invalides, the Rond-Point des Champs-Elysées, the Boulevard Haussmann, and the Boulevard Malesherbes. Moreover, special units were posted at the Elysée, the Palais Bourbon, and the major ministries.

Before long large groups of workers approached, carrying red banners, singing the "International," and chanting *"Vive Wilson!"* In successive waves of protesters more revolutionary slogans were heard, including *"A bas l'armée! A bas Clemenceau."* Since efforts to break into the sealed-off area were unsuccessful, the workers marched to other assembly points, all along battling security forces. There were serious incidents near the Place de l'Opéra, where Charles Lorne, an eighteen-year-old mechanic was killed by a pistol shot; near the Place de la République, where Léon Jouhaux, clubbed with a night stick, received a serious injury over his left eye; along the Boulevard Magenta, where Paul Poncet, a Socialist deputy from the Seine, was severely beaten and then treated by his colleague Pierre Laval; in front of the Bourse du Travail, where Louis Sellier, a municipal councillor, escaped with minor scars; and at the Gare de l'Est, where the bloodiest encounter took place, Alexander Auger, a forty-eight-year-old bill collector, being fatally shot. The number of wounded was estimated to have reached about 300, 31 of them serious cases, and about 107 demonstrators were arrested. The security forces suffered even heavier casualties. Some 400 police officers were said to have been injured, 12 of them requiring hospitalization.

Inevitably, the Left and the Right took opposite views of these events. The leaders of the SFIO and the CGT charged the government with deliberate provocation and excessive brutality. Work stoppages and demonstrations had taken place in all major cities, but in none but Paris were there any incidents, no doubt because the authorities had not intervened. In Paris alone was blood spilled, and only because security forces were drawn up so prominently and in such great strength and because the scheduled rally was forcibly prevented.

The Socialist deputies announced a "collective" interpellation for May 6. Meanwhile, at the request of the party executive, Fernand Bouisson and Compère-Morel, the last two Socialists in the Clemenceau administration, resigned in protest. Simultaneously Jouhaux resigned from the French Peace Delegation because Clemenceau "had prohibited a demonstration which he knew would be peaceful" and because his security forces had treated the demonstrators—including children, women, and disabled veterans—with "unspeakable brutality."[2]

The Right blamed the decision to take to the streets on a small band of dangerous extremists in the CGT and the Socialist Party. The *Temps* and the *Figaro* tended to credit Jouhaux with having tried his best to restrain these; the *Action Française* charged him with lack of forcefulness and courage. All three dailies, however, took an essentially conspiratorial view of the disorders as such. Accordingly, the agitators were not French workers but foreign as well as professional revolutionaries, anarchists, and Bolsheviks—Belgians, Turks, Italians, Russians, and Armenians. Since no such unsavory types had infiltrated the labor movement in the provinces, these were spared all disorders. And, of course, the peasantry never came close to being involved.[3]

On May 6 Cachin, Poncet, and Lafont carried the Socialist case to the *chambre*. The entire Socialist group stalked out before Pams started his defense: they would listen to and debate with the Premier only, not with a subordinate who merely executed orders.[4]

Pams again conceded that elaborate security precautions had been taken throughout the nation, particularly around "centers of restlessness," yet without causing incidents. There were disorders in Paris only because the Seine organization, by a narrow margin, had voted to stage street demonstrations. At that crucial meeting the initiative had come from a Mr. Bertho, alias Lepetit, who in April 1917 had been indicted for spreading defeatist propaganda; and none of the organizers, nor, for that matter, any other labor leaders, ever asked to discuss the projected demonstration with the authorities. In the interest of law and order the government had no alternative but to proscribe it; and it could only enforce this prohibition by setting up *des barrages*. In the morning of May 1 the government received word that the demonstrations would be turned into *"un effort de convulsion révolutionnaire."* Whereas the regular police carried revolvers that day, all other units were without firearms. Lorne was not killed by a police bullet and, given the high ratio of police casualties, the initiative to fire must have come from among the demonstrators.[5] As expected, the entire Right and Center uncritically accepted Pams's version. Only one negative vote was cast, by Jean Bon, the other dissident Radical Socialists preferring to retreat into abstention, while the Socialists persisted in their walkout.[6]

Perhaps Alfred Capus was not all that wrong in suggesting that no one was frightened when the Socialists walked out, probably to go home for a quiet family dinner. In his view these deputies were "moderates, for the most part capitalists and bourgeois, who were

2 *L'Humanité, le Populaire, le Temps,* and *le Figaro,* May 2–5, 1919.
3 *Le Temps, le Figaro,* and *l'Action Française,* May 2–5, 1919.
4 *JO,* May 6, 1919, 2196–208.
5 Ibid., 2208–10.
6 Ibid., 2210–11.

slightly embarrassed whenever their professional standing obliged them to anathematize the bourgeoisie and capitalism."[7] And, in fact, all they did at this juncture was to urge their followers "to buy *l'Humanité* every morning and *le Populaire* every evening."[8] Also, all the organizations that had participated in the events of May 1 called on the workers to join in the funeral procession for Charles Lorne, who was to be buried in the Pére-Lachaise cemetery on May 8. But this time only an estimated 100,000 workers answered the summons.[9]

[7] *Le Figaro*, May 7, 1919.
[8] Paul Faure in *le Populaire*, May 8, 1919.
[9] *L'Humanité* and *le Populaire*, May 6, 9–10, 1919.

20

Wilson's Fiume Appeal

PERHAPS IN ITALY domestic and foreign policy were more fatally intertwined than in the other three major victor nations. Her finances and economy were drastically shaken, and a greatly radicalized and rapidly expanding Socialist and labor movement thrived on this instability. But unlike in France, Britain, and the U.S., in Italy this postwar neurasthenia was aggravated by a *crise de régime*. The official Socialists wanted a Soviet-type regime. On the other hand, the Republicans, the Radicals, and the Reformist Socialists wanted to liquidate the monarchy in favor of a republic. They clamored for a constituent assembly, confident that an assembly elected by universal—including woman— suffrage would chart an essentially unicameral republic. Even large segments of the Center-right reluctantly abandoned the constitutional monarchy in the face of this party and popular rebellion. Rather than fight a losing battle, they concentrated on endowing this allegedly inevitable republic with minimum antidemocratic safeguards.

Italy's financial and economic crisis was worse than that of France. More than half of the estimated budget for 1919 could not be covered by current revenues. Her inter-Allied debts amounted to 700,000,000 pounds sterling. After the Armistice Italy was in no position to earn the foreign exchange with which to pay for vital imports of coal and industrial raw materials, so that she continued to be dependent on Allied loans. Also, if the Allies had not helped to stabilize the lira, it would have collapsed quickly instead of only falling gradually. Politically, of course, the high cost of living was most explosive. At the end of the war Italy's wholesale price index stood at 481, compared to 368 for France, 242 for Britain, and 206 for the U.S. Although it dropped to 358 in January, as of March it rose again, soaring to 451 by mid-1919. In early 1919 the retail price index in Milan stood at 399, or nearly 150 points higher than in Paris.[1]

Unemployment became an equally pressing problem. With the

[1] Ernest Lémonon: *L'Italie d'après guerre, 1914–1921* (Paris: Felix Alcan; 1922), 120–1; and Louis Hautecoeur: *L'Italie sous le ministère Orlando, 1917–1919* (Paris: Bossard; 1919), 206 ff.

sudden end of the war defense industries lost their government contracts. Whereas in 1913 heavy industry had employed 50,000 workers, in October 1918 it absorbed easily ten times that number. By the time that workers were dismissed, a flood of ex-servicemen poured into the bulging labor market. By early March 1919 some 1,700,000 soldiers had been demobilized. Reconversion was planless, disorganized, and slow. And whereas in 1913 close to 900,000 Italians had emigrated abroad, this escape channel was momentarily closed as well.[2]

This inflation and industrial unemployment were superimposed on chronic rural underemployment and on pent-up resentments against regressive consumer taxes. Instead of reducing the imbalances and tensions of Italy's modernizing capitalist economy, the war had magnified them. Simultaneously, it had intensified the attendant political unrest.

The first postwar year saw a spectacular growth in organized Socialist and labor strength: the membership of the ISP jumped from 25,000 to 83,000, the membership of the CGL from 249,000 to 1,160,000, and the circulation of *Avanti* from 18,000 to nearly 200,000. In the national elections of November 1919, the Socialist Party captured 156 seats with 1,835,000 votes, or nearly one third of the newly enlarged electorate, as compared to one quarter of the votes and 52 seats in the last prewar elections. And if Don Sturzo's Partito Popolare and the related Italian Confederation of Labor had not entered the field with a vigorous reform platform, the Socialists' electoral advance of 1919 undoubtedly would have been still more sweeping.[3]

Starting in January and until mid-1919 this left-wing expansion was dramatized by the growing number of and participation in local strikes. Individual trades staged one-day walkouts in Genoa, Milan, and Turin. Occasionally these stoppages were punctuated by mass demonstrations. Ten thousand workers paraded through the streets of Turin on January 24. But the first nationally advertised and commented-upon demonstration occurred in Milan on February 16. Between 25,000 and 30,000 workers answered the summons of the CGL and ISP for a demonstration for the eight-hour day and for electoral reform. Through March these strikes remained essentially industrial in nature; thereafter political considerations and purposes edged to the foreground. In the meantime the moderates in both the CGL and the ISP were completely overwhelmed by militant Maximalists.[4]

[2] See the speeches by Orlando and Nitti in *Camera*, March 1 and 6, 1919, 18071–4 and 18637–9.
[3] Maurice F. Neufeld: *Italy: School for Awakening Countries* (Ithaca, N.Y.: Cornell University Press; 1961), 368–9; and Federico Chabod: *A History of Italian Fascism* (London: Weidenfeld and Nicolson; 1963), 35–9.
[4] *Avanti*, January–March, 1919.

Unabated economic hardships—in particular the high cost of living
—provided much of the fuel for this left-wing upsurge. But the appeals
of militant Socialists and syndicalists transcended these immediate
discontents. These pressed their indictment of the interventionists who
had dragged the nation into a costly war for selfish class and political
reasons. At that, the interventionists' scheme had misfired: instead of
netting substantial fruits of victory, the war had left a legacy of worsen-
ing economic and social conditions to the workers. In 1915 the interventionists had resorted to war to contain the Left; in 1919 they looked
to an annexationist peace to shore up their battered prestige and cover
up the sterility of military victory. Incidentally, unlike their French and
British counterparts, the Italian interventionists could not convincingly
hold out hope for substantial reparations and indemnities.

In any case, in 1919 as in 1915 the fundamental issues were
domestic rather than diplomatic. The Left denounced the smoldering
horrors and uneven sacrifices of war in its campaign to discredit the
political forces, symbols, and institutions which were blocking wide-
ranging constitutional, economic, and social reforms. In turn, the Right
pointed up the disloyalty, the defeatism, and the *renunciarismo* of the
Left with a view to discrediting the political carriers of basic change.

To be sure, Benito Mussolini was not an advocate of the status quo.
Determined to build a mass movement, he fashioned promises and
slogans for the specific purpose of cutting into the surging Socialist
following. Mussolini knew that in the battle against Socialism "negative
action" would not be enough, that his "anti-party could not live as a
mere negation." Hence, he called for the perfection of political democracy through universal suffrage, proportional representation, a constituent assembly, and the abolition of the Senate. And since political
reforms alone could no longer satisfy, he also advanced a social-
economic program. Among immediate goals he gave highest priority to
the eight-hour day, social security, graduated capital levies, subsidized
housing—especially for veterans—and, as a counter to the call for
Soviets, the establishment of economic councils, to be elected by
professional groups.[5]

No doubt these planks eventually served to attract recruits to the
fascist movement, which presently became part of the overall assault on
the established order. In the first half of 1919, however, Mussolini's
primary thrust was against the Socialists, and as such he acted as one of
the shields of the existing power structure.

For the time being Mussolini did not bother to criticize the Orlando
administration, Parliamentary government as such, or the capitalist
economy. Instead, he aimed nearly all his fire at the Socialists. He

[5] *Il Popolo d'Italia,* March 30, April 13–14, and May 1, 1919, cited in Edoardo and
Duilio Susmel (eds.): *Opera Omnia di Benito Mussolini* (Florence: La Fenice;
1954), XIII, 16–19, 47, 52–4, 97.

accused them of first having opposed the war, of then having turned defeatist, and of now seeking to mangle the hard-won military victory with an unsatisfactory peace. Mussolini's charges against the official Socialists paralleled the accusations of traditional Rightists, except that the latter would never have claimed the revolutionary label for themselves.

> In Italy alone we interventionists have a right to talk about revolution. . . . Unlike the crowd of [Socialist] party members, we need not wait for the Revolution . . . [because] we have already fought this Revolution . . . in May 1915.
>
> That May was essentially and sublimely revolutionary and to the extent to which it broke an infamous domestic impasse and decided the outcome of the World War, to that extent we revolutionary *fasci di combattimento* take it as our point of departure. That was the initial act of the Revolution. It was the start. The Revolution [then] continued for forty months under the guise of war. It is not over yet. . . . It will continue with changing speed. . . . As for our means, we are not guided by rigid principles. We will use whatever means—both legal and illegal—may be required. The new historical era which is opening is one of mass politics or democratic hyperbole [which] we cannot [afford] to oppose.[6]

By thus sanctifying the war and making it the touchstone of political loyalty Mussolini, the new Rightist, ranged himself squarely with the traditional Right. Whatever his long-range political and social aims may have been, in the short run he led the *avant-garde* of the attack on the Socialists under the banner of jingoist nationalism and with the demand for a victor's peace. Needless to say, the Socialists exposed Mussolini for the counterrevolutionary that he was.

Shortly after the Scala incident[7] the new Right began to take organizational shape. On January 19, 1919, Captain Ferruccio Vecchi, an ex-*arditi*, and F. T. Marinetti, the Futurist poet, presided over a meeting at which the Association of Arditi of Milan was formally charted. In short order this association launched a weekly—*l'Ardito*—and inaugurated a new meeting house, Mussolini being present for the occasion. Moreover, between January 20 and mid-March branches of the Associazione Nationale di combattimento sprang up in many cities which also experienced anti-Socialist and pro-Fiume demonstrations, all organized by proto-Fascists.[8]

As of early March Mussolini decided that there was need for a central organization to mobilize and direct this burgeoning protest

---

[6] *Il Popolo d'Italia*, March 18, 1919, cited in Susmel (eds.): *Opera Omnia*, XII, 309–11.

[7] See pp. 219–20 above.

[8] G. A. Chiurco: *Storia della Rivoluzione fascista, 1919–1922* (Florence: Vallechi; 1929), I, 87–90.

movement. Through the *Popolo d'Italia* he announced that on March 23 the delegates of veterans' groups would meet in Milan to organize a nationwide anti-party and to formulate a program and strategy with which to fight "the misoneism of the Right and the destructiveness of the Left."[9]

On Mussolini's initiative the fascists and the *arditi* of Milan held a preliminary meeting on March 21, chaired by Vecchi. Mussolini took this opportunity to outline his plan to bring together all interventionists and front-line veterans in a nationwide organization for the sole purpose of "turning victory to full account." This projected anti-party or super-party would prepare an exclusively Italian revolution of distinct Roman and Latin imprint, free of "Tartar and Muscovite" influences. Before adjourning, this local caucus set up the Fascio di combattimento of Milan, designated Vecchi to preside at the larger meeting on the twenty-third, and chose Michele Bianchi to become the Secretary General of the national Fascio, effective April 1.[1]

This national Fascio di Combattimento was founded right after the executive of the ISP voted to abandon the Second for the Third International[2] and Béla Kun was catapulted into power in Budapest. Of course, Mussolini had chosen this Sunday, March 23, independent of these events. Nevertheless, there is no doubt that his step was a response to the radicalization of the Left and not to the zealous agitation of the "misoneistic" Right. In fact, by securing the use of the assembly hall of the local "Association of Industrial and Commercial Interests," Mussolini publicly attested to his right-wing affinities, if not affiliations.

A motley collection of less than a hundred enthusiasts assembled in that small hall on the first floor of the Palazzo Caetani in the Piazza San Sepolcro. In this congregation of Fascists of "the first hour"—later lionized as *sansepolcristi*—Futurists mingled with *arditi*, syndicalists with retailers, white-collar workers with professional men. Evidently, here were "interventionists of all social categories, with a preponderance of petit bourgeois."[3] On the square below, meanwhile, a group of *arditi* mounted the guard, thereby signifying the organizers' predilection for para-military methods.[4]

At the morning session Mussolini introduced and explained three public declarations. In the first he hailed all veterans and assured them that the Fasci would push programs favorable to them. In the second, after swearing opposition to imperialism and accepting the postulate of a League of Nations, he committed the Fasci to work for

[9] Chiurco: *Storia*, I, 94–6; and *Il Popolo d'Italia*, March 2–18, 1919, cited in Susmel (eds.): *Opera Omnia*, XII, 259–311.
[1] *Il Popolo d'Italia*, March 22, 1919, cited in ibid., 317; and Chiurco: *Storia*, I, 98–9.
[2] *Avanti*, March 20, 1919.
[3] Giorgio Pini and Duilio Susmel: *Mussolini*, I (Florence: La Fenice; 1953), 390.
[4] Laura Fermi: *Mussolini* (Chicago: Chicago University Press; 1961), 155.

the rounding out of Italy "along the Alps and along the Adriatic, including the claim to Fiume and Dalmatia." Finally, he announced that in the coming general elections the Fasci would oppose all neutralists, regardless of party affiliations.[5] During the afternoon session Mussolini delivered a major address in which he sketched his program for political, economic, and social reforms. Among these he attached particular importance to the eight-hour day and minimum pay.[6]

The superpatriotic *Idea Nazionale,* one of Sonnino's staunchest boosters, welcomed the Fasci as valiant defenders of the state against the assault of domestic Bolshevism. Unlike the fatally divided constitutional parties this new movement had the merit of embracing a positive program with which to counter the constantly mounting militancy of the Socialists. It proposed to fend off Bolshevism "not by defending the existing organization of the state and its ruling class, but by canalizing the revolutionary forces into the national camp, both economically and politically.[7]

In both the *camera* and the press this nationalist camp relentlessly pushed for an annexationist peace. During the first week of March 1919 Orlando interrupted his work in Paris in order to inaugurate the new session of the House. In his governmental declaration he focused heavily on the paralyzing financial and economic crisis. His outline of the magnitude of this crisis and of the administration's timid remedial program elicited only very sporadic and meager applause.[8] Only when he turned to foreign affairs did the House really become attentive. Since the resignation of Bissolati and Nitti, the Premier had made no official pronouncement about his plans at the Peace Conference.

Would Orlando endorse Sonnino's extravagant claims, or would he ask for Fiume plus the Treaty of London, or would he offer concessions in Dalmatia in exchange for Fiume, thereby hoping to pacify the Right as well as the Bissolatians?

Orlando equivocated by declaring that "Italy could not ignore the appeal which came from that most Italian city, the jewel of Quarnero," and vowed to pursue Italy's sacred rights without intransigence but with firm resolve, mindful that her rights had been consecrated by incalculable popular sacrifices and sufferings, including the death of hundreds of thousands of selfless Italians. In spite of the equivocation this was the only point at which all the deputies, except the Socialists, jumped to their feet for deafening and prolonged applause, interspersed with cries of *"Viva Fiume!"*[9] On the other hand, the *Idea Nazionale* and the *Resto del Carlino* were dissatisfied, suspecting Orlando of

[5] *Il Popolo d'Italia,* March 24, 1919, cited in Susmel (eds.): *Opera Omnia,* XII, 321–4.
[6] *Il Popolo d'Italia,* March 24, 1919, cited in ibid. 324–7.
[7] *Idea Nazionale,* March 24, 1919, cited in Chiurco: *Storia,* I, 103–4.
[8] *Camera,* March 1, 1919, 18071–7.
[9] *Camera,* March 1, 1919, 18076–7.

appeasement. Even the Treaty of London plus Fiume would not do; there was another all-Italian city, Spalato, which craved liberation.[1]

As yet the Italian claims were not being dealt with by the chiefs at the Peace Conference. Compared to the German and Russian problems the Austrian, Yugoslav, and Greek questions seemed altogether less urgent, particularly *before* the Hungarian coup. Just the same, Italians were becoming restless. The Paris timetable implied—once again—that their country was a second-class power, in the same category with far-distant Japan. In and of itself Sonnino's ready agreement to wait until last was not unreasonable. However, during the excruciatingly long wait from January through mid-April he did little to assert his nation's influence at the Conference or to give the Italian public a sense of confident expectation.

Sonnino was never really interested in the newly emerging structure of world power and politics, except as it impinged very directly on the Italian question. From the point of view of diplomatic strategy and tactics he failed to appreciate the value of supporting suitors and suppliants whose interests were not immediately involved with Italy's. He gradually isolated his delegation within the Conference, an isolation which produced damaging diplomatic as well as moral consequences. Blinded by Italy's confrontation with nascent Yugoslavia, Sonnino was either hostile or indifferent to the representations of Poland, Czecho-slovakia, and Rumania. Nor did he consider offsetting his disinterest in smaller nations through a rapprochement with one of the Big Powers. In his view America was the arch-villain: she blocked the establishment of a *mare nostrum* in the Adriatic. He also distrusted France. Paris not only failed to favor Italy's claims to Dalmatia and Fiume with the proper enthusiasm but also loomed as a new rival in the Balkans and among the Slavs. Sonnino would settle for nothing short of his maxi-mum aims, instead of exploring the possibility of freely yielding un-essential points in exchange for gaining those that he considered absolutely vital. He thought in oversimplified *territorial* terms and their *political* pay-off inside Italy, to the near neglect of economic and financial considerations.

Whereas Trent, Trieste, Pola, and even Fiume—which he and Salandra had conceded to Croatia in the Treaty of London—could rightfully be claimed under the nationality principle, each of his other territorial demands needed a different justification. Accordingly, south-ern Tyrol was essential for reasons of military security; the Dalmatian coast, southern Albania, and the Dodecanese Islands for reasons of naval security; and overseas possessions in Asia Minor and Africa for reasons of commerce, raw materials, and population settlement. Since

---

[1] *Resto del Carlino,* March 2, 1919, cited in *Bulletin Périodique de la presse italienne,* No. 106, March 22, 1919 (March 1–15, 1919), 7; and *Idea Nazionale,* March 2, 1919, cited in *Review of the Foreign Press, APS,* March 12, 1919, 415.

Sonnino was estranged from the Wilsonian ideology and rhetoric, he could not convincingly offer to have Italy act as a "selfless" trustee for the League in an internationalized Fiume or a mandated Anatolia. In fact, he made no concrete proposals of any kind. He preferred to wait patiently for the Big Three as well as smaller states to secure terms which violated the Wilsonian dispensation, confident that these infractions would legitimize and fortify the entire range of his own demands.

In brief, Sonnino ignored the rest of the world while pursuing Italy's territorial interests with parochial and unbending single-mindedness. There was but one exception to his insouciance about Europe at large. At the Conference he invariably sided with the advocates of a full-fledged military crusade against the Soviet regime. Actually he was ambivalent about Russia's plight: whereas he welcomed her paralysis as an active protector of the Slavs, Sonnino was genuinely terrified by the danger of ideological and political contagion, Italy being singularly vulnerable. This fear of Bolshevism drove him to support—and be defeated with—Churchill and Foch in mid-February and mid-March. Had Italy been in a position to provide the manpower, finance, and matériel for the Foch-Churchill crusade, Sonnino might have had a valuable diplomatic trump. However, given Italy's military and material depletion, he had no alternative but to settle for indirect intervention. Meanwhile reports about his brave but meretricious anti-Bolshevik stand in Paris endeared him still further to his uncritical Rightist supporters back home.

Of course, not Sonnino but Orlando headed the Italian government and Delegation. In his world outlook, political inclinations, and operational code the Premier was closest to Lloyd George. He was conscious of Europe's, including Italy's, critical agony; he tended to appease rather than defy radical nationalism or Socialism; and he conceived of domestic and foreign policy as a symbiotic unit and process.

Unfortunately Orlando never managed to get a tight rein on his Foreign Minister. In foreign policy questions Sonnino, unlike Balfour, considered himself an equal rather than a subordinate of his chief. He dexterously played on Orlando's irresolution in diplomacy. The latter's hesitation was a function of self-doubt concerning his own diplomatic judgments, reinforced by a grudging deference to Sonnino's expertise. More importantly, Sonnino had solid political support both inside and beyond the *camera*. Orlando was not nearly so well served. As compared to Lloyd George he could not even rely on the Socialist Left. He was at odds with Bissolati, whose influence and power were spent in any case. He had also broken with Nitti, who continued to be erratic. As for the Giolittians, they persisted in their devious role even after first Luigi Facta and then Camillo Corradini were taken into the cabinet.

Moreover, although the Reformist Socialists, the Republicans, the Democratic Liberals, and even a good many Giolittians were inclined to so amend the Treaty of London as to reduce Italy's claims in Dalmatia, they mounted a campaign for the annexation of Fiume. In his deperate search for a firm political base of his own Orlando embraced the cause of Fiume, probably with the hope that this maneuver would bring him the political support needed to break loose from the Treaty of London. He miscalculated. The hoped-for coalition never gelled: personal and party rivalries persisted; conflicts of interest were irreconcilable; and fear of Bolshevism at home increased the moderates' susceptibility to supernationalist blandishments. The Parliamentary Fascio, the jingoists outside Parliament, and Sonnino hastened to seize their opportunity. They locked the Premier into a course which committed him to the Treaty of London plus Fiume.

As of mid-March the specter of Bolshevism was of rapidly increasing importance. The Right in particular attributed every industrial disturbance to the subversive activities of militant extremists. The ISP's break with the Second International, its denunciation of Turati's moderate Parliamentary group, and the politicization of strikes gave considerable credence to this charge. Sonnino and his backers warned that unless Italy's peace terms were met in Paris, the internal crisis would go from bad to worse; popular faith in the government as well as the state would be fatally shaken; and the national idea would be so tarnished that it could no longer rally people in defense of the established order. Needless to say, according to Sonnino the Bolsheviks and not the Fascists were spreading disorder and instability as a prelude to hoisting themselves to power.

Once Orlando realized that his efforts to broaden his moderate political base were miscarrying and that the radicalization of the Left could not be stemmed or reversed with minor domestic concessions, he gave up all hope of restraining Sonnino. He knew that in the long run the return of stability waited on the implementation of substantive political and economic reforms. At this juncture, however, he was not prepared to risk denying Italy's sick power structure the tonic of national exhilaration. As a result, in the Council of Four Orlando himself repeatedly tried to exploit the Bolshevik specter over Italy to frighten the Big Three into satisfying his demands.[2]

The March-April crisis in the Peace Conference coincided with the aggravation of disorders in Italy. On February 20, four days after the massive demonstrations in Milan, a group of big industrial firms in Lombardy and Liguria signed an eight-hour-day agreement with the Federation of Metallurgical Workers, a key affiliate of the CGL.

[2] Cf. Baker: *Woodrow Wilson and World Settlement*, II, 138–9, 303; René Albrecht-Carrié: *Italy at the Paris Peace Conference* (New York: Columbia University Press; 1938), 89–90, 102–3, 432–3; Rodolfo Mosca (ed.): *Vittorio Emanuele Orlando: Memorie, 1915–1919* (Milan: Rizzoli; 1960), Pt. 2; and Luigi Salvatorelli and Giovanni Mira: *Storia d'Italia nel periodo fascista* (Turin: Einaudi; 1956), 73–5.

However, controversies over the interpretation of this agreement followed in no time, and the government delayed introducing an eight-hour bill until May 10. Furthermore, not only the metallurgical union but also those of most other trades impatiently pressed for wage increases to catch up with the high cost of living.[3] By mid-March strikes began to proliferate: the fourteenth, the textile workers in Turin; the sixteenth, the workers at Fiat; the twentieth, a general strike in Pavia; the twenty-fourth, the dressmakers in Genoa; the twenty-fifth, the barbers in Milan; the twenty-ninth, the tailors in Turin; April 1, a demonstration in Bologna; the second, the metalworkers in Turin, Roverto, and Brescia; and the eighth, the metalworkers in Turin.[4]

Meanwhile, on March 18–22, the executive of the ISP, by a decisive three to one majority, formally pledged the party to a Maximalist course. In a series of radical motions this executive denounced the "deceptive appearance of the bourgeois-Wilsonian ideology"; urged the local parties to be wary of all old and new members whose wartime defensism was incompatible with Socialism; and joined the Third International because the Berne Conference had been but a sham. More significantly still, the executive resolved to try to hold the reformist Parliamentary delegation to its instructions: Turati, Treves, and their colleagues were enjoined to expose the deceit of Wilsonianism, to protest against vindictive peace terms, and to oppose all annexations. Hereafter at all levels the ISP proposed to center its political campaign around agitation against intervention in Russia, possibly with a view to preparing a general strike to secure the withdrawal of Italian troops.[5]

The Center-left parties were not insensitive to this swelling militancy and during the first week of April urged that it be checked by tackling the domestic crisis that was furthering it. The Constitutional Liberals called for "the acceleration in the rhythm of the evolution required by the times, with due respect for [established] institutions and . . . with disciplined order." Similarly, at a joint congress the Republicans and Bissolati's Reformist Socialists emphasized that "the specter of Bolshevism should not be used as a pretext for holding up the advance of the working class and the fundamental renewal of national life," otherwise anarchy would spread. To achieve the "social Republic" Italy needed a quick Wilsonian peace, a constituent assembly, universal suffrage, and broadened regional autonomy. The executive of the Radical Party made this same plea for universal suffrage as the key to peaceful and legal change, particularly to the political and economic advancement of the working classes. Of the three Center-left parties

---

[3] Hautecoeur: L'Italie sous le ministère Orlando, 211–13; and Neufeld: Italy, 370–1.
[4] For the most convenient and complete calendar of left-wing strikes and demonstrations, as well as of fascist activities, see Chiurco: Storia, I, passim.
[5] Avanti, March 19–23, 1919.

only the Radicals specifically advocated the recognition of unions, minimum wages, maximum hours, and social security. Also, the Radicals appealed for a united front of all Italians from the legal Socialists to the democrats in support of this "Social Radicalism."[6]

While these Parliamentary parties reaffirmed and updated their reformist faith without, however, changing their political tactics, the Fascists were busy establishing branches throughout Italy. Within four weeks of *sansepolcristo* day Fasci were organized in Genoa, Turin, Verona, Treviso, Bergamo, Padua, Naples, Pavia, Trieste, San Remo, Mestre, Brescia, Recco, Vigevano, Bologna, Rome, Perugia, Camerino, Stradella, Feltre, Forli, Savona, Porto S. Stefano, Varese, Spezia, Venice, and Zara. The Fasci di combattimento acquired ready-made strength when three established patriotic societies decided to affiliate *en bloc:* The Comitato della difesa dei diritti d'Italia of Milan, the Unione Famiglie prigionieri di Parma, and, above all, the 20,000-strong Associazione fra gli Arditi d'Italia.[7]

In Milan—the nerve center of both Socialism and Fascism—the local Fascio met on April 2 to prepare its campaign against Leninism. Mussolini, Marinetti, Bianchi, Ferrari, and Monzini took charge of the propaganda effort while five colleagues were assigned to look after finances. The Genoa chapter also made plans to act in the streets and the piazzas rather than in the town halls.[8]

The militant Socialists and the new Fasci were headed for their first encounter—which came in the week of April 11–18.

It was on April 9 that the ISP, in conjunction with the *Camera del lavoro* of Rome, ordered a general strike to be held in the capital on the eleventh. According to *Avanti,* the leaders originally planned a peaceful mass demonstration as a general show of unity and strength. The right-wing press instantly claimed, however, that they were preparing a provocative political march to protest the bloody repression of Spartacism in Germany, to commemorate Liebknecht's assassination, and to celebrate Lenin's birthday. In any event, the city authorities prohibited this demonstration. Defiantly, the Socialists escalated their march to be part of a one-day general strike.[9]

The security forces easily and without bloodshed controlled—but did not prevent—the mass march and arrested a string of leaders (D'Amato, Vella, Della Seta, Edoardo della Torre, and others). Of greater signifiance was that these normal police measures were supplemented by an unsolicited and equally unauthorized counterdemonstration. Allegedly without advance notice or planning, a group of *arditi* assembled in the Piazza Colonna and through the Via Nazionale

[6] The full texts of these party manifestoes are cited in *Bulletin Périodique de la presse italienne,* No. 108, April 17, 1919 (March 30–April 11, 1919), 7–8.
[7] Chiurco: *Storia,* I, 117, 128–30.
[8] Ibid., 117–18.
[9] *Avanti,* April 12, 1919.

marched to the War Ministry, where they listened to a jingoist oration by Luigi Federzoni, the Nationalist deputy for Rome. Simultaneously, another band of ultranationalists staged a demonstration in the Piazza del Quirinale. Still a third group assembled in the Piazza Sciarra, the home of two major dailies: whereas the *Giornale d'Italia* was cheered, abusive slogans were directed against the *Corriere della Sera*. This day witnessed minor skirmishes between Socialists and superpatriots, leaving a few light casualties.[1]

Since some 100,000 workers had joined in the march *Avanti* boasted that the Left had scored an impressive success. It even twitted Orlando, suggesting that in all likelihood he was grateful for this demonstration: at the Peace Conference he could point to it as evidence of "a vague and distant Bolshevik menace" which would worsen unless Italy's territorial demands were satisfied.[2] And, in fact, the Premier acted in the predicted manner. In the Council of Four he referred to "a Maximalist demonstration in the streets of Rome which, even though it turned against its organizers and ended up as a big patriotic manifestation, nevertheless was a sign of the fermentation in the Italian public mind."[3]

Orlando's interpretation of the clash coincided with right-wing estimates. The *Giornale d'Italia* affirmed that most workers participated only with great reluctance and that they opposed all seditious activities. But whereas this daily accused the Socialists of "treason against the nation, the dead, and the war crippled" and of undermining the delegation in Paris, it welcomed the "nationalist and patriotic counter-demonstrations which occurred here and there." Even the "accompanying incidents of like origin, which fortunately were inconsequential," were not censured. Both proved that "Italy was not Russia, that Italy was victorious . . . and that the triumph of Leninism was still far-off." Still, this day had all the earmarks of "a general rehearsal." The *Idea Nazionale* characterized the demonstration as a total failure: thanks to Rome's workers, the strike "organized in honor of Lenin and Liebknecht was transformed into a patriotic tribute to the army and victory." Mussolini was equally ecstatic about the "piteous, noisy, and irreparable failure" of the general strike organized by 30,000 party members who were not even united among themselves. "Italy was not Russia" but Eternal Rome, the center of three world civilizations, and the people were rising against those who were trying to mutilate or sabotage Italy's victory.[4]

---

[1] Chiurco: *Storia*, I, 118; and *DR, APS*, April 30, 1919, 575.
[2] *Avanti*, April 12, 1919.
[3] Paul Mantoux: *Les Délibérations du conseil des quatre*, I (April 11, 1919, a.m.), 221.
[4] *Giornale d'Italia*, April 12, 1919, and *Idea Nazionale*, April 11–12, 1919, cited in *Bulletin Périodique de la presse italienne*, No. 109, April 30, 1919 (April 12–25, 1919), 1; and *Il Popolo d'Italia*, April 11–12, 1919, cited in Susmel (eds.): *Opera Omnia*, XIII, 43–6.

The scene now shifted to Milan, where on Sunday, April 13, the Socialists staged a mass rally in the Piazza Garigliano, in the working-class section behind the central railway station. As the police moved in to break up the meeting, which was being harangued by the anarchist Ezio Schiaroli, numerous scuffles took place. In the *mêlée* a worker—Giovanni Gregotti—was killed and several others were wounded, some at the hand of anti-Socialist vigilantes.[5]

To protest the breaking up of this rally the leaders of the local *Camera del lavoro* and the party scheduled a twenty-four-hour general strike for April 16, to be capped by a mass meeting in the Milan Arena. In a last-minute appeal Turati cautioned the rank and file against disorders without, however, withholding his support.

The morning of the sixteenth was calm and uneventful; the mammoth rally was set for three in the afternoon. In the Arena the major speakers were Michele Bianchi of the CGL, Franco Mariani of the *Camera del lavoro,* and Treves of the Parliamentary party. All three urged the enthusiastic crowd to remain calm, to ignore provocations, and to go back to work the following morning. At the conclusion of the meeting the assembled workers peacefully returned to their homes, except for a small band of militants. These formed into a column and marched through the Foro Bonaparte and Via Dante toward the Piazza del Duomo, chanting and shouting revolutionary songs and slogans along the way.

In the meantime excited superpatriots started to gather for a counterdemonstration in the Via Manzoni, in the very heart of the city. This rival band of *arditi,* officers, students, and soldiers, belonging to the Fasci di combattimento and other patriotic organizations, marched across the Piazza della Scala, ominously skirted the Socialist-controlled Palazzo Marino, and through the Galleria Victor Emanuel headed for the same Piazza del Duomo. There they gathered around the Victor Emmanuel Monument, cheering the patriotic speeches of their leaders.

The security forces failed to put up a wall between the rival bands when the Socialists reached the Piazza. In the ensuing free-for-all many demonstrators were injured, the casualties being particularly heavy among the Leftists, who were then forced to retreat along the Via Dante. Encouraged by this triumph, some hundred Nationalists set out for the headquarters of *Avanti* in the Via San Damiano. For the second time the security forces were overwhelmed. A few shots rang out and an army private was killed. Incensed by this fatal shooting, which they blamed on the Socialists who were firing from within the besieged building, the agitators pressed their attack. They stormed the building,

[5] *Corriere della Sera* and *Avanti,* April 14–15, 1919, as well as other dailies, cited in *Bulletin Périodique de la presse italienne,* No. 109, April 30, 1919, 1–2; and Pietro Nenni: *Storia di quattro anni* (Rome: Einaudi; 1946), 21–2.

wrecked the printing plant, and finally set fire to furniture and paper supplies. In addition to the one soldier, four civilians were killed and a great many others were injured.

Later that evening, to celebrate their victory, a group of demonstrators waving the black banner of the *arditi* as well as the national tricolor assembled at the headquarters of the *Popolo d'Italia*. Mussolini obligingly came out on the balcony to acknowledge the cheers below and to commend his followers for giving the "Leninist mob" renewed proof that "all Italians were determined to preserve the fruits of victory."

During the following two days there were sympathy strikes in a half dozen Italian cities, with general work stoppages in Turin and Naples. By April 19, however, this particular round of demonstrations and counterdemonstrations had run its course.[6]

Except for *Avanti* the entire press arraigned the ISP and the CGL executives for their reckless agitation as well as for their irresponsible decision to stage a test of strength first in Rome and then in Milan. But with regard to the skirmishes between Socialists and superpatriots, the press of the Center and Center-left hesitated to put all the blame on the Socialists.

The *Stampa* flatly charged that the sacking of *Avanti* had been "prearranged and premeditated." Although *Epoca* averred that neither side had deliberately unleashed violence, it censured the anti-Bolsheviks for exaggerating the importance of the "red armbands, the portraits of Lenin, and the wish to commemorate Berlin's Red Week." Notwithstanding *Avanti*'s "verbal violence," the strikes, and the rallies, to date there had been no revolutionary movement. In this same spirit the *Corriere*, while blasting the Leninists for their provocations, nevertheless maintained that the government and not the White terror had the responsibility for the maintenance of order.[7]

Yet the right-wing press had no such qualms. According to the *Resto*, the *Perseveranza*, and the *Idea Nazionale*, the aims and methods of the Socialists were unmistakably Bolshevik and those who struck back in the name of the nation did so in "legitimate self-defense." Indeed, the Italian people as a whole "was grateful to the Milanese citizens for having shown by their energetic behavior what deep-seated roots Italy had struck in the hearts of Italians." In Milan "the terror of the revolution was suffocated . . . , Bolshevism was crushed . . . , and the proletarian dictatorship drowned in the Naviglio with the furniture of the *Avanti* and the illustrated postcards of Lenin."[8]

[6] *Bulletin Périodique de la presse italienne*, No. 109, April 30, 1919, 2; *DR, APS,* April 30, 1919, 575–6; *Il Popolo d'Italia,* April 18, 1919, cited in Susmel (eds.): *Opera Omnia,* XIII, 60; Chiurco: *Storia,* I, 121–3.
[7] Cited in *Bulletin Périodique de la presse italienne,* No. 109, April 30, 1919, 2–3; and *DR, APS,* April 30, 1919, 582.
[8] Cited in ibid., 582.

As for Mussolini, he characterized the encounters in Milan "as the first episode of the civil war." According to him, the counteractions, in particular the storming of *Avanti,* had been altogether spontaneous. At the same time he proudly and boldly declared that even though the Fascists had not planned these forays, "they accepted full moral responsibility" for them. The column which set out for the Via San Damiano was made up not of reactionaries, bourgeois, or capitalists but of "authentic soldiers, authentic workers, and . . . *macerati* of the trenches," firmly dedicated to the infinite progress of the working masses. These Fascists were sworn to make every last sacrifice to defend liberty and to protect the nation from "violence and the new Asiatic tyranny." Theirs was an "anti-party without statutes and regulations." They were neither republicans nor monarchists, Catholics nor anti-Catholics, Socialists nor anti-Socialists. Rather, they were realists and pragmatists resolved to solve problems within the framework of their flexible program for national salvation.[9]

During this week of simmering civil war Italy's diplomatic problems also generated increasingly heated agitation. It was no secret that as soon as the Rhineland, the Saar, and the reparations were settled the Council of Four would turn to the final discussion of Italian claims. The ongoing radicalization of the Left merely reinforced the Right in its resolve to hold the government to an intransigent foreign policy course. Whereas for domestic consumption the anti-Socialist press incessantly repeated that Bolshevism could not engulf a victorious nation, for Parisian consumption it took the line that without the satisfaction of Italy's diplomatic demands Bolshevism would be difficult to resist.

Two dispatches from Paris served to arouse nationalist tempers. One was the text of an article by Steed, the other a rumor that Wilson was digging in his heels. In his article Steed suggested that with Italy on the brink of Bolshevism, Orlando lacked the strength to hold out for his maximum demands. Moreover, since Italy would be an unreliable partner in the containment of Bolshevism, it was doubly important to turn Yugoslavia into a firm anti-Bolshevik bulwark. The right-wing press hailed Steed's influential column as proof that the Left was sabotaging Italy's diplomatic position. Meanwhile Paris was told that provided Italy was not cheated out of her victory she would emerge as a solid anti-Bolshevik bastion and ally.[1]

Of greater consequence were the rumors that Wilson had decided to stand fast on Dalmatia and to make Fiume a free international port. As

[9] Mussolini's interview with the *Giornale d'Italia,* April 18, 1919, and *Il Popolo d'Italia,* April 18, 1919, both cited in Susmel (eds.): *Opera Omnia,* XIII, 61–6.

[1] *Daily Mail* (Paris), April 13, 1919; *Bulletin Périodique de la presse italienne,* No. 109, April 30, 1919, 6; *Il Popolo d'Italia,* April 15, 1919, cited in Susmel (eds.): *Opera Omnia,* XIII, 57–9; *DR, APS,* April 30, 1919, 576.

it was he opposed his experts, who wanted Fiume to go outright to Yugoslavia. The President's own entourage did much to spread word of his decision. Starting April 10, and with official encouragement, Italian correspondents in Paris sent back dispatches designed to sound the alarm and to mobilize public support for the impending diplomatic showdown.[2]

The mildest protest came from the *Corriere,* which held that a free and neutral Fiume would be a solution "without justice or wisdom, a weak and dilatory expedient destined to perpetuate dissension." Not surprisingly the *Giornale d'Italia* was not nearly so restrained. According to this Sonninoist organ, if Wilson had his way Italy would "end a little East of Pola." The President had better realize that Italy would not renounce Fiume, Zara, Sebenico, and the islands. By April 12 the *Giornale* declared that if need be the government would fall back on the hallowed formula of the Risorgimento: *l'Italia farà da sè.* While intoning such go-it-alone slogans the entire jingoist press taunted Wilson for his double standard: whereas he placated American supernationalism by incorporating the Monroe Doctrine into the Covenant—thereby emasculating it—he proposed to deny Italy's vital claims.[3]

Presently the minatory manifestoes of the British and French parliamentarians further encouraged the patriotic firebrands, who gleefully pointed out that not only American but also Allied patriots were successfully pressuring their governments to protect their respective national interests. Various papers[4] promptly urged that this was the time for the Italian Parliament to strengthen the hand of its plenipotentiaries, in order that there be no wavering or concessions. There even were suggestions that the government itself was asking for such a display of support.

Be that as it may, on April 14 Senator Mazziotti made a preliminary canvass of his colleagues with a view to issuing a collective statement; and he called a meeting of all legislators interested in endorsing such a manifesto for the fifteenth in Montecitorio. About 150 Senators and 250 Deputies, mainly from the Parliamentary Fascio, answered this call, agreeing that this was the time to speak up. Then and there they signed a telegram drafted by Deputy Raimondo to be sent to Orlando. This telegram solemnly declared that "no Government or Parliament could accept a peace which disregarded the clearly asserted will of Italianate cities and offended the sentiments and interests of the Italian people by refusing to satisfy its territorial claims, economic and financial reparations, and the security of its borders, not to mention the unquestionable claims to which it was entitled by right,

---

[2] Ibid., 575.
[3] *Bulletin Périodique de la presse italienne,* No. 109, April 30, 1919, 7.
[4] *Corriere della Sera, Gazetta del Popolo,* and *Stampa.*

by treaty, by sacrifice, and by victory."[5] Not a dissenting voice was heard, though the Socialists stood aside. In the *Giornale d'Italia* Vittorio Vettori, its Paris correspondent, asserted that both "the magnificent attitude of the Italian people in facing the murderous attempts of the Leninists . . . and the expression of the opinion of the Italian Parliament" proved the ardent patriotism of a victorious and united nation which would refuse to be "disarmed by abstractions and sophisms."[6] Neither deals nor compromises would be tolerated. The Italian Delegation would secure the Treaty of London plus Fiume, or else *l'Italia farà da sè*.

Against this background of mounting nationalist pressures the Council of Four turned to the Italian question on April 19.[7] Wilson argued that just as strategic and economic considerations had been overruled in the settlement of Danzig, so they would have to be passed over with regard to Fiume. Since in addition to serving Yugoslavia, Fiume served the commerce of Czechoslovakia, Hungary, and Rumania, there were compelling reasons for establishing "its free use as an international port"—particularly since Trieste was going to Italy. Besides, the Italian population in the city "was not connected with Italy by intervening Italian population." As for the security argument, with the destruction of Austria-Hungary, the demilitarization of the Dalmatian coast, and the protection of the League of Nations, Dalmatia would cease to be an offensive bastion. Certainly the Yugoslav navy would be no threat to Italy unless Italian hostility drove Yugoslavia to ally herself with more powerful states.

Clemenceau regretted that his Italian colleagues went beyond the Treaty of London which allotted Fiume to Croatia. France could not adhere to one clause of a treaty while at the same time renouncing another. He urged the Italian delegates to "make one last effort to come to an agreement," emphasizing that Italy would be the primary loser if they catered to passing popular exaltation at the risk of breaking with the Allies. Clemenceau hoped, therefore, that even if they left the Conference to consult their people, "the forces of reason would bring them back." Lloyd George endorsed this plea, insisting that "M. Clemenceau could no doubt evoke a great demonstration . . . and satisfy powerful elements by announcing that the French frontier was to rest on the Rhine." And yet he had agreed to a compromise solution.

Orlando indignantly rejected the implication that he was courting popular favor. A truncated peace would injure Italy quite as seriously as a break with the Allies. Orlando wanted his colleagues to know that

---

[5] For the build-up of this press and Parliamentary pressure, including the full text of the telegram, see *Bulletin Périodique de la presse italienne*, No. 109, April 30, 1919, 6.

[6] Cited in *DR, APS*, April 30, 1919, 576.

[7] This discussion of the debates of April 19, 1919 (a.m.), is based on *F.R.,P.C.,1919*, V, 80–94; and Mantoux: *Délibérations*, I, 277–91.

he "preferred to die with [his] nation" and, should it come to that, he hoped that "the great Italian corpse . . . would not poison the [rest of the] world."

The following morning, April 20—Easter Sunday—the Big Four had their second full-blown discussion of the Adriatic problem.[8] Orlando led off by formally declaring that provided the Conference guaranteed Italy "all the rights which the Treaty of London had assured her," he would not "break the Alliance" and would "abstain from every act or deed which could have this signification." In other words, he retreated to the Treaty of London, confident that Britain and France would honor their pledge. Even though he did not explicitly renounce Fiume, he certainly indicated that it might be expendable. Possibly in order to magnify the sacrifice he was about to make, he reaffirmed that if Fiume were "not granted to Italy there would be among the Italian people a reaction of protest and of hatred so violent that it would [soon] give rise to the explosion of violent contrasts . . . which would be extremely fatal, just as much to the interests of Italy as to the peace of the world."

Wilson was not about to compensate Orlando for abandoning a port that had never been his to abandon. In his response he ignored the feeler and limited himself to explaining once again that the U.S. was not bound by and could not accept the Treaty of London. In turn Orlando exclaimed that he was not bound by the Fourteen Points, reminding the President that at the time of the Armistice he had made explicit reservations with regard to their application to the Austro-Hungarian settlement. Wilson readily conceded this point, attributing their impasse to "a fundamental difference of policy between them." He, for his part, wanted not only Germany's but also Austria-Hungary's frontiers drawn along primarily ethnographic lines. Realizing the futility of further debate, Lloyd George proposed that the signatories of the Treaty of London meet separately "to consider President Wilson's grave decision."

This separate discussion took place in the morning of April 21.[9] The three premiers were accompanied by their Foreign Ministers. Here was the old wartime Entente, minus Russia. Clemenceau and Lloyd George jointly reassured the Italians that if no compromise could be worked out they were bound to uphold the Treaty of London. Having given this assurance, they set out in search of an accommodation.

Both Lloyd George and Clemenceau strained to convince Orlando and Sonnino that since Wilson had been accommodating regarding indemnities and the Saar, it was worth seeking a basis for compromise. Clemenceau pointed to himself as an example: he had given up the

---

[8] This discussion of the debate of April 20, 1919 (a.m.), is based on F.R.,P.C.,1919, V, 95–101.
[9] The minutes of this meeting can only be found in Mantoux: Délibérations, I, 301–6.

frontiers of 1814 as well as the permanent occupation of the left bank in the face of stiff domestic opposition. Italy should make similar concessions which would, in the end, leave her with considerably better borders than at the outbreak of war. Even if today Orlando secured only a few points in Dalmatia, he would still be in an excellent position vis-à-vis public opinion.

But Sonnino would not budge. As was his habit, rather than make concrete proposals of his own he waited for his two Allies or Wilson to make them. He preferred to simply rehearse his stock arguments. In spite of a half-million dead and a country in ruin, Italy was being denied those rewards for which she had entered the war. Moreover, for five months America had said nothing. "Only now, after having made perfectly legitimate concessions to the other Allies was she trying to recover her virginity at Italy's expense by invoking the purity of principles." If the Italian Delegation accepted a Wilsonian settlement his nation would be overcome not by Bolshevism but by "disorder and anarchy."

Orlando promptly expanded on this interplay of peace terms and domestic politics.

> If I went back to Italy with a peace which provoked a popular uprising, I would harm the entire world. Should President Wilson's view prevail, there would undoubtedly be a revolution in Italy. Recently, in Rome and in Milan, skirmishes took place between the Bolsheviks and the patriots. The Bolsheviks were defeated; in Milan, two of them were killed. Well now, these nationalist elements, which at this time were so stirred up, would make a revolution if they considered the peace terms bad, and this time the Bolsheviks would be on their side, because they were in favor of revolution, whatever its nature or pretext. Whereas a satisfied Italy would remain absolutely stable and calm, a disappointed and dissatisfied Italy would mean revolution and a danger for the entire world.
>
> If I return to Rome, alone against the entire world and tell our people, as I did after Caporetto, to "stand up! have courage! [so that] the nation could be saved," I might be able to rally all the national elements. . . .

Before taking this fatal step he was still open to a compromise proposal which would not call the annexation of Fiume into question. Should such a proposal not be forthcoming he would demand the execution of the Treaty of London, pure and simple.

Lloyd George and Clemenceau were astounded to find that since yesterday Orlando and Sonnino had hardened their stand on Fiume. The British Prime Minister nevertheless advanced a concrete offer: to satisfy her security concerns Italy would get the offshore islands, while the entire Dalmatian mainland, thoroughly demilitarized, would go to the Yugoslavs. Because Fiume was not included in this offer both Italian spokesmen excitedly refused to even entertain it as a basis of discussion. With disarming candor Sonnino asked whether Italy was really expected "to give up Dalmatia without compensation?"

At the beginning of this session Lloyd George had warned of the danger of America's refusing to sign the Austrian Treaty. In his view it was of the utmost importance to involve the Americans thoroughly in the new concert of power, since if they did not "put oil in the machine" Europe's economic recovery would be difficult, if not impossible. Balfour returned to this theme at the end, applying it specifically to Italy.

> M. Orlando is afraid of revolution in Italy. But suppose Italy falls out with the United States, I do not see how her economic life can continue, and, in that event, how would you avoid the social revolution? This danger seems every bit as great to me as your return to Rome with a treaty which, in my judgment, would be perfectly satisfactory. . . .

Balfour had touched a sensitive nerve, and Orlando showed it. However, since Orlando was too far committed to Sonnino's collision course he denied that "one of the dangers was greater than the other, and [claimed] that by staying with his country he still had a chance of avoiding the revolution."

The British and French Premiers pursued their mediation effort at an afternoon session with the President.[1] Neither the Foreign Ministers nor Orlando was present. Having received renewed confirmation that the Italians unequivocally rejected the strategic offshore islands as a sufficient basis for discussion, Lloyd George wondered whether Sonnino might not be bought off with concessions in Asia Minor. Since Italy was economically poor and lacked natural resources, a sphere of influence over most of Anatolia, with ample scope for economic development, should be quite attractive. After making sure that this sphere of influence would take the form of a League mandate and that Turkey would retain some form of political presence, Wilson reluctantly agreed that this proposal should be explored. Still, the Allied premiers had no illusions. They knew that even the most favorable deal in Anatolia could not deflect Italian politics and passions from the Adriatic.

The President then suggested that perhaps the Italian delegates should be encouraged to go home to consult their Parliament. Meanwhile, since the American Delegation was being blamed for the deadlock, he had drafted a manifesto explaining his position, which he planned to publish in the morning.

Fresh from his encounter with Commons, Lloyd George thought it inadvisable for the Italians to face their *camera* with empty hands. He

[1] This discussion of the session of April 21, 1919 (p.m.), is based on *F.R.,P.C.,1919*, V, 106–9; and Mantoux: *Délibérations*, I, 307–15.

would have hesitated to ask Commons for instructions on indemnities without first having settled them. Experience had taught him that unless they were guided with a firm hand parliaments "behaved like undisciplined crowds." Should Orlando and Sonnino quit the Conference Italy would be seized by "an explosion and delirium."

As for the manifesto, both premiers urged Wilson to postpone it. They argued that in addition to closing the door to compromise, his premature statement would "unleash a storm in Italy . . . and mobilize public opinion" against him. Even though the President still felt that his public explanation should precede Orlando's, "in deference to his colleagues he agreed not to publish it immediately."

The three chiefs had another round on the afternoon of April 22, again without the Italians.[2] Lloyd George reported that in a private conference Orlando had stood his ground even when told that the President "was immovable . . . and that he wanted to present his case to the public immediately." In response to the offer of the offshore islands and the internationalization of Fiume, the Italian Premier "harkened back to Zara, Sebenico, and Spalato." The Prime Minister pleaded for one last effort. He proposed that in addition to making Fiume a free city and ceding the strategic islands to Italy, Zara and Sebenico should become free cities under the League with a provision for plebiscite at some future date.

This time not only Wilson but also Clemenceau balked, even after Lloyd George cautioned that a crisis in Italy would return Giolitti to power, and that Giolitti would conspire with the Germans. Wilson once again wanted to publish his manifesto. But the British Prime Minister again warned that it would unleash a storm. Since Europe "was like a field strewn with mines," ready to explode, he begged that he be given time to make his proposal. Though Clemenceau agreed, Wilson held out a while longer. The President predicted that after an initial outcry over his statement the Italian people would come to their senses and opt for continued cooperation with America. For the first time he then aired his concern about satisfying the Italians at the expense of offending the Slavs. In that event "the road would be open to Russian influence and to the development of a Slav bloc hostile to Western Europe." In the end Wilson nevertheless yielded to Lloyd George's supplications.

When the same three met in the morning of April 23 Lloyd George sadly confessed that this last offer had also been rejected.[3] Whatever the arrangement for Fiume, Orlando and Sonnino insisted on Italian sovereignty; they also wanted an Italian mandate over Zara and

[2] This discussion of the session of April 22, 1919 (p.m.), is based on *F.R.,P.C.,1919*, V, 135–7; and Mantoux: *Délibérations*, I, 328–39.

[3] This discussion of the session of April 23, 1919 (a.m.), is based on *F.R.,P.C.,1919*, V, 149–51; and Mantoux: *Délibérations*, I, 340, 343–6.

Sebenico. Wilson's patience was running out. With renewed emphasis he asserted that the Peace Conference had to choose between "drawing the Southern Slavs to Western Europe and the League of Nations or of throwing them back on Russia and Bolshevism." As for the British and the French, what would they do if the Italians asked them simply to execute the Treaty of London, thus forcing them to separate themselves from America? Lloyd George and Clemenceau were confident that they would be spared this dilemma since the Italians would never give up Fiume. But even if they should do so, there was another out: by withdrawing from the Conference the Italians would break the Pact of London of 1914, which bound them not to make peace separately. In any event, Wilson finally announced that he intended to publish his manifesto that evening, and this time neither Lloyd George nor Clemenceau even tried to dissuade him.

On this occasion not only did they not object, but Lloyd George presented for discussion a memorandum, drafted by Balfour, which explained the position of France and Britain. In it the two Allies made it unmistakably clear that they sided with Wilson on the question of Fiume. After a few minor changes in the text the two Premiers decided to forward this memorandum to the Italian representatives. However, they did not set a firm hour or date for its transmittal.

In his manifesto Wilson merely repeated publicly what he had been saying behind closed doors since late December and more particularly since April 14. Accordingly, America was not bound by the private Treaty of London; the Austrian Treaty should be made on the same general principles as the German Treaty, with particular regard for the newly liberated smaller states; the collapse of the Austro-Hungarian Empire ended the threat to Italian security in the Adriatic and the eastern Mediterranean; the demilitarization of the Dalmatian coast and the limitation of armaments of the new states under the League offered additional safeguards; the Italian minorities would receive adequate internationally sanctioned guarantees; and hence Fiume should go neither to Yugoslavia nor to Italy, particularly since it should serve the commerce of Central and Eastern Europe. Even though the statement revealed that Italy would get the Brenner frontier, it gave no hint of the various compromise formulas which had been unsuccessfully proffered during the past five days.

Obviously, Wilson never intended his statement to serve as a basis for close diplomatic bargaining between and among parties that were close to agreement. He realized that he was issuing an appeal calculated to produce political effects, much as his Fourteen Points and subsequent pronouncements had done during the last year of war. At a minimum he sought to encourage the Italian moderates to pressure Orlando into liberating himself from Sonnino and the Right. Without such a political realignment inside Italy Wilson could see no way out of the impasse. Not that he wanted the Italian Delegation to surrender unconditionally. But at a minimum he expected Orlando to engage in the same give-and-take as Clemenceau. Needless to say, he also looked beyond the achievement of this minimum objective. Should this appeal succeed in rallying not only the Wilsonians of Italy but also those of Britain, France, and even America, the entire peace settlement might be unveiled in a cleansed ideological and moral atmosphere.

As at the time of the Fourteen Points address, so now, the President's inclination to assert his leadership was reinforced by advice and pressure from many quarters. Within the American Delegation there was a rift among the advisers as well as among the Commissioners.[4] One group of advisers wanted the President to make considerable concessions to Italy, even on Fiume. The most prominent members of this group, who worked in close harness with Colonel House, were Mezes, Auchincloss, Miller, and George Louis Beer. Of these only Beer was a territorial expert, notably on colonial questions. Mezes was a political appointee—he was House's brother-in-law—whose background was in college administration and not in international affairs, history, or political science. Auchincloss, who was House's son-in-law, was equally inexperienced, except that Miller, his law partner, knew enough international law to qualify both of them for high-level posts. Significantly, these advisers of the House entourage—especially Miller, Auchincloss, and Mezes—energetically opposed any concessions to Lenin at the same time that they advocated an accommodation with Sonnino.

Pitted against them and vying for the President's attention were the five experts most immediately concerned with the Italian question: W. E. Lunt, the Chief of the Italian Division; Clive Day, Chief of the Balkan Division; Charles Seymour, Chief of the Austro-Hungarian Division; Douglas Johnson, Chief of the Division of Boundary Geography; and Allyn A. Young, Chief of the Division of Economics and Statistics. Beginning in January and with unwavering resolution thereafter, all five rejected Italy's claims to the Dalmatian coast and Fiume. When it appeared that the House group was in the ascendancy and that the Italian question was about to be tackled by the Big Four, these experts decided to seek a hearing. On April 4 they advised Wilson that in their unanimous opinion "Fiume should be given to Yugoslavia without restriction and . . . that it was unwise to make Fiume a free city."[5] In his extended talk with Orlando on the fourteenth, the President ignored this advice on Fiume. By then, also, the campaign in Italy

---

[4] For these cross-currents within the American delegation see Paul Birdsall: *Versailles Twenty Years After* (New York: Reynal and Hitchcock; 1941), Ch. xi. In spite of the almost total neglect of the political situation in Italy, this chapter is the strongest in this pioneering work.

[5] The five experts to Wilson, April 4, 1919, Wilson Papers, VIII A:32.

for the Treaty of London plus Fiume—and more—was going into high gear.

Consequently on April 17 the experts sent a follow-up letter to the President, this time with the additional signature of Isaiah Bowman, the Chief Territorial Specialist. They again urged Wilson not to yield, basing their plea on his own injunction to them in December, while crossing the Atlantic on the S.S. *George Washington,* to tell him "what's right and I'll fight for it . . . [and for] guaranteed position[s]." Unlike the President's statement of April 23, which was cast in terse and almost businesslike language, this letter recreated Wilson's own inspirational rhetoric.

> The Italian representatives demand Fiume and part of Dalmatia in order to emerge from the Conference with loot. . . . These districts belong to Yugoslavia, not to Italy. . . . [By not making them] an integral part of the Yugoslav organization . . . it would be charged that the principle, "There shall be no bartering of peoples," had been publicly and cynically thrown aside.
>
> Italy entered the war with a demand for loot [and even though] France and England surrendered to her demand . . . the belligerent nations, including Italy, agreed to make peace on the President's principles. *Italy now insists that she must carry home an ample bag of spoils or the government will fall.*
>
> If Italy gets even nominal sovereignty over Fiume as the price of supporting the League . . . the League of Nations will be charged with the acceptance of the doctrines of Talleyrand and Metternich. . . . *The Italian Government may fall,* but the Italian people cannot long withstand the opinion of the world.
>
> Never in his career did the President have presented to him such an opportunity to strike a death blow to the discredited methods of old-world diplomacy . . . [by destroying], by a clean-cut decision against an infamous arrangement, the last vestige of the old order [italics mine].[6]

During the two weeks between the first and the second letter the experts had slightly eased their stand. They still wanted these districts to go to Yugoslavia. However, instead of arguing against the internationalization of Fiume as such, they now warned against Italy receiving "even nominal sovereignty"—a position Orlando subsequently claimed. In any case, by return letter Wilson assured all six that his "instincts responded" to their views and he expressed his deep obligation for their "reinforcement of judgment in a matter which, like yourselves, I regard as of the most critical importance."[7] All along the Yugoslav representatives inclined to let Wilson fight their battle for them.[8]

[6] The six experts to Wilson, April 17, 1919, Wilson Papers, VIII A:38, and cited in Baker: *World Settlement,* III, 278–80.

[7] Wilson to Bowman, April 18, 1919, Wilson Papers, VIII A:38.

[8] See Ivo J. Lederer: *Yugoslavia at the Paris Peace Conference: A Study in Frontier-making* (New Haven: Yale University Press; 1963), Ch. vii.

While House and his advisers continued to weal and deal, Lansing, Bliss, and White backed up the experts. On April 18, at a meeting of the four Commissioners, Lansing repeated his firm opposition to a compromise on Fiume; "White and Bliss said the same, and so did House."[9] Three days later, however, when the President met with the Commissioners to explain the Fiume situation, "House said little." On this occasion Wilson read the statement which he intended to publish. There was "no compromise in it [and] Bliss, White and I [Lansing] were strong for it."[1] That afternoon Bliss advised Wilson that "if a break should come and if your statement should be published after the break, it might possibly be regarded as a defense of the American attitude, whereas, if it were published in advance of the break it would appeal to the world as the statement of basic principle which would leave the break with [without?] any justification in the eyes of the honest part of the world."[2] For special emphasis Bliss added that "Lansing and White both seem to think well of this suggestion."[3] In the morning of the twenty-third Wilson replied that while the two Premiers advised against immediate publication because it "would end the possibility of agreement with Italy," he would stand up for his rights and "not hold it back too long."[4] And, indeed, he issued his declaration later that very afternoon.

In the meantime Henry White begged the President to counteract the propaganda campaign in the Allied nations and America that blamed him for the protracted deadlock of the Conference. White wanted Wilson to make it "known to the Council of Four as soon as possible that not one American soldier, dollar, or pound of supplies for military purposes would be furnished until peace was made."[5] From Washington Tumulty expressed the same uneasiness about Wilson being blamed for this aimless drift. In spite of all the risks, he thought that the President "ought in some way to reassert [his] leadership publicly."[6] A few days later, in a separate cable to Admiral Grayson, the President's physician and confidant, Tumulty struck a note of unrestrained urgency.

> In my opinion the President must in some dramatic way clear the air of doubts, misunderstandings, and despair which now pervade the whole world situation. . . . Only a bold stroke by the President will save Europe and perhaps the world. That stroke must be made

[9] Lansing Diary, April 18, 1919.
[1] Ibid., April 21, 1919.
[2] Later that same afternoon Wilson used this argument to counter the two premiers' admonition that a premature statement would do irreparable harm. Mantoux: *Délibérations,* I (April 21, 1919, 4:00 p.m.), 310, 315.
[3] Bliss to Wilson, April 21, 1919, Wilson Papers, VIII A:39.
[4] Wilson to Bliss, April 23, 1919, Wilson Papers, VIII A:40.
[5] Henry White to Wilson, April 12, 1919, Wilson Papers, VIII A:35.
[6] Tumulty to Wilson, March 30, 1919, Wilson Papers, VIII A:30.

regardless of the cries and admonitions of his friendly advisers. He has tried to settle the issue in secret, only publicity of a dramatic kind can now save the situation. . . .[7]

This cable arrived on April 6, when Wilson was confined to bed with acute influenza and when the Saar and the Rhine frontier, let alone Fiume, still divided the Big Four.

Early the following morning the President, who made a rapid recovery, took a first step to jolt the three premiers. He ordered the S.S. *George Washington,* which was being repaired in the U.S., to sail for Brest at the earliest possible date. This thinly disguised pressure instantly moved Clemenceau—but not Orlando—to a more conciliatory position. Between April 8 and 13, the Franco-American stalemate over the Saar, the Rhine frontier, and reparations was broken and the press campaign against Wilson began to subside.[8]

Especially since he could not foresee the effectiveness of this proto-ultimatum, Tumulty was unhappy with the manner Wilson had chosen to reassert his leadership.

> The ordering of the *George Washington* to return to France looked upon here as an act of impatience and petulance on the President's part and not accepted here in good grace by either friends or foes. It is considered as an evidence that the President intends to leave the Conference if his views are not accepted. I think this method of withdrawal most unwise and fraught with the most dangerous possibilities here and abroad, because it puts upon the President the responsibility of withdrawing when the President should by his own act place the responsibility for a break of the Conference where it properly belongs. The President should not put himself in the position of being the first to withdraw if his 14 Points are not accepted. Rather he should put himself in the position of being the one who remained at the Conference until the very last, demanding the acceptance of his 14 principles. Nothing should be said about his leaving France, but he ought when the time and occasion arrive to re-state his views in terms of the deepest solemnity and yet without any ultimatum attached and then await a response from his associates. In other words, let him by his acts and words place his associates in the position of those who refuse to continue the Conference because of their unwillingness to live up to the terms of the Armistice. Then the President can return to this country and justify his withdrawal. He cannot justify his withdrawal any other way. . . .[9]

[7] Tumulty to Grayson, April 5, 1919, Wilson Papers, VIII A:32, and cited in Joseph P. Tumulty: *Woodrow Wilson As I Know Him* (Garden City, N.Y.: Doubleday, Page; 1921), 524.

[8] Baker: *World Settlement,* II, 57 ff.

[9] Tumulty to Grayson, April 9, 1919, cited in Tumulty: *Woodrow Wilson As I Know Him,* 525.

In this instance, as in all others, Tumulty was first and foremost attuned to the home reaction to his chief's diplomacy. He desperately wanted to stem if not reverse the anti-Wilson and anti-Democratic trend which had been growing apace ever since the November elections. Whether or not an appeal of Fourteen-Point vintage could do the trick was another matter. Tumulty may well have misread American public and party opinion as much as Wilson eventually misjudged the political situation in Italy.

In any case, given his success with public appeals during the war, the President never really considered precipitating a rupture without issuing a fiery manifesto. Tumulty's cables merely drove home the advantage of forcing his associates to walk out rather than walking out himself.

As of late March and with increasing frequency in early April, Ray Stannard Baker discussed with Wilson the timeliness of a public appeal.[1] In the early evening of April 7—hence some 12 hours after the *George Washington* was summoned—the two once again weighed the expediency and timing of an open declaration. At this juncture the President was still most immediately concerned with French obstructionism. If Baker pressed the Italian issue it was because of his long-standing involvement in it.

> I went up to see Mr. Wilson at 6:30 [p.m.]—the first time since he fell ill—and had a long talk. . . . What he said put new courage into me. He is going to fight, and fight to the end. . . .
> I told the President about the effect of his announcement regarding the *George Washington*.
> "Well, the time has come to bring this thing to a head," he said. "House was just here and told me that Clemenceau and Klotz had talked away another day. . . ."
> I then agreed, as I have done before, that a statement be issued at once—and with specific applications of his principles. This we discussed, he being doubtful about too detailed a statement upon the specific issues. *He said, if he had not fallen ill, the time for meeting the situation would have been today.* He proposed to stand upon his principles.
> "Then Italy will not get Fiume."
> "Absolutely not—so long as I am here," he said sharply.
> "Nor France the Saar."
> "No. We agreed among ourselves and we agreed with Germany upon certain general principles. . . ."
> . . . I told him how I had answered the Italians who declared they were going home if they did not get Fiume.
> "That is interesting," I said, "it would relieve us of a great responsibility."

[1] See pp. 571–2 above.

"How is that," they said.

"Well, we are now stabilizing your lira at 6.32. Of course, if you withdraw from the Conference, you cannot expect us to go forward doing that. . . . And our merchants are now shipping much wheat and other food to Italy. I presume they will not care to do this unless they are well assured of their pay." . . .

"That was exactly what you should have said," the President remarked [italics mine].[2]

By the time Wilson was well enough to return to the Council of Four—starting with the afternoon session of April 8—Clemenceau's inclination to strike a compromise began to be apparent. The time to take the Saar-Rhine-reparations issue to the public had passed.

Given Orlando's unwavering obstinacy on Fiume, it is hardly surprising that the Italian question should have become the occasion and pretext for the projected public blast. On the other hand, what if Orlando had accepted Wilson's offer of making Fiume a free city and Lloyd George's proposal for the offshore islands and Anatolia? And would Wilson have precipitated matters on the twenty-third had he not been told that Orlando was about to release a statement of his own,[3] and had there not been rumors that Orlando might leave Paris that night with the intention of proclaiming the annexation of Fiume upon his arrival in Rome?[4]

Anyway, after the statement was out, rather than quit in a huff the Italian Premier attended the Council of Four until shortly before his train left Paris in the early evening of April 24.[5] At this session Orlando convincingly argued that Wilson's declaration had pushed territorial issues into the background. The President was appealing "to the people of Italy and to the people generally" to question the wisdom and policy of his government and delegation. He had no alternative but to try to mend his political fences by going to Rome to enlighten the public at large and to consult Parliament. Orlando made a point of stressing that he was not breaking off negotiations. He was merely "returning to consult the source of his authority," much as his colleagues had done recently. After all, it was useless to continue these conversations since his three colleagues were agreed on Fiume. At the same time, no one should underestimate the difficulties facing him at home: "speaking among friends, the fact was that Italy had made Fiume a national question."

This time Lloyd George did not play the role of mediator. He freely admitted that he could not question Orlando's decision to go to Rome

[2] Baker Diary, Book XXII, April 7, 1919, 152–5.
[3] See Luigi Aldrovandi Marescotti: *Guerra diplomatica* (Milan: Mondadori; 1938), 257–60.
[4] Cf. Wickham Steed: *Through Thirty Years,* II, 328–9.
[5] This discussion of the afternoon meeting of April 24, 1919, is based on *F.R.,P.C.,1919,* V, 210–22.

since he himself "had felt it necessary to go to London in much less serious circumstances." Meanwhile, would the Italian government be represented in the first meeting with the Germans, who were about to arrive in Versailles, and in inter-Allied negotiations pertaining to reparations, coal, and the economic rehabilitation of Europe? When Clemenceau also asked, in a rather peremptory fashion, whether or not Italy would be represented at the meeting with the Germans, it was quite clear that the three were standing firm, were encouraging Orlando to go home for consultations, and were preparing to put the legal onus for any break on Italy.

Sonnino—the only Foreign Minister who regularly accompanied his chief to the Council of Four—was alone in speaking as if this session were merely another round of diplomatic bargaining. But rather than submit negotiable terms himself, he once again challenged the Big Three to offer a concrete formula on which they were agreed among themselves for submission to the Italian Parliament. In the hope of sowing discord among the three, Sonnino charged that judging by Wilson's statement the President was not aware or did not approve of "certain additional proposals" which had been made during the last few days. Lloyd George instantly interjected that even though the President was not keen on these proposals, "as he understood the matter he [Wilson] was prepared to accept them if his Italian colleagues would agree." In turn, Wilson himself all but confirmed this interpretation. He claimed that when he asked Lloyd George to "ascertain if the Italians would be ready to discuss on this basis, the reply he had received was that they were not." Even at this point "he did not want his Italian friends to think that he would not discuss any aspect of the question," and therefore offered "to go over the ground a hundred times, if necessary." However, he would not "make a proposal for Mr. Orlando to present to Parliament." In his judgment the Italian Premier should seek authority to work out the best possible compromise solution. Whereas Sonnino countered that "if only a compromise could be agreed to now, Parliament could [then] be asked to accept it," Orlando agreed that he should merely ask for a general mandate.

With that Orlando announced that in order to make his train he had to start for the railway station at once. It was at this point, just before leaving Lloyd George's study in the rue Nitot, where this meeting was held, that Maurice Hankey handed him the Balfour note, signed by both Clemenceau and Lloyd George.

In early January Wilson had made a triumphal visit to Italy. Now it was Orlando's turn to rally the crowds. Overnight he became a national hero *malgré soi,* completely supplanting Sonnino as symbol and champion of territorial fulfillment. All along his rail route to Rome there were enthusiastic popular demonstrations, notably in Turin, Alessandria, Genoa, and Pisa. On his arrival in the Eternal City church bells rang out, airplanes blanketed the streets with patriotic fliers, and during his automobile ride from the station he was hailed with cries of *"Viva Orlando! Viva Fiume! Viva l'Italia!"*

Of course, in his countermanifesto, which in Italy was published alongside Wilson's declaration, Orlando reiterated all the stock arguments in support of the Treaty of London plus Fiume, justifying the claim to this latter port with Wilson's own principle of self-determination. Moreover, his reply was directed against Wilson and made but a passing reference to the joint Anglo-French note. In other words, Orlando created the impression that he proposed to fight for Sonnino's full program without revealing the degree to which Italy was isolated in the Conference, particularly on the Fiume issue.[6]

But even assuming Orlando's countermanifesto had been modulated, it could not have checked the passionate anger which swelled up against Wilson or the national apotheosis of Fiume. The Italian Premier knew better than the American President that there were few politically organized moderates or Wilsonians to be found and that many of these few wanted Fiume for Italy, even though they rejected the extravagant claims on the Dalmatian coast as well as in southern Tyrol.

Unlike in Britain and France even the Socialist party was not in Wilson's corner. The Maximalists, whose strength was outside Parliament, bluntly declared that they "never believed that the American President, with his Fourteen Points, took up the cudgels for the good of humanity or the rights of people, any more than [they] believed that in his current opposition to Italian aspirations in the Adriatic he was idealistically motivated." In fact, they prided themselves in "not being Wilsonians." As Socialists they had opposed Italy's entrance into the war four years before; and some four months ago they had boycotted the deafening welcome to Wilson during his Italian visit. At this juncture "they could not fight for either one of the opposing theses" because each was equally antithetical to the true interests of the proletariat.

Exhilarated by Wilson's blast, the British Labour Party sent a telegram urging the Italian Socialists to do battle for a peace based on the Fourteen Points. Significantly, the essentially reformist Parliamentary group joined with the Maximalist Executive in sending a barbed response: "we thank you for your telegram, but we note that Wilsonian principles are every day more and more wrecked by the policy of capitalist governments, including the American and British governments, which compete in being Wilsonian only when countries other than their own are in question, otherwise they are imperialistic." Sarcastically, they declared their readiness to join their British colleagues in condemning capitalist policies and in "hastening the

[6] See Albrecht-Carrié: *Italy at the Paris Peace Conference*, 144–9.

complete and general resumption of contacts among all the proletariats on the basis of the principles adopted at Zimmerwald." Even Turati and Treves did not abstain on a declaration in which the Left maintained that it was "not surprised to witness the bankruptcy of the [Wilsonian] ideology which had fostered the utopian illusion of being able to tame the capitalist interests unchained by the War." This illusion that the men in Paris had a choice "between Wilson and Lenin" was fading rapidly and inexorably.[7]

In view of the recent radicalization of the Left, this refusal to come out fighting for Wilson was not particularly surprising. Besides, Bissolati rather than Turati was the logical rallying point for moderates of the Left and Center-left. However, Wilson's declaration was totally unsuited for this purpose, notably because it clashed with Bissolati's position on Fiume. Granted, the Reformist Socialist leader refrained from urging all Italians to close ranks around their government. Even so, harking back to his January speech in Milan, he appealed for a compromise in Dalmatia "in exchange for an Italian Fiume with an autonomous Zara, supplemented by guarantees for Italian nationals along the Adriatic shores."[8] Since by now the claim for Fiume had crystallized into the battle cry of all jingoists, Bissolati's appeal was widely—and not inaccurately—hailed as an endorsement of the seething nationalist insurgence.

The Democratic and Liberal press also was up in arms. Editorial writers and columnists in the *Stampa, Secolo, Tribuna,* and *Corriere della Sera*—not unlike Sonnino—charged Wilson with trying to recapture his moral virginity and political popularity at Italy's expense. The President had gone from compromise to compromise, from concession to concession with Britain, France, Poland, and Czechoslovakia. Moreover, out of sheer political expediency he had dictated the Monroe Doctrine clause and vetoed the principle of racial equality. Italy refused to offer herself as a sacrificial lamb for the principles of diplomatic purity that were violated for the benefit of all other nations: the principles that were compromised in Paris could not be cleansed in the Adriatic. Though the Giolittian organs conceded that Italy's delegates may well have committed grave tactical blunders, they proclaimed that this was the time not for criticism but for loyal support of the government. There were two keys to the situation: the degree of Parliamentary support for the cabinet and the degree of Allied support for Italy in her disagreement with Wilson.[9]

[7] *Bulletin Périodique de la presse italienne,* No. 110, May 10, 1919 (April 26–May 5, 1919), 3; *DR, APS,* May 7, 1919, 15; *Critica Sociale,* Vol. XXIX, No. 8, April 16–30, 1919, 85–7.

[8] Cited in Leonida Bissolati: *La Politica estera dell'Italia dal 1897 al 1920* (Milan: Fratelli Treves; 1923), 415.

[9] *Bulletin Périodique de la presse italienne,* No. 109, April 30, 1919, 15, and No. 110, May 10, 1919, 1–4.

The alienation of the moderates from Wilson was most glaringly reflected in Salvemini's bitter broadside. With sharp sarcasm he inquired why the President wanted to impose "absolute justice" on Italy alone? Why did he not appeal to the British people about the German colonies, the French people about the Saar, the Yugoslav people about Pola, and the American people about the Monroe Doctrine? Furthermore, because the security arrangements of the League were still untested, Wilson was not asking Britain to abandon Gilbraltar, Malta, and Suez. Indeed, he was even recognizing the British protectorate in Egypt. Hence, "why not recognize Italy's right to protect herself in the Adriatic by occupying those islands off the Dalmatian archipelago which would make her coast secure?" If Italy was to be barred from Dalmatia because it was Slav territory, then the Slavs should renounce Fiume, which was "2/3 Italian." As for the argument that the Slavs needed Fiume for their commerce, Article 21 of the Covenant enjoined all states to guarantee free passage and equitable treatment for the commerce of all member nations. Whereas the Slavs seemed entitled to doubt the League's ability to see to it that Italy would provide freedom of transit in Fiume, Italy was expected to trust the League to protect the rights and interests of the Italian population of that port. Salvemini held that this unequal treatment of Italy had called forth popular disillusionment, hostility, irritation, and even revolt.[1]

Wilson must have known—certainly he should have known—that except for these discordant Center-left and Center parties and factions no one could conceivably give Orlando a political base and mandate for accommodation in the eastern Adriatic. Unquestionably they alone were willing to shed "the shirt of Nessus—the Treaty of London—which Sonnino had put on Italy's back." However, given their determination to hold the middle ground between the radicalized Left and Right, they could not agree that Italy go without any shirt. In exchange for the shirt of Nessus they wanted Fiume, which Wilson's manifesto denied them.[2]

Perhaps Wilson would have elicited a better response had he issued an appeal explaining that the Italian Delegation had stubbornly rejected both the internationalization of Fiume and a special regime for the offshore islands. On the other hand, such a statement would have pushed the Center-right toward the extreme nationalists, thereby further undermining the Orlando ministry.

As it was, these extreme nationalists did their best to create an ugly and intransigent atmosphere with their racy editorials, manifestoes, and demonstrations. Vittorio Vettori of the Giornale d'Italia accused Wil-

---

[1] "Il Messagio di Wilson," in Unità, May 3, 1919, cited in Salvemini: Dal Patto di Londra alla pace di Roma (Turin: Piero Gobetti; 1925), 270–4.

[2] Cf. Unità, May 3, 1919, cited in DR, APS, May 14, 1919, 40.

son of falling back on his late demagogic and subversive tactics of wartime.

> Drunk with the success of his direct appeals to the German people he thought these same tactics would work with the Italian people. . . . [But] he was gravely misinformed about Italy's internal situation, since he sincerely proceeded on the ridiculous assumption that Bissolati might return to power, forgetting that Bissolati himself attached major importance to the annexation of Fiume.

Sonnino's organ intensified this jingoist incitement, implying that, if need be, all good citizens would favor outright annexations under the motto *l'Italia farà da sè*.

The *Idea Nazionale* actually called on the government to decree the annexation not only of Fiume but also of the Adige, all of Istria, and Dalmatia, including Zara, Sebenico, and Spalato. To be sure, Italy had neither wheat, coal, nor gold. But her profound consciousness of her rights made up for this material weakness. Moreover, she could easily hold these annexations, since only the Yugoslavs would want to contest any of them with arms, and they lacked the military capacity to do so. Besides, except for Spalato, all these territories were already being controlled by Italian occupation forces under the Armistice agreement. All the nationalist and jingoist organs—*Giornale d'Italia, Idea Nazionale, Gazzetta del Popolo, Perseveranza,* and *Resto del Carlino* —insisted that at a minimum the government should arbitrarily annex all disputed territories that were under Italian occupation.[3]

Through the *Popolo d'Italia* Mussolini nourished this boisterous campaign. He assured the nation that even though the Fascists "were busy guarding Milan they would not neglect Paris." By trying to cut the Croats, Slovenes, and Bosnians in on the spoils, Wilson was preparing to defraud Italy. Worse still, Italy's Allies seemed to be siding with him. Was the Treaty of London but one of those "scraps of paper," to be torn up at will? In any case, Cairoli's policy of *mani nette* may have been acceptable in 1878, when Italy's national conscience was still young. Today, forty years later, at the Paris Conference, a fully awakened nation expected equal treatment with the other Great Powers.[4]

Mussolini lambasted Wilson's manifesto as an infamous trick, swindle, and *parecchio*. The President of the vast continental nation was contemptuous of "little Italy." Furthermore, his narrow American mentality—which was both anti-European and anti-Latin—was incapable of understanding European affairs. Most important, Mussolini saw a direct relationship between Wilson's message and the "mysteri-

---

[3] Excerpts from the right-wing press cited in *Bulletin Périodique de la presse italienne,* No. 109, April 30, 1919, 10–12, and No. 110, May 10, 1919, 1–2; and *DR, APS,* May 7 and May 14, 1919, 14, 36.
[4] *Il Popolo d'Italia,* April 20–25, 1919, cited in Susmel (eds.): *Opera Omnia,* XIII, 70–81.

ous, ignoble, and vulgar" appeasement campaign which in Italy was directed against Sonnino and the Treaty of London. But Wilson vastly overestimated the influence and power of the *renunciatori*, whom the Fascists were fighting with all their strength, if need be by occupying the piazzas. In any case, the Italian people could not be insulted with impunity; and more than ever they were determined to resist external pressure. As it was, their delegates were excessively conciliatory. Italy was entitled to Ragusa, Cattaro, and Spalato, let alone to Fiume, Zara, and Sebenico. On April 27 Mussolini joined the nationalist press in asking for the outright annexation of Fiume and Dalmatia. In his view the risks were minimal. The Yugoslavs could only "grit their teeth" and issue "more or less vibrant diplomatic protests," since they were without "field artillery, machine guns, airplanes, ammunition, provisions, and . . . internal cohesion."[5]

The jingoist uproar was not confined to these incendiary editorial pages. There were incessant pro-Italy demonstrations in Fiume, where the local "Young Italy Society" fashioned the battle cry "Italy or death!" and pledged to destroy the city rather than live under Slav or international yoke. By April 26 the National Council of Fiume proclaimed the port city's annexation to the motherland and demonstratively transferred power to General Franceso Grazioli, the ranking official of the Italian occupation authorities. The annexationist clamor reached a comparable pitch among irredentists in Trieste, Pola, Zara, and Trent.[6]

Of course, in Italy proper, the protest movement against renunciations and against Wilson predated the President's manifesto. On April 22 the Milanese Fascio di combattimento held a public rally in the Piazza San Sepolcro which not only berated all Leninists but also exhorted Sonnino to make a firm stand for Fiume and Spalato.[7] The following day, April 23, Rome was treated to a sizable parade in which even a number of Deputies and Senators marched behind banners bearing the inscription *Viva Fiume! L'Italia farà da sè!*[8]

Naturally Wilson's appeal poured oil on this smoldering fire of direct action. On April 27 a capacity crowd wildly cheered yesterday's self-decreed annexation of Fiume. On the twenty-eighth various national organizations, in conjunction with the Fascists, held mass meetings in Milan and Turin, urging the government to act boldly in Dalmatia. During these same two days locals of the Fasci di com-

[5] *Il Popolo d'Italia*, April 26–29, 1919, cited in ibid., 82–90.
[6] *Idea Nazionale*, April 26, 1919, and *Tribuna*, April 27, 1919, cited in ibid.; DR, APS, May 7, 1919, 15; and *Corriere della Sera*, April 27, 1919, cited in *Bulletin Périodique de la presse italienne*, No. 110, May 10, 1919, 2.
[7] Chiurco: *Storia*, I, 130; and *Il Popolo d'Italia*, April 23, 1919, cited in Susmel (eds.): *Opera Omnia*, XIII, 74.
[8] *Review of the Foreign Press*, APS, May 7, 1919, 14.

battimento staged pro-Fiume and pro-Dalmatia demonstrations in Savona, Stradella, Forli, Cremonia, Bari, Perugia, and Brescia.[9]

All these activities were but a prelude to a dramatic national revival meeting at which Gabriele d'Annunzio officiated. As early as April 23 Federzoni sent a telegram to the eccentric poet begging him to come to the capital, where he was needed to help mobilize the national will. In preparation for his arrival the major patriotic and jingoist associations grouped themselves together in a "Central Action Committee for the Recovery of National Territories." Under the auspices of this committee 10,000 nationalist fanatics met in the Augusteo on May 4 to acclaim a motion calling for the immediate annexation of all the territories covered by the Treaty of London; the liberation of other enslaved Italian cities, notably of Fiume and Spalato; and the preparation of all measures necessary to ward off foreign reprisals. This motion, which was also endorsed at nationalist rallies throughout Italy, set the mood and stage for one of d'Annunzio's renowned apocalyptic orations.

> Our epic May begins. I am ready. We are ready.
>
> Four years ago we prepared the consecration of the Thousand at Quarto, with a military vigil. Today we consecrate more than 40 million Italians. . . . I repeat that today only Italy is great, that today she alone is pure. . . . Against us I see only big and small merchants, big and small usurers, big and small forgers. . . . As in that other month of May we find before us the same coterie of bankers. . . .
>
> Annexation! Annexation! Such was the battle cry of all true Italians in 1859. . . . Isn't it ours? . . .
>
> In the face of criminal intrigues Italy must be bold. Powerless against defeated and disintegrating Russia, Germany, and Hungary, will the Peace Conference prevail over the most victorious of all nations, over the nation which saved all other nations? . . . Will the Triumvirate pronounce sentence against us, and in which tone? Are their peoples with them? . . . They couldn't be, unless Europe is Prussian and Pharisaic, and then the peace should be signed in Potsdam rather than in Versailles.
>
> Fiume, Zara, Sebenico, Traù, Spalato, Almissia, and—why not include your name—Ragusa? . . . Creatures of life, more alive today, in this Italian hour, than in all the past centuries of Rome and Venice, today more beautiful than yesterday and less so than tomorrow, impregnable flowers of Latin beauty, covered with the dew of blood and tears. . . .
>
> No, the race of George Washington and Abraham Lincoln cannot be allowed to be the echo and the heart of the Croatified Quaker.
>
> Down there, on the roads of Istria, on the roads of Dalmatia, all

[9] *Il Popolo d'Italia* and *Gazette del Popolo*, April 29, 1919, cited in *Bulletin Périodique de la presse italienne*, No. 110, May 10, 1919, 2; and Chiurco: *Storia*, I, 131.

of which are Roman, do you not hear the rhythmic footsteps of a marching army?

With the eagles and the Tricolour and without further delay let us rededicate this army's month of May so that Italy shall once again be in motion, setting out from the top of the Capitol.

It is up to us.[1]

In this supercharged atmosphere, with the word annexation written across many Roman walls, Orlando set out to rally Parliament behind him. Granted, he never tried to quell the nationalist turbulence with sobering speeches or manifestoes, possibly because he acknowledged the futility of such efforts. From his intimate experience with Giolittian political manipulations he had learned to tackle acute Parliamentary crises by calculated behind-the-scenes maneuvering. Hence he did not take his story and his appeal for support to the *camera* without first thoroughly preparing the ground.

On April 26 the two branches of the legislature designated 15 members each—representing all major parties and groups except the Socialists, who abstained—to sit on a joint commission to draft a statement expressing the Parliamentary consensus. On this commission, where Luzzatti spoke for the administration, the annexationists definitely had the edge. Under their sway a text was adopted that held the government to concrete and specific territorial claims, notably to the Treaty of London plus Fiume. Needless to say, such a motion would have riveted the government to a rigorous program, denying it all freedom of diplomatic give and take. On April 27 the commission met for more than two hours with Orlando, who insisted that a motion tying the delegation's hand so rigidly was totally unacceptable to him. What he demanded—and eventually secured—was an order of the day pure and simple, an open-ended mandate of the sort he and Wilson had agreed would be most practical and desirable. Perhaps it should be added that by this time even the *Idea Nazionale* began to worry lest the jingoist campaign drive the government into an irreparable break with the Peace Conference.[2]

When Orlando and Sonnino entered the *camera* in the early afternoon of April 29 they were greeted by a rousing standing ovation, punctuated by cries of *Viva Fiume! Viva la Dalmazia! Viva l'Italia!*[3] Before the Premier took the floor the Secretary read telegrams from Italian patriotic associations in Fiume, Spalato, Traù, Zara, Sebenico,

---

[1] Heavily censored text in *l'Idea Nazionale, Popolo d'Italia,* and *Giornale d'Italia,* May 5, 1919, cited in *Bulletin Périodique de la presse italienne,* No. 110, May 10, 1919, 8–10. See also Chiurco: *Storia,* I, 131–2.

[2] *Secolo, Stampa, Corriere della Sera, Giornale del Popolo, Il Giornale d'Italia,* and *Idea Nazionale,* April 27–29, 1919, cited in *Bulletin Périodique de la presse italienne,* No. 110, May 10, 1919, 2–3, and in *DR, APS,* May 14, 1919, 35–6.

[3] This discussion of the April 29 debate is based on *Camera,* April 29, 1919, 18849–63.

Abbazia, and the island of Brazza, all of them demanding annexation. Each wire brought forth wild cheers and throughout the reading "the whole House remained standing, with the exception of the Official Socialists, who stood up for Fiume and sat down for the rest."[4]

Eventually Orlando mounted the rostrum to deliver his eagerly awaited statement. Given his audience's agitated mood he thought it advisable to start with a plea for "calm and serenity" in this grave hour. As if to counter the raging nationalist tempest, he promised that his statement would be "an objective and impartial exposition of the facts."

According to Orlando's summary of the course of the negotiations in Paris, the trouble did not start until April 14, when President Wilson—in conversation and in a detailed memorandum[5]—barred Italy from the Dalmatian coast and the offshore islands, "granted Fiume only incomplete liberty," and even shattered the unity of Istria. After he told the President in unequivocal terms that these conditions were totally unsatisfactory, there followed intensive negotiations in the Council as well as concerted efforts by Britain and France to effect a conciliation.

At this point Orlando forced his historical narrative. Rather than give his listeners an inkling of Lloyd George's compromise package, he affected to have been completely surprised by Wilson's message in the midst of direct negotiations with the British Prime Minister. Once this message was issued he had no alternative but to come home to consult the country and Parliament. As for Italy's two Allies, they were ready to honor the Treaty of London, but with regard to Fiume they would go no further than to make that port "a city-state, free and independent." He softened the impact of this confession with the exaggerated assertion that the final session of April 24 had revealed continuing disagreements between the Allies and the President.

So much for the past. What about the future? In this concluding part of his speech Orlando said nothing to exacerbate nationalist sentiments or to feed annexationist expectations. Of course he promised to resist any proposal which would cut into the "essential requirements of national conscience and dignity." However, he studiously avoided defining the hard core of Italy's claims while stressing the importance of preserving alliances and friendships. Most important, he rejected the "spirit of blind intransigence," warned against yielding to "excitement and exaltation," and summoned the people to give proof of "prudent and austere calm." Orlando rounded out his presentation with an appeal for continuing the political truce of men and parties until after peace was made.

By prearrangement Luzzatti was the next speaker. He proceeded to

---

[4] *DR, APS,* May 14, 1919, 35.
[5] Orlando distributed a copy of this memorandum to all the Deputies and Senators.

move the joint commission's noncommittal motion, of which he was the chief architect.

> As guardian of the dignity and interpreter of the will of the Italian people, this Chamber reaffirms its solidarity with and full confidence in the Government to secure the supreme rights of Italy as an indispensable condition for a just and durable peace.

Probably in order to head off inflammatory oratory on the floor of the *camera* Luzzatti himself recommended the motion in rather extravagant terms. As he put it, by voting this text the *camera* would instruct the delegation to claim the Brenner frontier, all of Istria, Fiume, the Dalmatian towns promised in the Treaty of London—plus the right to protect those Italian settlements in the Adriatic that were not covered by any treaties.

Spokesmen for the Parliamentary Fascio—or even for the Fasci di combattimento—could not have asked for more. Hence, the Rightists kept quiet, also because they relied on Sonnino, Barzilai, and Salandra to continue keeping a sharp eye on the chief. It was left to Turati to close the debate. His address was heavy with irony and embarrassment.

Turati's speech was remarkable not for what it said about the annexationists but for its sarcastic treatment of Orlando, the Allied Left, and Wilson. After the Armistice the Premier had promised an equitable peace. Since then he had freely consented to oppressive terms favorable to his Allies, in the hope of being repaid in kind. Granted, Fiume should have the right to self-determination. But why should Socialists fight for this right in Fiume if the Italian government violated this same right in Russia?

Just as he could not support Orlando he could not make common cause with the British Labour Party or the French CGT. Whereas the former sanctioned British imperialism in Africa and Asia, the latter acquiesced in the Saar settlement. Having soiled their hands, they were now trying to recover their *verginità democratico-socialista* by siding with Wilson exclusively on Fiume, Dalmatia, and eastern Istria. "No, comrades, we will not drink from that cup."

Nor would he drink from Wilson's cup, because not unlike the Allied Left, the President was an accomplice of numerous injustices.

Having put the plague on all three—let alone on Barzilai, Sonnino, and the extreme Right—Turati warned that by refusing a reasonable compromise, by standing alone, Orlando would bring on "famine, revolt, civil war and disaster." He even begged him not to drive Italy into the abyss or to suicide before the International was mature enough to take his place! In any case, Turati announced that he and his friends would vote against the motion which was calculated to give the ministry a blank check.

Only the 40 Socialists cast a negative vote. *All* the other parties and factions solidly closed ranks, giving the government 382 votes. On this occasion Giolitti, Nitti, Labriola, Bissolati, and Bonomi called out a clear *si!* in unison with Barzilai, Salandra, and Federzoni and with the Senate, which adopted the same motion of confidence unanimously. The Italian Parliament proved once again that it was in step with the parliaments of Britain, France, and America.

Whereas the Center-left and Orlando were satisfied with the outcome, the jingoist press was sorely dissatisfied. The *Idea Nazionale* and the *Resto del Carlino* promptly stepped up their drive for annexation, insisting that the risk of military and economic reprisal was nil.[6] Naturally, Mussolini was the most uncompromising critic. In his judgment both Orlando's speech and Luzzati's motion were excessively vague, and therefore superfluous. There was an off chance that Wilson would have changed his attitude provided the motion "had given him a strong punch in the stomach," the only language the American mentality was equipped to grasp. As it was, the situation was "the same as yesterday and the Parliamentary vote had changed nothing." This was "a time for action"—for annexation—and not for ineffectual words. And to return to Paris without a firm promise of at least the Treaty of London plus Fiume would be equivalent to once again "taking the road to Canossa."[7] The mass meeting in the Augusteo at which d'Annunzio spoke was the most spectacular expression of surging right-wing protest.

As Orlando prepared his return to Paris, fortified by the popular and Parliamentary endorsement he had sought, he realized that of the two political extremes, the new Right exercised the most sustained and immediate pressure. It was effective not by virtue of its intrinsic strength and power but because it had so many well-wishers, partisans, and fellow travelers in the power structure—in Parliament, the constitutional parties, the army, the bureaucracy, the press, the church, and the power elite at large. By comparison, in spite of vast numerical and organizational resources, the Socialist and labor movements were impotent and vulnerable. Precisely because the power structure was frightened by the current and potential strength of the Left, the movement found itself isolated, ostracized, and watched over. The militants had to move with caution, for fear of provoking overpowering retaliation. Not surprisingly, other than a mass demonstration in Turin, May Day was calm throughout Italy. To mark the occasion *Avanti*—which, following the ransacking of its plant by Fascist toughs, was temporarily printed in Turin—resumed publication in Milan. But it could do no better than vow to make the month of May a month of "resurrection." After their return to Paris, then, the Italian delegates were no more

6 Cited in *Bulletin Périodique de la presse italienne*, No. 110, May 10, 1919, 4–5, and *DR, APS*, May 21, 1919, 72.
7 *Il Popolo d'Italia*, April 30 and May 3, 4, 7 and 19, 1919, cited in Susmel (eds.): *Opera Omnia*, XIII, 93–4, 98–9, 101–4, 137–9.

inclined to placate the Left—at the risk of further incensing the Right—with regard to Italian interests than were their British, French, and American colleagues with regard to theirs.

This is not to say that the Allied Left passed up this opportunity to measure its influence, as certain observers on the Right were quick to notice. Charles Maurras and Pertinax quite realistically warned that should Wilson and his supporters have their way in the Adriatic, they would then go on to assert themselves along the Rhine.[8]

In both Britain and France the political as well as the trade union arms of the labor movement formally and publicly endorsed the President's appeal, calling on their premiers to return to the straight and lofty path of the Fourteen Points. And, of course, the press of the forces of movement was ecstatic: "at last Wilson had struck!"[9]

In addition to this public support, Wilson was swamped with congratulatory letters and telegrams. Lansbury's letter was representative of these private testimonials.

> We are all trusting that at long last all the Allied statesmen will come into line. . . . There is a sort of unspoken longing for peace and for the commencement of that new social order of which we have all heard so much. But it is to you that everyone is looking who is taking part in affairs at all. . . .[1]

Felix Frankfurter wrote in a similar vein, on a letterhead of the Délégation Sioniste au Congrès de la Paix.

> Great gifts should not be accepted in silence. You will therefore forgive me if one more voice expresses its gratitude for the heartening message you addressed, not only to Italy, but to the liberal faith of the world. Surely no one familiar with the hopes and the feelings of the masses in England and France, as well as in the U.S., can doubt that they will respond to all the calls you may make upon them in the enforcement of your principles.[2]

C. P. Scott, Jane Addams, and Herbert Asquith, among others, also wrote in. Equally encouraging were the messages from such associations as the International Committee of Women for a Permanent Peace, the League of World Friendship, the League of Free Nations, and the Serbian National Defense League of the United States.[3]

Tumulty's cables provided further evidence of the impact of Wilson's statement, the more so since only recently his Secretary had

[8] L'Action Française, April 26, 1919; and Echo de Paris, April 24, 1919.
[9] L'Humanité, April 27–28, 1919; Daily Herald, April 24, 1919; The U.D.C., May 1919, 322.
[1] Lansbury to Wilson, April 24, 1919, Wilson Papers, VIII A:40.
[2] Felix Frankfurter to Wilson, April 29, 1919, Wilson Papers, VIII A:42.
[3] See Wilson Papers, VIII:41 and 42, passim.

censured his ordering of the *George Washington*. "Let the nations who believe in secret treaties follow Italy. The people of the world will back you up. This is your supreme hour and I have never been so proud of you. . . ." Convinced that this was the time "to use your heavy artillery" Tumulty even encouraged the President to "cast another die, this one in the direction of Japan."[4] He must have assumed—rightly or wrongly—that large segments of opinion, both inside and outside Congress, were waiting for a clarion call.

In this prepollster era Tumulty considered the press to be the most sensitive barometer of changing public reactions. And, judging by the editorial columns, a vast body of opinion upheld the President's opposition to Italy's excessive demands.[5] The Los Angeles *Times* (Republican) hoped that Italy would yield; the Houston *Post* (Democratic) proclaimed that Wilson had "all the arguments, all the morals, and all the respectability on his side"; the Chicago *Evening Post* (Independent) declared that whereas "Fiume was not vital to Italy it was vital to Yugoslavia"; the Springfield *Republican* (Independent)[6] predicted that Wilson would "never sign a treaty making Fiume an Italian seaport"; the New York *Evening Post* (Independent) characterized the situation as "pretty nearly a case of Italy *contra mundum*"; and the St. Louis *Post Dispatch* (Democratic) was grateful because the Italian Delegation's attitude revealed "what might have been the attitude of all European delegations but for the spirit and counsel which America brought to the Conference." It goes without saying that for the *Nation* and the *New Republic* this was an occasion for renewed hope: both commended Wilson for taking a firm stand.

Whether or not the President's Secretary read the opposition press with equal attention is another matter. Since the *North American Review* was far out in right field he probably dismissed its defiant prophecy that America and the world would get a "peace with victory."[7] But George Harvey's organ did not stand alone. Hearst's New York *American* argued that Italy had "at least a fair prima-facie case"; the Brooklyn *Citizen* (Democratic) claimed that Italy could make as good a security case for Fiume as America for Cuba; the Washington *Post* (Independent) was disappointed in Wilson's rigidity; the Boston *Transcript* (Republican) hailed the Italians for striking "a fair balance in government and diplomacy"; the Wheeling *Intelligencer* (Republican) affirmed that "even if all of Italy's claims were met her gains would be small compared to Yugoslavia's"; the St. Louis *Globe-*

---

[4] Tumulty to Wilson, April 24, 26, and 28, 1919, Wilson Papers, VIII A:40, 41, 42.

[5] The following survey of the U.S. press is based on *The Literary Digest*, May 10, 1919, 11–13.

[6] Tumulty watched this paper with special care on the assumption that it was one of the best indexes to independent and nonpartisan Democratic opinion outside the South.

[7] *The North American Review*, May 1919, 577–9.

Democrat (Republican) thought it "better to grant the Italian demands, even at some sacrifice of principle, than to destroy the whole fabric that had been built up at such great cost"; the Detroit *Free Press* (Independent) maintained that the settlement of Italy's claims was "not in any way or in any degree our business" and that although America may consider Italy "selfish and grasping, it was not our part to act as moral dictator for the whole earth"; the New York *Evening Sun* (Independent) was convinced that the issue was "not America's affair"; the Providence *Journal* (Independent) hailed Orlando's success at home for bringing "into sharp contrast Mr. Wilson's lack of mandate from America"; and the Philadelphia *Inquirer* (Republican) accused the President of wanting to "rule the Peace Conference just as he had ruled the Democratic Congress" and of again blundering as he had last November in his election appeal to the American people.

Not least important, Senator Lodge deliberately turned Fiume into a political issue. On April 29 he sent his "strictly non-partisan telegram" to all Republican Senators, requesting that they withold comment on the amended covenant until they could meet to discuss it. He did so for fear that many of them might make approbative statements now that Wilson and the Conference had yielded to his own principal reservation regarding the Monroe Doctrine. That same day, in a public letter to leading Italian-Americans in Boston, Lodge championed Italy's cause: in his view Italy should get Fiume if she was of the opinion that Fiume was necessary "to her safety and for her protection."[8] This letter was a preview of Lodge's bid for the support of all those hyphenated-Americans—Italian, German, Irish, Armenian— whose countries of origin were dissatisfied with the outcome of the Peace Conference, blaming Wilson for their national frustrations.

On the whole, then, on both sides of the Atlantic, the Fiume crisis cleared the air. Since the President's triumphal tour,[9] Wilsonians and anti-Wilsonians had had no synchronized occasion to take each other's measure. Now that they were doing so, it became apparent that the Allied and Associated forces of movement had lost further ground to their opponents.

Doubtless Wilson was disappointed that his appeal paid such meager political and diplomatic dividends, not only in Italy but throughout the victor world. Whether or not a Fiume-type statement would have produced better results five, four, or three weeks before is doubtful. However, at the time, Wilson's constituents did not hesitate to blame him for their own ineffectiveness. In America both the *Nation* and the *New Republic* lamented that his "flight of statesmanship

---

[8] Cited in *The Literary Digest*, May 10, 1919, 11. See also Karl Schriftgiesser: *The Gentleman from Massachusetts: Henry Cabot Lodge* (Boston: Little, Brown; 1944), 325–7.

[9] See Chs. 6–7.

[probably] came too late and was hampered by his grave inconsistencies."[1] Likewise in Britain the *Daily Herald* was afraid that Wilson's "stand had come too late, when Imperialism and greed had obtained such a hold that the Peace Conference of Capitalist Governments would end in disaster."[2] In France Cachin deplored that the President had waited too long to pound his fist on the table.

> [Nonetheless], the representatives of French and British labor would gather around Wilson to sustain his *last direct* appeal to the peoples of Europe. . . . The workers were waiting for the voice which would rally them. . . . The hour had struck and should this last opportunity be missed Europe would move to the edge of the abyss. . . . No one could accuse the SFIO of not having given maximum credit to the *grand bourgeois américain* who was straining to preserve traditional Anglo-Saxon Liberalism. If in spite of his pure intentions he could not restrain the appetites of his associates, others would step forward to do the necessary job [italics mine][3]

In a more distant future the Allied Socialists might well come to power, but even then primarily on the strength of internal developments in their respective nations. And at this juncture they were in limbo not because Wilson betrayed the Fourteen Points in Paris but because they were not up to challenging the Right at home. Their weakness undermined Wilson, and not vice versa.

[1] *The Nation,* May 3, 1919, 676; and *The New Republic,* May 3, 1919, 5. "Fear President's statement was issued too late to be effective. Should have been done a month ago." Lansing Diary, April 24, 1919.
[2] *Daily Herald,* April 24, 1919.
[3] *L'Humanité,* April 28, 1919.

21

Béla Kun in Power

ALL ALONG the Big Four kept a careful watch on developments in the defeated territories of the expired Austro-Hungarian Empire. The American Delegation was most attentive, having both the Coolidge Mission and Hoover's agents in the field. Perhaps because Coolidge was a conventional diplomat and political historian, it is not surprising that House and others should have become impatient with his "interminable dispatches dealing almost exclusively with the history of the pragmatic sanction."[1] Evidently the Harvard Professor needed to be sensitized to the nascent international civil war. On March 9, in a cable drafted by Allen W. Dulles, the Ammission requested information about Bolshevism in the territories of the Coolidge Mission's jurisdiction. "Is there evidence of Russian propaganda? Are there active revolutionary groups of importance? Are revolutionary outbreaks likely to occur? If so, will they succeed?"[2] Without even waiting for an answer, the Ammission summoned Coolidge to Paris as soon as he could conveniently absent himself from Vienna, for consultations.[3]

This telegram left Paris before the Hungarian explosion and reached Coolidge shortly after Vienna registered its first tremors. In view of the new situation in Budapest, Lansing sent an urgent follow-up message. He suggested that Coolidge use his own judgment "as regards the advisability of proceeding to Paris at the present time." The American Delegation thought that it "might be undesirable to abruptly break off all connection with the new Government in Budapest," since such a step "would inevitably tend to throw them into the arms of the Moscow Government." If possible, Lansing wanted a member of the mission to remain in the Hungarian capital.[4] Independent of this wire Coolidge advised his superiors that Roosevelt was on his way to report

[1] Stephen Bonsal: *Unfinished Business* (Garden City, N.Y.: Doubleday Doran; 1944), 118.
[2] Ammission to American Legation in Berne, for Coolidge, March 9, 1919, National Archives, Document 184.01102/191A.
[3] Ammission to Coolidge, March 20, 1919, National Archives, Document 184.011/139-A.
[4] Lansing to Coolidge, March 24, 1919 (10:00 p.m.), National Archives.

to them directly; that Brown would stay in Budapest at his own request; and that he himself would leave for Paris that day.[5]

On his arrival in Paris on March 26, Roosevelt submitted a brief on "The Hungarian Revolution." He told the American Delegation that the revolution "was precipitated by the presentation" of the Vix note; that it was "accomplished with comparative quiet"; that "the members of the Laborers' party" forced Béla Kun to insist "on a complete change"; that there was an "apparent accord between the Károlyi Government and the new Government"; and that there were unconfirmed rumors of German as well as Italian complicity. In Roosevelt's judgment the revolution was "essentially nationalistic, making use of Bolshevism for national ends." Hungary was openly defying a decision of the Peace Conference by "holding the club of Bolshevism over the Allies and asking 'What are you going to do about it?' " Actually there were three alternatives. The Czechs and Rumanians could advance and occupy the country, but this would be bloody and, besides, they might not be up to the job. Secondly, the Allies could undertake this task themselves; according to the chief of the British mission, 10,000 troops would suffice, certainly to hold Budapest. Last, the Allies could rely on a rigorous blockade, though it would take two months for the food situation to become critical. In any case, "immediate and vigorous" action was essential so as to prevent a "disastrous state of affairs in Central Europe which might take years to straighten out." Unless Hungary's defiance and her alliance with Bolshevism were checked, it would be "Germany's turn next."[6]

That same day, March 26, Philip Marshall Brown sent his first two dispatches from Budapest to Vienna by special courier. He reported that the new regime was styling itself on the Soviet Russian model and was busy "drafting Socialistic legislation covering every field of social interest." In foreign policy it was not aggressive, but was appealing to the European proletariat—especially the proletariat of neighboring nations—to oppose policies of territorial aggrandizement. Another appeal went out to Soviet Russia, but because the Red Army was too far away even the extreme Hungarian Communists did not expect much from that quarter. In Brown's judgment the mass of the people were "neither extreme nor even socialistic"; they were "intensely nationalistic"; and only the threat of dismemberment had brought about the "unnatural partnership . . . of nationalism and Socialism."

As to the policy to pursue, Brown thought that "firm but liberal" action could keep Hungary "from becoming completely Bolshevist." He was confident that in exchange for "clear assurance" that the principle

[5] Coolidge to Ammission, March 24, 1919, National Archives, Document 184.01102/262.

[6] The full text of Roosevelt's memorandum is cited in *F.R.,P.C.,XII*, 416–19. For his own ten-point summary see National Archives, Document 184.01102/254.

of self-determination would be respected in the territorial settlement, the new regime would "consent to a considerable rectification of the frontiers" with Rumania and Czechoslovakia. Should the Hungarian people nonetheless be turned over to Bolshevism, immediate and "active military intervention" might have to be considered. But a third course might be the wisest of all: "military intervention by British and American troops combined with conciliatory assurances." On the whole, though, speedy action was of essence if the "moderate radicals," whose "good intentions" he did not question, were to continue keeping the "extreme Communists" from gaining ascendancy.[7]

Brown himself telephoned a summary of his lengthy report to the Vienna headquarters of the Coolidge Mission. In turn, at 4:00 p.m. the Vienna office rushed a telegram to the American Delegation in Paris: "Brown emphasizes Government is conciliatory and moderate and desires understanding with Entente. Feeling that if right of self-determination given to Hungary country can still be saved and advises caution."[8]

Having completed his official reports, Brown felt the need to write a "personal word" to Coolidge. In this note he expressed considerably more anguish and anxiety:

> I regard the situation here as full of very unfortunate possibilities. It seems as if we were in the hands of inexorable fate. I do not question the motives of this present radical government. They are probably sincere socialists who scorn nationalism as well as capitalism. But they have only a tenuous hold over the forces they have let loose. The air is full of resentments and fears and fanaticism. War against the *bourgeoisie* has been declared and has begun in various acts, arrests of rich men, [etc.]. It is not difficult to prophesy where this may end.
>
> But in regard to staying here, . . . the new regime . . . has begged me to stay and report my impressions! It is possible that I might be the means of conveying important information to our Mission in Paris. Certainly the whole European situation is so very critical that I would hesitate to leave this storm center if . . . [I could contribute] to finding a way out of the present labyrinth. . . . I am glad you went to Paris. . . . The situation here is so delicate that it must be handled with great consideration and prudence. We certainly ought not to make a bad situation worse. I am sorry to say that I fear that Austria may go the same road if not handled with immense care.[9]

[7] The full text of both dispatches, both dated March 26, 1919, is cited in *F.R.,P.C.,1919*, XII, 419–23.

[8] Cited in ibid., 424. On March 27 Lansing brought this wire to President Wilson's attention.

[9] Brown to Coolidge, March 26, 1919, in National Archives, Document 184.01102/266. Unlike Brown's two reports and the wire from Vienna—all three dated March 26— his personal letter is not printed in *F.R.,P.C.,1919*, XII.

Brown did not for long reserve his pessimistic concern to private letters. In fact, the very next day, he called Vienna to say that Russians were stimulating the antibourgeois campaign and directing the expansion of the radical ranks. It all "looked like Red Terror." In Brown's view "this was not an amateur, but a professional revolution," and he asked for instructions about his staying on in Budapest.[1] From Paris Coolidge replied that the American Delegation considered his presence in Hungary "useful and desirable as long as in his discretion there were no strong reasons for leaving."[2]

For a few more days Brown continued to stress that the "Russian faction, which was in constant communication with Moscow," was pressing for "extreme measures"; and that unless prompt actions were taken the "extreme element under Russian influence may gain control." On March 29, he expressed doubts about the government's strength, stated his conviction that "the mass of Hungarians would welcome friendly intervention, if not too long delayed," and estimated that "not more than 30,000 troops would be required for this intervention," since the regime's recruitment drive had "met meager results."[3]

Overnight Brown became more hopeful and considerably less prone to accept a conspiratorial view of events. This change resulted from a long conversation with Kunfi, who called on him on March 30. It is not known whether the Commissioner of Education, who was the moderate holdover from the Károlyi cabinet, came on his own initiative or was instructed to seek out the American official. In any event, Kunfi told Brown that even though his government "could not formally accept . . . the new advanced demarcation line" of the Vix note, they "would not resist military occupation of the zone in question." Boundaries as such were not all that vital to Socialists, provided Hungary was "not strangled economically." Kunfi also assured him that a "Red Army" was being mustered for purposes not of aggression but "of maintaining the new regime in power." As for the best way of "avoiding excesses," Kunfi emphasized—with Brown's concurrence—the "importance of sending food and coal." Meanwhile, his colleagues were anxious for Béla Kun, the Commissar of Foreign Affairs, to serve as an intermediary "between the Entente and Lenin for the sake of reaching a friendly understanding."

At this point Brown asked Kunfi to clarify the distinction between Socialists and Communists.

> He said it was only a question of "tempo": that the Communists insisted on accelerating the process of Socialization, and that they

[1] Coolidge Mission (Vienna) to Ammission (for Coolidge), March 27, 1919, National Archives, Document 184.01102/276.

[2] National Archives, Document 184.011/144B.

[3] Coolidge Mission (Vienna) to Ammission (for Coolidge), March 29 and 30, 1919, National Archives, Documents 184.01102/282 and 286.

frankly had the ascendancy in the new Government. He assured me, however, that the Government would in no way approve of terrorization and bloodshed. [But] the *"bourgeoisie"* would have to accommodate itself to the new order or there would be excesses. . . .

In the light of this explanation, which he had confirmed by other sources, Brown relented in his suspicion even of the extreme Socialists. "Whatever their first *élan* and their expression of solidarity with the Russian Bolshevists, I am strongly inclined to believe that the Hungarian Government is not a Bolshevist Government."

As he turned to policy advice in his report, Brown conceded that only the day before he had pointed "to military intervention as the best" course. But that was before "Kunfi's *démarche* and before the actual trend of events" indicated the possiblity of "a friendly understanding." No doubt, properly handled, military intervention "probably would be easy," but would it permanently eliminate the Socialist government? Besides, Brown doubted that "the Entente would care to appear as the enemy of Socialism, though sworn to hostility against Bolshevism."[4]

Presently Brown also questioned the wisdom of those who opposed sending food because it would "strengthen the hands . . . and enhance the prestige" of the revolutionary government. He was convinced that food shipments, combined with a declaration of fair-minded purpose, would impress the Hungarian people in favor of the Entente and of moderation.[5]

Meanwhile both the Coolidge Mission and the Peace Conference were worried about the repercussions of the Hungarian Revolution on Austria. Before leaving for Paris, Coolidge wired that a high Austrian official had told him that the situation was "immediately very threatening [and that] Austria's only salvation was the sending of Allied troops." Another of his wires was equally alarming:

> Conservative and propertied classes apparently in state of panic. Newspapers take the tone that it is the natural result of the action of Conference in taking so long in coming to a decision while the situation in the Central Empire has steadily grown worse and the tension greater. . . .

Coolidge also revealed that the lead editorial in the *Arbeiter Zeitung*, expressing sympathy with the revolution, was inspired by the govern-

[4] The full text is cited in *F.R.,P.C.,1919*, XII, 425–7. This report reached Paris by special courier on April 2. But since he—and Roosevelt—considered Kunfi's *démarche* to be of urgent importance, Brown himself prepared a 100-word summary, which was sent in cipher from Vienna and was received in Paris at 11:30 p.m. on the thirty-first. The U. S. Delegation read Brown's dispatches with care, judging by a long cable of April 3 to Polk in Washington, drafted by Allen Dulles. National Archives, Documents 184.01102/287 and 305.

[5] Brown to Coolidge, April 6, 1919, cited in *F.R.,P.C.,1919*, XII, 428–9.

ment. According to this editorial, Austria's main reason for not imitating Hungary was her complete dependence on the Allies for food.[6]

The day of the overturn in Budapest, Otto Bauer called Cnobloch, the Austrian envoy in Hungary, instructing him to inform Béla Kun that Vienna wanted friendly relations with the new regime. He was also asked to stress, however, that in Austria a Soviet-type regime could not last more than a few days on account of her exposed economic and geographic position. On the twenty-third, the officially inspired editorial expanded on this double theme.

> Already many an eye shines brighter, already many a heart beats faster. Is our situation not the same as that of our Hungarian brothers? Is not here—in German-Bohemia and in the Sudetenland, in South Tyrol, Carinthia and Lower Styria—German soil threatened by an insolent victor who disposes of people as if they were cattle? . . .
>
> True, we could dethrone the bourgeoisie of our own country as easily and rapidly as they have done; a few battalions would suffice. *But in regard to the Entente bourgeoisie we are chained in a manner quite different from that of the Hungarian proletariat.* Dictatorship of the proletariat here would be equivalent to a provocation and a declaration of war. . . . *The Hungarians advise us to separate ourselves from Paris and to link up with Moscow; but Moscow is far away,* the Soviet armies are still more than a 1000 km. from us, Poland and the Ukraine shut us off from every contact with them. . . . The Entente bourgeoisie holds us in chains . . . and it holds protective hands over our own bourgeoisie. . . . Today we are powerless; but when the proletariat of the Entente countries rises against their bourgeoisie, then, in alliance with it, we too shall break our chains [italics mine].[7]

The Allies could take comfort from the fact that Austria's Social Democrats recognized the precariousness of Vienna's food supply, and thus made their own radicalism contingent on what their Allied counterparts would support. Even so, the situation might get out of hand.

On March 28, the Vienna office of the Coolidge Mission wired distressing news: a railway strike was spreading all over Austria; the government could not afford to raise wages; and the Communists were successfully denouncing Allied diplomacy. The following day Paris was notified, on the strength of a visit from Hoffinger, that even though the

---

[6] National Archives, Documents 184.01102/263 and 266A.

[7] The text of Bauer's oral instructions to Cnobloch as well as the text of the editorial in the *Arbeiter Zeitung* of March 23, 1919, are cited by Alfred D. Low: "The First Austrian Republic and Soviet Hungary," in *Journal of Central European Affairs*, XX, No. 2 (July, 1960), 178, 180. See also Otto Bauer: *Die Österreichische Revolution* (Vienna: Wiener Volksbuchhandlung; 1923), 136 ff. In the judgment of the German Ambassador in Vienna, Friedrich Solfer, and his colleagues, the editorial "very deftly" pointed to the danger of starvation should Austria plunge into Bolshevism. Wedel to Foreign Ministry, April 23, 1919, G.F.M.

strike was settled, the government "felt itself very weak" and was considering "resigning and handing power over to Councils of Workmen, Soldiers, and Peasants to avert extreme radicalism by giving way before the coming storm." While Karl Renner asked the Allies to provide higher food rations, Hoffinger called for a "definite statement from the Allies that they [would] oppose Bolshevism or for an Allied appeal to the present German-Austrian Government to assist in opposing it."[8]

But Colonel Thomas Cunningham, the chief British representative in Vienna, who had just returned from Budapest, estimated the situation to be so critical that he summoned the other Allied representatives to meet with him on April 1 to consider the advisability of military occupation.[9] Roosevelt wired to Coolidge in Paris that he planned to attend the meeting. Evidently Coolidge showed this telegram to Bliss, who, after consulting Lansing, promptly instructed Roosevelt "under no circumstances to discuss question of military occupation of Austria with anyone," but to obtain such information as he could "without taking part in any discussion."[1]

Although these instructions did not arrive in time, Roosevelt carefully avoided expressing any opinion on military occupation at the meeting. The British Colonel had close connections with conservative and liberal political circles which considered the Austrian Social Democrats to be every bit as radical and dangerous as the Bolsheviks. Both he and they were particularly incensed about Julius Deutsch and his *Volkswehr*, which they suspected of subversive intentions. Cunningham now proposed that 10,000 British or Americans occupy Vienna, and another 3,000 each Wiener–Neustadt, Graz, and Linz. Once on the spot these troops would help the government—which he claimed favored intervention—disarm the *Volkswehr* and organize new and "reliable" security forces. Cunningham "further explained that it would be his idea to bring these troops in under the pretext of operating against Hungary or of preserving the lines of communication for food distribution."

The Italian representative, General Segre, was altogether unen-

---

8 National Archives, Documents 184.01102/278 and 281.
9 Such requests were made even before the actual overturn in Budapest. "Director of Political Department asked me today to meet Swiss Minister at Vienna who is here [in Berne] for a few days. A member of the French Embassy and American Legation were also present at meeting. Swiss Minister said that there was a very serious danger of Bolshevik outbreak in Vienna next month. . . . He had discussion of situation in Vienna with Prefect of Police . . . who stated that if only one British, American or French regiment were sent to Vienna, he would guarantee that there would be no fear of a Bolshevik outbreak . . . Swiss Minister said that Volkswehr was unreliable. . . ." Rumbold (Berne) to Balfour, March 20, 1919, F.O. 608/16.
1 Roosevelt to Coolidge, March 31, 1919, and Bliss to Roosevelt, April 1, 1919, National Archives, Document 184.01102/288.

thusiastic about direct military intervention, pointing out that "operations against Hungary would not be a welcome [popular] pretext" for Allied soldiers in Austria. However, all three agreed—the French mission was not represented—that food should instantly be rushed in, and Cunningham pressed for special rations for the restless railway men. Before adjourning, it was decided that rather than send recommendations to Paris, each participant should acquaint his own government with these deliberations. Roosevelt's report of this conference, which reached Paris on April 3, prompted Bliss to append the following note for the benefit of his colleagues: "I am opposed, on principle, to associating ourselves in any more military expeditions. We have had enough of such."[2]

In the afternoon of April 1, and completely on his own, Roosevelt went to see Renner to feel him out about the Cunningham proposal. On this occasion the Chancellor assured him that there was "no cause for alarm." But he also said that sentiment against Allied military occupation was great, particularly because of popular suspicion that the Allies intended to use Austria as a base against Hungary. At the same time, he indicated that his government, following Károlyi's example, would resign if the country were dismembered, referring specifically to German Bohemia and German Tyrol. For good measure Renner added that only under such circumstances would Bolshevism pose a real threat. Significantly, in a covering note even Coolidge, who had just returned to Vienna, called the Ammission's attention to the fact that "the Chancellor's remarks differed from other reports one gets from the conservative classes."[3]

In the midst of this barrage of conflicting intelligence reports, the Big Four rushed through the restoration of trade with Austria. On March 31 instructions went out to the Coolidge Mission to advise the Austrian government of this decision and of the establishment of an Inter-Allied Trade Commission in Vienna, but specifying that re-exportations to Germany, Hungary, and Bolshevik Russia would continue to be prohibited. That the specter of Bolshevism was ever present in the minds of Allied officials was obvious from the concluding two paragraphs of these instructions:

> In case the Austrian Government should have fallen before this reaches you [Coolidge], it is left to your discretion whether above action should be taken or not.
>
> It had been contemplated to restore trade relations with Hungary at the same time as with German-Austria, but in view of Bolshevik

2 Roosevelt to Coolidge, April 1, 1919 (telegraphic summary), and Coolidge (Vienna) to Ammission, April 3, 1919 (transmitting Roosevelt's full report), National Archives, Documents 184.01102/296 and 302.

3 Roosevelt to Coolidge, April 1, 1919 (telegraphic summary), National Archives, Document 184.01102/297, and Coolidge (Vienna) to Ammission, April 3, 1919 (transmitting Roosevelt's full report), cited in *F.R.,P.C.,1919*, XII, 281–2.

conditions there, resumption of trade with Hungary will be considered later.[4]

By mid-April, Renner's government announced the doubling of the flour ration.[5]

But the Big Four had to go beyond providing German-Austria with antibodies and beyond building up the Rumanian armies for possible intervention in Hungary. They had to react formally to this first defiance by a defeated enemy. Moreover, since the Big Four resolved to continue pursuing a policy of intervention—however incoherent—against revolution in Russia, they had to stretch and adapt this policy to cover the revolution in Hungary.

It was on March 29 that Orlando initiated a discussion of the Hungarian problem in the Council of Four.[6] The new Italian Minister to Yugoslavia, Prince Borghese, happened to be passing through Budapest during the "alleged revolution." On March 24 the new regime approached him to say that this revolution had been precipitated by political rather than social causes and that the government was Socialist and not Bolshevik. After some hesitation, Borghese agreed to transmit an *aide-mémoire* from Béla Kun to the Peace Conference, which reached Orlando by special courier.

In this memorandum, which was now circulated, Béla Kun stated that for Hungary the nonacceptance of the Vix note in no way impinged upon the validity of the Armistice of November 3; that the alliance with Russia was an informal "*entente cordiale*" of two identically constituted governments which did not "in any way imply an aggressive combination"; that the Soviet republic was "ready to negotiate territorial questions on the basis of the principle of self-determination"; and that it would "gladly welcome a civil and diplomatic mission of the Entente in Budapest."[7]

Both Wilson and Lloyd George wanted to discuss the dispatch of a mission right then and there. But Clemenceau stalled. He was not inclined to deal with a government which was alleged to have arrested Colonel Vix and had offered an alliance to Soviet Russia. In turn, Lloyd George warned that the Allies should not treat Hungary as they had treated Russia, insisting that "one Russia was quite enough." After a while Clemenceau indicated that although he objected to a "regular mission," he might agree to sending "an investigator." The British Prime Minister seized this opening and promptly volunteered the serv-

[4] Ammission to Coolidge (very urgent), March 31, 1919, cited in *F.R.,P.C.,1919*, XII, 281.
[5] Coolidge to Ammission, April 16, 1919, National Archives, Document 184.01102/361.
[6] This discussion is based on the minutes of the session of March 29, 1919, p.m., in Paul Mantoux: *Les Délibérations du conseil des quatre*, I, 80–2.
[7] The text of this *aide-mémoire* is cited not in Mantoux: *Délibérations*, but in *F.R.,P.C.,1919*, V, 18.

ices of General Smuts.[8] Rather than make a final decision the Big Four agreed to use the weekend to consult their Foreign Ministers and to consider other candidates for the assignment.

On Monday, March 31, the four Foreign Ministers joined their chiefs for the deliberation of the Hungarian question.[9] As expected, Pichon was altogether intransigent. He held that although Budapest had been told that the demarcation line would not prejudice the final boundaries, Károlyi had agreed to the proclamation of a soviet republic. Worse still, the Allied missions were being harassed and as "its first act the new Government contacted Lenin." Budapest claimed that there was no formal alliance with Russia. But he could not forget that Béla Kun was "Lenin's friend and accomplice." Were the Allies proposing to establish relations with a soviet regime, and would such a step be "the prelude to negotiations with Russia?" He, for one, opposed such a course. Besides, the Allies could not side with hostile Hungary against friendly Rumania, "especially since now more than ever they were pledged to support her as a bulwark against Bolshevism." Rumania's claim to Transylvania had to be honored.

Lansing interjected that the demarcation line between Hungary and Rumania might not be altogether fair, that the Rumanians were the first to have crossed the Armistice lines, and that no Hungarian government could accept the frontiers of the secret treaty of 1916.[1] Lloyd George, Balfour, and Sonnino regretted that Colonel Vix had failed to make it sufficiently clear that the new lines would not prejudice the final boundaries. Sonnino added, however, that it would be a dangerous precedent for the other defeated powers if Hungary successfully used Bolshevism to blackmail the Allies into making concessions.

It was Wilson who reminded the Council that the proposed mission would not fix boundaries or establish regular relations but would merely investigate local conditions.

> It was important to avoid an excessively hard attitude which would push one country after another into Bolshevism. The same danger existed in Vienna: should we have to trace a line of demarcation [for Austria], Vienna might answer by throwing herself into Bolshevism. If such developments were to repeat themselves, there would be no one with whom to make peace. . . . He

---

[8] LLOYD GEORGE: "I know you don't like him after the letter I read to you." CLEMEN-CEAU: "I respect him, but I would prefer it if you sent some one else down there."

[9] This discussion is based on the minutes of the session of March 31, 1919 (p.m.), in Mantoux: *Délibérations*, I, 98–104. There are no "Hankey minutes" for this session.

[1] "[Council] discussed sending a representative to Budapest. I told them I thought the neutral zone in Transylvania was unjust and that the course we were pursuing was making Bolshevik governments. (It was directed at the French.) Finally agreed that General Smuts should go and Lloyd George draft instructions." Lansing Diary, March 31, 1919.

was ready to converse with any rascal, provided what the latter proposed was acceptable and left his honor intact.

. . . The confidence man . . . should go to Budapest to say to the Hungarians: "I have no powers from the Associated Nations, except on one point . . . explain your position, [especially] your assertion that you have no alliance with Bolshevism. . . ." Above all we must clarify the situation. The Budapest Government is not charged with the crimes which we hold against the Russian Bolsheviks. It is probably nationalist. It is a soviet government because that is the form of revolution which is in fashion; and there may well be different species of soviets.

Lloyd George supported Wilson's analysis as well as his proposal that the envoy should be a man of experience and stature and who enjoyed the full confidence of the Council.

After some further debate it was agreed that General Smuts—who was respected as both soldier and statesman—should be sent to Hungary to "investigate the treatment of our missions and to examine the question of the neutral zone."

Sir Henry Wilson thought it "a curious business that a Welshman was sending a Dutchman to tell a Hungarian not to fight a Rumanian."[2] But the nationality of the chief of this mission was less startling than its composition and instructions. In order to reserve the full veto power of the Conference, the mission was to be essentially British. As aides Smuts chose Allen Leeper and Harold Nicolson, of the Foreign Office; Colonel Heyward, of Military Intelligence; Cyril Butler, of the Food Control Commission; and Ernest Lane, his personal aide-de-camp. To provide himself with an inter-Allied aura, Smuts asked each of Britain's three Allies to designate one official to join his team. The French and Italians each sent an officer, while Colonel House deputized Major Stephen Bonsal, who went along in civilian clothing as a newspaperman.[3]

As for Smuts' instructions, they were rather open ended. He was to explain to the Hungarian government that the neutral zone was established "without any intention of prejudicing the eventual settlement of the boundaries between Hungary and Rumania"; he was empowered to "make any adjustments in the boundaries of the neutral zone or the method of its occupation by Allied troops" which might further "the objects of the Allied and Associated Governments"; and he was authorized "to proceed to any place . . . and to take any steps which may enable him to carry out these objects or others closely connected with

2 Callwell (ed.): *Henry Wilson*, II, 179. Wilson and Smuts had fought on opposite sides in the Boer War.
3 Harold Nicolson, *Peacemaking 1919*, 292, entry of April 1, 1919; House Diary, April 1, 1919; Bonsal: *Unfinished Business*, 119.

them."[4] Seizing upon this closing omnibus clause, and before leaving Paris in the early evening of April 1, Smuts proposed that Lloyd George invite a Soviet Russian delegation to meet him in Budapest, confident that he could recommend terms for "peace with Russia and thus round off the work of this Peace Conference."[5] Evidently Smuts was aware of the possibility of using Béla Kun as a line of communication with Moscow, as Kunfi had suggested through Brown. In any case, on the train to Budapest, Nicolson and Leeper got the impression that Smuts wanted them "to handle this side of the business on their own, without engaging *his* responsibility." In his diary Nicolson added that if this was "really so," and since neither he nor Leeper liked the idea or wanted "another Prinkipo," they would "do the stupid, and pretend not to understand what [was] expected of [them]."[6]

Smuts and his party arrived in Budapest in the morning of April 4, whereupon both sides began to jockey for position. Smuts was determined to avoid any gesture or word which might suggest approval or recognition of the new regime. He and his party refused to put up at the Ritz Hotel, preferring to stay in their railway cars and within the confines of the railway station. It was here, during the first interview, that Smuts refused to shake hands with Béla Kun. In turn, Béla Kun sought to use the mission to raise his and his government's prestige. He created the impression that the Soviet government had succeeded in getting the respect and attention of the Peace Conference and that the visit foreshadowed *de facto* recognition.

In his initial conference in his railway carriage with the Foreign Commissar, Smuts explained that the line suggested in the Vix note "was not intended to be a permanent political frontier." He went on to say that the neutral zone, to be occupied by the Allies in order to prevent disorders and military clashes, would "in no way prejudice the Hungarian case."[7] Smuts tried to make evacuation more palatable by promising removal of the blockade and friendly relations with the Allies.

Béla Kun countered that compliance with the note would precipitate the immediate fall of his government; and that even if he ordered the withdrawal of Hungarian troops—especially of the crack Székler Division—his order was likely to be ignored. Should the Allies insist on evacuation, thereby forcing his government to step back, "there was no

---

[4] For the full text of these instructions see Balfour to Curzon and Clemenceau to Franchet d'Esperey, April 1, 1919, F.O. 608/16. Clemenceau directed Franchet d'Esperey to comply with such directions as General Smuts might give.

[5] Cited in W. K. Hancock: *Smuts: The Sanguine Years, 1870–1919* (Cambridge: University Press; 1962), 516.

[6] Nicolson: *Peacemaking*, 293, entry of April 2, 1919.

[7] This discussion of the first Smuts–Béla Kun meeting is based on a paraphrased version of Smuts's wire to Balfour, April 4, 1919, cited in *F.R.,P.C.,1919*, V, 41–3. Cf. Nicolson: *Peacemaking*, 299–300, entry of April 4, 1919.

[other] party capable of assuming power" and of preventing chaos, so that the Allies would have to step in and rule the country themselves.

As a diplomat Béla Kun was at least as adept as Károlyi. He did not limit himself to rejecting the note, nor did he try to bargain for improved demarcation lines at this stage. Instead, he proposed, with Károlyi's endorsement, that the Entente call a meeting of representatives of Hungary, German-Austria, Czechoslovakia, Yugoslavia, and Rumania to settle borders on the basis of self-determination. This same conference, to be held in either Vienna or Prague, should also deal with the economic problems of the new states, which were at least as crucial as the vexing frontier questions.

Smuts was not unreceptive to this suggestion. In the same wire in which he reported Béla Kun's refusal to evacuate his troops, he recommended that the Allies have these representatives meet in Paris, where Bolsheviks would be easier to keep in check, at a minimum for preliminary discussions.

At 10:00 a.m. on April 5, during their second conference, Smuts made concrete concessions designed to win Béla Kun's approval.[8] According to this proposal the easternmost demarcation line was to be moved by 8 to 10 kilometers in some places, even by 20 kilometers in others, in Hungary's favor. This left Debrecen within Magyar borders. The Rumanians were not to advance beyond their present positions, leaving Arad, Nagy-Várad and Szatmár to the neutral zone, which, thus enlarged, was to be occupied by troops of the Big Four. Smuts "decisively pointed out" that these lines "would not influence" the shaping of final boundaries. He also promised to recommend to the Peace Conference that the blockade be lifted to allow fats and coal to be brought in and that representatives of the Hungarian government be invited to a conference of the successor states to discuss territorial and economic questions.

This proposal represented a major improvement over the Vix note. Smuts made important territorial and economic concessions; he held out a promise of territorial negotiations; and he implied a degree of recognition. Even so, when Béla Kun presented it to his Council of Commissars he advocated extreme caution. He warned that acceptance would provoke a nationalist reaction which might well lead to a counterrevolutionary coup. At the same time it would call for a break with Soviet Russia and thereby endanger the revolution. Besides, was it all that certain that these concessions represented more than Smuts's personal promises, subject to review, possibly to cancellation, by the Peace Conference? His own *enragés* helped pressure him into this very

---

[8] The text of Smuts's proposal was forwarded by Brown to Coolidge (for Paris), April 9, 1919, National Archives, Document 185.3123. See also Nicolson: *Peacemaking*, 302, entry of April 5, 1919; and Wilhelm Böhm: *Im Kreuzfeuer zweier Revolutionen* (Munich: Verlag für Kulturpolitik; 1924), 314–16.

guarded position; and even those commissars who tended to favor acceptance were under the spell of reports about revolutionary developments in Bavaria and the Ruhr as well as about the disruptive clash of Italy and Yugoslavia over Fiume.[9] There is no substantiated evidence that Béla Kun ever consulted Lenin before either confronting his fellow commissars or drafting his answer to Smuts.[1]

The crux of Béla Kun's counterproposal, which the entire Council of Commissars endorsed, was the demand that the Rumanian troops withdraw eastward to the Maros line as originally stipulated in the Belgrade Military Convention of November 13, 1918, while units of the Big Four occupy the vastly enlarged neutral zone. Otherwise he accepted Smuts's document. He "begged" that the blockade be lifted and asked that the conference of the successor states "take place speedily and if possible in Vienna or Prague."[2]

Accompanied by Garbai, Kunfi, and Bolgár, the Foreign Commissar handed this counterproposal to Smuts in that "half-lit dining-car" at 7:00 p.m. on April 5.[3] After reading it over twice Smuts decided that it was altogether extravagant, since the Conference would not and could not force the Rumanians back to the Maros line: "No, gentlemen, this is not a note which I can accept. There must be no reservations." Smuts reiterated his insistence on an unqualified acceptance of this morning's memorandum for a second time. While the General was determined to break off negotiations right then and there, Béla Kun and his colleagues expected him to propose some third line and to fix a fourth meeting for the following morning. To their consternation Smuts courteously broke off the conversation and at 8:00 p.m. ordered his train to move out of the station.

> As they stood the train gradually began to move. Smuts brought his hand to a salute. We glided out into the night, retaining in the retinas of our eyes the picture of the four bewildered faces looking up in blank amazement.

Smuts and his party returned to Paris via Prague and Vienna.

[9] Böhm: *Im Kreuzfeuer*, 316–18.
[1] Béla Kun "says he must consult his cabinet. That means he must consult Moscow." Nicolson: *Peacemaking*, 302, entry of April 5, 1919. "I can not but feel convinced that Lenin must have been consulted before Béla Kun definitely replied to General Smuts." Brown to Coolidge (for Paris), April 9, 1919, National Archives, Document 185.3123. "Kun, who had gone off to Csepal Island to get advice by 'wireless' from Moscow, suddenly reappeared at the railway station with quite a different case. . . ." Maxwell H. H. Macartney: *Five Years of European Chaos* (London: Chapman & Hall; 1923), 28.
[2] Brown transmitted the text of Béla Kun's counterproposal to Coolidge (for Paris), April 9, 1919, National Archives, Document 185.3123.
[3] This discussion of the third and final Smuts–Béla Kun encounter is based on a paraphrased version of Smuts's telegram to Balfour, April 6, 1919, cited in *F.R.,P.C., 1919*, V, 61–2; Nicolson: *Peacemaking*, 303–4, entry of April 5, 1919, from which all quotations are taken; Brown to Coolidge (for Paris), April 6 and 9, 1919, National Archives, Documents 864.00 and 185.3123.

The question arises as to why Smuts broke off negotiations so abruptly. During the morning session he had not presented his own proposal as an ultimatum, to be accepted or rejected without further discussion. During their sojourn at the railway station, Smuts and some of his assistants met with C. B. E. Ashmead-Bartlett of the *Daily Telegraph* and Maxwell H. H. Macartney of the London *Times*. Having arrived in Budapest a few days after the March revolution, both correspondents now took it upon themselves to enlighten their countrymen. They first spent an hour and a half with Reggie Nicolson, who subsequently noted that they told him that Béla Kun had "little influence outside the capital, and that the whole thing would collapse at the slightest push."[4] The two newspapermen were glad to discover that the young Foreign Office official "disapproved of the General's Mission and of giving recognition to the Soviet Government, and felt certain that no good would come of the journey." They even carried away the impression that like themselves, Nicolson "was all in favor of a military occupation of the capital, so as to give the constitutional parties a chance to establish a government." Later in the morning of the fourth, Ashmead-Bartlett and Macartney were invited to lunch with Smuts, so that they also had "the opportunity for a very long talk" with him.[5]

Brown reported to Coolidge that Smuts "apparently received no other people except myself and the two British newspapermen . . . both of whom had been advocating rather indiscreetly and in violent language, immediate military intervention." In his own contacts with the mission, Brown gained the impression that Smuts did not approve of the conference which Béla Kun wanted summoned for Vienna or Prague, preferring to have the Hungarians state their case in Paris. In large measure it would be "natural to believe that such a conference would serve principally for the purpose of Socialist propaganda and intrigue" by a government which "was not greatly concerned about questions of boundaries." In addition, Brown learned that Smuts and his entourage had formed the judgment that the regime "had not long to live any way" since it lacked the "ability . . . to hold power much longer."[6]

It is not too much to suggest, therefore, that the two newspaper correspondents as well as members of his own party helped convince Smuts that "Béla Kun and Hungarian Bolshevism were not a serious menace and could not last."[7] Significantly, in his first telegram, Smuts reported that he had "ascertained from many reliable sources" that the government's authority "was confined in main to town of Budapest

[4] Nicolson: *Peacemaking*, 300, entry of April 4, 1919.
[5] C. B. E. Ashmead-Bartlett: *The Tragedy of Central Europe* (London: Thornton Butterworth; 1923), esp. 109; and Macartney: *Five Years of European Chaos*, 23 ff.
[6] Brown to Coolidge (for Paris), April 6, 1919, National Archives, Document 864.00.
[7] Nicolson: *Peacemaking*, 307, entry of April 9, 1919.

and was but slight in provinces."[8] In his second wire he advised Paris that the regime was "weak" and torn by "internal divisions which were likely to lead to its fall at an early date." Hence, there was no need for direct military action, as suggested by the correspondents. The Allies should simply take a waiting attitude, while alternately wielding the carrot and the stick. The carrot would consist of "hearing the Hungarians' statement [of territorial demands] in Paris or some other place" and of letting through "the trainload of fats" which, though paid for, was being detained by Allied authorities at Agram. At the same time, there was to be no *de facto* recognition; nor should the blockade be raised "for the present." Not a word was said about restraining the Rumanians during this standoff period, and, of course, Smuts forgot all about using Béla Kun as a line to Moscow.[9]

Until it became clear that the Allies would sit tight and continue the blockade, the moderates in Vienna were up in arms. A high foreign office official excitedly confided to Coolidge that the government had kept the revolution in check "by arguing that if Austria went Bolshevik, food supplies would cease, but now Allied readiness to feed Hungary was weakening this argument." Another official confirmed that the government and public opinion, including conservatives and moderate Socialists were alarmed "by Smuts's offer to ship food and goods to Hungary," since they felt they were being "deprived of one of their best arguments for keeping people quiet."[1]

On his way through Vienna Smuts is likely to have been exposed to this line of reasoning, having conferred with Cunningham there. He may also have heard that the general situation remained discouraging and depressing, in spite of the lifting of the blockade. "It was not so much that anything got seriously worse but there were almost no signs of improvement." The krone continued to depreciate; industrial labor kept demanding higher wages; food and coal shortages were not remedied as yet; unemployment was as great as ever; the government was "weak and not too well united"; the *Volkswehr* was unreliable in that it was terrorizing the property-holding classes; and inspired by the Hungarian example, Bolshevism was growing. On the plus side of the ledger Coolidge, in agreement with General Alberti, the chief of the Italian mission, could only point to the "extraordinarily quiet, docile, and orderly, not to say apathetic character of the population"; and to the fact that the "approach of summer made the suffering from lack of light and fuel less severe." Otherwise, the Swiss and Czech (Mr. Tussar)

---

[8] This sentence is not alluded to in the paraphrased version of Smuts's telegram to Balfour of April 4, 1919, printed in *F.R.,P.C.,1919*, V, 41–3. It is taken from the original text in F.O. 608/16.

[9] Smuts to Balfour, April 6, 1919, cited in *F.R.,P.C.,1919*, V, 62.

[1] Coolidge to Ammission, April 7 and 8, 1919, National Archives, Documents 184.01102/329 and 335. See also Coolidge to Ammission, April 8, 1919, cited in *F.R.,P.C.,1919*, XII, 289.

ministers, as well as Allizé and Cunningham, shared his gloomy outlook.[2]

Whereas Cunningham and "the conservative elements" still advocated direct military intervention, Mr. Schobe, Vienna's Chief of Police, who all along wanted to disband Deutsch's *Volkswehr,* approached Coolidge with a proposal "for some sort of foreign intervention, though in as disguised a form as possible." In his view, by now anything like an outright threat to cut off food, without first having dissolved the *Volkswehr,* would be likely to "provoke an outbreak." However, "official Allied advice that they should be dissolved" might encourage and strengthen the government, especially if combined with increased supplies of food, coal and raw materials. In order to exercise a "reassuring effect on the population," future food trains should be accompanied by "a considerable guard . . . especially of American and English soldiers." Coolidge added his personal opinion that "Mr. Schobe was entirely right in his recommendations," which gave the "impression of strength as well as of good will, . . . [and] in any case no one could look this gift-horse in the mouth."[3]

Meanwhile, persistent rumors circulated that a Bolshevik uprising was planned for April 14, 17, 22, or May 1. It was widely suspected that Hungarian agents were slipping across the border to spark and direct this revolutionary enterprise, particularly since Béla Kun and his colleagues considered German-Austria to be the ripest and most convenient neighbor for a Bolshevik coup.[4]

On April 8, Orlando warned the Council of Four that according to his Ambassador in Berne a soviet republic would probably be proclaimed in Vienna on April 14, "unless the Allies occupied" the capital before then. With unconcealed anger Lloyd George asked who would be sent to occupy Vienna? And why stop with Vienna, since his agents in Berlin were using similar language in their dispatches about Germany? If we follow these suggestions, why not occupy all of Europe?"[5]

Not that either Wilson or Lloyd George was against preventive action; they only opposed outright military steps. With prior approval from Paris, first Hoover and then Cunningham issued minatory statements, which were not unwelcome to the Austrian government. In the Austrian press Hoover was widely and approvingly quoted as saying that even "the desperate and rebellious" elements should understand that rioting would endanger Allied supplies of food and coal. Especially

2 Coolidge to Ammission, April 6, 1919, National Archives, Documents 184.01102/316 and 319; and Coolidge to Ammission, April 7, 1919, cited in *F.R.,P.C.,1919,* XII, 287–9.
3 Coolidge to Ammission, April 7, 1919, National Archives, Document, 184.01102/328; and Coolidge to Ammission, April 7 and 8, 1919, cited in *F.R.,P.C.,1919,* XII, 285–7, 290.
4 Coolidge to Ammission, April 13 and 15, 1919, National Archives, Documents 184.01102/345 and 354.
5 Mantoux: *Délibérations,* I, 179.

Vienna "must be fed by the Allies, who were fighting Bolshevism."[6] According to Hoover, the food operation was "a race against both death and Communism"; he never managed to have more than "a ten days supply of food on hand in Vienna." In anticipation of troubles on May Day Hoover's agents prevailed on the municipal authorities to post on city walls a proclamation, signed by Hoover, to the effect that "any disturbance of public order would render food shipments impossible and bring Vienna face to face with absolute famine." In the first half of 1919, the Relief Administration "poured more food" into Austria, in proportion to population, than into any other defeated or liberated country.[7]

Similarly, on April 13, Cunningham issued a long statement through the editor of the *Arbeiter Zeitung*. He claimed that the "British section of the Paris Conference" had authorized him to declare emphatically "that political unrest would lead to the interruption of all imports, including food." Since there was such an acute food shortage in Europe, the Entente was inclined to deny rations to countries consumed by political disorders. Besides, quite apart from political and constitutional issues, the Conference considered Vienna a critical railway point for the supply and support of valued allies, particularly of Poland and Czechoslovakia.

In spite of these admonitions the expected outbreak occurred on April 17. Starting at 2:30 p.m. huge crowds of unemployed and invalids and a few *Volkswehr* assembled in front of City Hall. Waving red flags, they cheered speeches by university students, Hungarian agents, and an Austrian just back from Bavaria. These speeches alternately called for the relief of harsh living conditions and the establishment of a soviet government. At 4:00 p.m. the crowd moved up the Ringstrasse to the square in front of the Parliament Building. After listening to more speeches, militant activists tried to force the doors and windows of the building. But since on the basis of advance information, both the police and the loyal units of the *Volkswehr* had been alerted, these easily drove back the assailants, inflicting rather few casualties. In no time the swollen crowds dispersed and the revolt was quelled.

According to Walter R. Bundy, Vice-Consul on Coolidge's staff, the "whole affair had been carefully planned," the protest of the unemployed and disabled veterans serving as "a cover for gathering the crowd for an attempt to overthrow the Government and set up a councils-republic." From private sources he learned that the mastermind of the entire disturbance was Kadriansky, a Russian who a few days before had come from Budapest with 8.5 million kronen. But whereas Bundy kept denouncing the *Volkswehr* for their alleged disloyalty, Coolidge conceded that Deutsch and his units had saved the

[6] American Relief Administration: *Bulletin*, No. 9 (May 13, 1919), 30.
[7] Herbert Hoover: *Memoirs* (New York: Macmillan; 1951), I, 393.

day, and advised Paris that as long as the *Volkswehr* was behind the government chances of further disturbances were "greatly lessened." Coolidge also took comfort from the fact that Hungarian agents were being arrested. Bauer even informed him confidentially that although the new law for expelling or interning foreigners was being publicized as a food-saving measure, it was "primarily to enable the Government to arrest revolutionary agitators." In an interview with Coolidge, Chancellor Renner defended the new ban on public assemblies in similar terms.[8]

During the rioting in front of Parliament, Cunningham, accompanied by John Banister, head of the British Food Mission, called on Renner at the State Chancellery. They again threatened to halt the twelve food trains which crossed into Austria every day and reminded him that under the Armistice the Allies had the right to send in troops to maintain order. The next day placards were posted throughout the city advising the public of these veiled threats. Meanwhile the executive of the Social Democratic Party publicly warned that the bourgeoisie had for a long time been calling for Allied occupation because they were intent on staging a counterrevolution "under the protection of foreign bayonets." Yesterday's splendid performance by the *Volkswehr,* which proved that Austria was capable of maintaining order by herself, had foiled this scheme.[9]

In the second half of April the Hungarian Soviet Republic was hopelessly isolated. Russia's Red Army was a thousand kilometers from her borders; the Austrian government survived as a benign satellite of the Allies; Smuts strengthened the Big Four's resolve to keep up the quarantine; and three hostile neighbors were primed for further encroachments. The Rumanians in particular were eager to exploit this favorable situation, with or without French encouragement or connivance.

Brătianu fully realized that he held many trumps. The Big Four, having decided to give high priority to the feeding and equipping of his armies in their overall containment policy, made it clear that the Allies counted on Rumanian troops to step up the pressure along the Dniester front. By April 3 Brătianu had told the Conference that only by hastening the retreat of Hungarian troops beyond the neutral zone and compelling their complete demobilization, could Rumanian troops "successfully make resistance in the East."[1] He also readied his forces to march to Budapest to overthrow Béla Kun, should he or the Allies deem it opportune or necessary. Whereas for fighting Russian Bolshevism Brătianu expected Bessarabia as a reward, for checking Hun-

[8] Coolidge to Ammission, April 18–28, 1919, National Archives, Documents 184.01102/376, /380, /388, /392, /394, /401, /410, /413.
[9] *Arbeiter Zeitung,* April 18 and 19, 1918.
[1] See David Hunter Miller: *My Diary at the Conference of Paris,* XVII, 374–5.

garian Bolshevism he expected a Transylvanian award which would exceed the confines of the secret Treaty of Bucharest.

Within ten days after Smuts's visit, Rumanian troops started an offensive all along their western front. Béla Kun was not prepared for this onslaught. Following the inconclusive Smuts negotiations he set his mind to further diplomatic maneuvers, for his fledgling Red Army was far from combat-ready. Not surprisingly, therefore, the Rumanian forces, under General Marderescu, advanced swiftly. In short order they reached the Vix lines. With the Hungarian army in total disarray, Brătianu pressed his advantage. By May 1 his troops were encamped along the western bank of the Tisza, deep in Magyar territory and far beyond the neutral zone. They reached Szolnok, a key transportation center, and even crossed the river. While the Rumanian armies proceeded to occupy this line, which placed them within 80 miles of the capital, the Czechs renewed their advance. They not only moved southward into the coal and iron producing basin of Salgó-Tarján and Miskolo, but also eastward for a hook-up with the Rumanians at Csap. The Czech army in Slovakia was under the command of French officers, thereby lending further credibility to Béla Kun's charge that the French, if not the entire Entente, were accomplices in this effort to throttle the soviet republic.

As early as April 19, when Nagy-Várad was about to fall, Béla Kun publicly admitted the seriousness of the Rumanian attack as well as of the Hungarian reverses. In an address to the Workers' and Soldiers' Council in Budapest, he conceded that the Red Army was far from ready, that the Rumanians had superior numbers and equipment, and that it was just a matter of days before the Czechs and the Serbs would launch an attack on the northern and southern fronts. He had never conceived of Hungary's struggle in national terms, that is separate from the Russian and the World Revolution. But even though Russian troops had crossed into Eastern Galicia and were pushing toward Czernowitz they were still a long way off. Béla Kun proclaimed that until the international proletariat could come to Hungary's aid, the Hungarian proletariat would have to struggle alone against this Entente-inspired offensive, which was calculated to crush the Hungarian Soviet as the Paris Commune had been crushed. Three days later, in a message to Lenin, he foreshadowed a Hungarian Brest Litovsk.[2]

This perilous military emergency provoked sharp political repercussions. Left-extremists, notably Pogány and Számuely, proposed drastic measures for this battle for revolutionary survival. Pogány called on the government to address ringing revolutionary appeals to the European workers, including the enemy troops; to declare a *levée en masse;* and to impose a ruthless revolutionary terror. He vouched that the Hun-

[2] Speech of April 19, 1919, and letter to Lenin, April 22, 1919, both cited in Béla Kun: *La République hongroise des conseils* (Budapest: Cornive; 1962), 129–33.

garian bourgeoisie would be used as a hostage: every Rumanian advance would be answered with "cruel ordeals for the bourgeoisie here." In the Budapest Soviet Számuely ominously served notice that "he who is against us is our enemy! We will crush him, whoever he may be and regardless of his protestations."[3]

This was the beginning of a campaign by the ultras to stir up class hatred and root out internal counterrevolutionaries. In the excitement the air was heavy with charges that in the occupied provinces class enemies welcomed the advancing Rumanians with open arms; that throughout the rest of Hungary, while eagerly awaiting liberation by enemy armies, they were hatching dangerous counterrevolutionary plots. The fear of counterrevolution, whether real or imagined, called forth a terrorist response.

Following the arrest of prominent men of the *ancien régime* for allegedly counterrevolutionary activities, Brown warned that hereafter everything that "savored of resistance or counterrevolution could serve as a pretext for dreadful excesses . . . [and] that the Revolutionary Tribunals, with their provision for crude, swift, and pitiless 'justice' were ready at hand for sinister uses." He admitted, though, that counterrevolutionary movements were "always possible and might almost come unexpectedly," especially since the "average Hungarian" was not "really in favor" of Socialism and certainly was "violently opposed to Bolshevism."[4]

According to Von Fürstenberg, even though all middle- and upper-class Magyars profoundly despised the Rumanians, they nonetheless looked upon their advance as "the beginning of their liberation," particularly since they counted on the Entente to curb Bucharest's territorial appetites. Though the real danger was in the provinces, the tocsin against the counterrevolution was being sounded most loudly in Budapest. Numerous arrests were made in the capital, estimates ranging from 43 to 200. Moreover, coffeehouses were closed, private telephone service was suspended, public meetings were proscribed, and an evening curfew was proclaimed. Számuely was charged with maintaining order and security on the home front.[5]

All in all, the Rumanian attack and the internal tensions which it aggravated endangered the government. Coolidge wired that in his speech of April 19 Béla Kun had admitted the "collapse of Hungarian resistance" and had called the "situation very critical and tense." It was widely rumored that the Széklers had come to an understanding with

[3] The speeches of Pogány and Számuely at the April 19 session of the Workers' and Soldiers' Council in Budapest are cited in *Bulletin Périodique de la presse hongroise*, No. 32, May 12, 1919, 7.
[4] Brown to Coolidge (for Ammission), April 19, 1919, cited in *F.R.,P.C.,1919*, XII, 433–4.
[5] Von Fürstenberg to Wedel (for Foreign Ministry), April 18, 20, and 24, 1919, G.F.M.

the Rumanians and that the government had been overthrown.[6] On the twenty-second Von Fürstenberg also reported the situation to be "very critical," with a decisive turning in the offing.[7] The following day he reached the conclusion that the government could not survive the Rumanian offensive and predicted that a moderate cabinet, under Garami, would soon take over, as a first step to a negotiated settlement.[8] On April 24, Von Fürstenberg confirmed this forecast, adding that the regime had actually approached Colonel Cunningham to find out the conditions on which the Entente would settle. The Entente was said to insist that the resignation of the Communist government in favor of a "moderate Socialist" administration was the essential precondition for armistice negotiations.[9]

Actually Béla Kun as well as other members of the Soviet executive all along made more serious approaches to Brown than to Cunningham. Coolidge's deputy met repeatedly with the Foreign Commissar, even before the acute crisis. Shortly after Smuts's departure Kun called on Brown for a general exchange of views. Brown reported:

> I was greatly impressed by his immense vitality and shrewdness. Not impressive in personality, he is nevertheless a force to be reckoned with. He knows what he is after, is a sincere Socialist, and evidently most resourceful. His whole policy seems how to avoid, if possible, the regrettable excesses of the Russian Socialists, which have given the name Bolshevist so sinister a significance. Personally devoted to Lenin, he at this present moment is evidently guided in most of his decisions directly by the great Russian leader; not for any political reasons, but because of the affinity that binds all Socialists in common devotion to a fundamental ideal.[1]

Brown must have been fascinated and intrigued by the personality of this 32-year-old dictator, for following their next conversation on April 15, he gave an even more detailed pen portrait.

> Though not endowed with what we are accustomed to denote as "presence," and at first glance rather unimpressive and even repellent, Béla Kun ends by making a decided impression of immense vitality, resourcefulness and a certain self-mastery and poise that is quite extraordinary when one thinks of his utter lack of preparation for the position of dictator of a nation. It is only a few weeks ago that he was imprisoned . . . and his head still shows the wounds he received. . . .

[6] Coolidge to Ammission, April 20, 1919, National Archives, Document 184.01102/381.
[7] Von Fürstenberg to Wedel (for Foreign Ministry), April 22 and 23, 1919, G.F.M.
[8] Von Fürstenberg to Wedel (for Foreign Ministry), April 23, 24, 1919, G.F.M.
[9] Von Fürstenberg to Wedel (for Foreign Ministry), April 24, 1919, G.F.M. Cunningham was said to have arrived in Budapest on April 23.
[1] For the full text of the report on this interview see Brown to Coolidge (for Ammission), April 10, 1919, cited in *F.R.,P.C.,1919*, XII, 432–4.

. . . Though I believe him to be a sincere Socialist, he is not a fanatic nor an impractical dreamer, but is shrewd and practical, and ready to seize any and every opportunity to accomplish his aims. In other words, he is a good deal of a strategist, an opportunist who, like a good general, keeps his main end in view without faltering.

It seems to be quite clear that Béla Kun's policy is one of moderation. . . . So long as he maintains his ascendancy I think we may confidently expect that Hungary will not witness the terrorism and the excesses of Russian Bolshevism.[2]

Hereafter Brown never wavered in his estimate that as long as the Soviet Republic survived Béla Kun was the best foil against such left-Communists as Számuely.

Their conversation of the fifteenth of April was wide ranging. To a hypothetical inquiry about allowing "American representatives to take charge of the transportation and distribution of food and raw materials," Kun unhesitatingly answered that "this would be acceptable so long as there were no soldiers in uniform."[3] When pressed about political persecutions he acknowledged that "there had been a number of arrests" and that there "had been 43 arrests the night before." But he went on to say that they were meant to quell "a widespread counter-revolutionary plot, organized in Vienna and Switzerland"; that the men in question were "under detention rather than in strict confinement"; and that they were also designed to "prevent the mob from taking matters into their own hands." As for the manifestoes to proletariats of other countries, these were appeals urging them "not to take up arms against each other." The Soviet Republic would "refrain from carrying on propaganda provided foreign countries would not interfere here."

With regard to foreign policy, Béla Kun repeated his offer to serve as an intermediary with Lenin. When Brown informed him that his proposal for a conference of successor states was ill received because of "memories of Brest Litovsk, where Trotsky had preached Bolshevism," he replied that he was prepared to "confine himself strictly to business." In parting, Brown cautioned against the destructive consequences of class hatred and pleaded for moderation. After some reassuring words Béla Kun added that when the police beat him over the head "he merely remarked that they did not know what they were doing, and that he hoped that when they were getting blows on their heads they would take them as philosophically as he took his."[4]

[2] Brown to Coolidge (for Ammission), April 17, 1919, cited in ibid., 437–8.
[3] BROWN: "I then said that of course he must understand that it was far from my own thought to suggest anything of the nature of intervention, disguised or otherwise [sic!]."
[4] "Memorandum of a Conversation with Béla Kun," April 15, 1919, cited in F.R.,P.C., 1919, XII, 438–42.

With Rumanians approaching the Tisza River, Brown's conversation with Béla Kun as well as his acquaintance with Kunfi became the basis for a major *démarche*. On April 24, following intensive negotiations with moderate members of the government, Brown wanted to get an urgent message to Coolidge. Whereas heretofore he had used special couriers for this purpose, because of the explosive situation in Budapest he did not want to risk a written dispatch being intercepted. So he sent two assistants, Captain C. A. Scully and Lieutenant W. H. Osborn, with oral reports, which they were instructed to put into writing after their safe arrival in Vienna.[5]

According to these reports,[6] in the face of disastrous military reverses "the ground in Budapest was well prepared for the formation of a transitional government along moderate socialist lines," possibly with Garami, Böhm, Agoston, and Buchinger in the lead. However, such a transitional government could not be set up "without considerable bloodshed" unless Béla Kun were part of it.

> Béla Kun was unquestionably in control of the city. . . . It was he alone who was holding the radical revolutionary elements in the city in check. . . . He was extremely popular with the radical elements . . . but was exerting all his influence to keep down their excesses.

Quite clearly, he alone could secure support or at least acquiescence for this change among the "wilder element." Béla Kun himself was disposed to "form a transition government of the moderate socialist type . . . and to come to an understanding with Garami."

But there was another side to this plan, of which Béla Kun is not likely to have known. Probably on the advice of his Social Democratic interlocutors, Brown urged that Béla Kun, possibly accompanied by Kunfi or Agoston, be invited to Switzerland to meet with representatives of the Entente to discuss the Hungarian situation as well as to be an intermediary with Lenin.

In other words, since Kun was needed to launch the new government, he would be retained as a Minister. But soon afterwards he was to be whisked out of town: "the real reason" in back of the meeting in Switzerland "was to afford a plausible reason for Kun to leave the city and . . . give the new regime a chance to become installed without his presence."

On April 29, Brown sent Scully to Vienna again.[7] By this time "the

[5] Coolidge to Ammission, April 25, 1919, ibid., 442–3.
[6] The full text of the two memoranda of April 25—one signed by Osborn the other by Scully and Osborn—is printed in ibid., 444–7.
[7] The full text of Brown's dispatch of April 29, 1919, is printed in ibid., 449–52.

Rumanian advance had profoundly discouraged this Government and inflamed the extremists," who prior to that advance had been losing ground.

> There was undoubtedly a serious counterrevolutionary plot involving a very large number of people, including some of the old police force. It was most unskillfully managed with the result that there have been many arrests, some just and many unjust. I believe that only two of the leaders have been shot.
> Many of those placed under arrest are prominent persons suspected of being in sympathy with counterrevolutionary movements. Certainly many have been most indiscreet in openly showing their sentiments, and particularly in spreading rumors calculated to discredit this regime.
> Unfortunately, some of the government officials were so ill-advised as to speak of these *détenus* as "hostages." I immediately let them know that such an idea was utterly abhorrent, and was at once assured that the Government had no thought of resorting to such barbarous measures . . . and that many of these suspects would be immediately released. . . . I hear this morning that 30 were released in one bunch and that more will follow.

Brown and his staff repeatedly claimed credit for exerting a moderating influence. They were "encouraging the Government to purge itself of all Bolshevist taints" so that it should "inspire some confidence in the outside world." Presently Kun forced through the dismissal of Szamuely and Pogány.

In this report Brown again insisted that it was "fortunate . . . that Béla Kun [who was anxious to check extremism] was in control of the situation." Because he saw no one else who could "guarantee any sort of order and security . . . and prevent acts of terrorism," he once more emphasized the "impossibility of bringing about a transitional political transformation without the aid of Béla Kun." But he also reiterated that Kun's going abroad for the conference "was the key to the whole problem."

In conclusion, Brown expressed the hope that Coolidge and Gregory, Hoover's representative in Vienna, would support him in this policy on which they had agreed during recent meetings. In particular, provided he could do so "without violence to his own judgment," Coolidge should get an answer from Paris about the "conference in Switzerland along the lines already suggested by Smuts and myself."

Actually Brown and Coolidge differed profoundly in their estimates of the Hungarian imbroglio. On April 18 Coolidge had recommended to Paris that Brown and his staff be withdrawn from Budapest, allegedly because "the threatened counterrevolutionary intervention in Hungary . . . might cause the Béla Kun Government to hold Allied representatives . . . as hostages." On the twenty-first Brown hastened to Vienna to get his assignment prolonged. Presently Coolidge yielded to Brown, who thought that he might be able "to achieve important results, . . . especially perhaps to prevent something like a massacre." Even though Coolidge did not quite agree with him, he advised the Ammission that he had allowed Brown to return to Budapest because he was "a man of mature years and sound judgment and some experience in revolutions." The Commissioners did not object.[8]

During this same hurried meeting in Vienna, Coolidge, Gregory, and Brown agreed on the broad outlines of the plan to use American influence to assist the nonviolent transmogrification of the Soviet regime. It soon turned out, however, that although Brown was prepared to work with Béla Kun in pursuit of a moderate Socialist regime, Coolidge was reluctant to do so. Having digested the reports of Scully and Osborn, he wired Paris that "Béla Kun would be willing to use his influence in favor of a less radical government *and retire himself* if he could go as representative" to Switzerland to negotiate with Allies and mediate for negotiations with Moscow [italics mine].[9]

In the covering letter accompanying Scully's and Osborn's reports to Paris, Coolidge elaborated on his reservations. To be sure, Brown's reports were "full of interest"; he evidently was "doing work of much value"; and he was exercising "a restraining influence" which had "prevented excesses that might otherwise have taken place." Still, Coolidge was not so sure that the "movement of public opinion in Hungary was at present towards the right." According to Bauer, whom he had seen yesterday, "unless attacked from the outside," the regime could maintain itself for quite a while. Because the Bolshevik leaders were "thoroughly frightened" of an Allied advance on Budapest, an advance which they could not resist, they were "willing to make great concessions . . . to avert their own downfall." But could their promises be trusted, "especially in the matter of refraining from propaganda?"

Coolidge agreed that Béla Kun was "superior to most of his associates" and might be able to institute a "stable and relatively moderate" transitional government in order to ward off foreign intervention.

> If no such intervention is contemplated, he is the man that must be dealt with. An intervention will mean bloodshed and perhaps massacre. If, on the other hand, the only way to check definitely the spread of Bolshevism in this part of the world is to crush it out in Hungary at once, action to this effect should immediately be taken. . . . Until the Rumanian advance I had felt that it was better not to

[8] Ammission, Memoranda Nos. 236 and 247, April 22 and 25, 1919, and Coolidge to Ammission, April 22, 1919, National Archives, Documents 184.011/157 and 159 and 184.01102/391.
[9] Coolidge to Ammission, April 25, 1919, National Archives, Document 184.01102/397.

attempt intervention in Hungary. Since that advance I have believed
that prompt, decisive action would be the best course.

Coolidge confessed that within a week he might again change his mind,
but this was his position for the moment.[1]

On May 1, when transmitting Brown's follow-up dispatch, Coolidge was still very much of the same mind. Again, after praising Brown
for his admirable work under "trying circumstances," Coolidge demurred, this time under cover of the "domino theory."

> Professor Brown's evidence is almost entirely from one, interested
> side, and the fact that Béla Kun is wise enough, not only to maintain
> law and order but also to wish to establish decently civilized
> conditions, does not prove that he and his partisans are really
> moving to the right as far as their fundamental principles are
> concerned. I must admit too, that the idea of a "transitional"
> government groping towards something better appears to me a little
> nebulous. But even disregarding all such doubts, there are other
> considerations to be taken into account, and to be given even more
> weight than those mentioned by Professor Brown.
> The question as to how the Allies should treat the government of
> Béla Kun is of importance not only to Hungary. It also will affect
> Austria, Bohemia, Germany, Poland, and indirectly at least the
> whole world. To give public recognition and encouragement to the
> man whose name stands next to that of Lenin and Trotsky as the
> apostle of international Bolshevism and class warfare is a grave
> matter. To invite him to come on a special mission to treat as an
> equal with representatives of the Allied Powers, and perhaps to
> serve as an intermediary between them and Lenin would vastly
> enhance his present importance as well as tend to stabilize his
> government and what it stands for in Hungary. This would be going
> a great deal further than General Smuts' propositions, which were
> that Hungary should merely appear as one of several interested
> states in a general meeting, and there is no doubt that the mission of
> General Smuts did much to strengthen the hand and enhance the
> prestige of Béla Kun. At the same time it weakened the position of
> the government here, which had been telling its people that a
> Bolshevist revolution would mean the end of the Allied food supply
> which alone saved Vienna from starvation. Since then, in spite of
> the Smuts' Mission, the statement has been repeated and it has been
> explicitly and officially confirmed by the English and French repre-
> sentatives here, whose utterances on the subject have never been
> repudiated. The belief in its truth has unquestionably been an
> influence for the maintenance of order. Conversely, every encour-
> agement given to the present Hungarian regime weakens the hold of
> the Austrian government on its own more radical supporters.
> In the eyes of the Hungarian Bolshevists few things at this
> moment could be more desirable than a revolution here, which

[1] Coolidge to Ammission, April 25, 1919, cited in *F.R.,P.C.,1919*, XII, 442–4.

would establish in Vienna a system similar to that of Budapest. It would be one more great step in the progress of international revolution, a conquest in itself and one full of menace to the security of Bohemia, of Poland, of Germany and beyond. On the other hand, the collapse or the overthrow of the government of Béla Kun, whatever his merits as a statesman, would, provided it were succeeded by a moderate regime, depress revolutionists and strengthen the forces of law and order the world over. It is thus evident that the advisability of recognizing him does not depend solely on the likelihood of massacres in Budapest, however terrible. Large considerations have to be taken into account, and these considerations, whatever may be true tomorrow, are I believe decisive today against such action as recommended by Professor Brown.[2]

In an unaccustomed outpost in East Central Europe, two American intellectuals-*cum*-scholars, temporarily turned government experts, prescribed fundamentally different strategies of containment.

Needless to say, the Rumanian government was in full accord with the Coolidge thesis. Brătianu counted on the French to plead his case in Paris. He argued that now that Hungarian resistance was almost broken, Entente forces could occupy Budapest without difficulty.

> This occupation would . . . cut short any cooperation between Hungarian and Russian Bolsheviks. It would raise a barrier between the latter and their German counterparts. . . . At the same time, we could withdraw our troops from Transylvania in order to reinforce our defense on the Dniester . . . where we fight not only for our country, but for Europe herself and for civilization. It is not more than right, therefore, that our great Allies help us. . . . The occupation of Budapest would be of immense help, . . . supplemented by the disarmament of Bulgaria. . . .

In this *aide-mémoire* Brătianu claimed that Rumania would for many years have to be the "guardian of the European order." Therefore, she should have borders which would brace her for this all-important assignment: in the west the confluence of the Tisza and Danube, and in the north in Bukovina, a common border with both Poland and Czechoslovakia.[3]

Meanwhile, how were the Big Four reacting to the Rumanian-Czech offensive and to the impending collapse of the Hungarian Soviet regime? On April 26, Woodrow Wilson recommended that Rumania be asked to cease her "distinctly aggressive" action. He seemed particularly disturbed because she was the recipient of "considerable assistance

---

[2] Coolidge to Ammission, May 1, 1919, cited in ibid., 447–9.
[3] Brătianu to French Minister in Bucharest, April 28, 1919, Klotz Papers, 10(A-6). Also see Sherman D. Spector: *Rumania at the Paris Peace Conference* (New York: Bookman Associates; 1962), *passim*, esp. Chs. iii and iv.

from the Allies." The President's proposal to send a joint letter to Brătianu was defeated by Lloyd George and Clemenceau, who preferred to give the Rumanian statesman a chance to appear before them. Wilson did not press the point, either that day or thereafter, so that neither was the letter sent, nor was Brătianu summoned.[4] A direct wireless appeal by Garbai and Béla Kun to Wilson "to arrest immediately all warlike action against us" was equally unproductive.[5]

Around May 1, as the Rumanians reached the Tisza, the reeling Hungarian Soviet government asked Bucharest for a cessation of hostilities, indicating that it was prepared to make territorial concessions. A few days later Brătianu answered with what amounted to an ultimatum for unconditional surrender. Almost simultaneously General Hallier, the chief of France's military mission in Vienna, threatened Allied occupation of Budapest unless Béla Kun resigned.[6] Soviet authorities rejected both demands out of hand, Rumanian forces crossed the Tisza, and some Czech units were said to have penetrated to within 30 miles of the capital.[7]

In Paris, meanwhile, the Big Four considered inviting the Austrians to send delegates for peace talks to Chantilly. Woodrow Wilson had just received a joint note from his fellow American Peace Commissioners stressing the urgency of strengthening the elements of law and order in Austria and Hungary, recommending that Austrian representatives be "allowed to proceed to Paris immediately to present their case," and giving it as their combined opinion that this step would "go far towards encouraging the Austrians to resist the ever increasing propaganda of the Communists."[8]

Primed by this note, Wilson convinced the Council of Four to issue the invitation, the "principal reason [being] to steady" the Renner government, which was still being shaken by the "Hungarian ferment." Inadvertently a similar invitation went out to Allizé in Vienna, for presentation to the Hungarian government. The French chargé, appalled at this prospect, promptly wired for confirmation to Pichon, warning that such a step would strengthen Béla Kun. Pichon rushed to the Council of Four to say that the Allies could not negotiate with a

[4] F.R.,P.C.,1919, V, April 26, 1919, a.m., 291–2.
[5] For the full text of this appeal, dated April 28 or 29, 1919, see F.R.,P.C.,1919, XII, 453–4.
[6] On April 27, 1919, le Temps indicated that the Entente would consider an armistice on condition that the Soviet government step back in favor of "a government representing all classes."
[7] Von Fürstenberg to Wedel (for Foreign Ministry), May 4, 1919, G.F.M.; Calliope G. Caldis: The Council of Four as a Joint Emergency Authority in the European Crisis at the Paris Peace Conference 1919 (Thèse No. 93, Université de Genève: Institut Universitaire des Hautes Études Internationales; 1953), 116–17; Spector: Rumania at the Paris Peace Conference, 135.
[8] Lansing, White, Bliss, and House to Wilson, April 28, 1919, Wilson Papers, VIII A:42. They added that "similar measures could be taken in the case of Hungary as soon as a representative government existed there."

Soviet regime. Besides, the Béla Kun government "was tottering and the country was not behind it." On May 1, the Conference readily rescinded the invitation.[9]

Except for their refusal to send Allied infantry units to fight alongside the Rumanians, the Big Four—and not just the French—actively worked for the overthrow of Béla Kun. This became clear on May 5 when, at Hoover's request, the Supreme Economic Council recommended that the blockade of Hungary be lifted "as soon as the political situation permitted." When the recommendation came before the Council of Five on May 9, Hoover explained that the proposal was based on the "supposition that the Béla Kun Government would fall at once," though this had not happened to date.

> But the Supreme Economic Council [was asking] for a mandate to act as soon as that Government should disappear. The information available went to show that two days ago it appeared certain that the Béla Kun Government would be upset. Unfortunately, the invitation to Austria to attend the Peace Conference had been interpreted to include the Hungarian Government with the result that Béla Kun's Government had again been put on its feet.[1]

Pichon having suggested that the removal of the blockade be made contingent on "the reestablishment of order," Sonnino and McCormick interpreted this to mean the overthrow of Béla Kun. In any case, the Council of Foreign Ministers accepted Pichon's wording. On May 22, at the behest of the Supreme Economic Council, the Big Four authorized a public announcement to the effect that "the blockade of Hungary would be suspended as soon as a Government was installed there which gave some assurance of settled conditions." The Press Committee was asked to give this announcement wide publicity in the Allied and Neutral press.[2]

Quite clearly, the Big Four had no intention of dealing with a "transitional government" which included any Bolsheviks and perpetuated the Soviet Republic. But even if they had, there were insuperable obstacles at the Hungarian end. The Socialists and Communists were unable to come to an agreement about the composition of a new government. Béla Kun might have been amenable, possibly even to his own removal, but his left-Bolsheviks were up in arms. Moreover,

[9] *F.R.,P.C.,1919*, V, Sessions of April 26, 1919, a.m., and May 1, 1919, a.m., 291–2, 392–3, 406; Coolidge to Ammission, May 8, 1919, cited in *F.R.,P.C.,1919*, XII, 455–6; Alfred D. Low: "The Soviet Hungarian Republic and the Paris Peace Conference," in *Transactions of the American Philosophical Society*, New Ser., Vol. 53, Pt. 10 (1963), 64.

[1] On May 8 Hoover issued instructions to the Food Mission in Trieste to prepare two trainloads of fats "for transmission to Budapest without delay, immediately upon the collapse of Bela Cohen's [*sic!*] Government." American Relief Administration: *Bulletin G* (May 13, 1919), 11.

[2] *F.R.,P.C.,1919*, X, 228–9, 233–4, 247, 265, 293; and *F.R.,P.C.,1919*, V, 693–5, 813, 817.

prominent moderate Socialists, including Garami, were reported to be opposed to assuming the humiliating task of begging for Hungary's survival as a sovereign state.[3]

In sum, there was no alternative to a *levée en masse* under the direction of the existing government. Not only some of his fellow Commissars but also Lenin urged Béla Kun toward that course. On April 26, he had begged the Russian leader to step up the military pressure on the Rumanians in order to force them to divert troops from their Hungarian campaign. Lenin's answer reached him on May 2, at the peak of Kun's own despair.

> *Ne vous énervez pas.* The events on the Rumanian front are not as serious as you imagine. As soon as we have free troops available on our eastern front, we will try to hold back the Rumanians in Bukovina and Bessarabia. The mobilization of our Internationalists is in process at Kiev. Trust in the development of the world revolution of the proletariat, which is just a matter of time. Until then, fortify the city [Budapest], stock up munitions and food, arm the entire proletariat and have them join in the struggle. Hold until assistance reaches you. . . . Have confidence, our victory is certain.[4]

This telegram, though disappointing on the score of material aid, inspired Béla Kun to join with those advocating a last-ditch stand, at whatever cost.

Later that same day he issued a call to arms to all workers in a stirring address to the Workers' and Soldiers' Council in Budapest. He began by bluntly conceding the lack of discipline, the shortage of arms, and the demoralization of the Hungarian forces who were retreating in complete disarray before the Rumanians. Szolnok had fallen; and so had Miskolo. The retreating divisions were in no condition to resume the battle, so that Budapest was "at the mercy of a Rumanian offensive." But here in the capital there were battalions of industrial workers who could use the arms and equipment stored in the regular army barracks. The question was, then, whether "we will abandon Budapest . . . or whether the proletariat of the capital will fight to maintain its dictatorship there. If this dictatorship is swept away it will be because it was not invested with enough proletarian blood. Should we decide to fight the struggle will consist of rifle shots, bayonet charges, and organization—and not . . . of sermons." But before throwing themselves into battle, Béla Kun wanted the workers to know about Hungary's international situation.

Precisely because the military prospects were so hopeless, the Soviet government had tried to secure "a Brest Litovsk" peace at practically

[3] Von Fürstenberg to Wedel (for Foreign Ministry), April 30, 1919, G.F.M. (92/I/28) 13206.
[4] Cited in Arpad Szelpal: *Les 133 jours de Béla Kun* (Paris: Fayard; 1959), 176.

any price provided it could salvage a small territorial base in which to preserve the proletarian dictatorship. "It was no pleasure," Béla Kun confessed, "to send telegrams to the bourgeois governments of the surrounding countries, to Wilson, and to the Peace Conference in Paris." And yet we sent them in the hope of salvaging something. But probably the Entente wants to crush us here, which "will cost them less than in Russia."

At this point Béla Kun restated the choice before the Council: to abandon Budapest, which seemed to be the position of the vast majority of workers; or to defend the capital, which was the position of a "Lilliputian" minority of militarily insignificant but ideologically unified workers.

> I will tell you sincerely that my personal point of view—which perhaps is unjustifiable both militarily and even politically, but stems from my past—is that, if possible, well, then, let us defend our dictatorship, if necessary all the way to Wiener-Neustadt. . . .

With this realistic but defiant appeal Béla Kun, who usually was not a particularly effective speaker, rallied even the hesitant Social Democrats to the defense of the revolution, the regime, Budapest, and Hungary.[5]

With General Aurélien Stromfeld as his chief of staff, it was Böhm, the Commissar for Defense, who set about organizing this proletarian army. In less than three weeks more than 100,000 workers, especially trade unionists, were ready for battle. Inspired by the national rather than proletarian cause, army officers came forward to train and lead the Continent's second fledgling Red Army, in which discipline—not political reliability—was the touchstone of authority.[6]

On the home front war production went into high gear. At the same time, the government decreed a host of emergency measures, many of them designed to calm the restless urban masses. Accordingly, soup kitchens were organized; price controls instituted; private savings above a certain level confiscated; unused space in private homes made available at low rents; and large estates collectivized. Even though these and similar regulations were only partly ideological in inspiration —any *levée en masse* of necessity has a strong leveling edge—they tended to alienate further the *bourgeoisie,* the landowners, and other non-Socialist opponents of the regime.

This vast forced-draft mobilization was spurred on by a massive propaganda campaign. In newspapers, on wall posters, on fliers, and in platform speeches, nationalist and Socialist appeals were variously combined, all depending on the intended audiences. Hungarians were

[5] For the full text of this speech of May 2, 1919, see Béla Kun: *La République hongroise des conseils,* 135–40. See also Géza Herczeg: *Béla Kun: Eine historische Grimasse* (Berlin: Verlag für Kulturpolitik; 1928), 102–12.
[6] Böhm: *Im Kreuzfeuer,* 357–60.

summoned to fight against both imperialism and capitalism. The invading Rumanian and Czech armies, composed of servile soldiers, were portrayed as the catspaws of the Entente, the world directorate of predatory capitalism. The preliminary peace terms presented to the Germans on May 7 were pointed to as a clear demonstration of the hollowness of Wilsonianism and the corresponding rapacity of Clemencism.

Another dimension of this ideologically infused *levée en masse* was the campaign against internal enemies. These were said to be working hand in glove with the invaders as well as with the French. This charge gained in credibility when the French sponsored and supported the rival government first in Arad and then in Szeged where it was establishing its authority over the liberated areas. Headed by Count Julius Károlyi, and as of early June with Nicholas Horthy as Minister of War, the composition and the purposes of this government were unmistakably counterrevolutionary. In fact, the titled *"émigrés"* in and around this "government-in-exile," as well as those making up its Vienna outpost, were such extreme reactionaries that even their French patrons soon became impatient with them[7]

Meanwhile there were numerous arrests, notably in the war zones, and for a while Joseph Cserny's "Lenin Boys" were able to take advantage of the counterrevolutionary scare to spread their terror, first in the capital and then in the western provinces.

This, then, was the domestic underpinning for the projected counteroffensive of the inexperienced but vigorous Red Army. Böhm and his military advisers had made good use of the present halt of the invading armies. To be sure, during the first ten days in May the Rumanians established a number of bridgeheads on the right bank of the Tisza. But Brătianu's military advisers hesitated to press on directly to Budapest: their supply lines were overextended; they disposed of only some three divisions; and the Dniester front might at any moment drain away some of these limited effectives. Moreover, on May 31 the Peace Conference turned down Brătianu's proposal that his troops march on the Hungarian capital.[8] While regrouping his forces Brătianu pressed the French either to commit their own troops or to prevail on the Yugoslavs and the Czechs to join in this venture.

Probably for the same reasons that he would not send additional troops to Russia, Clemenceau refused to assign units of Franchet d'Esperey's eastern armies to this intervention. Besides, he fully expected Béla Kun's regime to crumble under the combined pressure of the surrounding states, given the internal state of affairs and its aggravation by the blockade. As for the Yugoslavs, they used their military re-

---

[7] See Louis Varjassy: *Révolution, Bolchevisme, réaction: Histoire de l'occupation française en Hongrie, 1918–1919* (Paris: Jouve; 1934), 55 ff.; and Böhm: *Im Kreuzfeuer*, 407–14.

[8] *F.R.,P.C.,1919*, VI, 133.

sources to mount the guard against the Italians and the Bulgarians until the Peace Conference finally granted them satisfactory borders.

With the southern front relatively safe, the Hungarians faced the question of moving either against the Rumanians or the Czechs, the Red Army being in no position to muster sufficient power to tackle both. An advance against the Rumanians was ruled out because they could establish a formidable defensive line along the eastern shores of the Tisza. An attack on the northern front promised the quickest and most dramatic results, and a quick victory would give a tremendous boost to the shaky regime. The Czech forces were reported to be considerably weaker than the Rumanian units; the territory to be recovered was unmistakably Magyar and contained important coal districts; the junction between the Czechs and the Rumanians might be broken; and whatever small chance there was of a link-up with Russia's Red Army across the Carpathians lay in the northern direction.[9]

The counteroffensive against the Czechs started on May 19. Within five days Miskolo was recaptured. During the following two weeks the Red Army easily advanced beyond the original demarcation line into southern Slovakia, thereby driving a wedge between the Czechs and the Rumanian army. At the same time, the Rumanians sensed that the enemy's defensive line was stiffening and accordingly decided to dig in on the eastern bank of the Tisza.

This remarkable military achievement strengthened Béla Kun's government. By May 23—the day Miskolo was retaken—Von Fürstenberg reported that "in general most people were inclined to believe that this regime would last longer than one would have supposed a few weeks ago." Two days later he repeated that "predictions of an imminent overturn were premature" because Allied forces were not expected to intervene directly and the government-in-exile was too weak for action.[1]

[9] Cf. Böhm: *Im Kreuzfeuer,* 364.
[1] Von Fürstenberg to Wedel (for Foreign Ministry), May 23 and 25, 1919, G.F.M.

Part Six

THE WAGES OF VICTORY

22

The Versailles Treaty

IT MAY well be that between the Armistice and the signing of the Versailles Treaty on June 28, 1919, conditions in Germany were never really revolutionary. To many contemporaries, however, she repeatedly seemed to hover on the brink of disaster. Certainly Lloyd George and Wilson, as well as their chief advisers, were profoundly troubled by the prospects for political stability first in November–December, then in early January, and again in March–April. In early April they tended to take the same grave view as Brockdorff-Rantzau and Groener, who were convinced that Germany was about to be shaken by a "third revolutionary wave." To be sure, by then the blockade had been eased to the point that massive shipments of food could be sent into the country, but what effect this would have remained to be seen. Everyone was afraid that this third wave would be far worse than the two preceding ones. They knew that it took time to distribute food, to carry it from the ports to the urban centers; that, because of an acute raw materials shortage, unemployment continued at a high level; and that radicals of the Left and Right were emboldened by the Hungarian overturn.[1]

Especially those British officials who were investigating economic and financial conditions in Germany sent in alarming reports, even after the food blockade had been lifted.[2] In their view the Ebert-Scheidemann regime and the National Assembly were the only "possible alternative to a Soviet Government." To strengthen them the Allies should immediately rush in foodstuffs and raw materials, should reopen

[1] Cf. Minutes of the conversation between Brockdorff-Rantzau and Groener, held in Berlin on April 4, 1919, G.F.M. (H234106–21); and the editorial "Playing With Bolshevism," in *Die Freiheit,* April 3, 1919.

[2] *Further Reports by British Officers on the Economic Conditions Prevailing in Germany,* March and March/April 1919, H.M.S.O., Command Papers 54 and 208; *Report on Food Conditions in Germany* (by Ernest H. Starling, et al.), 1919, H.M.S.O., Command Paper 280; memorandum on "Conditions in Germany," April 15, 1919, transmitted to the French Delegation by the British Military Section, in Klotz Papers, 18(2).

the channels of trade, and should extend long-term credits. In a blunt personal note, Major C. L. Kuyvett, head of the British Economic Mission, advised Lieutenant-General Sir Richard Haking, chief of the British Section of the Armistice Commission at Spa, that there was "a great danger—an immediate one—of the utter ruin of Germany through Bolshevism, and [that he felt] sure that if this happened it must spread to France and eventually to England." E. F. Wise also urged that since "Germany's danger was a danger to the entire democratic world . . . and since it was a struggle between the proposed League of Nations and Lenin," the Allies should support the present Ebert-Scheidemann government as long as they were satisfied that it was not militarist.

Of all such warnings, General Haking's was the most sweeping. He told the Allies to stop ranging themselves "against a danger that was past." Now that "one war was over" they should "prepare to act victoriously against the next," which meant rearranging "their former forces and creating an alliance with any people, in or out of Europe, who were prepared to join hands with them to defeat the international power of Bolshevism." Haking even went so far as to suggest that France "be left out of calculation and told not to interfere" if she opposed the strengthening of Germany "for the fight against Bolshevism in her own country and on her frontiers."[3]

In late March and early April British officials went beyond providing their own delegation with information, impressions, and advice. When Wise and Gibson called on Brockdorff-Rantzau, they told him that before leaving Paris Lloyd George had instructed them to assure Berlin that "the British Government had no intention whatever to destroy Germany; on the contrary, it wished for her reconstruction and prosperity." But the German Foreign Minister refused to be put off by empty phrases. He wanted concrete proof of this attitude, insisting once again that a nation of 70 million could not be destroyed. He did not believe in using Bolshevism as a threat, but all sensible politicians would have to agree that "with their policies to date the Allies were fostering the Bolshevik cause." Thereupon Wise revealed that he was charged with investigating whether or not Germany could put up collateral for an Anglo-American loan. Brockdorff-Rantzau attached great importance to this feeler, which he construed as evidence of Anglo-American rivalry for political and economic influence in Germany.[4] Almost simultaneously Haking told Von Hammerstein and Von Lersner in Spa that once peace was signed Britain would seek close relations with Germany, "since she

3 Haking's "The Defeat of Bolshevism," March 31, 1919, transmitted to the War Cabinet by Churchill on April 8, 1919, G.T. 7086, Cabinet 24/77.
4 Secret Memorandum on Brockdorff-Rantzau's Conversation with Wise and Gibson, March 30, 1919, G.F.M. (H234929–32).

always stood with the weaker party in Europe." Again Von Lersner challenged the British to prove their good intentions by working for the complete removal of the blockade, lest America and Hoover get all the credit.[5]

A few days later, at a formal session with two Allied mission chiefs and their staffs in Spa, Von Hammerstein presented a stern oral report about internal developments in Germany. He warned that "storm signals" were increasing rapidly: there was no ordered government in Bavaria; Württemberg was in the grip of a general strike; there were renewed disorders in the Ruhr; and the Workers' Council of Berlin had sent a congratulatory message to the new government in Budapest.

> The despair of the German people was growing visibly. Admittedly the food supplies, which had been promised ever since November, had finally been cleared. However, they were arriving so gradually that the population experienced no improvement as yet. Meanwhile the blockade continued . . . [so that] the Entente was still substantially hindering the government's battle against Bolshevism. Requests and representations here in Spa to allow Baltic shipping toward Courland continued to be ignored. At vast expense Germany was trying to create a volunteer army to fight both the external enemies in the East and insurgency at home. . . . And yet on March 18 Noulens insisted that only regular troops could guard the demarcation line at Posen. Moreover, the Allies refused to sanction the withdrawal of volunteers from the occupied territories for the formation of Freikorps earmarked for the Eastern Frontier. They kept dodging the question of coal imports into Eastern Germany. . . . The Hungarian example was beginning to impress even moderate circles. The phrase "rather Red than Entente slave and dead" was being heard with greater frequency.

This declaration, coming on top of other reports, impressed even General Nudant, to say nothing of the Red-fearing General Haking.[6]

On April 7 Lloyd George told the Council of Four that his military agents in Germany reported that Spartacism was growing rapidly, that a *coup* was expected that week, and that the German government had only 80,000 men in readiness—25,000 in Berlin, 6,000 in Halle, 6,800 in the Ruhr basin, some 10,000 in Silesia, and the rest along the Polish border.[7] Both Clemenceau and Foch confirmed that this information corresponded to theirs. After reading Foch's report on his recent negotiations in Spa, the British Prime Minister sardonically commented

---

[5] Von Lersner to Foreign Ministry, March 28, 1919, G.F.M. (D 924678–9).

[6] Von Hammerstein to Erzberger and others, April 2, 1919, G.F.M. (D 925133–35).

[7] This discussion of the meeting of the Council of Four, April 7, 1919 (p.m.), is based on Paul Mantoux: *Les Délibérations du conseil des quatre*, I, 167–9; and *F.R.,P.C.,1919*, V, 39.

that whereas his military men in Berlin wanted the Allies to occupy Germany, Matthias Erzberger called for the occupation of any place except Germany, notably Budapest and Vienna.

The following morning Lloyd George was, if anything, still more agitated.[8] He had just heard that a soviet republic had been set up in Bavaria. Haking and General Wilson were agreed that the situation in Germany was going from bad to worse and that a catastrophe was fast approaching. Time was working against the Allies. Either there would be no German government left to sign the peace, or else it might refuse to do so, and the military representatives should make plans for both eventualities. Meanwhile the Council should speed up the completion of the draft-treaty without getting lost in details. Clemenceau agreed that they should "proceed as rapidly as possible," and House urged that the Germans be notified of the date for their appearance right away, since this invitation itself would be of help to the Berlin government.

It was at this juncture that Lloyd George's War Minister entered the picture with his apocalyptic view that without a stable Germany it would be difficult to carry forward the struggle against "bankruptcy, anarchy and revolution," which was threatening Europe's victors as well as vanquished.

> All the information I receive from military sources indicates that Germany is very near collapse. All my military advisers, without exception, have warned me that the most vital step we ought to take immediately . . . [is to provide Germany with food and raw materials].
>
> The situation in Germany is grave. The Socialist Government of Scheidemann and Ebert and Noske is tottering, and if it falls no one knows what will take its place. If Germany sinks into Bolshevist anarchy she will no doubt be skinned alive, and not only will there be no indemnity, but we shall ourselves be impoverished, and our trade revival will be paralyzed by the increasing disorder and ruin of the world. . . .

Churchill wanted the Allies to appease Germany as part of their search for a stable and prosperous European and world community. Simultaneously he told Germany how to atone for her past sins and prove herself worthy of considerate treatment: "by combating Bolshevism, by being the bulwark against it, Germany may take the first step toward ultimate reunion with the civilized world."[9]

Against this background of mounting anxiety, British agents once again called on Brockdorff-Rantzau in Weimar. This time, on April 10,

---

[8] This discussion of the meeting of the Council of Four, April 8, 1919 (a.m.), is based on Mantoux: *Délibérations,* I, 178–81; and *F.R.,P.C.,1919,* V, 59–60.

[9] For the text of Churchill's luncheon address to the Aldwych Club, April 11, 1919, see *The Times* (London), April 12, 1919, cited in Suda L. Bane and Ralph H. Lutz (eds.): *The Blockade of Germany After the Armistice, 1918–1919* (Stanford: Stanford University Press; 1942), 762.

Thornely Gibson was accompanied by Major Dunsey, who had just arrived from Paris. They declared that their government "felt that it had to give some support to the German Government." Following consultations with American and British representatives in Paris, Lord Robert Cecil had drafted a statement which Dunsey was instructed to transmit to the German government with the request that it be publicized. Cecil's statement summarized the steps that had been taken to supply Germany with food. It particularly emphasized that 100,000 tons had already been delivered or were in the course of being unloaded at Rotterdam, Antwerp, and Copenhagen; that 300,000 tons were on their way for April delivery; and that arrangements would immediately be made "to provide certain materials urgently required to restart German economic life." The statement closed with the by now standard litany designed to strengthen recipient governments, that it "must of course be understood that the successful execution of these proposals must depend upon the maintenance of a stable government and the preservation of social order in Germany." Brockdorff-Rantzau professed that Lord Cecil's communiqué offered nothing new, but that he wanted time to consider it further.

Within three days the two agents renewed their representations, this time in Berlin. Although Brockdorff-Rantzau agreed to publish the communiqué through the *Hamburger Fremdenblatt,* he reiterated that it merely recorded the results of the Brussels negotiations, without even touching on the vital issue of the payment for foodstuffs. In reply Gibson stressed that, after all, the closing paragraph—the litany—was not an insignificant "bribe." But Brockdorff-Rantzau stood his ground. He repeated that little could be achieved with such *Mittelchen,* adding that, if "the blockade was not lifted, and at once, he could take no responsibility for the course of internal developments in the direction of Bolshevism." With that Brockdorff-Rantzau pulled out an editorial from the *Daily Mail* of April 11, which charged him with advocating that Germany use sham Bolshevism to frighten the Allies and that in line with this policy Weimar had secretly fomented the outbreak in Bavaria.[1] The Foreign Minister indignantly but forcefully protested that this was the exact reverse of his position. To prove his point he revealed that on assuming his post, he had told his fellow ministers at a secret cabinet session that "the struggle against Bolshevism was the only formula which could enable Germany to resume tolerable relations with her enemies." He also reminded his interlocutors that in late February he had advised Haking of his readiness "to work with England against Bolshevism and to transmit to the British the materials found on Radek." He was eager to continue this cooperation, though for reasons of domestic politics he could not meet Britain's informal request to transfer Karl Radek from the capital to a jail in Cologne,

[1] *Daily Mail* (Paris), April 11, 1919.

where he might be safer. Brockdorff-Rantzau indicated, however, that a formal and written request might receive more favorable consideration. The British agents readily agreed to pass this suggestion on to their government, with the additional suggestion that perhaps the Big Four rather than Britain alone request Radek's transfer.[2]

There was one further British move before the German Delegation left for Versailles. On May 1, Haking, who himself was leaving for Paris that night, invited Von Hammerstein for a "private and personal" conversation in Spa. He was anxious to get an up-to-the minute estimate of prospects for a strong and stable government in Berlin. By now Von Hammerstein conceded that the worst of the "spiritual epidemic" was over. Still, Germany's "sickness" was far from cured, because the most important drugs—food and employment—were still in short supply and had not taken effect yet. Haking agreed with the diagnosis, implying that Britain would help her former foe to restore her economy. To give his view additional weight, Haking referred to Churchill's Aldwych speech—which was known to Von Hammerstein—emphasizing that he was in full agreement with Churchill, who had a "very strong following" in Britain and who, like himself, was pressing for concessions to Germany.[3]

In early April the American Delegation became every bit as alarmed as the British. On April 2, U. S. Army Intelligence reported unsettled internal conditions underneath a "superficial relative calm;" on the fifth, an "increase in radical strength"; and on the eighth, growing party bitterness in Berlin, the establishment of a soviet republic in Munich, and chances for disturbances elsewhere. Even though the reports expressed confidence in Noske's ability to cope with this rising unrest without Allied aid, the delegation decided to have another high-level civilian mission study the political situation on the spot and renew contact with the Ebert-Scheidemann government.[4]

The very fact of sending Dresel for a second time was calculated to reassure Berlin, which hastened to say that it had "no objections" to his visit.[5] At first the Commissioners thought of sending along Buckler. But instead Lithgow Osborne, a Second Secretary of Embassy, was chosen to accompany Dresel, while Buckler was assigned "to keep watch" over telegrams from Germany and "to stir up the Commission if Dresel and Osborne send recommendations."[6]

2 Secret memoranda by Brockdorff-Rantzau, April 10 and 13, 1919, G.F.M. (D 925464–67, H 234157–62).

3 Von Hammerstein to Brockdorff-Rantzau, May 1, 1919, G.F.M. (E 212247–48).

4 G-2-B, G.H.Q., A.E.F., Memoranda for General Bliss, Nos. 8–16, April 2–10, 1919, in House Papers, 29:139A.

5 Stovall (Bern) to Dresel, April 5, 1919, in National Archives, Document 184.0131/9.

6 Buckler to Georgina Buckler, April 12, 1919, in Buckler Papers; and F.R.,P.C.,1919, XII, 82. Bliss suggested that before leaving Dresel seek an appointment through House with the President (who was sick just then) "to receive such instructions as might enable him to conduct his Mission in Berlin more satisfactorily."

The Second Dresel Mission[7] arrived in the German capital on April 18. The following evening Dresel made his first official call on no lesser a personage than Brockdorff-Rantzau. Dresel informed Paris that the Foreign Minister was depressed and irritated over the previous day's abrupt summons to the German government to send a delegation to Versailles on April 25 to "receive" the treaty, an invitation which suggested that the Allies intended to dictate rather than negotiate. Brockdorff-Rantzau indicated that he would refuse terms which would reduce Germany to "abject slavery," notably the amputations of the Saar and of Upper Silesia. When asked how Germany would face the ruinous economic consequences of refusal, "he made no definite answer and repudiated [Dresel's] suggestion that possibly an arrangement with Russia might be attempted." Not unlike his British counterparts, Dresel kept stressing that following the conclusion of peace America would cooperate in the economic rehabilitation of Germany.[8]

Dresel's record of this interview is not nearly as full and dramatic as Brockdorff-Rantzau's. According to the latter, the American official claimed to speak for Colonel House, who wanted him to know "that America had the warmest sympathy for Germany and would do everything in her power to promote the reconstruction and economic rehabilitation of Germany." Even before their meeting, Dresel had given the official news agency a schedule of the food supplies and raw materials America projected for Germany, as evidence of Washington's concern for "the quick recovery of her overall internal situation."

Then the conversation turned to the impending peace negotiations. Dresel said that even though he was not authorized to speak officially, he nevertheless was in a position to provide "authentic" information. Thereupon Brockdorff-Rantzau learned that France would recover Alsace-Lorraine outright; that the French would occupy the Saar for fifteen years, following which there would be a plebiscite; that Danzig would be a free port under Polish administration; that north and central Schleswig would be given to Denmark; and that the fate of Upper Silesia had not yet been settled.

Brockdorff-Rantzau's immediate retort was that any government that accepted these terms would be "swept away by public opinion." He did suggest, however, that provided Germany were not amputated or castrated territorially, she would be in a position to pay a large sum for reparations and indemnities.

But Dresel held out no hope that territories could be traded for marks, or that territorial issues were even negotiable. Instead, he

---

Whether or not he saw the President is not known; but he did confer at length with House. *F.R.,P.C.,1919,* XI, 146–7, 153.

[7] Besides Dresel and Osborne, the party included Morris Medofsky, David L. Ullman, and James Mannion, all three performing essentially secretarial duties.

[8] Dresel to Ammission, April 20, 1919, in *F.R.,P.C.,1919,* XII, 82–3.

declared that it would be very regrettable indeed "if territorial questions wrecked the peace," arguing that the American Delegation "was of the opinion that peace should be made quickly and that [these] conditions were altogether acceptable." As it was, America had thwarted France's demand for more than 300 billion marks and for the left bank of the Rhine.

Brockdorff-Rantzau snapped back that France might as well have asked for 1000 billion and all of Brandenburg! In any case, in the interest of the future of civilization, he would not sign a dictated peace that would give birth to infinitely stronger *revanchist* feelings than the peace of 1871. He also disputed Dresel's observation that the German masses and with them the Independent Socialists wanted peace at any price. The Allies should know that if they persevered in their vindictive course they "would drive his country into Bolshevism, which would not stop at Germany's borders." This was not a threat but a fact, and they would have to assume "full responsibility for the world revolution."

For himself and his associates, Brockdorff-Rantzau recorded the impression that the Allies were worried that Germany might not sign and did not know what to do about a refusal; that Dresel was in Berlin "to prime the people and the government for an acceptance"; and that he had made it "unmistakably clear to Dresel that he [Brockdorff-Rantzau] would under no circumstances sign such a peace."[9]

Dresel was undaunted in his belief, stemming from his preceding mission, that there was no alternative to strengthening the SPD-dominated coalition against the Spartacists and for acceptance of the treaty. Between April 19 and May 3 he and Osborne pored over German newspapers whenever they could spare time from interviews with the leaders of Germany's political class, men such as Bernstein, Kautsky, Haase, Oscar Cohn, Theodor Wolff, Rathenau, Bernstorff, Melchior, Erzberger, Harden, Noske, and Dernburg.[1]

On the strength of these soundings and as early as April 21, Dresel reassured Paris that there was not "much danger of the Spartacists getting the upper hand."[2] Not that he dismissed the government's stiff-necked opposition to the terms as reported in the press. He conceded that this opposition was being endorsed enthusiastically by nationalists, conservatives, the regular army, the *Freikorps,* the peasantry, and the "large inert mass of bourgeoisie."

Even so, did these forces of order have a real alternative? They realized that the Independents were rapidly gaining in strength throughout the industrial centers at the expense of the SPD. These Independents and the Spartacists favored acceptance, confident that before

9 Secret Memorandum by Brockdorff-Rantzau, April 19, 1919, G.F.M. (H234180–93).
1 See *F.R.,P.C.,1919,* XII, 117. The memoranda on these and other interviews have not been printed but are attached to National Archives, Document 184.013102/58.
2 Dresel to House, April 21, 1919, in House Papers, 5:13.

too long the Socialist and radical forces in the Entente, in cooperation with Soviet Russia, would force a revision of the terms. To be sure, the Independents had "little cohesion, . . . few practical men, . . . and a destructive rather than constructive" outlook. Even so, their radicalism, backstopped by Spartacist militancy, frightened all those non-Leftists who saw the merits of a continuing revolution from above.

In any case, Dresel could not convince himself that an overthrow of the government "was imminent in spite of the undoubted increase in USPD strength." He suspected that as long as the government had at its "disposal the only organized military forces in Germany it would continue to have the support of the bourgeoisie, the conservatives, and very great numbers of people who saw nothing ahead but Bolshevism as an alternative for the present government." Actually, compared to December-January,[3] the danger of "a reactionary, counter-revolutionary uprising . . . seemed much nearer . . . than the danger of a new Spartacist revolt, though the one would provoke the other."

In other words, the Allies should support the genuine "reformists" in and out of the government, whose nationalist bark was louder than their bite. In the end they would sign and execute the treaty, provided the Allies were conciliatory on nonessentials, made a few territorial concessions, arranged for a semblance of negotiations, and held out economic aid.[4] Before leaving Berlin Dresel also advised Paris that he had heard that for the moment the cabinet had decided not to seek an agreement with the Soviet Russian government, "out of fear of the effect which this action would have on the peace terms."[5]

Osborne was altogether less sanguine than Dresel about the viability of a reformist coalition in a nation increasingly torn between right-wing nationalism and left-wing Socialism. In his judgment the Ebert-Scheidemann regime was "pseudo-democratic" at best. It had "compromised itself with the Left by its lack of socialism and . . . its dependence on old-time militarists and the financial help of the Big Business interests"; it was composed of "pseudo-Socialists, still milder pseudo-Democrats and persons who pretended to base their democracy on Catholicism"; and it used the administrative and military machinery of the *ancien régime* to execute temporizing and opportunistic policies. In other words, the present government was "a fake as far as democracy was concerned," and whether it signed or not, "democracy, as we think of it, was finished."

While Dresel was resigned to working in harness with this "dishonest" regime in order to contain the militant Independents and the Spartacists, Osborne was reluctant to pursue this containment of the

---

[3] See pp. 281–2 above.
[4] Dresel to Ammission, April 28 and 30, May 2 and 3, 1919, in *F.R.,P.C.,1919*, XII, 85–93; and Dresel to House, April 29, 1919, in House Papers, 5:13.
[5] Dresel to Ammission, May 2, 1919, National Archives, Document 184.013102/41.

extreme Left at the price of strengthening the nationalist, militarist, and revanchist elements. He was inclined to recommend that the Allies actively encourage and support the formation of a coalition of Majority and Independent Socialists, even if this meant dropping "compromised" Majoritarians like Noske, who were unacceptable to the Independents. Only such a coalition Socialist government could check the radical Right as well as the radical Left and its line to Moscow.[6] Just then Hoover advocated a similar course: in case the Scheidemann government refused to sign the treaty, "Ebert should be guided to create an Independent Socialist Cabinet," since the Independents were "not Bolshevists in the ordinary sense of the word" and stood a "better chance of preserving order" than the Scheidemann cabinet.[7]

On their return to Paris on May 5, Dresel and Osborne submitted a joint report to the American Commissioners, including the President.[8] This report had Dresel's rather than Osborne's imprint, in that it held that "whatever the shortcomings of the present Government, it was sincerely democratic." Moreover, rather than urge support for a coalition of Independents and Majoritarians, it noted that all efforts in this direction had failed, primarily because the rank and file of the Independents "had become too radical." On the other hand, they predicted that in the likely event that the present government refused to sign and an Independent Socialist government took over, the latter would have to face a strong dictatorial reaction and militarist revival. Still, when all was said and done, the present government was "the only combination in sight which had elements of stability sufficient to guarantee the carrying out of the peace terms." Hence Dresel and Osborne recommended the dispatch of informal diplomatic, financial, and economic missions to give "such assurances as may be possible." Also the Allies should give "such moral encouragement as was possible" to the Ebert-Scheidemann regime, which at least "in theory" was democratic and representative, while making it known that a "non-representative government, whether of the Right or Left, could count on neither recognition nor assistance."[9]

The mounting disorders of late March and early April—symbolized by the Bavarian revolt—prompted the Big Four to hasten their invita-

---

[6] See Osborne's memoranda of April 24 and 30, 1919, cited in *F.R.,P.C.,1919*, XII, 94–103.

[7] Hoover to Wilson, April 21, 1919, cited in Bane and Lutz (eds.): *Blockade of Germany*, 384–6. On April 20, 1919, Lloyd George read to the Council of Four a memorandum from a British agent who also urged Allied support for a "purely Socialist Government" in which the Independents would agree to having the troops maintain order, though not under Noske's command. See *F.R.,P.C.,1919*, V, 101–5.

[8] See Wilson Papers, VIII A:45.

[9] Dresel and Osborne (Paris) to Ammission, May 5 and May 10, 1919, in *F.R.,P.C., 1919*, XII, 103–17.

tion summoning the Germans to Versailles for April 25, to send agents to study the situation firsthand, and to reassure the Berlin government. All three steps were motivated by Anglo-American fears that the presentation of harsh peace terms might precipitate a Hungarian-style coup in Germany.

But this fear turned out to be vastly exaggerated. To be sure, most signs pointed toward a refusal by the incumbent government, including its Foreign Minister. In Germany, however, such a refusal was not about to be combined with a swing toward Spartacism and Moscow. The Ebert-Scheidemann regime had solid moorings in the Ebert-Hindenburg and Stinnes-Legien agreements; the Spartacists had been in retreat since January; food, raw materials, and credits could only be supplied by the West; and the Poles stood in the way of a juncture with the Red Army. Even if the Scheidemann cabinet resigned and left the field to the USPD, that party was not all that dangerous. Haase and Kautsky would not rush to the teletype to seek instructions from Lenin. Nor would they be inclined or even able to challenge the regular army and the *Freikorps,* which for a transitional period might make themselves available to enforce internal order. Besides, the Independents advocated accepting even a Carthaginian peace in order to get on with economic reconstruction and reform, for which they were likely to look to the West for aid.[1]

In any case, by April 20, when Brockdorff-Rantzau defiantly replied that he would send three subordinates to fetch the text of the preliminary terms, the third wave of unrest was fast subsiding, only Bavaria remaining to be pacified.[2] For purposes of foreign policy, Noske was doing his job too efficiently and too fast, in that the blackmail value of the Red specter was losing its force. When Lloyd George and Wilson presented Gibson's and Dresel's findings to the Council, they no longer had grounds for scaring Clemenceau with a German Soviet. They themselves were confident that Brockdorff-Rantzau's unpliant attitude was being counterbalanced by industrialists who were eager to get on with economic reconstruction and by an exhausted and peacemongering population.

In sum, the Big Four did not hesitate to force Brockdorff-Rantzau's hand by requiring Berlin to send fully authorized plenipotentiaries

[1] See Kautsky's article "Die Friedensverhandlungen" in *Die Freiheit,* April 24, 1919.
[2] "It has been suggested to us on behalf of the Hoffmann [Bavarian] Government that it would be desirable to have supplies (milk and fats especially) at some convenient place, such as Mannheim or Nürnberg, in readiness to provision Munich on its capture. From a political point of view, it seems to us that it might be of distinct advantage that the arrival of Entente food supplies should be the immediate result of the overthrow of the Bolshevist regime." Captain J. E. Broad, April 26, 1919, in *Further Reports by British Officers on the Economic Conditions Prevailing in Germany, March–April 1919,* H.M.S.O. Command Paper 208, 44.

rather than mere messengers. Nor did they see any pressing need to water down the preliminary terms. For the time being, appeasement would be limited to continuing food shipments and to allowing a "certain amount of discussion" with the German Delegation. Probably with one eye on the Republican opposition at home, even Wilson agreed that this "discussion should take place in writing."[3]

The publication of the preliminary peace terms on May 7 raised a storm of bitter anger, indignation, and protest throughout Germany. For some ten days all the parties except the USPD joined in a government-fostered campaign of nationalist breast-beating and proclamation that the treaty was totally unacceptable. But even at the height of this wave of self-pity the threat of Bolshevism, National Bolshevism, and cooperation with Lenin was muted. The Independents, not the Spartacists, represented the most consequential challenge to the precarious consensus of nonacceptance, and they appealed for help to the proletariat of the Allied nations and the Berne International rather than to the Russian proletariat and the Third International.

Needless to say, the Right opposition took a stand for absolute irreconciliation. The entire conservative press agitated for unconditional refusal, blustered about a nationalist revival, and denounced the Socialists and Democrats for having brought Germany to this pass with their treacherous revolution and their naïve faith in Wilson.

The tone of the government press was no less strident than that of the *Tägliche Rundschau* or the *Deutsche Allgemeine Zeitung*. Banner headlines in the *Berliner Tageblatt* declared the peace proposal to be *"unerträglich, undurchführbar, und unannehmbar."* Unless the Allies agreed to fundamental revisions, Germany would arise in all-out resistance. Theodor Wolff was prepared to evacuate the populations of the starvation-threatened urban centers to the countryside in order to steel the nation for a renewed food blockade. "The world can and must be denied tranquility as long as Germany does not get another peace." Let Wilson, Lloyd George, and Clemenceau convince their electorates of the need to postpone demobilization in order to keep mounting the guard on a turbulent Continent. National resistance and not accommodating compliance by the Independents would stimulate revisionist pressures in the Allied countries. Wolff warned that if the Democratic Republic ever signed such an extortionist peace it would soon be overcome by a wave of "reactionary, anti-republican nationalism." In an impoverished country, Bolshevik or semi-Bolshevik slogans could not compete with nationalist appeals "to wounded passion."[4] Although Friedrich Naumann conceded that Germany was in no position to offer

[3] See the minutes of the Council sessions of April 20–24, 1919, in *F.R.,P.C.,1919*, V, 101–2, 151–2, 204–5; and Mantoux: *Délibérations*, I, 312–13, 351–2.
[4] *Berliner Tageblatt*, May 7–12, 1919.

effective resistance to the Allies, he swore that she simply "would not sign her own death warrant."[5]

For the *Vorwärts* this "peace of destruction exceeded all bounds," leaving no meaningful choice between acceptance and rejection, but a choice between two modes of death: "to go up in flames or to jump out of the window." Of course, the cost of not signing would be steep. In particular, economic reconstruction would be delayed if Germany were cut off from the developed capitalist West, economic relations with the underdeveloped Bolshevik East being a poor substitute. Stampfer alone continued to brandish the specter of Spartacism, though not convincingly. But he, too, defied the Allies to occupy all Germany, confident that such a course would "strain their external and internal unity." Not unlike the Kaiser and Bethmann-Hollweg in July 1914, SPD leaders called for a political truce to strengthen the hand of the government in this hour of crisis.[6] *Germania,* the Catholic Center organ, was also in tune with the spirit of noncompliance.

In other words, in terms of nationalist wrath, the press of the coalition parties compared favorably with that of the conservatives and the nationalists. But unlike these latter, the coalition press called for negotiations.

Meanwhile, in an effort to frighten the Allies into negotiations, the government encouraged and organized a variety of protest activities in all parts of Germany. On May 8, Ebert issued a formal statement accusing the Allies of presenting terms which, besides violating the pre-Armistice agreement, were "unbearable" and "unrealizable"; the next day Scheidemann declared a week of national mourning to be expressed through mass meetings; on May 10, the Prussian House convened to endorse a remonstrance; and the *Zentrum* and Socialist parties issued appeals respectively to Catholics and Socialists outside Germany.

The single most dramatic protest was the special session of the National Assembly held in the Aula of the University of Berlin on May 12. This new assembly displayed the same unanimity and pitch of national fervor as had the defunct Reichstag on August 4, 1914. By prearrangement Fehrenbach, the President, recognized one speaker for each of the six major parties as well as one spokesman for each of the "threatened territories"—Schleswig-Holstein, West Prussia, Posen, Silesia, the Saar, and Eupen-Malmédy. On this occasion it was Chancellor Scheidemann who delivered the hardest-hitting address, a speech that had been cleared and even toughened by his cabinet. He refused even to measure the terms of the treaty against Wilson's

[5] Cited in Theodor Heuss: *Friedrich Naumann* (Stuttgart: Deutsche Verlagsanstalt; 1937), 640.
[6] *Vorwärts,* May 8–18, 1919.

program. Instead, he simply charged the Allies with asking the German people to "consent to their becoming slaves and helots, and to doing forced labor behind barbed wire and prison bars." In the name of his government, Scheidemann declared this peace treaty to be "unacceptable" and called on all Germans, regardless of party, to stand up against this "death plan" (*Mordplan*). Not even Count Posadowsky-Wehner, of the far-Right National party, could improve upon this indictment, though he admonished the Allies not to sow dragons' teeth which some day would turn into armed men bent on reclaiming Germany's freedom.[7]

In the press, at public meetings, and in the National Assembly, the Independent Socialists alone campaigned in favor of accepting even hard and oppressive terms. But they, too, protested this peace of violence, insisting that only they, who had opposed Germany's own imperialist policies throughout the war, were entitled to protest now. Haase and Kautsky were convinced that nonacceptance, intimidation, and revenge-mongering would get Germany nowhere. To begin with, whereas Germany could at best offer passive resistance, the Allies had it in their power to tighten the blockade and occupy economically and strategically vital provinces, both east and west. The workers would be hardest hit by the resulting unemployment, famine, and national decomposition. Should Germany refuse to sign, within weeks she would be compelled to capitulate, accepting even worse conditions. In other words, the issue was less one of will than of power.

This being so, the government should appeal to reason and the solidarity of the workingmen of the Western world rather than to fear. Besides, by whipping up this nationalist hysteria, Scheidemann was creating a jingoist atmosphere reminiscent of August 1914, which then as now played into the hands of the counterrevolution. The same day that he called for a new *Burgfrieden,* Noske's troops were unseating the all-Socialist regime in Leipzig. No, they could not rally behind the allegedly democratic Ebert-Scheidemann-Noske regime which harbored imperialist Social Patriots, stifled the German revolution, promoted militarism, practiced the Old Diplomacy, and pursued a counterrevolutionary course in the East.

The Independents even had the courage to suggest that the conditions of the treaty did not spell utter ruin. Germany would lose only 7,500 square kilometers out of 465,000, and six to seven million souls out of sixty. The economic importance of the Saar should not be exaggerated. Although the losses in the East would be considerably heavier, those losses might do more to shake the Prussian power elite than to weaken the rest of the nation. To be sure, it would be difficult to abandon the coal mines of Upper Silesia, but those of the Ruhr, the best

---

[7] For this Reichstag session of May 12, 1919, see *Verhandlungen der verfassungsgebenden Nationalversammlung.* Reichstag: Stenographische Berichte. Vol. 327, 1081 ff.

in Europe, would remain Germany's property. Moreover, by using modern production methods and by socializing key industries Germany could meet reparations payments, which in any case would be subject to revision. And certainly the nation that before the war had built 600,000 to 700,000 tons of shipping annually should be able to manage the 200,000 tons to be delivered over a period of five years.[8]

Incidentally, the Draconian terms could not have come as a complete surprise either to the government or to the political class. There had been ample warnings from Gibson and Dresel, from informed sources in neutral countries, and from the Allied press. On the eve of leaving for Versailles, Brockdorff-Rantzau had told Ebert that although he did not face his assignment with "unqualified pessimism," he was going in a very "skeptical" frame of mind. On the basis of unimpeachable information he knew that the original conditions would be so "exorbitant that even if they were mitigated by 10%" the peace would still be unsatisfactory. He fully intended to make "practical counterproposals." In the event that these failed, the government might finally decide to sign anyway, but he could not put his signature to a treaty which he knew could not be executed and which clashed with his own public pronouncements.[9]

In the afternoon of May 7, in the great hall of the Trianon Palace, the German plenipotentiaries at long last were handed the bulky volume containing the text of the peace terms. As expected, both Clemenceau and Brockdorff-Rantzau remained in character throughout the one-hour confrontation. For the former, "the time had come for a heavy reckoning of accounts." Unceremoniously, Clemenceau told the Germans that they had two weeks in which to submit written, not oral, observations.

Brockdorff-Rantzau's reply was equally brusque, in both manner and content. He chose to remain seated to deliver a speech which was pugnacious and defiant. He began by registering the victors' intense and passionate hatred for the vanquished, who, in line with their guilt, were to be punished. He then went on to contest Germany's war guilt, and stressed that only a peace consonant with Wilson's principles and the pre-Armistice agreement could be just and lasting. Even in a more congenial atmosphere, given his general background, bearing, and personality, Brockdorff-Rantzau would not have been particularly compliant and ingratiating. If his demeanor and speech were abrasive, perhaps the fault was less his own than that of the government of the

[8] *Freiheit*, May 8–22, 1919. The *Bund Neues Vaterland* also advocated signing under protest. For future revision it trusted not in *revanche* but on the advance of democracy, Socialism, and pacificism, essential preconditions for an effective League of Nations. See Otto Lehmann-Russbüldt: *Der Kampf der deutschen Liga für Menschenrechte für den Weltfrieden, 1914–1927* (Berlin: Hensel; 1927), 80–1.
[9] Secret Memorandum by Brockdorff-Rantzau, April 27, 1919, G.F.M. (H 234980–88).

young republic, which had chosen a proud diplomat of the old school as its representative. Brockdorff-Rantzau spoke as Solf[1] or Von Bernstorff would have spoken.[2]

Moreover, the cabinet's first inclination was to encourage Brock-dorff-Rantzau in his defiance. Before leaving Berlin he was afraid that internal political concerns would cause the Social Democrats, including Noske, to waver prematurely. But now, on May 8, he received a wire from Ebert requesting him to notify the Allies formally that the terms were "unfulfillable, unbearable, and ruinous for Germany."[3]

Not surprisingly the German Delegation, charged with a heavy diplomatic assignment, resisted the temptation either to send a blistering note or to pack up and return home. On May 8 Brockdorff-Rantzau met with his associates for a free-wheeling exchange of views. Even though they all considered the terms unbearable, with two insignificant exceptions the assembled delegates and experts agreed to make counterproposals and to seek negotiations.

Emotions ran as high in the *Hotel des Réservoirs,* the German Delegation's headquarters, as in Berlin. For some these terms spelled *finis Germania;* for others "a death warrant"; for still others "vassalage." Even so, Germany was in no condition to resist. Eventually she might have to sign under protest in order to avoid a complete catastrophe. Meanwhile, expert committees would draft notes commenting on specific aspects of the treaty, to be submitted to the Allies in the order in which they were completed. At the same time the delegation would check with Berlin.[4]

Between May 9 and 29, under immense pressure of time, the delegation submitted fifteen separate notes: on the Covenant, the I.L.O., war prisoners, reparations and responsibility, economic and territorial questions, the Saar, German missionaries, and the liquidation of private property abroad.[5] From the point of view of diplomatic strategy it may not have been wise to nettle the Allies with a stream of notes contesting all provisions of the treaty with equal force. There were two other alternatives: to concentrate in one or more notes on those few issues that were truly vital or to forego all exchanges in favor of an overall counterproposal at the end of May.[6] The former alternative might easily have commended itself since the delegation seemed agreed that

---

[1] On November 8, 1918, Solf instructed his staff that now that Germany could no longer count "on either a victorious or a status quo peace" it should "prepare for the peace negotiations on the basis of the programmatic points proclaimed by President Wilson." G.F.M. (P.R.O. 4069/1).

[2] For the developments at and surrounding the historic session in the Trianon Palace on May 7, 1919, see Alma Luckau: *The German Delegation at the Paris Peace Conference* (New York: Columbia University Press; 1941), 61–9 and 213–24.

[3] Cited in Luckau: *German Delegation at Paris,* 71.

[4] Minutes of the delegation's discussion, May 8, 1919, G.F.M. (E 212380–99).

[5] For the full text of these notes see Luckau: *German Delegation at Paris,* 225–302.

[6] Ibid., 73.

it was more important to achieve a revision of territorial than of economic terms.

Ironically, this staunchly traditional delegation opted for "brief and forceful notes" because these were first and foremost intended to "influence public opinion in [Germany's] favor." The first two notes, one dealing with the League of Nations and the other with the International Labor Organization, were specifically calculated to win the sympathy of Europe's forces of movement. The former protested Germany's not being invited to join the League; the latter asked that the resolution of the trade union conference in Berne form the basis for another international syndicalist meeting to be convened in Versailles. On the other hand, notes on territorial questions were hurried along "for reasons of domestic politics, in Germany, where they expected the Delegation to dispose of the most pressing issues." In sum, political rather than purely diplomatic considerations influenced the mode and style of articulation. Besides, Von Haniel and Von Stockhammern, of the Foreign Ministry, explicitly stated that from the diplomatic point of view "the primary aim was to bring about oral negotiations, to which these brief notes were the best bridge." To further this aim the delegation resolved to ask the cabinet to issue a directive to the German press "not to stress the alternative between signing and not signing, but to demand negotiations which would bring about tolerable conditions."[7]

Meanwhile, Brockdorff-Rantzau initiated consultations with the cabinet. On May 12 he sent Otto Landsberg and Josef Giesberts to Berlin, where they were greeted with criticism for the intractable spirit pervading the note on reparations and responsibility. In this note of May 13 the delegation affirmed that the Berlin government accepted the obligation to pay reparations "independently of the question of responsibility," claimed that the German people all along "remained convinced that this war was for them a defensive war," and challenged the Allies to publish the report of the international commission chartered to establish responsibility. When Bernstorff notified Brockdorff-Rantzau that hereafter all notes should be submitted for prior clearance to the cabinet, the delegation supported its chief's outright refusal.[8]

Direct personal contact with the cabinet seemed advisable, and on May 17 Brockdorff-Rantzau himself traveled to Spa to confer with Bernhard Dernburg, Rudolf Wissel, and Albert Südekum. Before leaving, Melchior asked him to impress on Dernburg, and through him on the cabinet, that "in order to save Upper Silesia, Danzig, and the connection with East Prussia it would be necessary to make considerable territorial concessions in Posen and West Prussia." Melchior indicated,

---

[7] Minutes of the meeting of the German Peace Delegation May 10 (a.m.) and 11 (p.m.), 1919, G.F.M. (E 212403–6).

[8] Delegation to Paxkonferenz, May 11, 1919; Bernstorff to Brockdorff-Rantzau, May 14, 1919; and Brockdorff-Rantzau to Bernstorff, May 15, 1919, G.F.M. (E 211588–91, E 211821–23).

furthermore, that the economic experts and advisers of the delegation
advocated "financial sacrifices in order to avoid intolerable territorial
losses, . . . the size of the overall sum being less important than the
amount of the yearly annuities." Cuno joined Melchior in trying to convince the delegation as well as the politicians back home "that extreme
sacrifices should be made in the economic and financial sphere so as to
save the essentials for German survival in the territorial sphere."[9]

At Spa Brockdorff-Rantzau reiterated that even though he would
keep the cabinet abreast of all important developments he would "tolerate" no interference with his conduct of affairs in Versailles. In concert
with the entire delegation he proposed to make decisions without being
"influenced by internal political considerations, as was likely to be the
case in Berlin." Dernburg assured the Foreign Minister that except for a
segment of the Independent Socialists, the entire nation would support
rejection of the terms unless "really far-reaching and fundamental
concessions" were made. Rather than accept impossible terms the
people were prepared to shoulder the burden of further Allied occupations and a resumption of the food blockade. At this point Wissel demurred, suggesting that the pressure of the blockade would rapidly sap
the spirit of resistance. Brockdorff-Rantzau hoped to avoid this test of
German resistance, there being a good chance that provided Germany
"held out for another two months an acceptable peace could be
achieved." On balance Dernburg and Südekum conveyed the impression that the cabinet was inclined to ask for greater concessions than
even Brockdorff-Rantzau thought reasonable: they envisaged retaining
Posen and pressing for an army of 350,000 men, to be reduced gradually. Brockdorff-Rantzau viewed their self-confidence with skepticism
and reserved the right not to act upon impracticable and unrealistic proposals.[1]

All the time that the delegation bombarded the Peace Conference
with politically motivated preliminary notes it also worked on a comprehensive diplomatic brief. Having secured a one-week extension,
Brockdorff-Rantzau and his associates had until May 29 to complete
this all-important memorandum outlining Germany's concrete counterproposals. When these were published it was clear that the delegation
had decided to be pliable on economic and military clauses while
standing firm on territorial matters. Unfortunately Walter Schücking's
moralizing introduction aggravated the damage done by Brockdorff-
Rantzau's Hectorian performance on May 7 and by the petulant notes
since that time. In rather blunt language he laid bare those clauses
that violated the wartime and pre-Armistice pledges. But, again, the

[9] Minutes of the meeting of the German Peace Delegation, May 17, 1919 (p.m.), and
   Melchior to Brockdorff-Rantzau, May 20, 1919, G.F.M. (E 212415–16, E 211885).
[1] Brockdorff-Rantzau's memorandum on the Spa meeting, May 19, 1919, G.F.M.
   (E 211859–70). In his opinion "Minister Südekum spoke like a reactionary minister of former times."

fault was not his, since Schücking's associates in the delegation as well as the cabinet approved his draft, no doubt in order to impress public opinion at home and abroad.[2]

While the German government and Delegation denounced the Independent Socialists' acceptance campaign, they cheered the protest against the draft-treaty by the Left-opposition in the Allied camp. The one threatened to undermine Berlin's capacity to withstand Allied pressure; the other promised to make Paris more conciliatory. This protest by the Allied forces of movement seemed particularly encouraging because just then Britain, France, and Italy were experiencing a new wave of labor unrest over economic grievances, demobilization, and intervention in Russia and Hungary.

In England the *Daily Herald* was scandalized by the preliminary treaty: the terms of peace violated every pledge; the League was a mechanical League of Victors without a soul; and the Entente's attitude toward Soviet Russia and Hungary remained unsettled. Wilson, on whom the Allied Labour and Socialist parties had "pinned their faith, was beaten." Would the workers, in the future as in the past, be satisfied with passing "magnificent resolutions," or would they show their courage before it was too late?[3] In a hastily drafted manifesto the National Executive of the Labour Party charged that the terms were "opposed to the declaration of President Wilson, the Inter-Allied Conferences and the Berne Conference." Germany was discriminated against with regard to mandates and trade; the reparations clauses ignored Germany's "obligation to meet the needs of her own population"; the disarmament provisions were unilateral; the political and economic controls over the Saar were objectionable; and plebiscites were not provided for Alsace-Lorraine, Malmédy, and the Polish and Czech frontiers.[4]

Further to the left the ILP's *Labour Leader* exclaimed that Wilson's Fourteen Points were being treated with "callous contempt." It was both "hypocritical and insulting" to incorporate a League into this victor's treaty. Germany was to be "deprived of three-quarters of her iron supply, of about half of her coal supply, and all her tropical possessions." Her trade was to be hampered and a "huge and indeterminate indemnity" was to be levied upon her. Even if Germany signed under duress this "truce of war" would have no "moral, binding, or lasting effect." Meanwhile, would the International simply stand aside and be content with a mild protest? For Ponsonby this vindictive, dishonorable, and deceitful treaty, if adopted, would be the "precursor of a century of strife and conflict." Should the Big Four fail to come to their senses during the critical weeks ahead, perhaps the East was the

[2] See Luckau: *German Delegation at Paris*, 84–7.
[3] *Daily Herald*, May 8, 1919.
[4] The full text of this manifesto is cited in *Daily Herald*, May 19, 1919.

only remaining hope. Rather than make detailed criticisms, Ramsay MacDonald contemplated the broad picture, seeing the terms as "an act of madness unparalleled in history" involving not only Germany but all of mankind.[5] UDC castigated the draft-treaty as a *Betrayal of the Peoples*,[6] while the *Nation*, "troubled by a sense of an endangered future, [looked] to organized Labour for help."[7]

In France, the Left was equally agitated. Jean Longuet compared the draft-treaty to Tilsit, Vienna, and Brest Litovsk. Under the title "Wilson's Defeat" Daniel Renoult credited the President with having put up an honorable and noble fight, in which he counted upon Socialist support. He no doubt considered breaking off the Conference, but as a great bourgeois leader he could not risk the revolutionary consequences of such a step. As for Mayéras, he warned that with these harsh terms, calculated to appease the Allied Right, Germany's 100,000-strong professional army of noncommissioned officers would become the nucleus and cadres *pour la levée en masse de la revanche!*[8] The Executive Committee of the SFIO and the Parliamentary delegation each appointed twelve members to sit on a joint committee to frame a critique of the draft treaty and to plan future action.[9]

In Italy, *Avanti* gleefully spoke of a "diplomatic Caporetto," decried the "general bankruptcy of the vanquished among the victors," and contemptuously pronounced the collapse of the democratic ideology which the capitalist governments used to justify a world cataclysm that cost 12 million dead.[1] Treves predicted that the betrayal of Versailles would turn the people toward Zimmerwald, while the death of the Fourteen Points would breathe life into the Kienthal theses.[2]

Without losing any time, Branting and Huysmans called an emergency meeting of the Berne International's Peace Committee, to assemble in Paris on May 11 and to remain in session until peace was signed. In a manifesto drafted by MacDonald, Stuart-Bunning, and Renaudel, this committee declared that the faults of these peace terms were so serious that "they were not our terms and that the nations were still threatened by the policy of victors sharing the spoils without worrying about the inevitable consequences." Significantly, Wilson's name was not mentioned in the text.[3]

---

[5] *Labour Leader*, May 15, 22, and 29, 1919.
[6] UDC Pamphlet No. 37a, issued by the Executive Committee on May 8, 1919.
[7] *Nation* (London), May 24, 1919, 220–1.
[8] *Le Populaire*, May 10, 11, 14, and 18, 1919.
[9] *L'Humanité*, May 11 and 18, 1919.
[1] *Avanti*, May 10 and 12, 1919.
[2] *Critica Sociale*, May 16–31, 1919, 111.
[3] *Le Populaire*, May 11–13, 1919. The full text of the memorandum is printed in the edition of May 13.

Not surprisingly, in America radical disillusionment took the form of an infamous assault on the President. For the *Nation,* Wilson revealed himself as an "arrogant autocrat and a compromising politician" by agreeing to terms which betrayed all his pledges. To consent to this treaty, which was sheer "madness," the American people would have to display "blindness and moral callousness beyond belief."[4]

In less personal and moral terms, the *New Republic* charged that this Punic treaty could only be "the prelude to quarrels in a deeply divided and hideously embittered Europe." This being so, Americans "should decide cooly just how to limit their obligations and commitments under the Covenant" in order to guarantee the preservation of this unstable settlement. They would be "fools to permit themselves to become entangled in a system of European alliances." Besides, liberalism would "commit suicide" if it did not protest the sell-out of the higher purposes for which this war had been fought. Liberalism in the Allied nations was determined to avoid the fate that overtook it in Russia and Imperial Germany respectively, where it was "ground between the upper and the lower millstones of reaction and revolution."[5]

Needless to say, Allied conservatives and right-liberals had cause to rejoice. Germany would be punished and rendered harmless, the victors compensated. Still, what about enforcing this treaty, since Germany survived as a major power with great potential for upsetting the new status quo? The London *Times,* the *Journal des Débats,* and *Figaro* all stressed the crucial importance of America's guarantee—as yet unratified—of France's borders. Moreover, the *Times* noted that by comparison with France, Poland and Czechoslovakia were in a much weaker and more exposed position. Especially since Germany was likely to try to compensate for her defeat in the West by striking out toward the brittle East, what was the strength of the eastern barrier, which would not be covered by the American guarantee?[6]

In England even the *Morning Post,* the *Daily Mail* and the *Chronicle* conceded that on the whole the naval, military, territorial, and colonial terms were better than expected. They merely complained that the financial provisions fell short of the khaki election pledges and warned against concessions to the German Delegation at Versailles.

In France the ultranationalist wing was not nearly so satisfied. Jacques Bainville proclaimed the peace to "be too soft for being so hard." That the terms were a "compromise between the Allied program of restitutions, reparations, and guarantees and the Wilsonian program" was a flaw rather than a merit. The dismemberment of Germany

[4] *The Nation,* May 17, 1919.
[5] *The New Republic,* May 17, 24, and 31, 1917, esp. 70–71, 101–2, 135.
[6] *The Times* (London), May 10, 1919; *Journal des Débats,* May 9–10, 1919; *Figaro,* May 8, 9, 12, and 15, 1919.

at a few select points would eventually stimulate her desire for complete reunion. Admittedly, in the immediate future, France and her Allies would get satisfaction. But what about long-range considerations?

Germany would survive as a great power which, with a bit of patience, could someday hope to free herself from the conditions that military defeat compelled her to accept. According to Bainville for fifteen years Germany would bow her head and meet her obligations. But then, with the end of foreign occupation and the Rhine unshackled, her tribute would strike her as unbearable and the temptation to seek deliverance would take hold. Project yourself to the place of the Germans in 1934: which people, in their situation, would not look about to see whether the hour of liberation was at hand? The draft terms did not take into account the facts that at the end of fifteen years the Franco-German border would be that of 1870, thus allowing Germany to invade France without going through Belgium; and that the Germans would be 70 million strong and united in the center of Europe. Meanwhile, what about Russia? Were the Allies doing all they could to restore her as a counterweight?

In other words, Bainville predicted that 1934 would be the "climacteric" year in which the settlement would be put to the test. Along with the London *Times,* he cautioned that Germany would take her vengeance against Poland and Czechoslovakia rather than France. These countries were young and weak, and unless they received assurances over and above those of the untried League, their existence would be "problematical."[7]

Naturally enough, in Italy the non-Socialist papers, including the organs of the ultranationalists, wailed about their country being shortchanged in the proposed treaty. The Orlando-Sonnino team was upbraided for permitting the veto on Austria joining Germany, for losing out on African mandates, for recognizing the exclusive domination of France in Morocco and Britain in Egypt, for allowing the I.L.O. charter to discriminate against Italian emigrants, and, above all, for not securing Italy's inclusion in the Anglo-French-American directorate of the League.[8] According to Mussolini the Allies had reduced Italy to the same rank as Portugal at a conference that consecrated their crushing military victory without regard for idealistic principles. He tersely warned that the entire edifice, resting on an unadulterated "Parliamentary Bonapartism, . . . would crumble miserably at the first Italian or German 'no'."[9]

The Big Four kept a careful eye on their home fronts as the

---

[7] See Bainville's columns in *l'Action Française,* May 7, 8, 11, 12, 16, and 19, 1919.
[8] The Italian press for the week of May 6–12, 1919, is surveyed in *Bulletin Périodique de la presse italienne,* No. 111, May 15, 1919, 7–8.
[9] *Popolo d'Italia,* May 9, 20, 24, and 29, 1919, cited in Edoardo and Duilio Susmel (eds.): *Opera Omnia di Benito Mussolini* (Florence: La Fenice; 1953), XII, esp. 141 and 148.

German counterproposals came before them. For a brief while it looked as if they might have to consider making substantial concessions. The Germans seemed to be intransigent at the same time that the Allied Left went into renewed opposition. Should this opposition build up tangible momentum, the Allied Governments had one of two choices: either move toward appeasing both the Germans and the Left, even at the risk of further infuriating the Right extremists, or stand fast, even at the expense of paying off the ultra-Right, for fear that appeasement would dangerously embolden the Left.

By itself the Labour and Socialist indignation over the draft-treaty could easily have been ignored. Especially in Britain and France—but also in America—anti-German feelings continued to run high and, if need be, could be inflamed still further. If the Left was to make any headway it had to demonstrate that the extortion of Germany, the intervention in Russia and Hungary, and the postponement of domestic reforms were part and parcel of the same conservative, if not reactionary, thrust.

In Britain, a mounting protest against intervention in Russia served as the wedge for the Labour attack. The Triple Industrial Alliance of miners, transport workers and railwaymen, impatient with resolutions and deputations to ministers, petitioned the Parliamentary Committee of the T.U.C. to call a special conference to decide how to compel the government to withdraw from Russia. This was the very time when the *Daily Herald* caused a sensation by publishing the secret War Office circular asking all commanding officers to determine whether their troops could be relied on to break strikes and to serve overseas, notably in Russia, and whether trade unionism was growing among them.[1]

In any case, the Party Executive and the Parliamentary Committee of the T.U.C. could no longer disregard the pressure from the Triple Alliance, the *Herald,* the *Labour Leader,* and the Labour Party's Advisory Committee on International Questions. As a first step they appointed a deputation from the Parliamentary Committee of the T.U.C. to call on Bonar Law in the evening of May 22, to secure clarification on those issues that agitated Labour most. Stuart-Bunning, the spokesman for this fourteen-man delegation,[2] opened the interview by telling the Deputy Premier that he and his colleagues were "being pressed very strongly by some important bodies of Trade Unionists to take certain steps, which might result in a very serious dislocation of trade in this country, and that the movement behind [them] was a serious movement."

Having marked the gravity of the occasion, Stuart-Bunning proceeded to an exposition of Labour's grievances. In one or two sentences he called for the prompt release of conscientious objectors and urged

[1] See pp. 617–19 above. See also *Labour Leader,* May 22, 1919.
[2] C. W. Bowerman acted as secretary.

that if the blockade of Germany could not be entirely lifted it should be "rendered as little stringent as possible." But the bulk of his presentation focused on Russia. Why intervene now, when the Russian people were forging a government of their own, particularly since we "never interfered in the old tsarist days"? Was this intervention an excuse for "retaining conscription"? And if it was "really necessary to go to Russia, why can't we have a voluntary army?" Bonar Law interrupted Stuart-Bunning in order to take the edge from these questions: the conscript army was still needed for occupation duty in Germany, and volunteers were replacing conscripts in Archangel. When pressed on the War Office circular, he again interrupted to ask whether it was "not true that the old soldiers could have been relied on with much more certainty than the present army?"

Rather than argue, Stuart-Bunning insisted that unless he and his associates received satisfactory answers to be relayed to their constituents, an emergency Trades-Union conference was likely to be called, and such a conference "would almost certainly decide in favor of a general strike."

Especially since this thinly disguised threat was part of an otherwise mild presentation, Bonar Law would not let it pass. In fact, his comments on the specific issues raised were completely overshadowed by his reaction to "purely political questions being taken out of the hands of the House of Commons and put in those of the Trades-Union Congress." Should an attempt of this sort be made, constitutionalism would be seriously jeopardized. In fact, "if such a movement succeeded, the Government created in that way would be a revolutionary Government." Bonar Law was confident that most of the Labour Members of Parliament would not favor such a course. Moreover, in defending the secret army order, he referred to his recent statement that in "the event of a real conflict between the Government and a great power in the Trades Unions, all the forces of the State must be used to put it down." Bonar Law further proved his resolve not to be intimidated by defending the government's Russian policy even to the point of contesting Labour's charge that Kolchak was not "to be trusted because he was a reactionary."[3]

Both this special deputation and the T.U.C. Parliamentary Committee were caught between a pugnaciously intransigent Bonar Law and the militants of the Triple Alliance. After agonizing consultations the Parliamentary Committee finally held a formal meeting on May 28, under the chairmanship of Stuart-Bunning. This meeting decided that Bonar Law's "replies . . . were sufficiently satisfactory to justify them in not acceding to the suggestion of the Triple Alliance that a special conference should be held." At the same time the committee felt that

[3] For the minutes of this interview, which the government never challenged, see *Daily Herald*, May 30, 1919.

the Labour Party should continue to press the issues under discussion in Commons and with the Deputy Premier.[4]

Meanwhile, the Executive of the National Union of Railwaymen had met to protest the War Office circular and to record its "disgust at the pettifogging manner in which the Parliamentary Committee . . . [had] dealt with the whole question of conscription." But whereas the leaders of the railwaymen wanted the Triple Alliance to move toward direct action on political issues, in particular, the leaders of the transport workers, but also those of the miners, were considerably more cautious.[5] In other words, even the Triple Alliance—the only consequential militant outpost in the entire labor movement—was far from united on the issue of industrial action for political objectives. This being the case, the high command of the Labour Party, the T.U.C., and the Parliamentary Delegation, which was overwhelmingly moderate in outlook and disposition, were not inclined to break with the time-honored distinction between and separation of political and industrial action. At the Southport Conference in late June 1919 all the prominent leaders, except Smillie and Hodges, either opposed direct action to stop intervention in Russia or advocated extreme caution. They were not even particularly disturbed when by 1,893,000 votes to 935,000 the conference, which was dominated by trade unionists, adopted a resolution calling for the "immediate cessation of intervention" and instructing "the National Executive to consult the Parliamentary Committee of the Trades-Union Congress, with a view to effective action being taken to enforce these demands by the unreserved use of their political and industrial power."[6]

The government must have been fully informed about these crosscurrents in the Labour movement. Because he did not want to provoke the direct-actionists, Lloyd George was reluctant to go along with policies in either Germany or Russia which might necessitate additional troop commitments. But short of this he knew that Labour was in no position to force a Wilsonian settlement or an instant withdrawal from Archangel and the Caucasus. Needless to say, whenever it suited his purposes, he exaggerated the intensity of the Labour threat, notably in his last-minute efforts to soften the terms of the German treaty.[7]

Between mid-May and mid-June the pressure to use syndical action for political ends was, if anything, more intense in France than in England. This was so because just then industrial unrest came to a head in Paris. The cost of living was still rising. At the same time, the employment picture was clouded due to slow reconversion and rapid demobilization. Moreover, employers tended to be uncompromising in

[4] *Daily Herald*, May 23 and 29, 1919.
[5] *Daily Herald*, May 29 and June 7, 1919.
[6] See Labour Party: *Report of the Nineteenth Annual Conference* (Southport, 1919), 113–23, 156–61. Cf. Stephen Richards Graubard: *British Labour and the Russian Revolution, 1917–1924* (Cambridge: Harvard University Press; 1956), 72–6.
[7] See pp. 796–9 below.

their opposition to the eight-hour day while continuing to fight higher direct taxes in the expectation that reparations would cover mounting budget difficulties.

A sense of nervous restlessness was first manifest at the national convention of the railwaymen on May 13–14, when the delegates refused to limit themselves to the consideration of wages, hours, and nationalization. They proceeded to vote motions congratulating their comrades in Central and Eastern Europe, calling for the withdrawal of troops from Russia, protesting the preliminary peace terms, and condemning the continued state of siege in France. They also urged direct action in conjunction with the CGT.[8]

Within ten days serious trouble developed in the all-important nationwide metalworkers union. On May 24 Merrheim and industry leaders signed an agreement implementing the convention of April 17: the union was recognized as the sole bargaining agent and the work week was set at 48 hours, to be spread over six days. But the syndicalist leaders of the Paris region, organized in an *ad hoc comité d'entente,* rejected these terms, demanding a 44-hour and a five-and-a-half-day week, without cut in pay. When both Merrheim and the industrialists stood their ground, the *comité* called a strike of all metallurgists in the Seine and Seine-et-Oise.[9]

This strike, which started on June 2, inaugurated two weeks of serious labor unrest in Paris and the *grande banlieue.* The membership of the striking metalworkers unions jumped from 10,000 to 80,000 during this fortnight. These metalworkers were joined by workers in the automobile, aircraft, chemical, and construction industries; workers in public transport (subway, bus, trolley); house painters; tailors; and the employees of banks and of *Le Printemps.* Outside the capital 50,000 miners struck in the Pas-de-Calais and 30,000 textile workers in Rouen.[1]

Encouraged by the scope of this movement the *comité d'entente* raised its sights. Some of the Parisian militants made every effort to bring about a general strike for economic as well as political ends. In particular, they pressured the national leadership of the Metal Federation to join their strike, hoping thereby to activate the *cartel interfédéral* of the seven key unions, which was modeled after Britain's Triple Industrial Alliance.[2]

Simultaneously the Executive of the CGT came under strong pressure to play an active and leading role. On May 27, on the eve of this strike wave, its National Committee had issued a formal statement

[8] *Le Populaire,* May 15, 1919.
[9] Edouard Dolléans: *Histoire du Mouvement ouvrier,* 2 vols. (Paris: Colin; 1953), II, 302–3.
[1] See *l'Humanité,* June 1–15, 1919.
[2] Dolléans: *Histoire du Mouvement ouvrier,* II, 305–6.

calling for the restoration of civil liberties, rapid and total demobilization, political amnesty, and the end of intervention in Russia and Hungary. But Jouhaux and his associates, not unlike their British counterparts, were reluctant to fall in with the "insurgent" labor leaders and intellectuals who counted so many recent and therefore undisciplined converts to syndicalism among their eager followers. They were afraid that precisely because conditions in victorious France were not sufficiently revolutionary, the government could easily crush a politically motivated general strike, crippling the labor movement for many years to come.[3]

In any case, still following the British example, Jouhaux headed a delegation of fourteen trade unionists which on May 29 called on Clemenceau to present the CGT's views on demobilization, political amnesty, and intervention in Russia. Whereas the Premier gave satisfaction on the first two points, on the Russian question he was obdurate. He took the position that French soldiers would have to stay there until the Red armies ceased their assault on France's eastern allies and Russia's neighbors.[4]

After the strikes flared up the CGT leaders could do no less than issue a proclamation explaining their own position. In their pronouncement of June 6 they made no effort to disguise their own qualms and hesitations in the face of a strike movement which, without their encouragement and guidance, had mushroomed to unexpected proportions.[5] They stressed that its underlying causes were industry's resistance to the eight-hour day and the steep rise in the living cost. To the extent that the strikers pressed for bona fide economic grievances, the CGT supported them. As for the attendant political and social claims, there was need for caution. The proclamation reminded the workers that the CGT's own national committee had recently—on May 27—formulated such demands and that a major propaganda drive was about to get under way. Meanwhile, however, it was up to the national executive, and not to local organizations, to decide on other ways and means of pushing them.[6]

This reticent proclamation merely stimulated the insurgents to redouble their efforts as well as their assault on the national leadership of the CGT. The *cartel interfédéral* met on June 10. Even though it, too, was split, it agreed to explore the possibilities for joint action at home and for coordinated action with Allied labor organizations abroad.

[3] See Bernard Georges and Denise Tintant: *Léon Jouhaux: Cinquante ans de syndicalisme* (Paris: Presses Universitaires; 1962), 365–6.
[4] *L'Humanité,* May 30, 1919; and *Le Temps,* May 31, 1919.
[5] "The internal situation continues to be serious. There was a military mutiny in Toulouse this morning. Should there be a general strike, is it certain that order can be maintained?" Alexandre Ribot: *Journal et Correspondances inédites* (Paris: Plon; 1936), 274, entry of June 2, 1919.
[6] For the full text of this proclamation see *l'Humanité,* June 7, 1919.

Moreover, the leaders of the SFIO became increasingly eager not to waste the momentum that was building up.[7]

Just the same, the CGT refused to give way to the militants in the *comité d'entente,* the *cartel interfédéral,* and the SFIO. According to Dumoulin, the general strike was too "powerful and delicate a weapon" to be ordered "spontaneously" by a local union and to be conjured or used in every industrial dispute. Had the strikers avowed their political objectives from the very start, the CGT would have asked them to wait.

> Why this storm of impatience against the CGT? No doubt be-
> cause the CGT's wait-and-see attitude was in opposition with
> the impatience and irritation of those masses which had spontane-
> ously joined the organization and the strike. . . . But those of us
> who knew . . . that the underlying causes of the general unrest
> could not be remedied except by efficient and revolutionary methods
> *were duty-bound not to let ourselves be blinded by spontaneous
> impatience and irritation.* . . . [italics mine].[8]

This unwavering refusal to condone or back any further expansion of these politically infused strikes assured the defeat of a general-strike motion at the meeting of the executive of the *cartel interféderal* on June 25.[9]

The anti-Socialist press was up in arms, notably because of the political edge of the movement. While conceding that the soaring cost of living was contributing to the unrest, the *Temps* attached particular importance to the fact that there were leaders who were determined to "exploit these conditions for purely political purposes." In cooperation with Socialist and labor leaders in Britain and Italy these leaders were out to secure a soft peace and the survival of the Russian Revolution, motivated by the fear that the defeat of Bolshevism in Russia and Hungary would involve a setback for Socialism throughout Europe.[1] The entire non-Socialist press raged because these disturbances encouraged those Germans who argued that the Allied Governments were in no position to enforce their terms.

As soon as it became evident that the CGT would act as a brake the bourgeois press began to hail Jouhaux as another Gompers. By mid-June both the government and the editorialists realized that the divisions in the Left were so deep that a demonstration of consequence was most unlikely, certainly before the signing of the German peace.

While the trade unionists were preoccupied with the scope and direction of the strike movement, the Socialists mounted a campaign for withdrawal from Russia in the press and in Parliament. Needless to

[7] *Le Temps,* June 12, 1919.
[8] Cited in *l'Humanité,* June 21, 1919.
[9] Dolléans: *Histoire du Mouvement ouvrier,* II, 305–10.
[1] *Le Temps,* June 4 and 8, 1919.

say, for a while the expansion and politization of the strikes gave exceptional force to their representations.

The mutiny by the sailors of the Black Sea Fleet precipitated this renewed critique of the government's Russian policy. The Executive of the SFIO as well as of the CGT demonstratively congratulated the mutinous sailors for refusing to fight against the Russian Revolution and notified the government that should they be prosecuted the Socialist and labor movement would resolutely defend them.[2]

The SFIO Executive chose June 2, the day the strikes started, to issue a proclamation against intervention in Russia. It called on the workers and peasants of France not to permit the Russian and Hungarian revolutions to be crushed, for otherwise a wave of reaction would sweep away their own hopes of liberation. The sailors in the Black Sea had shown the way, and the Triple Alliance in Britain as well as the Italian Socialist Party were getting ready to demonstrate. French Socialists were urged to prepare their own protest by distributing tracts and pamphlets and by holding public meetings.[3]

These appeals were designed to support and focus attention on a major assault on the government's Russian policy in the *chambre*. At first the date for the debate was fixed for June 6.[4] But it was postponed to the tenth—by a vote of 274 against 159—to avoid "pouring oil on the fire . . . and aggravating the nation's particularly critical situation."[5]

Maurice Viollette, Republican Socialist who stood close to the SFIO, opened the unusually fierce discussion which took up four full sessions. He accused the government of having circumvented its promise of late March not to dispatch additional French recruits or volunteers,[6] by sending colonial units and by arranging for Greek reinforcements. Admittedly these never took up their positions, but only because they reached the Black Sea after the French command had been forced to evacuate Odessa and Sebastopol.[7]

The Radical Socialist de Kerguézec, who had just returned from an inspection tour of the Black Sea front, then described the circumstances of the evacuation. He insisted that an acute food shortage in these port cities turned the population against the Allies, leaving no other alternative. On April 13 Kerguézec himself had wired to Clemenceau that the morale of all French units of the *armée de l'orient* was so low that Paris should instantly withdraw them in favor of a forced-draft build-up

---

[2] *L'Humanité* and *le Populaire*, May 28, 1919; *le Temps*, May 31, 1919; Parti Socialiste: *Rapport du Secrétariat: la vie du parti d'octobre 1918 à janvier 1920* (Paris, 1920), 77–80.

[3] Full text cited in *l'Humanité*, June 3, 1919.

[4] *JO* (May 23 and 28, 1919), 2393–4.

[5] *JO* (June 5, 1919), 2556–8.

[6] See pp. 656–9 above.

[7] *JO* (June 10, 1919), 2593–4.

of the Rumanian forces. When Kerguézec complained that the government's Rumanian policy was too dilatory, Pichon gave a forceful rejoinder. He assured the *chambre* that France had reorganized Rumania's army, had agreed to advance material aid up to one billion francs, and championed her interests at the Peace Conference. In any case, Kerguézec went on to develop the thesis that among the mutinous sailors who were appalled at the plight of Odessa "there were no Bolsheviks," but only men who were exhausted, badly fed, denied home leave, and opposed to fighting Bolsheviks.[8]

In the name of the Socialists Emile Goude even charged that to the extent that there was political excitement on board the warships, it was provoked by the government. Specifically, political debates started following the distribution of a government tract entitled "The Bolshevik Tyranny," reproducing excerpts from Pichon's speech of March 26. Moreover, the men on the *Jean-Bart* and the *France* were infuriated by newspaper stories which claimed that they were volunteers. Goude, followed by Cachin, served notice that the Socialists were determined to prevent sanctions from being applied against the rebel sailors who at all times kept the French flag aloft next to the red banner.[9]

At the end of three days of debate Cachin explicitly asked the Navy Minister to promise that none of the sailors would be punished and the Foreign Minister to issue orders for the immediate recall of all French troops from the Dniester front, where they had no further business. He added that these two steps would help reduce the country's neurasthenia which currently found expression in the strike movement.[1]

But Georges Leygues, the Minister of Navy, was not in the least conciliatory. Even though the sailors had some legitimate grievances, grievances by themselves could not explain the mutinies. Revolutionary propaganda preyed on this irritated state of mind, and this Bolshevik poison was deliberately introduced by German agents at a time when the Peace Conference was completing the draft-treaty. Moreover, the nation should not forget that in Austria, Russia, and Germany "mutinies by naval crews had been the prelude to catastrophe."[2]

After once again feigning that the government "had never premeditated, wanted or undertaken any military expedition in Russia," Pichon tried to minimize the extent of France's commitments. Of 400,000 Russian (*sic*) and Allied troops in Siberia, only 500 were French; and of 40,000 Allied troops in Murmansk and Archangel, less than 2000 were French. Granted, three French divisions were posted along the Bessarabian border, but Bessarabia was not Russia

[8] Ibid., 2624–8.
[9] *JO* (June 12–13, 1919), 2649–53, 2671.
[1] *JO* (June 13, 1919), 2674.
[2] Ibid., 2675, 2678.

proper. Moreover, whereas one of these divisions had already left for Bulgaria, the remaining forces would be withdrawn as soon as the Rumanians were capable of defending their borders.

Even so, the fact that France abstained from military intervention should not be construed as a lack of interest in Russia. For the future peace to be lasting, Russia would have to be "reconstituted in such a way as to prevent German colonization and to permit the complete restoration of her ties of alliance" with Paris. Unlike Germany, France did not want a fragmented but a united and powerful Russia, organized along federative lines. Kolchak was helping to achieve this goal. Pichon concluded that if the Socialists persisted in denouncing this policy for being reactionary he wanted them to know that France was pursuing it in complete unison with the Americans and the British.[3]

As expected, this debate closed with a comfortable vote of confidence for the government, the opposition never gathering more than 140 votes.[4] Meanwhile, however, for a week, with industrial disorders at a peak, the widely reported Parliamentary shouting match exercised a moderating influence on Clemenceau's Russian and Hungarian policy.

In late spring and early summer of 1919 the Italian government came under more severe pressure than either the British or the French. Orlando and Sonnino returned to Paris just in time to be present for the presentation of the draft-treaty to the Germans on May 7. But since their return was unconditional and motivated by the fear of a break with the Conference, it did not strengthen the ministry's position in Italy. Rightist criticism of the government reached a new peak as it became evident that the Conference continued to block Italy's Adriatic aspirations, particularly now that France and England were about to receive full satisfaction of claims.

However, Italian ultranationalist agitation in the press, at public meetings, and in Parliament was soon overshadowed by serious labor unrest. Rising prices, food shortages, low wages and industry's refusal to implement the eight-hour day taxed the patience of even the most moderate Socialist and union leaders. Particularly the urban proletariat and lower middle classes chafed under the high cost of essential foods and manufactures. In April the price index started to climb again. The second half of May witnessed strikes of limited scope in Florence, Genoa, Rome, Livorno, and Turin, and a general strike in Biellese and Salerno.

These limited work stoppages of late May were the prelude to a vast wave of labor unrest which engulfed most of the peninsula in June and early July. At one time or another most of the major cities were the scene of strikes, demonstrations, riots, and the sacking of stores and

---

[3] *JO* (June 17, 1919), 2699–2704.
[4] Ibid., 2715.

warehouses: June 2 , street demonstrations in Naples; June 4, strike by the railway personnel in Rome; June 6, agitation for a general strike in Naples, Salerno, and Fratte; June 7, general strike in Naples and Verona; June 8, walkout by office employees in Rome; June 11, nationwide strike of 50,000 out of 70,000 schoolteachers and looting of stores in Spezia; June 12, general strike in Genoa; June 13, a half-day general strike in Milan and Turin; June 14, strike in Reggio Emilia; June 15, disorders in Bologna. After a brief respite during the last days of June and the first week of July serious disorders paralyzed industry, commerce, and local government in Forli, La Spezia, most major cities in Tuscany, Romagna, and Emilia, as well as in Palermo, Milan, Rome, and Naples.[5] From these urban centers the turmoil penetrated into the surrounding countryside.

The Executive of the Confederation of Labor and the Directorate of the Socialist Party neither instigated nor directed this agitation. Most of the disorders and strikes were spontaneous outbursts against local conditions, though eventually the Chambers of Labor provided some guidance and the general atmosphere became highly contagious.

According to the *Idea Nazionale* the high cost of living was but the pretext for these Bolshevik-inspired outbreaks, which undermined the Italian cause at Versailles.[6] For Mussolini, however, the high cost of living and the disillusionment over the peace negotiations combined to foster this upsurge of general discontent. On June 11 he characterized the situation as highly critical, predicting a quasi-total paralysis of the nation. Shaken by the scope of the labor rebellion, Mussolini reactivated his leveling platform. This was the moment for heroic sacrifices by rich and poor alike. The wealthy in particular should be subjected to a progressive capital levy, to the confiscation of excess war profits, and to heavy inheritance taxes.[7]

In any case, there was growing uneasiness in Parliamentary circles. The air was thick with rumors about impending cabinet resignations, and the government was being pressed to take immediate and dramatic action to reduce the cost of living and various shortages.

By June 8 the situation in Parliament and outside was so alarming that in the midst of delicate negotiations Orlando stole away from Paris to Oulx for an emergency conference with Gaspare Colosimo, the Vice-President of the cabinet. Colosimo lacked the drive, authority, and Parliamentary support to take energetic measures of any sort. The crisis hit at a time when Orlando, who was also Minister of the Interior, had to be in Paris; when Crespi, who was also in Paris, had not been replaced

[5] *Avanti*, May 15–July 10, 1919, *passim*.
[6] *Idea Nazionale*, June 7, 1919, cited in *DR, APS*, June 18, 1919, 210–11.
[7] *Popolo d'Italia*, June 11 and 14, and July 6, 1919, and speech in Milan on June 9, 1919, all cited in Susmel (eds.): *Opera Omnia*, XII, 177–9, 186, 223–4.

as Minister of Food and Supplies; and when Stringher, the Minister of Industry, submitted his resignation. At Oulx, Orlando instantly realized that this time domestic disorders were about to precipitate a cabinet crisis, but he could do no more than instruct his deputy to convene the *camera* for June 19 and to announce his early return to Italy.[8]

Back in Paris Orlando could not conceal Italy's internal crisis from the Big Three. A striking diplomatic triumph might have steadied his cabinet, but his political weakness undermined his bargaining position still further. On June 12 he told the Council of Four that because he was faced with a cabinet crisis and with Socialist disorders he might have to leave for Rome at any moment. The current labor troubles, which were above all due to skyrocketing prices, had developed into a riot in Spezia in which one person was killed and two others wounded. This being the height of the strike movement in Paris, Clemenceau confessed that there was also cause for concern in France. Lloyd George reported that Ramsay MacDonald, on a recent trip to Rome, had discovered that the Italian Socialists favored direct action in cooperation with British and French workers, but that MacDonald had discouraged them.[9]

When Orlando faced the *camera* on June 19 he realized that chances for his cabinet's survival were slim, indeed. Nationalists of all persuasions were critical of his government's diplomacy; most Radicals and Liberals inveighed against his subservience to Sonnino and his lack of direction in domestic affairs; the Socialists were altogether disaffected. To make matters worse, he had little, if anything, to offer. He could not serve up any diplomatic gains, and he was baffled by Italy's economic plight. And the standard plea to close ranks for the duration of the peace negotiations had started to wear thin even before the domestic situation had reached such an explosive impasse.

Just the same, Orlando took cover behind the primacy of foreign policy by asking the *camera* to vote to go into secret session to debate foreign policy, while offering to discuss the domestic crises in the open. But the motion was defeated by 259 against 78 votes. An unholy alliance of Fascists, Catholics, Radicals, Giolittians, Reformists, Republicans, and Socialists threw Italy into a cabinet crisis when Orlando decided to make this procedural vote into a question of confidence. Perhaps by design the *camera* was thus spared a debate which could only have widened the prevailing cleavages.[1]

The King promptly summoned Nitti to form a new cabinet. Judg-

---

[8] See the coverage of the Italian press, June 5–15, 1919, in *Bulletin Périodique de la presse italienne*, June 21, 1919, No. 114 (June 2–16, 1919), 10–11; and *DR, APS,* June 25, 1919, 240–1.

[9] Compare the minutes of the Council of Four, June 12, 1919 (p.m.), in *F.R.,P.C.,1919,* VI, 355, and Mantoux: *Délibérations,* II, 400–1.

[1] *Camera,* June 19, 1919, 18866–73.

ing by the team he assembled, Nitti was determined to explore the avenue of appeasement both at home and in Paris. Of fifteen cabinet posts, seven went to politicians who were either loyal or sympathetic to Giolitti, one to the leader of the Radicals, and two to liberal conservatives. Tittoni became Foreign Minister, a post in which he had served Giolitti intermittently during the first decade of the century, as well as head of the peace delegation. Quite clearly, Nitti placed the peace negotiations in Tittoni's hands in order to be free to devote himself fully to domestic affairs.

According to *Stampa,* the new cabinet was "a combination of the [non-Socialist] Left with a slight thrust towards the Right." Except for allowing Scialoja to join the peace delegation, allegedly for reasons of national interest, the Parliamentary Fascio as well as the extraparliamentary ultranationalists vigorously fought the Nitti government. In their eyes Nitti and Giolitti, while balancing each other, were out to recover the political hegemony they had lost in 1915. They were accused of allowing themselves to become the instruments of the official Socialists for an offensive against all interventionists. For Mussolini the Premier was "a Giolittian by conviction and temperament." Moreover, in addition to having Giolitti's "Parliamentary cynicism" he had Orlando's "oratorical skills as well as his mania for compromise."[2]

Curiously enough, the Socialists agreed that the new ministry marked the revenge of Giolittism. It was a first step towards "the comeback of that fraction of the bourgeoisie which, more or less sincerely averse to the war," had been in eclipse ever since 1915. *Avanti* claimed that now that the revolution was on its doorsteps the entire bourgeoisie realized that "only Giolitti could be its savior." But precisely because the Socialists had no interest in assisting this salvage operation they, too, were opposed to Nitti.[3]

Needless to say, the German government carefully scrutinized this unrest inside the Allied nations. On June 5 Adolf Müller notified Berlin that Longuet and MacDonald had just been in Berne for consultations with Swiss Socialist leaders and that both testified to the upswing of left-wing activism in their respective countries. They were preparing the ground for a twenty-four-hour general strike against intervention in Russia. Because the French Socialists were still too weak to act by themselves, Longuet advocated that this demonstration be directed against the peace treaty as well. Whereas the Italians and Swiss approved this

2 *Stampa* and *Gazetta del Popolo* of June 23, 1919, cited in *Review of the Foreign Press, APS,* July 9, 1919, 306; *Popolo d'Italia,* June 22–27 and July 3, 1919, cited in Susmel (eds.): *Opera Omnia,* XIII, 198–222; Luigi Salvatorelli and Giovanni Mira: *Storia d'Italia nel periodo fascista* (Turin: Einaudi; 1956), 28–9. For the Fascist demonstrations against Nitti in Rome, Milan, Florence, Genoa, and Turin, see G. A. Chiurco: *Storia della Rivoluzione fascista* (Florence: Vallechi; 1929), I, 141–3.

3 *Avanti,* June 20–25, 1919.

plan, the British were as yet uncertain. But MacDonald was off to London to win over his colleagues. Should the British labor movement go along with the plan, this demonstration might take place within five or six days.[4]

Four days later Brockdorff-Rantzau, in a top secret wire, notified Ebert that recently "internal conditions" in the Entente countries had taken "a strong turn" in Germany's favor. Though the French strikes had economic causes, they were aimed against Clemenceau's overall domestic, fiscal, and foreign policies. In fact, they might well be the "prelude to a revolutionary crisis of vast proportions." The working class was making "common cause" with the Black Sea sailors. Moreover, both the serious mutiny in Toulouse and the Paris railway workers' decision to halt troop trains were protests against military intervention in Russia, Hungary, and Germany. In Belgium especially the Flemish workers were getting restless. In England the Labour and Liberal opposition to the peace terms and the renewal of the blockade "was growing to such an extent that Lloyd George was being forced to take a strong stand against Clemenceau and Wilson." Meanwhile Denmark, Norway, Sweden, and Switzerland had refused an Allied request to participate in a blockade to force Germany to sign the treaty.

According to Brockdorff-Rantzau, even though this Allied opposition would not be strong enough to restrain the victors from having recourse to countermeasures against a recalcitrant Germany, "it could certainly force them to halt before long." However, should "unjust conditions find support among the German proletariat" this Allied opposition would falter, leaving the Conference free to rely on outright threats. The Foreign Minister urged Ebert to advise the executives of both the SPD and the USPD of these developments and to impress them with the importance of standing firm.[5]

Max Warburg took advantage of Carl Melchior's trip to Berlin to send a confidential letter to Ebert about this same subject. He claimed that the delegation's interim notes had been favorably received throughout the entire Allied world. Symbolic of this response was the resignation of influential members of the American Peace Delegation.[6] Warburg briefly elaborated on the outcome of recent by-elections in England, the strikes in France, the pressure for demobilization in all Allied countries, the "hopeless" financial situation of France, and the intractability of the neutrals. All these developments proved that "time was working for Germany" and that the government should continue to be tenacious. Otherwise, by accepting the proffered terms, "we would dig our own grave, demoralize the whole people, kill Democracy and

[4] Adolf Müller to Foreign Ministry, June 5, 1919, G.F.M. (D 934340–41).
[5] Brockdorff-Rantzau to Ebert, June 9, 1919, G.F.M. (D 934380–83).
[6] See pp. 799–801 below.

Socialism in Germany for decades to come," and pave the way toward either reaction or revolution. Provided the spirit of acceptance was checked in Germany, propaganda—"the only weapon we still possess" —could continue to be used to good advantage.[7]

After speaking with Melchior in Berlin and reading press dispatches about internal developments in France, Cuno was convinced that Clemenceau wanted to put over a tough peace at the earliest possible moment. He told Brockdorff-Rantzau that the Tiger needed an "external success which would rally chauvinist circles around him" for his struggle against labor unrest at home. Hence, Germany should play for time so that the internal conditions in France, which were grave, would dispose Clemenceau's government to become conciliatory. A declaration that Germany was ready to disarm and to pay reparations not only might make it difficult for the Allies to refuse oral negotiations but also would favorably influence Allied opinion.[8]

Erwin Barth, Stampfer's co-editor at the *Vorwärts,* saw an upheaval in the offing in France "which would change the political situation on the Continent." Germany had to make every effort to provide the time for this change to work itself out. His particular stratagem was a popular referendum on the peace terms. Should the Allies agree to one, it could be delayed for quite a while. In the meantime, a referendum would make a good impression on the outside world, including the neutrals. It would also force the hand of the Independents, who could hardly reject a procedure which fitted in so perfectly with their own democratic credo. On the other hand, by spurning the referendum proposal the Allies would damage themselves in the eyes of democratic and Socialist opinion.[9]

When he returned to Weimar to plead for the rejection of the final treaty Brockdorff-Rantzau presented a survey of domestic conditions in the Allied countries to the cabinet and to other groups. He reported that in France the strikes had a political character; that the workers were increasingly resolute in their opposition to a dictated peace; that according to Adolf Müller, Longuet predicted a continuing radicalization of the proletariat; that a constantly expanding group of *Wirtschaftspolitiker* was pressing for ameliorated conditions; and that war weariness and lack of discipline were eating into the Allied armies. Furthermore, judging by Lloyd George's wavering behavior, in England Labour and Liberal pressure for revision was not negligible. Brockdorff-Rantzau claimed to have strong grounds to assume that "if given the opportunity, the British Left would certainly continue" its

[7] Max M. Warburg to Ebert, June 6, 1919, G.F.M. (E 211984–88).
[8] Cuno to Brockdorff-Rantzau, June 11, 1919, G.F.M. (E 212167–72).
[9] Erwin Barth to Brockdorff-Rantzau, June 11, 1919, G.F.M. (E 212197–200). Actually Barth's proposal did not reach the Foreign Minister until June 19, by which time he was back in Berlin.

protest. Public opinion would vigorously oppose a tightening of the blockade, without which "British military policy was like a knife without a blade." He did not think that the blockade threat was particularly credible, a view apparently shared by the neutrals. As for the opposition in America, though it was not motivated by good will for Germany, it nevertheless exercised a salutary influence. Certainly, America would oppose renewal of the blockade; important economic interests were eager to renew trade relations with Berlin; other circles relied on Germany to help in the containment of Russian Bolshevism; and U. S. troops desperately wanted to return home. To be sure, Italy was of least importance. Still, she certainly was in no condition to attack southern Germany. In brief, the Foreign Minister argued that the Allies were not likely instantly to enforce their ultimatum and that provided the home front held in Germany, there was a good chance that within two or three months the Allies would agree to oral negotiations about Germany's counterproposals.[1]

Walter Simons eventually summarized the place of domestic developments in the Allied nations in Brockdorff-Rantzau's diplomatic calculations.

> During the month of May in France and England the mood of the Government organs became increasingly uncertain and nervous and the views of leading personalities increasingly divergent. To the same degree the opposition papers became constantly more strident and open in their attacks on their Governments' peace policies. In France, Belgium and England there emerged strong currents against the application of force for the imposition of peace conditions.
>
> These symptoms reached their apogee during the month of June. There were important demonstrations against the hunger blockade in England; the Conference of the Belgian Socialist Party passed a resolution against a vindictive peace; in France there was a politically oriented strike movement as well as mutinies in regiments assigned to march into Toulouse. Had German public opinion been united and had Germany's Left-Socialists supported a pungent propaganda drive against an oppressive peace, these movements would have grown to such proportions that any extended application of coercive measures would have been impossible. . . . The [Allied] Socialist Parties were afraid to fall between two chairs and did not want to be more Catholic than the Pope, particularly since the Independent Party of Germany fervently advocated the signing of the treaty. . . .[2]

Perhaps a *new-style* diplomat representing a *genuine* Socialist government could have cultivated and enlisted the Socialist and labor protest in the Allied world for Germany's benefit. As it was, neither the

---

[1] Résumé presented to the cabinet on June 18, 1919, and Brockdorff-Rantzau's memorandum of July 2, 1919, G.F.M. (E 212220–25, E 235529–44, esp. E 235541).

[2] Memorandum, [no date], G.F.M. (H 235547–55).

Scheidemann administration nor Brockdorff-Rantzau was a particularly convincing apostle of the Wilsonian and Socialist gospels. To be sure, they emulated Lenin's and Trotsky's diplomatic style of direct appeals to the peoples of Europe. Ebert issued a manifesto while many of Brockdorff-Rantzau's notes were couched in anticapitalist and social-reformist rhetoric.

But the *Rote Fahne* and the *Freiheit* rightly noted that Allied Socialists were not likely to exert themselves for a government that gave free rein to the Noske guards, allowed Von der Goltz to participate in the anti-Bolshevik crusade in the Baltic, and kept postponing socialization measures at home.

In any case, this unrest and dissent in the victor nations never reached sufficient proportions in June to influence significantly the acceptance debate in Germany. As the *Frankfurter Zeitung* suggested, Germany could not count on external developments, notably on the strikes, to favor her cause: "neither the break-up of the Entente nor revolutionary turmoil in the Allied nations was close at hand." Admittedly, the question as to whether or not there would be a revolution in the West was of "deadly earnest importance." However, in Germany's immediate predicament "erroneous estimates could spell destruction and vague phrases were dangerously poisonous."[3]

The government and the parties simply would have to make their decision in the light of *internal* rather than *external* considerations. This being so, the *Frankfurter Zeitung* made a consistently convincing case for the wisdom if not inevitability of acceptance. Germany was powerless, her people exhausted, and her armies inadequate for renewed warfare. Moreover, Germany's unity would be endangered by either the threat or the reality of punitive occupations, especially in the south and west. But there was also an all important political consideration. Reactionaries of all stripes were taking advantage of this crisis "to agitate not only against the existing government, but above all against the German Revolution and its constitution." Accordingly, the revolution was being denounced for having caused first the military defeat and then a humiliating peace. Not that the treaty could possibly make anyone popular, and the supernationalists would in any event put all the blame on the revolution and on democracy. Meanwhile, however, time might work in favor of moderation at home and abroad.[4]

The Independents kept advancing most of these same arguments. Should Germany refuse, the Allies had it in their power to occupy key industrial and mining centers, to blockade all ports, to cut off food imports, to paralyze transport and production, and to promote separatism in the Rhineland and Bavaria—all at the expense of the lower

[3] *Frankfurter Zeitung,* June 10, and 11, 1919.
[4] *Frankfurter Zeitung,* June 5–18, 1919.

classes. Only the militarists, the nationalist parties, and the capitalists would know how to exploit the resulting chaos, misery, destruction, and decomposition. The USPD urged acceptance under protest while pledging to seek revision in cooperation with the masses of the victor countries, who themselves were suffering from the consequences of their rulers' extreme victory.[5]

Through the *Berliner Tageblatt* the Democratic party voiced an equally strong fear of an ultranationalist comeback. But unlike the *Frankfurter* and the Independents Theodor Wolff argued that the only way to ward off this danger was for the German government parties to reject the settlement, thereby denying the counterrevolution a monopoly on the appeals of nationalism. The Democrats wanted the coalition to head a political truce and, if need be, a *levée en masse,* in opposition to Allied depredations.

There were strong pressures for this same nationalist-oriented policy of refusal in the SPD. At the party congress of June 10–15 Bernstein, who worked for a fusion of the SPD with the moderate Independents in favor of acceptance, warned of playing into the hands of the Right by whipping up a nationalist hysteria over a treaty which was "9/10 inevitable." He was promptly and viciously taken to task by unreconstructed Social Patriots who gave free expression to their lingering anti-Semitism. Adolf Braun struck out against Bernstein's "talmudic political methods." He was followed by Hermann Müller who protested that in day-to-day politics "not all things could be viewed from the perspective of a rabbi from Minsk" or treated in the manner of a *Hosenhändler* to whom first 9/10 and then 8/10 of the treaty would be acceptable. According to Scheidemann, the high priest of revisionism had turned into "the devil's advocate."[6] Still, even the *Vorwärts* eventually concluded that a cabinet committed to rejection would be out of the question "because it would have to rely on the support of the *Deutschnationalen* and the *Deutsche Volkspartei,* and it would be so bourgeois and rightist that for internal reasons it would be unbearable for the German people."[7]

Incidentally, the *Deutschnationalen* and key segments of the *Volkspartei* were stepping up their campaign against the government as well as against Brockdorff-Rantzau, whose diplomacy they compared unfavorably with Talleyrand's. They threatened that the "German East" would overthrow the government if it decided to sign the treaty.[8] Presently Walter Reinhardt, the Prussian Minister of War, a fiery

---

[5] See, e.g., the USPD manifesto of June 17, 1919, in *Freiheit,* June 18, 1919.
[6] Sozialdemokratische Partei Deutschlands: *Protokoll über die Verhandlungen des Parteitages,* Weimar, June 10–15, 1919, 240–81.
[7] *Vorwärts,* June 20, 1919.
[8] See the article "Enough Words Have Been Exchanged," in the *Deutsche Zeitung,* June 6, 1919. This article prompted Noske to proscribe this paper for six days.

advocate of rejection and resistance, prepared to hold the eastern provinces, the heartland of the Prussian state, even at the expense of either the occupation or separation of the south and west.[9]

As early as June 3 and 4—hence nearly two weeks before the Allies answered Brockdorff-Rantzau's counterproposals—Erzberger forced the cabinet to give preliminary consideration to the question of acceptance vs. rejection. By then he was persuaded that whatever concessions might be forthcoming would not satisfy the antisigners. For the occasion of this cabinet debate he drafted a working paper summarizing the arguments on both sides of the question, paying particular attention to the domestic consequences of either course.

In case of acceptance the foreign policy gains seemed self-evident: the blockade would be eliminated, production and trade would resume, the war prisoners would return home, Poland would abandon her aggressive designs, and German unity would survive. These developments, especially the resumption of economic life, would help restore order internally and undercut the appeals of Bolshevism. Consolidation on the Left, which would benefit from the profound peace-hunger of the great majority of the population, would strengthen the existing coalition to stand up to the Right, which would be the real threat. This Right, including "a segment of the liberal bourgeoisie," was likely to launch a bitter attack on the government. It might not even shy back from a military coup, whose center of gravity would be in the eastern provinces. However, this movement would probably evaporate quickly, particularly because of the apparent internal improvements attendant on the acceptance of the treaty.

As an early and leading advocate of acceptance within the government, Erzberger intentionally painted an overly lurid picture of the consequences of rejection. Accordingly, in terms of foreign policy, the Allied armies, including the U. S. units, would instantly advance to a line parallel to the Rhine as far inland as Kassel, occupying above all the entire Ruhr basin; the blockade would be tightened; men of draft age would be subject to deportation; requisitions would be stepped up; and the Poles would advance from the east. Domestically, these sanctions would paralyze the economy, endanger daily rations, and promote inflation. As in Russia the resulting anomie would lead to civil war, especially in Berlin and the big cities, with the bourgeois elements caught between the extreme Left and the extreme Right. Moreover, the unity of Germany would be endangered by separatist movements in Bavaria, the Rhineland, and the East. Eventually the Allies would seal this national decomposition by signing separately with the several German states. In sum, rejection would lead to the over-

[9] John W. Wheeler-Bennett: *The Nemesis of Power: The German Army in Politics, 1918–1945* (New York: St. Martin's Press; 1954), 53.

throw of the government by Independents and Communists, to the dissolution of the army, and to the breakdown of order throughout the country.[1]

Except for Noske and David the entire cabinet, but especially the Democratic members, stubbornly upheld the antiratification position. If Noske began to incline toward signing he did so because the USPD was making serious inroads among the urban workers and because he realized that the army was in no condition to resume military operations against the Allies. This latter judgment was shared by General Groener, who had made a point of sounding out his officers on the morale and readiness of their units.[2]

Outside the cabinet, sentiment in favor of signing was mounting rapidly. Except for the *Deutschnationalen* at the extreme Right and the Independents and Spartacists at the opposite extreme of the political spectrum, all the parties, even the *Volkspartei,* became increasingly divided as the hour of decision approached. Of the three government parties, the Democrats were most united in opposition to ratification. Only a few deputies, mostly from the exposed southwest and led by Von Payer, favored acceptance. In the SPD, even though the top leadership was resolutely opposed to signing, a substantial majority of deputies, sensitive to the peace urge among the rank and file, would not follow Scheidemann. And in the Center party Erzberger broke the antiratification majority by agreeing to make acceptance conditional on concessions with regard to war guilt and extradition of war criminals.[3]

The moment Brockdorff-Rantzau heard about these divisive partisan squabbles he pressed Ebert and Scheidemann to dampen them. Since he would not settle for minor concessions, he needed a united home front in order to prevail on the Allies to negotiate about the entire range of counterproposals. Therefore "complete calm, cold blood, and self-control" should take the place of boisterous protestations of nonacceptance and of premature declarations of concessions. Brockdorff-Rantzau asked his principals to instruct the press to counter the rumors that in the cabinet as well as in the Reichstag the view was gaining that not to sign would be to let Germany in for a *va banque Spiel*—for brinksmanship. On another occasion, after Melchior informed him that Bernstorff now also inclined toward unconditional acceptance, he asked his cousin to suspend judgment until his return home. But Bernstorff wired that he had merely asked Melchior to inform Brockdorff-Rantzau about the domestic political situation so that he

---

[1] For the full text of this memorandum see Matthias Erzberger: *Erlebnisse im Weltkrieg* (Stuttgart and Berlin: Deutsche Verlagsanstalt; 1920), 371–3.

[2] Erzberger: *Erlebnisse,* 273–5; and Wilhelm Groener: *Lebenserinnerungen* (Göttingen: Vandenhoeck and Ruprecht; 1957), 495–6. See also Klaus Epstein: *Matthias Erzberger and the Dilemma of German Democracy* (Princeton: Princeton University Press; 1959), 317–18.

[3] See Epstein: *Matthias Erzberger,* 318–19.

should not have "excessive hopes." The Socialists knew that in case of refusal the majority of their followers would immediately join the Independents in a strike, the army would not be able to handle the situation, and Bolshevism would follow. Bernstorff expected, therefore, that the Socialists would declare the enemy concessions satisfactory in order to be able to sign under protest. The *Zentrum* and at least a faction of the Democrats would be likely to go along.[4]

Between May 29 and mid-June, while considering the German counterproposals, the Big Four kept one eye on the acceptance debate in Germany and the other on party and opinion pressures in their own countries. A concerted effort was made to secure an up-to-date reading of the enemy's political pulse: the German press was scanned thoroughly, agents took straw polls, emissaries interviewed German officials, and the telegrams between the German Delegation in Versailles and Berlin were intercepted.

The American Delegation received daily reports from Army Intelligence in Germany.[5] These were supplemented by occasional reports from Conger, the intelligence officer on Pershing's staff who had direct contacts with Erzberger as well as an indirect line to Groener.[6] But perhaps the Dyar Mission was the most consistent and reliable source of information.

Charles B. Dyar was a State Department clerk "with wide experience in the former Berlin and other Embassies."[7] When Dresel concluded his second mission to Berlin on May 3 he left Dyar behind, in charge of an efficiently organized press bureau and authorized to transmit "information received through other channels."[8] Throughout May and June Dyar filed almost daily reports on political developments in Germany as well as detailed surveys of the German press.[9]

All along Dyar stressed that the antiratification campaign was serving the purposes of the Right. By June 7 he pointed to the renewed campaign against Erzberger "as fresh proof of the strength of the reactionary movement." On the twelfth he reported that in an interview Oscar Cohn had expressed the opinion that "the danger of counterrevolution was very real." The USPD leaders urged that the Allies help arrest this trend by encouraging the proratification elements

---

[4] Brockdorff-Rantzau to Von Langwerth, June 6 and 12, 1919, Brockdorff-Rantzau to Bernstorff, June 14, 1919, and Bernstorff to Brockdorff-Rantzau, June 15, 1919, in G.F.M. (D 934349–50, E 212144–46, E 212161–63).

[5] G-2-B, G.H.Q., A.E.F., Memoranda for General Bliss: Germany, May 15–June 15, Nos. 50–82, in House Papers, 29:139A.

[6] See *F.R.,P.C.,1919,* XII, 124–35; and Brockdorff-Rantzau to Von Langwerth, June 12, 1919, G.F.M. (D 934391, D 934408–9).

[7] Dresel to American Commissioners, February 15, 1919, National Archives, Document 184.012/37.

[8] Dresel to Ammission, April 29, 1919, National Archives, Document 184.0131/30.

[9] See National Archives, Documents 184.0132/ff and 184.013202/ff. Dyar was assisted by two translators, one stenographer, and one code clerk.

—notably Erzberger in the cabinet—with the immediate admission of Germany to the League and the concession of a plebiscite in Upper Silesia.[1]

Meanwhile Dyar had also been received by both Bernstorff and Erzberger. The former was quite certain that "the Germans would eventually sign if concessions were granted regarding admission to the League, plebiscite in East Germany and reorganization of the Reparations Committee." Bernstorff even indicated that it was quite likely that the peace delegation would resign, followed by resignations from the cabinet, "probably Scheidemann and Giesberts." This could mean that a new delegation representing the three major parties of a reconstituted cabinet would be sent to Versailles.

As for Erzberger, he also reiterated the "absolute necessity of admitting Germany to the League (perhaps not now) and of holding a plebiscite in Upper Silesia, Posen, and West Prussia." In addition, he characterized the functions of the Reparations Commission as too far-reaching, criticized the absence of a fixed sum of reparations, and insisted that Germany could not sign a settlement with the two humiliating honor clauses.[2]

All signs pointed toward acceptance by a government—possibly a reconstituted government—resolved to check the nationalists on the Right and the Independents on the Left. Significantly, no leader, party, or faction of consequence proposed a common front with Soviet Russia against the overbearing West, if need be along with the enthronement of national Bolshevism in Germany. Actually, Brockdorff-Rantzau was much more inclined to proffer loyal cooperation in the containment of Russian Bolshevism in Courland than to frighten the Allies with an alliance with Moscow, all the more so since he and the entire government were irrevocably committed to the extermination of Bolshevism within Germany.[3] Incidentally, this reluctance to play the Soviet Russian card may well have been reinforced by the fact that beginning in late April the Red Army suffered severe reverses at the hands of Kolchak and the fall of Petrograd seemed imminent.[4] For the moment the Allies were as little apprehensive about the specter of German-Soviet cooperation as they were about the possibility of a Spartacist take-over in Berlin.[5]

---

[1] Dyar to Ammission, June 7 and 12, 1919, National Archives, Documents 184.013202/59 and 68A.

[2] The memorandum on these two interviews as well as other reports and surveys by Dyar came to President Wilson's attention. See Grew to Close, June 14 and 17, 1919, and Grew to Wilson, June 16, 1919, in Wilson Papers, VIII, A:62.

[3] See Brockdorff-Rantzau to Von Langwerth, May 3, 1919; memorandum by Von Romberg, May 8, 1919; and Von Langwerth to Brockdorff-Rantzau, May 9, 1919, in G.F.M. (H 235264–65, E 211763–66, E 211769).

[4] See pp. 813–5 below.

[5] "On the whole the position as regards Bolshevism is less menacing than it was three weeks ago. . . ." Directorate of Intelligence, Weekly Review of the Progress of

Consequently, whereas at Fontainebleau the Red specter on the Continent had precipitated Lloyd George's turn to appeasement, such was not the case in early June. The German counterproposals became the occasion for another effort at revision, perhaps as much in order to make the peace acceptable to the Germans as to quiet domestic and imperial dissent. Moreover, satisfied with the colonial, naval, and trade terms, Lloyd George wanted to make a last-minute effort to reduce those French-dictated demands that were most likely to leave a legacy of rancor and instability and to become a source for future British entanglements on the Continent.

The British Prime Minister thought it best to try to strengthen his hand for this final but difficult round with Clemenceau and Wilson over Germany's proposals. For this purpose he invited nine principal members of his Cabinet and all the Dominion Premiers to meet with him. For three long consultative sessions—one on May 30 and two on June 1 —Lloyd George presided over what he himself characterized as "one of the most remarkable Cabinet Councils ever held by the British Empire."[6] From correspondence or conversations with Smuts, Barnes, Churchill, and Cecil he knew that he could expect considerable support for a sympathetic reexamination of the treaty in the light of the German reply.

In these deliberations Smuts, whose basis of power and range of influence were circumscribed, was the advocate of the most comprehensive and far-reaching revisions. In his judgment the preliminary draft was a "war treaty" under which Europe, rather than find peace, would sink into an intolerable situation and "a revolution must come, or again, in due course, an explosion into war." As early as May 14 he implored Lloyd George and Wilson, in the name of "the silent masses who had suffered so mutely, . . . to use their unrivalled power and influence to make the final treaty more moderate and reasonable." Within a week, alarmed at the prospect of a German refusal, he called for "alterations and compromises . . . [through] oral discussion." He warned that any treaty that was signed at gun point would be in danger of "moral repudiation by the German people." By May 30, after the German reply, his indignation reached a still higher pitch. For Smuts the Germans were justified in their charge that the terms were not "within the 4 corners of the Wilson Points and Speeches." He, for one, would be no party to ending the war as it had begun, "with another

---

Revolutionary Movements Abroad, Report No. 1, May 1, 1919, G.T. 7196, Cabinet 24/78. "The horizon is less low this week than it has been for months. . . ." Ibid., Report No. 2, May 7, 1919, G.T. 7217, Cabinet 24/79.
[6] See W. K. Hancock: *Smuts: The Sanguine Years, 1870–1919* (Cambridge: Cambridge University Press; 1962), 529.

'scrap of paper.' " As he told Wilson in their last exchange of letters, if this peace was not substantially revised it might turn into "an even greater disaster to the world than the War was."[7]

General Smuts was the first to speak at the marathon meeting of the British Empire Delegation. Following a brief recapitulation of his objections of principle, he advanced five specific and major points for revision. He called for the abolition of the proposed fifteen-year military occupation of the Rhineland; the elimination of such "pin-pricks" as the internationalization of German rivers; the immediate admission of Germany to the League; the thorough modification of the eastern borders, possibly through plebiscite;[8] and the stipulation of a fixed and reasonable, though high, reparations bill.[9]

Barnes backed Smuts on three of these points. In his view, especially with the Anglo-American guarantee, the occupation provisions were altogether exaggerated; Germany should instantly be admitted to the League, otherwise she would set up "another League of Nations with Russia"; and it was wrong not to claim a fixed amount for reparations.[1]

It is not surprising that Smuts and Barnes should have been the most radical revisionists. Both were Wilsonians committed to the appeasement of the vanquished and of the social revolution. Both were prepared, furthermore, to strain relations with France in order to conciliate the anti-acceptance forces in Germany as well as the forces of movement throughout the Western world.

Churchill seems to have shared their excessive fear of German rejection. As War Secretary his particular concern was with the disposition of Britain's dwindling army strength, at a time that the demobilization and anticonscription campaigns were at their height. He wanted Lloyd George to "split the outstanding differences," for fear that the Allies would have to reimpose the blockade and occupy further parts of Germany. Moreover, in the short as well as in the long run, Churchill —like Smuts—worried about the debilitating effects on the Empire of

[7] The quotations are from letters of Smuts to Lloyd George, Wilson, and Smuts's wife, May 14–30, 1919, all cited in Hancock: *Smuts,* 522–5, 528.

[8] "The new Poland will include millions of Germans (and Russians). . . . It is reasonably certain that both Germany and Russia will again be great Powers, and that sandwiched between them the new Poland could only be a success with their good will. How, under these circumstances, can we expect Poland to be other than a failure, even if she had that ruling and administrative capacity which history has proved she has not? Even now, while the Conference is sitting, the Poles are defying the Great Powers. What is going to happen in the future with the Great Powers divided and at loggerheads? I think that we are building a house of sand." Smuts to Lloyd George, May 22, 1919, cited in Baker: *Woodrow Wilson and World Settlement,* III, 461.

[9] See David Lloyd George: *The Truth About the Peace Treaties,* I, 691–3; and Smuts to Lloyd George, June 2, 1919, cited in Hancock: *Smuts,* 530–1.

[1] Lloyd George: *Truth,* I, 716–17.

festering tensions on the Continent: Britain would have to divert resources from India, Egypt, the Middle East, and Turkey, where "formidable preoccupations were arising."[2] Churchill may also have favored concessions as part of his anti-Bolshevik project.

As for Robert Cecil, he reminded his chief that the terms were "out of harmony with the spirit, if not with the letter, of the professed war aims" in the Allied Note to Wilson of January 1917, Lloyd George's T.U.C. address of January 1918, and the Fourteen Points. The provisions concerning the Saar, Poland, and reparations could not be squared with any of these pronouncements and were not "suitable for a lasting pacification of Europe." Apart from worrying about future Anglo-American cooperation, Cecil felt that "in these negotiations our moral prestige had greatly suffered," one of his friends having described the treaty "as the moral bankruptcy of the Entente." With Churchill, Fisher, Barnes, and Milner he wanted "to go furthest in the direction of amendment." They advocated giving up Upper Silesia and the Polish corridor to the Baltic; shortening the Saar occupation; modifying the occupation of the Rhine provinces; admitting Germany to the League at an early date; and drastically revising the reparations clauses, "providing for no payment for the first year or so, and a definite sum, such as 5 billion pounds as the total liability."[3]

Except for Premier Hughes of Australia, who was as intransigent as ever, all the other participants—including Austen Chamberlain and General Botha—were strongly of the opinion that certain changes were necessary, though no one would go quite so far as Smuts. At the end of the deliberations Lloyd George summarized the consensus which from the start he knew would emerge. Accordingly he took it to be the sense of the delegation that he had full discretion to press for revisions with regard to the eastern frontiers, Germany's early admission to the League, the occupation clauses, and the reparations settlement. Furthermore, in case of resistance in the Council of Four he could threaten to refuse the services of the British Army and Navy to coerce Germany with the present treaty.[4] Needless to say, not even Smuts suggested that Britain or the Empire freely offer "to sacrifice anything of importance to themselves either to encourage French concessions or to meet the German counter-proposals."[5]

On June 2 Lloyd George took his case to the Council, elaborating at some length on all four major points. But more important than the

---

[2] See "Memorandum by Mr. Churchill," May 21, 1919, cited in Harold I. Nelson: *Land and Power: British and Allied Policy on Germany's Frontiers, 1916–19* (London: Routledge; 1963), 328–9; and Churchill: *Aftermath*, 217–18.

[3] Cecil to Lloyd George, May 27, 1919, in Cecil Papers, 51076; and Cecil Diary, May 31, 1919.

[4] Lloyd George: *Truth*, I, 694, 714, 718–19.

[5] Nelson: *Land and Power*, 337.

specific details was his insistence that "unless certain defects in the Peace Treaty were put straight" the Empire Delegation and the Cabinet were not prepared to resume military operations and reimpose the blockade. He claimed that neither Barnes nor Botha and Smuts would sign the present treaty.

Clemenceau impatiently replied that whereas in England "the view seemed to prevail that the easiest way to finish the war was by making concessions, in France the contrary view was held that it was best to act quickly and with firmness." With undisguised sarcasm the Tiger noted that of course British public opinion was not objecting to Germany being asked to give up all her colonies and her entire fleet! Still, he agreed with Wilson that "the objections raised . . . were of such importance" that they, too, wanted to consult their delegations.[6]

Wilson in particular came under pressure to ease the terms. Protests and caveats came from all directions, and all of them reminded the President that the draft treaty violated his own principles and promises. Wilsonians on both sides of the Rhine issued manifestoes; Smuts kept sending urgent letters; Lloyd George pressed for reexamination; and in America the *New Republic* and the *Nation* abandoned "their" Wilson.

But most imminently disturbing was the simmering rebellion in the American Delegation. Shortly before Wilson's return from his visit home the U. S. Commissioners had accepted Bliss's suggestion that the American delegate on each of the various committees of the Conference "be instructed to report . . . in what respect (if any) the report of his Committee violates (if it does violate) any of the President's declarations, and what is the justification for it."[7] Whether or not these reports were ever submitted, this circular reveals that American officials felt bound to keep measuring day-to-day decisions against the Wilsonian decalogue. Until May 7 delegates were inclined to excuse particular violations, convinced that they were minor and exceptional. But once the complete draft-treaty was in their hands they were struck by the scope and intensity of its departure from their cherished norms.

The first sign of revolt came at the lowest echelon of the mission. On May 14–15 five young experts vigorously registered their fundamental disagreement with the announced terms, and offered to resign. For John Storck the treaty would make Germany "eager for revenge," would "foster the Prussian spirit" in the victor nations, and would "stand as a monument of shame above the graves of the millions who [had] suffered and died." Adolf A. Berle not only denounced the wholesale abandonment of the letter and spirit of Wilson's fundamental principles but also the endangerment of America's interests, notably in the Japanese clauses. Joseph V. Fuller voiced his conviction that America would dishonor herself by signing and guaranteeing a settle-

---

[6] See minutes of Council of Four, June 2, 1919 (p.m.), in *F.R.,P.C.,1919*, VI, 139–46.
[7] Bliss to U.S. Commissioners, March 11, 1919, cited in *F.R.,P.C.,1919*, XI, 110.

ment in which she "bartered away her principles in a series of compromises with interests of imperialism and revenge." And while Samuel Eliot Morison chafed at the violation of American interests, ideals, and principles, George Bernard Noble predicted that this peace, in which American ideals were "sacrificed on the altar of imperialism, . . . would be provocative of future wars."[8]

All five left it to the Commissioners to decide whether, in spite of their disagreement with Administration policy, they were wanted to stay on in their posts. Such a "collective" resignation might cause a stir, affront the President, and set off other protests. For example, Ray Stannard Baker, who was in a quandary about his own course, might have joined the rebellion.[9] In any case, the Commissioners sought to bank the fires by asking the writers for time "in which to consider what course should be pursued under the circumstances."[1] The eventual recognition of Kolchak in mid-June prompted Morison and Berle to insist that their resignations be accepted.[2]

Meanwhile another Young Turk would not leave the decision to the Commissioners. On May 17 William Bullitt sent a formal letter of resignation to Secretary Lansing, who promptly accepted it. That same day Bullitt also wrote to the President explaining the reasons for this drastic step. He commended himself as "one of the millions" who had trusted in Wilson to secure a principled and lasting peace. Instead, principle and prudence were violated with regard to Russia, Shantung, Tyrol, Thrace, the Saar, Hungary, East Prussia, Danzig, and the freedom of the seas. These oppressions and dismemberments foreshadowed "a new century of war" which the League would be "powerless" to prevent. He urged that the U.S. avoid involvement and entanglement by refusing to sign the treaty, to join the League, or to guarantee France's borders.

In this letter, as on so many other occasions, Bullitt did not hesitate to speak as if he were a ranking member of the delegation. After crediting the President for "personally [having] opposed most of the unjust settlement" he took it upon himself to lecture him caustically on how this fiasco could have been prevented.

> It is my conviction that if you had made your fight in the open, instead of behind closed doors, you would have carried with you the public opinion of the world, which was yours; you would have been able to resist the pressure and might have established the "new international order . . ." of which you used to speak. I am sorry you did not fight our fight to the finish. . . .

[8] For the full text of these five letters to the Secretary General of Ammission (Grew) see ibid., 569–72.
[9] See Lansing Diary, May 18 and 19, 1919, in Lansing Papers.
[1] F.R.,P.C.,1919, XI, 179.
[2] See ibid., 235–6, 238–9, 244, 591–2.

Bullitt's disillusionment and anger were complete and his break irrevocable.[3]

Since Bullitt asked House to bring this letter to the President's attention,[4] the Colonel summoned him for a long interview. Rather than transmit the letter, House indicated that he would "ask the President whether he had received the copy which [Bullitt] sent him." Throughout the interview House kept stressing that the League would be a valuable and effective instrument for peaceful change, particularly once more "radical" governments ruled throughout Europe as well as in America. He also defended the President for not pulling out of the Conference, otherwise there would have been "revolution in every country in Europe, and . . . the President was not ready to take this responsibility."[5]

Neither Lansing nor House pressed Bullitt to stay on. On the other hand Bliss, who was the most sympathetic of the four Commissioners, argued that the time for criticism was not now but would come when everyone would be called before the Senate Foreign Relations Committee. Since negotiations with the Germans were in the offing Bliss thought it unfortunate that men of Bullitt's persuasion were leaving "because, although we do not have much effect on the decisions of the President, at least as long as we are here we can hang on to his coattail, while if we were all to go, there would be no one left to urge him to stand for the right things."[6]

Even though Wilson may never have seen the first five protests, Bullitt's letter is not likely to have escaped his notice. He knew who Bullitt was and was familiar with his work. Moreover, Bullitt's letter somehow got into the press, where it caused much comment. The *Morning Post* feigned less surprise about the resignation of the "Bolshevizing and Germanophile" Bullitt than about his original appointment to the commission. Ironically, the *Populaire* thought that Bullitt was excessively hard on the President, for by himself Wilson could not have reversed the course even in public discussions. Besides, he had tried open diplomacy in his appeal to the Italian people. No doubt Wilson repeatedly thought of pulling out. But at the last moment he always shied back because "as President of a great capitalist state he was hardly likely to take a step which could lead to general revolution against international capitalism."[7]

None of the more prominent members of the American Delegation

[3] Bullitt to Lansing, May 17, 1919, in Bullitt Papers; and Bullitt to Wilson, May 17, 1919, *F.R.,P.C.,1919*, XI, 573–4.

[4] Bullitt to House, May 17, 1919, Bullitt Papers.

[5] See Bullitt's "Conversation with Colonel House," May 19, 1919, in Bullitt Papers.

[6] See Bullitt to Bliss and Bullitt's "Memorandum on a Conversation with General Bliss," May 19, 1919, in Bullitt Papers.

[7] *Morning Post*, May 23, 1919; and Daniel Renoult's "Les Wilsoniens contre Wilson," in *le Populaire*, May 25, 1919.

ever considered resigning. Even so, there was mounting restlessness as Germany's notes and counterproposals poured in. In particular Hoover, who knew of Smuts's position, went about saying that the blockade could not be renewed to impose unreasonably hard terms. Even if the Germans signed, such terms would not "secure stability," while if she refused the Allies would extinguish "the possibility of democracy in favor of either Communism or reaction." Hoover urged the President to take advantage of "the British change of heart . . . to absolutely insist on his original contentions, even at the risk of disruption of the Conference." He, for one, considered such a disruption, which he did not believe would happen, as "the least of evils," largely because every European politician would in any case use America "as a foil."[8]

It was at Hoover's suggestion that on May 27 Lansing, Bliss, White, and House sent a joint note to their chief suggesting that he call a special meeting of all the American Commissioners, technical experts and advisers to confer with them about the German reply. House, who himself questioned the wisdom of "seriously modifying" the treaty at this late date,[9] urged the President to agree to such a meeting, otherwise "some of them would be disgruntled and perhaps make trouble."[1]

In his reply Wilson claimed that such a meeting was "just what [he himself] had in mind"[2] and following Lloyd George's challenge it convened late in the morning of June 3 at the Hotel Crillon.

The President told the 38 assembled officials that he had come to hear and not to express opinions and that he wanted them to air their general impressions.[3] After listing the four points which had made the "greatest impression on our British colleagues," he suggested that they start with reparations, which were the "biggest point."

Both Norman Davis and Thomas Lamont thought that by "coming back with a fixed sum" the Germans offered a basis for negotiations parallel to their own. A fixed sum was needed to restart Germany's economic and industrial life with the help of foreign credits. It would also make it possible to reduce the scope of the Reparations Commission which the Germans found so intolerable. Both economic advisers urged the President not to agree to delay setting a definite sum, even for a few months, since Lloyd George was "simply trying to postpone the evil day, as far as public opinion is concerned."

[8] Lansing Diary, May 21, 1919, in Lansing Papers; and Hoover to Wilson, June 4, 1919, and Hoover's "Memorandum on the Peace Treaty," June 5, 1919, printed in Suda L. Bane and Ralph H. Lutz (eds.): *Organization of American Relief in Europe, 1918–1919* (Stanford: Stanford University Press; 1943), 536–8.
[9] House Diary, May 30, 1919.
[1] The four Commissioners to Wilson and House to Wilson, May 27, 1919, in *F.R.,P.C., 1919*, XI, 587–8.
[2] Wilson to Lansing, May 29, 1919, in ibid., 588.
[3] This discussion is based on the stenographic report of this meeting in ibid., 197–222.

At this point Lansing interjected the proposal that the President ask each group to "prepare a memorandum of what might be conceded." But for fear of opening the floodgates of criticism, Wilson demurred. Whereas he was prepared to reconsider those points which could be shown to be unjust and contrary to principle, he was not inclined to review points which simply struck the Germans as excessively hard. Also, he was anxious to avoid "sharp lines of division" among the Allies.

With great clarity and directness Hoover posed *the* decisive question: in order to get the Germans to sign "apart from all questions of justice, how far does the question of expediency come in?" In these times it was "pretty difficult" to weigh justice and injustice. Justice would require that the Germans foot the entire bill and hand over the Saar and the Silesian coal mines. But in order to "get something rather than lose all" it might be expedient to make changes in the reparations, Saar, and Silesian terms. More than that, such changes would not even "contravene the principles of justice." Thereupon White and Haskins suggested that "two or three minor modifications" would square the Saar clauses, while Davis was hopeful that provided the Allies went along, the financial and economic clauses could be composed with the Germans.

As compared to the debates of the British Empire Delegation, the American debates were disorganized and diffuse. Moreover, the economic and financial spokesmen tended to dominate the proceedings. Besides, Wilson's nerves were frayed; he did not appreciate being reminded of compromises which had pained him at the time they were made; and he was not inclined to accept advice which could reopen time-consuming negotiations.

Rather defensively he tried to justify his own reluctance to seek substantial modifications.

> The time to consider all these questions was when we were writing the treaty, and it makes me a little tired for people to come and say now that they are afraid the Germans won't sign, and their fear is based upon things that they insisted upon at the time of the writing of the treaty; that makes me very sick.
>
> And that is the thing that happened. These people that overrode our judgment and wrote things into the treaty that are now the stumbling blocks, are falling over themselves to remove these stumbling blocks. Now, if they ought not to have been there, I say, remove them, but I say do not remove them merely for the fact of having the treaty signed. . . .
>
> Here is a British group made up of every kind of British opinion, from Winston Churchill to Fisher. From the unreasonable to the reasonable, they are all unanimous, if you please, in their funk. Now that makes me very tired. They ought to have been rational to begin

with and they would not have needed to have funked at the end. . . . Though we did not keep them from putting irrational things in the treaty, we got very serious modifications out of them. If we had written the treaty the way they wanted it the Germans would have gone home the minute they read it.

This abrupt closing statement signified that the President was not about to throw in his lot with Lloyd George, who could not be trusted to persevere in his present course.

Perhaps it is worth stressing that there was no Smuts or Barnes in the American Delegation. Except on the occupation issue Bliss remained silent throughout these deliberations, and he did not approach the President on his own. Though House also conceded that the treaty was too severe, he was opposed to unraveling it for fear of not being able to stop the revision process.[4] Likewise, White felt that oral discussions with the Germans, which were required to achieve meaningful changes, "would materially postpone the signature . . . and the consequent restoration of peace, which is now so eminently desirable, in view of the present state of unrest in nearly every country of the world."[5] Lansing did suggest the preparation of memoranda, but his overall posture was hardly that of an indignant Wilsonian.

In the second echelon there were no flaming critics either. Vance McCormick and Baruch thought the treaty was "just and workable." To be sure, there was Hoover's protest, but even he wanted the President "to feel that whatever the course you may choose I am, for what I am worth, prepared to stand by."[6] And on the basis of Dyar's reports Dresel advised Wilson that Germany's immediate admission to the League would not only induce the German government to sign but also would at once and immensely "strengthen the parties of order and true democracy."[7]

Within less than three hours after Wilson recessed the meeting of his delegation the Big Four plunged into a detailed consideration of the four major terms which Lloyd George had proposed for revision.[8] At Wilson's suggestion they turned to the question of Upper Silesia first. He opposed a plebiscite because German capitalists and landed magnates would hamper a free vote and because when he spoke of "unmistakably" Polish territory in his Thirteenth Point "he included generally Upper Silesia." But the British Prime Minister persisted, insisting that of all the points the German government attached the greatest

[4] House Diary, May 30, 1919.

[5] Henry White to Wilson, June 5, 1919, Wilson Papers, VIII A:56.

[6] McCormick Diary, June 14, 1919, cited in Suda L. Bane and Ralph H. Lutz (eds.): *Organization of American Relief* (Stanford: Stanford University Press; 1943), 527, 535.

[7] Dresel to Wilson and Wilson to Dresel, June 5 and 7, 1919, Wilson Papers, VIII A:57.

[8] This discussion of the debate of June 3, 1919 (p.m.), is based on *F.R.,P.C.,1919*, VI, 147–60.

importance to this one, with which Wilson agreed. In passing Lloyd George claimed that he was "simply fighting through" Wilson's Fourteen Points. For the rest he concentrated on persuading the President that a League of Nations Commission and Allied troops—preferably U.S. troops—could easily safeguard a popular consultation in which intimidation would be kept to a minimum. Clemenceau, who wanted no change whatever, kept himself in the background. He merely warned that if Allied troops supervised the plebiscite "the Germans would simply allege that pressure had been exercised to avoid a free vote."

The most dogged opposition came from Paderewski, who was summoned for June 5. He affirmed that the proposed change might "endanger the whole situation, not of my country alone, but of Eastern Europe . . . [where] for the past few months Poland had been the stronghold of peace and order . . . and where there was no sign of revolution, no sign of Bolshevism." If "something were taken away" from the Polish people, they would lose faith in him as well as in the Big Four, and there would be revolution.

This inflexible and insolent response provoked Lloyd George into venting his impatience with all the successor states on Poland and her spokesman. Throughout the war the Poles actually fought "against their own freedom" in so far as they fought at all. They got their freedom "not by their own exertions" but by "the blood" of millions of Frenchmen, Englishmen, Italians, and Americans. And rather than show gratitude the Poles, who never had "the slightest hope of getting freedom," were losing faith in their liberators and were "more imperialist than either England and France, than certainly the United States."[9]

Perhaps if Clemenceau himself had been as intractable as Paderewski the President, encouraged by Robert H. Lord, would have let it come to a showdown with Lloyd George. As Clemenceau put it, "as against the Germans he was pro-Pole with all his heart." But the Tiger relented. He calculated that even if the plebiscite would not induce the Germans to sign, it would make it easier to marshal popular support for the coercion of Berlin.[1] Also, quite apart from being confident of the outcome in the industrial and mining districts, he preferred to make his stand on the occupation terms.

The President reluctantly sided with Lloyd George. On the recommendation of an expert committee, the Council finally decided to provide for a plebiscite within six to eighteen months after the establishment of an inter-Allied commission which would administer Upper Silesia during the interim.[2]

With regard to reparations, Wilson and his advisers took the lead.

9 For the Paderewski-Lloyd George exchange, see ibid., 191–201.
1 Ibid., 159, 303; and Mantoux: *Délibérations*, II, 349.
2 *F.R.,P.C.,1919*, VI, 311–13, 316–17, 449–51.

Lloyd George provided them with another opportunity to press for a fixed sum to be included in the treaty. Wilson noted that the Germans and the Allies were not that far apart: whereas the former offered five-billion pounds sterling, the "fixed-sum" advocated among the Allies contemplated the same figure, plus interest. Moreover, there was general agreement that a fixed sum was the essential precondition for credits. But the Big Four and their expert committee continued to be deadlocked. With perfect candor Lloyd George confessed that "any figure that would not frighten the Germans would be below the figure with which he and M. Clemenceau could face their peoples in the present state of public opinion." Besides, at this time a definite figure would "raise inconvenient questions between the Allies," notably between Britain and France. With the British and French Premiers unwilling to pacify the Germans with more than "some general assurance" that the Allies had no "desire to crush Germany," the Council again avoided a specific amount. Instead, at Lloyd George's suggestion, the Council agreed to give Germany four months in which to offer an overall sum or any plan—provided it was practicable, reasonable, unambiguous, precise, clear, earnest—for restitution and reparation of already-agreed-upon categories of damages. In turn, the Allies promised to reply to this offer within two months after receiving it.[3]

Lloyd George and Wilson were least divided over the former's proposal that Germany be admitted to the League at an early date. Again, both thought that a "general assurance" was all that was required. Certainly the Prime Minister was not about to press Smuts's call for immediate admission. As for Wilson, apparently he still wanted proof that the change in the system of government in Germany was "sincere" and that the new government was "stable." As late as June 5 Dresel once again felt called upon to contradict charges that the "existing Government was merely a cloak for German militarism and that its members were arch-hypocrites." He assured Wilson that in spite of "many faults" the Ebert-Scheidemann regime was "clearly democratic in form and sentiment" and that it stood "unquestionably for a republican form of government."[4] Even Clemenceau could not object to the final draft according to which Germany would be admitted "in the early future" provided her government "clearly proved its stability" and its desire to honor her international obligations.[5]

But with regard to the 15-year, three-stage occupation of the Rhineland Clemenceau would not yield ground. Both Lloyd George and Wilson argued that the motivation for the 15-year period was

[3] *F.R.,P.C.,1919,* VI, 155–7, 261–4, 267–71, 272–9, 290–4, 295–300. "Lloyd George was curiously reluctant to make any changes in the reparations proposals." Cecil Diary, May 31, 1919.
[4] Dresel to Wilson, June 5, 1919, Wilson Papers, VII A:57.
[5] *F.R.,P.C.,1919,* VI, 157–8, 325, 327, 339–42.

political, to quiet public opinion, since this occupation would come to an end at the precise moment when Germany's military strength was likely to have recuperated. Clemenceau avoided joining this issue by insisting that foreign troops were needed on German soil "as a guarantee for the payment of the indemnity, . . . as a reminder to the Germans that they owed money which they should pay." Lloyd George then pleaded his own political difficulties. Parliament would want to know why France should have a prolonged occupation as well as a guarantee. Still, Clemenceau would go no further than a promise, in a separate declaration, that if Germany gave proof of "goodwill and satisfactory guarantees to assure the fulfillment of her obligations" the Allied and Associated Powers would "be ready to come to an agreement . . . for the earlier termination of the period of occupation," and that as soon as Germany fulfilled the disarmament conditions the annual cost of occupation to Germany would not exceed $60 million.[6]

These four concessions were communicated to the Germans on June 16 in the form of a reply to their counterproposals and accompanied by a five-day ultimatum.[7] In Germany the acceptance debate, which had started on May 7, now entered its closing but decisive phase.

Brockdorff-Rantzau and his delegation had instructions to return to Weimar, where they arrived in the early morning of Wednesday, June 18. In the course of their journey they decided that the modifications were insufficient to make the treaty acceptable and workable. Hence, in Weimar the delegation became a precious ally of the antiratification forces, whose press—from the *Berliner Tageblatt* to the *Deutsche Zeitung*—rejected the concessions out of hand.[8]

The cabinet met at 10:00 a.m. on the eighteenth to hear Brockdorff-Rantzau and to begin a round of feverish debates and consultations. The Foreign Minister conceded that he had expected the Allies to accept only a small fraction of his counterproposals; that the Allies, but especially France and Belgium, were prepared to enforce harsh terms; and that inter-Allied unity would survive a German refusal. Even so, he urged the cabinet to persevere because "time worked in Germany's favor." He held out the hope of oral negotiations within the next two to three months. These would not only secure concessions far beyond those granted thus far, but would also end Germany's status as a pariah among nations. Brockdorff-Rantzau calculated that the Allies would move to the conference table under the pressure of internal developments,[9] because of the Anglo-American reluctance to reimpose the

[6] Ibid., 327–9, 377–94, 521–2.

[7] For the full text of this reply see ibid., 926–96.

[8] See the review of the German press of June 17–18, 1919, in the *Frankfurter Zeitung*, June 18, 1919, cited in *Bulletin Périodique de la presse allemande*, No. 126, July 4, 1919 (June 17–23, 1919), 2.

[9] See pp. 788–9 above.

blockade and resume war operations, and because of inter-Allied rivalries over future economic influence in Germany.[1] Brockdorff-Rantzau at no time, either that morning or during the ensuing crucial days, faced up to the consequences of an Allied refusal to fall in with such dilatory tactics.

Within the cabinet he could count on the steadfast support of Scheidemann, whose speech of May 12 committed him to nonacceptance; of Landsberg, his colleague on the delegation, who ever since November had been a champion of unmitigated Social Patriotism in the highest councils of the SPD; and of all three Democratic Ministers.

Ranged against these six irreconcilables were Erzberger, Giesberts, and Bell, as well as four Socialists, led by Noske. The first three were of the Catholic *Zentrum,* which was particularly sensitive to proacceptance sentiment in the south and the west and which was bidding for lower-class votes in the cities. As for Noske, even though he was far from firm, under General Groener's influence he never really abandoned the partisans of acceptance. Himself from Württemberg, Groener insisted that although the army could hold in the east and even reconquer Posen, it was in no condition to hold in the west, where the Allies would have to be checked. Groener won Hindenburg over to his view as against Generals Reinhardt, Von Below, and Von Lossberg. Should the cabinet and the assembly sign, these three generals wanted the High Command to spark and direct an insurrection whose geographic center would be in the eastern provinces, even at the cost of dismantling Bismarck's national structure.[2]

Clearly, the Allied ultimatum precipitated or forced the break-up of the coalition cabinet. Whereas on June 3–4, following consideration of Erzberger's memorandum, the cabinet split ten to four against acceptance, now it was almost evenly divided. Not only was there no clear majority either for or against ratification, but Scheidemann, the Chancellor and chief champion of nonacceptance, lost the support of his own party. In the evening of June 18 a straw vote of the Parliamentary delegation of the SPD revealed that 75 were in favor of signing, while only 39 were against.[3] On Thursday the other Parliamentary delegations were polled. The *Zentrum* voted four fifths in favor of acceptance provided the honor clauses were eliminated. Erzberger routed Spahn only by agreeing to a condition which he knew was not likely to be met. Following a rousing and truculent address by Schücking, the Democrats voted 56 against acceptance and only one—Von Richthofen—for signing, with eight undecided but leaning toward acceptance. Needless

[1] "Secret Memorandum" by Simons, July 2, 1919, in G.F.M. (H 235529–55).
[2] For the split in the military and Noske's relation to it, see Wheeler-Bennett: *The Nemesis of Power,* 53–9; Groener: *Lebenserinnerungen,* 500–8; Gordon Craig: *The Politics of the Prussian Army, 1640–1945* (New York: Oxford; 1955), 364–73.
[3] *Vorwärts,* June 19, 1919.

to say, the *Deutschnationalen* and the *Volkspartei* were as unanimously opposed to as the Independents were in favor of swallowing this bitter pill of defeat and humiliation.[4]

Shortly after midnight on the twentieth Scheidemann formally submitted the resignation of the entire cabinet to Ebert. Actually, the President sympathized with the anti-signers. But he could not afford to call on an anti-signer to form a new cabinet. At best an antiratification government would be confirmed by a majority of a very few votes. In other words, a policy of resistance, which to be successful required a high degree of national unity, would have to be carried forward with a slim Parliamentary majority, against the 45 per cent of the electorate that followed the SPD and the USPD, and with the support of the antirepublican nationalists and militarists. Like everyone else, in the press of time Ebert was less concerned with the concrete terms of the treaty—including present and prospective revisions—than with the general political situation *within* Germany.

On June 21 Ebert asked the moderate Socialist Gustav Bauer, former Minister of Labor, to form a cabinet which would seek Parliamentary approval for a policy of acceptance. Since the Democrats stubbornly refused to sanction the participation of any of their politicians, Bauer was reduced to building an SPD-*Zentrum* coalition. Erzberger became Vice Chancellor and Finance Minister; Noske resumed the Defense Ministry; and the Foreign Office went to Hermann Müller, who only a few days before had Jew-baited Eduard Bernstein for advocating acceptance.[5] Being so heavily beholden to the Center party, Bauer went to the Reichstag for authorization to sign the treaty, conditional on securing the modification of Articles 227 to 231.

It was shortly after mid-day on Sunday June 22, 1919, that Fehrenbach called the Reichstag to order and recognized the new Chancellor. Bauer was diffident without being spineless: he and his colleagues were shouldering this burden because it was "their damned duty and obligation to try and salvage what could still be salvaged."[6] As for the domestic program of this SPD-Center coalition, it would be the same as that of the defunct Scheidemann administration.

Apart from this general reference to program, Bauer made no mention of internal affairs. Time was running out and he needed authority to wire an acceptance to Paris. First came the usual protests against this treaty of "violence and destruction," against this "mockery of self-determination," against this "enslavement of a great and good people," and against this "threat to world peace under the guise of a festive peace treaty." There then followed the solemn declaration that

---

[4] See *Vorwärts* and *Freiheit,* June 20, 1919.
[5] See Epstein: *Erzberger,* 320–1. Other cabinet posts were taken by David (Interior), Wissell (Economics), Giesberts (Post Office), and Bell (Communications).
[6] This discussion of the Reichstag session of June 22, 1919 is based on *Verhandlungen der verfassungsgebenden deutschen Nationalversammlung,* Vol. 326, 1113–39.

"no signature would invalidate this protest which we—democrats, Socialists, and pacifists—raise and swear for all time."

Insisting that Germany's resistance was broken, Bauer propounded that "a *no* would mean but a brief postponement of a *yes*." This being so, the government was prepared to fulfill the dictated peace conditions to the extent that they could be carried out, provided Germany was not charged with sole war guilt and on the understanding that no German nationals would be extradited for war-crimes trials abroad.

For the SPD Paul Löbe stressed many of these same points, particularly Germany's helplessness. In his view, not to sign would be much worse than to accept under protest, since the people "neither wanted to nor could resume fighting." After a short interlude, with the whole economy paralyzed and enemy troops advancing, Germany would have to submit to even worse conditions. Löbe concluded with the ringing nationalist assertion that the more the German *Volk* was suppressed, the more faithfully the German workers would stand up and be counted. With Marx, Engels, Bebel, and Liebknecht—and against Bismarck—the SPD was *grossdeutsch*, was for the "unity of all who learned to speak from German mothers along the Danube and the Etsch, and at the mouth of the Weser, the Elbe, the Oder, and the Weichsel." Löbe even "eagerly looked ahead to better times when Germans would be reunited with those of their brothers and sisters who would be suppressed in the Sudetenland, in Vienna, in Klagenfurt, in Bozen, and in Meran."

Similarly, in the name of the *Zentrum*, Gröber rejected *la politique du pire*. Acceptance would not only avoid a resumption of war under unfavorable conditions, it would also bring home war prisoners, prevent starvation, start up economic reconstruction, and preserve national unity. Of course, the humiliating clauses would have to go.

The spokesman for the Democrats conceded that especially the plebiscite for Upper Silesia was an improvement over the original terms. Even so, for Schiffer "this was not sufficient," and should this treaty be signed, "the greatest war in world history would terminate in the greatest crime ever perpetrated on a people." The Democrats, for their part, would prefer "to go down with honor," and therefore would stand by their position of May 12.

Count Arthur von Posadowsky-Wehner agreed that nothing had changed since that magnificent session in the Aula of the Berlin Academy. The treaty was unacceptable because Germany would be left defenseless; would be raped of territory "three quarters the size of Great Britain with some 8 million inhabitants," not to speak of the colonies; and would lose 70 per cent of her iron ore, 30 per cent of her hard coal, all her tin mines, and 12 per cent of her food resources. In addition, Germany would humiliate herself by even considering the clauses bearing on reparations, war guilt, and the extradition of the

Kaiser. At the conclusion of Von Posadowsky-Wehner's indictment Bauer rather defensively reminded the Reichstag that the speaker had failed to "spell out the ways and means which would enable Germany to reject this brutal treaty." Neither this spokesman for the Nationalists nor Dr. Wilhelm Kahl, the spokesman for the *Deutsche Volkspartei,* ever took up Bauer's challenge.

Finally, it was Haase's turn. He was totally out of tune with this atmosphere of national self-righteousness. Rather than once again reiterate the USPD's arguments for signing, he concentrated on the conditional nature of Bauer's proposal for acceptance. He charged the new government with continuing the policy of "dangerous illusions," the Allies being in no mood to accept qualifications. Besides, the time had come for Germany to admit that though all capitalist governments shared in the responsibility for the outbreak of the war, "the Habsburg government, with the approbation of the German government, had set the fuse to the powder keg, thereby detonating the world conflagration." There was no alternative to signing and counting on the world revolution to bring about revisions. But as if to contravene Brockdorff-Rantzau, Haase warned that notwithstanding recent developments in the Allied countries, it would be "altogether foolish to bank on the outbreak of the world revolution in the near future, during the next few weeks."

The time for the vote was at hand. The deputies were asked to signify their "agreement with the signature of the peace treaty," no mention being made of the twin qualifications. By 237 to 13 votes, with five abstentions, the Reichstag decided in the affirmative. There then followed a vote of confidence, which went 236 against 89, some 68 Democrats abstaining rather than voting against the Bauer-Erzberger team.

Meanwhile, even before these two votes were tallied and in order to stay within the deadline, Bauer had wired Paris that his government would "sign the Treaty of Peace without, however, recognizing thereby that the German people was the author of the War, and without undertaking any responsibility for delivering persons in accordance with Articles 227 to 230."[7]

But the Big Four would tolerate no further exchanges, particularly since they had just learned of the scuttling of the German fleet at Scapa Flow. By return telegram Berlin was notified that "the time for discussion had passed," that no "qualification or reservation" could be accepted, and that "less than 24 hours remained" for final acceptance or rejection.[8] Early Monday morning, June 23, the Big Four refused Von Haniel's request for a forty-eight-hour extension.[9]

[7] Cited in *F.R.,P.C.,1919,* VI, 611.
[8] Ibid., 612.
[9] Ibid., 615–16.

As Haase had predicted, the season of illusions was drawing to a close. Even though Bauer and the SPD were willing to sign unconditionally, the *Zentrum* party was bound by its resolution of June 19. And in the morning of June 23 all but 14 of the Centrist deputies, including a depressed Erzberger, voted to reject the Allied demand for unqualified acceptance. Not only the cabinet was in danger, but also the majority in the Reichstag. At an emergency meeting of party leaders, presided over by Ebert, Erzberger bluntly asked the spokesmen of the Democrats, the People's Party, and the Nationalists whether they were prepared to form a government which would reject the treaty and face the consequences. All three answered in the negative. Even the Nationalists shied back, no doubt largely because Groener and Hindenburg had successfully contained the simmering officers' rebellion.[1]

Rather than let it come to another vote in the Reichstag (there was no time for another debate!) the party leaders agreed to construe yesterday's motion as also authorizing the government to sign unconditionally. Moreover, they also agreed that the spokesmen for the three major antiratification parties—Schiffer for the Democrats, Schultz-Bromberg for the *Deutschnationalen,* and Heinze for the *Deutsche Volkspartei*—would rise in the Reichstag in the afternoon of the twenty-third to declare that the patriotism of the pro-signers was above reproach.[2] Thus the signers sought to hedge against the inevitable recriminations by the opposition which would seek to monopolize the high ground of superpatriotism.

This same concern permeated the final acceptance telegram. Müller notified the Allies that the German Republic was ready to sign the conditions "imposed" by the Allies. But he also proclaimed that in "yielding to overwhelming force" the German people would neither tarnish its honor nor cease to consider the peace terms as an "injustice without parallel."[3]

There followed the ceremony in the Hall of Mirrors on June 28.

[1] Epstein: *Erzberger,* 322.
[2] For the text of the three statements, of which Schultz-Bromberg's was the most reserved, see *Verhandlungen der verfassungsgebenden deutschen Nationalversammlung,* Vol. 327, 1139–41.
[3] Cited in *F.R.,P.C.,1919,* VI, 644.

23

Recognition of Kolchak

IN MARCH–APRIL, the prospects, as seen from Paris, for an early overthrow of Lenin were rather discouraging. The evacuation of Odessa and Sebastopol signaled an unfavorable turn in the Russian Civil War and intervention. On the Dnieper, Denikin was floundering, his energies consumed in internecine struggles with Petlura. Similarly, on the Baltic front, the anti-Soviet campaign was undermined by the irreconcilable clash of Yudenich and Mannerheim over the future of Finland. Admittedly, Kolchak was advancing into the Volga region; however, the Allies still considered the Siberian front a sideshow. Even though the fall of Petrograd would be a serious blow for the Soviets, this northern theater also rated low as compared to the southern front—the Ukraine, the Crimea, and the Caucasus.

All this time Allied policy was indecisive. Except for massive material aid for Kolchak and Denikin and the tight naval ring, the Big Four offered little encouragement. Domestic political pressures not only prevented the dispatch of Western conscripts but also sparked rumors of an imminent withdrawal from Archangel and Murmansk. Anglo-French rivalries and budgetary stringencies delayed an advance promise of food for Petrograd should that city be liberated. And diplomatic efforts to convince the Finns and the Estonians to work with Yudenich failed.

Especially following the fall of Budapest and with the Red Army at the East Galician border, the Allies thought in essentially defensive terms. Clemenceau sternly turned down Franchet d'Esperey's proposal to occupy the Hungarian capital. Instead, the same day that Franchet d'Esperey was ordered to evacuate Odessa he was told that hereafter, on the "Bessarabian and the Hungarian front, his mission was exclusively to check any Bolshevik advance." To make this containment effective, notably along the Dniester, the Allies decided to provide the Rumanians with all the necessary material aid;[1] they also expedited the

[1] Clemenceau to Franchet d'Esperey, March 29, 1919, Quai d'Orsay, 3216 BS/3 and 3226 BS/3.

transfer of Haller's division to bolster the Polish front. Though the Bullitt scheme was defeated, his mission as well as the Nansen Plan were symptomatic of a scandalous failure of nerve in the eyes of the Allied Right.

Almost overnight this picture changed. To every one's surprise it was Kolchak who scored a dramatic breakthrough. By late April his troops had advanced along a broad front running from Perm to Orenburg to some 30 miles short of Kazan and Samara. Kolchak was headed for Moscow as well as for a juncture with General Eugene Miller, who was moving southeastward from his Archangel enclave.

Although between April 24 and 27 the Red Army struck a debilitating blow at Kolchak's left wing, it was not until mid-May that this offensive was finally checked. To achieve this result the Bolshevik high command had to draw troops and supplies from the southern front. As a result, the Soviet leaders were forced to abandon any thought of helping Béla Kun either by rolling back Petlura for a breakthrough between Lvov and Czernovicz or by pressing toward Bessarabia. Moreover, Denikin and Krasnov began probing the weakened Red lines prior to launching a major three-pronged offensive in mid-May. Paradoxically, at the precise moment that the Soviet armies first stopped and then pushed back Kolchak's troops, Denikin started his big push. By the end of June his Volunteer Army had captured Kharkov and Tsaritsin. Equally dramatic was the advance by both Yudenich and the Finnish Volunteers from Estonia and Karelia to within easy striking distance of Petrograd.

These uncoordinated but nevertheless perilous offensives consumed all the energies and resources of the fatally isolated Soviet regime. Lenin and Trotsky poured every last resource into the defense of their besieged and shrinking citadel. Except for revolutionary manifestoes to the peoples of Europe, the Bolshevik leaders had no means to spare for intervention in Hungary or elsewhere.

The point to note is that this nadir of the Revolution's military fortunes coincided with the exchange of notes and proposals between the Allies and the German Delegation. As a result, during this critical confrontation Berlin was unable to enlist the specter of Bolshevism. At home, for the time being, the Spartacists were in complete disarray and the security forces in full preparedness, so that a plea or threat for leniency in order to avoid a Bolshevik take-over would have sounded hollow. Likewise, precisely because the various White armies, lavishly supported and advised by the Allies, were so successful, the Big Four were not about to soften their terms in exchange for German help in the containment or overthrow of Russian Bolshevism. At best the Allies would be slow to enforce their demand for the recall of Von der Goltz.

In any case, as of early May the right-wing press became ecstatic about the progress of the counterrevolution in Russia. The London

Times celebrated "the break-up of Bolshevism," prematurely hailing the fall of Béla Kun as well. Kolchak was said to have "no motives other than our own." As for the impending capture of Petrograd, it would be a pity if the Finns got there first or alone: a Finnish occupation of Petrograd would do as much harm as an Irish occupation of Liverpool! Since the difficulty was not so much to take the city as to revictual it, perhaps the Allies should use their economic power to give the edge to Yudenich. The time for action was now, otherwise "when Bolshevism in Russia went under, the new Government would have no cause for gratitude to us and would thank us for nothing."[2]

Before long the *Times* boasted of Britain's contribution while at the same time calling for a supreme effort. The Murmansk army under General Maynard was pushing toward the head of Lake Onega; Britain was supplying Denikin with "complete equipment for 250,000 men"; the British fleet was helping with landing operations on the southern shores of the Gulf of Finland; and Britain had recognized the independence of Finland. This increased British activity in the Baltic and the Black Sea areas revealed that at long last the period of vacillation was over. The next step was to recognize Kolchak, prevail on him to recognize Finland, and have the Finns help in the liberation of Petrograd at his invitation, backed by a British promise of food for the civilian population.[3]

For the *Daily Mail* the center of interest also shifted from the question of German acceptance to the Russian problem. The Allies should resolutely and swiftly recognize Kolchak's organization as the provisional government of Russia while simultaneously supporting "the Russo-Finnish enterprise for the liberation and subsequent revictualing of Petrograd."[4]

In the French press Kolchak's widely publicized military advances were taken to show that no real peace was possible as long as Russia was unsettled. Of course, the emphasis was less on the Baltic than on Kolchak, who relied on General Janin for military counsel, and on Denikin. Whereas Britain favored the independence of the Baltic provinces and a federated Russia, France still hoped for a Russian colossus to help countervail Germany.

Once again Bainville gave a particularly incisive statement of the East European problem.

> In the East it is proposed to make peace in the absence of Russia. That is rather simple-minded. It would not be possible to award Poland and Rumania such [generous] eastern limits if there still were a Russian state and if that state were our ally. The same would hold true with regard to Galicia and the Ruthenians. . . . In brief,

[2] *The Times* (London), May 3 and 5, 1919.
[3] Ibid., May 15 and 21, 1919.
[4] *Daily Mail* (Paris), May 15, 1919.

these allocations are being made without either Muscovite or Kievan Russia being consulted.

Such are the conditions in which the Conference establishes that barrier of new states on which an entire school counts to contain Germany in the East. And, in fact, to contain Germany on the slope opposite ours, there is need for a greater Poland, a greater Bohemia, and a greater Rumania. These three states can have no consistency, cannot support each other without annexing Russian territories or Slav populations traditionally under Ukrainian or Muscovite influence.

Accordingly, such a settlement will last only as long as Russia can be ignored or continues to be asleep. The establishment of this "barrier" postulates an eternal sleep. The day the Russian state reawakens and is again capable of having a foreign policy, it will automatically team up with Germany against the nations formed at their mutual expense. As in the past, Poland will unfortunately be caught in a crossfire.[5]

In brief, Bainville was for leaving Kolchak a free hand as against pressuring him to give Karelia to the Finns, White Russia to the Poles, and Bessarabia to the Rumanians. Furthermore, no Russia worth her salt would ever accept the "secession" of the Baltic provinces and the Ukraine. For France to recognize the independence of such "states" would be as friendly an act as for Russia to recognize, under similar circumstances, the secession of the "Channel, Atlantic, and Mediterranean provinces" from France![6]

Pertinax also wanted the Allies to support Kolchak's drive to rally the demoralized Czechs to his cause, and to aid Yudenich as over Mannerheim in the storming of Petrograd. The Omsk government should be recognized unconditionally and Sazonov, Kolchak's delegate in Paris, should be admitted to the Conference. Only by associating responsible Russian spokesmen with the European settlement could the danger of German revenge be banished effectively.[7]

In *Figaro* Alfred Capus, Raymond Recouly, and Joseph Reinach took turns stressing that no control of Germany could be lasting without the reentry of Russia into European life. Obviously, Lenin could not be overthrown by the Whites without external aid, and the bulk of this aid should go to Kolchak, the only counterrevolutionary leader of real stature. Besides, since the regime's capital was in Moscow, the liberation of Petrograd would not spell the end of Bolshevism. Moscow had to be taken, and Kolchak could do the job in no time, particularly once order- and freedom-loving Russians rallied around

[5] *L'Action Française,* May 10, 1919.
[6] Ibid., May 28, 1919.
[7] See Pertinax's article "It is up to us to finish off the Bolsheviks," in *l'Echo de Paris,* May 15, 1919.

this *"grand chef,* this Siberian Washington, this great man of Plutarch-like, republican virtues."[8]

The *Temps* agreed that without Russian participation the frontiers of Europe could not be drawn properly. The Omsk government was entitled to recognition, Kolchak having proven himself militarily as well as by cooperating loyally with Janin, Knox, and Stevens. Moreover, the Russian Political Conference represented Kolchak in Paris. Naturally Kolchak and Sazonov were equally loath to consider any dismemberment of Russia. But perhaps a transitional arrangement could be worked out whereby Kolchak—in agreement with Denikin and Yudenich—would put the border provinces in trust with the League.[9]

Within the Conference there was a brief hiatus in the discussion of the Russian problem following the dispatch of the Nansen proposal in April. But as soon as word reached Paris that Kolchak was approaching Kazan and Samara, interest flared up again. Since the Big Four and, more especially, some of their chief advisers were always prone to exaggerate the victories of the Whites and the defeats of the Reds, the developments on the Siberian front filled them with confidence. It looked as if the policy of providing material, technical, and financial aid to the Russian counterrevolutionaries was beginning to pay off at last. To be sure, the British sent relief units to Archangel and instead of withdrawing these refreshed forces London ordered them to march toward Kotlas, in the hope of linking up with Kolchak. Even so, the issue before the Conference was not the allocation of additional matériel, cadres, or infantry units.

Rather, the Big Four—in this instance America, Britain, France, and Japan—felt called upon to throw their diplomatic and moral weight behind a promising onslaught against Lenin. They would do so not only in order to help the enterprise but also for fear that if it succeeded without their blessings their influence with the successor regime would be damaged seriously, possibly to Germany's advantage. At the same time, whereas reactionaries and conservatives had no qualms about the nature of the post-Leninist regime, under Socialist pressure all Wilsonians caviled at the prospect of an imperial and autocratic restoration in Russia.

On May 7, a few hours before the draft-treaty was handed to the Germans, Lloyd George urged the Council of Four to turn to the Russian problem at the first possible moment.

> There had been a curious collapse of the Bolsheviks . . . and Kolchak had made such progress that he might soon be in a position to join hands with the forces based on Archangel. On the other

[8] *Le Figaro,* May 4, 17, 25, 26, 30, and June 6, 1919.
[9] *Le Temps,* May 17, 1919.

hand, it was possible that he might march direct on Moscow. . . .
Hence, in a short time the Allied and Associated Powers might be
faced with a Kolchak Government in Moscow.

Lloyd George went on to say that both Chaikovsky and Paderewski
considered Kolchak as nothing more than a soldier, were suspicious of
pro-German influences at Denikin's headquarters, and were anxious
about the rebirth of an imperial Russia. Actually, he himself was more
afraid of the rebirth of an imperial Russia than of Bolshevism. In any
case, the Allies should give thought to "imposing conditions on Kolchak and Denikin" before furnishing further supplies.

While Clemenceau claimed to be equally fearful of an imperial and
of a Bolshevik Russia, Wilson agreed with Lloyd George that the revival
of an imperial Russia was the greater of the two dangers. And he, too,
suggested that the Allies make their continued support contingent on a
"program of reform."[1]

During the last week of April the American Delegation began to
debate the advisability of provisionally recognizing Kolchak. Some
officials were opposed because "the Omsk Government seemed to be a
military dictatorship." In an interview with one of these officials Kerensky confirmed this diagnosis, warning that Kolchak would "inaugurate
a regime hardly less sanguinary and repressive than that of the Bolsheviks." The mission asked Polk and Ambassador Morris about chances
of inducing the Admiral to promise to summon a constituent assembly.
Wilson himself eventually inquired what "kind of men and influences
[were] surrounding Kolchak . . . and was he strong and liberal
enough to control them in the right direction?"[2]

Polk was confident that once aware that recognition "was at hand"
the Omsk government would "willingly issue a satisfactory statement"
with regard to a constituent assembly, civil liberties, property rights,
and the protection of foreign interests. But Morris was more reluctant,
having advised against provisional recognition as recently as April 12.
He would have preferred to wait until the Kolchak regime "showed
more willingness to define its purposes and policy and less subserviency
to reactionary influences." Still, if Britain and France pressed for
immediate conditional recognition, the U.S. as well as Japan should go
along, since "unity of action in Siberia was more important than the
character of the action."[3]

On May 9 Wilson reopened the Russian question in the Council of
Four. He reported that the Omsk government was impatient with U. S.
representatives in Siberia because unlike their British and French

[1] Minutes of the session of May 7, 1919 (a.m.), in *F.R.,P.C.,1919*, V, 497–8. Cf. Paul
Mantoux: *Les Délibérations du conseil des quatre*, I, 505–6.
[2] See *F.R.,Russia,1919*, 336–8, 349.
[3] Ibid., 339–41.

counterparts they did not support Kolchak. Wilson conceded that his government did not "believe" in Kolchak. However, he also realized that given the civil war and the danger of collision between U. S. and White troops Washington had only two alternatives: siding with Kolchak or withdrawing altogether. Lloyd George proposed that this question be resolved in the context of a common Allied policy which was urgently needed now that Kolchak was advancing so rapidly. Whereas Lloyd George approvingly reported that Chaikovsky was of the view that the Allies could extract conditions from the Admiral, Wilson doubted that Kolchak could be forced to abide by them. Nevertheless, the President agreed to start the search for a common Russian policy by hearing Chaikovsky the next day, thereby indicating that he was reluctant to withdraw and leave Siberia to the Western Allies, let alone to the Japanese.[4]

When the former head of the Archangel government was introduced Wilson told him that the Allies were taking up the Russian question because of Kolchak's "growing strength and rapid advance westward" and because they were fearful that Kolchak's leadership "would result in a policy of reaction and military power." Wilson and Lloyd George took turns probing Chaikovsky's assessment of the "liberality" of Kolchak, Denikin, and Yudenich.

Chaikovksy was prepared to reassure the Big Four. Granted, Kolchak's position on land reform was not all that clear, but in Siberia "the land question was not nearly as acute as in European Russia." As for the constituent assembly, what more could one ask than Kolchak's recent promise to resign "immediately there was a chance of getting" one. Besides, he kept "announcing democratic measures" because except for the military there were no reactionaries in Siberia and "most of his Ministers were former Socialists." With regard to the border states, it would be well to remember that should they gain independence, they would be so weak economically that they would "inevitably fall into dependence on someone else." Certainly, since the Finns were claiming Russian territories they should not liberate Petrograd without Russian forces at their side. In addition, he and his friends could see to it that Yudenich maintained democracy there. All in all, the White leaders were likely to strive to give Russia a constitutional monarchy, which he was confident would soon be succeeded by a federated republic.[5]

Wilson was not impressed by this testimony and he refused to depend on the advice of British and French military leaders in Siberia, most of whom were partisans of Kolchak. He told the Council that he

---

[4] Minutes of the session of May 9, 1919 (p.m.), in *F.R.,P.C.,1919*, V, 528–30; and Mantoux: *Délibérations*, II, 16–19.

[5] Minutes of the session of May 10, 1919 (a.m.), in *F.R.,P.C.,1919*, V, 544–51; and Mantoux: *Délibérations*, II, 27–31.

felt the need for a "fresh view," and for this purpose he would ask Ambassador Morris to proceed to Kolchak's headquarters. Morris was instructed to secure "official and definite assurances" with regard to land reform, suffrage, and a constituent assembly; he was also to "learn as definitely as possible the influences that Kolchak was under." At the suggestion of the British, Morris was asked to check his own findings with Colonel John Ward, the Commander of the Middlesex Battalion, who was a Labour Member of Parliament; and with Colonel R. A. Johnson of the Fifth Hants, who was a former editor of the *Westminster Gazette*. The Anglo-Americans could think of no way of getting a reappraisal of Denikin, which suited Clemenceau, who had kept quiet all this time.[6]

At this point, on May 20, the Big Four had Chicherin's reply to Nansen before them. Clemenceau was especially indignant that Lenin should set such stiff conditions for the acceptance of an overly generous proposal at a time when the Bolsheviks were "going down hill." But above all he wanted to make sure that no conciliatory step be taken which would undercut the current momentum and élan of the Whites.

Wilson and Lloyd George had a few pangs of conscience, having strayed so far from the Nansen, let alone the Bullitt course. The President recognized that Lenin was "perfectly correct" in claiming that instead of pressuring Kolchak and Denikin into stopping their campaign the Allies were supporting them. He even admitted that "if supplies were stopped" the counterrevolutionaries could not carry on. Besides, originally American troops had gone into Siberia to get the Czechs out and not to intervene in a civil war. Half apologetically Lloyd George repeated the standard rationalization that whatever the original objectives, the Allies could not leave those who had supported them in a lurch. He had to confess, however, that the Allies had little confidence in those who were "trying to squash . . . [that] lunatic revolution." Both he and Clemenceau then endorsed Wilson's proposal that the Allies secure pledges from the major White groups in exchange for continuing assistance. Philip Kerr was charged with preparing a draft-letter, using as a guide a statement prepared by Kerensky's exile group.[7]

In fact, the idea of securing pledges from the White governments was being promoted by most if not all *émigrés* in Paris. Right-wing exiles advocated guarantees just strong enough to induce Wilson and Lloyd George to recognize Kolchak and continue aid. On the other hand, the *émigrés* of democratic, liberal, and Socialist persuasion urged the Big Four not to be satisfied with vague and empty promises.

---

[6] Minutes of the sessions of May 10 (p.m.), 14 (p.m.), and 17 (p.m.), 1919, in *F.R.,P.C.,1919*, V, 560, 608, 687–8; and Mantoux: *Délibérations*, II, 36–7. For the instructions to Morris see *F.R.,Russia,1919*, 349.

[7] Minutes of the session of May 20, 1919 (a.m.), in *F.R.,P.C.,1919*, V, 734–48.

Through its major organ the Union for the Regeneration of Russia called for an *union sacrée* of all counterrevolutionaries behind Kolchak and Denikin. The Union argued that precisely because both leaders and their entourages were decidedly reactionary, it was up to the Allies to democratize the counterrevolution, to take it out of reactionary hands. The *émigrés* denied that there was any inevitability to the polarization of Red Bolshevism and White reaction, provided the Allies made it clear that their aid both now and after the overthrow of Lenin was contingent on the promise that an all-Russian constituent assembly would be elected by universal suffrage. The nondemocratic anti-Bolshevik governments would have to meet this demand since without Allied aid they could neither fight nor survive. Needless to say, these advocates of a counterrevolutionary political truce, who supported the Russian Political Conference, were eager to avoid spelling out the political and economic planks of their platform for fear of splitting their united front and of exposing their conservative as well as imperialist natures.[8] Even after the overthrow of Béla Kun led to a White terror in Hungary the Union insisted that a counterrevolution need not lead to reaction. "Such a triumph of reaction was not a historical law or fatality . . . and the Russian Revolution need not repeat the vulgar rhythm of other revolutions, as if it were a theatrical play rather than a living tragedy."[9]

The Ligue Républicaine Russe, of which Kerensky was the most prominent spokesman, at first refused to throw its weight behind Kolchak and Denikin, even as they seemed slated for victory. Quite unrealistically these "democratic" counterrevolutionaries—Mensheviks, Social Revolutionaries, and Cadets—urged "the restoration of a genuinely democratic government, based upon a coalition of all parties who stood for the principles of the March Revolution of 1917 (i.e., excluding the Bolshevists at one extreme and the monarchical reactionaries on the other)."[1] In their view military force alone could not prevail over the Bolsheviks. To fight this civil war effectively the "demagogic ideals of the Bolsheviks would have to be countered by a genuine ideal of social justice . . . , by an essentially reformist Wilsonianism."[2]

The ideological pronouncements of the Russian Political Conference simply would not do, both because they were excessively vague and because of the political background of their sponsors. The Ligue and Kerensky refused to trust Sazonov, "that last-minute convert to democracy" who before the war had been associated with "that hang-

<hr>

[8] See *La Russie Démocratique,* April 23, May 15, and June 12, 1919.
[9] See the article "The Law of Reaction" by Delevsky, Secretary General of the Union for the Regeneration of Russia, in *La Russie Démocratique,* August 11, 1919, 4.
[1] Memorandum of a conversation with Kerensky by an U.S. official, May 4, 1919, cited in *F.R., Russia, 1919,* 337–8.
[2] *La République Russe,* April 15, 1919.

man Stolypin, that scoundrel Chtcheglovitov, and that debauched Rasputin." All alike had countered the demands of prewar reformists with the well-known phrase "first pacification and then reform." Presently they were dishing up another version of this same slogan: "let us first destroy Bolshevism and then worry about the shape of the future." No, unlike in international war, in civil war there could be no political truce, particularly since the forces that originally raised and now controlled Kolchak would never relax their grip of their own free will. A few liberal personalities like Chaikovsky and V. Bourtsev could at best spread a thin democratic veneer over this blatantly retrograde enterprise.[3]

Even so, as the campaign in favor of Kolchak gained momentum, Kerensky and his faction abandoned their rigid stand to become ardent champions of conditional recognition. The American Delegation became their preferred channel to the Council of Four. On May 4 Kerensky presented an outline of pledges to be exacted to a U.S. official; on May 14 he left a letter for the President with Colonel House; and on May 19 Wilson told the Council of Four that Kerensky's proposal that Kolchak pledge himself "to a certain progressive policy" in exchange for continuing aid "provided the rudiments of a policy."[4]

On May 21, through *Humanité*, these private representations were supplemented by a public "appeal to world Democracy," thereby strengthening the opposition to unqualified recognition. This manifesto called on the Allies to declare categorically that they would abandon any provisional government that refused to "undertake to summon a constituent assembly of all Russia as soon as civil war ends, in the interim holding elections of legislative regional assemblies on a truly democratic basis." To demonstrate the seriousness of their purpose, the Allies should send a special mission, including delegates of organized labor and Socialism, to interpret their intentions. These policy recommendations were reinforced by the warning that should Russia fall prey to reaction she would head up a drive to transform the League of Nations into a Sainte Alliance.[5]

This manifesto forced the issue of recognition into the open, particularly since it was widely assumed that by holding out for pledges, Wilson was trying to postpone action. The *Temps* asked "why the Allied governments should ask a Russian government to forget the war in favor of domestic politics when they themselves had not held elections in wartime?" The primary objective was to overthrow the Bolshevik autocracy. Hence, Kolchak could not be expected to promise anything beyond the free election of a constituent assembly "as promptly as

[3] *La République Russe*, April 15, May 3, and June 5, 1919.
[4] *F.R., Russia, 1919*, 338; House Diary, May 14, 1919; Minutes of session of Council of Four, May 19, 1919 (p.m.), in *F.R.,P.C.,1919*, V, 725.
[5] See also *La République Russe*, May 22, 1919.

possible." Meanwhile France should step up her assistance. The Russian field simply could not be left to the British who were taking a commanding lead in the Baltic and at Archangel. Indeed, "why was Great Britain, notably Churchill, liberating Petrograd when France could not save Odessa?" In pressing for the recognition of Kolchak, France should not dictate internal policies. Instead, she should persuade the Russians that she sincerely favored the independence and integrity of their nation and was eager to help prepare the ground for an understanding between Russia and her two neighbors, Poland and Rumania, which were tied to France by special interests.[6]

Jacques Bainville was still more impatient than the *Temps* with delays and preconditions. He advised Kolchak to "say amen to all Allied conditions" and then do as he pleased. Russia was far away and no one would ask him for an accounting. Besides, it was not up to France to tell her former ally which form of government to live by. And it might also be well to keep in mind that the day Russia recovered "she would not ask for democratic guarantees but for evidence that her national unity was and would be respected."[7] Similarly, the *Morning Post* did not believe "in forcing our particular brand of political religion upon parts of the world in which democracy was not indigenous." The enthusiasts of Russian liberalism had had their chance: their drive for constitutionalism had turned into a revolution of violence. Judging by her history, Russia was best suited for "a strong but benevolent despotism."[8]

Against this background of mounting public debate Kerr completed the draft-memorandum for Kolchak. Since Denikin and Miller had meanwhile declared their allegiance to the Admiral, this memorandum was also expected to be acceptable to them. Actually, like Kerensky, Kerr skirted the issue of recognition: the most he would promise was "the continuation of assistance" in exchange for a host of constitutional, political, and diplomatic pledges. This formula put Wilson in a quandry, since except for helping the Czechs and guarding the Trans-Siberian railway the U.S. provided no aid. Clemenceau was equally reticent, France's contribution having been minimal. Britain was the principal source of supply: Kerr's original draft quite properly claimed that to date England had provided £50 million worth of war matériel and provisions to the various anti-Bolshevik governments of Russia.[9] In any case, Wilson and Clemenceau asked for time to consult their advisers about the proposed formula.[1]

[6] *Le Temps,* May 23 and 28, 1919.
[7] *L'Action Française,* May 28, 1919.
[8] *Morning Post,* May 25 and 27, 1919.
[9] See *Cost of Naval and Military Operations in Russia, from the Date of the Armistice to the 31st July 1919,* Command Paper 307 (1919).
[1] Minutes of the session of May 23, 1919 (p.m.), including the text of Kerr's first draft, in *F.R.,P.C.,1919,* V, 901–3 and 909–11; and Mantoux: *Délibérations,* II, 190–2.

In the second draft Kerr wanted to remind Kolchak that since the Armistice all the Allies, including Japan, had provided munitions and supplies in excess of 100 million pounds sterling. But at Lloyd George's own suggestion the words "at a very considerable cost" were substituted for this specific figure. Concern for Allied public opinion prompted this change just as it also led the Big Four not to hold out any hope for volunteers.[2]

What, then, did the Allies say to Kolchak? They once again professed to have no inclination to interfere in the internal affairs of Russia, though they were interested in seeing peace restored there. Since the Soviet government had turned down both the Prinkipo invitation and the Nansen proposal they were convinced that it was not possible to achieve this objective by dealing with Lenin. The Allies were disposed, therefore, to continue to assist Kolchak and his associates on the following conditions: that immediately upon reaching Moscow they would either organize the "free, secret, and democratic" election of a constituent assembly or summon the Assembly of 1917 as a stopgap; that until then they would allow free elections "for all local and legally constituted assemblies such as municipalities and Zemstvos"; that they would "not revive the special privileges of any class or order" nor restore the "former land system"; that they would support civil and religious liberty, and would not "reintroduce the regime which the revolution had destroyed"; that they would recognize the independence of Finland and Poland; that Russia's relations with the border territories would be settled "in consultation and cooperation" with the League; that Russia's international debts would be honored; and that they "would undertake to form a single government and army command" as soon as possible.[3]

In his answer Kolchak very shrewdly made most of his promises contingent on the wish of the Russian people, as expressed through a constituent assembly. Even though he refused to reconvene the Assembly of 1917, he assured the Allies that his "first thought at the moment when the Bolsheviks were definitely crushed would be to fix the date for elections . . . on the basis of universal suffrage." This new representative body would have to ratify all questions involving modifications of the territorial frontiers and of external relations. Meanwhile, his government would confirm the independence of Poland and was disposed to recognize the *de facto* government of Finland, both subject to final ratification by the assembly. Likewise, the assembly would have to ratify the autonomy—not independence—which would be worked out

[2] Minutes of the session of May 24, 1919 (p.m.), including text of Kerr's second draft, in *F.R.,P.C.,1919*, VI, 15–19 and 22–23.

[3] For the final text of the message to Kolchak, dated May 26, 1919, see ibid., 34–6.

with Estonia, Latvia, Lithuania, the Caucasian and Transcaspian countries, and Bessarabia.

With regard to internal politics Kolchak repeated that there "could not be a return to the regime which existed in Russia before February 1917." But he would not go beyond this general assurance either on the agrarian question or on the political regime to be applied in the White-controlled and liberated territories. On both foreign and domestic questions he claimed to "speak in the name of all National Russia."[4]

Without much debate the Big Five advised Kolchak and his associates of their willingness to continue extending aid because the "tone" of his reply was "in substantial agreement with the propositions which they had made, and . . . contained satisfactory assurances for the freedom, self-government, and peace of the Russian people and their neighbors."[5] Much to Baron Makino's chagrin, the Big Four would not go so far as to extend *de facto* recognition to the Omsk government either over the Siberian territories or over the whole of Russia. Perhaps the powers would have been less reticent if in mid-June Kolchak's troops had still been advancing toward Moscow and Kotlas. But by this time his thrust had failed and Denikin's exploits as well as the encirclement of Petrograd became the new hope of all anti-Bolsheviks.

Even so the London *Times* regretted the excessive timidity of this new Russian policy, particularly since Kolchak's reservations were perfectly constitutional. On the other hand, the *Daily Mail* thought that the promise of continuing assistance was a "far more valuable pledge . . . than any official act of recognition, unbacked by active support." As for the *Morning Post,* it was scandalized by this ill-concealed interference in Russia's internal affairs, which was due to the Big Four's fear of offending the Allied Socialists. All the Allies should ask for was a determined pursuit of the Bolsheviks. It would be time enough to talk of other matters once a provisional government held Moscow and Red rule was ended.[6]

In France the *Temps* explained that while the Allies had no right to dictate Russia's domestic arrangements, any discussion of territorial issues would be premature. First Russia had to be liberated from Bolshevism. Meanwhile no Frenchman should ever forget that "the invasion of East Prussia helped win the battle of the Marne." The editorialists of this prestigious daily agreed with Pertinax that France should use her good offices to smooth out Russia's relations with Poland and Rumania while seeking to influence all the other border provinces, including Finland, to accept at least Russian suzerainty. In any case,

---

[4] For the full text of Kolchak's reply see ibid., 321–3.
[5] For the full text of this reply, also drafted by Kerr, see ibid., 356.
[6] *The Times* (London), June 14, 1919; *Daily Mail* (Paris), June 14, 1919; *Morning Post,* June 19, 1919.

nothing final should be decided until after Russia "had resumed her place among the great powers." Bainville doubted the wisdom of the entire exchange. Even though the only Russia they ever knew had been autocratic, bureaucratic, and centralized, the Allies proposed to transform her, by fiat, into "a democratic and liberal as well as federative nation."[7]

This was precisely the transformation that Wilson and Europe's forces of movement craved. The *Populaire* sneered that Plehve, Stolypin, Stürmer, and Sazonov could have drafted Kolchak's reply: "the vanquished of Ufa" accepted the constituent assembly much as Nicolas II had accepted the Duma. Moreover, he put off the fixing of all frontiers and reserved the right to reimpose Russian domination on Finland.[8] The *République Russe* was equally critical, indicting the Council of Four for declaring war on the Great Russian Revolution.

> The recognition of Kolchak is the logical culmination of the Quai d'Orsay's Russian policy. . . . The Quai knows very well what Kolchak is up to, Sazonov being there to provide information. . . . The government which loaned the Tsars its police and its bourgeoisie's capital and left Kerensky to flounder in the worst of difficulties could not have done otherwise than to continue dealing with Kolchak.

A possible alternative would have been to stop all fighting and allow those parts of Russia that were not under Soviet control to become demonstration areas of political, economic, and social development. Incidentally, the French censor would not clear the issue of the *République Russe* in which this editorial appeared, so that the Ligue des Droits de l'Homme put it out under the title *Nos Libertés.*[9]

Within a few weeks Bourtsev congratulated the Allies for putting an end to Béla Kun and called on them quickly to "do for Russia what they had done for Hungary."[1] This appeal vindicated Kerensky and his associates. It was true, then, that the Bolsheviks could only be overthrown at the cost of large-scale looting, massive pogroms, a fierce White terror, and the enthronement—by Allied missions—of a liberator who for a brief spell would pose as a democrat.[2] Indeed, in revolutionary times the moderate middle was in disrepute. Russia's moderates were being told that there was no choice other than that between Lenin and Kolchak.

[7] *Le Temps,* June 14, 1919; *l'Echo de Paris,* June 13, 1919; *l'Action Française,* June 19, 1919.
[8] *Le Populaire,* June 15, 1919.
[9] *La République Russe (Nos Libertés),* July 1, 1919.
[1] *La Cause Commune,* August 9, 1919.
[2] *La République Russe,* September 13, 1919.

24

Overthrow of Béla Kun

THE UNEXPECTED and successful Hungarian counterblow came to the attention of the Peace Conference on June 5, when the Big Four asked their military advisers to assess its implications.[1] Within two days, and before these advisers had completed their study, Clemenceau alerted the Council of Four that after finding out that the Rumanians "were being held back," the Magyars had concentrated their forces against the Czechs, who were in full retreat into Slovakia. Under the impression that the fall of Pressburg (Bratislava) was imminent the Council authorized Clemenceau to rush a minatory wire to the government in Budapest. In this wire he claimed, rather disingenuously, that this "unjustified attack" came at a time when Hungarian delegates were "on the point of being summoned" to present their views to the Conference; that the Allies had twice stopped the Rumanian armies after they had crossed the Armistice line and the neutral zone and had "prevented them from continuing their march on Budapest"; and that the Allies had also "stopped the Serbian and French Armies on the Southern Hungarian front." Almost as a *quid pro quo*, Béla Kun's government was asked to stop immediately the attack and reply within forty-eight hours, otherwise the Allies would take "extreme measures . . . to make their injunctions respected."[2]

Monday morning, June 9, the Big Four met with their military advisers.[3] General Sir Henry Wilson bluntly indicted the Czechs for having been the first to overstep their boundary, with the result that the Hungarians, who were striking back, now had a good chance of beating them. Lloyd George elaborated on the sequence of events, in that he charged the Czechs with advancing to occupy Hungary's last remaining coal districts only after the Rumanians had crossed Hungarian borders

[1] *F.R.,P.C.,1919*, VI (June 5, 1919, a.m.), 189.
[2] Council of Four, Session of June 7, 1919 (p.m.), in *F.R.,P.C.,1919*, VI, 240-1 and 246-7; and Paul Mantoux: *Les Délibérations du conseil des quatre*, II, 339.
[3] This discussion is based on *F.R.,P.C.,1919*, VI, 254-61.

once again. Even after General Belin warned that Pressburg was in danger, both the Prime Minister and Wilson emphasized that the Rumanians and Czechs "were wholly to blame" and that it was the "duty of the Council to be fair, even to their enemies." They proposed that the Allies suspend their heavy military and economic aid to the Rumanians until such time as they returned to and stayed within their lines. When Clemenceau interjected that they had stopped their advance on orders from the Supreme Council, Lloyd George snapped back that "it would be more correct to say that they had been stopped by Hungarian forces." In any case, he was quite sure that the Hungarians "would withdraw from Czechoslovakia if the Rumanians could be made to withdraw from Hungary."

Meanwhile, there was renewed pressure for the quick strangulation of the Soviet regime, especially now that Béla Kun had confounded his detractors with this bold military stroke. The *Temps* would settle for nothing less than his overthrow.[4] Alonzo Taylor warned Hoover that the Hungarian success was "actually and potentially much greater than openly indicated." At the same time, T. C. Gregory urged his chief to recommend that there be "an immediate combined advance from all quarters"; that the Allies promise foodstuffs and coal "as soon as the city of Budapest was taken or the present government ousted"; and that this policy be promptly executed "to support a new and more conservative government when it goes in." Hoover forwarded these dispatches from his principal lieutenants to President Wilson, with an unqualified supporting note.

> I must agree with them that unless something can be done to the Hungarian situation and at once, the adjacent orderly Governments will fall into chaos. As much as I dislike to suggest it, I can see but one solution, and that is for the French troops which are now in Yugoslavia to advance on Budapest without delay. Otherwise, it appears to us, that both the Czechoslovakian and the German-Austrian Governments will surely fall.

The President assured Hoover that the Big Four realized "how very critical the whole matter" was, but that they were "deeply perplexed" about what to do.[5]

On June 10 Brătianu and Misu as well as Kramař and Beneš appeared before the Big Four to explain their armies' transgressions.[6] As expected, Brătianu was arrogant and unyielding. He once again argued that the "Bolshevik movement in Hungary had been organized

[4] *Le Temps,* June 11, 1919.
[5] Hoover to Wilson, June 9, 1919, and Wilson to Hoover, June 10, 1919, in Wilson Papers, VIII A:60. Two days earlier Lewis Strauss had sent the same letter from Gregory to the President.
[6] This discussion of the session of June 10, 1919 (p.m.), is based on *F.R.,P.C.,1919,* VI, 281–9.

just as much by Károlyi as by Béla Kun." Such was his justification for the successive advances which eventually took his troops to the Tisza, "the only decent military line of defense," to be occupied until peace was signed.

After fully supporting Brătianu's indictment of Károlyi, the Czech Premier claimed to have "no knowledge of any aggressive movements" bv Czech troops, who had merely defended themselves against the Bolshevik movement. Actually, like the Rumanians, the Czechs deserved credit for having ignored the pleas of the Hungarian *bourgeoisie* "to advance and crush Bolshevism." He urged the Allies to order the Red Army to stop and to supply his armed forces with arms and ammunition, which they would use exclusively for defensive purposes.

The Anglo-American statesmen countered that it "would take a great deal to convince [them] that Károlyi had encouraged the Bolshevik movement." They went on to charge that predatory military moves were powerful stimulants of Boshevism. After being told that the Czech and Rumanian delegations had not been officially informed of their permanent boundaries with Hungary, they were asked to confer forthwith with the Council of Foreign Ministers. Once these lines were fixed, all parties, including the Hungarians, would have to withdraw behind them.

The following afternoon the Foreign Ministers recommended to their chiefs that the Hungarian-Rumanian frontier, as adopted on May 12, be accepted, and that the Hungarian-Czech border also be accepted, subject to a small change incorporating the "junction of the Korpona railway with the Losoncz railway line" into Czechoslovakia.[7] Clemenceau doubted that the Allies could induce the Rumanians to withdraw behind lines unacceptable to them. But there was no time for debate. The Hungarians had to be stopped. Hence, in spite of this rather ominous caveat, the Big Four agreed to notify all three governments of their permanent boundaries, at the same time insisting on the cessation of hostilities and withdrawal behind the new lines.

Balfour was asked to draft the three telegrams which the Big Four approved and sent out on the thirteenth, over Clemenceau's signature.[8] In the wire to Budapest, Béla Kun was given four days in which to start withdrawing behind the permanent Hungarian-Czech line, otherwise the Allies held themselves "free to advance on Budapest." But he was also assured that once his troops had evacuated Czechoslovakia, Rumanian troops would "withdraw from Hungarian territory."

This message from the Peace Conference, which was a vast improvement over that of June 9, caused a sensation in Budapest. In the

---

[7] This discussion of the session of the Council of Four of June 12, 1919 (p.m.), is based on ibid., 351–2, 358–60.

[8] For this approval as well as the full text of the telegrams see ibid., 399, 412–13. Cf. Mantoux: *Délibérations*, II, 415–16.

government as well as in the Workers' and Soldiers' Councils Béla Kun instantly argued in favor of accepting Clemenceau's terms, in large part because the threat of a march on Budapest struck him as real and also because the Red Army was strained to the limit. Admittedly, he had opposed a similar deal when offered by Smuts. But conditions had changed, and he accepted Liebknecht's old adage that Communists "must be prepared to change tactics 24 times in 24 hours." In brief, the time for a Brest Litovsk was at hand. During this breathing space revolutionary conditions would develop in the surrounding countries; dissension within the Entente would grow; the harsh peace terms would promote radicalism in Germany and Austria; and the regime could consolidate its political, economic, and military position. For the Social Democrats Kunfi also advocated an accommodation with the Entente, though primarily in order to get on with internal reconstruction and to escape the pressures of the *levée en masse*. Alone the left-Communists wanted the government to ignore Paris, take advantage of the favorable military situation, and gamble on the Entente's lack of unity for a concerted attack on Budapest.[9]

In any case, whatever Béla Kun's reasons, the overwhelming majority of the Left cheered him on in his widely publicized negotiations with the Big Four, negotiations that suggested a measure of recognition for the Soviet Republic. On June 16 he wired Clemenceau that in response to his telegram the Hungarian forces had ceased all hostilities and were preparing their withdrawal, pending arrangements to be made directly between his military authorities and the Czech and Rumanian commanders. He used this occasion to renew his proposal that all the successor states meet in a special conference to discuss and settle their common problems.[1]

When this wire reached Paris, the Big Four instructed General Bliss to work out the arrangements for the troop withdrawals in consultation with the Czech and Rumanian delegates.[2] Beneš refused outright to allow his military chief to have any negotiations with his Hungarian counterpart: he was "absolutely persuaded that the reply of the Hungarian Bolsheviks was not in good faith." The Czech Foreign Minister convinced Bliss that since four French generals were in command of the Czech Army in Slovakia that entire front was controlled by Allied officers! Accordingly, Marshal Foch, the Supreme Commander, was asked to issue orders to General Pellé, his representative in Prague and

---

[9] For the full text of Béla Kun's speech of June 19, 1919, to the National Congress of the Workers' and Soldiers' Councils, see Béla Kun: *La République hongroise des conseils* (Budapest: Cornive; 1962), 189–206. See also Wilhelm Böhm: *Im Kreuzfeuer zweier Revolutionen* (Munich: Verlag für Kulturpolitik; 1924), 472–4; and Von Fürstenberg to Foreign Ministry, June 18 and 20, 1919, G.F.M.
[1] For the full text of this telegram see *F.R.,P.C.,1919*, VI, 518–20.
[2] Ibid., 513–14; and Mantoux: *Délibérations*, II, 440.

Commander in Chief of the Czech Army, to make all necessary arrangements.[3]

General Pellé informed the Hungarian government on June 22 that at a date about to be set it would be given 72 hours in which to evacuate all territory south of its northern frontiers, following which the Czechs would advance to their southern borders. Böhm tried to get a postponement for the start of this evacuation until after Pellé or Clemenceau had provided explicit guarantees that the Rumanians would follow suit by withdrawing their troops. No additional guarantee beyond the original wire of June 13 was ever received, and the Allies ignored Béla Kun's request for a conference of the successor states. Even so, the Red Army began to evacuate Slovakia on June 30.[4]

In the meantime, on June 20, Béla Kun received a telegram in which Lenin, "in his own name," approved of his negotiations with the Allies.

> These negotiations must be taken up and continued and it is necessary to seize every opportunity to achieve either a temporary armistice or peace, so that the people should be able to catch their breath. But do not trust the Entente Powers for an instant. They are deceiving you and only seek to gain time in order to better strangle both you and us.

Lenin rightly suggested that *both* sides had need of a temporary breathing spell. In his reply, Béla Kun left no doubt that he, too, was aware of this.

> I am very proud to be one of your best pupils, but I think that in one point I am superior to you, namely, in the question of *mala fides*. I think I know the Entente very well. I know that they will fight us to the end. In this war, only a state of armistice can occur but never peace. This is an out and out fight.

This exchange of telegrams was intercepted by the British and the Austrians. On July 5, Hoover dramatically read them to the Council of Four as irrefutable evidence of Boshevik villainy and duplicity.[5]

The Food Tsar had long ago decided that Bolshevism was a deadly scourge; and he and his policy proposals justified Lenin and Béla Kun in their suspicions. On July 1, at the request of the Supreme Economic Council, Hoover prepared a memorandum for submission to the chief delegates. In it he argued that because of Hungary's "special geographic and economic position . . . the whole economic destiny of

---

[3] *F.R.,P.C.,1919*, VI, 550–7; and Mantoux: *Délibérations*, II, 465.

[4] *F.R.,P.C.,1919*, VI, 706–7; Mantoux: *Délibérations*, II, 440, 525; Böhm: *Im Kreuzfeuer*, 477.

[5] This interchange of telegrams is cited in Béla Kun: *La République hongroise des conseils*, 209; and *F.R.,P.C.,1919*, VII, 22.

the surrounding States was almost absolutely in [Béla Kun's] hands."
After consulting his officials throughout the old Austrian Empire, he
concluded that there were four courses to choose from: military occupation and expulsion of the Soviet government; economic negotiations
through commissions which would raise the blockade without recognizing Béla Kun; economic agreements with Kun together with policing by
Allied troops; and full recognition.[6]

Significantly, when meeting with the American Commissioners,
Hoover came out vigorously for this first alternative, possibly because
Wilson was on his way back to Washington.

> The time had come when the Allied and Associated Powers would
> either have to negotiate with Béla Kun or else throw him out by
> force of arms. All of the British and American economic and food
> relief experts were strongly of the opinion that he should be thrown
> out. . . . Hoover was convinced that the two French divisions at
> present in the southeast of Europe were fully capable of accomplish-
> ing this act.

Borrowing a word from Wilson's letter of June 10, he conceded that it
would be "inopportune" to allow the Czechs, Yugoslavs, or Rumanians
to do the job.[7]

When the heads of delegations met on July 5, they had Hoover's
memorandum before them.[8] Moreover, Hoover himself was there to
press direct military intervention, insisting that it was no longer just a
question of Hungary blocking the economic rehabilitation of Central
and Southeastern Europe. There was also a political aspect. Bolshevik
ideas were infecting the working classes throughout this area. Béla
Kun's government was spreading this infection by "sending a great
deal of money or sending Bolshevik missionaries to industrial centers
outside Hungary." Hereafter the regime "was not likely" to refrain
from spreading its theories abroad with "military force," Czechoslovakia and Austria being the "next probable" victims. Hoover concluded
that of the four possible policies, "no doubt the military occupation of
Budapest would be the best."

Rather surprisingly, Arthur Balfour readily agreed that the case
had to "be approached from the military side." But the British Foreign
Secretary was interested not in the economic revival of the Danubian
basin, but in compliance with the Conference's instructions by the
different parties to the Hungarian imbroglio. Brătianu had just told
him privately that because the Hungarians were withdrawing their
troops from Slovakia and were continuing to build up their army, the

---

[6] Hoover to Lansing, July 1, 1919, cited in *F.R.,P.C.,1919*, VII, 29–30, and X, 460–61.
[7] Minutes of meeting of U.S. Commissioners Plenipotentiary, July 1, 1919, cited in
F.R.,P.C.,1919, XI, 259–60.
[8] This discussion of the meeting of the heads of delegations, July 5, 1919 (p.m.), is
based on *F.R.,P.C.,1919*, VII, 20–8.

Rumanians were in greater danger than before. Therefore they "could not and would not retire from the Tisza, . . . which they could defend, . . . until after the Hungarians had disarmed." Balfour thought there was much force in this argument, reminding the Council that under the Armistice Hungary was limited to six divisions. In brief, the Allies should order Béla Kun to abide by the Armistice, after which the Rumanians would retire. He hoped that the threat of force would do the trick. But if not, it would be necessary to take military action with the "Rumanian, Czech, Serbian, and French troops at hand."[9]

Next it was Clemenceau's turn. The situation reminded him of La Fontaine's fable about an assembly of rats which was agreed to bell a cat but knew not how to go about it. He agreed with all that had been said thus far, including Mr. Balfour's proposal. There was only one point he wished to stress.

> France was demobilizing and could not stop the process. . . . The French Army would [soon] be on a peace footing. The French Chamber was resolutely opposed to intervention in Russia. He thought the Chamber was right, seeing the results hitherto obtained; a million or so was being thrown away on the expedition in Siberia. . . . If Parliament, therefore, declines to fight Bolshevism in Russia, it would equally refuse to fight it in Hungary. . . .
>
> What troops did Mr. Balfour mean to use to coerce the Hungarians? He had mentioned Czechs, Rumanians and [Serbs]. . . . They would require money. He for one could not supply any. . . . [Besides] he had some doubts about the capacity of the Czechs to fight the Hungarians. The Rumanians might or might not be willing. At the present time they seemed considerably dissatisfied with the Peace Conference. There were no British or American troops available. French and Italian troops therefore seemed called upon to do the work. He must state clearly that for his part he could not undertake it. . . .
>
> The fact was that the peoples of the Entente countries were anxious to settle the crisis more quickly than was really possible. After the vast upheaval of the War and the pulverization of military forces, and, on top of it, the universal inclination towards social revolution, it was hardly possible to produce order in short time. . . . The evil had spread. Italy . . . had been shaken up. Great Britain and France had had their troubles. There had been disaffection in the French Navy and even in the Army. The world was sick of fighting. The Conference had therefore to deal with revolutions in military power, alterations of frontiers, and social revolutions inspired by no ideas. . . . All intervention to assist [the Russian

---

[9] At this time Britain was reported to be taking an interest in petroleum rights in Rumania and in Danubian shipping lines as well as in certain railways in Hungary. See Sherman D. Spector: *Rumania at the Paris Peace Conference* (New York: Bookman Associates; 1962), 163; and Von Fürstenberg to Foreign Ministry, June 14, 1919, G.F.M.

people] . . . had been in vain. Now the evil had attacked Hungary, which had not been anticipated, as it was a country of peasants and relatively rich . . . [and relatively impervious to economic blockade].

The policy he had to offer was not one of which he was proud. It was simply this—to hold the issues and to wait. He said this after taking into consideration the feelings of the Entente Peoples, and of their Parliaments. . . . He would follow Mr. Balfour's policy so far as to threaten Hungary with intervention should they not observe the armistice. . . . If military action had to be undertaken . . . and the Generals recommended a plan similar to that shown him some months ago by Marshal Foch, he felt sure that no Government would undertake the task of coercing Hungary. . . .

In sum, the Tiger proposed that the Allies "temporize," surrounding Hungarian Communism with the same *cordon sanitaire* which was meant to wear down Russian Bolshevism.

But once Lansing agreed to the use of military pressure, the Council nevertheless rallied around Balfour's proposal that the military representatives and Marshal Foch "examine the military possibilities" of forcing Hungary to respect the Armistice.

The military representatives presented a preliminary report on July 9.[1] They estimated that Hungary's Red Army could field between 100,000 and 120,000 good troops for defensive purposes. In addition, Budapest had been transformed "into a veritable fortress" which could be captured only with great effort. Conditional on the agreement of the governments involved, the Allies could oppose this Hungarian effort with 60,000 Rumanians, 8,000 Serbians, 20,000 Czechs, and 8,000 Frenchmen, or a total force of 100,000 to 110,000 men, who, to be at all effective, would have to operate under a unified command.

Balfour again warned that Béla Kun "was turning Hungary into a military stronghold of revolution"; that he was spreading propaganda both East and West; and that the European situation would become critical "if it were manifest that the Conference could not control a small and defeated nation, which was not only breaking the terms of the Armistice, but, in alliance with the Russian Soviet Government, was attempting to cause general revolution." After fully endorsing Balfour's statement, Lansing proposed that the Allies summon the delegates of Hungary's neighbors "to find out what these States could do to help." This suggestion was accepted, but only after Clemenceau reiterated that apparently no British and American troops would be available.

Rumanian, Yugoslav, and Czech delegates, as well as Foch, Weygand, and the military representatives met with the Council on July

[1] For the text of this report as well as the minutes of its discussion by the heads of delegations see *F.R.,P.C.,1919*, VI, 59–61, 67–71.

11.[2] Ironically, they had before them a telegram from General Pellé reporting the completion of the Red Army's withdrawal from Czech territory. But even Pellé was suspicious of the reasons behind this retreat, which he thought was "momentary." He took it upon himself to warn that if the Entente continued to tolerate the growth of Bolshevism in Hungary it would soon seize Vienna, whence it would "threaten Italy and Switzerland or rejoin Bavaria." He had no doubt that "military intervention against Hungary by the Entente . . . [was] an inevitable necessity."

No one took exception to Pellé's intrusion into the political realm. Instead, Foch insisted that because of the very limited forces available for intervention there was need for a political understanding between the participant states, for a single command, and for a careful plan of operations, all of which remained to be worked out.

For the Rumanians Misu indicated that they had seven divisions in Hungary, were forming two additional army corps in Transylvania, and maintained four divisions on the Russian front; and that "two more were being mobilized with the help of equipment supplied by the Allies." On behalf of his government he "felt entitled to say that a very willing spirit would be shown."

However, Milenko Vesnić was not nearly so eager. He offered only one Serbian division, and that one only on condition that during the campaign the Allies guarantee Yugoslavia's protection from the Bulgarians.

Even Kramař felt compelled to say that "the present moment was not propitious" for action: "The Hungarians had observed the [Czech-Hungarian] Armistice and had evacuated Czecho-Slovakian territory. What pretext, therefore, was there for the Czechs to attack the Hungarians?" When pressed, Kramař acknowledged that Czechoslovakia had available more than the 20,000 men suggested in the preliminary report of the military representatives. Just the same, on this whole matter he could not act without prior consultation with Prague. Incidentally, their claims to Hungarian territory having long since been satisfied, Prague and Belgrade were not open to bribery.

Crespi was equally reticent, claiming that "Italy was threatened by her own Bolsheviks." As a result, Italy was in danger of a general strike should she act against Bolshevism either in Russia or elsewhere. Still, he would reserve his position until after Tittoni's return from Rome.

As Clemenceau noted, this discussion did not furnish Foch with "a very coherent force." All he could count on were nine divisions: six Rumanian, two French, and one Serbian, plus "a doubtful quantity" of Czechs. Clemenceau then urged Balfour to find out from London what

[2] This discussion of the session of July 11, 1919 (p.m.), is based on *F.R.,P.C.,1919*, VII, 103–8, 114–15.

contribution Britain might make before instructing Foch to present a tentative plan of operations within a week.

While actual or presumed internal pressures and developments restrained the Great Powers from decisive and direct military intervention, they eventually pushed Béla Kun into foreign policy activism. No doubt, Clemenceau's promise that in exchange for evacuating Slovakia the Rumanians would withdraw from the Tisza gave the besieged regime a welcome lift. Béla Kun seemed to be succeeding where Károlyi had failed. Now that he was paving the way for an accommodation with the Entente, broad segments of the political class, including the Social Democrats, were inclined to ignore the revolutionary rhetoric with which he justified it.

But this euphoria was short-lived. The Rumanians made no move to withdraw; and the Peace Conference made no effort to compel Brătianu to carry out its orders. Quite the contrary. No sooner had the danger to Slovakia subsided and Béla Kun staked his prestige on a policy of fulfillment than the Allies resumed their irreconcilable attitude, culminating in the demand for a reduction of the Red Army to six divisions as a precondition for Rumania's compliance with the order of June 13.

But even without this conspicuous rebuff in foreign policy, internal conditions would have deteriorated before taking an upward turn. Béla Kun, like Károlyi before him, inherited a broken-down economy and fiscal system. As time went on, Budapest in particular experienced acute food shortages and high prices. The growing Red Army made increasingly heavy food requisitions in the war zones. Moreover, the peasantry, quite apart from being hostile to the regime, would not deliver surpluses except in exchange for manufactured goods, which were at a premium. Stocks were exhausted, there were no imports, and industry was geared to war production.

Concurrently the monetary situation became critical. The krone kept falling because of heavy but uncovered government expenditures and rising wages. When the printing presses began to turn out 200- and 250-kronen emergency notes these failed to win acceptance and drove the old currency out of circulation.

The blockade and the loss in productivity due to revolutionary reforms merely intensified this economic crisis which hit the wage- and salary-earning urban classes with particular force. Except for the hardcore Bolsheviks, these groups rapidly turned against the incumbent government, particularly against Béla Kun, for failing to take effective remedial measures. At the same time that so many of the workers, who in March had expedientially embraced Bolshevism, switched back to Social Democracy, Béla Kun continued to be at odds with the peasants over the disposition of the large landed properties which had been confiscated and which they wanted distributed. This disaffection on the home front contributed to restlessness among the rank and file in the Red Army.

Those bourgeois and aristocratic elements that had rallied to the regime for patriotic reasons began to defect with the unrewarded withdrawal from Slovakia. Hereafter they moved ever closer to the counterrevolutionary camp whose external headquarters were in Vienna and Szeged. Both before and after the unsuccessful putsch of June 25, in which some officers and workers cooperated, counter-revolutionary agitation was carried forward with the help of the clergy, which did not hesitate to use anti-Semitic slogans. The lines were beginning to be drawn between the Social Democrats and the Whites for the succession to the beleaguered Soviet system.

Around July 10, both internal and external considerations prompted Béla Kun to consider another dramatic foreign policy foray, this one to take the form of an offensive against the Rumanians along the Tisza. A foreign policy success was needed to bolster his regime; a military victory, to halt the disintegration and boost the morale of the army; and an advance into the fertile Rumanian-held great plains, to procure the desperately needed grain harvest.

These internal calculations were fortified by rumors that Paris was close to sponsoring a direct military intervention. Judging by his telegram to Lenin, Béla Kun never let down his guard, knowing that the next attack was just a question of time. Should the Red Army helplessly wait for the inevitable blow or were there circumstances under which a pre-emptive strike might be considered?

By mid-July the government-controlled press carried a detailed analysis of Allied intentions. According to the *Pester Lloyd* there was "no doubt whatever" that the Conference was debating the question of intervention and that important circles had a strong preference for military measures. However, according to the Chicago *Tribune,* the Great Powers were least disposed to shoulder the material and physical cost of this enterprise: "Whereas America and England were not willing, France and Italy were not able." In all four countries there was unabated pressure for the rapid completion of demobilization and popular opposition to military intervention. With the preparations for the demonstrations of July 21 in full swing, a "march against Hungary would be a risky undertaking." Judging by the recent exchanges with Clemenceau it seemed quite clear that Rumania had been chosen to strangle the Soviet Republic, since none of the Great Powers wanted to serve as hangmen themselves. The *Pester Lloyd* declared that the country faced this attack with calm and confidence.[3]

Béla Kun himself repeatedly referred to the advantages deriving from the pressure for demobilization in the Entente, the strikes sched-

[3] *Pester Lloyd,* July 15, 1919, cited in *Bulletin Périodique de la presse hongroise,* No. 35, August 23, 1919 (July 12–August 3, 1919), 2.

uled for July 21, and the rivalries among the powers. On July 8 he claimed not to fear an Entente offensive because "the internal political situation in the Allied countries did not allow them to raise sufficient manpower; . . . even the British working class . . . was organizing a general strike for July 21, in order to protest against intervention in Russia and Hungary."[4] A week later, on July 15, he frankly conceded that the Soviet Republic's situation was "much more favorable" in foreign policy than in home affairs.

> It is undeniable that the actions of the Russian and Hungarian proletariat are at the bottom of the mushrooming international revolutionary movement which manifests itself in the mass strike scheduled for July 21 in Italy, France, England, Switzerland, Holland, and Sweden. . . . I do not say that these revolutionary actions overnight can enable us to lift the blockade which weighs on our borders, . . . or break the bayonets of the imperialist troops of the Entente. Nonetheless, from the point of view of the Entente's overall policy, this coordinated international action unquestionably is an important factor today, and will be more so hereafter. I have often stressed that the Entente has not strangled us not because she did not want to but because she was unable to. She cannot do it both because she lacks reliable troops and because the requisite internal political conditions are wanting.[5]

At this juncture he counted more on the restraining influence of the Entente proletariat than on the actual assistance of Russia's Red Army, which was busy fighting the Poles as well as Petlura.

Apparently, then, in Béla Kun's estimate Allied soldiers were not likely to be thrown into the battle against him. On the other hand, he expected the Allies to keep up a tight economic blockade and to supply and encourage the neighboring armies—notably the Rumanian army—for an early offensive. He must have considered the advisability of striking a preventive blow before the Rumanians could complete their own build-up for an offensive. And since the attack across the Tisza was launched on July 21, it is more than likely that this date was chosen to coincide with the European Left's demonstration against military intervention.

Possibly to prepare opinion for his preventive move, on July 12 Béla Kun sent a wire to Clemenceau reminding him that whereas Hungarian forces had completed the evacuation of Slovakia, Rumanian troops continued to ignore the Entente's orders by not withdrawing from the Tisza.[6] He asked that the Conference make its wishes respected, otherwise his government would find it difficult to "justify its conciliatory attitude in the eyes of its supporters." At the Council

---

[4] Cited in Béla Kun: *La République hongroise des conseils*, 214.
[5] Ibid., 219.
[6] For the text and the discussion of this telegram see *F.R.,P.C.,1919*, VII, 120–1, 125–7.

session Balfour promptly repeated that Hungary was in violation of the Armistice and that Brătianu was right not to withdraw, emphasizing that Rumania was threatened by Bolshevism on both her eastern and western frontiers. Anyway, he proposed and the Council agreed to notify Béla Kun that it could not discuss "any matter" with him as long as he violated the Armistice conditions.

Within three days the heads of delegations met to consider Béla Kun's reply, which reiterated that the Czech and Rumanian troops had been the ones to cross the demarcation lines in violation of the Armistice and that "everything which happened afterwards was the direct consequence of this offensive."[7] Following the instructions of June 13, it was "not a question of negotiation but of the Rumanians' observance of Monsieur Clemenceau's promise and of the order of the Peace Conference."

At last Clemenceau conceded that "Béla Kun had right on his side" and that the Council "would be in a bad position" if the Rumanians, for whatever reason, continued to balk. Though Balfour agreed that the honor of the Council might be at stake, he thought it would be in a worse position if it ordered the Rumanians to withdraw from the Tisza. In line with their inclination to temporize, Béla Kun's telegram was referred to Foch for yet another report on the infractions of the Armistice by all parties concerned.

While Foch was preparing an operational plan, two members of the American Relief Administration, who had recently visited Budapest, submitted a project of a less blatantly military nature. Their idea was based on the premise that the vast majority of Hungarians were as hostile to White counterrevolutionaries as they were to Red revolutionaries. Lieutenant Emory Pottle and Dr. E. Dana Durand proposed a four-step operation.

First, airplanes were to saturate Hungary with a manifesto—also to be published in the press for the benefit of the rest of the world—setting forth that the Allies were occupying parts of the country with the sole aim of maintaining order and establishing a representative and stable government "competent to negotiate a binding peace" with the Entente. Immediately after arriving, the Allied forces would appoint a "temporary directorate" which would "as promptly as possible" hold elections, by universal suffrage, for a constituent assembly. Moreover, the Entente would promise a fair hearing with regard to Hungary's borders and protection against aggression; the safety of the members of the present government; the provision of food, coal, clothing, and the necessary credits; and the prohibition of "revolutionary movement on the part of the Reds and counter-revolutionary movement on the part of the Whites."

---

[7] For the text and the discussion of this telegram see ibid., 129–31, 139–40.

Second, the day following the distribution of this manifesto a small flotilla of British monitors should come down the Danube and land 400 to 500 British and American troops, who would instantly proceed to the Royal Palace to run up Allied flags and to establish a command post from which the city would then be policed.

Third, the Allied commander should immediately summon Béla Kun and his associates and hold them and their families at the Palace.

Fourth, as a sign of good faith, the occupation forces should bring Garami along with them. After their arrival they should issue a manifesto announcing his presence and declaring that he would head and form the new directorate.

The manifesto of intent as well as the presence of Garami would be calculated not only to rally popular support for this intervention in Hungary but, "more important still, [to] disarm the opposition to such intervention on the part of the proletariat of the Allied nations." Of course, in order not to endanger this small task force, it would be well to let it be known that Allied troops were massed at Hungary's borders, "ready to march in."[8]

On July 17, Foch presented his operational prospectus to the heads of delegations and to the delegates of Hungary's three neighbor countries, following consultations with Generals Pellé (Czech Army), Pechitch (Yugoslav Army), Prezan (Rumanian Army), and Franchet d'Esperey.[9] By now Masaryk had agreed to contribute all the armed forces of the Czech Republic, or 100,000 men. These were ready to resume offensive operations, but on condition that the Allies prevail on Vienna to provide artillery shells, which were in short supply.[1] The Belgrade government was prepared to assign some "18 to 20 thousand excellent soldiers who [would be] ready and on a war footing" starting July 18. Although there was no final word from Bucharest, it was safe to count on the entire Rumanian Army of the West, encamped along the Tisza and 75,000 strong, assuming the British and the Americans would continue to provide material aid with which new reserves could be organized for the interior. As for the French, they might put in a mixed force of 25,000 men, which could draw supplies from the Army of the East.

In sum, within a few days the Allies could field a combined army of some 160,000 combatants, composed of seventeen and a half infantry and two and a half cavalry divisions. Accordingly, the invading forces

[8] For the full text of this plan, accompanied by a memorandum on conditions in in Hungary, see *F.R.,P.C.,1919*, XI, 312–22. Among others, White, Bliss, and A. W. Dulles were present when these materials were discussed.

[9] For the text and the discussion of Foch's "Note on Possible Action in Hungary" see *F.R.,P.C.,1919*, VII, 177–83, 187–90.

[1] The Austrian government was informed that hereafter the supply of food and raw materials would be contingent on the prompt delivery of arms and ammunition to Czechoslovakia. See ibid., 174–7.

would have a numerical superiority of about 60,000 troops. Further-more, on condition that they operated under a single command, they would enjoy a strategic advantage in that they would move in from four different directions.[2]

Since Foch expected this inter-Allied force to capture Budapest within a few days, he urged that preparations be made to set up in Hungary "a government of order, with which the Entente would be able to sign a peace corresponding with its intentions." As for relief, it would be under the direction of the British, who would also be in charge of navigation on the Danube.

In the ensuing debate it rapidly appeared that now that the military picture seemed so promising the delegates were above all concerned about the political aspects of this enterprise. Balfour was apprehensive about setting up a puppet government which would furnish a weapon to all the enemies of the Entente. Likewise, Tittoni was worried that the attack by neighboring troops would enable Béla Kun "to drape himself in national colors," even though the overwhelming majority of the nation was opposed to him. Moreover, all the participant governments would be subject "to the criticism and opposition of [their] Labour parties." To counteract both developments, he wanted the Allies to "act in concert with the Szeged Government," thereby giving the appearance of delivering the country from tyranny.

Even though Beneš, Kramař, and Vaida-Voevod recognized the danger of further elevating Béla Kun as a champion of Magyar nationalism, they would not agree to cooperation "with any Hungarian Party," since all alike refused to admit their defeat. They wanted the armies "to march under the banner of 'respect for the Armistice.' "

With his usual candor Bliss expostulated that whatever the disguise, this plan proposed to renew war on Hungary "with the object of destroying its present Government." He cautioned against using the violation of the Armistice as a "pretext," since the reconstitution of Hungary's army beyond six divisions did not occur until after Rumania's "unwarranted invasion."

Balfour bristled with indignation at the implication that the breach of the Armistice was but a pretext for attacking the Soviet regime.

> He wished it to be understood that he was not animated by any consideration of Hungarian internal politics, little though he might approve of Béla Kun. He agreed with Mr. Kramarcz that it was intolerable to allow the Hungarian State to become a military stronghold, from which economic and political disturbances radiated over Central Europe.

[2] On July 10 Colonel Cunningham wired from Vienna that "to liberate Hungary from Communism in one week a force of 8 infantry divisions, one cavalry division, 100 airplanes and as many armored cars as possible would suffice." See ibid., 177.

Clemenceau recalled that on July 12 no objections had been raised when the Council informed Béla Kun that no discussions with him were possible because he was not respecting the Armistice. With equal impatience Kramař and Pašić reiterated that whatever the legal aspects might be, their countries were threatened and Béla Kun should be forced to fulfill existing obligations. But since both London and Washington remained to be consulted, the final decision was put off.

Literally overnight Balfour developed qualms: he was either re-buffed by Lloyd George or he never even consulted him. For the following morning he suddenly claimed that his own "advocacy of military action was based on the hypothesis . . . that the Hungarians were trying to collect an aggressive force to attack their neighbors." Should this hypothesis be untrue, then "the policy built upon it natu-rally [had to] be abandoned" and he would hesitate to recommend military action to his government. At Clemenceau's suggestion the Council then decided to send a commission of four general officers to Hungary to verify her military capabilities and intentions, pending approval of this procedure by Washington and London.[3]

But this interim, temporizing step was overtaken by events. On July 21, Clemenceau shook the Council with a radio message from Béla Kun announcing that his forces were crossing the Tisza "to try to make the will of the Entente respected by the Rumanians." Quite apart from the fact that Henry White—unlike Balfour—was still without authori-zation from his government, the commission of inquiry was put on ice. Instead, at Tittoni's suggestion, it was decided to instruct Allied repre-sentatives in Vienna to verify and evaluate reports that Böhm had resigned, was visiting the Austrian capital, and was looking for a way to transform Béla Kun's Bolshevik regime into a Socialist government.[4]

Actually, Böhm had stepped down as War Minister on July 10, and Béla Kun had posted him as envoy to Vienna. There he immediately went into consultation with Bauer—a fellow Social Democrat—to explore ways of approaching the Allies. Bauer called in Cunningham to inquire whether he "would be permitted to negotiate with Böhm with a view to throwing Béla Kun and the radical leaders out of the Government and making it a Social Democratic Government." The British official, who beforehand had consulted Albert Halstead, the U. S. Minister in Vienna, answered that even though he was not authorized to negotiate, he might entertain provisional and unofficial soundings on condition that the terror cease and with it the foreign

---

[3] For the minutes of the Council meeting of July 18, 1919 (a.m.), see *F.R.,P.C.,1919*, VII, 198–200. See also White to State Department, July 19, 1919, in David Hunter Miller: *My Diary at the Conference of Paris*, XX, 353.

[4] For the text of Béla Kun's message and the attendant discussion see *F.R.,P.C.,1919*, VII, 236, 248–9.

propaganda, that all contacts with Lenin be severed, and that all Bolsheviks leave the government.[5]

Ironically, Brown had been recalled to Paris,[6] so that it fell to others to revive his earlier scheme. On July 22, following a trip to Budapest, Böhm called on Cunningham. In their conference Böhm indicated that a possible solution would be "the overthrow of Communism and the establishment of a temporary military dictatorship under Böhm, Haubrich and Agoston, with an Allied Commission to assist it." Cunningham and Halstead seemed agreed that this Allied supervision, possibly supplemented by a consultant body composed of local non-Socialists, might serve to get rid of Bolshevism without paying the divisive price of an aristocratic restoration.

On the morning of the twenty-third, Cunningham met with Borghese, Gregory, and Halstead to work out a set of tentative propositions to be accepted by Böhm.

> First: Assuming of dictatorship in which complete powers of Government are vested in names to be discussed: Haubrich, Agoston, Garamy. Second: Dismissal of communistic Kuhn Government, repudiation of Bolshevism and complete cessation of Bolshevistic propaganda. Third: Dictatorship to bridge over until formation of Government representative of all classes. Fourth: Immediate cessation of all terroristic acts, confiscations and seizures. Fifth: Immediate call of Entente advisory body. Sixth: Raising of blockade and immediate steps to be undertaken by Entente to supply food, coal and assistance in opening Danube river. Seventh: No political prosecutions. Eighth: Ultimate determination of socialization to be left to permanent Government.

Böhm accepted these propositions in the afternoon, subject to consultation with his fellow conspirators.

That night at 10:30 these Allied officials finally let Allizé, their French colleague, in on their project. He, too, agreed. By the following morning, when Cunningham confirmed to Böhm that instructions were being sought from Paris, Jakob Weltner and Karl Peyer had arrived to help in the search for a negotiated settlement, the Rumanians having repulsed the Red offensive.[7]

Although each Allied representative eventually wired the outline

[5] Albert Halstead to Ammission, July 18 and July 24, 1919, cited in *F.R.,P.C.,1919*, XII, 544, 548–9, 615–17.
[6] He arrived in Paris in mid-May. "Brown thinks that the Allied army should go in at once and police Budapest to avoid terrorism." Buckler to Georgina Buckler, May 16, 1919, Buckler Papers. "[Saw] Brown on necessity of allowing French to overthrow Béla Kun's Government. Referred him to Bliss." Lansing Diary, May 20, 1919.
[7] For the course of these negotiations and the text of the eight propositions see Halstead to Ammission, July 24, 1919, in *F.R.,P.C.,1919*, XII, 614–18; and Böhm: *Im Kreuzfeuer*, 496–502.

proposal to his own government, Gregory beat them to it. At 9:00 p.m. on the twenty-third, he wired the draft-outline to Hoover with the request that he find out whether the plan was "acceptable . . . as a working basis for business about which we have been talking."[8] On the morning of July 25, Hoover asked the American Commissioners to recommend urgently to the Council of Five that the Allied representatives in Vienna—not the French military—be authorized to inform Böhm that if the Social Democrats "set up a government of law and order" and promise instant general elections the Conference would "undertake to treat with them for peace, open the Danube, and lift the blockade."[9]

To simplify matters, White took Hoover along to the afternoon session of the Council.[1] There he did not elaborate on the plan, except to say that Böhm would be temporary dictator, Béla Kun deposed, terrorist actions ended, and order restored. Perhaps Hoover was so sketchy because the previous evening he had briefed the British Foreign Secretary, the chief protagonist of military measures.

> [Balfour] now wondered whether the best way of getting rid of Béla Kun was by means of military intervention. It was now possible that the best solution lay in adopting the suggestions contained in Mr. Hoover's telegram. . . . [But] was it possible to place full confidence in General Böhm? . . . He [Balfour] would not be disposed to enter into an elaborate political arrangement with him. . . . It would be best to . . . tell him to confine his action to establishing some kind of military dictatorship [with the army he claimed he controlled] with a view to calling a Constituent Assembly. . . .
>
> Such a solution had a great advantage. In each of our countries there are sections of opinion which, without being actually Bolshevik, have none the less a certain sympathy for Bolshevik programs. Those portions of the public were most strongly opposed to military action against the Bolsheviks. All these disadvantages would be avoided by proceeding through General Böhm . . . who would be given the moral support of the Allies. . . .

But Balfour kept emphasizing that everything hinged on Böhm's reliability and on his support inside Hungary. Coolidge, who was also present, readily vouched not only for Böhm, but also for the other three Social Democrats mentioned in the Vienna plan.

Before committing themselves, the delegates called in Foch for his

[8] Gregory to Hoover, July 23, 9:00 p.m., 24, and 25, 1919, cited in *F.R.,P.C.,1919*, XI, 348–9, and VII, 310–11. Gregory as well as Halstead advised against the projected military mission, which would raise the prestige of the tottering regime.
[9] *F.R.,P.C.,1919*, XI, 348–9.
[1] This discussion of the meeting of the heads of delegations, July 25, 1919 (p.m.), is based on *F.R.,P.C.,1919*, VII, 254–6.

opinion on the morning of the twenty-sixth.[2] Balfour wanted his judgment as to whether Böhm "had sufficient influence with the Hungarian Armies to crush Béla Kun . . . without the Allies being called upon to strike a blow." The Marshal claimed complete ignorance about Böhm and his plan, which he thought to be of "a purely political nature," and therefore outside his province. He took this occasion, however, to make the Council aware that the surrounding countries "would shortly take an initiative of some kind," since they were not likely to "keep their armies mobilized indefinitely."

Pichon, White, and Hoover then took turns impressing on Balfour that the Allied representatives in Vienna were of the opinion that Böhm should be taken seriously. But they also agreed that this gave little guidance on how to go about expressing support for his intended coup.

Cautioning the delegates against "open negotiations with secret agents," Hoover proposed that the Allies issue a public declaration to the effect that "economic assistance would be given to a properly constituted government," leaving it to Böhm "to make his own deductions from it." Before adjourning, the delegates asked Hoover to confer with Balfour, who agreed to draft such a statement for discussion at the afternoon meeting.

The critical paragraph of this statement served notice that "if food and supplies were to be made available, if the blockade was to be removed, if economic reconstruction was to be attempted, if peace was to be settled, it could only be done with a Government . . . which carried out the letter and spirit [of its] engagements . . . and which represented the Hungarian people, and not with one that rested its authority upon terrorism."[3] The text as such was acceptable. What provoked another extended debate was Balfour's suggestion that Marshal Foch be instructed to continue military preparations in the event that this economic pressure produced no results.

Tittoni again felt compelled to say that he could contribute no troops for fear that because of Italy's "economic crisis and its political consequences . . . any campaign against Hungary would produce a general strike." After castigating Balfour for not making any British troops available, Clemenceau claimed that "his situation, though not as serious as Mr. Tittoni's, had some analogies with it."

When Balfour asked Clemenceau for his alternative, the French Premier suggested that Hungary be left to her own devices.

> The war was over, the American Army had been withdrawn very rapidly, the British army nearly as rapidly, and the French army was being demobilized. He was forced to demobilize very quickly. . . .
> He could not, therefore, contemplate the sending of two French divisions into Hungary unsupported by their [English, Italian, and

2 The discussion of this session is based on ibid., 304–8.
3 For the text and discussion of this statement see ibid., 317–22.

American] Allies. . . . He could not ask his people to go to war
again. . . . Any check would have serious results in Italy . . . , in
France and also probably in Great Britain. He did not wish to run
this risk. . . . In any case, he was not ready to begin fighting
again.

He felt inclined to adopt the proposals made by Mr. Balfour and
Mr. Hoover. He would encompass Hungary with a ring of hostile
States, and rely on her to rid herself of a minority in her own
way. . . . He believed Mr. Hoover held the key to the situation.
The offer of food in return for good behavior would be a very
effective weapon. The case was similar to that of Russia, but in the
case of Russia, there were no means of coercion, against the
Hungarians there were. They could be surrounded and in time
would have to come to terms. . . . The plans of General Böhm
offered for the moment a better outlook than existed a week ago. If
the Hungarians were really in the majority opposed to Béla Kun
they might under the stress of Mr. Hoover's blandishments overthrow the Béla Kun Government. There might then occur a favorable opportunity of which Marshal Foch could avail himself.

That Clemenceau was not exaggerating the debilitating effect of
France's rapid demobilization became evident within forty-eight hours,
when he announced the withdrawal of 45,000 men from his *armée
d'orient,* leaving a bare three *brigades mixtes* near Hungary's borders.[4]

Since England was in no position to take up the slack, Balfour
finally conceded that "without a French Commander-in-Chief and
without the cooperation of the two French divisions . . . there was
little prospect of success." To be sure, there remained the "economic
weapon." But otherwise the authority of the Conference was eroded,
largely because of the speed with which armies of 15 million men had
been demobilized to the point that it "was difficult to lay hands on a
single battalion." His fear was that if Béla Kun found out about this
impotence, he would exploit it to the full. Even so, he had to "content
himself with half of the policy he had proposed." Balfour would have
been depressed, indeed, except for Foch's reassurance that the "Rumanians were not alarmed by the Hungarian attack." Hence, he was able to
close the session with the prayerful speculation that if the Hungarian
offensive failed Béla Kun "might fall of his own weight, [which] would
certainly be better than if he were overthrown by the Allies."

The next day, July 27, the statement drafted by Balfour was
released by wireless and through the press. As White and Bliss reported
to Washington, this statement was issued as "an alternative to an attack
upon Béla Kun by Rumanian and Czech troops, or the parts of two
French divisions, which Marshal Foch seemed to think would bring
about his fall, but Clemenceau expressed himself very strongly as to his
unwillingness to risk the life of a single French soldier in such an

4 Ibid., 348.

enterprise, inasmuch as no assistance would be forthcoming from us or from Great Britain, and a French nation pressing for rapid demobilization."[5] Within a week, on August 2, word reached the heads of delegations that in spite of their procrastination and pusillanimity Béla Kun had been forced to resign, to flee abroad with his associates, and to hand over the reins to an all-Socialist government, headed by the very moderate Julius Peidl.[6]

According to Halstead the note of July 27, combined with the unofficial negotiations in Vienna, hastened and precipitated the overthrow, whose underlying causes were discouragement over the withdrawal from Slovakia, the economic and political consequences of the blockade, and the defeat of the Red Army by the Rumanians.[7]

Whatever the ultimate reasons for Béla Kun's ouster, the successor government instantly notified the Peace Conference that it was sworn to a policy of fulfillment and accommodation. Peidl assured Clemenceau that he and his colleagues accepted the "proposals of the Allied Powers in the form in which they were agreed to" in the unofficial negotiations in Vienna. Moreover, he requested that, pending further dispositions by the Conference, hostilities be suspended and the armistice line for the Rumanian Army be fixed at the Tisza.[8] Judging by this last point the advance of the Rumanian forces rather than Böhm's manipulations or Hoover's economic blackmail was the immediate cause for this disconcertingly swift overturn.

Once the Rumanian troops had turned the tide of the battle and had crossed the Tisza, their advance towards Budapest was swift. The Peidl government reeled under the impact of the imminent capture of Budapest and the upsurge of counterrevolutionary forces, whose ranks now were swelled by public servants, officers, the middle classes, the aristocracy, the clergy, and defectors from the army.

In an eleventh-hour effort to save the October Revolution, Peidl and Agoston, the new Foreign Minister, instructed Böhm to impress again on Cunningham, Borghese, and Allizé that the Social Democratic administration was complying with the full range of Allied conditions.

Böhm rushed to the three Allied representatives to say that the Hungarian government had stopped political persecutions and released political prisoners, was committed to democratic institutions and liberties, would shortly hold free elections for a national assembly, recog-

[5] Ammission to Lansing, July 27, 1919, cited in *F.R.,P.C.,1919*, XII, 619.
[6] Foreign Affairs, Peter Agoston; Commerce, Anton Dovcsák; Education, Garbai; Justice, Garami; Minorities, Gyozö Kraller; Interior, Peyer; and War, Haubrich.
[7] Halstead to Lansing August 2 and 5, 1919, cited in *F.R.,P.C.,1919*, XII, 622–4, 627.
[8] Peidl's communication of August 1, 1919, reached Clemenceau in the form of a wireless from Lieutenant Colonel Romanelli, the Chief of Italy's Military Mission in Budapest. For the full text and the discussion of this message see *F.R.,P.C.,1919*, VII, 480–3, 489–90.

nized and would abide by the Armistice of November 13, suspended all relations with the Soviet government in Moscow, put an end to Bolshevik agitation at home and abroad, rescinded all terrorist decrees, and pursued "order and tranquility in order to normalize economic life." The Allies were implored to help by recognizing the government, lifting the blockade, and curbing the Rumanians.[9]

But at first the Allies made no particular effort to help consolidate the new regime. In reply to Peidl's urgent plea the Council of Five sent word that it saw no "reason for interfering in the domestic politics of the Hungarian Republic." Therefore the proposals of Allied representatives in Vienna could not be taken into account and future relations would have to be based on the November Armistice and the June note. Meanwhile, the Rumanians could not be ordered back either to the Tisza or to the lines of the June note until after the new government "conformed strictly with the terms of the Armistice." They would be asked to stop in their present position.[1]

This hardened response reached Böhm and Peidl—and Brătianu— on August 3. By then the Rumanian forces had reached the outskirts of Budapest, where they now stopped, presumably in compliance with Paris. General Holban, the Rumanian commander, entered into negotiations with Haubrich (Minister of War) and Franz Harrer (Mayor of Budapest) for the disarmament and dissolution of the Hungarian forces in exchange for sparing Budapest from enemy occupation. But these negotiations never got very far. A self-appointed Hungarian delegation, representing the Right and headed by General Franz Schnetzer, went to Rumanian headquarters to request that the city be occupied in order to eliminate the Bolshevik-infected regime. The Rumanians could not have been very serious either about their pause outside the capital or about the negotiations, for on August 4 they marched into Budapest under the anti-Bolshevik banner.[2]

Two intimately related issues now faced the big powers: how to prevent an outright White terror in Hungary and how to restrain the Rumanians.

U. S. officials in particular urged the importance of demonstrating the viability of a regime which was neither Bolshevik nor reactionary. Unlike so many Rightists, Halstead, Gregory, and Hoover did not consider moderate Socialism as a subterfuge or as the *avant-garde* of Bolshevism, but rather as an essential preparation for a centrist solution. To be sure, the Peidl cabinet was far from ideal. According to Hoover the new government, which represented the trade unions, was "very radical," and eventually should be made more representative by the inclusion of peasant and bourgeois leaders. Meanwhile, however,

---

[9] Böhm: *Im Kreuzfeuer,* 526–8.
[1] The full text of this communication is cited in *F.R.,P.C.,1919,* VII, 490–1.
[2] Böhm: *Im Kreuzfeuer,* 528–9.

"trade unionism was the instrument that should be used to upset Bolshevism," in large measure in order to point the democratic forces of change in Russia and the rest of Europe toward a reformist alternative. On August 4, before Paris knew about the occupation of Budapest, even Polk cautioned the Council that either a nationalist reaction or Rumanian looting, or both, would undermine "the whole effect of the overthrow of Béla Kun" on Russia.[3]

Impressed by this line of reasoning and by Pichon's objections, the Council followed up its stern note of August 2 with a promise that provided the new government gave evidence of promptly complying with the Armistice, the blockade would be lifted, the Danube opened, and food surpluses from the Banat rushed in. At the same time, an inter-Allied military mission was sent to Budapest less to check up on the Hungarians than to prevail on the Rumanians to behave themselves, the latter to be threatened with economic sanctions in the event of excesses.[4]

But these steps could not and did not prevent the Rumanian advance into the capital and beyond, Brătianu's presentation of Draconian and unacceptable economic terms to Peidl, or the bloodless coup of August 6, which returned Archduke Joseph as head of state in combination with the solidly conservative but not outright reactionary Stephen Friedrich Ministry. Presently the peace delegations received the first reports about Rumanian terrorism, looting, and destruction, which exceeded even their worst fears and predictions.[5]

The Americans were up in arms. Like it or not, the world at large would associate the Allied and Associated Powers with these counter-revolutionary developments. Polk predicted that this "setting up of a reactionary Government in Hungary in place of a moderate Socialist Government" would give a powerful new stimulus to Bolshevism: "Lenin would point to the example of what had taken place on the downfall of the Soviet Government in Hungary, in order to scare Russia and preserve his own regime." With the return of a Habsburg even Pichon murmured something to the effect that the setting up of a "reactionary Government was contrary to Allied policy," while Clemenceau added that "the public of the Entente countries would not allow" the Conference to back such a reactionary regime.[6]

Reports about the naked plundering of the Rumanian troops continued to pour into Paris. Certainly Bucharest would have to be tamed

---

[3] "[In the Council] we took the position that the way we treated the Hungarians would not only affect future peace in Hungary, but have great influence on Russia." Polk to Wilson, August 5, 1919, cited in Miller, *My Diary,* XX, 378–80.

[4] For the meeting of August 4, 1919 (p.m.), see *F.R.,P.C.,1919,* VII, 504–11, 516–18.

[5] See three telegrams from General Reginald Gorton, head of British Military Mission and member of newly constituted inter-Allied Military Mission in Budapest, to Supreme Council, August 6, 1919, cited in ibid., 604–5.

[6] See the debates of August 7 and 13, 1919, in ibid., esp. 605–6, 679.

as a prelude to ousting the Archduke in favor of a coalition, representative regime. The Allies lacked the military contingents and the diplomatic resolve to dislodge the Rumanians from the unassigned regions occupied by them. As on so many other occasions, with Hoover's help they simply proposed to threaten both Brătianu and Joseph with economic sanctions.

On the strength of dispatches from his agents, Hoover denounced the Rumanians for working in collusion with associates of the Archduke as well as with members of the ultrareactionary Szeged group, thereby giving aid and comfort to Bolshevism, however unintentionally.

> While the *coup d'état* . . . was not an entirely Rumanian affair, nevertheless Rumanian troops had surrounded the meeting place of the [Peidl] Ministry and had turned their machine guns on the building in which they were. This event had immediate repercussions throughout Poland and Eastern Europe and the Bolsheviks were making much of it and claiming that the Alliance was trying to reestablish a reactionary government in its worst form and this had done more to rehabilitate the Bolshevist cause than anything that had happened for a long time. The Social Democrats refused to have anything to do with the new Government and Garami, the leader of this group, thought that if things were allowed to continue as they were, the old reactionary party would be well established in ten days and the Allied and Associated Powers would have to be prepared to see the House of Habsburg begin to reestablish itself throughout all its former dominions. . . .

Anyway, Hoover proposed that the inter-Allied Military Mission unequivocally tell the Archduke to resign—a demand fiercely echoed by the Czechs and Yugoslavs—and that all aid to Rumania, including military supplies, be cut off.[7]

Once again, because he was so deft at drafting diplomatic notes, Balfour was commissioned to formulate the telegram that went out to the Allied Generals in Budapest, for publication there. In this wire of August 22, the Allies, who still pretended to uphold a policy of noninterference, told the Archduke that they could not negotiate peace with or give economic support to a government brought into existence "by a *coup d'état* carried out by a small body of police under the protection of a foreign army." They suggested that he resign so that a "Government in which all parties were represented should [be able] to appeal to the Hungarian people."[8] Under this pressure the Archduke resigned instantly. But Friedrich continued as Premier of his bourgeois cabinet, changing only three of his 14 Ministers and scheduling elections for September 28.[9]

---

[7] See the debates of August 21, 1919, in ibid., esp. 774–8.
[8] The text of this wire is cited in ibid., 803.
[9] Inter-Allied Military Mission to Supreme Council, August 23, 9:00 a.m., and 28–30, 1919, cited in *F.R.,P.C.,1919*, VII, 855, and VIII, 71–73.

Incidentally, the right-wing press in Paris expressed strong reservations about this policy of intervention. According to Pertinax, if the Allies declared that in Central Europe they would only "deal with governments that were half ways between Bolshevism and the *anciens régimes,*" they would be condemning themselves to never finding acceptable interlocutors. He accused the Americans, in particular Hoover, of embracing the simplistic view that by imposing a democratic regime on Budapest they would forever destroy the mainsprings of Magyar *revanchism.* This policy, which called for continuing intervention in the internal affairs of the vanquished, was risky because it was not at all clear that there was a viable middle ground between "the revanchist patriotism which threatened Europe's political order, and Bolshevism, which threatened the political as well as the social order." At this juncture the choice should be for Germanism over Bolshevism, particularly with Germanism presenting itself in the superficial form of a Habsburg Grand Duke, precariously installed in Budapest. Besides, the Allies never looked to achieve their security at the cost of ruined and impotent enemies: "there was a solidarity between the elements of social order and economic production of all nations, both allied and enemy."[1]

But whereas the pitiful Habsburg readily yielded, the headstrong and victory-drunk Brătianu continued to defy the Allies. The Conference repeatedly decided to impose an embargo on military supplies as well as economic aid.[2] Due to French and Italian obstruction, however, this decision was not implemented until late September, by which time the Rumanians had drained Hungary of rolling stock, military and industrial equipment, and livestock.[3] Even at the risk of being excluded from the "victor club," Brătianu was determined to try for his maximum territorial aspirations, which reached to the line of the Tisza.

As late as September 3, he repeated his refusal to withdraw beyond the Tisza, warning that such an evacuation would renew the struggle between "Bolsheviks and monarchical reactionaries," thereby plunging this region into further chaos. He implied that the Allies should readily grant his thinly veiled claim to the Tisza line since "by the occupation of Budapest and the destruction of Bolshevism, Rumania had rendered a great service to the general cause."[4]

Right down to early November, when the Rumanians finally began their evacuation of Budapest and their withdrawal to the Tisza, Brătianu played his diplomatic cards with consummate skill.[5] He took advantage of the rivalries among the Great Powers, the Entente's military impotence, France's security-motivated search for a reliable

[1] *L'Echo de Paris,* August 10, 23, and 24, 1919.
[2] E.g., August 23 and 25, 1919. See *F.R.,P.C.,1919,* VII, 813, 838.
[3] *F.R.,P.C.,1919,* X, 561.
[4] Cited in *F.R.,P.C.,1919,* VIII, 110.
[5] See Spector: *Rumania at the Paris Peace Conference,* 178–213, 233–7.

partner in East Central Europe, Italy's diplomatic isolation, and America's eagerness to withdraw militarily and diplomatically from Europe. All his conventional diplomatic maneuvers—bargaining, delaying, promising, threatening, lying—drew additional punch from his unrelenting exploitation of Russia's eclipse and the Allied fear of the Bolshevik specter. The Entente eagerly compensated him with Bessarabia and northern Bukovina for his contribution to the containment of Lenin. Moreover, from September through October Brătianu confidently disregarded all evacuation orders, knowing that the Allies did not really want him to pull out of Budapest until after reliable internal security forces had been organized by an otherwise cowed Hungarian government. And when the Rumanians finally did leave the capital they turned over control to Admiral Horthy, the commander of troops who shared his loyalty to the Whites of Szeged rather than to Friedrich.

Admittedly, Karl Huszár, who headed the new Provisional Government installed on November 25, was a moderate clerical and secured the cooperation of some right-wing Socialists. Even so, he was dependent on Horthy's protection and on the Whites, particularly on right-wing Nationalists and Christian Nationals. Over the scruples and objections not only of Huszár but also of more radical counterrevolutionaries, Julius Gömbös and Tibor Eckhardt masterminded a savage White terror. The Jews were the special victims of this terror, which perpetrated infinitely more brutal and more numerous atrocities, including murders, than Szamuely's Red terror, which it presumed to avenge.

25

Abortive General Strike

FOLLOWING the Berne Conference the leaders of the Second International continued to be disinclined either to mount political strikes or to apply for membership in the Third International. Instead, they adopted the posture of a loyal opposition to the peacemakers. They set out to influence the course of the peace negotiations by encouraging and supporting especially Wilson but also Lloyd George against Clemenceau, the military, and the supernationalists of the Allied nations. Their overall aim was minimal: to mitigate the Carthaginian terms which they knew could not be eliminated altogether. As for their methods, they were unexceptionable. At one time or another they sought and secured interviews with Lloyd George and Clemenceau to present their critical views; they capitalized on their personal contacts with second and third echelon officials, notably in the American and British delegations;[1] through the dissident press they disseminated their resolutions and proposals; and they used the Parliamentary platforms to dramatize their plea for moderation. Now and then strikes, mass demonstrations, and public rallies reinforced the representations and votes of Labour and Socialist parliamentarians. This extraparliamentary agitation tended to be sparked by leaders and groups that were impatient with the bended-knee begging of prominent party and trade-union officials.

At Berne the delegates had charted a Committee of Action to watch over the Peace Conference, to plan future meetings, and to draft recommendations on major international issues as well as on the reconstruction of the International. Soon after starting its vigil in Paris,

1 "Henderson, Stuart-Bunning, and MacDonald will arrive here from London in the evening of the 28th, and will telephone me their address on Saturday morning. They are to confer here with Branting, Huysmans, Renaudel and Longuet, who with them form the 'Paris Committee' of the Berne Conference. . . . If you wish to see any of them or would like any communication to be made to them on the subject of the proposed amendments to the Covenant, I should be glad if you would kindly let me know." Buckler to House, March 24, 1919, in Buckler Papers.

this committee summoned the Permanent Commission to meet in Amsterdam from April 26–29, 1919.[2]

The very moderate elements were even more conspicuous in Amsterdam than in Berne, the delegates of the Belgian and Australian parties being there to reinforce them. On the other hand, by now these moderates were no longer quite so obsessed by their hatred of the German Majoritarians. In most nations the Centrists were rapidly increasing their following thanks to continuing economic frustrations, inspiration by revolutionary developments in Central and Eastern Europe, and disenchantment with the Big Four's peacemaking and interventionism. As a result, even Renaudel struck a somewhat more militant note in the hope of slowing down defections from the Majoritarian to the Independent camp in the national movements as well as within the Second International, and from the Berne to the Moscow International.

The first item of the agenda—fixed by Camille Huysmans, the Secretary—was the question of "the extent to which the Paris Conference was taking account of the Berne resolutions."[3] Of course, by late April the draft treaty had not been released. Only the charters of the League and the I.L.O. had been published, so that the delegates could scrutinize only them. With regard to the Covenant MacDonald reported that the Action Committee had called on Lord Robert Cecil. In this interview the committee had stressed three points: the early admission of Germany and Russia, disarmament, and popular representation in the central organ of the League. Whereas Cecil seemed conciliatory on the first point, he gave no satisfaction on the other two.[4]

It was Renaudel who came forward to confess that the International's "intercessions with Lord Robert Cecil, Clemenceau, etc. had been unsuccessful." He urged the delegates to publicize this failure alongside a reminder that the Allied Left was sworn to oppose a peace of violence, thereby trying to frighten the Big Four into taking the Second International seriously. Even though Longuet and Troelstra favored a stronger stand they failed to improve on Renaudel's formula for seeking yet another interview.

[2] For the composition and functions of Berne's Executive Committee, Committee of Action, and Permanent Commission as well as for the first representations in Paris by the Committee of Action, see p. 405 above.

[3] For the most complete compte-rendu of the Amsterdam Conference see Bulletin der Zweiten Internationale, No. 2, July 1919, 1–12. The full text of the resolutions adopted at Amsterdam is cited in ibid., No. 1, May 1919, 1–5, and in Labour Party: Report of the 19th Annual Conference (Southport, 1919), 206–11. Unless otherwise indicated in this discussion of the Amsterdam Conference all quotations are from Bulletin der Zweiten Internationale, Nos. 1–2.

[4] "This morning I had an interview with Arthur Henderson, Ramsay MacDonald, Stuart-Bunning, Renaudel, Longuet, Huysmans, and Branting, who gave me some compliments. They came to talk about the League of Nations, and were on the whole very reasonable. Indeed, with most of their suggestions I heartily agreed. . . ." Cecil Diary, March 31, 1919.

In his report on the I.L.O. Henderson struck an extremely satisfied note. He had no criticism of the composition of the national delegations —two representatives for the government, one for the employers, one for organized labor—and was particularly gratified that the eight-hour day (forty-eight-hour week) figured at the head of the agenda for the first I.L.O. congress scheduled for October 1919. Even though not all of labor's demands were about to be met, "through energetic agitation and organization" the Second International could see to it that "this inaugural session adopt more far reaching reforms."

The delegates then turned to the Action Committee's report on territorial questions. Since there were no concrete treaty terms to evaluate, they simply endorsed a rigorous application of self-determination through plebiscites for Finland, Georgia, Estonia, Armenia, the Ukraine, German-Austria, the Polish-German frontier areas, and Ireland. They opposed the detachment from Germany of the Palatinate and the left bank of the Rhine; and though they agreed that reparations should be extracted from the Saar, the delegates warned against using "economic annexation to bring about political annexation." Whereas the Socialist parties of Estonia, Georgia, and the Ukraine were represented, the Italians again stayed away, thereby allowing the conference to dodge the Adriatic question. As for overseas possessions, the delegates wanted "all colonies and dependencies . . . and not merely the German colonies" to become subject to the mandate system.

Having been refused passports for its study mission to Russia, the International proposed to make one more *démarche* with the Allied Governments. Should the Allies stick to their refusal, a mission composed of Socialists from neutral countries would be dispatched, thereby circumventing passport restrictions. And even though the assembled Socialists did not renew their protest against intervention in Russia, they did protest against the intervention in Hungary.

Before recessing it was decided to call a general congress of the Second International for February 2, 1920; to hold the next meeting of the Permanent Commission of the Berne Conference in Lucerne on August 1, 1919; and to reconvene the Action Committee in Paris on May 10. This latter committee was instructed to present the Amsterdam resolutions to the Peace Conference; to secure passports for the mission of inquiry to Russia or, in case of refusal, to appoint a mission of neutrals; to examine the territorial provisions of the draft treaty; to prepare a charter for "the new International" in consultation with the trade unions and co-operative organizations; and to draft a reply to the Third International to be examined in Lucerne.

The Action Committee—Longuet, Renaudel, Henderson, MacDonald, Stuart-Bunning, and Huysmans (Secretary)—convened in Paris just three days after the preliminary treaty was handed to Brockdorff-Rantzau. Overnight, on May 11, they issued a relatively mild manifesto criticizing these draft terms from the point of view of the International's principles.[5] Apparently at Renaudel's insistence[6] the committee resolved to seek an audience with the Council of Four, Henderson being charged with approaching Lloyd George for this purpose. Without as much as a debate the statesmen bluntly notified Henderson that since the "summary of the Peace Terms was already published and had been communicated to the German plenipotentiaries . . . no useful object would now be served by [receiving] the proposed deputation."[7]

This unceremonious rebuff was a severe blow to the moderates, in that it dramatized the ineffectiveness of their strategy. Neither Henderson nor Renaudel were bothered by Zinoviev's charge that they never even got beyond the "ante-chamber" of the Peace Conference.[8] On the other hand, they could not lightly dismiss the attacks of their more militant colleagues within the Second International. They came under heavy fire for still nursing the illusion that the Berne Socialists could influence the Big Four with measured petitions, polite representations, and inoffensive speeches. The time had come to steer the International into a more radical course. Perhaps the best way to do this was to hold a full-scale congress now, instead of next February, at which the Italian and Swiss delegates would team up with the left wing led by MacDonald, Longuet, Haase, and Troelstra. But what guarantee was there that the Italians and the Swiss, not to speak of the Russians, would accept an invitation to a congress summoned by Henderson, Branting, and Huysmans? To avoid aggravating the mutilation and disequilibrium of the International it might be expedient to seek unity through action rather than through formal organization.[9]

Presently, on May 19, *Avanti* proposed that instead of issuing a steady but ineffectual barrage of protests against intervention in Russia, Allied Socialists should have recourse to the general strike. By the end of May this suggestion had been endorsed by the executive of the SFIO, the CGT, and the British Triple Alliance, as well as by the Italian movement. But before going any further with this plan of action there would have to be consultations between and among the prospective participants.

As it was, in the wake of the latest rebuff by the Big Four the

---

[5] For the full text see Labour Party: *Report of the 19th Annual Conference*, 212–13. See also p. 772 above.

[6] See *le Populaire*, May 25, 1919.

[7] *F.R.,P.C.,1919*, V, 607–8, 621; and *Bulletin der Zweiten Internationale*, No. 1, May 1919, 8.

[8] See the text of Zinoviev's manifesto "Boycott of the Yellow International," June 15, 1919, in *Bibliothek der Kommunistischen Internationale: Manifest, Richtlinien, Beschlüsse des ersten Kongresses; Aufrufe und offene Schreiben des Exekutivkomitees bis zum Zweiten Kongress* (Hamburg: Verlag der Kommunistischen Internationale; 1920), 119–23.

[9] See articles by Frossard, Verfeuil, and Longuet in *le Populaire*, May and June, 1919.

Action Committee instructed Longuet and MacDonald to go to Rome and Milan to woo the Italians back into the Berne International.[1] Immediately upon arrival in the Eternal City on May 30 they discovered that their Italian comrades were much less interested in protesting the Peace Treaty or in reconstituting the International than they were in united action designed to save the Russian—and Hungarian—revolutions.

On May 30–31, in Rome, MacDonald held preliminary discussions with a group of Socialist parliamentarians headed by Turati. Both MacDonald and this group then took the train to Milan for another two days of meetings. There they were joined by Longuet; by Serrati and two other members of the party executive; by D'Aragona, the Secretary of the Confederation of Labor; and by two members of the Milanese section of the ISP.

MacDonald and Longuet took turns stressing the danger of allowing the European Left to be torn between two rival Internationals, insisting that a decidedly more militant majority would have triumphed at Berne if only the Italians, the Swiss, and the Russians had been there. Moreover, they reported on the recent turn in favor of protesting interventionism in the British and French labor movements.

Turati, who presided over this conclave, implied that the differences between the Italians and the Second International "were more formal than real." But even he advocated seeking unity through common action, though he thought in terms of coordinated Parliamentary maneuvers. As compared to the Socialist parliamentarians, the spokesmen for the Italian party and trade unions called for altogether more direct and energetic action. They drew courage from the doubling of the party membership, the tripling of the union ranks, and the eruption of the strike wave. In their view, regardless of the blemishes of Bolshevism, the Russian Revolution could not be allowed to go under, for the defeat of Lenin and Béla Kun would almost certainly be followed by the strangulation of Socialism from the Urals to the Atlantic. Serrati, Vella, and D'Aragona did not equivocate: "Italian Socialists would stand with the Berne International only provided it decided for concrete and immediate action in favor of the Russian Revolution." Whereas they declared that both the party and the unions were ready for a general work stoppage to protest intervention in Russia and Hungary, MacDonald pointed out the difficulty of rallying British trade unionists for a political strike, even one limited to twenty-four hours.

Even so, the conferees decided to return to their respective principals to secure agreement for an internationally coordinated general

[1] This discussion of the Longuet-MacDonald mission to Italy is based on Charles Roden Buxton: "Messengers of the International," *Labour Leader*, June 12, 1919, 3; *Avanti*, June 2–3, 1919; *l'Humanité*, June 4, 1919; *The Times* (London), June 2, 1919. Buxton acted as interpreter. Originally Huysmans was scheduled to go along, but at the last moment he begged off.

strike of twenty-four hours. Armed with these authorizations, delegates of the three Allied labor movements would then meet in Paris to synchronize this ambitious enterprise.

To punctuate this new departure the Milanese section called a special mass meeting in the People's Theater. On a few hours' notice at least 10,000 workers came to hear MacDonald, Longuet, Turati, and Serrati speak in defense of the Russian Revolution and against the dictated, imperialist peace. The overflow audience wildly cheered Serrati's motion "inviting comrades Longuet and MacDonald to interpret the sentiments of the Italian workers to the French and British proletariat; and expressing the hope that the concordant, joint and energetic action decided during the Socialist meetings in Rome and Milan take place as soon as possible for the safety of the eastern Republics and the future of Socialism."

Longuet and MacDonald had gone as emissaries of the Action Committee to convince the Italians to stay in step with the Berne International; they returned to their respective national organizations and movements rather than to the International as advocates of the Italian line. Perhaps Italy's overheated atmosphere helped convince them that *la révolution est un bloc*. They may also have appreciated the advantage of challenging their governments on their halting and publicly suspect interventionism rather than on the immeasurably more popular punishment of the Central Powers. Needless to say, in each of the Allied nations, maximum support for such a foreign policy assault could only be mustered by also billing it as an expression of domestic grievances.

The *cartel interfédéral*—the grouping of seven major trades modeled on Britain's Triple Alliance—and the Administrative Committee of the CGT met on June 11 to take stock of the current strike wave.[2] This same meeting decided that direct action in France for economic as well as political ends should be coordinated with parallel actions in England and Italy. The *Temps* instantly voiced the suspicion that the recent Milan conclave had stimulated the fusion of "these two movements, one national, the other international, one economic, the other political."[3] The following two days the top leaders of the SFIO and the CGT agreed to go forward with common action, but with each side maintaining "maximum autonomy and independence." In turn, they committed themselves to meet on June 15 with their Italian and British counterparts to coordinate this French action with an international demonstration in defense of the Russian Revolution.[4] Again the *Temps* was up in arms: although the CGT had maintained its autonomy in principle, in practice it was "about to abandon its corpo-

2 See pp. 778–80 above.
3 *Le Temps,* June 12, 1919.
4 *L'Humanité* and *le Populaire,* June 13, 1919.

rative stance in order to also throw itself into the essentially political adventure of an international demonstration."[5]

That the project of a twenty-four-hour strike would be least acceptable to the British Left was confirmed when Henderson wired that the Labour Party was not yet ready to participate in the Franco-Italian talks of June 15–16 and that "the Italian proposition could only be implemented after a referendum by the Trade Unions."[6]

Meanwhile D'Aragona, Lazzari—the Secretary of the ISP—and Serrati had arrived in Paris and settled down to conversations with Longuet, Bracke, Frossard, Verfeuil, Paul Faure, Rappoport, Jouhaux, and Dumoulin. With the strikes in Italy and France at their peak, militant Centrists and radicals seemed to be taking charge, to the exclusion of Renaudel and Turati. In no time they agreed that an international—inter-Allied?—general strike of twenty-four hours should be held at the earliest possible moment. However, the final decision and the choice of a date were made contingent on consultations with the British on June 25–26 in Southport, where the annual conference of the Labour Party as well as Berne's Action Committee were scheduled to convene.[7]

Jouhaux, Dumoulin, Renaudel, and D'Aragona left for England on June 21. On their arrival in London the first two were taken to Scotland Yard to be searched and interrogated, and they were placed under surveillance at their hotel before being allowed to proceed to Southport. Longuet and Frossard, who left on the twenty-third, never got beyond Folkstone, where in spite of valid passports and visas they were turned back. Longuet sent an indignant telegram to Lloyd George who replied apologetically that the decision to bar him and Frossard had not been a cabinet decision. However, by the time the immigration officers at Folkstone received the Prime Minister's instructions to admit the two Frenchmen, they were on their way back home.[8]

Unity through action was making considerable strides. In the evening of June 25 and again in the evening of June 26 at Southport Allied Socialists and trade unionists conferred with both the Action and the Executive Committee of the Berne International. Britain was represented by the Executive Committee of the Labour Party; France by Jouhaux, Dumoulin, and Renaudel; Italy by D'Aragona; and the International by Branting and Huysmans.[9] Whereas the nonappearance of Longuet and Frossard was fully aired, even D'Aragona never explained why Lazzari and Serrati stayed away. Certainly the absence of these four militant Socialists combined with the overrepresentation of British

[5] *Le Temps,* June 14, 1919.
[6] Henderson to Jouhaux and Frossard, June 14, cited in *l'Humanité,* June 17, 1919.
[7] *L'Humanité* and *le Populaire,* June 15–17, 1919.
[8] *Le Populaire,* June 26 and 28, 1919.
[9] This discussion of the Southport consultations of June 25–26, 1919, is based on Labour Party: Minutes of the Executive Committee, 18.

Labour skewed the composition of this meeting to the disadvantage of the *enragés,* and this at a time when the labor disorders were subsiding.

Jouhaux made the opening statement. He reported that at their meeting in Paris French and Italian delegates had endorsed the proposal of a twenty-four-hour strike as a demonstration "against Allied intervention in Russia, in favor of a political amnesty, and for speedier demobilization." Moreover, they had instructed the French and Italian delegates now present to proceed to England to confer with representatives of the British movement, who seemed to be dragging their feet. Since his arrival he had conferred with Mr. Bowerman, Secretary of the T.U.C. Parliamentary Committee. Bowerman indicated that the English working classes were "not prepared to take strike action on the subjects indicated; that in any case a National Conference would be necessary; and that up to this moment the Parliamentary Committee had opposed the holding of a special conference on the subject." Renaudel and D'Aragona supported Jouhaux in his contention that the French and Italian movements were committed to action, but that "this action would be less weighty if the British movement did not associate with it." Moreover, after emphasizing that the British public in particular was wrought up about intervention in Russia, Jouhaux warned that the proposed ballot might entail a fatal delay.

At this point the foreign delegates withdrew to enable the Labour Executive to deliberate in private. It rapidly became clear that this executive would not be shaken in its view that "the organization of industrial action in pursuit of political objectives was not within the scope or powers of the Labour Party." Of course, should the trade unions decide to act, which was most unlikely, the party would support them. Meanwhile, the executive was prepared to organize a series of nationwide demonstrations of protest against Allied intervention in Russia on a date to be agreed upon with the Allied delegates.

Late in the night of the twenty-fifth the foreign delegates rejoined their British colleagues. Henderson urged them to accept the executive's compromise proposal. C. T. Cramp, President of the National Union of Railwaymen, put the weight of the more cautious elements in the Triple Alliance behind this scheme, insisting that should this Alliance ever strike it would do so "to achieve certain definite objectives" and not for simply "demonstrative" purposes.

When the meeting reconvened at 6:00 p.m. on the twenty-sixth, the foreign delegates reluctantly accepted Labour's proposal. So as to cover up internal disagreements a public announcement would stress that the workers in each country would hold their own demonstration "in the form best adapted to their circumstances and to their method of operation." This announcement would also make it clear that apart from protesting intervention, the demonstrations were aimed at "the specific political or economic objects demanded by circumstances in each country."

The discussion then turned to a search for a mutually acceptable date. Jouhaux and Dumoulin pressed for July 2, but the Italians claimed they could not get ready on such short notice. Because the French were afraid of the nationalist groundswell at the annual celebration of Bastille Day (July 14), the delegates finally scheduled the Continental strikes and the British demonstrations for July 20 and 21. Quite obviously, precious time was being lost. The excitement and activism of the May–June strikes had faded and the organizers faced the formidable task of regenerating them, particularly in France and England.[1]

Before adjourning, the much enlarged and Anglicized Action Committee of the Berne International agreed on a resolution drafted by Ramsay MacDonald, Sidney Webb, and Robert Williams—to be read at all strikes and demonstrations on the appointed day. Not surprisingly, this manifesto was rather mild. In sweeping and undifferentiated strokes it welcomed the "Revolutions which had destroyed the old order in Russia, Germany, Austria, Hungary and elsewhere," called for an end to military intervention and to the extension of material aid to the "leaders of the counterrevolutions in these countries," and served notice that these manifestations would be reinforced by Parliamentary pressures.

At the Labour Party Conference, meanwhile, a heated debate raged about the wisdom, legitimacy, and expediency of using the strike weapon for political purposes. In his keynote address the chairman, John McGurk, argued that it would be both "unwise and undemocratic, because we fail to get a majority at the polls, to turn around and demand that we should substitute industrial action."[2] With the proposed strike action against intervention foremost on their minds Sexton, Tillett, and Clynes took turns bolstering McGurk's caveat. Clynes even warned that the use of the strike to terrorize the government and other classes, which would signify the abandonment of constitutional methods, could only result in "tears and blood."[3]

Hodge, Smillie, Williams, and Bromley—the top leaders of the Triple Alliance—set out to explode the Clynes thesis. All four were restless because ever since mid-April the right-wing majority of the T.U.C. Parliamentary Committee had ignored their repeated pleas for a

---

[1] See Edouard Dolléans: *Histoire du Mouvement ouvrier*, 2 vols. (Paris: Colin; 1953), II, 312–13.

[2] Labour Party: *Report of the 19th Annual Conference*, 113; and *The Times* (London), June 26, 1919.

[3] Labour Party: *Report of the 19th Annual Conference, passim*, esp. 160–1; and *The Times* (London), June 26, 1919.

firm stand against intervention in Russia. They now tried to enlist the Labour Conference on their side with the argument that Parliamentary and industrial action, far from being mutually exclusive, actually were calculated to reinforce each other. Eventually, with the help of bloc voting, they secured 1,893,000 against 935,000 votes in favor of a resolution protesting intervention. This same resolution instructed the Labour Executive to consult with the Parliamentary Committee of the T.U.C. "with a view to taking effective action to enforce . . . [this protest] by the unreserved use of their political and industrial power."[4]

This vote was taken after Henderson had cautioned the delegates that if the British labor movement were to initiate a general strike for political objectives not the party but the trade unions, whose members and treasuries would have to carry the burden, should themselves "realize the responsibilities . . . and determine the plan of any such new campaign." But by balloting time Henderson had also informed the conference about the consultations and agreement with the French and Italian representatives, and had pledged the executive to "begin at once to organize these simultaneous demonstrations to be held throughout the country."[5]

That the conference resolution would be interpreted restrictively became evident at the meeting of the new executive on June 27. Once Henderson had read "a list of the suggested constituencies for holding demonstrations," the members unanimously resolved "that two speakers should be supplied to each of the places accepting the *suggestion* [to hold such a demonstration], and that the general arrangements for same be left with the head office [italics mine]."[6] Apparently the Labour leaders did little to stir the Parliamentary Committee of the T.U.C. into active cooperation. In fact the top echelons of the Labour Party, the Parliamentary Labour Party, and the T.U.C. Committee were equally reticent to risk any serious confrontation with the government. Only the leaders of the Triple Alliance—with notable exceptions like J. H. Thomas—and the British Socialist Party kept clamoring for industrial action to end intervention in Russia and conscription at home.[7]

On July 1, in Paris, the Executive of the CGT, Frossard and Paul Faure for the SFIO, and Serrati for the ISP, formally approved the July 20–21 movement, as outlined by their four-man delegation to Southport. Accordingly, the British labor movement would stage massive popular demonstrations throughout England on July 20, a Sunday; while the French and Italian proletariat would stage a general strike of

---

[4] Labour Party: *Report of the 19th Annual Conference,* 116–23, 156–61.
[5] Ibid., 116, 156.
[6] Labour Party: Minutes of the Executive Committee, 18, June 27, 1919.
[7] See Alan Bullock: *The Life and Times of Ernest Bevin,* I (London: Heinemann; 1960), 105–6.

twenty-four hours on July 21, a full working day. Moreover, the anti-interventionist theme would be interwoven with the most burning domestic issues peculiar to each Allied nation.

In France Jouhaux and his colleagues, who took full charge of the organization of the projected strike, decided to give priority to domestic over foreign issues in their summons to the workers. They were asked to lay down their tools in support of the CGT's long-standing but thus far abortive campaign against the high cost of living; for speedier demobilization; for the restoration of civil liberties; and for an across-the-board amnesty of political prisoners. The protest against intervention in Russia and Hungary was mixed in with—nearly submerged by—this bill of domestic particulars; and the Versailles Treaty was not even mentioned.[8]

Meanwhile the secretaries of the member federations were notified that the projected strike was an implementation of the decision taken by the CGT's National Council on May 23–24. They were asked to convene their administrative committees to examine and organize the work stoppage in their respective trades and industries and to use the executive's proclamations as guidelines for propaganda. Similar instructions went out to the secretaries of each of the departmental organizations, with a reminder to use Sunday, July 20, for the last-minute coordination of all strike activities in their region. All alike were asked to enforce rigorous discipline and to limit the strike to twenty-four hours.[9] Between July 8 and 18 the executives of most of the affiliated federations—including those of the railwaymen, miners, dockers, and textile workers—announced their participation and urged their sections to maximum effort. The railwaymen as well as the postal employees decided for the strike in spite of official threats that they would endanger their jobs.[1]

On July 13–14, in the midst of these syndical preparations and of France's main national holiday, the National Council of the SFIO convened in Paris. Its principal purpose was to fix the party's attitude toward the Versailles Treaty. From the start the ex-*minoritaires* were in a commanding position. Out of a total of 1986 ballots, 1420 were cast for the resolution asking the Parliamentary delegation to vote against ratification of the treaty. Even Grumbach, speaking for Alsace-Lorraine, voted with Longuet, Mayéras, Faure, Frossard, and Mistral. Moreover, the left-radicals—Loriot, Saumoneau, Mayoux—provided additional support for the antiratification stand, without muting their call for instant accession to the Third International. The ex-*majoritaires* were swamped. They rallied a mere 168 votes, 114 votes for

[8] See the communiqué about the July 3 session of the CGT's Executive Committee, Jouhaux's own justification for the strike, and the CGT's formal appeal of July 14, in *l'Humanité*, July 4, 13, and 15, 1919.
[9] See the text of these instructions in *l'Humanité*, July 6, 1919.
[1] See *l'Humanité* and *le Populaire*, July 8–19, 1919.

abstention and 54 in favor of qualified approval. However, on the critical question as to whether to make the injunction to vote against ratification subject to formal party discipline, the imbalance was not nearly so great. Only 1133 advocated the use of the party whip; with Renaudel another 437 favored leaving the Socialist deputies a choice between rejection and abstention; and still another 319 simply "invited" the deputies to vote against ratification.[2]

But in the concluding night session these fissures were momentarily papered over when Longuet moved a resolution urging all Socialists to support the general strike of July 21, which he insisted was called and organized by the CGT. Renaudel seconded this motion, which was carried unanimously.

While in France the CGT took complete charge of the preparations of the strike, the SFIO merely providing moral and ideological encouragement, in Italy the Socialists and the syndicalists worked hand in hand from the very start. On July 5–6 D'Aragona met with representatives of the executives of the ISP, the CGL, and the all-important Union of Railwaymen to ratify the Southport plan. All agreed to strive for a complete standstill of the economy, accompanied by vast street demonstrations. Unlike either the British or the French, they were willing to chance a test of strength with the untried Nitti government. This being so, the Italian leaders recognized the need for an emergency committee of Socialists and syndicalists to direct and control the July 21 movement. Moreover, mixed committees were formed on the local level.[3]

In the communiqué in which D'Aragona and Lazzari announced the Italian movement's "energetic and coordinated" participation in the international strike, the protest against intervention in Russia and Hungary received first priority.[4] Shortly thereafter, in their formal appeal to the workers to strike from midnight on the nineteenth through midnight on the twenty-first—hence, forty-eight hours—there was not even a passing reference to economic grievances. The Italian workers were simply summoned to join their French comrades in a "complete general strike," which would be coordinated with powerful trade-union demonstrations in England, in order to prevent the three Allied Governments from strangling Lenin and Béla Kun.[5]

The specter of a general strike began to haunt Italy's political class. Memories of the general strike of 1911 and of Red Week in 1914 were still fresh. Admittedly, thus far the post-Armistice labor unrest had

[2] For the complete minutes of this National Council see l'Humanité and le Populaire, July 14–16, 1919; for a brief précis see Parti Socialiste: Rapport du Secrétariat: la vie du parti d'octobre 1918 à janvier 1920, 14–16.

[3] Avanti, July 7, 1919.

[4] Cited in Avanti, July 7, 1919.

[5] Cited in Avanti, July 13, 1919.

been amorphous and erratic. But with the ongoing economic and financial crisis generating widespread discontent, this protest against intervention might become the occasion for the coordination of hitherto unconnected outbursts.

Mussolini seized on the July 20–21 movement as the perfect illustration of the unconscionable recklessness of Italy's Socialists. They alone were aiming at a forty-eight-hour stoppage in the nation that could least afford it. The British Left planned to restrict itself to Sunday demonstrations; and the French intended to stay out only twenty-four hours. Besides, the main purpose could not be to impair the intervention in Russia and Hungary, since the Italian government had no active part in it. All the talk about saving the Eastern revolutions was designed to conceal the real purpose, which was to seize power for a cabal of unscrupulous and determined politicians. This being so, all Fascists were urged to be vigilant. They would protect the nation without, however, defending the established order, whose panic-stricken bourgeoisie was deserting the cities. As in 1917, the Fascists would defeat "this second criminal Caporetto-like assault." All the interventionists who had suffered in the trenches were summoned to check once and for all this "bastard breed" of Bolsheviks which was out to rob Italy of her hard-won fruits of victory to save the nation from dishonor. Until the emergency was over a special committee of the Fasci di combattimento, sitting in Milan, as well as local committees, would mount the guard.[6]

The *Corriere della Sera,* not to speak of the *Gazzetta del Popolo,* joined Mussolini in trying to instigate distrust of the militant leaders among the workers. "Why should the Italian proletariat make twice as many sacrifices for Lenin and Béla Kun as the English and French proletariat," particularly since Italy "not only had done nothing against the Bolsheviks but was even being accused of having helped them in Hungary?"[7]

Presently Nitti told the *camera* that Italy was not intervening against the Bolshevik regimes in Russia and Hungary any more than she had intervened against tsarist despotism before the war. At the same time, in a widely publicized circular, he advised all prefects that the projected strike "had no legitimate aim"; that the vast majority of workers realized that in Italy the strike had no concrete objective; and that only "small groups and noisy minorities were hoping to take advantage of the strike to provoke disorders." In any event, "order would have to be maintained at any price, against whoever it may be." Significantly, the Premier was not exclusively concerned about left-

---

[6] See the *Popolo d'Italia,* July 12–18, 1919, cited in Edoardo and Duilio Susmel (eds.): *Opera Omnia di Benito Mussolini* (Florence: La Fenice; 1954), XIII, 234–45; and G. A. Chiurco: *Storia della rivoluzione fascista, 1919–1922* (Florence: Vallecchi; 1929), I, 152–3.

[7] Cited in *Bulletin Périodique de la presse italienne,* No. 117, August 2, 1919 (July 12–27, 1919), 8. See also *Avanti,* July 16, 1919.

wing troublemakers. For he also notified the prefects that it would be "the height of folly to allow certain demonstrations which on the surface seemed patriotic . . . but in reality were not of good faith, to coincide with the general strike."[8] As in France, state employees were threatened with the loss of their jobs.

This press and cabinet campaign furthered dissension within the labor ranks. On July 16 the three-man Executive Committee of the Railway Syndicate, meeting in Rome, urged all sections to forsake the strike against the government's foreign policy in favor of simply going on record as endorsing the Labour Party's manifesto. *Avanti* promptly denounced Durando Emilie, Faggiano Luigi, and Fanti Ferdinando for yielding to Nitti's rhetoric and blandishments. Moreover, a rival committee hastily convened in Turin, as well as numerous local sections, appealed for continuing militancy. Even so, the majority of sections and railway workers swung behind the Executive Committee. Simultaneously the defection spread to the post office workers, the other major unionized sector of government employees.[9]

Mussolini hailed the pullback of the railway workers' executive under the caption "Daybreak" and congratulated the syndicalists for rebelling against the ISP, which had turned Leninist. Not that he objected to revolution as such. But for him, a revolution was not in the nature of *un ballo di S. Vito* or an improvised fit of epilepsy. It was the methodic use of violence in the pursuit of clear objectives. The projected strike failed to meet these criteria. And in any case, by now it was perfectly obvious that it would "neither be international nor general in Italy."[1]

Lazzari desperately tried to ward off hostile propaganda and to stem the defections. In one manifesto he countered the claim that Italy had no hand in the intervention, stressing that the government had recognized Kolchak, dispatched troops to Murmansk and Siberia, collaborated in the overthrow of the Archangel Soviet, and participated in the blockade. In another appeal he sought to embolden wavering spirits by stirring their pride in the Italian party's initiative in the rebirth of international working class cooperation. In still another he expressed his confidence that the workers would answer the strike call in spite of "mounting pressure, intimidation, and maneuvering by all declared and concealed enemies of the Socialist cause."[2]

In the course of July 19, the day immediately preceding the strike, the organizers suffered another severe blow. The press disseminated

---

[8] The text of Nitti's telegraphic circular to the prefects, released to the press by the Stefani Agency on July 18, 1919, is cited in *Bulletin Périodique de la presse italienne*, No. 117, August 2, 1919, 8–9.

[9] *Avanti*, July 17–19, 1919.

[1] *Popolo d'Italia*, July 17–19, 1919, cited in Susmel (eds.): *Opera Omnia*, XIII, 243–51.

[2] For the text of Lazzari's appeals see *Avanti*, July 16–18, 1919.

and Nitti confirmed reports that the Confederation of Labor in France had just called off its strike and that Jouhaux had notified his Italian colleagues of this decision.[3]

The turnabout by the French CGT came during the final week of preparations. With the threat of the general strike in the offing the Socialists served notice that on July 15 they would question the government about the high cost of living which agitated ever wider circles.[4] In fact, that day the Republican Socialists and the left wing of the Radical Socialists stole the initiative from the SFIO. It was Augagneur who moved a motion critical of the government's overall economic policy. In particular, this motion charged that whereas in France the cost of living had steadily risen since January 1919 it had been cut by one half in Belgium and by one quarter in England. No doubt after consulting Clemenceau or other cabinet colleagues, Victor Boret, the Minister of Agriculture, came forward on July 18 to brand the order of the day as unacceptable and to urge the *chambre* to reject it. Much to his dismay, the Augagneur motion passed by 227 against 213 votes. In turn, Boret submitted his resignation to Clemenceau, who promptly accepted it.[5]

Since in calling for the defeat of the Augagneur motion the government had not posed the question of confidence, Clemenceau had no intention of submitting his cabinet's resignation. The Socialists maintained, however, that the issue on which the government had been voted down was so vital that Clemenceau could not regain the legislature's confidence by merely sacrificing his Minister of Agriculture. In brief, they convinced themselves and set out to convince others that France was on the verge of a serious cabinet crisis.[6]

Undaunted and with the deadline for the general strike approaching, the government was determined to stand fast. In the morning of July 18 the Premier's office notified Jouhaux, Dumoulin, and Laurent that Clemenceau expected them at 7:30 p.m. that same day. The CGT leaders never even considered ignoring this summons. They obligingly postponed the meeting of the Executive Committee—at which the final strike manifesto was to be approved and issued—from 4:00 in the afternoon until after their unexpected but momentous interview.

In this interview Clemenceau held out the promise of an across-the-board amnesty and indicated that demobilization would be completed by the end of September. But having made these concessions, the Premier warned that because the projected strike was of an essentially political nature his government was prepared to use all necessary means to maintain order as well as to operate the public services.

---

[3] See *Bulletin Périodique de la presse italienne,* No. 117, August 2, 1919, 9.
[4] See Cachin's article in *l'Humanité,* July 13, 1919.
[5] *JO* (July 15 and 18, 1919), 3477–91 and 3597–614.
[6] See the commentaries by Cachin and C.-E. Labrousse in *l'Humanité,* July 19, 1919.

According to one report, at the time that Clemenceau notified the CGT leaders of this resolve they had learned that "military trucks driven by Annamites were drawn up around the capital, ready to converge on the center with loyal troops."[7]

Jouhaux and his colleagues immediately went to the Executive of the CGT which was waiting for their report. After a long and heated debate and apparently without consulting the SFIO, in the early hours of July 19 the executive issued a communiqué announcing the indefinite postponement of the strike. By then the syndicalists were in a position to justify this drastic reversal with the claim that the threatened strike had already produced important results: the *chambre* had condemned the government's economic policies and assurances had been extracted with regard to both the amnesty and the demobilization. On the twenty-first, instead of a strike, the National Council would meet in special session to take stock of the new situation.[8]

At this session Jouhaux reported that "the mass of workers" had not responded as enthusiastically as he had hoped and that Clemenceau had left the impression that "the government intended to use all necessary means to suppress the movement." Even so, the strike order would have been maintained except for the vote by which the *chambre* demonstrated its determination to "act against the high cost of living," which all along had been the principal issue.[9]

Actually Jouhaux had to answer two sets of critics. Even though the anti-Socialist press once again praised him for his statesmanlike moderation, it questioned his explanation for the last-minute cancellation. The *Temps, Figaro,* and the *Journal des Débats* insisted that rather than pretend that the strike was merely being postponed, Jouhaux should admit that the general strike was canceled because it was doomed to fail. Public opinion at large was hostile; the mass of workers neither understood nor approved the movement; the syndicalist leaders were seriously divided among themselves on the issue of political strikes; and the British and the Belgian workers refused to join their French and Italian comrades.[1]

Another set of charges was leveled by the militants within both the CGT and the SFIO. Jouhaux, and even more so Laurent and Dumoulin, were accused of being afraid of Clemenceau, of having lost touch with the masses, of having a narrow bread-and-butter outlook, and even of seeking to discredit the advocates of direct action. They

---

[7] Since thus far no minutes of this interview have turned up this discussion is based on press reports in *l'Humanité, le Populaire, le Figaro,* and *le Temps,* July 19–21, 1919.

[8] The text of this communique is cited in *l'Humanité,* July 19, 1919.

[9] See *l'Humanité* and *le Populaire,* July 23–24, 1919.

[1] *Le Temps,* July 20 and 23, 1919; *le Figaro,* July 20, 1919; *Journal des Débats,* July 23, 1919; *l'Action Française,* July 19, 1919.

were indicted for failing to take advantage of the prerevolutionary crisis that consumed France in mid-1919. The chiefs of the CGT also had demonstrated bad tactical judgment: whereas in mid-June, at the height of the economic crisis, they warned against a political strike, within a few weeks, when this economic crisis was subsiding, they changed their minds—only then to reverse themselves again. According to Monatte, the high command of the CGT "refused action when it was possible while appearing to favor it once it no longer was."[2]

Jouhaux became particularly vulnerable to left-wing attack after July 22. That was the day that Clemenceau appeared in the *chambre* with Joseph Noulens, his new Minister of Agriculture. The choice of Noulens offended the Socialists, who remembered his anti-Kerensky and anti-Bolshevik role while Ambassador to Russia. More important, the *chambre* now reversed itself. By a vote of 272 against 181 it rejected the same Augagneur motion that it had approved just a few days ago and by a vote of 289 against 176 renewed its confidence in Clemenceau.[3]

The cabinet crisis from which the Left expected so much never materialized, and Jouhaux could no longer use the vote of July 18 as a justification for calling off the strike. He and his colleagues now conceded that the leaders of many federations objected to striking for political purposes, that there was a profound gulf between reformist and revolutionary leaders, that the rank and file were slow to answer the summons, and that the coordinating machinery was inadequate. Above all, he stressed that it was dangerous to raise barricades and launch a general strike before the blueprints and cadres for postrevolutionary politics were ready, because a revolution culminating in famine was condemned to self-destruction.[4]

In both England and France, then, the July 20–21 movement collapsed ignominiously, this retreat being a consequence of divisions and hesitations within the Left rather than of the threat of government repression. Across the Channel "the only strikes of importance were these of the London Dockers, the Norwich Boot and Shoe Operatives, and the Merthyr Miners." As for demonstrations, which the Party Executive had sanctioned, they achieved varying degrees of success. In London there were two rallies, one at Trafalgar Square and another in Victoria Park, both being poorly attended as well as marked by friction

---

[2] See Frossard's articles in *le Populaire*, July 26, 1919, and in *l'Humanité*, July 30, 1919, as well as Pierre Monatte's article "The Fault of the Masses?" in *la Vie Ouvrière*, July 23, 1919.

[3] *JO* (July 22, 1919), 3626–37.

[4] See the text of Jouhaux's address to the National Council of the CGT as well as Cachin's editorial endorsement of Jouhaux's thesis in *l'Humanité*, July 26, 1919. See also Dolléans: *Histoire du Mouvement ouvrier*, II, 313–15; and Bernard Georges and Denise Tintant: *Léon Jouhaux* (Paris: Presses Universitaires; 1962), 368–71.

with counterdemonstrators. In a "great many other towns" the official party resolution was solemnly passed.[5]

The leaders of the Italian strike movement were outraged by the French CGT's counterorder which, however unintentionally, was a "strong and treacherous blow" against them.[6] Coming on top of the reticence of the British trade unions, it reinforced the defectors within their own ranks while at the same time playing into the hands of the opposition press. Certainly the government workers felt encouraged to abide by their decision to bolt. Significantly, by keeping the railroads running on both July 20 and 21, the railwaymen forestalled what might otherwise have been an all-encompassing general strike—for on Monday, July 21, the work stoppage was nearly complete in the private sector of Italy's industrial and urban economy. In any case, with the public services in full operation, neither the government nor the Fasci had either cause or excuse for interfering, so that the day passed without serious incidents.

Still, Turati was bitter about being abandoned by the Allied Left. At a public rally in Rome he struck out at the British Labourites for being "the bourgeoisie of the international proletariat." With D'Annunzian overtones he denounced them for welcoming the Versailles Treaty which, by strengthening England's maritime and colonial mastery, enabled them to "eat five meals a day and work seven hours." As for the French proletariat, it also readily accepted a treaty which recovered Alsace-Lorraine and secured the wealth of the Saar basin. D'Aragona, who had played a leading role in the launching and co-ordination of the all-European protest movement, confessed to an over-flow crowd at the People's Theater in Milan that he was baffled by the desertion of his French colleagues.[7]

Whatever the reasons for the Anglo-French defection, the damage was done. The *Corriere* and the *Stampa* agreed with Turati that the "international strike failed because there was no International." But whereas the *Corriere* welcomed this bankruptcy of an International devoid of realism and contemptuous of nationalism, the *Stampa* half-regretted it, primarily because it preferred attacking the Versailles settlement with a united front of the Left instead of the Right.[8]

The conspicuous collapse of the July 20–21 movement produced mixed reactions among the members of the Permanent Commission of the Berne International, which met in Lucerne from August 3–10.[9]

[5] Report on Revolutionary Organizations in the U.K., No. 13, July 24, 1919, G.T. 7790, Cabinet 24/84.

[6] *Avanti,* July 22, 1919.

[7] *Avanti,* July 22–23, 1919.

[8] *Corriere della Sera* and *Stampa,* July 22, 1919, cited in *Bulletin Périodique de la presse italienne,* No. 117, August 2, 1919, 9.

[9] Since there is no *compte-rendu* of the Lucerne Conference, the story must be pieced together from press reports and commentaries between August 3 and 15, 1919.

The moderates, including the executive and the Bureau of the International, seized upon it as justification for past and future caution, insisting that neither the workers nor prevailing conditions were anywhere near the revolutionary threshold and that the governments were ready, able, and eager to crush any challenge from below. On the other hand, the radicals, without completely rejecting this diagnosis, denounced the moderates for their excessive caution as well as for their alternating faith in and fear of the established governments. Even Cachin, who occupied a middle position between Renaudel and Longuet, could no longer contain his impatience with the arid diplomatic strategy and tactics of the International's Bureau and executive, which had kept singularly aloof from the general strike movement.

In any case, even though Longuet, Fritz Adler, Hilferding,[1] Troelstra, and MacDonald gave the non-Communist left wing greater coherence and driving force than it had mustered at the Berne Conference, the right wing retained a controlling majority in both the plenary and the major committees at Lucerne. Branting, Huysmans, and Henderson, who ran the "apparatus," had all draft-resolutions prepared by moderate, pro-Allied, and anti-Bolshevik Socialists. They actually entrusted the drafting of the all-important resolution on "The General Political Situation" to the safe and sober British delegation.

This majority resolution did not enter a flaming protest against the Versailles Treaty.[2] Rather, it welcomed "the formal conclusion of peace" for preparing the atmosphere in which the International could effectively appeal to the victorious peoples to press their governments into making the peace treaties "more favorable" to international reconciliation. Moreover, instead of execrating the League as a capitalist and bourgeois institution, the majority hailed it as "the first effective international organ," whose role would be the more effective "in the degree to which it was penetrated by Socialism."

The minority was appalled by the resigned and cowardly tone and purpose of this document. As if oblivious to the recent strike fiasco, in a rival draft they summoned the conference "to turn to account revolutionary situations created by the war, in order to gain and exercise political power everywhere for the realization of socialism and the abolition of the classes." It was the duty of the International to take a

---

The most complete coverage of the debates in the plenary sessions is in the *Journal de Genève*. The dispatches by Amédée Dunois and Henri Dumont, special correspondents of *l'Humanité* and *le Petit-Parisien* respectively, are quite informative. There are also revealing commentaries by Cachin, Frossard, Renoult, and Longuet in *l'Humanité* and *le Populaire*.

[1] USPD leader who was editor of the influential *Freiheit*. Sickness prevented Haase from attending; the reasons for Kautsky's absence are not clear.

[2] For the full text of all resolutions—majority, minority, joint, and special—see Labour Party: *Report of the 19th Annual Conference*, 218–30.

vigorous stand on two key questions—the peace treaty and the victors'
intervention against the Bolshevik regimes in Russia and Hungary.
With regard to the treaty, the "signal rebuff to the Wilsonian proposals
at the Peace Conference was sufficient proof that the capitalism of the
Entente States was resolved to defend the fruits of its victory," and
the peoples could not be pacified by vague and empty promises of early
revisions.

On the issue of intervention, which the majority resolution dodged
altogether, the minority bluntly asked that the Lucerne Conference
continue the vigorous protest initiated by the "recent common decisions of the Socialist Parties of France, England, and Italy." Not that
Longuet, Adler, Hilferding, MacDonald and Troelstra even by implication meant to endorse the Bolshevik theory and practice. As if to avoid
commitment to both the atrophying Berne International and the untried Third International they explicitly refused to pronounce themselves "on the methods of the Russian Bolsheviks" and urged that all
"questions of tactics" be reserved for subsequent debate. In the meantime, the International had a solemn duty to defend the Russian
Revolution and to protest the strangling of the Hungarian Socialist
Republic and nation by the Entente-supported Rumanian oligarchy,
which was the *avant-garde* of the "new capitalist Holy Alliance." But
even the two-and-a-half Internationalists could do no more than place
the International's *moral* force at the disposal of the Russian and
Hungarian peoples.

Even so, the gulf between the Social Patriots and the Independents
was too wide to be bridged. Renaudel, Vandervelde, Müller, and, only
to a slightly lesser extent, Henderson were not about to avow the
bankruptcy of their loyal defensism in wartime and their compliant
remonstrances during the Peace Conference. Besides, in addition to
genuine ideological, programmatic, and tactical differences, the
Lucerne Conference was torn asunder by sharp personality conflicts as
well as by the jockeying for position by the rival factions of national
delegations. The Renaudel-Longuet duel was symbolic of this double-
barreled incipient schism. In the SFIO Renaudel's faction had long
since yielded control to the increasingly militant ex-*minoritaires*. He
was much weaker at home than in the International, which he sought to
bring into play to recover ground for the flagging ex-*majoritaires*. As
for the British and the German Majority leaders, they were eager to use
the leverage of international solidarity to maintain their supremacy at
home against the radicalized Independents. In the Permanent Commission at Lucerne, in which nineteen nations were represented, the Social
Patriots of the major victor and vanquished nations, together with the
Belgians, fought their rear-guard action with the help of the Swedish
and Danish majority, the Dutch right-wing minority, the Russian
Mensheviks and Social Revolutionaries, and such small or dependent

nationalities as the Estonians, Lithuanians, Georgians, Ukrainians, and Armenians.

This inchoate block, dedicated to the survival of a *reformist* International, was under heavy attack by France's ex-*minoritaires,* the USPD, the Austrian Social Democrats, the British minority, and the Dutch majority. Especially when Renaudel once again tried, as he had at Berne, to put the Bolshevik dictatorship on trial for its oppression of Socialist parties and attacks on the Socialist governments of border states, the breach between the two opposing groups became irreparable. The Independent leaders, sensitive to the ongoing radicalization of their own followers, were not willing to sanction a break between the Second and the Third International, particularly since they wanted no part of a Second International dominated by Social Patriots. In spite of Lenin's uncompromising conditions for cooperation with the Independents, Longuet and Adler were determined to work for an all-inclusive International in which an Independent-Bolshevik axis would keep the reformists at bay. They were strengthened in this resolve by the knowledge that both the Italian and the Swiss Socialist parties, which were not represented at Lucerne, favored such a course.

At any rate, there was too little common ground between the opposing blocks for them to agree on a compromise of the two resolutions on "The General Political Situation." Both were allowed to stand, while the conference rallied around a joint resolution repeating the criticisms of the peace treaty which the Action Committee had voiced in May.

Of the seventeen special resolutions adopted at Lucerne the ones on Russia and Hungary were of greatest importance. Hilferding and Irakly Tseretelli drafted the resolution which protested intervention in Russia and invited all Socialist parties to agitate for the withdrawal of troops, without any censure whatever of Bolshevik methods. Just then the overthrow of Béla Kun caused a mixture of consternation and rage among the delegates. For fear of further uniting Centrists like Cachin with the Independents, the Social Patriots decided not to press their condemnation of the Soviet dictatorship and their glorification of parliamentarism. In fact, at the very last moment Renaudel himself drafted and moved the resolution on the Hungarian situation. He held the Allies responsible for the outright "counter-revolutionary regime" which followed the withdrawal of the Soviet government, perhaps implying that intervention would have been acceptable provided the Hungarian Social Democrats had inherited the state. The return of the Archduke Joseph, which was even too brazen for the Big Four, smoothed the way for the unanimous acceptance of Renaudel's indictment that "in their desire to bring to naught all revolutionary conquests, the Allied Governments did not even hesitate to restore the ancient dynasties which were responsible for the war."

Epilogue:
Disillusioned Intelligentsia

THE FIRST WORLD WAR brought about an unintentional and radical transformation in both national and international politics. The concert of powers that had controlled European affairs until 1914 was gravely mutilated. Its reconstruction was complicated, if not thwarted, by the decomposition of Austria-Hungary, the Revolution in Russia, and the exhaustion of the three Allied powers.

None of the successor states, which from the start were consumed by unsettling border and minority conflicts, were promising candidates for Austria-Hungary's place in the directory of powers. Their vicissitudes, congenital with new nation states, threatened to become a source of chronic instability, thereby undermining rather than steadying the new international system.

But this disturbance would have been less sweeping and easier to regulate if Russia had survived as a major power in good standing. With France able to rely on Russia as the chief counterweight to Germany, Poland's ambitions would have been kept in check. Moreover, the proximity of Russian military power would have compensated for the distance that separated the weak and vulnerable successor states from their Western protectors. In more general terms, with Russia in the picture, France could have afforded to be more lenient with Germany.

Incidentally, Russia did not withdraw from the European system; she was excluded from it. This exclusion was ideologically and politically motivated, particularly with statesmen and generals who otherwise advertised their unswerving allegiance to the canons of the balance of power. The further to the right they stood on the political spectrum, the greater their opposition to any diplomatic *rapprochement* with

Lenin. In the last analysis, then, Russia was ostracized and quarantined because of her revolutionary transgression, and this transgression became both cause and excuse for treating Russia as if she were a decaying empire. Not that Lvov or Kerensky could have salvaged the full territorial integrity of prewar Russia, assuming they had wanted to. But in all likelihood they would have been asked to send delegates to the Peace Conference. In that event Poland and Rumania would have had to moderate their demands and the entire settlement in the borderlands separating Russia and Germany would not have been made so heavily at Russia's expense.

Because of their own military and economic exhaustion the Allies, in particular France, could ill afford this violation of the rules of power politics. That they had overreached themselves became even more apparent once the Unied States recoiled from Europe. Again, America's withdrawal, not unlike Russia's expulsion, was activated by political considerations in foreign policy and not by considerations of *raison d'état*.

The end of the war emergency and the intensifying contest between revolution and counterrevolution pushed the primacy of foreign policy into the background. Whereas the Big Four succeeded in arranging a brittle truce in Europe's international politics, it was beyond them to calm domestic affairs. The legacy of disorder, frustration, and exhaustion actually intensified political tensions beyond what they had been before the war; and disappointments with the outcome of the Peace Conference intensified these tensions still further. The signing of a diplomatic document could not lessen or liquidate the massive world crisis whose locus shifted from the international to the internal arena. Hereafter foreign policy issues became caught up in partisan politics; foreign policy and diplomacy became pawns in the domestic struggle for power. In Italy, Germany, and France the old and the new Right combined to indict their governments for selling out at Versailles, thereby laying the groundwork for the Fascist and National Socialist insurgency. Throughout Europe and America the non-Communist Left, shaken by the failure of Wilsonianism, was torn between retreat from politics and sympathy with the Third International.

Whereas Paul Birdsall credits Wilson with having prevented the worst,[1] Harold Nicolson maintains that a "hypocritical compromise" was worse than either a Wilsonian or a Carthaginian settlement. This being so, he would have had the Big Four organize the Conference "upon a basis of greater reality."[2] What Nicolson considered greater realism is not clear. But perhaps he shared Churchill's estimate that Wilson "gained as an antagonist and corrector results which were piti-

[1] Paul Birdsall: *Versailles Twenty Years After* (New York: Reynal and Hitchcock; 1941), 9, 295.
[2] Harold Nicolson: *Peacemaking 1919* (New York: Harcourt, Brace; 1939), 95.

fully poor compared to those which would have rewarded . . . his making common cause with Lloyd George and Clemenceau."[3] Needless to say, had Wilson taken this course of least resistance, in all likelihood the treaty would have been even more than less severe.

But even assuming the peace had been concluded somewhat more swiftly and the terms had been less exacting, would it have mattered? Colonel House quite rightly conjectured that "the same forces that had been at work in the making of this peace would be at work to hinder the enforcement of a different kind of peace."[4] In the victor as well as in the vanquished nations the superpatriots were poised to attack the treaty, whatever its terms. The wrath of the German Right could only have been attenuated at the cost of arousing the French and British jingoists. Though a diplomatic and legal instrument, the treaty, including the covenant, was forged into a salient political issue.

Meanwhile, whereas Wilson's arrival in Europe had been marked by wild popular enthusiasm, his departure for America was barely noticed. Few, if any, of the original enthusiasts remained loyal to the President. Though the treaty filled him with despair, G. Lowes Dickinson was one of the few to take the trouble to assure Wilson that he knew that the hope-inspiring covenant was "due in the main to your faithful and untiring efforts."[5] William Allen White was equally reluctant to blame him for the outcome. He watched the "slowly gathering forces" close in on Wilson, who "was bound to the rocks, with the vultures forever at his entrails." These "damned vultures" had "taken the heart out of the peace . . . and the joy out of the great enterprise of the War, and made it a sordid malicious miserable thing like all the other wars in the world." From London White wrote Baker that it would break his heart "to know how the radicals of the world had left him, how they jeered and hooted at his name."[6]

The UDC, Wilson's most authentic and prestigious booster, also was fast abandoning its hero.

> The odds were gigantic—true. He was inadequately supported—true. But how much better to have fought to the last, to have gone down fighting, if need be, for the principles in which he believed; to have flung out a last appeal to the peoples . . ., if necessary to have resigned the Presidency of the United States, rather than to be false to himself and to betray humanity. . . . Humanity can evolve an antidote for the tyrant and the despot. It recovers hardly from the statesman who proclaims a high ideal, only to stand impotently by while it is shattered to pieces before his eyes.[7]

[3] Churchill: *Aftermath*, 450.
[4] House Diary, June 29, 1919.
[5] G. Lowes Dickinson to Wilson, May 20, 1919, in Wilson Papers, VIII A:55.
[6] William Allen White to Ray Stannard Baker, June 3, 1919, in Baker Papers, Series Two, Box 125, attached to notebook XXIV, 1919.
[7] *The U.D.C.*, June 1919, 330.

The few genuine Wilsonians in Germany were similarly shaken. They considered his bankruptcy their own and, like their Anglo-American counterparts, looked to Socialism for guidance.[8]

Democratic Socialists, while conceding that Wilson had served their cause for a while, proclaimed that it was beyond the last of the *grand bourgeois* to prevent the inevitable debacle. His defeat was the defeat of bourgeois idealism which was "occasionally sincere but always powerless." By late July Marcel Cachin confessed that Socialists no longer "dared" invoke their Wilsonian dreams.[9]

In France Alfred Rosmer, in Britain Neil Maclean, and in America Max Eastman struck an altogether more belligerent tone. According to Rosmer, in Paris Wilson served no purpose except to spread an idealistic veneer over a predatory treaty. Maclean denounced Wilson as a "commercial traveler for American capitalism" whom European labor could not trust as long as he kept American Socialists in jail. As for Eastman, he concurred that Wilson's "disinterested idealism . . . amounted to a heroic determination to surround himself and the general public with a blinding vapor of self-righteous emotion all the time that the job was being done."[1]

Once again Léon Blum issued an exceptionally moving cry of despair. Although in 1918 he had refused to choose between Wilson and Lenin, preferring to remain loyal to the memory of Jaurès, his cultivated mind went on being seduced by the elegance and *élan* of the President's ideology and rhetoric. He confessed that he had really believed that this war was *la guerre du droit,* and that the capitalist regime, notwithstanding all its iniquities, was the carrier of precious principles of individual rights, of public law, and of international law and morality. Consequently, when aggression endangered these values in 1914, French Socialists had to come forth to fight for them, much as they had done during the Dreyfus Affair. But now the punitive peace terms raised grave doubts in Blum's mind: had he rallied to the bourgeois-capitalist state under the hypnotizing spell of the romantic republicanism which had informed his youth? Granted, war was a generator of national and individual egotisms. Even so, the Carthaginian outcome was not foreordained. According to Blum, the libertarian political morality and legal conceptions which existed outside Socialism could have been advanced by "maintaining close contact with *l'âme populaire;* by heeding the voice of Berne; and by following the pure glow which flowed from Wilson's messages and arrival in Europe." But instead of keeping their tacit agreement to remove the

---

[8] Alfred H. Fried: *Mein Kriegs-Tagebuch* (Zurich: Max Rascher Verlag; 1920), IV, 396–7, 409, 413, entries of April 18, May 10 and 17, 1919.
[9] See Daniel Renoult, "M. Wilson s'en va," and Cachin, "Bilan," in *l'Humanité,* June 28 and July 28, 1919.
[1] *La Vie Ouvrière,* May 14, 1919; Labour Party: *Report of the 19th Annual Conference* (Southport, 1919), 115; *The Liberator,* June 1919, 5.

seeds of war in exchange for the Socialists' wartime loyalty, the Allied Governments disavowed not only the men of the Left and of good will but also the libertarian idea, morality, and faith. This dual disavowal was at the heart of "the *crise de conscience*" into which Blum felt himself thrown by the statesmen of Versailles.[2]

Socialists and radicals of all persuasions only gradually realized that America was becoming a chief pillar of unreconstructed capitalism. As Bertrand Russell suggested, "so long as America was content to believe in the Liberal ideas of 1776, so long not only Bolsheviks or Spartacists, but even conventional Socialists, could not hope to maintain themselves for more than a moment in any important country: their existence would be inconvenient to American capital and therefore, through the usual channels for educating public opinion, odious to the American nation."[3] But whereas Russell maintained that unless the forces of social reconstruction conquered America they would be thwarted in Europe, for the *Dial* the needs of the impoverished and prostrated old world rather than the wealth and liberalism of the new would have to stoke the engines of reconstruction.[4] By capitulating to the Allied Premiers for fear of precipitating revolution, notably in France, Wilson "only made the revolution more certain." In fact, he might well have driven "the last nail into the coffin of European capitalism" by convincing the disillusioned masses that only radical change could secure the ideals that Wilson espoused but failed to attain.[5]

The President is not likely to have been insensitive to the domestic reforms which would have to be consummated in America as well as in the Allied nations if a new start were to be made in international relations. Even during the Conference Wilson was repeatedly urged to translate this sensitivity into action. At Tumulty's suggestion George L. Record bluntly told Wilson that he would have to tackle questions of national reconstruction at the same time that he fought for the League. In the wake of the Eastern and Central European revolutions the glorification of *political* democracy would earn him few plaudits, especially in the Western nations, where it had long since been secured. Under the challenge of Socialism the issue of *economic* democracy simply had to be faced.

> The only way to meet this menace of socialism, if menace it is, is by offering a better program for the removal of injustice in our industrial and social relations . . . You should now undertake a job worthy of your great abilities. You should become the real leader of the radical forces in America, and present to the country a constructive program of fundamental reform, which shall be an

2 See his "La Victoire et la paix," in *l'Humanité*, July 19, 1919.
3 Cited in *The Dial*, June 28, 1919, 631.
4 *The Dial*, July 12, 1919, 26–7.
5 Robert Dell writing in *The Dial*, June 28, 1919, 634.

alternative to the program presented by the socialists, and the Bolsheviki, and then fight for it. . . . This program would gather around you at once, as if by magic, the forces of intelligent and orderly radicalism who have been looking in vain to you for leadership, and are now in a state of profound discouragement.

Record called on Wilson to place his reform program before a special session of Congress, thereby turning the flank of the Republicans and putting them on the defensive. Probably not only the Republican but also the Democratic party would split; and a third party might form around this program. Granted, the odds were against the success of such a flanking operation. Even so, Wilson had to try it, if only to secure his place in history. The League, without this underpinning, would not justify his being recognized as "a truly great man."[6]

But Wilson gave no sign of being attentive to questions of domestic reform. He was absorbed in peacemaking and he was fearful of endangering the League by stirring up additional political controversy. He may not have realized the extent to which rising prices, strikes, and political intolerance were stirring the nation. Moderates of both parties were unable to deny the political initiative to militants of the Right and Left. There was need for presidential leadership as much in domestic as in foreign affairs.

In early June Tumulty took it upon himself to press his chief into facing up to his home front, where the progressive forces were as much in retreat as they were in the Allied nations.

> It is clear to me, as it must be to you after witnessing the aftermath of war in Europe and the reaction in this country, that something vitally reconstructive must be done to save the world from something more terrible than European war. What happened in Washington last night in the attempt upon the Attorney General's life[7] is but a symptom of the terrible unrest that is stalking about the country. Very few people, and especially the gentlemen on the Hill, realize the absolute seriousness of the whole situation. As a Democrat I would be disappointed to see the Republican Party regain power. That is not what depresses one so much as to see growing steadily from day to day, under our very eyes, a movement that, if it is not checked, is bound to express itself in attack upon everything that we hold dear. In this era of industrial and social unrest both parties are in disrepute with the average man. . . . It is, therefore, your duty as the leader of the liberal forces of the world to speak the truth about the whole situation and to propose the remedy.

[6] For the full text of Record's letter to Wilson, dated March 31, 1919, see James Kerney: *The Political Education of Woodrow Wilson* (New York: Century; 1926), 438–46.
[7] On the night of June 2, 1914, an anarchist exploded a bomb in front of the Washington home of A. Mitchell Palmer.

Tumulty recommended that the President convene a national industrial conference at which representatives of business and labor would chart guidelines for a national plan for the improvement of the relations between capital and labor. Guided by Britain's Whitley program,[8] he envisaged giving labor a share in the profits and a voice in management. Moreover, he wanted the conference to consider such questions as the public ownership of railroads, the control of public utilities, the "reasonable" return on industrial investments, and the "control of fundamental necessities like oil, steel, and coal."

Tumulty conceded that by pushing this kind of program the President might provoke "a realignment of parties and a fight between Federalist and Anti-Federalist, Whig and Tory, Democrat and Republican, Bull Moose and Stand Pat." In the meantime, however, the conference would *"invite industrial peace by exposing the rainbow of promise rather than intensify the cloud of hopelessness* [italics mine]."[9]

At about this same time Lincoln Steffens, who had recently been to Russia, placed his concern about the American scene before Colonel House. After noting that public opinion was "confused, impatient, and apt to break into acts of violence," Steffens urged that it be dealt with as soon as peace was signed. As a first step he advocated a most generous and sweeping pardon of all political prisoners. Then, once the "shock of extreme pardon had forced attention to a better spirit," the government should relieve this shock with "a plan for a reasonable consideration of ways out of the difficulties." This two-phase program was designed to thwart Bolshevism by fighting it in a spirit other than the Bolshevik spirit. Steffens championed the use of reason "so far as it may be used to avoid the class struggle."[1]

Significantly, the very day that the treaty was signed in Versailles Wilson asked Tumulty to express to Palmer and Burleson the President's "earnest desire to grant complete amnesty and pardon to all American citizens in prison or under arrest on account of anything they have said in speech or in print concerning their personal opinions with regard to the activities of the Government" during the war. Wilson thought it only fitting that such a generous and just act "accompany the signing of the peace."[2]

But Palmer thought otherwise. Protesting that no one had been convicted "for mere expression of opinion," but rather for "obstructing the war under statute," the Attorney General successfully prevailed on

---

[8] Councils for each industry, composed of representatives of capital and labor, to discuss industrial problems, including wages and hours.

[9] For the full text of Tumulty's letter to Wilson, dated June 4, 1919, see Wilson Papers, VIII A:56. Except for a few rather crucial sentences this letter is cited in Kerney: *Political Education*, 446–8.

[1] "Memorandum Submitted by Lincoln Steffens to Colonel House" (no date; mid-June 1919?), in Wilson Papers, VIII A:69.

[2] Wilson to Tumulty, June 28, 1919, in Wilson Papers, VIII A:68.

Wilson to postpone consideration of amnesty and pardon until after his return.[3] During the weeks following Wilson's return the sentences of some 100 persons convicted under the Espionage Acts were commuted. But Palmer balked again when Wilson asked for the release of Eugene V. Debs. He admitted readily that the ten-year sentence was excessive. On the other hand, Debs continued to be defiant and unrepentant. More important, his release would "be used by many opponents of the peace treaty as evidence of too great leniency toward law violators of the radical element in the labor classes, in a way that would prejudice many people against the liberal labor provisions of the treaty." Wilson meekly accepted Palmer's judgment that consideration of all remaining cases, including the case of Debs, should be postponed until after the treaty actually went into force.[4]

By the time Wilson came home from Europe the treaty-*cum*-covenant had developed into a highly political issue. Even though he scrupulously refrained from making programmatic pronouncements about domestic reconstruction and reform, he was widely suspected of planning to use the putatively apolitical Covenant to marshal a coalition whose unity and *élan* subsequently could be harnessed for reform purposes. Whereas Lodge, Root, and even Taft were determined to check Wilson because he was too radical for their taste, Borah and LaFollette opposed him because of his sham progressivism.

Indeed, the League was a perspicuous symbol of the spirit, program, and forces of progressive liberalism. It provided for the limitation of armaments, the removal of tariff walls, the amelioration of labor conditions, and the termination of go-it-alone colonial imperialism. Both Taft and Root, who together with their conservative Republicans were the mainstays of the League to Enforce Peace, eagerly championed an international organization designed to facilitate the peaceful settlement of diplomatic disputes between and among nations. But that was before Lodge spelled out the full political implications of Wilson's world project. Hereafter all three set out "not only to discredit the League in order to discredit Wilson, but also particularly . . . to discredit Wilson's reform program."[5]

As for the American forces of movement, they opposed Wilson for precisely the opposite reasons. Before the Armistice they balked at the rigorous application of the Espionage Acts and at Burleson's censorship; after November 1918 they denounced the officially sanctioned Red Hunt. They were suspicious of Wilson because he failed to reinforce his pronouncements about a utopian peace with promises of a new deal at home. But even if he had done so, their suspicions would

[3] Tumulty to Wilson, June 28, 1919, in Wilson Papers, VIII A:68.
[4] A. Mitchell Palmer to Wilson, July 30, 1919, and Wilson to Palmer, August 1, 1919, in Wilson Papers, Box 611.
[5] Ruhl J. Bartlett: *The League to Enforce Peace* (Chapel Hill: University of North Carolina Press; 1964), 211–14, esp. 213.

not have been allayed readily. The country had once before "been drugged by words about 'The New Freedom' and true democracy" and radicals, not to speak of Socialists, were not about to succumb to Wilson's "hypnotic powers" for a second time.[6]

Still, until the preliminary draft of the treaty crushed their spirits in mid-May, they continued to put great stock in the League project. In fact, they tended to consider it their own. As of mid-1918 these liberal internationalists began to fight for the soul of this League with the conservatives, who dominated the League to Enforce Peace. By November 1918 a rival League of Free Nations Association had been chartered, sponsored by John R. Commons, John Dewey, Charles and Mary Beard, Thomas W. Lamont, Frank P. Walsh, Felix Frankfurter, Learned Hand, Herbert Croly, Jacob Schiff, E. R. A. Seligman, and Ida Tarbell. These liberals declared that the League would have to secure for each nation not only security but also equal economic opportunity. To achieve this dual goal national sovereignty would have to be curtailed. Accordingly, the member nations would pool their arms for purposes of collective security; and the inter-Allied war agencies for shipping, food, raw materials, and finance would be "continued during the very considerable period of demobilization and reconstruction." The new association also stipulated that membership be limited to nations with governments "responsible to the people" and that there be "effective popular representation" in the League's legislative organ.[7] Here lurked the anticipation that the League would become the international expression of democratic and progressive regimes. As the Peace Conference convened, the association summoned the American people to support Wilson against Clemenceau, Smuts against Lodge, Cecil against Reed, economic freedom against rival armaments, the League of Nations against the balance of power.[8]

This appeal found little if any resonance in either of the two major parties. At this stage liberals could at best look for a sympathetic hearing to several of the larger but nonpolitical labor unions, to the moderate wing of the Socialist party, to the Non-Partisan League, to the National Conference of Social Work, and to a host of religious groups.

In mid-March they resolved to seek a more solid political base by rallying radicals of all persuasions around a common program and organizing them for common political action. Some of the same men who sponsored the League of Free Nations Association—notably Allen T. Burns, Lincoln Colcord, and Will Durant—founded the Committee

---

[6] *The Nation*, July 5, 1919, 4.

[7] For the statement of principles of the League of Free Nations Association see *The Nation*, November 30, 1918, 650–1.

[8] See the Association's advertisement "Which Shall it Be?", in *The Dial*, January 25, 1919, 97.

of Forty-Eight for this purpose. Their initial manifesto was a call for a party to oppose reconstruction both to reaction and to revolution.

> Despite America's splendid success in a war waged against foreign autocracy, our country is menaced by the growing power of an autocratic and reactionary minority at home. . . . The very classes whose labors in factory and field are the basis and substance of our economic power, find no effective political medium through which to express their economic demands, but by deceptive diversions of our party-system are denied their proper representation. . . . America cannot grow much more in these old [party] skins. Rather must reconstruction derive its impetus and direction from the political organization of the manual and mental workers. . . .

The committee summoned the leaders of "liberal thought and all forward looking citizens" to meet in special conference and show the way to the "leaders of the new labor parties and of the organized farmers."[9]

This second party proposed to do battle for "a new deal" against both Republicans and Democrats, who represented one and the same "party of order and stability," while at the same time stealing the march on the radical Left.[1] But by the time the national conference finally met in St. Louis in December 1919 the dream of such a realignment had long since evaporated. Even after Wilson's refusal to turn Left was apparent to all, the Committee of Forty-Eight never managed to mobilize and unify "the independent radical fringe," which continued to be fragmented into so many cults, movements, and organizations of a radical nature.[2]

On both sides of the Atlantic this contraction of the vital political center, punctuated by Wilson's defeat at Paris, left the intelligentsia in a serious quandary. With a few notable exceptions, intellectuals— scholars, writers, artists, scientists, and professionals—had supported the war effort of their respective countries. Some had done so with pristine enthusiasm; others with a troubled conscience. As of 1917, when war and revolution became enmeshed, they could no longer simply rally to the flag. Within each nation the prewar fissures re-appeared, and they were forced to locate themselves on the political spectrum. Hereafter they opposed each other across trenches as well as across party lines.

To many of the brainworkers in both belligerent camps Wilson came as a godsend. Especially those who never ceased to be troubled about having enlisted in a narrow national cause found comfort in the

[9] See the full text of the manifesto "Revolution or Reconstruction" in *The Dial*, March 22, 1919, 274.

[1] Committee of 48, Pamphlet No. 1: Allen McCurdy, *Wanted—A Ballot Box*, 6–8. See also "A New Political Alignment," in *The Nation*, March 22, 1919, 460–1.

[2] Lincoln Colcord, "The Committee of Forty-Eight," in *The Nation*, December 27, 1919, 821–2.

universal moral purpose of his manifestoes. Moreover, his call for a moderate peace appealed to them because it was premised on the primacy of reason and rationality over passion.

In 1917–18 conscience-stricken intellectuals seized upon Wilson's ideology to rationalize their loyalty and service to the warfare state; after the Armistice they transmuted it into a world view with which to make sense of a crisis-torn universe. Unlike Leninism and Socialism, Wilsonianism did not require its followers to subscribe to a political orthodoxy or to affiliate with a political party. It enabled intellectuals to eschew hard and fast political commitments without, however, opting out of the struggle between darkness and light. Through Wilson they ranged themselves on the side of progress and reform.

Once the fighting had stopped these intellectuals, who were chary of political affiliations, craved to reestablish contact with their colleagues in other countries. In December 1918 the Committee for the Federation of Peoples, with headquarters in Holland, circulated an appeal for a constructive peace which gathered some 100 signatures, among them Jane Addams, Albert Einstein, Sigmund Freud, John Galsworthy, Upton Sinclair, Israel Zangwill, and Romain Rolland.[3]

At about this same time E. D. Morel began to think about "internationalizing" the British Union of Democractic Control. When asking Romain Rolland to head up a French section he assured him that even though several UDC leaders were members of the ILP, the UDC as such "had no position on questions of domestic politics." However, the workers had to be the primary target of UDC-type propaganda, since they needed to be convinced that popular control of foreign policy "was intimately tied to the progress of democracy in internal affairs." Morel wanted all "realistic pacifists" to pool their efforts in support of the international program of Socialism. As a first step he proposed the release of a manifesto expounding UDC's ideal of international reconciliation and popular control, to be signed by "a small number of men and women, who represent an activist intellectuality."[4]

But by far the most stirring initiative originated with G. F. Nicolai, the biologist, and Romain Rolland, the writer. To protest the intelligentsia's sellout to the nation at war, both had gone into voluntary exile, the one from Germany to Denmark, the other from France to Switzerland. In October 1918 Nicolai launched a new periodical, *Das werdende Europa*, with an appeal to intellectuals to put their Europeanism ahead of national loyalties. He invited Rolland, who considered himself "a European of the first hour," to contribute an article to the second issue. Rolland agreed to do so, but not without first

[3] Text and signatures cited in Romain Rolland: *Journal des Années de guerre, 1914–1919* (Paris: Albin Michel; 1952), 1670.

[4] The full text of Morel's letter to Romain Rolland, dated February 19, 1919, cited in Rolland: *Années de guerre*, 1748–51. See also Herbert W. Horwill, "Toward a New International," in *The Nation*, May 41, 1919, 864–5.

asking that "the limits of the City be extended beyond Europe." Fearful that tomorrow Europe and America—the white world—would be pitted against Asia—the colored world—Rolland wanted the appeal to be addressed to the "intellectual élite of Asia" as well.[5]

In his article for Nicolai's journal Rolland challenged the intelligentsia to reaffirm its freedom.

> The states as well as the social parties make intellectuals into servants and instruments. Such was the case in the autocracies; such is the case in the bourgeois democracies; and such will be the case in the proletarian revolutions. Recently I read in [a] . . . Bolshevik organ that the collaboration of the intellectuals with the working class would be accepted provided the intellectuals submitted to the iron discipline and will of the Soviet Government.—Will art and science allow themselves to be domesticated? Will thought become a State Ministry, and thinkers state functionaries? Let us protest! Thinkers of all countries, let us issue our freedom charter, the Declaration of Intellectual Independence. We are at the service neither of reaction nor of revolution—but of reason. We are on earth not to contribute to human conflicts, but to unite and to harmonize. . . .[6]

At this juncture Rolland was equally fearful of the corroding influence of revolution and counterrevolution. In a letter to Stefan Zweig he foresaw a "hideous crusade against the Russian Revolution by Europe's 'liberal,' 'democratic,' and 'republican' bourgeoisie." Upon completion of this shameful enterprise a "dishonored Europe would languish in her own filth: the bourgeois hypocrisy of great principles and big 'democratic' capital would enslave not only the masses, but also the élite, the body, and the intellect."[7] Meanwhile, although he expected Wilson to join in this crusade, for the time being Rolland advocated support for the President in the peace negotiations. Wilson alone might be able to check the "ferocious appetites and the instincts of vengeance" among the victors, thereby establishing a "provisionally tolerable and relatively equitable modus vivendi in Europe, without first unleashing social violence."[8]

In mid-March Nicolai visited Rolland in Switzerland. Once again Rolland complained that Nicolai's "heart shuddered only for the suffering of the white races and that his humanitarianism stopped at the borders of the yellow peoples."[9] Eventually they agreed that Rolland should draft a manifesto to the intellectuals of the world and not just of Europe or the West.

[5] Rolland: Années de guerre, 1623–4.
[6] Cited in ibid., 1637.
[7] Rolland to Zweig, November 2, 1918, cited in ibid., 1635.
[8] Rolland to Enrico Bignami, November 17, 1919, cited in ibid., 1654.
[9] Ibid., 1761.

This Declaration of Intellectual Independence called on the brain-workers, who "for five years were separated by armies, censorship, and mutual national hatreds," to forge more solid bonds than had existed before 1914.

The War threw confusion into our ranks. Most intellectuals put their science, art, and reason in the service of their governments. We neither accuse nor rebuke any one. We know the weakness of the individual soul and the elemental force of great collective currents: the latter swept the former aside with ease because no preventive measures had been taken in advance. Let this be a lesson to us for the future.

Let us take stock of the disastrous consequences of the near-complete abdication of the world's intelligence and its voluntary enslavement to unchained forces. Thinkers and artists added a vast quantity of poisonous hatred to the scourge which is gnawing at Europe's body and soul. They searched their arsenal of knowledge, memory, and imagination for old and new historical, scientific, logical, and poetic reasons to hate. They labored to destroy mutual understanding among men. And, in so doing, they disfigured, debased, humbled, and degraded thinking as such, which they represented. They transformed thought into the instrument of passion and (perhaps unintentionally) of the selfish interests of some political or social caste, of some state, nation, or class. . . .

Stand up! Redeem the Intellect from the compromises, from these humiliating alliances, from this concealed bondage! The Mind knows no master. We are the servants of the Mind! We recognize no other master. We exist to carry and defend its light, to rally around it all misguided men. It is our function and duty to maintain a fixed point, and to point to the lodestar when the whirlwind of passion sweeps over the right. We do not choose between these passions of arrogance and mutual destruction; we reject them one and all. We vow to serve only Truth unfettered by frontiers, limits, and prejudices of race or caste. To be sure, we are not disinterested in Humanity. Indeed, it is for Humanity that we work, but for the *whole* of Humanity. We do not recognize different peoples. We know only *the* People—one and universal—the People that suffers, struggles, falls only to rise again, and forever marches forward on the rough road drenched with its sweat and blood—the People of all men, all equally our brothers. . . .[1]

Rolland and Nicolai proposed to get three world-renowned sponsors from each nation. Eventually the list of signatories included Benedetto Croce, Zweig, Hermann Hesse, Heinrich Mann, Jean-Richard Bloch, Georges Duhamel, Einstein, Ernst Bloch, Bertrand Russell, and Israel Zangwill.

Some accepted the text as it stood; others signed only after trying,

[1] The full text of this declaration is cited in ibid., 1769–71. A translation was published in *The Liberator*, December 1919, 23.

unsuccessfully, to get the text modulated. Zangwill signed with enthusiasm, as both Englishman and Jew; Croce wanted it understood that for him the "war was sacred, but that Truth was also sacred and should not be used as an instrument of war"; Heinrich Mann would have preferred a change from "we do not recognize different peoples" to "we recognize different peoples, but above them we recognize . . ."; and Bertrand Russell objected to condemning intellectuals for their wartime transgressions for fear of complicating their reconciliation with those who had remained above the battle.[2]

At Russell's suggestion Rolland invited George Bernard Shaw to associate himself with this "challenge to world-wide reaction and to the self-enslavement of nearly the entire European élite." In line with Russell's caveat Shaw asked "for a confession rather than a censure, otherwise we will look like Pharisees or even snobs." But whereas Russell left no doubt that in the last analysis he was prepared to accept Rolland's original wording, Shaw was not nearly so accommodating. In fact, he took it upon himself to revise the text drastically, making his signature contingent on the acceptance of his position.

> The War threw confusion into our ranks. It constrained us to put our science, our art, our reason in the service of our governments. In a war, as in a shipwreck, one ceases to be a scholar, an artist, or a philosopher and becomes a soldier, a sea-dog, a patriot: for national defense one must sacrifice and even prostitute not only one's life, but also one's soul, intellect, and conscience, and wield lies as unscrupulously as bayonets and bombs, . . . Let us submit that under the yoke of this odious necessity we, artists and thinkers, contributed to the scourge. . . .

Needless to say, Rolland impassionately rejected Shaw's proposition that of necessity the requirements of war fatally sweep everything before them. He would never admit that even in wartime an intellectual's first duty is to national defense. For Rolland, at all times—in peace, prewar, and war—the "defense of thought" retained absolute precedence over nation and even home. He was equally quick to disagree with Shaw's exhortation that now that "peace gave them back their freedom" the intelligentsia should take full advantage of it, insisting that neither of them had "waited for the return of peace to speak freely."[3]

In America Max Eastman had other grounds for not joining Nicolai and Rolland. Even though he shared their indignation about

---

[2] Rolland:*Années de guerre,* 1818–20, 1790–2, and *passim.* The complete list of signatories seems difficult, if not impossible, to reconstruct. For example, according to Rolland's diary the text went out to Tagore and to George Brandes, but their response is not recorded.

[3] For the Rolland-Shaw exchange see ibid., 1796, 1815–17.

the intellectuals' "wanton perversions of judgment" during the war, he demurred at making "intellectuality in the abstract [into] a far more sovereign and inclusive ideal than truth itself warrants." Actually, Eastman charged that all the time that Rolland glorified this unfettered mind he presupposed that this mind would serve the ideal purposes which he himself had chosen. In other words, by implication Rolland conceded that the mind could serve either tyranny and reaction or liberty and democracy. This being the case, the time had come to harness the mind to the "science of revolution based upon the Economic Interpretation of History." For according to the postulates of that science, if liberty and democracy were to be achieved, intellectuals had to place themselves and all their powers "unreservedly upon the side of the working class in its conflict with the owners of capital." Eastman wanted the intelligentsia, in its social guise, to "adopt a fighting mentality . . . and to engage in a conscious class struggle." To widen further the gulf between himself and Rolland, Eastman repudiated the distinction between on the one hand, a "separate class" and a "superior cult" of intellectuals representing "higher thought" and, on the other, the lower orders.[4] Later, when refusing his cooperation to the *Clarté* movement, Eastmen flatly declared that liberty and peace would be won not "by intellectuality, reason, [and] 'the power of thought' . . . [but by] the self-protective will of the exploited classes."[5]

Clarté was another attempt to enlist forward-looking intellectuals in the struggle for a better world. The original impetus came from Henri Barbusse, author of the superrealistic antiwar novel *Le Feu* and president of a vast association of progressive war veterans in France. In January 1919 he and some ten second-string writers issued an appeal "To the Fighting Intellectuals of the World." They appealed to those who, unlike "the great intellectuals who failed in their moral mission, . . . kept their faith in man's dignity and . . . the power of reason [even under] the clash of fire and steel." These brainworkers of the trenches, whose patriotism and valor were beyond reproach, were asked to rally around Wilson: "his voice is ours and our voice is his, in spite of everything and everybody."[6] Barbusse and his co-founders— notably Cyril-Berger and Vaillant-Couturier—remained loyal to Wilson through mid-June, by which time some 300 French writers, artists, journalists, and actors had gathered about them. Rolland refused to lend his name not so much because his faith in Wilson had run out but because he doubted the sincerity and reliability of these

[4] Max Eastman: "A Letter to Romain Rolland," in *The Liberator,* December 1919, 24–5.
[5] *The Liberator,* April 1920, 41.
[6] *Le Populaire,* January 17, 1919.

heterogeneous, latter-day converts to internationalism, whom he seemed to scorn intellectually, morally, and socially.[7]

Barbusse nevertheless continued his campaign to make *Clarté* into a worldwide "League of Intellectual Solidarity for the Triumph of the International Cause." By the end of the year he had assembled a 30-man international executive committee which included such notables as George Brandes, Georges Duhamel, Anatole France, Charles Gide, Thomas Hardy, E. D. Morel, Jules Romains, Upton Sinclair, H. G. Wells, and Stefan Zweig. The next step consisted of establishing national sections in the principal countries to work in close harmony with the executive committee, whose seat was in Paris.[8]

Ironically, even though it assumed an undisguised political and revolutionary position, *Clarté* momentarily attracted even some of the more cautious minds, including George Bernard Shaw. This may have been so because as compared to Rolland's declaration, which was circulated between March and June 1919, *Clarté's* organizational drive occurred in the second half of that year. By then the Versailles Treaty had shattered all remaining illusions, notably among the radical intelligentsia.

In his manifesto Barbusse pointed to Wilson's tragic fall as the agonizing symbol of this disillusionment and bankruptcy.

> The figure of Wilson epitomizes the disability and impotence of all liberals and semi-clairvoyants. There was a time when Wilson issued social pronouncements whose lucidity touched on the sublime. He proclaimed that the struggle between democracy and autocracy was under way throughout the world; that governments should be the servants of the people, and not vice versa; that the people had the right to dispose of themselves; that trade and the seas should be free; and, above all, that the general interest should supersede the national interest. Revolutionaries, intransigents, and rationalists, all of us excitedly hailed these great utterances when they reverberated around the world.
>
> Since then Wilson has become an accomplice of the authors of the Versailles Treaty which systematically negates the Wilsonian principles. Was Wilson bewildered and paralyzed by the secret treaties . . . ? Did he consider it expedient to try and save appearances instead of protesting boldly and peremptorily . . . ?
>
> No, the truth lies elsewhere. *Wilson never really understood what he had said.* He never attributed the complete and splendid meaning to his pronouncements that we did. He never thought about the demolition and reconstruction which the integral implementation of his propositions would require. Instead, he quite sincerely allowed his high moral and social commandments to be translated into half-

[7] Rolland: *Années de guerre,* 1824–5, 1828–31.

[8] For the full membership of this executive committee and the formal statutes of the League, which continued to be known as the *Clarté* movement, see Henri Barbusse: *La Lueur dans l'abîme: Ce que veut le Groupe Clarté* (Paris, 1920), 147–53.

measures which annihilated them openly or on the sly. In truth, was Wilson worthy of the insult which Clemenceau intended him when he spoke of his exalted candor? [italics mine].[9]

For Barbusse and the *avant-garde* of intellectuals the perfidious treaty was only the diplomatic manifestation of an overall retrogression. It was cut of the same political and social cloth as a host of other developments that the victors promoted, encouraged, or condoned: the intervention in Russia; the White terror in Hungary; and the retreat of Social Democracy or Radical Democracy in Germany, Poland, Austria, Luxembourg, and Finland.[1] The triumph of the old and the new Right in America, Britain, France, and Italy completed the picture.

The great promises of 1917–18 turned out to have been a pipe dream. Obsessed by the flaws in the treaty, the war and blockade against Soviet Russia, and the counterfeit domestic reconstruction and reform, the dazed intelligentsia simply discounted the League as a combination victors' club, Holy Alliance, and capitalist directorate, all rolled into one. Internationally Wilson was discredited, as Lenin had predicted he would be; and his campaign for the Covenant in America could not rehabilitate his stature. At the same time, in America and throughout Europe the political parties and social forces with which the Radical intelligentsia historically felt most at home were decimated, pushed further to the right, or in full retreat—the progressives in the U.S., the Liberal Party in England, the advanced Radical Socialists in France, and the Liberals and Radicals in Italy. Even in Germany, between January 1919 and January 1920 the Democratic Party's percentage of the popular vote fell from 18.6 to 8.3, foreshadowing its uninterrupted decline down through March 1933, when it plummeted to 0.8 per cent. Meanwhile, even though the Catholic parties in both Italy and Germany had vital progressive wings, they were unlikely havens for confirmed secular intellectuals.

These could have turned, of course, to the Socialist and labor parties, which were growing rapidly in size, strength, and influence. But so many of them were less willing to forgive the Socialist than the Liberal leaders for their wartime contraventions. After all, the former had long been sworn explicitly to put their allegiance to internationalism ahead of national loyalty. When the test came in July–August 1914, and until 1917, the Majoritarian leaders, undeterred by the rank and file, dutifully championed the cause of national defense. Only in the wake of war weariness, the Russian Revolution, and Wilson's liberalizing intervention were the European Social Patriots forced to make grudging concessions to the Independents, who all along had tried to hold aloft the banner of internationalism.

[9] Ibid., 115–17.
[1] Ibid., 37–43.

After the Armistice the internecine struggle between Majoritarians and Independents redoubled in intensity. They battled for supremacy not only in the various Socialist and labor movements but also in the renascent Second International. The Majoritarians pugnaciously justified their unconditional wartime defensism, advocated minimum economic and social reforms, and pressed for an irrevocable break with Bolshevism. Especially once the Versailles Treaty and the continuing intervention in Russia had wrecked their Wilsonian premises and pretensions, they lost the initiative to their Independent rivals.

The Wilsonian debacle also unsettled the Independents, though less fatally, or so it seemed. They had been Wilsonians of the first hour, in that they began to champion enlightened war aims before Wilson. Moreover, their defensism never ceased to be highly qualified. As a result, the outcome of Versailles, like the revelation of the secret treaties before, came as a vindication of their nurtured skepticism and opposition. Wilson's defeat did not come as a real shock, since they never really expected conservative and bourgeois governments and autocratic empires to implement left-Socialist foreign policy programs. Lenin's strictures against the Independent renegades were vastly overdrawn. Admittedly, they were not direct-action revolutionaries, but neither did they *consciously* and *intentionally* delude themselves and the proletariat about the anticapitalist and anti-imperialist thrust of the war, short of defeat on the scale experienced by Russia.

In fact, Lenin was their surrogate conscience all the time that they rode Wilson's coattails. With Wilson gone, the Independents became particularly vulnerable to Lenin's broadsides against them. This vulnerability had two sides: psychological, in that they could not reject out of hand the Bolshevik charge that they were approaching bankruptcy; political, in that they were determined to turn left to compete with the Bolsheviks for the allegiance of the radicalized workers, who were turning away from the stand-pat Majoritarians. Philosophically, morally, and ideologically the Independents were at least as repelled as their right-Socialist rivals by the excesses of Bolshevik theory and practice. Besides, they expected backward Russia to be as violent in revolution as she had been in reaction. In any case, at this point the Independents were not inclined to censure Bolshevik excesses without at the same time denouncing the intemperance of the advancing counterrevolution. It was Jaurès who, in speculating about the aftereffects of war in 1905, forewarned of "crises of counterrevolution, of violent reaction, of exasperated nationalism, of stifling dictatorship, of monstrous militarism, a long chain of retrograde violence and enslavement."[2] The Independents also grudgingly admired the Russian Bolsheviks for their

---

[2] Cited in Milorad Drachkovitch: *Les Socialismes français et allemand et le problème de la guerre, 1870–1914* (Geneva: Droz; 1953), 108.

revolutionary *élan,* their fanatic dedication to an utopian ideal, and their heroic courage.

Whereas the Majoritarians were inclined to fellow-travel with preservative forces and governments, the Independents were disposed to fellow-travel with the Bolsheviks and the Third International. To do so was not to accept or consent to the Soviets' operational code, especially not as it applied to matters of internal politics. Quite the contrary. Eventually they hoped to temper the Bolsheviks and to emerge as the rallying focus for a united Socialist front. In the meantime, they compensated for their own self-defeating compromises by energetically protesting the intervention, which they blamed for the rigidification of Soviet politics and administration.

The radical intelligentsia shared much of this Independent Socialist outlook. Above all, both Rolland and Barbusse were staunch internationalists with a strong repugnance for national loyalties, particularly because just then these served the conservative, if not the counter-revolutionary, cause. Moreover, in their desperation about the crisis in advanced industrial civilization and their agony about the senseless and crippling slaughter of the recent war, they turned to the Russian Revolution as the one *lueur dans l'abîme. Clarté* "wanted to make a revolution in the minds of men"[3] to pave and ease the way for a fundamental political, social, and economic transformation of society in accordance with vaguely conceived Socialist blueprints. The details of these plans were less important than their overall direction. These disaffected intellectuals were neither temperamentally nor morally disposed to forsake the world, steep themselves in scholarly pursuits, and leave it to others to worry about the commonweal. Nor were they about to escape into dreams of a sublime and perfect past which they knew were the stock-in-trade of revolutionaries from the Right. These men of thought never even questioned the desirability and feasibility of improving political, economic, social, and moral institutions and conditions through rational action.[4] It was faith in rational progress that attracted Rolland and Barbusse first to Wilson and then to Lenin. Whatever disillusionments and betrayals they experienced along the way were the price they paid for the courage of believing in rational man in history.

[3] See the motto on the cover and title page of Barbusse: *La Lueur dans l'abîme.*
[4] Cf. J. Huizinga: *The Waning of the Middle Ages* (New York: Anchor; 1954), 37–9.

Bibliography

I. UNPUBLISHED DOCUMENTS AND PAPERS

A. *Official Documents of the German Government*

Protokolle des Rats der Volksbeauftragten, Vols. I and II (November–December 1918), in the International Institute for Social History, Amsterdam.

Microfilm files of the German Foreign Ministry. G.F.M. 2: 1688–1692, 4069, 4080, 4097–4099, 4121, 4627, 4662–4665, 9101, 9105; G.F.M. 6: 38, 39, 102; G.F.M. 131. Foreign Office Library and the Public Record Office, London.

B. *Official Documents of the Government of the United Kingdom*

Minutes of the War Cabinet; Minutes of the Imperial War Cabinet; Minutes of the British Empire Delegation at the Paris Peace Conference; War Cabinet Papers G.T. 5700–7700, in the Public Record Office, London.

General Staff, War Office: Appreciation of the Internal Situation in Russia, January 12, 1919 (Secret: For use at the Peace Conference), in Wilson Papers, VIII A: 10.

C. *Official Documents of the United States Government in the National Archives, Washington, D.C.*

State Department Files, in the Foreign Affairs Section, files No. 183.9 (Russia); 184.01 (Coolidge Mission); 184.012 (Gherardi Mission); 184.013 (Dresel Missions); 184.0132 (Dyar Mission); 184.014 (Field Mission); 184.015 (Green Mission); 184.022 (Bullitt Mission); 763.72; 841.504; 851.00; 861.00.

D. *Private Papers*

In the Library of Congress:
Ray Stannard Baker Papers
Tasker H. Bliss Papers
Robert L. Lansing Papers
Henry White Papers
Woodrow Wilson Papers
In the Sterling Memorial Library of Yale University (Edward M. House Collection):
Gordon Auchincloss Papers
William H. Buckler Papers
William C. Bullitt Papers

Walter Goodwin Davis Papers
Edward M. House Papers
Frank L. Polk Papers
William Wiseman Papers
In the Firestone Library of Princeton University:
Ray Stannard Baker Papers
In the Hoover Institution of Stanford University:
V. A. Maklakov Papers
Vance C. McCormick Diary
In the Oral History Collection of Columbia University:
The Reminiscences of Sir Norman Angell
The Reminiscences of Boris A. Bakhmeteff
In the British Museum Library:
Arthur Balfour Papers
Cecil of Chelwood Papers
In the Library of the London School of Economics:
George Lansbury Papers
E. D. Morel Papers
In the Bibliothèque de Documentation Internationale Contemporaine:
Louis-Lucien Klotz Papers

E. *Party and Society Archives*

Archives of the Labour Party, Transport House, London. Minutes of the Executive Council (Vols. 14–18, August 21, 1918–December 8, 1919); Memoranda as well as Minutes and Agenda of the Advisory Committee on International Questions, 1918–1920; Correspondence concerning Peace Conference and International Meetings (1 box); Materials Bearing on the Berne Conference, 1919 (3 boxes); Materials Bearing on the Lucerne Conference, 1919 (1 box).
Archives of the Conservative Party, London. Minutes of the Executive Committee of the National Unionist Association of the Conservative and Liberal Unionist Organizations; Minute Book of the Council of the National Unionist Association; Minutes of the Labour Sub-Committee.

II. PRINTED AND PUBLISHED GOVERNMENT PUBLICATIONS

A. *France*

Journal Officiel de la République Française, Chambre des Députés, *Débats Parlementaires*, Session Ordinaire, 1918–19.
Mantoux, Paul: *Les Délibérations du conseil des quatre*. 2 vols. Paris: Éditions du Centre de la Recherche Scientifique; 1955.

B. *Germany*

Amtliche Urkunden zur Vorgeschichte des Waffenstillstandes, 1918. Berlin: Deutsche Verlagsgesellschaft für Politik und Geschichte; 1928.
Marhefka, Edmund, ed.: *Der Waffenstillstand: Das Dokumentenmaterial der Waffenstillstandsverhandlungen*. 3 vols. Berlin: Deutsche Verlagsgesellschaft für Politik und Geschichte; 1928.

Allgemeiner Kongress der Arbeiter- und Soldatenräte Deutschlands, am 16. bis 21. Dezember 1918: Stenographische Berichte. Berlin, 1918.
Zweiter Kongress der Arbeiter-Bauern-und Soldatenräte Deutschlands, am 8. bis 14. April 1919: Stenographisches Protokoll. Berlin, 1919.
Verhandlungen der Verfassungsgebenden Deutschen Nationalversammlung. Reichstag: Stenographische Berichte. Vols. 326–30. Berlin, 1919.

C. *Great Britain*

House of Commons: *Parliamentary Debates.* 5th ser., 1918–19, Vols. 110–123.
Woodward, E. L., and Butler, R., eds.: *Documents on British Foreign Policy 1919–1939.* 1st ser., Vol. 2. London: H.M. Stationery Office; 1952.
Bolshevism in Russia or Revolutionary Socialism in Practice: Extracts from Reports to British Foreign Office on Bolshevism in Russia, Cmd. 8 (April 1919).
Reports by British Officers on the Economic Conditions Prevailing in Germany, Cmd. 52, 54, 208, 280 (December 1918–April 1919).
Cost of Naval and Military Operations in Russia from the Date of the Armistice to the 31st July, 1919, Cmd. 307 (1919).
Cost of Naval and Military Operations in Russia from the Date of the Armistice to the 31st October, 1919, Cmd. 395 (1919).
Some Considerations for the Peace Conference Before They Finally Draft Their Terms [Fontainebleau Memorandum], Cmd. 1614 (1922).
Ministry of Labour: *Labour and the Peace Treaty.* London, 1919.

D. *Italy*

Atti del Parlamento Italiano. Camera dei Deputati. Legislatura XXIV. Discussioni, esp. Vols. XVI–XIX.

E. *United States*

American Relief Administration: *Bulletin,* Nos. 1–22.
Congressional Record, Third Session of the Sixty-Fifth Congress (Vol. 57: December 2, 1918–March 4, 1919) and First Session of the Sixty-Sixth Congress (Vol. 58: March 4, 1919–November 19, 1919).
Department of State: *Papers Relating to the Foreign Relations of the United States, 1918, Supplement I, The World War.* 2 vols. Washington, D.C.: U.S. Government Printing Office; 1933.
———: *Papers Relating to the Foreign Relations of the United States. Russia, 1918.* 3 vols. Washington, D.C.: U. S. Government Printing Office; 1931–32.
———: *Papers Relating to the Foreign Relations of the United States. The Paris Peace Conference, 1919.* 13 vols. Washington, D.C.: U. S. Government Printing Office: 1942–7.
———: *Papers Relating to the Foreign Relations of the United States. Russia, 1919.* Washington, D.C.: U. S. Government Printing Office; 1937.

III. PARTY AND SOCIETY DOCUMENTS AND
PUBLICATIONS

A. *France*

Bulletin des Droits de l'Homme, 1918–19.
Bulletin du Parti Républicain Radical et Radical Socialiste: Organe officiel du comité exécutif, 1918–19.

Parti Socialiste (SFIO): *Rapport du Secrétariat: La vie du parti d'octobre 1918 à janvier 1920.* Paris, 1920.

———: *17ème Congrès National tenu à Strasbourg 25–29 février, 1920: Compte rendu sténographique.* Paris, 1920.

———: *Rapport sur les négociations conduites à Moscou avec l'Internationale Communiste présenté à la Commission Administrative Permanente par le citoyen Louis Frossard.* Paris, 1920.

———: *Les Résolutions de la Conférence Internationale Ouvrière et Socialiste de Berne,* February 3–10, 1919. Paris, 1919.

B. Germany

Sozialdemokratische Partei Deutschlands (SPD): *Protokoll der gemeinsamen Sitzung des Parteiausschusses und der Reichstagsfraktion,* in Berlin, September 23, 1918. Printed but unpublished copy in the International Institute for Social History, Amsterdam.

———: *Protokoll über die Verhandlungen des Parteitages,* in Weimar, June 10–15, 1919.

Unabhängige Sozialdemokratische Partei Deutschlands (USPD): *Protokoll über die Verhandlungen des ausserordentlichen Parteitages,* in Berlin, March 2–6, 1919.

Kommunistische Partei Deutschlands: *Bericht über den Gründungsparteitag,* in Berlin, December 30, 1918–January 1, 1919.

Deutsche Demokratische Partei: *Allgemeine Werbeflugschriften,* 1918–19.

Deutschnationale Volkspartei: *Flugschriften,* Nos. 1–20.

Bund Neues Vaterland: *Flugschriften,* Nos. 1–15.

Generalsekretariat zum Studium zur Bekämpfung des Bolschewismus: *Revolutionäre Streitfragen,* Nos. 1–14.

———: *Revolutions-Streitfragen* (new edn.), Nos. 1–10.

Institut für Marxismus-Leninismus: *Dokumente und Materialien zur Geschichte der deutschen Arbeiterbewegung.* Ser. II, Vol. 2. Berlin: Dietz Verlag; 1957.

C. Great Britain

Independent Labour Party (ILP): *The I.L.P. in War and Peace: A Short Account of the Party from Its Foundation to the Present Day.* London, 1942.

(1) Labour Party

Inter-Allied Labour and Socialist Conference: *The Replies of the Socialist Parties of the Central Powers to the 'Memorandum on War Aims.'* London, mid-1918.

———: *Report on Conference held in Central Hall, London, September 17–21, 1918* (n.p., n.d., galley proofs in the Archives of the Labour Party).

Notes for Speakers (for the General Election of December 1918).

Report of the Executive Committee to the Emergency Conference on the General Election held in Central Hall, London, November 14, 1918.

Report of the Seventeenth Annual Conference, Nottingham and London, 1918.

Report of the Eighteenth Annual Conference, London, 1918.

Report of the Nineteenth Annual Conference, Southport, 1919.

(2) Liberal Party

The Liberal Magazine. Vols. 18–19. London, 1919–20.

(3) National Unionist Association
Gleanings and Memoranda. Vols. XLIX–L, November 1918–December 1919.
Pamphlets and Leaflets issued during the General Election of 1918, Nos. 1830–1874.

(4) Union of Democratic Control
The U.D.C. Vol. 4, November 1918–June 1919.
The Betrayal of the Peoples. Pamphlet No. 37a (criticizing the preliminary draft of the peace treaty).

D. *Italy*

Partito Socialista Italiano: *Resoconto Stenografico del XV congresso nazionale,* in Rome, September 1–5, 1918.
———: *Rescoconto Stenografico del XVI congresso nazionale,* in Bologna, October 5–8, 1919.
Pedone, Franco, ed.: *Il Partito Socialista Italiano nei suoi congressi.* Vol. III: 1917–26. Milan: Edizioni Avanti!; 1963.
Arfé, Gaetano, ed.: *Storia dell'Avanti.* Vol. I: 1896–1926. Milan: Edizioni Avanti!; 1956.
Partito Popolari Italiano: *La Vita del Partito Popolare Italiano nei suoi tre primi congressi.* Rome, 1923.

E. *United States*

American Federation of Labor: *American Federationist,* 1918–1919.
———: *Report of the Proceedings of the Thirty-Ninth Annual Convention,* in Atlantic City, New Jersey, June 9–23, 1919.
American Legion, Proceedings and Committees, in St. Louis, Missouri, May 8–10, 1919.
American Protective Tariff League: *American Economist,* 1918–19.
Committee of 48. Pamphlets, Nos. 1–5.
League to Enforce Peace: *The League Bulletin,* Nos. 105–65.
National Security League: *National Security League Organizes Entire Nation for War on Bolshevism.* Leaflet, June 23, 1919.
———: *Handbook of War Facts and Peace Problems.* New York, 1919.

F. *Second International*

Bulletin der Zweiten Internationale. Amsterdam, Nos. 1–3, May–September 1919.
International Labour and Socialist Conference held in Berne. Press Committee, *Official Bulletin.* Vol. I, Nos. 1–8, February 3–21, 1919.
Renaudel, Pierre: *L'Internationale à Berne: Faits et documents.* Paris: Grasset; 1919.

G. *Third International*

Bibliothek der Kommunistischen Internationale: *Manifeste, Richtlinien, Beschlüsse des ersten Kongresses; Aufrufe und offene Schreiben des Exekutivkomitees bis zum zweiten Kongress.* Hamburg, 1920.
Degras, Jane, ed.: *The Communist International, 1919–1943.* Vol. I. London: Oxford University Press; 1956.
Der I. Kongress der Kommunistischen Internationale: Protokoll der Verhandlungen in Moskau vom 2. bis zum 19. März 1919. Petrograd: 1920.
Der I. und II. Kongress der Kommunistischen Internationale: Dokumente der Kongresse und Reden W. I. Lenins. Berlin: Dietz; 1959.

IV. THE PRESS

A. *Daily Press*

(1) France
L'Action Française
Echo de Paris
Le Figaro
L'Humanité
Journal des Débats
Le Petit Parisien
Le Populaire
Le Temps

(2) Germany
Berliner Tageblatt
Deutsche Allgemeine Zeitung
Deutsche Zeitung
Frankfurter Zeitung
Die Freiheit
Die Rote Fahne
Vorwärts

(3) Great Britain
Daily Mail (Paris Edition)
Daily News
The Herald (*Daily Herald* as of March 31, 1919)
Morning Post
The Times (London)

(4) Italy
Avanti
Corriere della Sera
Idea Nazionale
Popolo d'Italia

(5) United States
The New York Times
The Sun (New York)

(6) Russian Émigré
La Russie Nouvelle

B. *Special Collections*

Review of the Foreign Press. Issued by the General Staff of the British War Office, and based on a systematic reading of the Allied, enemy, and neutral press. London, 1918–19:
Daily Review of the Foreign Press
Daily Review of the Foreign Press: Allied Press Supplement
Daily Review of the Foreign Press: Enemy Press Supplement
Bulletin de la Presse Étrangère. Issued by the Ministère des Affaires Étrangères et de la Guerre. Paris, 1918–19 (incomplete in House Papers):

Bulletin Quotidien de la Presse Étrangère
Bulletin Périodique de la Presse
 Allemande
 Américaine
 Anglaise
 Hongroise
 Italienne
Press Review. Issued by the 2nd Section, General Staff, G.H.Q.A.E.F.
Literary Digest [of the American Press]. New York: Funk and Wagnalls; 1918–19. (Weekly.)

C. *Periodicals*

(1) Germany
 Deutsches Volkstum
 Neue Zeit
 Preussische Jahrbücher
 Sozialistische Monatshefte
 Welt-Echo
(2) Great Britain
 Labour Leader
 Nation (London)
(3) Italy
 Critica Sociale
 L'Ordine Nuovo
 Politica
(4) United States
 The Dial
 The Liberator
 Nation (New York)
 New Republic
 North American Review
(5) Russian Émigré
 La Cause Commune (pro-Kolchak)
 Bulletin de la Ligue Républicaine Russe. As of March 1, 1919, continued as
  La République Russe (neither Kolchak nor Lenin)
 La Russie Démocratique (anti-monarchist but pro-Kolchak)
(6) Others
 Bulletin d'Informations Roumaines
 L'Indépendence Polonaise
 La Nation Tchèque
 New Europe (London)
 Revue Baltique

v. WORKS ON THE PARIS PEACE CONFERENCE

Albrecht-Carrié, René: *Italy at the Paris Peace Conference.* New York: Columbia University Press; 1938.
Berger, Marcel, and Allard, Paul: *Les Dessous du traité de Versailles.* Paris: Portiques; 1933.

Binkley, Robert C.: "New Light on the Paris Peace Conference." *Political Science Quarterly.* Vol. 46 (1931), pp. 335–61, 505–47.
———: "Ten Years of Peace Conference History." *Journal of Modern History.* Vol. I (1929), pp. 607–29.
Birdsall, Paul: *Versailles Twenty Years After.* New York: Reynal and Hitchcock; 1941.
Bonsal, Stephen: *Suitors and Suppliants: The Little Nations at Versailles.* New York: Prentice-Hall; 1942.
Caldis, Calliope G.: *The Council of Four as a Joint Emergency Authority in the European Crisis at the Paris Peace Conference 1919.* Geneva: Thesis No. 93, Graduate Institute of International Studies, 1953.
Deák, Francis: *Hungary at the Paris Peace Conference.* New York: Columbia University Press; 1942.
Dillon, E. J.: *The Inside Story of the Peace Conference.* New York: Harper; 1920.
Gathorne-Hardy, G. M.: *The Fourteen Points and the Treaty of Versailles.* Oxford Pamphlet on World Affairs, No. 6. London: Clarendon Press, 1940.
Hankey, Lord: *The Supreme Control of the Paris Peace Conference, 1919.* London: George Allen and Unwin; 1963.
Jordan, W. M.: *Britain, France and the German Problem, 1918–1939.* London: Oxford University Press; 1943.
Keynes, John Maynard: *The Economic Consequences of the Peace.* New York: Harcourt, Brace; 1920.
Lederer, Ivo J.: *Yugoslavia at the Paris Peace Conference.* New Haven: Yale University Press; 1963.
Luckau, Alma: *The German Delegation at the Paris Peace Conference.* New York: Columbia University Press; 1941.
Marston, F. S.: *The Peace Conference of 1919: Organization and Procedure.* New York: Oxford University Press; 1944.
Mermeix (pseud. G. Terrail): *Le Combat des trois.* Paris: Ollendorff; 1922.
Nelson, Harold I.: *Land and Power: British and Allied Policy on Germany's Frontiers, 1916–19.* London: Routledge; 1963.
Nicolson, Harold: *Peacemaking 1919.* New York: Harcourt, Brace; 1939.
Noble, G. Bernard: *Policies and Opinions at Paris.* New York: Macmillan; 1935.
Nowak, Karl Friedrich: *Versailles.* New York: Payson and Clarke; 1929.
Rudin, Harry: *Armistice 1918.* New Haven: Yale University Press; 1944.
Satow, Sir Ernest: "Peacemaking, Old and New." *The Cambridge Historical Journal.* Vol. I, No. I (1923), 23–60.
Shotwell, James T., ed.: *The Origins of the International Labor Organization.* 2 vols. New York: Columbia University Press; 1934.
Spector, Sherman D.: *Rumania at the Paris Peace Conference.* New York: Bookman Associates; 1962.
Stein, Boris E.: *Die Russische Frage auf der pariser Friedenskonferenz, 1919–1920.* Leipzig: Koehler und Amelang; 1953.
Temperley, H. W. V., ed.: *A History of the Peace Conference of Paris.* 6 vols. London: Frowdy, Hodder, and Stoughton; 1920–24.
———: "The Congress of Vienna, 1814–1815 and the Conference of Paris, 1919: Attempts at International Government in Europe." *The Historical Association,* Leaflet No. 56. London, 1923; 14–23.
Thompson, John M.: *Russia, Bolshevism, and the Versailles Peace.* Princeton: Princeton University Press; 1966 (published after this study was completed).
Tillman, Seth P.: *Anglo-American Relations at the Paris Peace Conference of 1919.* Princeton: Princeton University Press; 1961.
Torre, Augusto: *Versailles; Storia della conferenza della pace.* Milan, 1940.

Webster, Charles K.: "The Congress of Vienna, 1814–1815, and the Conference of Paris, 1919: A Comparison of Their Organization and Results." *The Historical Association,* Leaflet No. 56. London, 1923; 2–13.
———: *The Congress of Vienna, 1814–1815.* London: G. Bell; 1945.
Wolfers, Arnold: *Britain and France Between Two Wars.* New York: Harcourt, Brace; 1940.
Ziegler, Wilhelm: *Versailles: Die Geschichte eines missglückten Friedens.* 4th rev. edn. Hamburg: Hanseatische Verlagsanstalt; 1933.

VI. AUTOBIOGRAPHIES, BIOGRAPHIES, DIARIES, LETTERS, MEMOIRS AND SPEECHES

A. *France*

Cambon, Paul: *Correspondance, 1879–1912.* Paris: Bernard Grasset; 1946. Vol. III.
Clemenceau, Georges: *Grandeurs et Misères d'une victoire.* Paris: Plon; 1930.
Colton, Joel: *Léon Blum: Humanist in Politics.* New York: Knopf; 1966.
Foch, Ferdinand: *Mémoires pour Servir à l'histoire de la guerre de 1914–1918.* 2 vols. Paris: Plon; 1931.
Frossard, L.-O.: *De Jaurès à Lénine: Notes et souvenirs d'un militant.* Paris: Bibliothèque de Documentation Sociale: Éditions de la "Nouvelle Revue Socialiste"; 1930.
———: *De Jaurès à Léon Blum: Souvenirs d'un militant.* Paris: Flammarion; 1943.
Georges, Bernard, and Tintant, Denise: *Léon Jouhaux: Cinquante ans de syndicalisme.* Paris: Presses Universitaires de France; 1962.
L'Hôpital, Commandant: *Foch, l'armistice et la paix.* Paris: Plon; 1938.
Marcellin, L.: *Politique et Politiciens d'après guerre.* Paris: Renaissance du Livre; 192[2?].
Millet, Raymond: *Jouhaux et la C.G.T.* Paris: Éditions Denoël; 1937.
Mordacq, Jean Jules Henri: *Le Ministère Clemenceau: Journal d'un témoin.* 4 vols. Paris: Plon; 1930–1.
Paul-Boncour, Joseph: *Entre deux Guerres: Souvenirs sur la Troisième République.* Paris: Plon; 1945. Vol. II.
Poincaré, Raymond: *Au Service de la France.* Vol. X, *Victoire et Armistice, 1918.* Paris: Plon; 1933.
Rolland, Romain: *Journal des Années de guerre, 1914–1919.* Paris: Albin Michel; 1952.
Schaper, B. W.: *Albert Thomas: Trente ans de réformisme social.* Assen: Van Gorcum; 1959.
Suarez, George: *Briand, Sa vie—Son oeuvre.* Paris: Plon; 1940–1. Vols. IV and V.
Tardieu, André: *La Paix.* Paris: Payot; 1921.
Xydias, Jean: *L'Intervention française en Russie, 1918–1919: Souvenirs d'un témoin.* Paris: Editions de France; 1927.

B. *Germany*

Barth, Emil: *Aus der Werkstatt der deutschen Revolution.* Berlin: A. Hoffmann's Verlag; 1919.

Brockdorff-Rantzau, Graf Ulrich: *Dokumente und Gedanken um Versailles.* Berlin: Verlag für Kulturpolitik: 1925.

Eichhorn, Emil: *Januar-Ereignisse: Meine Tätigkeit im Berliner Polizeipräsidium und mein Anteil an den Januar-Ereignissen.* Berlin: Verlagsgenossenschaft "Freiheit"; 1919.

Epstein, Klaus: *Matthias Erzberger and the Dilemma of German Democracy.* Princeton: Princeton University Press; 1959.

Erzberger, Matthias: *Erlebnisse im Weltkrieg.* Berlin: Deutsche Verlagsanstalt; 1920.

Fechter, Paul: *Moeller van den Bruck: Ein politisches Schicksal.* Berlin: Frundsberg; 1934.

Freytagh-Loringhoven, Arel Freiherrn von: *Politik.* Munich: J. Lehmanns; 1919.

Fried, Alfred H.: *Mein Kriegs-Tagebuch.* Zurich: Max Rascher; 1920. Vol. IV.

Ebert, Friedrich: *Schriften, Aufzeichnungen, Reden.* Dresden: Carl Reissner; 1926. Vol. II.

Groener, Wilhelm: *Lebenserinnerungen.* Göttingen: Vandenhoeck und Ruprecht; 1957.

Goltz, Graf Rüdiger von der: *Als politischer General im Osten: 1918 und 1919 in Finnland und im Baltikum.* Leipzig: K. F. Koehler; 1936.

Haase, Ernst: *Hugo Haase: Sein Leben und Wirken.* Berlin: J. J. Ottens; n.d.

Heuss, Theodor: *Friedrich Naumann.* Stuttgart: Deutsche Verlagsanstalt; 1937.

Maximilian, Prince of Baden: *The Memoirs of Prince Max of Baden.* New York: Scribner's; 1928. Vol. II.

Mommsen, Wolfgang J.: *Max Weber und die deutsche Politik.* Tübingen: J. C. B. Mohr; 1959.

Müller, Hermann: *Die November Revolution: Erinnerungen.* Berlin: Der Bücherkreis; 1928.

Müller, Richard: *Vom Kaiserreich zur Republik.* Wien: Malik; 1925. Vol. II.

Nadolny, Rudolf: *Mein Beitrag.* Wiesbaden: Limas; 1955.

Naumann, Victor: *Dokumente und Argumente.* Berlin: Ernst Rowohlt Verlag; 1928.

Noske, Gustav: *Von Kiel bis Kapp.* Berlin: Verlag für Politik und Wirtschaft; 1920.

Rabenau, Friedrich von: *Seeckt: Aus seinem Leben, 1918–1936.* Leipzig: V. Hase und Koehler; 1940.

Scheidemann, Philipp: *Memoiren eines Sozialdemokraten.* Dresden: Carl Reissner; 1928. Vol. II.

————: *Der Zusammenbruch.* Berlin: Verlag für Sozialwissenschaft; 1921.

Stadtler, Eduard: *Als Antibolschewist, 1918–1919.* Düsseldorf: Neuer Zeitverlag; 1935.

Stampfer, Friedrich: *Die vierzehn Jahre der ersten deutschen Republik.* Karlsbad: "Graphia"; 1936.

Thimme, Annelise: *Gustav Stresemann.* Hannover and Frankfurt: Norddeutsche Verlagsanstalt; 1957.

————: *Hans Delbrück als Kritiker der Wilhelminischen Epoche.* Düsseldorf: Droste; 1955.

C. Great Britain

Blake, Robert: *The Unknown Prime Minister: The Life and Times of Andrew Bonar Law, 1858–1923.* London: Eyre & Spottiswoode; 1955.

Bullock, Alan: *The Life and Times of Ernest Bevin.* London: Heinemann; 1960. Vol. I.

Butler, J. R. M.: *Lord Lothian [Philip Kerr], 1882–1940.* London: Macmillan; 1960.
Callwell, Major-General Sir C. E., ed.: *Field-Marshal Sir Henry Wilson: His Life and Diaries.* London: Cassell; 1927. Vol. II.
Churchill, Winston S.: *The Aftermath,* being a sequel to *The World Crisis.* London: Macmillan; 1941.
Cole, Margaret I., ed.: *Beatrice Webb's Diaries, 1912–1924.* London: Longmans, Green; 1952.
Croft, Brigadier-General the Lord Page: *My Life of Strife.* London: Hutchinson; 1948.
Dugdale, Blanche E. C.: *Arthur James Balfour.* London: Hutchinson; 1936. Vol. II.
Gollin, A. M.: *Proconsul in Politics: A Study of Lord Milner in Opposition and in Power.* London: Anthony Blond; 1964.
Hamilton, Mary Agnes: *Arthur Henderson.* London: William Heinemann; 1938.
Hammond, J. L.: *C. P. Scott of the Manchester Guardian.* London: G. Bell; 1934.
Hancock, W. K.: *Smuts: The Sanguine Years, 1870–1919.* Cambridge: Cambridge University Press; 1962.
Hewins, W. A. S.: *The Apologia of an Imperialist: Forty Years of Empire Policy.* London: Constable; 1929. Vol. II.
The History of The Times. The 150th Anniversary and Beyond. 1912–1948. Part 1, Chapters I–XII, 1912–1920. London: written and published at the office of *The Times,* Printing House Square; 1952.
Jenkins, Roy: *Asquith.* New York: Chilmark Press; 1964.
Jones, Thomas: *Lloyd George.* London: Oxford University Press; 1951.
Lansbury, George: *My Life.* London: Constable; 1931.
Lloyd George, David: *The Truth About the Peace Treaties.* 2 vols. London: Victor Gollancz; 1938.
Owen, Frank: *Tempestuous Journey: Lloyd George, His Life and Times.* New York: McGraw-Hill; 1955.
Postgate, Raymond: *The Life of George Lansbury.* New York: Longmans, Green; 1951.
Pound, Reginald, and Harmsworth, Geoffrey: *Northcliffe.* New York: Praeger; 1960.
Riddell, George Allardice: *Lord Riddell's War Diary, 1914–1918.* London: Ivor Nicholson and Watson; 1933.
————: *Lord Riddell's Intimate Diary of the Peace Conference and After, 1918–1923.* New York: Reynal & Hitchcock; 1934.
Snowden, Philip Viscount: *An Autobiography, 1864–1934.* London: Ivor Nicholson and Watson; 1934. Vol. I.
Steed, Henry Wickham: *Through Thirty Years, 1892–1922.* London: William Heinemann; 1924. Vol. II.

D. *Italy*

Aldrovandi Marescotti, Luigi: *Guerra diplomatica: Ricordi e frammenti di diario, 1914–1919.* Milan: Mondadori; 1938.
————: *Nuovi ricordi e frammenti di diario.* Milan: Mondadori; 1938.
Bissolati, Leonida: *La politica estera dell'Italia dal 1897 al 1920: Scritti e discorsi.* Milan: Fratelli Treves; 1923.
Bonomi, Ivanoe: *Leonida Bissolati e il movimento socialista in Italia.* Rome: Sestante; 1945.

————: *From Socialism to Fascism: A Study of Contemporary Italy*. London: Martin Hopkinson; 1924.

Corradini, Enrico: *Scritti politici, 1902–1923*. Florence: Vallecchi; n.d. (1923?).

Crespi, Silvio: *Alla difesa d'Italia in guerra e a Versailles: Diario 1917–1919*. Milan: Mondadori; 1937.

De Felice, Renzo: *Mussolini il rivoluzionario*. Turin: Einaudi; 1965 (published after this study was completed).

Dorso, Guido: Mussolini alla conquista del potere. Turin: Einaudi; 1949.

Fermi, Laura: *Mussolini*. Chicago: University of Chicago Press; 1961.

Kirkpatrick, Sir Ivone: *Mussolini: A Study of a Demagogue*. London: Odham Books; 1964.

Malagodi, Olindo: *Conversazioni della guerra, 1914–1919*. Milan: Ricciardi; 1960. Vol. II.

Monelli, Paolo: *Mussolini: An Intimate Life*. London: Thames & Hudson; 1953.

Mosca, Rodolfo, ed.: *Vittorio Emanuele Orlando: Memorie, 1915–1919*. Milan: Rizzoli; 1960.

Pini, Giorgio, and Susmel, Duilio: *Mussolini: L'uomo e l'opera*. Florence: La Fenice; 1953–4. Vols. II and III.

Susmel, Edoardo and Duilio, eds.: *Opera Omnia di Benito Mussolini*. Florence: La Fenice; 1953–4. Vols. XI–XIII.

Tamburrano, Giuseppe: *Antonio Gramsci*. Manduria: Lacaita; 1963.

Treves, Claudio: *Polemica socialista*. Bologna: Nicolà Zanichelli; 1921.

E. *United States*

Bailey, Thomas A.: *Woodrow Wilson and the Lost Peace*. New York: Macmillan; 1944.

Baker, Ray Stannard: *Woodrow Wilson: Life and Letters*. 8 vols. New York: Doubleday, Doran; 1927–39.

————: *Woodrow Wilson and World Settlement. Written from His Unpublished and Personal Material*. 3 vols. Garden City, N.Y.: Doubleday, Page; 1923.

————, and Dodd, William Edward, eds.: *The Public Papers of Woodrow Wilson*. 6 vols. New York: Harper; 1925–7.

Blum, John M.: *Woodrow Wilson and the Politics of Morality*. Boston: Little, Brown; 1956.

Bryn-Jones, David: *Frank B. Kellogg: A Biography*. New York: Putnam; 1937.

Dodd, William E.: *Woodrow Wilson and His Work*. Garden City, N.Y.: Doubleday, Page; 1920.

Freud, Sigmund, and Bullitt, William C.: *Thomas Woodrow Wilson*. Boston: Houghton, Mifflin; 1967 (published after this study was completed).

Gitlow, Benjamin: *I Confess: The Truth About American Communism*. New York: E. P. Dutton; 1940.

George, Alexander L. and Juliette L.: *Woodrow Wilson and Colonel House: A Personality Study*. New York: John Day; 1956.

Gompers, Samuel: *Seventy Years of Life and Labor*. New York: E. P. Dutton; 1925. Vol. II.

Green, Horace, ed.: *American Problems: A Selection of Speeches and Prophecies by William E. Borah*. New York: Duffield; 1924.

Hapgood, Norman: *The Advancing Hours*. New York: Boni & Liveright; 1920.

Harvey, George: *Henry Clay Frick: The Man*. New York: Scribner's; 1928.

Haywood, William D.: *Bill Haywood's Book: The Autobiography of William D. Haywood*. New York: International Publishers; 1929.

Hicks, Granville: *John Reed: The Making of a Revolutionary.* New York: Macmillan; 1936.

Hoover, Herbert: *Memoirs.* New York: Macmillan; 1951. Vol. I.

————: *The Ordeal of Woodrow Wilson.* New York: McGraw-Hill; 1958.

Howe, Frederick C.: *The Confessions of a Reformer.* New York: Scribner's; 1925.

Jessup, Philip C.: *Elihu Root.* New York: Dodd, Mead; 1938. Vol. II.

Johnson, Claudius O.: *Borah of Idaho.* New York: Longmans, Green; 1936.

Johnson, Willis Fletcher: *George Harvey: A Passionate Patriot.* Boston: Houghton Mifflin; 1929.

Kerney, James: *The Political Education of Woodrow Wilson.* New York: The Century Co.; 1926.

Lansing, Robert L.: *The Peace Negotiations.* Boston: Houghton Mifflin; 1921.

Longworth, Alice Roosevelt: *Crowded Hours: Reminiscences.* New York: Scribner's; 1933.

Marburg, Theodore, and Flack, Horace E., eds.: *Taft Papers on the League of Nations.* New York: Macmillan; 1920.

Miller, David Hunter: *My Diary at the Conference of Paris.* 21 vols. Privately printed. New York: Appeal Printing; 1924.

Nevins, Allan: *Henry White: Thirty Years of American Diplomacy.* New York: Harper; 1930.

Palmer, Frederick: *Bliss, Peacemaker: The Life and Letters of General Tasker Howard Bliss.* New York: Dodd, Mead; 1934.

Pringle, Henry F.: *The Life and Times of William Howard Taft.* New York: Farrar & Rinehart; 1939. Vol. II.

Seymour, Charles, ed.: *The Intimate Papers of Colonel House.* 4 vols. Boston: Houghton Mifflin; 1926–8.

Schriftgiesser, Karl: *The Gentleman from Massachusetts: Henry Cabot Lodge.* Boston: Little, Brown; 1944.

Sparks, George F.: *A Many-Colored Toga: The Diary of Henry Fountain Ashurst.* Tucson: University of Arizona Press; 1962.

Tumulty, Joseph P.: *Woodrow Wilson As I Know Him.* Garden City, New York: Doubleday, Page; 1921.

Villard, Oswald Garrison: *Fighting Years: Memoirs of a Liberal Editor.* New York: Harcourt, Brace; 1939.

Vinson, John Chalmers: *William E. Borah and the Outlawry of War.* Athens, Ga.: University of Georgia Press; 1957.

Walworth, Arthur: *Woodrow Wilson.* 2 vols. New York: Longmans, Green; 1958.

Watson, James E.: *As I Knew Them.* Indianapolis and New York: Bobbs-Merrill; 1936.

F. *Hungary*

Apponyi, Albert: *Erlebnisse und Ergebnisse.* Berlin: Keil; 1933.

Böhm, Wilhelm: *Im Kreuzfeuer zweier Revolutionen.* Munich: Verlag für Kulturpolitik; 1924.

Herczeg, Géza: *Béla Kun: Eine historische Grimasse.* Berlin: Verlag für Kulturpolitik; 1928.

Károlyi, Michael: *Gegen eine ganze Welt.* Munich: Verlag für Kulturpolitik; 1924.

————: *Faith Without Illusion.* New York: E. P. Dutton; 1957.

Kun, Béla: *La République hongroise des conseils.* Budapest: Editions Cornive; 1962.

G. Others

Deutscher, Isaac: *The Prophet Armed: Trotsky, 1879–1921.* New York: Oxford University Press; 1954.
Fischer, Louis: *The Life of Lenin.* New York: Harper & Row; 1964.
Hannak, Jacques: *Karl Renner und seine Zeit.* Vienna: Europa Verlag; 1965.
Troelstra, P. J.: *Gedenkschriften.* Amsterdam: N. V. E. M. Querido Uitgevers-Maatschappij; 1931. Vol. IV.

VII. HISTORIES, TREATISES, AND SPECIAL STUDIES

A. France

Bardoux, Jacques: *De Paris à Spa: La bataille diplomatique pour la paix française.* Paris: Félix Alcan; 1921.
Barthou, Louis: *Le Traité de paix.* Paris: Charpentier; 1919.
Beau de Loménie, Emmanuel: *Les Responsabilités des dynasties bourgeoises.* Paris: Editions Denoël; 1954. Vol. III.
——: *Le Débat de ratification du traité de Versailles à la chambre des députés et dans la presse en 1919.* Paris: Éditions Denoël; 1945.
Bonnefous, Édouard: *Histoire Politique de la Troisième République.* Paris: Presses Universitaires de France; 1959. Vol. III.
Bourgeois, Léon: *Le Traité de paix de Versailles.* Paris: Félix Alcan; 1919.
Brizon, Pierre: *La Grande trahison.* Paris: *"La Vague";* 1919.
Chastenet, Jacques: *Les Années d'illusions, 1918–1931. Histoire de la Troisième République.* Paris: Librairie Hachette; 1960.
Cornilleau, Robert: *Du Bloc national au front populaire.* Paris: Spes; 1938. Vol. I.
Deygas, Capitaine F.-J.: *Gloires et Misères de l'armée d'orient, 1915–1919.* Paris: Payot; 1932.
Dolléans, Édouard: *Histoire du Mouvement ouvrier, 1871–1920.* Paris: Armand Colin; 1953. Vol. II.
——, and Dehove, Gérard: *Histoire du Travail en France: Mouvement ouvrier et législation sociale, de 1919 à nos jours.* Paris: Domat; 1955.
Ebray, Alcide: *La Paix malpropre: Versailles.* Milan: *"Unitas";* 1924.
Faure, Paul: *La Scission socialiste en France et dans l'internationale.* Paris: Librairie Populaire; 1921.
Ferrat, André: *Histoire du Parti communiste français.* Paris: Bibliothèque du Mouvement Ouvrier; 1931.
Gaucher, François: *Contribution à l'Histoire du socialisme français, 1905–1933.* Paris: Les Presses Modernes; 1934.
Gide, Charles, and Oualid, William: *Le Bilan de la guerre pour la France.* Paris: Presses Universitaires de France; 1931.
Goguel, François: *Géographie des Élections françaises de 1870 à 1951.* Paris: Armand Colin; 1951.
——: *La Politique des partis sous la IIIe République.* Paris: Éditions du Seuil; 1946.
Guilbeaux, Henri: *Du Kremlin au Cherche-Midi.* Paris: Gallimard; 1933.
Haig, Robert Murray: *The Public Finances of Post-War France.* New York: Columbia University Press; 1929.
Jouvenel, Bertrand de: *D'une Guerre à l'autre.* Paris: Calmann-Lévy; 1940. Vol. I.

Kriegel, Annie: *Aux Origines du communisme français, 1914–1920.* 2 vols. Paris: Mouton; 1964.

Lachapelle, Georges: *Élections Législatives du 16 novembre 1919.* Paris: Librairies des Publications Officielles Georges Roustan; 1920.

————: *Les Finances de la IIIème République.* Paris: Flammarion; 1937.

Lefranc, Georges: *Le Mouvement socialiste sous la troisième république, 1875–1940.* Paris: Payot; 1963.

Ligou, Daniel: *Histoire du Socialisme en France, 1871–1961.* Paris: Presses Universitaires de France; 1962.

Manévy, Raymond: *Histoire de la Presse, 1914 à 1939.* Paris: Corréa; 1945.

Marin, Louis: *Le Traité de paix.* Paris: H. Floury; 1920.

Martin, Germain: *Les Finances publiques de la France et la fortune privée, 1914–1925.* Paris: Payot; 1925.

Marty, André: *La Révolte de la Mer Noire.* 2 vols. Paris: Bureau d'Éditions de Diffusion et de Publicité; 1927, 1929.

Moulis, E., and Bergonier, E., eds.: *La Guerre entre les alliés et la Russie, 1918–1920.* Paris: Librairie Générale de Droit et de Jurisprudence; 1937.

Mont, Jules: *L'Allemagne et la paix: La lutte contre les conséquences de sa défaite.* Paris: Librairie Académique; 1920.

Prélot, Marcel: *L'Évolution politique du socialisme français, 1789–1934.* Paris: Spes; 1939.

Rémond, René: *La Droite en France: De 1815 à nos jours.* Paris: Aubier; 1954.

Shapiro, David, ed.: *The Right in France, 1890–1919: Three Studies.* London: Chatto and Windus; 1962.

Slovès, H.: *La France et l'Union Soviétique.* Paris: Rieder; 1935.

Sokolov, Boris: *Le Voyage de Cachin et de Frossard dans la Russie des Soviets.* Paris: J. Povolozky; n.d.

Walter, Gérard: *Histoire du Parti communiste français.* Paris: Aimery Somogy; 1948.

Weygand, Général: *Le II novembre.* Paris: Flammarion; 1932.

Wohl, Robert: *French Communism in the Making, 1914–1924.* Stanford: Stanford University Press; 1966 (published after this study was completed).

Zévaès, Alexandre: *Histoire du Socialisme et du communisme en France de 1871 à 1947.* Paris: Éditions France-Empire; 1947.

————: *Le Socialisme en France depuis 1904.* Paris: Fasquelle; 1934.

B. *Germany*

Ahnert, Kurt, ed.: *Die Entwicklung der deutschen Revolution und das Kriegsende in Leitartikeln, Extrablättern, Telegrammen, Aufrufen und Verordnungen nach den führenden deutschen Zeitungen.* Nürnberg: Burgverlag; 1918.

Bessmertny, A., and Neven du Mont, M., eds.: *Die Parteien und das Rätesystem.* Charlottenburg: Deutsche Verlagsgesellschaft für Politik und Geschichte; 1919.

Berthold, Lothar, and Neef, Helmut: *Militarismus und Opportunismus gegen die Novemberrevolution.* Berlin: Rütten & Loening; 1958.

Beyer, Hans: *Von der Novemberrevolution zur Räterepublik in München.* Berlin: Rütten & Loening; 1957.

Buchner, Eberhard: *Revolutionsdokumente: Die deutsche Revolution in der Darstellung der zeitgenössigen Presse.* Berlin: Deutsche Verlagsgesellschaft; 1921. Vol. I.

Craig, Gordon A.: *The Politics of the Prussian Army, 1640–1945.* New York: Oxford University Press; 1955.

Dehio, Ludwig: *Germany and World Politics in the Twentieth Century.* New York: Knopf; 1960.

Euler, Heinrich: *Die Aussenpolitik der Weimarer Republik, 1918–1923.* Aschaffenburg: Pattloch Verlag; 1957.

Fischer, Ruth: *Stalin und der deutsche Kommunismus: Der Übergang zur Konterrevolution.* Frankfurt: Verlag der Frankfurter Hefte; 1948.

Flechtheim, Ossip K.: *Die kommunistische Partei Deutschlands in der Weimarer Republik.* Offenbach: Bollwerk-Verlag Karl Drott; 1948.

Franz, Georg: "Munich: Birthplace and Center of the National Socialist German Workers' Party." *Journal of Modern History.* Vol. XXIX, No. 4 (December 1957), 319–34.

Freund, Gerald: *Unholy Alliance: Russian-German Relations from the Treaty of Brest-Litovsk to the Treaty of Berlin.* London: Chatto and Windus; 1957.

Gumbel, E. J.: *Vier Jahre Politischer Mord.* Berlin: Verlag der Neuen Gesellschaft; 1922.

Hertzman, Lewis: "The Founding of the German National People's Party (DNVP), November 1918–January 1919." *Journal of Modern History.* Vol. XXX, No. 1 (March 1938), 24–36.

Kautsky, Karl: *Die Diktatur des Proletariats.* Vienna: Verlag der Wiener Volksbuchhandlung Ignaz Brand; 1918.

————: *Richtlinien für ein sozialistisches Aktionsprogramm.* Berlin: January 12, 1919.

————: *Vergangenheit und Zukunft der Internationale.* Vienna: Verlag der Wiener Volksbuchhandlung; 1920.

————: *Die Wurzeln der Politik Wilsons.* Berlin: Verlag Neues Vaterland; 1918.

Klein, Fritz: *Die diplomatischen Beziehungen Deutschlands zur Sowjetunion, 1917–1932.* Berlin: Rütten & Loening; 1952.

Klemperer, Klemens von: *Germany's New Conservatism: Its History and Dilemma in the Twentieth Century.* Princeton: Princeton University Press; 1957.

Klingmann, Georg: *Die erste Regierung der Sozialdemokratie in Deutschland.* Würzburg: Konrad Triltsch; 1939.

Kochan, Lionel: *Russia and the Weimar Republic.* Cambridge: Bowes & Bowes; 1954.

Kolb, Eberhard: *Die Arbeiterräte in der deutschen Innenpolitik, 1918–1919.* Düsseldorf: Droste; 1962.

Koszyk, Kurt: *Zwischen Kaiserreich und Diktatur: Die sozialdemokratische Presse von 1914 bis 1933.* Heidelberg: Quelle & Meyer; 1958.

Lauffenberg, Dr. Heinrich: *Zwischen der ersten und zweiten Revolution.* Hamburg: Willaschek; 1919.

Lehmann-Russbüldt, Otto: *Der Kampf (der Deutschen Liga für Menschenrechte, vormals Bund Neues Vaterland) für den Weltfrieden, 1914–1927.* Berlin: Hensel; 1927.

Liebe, Werner: *Die Deutschnationale Volkspartei, 1918–1924.* Düsseldorf: Droste; 1956.

Matthias, Erich: *Die deutsche Sozialdemokratie und der Osten, 1914–1945.* Tübingen: 1954.

Moeller van den Bruck, Arthur: "Das Recht der jungen Völker." *Deutsche Rundschau,* November 1918, 220–35.

Neumann, Sigmund: *Die deutschen Parteien: Wesen und Wandel nach dem Kriege.* Berlin: Junker und Dünnhaupt; 1932.

Norden, Albert: *Zwischen Berlin und Moskau.* Berlin: Dietz; 1954.

Purlitz, Friedrich: *Deutscher Geschichtskalender: Die deutsche Revolution.* 2 vols. Leipzig: Felix Meiner; 1919.

Richter, Werner: *Gewerkschaften, Monopolkapital, und Staat im ersten Welt-krieg und in der Novemberrevolution, 1914–1919.* Berlin: Verlag Tribüne; 1959.

Rosenfeld, Günter: *Sowjetrussland und Deutschland, 1917–1922.* Berlin: Akademie; 1960.

Salomon, Felix, ed.: *Die deutschen Parteiprogramme.* Leipzig and Berlin: B. G. Teubner; 1926.

Schüddekopf, Otto-Ernst: *Linke Leute von Rechts: Die nationalrevolutionären Minderheiten und der Kommunismus in der Weimarer Republik.* Stuttgart: W. Kohlhammer; 1960.

Schultze-Pfaelzer, Gerhard: *Von Spa nach Weimar.* Leipzig: Grethleim; 1929.

Tormin, Walter: *Zwischen Rätediktatur und sozialer Demokratie.* Düsseldorf: Droste; 1954.

Troeltsch, Ernst: *Spektator-Briefe: Aufsätze über die deutsche Revolution und die Weltpolitik, 1918–1922.* Tübingen: J. E. B. Mohr; 1924.

Volkmann, Erich Otto: *Revolution über Deutschland.* Oldenburg: Gerhard Stalling; 1930.

————: *Der Marxismus und das deutsche Heer im Weltkriege.* Berlin: Reimar Sobbing; 1926.

Waite, Robert G. L.: *Vanguard of Nazism: The Free Corps Movement in Post-war Germany, 1918–1923.* Cambridge: Harvard University Press; 1952.

Waldman, Eric: *The Spartacist Uprising of 1919.* Milwaukee: Marquette University Press; 1958.

Weber, Max: *Gesammelte politische Schriften.* Munich: Drei Masken; 1921.

Werner, Paul: *Die Bayrische Räterepublik: Tatsachen und Kritik* (2nd edn.). Leipzig: Frankes; 1920.

Wheeler-Bennett, John W.: *The Nemesis of Power: The German Army in Politics: 1918–1945.* New York: St. Martin's Press; 1954.

C. Great Britain

Arnot, R. Page: *The Miners: Years of Struggle.* London: George Allen & Unwin; 1953.

Beer, Samuel H.: *British Politics in the Collectivist Age.* New York: Knopf; 1965.

Coates, W. P., and Zelda, K.: *Armed Intervention in Russia 1918–1922.* London: Victor Gollancz; 1935.

————: *A History of Anglo-Soviet Relations.* London: Lawrence & Wishart; 1944.

Cole, G. D. H.: *A History of the Labour Party from 1914.* London: Routledge & Kegan Paul; 1948.

————: *Labour in the Coal-Mining Industry.* Oxford: Clarendon Press; 1923.

Crosby, Gerda Richards: *Disarmament and Peace in British Politics, 1914–19.* Cambridge, Mass.: Harvard University Press; 1957.

Davies, Ivor R. M.: *Trial By Ballot.* London: Cristopher Johnson; 1950.

Graubard, Stephen R.: *British Labour and the Russian Revolution.* Cambridge, Mass.: Harvard University Press; 1957.

Guttsman, W. L.: *The British Political Elite.* New York: Basic Books; 1963.

Hutt, Allen: *The Post-War History of the British Working Class.* London: Victor Gollancz; 1937.

Ironside, Edmund: *Archangel 1918–1919.* London: Constable; 1953.

Jennings, Sir Ivor: *Party Politics.* Cambridge: Harvard University Press; 1961. Vol. II.

Kellogg, Paul M., and Gleason, Arthur: *British Labor and the War: Reconstruction for a New World.* New York: Boni and Liveright; 1919.

Kirkaldy, A. W., ed.: *British Finance During and After the War: 1914–1921.* London: Isaac Pitman & Sons; 1921.

Maccoby, S.: *English Radicalism: The End?* London: George Allen & Unwin; 1961.

McCallum, Ronald B.: *Public Opinion and the Last Peace.* London: Oxford University Press; 1944.

McEwen, John M.: "The Coupon Election of 1918 and Unionist Members of Parliament." *Journal of Modern History.* Vol. XXXIV, No. 3 (September 1962), 294–306.

McKenzie, Robert T.: *British Political Parties.* New York: St. Martin's Press; 1955.

Mowat, Charles Loch: *Britain Between the Wars.* London: Methuen; 1959.

Pelling, Henry: *The British Communist Party: A Historical Profile.* London: Adam & Charles Black; 1958.

Snyder, Rixford K.: *The Tariff Problem in Great Britain, 1918–1923.* Stanford: Stanford University Press; 1944.

Storey, Harold: *The Case Against the Lloyd George Coalition.* London: George Allen & Unwin; 1920.

Stuart, Sir Campbell: *Secrets of Crewe House: The Story of a Famous Campaign.* New York: Hodder and Stoughton; 1920.

Wells, H. G.: *In the Fourth Year: Anticipations of a World Peace.* London: Chatto and Windus; 1918.

Willis, Irene Cooper: *England's Holy War.* New York: Knopf; 1928.

Wilson, Trevor: *The Downfall of the Liberal Party, 1914–1935.* London: Collins; 1966.

———: "The Coupon and the British General Election of 1918." *Journal of Modern History.* Vol. XXXVI, No. I (March 1964), 28–42.

Wintringham, T. H.: *Mutiny: Being a Survey of Mutinies from Spartacus to Invergordan.* London: Stanley Nott; 1936.

D. *Italy*

Alatri, Paolo: *Nitti, D'Annunzio e la questione adriatica, 1919–1920.* Milan: Feltrinelli; 1959.

Alazard, Jean: *Communisme et "Fascio" en Italie.* Paris: Bossard; 1922.

Chabod, Federico: *A History of Italian Fascism.* London: Weidenfeld and Nicholson; 1963.

Chiurco, Giorgio Alberto: *Storia della revoluzione fascista.* Florence: Vallecchi; 1929. Vols. I and II.

Currey, Muriel: *Italian Foreign Policy, 1918–1932.* London: Ivor Nicholson & Watson; 1932.

Dresler, Adolf: *Geschichte der italienischen Presse.* Munich and Berlin: R. Oldenburg; 1934. Vol. III.

Fabbri, Luigi: *La controrivoluzione preventiva: Saggio di un anarchico sul fascismo.* Bologna: Cappelli; 1922.

Flores, Enrico: *Eredità di guerra.* Rome: Edizioni di Politica; 1947.

Gobetti, Piero: *La rivoluzione liberale.* Bologna: Cappelli; 1924.

Howard, Edith Pratt: *Il Partito Popolare Italiano.* Florence: La Nuova Italia; 1957.

Jacini, Stefano: *Storia del Partito Popolare Italiano.* Milan: Garzanti; 1951.

Meda, Filippo: *Il socialismo politico in Italia.* Milan: "Unitas"; 1924.

Missiroli, Mario: *Una battaglia perduta.* Milan: "Corbaccio"; 1924.

Mondolfo, R., ed.: *Il fascismo e i partiti politici.* Bologna: Cappelli; 1922. Volumes by Grandi, Mondolfo, and Zibordi.

Morandi, Carlo: *I partiti politici nella storia d'Italia.* Florence: Felice Le Monnier; 1945.

Nenni, Pietro: *Storia di quattro anni, 1919–1922.* 2nd edn. Rome: Einaudi; 1946.

————: *La Lutte des classes en Italie.* Paris: Bibliothèque de Documentation Sociale; 1930.

Pernot, Maurice: *L'Expérience italienne.* Paris: Bernard Grasset; 1924.

Perticone, Giacomo: *La politica italiana nell' ultimo trentennio.* Rome: Leonardo; 1945. Vols. I and II.

Prezzolini, Giuseppe: *Fascism.* London: Methuen; 1926.

Rigola, Rinaldo: *Storia del movimento operaio italiano.* Milan: Domus; 1947.

Rocca, Massimo: *Le Fascisme et l'antifascisme en Italie.* Paris: Félix Alcan; 1930.

De Rosa, Gabriele: *Storia del Partito Popolare.* Bari: Laterza; 1958.

Rosen, Edgar R.: "Italiens Kriegseintritt im Jahre 1915 als innenpolitisches Problem der Giolitti-Ära." *Historische Zeitschrift,* Vol. 187, No. 2 (April 1959), pp. 289–363.

De Rossi, Giulio: *Il Partito Popolare Italiano dalla origini al congresso di Napoli.* Rome: Francesco Ferrari; 1920.

Salvatorelli, Luigi, and Mira, Giovanni: *Storia del fascismo: l'Italia dal 1919–1945.* Rome: Novissima; 1952.

————: *Storia d'Italia nel periodo fascista.* Turin: Einaudi; 1956.

Salvemini, Gaetano: *Dal patto di Londra alla pace di Roma.* Turin: Piero Gobetti; 1925.

————: *Tendenze vecchie e necessità nuove del movimento operaio italiano.* Bologna: Cappelli; 1922.

————: *The Fascist Dictatorship in Italy.* New York: Holt; 1927.

Silone, Ignazio: *Der Faschismus: seine Entstehung und seine Entwicklung.* Zurich: Europa-Verlag; 1934.

Sturzo, Luigi: *Italy and Fascismo.* London: Faber and Gwyer; 1926.

Tasca, Angelo [pseud. A. Rossi]: *The Rise of Italian Fascism, 1918–1922.* London: Methuen; 1938.

————: *Nascita e avvento del fascismo: L'Italia dal 1922.* Florence: La Nuova Italia; 1950 (with bibliographical notes not included in Eng. ed. above).

Valeri, N.: *Da Giolitti a Mussolini.* Florence: Parenti; 1956.

Valiani, Leo: "Il Partito Socialista Italiano dal 1900 al 1918." *Revista Storica Italiana.* Vol. LXXV, No. II (1963), 269–326.

Webster, Richard A.: *The Cross and the Fasces.* Stanford: Stanford University Press; 1960.

————: "From Insurrection to Intervention: the Italian Crisis of 1914." *Italian Quarterly.* Vols. 5–6, Nos. 20–21 (Winter 1961–Spring 1962), 27–50.

E. *United States*

Adler, Selig: *The Isolationist Impulse.* New York: Abelard-Schuman; 1957.

————: "The Congressional Election of 1918." *South Atlantic Quarterly.* Vol. XXXVI, No. 4 (October 1937), 447–65.

Bane, Suda Lorena, and Lutz, Ralph Haswell, eds.: *The Blockade of Germany After the Armistice, 1918–1919.* Stanford: Stanford University Press; 1942.

————: *Organization of American Relief in Europe, 1918–1919.* Stanford: Stanford University Press; 1943.

Bartlett, Ruhl J.: *The League to Enforce Peace.* Chapel Hill, N.C.: Univ. of North Carolina Press: 1944.

Berdahl, Clarence A.: "Myths About the Peace Treaties of 1919–1920." *International Conciliation.* No. 383 (October 1942), 441–522.

————: *The Policy of the United States With Respect to the League of Nations.* Geneva: Kundig; 1932.

Bullitt, William C.: *The Bullitt Mission to Russia: Testimony before the Committee on Foreign Relations, United States Senate.* New York: Huebsch; 1919.

Coben, Stanley: "A Study in Nativism: The American Red Scare of 1919–1920." *Political Science Quarterly.* Vol. LXXIX, No. I (March 1964), 52–75.

Commons, John R., ed.: *History of Labor in the United States, 1896–1932.* New York: Macmillan; 1935. Vol. IV.

————: *Trade Unionism and Labor Problems.* Boston: Ginn; 1921.

Creel, George: *The War, the World and Wilson.* New York: Harper; 1920.

Draper, Theodore: *The Roots of American Communism.* New York: Viking; 1957.

Fine, Nathan: *Labor and Farmer Parties in the United States, 1828–1928.* New York: Rand School of Social Science; 1928.

Gelfand, Lawrence E.: *The Inquiry: American Preparations for Peace, 1917–1919.* New Haven: Yale University Press; 1963.

Herron, George D.: *The Defeat in the Victory.* London: Cecil Palmer; 1921.

————: *The Greater War.* New York: Mitchell Kemerley; 1919.

Higham, John: *Strangers in the Land: Patterns of American Nativism, 1860–1925.* New Brunswick: Rutgers University Press; 1963.

Holt, W. Stull: *Treaties Defeated by the Senate.* Baltimore: Johns Hopkins Press; 1933.

Howe, Irving, and Coser, Lewis: *The American Communist Party: A Critical History, 1919–1957.* Boston: Beacon Press; 1957.

James, Marquis: *A History of the American Legion.* New York: William Green; 1923.

Jones, Richard Seelye: *A History of the American Legion.* Indianapolis and New York: Bobbs-Merrill; 1946.

Lippmann, Walter, and Merz, Charles: "A Test of the News." A Supplement to *The New Republic,* August 4, 1920.

Lockwood, George B.: *Americanism.* Washington, D.C.: The National Republican Publishing; 1921.

Lorwin, Lewis L.: *The American Federation of Labor.* Washington, D.C.: The Brookings Institution; 1933.

Lovenstein, Meno: *American Opinion of Soviet Russia.* Washington, D.C.: American Council on Public Affairs; 1941.

Mamatey, Victor S.: *The United States and East Central Europe: A Study in Wilsonian Diplomacy and Propaganda.* Princeton: Princeton University Press; 1957.

Moya, Clarence B.: *The Congressional Election of 1918.* Unpublished Senior Thesis, Princeton University, 1962.

Murray, Robert K.: *The Red Scare: A Study in National Hysteria.* Minneapolis: University of Minnesota Press; 1955.

Nearing, Scott: *Labor and the League of Nations.* New York: The Rand School of Social Science; 1919.

Samuelson, Paul A. and Hagen, Everett E.: *After the War, 1918–1920: Military and Economic Demobilization of the United States and Its Effect upon Employment and Income.* Washington, D.C.: U. S. Government National Resources Planning Board; June 1943.

Schuman, Frederick L.: *American Policy Toward Russia Since 1917.* New York: International Publishers; 1928.

Shannon, David A.: *The Socialist Party of America.* New York: Macmillan; 1955.

Soule, George: *Prosperity Decade: From War to Depression, 1917–1929.* New York: Rinehart; 1947.

Stearns, Harold: *Liberalism in America: Its Origin, Its Temporary Collapse, Its Future.* New York: Boni and Liveright; 1919.

Surface, Frank M., and Bland, Raymond L.: *American Food in the World War and Reconstruction Period.* Stanford: Stanford University Press; 1931.

Taft, Philip: *The A.F. of L. in the Time of Gompers.* New York: Harper; 1957.

Viereck, George Sylvester: *The Strangest Friendship in History: Woodrow Wilson and Colonel House.* New York: Liveright; 1932.

Wheat, George Seay: *The Story of the American Legion: The Birth of the Legion.* New York: G. P. Putnam's Sons; 1919.

Williams, William Appleman: *American Russian Relations, 1781–1947.* New York: Rinehart; 1952.

F. *Austria*

Bauer, Otto: *Die Österreichische Revolution.* Vienna: Wiener Volksbuchhandlung; 1923.

Glaise-Horstenau, Edmund von: *Die Katastrophe der Zertrümmerung Österreich-Ungarns und das Werden der Nachfolgerstaaten.* Zurich-Leipzig-Vienna: Almathea; 1929.

Gulick, Charles A.: *Austria from Habsburg to Hitler.* Berkeley: University of California Press; 1948. Vol. I.

MacDonald, Mary: *The Republic of Austria, 1918–1934.* London: Oxford University Press; 1946.

Strong, David F.: *Austria: Transition from Empire to Republic, October 1918– March 1919.* New York: Columbia University Press; 1939.

G. *Hungary*

Ashmead-Bartlett, Ellis: *The Tragedy of Central Europe.* London: Thornton Butterworth; 1923.

Bizony, Ladislaus: *133 Tage ungarischer Bolschewismus: Die Herrschaft Béla Kuns und Tibor Szamuelys.* Leipzig and Vienna: Waldheim Eberle; 1920.

Jászi, Oskar: *Magyariens Schuld, Ungarns Sühne: Revolution und Gegenrevolution in Ungarn.* Munich: Verlag für Kulturpolitik; 1923.

Kaas, Baron Albert, and Lazarovics, Fedor de: *Bolshevism in Hungary: The Béla Kun Period.* London: Grant Richards; 1931.

Koerfer, Stefan: *Die Folgen des Weltkrieges in Ungarn.* Vienna: Moritz Perles; 1919.

Low, Alfred D.: "The First Austrian Republic and Soviet Hungary." *Journal of Central European Affairs.* Vol. XX, No. 2 (July 1960), 174–203.

————: *The Soviet Hungarian Republic and the Paris Peace Conference.* Philadelphia: Transactions of the American Philosophical Society, New Series, Vol. 53, Pt. 10; 1963.

Macartney, Maxwell H. H.: *Five Years of European Chaos.* London: Chapman & Hall; 1923.

Nemény, Wilhelm: *133 Tage Bolschewistenherrschaft.* Berlin: Kulturliga; 1920.

Nyiri, Jules: *Ce que fut la Révolution d'octobre 1918 en Hongrie.* Paris: André Delpeuch; 1926.

Szantó, Béla: *Klassenkämpfe und die Diktatur des Proletariats in Ungarn.* Vienna: "Neue Erde"; 1920.

Szatmari, E.: *Im Roten Budapest.* Berlin: Kulturliga; 1919.

Szelpal, Arpad: *Les 133 jours de Béla Kun.* Paris: Fayard; 1959.

Varjassy, Louis: *Révolution, Bolshevisme, Réaction: Histoire de l'occupation française en Hongrie, 1918–1919.* Paris: Jouve; 1934.

H. *U.S.S.R.*

Brinkley, George A.: *The Volunteer Army and Allied Intervention in South Russia, 1917–1921.* Notre Dame: University of Notre Dame Press; 1966 (published after this study was completed).

Bunyan, James, ed.: *Intervention, Civil War, and Communism in Russia: April–December 1918: Documents and Materials.* Baltimore: Johns Hopkins Press; 1936.

Carr, Edward Hallett: *The Bolshevik Revolution: 1917–1923.* London: Macmillan; 1953. Vol. III.

Chamberlin, W. H.: *The Russian Revolution: 1917–1921.* 2 vols. New York: Macmillan; 1957.

Chicherin, George: *Der Friede von Versailles: Ein Brief an die deutschen Arbeiter.* Hamburg: Buchverlag Willaschek; 1919.

——: *Two Years of Foreign Policy, 1917–1919.* New York: The Russian Soviet Government Bureau; 1920.

Footman, David: *Civil War in Russia.* London: Faber & Faber; 1961.

Fischer, Louis: *The Soviets in World Affairs. A History of the Relations Between the Soviet Union and the Rest of the World, 1917–1929.* 2nd edn. Princeton: Princeton University Press; 1951. Vol. I.

——: *Men and Politics: An Autobiography.* New York: Duell, Sloan & Pearce; 1941.

Kazemzadeh, Firuz: *The Struggle for Transcaucasia, 1917–1921.* New York: Philosophical Library; 1951.

Kennan, George: *Russia and the West under Lenin and Stalin.* Boston: Little, Brown; 1960.

Stewart, George: *The White Armies of Russia: A Chronicle of Counterrevolution and Allied Intervention.* New York: Macmillan; 1933.

Tiedemann, Helmut: *Sovietrussland und die Revolutionierung Deutschlands, 1917–1919.* Historische Studien, Heft 296. Berlin; 1936.

I. *Baltic Countries*

Bilmanis, Alfred: *A History of Latvia.* Princeton: Princeton University Press; 1951.

Page, Stanley W.: *The Formation of the Baltic States: A Study of the Effects of Great Power Politics upon the Emergence of Lithuania, Latvia, and Estonia.* Cambridge, Mass.: Harvard University Press; 1959.

Rintala, Marvin: "The Politics of Gustaf Mannerheim." *Journal of Central European Affairs.* Vol. XXI, No. 1 (April 1961), 67–83.

Senn, Alfred Erich: *The Emergence of Modern Lithuania.* New York: Columbia University Press; 1959.

Smith, Clarence J.: *Finland and the Russian Revolution, 1917–1922.* Athens, Ga.: University of Georgia; 1958.

J. *Second International*

Cole, G. D. H.: *Communism and Social Democracy, 1914–1931.* 2 vols. London: Macmillan; 1958.

Fainsod, Merle: *International Socialism and the World War.* Cambridge, Mass.: Harvard University Press; 1935.
Kautsky, Karl: *Sozialisten und Krieg.* Prag: Orbis; 1937.
Kay, John de: *L'Esprit de l'Internationale a Berne.* Lucerne; 1919.
Louis, Paul: *La Crise du socialisme mondiale.* Paris: Félix Alcan; 1921.
Meynell, Hildamarie: *The Second International, 1914–1923.* Unpublished Dissertation: St. Hilda's College, Oxford; 1958.
Sokolova, Marie: *Les Congrès de l'Internationale Socialiste entre les deux guerres mondiales.* Paris: 1953.
Van der Esch, Patricia: *La Deuxième Internationale, 1889–1923.* Paris: Marcel Rivière; 1957.
Van der Slice, Austin: *International Labor, Diplomacy, and Peace.* Philadelphia: University of Pennsylvania Press; 1941.

K. *Third International*

Borkenau, Franz: *The Communist International.* London: Faber & Faber; 1938.
Carr, E. H.: "Radek's Political Salon in Berlin, 1919." *Soviet Studies.* Vol. III, No. 4 (April 1952), 411–30.
Hulse, James W.: *The Forming of the Communist International.* Stanford: Stanford University Press; 1964.
Jackson, George D., Jr.: *Comintern and Peasant in East Europe, 1919–1930.* New York: Columbia University Press; 1966.
Radek, Karl: *Die Entwicklung der Weltrevolution und die Taktik der kommunistischen Parteien im Kampfe um die Diktatur des Proletariats.* Berlin: November, 1919.
————: *Proletarische Diktatur und Terrorismus.* Berlin: 1919.
Rappoport, Charles: *La Révolution mondiale.* Paris: Édition de la Revue Communiste; 1921.

VIII. PERSPECTIVES

Arendt, Hannah: *The Burden of Our Time.* London: Secker and Warburg; 1951.
Aron, Raymond: *The Dawn of Universal History.* New York: Praeger; 1961.
Barraclough, Geoffrey: *An Introduction to Contemporary History.* London: C. A. Watts; 1964.
Carr, E. H.: *What Is History?* New York: Knopf; 1962.
Godechot, Jacques: *La Contre-Révolution, 1789–1804.* Paris: Presses Universitaires; 1961.
Halévy, Élie: *The World Crisis of 1914–1918.* London: Oxford University Press; 1930.
Hughes, H. Stuart: *Contemporary Europe.* Englewood Cliffs, N.J.: Prentice-Hall; 1961.
Holborn, Hajo: *The Political Collapse of Europe.* New York: Knopf; 1951.
Kehr, Eckart: *Der Primat der Innenpolitik.* Berlin: de Gruyter; 1965.
Kornhauser, William: *The Politics of Mass Society.* Glencoe, Ill.: Free Press; 1959.
Laski, Harold: *Reflections on the Revolution of Our Times.* New York: Viking; 1943.
Lukács, Georg: *Die Zerstörung der Vernunft.* 2d ed. Budapest: Luchterhand; 1961.

Mann, Thomas: *Betrachtungen eines Unpolitischen*. Berlin: S. Fischer; 1918.
Mayer, Arno J.: *Political Origins of the New Diplomacy, 1917–1918*. New
    Haven: Yale University Press; 1959.
Morgenthau, Hans J.: *Politics Among Nations*. 3rd ed. New York: Knopf; 1960.
Neumann, Sigmund: *Permanent Revolution*. New York: Harper; 1942.
Motherwell, Robert, ed.: *The Dada Painters and Poets*. New York: Wittenborn,
    Schultz; 1951.
Nolte, Ernst: *Der Faschismus in seiner Epoche*. Munich: Piper; 1963.
Palmer, Robert R.: *The Age of Democratic Revolution*. 2 vols. Princeton: Prince-
    ton University Press; 1959, 1964.
Rühle, Jürgen: *Literatur und Revolution*. Munich: Th. Knauer; 1963.
Rogger, Hans, and Weber, Eugen, eds.: *The European Right*. Berkeley: Univer-
    sity of California Press; 1965.
Toynbee, Arnold: *The World After the Peace Conference*. New York: Oxford
    University Press; 1925.

Index

A NOTE ABOUT THE AUTHOR

ARNO J. MAYER, who is professor of history at Princeton University, was born in the Grand Duchy of Luxembourg in 1926. He came to the United States in 1941, and received his B.B.A. from the City College of New York in 1949, his M.A. from Yale University in 1950 and his Ph.D., also from Yale, in 1954. He also pursued advanced studies in Geneva, Switzerland. Dr. Mayer was assistant professor of politics at Brandeis University, from 1954 to 1958, assistant professor of history at Harvard University, 1958 to 1961, and in addition to his position at Princeton, has been visiting professor of history at Columbia University. The recipient of fellowships from the American Council of Learned Societies, the Rockefeller Foundation, the Social Science Research Council, and the Guggenheim Foundation, Professor Mayer is the author of *Political Origins of the New Diplomacy, 1917–1918,* published by Yale University Press in 1959, and is a contributor to the *American Historical Review, Book Week,* and other publications. He resides in Princeton, New Jersey, and has two sons.

A NOTE ON THE TYPE

THE TEXT of this book was set on the Linotype in a face called TIMES ROMAN, designed by Stanley Morison for *The Times* (London), and first introduced by that newspaper in 1932.

Among typographers and designers of the twentieth century, Stanley Morison has been a strong forming influence, as typographical advisor to the English Monotype Corporation, as a director of two distinguished English publishing houses, and as a writer of sensibility, erudition, and keen practical sense.

Typography and binding design by Kenneth Miyamoto. Composed, printed, and bound by American Book–Stratford Press, Inc., New York, New York.